Managing Strategic

SHEFFIELD HALLAM UNIVERSITY
LEARNING CENTRE
CITY CAMPUS, POND STREET,
SHEFFIELD, S1 1WB.

101 775 099 8

KT-221-097

SHEFFIELD HALLAM UNIVERSITY
LEARNING CENTRE
WITHDRAWN FROM STOCK

ONE WEEK LOAN

2 2 JAN 2007

1 2 APR 2010

MANAGING STRATEGIC INNOVATION AND CHANGE

A Collection of Readings

SECOND EDITION

Edited by

MICHAEL L. TUSHMAN
Graduate School of Business
Harvard University

PHILIP ANDERSON
INSEAD

New York   Oxford
OXFORD UNIVERSITY PRESS
2004

Oxford University Press

Oxford   New York
Auckland   Bangkok   Buenos Aires   Cape Town   Chennai
Dar es Salaam   Delhi   Hong Kong   Istanbul   Karachi   Kolkata
Kuala Lumpur   Madrid   Melbourne   Mexico City   Mumbai   Nairobi
São Paulo   Shanghai   Taipei   Tokyo   Toronto

Copyright © 1997, 2004 by Oxford University Press, Inc.

Published by Oxford University Press, Inc.
198 Madison Avenue, New York, New York 10016
www.oup.com

Oxford is a registered trademark of Oxford University Press

All rights reserved. No part of this publication may be reproduced,
stored in a retrieval system, or transmitted, in any form or by any means,
electronic, mechanical, photocopying, recording, or otherwise,
without the prior permission of Oxford University Press.

Library of Congress Cataloging-in-Publication Data
Managing strategic innovation and change : a collection of readings / edited by Michael L.
   Tushman and Philip Anderson.—2nd ed.
      p. cm.
   Includes bibliographical references and index.
   ISBN 0-19-513577-6 (alk. paper) — ISBN 0-19-513578-4 (pbk. : alk. paper)
      1. Industrial management. 2. Technological innovations. 3. Creative ability in business.
   4. Organizational change. I. Tushman, Michael. II. Anderson, Philip, 1956–
HD31.M29425 2004
658.4′063—dc22   2003061008

Printing number: 9 8 7 6 5 4 3 2 1

Printed in the United States of America
on acid-free paper

SHEFFIELD HALLAM UNIVERSITY
WL
658·4063
MA
ADSETTS CENTRE
L5

To
Marjorie, Rachel, and Jonathan
and
Rhonda, Spencer, and Olivia

CONTENTS

Preface, xi
Contributors, xvii

I. Introduction and Overview, 1

1. Innovation Streams, Organization Designs, and Organizational Evolution, 2
   Michael L. Tushman and Wendy K. Smith

2. Capabilities, Cognition, and Inertia: Evidence from Digital Imaging, 18
   Mary Tripsas and Giovanni Gavetti

II. Innovation over Time and in Historical Context, 33

Technology Cycles

3. Managing Through Cycles of Technological Change, 35
   Philip Anderson and Michael L. Tushman

4. Technological Discontinuities and Flexible Production Networks: The Case of Switzerland and the World Watch Industry, 42
   Amy Glasmeier

Discontinuous Innovation, Disruptive Technology, and Technological Substitution

5. Gunfire at Sea: A Case Study of Innovation, 59
   Elting Morison

6. Customer Power, Strategic Investment, and the Failure of Leading Firms, 70
   Clayton M. Christensen and Joseph L. Bower

7. Architectural Innovation: The Reconfiguration of Existing Product Technologies and the Failure of Established Firms, 92
   Rebecca M. Henderson and Kim B. Clark

8. The Dynamics of Standing Still: Firestone Tire & Rubber and the Radial Revolution, 108
   Donald N. Sull

Dominant Designs

 9. The Panda's Thumb of Technology, 129
     Stephen Jay Gould

10. The Art of Standards Wars, 135
     Carl Shapiro and Hal R. Varian

11. Managing in an Age of Modularity, 151
     Carliss Y. Baldwin and Kim B. Clark

Era of Incremental Change

12. Nobody Ever Gets Credit for Fixing Problems That Never Happened: Creating and Sustaining
     Process Improvement, 161
     Nelson P. Repenning and John D. Sterman

13. Tailoring Process Management to Situational Requirements: Beyond the Control and
     Exploration Dichotomy, 178
     Kathleen M. Sutcliffe, Sim B. Sitkin, and Larry D. Browning

III.   Organizational Architectures and Managing Innovation, 193

14. Managerial Problem Solving: A Congruence Approach, 194
     Michael L. Tushman and Charles O'Reilly III

15. Building Your Company's Vision, 206
     Jim Collins and Jerry I. Porras

16. Managing Professional Careers: The Influence of Job Longevity and Group Age, 219
     Ralph Katz

17. Strong Cultures and Innovation: Oxymoron or Opportunity?, 234
     Francis J. Flynn and Jennifer A. Chatman

18. Understanding Power in Organizations, 252
     Jeffrey Pfeffer

19. The Weird Rules of Creativity, 267
     Robert I. Sutton

20. The Ambidextrous Organization: Managing Evolutionary and Revolutionary Change, 276
     Michael L. Tushman and Charles O'Reilly III

21. Core Capabilities and Core Rigidities: A Paradox in Managing New Product Development, 292
     Dorothy Leonard-Barton

IV. Innovation and Business Strategy, 307

22. Dynamic Capabilities and Strategic Management, 308
     David J. Teece, Gary Pisano, and Amy Shuen

23. Strategy, Value Innovation, and the Knowledge Economy, 333
     W. Chan Kim and Renée Mauborgne

24. Crafting R&D Project Portfolios, 347
     Ian C. MacMillan and Rita Gunther McGrath

V. Knowledge, Learning, and Intellectual Capital, 361

25. Making the Most of Your Company's Knowledge: A Strategic Framework, 363
     Georg von Krogh, Ikujiro Nonaka, and Manfred Aben

26. Crisis Construction and Organizational Learning: Capability Building in Catching-Up at Hyundai Motor, 375
     Linsu Kim

27. Learning from Collaboration: Knowledge and Networks in the Biotechnology and Pharmaceutical Industries, 393
     Walter W. Powell

28. Organizing Knowledge, 402
     John Seely Brown and Paul Duguid

VI. Managing Linkages, 417

Cross-Functional Linkages

29. Organizing and Leading "Heavyweight" Development Teams, 419
     Kim B. Clark and Steven C. Wheelwright

30. Making Teamwork Work: Boundary Management in Product Development Teams, 432
     Deborah Gladstein Ancona and David F. Caldwell

Organizational Linkages

31. Strategic Linking, 441
     David A. Nadler and Michael L. Tushman

32. Coevolving: At Last, a Way to Make Synergies Work, 457
     Kathleen M. Eisenhardt and D. Charles Galunic

33. Strategies for Managing Internal Competition, 468
Julian Birkinshaw

Extra-Organizational Linkages and Venturing

34. Technology Brokering and Innovation in a Product Development Firm, 480
Andrew Hargadon and Robert I. Sutton

35. Involving Suppliers in New Product Development, 506
Robert B. Handfield, Gary L. Ragatz, Kenneth J. Petersen, and Robert M. Monczka

36. Creating New Ventures from Bell Labs Technologies, 523
Henry W. Chesbrough and Stephen J. Socolof

VII.   Executive Leadership and Managing Innovation and Change, 529

37. Convergence and Upheaval: Managing the Unsteady Pace of Organizational Evolution, 530
Michael L. Tushman, William H. Newman, and Elaine Romanelli

38. Time Pacing: Competing in Markets That Won't Stand Still, 541
Kathleen M. Eisenhardt and Shona L. Brown

39. Implementing New Designs: Managing Organizational Change, 552
David A. Nadler and Michael L. Tushman

40. Beyond the Charismatic Leader: Leadership and Organizational Change, 563
David A. Nadler and Michael L. Tushman

41. Strategy as Vector and the Inertia of Coevolutionary Lock-In, 577
Robert A. Burgelman

42. Change in the Presence of Fit: The Rise, the Fall, and the Renaissance of Liz Claiborne, 605
Nicolaj Siggelkow

Index, 627

PREFACE

Why are we economically better off than our parents were? The economist Josef Schumpeter asked this question more than fifty years ago and arrived at a powerful insight: The prime driver of economic progress is technological innovation. In his day, economic orthodoxy suggested that the goal of policy was to promote more perfect market competition, thought to be the high road toward improving society's lot. Schumpeter, in contrast, pointed out that people were better off in the 1940s than they had been at the turn of the century because of technical advances, not because more industries had come to approach the perfectly competitive ideal. Modern life is a triumph of innovation, not antitrust policy; the refrigerator, the air conditioner, the radio, the closed-body automobile, synthetic rubber, and a host of other breakthroughs created a better life and ultimately made possible a mass consumer society. In the twenty-first century, Schumpeter's insight holds more firmly than ever. One goal of both societies and organizations should be to foster the fastest rate of technical progress possible, since technical progress is the key to elevating everyone's economic well-being.

Generally, firms try to increase revenues and profits, and innovation usually accelerates the expansion of both. Why, then, is successful innovation difficult, so much so that enhancing a firm's ability to innovate is often one of the top two or three concerns of senior executives? Lack of creativity is seldom the problem; managers often tell us that there already exist within their companies more great ideas than they know how to implement.

An innovation is more than an invention. It advances a novel idea to the next level, reducing it to practice in a way that creates economic value for some group of customers. An innovation may lower the cost of producing what a company already produces, enhance the value of the company's output, or allow the company to reach new customers. It may either enhance or replace existing products, and it may do so by altering a product, a set of processes, or both.

Frequently, one or more of four different barriers defeat attempts at innovation. First, innovations involve doing something new, and sometimes companies cannot bring new technology to market in a cost-effective way. Second, innovations offer customers something new, and sometimes it turns out that they are not willing to pay enough to make an innovative product or service profitable. Third, competing companies often introduce rival innovations, and sometimes one innovation fails because another gains superior market acceptance (perhaps because of the way it fits better into a complex system of technologies). Fourth, when companies innovate, they often must also change. A company that is configured for one type of output or set of routines may have to be reconfigured if either its outputs or its tasks change. Transforming an organization is often much more difficult and costly than introducing a new product or process.

Managing innovation to create value is a complex, cross-functional, historically dependent endeavor. It is not the same as managing research and development (R&D), "high-tech management," new product development, project management, or implementing change. This book focuses on managing innovation as an organizational problem, not simply a technical problem. We have entitled it *Managing Strategic Innovation and Change* because bringing an innovation to market involves more than creating something new. It is a *strategic* challenge because innovations succeed when they reach the right market at the right time with the right competitive positioning. It requires the management of *change* because innovations succeed when new ways of operating are aligned with new value propositions.

The key themes of managing strategic innovation and change are reflected in the way we have organized the seven sections of this book:

I. Building and running an organization that consistently generates innovation is our subject. It is a difficult task because executive leaders must overcome powerful forces that inherently hinder innovation. Paradoxically, these forces often grow stronger the more efficient, capable, and successful an organization becomes.

II. The kinds of innovation that lead to success vary over time in a recurring cycle. Because the technical and strategic challenges that firms encounter change across this cycle, there is no "one best way" to manage innovation over time. Breakthrough concepts lead to a period of ferment, in which variants of a technology compete with one another, even as their proponents try to displace the previously dominant technology. This can lead to disruption in some cases, but it may reinforce the position of dominant firms in other cases. Eventually, the original innovation culminates in a dominant design, a standard configuration or architecture. It is seldom the case that three or four standards coexist with roughly equal market shares—typically, one captures far more customers than does any other. What firms must do to attract early adopters and start a wave of technological substitution is often quite different from what they must do to establish a standard. Once a dominant design is established, competitive requirements change again, as efficiency and process improvement become more important. An organization's historical context also matters because organizations often find that their previous successes are the very things that

hinder adaptation during the next phase of a cycle. The new must spring from, yet ultimately break free of, the old.

III. Managing innovation is an *organizational* problem. The design and operation of a firm affects its capacity to innovate and to adapt to the environmental changes that innovation brings. There is no single best way to organize a company that succeeds at innovation, and managers must maintain congruence among many different aspects of the organization. An organization's vision, culture, power structure, career paths, organizational design, and ability to transcend its own previous competences are all important. Furthermore, innovative organizations must sustain different, parallel structures, some that are designed to win today's competitive game and others that are configured to lead the next turn of the wheel.

IV. Successful innovators do more than optimize the next innovation they intend to introduce— they think strategically. In addition to positioning individual new products and services, strategists think in terms of innovation *streams*. Today's innovations must exploit today's competitive advantages, and they must enhance the firm's dynamic capabilities, its capacity to build new sources of competitive advantage for tomorrow. Tomorrow's innovations should not take today's terms of competition for granted—value innovations are important because they change the rules by altering the logic that customers use to choose one vendor over another. Companies master these challenges by managing a balanced *portfolio* of innovation projects.

V. Organizations innovate by increasing their knowledge base and deploying it in new directions. They expand their stock of intellectual capital by balancing exploration (enlarging the domain of what they know) with exploitation (developing new ideas by building on what they already know). Often, both types of learning involve giving to and gaining from "communities of practice," informal groupings of people and organizations who contribute to a common body of knowledge. Companies accelerate their ability to learn from such communities by building a web of relationships with complementary knowledge producers and developing their "absorptive capacity," the ability to acquire skills in a given arena. By developing mechanisms that promote the sharing of knowledge across organizational boundaries, they foster innovation that springs from the recombination of ideas that are developed in different settings.

VI. Because recombination is such an important source of innovations, managing linkages across organizational boundaries—whether they separate functions, business units within a firm, or separate companies—is of vital importance. Frequently, innovations are brought to market by cross-functional teams, and managing such teams is a core managerial skill. Within an organization, executives forge and support linkages between subunits and manage competition among them, promoting active experimentation and flexibility instead of destructive internal rivalries. Business units also coevolve with one another, deciding in a decentralized fashion how and with whom they can best collaborate. Across organizational boundaries, firms innovate horizontally by acting as technology brokers, combining existing knowledge from disparate industries. They innovate vertically by partnering upstream with their suppliers and downstream with their distribution channels to develop new products and services that draw on competences that are distributed throughout the supply chain. They can also benefit from creating artificial organizational boundaries to incubate new internal ventures in an environment that benefits from a parent firm's strength but transcends its inertial tendencies. In each of these seemingly disparate situations, innovation springs from managers' ability to bring ideas and capabilities together across organizational boundaries.

VII. Many of the activities just described fly in the face of any organization's tendency to contin-

ue doing what has worked in the past. Organizations have difficulty following through and changing their fortunes via innovation because so many other simpler, less disruptive activities compete for limited time, resources, and talent. It takes strong executive leadership to overcome natural biases in favor of maintaining existing goals, processes, and organizational arrangements. Great leaders maintain a sense of urgency, pacing companies through cycles of convergence that are punctuated by necessary upheavals. They impart a unifying vision that motivates employees to pursue innovations because they fulfill a shared purpose, even when change is uncomfortable. At the same time, they encourage initiatives that lie outside accepted trajectories because they understand the risks of pursuing a vision so firmly that the organization loses the ability to transcend its own past and its own strengths. Maintaining congruence as an organization changes from what it has been to what it will become requires managing the dual challenge of efficiency and adaptiveness, creating change without a debilitating degree of chaos. Visionary leaders and strong executive teams surmount these problems; structures and systems alone do not.

Clearly, one needs a broad, multidisciplinary conceptual tool kit to manage the intertwined problem of creating value through strategic innovation and managing the organizational changes that flow from innovation. General managers draw upon many different types of insight and knowledge to run an organization that can repeatedly use innovation to change the terms of competition in its favor. This book of readings will introduce you to a variety of perspectives, tools, and frameworks. Each reading is meant to stretch your ability to think about an important aspect of a wide-ranging set of skills in a conceptually sophisticated, yet practical, way.

All of the selections are anchored in research that speaks to pragmatic problems while transcending individual cases. Although they contain many rich examples that are drawn from business experience, they are more than a collection of best practices. There is no recipe for managing innovation, because the challenges innovation poses change over time and reflect an organization's unique history. The readings do not provide innovation templates to be copied; they provide stimuli for original thinking. The research-anchored models they convey should accelerate your learning and enhance your ability to penetrate the surface of things, to distinguish symptoms from problems and incidents from principles.

We have selected readings that reflect the frontiers of thinking in this area, and the leading edge of any discipline is seldom tidy. Important ideas lead to new lines of inquiry that foster extensions and revisions of breakthrough concepts. This volume captures the key themes and most important debates that are taking place in the field of innovation management today. Those who contribute to these debates think critically about the ideas contained in this book, and we encourage you to do the same. Transcending received wisdom is the essence of innovation. You will get the most out of this book if you see yourself as a participant in an ongoing discussion who creates new concepts by recombining your own thoughts with those you encounter as you read.

In refining your own conceptual views, you will benefit from a common thread that connects most of the readings: They take a *dynamic* approach to thinking about processes that play out over time. Innovation is sensitive to history, timing, cycles, and the constant tension between environmental pressures for stability and change. Thinking about *streams* of innovation, as opposed to individual new products or services, causes one to think about the way in which different eras succeed one another as part of a larger cycle. A dynamic perspective starts with the past, with understanding how history and the trajectory of previous technological change shape today's possibilities. It also focuses on the present, asking how the current era creates opportunities to revolutionize today's value propositions and how an organization would need to change to take advantage of them. Simultaneously, it takes

into account the future. The capabilities and knowledge created by today's innovations may enable the firm to continue innovating successfully, yet will surely create inertial pressures that can constrain future adaptation unless strong leaders counteract these forces.

The book sets the stage for this dynamic view in Section I. The initial selection describes how innovation occurs in streams, which influence the ongoing evolution of innovating organizations. It introduces the idea that success often sets the stage for subsequent failure, which is why "radical" change often undermines industry leaders. The point is illustrated in the second selection, which examines Polaroid's difficulties in adapting to the transition from instant film to digital imaging. The ideas of its powerful, charismatic founder had a lasting effect on Polaroid's capabilities and accepted ways of thinking, causing trouble when environmental shifts undermined its once-successful business model.

Section II introduces a way of thinking about innovation as a historical, cyclical process that throws up different challenges as an industry passes from one era to another. Technologies change via a "punctuated equilibrium" pattern. A long period of routine evolution is typically interrupted by a breakthrough advance. Several variants of the original breakthrough emerge, until one becomes the dominant design, the standard expression of a new technology. Incremental change ensues until the next advance. This section illustrates the progress of a technology cycle using the example of the global watch industry and then considers when and how breakthrough innovations overturn established industry leaders. We then examine how dominant designs emerge, how firms jockey to establish their variant of a technology as the standard, and how platform leaders exploit their control of key standards. We finally explore the challenges of winning via process innovation during an era of incremental change, when efficiency and reliability are keys to competitive success.

In Section III, we turn to the problem of creating organizational architectures that can adapt to and exploit the shifting opportunities created by innovation and change. Flexible organizations create new products and services by aligning people and purpose. We introduce a congruence model that lies at the root of our approach to the strategic management of innovation and change. This methodology has been used in helping managers around the world diagnose and solve innovation problems. We then look at how to operate the levers that managers use to overcome natural resistance to change and fear of uncertainty. They include shared vision, strong cultures, career management systems, power and influence, and creative stimuli. We then examine how to design innovative organizations, focusing on *make* versus *outsource* choices and on creating ambidextrous structures to deal with today's and tomorrow's different requirements. We close by considering how firms overcome the paradox where their very strengths trap them when the environment shifts.

Section IV addresses setting and executing innovation strategies. Innovation advantage rests, in large part, on a firm's distinctive processes, which are shaped by its unique assets and its idiosyncratic trajectory of development. Firms with extraordinary dynamic capabilities are better at creating new competences than their rivals are; today's innovation projects create tomorrow's competitive strengths. Technological progress is only one aspect of innovation strategy; conceiving and executing innovations that introduce new competitive dimensions can dramatically enhance growth and profitability. Innovation strategy also includes crafting and balancing a portfolio of innovation projects that creates valuable options.

Section V shifts the spotlight to the related problem of accelerating the rate at which a firm generates and deploys knowledge. Intellectual capital is well along the path of displacing land, labor, and physical capital as the prime source of value in many industries. This section introduces a strategic framework for knowledge management and then addresses the four most important themes in the burgeoning knowledge management literature. The first is how organizations can enhance their "absorptive capacity," their ability to learn from other firms and individuals. The second is how organizations can build patterns and portfolios of collaboration that give them access to a diverse array of knowledge sources. The third rests on the notion that knowledge is often created and transferred within communities of practice (both within and between organizations), communities that have unusual procedures and values that must be respected. The fourth is how to manage "competency traps," where the more efficient a firm becomes at exploiting what it already knows, the more exploration into new knowledge domains is inhibited.

In Section VI, we return to the theme of Section II, running organizations that generate and implement innovations effectively. Here, the focus is on managing linkages across organizational boundaries. Because innovation is a complex, cross-functional endeavor, transcending organizational divisions is essential. Recombining knowledge that is held in different organizational locations is perhaps the most important wellspring of innovation. We start by examining how to create innovation through cross-functional teams. Moving up a level of analysis, we examine how firms meld contributions from different business units into new value-creating combinations. Several different schools of thought contribute to this section, including approaches that stress competition between business units and others that emphasize decentralized, voluntary collaboration among them. We then examine the problem of coordinating innovation across separate, independently governed organizations, whether they are complementors, collaborators in a supply chain, or ventures that operate at arm's length from their parents.

Section VII, the capstone of the book, is concerned with the essential ingredient that catalyzes all others: leadership. Leaders impart vision, values, and purpose, all essential to managing shifting cycles, designing effective organizations, forging and implementing strategies, fostering learning, and transcending organizational silos. We first investigate how effective executives manage the rhythm of change, setting a pace of progress that keeps their organizations ahead of environmental shifts instead of constantly reacting to them. We then develop insights into how one can impart energy and help people understand the meaning of change, allowing an organization to shift from one type of fit to another, even though the journey produces anxiety and doubt. We conclude with two fascinating examples of the paradox of fit. Strong leaders and a history of success often produce the seeds of their own downfall because the lessons a firm learns from great achievements are so hard to undo. Intel and Liz Claiborne exemplify companies whose triumphs in one era made it difficult to adapt to the next. These two cases provide a point of departure for thinking about how to rejuvenate great companies in the face of a changing environment.

Many changes have been made for this second edition; almost three-fourths of the material is new. In part, these changes reflect the vitality of research on innovation; the majority of the readings we added were not in print when the first edition of this book was published in 1997. In part, it also reflects the mission we have undertaken: to keep our readers on top of emerging themes and debates in the arena of managing strategic innovation and change and to link these debates with vivid, well-researched examples. The biggest change from the first edition is the addition of Section V. Knowledge management was in its infancy in 1997; today, intellectual capital and organizational learning are among the most important topics that scholars and practitioners study. Those who are familiar with the first edition will also find that Section IV, on strategy, has been substantially revised, reflecting ideas that have become much more prominent in the past few years, such as dynamic capabilities and value innovation. Otherwise, the general outline of the first edition remains, along with many classic articles that have stood the test of time and remain both fresh and relevant.

As with the first edition, we have designed the book to meet the needs of both managers and future managers. We have built on the ideas in these readings to design MBA courses and executive programs on managing innovation at the California Institute of Technology, Stanford University, Chalmers University, Columbia University Graduate School of Business, Cornell University's Johnson Graduate School of Management, Dartmouth's Tuck School of Business, the Harvard Business School, INSEAD, and MIT's Sloan School of Management. We have also used them in consulting engagements for a variety of firms around the globe,

both large and small. We are particularly grateful for input and support from managers at Novartis, Bristol Myers Squibb, BOC, Ericsson, Pfizer, Arrow Electronics, IBM, Millennia Partners, the World Bank, Thompson, and Biogen. We hope that managers and students who are looking for a broad, yet integrated, approach to the strategic management of innovation and change will find fresh insights from a set of ideas that are seldom brought together in one volume.

ACKNOWLEDGMENTS

It would be impossible to thank everyone whose ideas and constructive criticism have contributed to this book. Both the Harvard Business School and INSEAD have generously underwritten our research and teaching. We also appreciate the continuing support and counsel of 3i PLC, Europe's largest private equity investment firm, whose sponsorship of the 3i Venturelab at INSEAD helped underwrite the revision of this volume. Charles O'Reilly, Jeff Pfeffer, Ralph Katz, David Nadler, David Garvin, Clay Christensen, Gary Pisano, Marco Iansiti, Lori Rosenkopf, James Brian Quinn, Claudia Schoonhoven, and Paul Danos have been companions in building, extending, and challenging our ideas on managing innovation and change. The book would not have been possible without the tireless assistance of Hendrika Escoffier and Tom Barrow. The resources of the Baker Library at Harvard Business School, the Doriot Library at INSEAD, and the Feldberg Library at the Tuck School of Business have been invaluable. We would also like to thank Martha Cooley at Oxford University Press for spurring us to produce a new edition of our book. Over the years, we have worked with several thousand executives and MBAs, and we have learned a great deal from them. Their feedback has constantly challenged us to reorganize and rethink the way we present this subject. Their patience and goodwill as we have tested hundreds of ideas and readings with them have made this volume possible.

CONTRIBUTORS

MANFRED ABEN
Unilever

DEBORAH GLADSTEIN ANCONA
Sloan School of Management, MIT

PHILIP ANDERSON
INSEAD

CARLISS Y. BALDWIN
Graduate School of Business,
Harvard University

JULIAN BIRKINSHAW
London Business School, England

JOSEPH L. BOWER
Graduate School of Business,
Harvard University

JOHN SEELY BROWN
Xerox PARC (emeritus)

SHONA L. BROWN
McKinsey & Company, Toronto

LARRY D. BROWNING
College of Communication, University of
Texas at Austin

ROBERT A. BURGELMAN
Graduate School of Business,
Stanford University

DAVID F. CALDWELL
Leavey School of Business, Santa
Clara University

JENNIFER A. CHATMAN
Haas School of Business, University of
California, Berkeley

HENRY W. CHESBROUGH
Haas School of Business, University of
California, Berkeley

CLAYTON M. CHRISTENSEN
Graduate School of Business,
Harvard University

KIM B. CLARK
Graduate School of Business,
Harvard University

JIM COLLINS
Self-employed, Boulder, Colorado

PAUL DUGUID
University of California, Berkeley

KATHLEEN M. EISENHARDT
Management Science and Engineering,
Stanford University

FRANCIS J. FLYNN
Graduate School of Business,
Columbia University

D. CHARLES GALUNIC
INSEAD

GIOVANNI GAVETTI
Graduate School of Business,
Harvard University

AMY GLASMEIER
Department of Geography, The Pennsylvania
State University

STEPHEN JAY GOULD
Harvard University

ROBERT B. HANDFIELD
College of Management, North Carolina
State University

ANDREW HARGADON
Graduate School of Management, University
of California, Davis

REBECCA M. HENDERSON
Sloan School of Management, MIT

RALPH KATZ
College of Business Administration,
Northeastern University

LINSU KIM
Korea University

W. CHAN KIM
INSEAD

DOROTHY LEONARD-BARTON
Graduate School of Business,
Harvard University

IAN C. MACMILLAN
Wharton School, University
of Pennsylvania

RENÉE MAUBORGNE
INSEAD

RITA GUNTHER MCGRATH
Graduate School of Business,
Columbia University

ROBERT M. MONCZKA
W. P. Carey School of Business, Arizona
State University

ELTING MORISON
MIT

DAVID A. NADLER
Mercer Delta Consulting, Inc.

WILLIAM H. NEWMAN
Graduate School of Business,
Columbia University

IKUJIRO NONAKA
Japan Advanced Institute of Science
and Technology

CHARLES O'REILLY III
Graduate School of Business,
Stanford University

KENNETH J. PETERSEN
W. P. Carey School of Business, Arizona
State University

JEFFREY PFEFFER
Graduate School of Business,
Stanford University

GARY PISANO
Graduate School of Business,
Harvard University

JERRY I. PORRAS
Graduate School of Business,
Stanford University

WALTER W. POWELL
School of Education, Stanford University

GARY L. RAGATZ
Eli Broad Graduate School of Management,
Michigan State University

NELSON P. REPENNING
Sloan School of Management, MIT

ELAINE ROMANELLI
McDonough School of Business,
Georgetown University

CARL SHAPIRO
   Haas School of Business, University of
   California, Berkeley

AMY SHUEN
   Silicon Valley Strategy Group

NICOLAJ SIGGELKOW
   Wharton School, University of Pennsylvania

SIM B. SITKIN
   Fuqua School of Business, Duke University

WENDY K. SMITH
   Graduate School of Business,
   Harvard University

STEPHEN J. SOCOLOF
   New Venture Partners, LLC

JOHN D. STERMAN
   Sloan School of Management, MIT

DONALD N. SULL
   Graduate School of Business,
   Harvard University

KATHLEEN M. SUTCLIFFE
   University of Michigan Business School,
   Ann Arbor

ROBERT I. SUTTON
   Management Science and Engineering
   and Graduate School of Business,
   Stanford University

DAVID J. TEECE
   Haas School of Business, University of
   California, Berkeley

MARY TRIPSAS
   Graduate School of Business,
   Harvard University

MICHAEL L. TUSHMAN
   Graduate School of Business,
   Harvard University

HAL R. VARIAN
   Haas School of Business, University of
   California, Berkeley

GEORG VON KROGH
   Institute of Management, University of
   St. Gallen, Switzerland

STEVEN C. WHEELWRIGHT
   Graduate School of Business,
   Harvard University

SECTION I

INTRODUCTION AND OVERVIEW

Dynamic capabilities are rooted in the ability of an organization both to explore and to exploit. These organizational challenges are themselves inconsistent and take place in the context of strong historically anchored forces for inertia. Our initial section reviews as well as illustrates the several themes of our book: the difficulties of sustained success in evolving environments, innovation streams, technology cycles, organizational architectures, strategy and value-nets, organizational learning, strategic linkages, organizational change, and executive leadership. Tushman and Smith provide a literature review of these domains, and Tripsas and Gavetti richly illustrate the phenomena of managing strategic innovation and change with their unusually detailed research on Polaroid.

Innovation Streams, Organization Designs, and Organizational Evolution

MICHAEL L. TUSHMAN
WENDY K. SMITH

TECHNOLOGICAL CHANGE, AMBIDEXTROUS ORGANIZATIONS, AND ORGANIZATIONAL EVOLUTION

Technical change is one of the core drivers of organizational fates (Tushman and Nelson, 1990; Nelson, 1995). While technological change accentuates organizational failure rates, there is substantial heterogeneity in organizational life chances (Barnett and Carroll, 1995). Some firms thrive during eras of ferment, other firms proactively destabilize their product class with technological discontinuities, even as most firms are swept away during Schumpeterian gales of creative destruction (e.g., Grove, 1996; Morone, 1993; Sorensen and Stuart, 2000; Carroll and Teo, 1996). The stream of research on organizational technology is interested in how organizations shape and are, in turn, shaped by technological change. This literature sheds substantial light on how organizational architectures, capabilities, and senior teams affect both a firm's ability to shape technological change and to compete effectively when technologies change.

Technology and resource-rich firms often fail to sustain their competitiveness at technology transitions. Consider SSIH, the Swiss watch consortium; Goodyear Tire; Polaroid; and Oticon, the Danish hearing aid firm. These organizations dominated their respective worldwide markets, SSIH and Goodyear through the 1970s and Polaroid and Oticon through the early 1990s. Each developed new technologies that had the capabilities to re-create their markets (e.g., quartz movements, radial tires, digital imaging, and in-the-ear [ITE] volume and tone control). But although SSIH, Goodyear, Polaroid, and Oticon had the technology and the resources to innovate, it was smaller, more aggressive firms that initiated new technology in these four industries. SSIH, Goodyear, Polaroid, and Oticon prospered until new industry standards—what we call dominant designs—rapidly destroyed their market positions (Glassmier, 1991, Sull, 1999, Tripsas and Gavetti, 2000). Similar liabilities of success have been found in disk drives (Christensen and Bower, 1996), business equipment (Rosenbloom, 2000), photolithography (Henderson and Clark, 1990), and typesetting (Tripsas, 1999), among others (Tushman and O'Reilly, 1997; Miller, 1994).

In the watch, tire, photography, and hearing aid markets, it was not new technology that led to the demise of the Swiss, Americans, or the Danes; indeed, SSIH, Goodyear, Polaroid, and Oticon were technology leaders. Nor was the rapid loss in market share due to the lack of financial resources or to governmental

Adapted from Chapter 17 "Organizational Technology," by Michael L. Tushman and Wendy K. Smith, in Joel A. C. Baum (ed.), *The Blackwell Companion to Organizations*, pp. 386–414, copyright © 2002. Reprinted with permission of Blackwell Publishers Ltd., UK.

regulations. Rather, the rapid demise of SSIH and Goodyear and the losses at Polaroid and Oticon were rooted in organizational complacency and inertia. These pathologies of sustained success stunted their ability to renew themselves. This success syndrome is particularly paradoxical in that each of these firms had the competencies, resources, and technologies to proactively drive innovation streams. Innovation streams are patterns of innovations, some that build on and extend prior products (e.g., mechanical watches, bias ply tires, and behind-the-ear [BTE] hearing aids) and others that destroy the very products that account for a firm's historical success (e.g., analog to digital imaging). Innovation streams focus theoretical and empirical attention away from isolated innovations and toward patterns of innovation over time.

This paradoxical pattern in which winners, with all their competencies and assets, become losers is found across industries and countries (see Hamel and Prahalad, 1994; Utterback, 1994; Christensen, 1998). It seems that building core competencies and managing through continuous improvement are not sufficient for sustained competitive advantage. Worse, building on core competencies (e.g., for the Swiss, precision mechanics) and engaging in continuous incremental improvement actually trap the organization in its past and lead to catastrophic failure as technologies and markets shift. Core competencies often turn into rigidities (Leonard-Barton, 1992; Benner and Tushman, 2000). Firms that are caught by historically anchored inertia are unable to build, extend, or destroy their existing competencies to develop innovations that would create new markets (as Starkey did with ITE hearing aids) or to rewrite the competitive rules in existing markets (as Seiko and Michlein did with quartz watches and radial tires). These inertial firms get selected out of their competitive arenas by basic ecological dynamics (Levinthal, 1997; Sorensen and Stuart, 2000; Carroll and Hannan, 2000).

But liabilities of success are not deterministic; core competencies need not become core rigidities. Some organizations are capable of proactively shifting bases of competition through streams of innovation (Brown and Eisenhardt, 1998; Tushman and O'Reilly, 1997). These firms are able to develop incremental innovation, as well as innovations that alter industry standards, substitute for existing products, and/or re-configure products to fundamentally different markets. For example, in the watch industry, Seiko was not only able to compete in mechanical watches, but was willing to experiment with quartz and tuning-fork movements. On the basis of these technological options, Seiko managers made the decision to substitute quartz movements for their existing mechanical movements. In retrospect, the switch to the quartz movement led to fundamentally different competitive rules in the watch industry. Similarly, Starkey (a U.S. hearing aid company) was able to move beyond BTE hearing aids to ITE hearing aids by simply reconfiguring the existing components of hearing aids. This seemingly minor architectural innovation led to a new industry standard and to different industry rules that are anchored on sound quality and fashion.

Dynamic capabilities are rooted in driving streams of innovation. Firms that survive technological transitions compete through patterns of innovation over time: incremental, competence-enhancing innovation (e.g., thinner mechanical watches); architectural innovation (e.g., Starkey's ITE hearing aid); taking existing technologies to new customer segments, and fundamentally new, often competence-destroying, innovation (e.g., Seiko's quartz movement). By driving streams of innovation, senior teams increase the probability that their firm will be able to shape industry standards, take advantage of new markets for existing technology, and proactively introduce substitute products that, as they cannibalize existing products, create new markets and competitive rules (Teece, 1996; Burgelman and Grove, 1996; Hurst, 1995; Brown and Eisenhardt, 1998).

These dynamic capabilities are rooted in a firm's ability to be ambidextrous—both to learn and incrementally build on its past even as it simultaneously creates technological options from which senior teams make strategic bets (Duncan, 1976; Tushman and O'Reilly, 1997). Because of powerful inertial processes that are accentuated in those most successful firms, these strategic bets must be coupled with discontinuous organizational changes (Sastry, 1997; Romanelli and Tushman, 1994; Gavetti and Levinthal, 2000). We discuss the topics of technology cycles, innovation streams, ambidextrous organizations, senior teams, and discontinuous organizational change in turn.

TECHNOLOGY CYCLES AND DOMINANT DESIGNS

Technology cycles are composed of technological discontinuities (for example, quartz and tuning-fork movements in watches) that trigger periods of technological and competitive ferment. During eras of ferment, rival technologies compete with each other and with the existing technological regime. These turbulent innovation periods close with the emergence of an industry standard or dominant design (Utterback, 1994; Anderson and Tushman, 1990). For example, in early radio transmission, continuous-wave transmission was a technological discontinuity that threatened to replace spark-gap transmission. Continuous-wave transmission initiated competition not only between this new innovation and spark-gap transmission, but among three variants of the innovation: alternating-wave, arc,

and vacuum tube transmission. This period of technological ferment led to vacuum tube transmission becoming the dominant design in radio transmission (Aitken, 1985; Rosenkopf and Tushman, 1994). The emergence of a dominant design ushers in a period of incremental as well as architectural technological change, a period that is broken at some point by the next substitute product. The subsequent technological discontinuity then triggers the next wave of technological variation, selection, and retention (see Figure 1.1).

Technology cycles are seen most directly in nonassembled or simple products (e.g., glass, chemicals, skis, tennis racquets). For example, in crop fungicides, Ciba-Geigy's Tilt (propiconazol) was a new chemical entity that challenged Bayer's and BASF's products. Tilt triggered competition among chemical entities, as well as among a vast number of propiconazol formulations. Ciba eventually created its EC 250

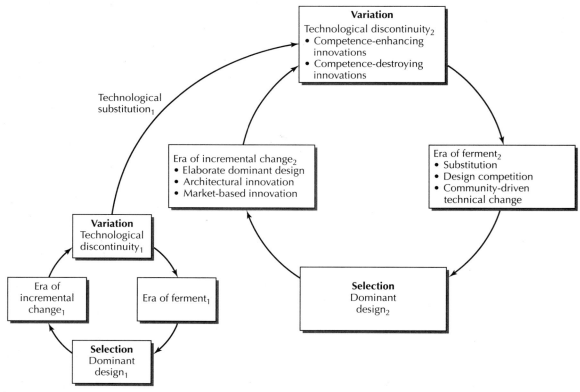

Figure 1.1. Technology cycles over time (adapted from Rosenkopf and Tushman, 1994).

version, which became the industry standard in crop fungicides. Ciba's Crop Protection Division then initiated several product substitutes (including genetically engineered seeds) to cannibalize and replace propiconazol. These fundamentally new crop-protection products initiated the next technology cycle in the crop-protection market (Rosenkopf and Tushman, 1994).

In more complex assembled products (e.g., computers or watches) and systems (e.g., radio or voice mail), technology cycles apply at the subsystem level. Landes (1983) and Hughes (1983) provided rich historically anchored details on the watch and electric power industries from their respective births. These comprehensive histories illustrate the interplay among technology, organizations, and communities. Watches, for example, are assembled products made up of at least four subsystems: energy source, oscillation device, transmission, and display. Each of these subsystems has its own technology cycle. In watch oscillation, the pin-lever escapement became the dominant design in the late nineteenth century. Escapements became better and better through incremental changes in the same fundamental design until the late 1960s. Between 1968 and 1972, escapements were threatened by both tuning fork and quartz oscillation. This period of technological competition among escapements, tuning-fork oscillation, and quartz movement ended with the emergence of quartz oscillation as the dominant design in the subsystem. As with mechanical escapements, the emergence of quartz movements as the dominant design led, in turn, to numerous incremental improvements in the quartz movement and sharp decreases in innovation in tuning-fork and escapement oscillation devices.

Not all subsystems are equivalent. Rather, a product is composed of hierarchically ordered subsystems that are coupled by linking mechanisms that are as crucial to the product's performance as are the subsystems themselves (Clark, 1985; Henderson and Clark, 1990; Baldwin and Clark, 2000). The more core subsystems are either tightly coupled to other subsystems or are strategic bottlenecks (Hughes, 1983; Schilling, 2000; Tushman and Murmann, 1998). In contrast, peripheral subsystems are weakly connected to other subsystems. Shifts in core subsystems have cascading effects on other more peripheral subsystems (Ulrich and Eppinger, 1995). Furthermore, subsystems shift in rela-

tive strategic importance as the industry evolves. In watches, oscillation was the key strategic battlefield through the early 1970s; then, once the quartz movement became the dominant design, the locus of strategic innovation shifted to the face, energy, and transmission subsystems. Similar dynamics of subsystem and linkage technology cycles have been documented in a variety of industries (Hughes, 1983, Van de Ven and Garud, 1994; Baum, Korn, and Kotha, 1995).

The technological discontinuities that initiate technology cycles are relatively rare, unpredictable events that are triggered by scientific advance (e.g., battery technology for watches) or through a recombining of existing technology (e.g., Sony's Walkman or continuous-aim gunfire) (Morison, 1966; Sanderson and Uzumeri, 1995). Technological discontinuities rupture existing incremental patterns of innovation and spawn periods of technological ferment that are confusing, uncertain, and costly to customers, suppliers, vendors, and regulatory agencies. Absent governmental regulation, a single dominant design emerges from periods of variation or eras of technological ferment (see Noble, 1984, Cusumano, Mylonadis, and Rosenbloom, 1992; Anderson and Tushman, 1990). During windows of opportunity at the emergence of dominant designs, competing firms must switch to the new standard or risk getting locked out of the market (Christensen, Suarez, and Utterback, 1998; Tegarden, Hatfield, and Echols, 1999).

How do dominant designs emerge? Except for the most simple nonassembled products, the closing on a dominant design is not technologically driven because no technology can dominate all possible dimensions of merit. Nor does the closing on a dominant design take place through the invisible hand of the market (Noble, 1984; Pinch and Bijker, 1987). Rather, it occurs through social, political, and organizational competition among the alternative technological variants (Hughes, 1983; Baum, Korn, and Kotha, 1995; Tushman and Rosenkopf, 1992). Dominant designs emerge out of the struggle between alternative technological trajectories that are initiated and pushed by competitors, alliance groups, and governmental regulators— each with its own political, social, and economic agendas. This social construction of technology has been thoroughly documented in a range of industries (see Bijker, Hughes, and Pinch, 1987). In an unusually rich process-oriented case study, Van de Ven, Angle, and

Poole (1988) provide details on the complex regulatory, organizational, and physician dynamics in the evolution of industry standards in the cochlear implant industry. This case describes not only the evolution of standards at the subsystem level, but how one firm, 3M, worked outside its boundaries to shape industry standards.

Similarly, the emergence of the VHS over Beta as a dominant design in the videocassette recorder industry illustrates the process of technology cycles and the social and political influences on this process. Cusumano, Mylonadis, and Rosenbloom (1992) used historical data on technological capabilities, mass market demands, and organizational strategies for six key companies that developed videocassette recorders between 1975 and 1988. They demonstrated that although initially Beta was more technologically advanced (e.g., the tapes held greater amount of information with a higher resolution) and initially captured more of the market, JVC was able to beat Sony through proactive alliances with strong producers and distributors.

Dominant designs are watershed events in a technology cycle. Before a dominant design emerges, technological progress is driven by competition between alternative technologies. After a dominant design emerges, subsequent technological change is driven by the logic of the selected technology itself (see Figure 1.1). The closing on a dominant design shifts innovation from major product variation to major process innovation and, in turn, to incremental innovation—to building on, extending, and continuously improving the selected variant. These periods of incremental innovation lead to profound advances in the now-standard product (Hollander, 1965; Myers and Marquis, 1969; Abernathy, 1978). In contrast, the consequences of betting on the wrong design are devastating—particularly if that design is a core subsystem (e.g., IBM's losing control of the microprocessor and operating system in PCs to Intel and Microsoft).

Technology cycles apply both to product subsystems and to linking technologies, and they apply across product classes—the only difference between high-tech (e.g., disk drive) and low-tech (e.g., concrete) industries is the length of time between the emergence of a dominant design and the subsequent discontinuity. Technology cycles highlight the points at which senior teams have a substantial impact on firm and product class evolution versus where they only have minor impacts (Christensen, Suarez, and Utterback, 1998; Hambrick and Finkelstein, 1996). During eras of ferment, actions by senior teams affect both the nature of technical change as well as organizational fates. During eras of incremental change, however, managerial influence on technical progress in the existing trajectory is sharply limited. Senior teams can, however, destabilize their product class by initiating different types of innovation—by driving innovation streams.

INNOVATION TYPES AND INNOVATION STREAMS

For complex products, the locus of innovation occurs both within subsystems and with the technologies that link subsystems together (Baldwin and Clark, 2000; Schilling, 2000). Decomposing products into components and linking mechanisms and clarifying target markets/customers helps untangle incremental, architectural, discontinuous, and market types of innovation (Henderson and Clark, 1990; Christensen, 1998; Tushman and Murmann, 1998) (see Figure 1.2).

Incremental Innovations
Incremental innovations are innovations that push the existing technological trajectory for existing subsystem and linking mechanisms. Such innovations are associated with significant improvements in products and enhanced customer satisfaction over time (Myers and Marquis, 1969; Hollander, 1965).

Architectural Innovations
Architectural innovations involve shifts in subsystems and/or linking mechanisms (Henderson and Clark, 1990). These relatively simple types of innovations are often initially targeted to new markets. Henderson and Clark (1990) identified architectural and modular innovation and explored their impacts on firms in the photolithography industry. Archival data and extensive interviews with the senior management teams of incumbents and new entrants indicated that the contact aligner and its successor, the proximity aligner, were exactly the same in their component subsystems, but altered the way that these subsystems interacted with one another. Over four such architectural innovations,

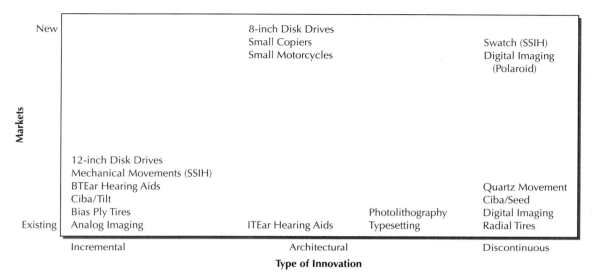

Figure 1.2. Innovation streams (adapted from Tushman and O'Reilly, 1997).

incumbents treated the innovation as if it were an incremental innovation. Established organizations failed to recognize the need to restructure their organization, to seek new markets, or to alter their production processes. In each case, incumbents failed to adapt to seemingly minor technical change. Similarly, Starkey's move into the fashion hearing aid market, Honda's early move to smaller motorcycles, the migration of disk drive technology from mainframes to personal computers, and Canon's smaller copiers are examples of architectural innovations that transformed their product classes. While these innovations were technologically simple, in each case, incumbents fumbled their future (Kearns and Nadler, 1992; Henderson, 1995; Christensen, 1998).

Discontinuous Innovation

Discontinuous innovation involves discontinuous technological change in a core subsystem. Such technical shifts trigger cascading changes in other less-core subsystems and linking mechanisms (Tushman and Murmann, 1998). For example, in the photography industry, digital imaging was a competence-destroying change in the camera's core subsystem. Tripsas and Gavetti (2000) documented, via interviews and industry data, how Polaroid, a leading incumbent, was able to generate the technological know-how but was unable to go to

market with digital cameras because of profound organizational inertia and stunted senior team cognitive models. Sull, Tedlow, and Rosenbloom's (1997) and Sull's (1999) historical analyses of the tire industry demonstrated how difficult it is for incumbents to initiate discontinuous innovation even when they have all the requisite technical competencies.

Whereas incremental, architectural, and discontinuous innovations are defined by their technological impact on subsystems and/or linking mechanisms, *market*-based innovations are those innovations that are targeted to new markets or customer segments. These often-technically simple innovations are frequently missed by incumbents at their considerable peril. Christensen (1998) conducted a census of all disk drive producers from 1974 to 1990. He found that in the transitions from 14-inch to 3.5-inch disk drives, incumbents were displaced by new players in every case. Each of these architectural innovations was initially most useful to newer, less-demanding customers from the incumbents' perspective. In every case, incumbents ceded these new markets to new players, and in every case, these new players proceeded subsequently to move up market. Christensen (1998) observed that these technologically simple innovations are disruptive to an incumbent's existing organizational architectures (note that they are not technologically disruptive).

Building on products as composed of subsystems and linking mechanisms, Sanderson and Uzumeri (1995) developed the notion of product platforms and families. A platform is a set of core subsystems; a product family is a set of products that are built from the same platform. These product families share traits, architecture, components, and interface standards. For example, once Sony closed on the WM-20 platform for its Walkman, it was then able to generate more than 30 incremental versions within the same family. Over a ten-year period, Sony was able to develop four Walkman product families and more than 160 incremental versions of those four families. Devoting sustained attention to technological discontinuities at the subsystem level (e.g., the flat motor and the miniature battery), closing on a few standard platforms, and generating incremental product proliferation helped Sony control industry standards and outperform its Japanese, American, and European competitors in this product class (Sanderson and Uzumeri, 1995).

Thus lying behind S-shaped product life-cycle curves are fundamentally different innovation dynamics (Klepper, 1996). Eras of ferment are associated with discontinuous product variants. Dominant designs are associated with fundamental process innovation. After dominant designs emerge, the subsequent eras of incremental change are associated with product modularization and are fertile periods for incremental, architectural, discontinuous, and market-based innovation. Given the nature of technology cycles, then, the roots of sustained competitive advantage may lie in a firm's ability to initiate proactively multiple types of innovations—to initiate streams of innovation. Yet the external push for innovation streams runs counter to internal inertial forces. Incumbents, even when armed with technological capabilities, are held hostage to their successful pasts. It seems to be difficult for incumbents to develop the diverse competencies and organizational capabilities to shape and take advantage of dominant designs, to shape architectural innovation, to move to less demanding markets, or to introduce substitute products before the competition.

AMBIDEXTROUS ORGANIZATIONS

A firm's dynamic capabilities are rooted in its ability to drive innovation streams—to create incremental, architectural, market, and discontinuous innovations simultaneously (Tushman and O'Reilly, 1997; Teece, 1996). Ambidextrous organizations are complex organizational forms that are composed of multiple internally inconsistent architectures that are collectively capable of operating simultaneously for short-term efficiency and long-term innovation (Duncan, 1976; Weick, 1979; Bradach, 1997). Such heterogeneous organizational forms build in the experimentation, improvization, and luck associated with small organizations, along with the efficiency, consistency, and reliability associated with larger organizations (Eisenhardt and Tabrizi, 1995; Imai, Nonaka, and Takeuchi, 1985).

Organizational architectures for incremental innovation are fundamentally different from those for all other innovation types. Continuous incremental improvement in products and processes and high-volume throughput are associated with organizations with relatively formalized roles and linking mechanisms, centralized procedures and processes, efficiency-oriented cultures, and highly engineered work processes (Eisenhardt and Tabrizi, 1995; Burns and Stalker, 1961; Nadler and Tushman, 1997). Efficiency-oriented units drive continuous improvement, exploitation, and the elimination of variability and have relatively short time horizons (Levitt and March, 1988; Levinthal, 1997). Such units are often relatively large and old, with highly ingrained, taken-for-granted assumptions and knowledge systems (Milliken and Lant, 1991) (see Figure 1.3).

In contrast to incremental innovation, discontinuous innovation emerges from entrepreneurial organizational architectures. Entrepreneurial units/organizations are relatively small; they have loose, decentralized product structures, experimental cultures, loose work processes, strong entrepreneurial and technical competencies, and relatively young and heterogeneous human resource profiles (McGrath and MacMillan, 2000). These units generate the experiments/options from which the organization's senior team can learn about the future (Levitt and March, 1988; McGrath, 1999; Leonard-Barton, 1995). These units build new experience bases, knowledge systems, and networks to break from the larger organization's history. They generate variants from which the senior team can make bets on possible dominant designs, new customer segments, and technological discontinuities

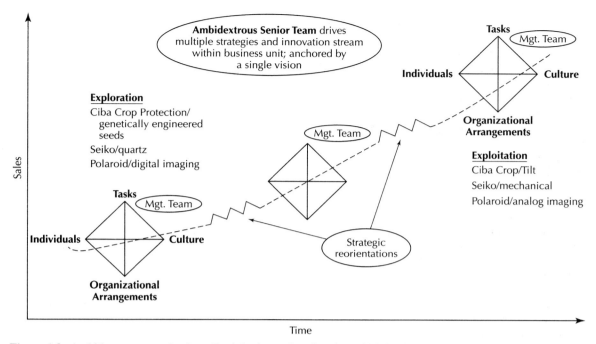

Figure 1.3. Ambidextrous organizations: Exploitation and exploration within business units.

(Burgelman, 1994; Nonaka, 1988). In contrast to the larger, more mature, efficiency-oriented units, these small entrepreneurial units are inefficient and rarely profitable and have no established histories (see Figure 1.3). These entrepreneurial units may be created internally or acquired externally through acquisition, contract research, joint ventures, or alliances (Teece, 1996; Roberts and Berry, 1985; Silverman, 1999).

Architectural innovations take existing technologies and link these technologies in novel ways; they are built not on new technological breakthroughs, but on integrating competencies from both the efficiency-oriented and the entrepreneurial subunits. While technologically simple, architectural innovations require fundamentally different linking structures, incentives, competencies, and cultures from the existing architecture (see Iansiti and Clark, 1994). Because of the difficulties of building linkage capabilities in the context of incremental innovation, architectural innovations are often not initiated by incumbent industry leaders (Brown and Eisenhardt, 1995; Henderson, 1995). Similarly, taking existing products to new markets must deal with the resistance of a firm's current customers

and existing resource-allocation processes. These sources of inertia often hold successful incumbents hostage to their pasts (Christensen, 1998; Rosenbloom and Christensen, 1994).

Although incremental, architectural, and discontinuous innovations require fundamentally different organizational architectures, to drive streams of innovation, these contrasting architectures must reside within a single business unit. Senior management's challenge is to build into a single organization multiple internally consistent organizational architectures that are themselves inconsistent from each other (see Figure 1.3). In ambidextrous organizations, single organizations host multiple cultures, structures, processes, management teams, and human resource capabilities to be incrementally innovative and, at the same time, create products that may make the existing product line obsolete (Bradach, 1997; Duncan, 1976; Tushman and O'Reilly, 1997).

Ambidextrous organizational forms build in organizational capabilities to simultaneously explore and exploit, to decrease variance as well as to increase variance at the same time. March (1991) suggested that organizational learning is accentuated when both exploitation and exploration are done simultaneously. Exploitation of knowledge extends existing knowledge, resulting in predictable, positive returns (at least in the short term.) In contrast, exploration is inherently experimental and often inconsistent with previous knowledge. Exploration accentuates variation, which is risky in the short term. Using a computer simulation that includes internal strategic pressure and external competitive pressure, March demonstrated the survival value of balancing these inconsistent learning modes.

Similarly, Burgelman (1991) identified contrasting learning modes in his field study of innovation at Intel. Induced strategic processes involve the continuation of current organizational strategy. These tended to be incremental changes, such as the continued development of memory chips. In contrast, autonomous strategic processes, which created the possibility of new products often to different customers, were typically outside the scope of the extant strategic initiative. Intel's senior team was less enthusiastic about funding these ventures because the uncertainty of market success was higher. Burgelman's analyses documented how innovation streams require fundamentally different learning modes that operate in parallel.

Ambidextrous organizations build in cultural, structural, and demographic contradictions. These internal contradictions are necessary if the organization is to be able to produce streams of innovations. Yet these contradictions create instability and conflict among the different organizational units—between the historically profitable, large, efficient, older, cash-generating units and the young, entrepreneurial, experimental, cash-absorbing units. Because the power, resources, and traditions of organizations are usually anchored in the older, more traditional units, these units usually work to ignore, sabotage, or otherwise trample entrepreneurial units (Cooper and Smith, 1992; Leonard-Barton, 1992; Miller, 1994; Morone, 1993; Hamel and Prahalad, 1994). Independent of the firm's boundary, ambidextrous organizations require subunits that are highly differentiated, weakly linked internally, but tightly integrated through the senior team (Tushman and O'Reilly, 1997).

The certainty of today's incremental advance often works to destroy the potential of tomorrow's architectural, market, or discontinuous advance. For example, Tripsas and Gavetti's (2000) inductive analysis of

Polaroid's experience with digital cameras documented the senior team's difficulties in building these complex organizational forms. As the market leader in the instant-photography industry, Polaroid developed incremental innovations of its hallmark SX-70 instant camera (e.g., improving the photo-quality subsystem), while it sought new markets with digital imaging cameras. Such a discontinuous innovation had the potential to disrupt Polaroid's exiting film/analog franchise. The incremental improvements in the instant camera occurred within an existing organizational structure, while the development of the digital camera technology occurred in its own separate laboratory, with 90 percent of its employees hired new for this project. Although the products and technology were available, Polaroid's senior team was unable to take the strategic actions to capitalize on their digital investments. Because Polaroid's senior team was unable to change their organizational, strategic, and cognitive models, Polaroid remained trapped in its historically rooted analog market.

Given the inertial, defensive, and political dynamics that exist in successful organizations, senior management teams must not only separate, protect, and legitimate entrepreneurial units, they must also make the strategic and organizational decisions to take advantage of this internal and/or external experimentation. While ambidextrous organizational forms can enhance dynamic organizational capabilities, they are difficult to implement. In industry after industry, either exploitation drives out exploration or today's customer trumps tomorrow's. To drive innovation streams, senior teams must build in and sustain internally inconsistent architectures even as they are the locus of strategic integration.

AMBIDEXTROUS SENIOR MANAGEMENT TEAMS

Strategic integration across innovation streams is anchored in a senior team's understanding of these innovation and organizational dynamics and their symbolic and substantive actions (Tripsas and Gavetti, 2000; Pfeffer, 1981). Internal structural heterogeneity provides the senior team with the ability to improvise in the present even as it experiments for the future (Gavetti and Levinthal, 2000; Brown and Eisenhardt,

1998; Iansiti and Clark, 1994). If these diverse capabilities can be integrated, they permit the organization to innovate for both today and tomorrow, but without integration, the potential of an ambidextrous organization is lost.

A clear, emotionally engaging vision provides a strategic anchor from which senior teams can balance the contrasting requirements of innovation streams (Hamel and Prahalad, 1994; Collins and Porras, 1994). Simple, direct competitive visions create a point of clarity within which an organization can simultaneously host incremental and discontinuous innovations (Nonaka, 1988; Hurst, 1995). Sustained, consistent commitment to a unit's vision, even when strategies and objectives change, reinforces that vision. Commitment is further reinforced by senior management's continuity and by its consistent behaviors in support of the vision (Pfeffer and Sutton, 2000). Through such clarity and consistency of vision, the senior team can support the internally contradictory organizational architectures that are associated with ambidextrous organizations and still be seen as consistent and credible. For example, in Ciba's Crop Protection Division, the senior team's aspiration of "keeping crops healthy" permitted the division to work simultaneously on chemical and biological technical trajectories.

The senior team's composition and demography and its ways of working together are also powerful tools for achieving integration in ambidextrous organizations (Hambrick, 1998). A study of the top management teams in twenty-four firms in the electronic industry suggested that homogeneity in age and tenure but heterogeneity in expertise in top management teams lead to more positive team dynamics and an increased ability to make adaptive changes (O'Reilly, Snyder, and Booth, 1993). While there are benefits in the continuity of senior management, there are also benefits in creating highly heterogeneous, demographically young senior teams. Such teams have the benefit of consistency in vision from the top, along with the ability to import new team members with different competencies and expertise (Smith et al., 1994; Virany, Tushman, and Romanelli, 1992). For example, as Microsoft grew, Bill Gates broadened his senior team with managers from outside Microsoft who had marketing, organizational, and technical skills (Cusumano and Selby, 1995).

Highly effective senior teams have diverse competencies to handle the contrasting innovation demands of ambidextrous organizations. In contrast, senior teams that are demographically old and homogeneous are typically dominated by historically anchored perspectives and simple cognitive models (Milliken and Lant, 1991; Miller, 1994). Inertial senior teams get stuck in routinized processes and are unable to deal with the contrasting demands imposed by innovation streams (Hambrick and D'Aveny, 1988; Boeker, 1989; Louis and Sutton, 1989). An organization can develop diverse senior team competencies by importing executives from outside the firm, by creating diverse career experiences internally, by building heterogeneous teams within the organization, and often by encouraging turnover in the executive team (Hambrick, 1994, 1998; Zajac and Westphal, 1996).

Effective senior teams are also able to work together in a way that takes advantage of their internal differences. They have internal processes that enable them to handle greater information and alternative decisions and to deal with diverse points of view and contrasting opinions (Edmondson, 1999; Eisenhardt, 1989). In a survey of fifty-three management teams, Smith et al. (1994) demonstrated that senior team processes, such as formal communication, informal communication, and social integration, have an impact upon the senior team's successful performance independent of the demographics of the senior team. Diverse, self-critical senior teams with effective group processes not only get their own work accomplished, but model appropriate ways to deal with conflict and cross-cutting priorities in the larger organization. In contrast, senior teams that send mixed messages, that cannot resolve their own conflicts, and that do not collaborate internally create highly unstable, politically chaotic organizations (Williams and O'Reilly, 1998; Pfeffer and Sutton, 2000).

Finally, senior management teams can create formal roles, structures, processes, and rewards to facilitate strategic integration. Particularly for architectural innovation, the development roles and formal linking mechanisms encourage integration within the senior team and across diverse parts of the organization. Team-based rewards that measure and value diverse types of innovation and collaborative team behaviors motivate team members to work together (Nadler and Tushman, 1997; Iansiti and Clark, 1994; Brown and Eisenhardt, 1995).

INNOVATION STREAMS
AND DISCONTINUOUS
ORGANIZATIONAL CHANGE

Within ambidextrous organizations, entrepreneurial units provide learning-by-doing data, variation, and luck to drive possible new dominant designs, architectural innovations, and/or product substitutions. Whether done internally, through alliances or acquisitions, the senior team can learn about alternative futures from these entrepreneurial units. In contrast, the more mature units drive sustained incremental innovation and short-term learning. The senior management team can then draw upon these diverse types of innovation and learning to make strategic decisions—when to initiate a dominant design, when to move on new customers, what product variant to bet on, when to initiate an architectural innovation, and/or when to introduce a product substitute.

The success of strategic choices of dominant designs, new customers, architectural innovation, and/or product substitutes is known only after the fact. Through building ambidextrous organizational capabilities, the senior management team maximizes the probability that they will have both the expertise and the luck from which to make industry-shaping decisions proactively rather than reactively. Ambidextrous organizations create options from which the senior team makes informed bets on the future (Burgelman and Grove, 1996; McGrath, 1999). While correct strategic bets can be known only in retrospect, managerial action within the firm—and with collaborators, alliance partners, and governmental agencies—can affect the ultimate closing on an industry standard or the success of a product substitute (Teece, 1987; Rosenkopf and Tushman, 1998; Cusumano and Yoffee, 1998).

At the closing of a dominant design, the strategic innovation requirements within the firm shift from a focus on major product variation to major process innovation and then to sustained incremental innovation (Abernathy and Clark, 1985; Utterback, 1994). At product-substitution events, for architectural innovations, and/or for taking an existing product to new markets, strategic management shifts from incremental innovation to major product, market, or architectural innovation. As strategic innovation requirements shift at these junctures, so, too, must the dominant organizational capabilities (Sorensen and Stuart, 2000). The organizational architectures—structures, roles, cultures, processes, and competencies—that were appropriate during eras of ferment are no longer appropriate during eras of incremental change. Similarly, the organizational architectures that were appropriate during eras of incremental change are no longer appropriate during eras of ferment (Foster, 1987; Benner and Tushman, 2000).

Because structural and social inertia are so powerful, managers can attempt to rewrite their industry's rules only if they are willing to rewrite their organization's rules. At these strategic junctures, shifts in a firm's innovation stream can be executed only through discontinuous organizational change (Tushman and Romanelli, 1985; Greenwood and Hinnings, 1993; Miller, 1994; Rosenbloom, 2000). For example, IBM's 360 decision in mainframes was coupled with sweeping shifts in IBM's structure, controls, systems, and culture. In contrast, bold strategic moves or great technology that is uncoupled from organizational capabilities leads to underperformance (Tripsas and Gavetti, 2000; Virany, Tushman, and Romanelli, 1992). Similarly, Sony's superior Beta technology format was unable to counter JVC's combination of an adequate VHS technology, coupled with brilliant organizational capabilities and strategic alliances (Cusumano, Mylonadis, and Rosenbloom, 1992). Innovation streams then, are, rooted as much in reconfigured organizational architectures as in technological prowess (Sull, 1999; Rosenbloom and Christensen, 1994; Rosenbloom, 2000).

Innovation streams and the associated framebreaking organizational changes are often initiated by transformed senior teams (Meyer, Brooks, and Goes, 1990; Ancona, 1990; Virany, Tushman, and Romanelli, 1992; Romanelli and Tushman, 1994). While reorientations are risky and often done incompetently (see, e.g., Carroll and Teo, 1996; Henderson, 1993), persistence in the face of a changing innovation stream is even more so. Furthermore, if strategic reorientations are not done proactively, they have to be done reactively—as with Burroughs in mainframes, SSIH in watches, Polaroid in digital cameras, and Oticon in hearing aids. Reactive reorientations (turnarounds) are more risky than are proactive reorientations because they must be implemented under crisis conditions and under considerable time pressure (Hambrick, Nadler, and Tushman, 1998).

Senior management's challenge in leading discontinuous change is fundamentally different from its challenge in leading incremental change (Weick and Quinn, 1999). Senior teams must build the capabilities to manage both if they are to manage effectively across an innovation stream (Nadler, Shaw, and Walton, 1995; Barnett and Carroll, 1995). Those more effective discontinuous changes are initiated and directed by the senior team, are shaped by an integrated agenda for change, and are rapidly implemented—driven by the senior team's vision and consistent actions (Nadler, 1998). These challenges are often associated with shifts in the senior team and within middle management (Kanter, Stein, and Jick, 1992; Pettigrew, 1985).

If implemented through incremental change methods, reorientations run the risk of being sabotaged by the politics, structures, and competencies of the status quo (Virany, Tushman, and Romanelli, 1992; Kearns and Nadler, 1992). For example, in Ciba's Crop Protection Division, the transition from fundamentally different fungicides to EC-50 (Ciba's bet on a dominant design) was executed through sweeping changes in the division and through a new fungicide team. In contrast, breakthrough innovations at Xerox in the late 1970s and early 1980s and Polaroid in the 1990s were not coupled with corresponding organizational shifts. The politics of stability held Xerox and Polaroid hostage to their pasts (Smith and Alexander, 1990; Tripsas and Gavetti, 2000).

Managing innovation streams is about managing internal paradoxes in the context of innovation streams: managing efficiency *and* innovation, tactical *and* strategic, incremental *and* discontinuous, today *and* tomorrow (Gavetti and Levinthal, 2000; Brown and Eisenhardt, 1998; Quinn and Cameron, 1988). Managing innovation streams is about consistency and control, as well as variability, learning by doing, and the cultivation of luck. It is the crucial role of the senior team to embrace these contradictions and take advantage of the tensions and synergies that emerge from juggling multiple competencies simultaneously (Van de Ven, Angle, and Poole, 1988; Hurst, 1995; Tushman and O'Reilly, 1997). It is the senior team's role to bind these paradoxical requirements together through their substantive and symbolic actions.

CONCLUSION

Even if periods of incremental change do build organizational inertia, organizations can create and shape innovation streams. Through building ambidextrous organizational forms and creating options from which

the senior team initiates proactive strategic change, organizations can manage the rhythm by which each expiring strength gives birth to its successor. Prior organizational competencies provide a platform so that the next phase of an organization's evolution does not start from ground zero; evolution involves, then, learning as well as unlearning (Weick, 1979). Organizations can renew themselves through a series of proactive strategic reorientations that are anchored by a common vision. Like a dying vine, the prior period of incremental change provides the compost for its own seeds, its own variants, to thrive following a reorientation in the subsequent period of incremental change.

In this review, we have taken a strong point of view on organizational evolution. Since dynamic capabilities are not rooted in technology cycles, organizational architectures, senior teams, or change dynamics alone, our understanding of the nature of dynamic capabilities must be rooted in a deep understanding of these modules of evolution and how they interact with each other. Yet each module is open to much debate—the nature of technology cycles, the nature of organizational architecture, the role of senior teams, and the nature of organizational change are all contested domains. Yet this energy is well founded, for these issues are both professionally interesting and managerially crucial. There is a significant opportunity, therefore, in digging deeply into those controversies in technology cycles, organizational architectures, senior teams and change, and perhaps even more so in building integrative theory and research across these interdependent domains.

ACKNOWLEDGMENTS

We thank Lori Rosenkopf, Mary Tripsas, and Joel Baum for their reviews and critical comments.

REFERENCES

Abernathy, W. *The Productivity Dilemma.* Baltimore: Johns Hopkins University Press, 1978.

Abernathy, W., and K. Clark. "Innovation: Mapping the Winds of Creative Destruction." *Research Policy* 14 (1985): 3–22.

Aitken, H. *The Continuous Wave.* Princeton, N.J.: Princeton University Press, 1985.

Aldrich, H. *Organizations Evolving.* London: Sage Publications, 1999.

Ancona, D. "Top Management Teams: Preparing for the Revolution." In *Applied Social Psychology and Organizational Settings,* edited by J. Carroll, 99–128. Hillsdale, N.J.: Lawrence Erlbaum Associates, 1990.

Anderson, P., and M. Tushman. "Technological Discontinuities and Dominant Designs: A Cyclical Model of Technological Change." *Administrative Science Quarterly* 35 (1990): 604–633.

Baldwin, C., and K. Clark. *Design Rules: The Power of Modularity.* Cambridge, Mass.: MIT Press, 2000.

Barnett, W., and G. Carroll. "Modeling Internal Organization Change." *American Review of Sociology* 21 (1995): 217–236.

Baum, J., H. Korn, and S. Kotha. "Dominant Designs and Population Dynamics in Telecommunications Services." *Social Science Research* 24 (1995): 97–135.

Baum, J., T. Calabrese, and B. S. Silverman. "Don't Go It Alone: Alliance Networks and Startup Performance in Canadian Biotechnology." *Strategic Management Journal* 21, no. 3 (2000): 267–294.

Benner, M., and M. Tushman. "Process Management and Organizational Adaptation: The Productivity Dilemma Revisited." Working Paper. Boston: Harvard Business School Press, 2000.

Bijker, W., T. Hughes, and T. Pinch. *The Social Construction of Technological Systems.* Cambridge, Mass.: MIT Press, 1987.

Boeker, W. "Strategic Change: Effects of Founding and History." *Academy of Management Journal* 32 (1989): 489–515.

Bradach, J. "Using the Plural Form in the Management of Restaurant Chains." *Administrative Science Quarterly* 42 (1997): 276–303.

Brown, S., and K. Eisenhardt. "Product Development: Past Research, Present Findings and Future Directions." *Academy of Management Review* 20 (1995): 343–378.

Brown, S., and K. Eisenhardt. *Competing on the Edge: Strategy as Structured Chaos.* Boston: Harvard Business School Press, 1998.

Burgelman, R. "Intraorganizational Ecology of Strategy Making and Organizational Adaptation." *Organization Science* 2 (1991): 239–262.

Burgelman, R. "Fading Memories: A Process Theory of Strategic Business Exit." *Administrative Science Quarterly* 39 (1994): 24–56.

Burgelman, R., and A. Grove. "Strategic Dissonance." *California Management Review* 38 (1996): 8–28.

Burns, T., and G. Stalker. *The Management of Innovation.* London: Tavistock, 1961.

Carroll, G., and M. Hannan. *The Demography of Corporations and Industries.* Princeton, N.J.: Princeton University Press, 2000.

Carroll, G., and A. Teo. "Creative Self Destruction Among Organizations: An Empirical *Study* of Technical Innovation and Organizational Failure in the American Automobile Industry, 1885–1981." *Industrial and Corporate Change* 5, no. 2 (1996): 619–643.

Chatman, J., and S. Barsade. "Personality, Organizational Culture, and Cooperation." *Administrative Science Quarterly* 40 (1995): 423–443.

Chesbrough, H. "The Organizational Impact of Technological Change: A Comparative Theory of National Factors." *Industrial and Corporate Change* 8, no. 3 (1999): 447–485.

Christensen, C. *The Innovator's Dilemma.* Boston: Harvard Business School Press, 1998.

Christensen, C., and J. Bower. "Customer Power, Strategic Investment, and the Failure of Leading Firms." *Strategic Management Journal* 17 (1996): 197–218.

Christensen, C., and M. Overdorf "Meeting the Challenge of Disruptive Change." *Harvard Business Review* 78, no. 2 (2000): 66–77.

Christensen, C., F. Suarez, and J. Utterback. "Strategies for Survival in Fast-Changing Industries." *Management Science* 44, no. 12 (1998): S207–S220.

Clark, K. "The Interaction of Design Hierarchies and Market Concepts on Technological Evolution." *Research Policy* 14 (1985): 235–251.

Collins, J., and J. Porras. *Built to Last.* New York: Harper Business, 1994.

Cooper, A., and C. Smith. "How Established Firms Respond to Threatening Technologies." *Academy of Management Executive* 6, no. 2 (1992): 55–70.

Cusumano, M., Y. Mylonadis, and R. Rosenbloom. "Strategic Maneuvering and Mass Market Dynamics: The Triumph of VHS over Beta." *Business History Review* 66, no. 1 (1992): 51–93.

Cusumano, M., and R. Selby. *Microsoft Secrets.* New York: Free Press, 1995.

Cusumano, M., and D. Yoffee. *Competing on Internet Time.* New York: Free Press, 1998.

Duncan, R. "The Ambidextrous Organization: Designing Dual Structures for Innovation." In *The Management of Organizational Design,* edited by R. Kilman and L. Pondy, 167–188. New York: North Holland, 1976.

Edmondson, A. "Psychological Safety and Learning Behavior in Work Teams." *Administrative Science Quarterly* 44, no. 4 (1999): 350–383.

Ehrenberg, E. "On the Definition and Measurement of Technological Discontinuities." *Technomation* 5 (1995): 437–452.

Eisenhardt, K. "Making Fast Strategic Decisions in High Velocity Environments." *Academy of Management Journal* 32 (1989): 543–576.

Eisenhardt, K., and B. Tabrizi. "Acceleration Adaptive Processes." *Administrative Science Quarterly* 40 (1995): 84–110.

Finkelstein, S., and D. Hambrick. *Strategic Leadership: Top Executives and Their Effect on Organizations.* New York: West, 1996.

Foster, R. *Innovation: The Attacker's Advantage.* New York: Summit Books, 1987.

Galunic, C., and K. Eisenhardt. "Reviewing the Strategy-Structures-Performance Paradigm." In *Research in Organizational Behavior,* edited by B. Staw and L. Cummings, 255–282. Greenwich, Conn.: JAI Press, 1994.

Garud, R., and D. Ahlstrom. "Technology Assessment: A Socio-cognitive Perspective." *Journal of Engineering and Technology Management* 14, no. 1 (1997): 25–50.

Gatignon, H., M. Tushman, P. Anderson, and W. Smith "A Structural Approach to Measuring Innovation." Working Paper. Boston: Harvard Business School, 2000.

Gavetti, G., and D. Levinthal. "Looking Forward and Looking Backward: Cognitive and Experiential Search." *Administrative Science Quarterly* 45 (2000): 113–137.

Glassmier, A. "Technological Discontinuities and Flexible Production Networks: The Case of Switzerland and the World Watch Industry." *Research Policy* 20 (1991): 469–485.

Greenwood, R., and H. R. Hinnings. "Understanding Strategic Change." *Academy of Management Journal* 6 (1993): 1052–1081.

Grove, A. *Only the Paranoid Survive: How to Exploit the Crisis Points That Challenge Every Company and Career.* New York: Currency Doubleday, 1996.

Hambrick, D. "Top Management Groups: A Reconsideration of the Team Label." In *Research in Organizational Behavior,* edited by B. Staw and L. Cummings, 171–214. Greenwich, Conn.: JAI Press, 1994.

Hambrick, D. "Corporate Coherence and the Top Team." In *Navigating Change,* edited by D. Hambrick, D. Nadler, and M. Tushman, 123–140. Boston: Harvard Business School Press, 1998.

Hambrick, D., and R. D'Aveni. "Large Corporate Failures as Downward Spirals." *Administrative Science Quarterly,* 33 (1988): 1–23.

Hambrick, D., D. Nadler, and M. Tushman, eds. *Navigating Change.* Boston: Harvard Business School Press, 1998.

Hamel, G., and C. Prahalad. *Competing for the Future.* Boston: Harvard Business School Press, 1994.

Henderson, R. "Underinvestment and Incompetence as Responses to Radical Innovation: Evidence from the Photolithographic Alignment Equipment Industry." *Rand Journal of Economics* 24 (1993): 248–269.

Henderson, R. "Of Life Cycles Real and Imaginary: The Unexpectedly Long Old Age of Optical Lithography." *Research Policy* 24 (1995): 631–643.

Henderson, R., and K. Clark. "Architectural Innovation: The Reconfiguration of Existing Product Technologies and the Failure of Established Firms." *Administrative Science Quarterly* 35 (1990): 9–30.

Hollander, S. *Sources of Efficiency.* Cambridge, Mass.: MIT Press, 1965.

House, R., W. Spangler, and J. Wyocke. "Personality and Charisma in the U.S. Presidency." *Administrative Science Quarterly* 36 (1991): 364–396.

Hughes, T. *Networks of Power.* Baltimore: Johns Hopkins University Press, 1983.

Hunt, C., and H. Aldrich. "The Second Ecology: The Creation and Evolution of Organizational Communities in the World Wide Web." In *Research in Organizational Behavior,* edited by B. Staw and L. Cummings, Vol. 20, 267–302. Greenwich, Conn.: JAI Press, 1998.

Hurst, D. *Crisis and Renewal.* Boston: Harvard Business School Press, 1995.

Iansiti, M., and K. Clark. "Integration and Dynamic Capability." *Industry and Corporation Change* 3 (1994): 557–606.

Imai, K., I. Nonaka, and H. Takeuchi. "Managing the New Product Development Process: How Japanese Firms Learn and Unlearn." In *The Uneasy Alliance,* edited by K. B. Clark, R. H. Hayes, and C. Lorenz, 337–376. Boston: Harvard Business School Press, 1985.

Kanter, R., B. Stein, and T. Jick. *The Challenge of Organizational Change.* New York: Free Press, 1992.

Kearns, D., and D. Nadler. *Prophets in the Dark.* New York: Harper, 1992.

Kets de Vries, M. "Vicissitudes of Leadership." In *Navigating Change,* edited by D. Hambrick, D. Naylor, and M. Tushman, 38–69. Boston, Mass.: Harvard Business School Press, 1998.

Klepper, S. "Entry, Exit, Growth, and Innovation over the Product Life Cycle" *American Economic Review,* 86 (1996): 562–583.

Klepper, S., and S. Sleeper. "Entry by Spinoffs." Working Paper. Pittsburgh, Penn.: Carnegie Mellon, 2000.

Landes, D. *Revolution in Time.* Cambridge, Mass.: Harvard University Press, 1983.

Leonard-Barton, D. "Core Capabilities and Core Rigidities: A Paradox in Managing New Product Development." *Strategic Management Journal* 13 (1992): 111–125.

Leonard-Barton, D. *Wellsprings of Knowledge.* Boston, Mass.: Harvard Business School Press, 1995.

Levinthal, D. "Three Faces of Organizational Learning: Wisdom, Inertia, and Discovery." In *Technological Innovation: Oversights and Foresights,* edited by R. Garud, P. Nayyar, and Z. Shapira, 167–180. Cambridge, England: Cambridge University Press, 1997.

Levitt, B., and J. March. "Organization Learning." *American Review of Sociology* 14 (1988): 319–340.

Louis, M., and R. Sutton. "Switching Cognitive Gears: From Habits of Mind to Active Thinking." In *Advances in Organizational Sociology,* edited by S. Bacharach, 55–76. Greenwich, Conn.: JAI Press, 1989.

March, J. "Exploration and Exploitation in Organizational Learning." *Organization Science* 2 (1991): 71–87.

McGrath, R. "Falling Forward: Real Options Reasoning and Entrepreneurial Failure." *Academy of Management Review* 24 (1999): 13–30.

McGrath, R., and I. MacMillan. *The Entrepreneurial Mindset: Strategies for Continuously Creating Opportunity in an Age of Uncertainty.* Boston: Harvard Business School Press, 2000.

Meyer, A., G. Brooks, and J. Goes. "Environmental Jolts and Industry Revolutions." *Strategic Management Journal* 11 (1990): 93–110.

Miller, D. "What Happens After Success: The Perils of Excellence" *Journal of Management Studies* 31, no. 3 (1994): 325–358.

Milliken, F., and T. Lant. "The Effect of an Organization's Recent History on Strategic Persistence and Change." In *Advances in Strategic Management,* Vol. 7, edited by J. Dutton, A. Huff, and P. Shrivastava, 129–156. Greenwich, Conn.: JAI Press, 1991.

Miner, A., and P. Haunschild, "Population Level Learning." In *Research in Organizational Behavior,* edited by B. Staw and L. Cummings, 115–166. Greenwich, Conn.: JAI Press, 1995.

Morison, E. *Men, Machines, and Modern Times.* Cambridge, Mass.: MIT Press, 1966.

Morone, J. *Winning in High Tech Markets.* Boston: Harvard Business School Press, 1993.

Myers, S., and D. Marquis. *Successful Industrial Innovation.* Washington, D.C.: National Science Foundation, 1969.

Nadler, D. *Champions of Change.* San Francisco: Jossey-Bass, 1998.

Nadler, D., R. Shaw, and E. Walton, *Discontinuous Change.* San Francisco: Jossey-Bass, 1995.

Nadler, D., and M. Tushman. *Competing by Design: The Power of Organizational Architectures.* New York: Oxford University Press, 1997.

Nelson, R. "The Co-evolution of Technology, Industrial Structure, and Supporting Institutions." *Industrial and Corporate Change* 3, no. 1 (1994): 47–63.

Nelson, R. "Recent Evolutionary Theorizing About Economic Change." *Journal of Economic Literature* 33 (1995): 48–90.

Noble, D. *Forces of Production.* New York: Alfred A. Knopf, 1984.

Nonaka, I. "Creating Order Out of Chaos: Self-Renewal in Japanese Firms." *California Management Review* 3 (1988): 57–73.

Nonaka, I., and H. Takeuchi. *The Knowledge Creating Company.* New York: Oxford University Press, 1995.

O'Reilly, C., R. Snyder, and J. Booth. "Effects of Executive Team Demography and Organizational Change." In *Organizational Design and Change,* edited by G. Huber and W. Glick, 147–175. New York: Oxford University Press, 1993.

Pettigrew, A. *The Awakening Giant: Continuity and Change at ICI.* Oxford, England: Blackwell, 1985.

Pfeffer, J. "Management as Symbolic Action." In *Research in Organizational Behavior,* Vol. 3, edited by L. Cummings and B. Staw, 1–52. Greenwich, Conn.: JAI Press, 1981.

Pfeffer, J., and R. Sutton. *The Knowing-Doing Gap.* Boston: Harvard Business School Press, 2000.

Pinch, T., and W. Bijker. "The Social Construction of Facts and Artifacts." In *The Social Construction of Technological Systems,* edited by W. Bijker, T. Hughes, and T. Pinch, 17–50. Cambridge, Mass.: MIT Press, 1987.

Podolny, J., and T. Stuart. "A Role Based Ecology of Technological Change." *American Journal of Sociology* 100, no. 5 (1995): 1224–1260.

Powell, W., K. Koput, and L. Doerr. "Interorganizational Collaboration and the Locus of Innovation." *Administrative Science Quarterly* 41 (1996): 116–145.

Quinn, J. B. *Intelligent Enterprise.* New York: Free Press, 1992.

Quinn, R., and K. Cameron. *Paradox and Transformation.* Cambridge, Mass.: Ballinger, Publications, 1988.

Rajagopalan, N., and G. Spreitzer. "Toward a Theory of Strategic Change." *Academy of Management Review* 22, no. 1 (1997): 48–79.

Roberts, E., and C. Berry. "Entering New Businesses: Selecting Strategies for Success." *Sloan Management Review* 26, no. 3 (1985): 3–17.

Romanelli, E., and M. Tushman. "Organization Transformation as Punctuated Equilibrium." *Academy of Management Journal* 37 (1994): 1141–1166.

Rosenbloom, D., and C. Christensen. "Technological Discontinuities, Organization Capabilities, and Strategic Commitments." *Industry and Corporate Change* 3 (1994): 655–686.

Rosenbloom, R. "Leadership, Capabilities, and Technological Change: The Transformation of NCR." *Strategic Management Journal* 21 (2000): 1083–1103.

Rosenkopf, L., and M. Tushman. "The Coevolution of Technology and Organization." In *Evolutionary Dynamics of Organizations,* edited by J. Baum and J. Singh, 403–424. New York: Oxford University Press, 1994.

Rosenkopf, L., and M. Tushman. "The Co-evolution of Community Networks and Technology: Lessons from the Flight Simulation Industry." *Industrial and Corporate Change* 7 (1998): 311–346.

Sanderson, S., and M. Uzumeri. "Product Platforms and Dominant Designs: The Case of Sony's Walkman." *Research Policy* 24 (1995): 583–607.

Sastry, A. "Problems and Paradoxes in a Model of Punctuated Organizational Change." *Administrative Science Quarterly* 42 (1997): 237–277.

Schilling, M. "Toward a General Modular Systems Theory and Its Application to Interfirm Product Modularity." *Academy of Management Review* 25 (2000): 312–334.

Silverman, B. S. "Technological Resources and the Direction of Corporate Diversification: Toward an Integration of the Resource-Based View and Transaction Cost Economics." *Management Science* 45, no. 8 (1999): 1109–1124.

Smith, D., and R. Alexander. *Fumbling the Future*. New York: Harper, 1990.

Smith, K., J. Olian, H. Sims, and J. Scully. "Top Management Team Demography and Process." *Administrative Science Quarterly* 49 (1994): 412–438.

Sorensen, J., and T. Stuart. "Aging, Obsolescence, and Organizational Innovation." *Administrative Science Quarterly* 45 (2000): 81–112.

Stuart, T. "A Structural Perspective on Organizational Innovation." *Industrial and Corporate Change* 8 (1999): 745–775.

Sull, D. "The Dynamics of Standing Still: Firestone and the Radial Revolution." *Business History Review* 73 (1999): 430–464.

Sull, D., R. Tedlow, and R. Rosenbloom. "Managerial Commitments and Technology Change in the U.S. Tire Industry." *Industrial and Corporate Change* 6 (1997): 461–500.

Teece, D. "Profiting from Technological Innovation." In *The Competitive Challenge*, edited by D. Teece, 185–219. New York: Harper & Row, 1987.

Teece, D. "Firm Organization, Industrial Structure, and Technological Innovation." *Journal of Economic Behavior and Organizations* 31 (1996): 193–224.

Tegarden L., D. Hatfield, and A. Echols. "Doomed from the Start: What Is the Value of Selecting a Future Dominant Design?" *Strategic Management Journal* 20 (1999): 495–518.

Tripsas, M. "Unraveling the Process of Creative Destruction: Complementary Assets and Incumbent Survival in the Typesetter Industry." *Strategic Management Journal* 20 (1999): 119–142.

Tripsas, M., and G. Gavetti. "Capabilities, Cognition, and Inertia: Evidence from Digital Imaging." *Strategic Management Journal* 21 (2000): 1147–1161.

Tushman, M., and P. Anderson. "Technological Discontinuities and Organization Environments." *Administrative Science Quarterly* 31 (1986): 439–465.

Tushman, M., and J. Murmann. "Dominant Designs, Technology Cycles, and Organizational Outcomes." In *Research in Organizational Behavior*, Vol. 20, edited by B. Staw and L. Cummings, 213–266. Greenwich, Conn.: JAI Press, 1998.

Tushman, M., and R. Nelson. "Technology, Organizations, and Innovation: An Introduction." *Administrative Science Quarterly* 35 (1990): 1–8.

Tushman, M., and C. O'Reilly. *Winning Through Innovation*. Boston: Harvard Business School Press, 1997.

Tushman, M., and E. Romanelli. "Organizational Evolution: A Metamorphosis Model of Convergence and Reorientation." In *Research in Organizational Behavior*, Vol. 7, edited by B. Staw and L. Cummings, 171–222. Greenwich, Conn.: JAI Press, 1985.

Tushman, M., and L. Rosenkopf. "On the Organizational Determinants of Technological Change: Towards a Sociology of Technological Evolution." In *Research in Organizational Behavior*, Vol. 14, edited by B. Staw and L. Cummings, 311–347. Greenwich, Conn.: JAI Press, 1992.

Ulrich, K., and S. Eppinger. *Product Design and Development*. New York: McGraw-Hill, 1995.

Utterback, J. *Mastering the Dynamics of Innovation*. Boston: Harvard Business School Press, 1994.

Van de Ven, A., and R. Garud. "The Coevolution of Technical and Institutional Events in the Development of an Innovation." In *Evolutionary Dynamics of Organization*, edited by J. Baum and J. Singh, 425–443. New York: Oxford University Press, 1994.

Van de Ven, A., H. Angle, and M. Poole. *Research on the Management of Innovation*. New York: Harper, 1988.

Virany, B., M. Tushman, and E. Romanelli. "Executive Succession and Organization Outcomes in Turbulent Environments." *Organization Science* 3 (1992): 72–92.

Weick, K. *The Social Psychology of Organizing*. Reading, Mass.: Addison-Wesley, 1979.

Weick, K., and R. Quinn. "Organizational Change and Development." *Annual Review of Psychology* 50 (1999): 361–386.

West, J. "Institutions, Information Processing, and Organization Structure in R&D." *Research Policy* 29 (2000): 349–373.

Williams, K., and C. O'Reilly. "Demography and Diversity in Organizations: A Review of Forty Years of Research." In *Research in Organizational Behavior*, Vol. 20, edited by B. Staw and L. Cummings, 77–140. Greenwich, Conn.: JAI Press, 1998.

Zajac, E., and J. Westphal. "Who Shall Succeed? How CEO Board Preferences Affect the Choice of New CPO's." *Academy of Management Journal* 39: (1996): 64–90.

2

Capabilities, Cognition, and Inertia
Evidence from Digital Imaging

MARY TRIPSAS
GIOVANNI GAVETTI

There is empirical evidence that established firms often have difficulty adapting to radical technological change. Although prior work in the evolutionary tradition emphasizes the inertial forces associated with the local nature of learning processes, little theoretical attention has been devoted in this tradition to understanding how managerial cognition affects the adaptive intelligence of organizations. Through an in-depth case study of the response of the Polaroid Corporation to the ongoing shift from analog to digital imaging, we expand upon this work by examining the relationship between managers' understanding of the world and the accumulation of organizational capabilities. The Polaroid story clearly illustrates the importance of managerial cognitive representations in directing search processes in a new learning environment, the evolutionary trajectory of organizational capabilities, and ultimately processes of organizational adaptation.

INTRODUCTION

Organizational change is difficult. Even when established firms recognize the need to change in response to shifts in their external environment, they are often unable to respond effectively. Technological change has proven particularly deadly for established firms, with numerous examples of established firm failure in the face of radical technological change (Cooper and Schendel, 1976; Majumdar, 1982; Tushman and Anderson, 1986; Henderson and Clark, 1990; Utterback, 1994; Tushman and O'Reilly, 1996; Christensen, 1997). Existing explanations for failure to adapt to radically new technology have focused on the nature of a firm's capabilities.[1] In this paper we expand upon this work by examining how managerial cognition influences the evolution of capabilities and thus contributes to organizational inertia.

In the tradition of evolutionary economics, much research has focused on how existing technological capabilities, codified in the routines, procedures, and information processing capabilities of the firm, limit its adaptive intelligence (Arrow, 1974; Nelson and Winter, 1982; Teece, Pisano, and Shuen, 1997). A firm's prior history constrains its future behavior in that learning tends to be premised on local processes of search (March and Simon, 1958; Levitt and March, 1988; Teece, 1988). When learning needs to be distant, and radically new capabilities need to be developed, firms often fall into competency traps, as core competencies become "core rigidities" (Leonard-Barton, 1992). A firm's nontechnological assets also influence

Reprinted from *Strategic Management Journal,* Vol. 21, Mary Tripsas and Giovanni Gavetti, "Capabilities, Cognition, and Inertia: Evidence from Digital Imaging," pp. 1147–1161, copyright © 2000. Reproduced by permission of John Wiley & Sons Limited.

the direction of its technological trajectory (Dosi, 1982). Firms are more likely to develop technologies that can utilize existing complementary assets—assets essential for the commercialization of the technology (Teece, 1986; Helfat, 1997). For instance, a firm's existing marketing capability, particularly its knowledge of customers, makes it more likely to develop technologies that appeal to existing customers as opposed to a new set of customers (Christensen, 1997).

Empirical evidence supports the importance of capabilities in explaining incumbent inertia and subsequent failure. When a new technology is "competence destroying" in that it requires mastery of an entirely new scientific discipline, established firms are more likely to fail (Tushman and Anderson, 1986). More subtly, when a new technology destroys the "architectural knowledge" of the firm—knowledge about interfaces among product components—established firms also suffer (Henderson and Clark, 1990). Finally, when technological change destroys the value of a firm's existing complementary assets, the firm is more likely to fail (Mitchell, 1989; Tripsas, 1997).

While most innovation scholars have emphasized the role of capabilities, others have focused on the role of cognition in explaining organizational inertia (Garud and Rappa, 1994). Since managers are boundedly rational, they must rely on simplified representations of the world in order to process information (Simon, 1955). These imperfect representations form the basis for the development of the mental models and strategic beliefs that drive managerial decisions. They influence the manner in which managers frame problems and thus how they search for solutions.

Cognitive representations are typically based on historical experience as opposed to current knowledge of the environment (Kiesler and Sproull, 1982). For instance, as senior managers work together over time, they often develop a set of beliefs, or "dominant logic," for the firm based on their shared history (Prahalad and Bettis, 1986). These beliefs include a shared sense of who the relevant competitors are (Reger and Huff, 1993; Porac et al., 1995; Peteraf and Shanley, 1997). Firm founders also play a significant role in establishing beliefs, leaving their imprint on the organization long after their departure (Baron, Hannan, and Burton, 1999). Given the influence of the historical environment on the development of beliefs, in rapidly changing environments top managers often have difficulty

adapting their mental models, resulting in poor organizational performance (Barr, Stimpert, and Huff, 1992; Brown and Eisenhardt, 1998).

Our goal in this paper is to explore how the combination of capabilities and cognition helps to explain organizational inertia in the face of radical technological change. We focus on cognition at the level of the senior management team, given the critical influence of top management teams on strategic decision making (Mintzberg, 1979; Hambrick and Mason, 1984). We examine how managerial cognitive representations may play a central role in terms of constraining organizational behavior and, ultimately, the development of a firm's capabilities (Zyglidopoulos, 1999; Gavetti and Levinthal, 2000). In order to explore the relationship between capabilities, cognition, and inertia, we perform an in-depth historical case study of a firm undergoing a radical transition. We analyze how the Polaroid Corporation has responded to the ongoing shift from analog to digital imaging.[2] The firm provides a particularly compelling example in that, despite early investments and leading-edge technical capability in areas related to digital imaging, the firm has so far not performed well in the digital imaging market. We explore why Polaroid has had difficulty, with an emphasis on understanding the role of both capabilities and cognition in explaining organizational inertia.

We find that by restricting and directing search activities related to technology development, managerial cognition influences the development of new capability. For instance, given Polaroid senior management's belief in pursuing large-scale "impossible" technological advances, the firm made significant investments in developing technical capability related to digital imaging. At the same time, their belief in a razor/blade business model delayed commercialization of a stand-alone digital camera product. Understanding processes of organizational change thus requires examining not only the central inertial forces associated with developing new capabilities, but also the impact that cognition has on such processes.

METHODS AND DATA

This research is based on an in-depth, inductive case study of the Polaroid Corporation's historical involvement in digital imaging. Given the open-ended nature of our questions regarding the relationship among capabilities, cognition, and inertia, we felt that this approach would be most useful for theory building (Glaser and Strauss, 1967; Miles and Huberman, 1994; Yin, 1984). In addition, by taking a long-term historical perspective we gain insight into the evolutionary nature of both capabilities and cognition. A combination of public data, company archives, and interview data were collected on the evolution of Polaroid's activities related to both digital imaging and the traditional instant photography business.

Publicly available data included a complete set of historical annual reports, financial analyst reports, prior studies of Polaroid's history, and business press articles on both Polaroid and the digital imaging industry. We were greatly aided by extensive prior historical work on Edwin Land and Polaroid's position in instant photography (McElheny, 1998). Company archives supplemented publicly available data. Historical strategic plans, organization charts, internal memos, and technical papers helped to document the evolution of the organization.

Finally, we interviewed a sample of current and ex-Polaroid employees. Our sample varied along three dimensions. First, it included individuals from multiple levels of the organizational hierarchy. We interviewed ex-CEOs, other senior managers, mid-level project managers, and first-line research scientists and marketing specialists. Second, we included individuals from multiple functional areas. Research and development, marketing, and manufacturing were all represented in our sample. Third, we included individuals present at different points in Polaroid's history in order to understand how the organization had evolved. In many cases this process involved interviewing retired employees, as well as employees who had moved to other companies. We interviewed individuals present during the "Land era" (before 1980) as well as outsiders brought in at various points in time in order to facilitate digital imaging efforts. Every key manager involved in Polaroid's digital imaging efforts was contacted and interviewed. Some individuals were contacted multiple times as we worked through the iterative process of data collection and theory development. In total, we conducted 20 interviews with 15 individuals. We stopped interviewing/collecting material when a level of saturation was reached (Glaser and Strauss, 1967).

Interviews were open ended, but based on a common set of questions. Interviewees were first asked to discuss their specific role in the company, and how it changed over time. We then asked them to broadly discuss the evolution of digital imaging activities vis-à-vis the evolution of activities in the traditional instant imaging business. A third set of questions specifically dealt with the emergence of strategic beliefs in the digital competitive arena, and the factors that constrained or inhibited this process. Interviews lasted from 1 hour to all day.

Data collection, data analysis, and conceptualization have been iterative (Glaser and Strauss, 1967). Analysis began with a cluster methodology (Aldenderfer and Blashfield, 1984) where each researcher identified common words and topics for clustering. Cluster labels included both firm capabilities and managerial beliefs/mental models. Researchers then met, compared differences, and repeated the clustering, resulting in a final set of groupings related to both capabilities and cognition.

POLAROID IN DIGITAL IMAGING

Polaroid's Foundations: 1937–80

Polaroid was founded in 1937 by Edwin Land, based on his invention of light-polarizing filters. It was Land's work in instant photography, however, that made Polaroid a household word. Polaroid introduced the first instant camera, a 5-pound device that produced low-quality brown and white pictures, in 1948. From that point forward, Polaroid focused on making improvements to the instant camera. Through ongoing research, Polaroid was able to significantly improve the picture quality, decrease the development time required, introduce color, and enable one-step development (see Table 2.1 for a list of major instant photography developments). Firm performance was exceptional, with average annual compounded sales growth of 23 percent, profit growth of 17 percent, and share price growth of 17 percent between 1948 and 1978.

This period of strong performance culminated in a clear set of firm capabilities and managerial beliefs resulting from both Land's imprint on the firm and years of innovation related to instant photography. We next review what these capabilities and beliefs were

Table 2.1. Polaroid's Major Instant Photography Developments, 1948–80

Year	Advance
1948	First instant camera: sepia (brown and white) film
1950	First black-and-white film
1963	First instant color print film
1964	Colorpack camera
1965	Polaroid Swinger, first low-priced camera (under $20)
1972	SX-70 (one-step developing with no waste)
1978	Sonar automatic focusing

and how they influenced subsequent search activities related to digital imaging (see Figure 2.1).

Capabilities: 1980

As one would expect, Polaroid's capabilities centered around its dominant position in instant photography. The firm's knowledge of the technologies relevant to instant photography technology was unsurpassed in the industry. Land himself held over 500 patents. The firm's patent position was so strong that when Kodak entered the instant photography market in 1976 Polaroid successfully sued them for patent infringement and was able to exclude Kodak from the U.S. market.[3] Polaroid's knowledge included not only a strong understanding of silver halide chemistry, but also a foundation in optics and electronics. For instance, Polaroid spent over $2 million on the development of the eyepiece for the SX-70 camera in the mid-1970s. The firm also used sonar technology to add an autofocus feature to some of its cameras.

Manufacturing was another of Polaroid's strengths. While manufacturing of both cameras and film was originally subcontracted, at the end of the 1960s Land decided to bring manufacturing in-house. For this purpose, both a camera manufacturing plant and a color negative plant were built. The evolution of these plants over time resulted in two distinct manufacturing capabilities: one in precision camera assembly and another in thin film coating.

Finally, the firm had strong distribution through mass market retailers such as K-Mart and Wal-Mart. This innovative use of channels contributed to Polaroid's success. By avoiding direct competition with traditional cameras, which were sold primarily through specialized camera stores, Polaroid was able to establish a strong presence without inciting a competitive response.

Beliefs: 1980

Land was a strong character, notorious for his autocratic manner and strong control of Polaroid as well as his absolute commitment to both science and instant photography (McElheny, 1998). His imprint can be codified in a number of beliefs that dominated the senior management team at the end of this period.

Polaroid was clearly a technology-driven, not market-driven company. Land considered science to be an instrument for the development of products that satisfy deep human needs—needs that could not be understood through market research. He therefore did not believe in performing market research as an input to product development; Polaroid's technology and products would create a market.

Consistent with this philosophy, Polaroid management firmly believed that success came through long-term, large-scale research projects. This philosophy was summarized by Land in the 1980 Annual Report's Letter to Shareholders, where he wrote, "Do not undertake the program unless the goal is manifestly important and its achievement nearly impossible. Do not do anything that anyone else can do readily." A member of senior management during that time commented in an interview. "What we were good at was major inventions. Large-scale, lengthy projects that other firms would hesitate to tackle." Several projects during this period were exemplary of this belief. For instance, in 1972, the firm announced the SX-70 instant camera after spending half a billion dollars on its development over an 8-year period. The camera was revolutionary in that it was waste free: after exposing the film, it ejected a picture that developed as the customer watched. The one-step SX-70 camera was a huge commercial success and served to reinforce the firm's belief in funding major inventions.

Another firmly held belief of management was that customers valued a physical instant print. For this reason, products such as video camcorders were not considered competition. As Land wrote to shareholders in 1981, "None of the electronic devices which prepare tapes or magnetic records to be viewed in television satisfied the conditions imposed by that early dream [of an instant print]." The success of the Po-

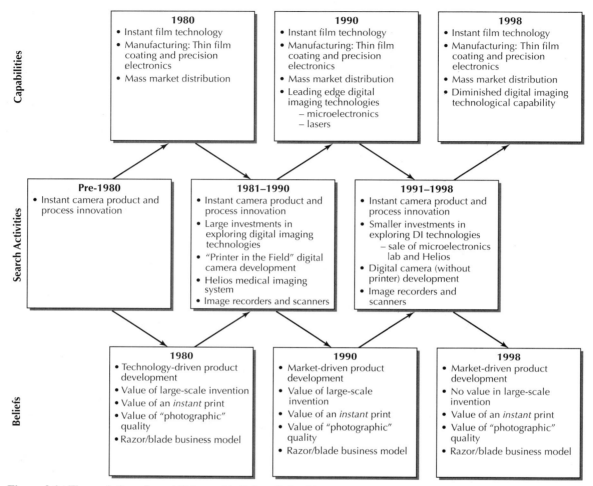

Figure 2.1. The evolution of capabilities and beliefs at Polaroid.

laroid instant camera was taken as prima facie evidence of this need.

Throughout this period there was also an obsession with matching the quality of traditional 35 mm prints, driven by a belief that customers required "photographic" quality. As the 1982 Annual Report's Letter to Shareholders stated, "Our research and engineering efforts continue to be challenged to bring our amateur systems to a level of performance consistent with the best in photography."

Finally, there was a strong belief in the razor/blade business model. While Polaroid had initially made money on both camera hardware and film in 1965 with the introduction of the "Swinger" model,

a decision was made to adopt a razor/blade pricing strategy. The firm dropped prices on cameras in order to stimulate adoption and subsequent demand for film. Film prices and thus margins were then increased. This strategy was extremely successful, and over time a fundamental, commonly held belief developed: Polaroid could not make money on hardware, only software (i.e., film). In one of our interviews, an ex-CEO began his comments with the following:

One of the things that's terribly important, and I think most people understand it but maybe not as fully as they should, is that in the photographic business all the money is in the software, none of it's in the hardware. . . . We were good at making hardware but we never made money on it. . . . So the fundamental objective in these things was to find ways to advance products but that would be useful for improving the software sales.

BEYOND INSTANT PHOTOGRAPHY— DIGITAL IMAGING SEARCH: 1981–89

The capabilities and beliefs articulated above had a profound influence on Polaroid's approach to digital imaging. These digital imaging search efforts were led by a new CEO, Bill McCune, who took over for Land in mid-1980. McCune, a Polaroid employee since 1939, had taken over the presidency in 1975 and was a long-time research colleague of Land's.

McCune began by committing substantial investment dollars to digital imaging technologies. An electronic imaging group was formed in 1981, and as part of this effort work began on a microelectronics laboratory. The microelectronics laboratory opened up in 1986 after a capital investment of about $30 million, and with an operating budget of about $10 million/year. By 1989, 42 percent of R&D dollars were devoted to exploring a broad range of digital imaging technologies. A 1981 strategic planning document identifies the following technological areas for exploration: microelectronics, IC design, advanced optical design, image processing, software design, PC board design, surface mount assembly, CAD/CAM/FEA design, and fiber optics.

While peripherally related to prior technical capabilities (e.g., to knowledge of electronics for instant cameras), these technologies primarily covered new scientific ground for Polaroid. For instance, about 90 percent of the employees in the microelectronics lab were newly hired. Developing radically new technical capability, however, was quite consistent with Polaroid's belief in the primacy of technology. As ex-CEO McCune stated in one of our interviews, "If you have good technical people you shouldn't be afraid of going into whole new technical areas." Similarly, one of the individuals involved in electronic imaging development commented, "We compared ourselves to Bell Labs. Our orientation was 'technical challenge—we can do it."

The Electronic Imaging group's exploratory efforts were guided by a desire to eventually develop an instant digital camera/printer product termed "PIF" for Printer In the Field. This product concept combined electronic semiconductor (CCD) sensors for image capture, software for image enhancement, and instant film for image output. As the 1984 Annual Report's Letter to Shareholders stated, "We believe that there is considerable potential in developing new hybrid imaging systems that combine instant photography and electronics." This work culminated in a 1990 patent (U.S. #4,937,676) for an "electronic camera system with detachable printer."

The PIF concept built on both Polaroid's prior capabilities and beliefs. Since the output was to be on instant film, it leveraged the firm's strong film-manufacturing capabilities. It was also, however, consistent with the firmly held belief in a razor/blade model. Since the digital camera was bundled with instant film output, there was a clear consumable/software piece of the product. In addition, the product was consistent with the belief that consumers valued an instant physical print. Rather than provide customers with the capability to view images on something like an LED screen, they were provided with an immediate print.

The second major area of digital imaging investment during this period was in a medical system called Helios. Helios used a high-energy laser to expose a dry film material. It was targeted at radiologists as a higher-resolution substitute for X-rays. Like the PIF concept, the development of Helios was influenced by both prior capabilities and beliefs. Although the media was not instant film, its development still leveraged Polaroid's chemical knowledge base. In addition, manufacturing of the Helios media was quite consistent with the thin film coating capabilities utilized in the manufacture of instant film.

The Helios business model was also consistent with the belief in the razor/blade model used in instant imaging. The majority of the profit stream was to come from the sale of high-margin media following the sale of the hardware. In commenting on the broad support for Helios, one manager in the electronic imaging area told us, "[Helios] was not, in their [senior management] minds . . . an electronic imaging thing. It had an electronic front end, but it's a film product and you make the money on the film. So it fell into the conventional wisdom. This is why it was always well funded and well taken care of." A member of senior management at the time confirmed this perspective commenting, "I haven't found many people that can make a buck outside of the consumable area . . . and so I think that Helios was part of that same business model. It fit comfortably into it." Helios also fit the belief in large-scale invention. In reflecting on the large investments made in Helios, a senior manager said, "The technology . . . was too costly. It took us too long . . . but it did miracles. . . . We were three years late, and we never got the hardware costs in line. But by God, we tried to bite off the whole world . . . new media, new lasers, new this, new that. And that goes back to doing the impossible."

In addition to working on PIF and Helios, a small number of electronic imaging products were developed and shipped during this period. A series of image recorders was sold, starting in 1983. These machines were used to print images from computer or video input onto instant film, slides, or transparencies. Targeted at specialized vertical markets such as graphic arts, these machines were never sold in large quantities. These products were once again building on existing knowledge of chemistry for the output media, although the electronic front-end was clearly based on newly acquired knowledge. The potential for an ongoing stream of media sales also made these products consistent with the razor/blade business model.

While the beliefs of senior management clearly influenced search activities that did take place, they also had a direct influence on activities that did not take place. In particular, there were three important areas of capability that Polaroid did not invest in: low-cost electronics manufacturing capability, rapid product development capability, and new marketing and sales capability.

In order to compete successfully in the hardware arena using a business model different from the traditional razor/blade approach, Polaroid would have to have developed low-cost electronics manufacturing capability and rapid product development capability—two areas in which Polaroid was particularly weak. Strong, low-cost electronics manufacturing capability would have been fundamental to increasing the typically smaller margins in the hardware business. At the same time, fast product development capability would have been necessary to permit the timely introduction of innovative products in a market where product life cycles were measured in months, as opposed to the years Polaroid was accustomed to for its instant imaging products. Polaroid's weakness in product development was characterized by one digital imaging manag-

er as follows: "Polaroid didn't have a sense of the distinction between research and product development. It was all mixed up. Many people were totally oblivious to what it means to get a product really developed and make it ready for the marketplace." Although it is unclear whether Polaroid could have been successful at developing either of these capabilities, senior management's belief in the razor/blade business model and their resistance to supporting activities that were not fully consistent with this view precluded any investment in them.

Senior management beliefs also influenced the evolution of marketing capability. Consistent with the belief that technology was dominant, Polaroid's top management viewed the transition to digital imaging through a technology-focused filter. Digital imaging was therefore viewed primarily as a technological, not a market shift, with the majority of digital imaging investment directed towards the development of new technical capabilities. As a consequence, the firm never invested in developing any sales or marketing capability specific to digital imaging. For instance, rather than establish new distribution channels, the existing sales force was chartered with selling electronic imaging products. This approach was taken despite the protests of those directly involved in digital imaging product development who were aware of the profound market differences between instant and digital imaging. As one member of the electronic imaging group in the mid-1980s told us, "We were not really happy about it, but there was not much else we could do."

Resulting Capabilities and Beliefs: 1990

The actions taken from 1980 to 1989 were influenced by prior capabilities and beliefs, but also resulted in a gradual shift in those same capabilities and beliefs. By the end of 1989 Polaroid had not only continued to evolve its expertise in technologies related to traditional instant photography, but also the firm had developed leading-edge technical capability in a number of areas related to digital imaging. Whereas the percentage of the firm's patents related to electronics between 1976 and 1980 was only 6 percent, between 1986 and 1990 that had increased to 28 percent.

Polaroid's image sensor technology was particularly strong with a number of clear advantages over competing sensors. By producing a higher-quality raw input file, Polaroid's sensors were able to generate a resolution of 1.9 million pixels when the majority of the competition had sensors that generated only 480,000 pixels. Polaroid also held a patent on the ability to use rectangular rather than square pixels. This technology improved color recovery. Finally, whereas most compression algorithms resulted in loss of information and thus a decrease in image quality, Polaroid had developed proprietary lossless compression algorithms. Polaroid was therefore well positioned by 1989 to develop a leading-edge digital camera.

During this time period the composition of the senior management team remained relatively unchanged. In 1986 McCune stepped down as president and CEO (although he remained chairman), but his successor, MacAllister Booth, had been with Polaroid since 1958 and was a long-time member of senior management. In addition, seven of the nine officers on the Management Executive Committee in 1989 had been members in 1980. It is not surprising, therefore, that the overall beliefs of senior management remained relatively static during this period.

In particular, the belief in the razor/blade business model remained firmly ensconced. Clearly, this business model was still appropriate for the traditional instant photography business. It was also continuing to be applied to digital imaging. An employee who joined the firm's electronic imaging group in 1989 commented on what he found: "What's the business model? It's the razor/blade . . . so we make money with the film. They [senior management] wanted to duplicate that in the electronic domain. This idea was pervasive. It was an idea they could easily relate to because it was continuing the instant photography business model. Right?"

There was also still a strong sense that customers wanted instant prints. The 1985 Letter to Shareholders states, "As electronic imaging becomes more prevalent, there remains a basic human need for a permanent visual record." Similarly, an employee who joined the firm's electronic imaging area in 1990 commented, "Another truth [I encountered] was that people really value an instant print. This was also an ontological truth."

Finally, there was still a strong emphasis on matching the quality of 35 mm cameras, in both the instant and digital imaging domains. A number of new films for instant cameras were announced in the 1980s, including new high-contrast and high-speed films. The electronic imaging group was also working on developing a mega-pixel sensor that would enable a photo-

graphic-quality image to be produced from a digital camera. As one employee in the electronic imaging area commented, "Polaroid was always stung by the assessment that instant photography was really cool, too bad the quality stunk . . . the entire motivation as near as I could detect for the investments that they put into sensor technology and so on was to counteract the 35 mm quality deficit."

The most significant change in senior management's beliefs was a shift away from being a purely technology-driven company. Polaroid faced stagnant growth for the first time in the 1980s with waning demand in the traditional instant photography market. After having achieved double digit annual sales growth for 30 years, total sales actually decreased between 1980 and 1985. Faced with this situation, management placed an increased emphasis on marketing, and a formal market research function was established. Market input also became an official part of the product development process. In the 1989 Letter to Share-holders Booth stated, "We have studied the needs of our customers in each market segment and those needs are driving the development of our new products." This statement is in direct contrast to the philosophy articulated by Land.

REFOCUSING ON DIGITAL IMAGING—SEARCH ACTIVITIES: 1990–98

In 1990, electronic imaging moved up in the corporate hierarchy as part of a major reorganization. Three market-focused divisions—Consumer, Business, and Scientific/Technical Imaging—were formed in addition to a fourth: Electronic Imaging Division. The Electronic Imaging Division was intended to feed products to each of the three market-focused divisions. At the same time, the exploratory investments of the 1980s were curtailed in 1990 when research into fiber optics, solar cells, and disk drives was cut. This decision was made in order to focus research efforts on those technologies directly related to products under development. In addition, in 1993 the Microelectronics Lab was sold to MIT, ending the majority of Polaroid's more basic research in microelectronics.

The composition of the electronic imaging group also changed dramatically after 1990. While a long-time Polaroid employee was initially in charge of the group, the majority of members were new hires with experience in digital imaging and other high-technology industries. Consistent with the new belief in being more market driven, an electronic imaging marketing group, comprised entirely of new hires, was established. This group was given the charter to develop a digital camera product concept. Once this concept was defined, a new hire was put in charge of the overall development project. And in 1994 another outsider was brought in to head up the entire group. This individual brought in yet more outsiders, assigning them to key strategic positions within the electronic imaging group.

Clearly, these new individuals, with no prior Polaroid experience, had a different perspective from that of senior management. The digital camera product concept developed by the group was therefore quite different from the prior PIF concept. While this digital camera could eventually be bundled with a Polaroid instant film printer, the initial concept included just a high-resolution camera, targeted at professionals in industries such as real estate that had a need for "instant verification," not necessarily an instant print. Given Polaroid's leading position in sensor technology development, the marketing group felt that Polaroid could offer a significant price/performance advantage over the competition. By 1992, there was a working prototype of the camera.

One can best characterize the period from 1990 to 1996 as one of cognitive dissonance between senior management and the newly hired members of the Electronic Imaging Division. This clash was driven by fundamentally different beliefs. First, there was disagreement about the appropriate business model for digital imaging. One of the newly hired individuals described to us the ongoing dialogue with senior management as follows:

> The catch [to our product concept] was that you had to be in the hardware business to make money. "How could you say that? Where's the film? There's no film?" So what we had was a constant fight with the senior executive management in Polaroid for five years . . . We constantly challenged the notion of the current business model, the core business, as being old, antiquated, and unable to go forward. . . . What was fascinating to me was that these guys used to turn their noses up at 38 percent margins. . . . But that was their big argument,

"Why 38 percent? I can get 70 percent on film. Why do I want to do this?"

Senior management, on the other hand, felt that the electronic imaging group did not understand the limitations of Polaroid's manufacturing and product development capabilities. As discussed earlier, given the strong belief in the razor/blade model, Polaroid had not invested in developing the manufacturing capability necessary to make money on "razors." In addition, the belief in large-scale projects with lengthy development cycles had precluded investment in fast product development capability. Management did not, therefore, feel comfortable competing with firms that possessed these capabilities. As one senior manager noted, "We're not just going to be up against Kodak, Fuji, etc. We're going to be up against 30 consumer electronic companies—the Sonys, Toshibas, Hitachis, the Intels, etc. We need to have a unique idea that corresponds to our core capabilities and the way we relate to the marketplace." There was also concern about Polaroid's ability to simultaneously manage very different businesses, as voiced by another senior manager: "Can we be a down and dirty manufacturer at the same time we're an innovator over here? Can you have two different philosophies running simultaneously in the company?"

As a result of this ongoing clash between senior management and the Electronic Imaging Division, there were continuous delays in development related to the digital camera, an inability to commit to relationships with potential strategic partners, and ultimately a lengthy delay in the commercialization of a digital camera product. Despite having a prototype in 1992, Polaroid did not announce its PDC-2000 mega-pixel camera until 1996. By that point in time there were over 40 other firms on the market selling digital cameras. The PDC-2000 received a number of awards for its technical achievement (the *Net-guide Magazine* State-of-the-Art Award, *Publish* magazine's Impact Award, and the European Technical Image Press Association's Best Digital Product of 1996), but it did not do well in the market. Although Polaroid was more "market driven" in the sense of using customer needs as an input to development, senior management still did not perceive the need for different sales channels. The Electronic Imaging Division requested separate sales support for the PDC-2000, but was told that they had to use the instant photography sales force. As one frustrated individual commented, "We had products in the $1,000 range and these people were used to going to K-Mart and Wal-Mart." In 1997 a follow-on PDC-3000 was announced, after which development activity ceased. By this point in time, the majority of the individuals hired to staff the Electronic Imaging Division in the early 1990s had left Polaroid.

Other activities of the Electronic Imaging Division also encountered senior management resistance throughout the early 1990s. Given the belief in a razor/blade model, one obvious avenue for Polaroid to explore was the development of alternative hardcopy technologies, such as ink jet or thermal dye sublimation. The belief that consumers needed "photographic quality," however, kept senior management from committing to these alternatives. As one member of the Electronic Imaging Division commented, "We had the capability . . . but there was disbelief that ink jet could be near photographic quality. Mathematical models and demos couldn't convince people." A member of senior management explained their reluctance to accept a lower-quality ink-jet output as follows: "I spent an awful lot of my life, [Sr. Manager X] spent almost all of his life—a lot of us . . . [Sr. Manager Y] spent an awful lot of his life focusing on improving the quality of the instant image. . . . So that was an everyday, all-day part of our lives . . . so that can't help but have been indelible in the DNA or something."

The one digital imaging product that received consistent, ongoing support throughout this period was the Helios medical imaging system. In fact, Helios was such a large project, with an annual investment of about $120 million in development (compared to $30–$40 million for the Electronic Imaging Division), that it was not organized as part of the Electronic Imaging Division, but was a separate group. As discussed earlier, Helios continued to receive such strong support because it was consistent with both Polaroid's capabilities and the beliefs of senior management. In addition a spin-off of the Helios technology, dry-output film for the graphic arts, also received support for the same reasons. Helios finally reached the market in 1993 after almost 10 years of development effort. Unfortunately, despite its technical achievement, Helios was not successful in the market. This failure was attributed to a number of factors including the lack of strength in distribution as well as misreading of the

film size required by radiologists. Digital imaging losses of $180 million in 1994 and $190 million in 1995 were primarily attributed to Helios. In 1996 the Helios division was sold to Sterling Diagnostic, although Polaroid still provides the film and lasers.

The sale of the Helios group was just part of an overall decrease in commitment to internal development of digital imaging technologies. In 1996 a new CEO, Gary DiCamillo, succeeded MacAllister Booth. DiCamillo was the first outsider to hold this position, and he brought with him a new top management team. Of 25 directors listed in the 1998 Annual Report, 15 had joined Polaroid after DiCamillo's arrival. With a background in consumer marketing, DiCamillo decreased the focus on technology even more. Soon after arriving at Polaroid he commented, "We're not in the business to get the most patents. We're not in the business to write the most research papers. And we're not in the business to see how many inventions we can come up with" (Convey, 1996). Consistent with this approach, research and development expenses were cut from $165.5 million in 1995 to $116.3 million in 1996. Not surprisingly, development of Polaroid's next-generation digital camera, the PDC-300 announced in 1997, was totally outsourced.

In conjunction with the decreased emphasis on technology, DiCamillo and his team placed renewed emphasis on marketing in both the instant photography and digital imaging domains. While the amount of money allocated to R&D decreased, the amount spent on advertising increased slightly from $124.1 million in 1995 to $134.6 million in 1996. Polaroid's marketing department created a new category called "photoplay," with products such as the Barbie instant camera introduced in 1998.

Resulting Capabilities and Beliefs: 1998

The series of digital imaging disappointments, combined with a new top management team, resulted in the evolution of capabilities and beliefs. By 1998 Polaroid's earlier strength in digital imaging technologies had significantly diminished. The firm had about 50 internal employees devoted to digital imaging research as opposed to a high of about 300 in 1992. Consistent with this decrease, the belief in the value of large-scale invention had disappeared. Instead Polaroid was focused on rapid incremental product development. "We have announced our intention of becoming a new products company . . . to bring 20 to 40 new products to market each year," DiCamillo stated in the 1998 Annual Report. The transition from a technology-driven to a market-driven company also seemed complete with the "photoplay" category taking on increased strategic importance.

Some parts of the senior management belief system, however, were surprisingly similar. DiCamillo supported the razor/blade business model, stating in a 1997 interview, "In the digital world we believe that hard copy is required. . . . Unless there is a consumable component, the business model falls apart. So we have to focus on what's consumable and what value-added we can provide that's unique" (Rosenbloom, 1997: 16) His commitment to photographic quality and therefore conventional film was also quite strong. "What are we? What are we good at? We're pretty good at creating images instantly. Not very many companies can do that . . . there's both a time and a skill required to take conventional film and make it look good. Substitute technology such as ink jet or thermal technologies are interesting, but they're not here yet" (Rosenbloom, 1997: 13).

Clearly the digital imaging market is still evolving, and it is uncertain what Polaroid's ultimate position will be. We believe it is fair to say, however, that having invested in and developed such strong technical capability in digital imaging in the 1980s, it is disappointing that Polaroid was unable to capitalize on its technical position in the marketplace. In addition, despite its early technological lead, Polaroid is ultimately left with quite limited technical strength in this emerging market.

DISCUSSION AND CONCLUSIONS

Our goal in this paper was to explore the relationship among capabilities, cognition, and inertia. While prior work in the evolutionary tradition has shown that failures to adapt to radical technological discontinuities often stem from the local nature of learning processes and, consequently, from the relative rigidity of organizational routines (Teece et al., 1994), little emphasis has been devoted, at least in this tradition, to understanding the role of managerial cognition in driving the dynamics of capabilities. Through the Polaroid story, we clearly demonstrate that search processes in a new

learning environment are deeply interconnected to the way managers model the new problem space and develop strategic prescriptions premised on this view of the world.

From a strictly evolutionary point of view, one would expect Polaroid to have had difficulty developing new, unrelated digital imaging technologies. Instead, we find that the firm had little problem overcoming the path dependencies normally associated with knowledge evolution. Indeed, thanks to the early investments in electronic technologies, Polaroid was able to develop leading-edge capabilities in a broad array of technological areas related to digital imaging. For instance, by the time the market for digital cameras started to take off in the early 1990s Polaroid had a working prototype of a high-resolution, mega-pixel digital camera that was a step function improvement in price/performance relative to other products in the market. Similarly, Helios, a medical imaging system aimed at replacing X-ray technologies, although a commercial failure, was a major technological achievement. Despite these capabilities, Polaroid failed to adapt to the radical changes that had occurred in the imaging competitive landscape. Understanding this paradoxical behavior requires us to go beyond explanations focusing on the localness of learning processes and on the inertia of a firm's competencies.

We argue that only by considering the role of cognition and its implication in terms of the learning dynamics of the organization can one gain insights into this apparent inconsistency. As previously documented, a number of strong beliefs were deeply diffused in the top management of the company, and remained substantially unaltered during its entire history. During the Land era, the company was characterized by a solid belief in the primacy of technology, according to which commercial success could only come through major research projects. There is little doubt that Polaroid's early exploration of the electronic domain, the basis for its state-of-the-art technological competencies in digital imaging, was legitimated by this view of the world. Despite the absence of a market for digital imaging applications, during the 1980s the company kept allocating considerable resources to this technological trajectory. For at least a decade, resource allocation in digital imaging was totally disjointed from any notion of performance. To put it simply, Polaroid did not experience major difficulties searching in a radically new technological trajectory and developing new technological competencies, largely due to the consistency of this purely exploratory behavior with the belief in the primacy of technology.

A second commonly held belief was that Polaroid could not make money on the hardware, but only on consumables, i.e., the razor/blade model. This business model, successfully developed and adopted in the instant imaging business, was applied to the company's activities in digital imaging, and we believe was a main source of Polaroid's inertia. At the beginning of the 1990s, when a market for digital imaging applications slowly started to emerge, senior managers strongly discouraged search and development efforts that were not consistent with the traditional business model, despite ongoing efforts from newly hired members of the Electronic Imaging Division to convince them otherwise. Digital camera development efforts, for instance, were stalled, given the inconsistency with a razor/blade business model. Similarly, Polaroid never attempted to develop the manufacturing and product development capabilities that would have been key had Polaroid decided to compete in digital imaging with a nonrazor/blade business model. (e.g., as a low-cost/high-quantity hardware producer.) In contrast, products such as Helios that were consistent with this view of the world received unconditional support on the part of senior managers.

In short, if on the one hand Polaroid's beliefs allowed the company to develop the necessary technological knowledge for competing in digital imaging, they became a powerful source of inertia when decisions were taken on how to further develop such knowledge in specific products and activities. This evidence points to the deep interrelationships between a manager's understanding of the world and the accumulation of organizational competencies. Although much current theorizing on the dynamics of capabilities emphasizes the inertial effects of the path dependencies associated with learning processes, we believe that understanding how capabilities evolve cannot neglect the role of managerial cognitive representations, especially in constraining and directing learning efforts. Importantly, emphasizing cognitive elements in the explanation of the genesis and evolution of capabilities raises both positive and normative issues that traditional explanations in the evolutionary realm largely overlook.

A particularly important issue is the question of how beliefs evolve within organizations. Can the top management team, for instance, simultaneously manage businesses with different dominant logics (Prahalad and Bettis, 1986)? In the Polaroid case, we find that senior management was able to develop new beliefs for digital imaging only as long as those beliefs were consistent with the instant photography business. For instance, they recognized the importance of being more market driven in both the instant photography and digital imaging domains. In contrast, they found it difficult to endorse a nonrazor/blade business model for digital imaging given that it was still the prevalent model for the instant photography business. In such situations Tushman and O'Reilly (1996) have found that successful organizations are "ambidextrous," simultaneously embracing multiple contradictory elements through an organizational architecture that combines a mix of autonomy and central control.

Turnover in the top management team is also an important driver of change. In particular, changes in both the CEO and executive team have been found to initiate discontinuous organizational change (Tushman and Rosenkopf, 1996). At Polaroid, the arrival of an outsider CEO, DiCamillo, combined with a new top management team, significantly changed elements of the belief system. The shift from lengthy, large-scale, technology-driven invention to rapid, incremental, market-driven product development is epitomized by Polaroid's new focus on products for the "photoplay" market. In rapidly changing environments, however, ongoing turnover of top management teams is likely to be impractical. In these situations, the development of "deframing" skills, the ability to question current strategic beliefs in an ongoing way, becomes increasingly important (Dunbar, Garud, and Raghuram, 1996).

These arguments suggest that a crucial challenge for organizations facing radical technological discontinuities is the ability to distinguish changes that require only the development of new technological capabilities from changes that also require the adoption of different strategic beliefs. For Polaroid, digital imaging represented an instance of the latter type of change: success in this new competitive landscape required fundamentally different strategic beliefs as articulated at the time by individuals in the digital imaging group. However, radical technological discontinuities do not always provoke mutations in the bases of competition. In fact, in some cases enduring belief systems can be a source of competitive strength (Collins and Porras, 1994; Porac and Rosa, 1996). In this situation, cognitive change can be highly dysfunctional for the organization, since strategic reorientations are costly and associated with high mortality rates (Tushman and Romanelli, 1985; Amburgey, Kelly, and Barnett, 1993; Sastry, 1997). In particular, changes in the basic strategic beliefs of a firm typically have short-term disruptive effects on organizational practices and routines (Gavetti and Levinthal, 2000). When environmental change does not render current strategic beliefs obsolete, the net effect of their modification is hardly positive for the organization.

A second issue that clearly emerges in this research is the role of hierarchy in cognition. Polaroid's difficulties in adapting to digital imaging were mainly determined by the cognitive inertia of its corporate executives. As we have documented, managers directly involved with digital imaging developed a highly adaptive representation of the emerging competitive landscape. They abandoned Polaroid's "software-oriented" view and adopted a "hardware-oriented" model that they were not free to put into practice. We speculate that the cognitive dissonance between senior management and digital imaging managers may have been exacerbated by the difference in signals that the two groups were receiving about the market. This evidence is suggestive not only of the presence of profound cognitive differences across hierarchical level, but also that there might be structural reasons underlying differences in cognitive adaptability across hierarchical levels (Gavetti, 1999).

Finally, this work raises important questions regarding the origins of both capability and cognition. The vast majority of research in each of these areas has focused on the capabilities and cognition of established firms, with limited understanding of their historical development. In the case of Polaroid, it appears that Edwin Land, the founder, had a profound and lasting influence on the development of both capabilities and cognition. However, given that that not all founders are as memorable as Land, one might ask what other initial factors are important. Work on organizational imprinting has demonstrated that a broad range of environmental conditions at organizational founding (e.g., the social, economic, and competitive

environments) have a lasting influence on organizational structure and culture (e.g., Stinchcombe, 1965; Kimberly, 1975; Boeker, 1988). How do these same environmental factors affect capabilities and cognition? By focusing future research efforts on start-up firms, in addition to established firms, we believe we can start to address these questions and significantly enrich our knowledge of both the origins and the evolution of firm capabilities and cognition.

ACKNOWLEDGMENTS

We are grateful to Hank Chesbrough, Connie Helfat, Dan Levinthal, Anjali Sastry, Mike Tushman, Steven Usselman, and the participants in the CCC/Tuck Conference on the Evolution of Capabilities for feedback on earlier versions of this paper. Financial support from the Huntsman and Reginald H. Jones Centers at the Wharton School is gratefully acknowledged.

NOTES

1. Since we are focusing on the distinction between capabilities and cognition, we use the term "capabilities" broadly to represent a number of noncognitive factors including capabilities, competencies, assets, and resources.

2. Digital imaging is the capture, manipulation, storage, transmission, and output of an image using digital technology. Digital imaging is competence destroying for analog photography firms in that it requires the mastery of new scientific domains such as semiconductors/electronics as well as the development of different distribution channels and new customer relationships. (For more detail on the technologies involved in digital imaging see Rosenbloom, 1997.)

There is also a great deal of uncertainty about the digital imaging competitive landscape with firms from the photography, consumer electronics, computer and graphic arts industries all converging on the industry. While the first digital cameras arrived on the market in the late 1980s, only recently has consumer demand for digital imaging skyrocketed. As of the end of 1998 there were over 70 firms that had entered the digital camera market with over 250 models available. The industry is growing rapidly, and the worldwide digital camera market is expected to reach $10 billion by the year 2000 (*Future Image Report*, 1997).

3. After a lengthy court battle, in 1991 Polaroid was awarded $924.5 million in damages from Kodak.

REFERENCES

Aldenderfer, M. S., Blashfield, R. K. 1984. *Cluster Analysis.* Sage: Beverly Hills, CA.

Amburgey, T., Kelly, D., Barnett, W. 1993. Resetting the clock: the dynamics of organizational change and failure. *Administrative Science Quarterly* **38**(1): 51–73.

Arrow, K. J. 1974. *The Limits of Organization.* Norton: New York.

Baron, J. M., Hannan, M. T., Burton, M. D. 1999. Building the iron cage: determinants of managerial intensity in the early years of organizations. *American Sociological Review* **64**: 527–547.

Barr, P. S., Stimpert, J. L., Huff, A. S. 1992. Cognitive change strategic action, and organizational renewal. *Strategic Management Journal,* Summer Special Issue **13**: 15–36.

Boeker, W. 1988. Organizational origins: entrepreneurial and environmental imprinting at the time of founding. In *Ecological Models of Organizations,* Carroll G (ed.). Ballinger: Cambridge, MA; 33–51.

Brown, S. L., Eisenhardt, K. M. 1998. *Competing on the Edge: Strategy as Structured Chaos.* Harvard Business School Press: Boston, MA.

Christensen, C. 1997. *The Innovator's Dilemma.* Harvard Business School Press: Boston, MA.

Collins, J. C., Porras, J. I. 1994. *Built to Last: Successful Habits of Visionary Companies.* HarperCollins: New York.

Convey, E. 1996. Polaroid chief charting new course for R&D. *The Boston Herald* 26 March: 32.

Cooper, A. C., Schendel, D. 1976. Strategic responses to technological threats. *Business Horizons:* 61–69.

Dosi, G. 1982. Technological paradigms and technological trajectories. *Research Policy* **11**(3): 147–162.

Dunbar, R. L. M., Garud, R., Raghuram, S. 1996. A frame for deframing in strategic analysis. *Journal of Management Inquiry* **5**(1): 23–34.

Future Image Report. 1997. Gerard, A. (ed.). Future Image, Inc: San Mateo, CA.

Garud, R., Rappa, M. 1994. A socio-cognitive model of technology evolution: the case of cochlear implants. *Organization Science* **5**(3): 344–362.

Gavetti, G. 1999. Cognition, capabilities and corporate strategy making. Working paper, The Wharton School.

Gavetti, G., Levinthal, D. 2000. Looking forward and looking backward: cognitive and experiential search. *Administrative Science Quarterly* **45**: 113–137.

Glaser, B. G., Strauss, A. L. 1967. *The Discovery of Grounded Theory.* Aldine: Chicago, IL.

Hambrick, D. C., Mason, P. 1984. Upper echelons: the organization as a reflection of its top managers. *Academy of Management Review* **9**: 193–206.

Helfat, C. E. 1997. Know-how asset complementarity and dynamic capability accumulation: the case of R&D. *Strategic Management Journal* **18**(5): 339–360.

Henderson, R. M., Clark, K. B. 1990. Architectural innovation: the reconfiguration of existing product technologies and the failure of established firms. *Administrative Science Quarterly* **35**: 9–30.

Kiesler, S., Sproull, L. 1982. Managerial response to changing environments: perspectives on problem sensing from social cognition. *Administrative Science Quarterly* **27**: 548–570.

Kimberly, J. 1975. Environmental constraints and organizational structure: a comparative analysis of rehabilitation organizations. *Administrative Science Quarterly* **20**(1): 1–9.

Leonard-Barton, D. 1992. Core capabilities and core rigidities: a paradox in managing new product development. *Strategic Management Journal,* Summer Special Issue **13**: 111–126.

Levitt, B., March, J. G. 1988. Organizational learning. *Annual Review of Sociology* **14**: 319–340.

Majumdar, B. A. 1982. *Innovations. Product Developments and Technology Transfers: An Empirical Study of Dynamic Competitive Advantage. The Case of Electronic Calculators.* University Press of America: Washington, DC.

March, J., Simon, H. 1958. *Organizations.* Wiley: New York.

McElheny, V. 1998. *Insisting on the Impossible: The Life of Edwin Land.* Perseus: Reading, MA.

Miles, M. B., Huberman, A. M. 1994. *Qualitative Data Analysis: An Expanded Sourcebook.* 2nd edn, Sage: Thousand Oaks, CA.

Mintzberg, H. 1979. *The Structuring of Organizations.* Prentice-Hall: Englewood Cliffs, NJ.

Mitchell, W. 1989. Whether and when? Probability and timing of incumbents' entry into emerging industrial subfields. *Administrative Science Quarterly* **34**: 208–234.

Nelson, R., Winter, S. 1982. *An Evolutionary Theory of the Firm.* Harvard University Press: Cambridge, MA.

Peteraf, M., Shanley, M. 1997. Getting to know you: a theory of strategic group identity. *Strategic Management Journal,* Summer Special Issue **18**: 165–186.

Porac, J., Rosa, J. A. 1996. In praise of managerial narrowmindedness. *Journal of Management Inquiry* **5**(1): 35–42.

Porac, J., Thomas, H., Wilson, R., Paton, D., Kanfer, A. 1995. Rivalry and the industry model of Scottish knitwear producers. *Administrative Science Quarterly* **40**: 203–227.

Prahalad, C. K., Bettis, R. A. 1986. The dominant logic: a new linkage between diversity and performance. *Strategic Management Journal* **7**(6): 485–501.

Reger, R. K., Huff, A. S. 1993. Strategic groups: a cognitive perspective. *Strategic Management Journal* **14**(2): 103–123.

Rosenbloom, R. 1997. Polaroid Corporation: digital imaging technology in 1997. Harvard Business School Case #9-798-013.

Sastry, A. 1997. Problems and paradoxes in a model of punctuated organizational change. *Administrative Science Quarterly* **42**(2): 237–276.

Simon, H. A. 1955. A behavioral model of rational choice. *Quarterly Journal of Economics* **69**: 99–118.

Stinchcombe, A. 1965. Social structure and organizations. In *Handbook of Organizations,* March, J. G. (ed.). Rand McNally: Chicago, IL; 153–193.

Teece, D. 1986. Profiting from technological innovation: implications for integration, collaboration, licensing and public policy. *Research Policy* **15**: 285–305.

Teece, D. J. 1988. Technological change and the nature of the firm. In *Technical Change and Economic Theory,* Dosi, G., Freeman, C., Nelson, R., Silverberg, G., Soete, L. (eds.). Pinter Publisher: London; 256–281.

Teece, D. J., Pisano, G., Shuen, A. 1997. Dynamic capabilities and strategic management. *Strategic Management Journal* **18**(7): 509–553.

Teece, D. J., Rumelt, R., Dosi, G., Winter, S. 1994. Understanding corporate coherence. *Journal of Economic Behavior and Organization* **23**: 1–30.

Tripsas, M. 1997. Unraveling the process of creative destruction: complementary assets and incumbent survival in the typesetter industry. *Strategic Management Journal,* Summer Special Issue **18**: 119–142.

Tushman, M. L., Anderson, P. 1986. Technological discontinuities and organizational environments. *Administrative Science Quarterly* **31**: 439–465.

Tushman, M. L., O'Reilly, C. A. 1996. Ambidextrous organizations: managing evolutionary and revolutionary change. *California Management Review* **38**(4): 8–30.

Tushman, M. L., Romanelli, E. 1985. Organizational evolution: a metamorphosis model of convergence and reorientation. In *Research in Organizational Behavior,* Cummings, I. L., Staw, B. M. (eds.). Vol. 7: JAI Press: Greenwich, CT; 171–222.

Tushman, M. L., Rosenkopf, L. 1996. Executive succession, strategic reorientation and performance growth: a longitudinal study in the U.S. cement industry. *Management Science* **42**(7): 939–953.

Utterback, J. 1994. *Mastering the Dynamics of Innovation.* Harvard University Press: Cambridge, MA.

Yin, R. K. 1984. *Case Study Research: Design and Methods.* Sage: Beverly Hills CA.

Zyglidopoulos, S. 1999. Initial environmental conditions and technological change. *Journal of Management Studies* **36**(2): 241–262.

SECTION II

INNOVATION OVER TIME AND IN HISTORICAL CONTEXT

Technological innovation sets the stage within which organizations compete. Firms compete to prevail in a particular context, but also to shape the competitive context itself. This section provides a research-based point of view on the nature of technological change. Technology cycles are initiated by technological discontinuities that usher in a period in which the new technology (and its associated variants) competes with the incumbent technology. This era of ferment is closed with the emergence of a dominant design or industry standard. The closure on standards ushers in a period of incremental technical change that is, in turn, destabilized by the subsequent technological discontinuity. Each phase of a technology cycle is associated with different innovation challenges and innovation types. These innovation streams are at the roots of dynamic organizational capabilities and are amenable to managerial action. However, they are often resisted by organizational inertia and active resistance to change.

Anderson and Tushman articulate the notion of technology cycles, and Glasmeier richly illustrates the dynamic of innovation cycles in the global watch industry. Her article describes the strategic and organizational consequences of getting stuck in a technology trajectory and being unable to traverse innovation streams. The theme of innovation streams and organizational inertia is also discussed in Morison's case of gunfire at sea. This example illustrates dynamic conservatism: how a truly breakthrough architectural innovation was strongly resisted in the U.S. Navy. Similarly, the Christensen and Bower article shows the impact of disruptive technologies on incumbents, while the Henderson and Clark article illustrates how architectural innovations impact incumbents. Finally, the Sull article discusses the impact of competence-destroying technical change on incumbents in the tire industry. These articles illustrate the challenge that incumbent organizations have in driving innovation streams—even when they have all the capabilities to do so.

Dominant designs are crucial strategic events in the evolution of a product class. Firms that control standards in core subsystems thrive, while those that lose the battle among possible standards either shift to the standard or underperform. We illustrate these issues in the Gould and the Shapiro and Varian articles. Whereas the Gould article is the classic example of standards emerging within subsystems of a typewriter, the Shapiro and Varian article is a more current piece on the dynamic of standards across a set of industries. This group of readings ends with the Baldwin and Clark article, which focuses on products and services as being made up of modules and associated interfaces. Baldwin and Clark bring the notion of standards to the module level of analysis and introduce the notion that some modules and interfaces are more strategically central than are others.

The final set of articles in this section focus on innovation issues during periods of incremental change. Both deal with process innovation and managing exploitative innovation. The Repenning and Sterman article focuses on the costs and benefits of process improvement programs, whereas the Sutcliffe, Sitkin, and Browning article presents a contingency approach to process management activities. These articles highlight how important it is to manage incremental, variance reducing, innovation effectively. Yet these process innovations are also associated with potential organizational pathologies that, if left unmanaged, stunt more exploratory innovation.

3

Managing Through Cycles of Technological Change

PHILIP ANDERSON
MICHAEL L. TUSHMAN

". . . industrial mutation . . . incessantly revolutionizes the economic structure from within. This process of Creative Destruction is the essential fact about capitalism."

—JOSEF SCHUMPETER, 1942

We are managing in what Peter Drucker has termed "the age of discontinuity." Examples of revolutionary technological changes that transform industries abound. Ceramic engine parts will replace metal engine parts in the next decade, thanks to their high strength-to-weight ratio and resistance to heat. Flat-screen displays will obsolesce today's bulky cathode-ray tubes in television screens and computer monitors. Optical disks capable of storing billions of bytes will supplant today's magnetic fixed disks for mass computer storage. Lithium batteries will supersede today's lead-acid technology.

It is precisely this sort of discontinuous change that brings about "creative destruction," the over turning of established industry structures which Schumpeter saw as the fundamental engine of capitalist progress. Building on a tradition extending back to the 1950s (see, for example, Strassmann, 1956, and Bright, 1964), Richard Foster (1986) argues that industry leaders become losers because they have difficulty managing technological discontinuities—movements from one technology to another with inherently higher limits.

Examples of creative destruction based on both product and process revolutions abound: the shift from vacuum tubes to semiconductors overturned the dominance of firms such as RCA and Sylvania; with the installation of new, energy-saving cement manufacturing technology, eight of the ten largest American cement makers were acquired by foreign firms between 1973 and 1980.

Managing through periods of upheaval and transformation requires that we develop a useful model of technological change. Are there predictable patterns of innovation that recur time and time again in industry after industry? Are there predictable consequences of technological discontinuities? Who pioneers discontinuous innovations? When do leaders become losers?

Foster's depiction of technological progression through a series of S-curves suggests that technological change follows a cyclical pattern. The best-known model of technological change, the Abernathy/Utterback model, originally viewed technological progress as a single cycle, leading toward more process and less product innovation and culminating in the "productivity dilemma." Yet more recent updates of this framework in the early 1980s also conclude that technological change is cyclical—"dematurity" can in effect set the clock back and return an industry from a "specific" to a "fluid" state.

Our study of the entire history of three industries (see editorial box, next page) leads us to conclude that technology progresses in a series of cycles, hinging on

Reprinted from *Research · Technology Management,* May–June 1991, Philip Anderson and Michael L. Tushman, "Managing Through Cycles of Technological Change," pp. 26–31. Reprinted by permission of Industrial Research Institute, Inc.

How the Study Was Conducted

Lehigh University's Center for Innovation Management Studies and Columbia University's Strategy Research Center funded our three-year investigation of the entire history of the U.S. minicomputer, cement, and glass (containers, plate and windows) industries. We tracked the entry and exit of firms in these industries from their inception via directories extensively cross-checked with archival sources and data from trade associations and consultants. We also tracked a single key performance measure for each industry to empirically identify discontinuities: we focused on kiln capacity for cement, machine capacity for glass containers and flat glass, and CPU speed for minicomputers. To measure dominant design, we looked at new process installations for glass and cement and sales by model for minicomputers. A dominant design was considered to have emerged when one fundamental architecture accounted for 50 percent or more of new product sales or process installations for three straight years. Complete details of the data

sources, methodology, and statistical analyses performed are contained in Anderson (1988), available from University Microfilms.

Important limitations to the study should be noted. First, due to the length of the time series examined, only three industries are included; it would be unwise to overgeneralize the results. In particular, these findings may not completely apply to service industries or sectors where an oligopoly exists, where regulation is an important factor, or where strong patent positions are common. Furthermore, the study looked at only one performance measure per industry (due to limitations of historical data); in most industries, one would measure the technical frontier using several parameters. We were only able to examine survival and exit rates; the study draws no conclusion about the effect on firm performance of being first-to-innovation or first-to-standard.

—*P.A. and M.T.*

technological discontinuities and the emergence of dominant designs. Here, we discuss

- The cyclical nature of technological change.
- The influence of "competences."
- The empirical character of observed technology cycles.
- Who pioneers discontinuities and dominant designs.
- The process of "creative destruction."
- The implications of technology cycles for managers.

TECHNOLOGY CYCLES

As Foster's notion of a series of S-curves suggests, an industry evolves through a *succession* of technology cycles. Each cycle begins with a *technological discontinuity*. Discontinuities are breakthrough innovations

that advance by an order of magnitude the technological state-of-the-art which characterizes an industry. They are based on new technologies whose technical limits are inherently greater than those of the previous dominant technology, along economically relevant dimensions of merit.

To illustrate, examine Figure 3.1. The manufacture of window glass has been characterized by three great discontinuities. In the 19th century, skilled artisans blew molten glass into long cylinders, which were cut with a wire and flattened into glass sheets. In 1903, the Lubbers process substituted an automatic blowing machine for the artisan. In 1917, the Colburn machine, which drew a continuous ribbon from a tank of molten glass, was introduced. In 1963, the Pilkington float glass process was introduced in the United States, producing a continuous ribbon by floating molten glass across a bed of molten alloy. In each case, a process with inherently higher limits redefined the state of the art, increasing machine capacity by an order of magnitude while lowering costs and improving quality.

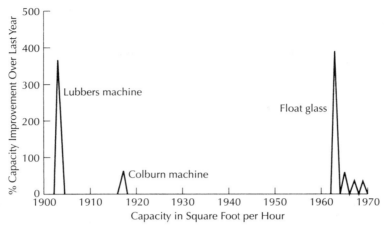

Figure 3.1. Three great discontinuities mark the development of machinery for manufacturing window glass in the United States.

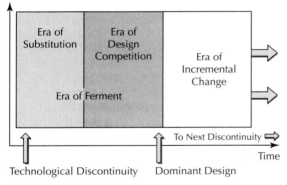

Figure 3.2. Industries evolve through successions of technology cycles, each inaugurated by a technological discontinuity. (Reproduced with permission of copyright owner. Further reproduction prohibited.)

Each technological discontinuity inaugurates a *technology cycle* (Figure 3.2). The breakthrough initiates an *era of ferment,* characterized by two processes. First, the new technology displaces its predecessor during an *era of substitution.* Though Foster argues that new technologies appear only when the old technology reaches its technical limits, often the older technology improves markedly in response to the competitive threat. Gaslight technology, for example, im-

proved dramatically in the decade after the introduction of the Edison electric light; Apple has pushed the limits of 8-bit microcomputer technology forward dramatically since the appearance of 16-bit and 32-bit replacements for the once-dominant Apple II. Despite these improvements, Fisher and Pry (1971) demonstrate that in many cases, the substitution process proceeds with mathematical inevitability once a small initial penetration is achieved.

The second process partly overlaps the first. An era of *design competition* follows a discontinuity. Radical innovations are usually crude, and are replaced by more refined versions of the initial product or process. Typically, several competing designs emerge, each embodying the fundamental breakthrough advance in a different way. Examples include the tremendous proliferation of automobile designs following Duryea's first auto or the appearance of dozens of competing airplane models after the Wright brothers' invention.

The design competition culminates in the appearance of what Abernathy and Utterback (1978) term a "dominant design," also called a "technological guidepost" by Sahal (1981). This design is a single basic architecture that becomes the accepted market standard. Dominant designs are not necessarily better than competing designs, and they often pioneer no innovative features themselves. Rather, they represent a *combination* of features, often pioneered elsewhere, that sets a benchmark to which all subsequent designs are compared. Examples include the IBM 360 computer series, the Fordson tractor, and the Ford Model T automobile.

The emergence of a dominant design marks the end of the era of ferment and the beginning of a period of incremental change. Here, the rate of design experimentation drops sharply, and the focus of competition shifts to market segmentation and lowering costs (via design simplification and process improvement). Many scholars and R&D managers contend that it is the patient accumulation of small improvements that accounts for the bulk of technological progress. Though this may not be true in every case, there is little doubt that once a design becomes a standard, it establishes a trajectory for future technical progress and changes the basis of competition in the industry. This era of competition based on slight improvements on a standard design continues until the next technological discontinuity emerges to kick off a new technology cycle.

INFLUENCE OF "COMPETENCES"

The nature of the technology cycle is dramatically affected by the cutting dimension of *competence*. Some discontinuous innovations are *competence-destroying*. They obsolesce existing know-now; mastery of the old technology does not imply mastery of the new. Firms must embark on a new learning curve which is essentially unaffected by the firm's existing know-how, and technical professionals require new training. The transistor illustrates a competence-destroying product innovation; mastery of vacuum tube technology proved as much a hindrance as a help to engineers trying to understand semiconductor electronics, and the learning curve for firms struggling to master the technology was unaffected by the firm's vacuum tube know-how. Similarly, float glass is a competence-destroying process discontinuity; a firm's knowledge of Colburn drawing technology conferred little advantage in mastering the Pilkington float glass process.

Other discontinuous innovations are *competence-enhancing*. These breakthroughs push forward the state-of-the-art by an order of magnitude, but build on existing know-how instead of obsolescing it. Thus the turbofan jet engine is a competence-enhancing product innovation. It markedly improved engine performance, but built on existing know-how instead of overturning it. The introduction of process control in cement kilns was a competence-enhancing process innovation. Computerization made possible enormous kilns, allowing cement manufacturers to employ their existing cement-making know-how to make more and better cement than any human operator could produce.

Both product and process innovations may either enhance or destroy existing competences. Yet there is a fundamental difference between product and process innovations. Product innovations normally affect more links in the value chain than do process innovations. The customer must be made aware of new products; often, he is not aware of process innovations per se. New products often require distribution channels and suppliers different from those which serviced older products. Process innovations usually make the product better and cheaper without necessarily disrupting upstream and downstream linkages. Thus, a key factor is not only whether the core technical know-how of an industry is disrupted by an innovation, but whether links in the value chain are overturned or reinforced by the new technology.

CHARACTERIZING THE TECHNOLOGY CYCLE

Discontinuities are generally uncommon, and their frequency varies greatly by industry. Nonetheless, they characterize both young and mature industries. We tracked 24 years of minicomputer data, over 100 years of cement industry history, and nearly 200 years of glass industry history and located only 17 discontinuities. The minicomputer industry passed through three discontinuities in a quarter-century, while the cement and glass industry experienced 50-year periods of incremental change. However, *every* industry we studied experienced at least one discontinuity since 1960, and the "mature" cement industry witnessed two.

A *single* dominant design *always* emerged following a discontinuity, except in two situations. When one discontinuity follows another very rapidly (within 3–4 years), a dominant design may not have time to emerge before the second new technology displaces the first. When several producers each patent their own proprietary process and refuse to license to others, a dominant design may not emerge. Otherwise, in every case a single product or process architecture accounted for over 50 percent of new installations. Ultimately one standard prevails; we did not observe cases where two standards coexisted or where the position of dominance rotated among several competing designs.

The original discontinuous innovation *never* became a standard. Some improved version of the initial breakthrough became the basis of a dominant design in every case. Furthermore, more often than not dominant designs lagged behind the state-of-the-art at the time they were introduced. The winner of the design competition is seldom at the industry's performance frontier; typically, the industry pushes the state-of-the-art forward during the era of ferment, then standardizes on a design that is *behind* the leading edge of the technology.

The length of the era of ferment (the lag from introduction of the new technology to establishment of a dominant design with 50 percent of the market) depends on whether the discontinuity enhances or destroys existing know-how. It took longer for an industry to converge on a dominant design following a competence-destroying discontinuity than it took to converge on a dominant design following a competence-enhancing discontinuity. When existing know-how is reinforced, the industry arrives at a standard relatively rapidly; when it is overturned, it takes considerably longer for the design competition to culminate in a single technological guidepost. Furthermore, when a series of discontinuities enhance the same underlying competence, the length of the era of ferment grew shorter in each successive technological cycle, bolstering the argument that the more familiar the underlying know-how, the easier it is to reach a standard.

PIONEERS OF DISCONTINUITIES AND DOMINANT DESIGNS

A key competitive question is, when will a discontinuity overturn an industry—when will leaders become losers? Figure 3.3 summarizes our findings. Focusing on the first five firms to adopt an innovation, we observed that in general veterans—firms which competed in the industry before the discontinuity—are more likely to pioneer breakthrough innovations. This runs counter to the often-heard argument that revolutions usually come from outside an industry. It is often the

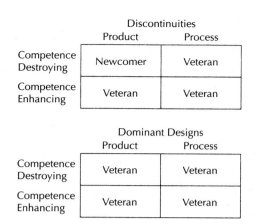

Figure 3.3. Veteran firms are more likely to pioneer each class of discontinuity and dominant design except the competence-destroying product innovation.

case that the *initial* innovator is a newcomer to the industry, but when we look at the group of first-movers, we usually find that veterans predominate.

It is easy to understand why this is so when an innovation builds on existing know-how. Firms which possess that know-how—the veterans—are most likely to build on that expertise. It is also easy to understand why competence-destroying innovations are pioneered by newcomers. The new technology obsolesces what the veterans know, temporarily knocking down barriers to entry. Veterans are reluctant to adopt the new technology because it wipes out their considerable investments and forces them to change in fundamental ways. It is in this case that leaders are most likely to become losers. However, competence-destroying process innovations are typically pioneered by veterans, despite the fact that they are obsolescing their own process know-how. We argue that veterans still are able to exploit strengths upstream and downstream in the value chain following a process discontinuity; only their core technical know-how is overturned. As a result, veterans are willing to write off investments in existing facilities and expertise to exploit the price/performance advantage of the new technology.

Finally, dominant designs are *always* pioneered by veterans, whether or not they build on or destroy competences. The revolutionary is seldom the standard-setter. Recall that dominant designs seldom are state-of-the-art, and that industry experience is needed to understand what the market needs in a standard.

CREATIVE DESTRUCTION

Industries are characterized by waves of foundings and failures. A period when the failure rate is unusually high is often termed a "shakeout." The conventional wisdom is that overcapacity or downturns in demand cause shakeouts. By analyzing mortality rates, we found no relationship between changes in demand and failure rates. Instead, failure rates were remarkably higher during eras of ferment than in any other period.

The inability to adapt to a new technical order seems to kill more firms than the inability to withstand a recession in the industry. Interestingly, only one American cement firm failed during the Great Depression; in contrast, dozens failed when confronted with the challenge of adapting to new kiln technology.

IMPLICATIONS FOR MANAGERS

The model of technology cycles provided here is one step toward developing what Foster terms "a language and a facility for talking about and directing technology." It allows managers in different industries to or-

---

How the Electric Auto Could Evolve

To see how the ideas developed in this research can help managers understand the probable evolution of a specific new technology, consider the predicted development of an electric automobile, a technology currently in its infancy:

A commercial electric automobile will become feasible following a breakthrough innovation, either in the power of electric motors (e.g., via superconductivity) or in power generation/storage technology (e.g., solar cells or improved batteries).

The initial electric automobile will be a crude design, which will be elaborated and altered by dozens of imitators (*unless* the innovation enjoys strong legal protection from the outset). The displacement of conventional automobiles by electric automobiles will follow a classic S-curve, whose takeoff will be greatly aided by one or two key sales (e.g., to government vehicle fleets or a major auto rental company). Rival versions of the initial breakthrough will compete for legitimacy and substantially improve the product's performance.

From the many versions of the initial innovation, one will emerge as the industry standard architecture, de facto or by regulation/agreement. This "dominant design" will account for over 50 percent of new electric automobile sales following its establishment.

Following the establishment of the dominant design, the competitive focus of this product class will shift from performance improvement via significant architectural variations to cost reduction, market segmentation, and development/elaboration of the infrastructure that supports electric automobiles. Improvements will be incremental, and virtually all successful models will incorporate the key features of the dominant design. This regime of continuous improvement will continue until another discontinuity overthrows this generation of electric automobiles.

If the discontinuity which paves the way for growth in this product class is a *process* discontinuity (e.g., superconducting power transmission), one should expect incumbent auto manufacturers and entrants from closely related fields (e.g., truck manufacture) to pioneer the new technology. The same would apply if the discontinuity is a component easily retrofitted to existing automobiles (e.g., a breakthrough battery). *Only* if the discontinuity involves a fundamental redefinition of automobile design (e.g., new concepts in motors, the body, power train, etc.) would we expect the process of "creative destruction" to replace today's vehicle makers with a new generation of companies spawned by the new technology.

—*P. A. and M. T.*

ganize their view of the industry's technical history, and to compare the effects of various types of innovations on the industry's structure. Beyond this, we draw four principal lessons for managers from this research.

1. Expect discontinuities. They do not happen frequently, but they do occur even in mature industries, and they are watershed events. When evaluating potential discontinuities on the horizon, consider whether they would enhance or destroy fundamental competences in your industry. Consider developing competences that survive technological revolutions, such as flexible manufacturing capability or strong distribution channels.

2. When a discontinuity appears, expect an era of ferment culminating in a single dominant design (with the two exceptions noted above). Expect several designs to compete; expect one to emerge as a winner. The dominant design will seldom be a state-of-the-art architecture; it is usually introduced by industry veterans, and the time it takes to reach a design depends on whether the discontinuity is competence-enhancing or competence-destroying.

3. Realize that technological revolutions may be introduced by an industry newcomer, but the group of firms that adopt it earliest typically includes a majority of veterans. Only in the case of competence-destroying product discontinuities do we observe a preponderance of newcomers in the pool of first-movers. It is worthwhile to monitor potential competitors from outside an industry, particularly when you suspect that a new product technology can obsolesce existing knowhow. But more often than not, the pioneers of discontinuities are competitors you already know, not newcomers to the industry.

4. Consider the implications of the finding that technological change, not downturns in demand, is associated with shakeouts. Top management always pays attention to industry recessions and is willing to make painful cost-cutting moves when demand drops. Yet it is not this form of competition that threatens the very survival of the firm and its rivals. Maintaining the or-

ganization's ability to navigate the rapids of creative destruction brought on by technological discontinuities is the key to fulfilling management's first duty to shareholders—preserving their capital by ensuring the continuance of the enterprise. The ability to direct the firm's marketing and financial operations helps top managers improve a firm's profitability. The ability to direct process and product innovation affects not only profitability but the viability of the firm itself in a world of technological upheaval.

REFERENCES

Abernathy, William. 1978. *The Productivity Dilemma.* Baltimore: Johns Hopkins University Press.

Abernathy, William and Clark, Kim. 1985. "Innovation: mapping the winds of creative destruction." *Research Policy,* 14:3–22.

Abernathy, William and Utterback, James. 1978. "Patterns of industrial innovation." *Technology Review,* 2:40–47.

Abernathy, William; Clark, Kim; and Kantrow, Alan. 1983. *Industrial Renaissance.* New York: Basic Books.

Anderson, Philip. 1988. *On the Nature of Technological Progress and Industrial Dynamics.* Unpublished Ph.D. dissertation, Columbia University.

Bright, James. 1964. *Research, Development and Technological Innovation.* Homewood, Illinois: Richard D. Irwin.

Clark, Kim. 1983. "Competition, technical diversity, and radical innovation in the U.S. auto industry." In Robert Rosenbloom (Ed.), *Research on Technological Innovation, Management, and Policy:* 103–149. Greenwich, CT: JAI Press.

Fisher, J. and R. Pry. 1971. "A simple substitution model of technological change." *Technological Forecasting and Social Change,* 3:75–88.

Foster, Richard. 1986. *Innovation: the Attacker's Advantage.* New York: Summit Books.

Sahal, Devendra. 1981. *Patterns of Technological Innovation.* Reading, MA: Addison-Wesley.

Schumpeter, Josef. 1942. *Capitalism, Socialism and Democracy.* New York: Harper & Brothers.

Strassman, Paul. 1956. *Risk and Technological Innovation.* Ithaca, NY: Cornell University Press.

4

Technological Discontinuities and Flexible Production Networks

The Case of Switzerland and the World Watch Industry

AMY GLASMEIER

The twentieth-century history of the Swiss watch industry illustrates how cultures and industrial production systems experience great difficulty adapting to external change at different points in time. The current emphasis on production networks—unique reservoirs of potential technological innovation realized through cooperation rather than competition among firms—lacks a detailed appreciation of historic networks, and in particular their fragile character in times of economic turmoil. While networks can and do promote innovation within an existing technological framework, historical experience suggests their fragmented, atomistic structure is subject to disorganization and disintegration during periods of technological change. An exclusive focus on "production" ignores other constraints that are powerful forces governing the reaction abilities of regions. Previous research has largely relied on a model of oligopolistic competition to explain how the Swiss lost control of the world watch industry. I conclude, on the contrary, that the Swiss experience must be understood from the standpoint of how technological change challenges previous ways of organizing production, industry, culture, and society. Technology shifts present a series of strategic turning points that industrial leaders must navigate during a period of technological change.

INTRODUCTION

The history of the Swiss watch industry is instructive as countries and regions experiment with network production systems in attempts to maintain and augment their competitiveness in a global economy. On the eve of the electronics revolution, the Swiss watch production system, centered in the mountainous Jura region, was flexible, cost-effective, and extremely profitable. Both horizontally and vertically disintegrated, the Swiss system offered enormous variety while maintaining quality and timeliness of delivery. "The multiplicity of enterprises, and the competition and emulation that characterized the industry, yielded a product of superior quality known the world over for high fashion, design, and precision" [21, p. 48].

Beginning in the 1970s, when foreign competition hurdled technological frontiers in watch movements, advancing from mechanical to electric, electronic, digital, and finally quartz technology, the Jura's undisputed dominance ended.[1] Massive job loss and

Reprinted from *Research Policy,* Vol. 20, Amy Glasmeier, "Technological Discontinuities and Flexible Production Networks: The Case of Switzerland and the World Watch Industry," pp. 469–485, copyright © 1991, with permission from Elsevier.

out-migration occurred as firms, unable or unwilling to adapt to new technologies, closed their doors. Today, while still world leaders in watch export value, Swiss watchmakers produce only a fraction of their pre-1970s output levels, and resources needed to invest in new product research and development are scarce [40]. In a span of less than 30 years, the world's dominant watch region yielded technological leadership (in watchmaking and micromechanics) to its Far Eastern rivals. What lessons can be learned about network production systems and technological innovation from the experience of Switzerland's watch region?

Industrial restructuring of the past 20 years has left once dominant manufacturing regions such as America's industrial heartland and Germany's Ruhr valley debilitated. Reincorporating technological innovation within production systems of deindustrialized regions has become a major concern. Even technologically vibrant regions such as Route 128, Silicon Valley, and Emilia Romagna confront uncertain figures in the current period of intense technological development and international competition. How can a region remain innovative during a period of technological change? Do network production systems offer a more flexible and permanent means of regional adaption? By examining the experience of the watch industry I hope to tie together empirical experiences of researchers asking similar questions concerning the relationship between structure of production, regional culture, technological change, the formation and maintenance of core skills, and state-led regional development in industrial hinterlands.

This article reviews the twentieth-century history of the Swiss watch industry. My purpose is to suggest that focusing solely on production transactions does not adequately explain how economic, social, and cultural conditions interact to form a complex of human relations that can remain flexible and innovative over time. While networks are quite proficient at production and innovation within an existing technological framework, disintegrated systems may neither accumulate profits nor demonstrate a collective will to make essential investments in research, marketing, and distribution in response to technological change. At a more refined level, this article suggests that the current emphasis on production networks—unique reservoirs of potential technological innovation realized through cooperation rather than competition among firms—

lacks a detailed appreciation of historic networks, and in particular their fragile character in times of economic turmoil [29, 30, 31, 32]. While networks can and do promote innovation within an existing technological system, historical experience suggests their fragmented, atomistic structure is subject to disorganization and disintegration during periods of major technological change [8, 9, 35].[2]

Interfirm networks are important ingredients of technologically innovative and flexible industrial production systems. This insight is an important addition to contemporary theoretical discussions about the relationship between regional and technology development. As the case of the Swiss watch industry suggests (within a particular structure of production and organization), a highly articulated system of production, tied together by elaborate cultural, institutional, and economic relationships, exhibits flexibility and adaptability within an existing technological framework. The case study also illustrates, however, that within any production system flexibility and innovativeness are time-dependent. Therefore, given specific historical circumstances, they are vulnerable.

The lack of coordination and organization within small firm complexes has precipitated discussions about the need for governing systems to regulate small firm atomistic behavior and to replicate functions performed by the vertically integrated corporation such as R&D, management training, marketing, and distribution. As Saxenian's work suggests, network production systems are vulnerable to technological threats from the outside [30]. Calls for institution-building must be tempered with the knowledge that coordinating organizations quickly become absorbed into the regional fabric and ossify over time. During the course of two centuries the Swiss watch industry established elaborate institutions, organized technological competitions and other social events, and supported diverse organizations to bolster the industry's innovative capabilities [8]. The strength of these institutions has been and still is significant. The Swiss Watch Industry Federation (FH) was the leading organization in trade negotiations for the world watch industry [24]. Long after the Swiss lost volume leadership, the FH continued to lead GATT negotiations [27]. Market share, quotas, and tariffs are still negotiated by the FH for the world watch industry. Yet despite its worldwide reputation, in the 1960s and 1970s the FH was unable to overcome resistance to new technology. While the organization sponsored Swiss R&D, it could not force members to incorporate new technologies into existing products.

This article departs from past treatments of the watch industry's postwar experience by examining the rise of world competition through the lens of technological shifts. Previous treatments have largely relied on a model of oligopolistic competition to explain how the Swiss lost control of the world watch industry. I conclude, on the contrary, that the Swiss experience must be viewed from another angle. How do technological shifts challenge previous ways of organizing production, industry, culture, and society? Fundamental changes in technology present a series of strategic turning points that industrial leaders must navigate. The Swiss were no exception.

This article first considers the historic evolution of the Swiss watch industry during the final decades of the last century and shows its early adaptability to new production innovations within the framework of mechanical watch technology. The bulk of the remaining discussion traces the evolution of the industry—illustrating the difficulties experienced in the face of radical technological developments.

The Swiss watch industry provides an important case study of an industrial and cultural system that retained technological supremacy for two centuries and that still holds its dominant position within the earlier mechanical paradigm. The industry has, however, yielded technological leadership to foreign competitors in a major geographical shift in world production [36]. The Swiss are now followers rather than leaders of industry trends.

THE EARLY TWENTIETH-CENTURY HISTORY OF THE SWISS WATCH INDUSTRY

Historically the Swiss industry has shown surprising resilience in the face of change. At the end of the last century (1876–1900) the industry was issued a major challenge by the U.S. watch production system. America's watch manufacturers developed machinery to produce watches at high volume with low cost, low skill, and relatively high levels of precision. Watch movements were drastically simplified and more economical to produce. While hand-adjustment was still required in final assembly, the overall skill content in American watches was drastically reduced.

The Swiss response to U.S. technological challenges was decisive. Over a period of 20 years (1885–1905) they proved more than capable of making needed technical progress [7]. While the Swiss lost considerable market shares in the U.S., the country's manufacturers did not yield control of global markets [19]. Over the course of two decades, the Swiss system adopted aspects of the American system that were cost-effective. The Swiss system shifted from its reliance on small-scale cottage production to an intermediate form that combined mechanization and partial vertical integration. Standard parts were mechanically manufactured at large scale in centralized factories, while flexibility was maintained in dispersed design and assembly activities. Even the more complicated parts were eventually mechanized using "versatile machines which were susceptible of all manner of adjustment, hence required some skill to operate . . ." [20, p. 40]. Thus within the existing mechanical technology system, the industry achieved new levels of profitability and international renown.

There is no doubt that by the 1910s Swiss mechanical watches dominated the world watch industry [18]. The Swiss controlled the micromechanical export industry by cost competitiveness, superior manufacturing competency, high levels of precision, and extraordinary attention to detail and style. The vertically integrated parts manufacturers achieved economies of scale through volume production. This benefit was passed on to assemblers in the form of low-cost movements. In the most labor-intensive aspects of the industry, the vertically disintegrated system of assembly and case manufacture kept overhead charges low.

International Economic Chaos and the Call for Regulation

The early 1920s was a period of great instability in the watch industry.[3] Disruptions in the watch market presented the Swiss with new and different problems [18]. Significant sums of capital had been invested to meet the American manufacturing challenge. Firms were larger, and the industry represented a larger share of gross national product [21]. The severity of the crisis forced family businesses to take drastic steps simply to reduce inventory. Opportunism, price-cutting, and increased export of movements and parts further destabilized the industry [39]. This unprecedented threat resulted in a call for industry regulation, and a cartel was formed.[4]

During the 1920s various associations were created to represent the interests of industry members. The Swiss Watch Industry Federation (FH) was organized to govern both firms assembling watches from component parts and the few firms with integrated manufacturing operations. The 17 manufacturers of ébauches (watch movements) were organized into a trust EBAUCHE S.A. Manufacturers of components other than ébauches (balance wheels, assortments, hair springs) were organized into the Union des Branches Annexes de l'Horlogerie (UBAH). In the late 1920s members of the various associations agreed to set levels of output and prices, and explicit rules were designed to restrict exportation of parts [18].

When this degree of collaboration proved insufficient to control opportunistic firms, the government intervened. In conjunction with industry and banking leaders, the federal government created the massive holding company ASUAG (which included EBAUCHE S.A. as well as other leading component producers). This final merger halted the exportation of parts and components to competitor countries [18].

The Statut de l'Horlogerie and the Codification of the Swiss System

The Statut de l'Horlogerie of the early 1930s established a regulatory system that governed Swiss watch manufacturing for more than 30 years. Through a combination of cartelization and government ownership, the Swiss industry was regulated to control vertical integration, foreign sourcing, and off-shore production. Swiss manufacturers could buy only from Swiss component producers, and component producers could sell only to Swiss firms. To further limit competition, government regulated the sale of machinery. The Statut de l'Horlogerie regulated the volume of Swiss watch production by requiring permits for the construction and expansion of production facilities [15].

The resulting industry structure consisted of the parts manufacturers who sold their output to assemblers, the assemblers, and the brand-name manufacturers. ASUAG could sell only to firms recognized by the Swiss government under the law. It could not export

parts or technology. Manufacturers fabricated complete watches but were restricted from selling movements and other parts to assemblers—thus eliminating competition with parts suppliers. They were also restricted from setting up production in other countries. Assemblers were prohibited from establishing production outside Switzerland, and they could buy parts from non-Swiss manufacturers only if prices were 20 percent below Swiss levels. The law's greatest effects were in regulating who was allowed to produce, what could be produced, and how much could be produced. By requiring export and manufacturing permits, the government essentially held supply below world demand and ensured Swiss firms handsome profit levels.

From 1933 to 1961 the Swiss watch industry experienced considerable stability matched by handsome growth. All industry sectors enjoyed the benefits. Under the Statut de l'Horlogerie, market shares were effectively stabilized. This predictably encouraged firms to reinvest profits in new process technology. High profits earned in this period allowed firms to develop a mechanical watch manufacturing system unparalleled in efficiency.

Abandoning Industry Regulation: Instituting Industrial Change

In the early 1960s three decades of stability once again gave way to uncertainty. Foreign competition ended the Swiss monopoly on mechanical watch production and the country's quasi-monopoly on the world watch industry. The slow erosion of Swiss world export market share met with cries from industry members to change laws that had regulated the industry for 30 years.

Reasons for industry discontent were numerous. The more profitable and better run firms lobbied against the cartel arguing that it protected firms that were producing low quality watches [39, 21]. Laws were also criticized for fixing the level of Swiss production at a time when other countries were making substantial inroads in the Swiss world export market share. In 1961 the Federal Assembly of the Swiss Confederation ratified a new decree eliminating the regulation of output and encouraging rationalization of the industry. The new law took effect in 1962, but it was not until the early 1970s that restrictions on watch manufacturing were entirely eliminated.

As expected, the watch industry underwent a series of unprecedented mergers. The healthier and larger establishments joined forces to match the sizes of their Far East Asian and American rivals. Within two years three firms were producing 32 percent of Swiss exports. SSIH (formed in the 1930s with the merger of Tissot and Omega to become a leading vertically integrated manufacturer) became the third largest watch manufacturer in the world (behind Timex and Seiko). In 1971 the ASUAG expanded beyond strictly component production by creating the General Watch Company, a holding organization of several brand names and component manufacturers [18]. A third holding company, Société des Garde-Temps (SGT), was created primarily to manufacture low-price and electronic watches.[5]

In addition to the three holding companies, there were a number of important groups. Rolex, although privately held, had 1972 sales estimated at 200 million Swiss francs (almost a quarter of Swiss exports by value) [17]. There were also four middle-sized groups including two subsidiaries of U.S. companies, Zenith and Bulova, and the prestige brands, Piaget, Patek Philippe and others. The remainder of the industry was made up of hundreds of small companies assembling and selling watches.

THE WORLD MARKET FOR WATCHES

At the end of the 1980s watch producers manufactured approximately 500 million watches annually worldwide (not including Eastern European production). The market for watches is made up of segments in a pyramid-like structure. The base of the pyramid consists of mass producers selling watches with a wholesale value of less than $50 (1990 dollars). These sales account for 90 percent of total volume. Although this segment of the market is dominated by Hong Kong producers, it also includes American Timex and the Swiss Swatch watch. The mid-price ($50–$500) watch market segment makes up 9 percent of all watch sales. Firms marketing in this segment include well known Swiss (Tissot, Omega, Longines, Rado), Japanese (Seiko and Citizen), and specialty American name brands (Hamilton).[6] The luxury market segment comprises only 1 percent. Luxury watch prices start at about $750. There are 20 brands in this category and

include such world-renowned names as Cartier, Ebel, Rolex, and Patek Philippe. Some firms span more than one market segment. These include firms such as Rolex that add value to the basic steel case watch model by altering the external parts of the watch (e.g., diamond-encrusted bezel).

Structure of the Swiss Watch Industry

The structure of the Swiss industry emerging after the collapse of the cartel maintains important vestiges of the old system. The Swiss watch industry reflects both horizontal and vertical disintegration of establishments. Although the number of individual producers has declined over time, the shares of establishments in the different industry segments have remained the same [25, 26]. The watch industry consists of four levels of production: movements and parts manufacturers; case and bracelet manufacturers; subcontractors; and assemblers and integrated manufacturers. Table 4.1 lists the number of Swiss watch firms and their employment by industry level.

Parts and Assemblers

Production of parts and components passes through various channels to arrive at final assemblers. Final assemblers assemble for all price segments of the watch market under nationally and internationally known brand names. Together, parts manufacturers, subcontractors, and assemblers employ approximately 20,000 workers with a turnover of more than 3 billion dollars, or 40 percent of total industry revenues (1990). Mid-price watch assemblers include such well known names as Chopard, Century, Corum, Eterna, and Raymond Weil. The luxury end of the assembly industry includes "international names" such as Cartier, Chanel, Christian Dior, Gucci, and Dunhill. These brand labels represent individual designers that sub-

Table 4.1. Industry Structure

	Houses	Employment
Movements and parts	40	8,000
Casing and bracelets	135	6,500
Subcontractors	135	6,000
Integrated manufacturers and assemblers	250	12,000

Source: Radja [26].

contract with Swiss component and case manufacturers to assemble their watches.[7]

Manufacturers

In contrast to the disintegrated structure of parts manufacturers and assemblers, the Swiss industry also includes enterprises that are vertically integrated. Manufacturers produce the entire product from movements through parts, casing, and final assembly. There are a dozen important integrated watch manufacturers. Rolex is the single largest manufacturer and enjoys 25 percent of total Swiss industry revenues. At the very high end luxury market segment are found the most prestigious integrated manufacturers, including Piaget, Patek Philippe, Audemars Piguet, Breguet, Ebel, and Blancpain. These firms produce watches that sell in the thousands of dollars and are produced in small numbers.

Movement Manufacturers

In response to economic instability in the 1930s, movement manufacturing was concentrated in a single firm (ASUAG). In the early 1980s reorganization further concentrated this activity. ASUAG was combined with a number of large previously independent manufacturers (Tissot, Rado, Longines, Omega, Certina, and Swatch) into SMH. SMH accounts for approximately 30 percent of all watch revenues and controls almost 25 percent of total watch employment. While SMH is the single largest supplier of parts and movements, there are a number of other movement producers including Fabrique D'Ebauches de Sonceboz et Ebosa, Piguet, and La Novelle Lemania et Laeger-Lecoultre. These firms cater to the luxury watch industry.

Movement production in the Swiss watch industry is the most vertically integrated. It is composed of 40 firms employing 8,000 workers with an average plant size of 200 employees. This component of production is the most technologically advanced and enjoys significant economies of scale. Parts and case makers, subcontractors, and independent manufacturers represent the majority of establishments but employ far fewer workers per firm (averaging 45 employees). Observing size of establishment verifies the disintegrated structure of production. Table 4.2 lists the number of firms by employee size category. The structure of the industry is essentially the same as it was in the 1970s.

Table 4.2. Firm Distribution by Size

Size Category	Number of Establishments	Number of Employees
1–9	200	1,500
10–19	130	2,000
20–49	100	4,000
50–99	70	5,000
100–199	34	5,000
200–499	32	10,000
500 plus	4	5,000

Source: Radja [26].

GLOBAL COMPETITORS AND THE WORLD MARKET FOR WATCHES

In the early 1970s the Swiss struggled to reorient their factories while nimble competitors flooded the field. But their production system was not easy to dismantle or rearrange. Japanese, American, and Hong Kong firms posed unique challenges to Swiss watchmakers. This new and rising competition and the advent of a new movement technology were both significant problems.

The Japanese industry were vertically integrated and therefore a low-cost producer [18, 22]. Seiko and Citizen made major inroads in the world watch market as both component and finished watch manufacturers. The Japanese made high quality low-priced movements that were sold to firms around the world. By the early 1970s, Japanese watch companies had succeeded in capturing 14 percent of the world watch market.

The Japanese increased their share of world export markets through various means. They had lower labor costs and an undervalued currency. They were vertically integrated and employed manufacturing automation. The Japanese developed the capacity to manufacture standardized movements and watch models. Japan was also selling large volumes of movements to the U.S. and Hong Kong. Although the Japanese produced models for every price range, they targeted the lucrative middle range, undercutting Swiss competitors.

Unlike the Swiss, the Japanese had the advantage of a large protected home market. Because other watch manufacturers were effectively locked out of their domestic market, Japanese producers enjoyed artificially high domestic prices that covered fixed costs. Thus in international markets watches could be sold close to or at marginal costs.[8]

Government regulation and financial assistance (R&D grants) accelerated Japanese penetration of the world watch industry. The Japanese watch industry continued to rationalize—undergoing further vertical integration that streamlined operations and reduced inefficiencies. The government encouraged vertical integration to "minimize the proliferation of marginal watch producers and to minimize the drain on foreign reserves caused by the importation of watch machinery" [18, p. 23]. In 1978, 88 percent of Japanese production was attributable to two firms. Switzerland's leading manufacturer accounted for only 9 percent of total national Swiss production [2].

The Structure of the Japanese Watch Industry

The level of vertical integration in the Japanese watch industry is high by national standards. High levels of vertical integration are primarily associated with the small number of industry competitors (Citizen, Seiko and Casio) and individual company product development strategies [10]. Citizen and Casio are primarily electronics firms which concentrate on digital watch manufacturing [3, 4]. Both companies pursued watch manufacturing to assure a market for their primary product, electronic components [8]. Seiko dominates Japan's watch industry. The company is responsible for 60 percent of the nation's output. Vertical integration was part of a conscious strategy to be the industry leader [34, 14]. After World War II (like other Japanese firms such as Honda), Seiko followed a product diversification strategy built around the company's core competence, precision manufacturing.[9]

The most critical advantage of Japan's capital-intensive system is the ability to manufacture components in huge volumes at low cost. The sale of movements and watch kits cemented the industry's 1970s world volume leadership.

The U.S. Market and American Watch Manufacturers

Japan was not the only significant challenger to the Swiss watch industry. The U.S. was both the world's largest and most competitive watch market [8]. The vast majority of American demand was satisfied by domestic firms. America's two stellar watch manufactur-

ers, Timex and Bulova, essentially controlled two-third's of the nation's market [19]. American watchmaking firms were dominant in the U.S. partly because of high tariffs that were based on the number of jewels in the watch movement and implemented to protect the domestic industry. Swiss manufacturers responded by redesigning their watches to include fewer jewels. But by redesigning watches, production was further fragmented with more models designed for the U.S. market. A bad side effect of this strategy was an inability to produce at volumes that would allow for productivity gains [27]. On the other hand, American firms enjoyed a loophole in trade policy which permitted offshore watch assembly by low-wage laborers. Because American firms could avoid paying duties, they could sell cheaper products than the Swiss.

Bulova and Timex presented significant problems for Japanese and Swiss manufacturers. Both corporations followed the American system of mass production. Employing a combination of sophisticated production technology and labor flexibility (through internationalization of production), Bulova produced a range of products spanning all price categories. Bulova's strength was the medium price range. The company produced hundreds of different styles in its Swiss factories. An international production system maximized site-specific advantages such as skill levels, technology, and markets.[10] The company's international orientation provided important opportunities to test-market new products. By having a strong brand policy and aggressively marketing products, Bulova moved into markets worldwide. At the high end, with its aggressively marketed tuning fork technology, Bulova was unique.

Alternatively, Timex sold a product that was cheap, simplified, and standardized. It was therefore easily mass produced. The company developed highly efficient, dedicated production equipment to produce huge volumes of standardized products. Timex also engineered true interchangeability. Parts could be exchanged not only within but between plants [21]. Because the U.S. lacked skilled watch workers, Timex pursued a capital-intensive production strategy. Machines were automated to reduce human involvement to a minimum. The company designed a dramatically simplified but well-manufactured watch with a relatively long life.[11]

But Timex did not confine itself to the low-price

market segment. By the early 1960s Timex had developed a low-priced higher quality jeweled watch line. In addition to its traditional and effective distribution channels (high traffic locations such as drug stores), Timex introduced its watches into jewelry stores and other, more conventional watch sales outlets. Within 20 years the company had gone from bankruptcy to control of 45 percent of the U.S. market and 86 percent of U.S. domestic watch production.[12]

The Hong Kong Industry[13]

While the Swiss were battling for market share with U.S. and Japanese firms, the Hong Kong industry emerged. From its experience as Japan's low-cost assembly location and a long standing preeminence in case and bracelet manufacturing, in less than 30 years the Hong Kong watch industry rose to become the world's volume leader. With little capital investment, Hong Kong watchmakers developed the capacity to produce thousands of watch models each year. Assembling in excess of 300 million units in 1988, Hong Kong produced more watches than any other nation. Based on value of exports, the country recently surpassed Japan to become the second largest watch producer, behind the Swiss.[14]

Early in the 1970s, with advances in diode technology, Hong Kong watchmakers moved into light-emitting diode (LED) display watches. LED watches dominated output for a short time, but declined when liquid crystal display watches emerged later in the decade. Until the early 1980s, this newer technology dominated the Hong Kong watch industry. In the early 1980s, the emergence of quartz analog watches breathed new life into the industry. Like other components of watch manufacturing, quartz analog watch production in Hong Kong relied upon foreign parts. And because it also required a higher level of capital investment, Hong Kong's production system took time to adjust.

But adjust it did. In the late 1980s quartz analog watches began to dominate the industry, and evidence of their growing importance is striking. In 1980 digital watches accounted for approximately 60 percent of the value of total watch output. Analogs made up only 8 percent, and mechanical watches accounted for the remainder. In 1984 quartz analogs and digitals each made up approximately 43 percent of total output value [13]. By 1988 quartz analog watches dominated the

market, accounting for 82 percent of total output by value. Digital watches made up only 12 percent. Because of its extremely fluid industrial structure, a rapid and complete transformation of the watch industry's product mix was possible [8, 13].

Hong Kong's flexibility to respond to technological change derives from the fact that its watchmaking industry is a user, not a producer, of new technology. Hong Kong has been unable to develop its own movement technology due to a lack of skills and capital investment. The "sweatshop" nature of the industry means that labor absorbs the cost of change. Watchmaking in Hong Kong is ephemeral. Like other low-wage assembly industries, Hong Kong's momentary advantage can evaporate with the slightest increase in wages. A significant portion of watch assembly is already done in mainland China. Thus, while at the moment watchmaking thrives in Hong Kong, the industry has little long-term attachment to the island.

TECHNOLOGICAL CHANGE AND INDUSTRIAL INSTABILITY

Until the 1970s, the world watch industry grew steadily, and production was shared among three countries, the U.S., Japan, and Switzerland.[15] Trade liberalization in the 1950s, coupled with GATT and U.S. tariff reductions in the 1960s, set the stage for enormous expansion of markets in the 1970s. In a span of 10 years the market for watches doubled from 230 to 450 million watches [41].

In the early 1970s world demand for watches was overwhelmingly for mechanical devices. Only 2 percent of export sales were electronic watches. But in just two decades, the structure of demand changed. The competitive terrain shifted from precision based on mechanical know-how to accuracy based on electronic engineering. By the late 1980s electronic products comprised 76 percent of world consumption—approximately 60 percent digital, and the remainder analog. While the Swiss were the first to develop electronic watch technology, competitors succeeded in commercializing it.

Science Replaces Art in Watch Manufacturing

The introduction of electronic watches in the early 1970s had a profound impact on the Swiss share of world markets (see Table 4.3). In 1974 Swiss watches made up 40 percent of the world export market (by volume). Ten years later this figure had fallen to 10 percent. The loss occurred almost entirely in the high volume, low- and medium-price watch market segments.

How was it that the Swiss share of world markets fell so precipitously? The watch cartel insulated Swiss manufacturers from the effects of interfirm competition. Enjoying (volume) control of the world market (based on mechanical devices), it was easy for firms to become myopic about external events and new technology introduced by distant competitors. Because ASUAG looked only to members of the Swiss Watch Industry Federation (FH) for market information, new developments outside Switzerland did not filter into existing information channels.

When pressured to incorporate radical technological innovations, the Swiss industry proved unprepared to commercialize new ideas. Although inventions were very frequent, industry leaders were often skeptical about the viability of new proposals—particularly if they implied a radical reorientation of existing timekeeping methods. As one leading watch family head commented on the industry's failure to capitalize on tuning fork technology: "Every day someone came to the factory door with a so-called innovation. Claims of new and different technologies were a dime a dozen. Given production pressures, problems, and uncertainties, what was one to do?" As Morgan Thomas notes, "many firms attempt to screen basic science and technical knowledge relevant to the firm's mission" [37]. This skeptical complacency proved costly when Hetzel, the Swiss inventor of tuning fork technology, was

ignored by Swiss watch manufacturers. After he successfully commercialized his new technology in the United States, the Swiss were forced into a defensive position just to gain access to the new technology.

The Organizational Structure of the Swiss Watch Industry

The tightly articulated network surrounding watch manufacturing strengthened the status quo. The watch industry was heavily geographically concentrated in the Jura Mountain region. To the outside world towns were identified by the factories of either major manufacturers (Longines in St. Emier; Tissot in Le Locle), or by specific watch products (Bienne and SMH formerly made ASUAG watch movements).

Regional institutions were interwoven into the fabric of the industry. Educational institutions were steeped in watchmaking tradition, turning out skilled workers who spent up to four years learning to make watches from start to finish. Machine tool firms such as Dixie, the originator of the jig bore, provided equipment to parts houses and claimed world preeminence in the manufacture of precision tools. Banking institutions were deeply implicated in the fortunes of the watch industry. In the early 1970s regional banks were known to have as much as 50 percent of their loanable funds invested in family-run watch-related enterprises. And the industry made heavy investment in collective R&D laboratories. The complicated web of watch manufacturing permeated the core of the region's social, political, and economic institutions.

Watch manufacturing's fragmented production structure also presented problems. Subcontracting levels were high, and the region's dominant firms could not exercise control over the myriad component producers. Fixation with precision had lulled the region's firms into believing they were invulnerable to external forces [5, 11]. Supreme precision, however, did not require a theoretical understanding of new scientific developments; rather it necessitated great attention to detail. As Pierre Rossel notes, "the region's firms were unprepared to overcome a technological paradigm shift that devalued the region's long-standing comparative advantage" [28].

Transferring a foreign technology into existing products was crippled by a manufacturing culture steeped in tradition. Rapid change was the antithesis of

Table 4.3. Export of Watch Movements and Completed Watches 1951–80 (thousands of units)

	Japan	Switzerland
1951	31	33,549
1955	19	33,742
1960	145	40,981
1965	4,860	53,164
1970	11,399	71,437
1975	17,017	65,798
1980[a]	68,300	50,986

[a]Includes movements [21].

watch culture which rewarded patient methodical actions within an existing technological trajectory. This was the key. The transition from mechanical to electronic movement manufacturing called into question the heart of the Swiss watch industry. To say that precision metal machining no longer ruled the sacred domain of timekeeping accuracy was simply too much for the centuries-old Swiss tradition to endure. Rather than embracing this new threat as they had done when confronted by the American system of mass production, they chose to diminish its significance—with grave consequence.

Invention Does Not Guarantee Innovation: Technological Discontinuity and the Advent of Quartz

Organizational limitations inhibited ASUAG, the major movement producer, from moving into quartz. Because its market was literally hundreds of mechanical watch assemblers, no individual firm's demand was enough to persuade ASUAG to commit to one quartz movement design. But neither did any single manufacturer have an incentive to switch technologies. And even when ASUAG recognized the importance of quartz technology, the company lacked the marketing capability to successfully sell a quartz product to its primary market, Swiss assemblers [38]. A captive producer (unable to sell movements outside Switzerland), ASUAG lacked the incentive, necessity, and the ability to develop the marketing skills to compete internationally. Simultaneously, key watch manufacturers such as SSIH were unable to decide upon a quartz model. They therefore invested in numerous efforts to develop a quartz movement.

As with other challenges, the Swiss responded initially to the new quartz threat. Convinced that quartz was a passing fancy, nonetheless the Swiss rose to confront the new menace. Setting technicians to the task, the Swiss produced the first quartz watch movement simply to show that it could be done. But the elaborate network then stopped in its tracks, confident that quartz would eventually be related (as the electric watch had been) to the status of curio.

By the time the Swiss developed an industry-wide response to quartz technology, they lagged two years behind the Japanese. Having developed the initial technology, they failed to commercialize it. The Swiss are not alone in this fate. As Hoffman notes, "an innovation may be a technical success but a commercial failure in the innovator firm but a commercial success in the imitator firm" [12]. While the Swiss could claim that they were the first to develop a quartz watch (1971), they had to buy the necessary accompanying semiconductor technology from the Americans. Increased investments in R&D could not overcome the Swiss lag in microelectronics technology. The Swiss failure to act in the face of quartz technology could perhaps be blamed on bad judgment. But the problem was more fundamental and went to the heart of its highly fragmented network system of production.

The Swiss did not anticipate that the new technology would dominate the market in such a short time. But as integrated circuit prices fell precipitously, quartz watches became increasingly affordable. Because the Japanese had been vertically integrated since the 1960s, companies such as Seiko were poised to take full advantage of manufacturing developments occurring at various stages in the watch manufacturing process—further cementing their technological lead. Simultaneously, they could cross-subsidize component manufacturing, reducing per unit prices while raising per unit performance. The late development of Swiss domestic production of integrated circuits in a freestanding enterprise could not take advantage of information passing between component producers and watch manufacturers.

Unlike the Japanese watch manufacturers who saw semiconductor technology as an end in itself, the Swiss' forays into microprocessor technology were oriented strictly toward watches. This end-market focus did not facilitate synergies between semiconductor manufacturers and a wide range of users. In contrast with Japanese watchmakers who had a commercial electronics industry to rely upon for market outlets, the Swiss watch industry had to go it alone. Given the size of the watch industry's demand for chips, it was difficult to operate a chip production facility at optimal scale. It also made investments in R&D very costly per unit of expected demand for chips. Based on the network tradition, companies such as SSIH attempted to overcome their lack of technological capacity through a joint R&D project with Battelle. FH also initiated a joint R&D project to lessen Swiss dependence on U.S. semiconductor technology. With the FH, Brown

Boveri and Philips of the Netherlands formed FASE-LEC, a laboratory to develop Swiss semiconductor production capacity. By the mid-1960s it was hard to judge the success of the venture because operations were never made public [18, 39].

Complicating matters further was the rapid development of digital display technology. The commercialization of digital watches occurred with lightening speed. Digital display technology increased demand for quartz watches, leading to further price declines. This time the competition included American semiconductor manufacturers producing their own brands. Price reductions were dramatic, and by 1975 Texas Instruments had introduced a very inexpensive digital watch in a plastic case for $19.95. Although problems with the battery momentarily resulted in high reject levels, and consumers really wanted watches with more visual appeal, it did not take long to solve these problems. Battery longevity was vastly increased, watch designs improved aesthetically, and within an astonishingly short period of time, digital watches took over a large share of the market.

The Swiss responded slowly to change in digital technology largely because when it was introduced, it was crude. Given what promised to be a reasonably long developmental period between the introduction of the quartz technology and its eventual market success, the Swiss were understandably skeptical. As Dosi characterizes this moment,

> Especially when a technological trajectory is very "powerful." it might be difficult to switch from one trajectory to an alternative one. Moreover, when some comparability is possible between the two (i.e., when they have some dimensions in common) the frontier on the alternative (new) trajectory might be far behind that on the old one with respect to some or all the common dimensions. In other words, whenever the technological paradigm changes, one has got to start (almost) from the beginning in the problem-solving activity [6, p. 154].

The quartz "problem" permeated the Swiss watch manufacturing network. Every segment of the industry was affected. The rapid development of quartz means there were now many sets of tools needed to produce cases and dials. Uncertainty in both technology and consumer preference forced the Swiss watch compa-nies to compete in three watch markets—digital, tuning fork, and quartz. The succession of innovations and new model development resulted in excess inventory. It seemed that just as a watch was developed, it became obsolete. During this period of rapid technological change, Swiss firms (and others) were forced to take back and in many cases write down inventory—an extremely costly endeavor [39]. The problems of the industry did not become widely apparent, however, until hidden reserves were consumed, and firms were forced to reveal their weakened position.

The Limits of the Network

The experience of the Swiss watch industry is indicative of the turmoil experienced when a new technological trajectory unfolds. Signals about which direction the technology will ultimately take are filtered through networks of institutions which often have competing short-term interests. In the case of the watch industry, firms had a vested interest in mechanical watchmaking. They were receiving positive signals about their existing product, and demand was strong. Therefore suggestions about a possible technological shift seemed misplaced. While the market provides a good focusing device after a decision is taken by industry participants, it is rarely helpful in deciding *ex ante* which direction the technology will ultimately take. As Dosi suggests,

> . . . the point we wish to stress, however, is the general weakness of market mechanisms in the *ex ante* selection of technological directions especially at the initial stage of the history of an industry. This is, incidentally, one of the reasons that militates for the existence of "bridging institutions" between "pure" science and applied R&D. Even when a significant "institutional focussing" occurs, there are likely to be different technological possibilities, an uncertain process of search with different organizations, firms and individuals "betting" on different technological solutions. With different competing technological paradigms, competition does not only occur between the "new" technology and the "old" one which it tends to substitute, but also among alternative "new" technological approaches [6, p. 87].

The introduction of the electronic watch resulted in unprecedented change in the organization of watch production. The differences between electronic and mechanical watches were dramatic. Whereas labor costs constituted as much as 70 percent of a mechanical watch, in electronic watches labor costs were very low (less than 10 percent). Another major difference was the control of technology. The Swiss effectively controlled mechanical watch technology (due to the watch statute), and Bulova controlled the tuning fork. Electronics were fundamentally different. The technology was widely available, thus increasing the likelihood of new competitors with little or no prior watchmaking experience. Given the evolution of electronics, it was almost a foregone conclusion that price declines would occur in tandem with increases in capability. Thus, even the cheapest watch could be a good watch.

Network Rigidities Hamper Industry Response

Internal industry organizational and cultural impediments hampered a rapid response to the electronic watch. For example, the production planning time horizon for mechanical watches differed radically from electronics. The manufacturing cycle was organized according to the lead time needed to manufacture tools and dies for the fabrication of a new caliber, or watch dimension. Once committed to a design, tools and dies were crafted to cut the necessary metal parts. After parts were manufactured, movements were assembled and sold. Introducing a new watch model took up to two years. With electronic watches there were fewer parts to be manufactured. Consequently the time needed to make a watch dropped dramatically. Thus, when the Swiss were faced with the need to shift to a new technology, they were already two years behind, given the differences in the manufacturing cycles.

Ironically, product variety further hampered the industry. Few factories specialized in a single caliber. Therefore, firms were unable to achieve economies of scale. And because most factories produced several calibers' parts, inventory overhead was costly. Parts were required for each caliber—resulting in huge volumes of work in process. And the manufacturing cycle had to be managed across a wide range of products from tool making to product assembly.

Manufacturers had no choice but to focus on quality to differentiate themselves from the assemblers. Moreover, marketing strategy dictated the need

to produce a family of watches to preserve firm market share. Since manufacturers could not sell movements, they could not achieve sufficient economies of scale to enjoy minimum efficiencies. Low volume of output led to high prices.

The effort required to overcome technological deficiencies associated with quartz technology required an industry-wide response. Given the industry's weakened condition, no single firm could afford the costs of developing such an uncertain technology. Numerous industry associations were formed to develop the technology. This new form of collaboration created serious problems, however, because no single firm could appropriate the fruits of collective research and translate it into a competitive advantage to capture new markets. Unlike times past, when pursuit of new innovation formed the basis of market share, collective research became collective knowledge. Firms were compelled to embark upon research to create technological differentiation based on the original quartz innovation. These efforts were costly, uncertain, and occasionally unsuccessful.

Distribution

The Swiss also had to contend with a centuries-old distribution system built around the watch as a piece of jewelry. Mechanical watches were traditionally distributed through jewelry stores, and jewelers made steady profits on repair. But quartz technology threatened to change all that.

Swiss distribution outlets initially balked at the quartz watch. Early rejection was partially attributable to awkward styling: electronic watches were bulky and unattractive [39]. But more importantly, watch distributors effectively stalled the introduction of Swiss quartz analog watches in defense of their own market for watch repair. Quartz watches were more accurate and relatively unbreakable compared with mechanical watches.

Unlike the Swiss, the Japanese did not have an age-old distribution system. Market channel conflicts did not confront Japanese quartz watch manufacturers. Indeed Japanese channel strategy selected outlets through which the benefits of quartz longevity and error-free operation were maximized. The quartz watch was easier to sell, and it was more accurate. Timing was also important. The Japanese quest for large markets occurred simultaneously with the retail revolution. Mass marketing greatly expanded the number of outlets for watches. By the 1970s consumers were more likely to buy a watch in a variety store than a jewelry shop.

By the mid-1970s the Swiss were running just to catch up. Major Japanese competitors introduced increasingly cheap, long-lived, and refined watches. They pursued a strategy of short production runs; each time improving upon previous designs and climbing the learning curve more rapidly. Because the manufacturing cycle for the electronic watch was much shorter than for the mechanical watch, the Japanese could experiment within a relatively short time period.

The final blow came when the benefits of quartz converged to produce a cheaper, smaller, thinner, stylish, and accurate woman's watch. Before quartz efforts at further miniaturization, women's watches had been less accurate and more costly to manufacture than men's. Now accuracy no longer distinguished cheap from expensive watches. The entire basis of Swiss market hegemony—precision—had evaporated.

Reorganization and Rationalization

By the early 1980s the Swiss industry was in disarray. The international recession dealt the final blow to the Swiss watch industry's historic organization. Faced with operating losses and massive inventories, SSIH was eventually a victim of industry reorganization. The company could not solve the equation of low prices, wide assortment, small volume, rapid change, short delivery time, and large model series [38]. Seiko, Japan's largest watch producer, was able to respond because it had the market volume to offer a wide assortment with economical series, low prices, and short delivery. A single statistic says it all, "on the average Japan produced, under each brand name, 6 million watches in the 1970s compared with fewer than 100,000 in Switzerland" [16, p. 221].

In the early 1980s SSIH and ASUAG were forced by the banks to merge. While the national significance of the Swiss watch industry could not be abandoned, neither could industry organization be allowed to continue as it had in the past. The merged SMH Group was taken over by powerful Swiss industrialists. One of the most dramatic changes arising from the merger was the introduction of a wholly new product, the "Swatch," propelling the Swiss back into the low-priced segment of the market [2, 23].[16]

SUMMARY, REFLECTIONS AND CONCLUSIONS

Over the course of the last 20 years the Swiss lost both volume market leadership and technological supremacy. Given the industry's well-tuned production system, high level of profitability, and persistent success in its traditional line of business, what precipitated this historic reversal?

Beginning in the late 1920s the industry organized as a cartel to reduce the opportunistic behavior of industry participants. The resulting structure, though highly efficient and profitable, outlived its usefulness. Following the rescission of the Statut de l'Horlogerie, the network structure of production, while efficient and flexible, was also fragmented. Faced with the need to shift from a technology based on mechanics to one based on electronics, a time-lag built into the fragmented system inhibited rapid information flow. Shifting technological systems required that institutions and other critical components of the existing system be substantially modified. But this task proved difficult. The 200-year dominance of the previous paradigm constituted an "outlook which focused the eyes and efforts of technologists, engineers, and institutions in defined directions" [6, p. 158]. Initially, the region did not have the training capacity to provide electronics engineers. These skilled workers had to be imported from outside. In the case of Swiss watches, the decades old distribution system promoted Swiss watches based on their mechanical precision. Other organizations which represented the industry, such as the FH, were still predicting mechanical watch supremacy as late as the early 1970s. Educational and technical institutions—the core of the region's production complex—took even longer to respond to the new technological regime.

Amid radical change, organizations could not form a single voice to respond. The watch industry's collective research efforts to pioneer new technology could not overcome organizational inertia and infighting that arose with the need to commercialize the new technology. Without detailed and prearranged specifications about how the benefits of research were to be distributed, institutional inertia slowed the process of change. Since no single firm could be the "first" to introduce the collectively developed innovation, each firm had to develop its own [39]. When industrial reorganization eventually occurred, efforts were insufficient to address the structural crisis. Longstanding inefficiencies embedded in the production system led many firms into bankruptcy, resulting in bank ownership of some of the region's most famous and successful firms.

As the Swiss case attests, elaborate network production systems suffer like any other organizational form in the face of unexpected technological change [36]. All prior means of governance are called into question. The peculiar advantage of decentralized systems are also potentially their greatest flaw. Extreme change often necessitates radical reorientation. In such instances the ability to respond rapidly dictates who will be the ultimate victors. Although watches represent a specific case, their longevity as a product should bring pause to pronouncements that network production systems are somehow immune to technological change.

APPENDIX: HISTORY OF WATCH TECHNOLOGY

Evolution of the Watch

Since its creation almost 300 years ago, the watch has remained remarkably the same. Up until the 1960s alterations in the watch occurred mostly to the exterior in response to fashion and consumer tastes. The internal mechanism remained stable. The advent of electronics represented the first significant departure in the internal functions of the watch. The impact of this new technological development was profound. Centuries-old traditions in the manufacture of watches were revolutionized over night. Prior to electronics, timekeeping accuracy was associated with the precision with which metal parts were cut, filed, and fitted together. The most accurate watches were made by a single craft worker who cut each part, polished each metal edge, and placed each tiny part in the watch movement. Tuning the watch to achieve accuracy required very careful attention to detail. A short description of the evolution of watches helps clarify the meaning of electronics to the industry. This section draws heavily from Knickerbocker's treatment of watch development [18].

The Standard Spring-Powered Watch

A standard mechanical watch consists of three groups of parts: the "ébauche," or movement blank; the regulating components; and other generic parts. The ébauche consists of the framework (or backbone) of the watch, the gear train, and the winding and setting mechanism. Regulating components make the movement work at a correct rate. The miscellaneous parts include the case, crystal, etc.

A mechanical watch is driven by a mainspring which transfers stored energy (in the spring coil) to the gears that move the hands. The release of energy is controlled by the escapement mechanism. Although numerous escapement models were developed over time, the mechanism is constrained by the anchor fork to give up a precise amount of energy. The anchor fork rocks back and forth allowing the escapement wheel to advance in tiny increments, and these increments are converted by other gears to the watch hands.

The anchor fork moves in conjunction with a balance wheel that moves back and forth. The balance wheel is motivated by a hairspring that coils and uncoils, keeping the balance wheel in motion. As the anchor fork disengages from the escapement wheel, it transmits enough power to the hairspring to coil it. As the hairspring uncoils, it rotates the balance wheel in the opposite direction. This motion rocks the anchor fork in the opposite direction, starting the next cycle of the regulating mechanism.

Not all watch movements are the same. Differences in movement quality relate to the technical composition of the parts used. Precision, ornamentation, and movement miniaturization differentiate a high from a low quality watch. Internal jeweling in watches does not reflect differences in quality. Jewels are used to reduce friction between touching metal parts. The majority of jewels used in the interior of a watch are made out of synthetic materials and do not add significant value to the watch. Within mechanical watches there is a qualitative difference between jeweled and pin lever watches. The pin lever watch contains a more simplified movement compared to a jeweled watch (an example is Timex). A pin lever watch has few moving parts and does not use jewels to reduce friction between metal parts.

The Electric Watch

In this century, the first major technological advance in watch movement manufacture was the introduction of the electric watch. The electric watch movement was made possible by World War II R&D developments in the miniaturization of motors and batteries. The electric watch was only a partial step away from the mechanical watch. The mainspring and many of the components of the escapement were eliminated and replaced by current from a battery that drove a tiny balance wheel motor. The electric watch was introduced in 1957 and was available world wide by the 1960s. Because electric watches were no more accurate than most mechanical watches, they did not make major inroads in the medium- and high-price watch markets.

The Tuning Fork Watch

The second major innovation in watch technology, the tuning fork, had a profound effect on the watch industry. The tuning fork is stimulated by an electric current from a battery. The current causes the tuning fork to vibrate at 360 cycles per second. A tiny strip of metal connected to the tuning fork transfers the vibration to a set of gears, which like a conventional watch, drives the watch hands. Because the tuning fork vibrates 31 million times a day, the mechanism is far more accurate than a mechanical watch. Tuning fork technology was invented in the early 1950s and became commercially available in the early 1960s. A women's version was eventually introduced in the early 1970s.

The Quartz Crystal Watch

The third, and most significant innovation in watch manufacturing occurred in the late 1960s with the use of quartz crystals to regulate increments of time. When electric current is passed through quartz it vibrates at a very high frequency. Microcircuitry subdivides the crystal's frequency into electric pulses which drive the watch. In some cases the quartz is used to power a stepping motor, which is connected to a gear train that moves the hands. Quartz technology can also be used to stimulate a tuning fork device. In solid state watches the pulses are fed into integrated circuits that convert the pulses into minute and second time increments. This last type of watch incorporates no moving parts. The face and hands of a solid state watch are replaced with different methods to display time.

Changes to the Watch Face

Prior to the introduction of the quartz crystal watch, changes in the timekeeping mechanism were com-

pletely internal to the watch. With the advent of the quartz crystal, time could be displayed by conventional means (analog) or by digital display. Two primary displays are important: light-emitting diodes (LED) and liquid crystal display (LC). LEDs are semiconductors that emit light (much like a lightbulb). Originally used in calculators, LEDs became fashionable in watches in the early 1970s. Because LEDs require considerable power they are not illuminated at all times. A push button activates the display. In contrast, an LC display consists of a glass sandwich with a thin coating of electrically sensitive chemical between the glass plates. When a current is passed through an LC, the chemical changes its crystalline structure. The altered crystals reflect light coming from an outside source. While less power consumptive than an LED, LC's brightness and precision depend on the brightness of the external illumination.

The advent of quartz altered both internal and external features of the watch. With high levels of accuracy, the quartz watch could also incorporate numerous functions. Within an incredibly small space, a quartz watch could include multiple timekeeping mechanisms including alarms and other sophisticated functions. In combination, quartz technology revolutionized the watch industry.

ACKNOWLEDGMENTS

This article is based on original research conducted in Japan, Hong Kong, and Switzerland. The assistance of Luc Tissot, Wendy Taillard Pierre Rossel, and Jocelyn Tissot, of the Tissot Economic Foundation, was greatly appreciated. The Foundation and its staff were instrumental in the successful completion of this research. A full elaboration of the argument presented in this article can be found in various working papers in the Graduate Program in Community and Regional Planning, Working Paper Series.

NOTES

1. The Appendix provides a brief review of watch technologies.
2. The use of the term "disintegration" is meant to imply chaos not the evolution of the spatial division of labor as used by Scott [32].

3. World War I created severe disruptions in the world watch market. Russia, a major Swiss market, closed its borders to international trade, while other countries raised protectionist barriers in attempts to preserve domestic industries. Demand for Swiss watches declined precipitously between 1916 and 1921.

4. It was the larger firms which had made the capital investments in equipment that wanted to inject order into the historically anarchistic industry. To recoup capital investments, the more advanced firms had to control the small firms that easily sprang up and produced cheap watches [15].

5. The SGT holding company also acquired two American watch companies, Waltham and Elgin.

6. The Hamilton Watch company is American in name only. The Swiss corporation SMH owns the brand.

7. Until recently these international brands did not operate their own manufacturing plants. Cartier (one of the largest international brands) previously subcontracted production to EBEL, a Swiss prestige manufacturer. The French firm recently opened a plant to manufacture its own products.

8. When domestic wages began to rise, the Japanese quickly shifted assembly to Hong Kong where wages were lower (creating a spatial division of labor to ensure low price and timely product delivery).

9. Today Seiko has major market share in certain types of semiconductors, micromachinery, miniature circuit board manufacturing, and small plastic and rare metal parts. The company has capitalized on the original core skill by pursuing markets and product niches in related fields.

10. For example, Accutron was made in the U.S. where technology levels were high despite lesser manual labor skills. Medium- and low-priced mechanical watches were manufactured by high-skilled Swiss workers.

11. Given that their watch was cheap, Timex made no pretense of providing after sales service. When the watch stopped running, it was simply thrown away and a new one purchased.

12. Like Bulova, Timex established international market presence and production capacity. The company had 20 plants scattered around the globe. Each market was carefully analyzed, and sales strategies were adjusted according to local customers [18].

13. In 1988 there were approximately 1,386 watch-making firms registered with the Hong Kong government. From 1983 to 1988 employment increased steadily from 25,200 to 26,444. Over 90 percent of firms employ fewer than 50 employees. The structure of the watch industry is remarkably similar to that of electronics in Hong Kong. A recent study by the Hong Kong Government Department of Industry indicated that many of the structural weaknesses evident in the watch industry are also apparent in electronics. These include lack of local brands and design

capacity, a fragmented production structure, and low levels of capital investment. Hong Kong watch prices (FOB) are extraordinarily low by world standards. The average wholesale price of a watch in 1988 U.S. dollars was $3.00. Advertised wholesale prices ranged from $4.00 to $10.00 per watch (with a lead time of between 25 and 60 days). Even jeweled watches cost a fraction of those manufactured in Switzerland. Orders can be as small as 100 watches, and in some cases firms have no minimum lot size.

14. Hong Kong is an established forerunner in innovation and exportation of watch parts, cases, bands, and accessories. The case and band industry is well-developed, and Hong Kong firms export finished products to major watch producing countries that include Japan, Switzerland, and the U.S. Surprisingly, even up-scale companies such as Cartier use Hong Kong watch bands. In 1984 (the latest year for which statistics are available), there were 484 case-making firms employing 9,200 workers in Hong Kong. This is almost four times the number of case producers in Switzerland.

15. We do not include Eastern Block country production in these figures. A considerable volume of watches is produced in the Soviet Union, East Germany, and other Eastern Block nations [18].

16. Swatch is a plastic watch manufactured at high volume using advanced automation and assembly-line methods. But the real innovation is in marketing the watch as a high fashion, mood-oriented product. Ownership of multiple models is stressed, and marketing is targeted toward specific age groups [1].

REFERENCES

1. J. Arbose, The Turnaround in Swiss Industry: How the Smokestack Crowd Learned Marketing, *International Management (UK)* 42 (1) (1987) 16–23.

2. *Business Month,* Up From Swatch (March 1988) 57.

3. Casio Computer, I. J. *Corporate Annual Reports* (1984–1988).

4. Citizen Watch Company (Japan), *Corporate Annual Reports* (1985–1988).

5. O. Crevoisier, M. Fragomichelakis, F. Hainard, and D. Maillat, *Know-how, Innovation, and Regional Development,* Paper presented at the 29th European Congress, Cambridge, England, September 1989.

6. G. Dosi, Technological Paradigms and Technological Trajectories, *Research Policy* 11 (1982) 147–162.

7. G. Dosi, Technological Paradigms and Technological Trajectories, in: C. Freeman (ed.), *Long Waves and the World Economy* (Butterworth, England, 1984).

8. A. Glasmeier, *The Hong Kong Watch Industry,* Final report to the Tissot Economic Foundation, Le Locle

Switzerland, Working Paper 14, Graduate Program in Community and Regional Planning, University of Texas at Austin, 1989.

9. A. Glasmeier, *The Japanese Small Business Sector,* Final report to the Tissot Economic Foundation, Le Locle, Switzerland, Working Paper 16, Graduate Program in Community and Regional Planning, University of Texas at Austin, 1989.

10. A. Glasmeier and R. Pendall, *The History of the World Watch Industry,* Preliminary report to the Tissot Economic Foundation, Le Locle Switzerland, Working Paper 13, Graduate Program in Community and Regional Planning, University of Texas at Austin, 1989.

11. F. Hainard, *Savoir-faire et culture technique dans l'Arc Jurassien* (UNESCO, Université de Neuchâtel, 1988).

12. W. D. Hoffman, Market Structure and Strategies of R&D Behaviour in the Data Processing Market—Theoretical Thoughts and Empirical Findings, *Research Policy* 5 (1976) 334–53.

13. Hong Kong Government Industry Department, Industrial Profile, Hong Kong's Watches and Clocks Industry (Hong Kong, October 1985).

14. *International Management,* Hattori Inspires Seiko to a High-Tech Future, *International Management* 39 (7) (July 1984) 20–25.

15. E. Jaquet and A. Chapuis, with the cooperation of G. A. Berner and S. Guye, *Technique and History of the Swiss Watch Industry* (Spring Books, London, 1970).

16. P. Katzenstein, *Small States and World Markets: Industrial Policy in Europe* (Cornell University Press, Ithaca, New York, 1985).

17. A. Knickerbocker, *Notes on the Watch Industries of Switzerland, Japan and the United States* (abridged) (Harvard Business School, Boston, 1974).

18. A. Knickerbocker, *Notes on the Watch Industries of Switzerland, Japan and the United States* (revised) (Harvard Business School, Boston, 1976).

19. D. S. Landes, Watchmaking: A Case Study of Enterprise and Change, *Business History Review* 53 (1) (Spring 1979) 1–38.

20. D. S. Landes, *Revolution in Time: Clocks and The Making of the Modern World* (Belknap Press, Cambridge, MA, 1983).

21. D. S. Landes, Time Runs Out for the Swiss, *Across the Board* 21 (1) (January 1984) 46–55.

22. D. Maillat, *Technology: A Key Factor for Regional Development* (Georgi Publishing Company, Saint-Saphorin, 1982).

23. L. Pilarski, Can New Management Team Keep Swiss Watches Ticking? *International Management* 40 (6) (June 1985) 57–58.

24. Conversation between Tihomil Radja and Amy Glasmeier, Switzerland (August 1989).

25. Conversation between Tihomil Radja and Amy Glasmeier, Switzerland (November 1990).

26. T. Radja, Unpublished tables (1990).

27. Conversation between Rene Retornaz and Amy Glasmeier, Neuchâtel, Switzerland (August 1989).

28. P. Rossel, Unpublished note, Tissot Economic Foundation, Le Locle Switzerland (1990).

29. C. Sabel, Reemergence of Regional Economies, in: J. Zeitlin and P. Hirst, *Reversing Industrial Decline? Industrial Structure and Policy in Britain and Her Competitors* (Berg, Leamington Spa, 1989).

30. A. Saxenian, *Regional Networks and the Resurgence of Silicon Valley,* Working Paper 508, Institute of Urban and Regional Development, University of California at Berkeley, 1989.

31. A. Saxenian, *The Origins and Dynamics of Production Networks in Silicon Valley,* Working Paper 516, Institute of Urban and Regional Development, University of California at Berkeley, 1990.

32. A. Scott, *Metropolis* (University of California Press, Berkeley, 1988).

33. A. Scott and M. Storper, High Technology Industry and Regional Development: A Theoretical Critique and Reconstruction, *International Social Science Journal* 112 (1989) 215–232.

34. Seiko, Hattori I. J. *Corporate Annual Report* (1985).

35. G. P. F. Steed, The Northern Ireland Linen Complex, 1950–1970, *Annals of the Association of American Geographers* 64 (3) (September 1974) 397–408.

36. M. Storper and R. Walker, *The Capitalist Imperative: Territory, Technology and Industrial Growth* (Basil Blackwell, Oxford, 1989).

37. M. Thomas, Growth and Structural Change: The Role of Technical Innovation, in: A. Amin and J. Goddard (eds.), *Technological Change, Industrial Restructuring and Regional Development* (Allen and Unwin, London, 1986).

38. Conversation between Luc Tissot and Amy Glasmeier, Zurich, Switzerland (August 1989).

39. Conversation between Luc Tissot and Amy Glasmeier, Austin, Texas (February 1990).

40. Union Bank of Switzerland, *The Swiss Watchmaking Industry,* UBS Publications on Business, Banking and Monetary Topics No. 100, Zurich (1986).

41. Union Bank of Switzerland, *Economic Survey of Switzerland* (1987).

5

Gunfire at Sea

A Case Study of Innovation

ELTING MORISON

In the early days of the last war when armaments of all kinds were in short supply, the British, I am told, made use of a venerable field piece that had come down to them from previous generations.[1] The honorable past of this light artillery stretched back, in fact, to the Boer War. In the day of uncertainty after the fall of France, these guns, hitched to trucks, served as useful mobile units in the coast defense. But it was felt that the rapidity of fire could be increased. A time-motion expert was, therefore, called in to suggest ways to simplify the firing procedures. He watched one of the gun crews of five men at practice in the field for some time. Puzzled by certain aspects of the procedures, he took some slow-motion pictures of the soldiers performing the loading, aiming, and firing routines.

When he ran these pictures over once or twice, he noticed something that appeared odd to him. A moment before the firing, two members of the gun crew ceased all activity and came to attention for a three-second interval extending throughout the discharge of the gun. He summoned an old colonel of artillery, showed him the pictures, and pointed out this strange behavior. What, he asked the colonel, did it mean. The colonel, too, was puzzled. He asked to see the pictures again. "Ah," he said when the performance was over, "I have it. They are holding the horses."

This story, true or not, and I am told it is true, suggests nicely the pain with which the human being accommodates himself to changing conditions. The ten-

dency is apparently involuntary and immediate to protect oneself against the shock of change by continuing in the presence of altered situations the familiar habits, however incongruous, of the past.

Yet, if human beings are attached to the known, to the realm of things as they are, they also, regrettably for their peace of mind, are incessantly attracted to the unknown and things as they might be. As Ecclesiastes glumly pointed out, men persist in disordering their settled ways and beliefs by seeking out many inventions.

The point is obvious. Change has always been a constant in human affairs; today, indeed, it is one of the determining characteristics of our civilization. In our relatively shapeless social organization, the shifts from station to station are fast and easy. More important for our immediate purpose, America is fundamentally an industrial society in a time of tremendous technological development. We are thus constantly presented with new devices or new forms of power that in their refinement and extension continually bombard the fixed structure of our habits of mind and behavior. Under such conditions, our salvation, or at least our peace of mind, appears to depend upon how successfully we can in the future become what has been called in an excellent phrase a completely "adaptive society."

It is interesting, in view of all this, that so little investigation, relatively, has been made of the process of change and human responses to it. Recently, psycholo-

Reprinted from *Men, Machines, and Modern Times,* by Elting Morison, pp. 17–44, copyright© 1966, with the permission of the publisher, The MIT Press.

gists, sociologists, cultural anthropologists, and econo-mists have addressed themselves to the subject with suggestive results. But we are still far from a full un-derstanding of the process and still further from know-ing how we can set about simplifying and assisting an individual's or a group's accommodation to new ma-chines or new ideas.

With these things in mind, I thought it might be interesting and perhaps useful to examine historically a changing situation within a society; to see if from this examination we can discover how the new ma-chines or ideas that introduced the changing situation developed; to see who introduces them, who resists them, what points of friction or tension in the social structure are produced by the innovation, and perhaps why they are produced and what, if anything, may be done about it. For this case study the introduction of continuous-aim firing in the United States Navy has been selected. The system, first devised by an English officer in 1898, was introduced in our Navy in the years 1900 to 1902.

I have chosen to study this episode for two rea-sons. First, a navy is not unlike a society that has been placed under laboratory conditions. Its dimensions are severely limited; it is beautifully ordered and articulat-ed; it is relatively isolated from random influences. For these reasons the impact of change can be clearly dis-cerned, the resulting dislocations in the structure easily discovered and marked out. In the second place, the development of continuous-aim firing rests upon me-chanical devices. It therefore presents for study a con-crete, durable situation. It is not like many other inno-vating reagents—a Manichean heresy, or Marxism, or the views of Sigmund Freud—that can be shoved and hauled out of shape by contending forces or conflicting prejudices. At all times we know exactly what continu-ous-aim firing really is. It will be well now to describe, as briefly as possible, what it really is. This will in-volve a short investigation of certain technical matters. I will not apologize, as I have been told I ought to do, for this preoccupation with how a naval gun is fired. For one thing, all that follows is understandable only if one understands how the gun goes off. For another thing, a knowledge of the underlying physical consid-erations may give a kind of elegance to the succeeding investigation of social implications. And now to the gun and the gunfire.

The governing fact in gunfire at sea is that the gun is mounted on an unstable platform, a rolling ship. This constant motion obviously complicates the prob-lem of holding a steady aim. Before 1898 this problem was solved in the following elementary fashion. A gun pointer estimated the range of the target, ordinarily in the nineties about 1,600 yards. He then raised the gun barrel to give the gun the elevation to carry the shell to the target at the estimated range. This elevating pro-cess was accomplished by turning a small wheel on the gun mount that operated the elevating gears. With the gun thus fixed for range, the gun pointer peered through open sights, not unlike those on a small rifle, and waited until the roll of the ship brought the sights on the target. He then pressed the firing button that dis-charged the gun. There were by 1898, on some naval guns, telescope sights which naturally greatly enlarged the image of the target for the gun pointer. But these sights were rarely used by gun pointers. They were lashed securely to the gun barrel, and, recoiling with the barrel, jammed back against the unwary pointer's eye. Therefore, when used at all, they were used only to take an initial sight for purposes of estimating the range before the gun was fired.

Notice now two things about the process. First of all, the rapidity of fire was controlled by the rolling pe-riod of the ship. Pointers had to wait for the one mo-ment in the roll when the sights were brought on the target. Notice also this: There is in every pointer what is called a "firing interval"—that is, the time lag be-tween his impulse to fire the gun and the translation of this impulse into the act of pressing the firing button. A pointer, because of this reaction time, could not wait to fire the gun until the exact moment when the roll of the ship brought the sights onto the target; he had to will to fire a little before, while the sights were off the target. Since the firing interval was an individual matter, vary-ing obviously from man to man, each pointer had to estimate from long practice his own interval and com-pensate for it accordingly.

These things, together with others we need not here investigate, conspired to make gunfire at sea rela-tively uncertain and ineffective. The pointer, on a mov-ing platform, estimating range and firing interval, shooting while his sight was off the target, became in a sense an individual artist.

In 1898, many of the uncertainties were removed from the process and the position of the gun pointer radically altered by the introduction of continuous-aim firing. The major change was that which enabled the gun pointer to keep his sight and gun barrel on the target throughout the roll of the ship. This was accomplished by altering the gear ratio in the elevating gear to permit a pointer to compensate for the roll of the vessel by rapidly elevating and depressing the gun. From this change another followed. With the possibility of maintaining the gun always on the target, the desirability of improved sights became immediately apparent. The advantages of the telescope sight as opposed to the open sight were for the first time fully realized. But the existing telescope sight, it will be recalled, moved with the recoil of the gun and jammed back against the eye of the gunner. To correct this, the sight was mounted on a sleeve that permitted the gun barrel to recoil through it without moving the telescope.

These two improvements in elevating gear and sighting eliminated the major uncertainties in gunfire at sea and greatly increased the possibilities of both accurate and rapid fire.

You must take my word for it, since the time allowed is small, that this changed naval gunnery from an art to a science, and that gunnery accuracy in the British and our Navy increased, as one student said, 3,000 percent in six years. This does not mean much except to suggest a great increase in accuracy. The following comparative figures may mean a little more. In 1899 five ships of the North Atlantic Squadron fired five minutes each at a light-ship hulk at the conventional range of 1,600 yards. After twenty-five minutes of banging away, two hits had been made on the sails of the elderly vessel. Six years later one naval gunner made fifteen hits in one minute at a target 75 by 25 feet at the same range—1,600 yards; half of them hit in a bull's-eye 50 inches square.

Now with the instruments (the gun, elevating gear, and telescope), the method, and the results of continuous-aim firing in mind, let us turn to the subject of major interest: how was the idea, obviously so simple an idea, of continuous-aim firing developed, who introduced it into the United States Navy, and what was its reception?

The idea was the product of the fertile mind of the English officer Admiral Sir Percy Scott. He arrived at it in this way while, in 1898, he was the captain of H.M.S. *Scylla.* For the previous two or three years he had given much thought independently and almost

alone in the British Navy to means of improving gunnery. One rough day, when the ship, at target practice, was pitching and rolling violently, he walked up and down the gun deck watching his gun crews. Because of the heavy weather, they were making very bad scores. Scott noticed, however, that one pointer was appreciably more accurate than the rest. He watched this man with care, and saw, after a time, that he was unconsciously working his elevating gear back and forth in a partially successful effort to compensate for the roll of the vessel. It flashed through Scott's mind at that moment that here was the sovereign remedy for the problem of inaccurate fire. What one man could do partially and unconsciously perhaps all men could be trained to do consciously and completely.

Acting on this assumption, he did three things. First, in all the guns of the *Scylla,* he changed the gear ratio in the elevating gear, previously used only to set the gun in fixed position for range, so that a gunner could easily elevate and depress the gun to follow a target throughout the roll. Second, he rerigged his telescopes so that they would not be influenced by the recoil of the gun. Third, he rigged a small target at the mouth of the gun, which was moved up and down by a crank to simulate a moving target. By following this target as it moved and firing at it with a subcaliber rifle rigged in the breech of the gun, the pointer could practice every day. Thus equipped, the ship became a training ground for gunners. Where before the good pointer was an individual artist, pointers now became trained technicians, fairly uniform in their capacity to shoot. The effect was immediately felt. Within a year the *Scylla* established records that were remarkable.

At this point I should like to stop a minute to notice several things directly related to, and involved in, the process of innovation. To begin with, the personality of the innovator. I wish there were time to say a good deal about Admiral Sir Percy Scott. He was a wonderful man. Three small bits of evidence must here suffice, however. First, he had a certain mechanical ingenuity. Second, his personal life was shot through with frustration and bitterness. There was a divorce and a quarrel with that ambitious officer Lord Charles Beresford, the sounds of which, Scott liked to recall, penetrated to the last outposts of empire. Finally, he possessed, like Swift, a savage indignation directed ordinarily at the inelastic intelligence of all constituted authority, especially the British Admiralty.

There are other points worth mention here. Notice first that Scott was not responsible for the invention of the basic instruments that made the reform in gunnery possible. This reform rested upon the gun itself, which as a rifle had been in existence on ships for at least forty years; the elevating gear, which had been, in the form Scott found it, a part of the rifled gun from the beginning; and the telescope sight, which had been on shipboard at least eight years. Scott's contribution was to bring these three elements appropriately modified into a combination that made continuous-aim firing possible for the first time. Notice also that he was allowed to bring these elements into combination by accident, by watching the unconscious action of a gun pointer endeavoring through the operation of his elevating gear to correct partially for the roll of his vessel. Scott, as we have seen, had been interested in gunnery; he had thought about ways to increase accuracy by practice and improvement of existing machinery; but able as he was, he had not been able to produce on his own initiative and by his own thinking the essential idea and modify instruments to fit his purpose. Notice here, finally, the intricate interaction of chance, the intellectual climate, and Scott's mind. Fortune (in this case, the unaware gun pointer) indeed favors the prepared mind, but even fortune and the prepared mind need a favorable environment before they can conspire to produce sudden change. No intelligence can proceed very far above the threshold of existing data or the binding combinations of existing data.

All these elements that enter into what may be called "original thinking" interest me as a teacher. Deeply rooted in the pedagogical mind often enough is a sterile infatuation with "inert ideas"; there is thus always present in the profession the tendency to be diverted from the *process* by which these ideas, or indeed any ideas, are really produced. I well remember with what contempt a class of mine which was reading Leonardo da Vinci's *Notebooks* dismissed the author because he appeared to know no more mechanics than, as one wit in the class observed, a Vermont Republican farmer of the present day. This is perhaps the expected result produced by a method of instruction that too frequently implies that the great generalizations were the result, on the one hand, of chance—an apple falling in an orchard or a teapot boiling on the hearth—or, on the other hand, of some towering intelligence proceeding in isolation inexorably toward some prefigured idea, like evolution, for example.

This process by which new concepts appear, the interaction of fortune, intellectual climate, and the prepared imaginative mind, is an interesting subject for examination offered by any case study of innovation. It was a subject, as Dr. Walter Cannon pointed out, that momentarily engaged the attention of Horace Walpole, whose lissome intelligence glided over the surface of so many ideas. In reflecting upon the part played by chance in the development of new concepts, he recalled the story of the three princes of Serendip who set out to find some interesting object on a journey through their realm. They did not find the particular object of their search, but along the way they discovered many new things simply because they were looking for *something*. Walpole believed this intellectual method ought to be given a name, in honor of the founders, serendipity; and serendipity certainly exerts a considerable influence in what we call original thinking. There is an element of serendipity, for example, in Scott's chance discovery of continuous-aim firing in that he was, and had been, looking for some means to improve his target practice and stumbled upon a solution by observation that had never entered his head.

Serendipity, while recognizing the prepared mind, does tend to emphasize the role of chance in intellectual discovery. Its effect may be balanced by an anecdote that suggests the contribution of the adequately prepared mind. There has recently been much posthaste and romage in the land over the question of whether there really was a Renaissance. A scholar has recently argued in print that since the Middle Ages actually possessed many of the instruments and pieces of equipment associated with the Renaissance, the Renaissance could be said to exist as a defined period only in the mind of the historians such as Burckhardt. This view was entertainingly rebutted by the historian of art Panofsky, who pointed out that although Robert Grosseteste indeed did have a very rudimentary telescope, he used it to examine stalks of grain in a field down the street. Galileo, a Renaissance intelligence, pointed his telescope at the sky.

Here Panofsky is only saying in a provocative way that change and intellectual advance are the products of well-trained and well-stored inquisitive minds, minds that relieve us of "the terrible burden of inert ideas by throwing them into a new combination." Educators, nimble in the task of pouring the old wine of our heritage into the empty vessels that appear before them, might give thought to how to develop such independent, inquisitive minds.

But I have been off on a private venture of my own. Now to return to the story, the introduction of continuous-aim firing. In 1900 Percy Scott went out to the China Station as commanding officer of H.M.S. *Terrible*. In that ship he continued his training methods and his spectacular successes in naval gunnery. On the China Station he met up with an American junior officer, William S. Sims. Sims had little of the mechanical ingenuity of Percy Scott, but the two were drawn together by temperamental similarities that are worth noticing here. Sims had the same intolerance for what is called spit and polish and the same contempt for bureaucratic inertia as his British brother officer. He had for some years been concerned, as had Scott, with what he took to be the inefficiency of his own Navy. Just before he met Scott, for example, he had shipped out to China in the brand new pride of the fleet, the battleship *Kentucky*. After careful investigation and reflection he had informed his superiors in Washington that she was "not a battleship at all—but a crime against the white race." The spirit with which he pushed forward his efforts to reform the naval service can best be stated in his own words to a brother officer: "I am perfectly willing that those holding views differing from mine should continue to live, but with every fibre of my being I loathe indirection and shiftiness, and where it occurs in high place, and is used to save face at the expense of the vital interests of our great service (in which silly people place such a child-like trust), I want that man's blood and I will have it no matter what it costs me personally."

From Scott in 1900 Sims learned all there was to know about continuous-aim firing. He modified, with the Englishman's active assistance, the gear on his own ship and tried out the new system. After a few months' training, his experimental batteries began making remarkable records at target practice. Sure of the usefulness of his gunnery methods, Sims then turned to the task of educating the Navy at large. In thirteen great official reports he documented the case for continuous-aim firing, supporting his arguments at every turn with a mass of factual data. Over a period of two years, he reiterated three principal points: first, he continually cited the records established by Scott's ships, the *Scylla* and the *Terrible*, and supported these with the accumulating data from his own tests on an American ship; second, he described the mechanisms used and the training procedures instituted by Scott and himself to obtain these records; third, he explained that our own mechanisms were not generally adequate without modification to meet the demands placed on them by continuous-aim firing. Our elevating gear, useful to raise or lower a gun slowly to fix it in position for the proper range, did not always work easily and rapidly enough to enable a gunner to follow a target with his gun throughout the roll of the ship. Sims also explained that such few telescope sights as there were on board our ships were useless. Their cross wires were so thick or coarse they obscured the target, and the sights had been attached to the gun in such a way that the recoil system of the gun plunged the eyepiece against the eye of the gun pointer.

This was the substance not only of the first but of all the succeeding reports written on the subject of gunnery from the China Station. It will be interesting to see what response these met with in Washington. The response falls roughly into three easily identifiable stages.

First stage: At first, there was no response. Sims had directed his comments to the Bureau of Ordnance and the Bureau of Navigation; in both bureaus there was dead silence. The thing—claims and records of continuous-aim firing—was not credible. The reports were simply filed away and forgotten. Some indeed, it was later discovered to Sims's delight, were half-eaten-away by cockroaches.

Second stage: It is never pleasant for any man's best work to be left unnoticed by superiors, and it was an unpleasantness that Sims suffered extremely ill. In his later reports, beside the accumulating data he used to clinch his argument, he changed his tone. He used deliberately shocking language because, as he said, "They were furious at my first papers and stowed them away. I therefore made up my mind I would give these later papers such a form that they would be dangerous documents to leave neglected in the files." To another friend he added, "I want scalps or nothing and if I can't have 'em I won't play."

Besides altering his tone, he took another step to be sure his views would receive attention. He sent copies of his reports to other officers in the fleet. Aware as a result that Sims's gunnery claims were being circulated and talked about, the men in Washington were then stirred to action. They responded, notably through the Chief of the Bureau of Ordnance, who had general charge of the equipment used in gunnery practice, as follows: (1) our equipment was in general as good as the British; (2) since our equipment was as good, the trouble must be with the men, but the gun pointer and the training of gun pointers were the responsibility of the officers on the ships; and most significant (3) continuous-aim firing was impossible. Experiments had revealed that five men at work on the elevating gear of a six-inch gun could not produce the power necessary to compensate for a roll of five degrees in ten seconds. These experiments and calculations demonstrated beyond peradventure or doubt that Scott's system of gunfire was not possible.

This was the second stage—the attempt to meet Sims's claims by logical, rational rebuttal. Only one difficulty is discoverable in these arguments; they were wrong at important points. To begin with, while there was little difference between the standard British equipment and the standard American equipment, the instruments on Scott's two ships, the *Scylla* and the *Terrible,* were far better than the standard equipment on our ships. Second, all the men could not be trained in continuous-aim firing until equipment was improved throughout the fleet. Third, the experiments with the elevating gear had been ingeniously contrived at the Washington Navy Yard—on solid ground. It had, therefore, been possible to dispense in the Bureau of Ordnance calculation with Newton's first law of motion, which naturally operated at sea to assist the gunner in elevating or depressing a gun mounted on a moving ship. Another difficulty was of course that continuous-aim firing was in use on Scott's and some of our own ships at the time the Chief of the Bureau of Ordnance was writing that it was a mathematical impossibility. In every way I find this second stage, the apparent resort to reason, the most entertaining and instructive in our investigation of the responses to innovation.

Third stage: The rational period in the counterpoint between Sims and the Washington men was soon passed. It was followed by the third stage, that of name-calling—the *argumentum ad hominem.* Sims, of course, by the high temperature he was running and by his calculated overstatement, invited this. He was told in official endorsements on his reports that there were others quite as sincere and loyal as he and far less difficult; he was dismissed as a crackbrained egotist; he was called a deliberate falsifier of evidence.

The rising opposition and the character of the opposition were not calculated to discourage further efforts by Sims. It convinced him that he was being attacked by shifty, dishonest men who were the victims, as he said, of insufferable conceit and ignorance. He made up his mind, therefore, that he was prepared to go to any extent to obtain the "scalps" and the "blood" he was after. Accordingly, he, a lieutenant, took the extraordinary step of writing the President of the United States, Theodore Roosevelt, to inform him of the remarkable records of Scott's ships, of the inadequacy of our own gunnery routines and records, and of the refusal of the Navy Department to act. Roosevelt, who always liked to respond to such appeals when he conveniently could, brought Sims back from China late in 1902 and installed him as Inspector of Target Practice, a post the naval officer held throughout the remaining six years of the Administration. And when he left, after many spirited encounters we cannot here investigate, he was universally acclaimed as "the man who taught us how to shoot."

With this sequence of events (the chronological account of the innovation of continuous-aim firing) in mind, it is possible now to examine the evidence to see what light it may throw on our present interest: the origins of and responses to change in a society.

First, the origins. We have already analyzed briefly the origins of the idea. We have seen how Scott arrived at his notion. We must now ask ourselves, I think, why Sims so actively sought, almost alone among his brother officers, to introduce the idea into his service. It is particularly interesting here to notice again that neither Scott nor Sims invented the instruments on which the innovation rested. They did not urge their proposal, as might be expected, because of pride in the instruments of their own design. The telescope sight had first been placed on shipboard in 1892 by Bradley Fiske, an officer of great inventive capacity. In that year Fiske had even sketched out on paper the vague possibility of continuous-aim firing, but his sight was condemned by his commanding officer, Robley D. Evans, as of no use. In 1892 no one but Fiske in the Navy knew what to do with a telescope sight any more than Grosseteste had known in his time what to do with a telescope. And Fiske, instead of fighting for his telescope, turned his attention to a range finder. But six years later Sims, following the tracks of his brother officer, took over and became the engineer of the revolution. I would suggest, with some reservations, this explanation: Fiske, as an inventor, took his pleasure in great part from the design of the device. He lacked not so much the energy as the overriding sense of social necessity that would have enabled him to *force* revolutionary ideas on the service. Sims possessed this sense. In Fiske, who showed rare courage and integrity in other professional matters not intimately connected with the introduction of new weapons of his own design, we may here find the familiar plight of the engineer who often enough must watch the products of his ingenuity organized and promoted by other men. These other promotional men when they appear in the world of commerce are called entrepreneurs. In the world of ideas they are still entrepreneurs. Sims was one, a middle-aged man caught in the periphery (as a lieutenant) of the intricate webbing of a precisely organized society. Rank, the exact definition and limitation of a man's capacity at any given moment in his career, prevented Sims from discharging all his exploding energies into the purely routine channels of the peacetime Navy. At the height of his powers he was a junior officer standing watches on a ship cruising aimlessly in friendly foreign waters. The remarkable changes in systems of gunfire to which Scott introduced him gave him the opportunity to expend his energies quite legitimately against the encrusted hierarchy of his society. He was moved, it seems to me, in part by his genuine desire to improve his own profession but also in part by rebellion against tedium, against inefficiency from on high, and against the artificial limitations placed on his actions by the social structure, in his case, junior rank.

Now having briefly investigated the origins of the change, let us examine the reasons for what must be considered the weird response we have observed to this proposed change. Why this deeply rooted, aggressive, persistent hostility from Washington that was only broken up by the interference of Theodore Roosevelt? Here was a reform that greatly and demonstrably increased the fighting effectiveness of a service that maintains itself almost exclusively to fight. Why then this refusal to accept so carefully documented a case, a case proved incontestably by records and experience? Why should virtually all the rulers of a society

so resolutely seek to reject a change that so markedly improved its chances for survival in any contest with competing societies? There are the obvious reasons that will occur to all of you—the source of the proposed reform was an obscure, junior officer 8,000 miles away; he was, and this is a significant factor, criticizing gear and machinery designed by the very men in the bureaus to whom he was sending his criticisms. And furthermore, Sims was seeking to introduce what he claimed were improvements in a field where improvements appeared unnecessary. Superiority in war, as in other things, is a relative matter, and the Spanish-American War had been won by the old system of gunnery. Therefore, it was superior even though of the 9,500 shots fired at various but close ranges, only 121 had found their mark.

These are the more obvious, and I think secondary or supporting, sources of opposition to Sims's proposed reforms. A less obvious cause appears by far the most important one. It has to do with the fact that the Navy is not only an armed force; it is a society. Men spend their whole lives in it and tend to find the definition of their whole being within it. In the forty years following the Civil War, this society had been forced to accommodate itself to a series of technological changes—the steam turbine, the electric motor, the rifled shell of great explosive power, case-hardened steel armor, and all the rest of it. These changes wrought extraordinary changes in ship design, and, therefore, in the concepts of how ships were to be used; that is, in fleet tactics, and even in naval strategy. The Navy of this period is a paradise for the historian or sociologist in search of evidence bearing on a society's responses to change.

To these numerous innovations, producing as they did a spreading disorder throughout a service with heavy commitments to formal organization, the Navy responded with grudging pain. For example, sails were continued on our first-line ships long after they ceased to serve a useful purpose mechanically, but like the holding of the horses that no longer hauled the British field pieces, they assisted officers over the imposing hurdles of change. To a man raised in sail, a sail on an armored cruiser propelled through the water at 14 knots by a steam turbine was a cheering sight to see.

This reluctance to change with changing conditions was not limited to the blunter minds and less resilient imaginations in the service. As clear and untrammeled an intelligence as Alfred Thayer Mahan, a prophetic spirit in the realm of strategy, where he was unfettered by personal attachments of any kind, was occasionally at the mercy of the past. In 1906 he opposed the construction of battleships with single-caliber main batteries—that is, the modern battleship—because, he argued, such vessels would fight only at great ranges. These ranges would create in the sailor what Mahan felicitously called "the indisposition to close." They would thus undermine the physical and moral courage of a commander. They would, in other words, destroy the doctrine and the spirit, formulated by Nelson a century before, that no captain could go very far wrong who laid his ship alongside an enemy. The fourteen-inch rifle, which could place a shell upon a possible target six miles away, had long ago annihilated the Nelsonian doctrine. Mahan, of course, knew and recognized this fact; he was, as a man raised in sail, reluctant only to accept its full meaning, which was not that men were no longer brave, but that 100 years after the battle of the Nile they had to reveal their bravery in a different way.

Now the question still is, why this blind reaction to technological change, observed in the continuation of sail or in Mahan's contentions or in the opposition to continuous-aim firing? It is wrong to assume, as it is frequently assumed by civilians, that it springs exclusively from some causeless Bourbon distemper that invades the military mind. There is a sounder and more attractive base. The opposition, where it occurs, of the soldier and the sailor to such change springs from the normal human instinct to protect oneself, and more especially, one's way of life. Military organizations are societies built around and upon the prevailing weapons systems. Intuitively and quite correctly the military man feels that a change in weapon portends a change in the arrangements of his society. Think of it this way. Since the time that the memory of man runneth not to the contrary, the naval society has been built upon the surface vessel. Daily routines, habits of mind, social organization, physical accommodations, conventions, rituals, spiritual allegiances have been conditioned by the essential fact of the ship. What then happens to your society if the ship is displaced as the principal element by such a radically different weapon as the plane? The mores and structure of the society are immediately placed in jeopardy. They may, in fact, be wholly destroyed. It was the witty cliché of the twenties that those

naval officers who persisted in defending the battleship against the apparently superior claims of the carrier did so because the battleship was a more comfortable home. What, from one point of view, is a better argument? There is, as everyone knows, no place like home. Who has ever wanted to see the old place brought under the hammer by hostile forces whether they hold a mortgage or inhabit a flying machine?

This sentiment would appear to account in large part for the opposition to Sims; it was the product of an instinctive protective feeling, even if the reasons for this feeling were not overt or recognized. The years after 1902 proved how right, in their terms, the opposition was. From changes in gunnery flowed an extraordinary complex of changes: in shipboard routines, ship design, and fleet tactics. There was, too, a social change. In the days when gunnery was taken lightly, the gunnery officer was taken lightly. After 1903, he became one of the most significant and powerful members of a ship's company, and this shift of emphasis naturally was shortly reflected in promotion lists. Each one of these changes provoked a dislocation in the naval society, and with man's troubled foresight and natural indisposition to break up classic forms, the men in Washington withstood the Sims onslaught as long as they could. It is very significant that they withstood it until an agent from outside, outside and above, who was not clearly identified with the naval society, entered to force change.

This agent, the President of the United States, might reasonably and legitimately claim the credit for restoring our gunnery efficiency. But this restoration by *force majeure* was brought about at great cost to the service and men involved. Bitternesses, suspicions, wounds were made that it was impossible to conceal and were, in fact, never healed.

Now this entire episode may be summed up in five separate points:

1. The essential idea for change occurred in part by chance but in an environment that contained all the essential elements for change and to a mind prepared to recognize the possibility of change.

2. The basic elements, the gun, gear, and sight, were put in the environment by other men, men interested in designing machinery to serve different purposes or simply interested in the instruments themselves.

3. These elements were brought into successful combination by minds not interested in the instruments for themselves but in what they could do with them. These minds were, to be sure, interested in good gunnery, overtly and consciously. They may also, not so consciously, have been interested in the implied revolt that is present in the support of all change. Their temperaments and careers indeed support this view. From gunnery, Sims went on to attack ship designs, existing fleet tactics, and methods of promotion. He lived and died, as the service said, a stormy petrel, a man always on the attack against higher authority, a rebellious spirit; a rebel, fighting in excellent causes, but a rebel still who seems increasingly to have identified himself with the act of revolt against constituted authority.

4. He and his colleagues were opposed on this occasion by men who were apparently moved by three considerations: honest disbelief in the dramatic but substantiated claims of the new process, protection of the existing devices and instruments with which they identified themselves, and maintenance of the existing society with which they were identified.

5. The deadlock between those who sought change and those who sought to retain things as they were was broken only by an appeal to superior force, a force removed from and unidentified with the mores, conventions, devices of the society. This seems to me a very important point. The naval society in 1900 broke down in its effort to accommodate itself to a new situation. The appeal to Roosevelt is documentation for Mahan's great generalization that no military service should or can undertake to reform itself. It must seek assistance from outside.

Now with these five summary points in mind, it may be possible to seek, as suggested at the outset, a few larger implications from this story. What, if anything, may it suggest about the general process by which any society attempts to meet changing conditions?

There is, to begin with, a disturbing inference half-concealed in Mahan's statement that no military organization can reform itself. Certainly civilians would agree with this. We all know now that war and the preparation for war are too important, as

Clemenceau said, to be left to the generals. But as I have said before, military organizations are really societies, more rigidly structured, more highly integrated, than most communities, but still societies. What then if we make this phrase to read, "No society can reform itself"? Is the process of adaptation to change, for example, too important to be left to human beings? This is a discouraging thought, and historically there is some cause to be discouraged. Societies have not been very successful in reforming themselves, accommodating to change, without pain and conflict.

This is a subject to which we may well address ourselves. Our society especially is built, as I have said, just as surely upon a changing technology as the Navy of the nineties was built upon changing weapon systems. How then can we find the means to accept with less pain to ourselves and less damage to our social organization the dislocations in our society that are produced by innovation? I cannot, of course, give any satisfying answer to these difficult questions. But in thinking about the case study before us, an idea occurred to me that at least might warrant further investigation by men far more qualified than I.

A primary source of conflict and tension in our case study appears to lie in this great word I have used so often in the summary, the word "identification." It cannot have escaped notice that some men identified themselves with their creations—sights, gun, gear, and so forth—and thus obtained a presumed satisfaction from the thing itself, a satisfaction that prevented them from thinking too closely on either the use or the defects of the thing; that others identified themselves with a settled way of life they had inherited or accepted with minor modification and thus found their satisfaction in attempting to maintain that way of life unchanged; and that still others identified themselves as rebellious spirits, men of the insurgent cast of mind, and thus obtained a satisfaction from the act of revolt itself.

This purely personal identification with a concept, a convention, or an attitude would appear to be a powerful barrier in the way of easily acceptable change. Here is an interesting primitive example. In the years from 1864 to 1871 ten steel companies in this country began making steel by the new Bessemer process. All but one of them at the outset imported from Great Britain English workmen familiar with the process. One, the Cambria Company, did not. In the first few years those companies with British labor established an initial superiority. But by the end of the seventies, Cambria had obtained a commanding lead over all competitors. The President of Cambria, R. W. Hunt, in seeking a cause for his company's success, assigned it almost exclusively to the labor policy. "We started the converter plant without a single man who had ever seen even the outside of a Bessemer plant. We thus had willing pupils with no prejudices and no reminiscences of what they had done in the old country." The Bessemer process, like any new technique, had been constantly improved and refined in this period from 1864 to 1871. The British laborers of Cambria's competitors, secure in the performance of their own original techniques, resisted and resented all change. The Pennsylvania farm boys, untrammeled by the rituals and traditions of their craft, happily and rapidly adapted themselves to the constantly changing process. They ended by creating an unassailable competitive position for their company.

How then can we modify the dangerous effects of this word "identification"? And how much can we tamper with this identifying process? Our security—much of it, after all—comes from giving our allegiance to something greater than ourselves. These are difficult questions to which only the most tentative and provisional answers may here be proposed for consideration.

If one looks closely at this little case history, one discovers that the men involved were the victims of *severely limited* identifications. They were presumably all part of a society dedicated to the process of national defense, yet they persisted in aligning themselves with separate parts of that process—with the existing instruments of defense, with the existing customs of the society, or with the act of rebellion against the customs of the society. Of them all the insurgents had the best of it. They could, and did, say that the process of defense was improved by a gun that shot straighter and faster, and since they wanted such guns, they were unique among their fellows, patriots who sought only the larger object of improved defense. But this beguiling statement, even when coupled with the recognition that these men were right and extremely valuable and deserving of respect and admiration—this statement cannot conceal the fact that they were interested too in scalps and blood, so interested that they made their case a militant one and thus created an atmosphere in which self-respecting men could not capitulate without

appearing either weak or wrong or both. So these limited identifications brought men into conflict with each other, and the conflict prevented them from arriving at a common acceptance of a change that presumably, as men interested in our total national defense, they would all find desirable.

It appears, therefore, if I am correct in my assessment, that we might spend some time and thought on the possibility of enlarging the sphere of our identifications from the part to the whole. For example, those Pennsylvania farm boys at the Cambria Steel Company were, apparently, much more interested in the manufacture of steel than in the preservation of any particular way of making steel. So I would suggest that in studying innovation, we look further into this possibility: the possibility that any group that exists for any purpose—the family, the factory, the educational institution—might begin by defining for itself its grand object and see to it that that grand object is communicated to every member of the group. Thus defined and communicated, it might serve as a unifying agent against the disruptive local allegiances of the inevitable smaller elements that compose any group. It may also serve as a means to increase the acceptability of any change that would assist in the more efficient achievement of the grand object.

There appears also a second possible way to combat the untoward influence of limited identifications. We are, I may repeat, a society based on technology in a time of prodigious technological advance, and a civilization committed irrevocably to the theory of evolution. These things mean that we believe in change; they suggest that if we are to survive in good health we must, in the phrase that I have used before, become an "adaptive society." By the word "adaptive" is meant the ability to extract the fullest possible returns from the opportunities at hand: the ability of Sir Percy Scott to select judiciously from the ideas and material presented both by the past and present and to throw them into a new combination. "Adaptive," as here used, also means the kind of resilience that will enable us to accept fully and easily the best promises of changing circumstances without losing our sense of continuity or our essential integrity.

We are not yet emotionally an adaptive society, though we try systematically to develop forces that tend to make us one. We encourage the search for new inventions; we keep the mind stimulated, bright, and free to seek out fresh means of transport, communication, and energy; yet we remain, in part, appalled by the consequences of our ingenuity, and, too frequently, try to find security through the shoring up of ancient and irrelevant conventions, the extension of purely physical safeguards, or the delivery of decisions we ourselves should make into the keeping of superior authority like the state. These solutions are not necessarily unnatural or wrong, but they historically have not been enough, and I suspect they never will be enough to give us the serenity and competence we seek.

If the preceding statements are correct, they suggest that we might give some attention to the construction of a new view of ourselves as a society which in time of great change identified with and obtained security and satisfaction from the wise and creative accommodation to change itself. Such a view rests, I think, upon a relatively greater reverence for the mere *process* of living in a society than we possess today and a relatively smaller respect for and attachment to any special *product* of a society, a product either as finite as a bathroom fixture or as conceptual as a fixed and final definition of our Constitution or our democracy.

Historically such an identification with *process* as opposed to *product,* with adventurous selection and adaptation as opposed to simple retention and possessiveness, had been difficult to achieve collectively. The Roman of the early republic, the Italian of the late fifteenth and early sixteenth century, or the Englishman of Elizabeth's time appears to have been most successful in seizing the new opportunities while conserving as much of the heritage of the past as he found relevant and useful to his purpose.

We seem to have fallen on times similar to theirs, when many of the existing forms and schemes have lost meaning in the face of dramatically altering circumstances. Like them we may find at least part of our salvation in identifying ourselves with the adaptive process and thus share with them some of the joy, exuberance, satisfaction, and security with which they went out to meet their changing times.

I am painfully aware that in setting up my historical situation for examination I have, in a sense, artificially contrived it. I have been forced to cut away much, if not all, of the connecting tissue of historical evidence and to present you only with the bare bones and even with only a few of the bones. Thus, I am also aware, the episode has lost much of the subtlety, vitality, and attractive uncertainty of the real situation. There has, too, in the process, been inevitable distortion, but I hope the essential if exaggerated truth remains. I am also aware that I have erected elaborate hypotheses on the slender evidence provided by the single episode. My defense here is only that I have hoped to suggest possible approaches and methods of study and also possible fruitful areas of investigation in a subject that seems to me of critical importance in the life and welfare of our changing society.

NOTE

1. This essay was delivered as one of three lectures at the California Institute of Technology in 1950. It has been reprinted in various truncated forms a good many times since.

6

Customer Power, Strategic Investment, and the Failure of Leading Firms

CLAYTON M. CHRISTENSEN
JOSEPH L. BOWER

Why might firms be regarded as astutely managed at one point, yet subsequently lose their positions of industry leadership when faced with technological change? We present a model, grounded in a study of the world disk drive industry, that charts the process through which the demands of a firm's customers shape the allocation of resources in technological innovation—a model that links theories of resource dependence and resource allocation. We show that established firms led the industry in developing technologies of every sort—even radical ones—whenever the technologies addressed existing customers' needs. The same firms failed to develop simpler technologies that initially were only useful in emerging markets, because impetus coalesces behind, and resources are allocated to, programs targeting powerful customers. Projects targeted at technologies for which no customers yet exist languish for lack of impetus and resources. Because the rate of technical progress can exceed the performance demanded in a market, technologies which initially can only be used in emerging markets later can invade mainstream ones, carrying entrant firms to victory over established companies.

Students of management have marveled at how hard it is for firms to repeat their success when technology or markets change, for good reason: there are lots of examples. For instance, no leading computer manufacturer has been able to replicate its initial success when subsequent architectural technologies and their corresponding markets emerged. IBM created and continues to dominate the mainframe segment, but it missed by many years the emergence of the minicomputer architecture and market. The minicomputer was developed, and its market applications exploited, by firms such as Digital Equipment and Data General. While very successful in their initial markets, the minicomputer makers largely missed the advent of the desktop computer: a market which was created by entrants such as Apple, Commodore and Tandy, and only later by IBM. The engineering workstation leaders were Apollo and Sun Microsystems, both entrants to the industry. The pioneers of the portable computing market—Compaq, Zenith, Toshiba, and Sharp—were not the leaders in the desktop segment.

And yet even as these firms were missing this sequence of opportunities, they were *very* aggressively and successfully leading their industries in developing and adopting many strategically important and techno-

Reprinted from *Strategic Management Journal*, Vol. 17, Clayton M. Christensen and Joseph L. Bower, "Customer Power, Strategic Investment, and the Failure of Leading Firms," pp. 197–218, copyright © 1996. Reproduced by permission of John Wiley & Sons Limited.

logically sophisticated technologies. IBM's leadership across generations of multi-chip IC packaging, and Sun Microsystems' embrace of RISC microprocessor technology, are two instances. There are many other examples, discussed below, of firms that aggressively stayed at the forefront of technology development for extended periods, but whose industry leadership was later shaken by shifting technologies and markets.

The failure of leading firms can sometimes be ascribed to managerial myopia or organizational lethargy, or to insufficient resources or expertise. For example, cotton-spinners simply lacked the human, financial, and technological resources to compete when DuPont brought synthetic fibers into the apparel industry. But in many instances, the firms that missed important innovations suffered none of these problems. They had their competitive antennae up; aggressively invested in new products and technologies; and listened astutely to their customers. Yet they still lost their positions of leadership. This paper examines why and under what circumstances financially strong, customer-sensitive, technologically deep, and rationally managed organizations may fail to adopt critical new technologies or enter important markets—failures to innovate which have led to the decline of once-great firms.

Our conclusion is that a primary reason why such firms lose their positions of industry leadership when faced with certain types of technological change has little to do with technology itself—with its degree of newness or difficulty, relative to the skills and experience of the firm. Rather, they fail because they listen too carefully to their customers—and customers place stringent limits on the strategies firms can and cannot pursue.

The term "technology," as used in this paper, means the processes by which an organization transforms labor, capital, materials, and information into products or services. All firms have technologies. A retailer such as Sears employs a particular "technology" to procure, present, sell, and deliver products to its customers, while a discount warehouse retailer such as the Price Club employs a different "technology." Hence, our concept of technology extends beyond the engineering and manufacturing functions of the firm, encompassing a range of business processes. The term "innovation" herein refers to a change in technology.

A fundamental premise of this paper is that patterns of resource allocation heavily influence the types of innovations at which leading firms will succeed or fail. In every organization, ideas emerge daily about new ways of doing things—new products, new applications for products, new technical approaches, and new customers—in a manner chronicled by Bower (1970) and Burgelman (1983a, 1983b). Most proposals to innovate require human and financial resources. The patterns of innovation evidenced in a company will therefore mirror to a considerable degree the patterns in how its resources are allocated to, and withheld from, competing proposals to innovate.

We observe that because effective resource allocation is market-driven, the resource allocation procedures in successful organizations provide impetus for innovations known to be demanded by current customers in existing markets. We find that established firms in a wide range of industries have tended to lead in developing and adopting such innovations. Conversely, we find that firms possessing the capacity and capability to innovate may fail when the innovation does *not* address the foreseeable needs of their current customers. When the initial price/performance characteristics of emerging technologies render them competitive only in emerging market segments, and not with current customers, resource allocation mechanisms typically deny resources to such technologies. Our research suggests that the inability of some successful firms to allocate sufficient resources to technologies that initially cannot find application in mainstream markets, but later invade them, lies at the root of the failure of many once-successful firms.

EARLIER VIEWS OF FACTORS INFLUENCING PATTERNS OF RESOURCE ALLOCATION IN THE INNOVATION PROCESS

Our research links two historically independent streams of research, both of which have contributed significantly to our understanding of innovation. The first stream is what Pfeffer and Salancik (1978) call *resource dependence*: an approach which essentially looks *outside* the firm for explanations of the patterns through which firms allocate resources to innovative activities. Scholars in this tradition contend that firms' strategic options are constrained because managerial discretion is largely a myth. In order to ensure the survival of their organizations, managers lack the power to do anything other than to allocate resources to innovative programs that are required of the firm by external customers and investors: the entities that provide the resources the firm needs to survive. Support for this view comes from the work of historians of technological innovation such as Cooper and Schendel (1976) and Foster (1986). The firms they studied generally responded to the emergence of competitively threatening technologies by intensifying their investments to improve the conventional technologies used by their current customers—which provided the resources the firms needed to survive over the short term.

The second stream of ideas, originally taught by Bower (1970) and amplified by Burgelman (1983a, 1983b), describes the resource allocation process internal to the firm. These scholars suggest that most strategic proposals—to add capacity or develop new products or processes—take their fundamental shape at lower levels of hierarchical organizations. Bower observed that the allocation of funding among projects is substantially shaped by the extent to which managers at middle levels of the organization decide to support, or lend *impetus,* to some proposals and to withhold it from others. Bower also observed that risk management and career management were closely linked in the resource allocation process. Because the career costs to aspiring managers of having backed an ultimately unsuccessful project can be severe, their tendency was to back those projects where the demand for the product was assured.

Our study links these two streams by showing how the impetus that drives patterns of resource allocation (and hence innovation) within firms does not stem from autonomous decisions of risk-conscious managers. Rather, whether sufficient impetus coalesces behind a proposed innovation is largely determined by the presence or absence of current customers who can capably articulate a need for the innovation in question. There seems to be a powerful linkage from: (1) the expectations and needs of a firm's most powerful customers for product improvements; to (2) the types of innovative proposals which are given or denied impetus within the firm and which therefore are allocated the resources necessary to develop the requisite technological capabilities; to (3) the markets toward which firms will and will not target these innovations; which in turn leads to (4) the

firms' ultimate commercial success or failure with the new technology.

A primary conclusion of this paper is that when significant customers demand it, sufficient impetus may develop so that large, bureaucratic firms can embark upon and successfully execute technologically difficult innovations—even those that require very different competencies than they initially possessed.[1] Conversely, we find that when a proposed innovation addresses the needs of small customers in remote or emerging markets that do not supply a significant share of the resources a firm currently needs for growth and survival, firms will find it difficult to succeed even at innovations that are technologically straightforward. This is because the requisite impetus does not develop, and the proposed innovations are starved of resources.

Our findings build upon the work of earlier scholars who have addressed the question of why leading firms may fail when faced with technological change. Cooper and Schendel (1976) found that new technologies often are initially deployed in new markets, and that these were generally brought into industries by entering firms. They observed that established firms confronted with new technology often intensified investment in traditional technical approaches, and that those that did make initial resource commitments to a new technology rarely maintained adequate resource commitments. Foster (1986) noted that at points when new technologies enter an industry, entrants seem to enjoy an "attacker's advantage" over incumbent firms. Henderson and Clark (1990) posited that entrant firms enjoyed a particular advantage over incumbents in architectural technology change.

We hope to add additional precision and insight to the work of these pioneering scholars, by stating more precisely the specific sorts of technological innovations that are likely initially to be deployed in new applications, and the sorts that are likely to be used in mainstream markets from the beginning; and to define the types of innovation in which we expect attackers to enjoy an advantage, and the instances in which we expect incumbents to hold the upper hand. By presenting a model of the processes by which resource commitments are made, we hope partially to explain a puzzle posed but not resolved by each of these authors: *why* have incumbent firms generally intensified their commitments to conventional technology, while starving efforts to commercialize new technologies—even while the new technology was gaining ground in the market? Finally, by examining why established firms do these things, we hope to provide insights for how managers can more successfully address different types of technological change.

RESEARCH METHODS

Three very different classes of data were used in this study, to establish solid construct validity (Yin, 1989). The first was a database of the detailed product and performance specifications for every disk drive model announced by every firm participating in the world industry between 1975 and 1990—over 1,400 product models in all. These data came from *Disk/Trend Report,* the leading market research publication in the disk drive industry, and from product specification sheets obtained from the manufacturers themselves. The tables and other summary statistics reported in this paper were calculated from this database, unless otherwise noted. This data set is not a statistical sample, but constitutes a complete census of companies and products for the world industry during the period studied.

The second type of information employed in the study relates to the strategies pursued, and the commercial success and failure, of each of the companies that announced the development of a rigid disk drive between 1976 and 1990. *Disk/Trend* reported each firm's rigid disk drive sales in each of these years, by product category and by market segment. Each monthly issue between 1976 and 1990 of *Electronic Business* magazine, the most prominent trade publication covering the magnetic recording industry, was examined for information about disk drive manufacturers, their strategies and products. We used this information to verify the completeness of the *Disk/Trend* data,[2] and to write a history of the disk drive industry describing the strategies and fortunes of firms in the industry (Christensen, 1993).

The third type of information employed in this study came from over 70 personal, unstructured interviews conducted with executives who are or have been associated with 21 disk drive manufacturing companies. Those interviewed included founders; chief executives; vice presidents of sales and marketing, engineering and finance; and engineering, marketing, and managerial members of pivotal product development project teams. The firms whose executives were interviewed together account for over 80 percent of the disk drives produced in the world since the industry's inception. Data from these interviews were used to reconstruct, as accurately as possible, the decision-making processes associated with key innovations in each company's history. Wherever possible, accounts of the same decision were obtained from multiple sources, including former employees, to minimize problems with post hoc rationalization. Multiple employees were interviewed in 16 of the 21 companies.

The *Disk/Trend* data enabled us to measure the impact that each new component and architectural technology had on disk drive performance. Furthermore, it was possible to identify which firms were the first to develop and adopt each new technology, and to trace the patterns of diffusion of each new technology through the world industry over time, among different types of firms. When analysis of the *Disk/Trend* data indicated a particular entrant or established firm had prominently led or lagged behind the industry in a particular innovation, we could determine the impact of that leadership or followership on the subsequent sales and market shares, by product-market segment, for each company.

Analysis of these data essentially enabled us to develop a theory of *what* will happen when different types of technological change occur—whether we would expect entrant and established firms to take leadership in their development. We then used our interview data to write case histories of key decisions in six companies to understand *why* those patterns of leadership and followership in technology development occur. These case studies covered entrant and established firms, over an extended period of time in which each of them made decisions to invest, or delay investing, in a variety of new technologies. These cases were selected in what Yin (1989) calls a multi-case, nested experimental design, so that through pattern-matching across cases, the external validity of the study's conclusions could be established.[3]

We studied the disk drive industry because its history is one of rapid change in technology and market structure. The world rigid disk drive market grew at a 27 percent annual rate to over $13 billion between 1975 and 1990. Of the 17 firms in the OEM industry in 1976, only one was still in operation in 1990. Over 130 firms entered the industry during this period, and more than 100 of them failed. The cost per megabyte (MB) of the average drive in constant 1990 dollars fell from $560 in 1976 to $5 in 1990. The physical size of a 100 MB drive shrank from 5,400 to 8 cubic inches over the same period. During this time, six architecturally distinct product generations emerged, and a new company rose to become market leader in four of these six generations. A description of disk drive technology that may be helpful for some readers is provided in Appendix 1.

TYPOLOGIES OF TECHNOLOGICAL CHANGE

Earlier scholars of technology change have argued that incumbent firms may stumble when technological change destroys the value of established technological competencies (Tushman and Anderson, 1986), or when new architectural technologies emerge (Henderson and Clark, 1990). For present purposes, however, we have found it useful to distinguish between those innovations that *sustained* the industry's rate of improvement in product performance (total capacity and recording density were the two most common measures), and those innovations that *disrupted* or redefined that performance trajectory (Dosi, 1982). The following two sections illustrate these concepts by describing prominent examples of trajectory-sustaining and trajectory-disrupting technological changes in the industry's history. The subsequent sections then describe the role these innovations played in the industry's development; the processes through which incumbent and entrant firms responded to these different types of technological change; and the consequent successes and failures these firms experienced.

Sustaining Technological Changes
In the disk drive industry's history, most of the changes in competent technology, and two of the six changes in architectural technology, sustained or reinforced established trajectories of product performance improvement. Two examples of such technology change are shown in Figure 6.1. The left-most graph compares the average recording density of drives that employed conventional particulate oxide disk technology and ferrite head technology, vs. the average density of drives that employed new-technology thin film heads and disks,

that were introduced in each of the years between 1976 and 1990. The improvements in the conventional approach are the result of consistent incremental advances such as grinding the ferrite heads to finer, more precise dimensions; and using smaller and more finely dispersed oxide particles on the disk's surface. Note that the improvement in areal density obtainable with ferrite/oxide technology began to level off in the period's later years—suggesting a maturing technology S-curve (Foster, 1986). Note how thin film head and disk technologies emerged to sustain the rate of performance improvement at its historical pace of 35 percent between 1984 and 1990.

The right-most graph in Figure 6.1 describes a sustaining technological change of a very different character: an innovation in product architecture. In this case, the 14-inch Winchester drive substituted for removable disk packs, which had been the dominant design between 1962 and 1978. Just as in the thin film-for-ferrite/oxide substitution, the impact of Winchester technology was to sustain the historically established rate of performance improvement. Other important innovations, such as embedded servo systems, RLL & PRML recording codes, higher RPM motors and embedded SCSI, SMD, ESDI and AT interfaces, also helped manufacturers sustain the rate of historical performance improvement that their customers had come to expect.[4] Hereafter in this paper, technological changes that have such a sustaining impact on an established trajectory of performance improvement are called *sustaining technologies*.

Disruptive Technological Changes
Most technological change in the industry's history consisted of sustaining innovations of the sort described above. In contrast, there were just a few trajectory-disrupting changes. The most important of these from a historical viewpoint were the architectural innovations that carried the industry from 14-inch diameter disks to diameters of 8, 5.25, and then 3.5 inches. The ways in which these innovations were disruptive are illustrated in Table 6.1. Set in 1981, this table compares the attributes of a typical 5.25-inch drive—a new architecture that had been in the market for less than a year at that time—with those of a typical 8-inch drive, which by that time had become the standard drive used by minicomputer manufacturers. Note that along the dimensions of performance which were important

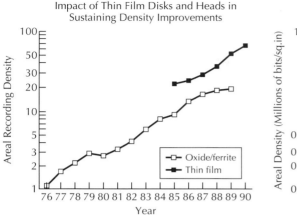
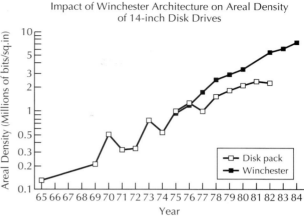

Figure 6.1. Examples of sustaining technological change in componentry (left) and product architecture (right). (*Source: Business History Review,* 1993, **67,** p. 557.)

to established minicomputer manufacturers—capacity, cost per megabyte, and access time—the 8-inch product was vastly superior. The 5.25-inch architecture did not address the needs of minicomputer manufacturers, as they perceived their needs at that time. On the other hand, the 5.25-inch architecture *did* possess attributes that appealed to the desktop personal computer market segment that was just emerging in 1980–82. It was small and lightweight—important features for this application. And it was priced at around $2,000, which means it could economically be incorporated in desktop machines. Hereafter in this paper, technologies

such as this, which disrupt an established trajectory of performance improvement, or redefine what performance means, are called *disruptive technologies.*

In general, sustaining technological changes appealed to established customers in existing, mainstream markets. They provided these customers with more of what they had come to expect. In contrast, disruptive technologies rarely could initially be employed in established markets. They tended instead to be valued in remote or emerging markets. This tendency consistently appears not just in disk drives, but across a range of industries (Rosenbloom and Christensen, 1995).

Table 6.1. The Disruptive Impact on Performance Improvement of the 5.25-Inch, vs. the 8-Inch Architecture

Attribute	8-Inch Drives	5.25-Inch Drives
Capacity (megabytes)	60	10
Volume (cubic inches)	566	150
Weight (pounds)	21	6
Access time (ms)	30	160
Cost per megabyte	$50	$200
Total unit cost	$3,000	$2,000

Key: Attributes valued highly in the minicomputer market in 1981 are presented in **boldface.** Attributes valued in the emerging desktop computing market in 1981 are shown in *italics.*
Source: Analysis of Disk/Trend Report data from Christensen (1992a: 90).

THE IMPACT OF SUSTAINING AND DISRUPTIVE TECHNOLOGIES ON INDUSTRY STRUCTURE

The history of sustaining and disruptive technological change in the disk drive industry is summarized in Figure 6.2. It begins in 1974, the year after IBM's first Winchester architecture model was introduced to challenge the dominant disk pack architectural design. Almost all drives then were sold to makers of mainframe computers. Note that in 1974 the median-priced mainframe computer was equipped with about 130 MB of hard disk capacity. The typical hard disk storage capacity supplied with the median-priced mainframe increased about 17 percent per year, so that by 1990 the typical mainframe was equipped with 1,300 MB of hard disk capacity. This growth in the use of hard disk memory per computer is mapped by the solid line emanating from point A in Figure 6.2. This trajectory was driven by user learning and software developments in the applications in which mainframes were used (Christensen and Rosenbloom, 1995).

The dashed line originating at point A measures the increase in the average capacity of 14-inch drives over the same period. Note that although the capacity of the average 14-inch drive was equal to the capacity shipped with the typical mainframe in 1974, the rate of increase in capacity provided within the 14-inch architecture exceeded the rate of increase in capacity demanded in the mainframe market—carrying this architecture toward high-end mainframes, scientific computers, and supercomputers. Furthermore, note how the new 14-inch Winchester architecture sustained the capacity trajectory that had been established in the earlier removable disk pack architecture. Appendix 2 describes how these trajectories were calculated.

The solid trajectories emanating from points B, C, and D represent the average hard disk capacity *demanded* by computer buyers in each market segment, over time.[5] The dashed lines emanating from points B, C, and D in Figure 6.2 measure trends in the average capacity that disk drive manufacturers were able to *provide* with each successive disk drive architecture. Note that with the exception of the 14-inch Winchester architecture, the maximum capacity initially available in each of these architectures was substantially *less* than the capacity required for the typical computer in the established market—these were *disruptive* innovations. As a consequence, the 8, 5.25, and 3.5-inch designs initially were rejected by the leading, established computer manufacturers, and were deployed instead in emerging market applications for disk drives: mini-computers, desktop PCs, and portable PCs, respectively. Note, however, that once these disruptive architectures became established in their new markets, the accumulation of hundreds of sustaining innovations pushed each architecture's performance ahead along very steep, and roughly parallel, trajectories.[6]

Note that the trajectory of improvement that the technology was able to *provide* within each architecture was nearly *double* the slope of the increase in capacity *demanded* in each market. As we will see, this disparity between what the technology could provide and what the market demanded seems to have been the primary source of leadership instability in the disk drive industry.

LEADERS IN SUSTAINING AND DISRUPTIVE TECHNOLOGICAL INNOVATIONS

To better understand why leading firms might successfully pioneer in the development and adoption of many new and difficult technologies, and yet lose their positions of industry leadership by failing to implement others, we compared the innovative behavior of *established* firms with that of *entrant* firms, with respect to each of the sustaining and disruptive technological innovations in the history of the disk drive industry. Building upon the approach employed by Henderson and Clark (1990), established firms were defined as firms that had previously manufactured drives which employed an older, established technology, whereas entrant firms were those whose initial product upon entry into the industry employed the new component or architectural technology being analyzed. This approach was used because of this study's longitudinal character, looking at the performance of incumbents and entrants across a sequence of innovations.

In spite of the wide variety in the magnitudes and types of sustaining technological changes in the industry's history, the firms that led in their development and adoption were the industry's leading, established firms. Table 6.2(a) depicts this leadership pattern for three representative sustaining technologies. In thin-film head technology, it was Burroughs (1976), IBM (1979), and other established firms that first successfully incorporated thin-film heads in disk drives. In the 1981–86 period, when over 60 firms entered the rigid disk drive industry, only five of them (all commercial failures) attempted to do so using thin-film heads as a source of performance advantage in their initial products. All other entrant firms—even aggressively performance-oriented firms such as Maxtor and Conner Peripherals—found it preferable to cut their teeth on ferrite heads in the entry products, before tackling thin-film technology in subsequent generations.

Note the similar pattern in the development and adoption of RLL codes—a much simpler development than thin-film head technology—which consumed at most a few million dollars per firm. RLL enabled a 30 percent density improvement, and therefore represent-

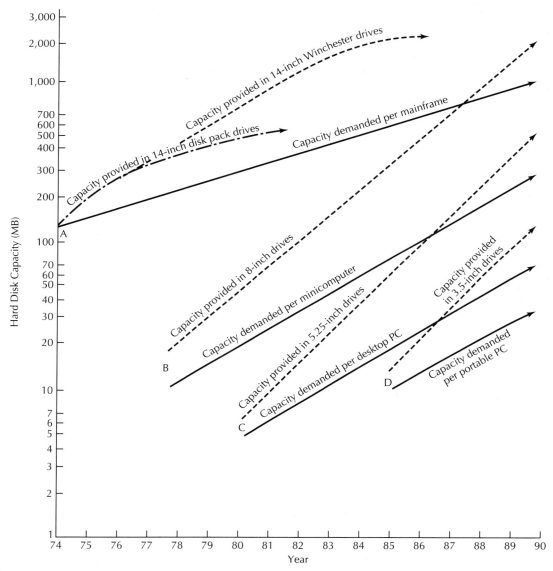

Figure 6.2. Patterns of entry and improvement in disruptive disk drive technologies. (*Source: Business History Review,* 1993, **67,** p. 559.)

ed the type of inexpensive path to performance improvement that ought to be attractive to entrant firms. But in 1985, 11 of the 13 firms which introduced new models employing RLL technology were established firms, meaning that they had previously offered models based on MFM technology. Only two were entrants, meaning that their initial products employed RLL codes. Table 6.2(a) also notes that six of the first

seven firms to introduce Winchester architecture drives were established makers of drives employing the prior disk pack architecture.[7]

The history of literally every other sustaining innovation—such as embedded servo systems, zone-specific recording densities, higher RPM motors, and the 2.5-inch Winchester architecture—reveals a similar pattern: the established firms led in the adoption of

Table 6.2. Trends in Technology Leadership and Followership in Sustaining vs. Disruptive Technologies

(a) Number of Established and Entrant Firms Introducing Models
Employing Selected Trajectory-Sustaining Technologies

		1974	1975	1976	1977	1978	1979	1980	1981	1982	1983	1984	1985	1986	1987	1988
Thin-film heads	Entrants								1		1	2	1		1	4
	Established			1			1	1	3	5	6	8	12	15	17	22
RLL codes	Entrants											1	2	3	6	8
	Established											4	11	20	25	26
Winchester	Entrants				1	4	9									
architecture	Established	1		3	3	7	11									

(b) Number of Established and Entrant Firms Introducing Models
Based upon Disruptive Architectural Technologies

		1974	1975	1976	1977	1978	1979	1980	1981	1982	1983	1984	1985	1986	1987	1988
8-inch	Entrants					1	4	6	8							
	Established					0	2	5	5							
5.25-inch	Entrants							1	8	8	13					
	Established							1	2	8	11					
3.5-inch	Entrants											1	2	3	4	
	Established											0	1	1	4	

Note: Data are presented in these tables only for those years in which the new technologies were gaining widespread acceptance, to illustrate tendencies in technology leadership and followership. Once the technologies had become broadly accepted, the number of firms introducing models using them is no longer reported. Twelve years are covered in the thin-film head category because it took that long for thin-film heads to become broadly used in the marketplace. Only 5 years of history are reported for RLL codes because by 1988 the vast majority of established *and* entrant firms had adopted RLL codes. Four years of data are shown for new architectures, because any established firms that had not launched the new architecture within 4 years of its initial appearance in the market had been driven from the industry.

sustaining technology be it in componentry or architecture. Entrant firms followed. In other words, the failure of leading firms to stay atop the disk drive industry generally was not because they could not keep pace with the industry's movement along the dashed-line technological trajectories mapped in Figure 6.2. The leading incumbent firms effectively *led* the industry along those trajectories even though many of these were competency-destroying progressions in terms of technologies, skills, and manufacturing assets required (Tushman and Anderson, 1986).

In contrast, the firms that led the industry in introducing *disruptive* architectural technologies—in the moves to points B, C, and D in Figure 6.2—tended overwhelmingly to be *entrant,* rather than established firms. This is illustrated in Table 6.2(b). It shows, for example, that in 1978 an entrant offered the industry's first 8-inch drive. By the end of the second year of that architecture's life (1979), six firms were offering 8-inch drives; two-thirds of them were entrants. Like-

wise, by the end of the second year of the 5.25-inch generation's life, eight of the 10 firms offering 5.25-inch drives were entrants. Entrants similarly dominated the early population of firms offering 3.5-inch drives. In each of these generations, between half and two-thirds of the established manufacturers of the prior architectural generation *never* introduced a model in the new architecture. And those established drive makers that did design and manufacture new architecture models did so with an average two-year lag behind the pioneering entrant firms. In this fast-paced industry, such slow response often proved fatal.

These patterns of leadership and followership in sustaining and disruptive technologies are reflected in the commercial success and failure of disk drive manufacturers. The ability of established firms to lead the industry in the sustaining innovations that powered the steep technological trajectories in Figure 6.2 often were technologically difficult, risky, and expensive. Yet in the history of this industry, there is no evidence that the firms that led in sustaining innovations gained market share by virtue of such technology leadership (Christensen, 1992b). This leadership enabled them to maintain their competitiveness only within specific technological trajectories. On the other hand, entrant firms' leadership advantages in disruptive innovations enabled them not only to capture new markets as they emerged, but (because the trajectories of technological progress were steeper than the trajectories of performance demanded) to invade and capture established markets as well.

Hence, all but one of the makers of 14-inch drives were driven from the mainframe computer market by entrant firms that got their start making 8-inch drives for minicomputers. The 8-inch drive makers, in turn, were driven from the minicomputer market, and eventually the mainframe market, by firms which led in producing 5.25-inch drives for desktop computers. And the leading makers of 5.25-inch drives were driven from desktop and minicomputer applications by makers of 3.5-inch drives, as mapped in Figure 6.2.

We began this paper by posing a puzzle: why it was that firms which at one point could be esteemed as aggressive, innovative, customer-sensitive organizations could ignore or attend belatedly to technological innovations with enormous strategic importance. In the context of the preceding analysis of the disk drive industry, this question can be sharpened considerably. The established firms were, in fact, aggressive, innovative, and customer-sensitive in their approaches to sustaining innovations of every sort. But why was it that established firms could not lead their industry in disruptive architectural innovations? For it is only in these innovations that attackers demonstrated an advantage. And unfortunately for the leading established firms, this advantage enabled attacking entrant firms to topple the incumbent industry leaders each time a disruptive technology emerged.[8]

To understand why disruptive technological change was so consistently vexing to incumbent firms, we personally interviewed managers who played key roles in the industry's leading firms, as incumbents or entrants, when each of these disruptive technologies emerged. Our objective in these interviews was to reconstruct, as accurately and from as many points of view as possible, the forces that influenced these firms' decision-making processes relating to the development and commercialization of disruptive architectural technologies. We found the experiences of the firms, and the forces influencing their decisions, to be remarkably similar. In each instance, when confronted with disruptive technology change, developing the requisite *technology* was never a problem: prototypes of the new drives often had been developed before management was asked to make a decision. It was in the process of allocating scarce resources among competing product and technology development proposals, however, that disruptive projects got stalled. Programs addressing the needs of the firms' most powerful customers almost *always* pre-empted resources from the disruptive technologies, whose markets tended to be small and where customers' needs were poorly defined.

In the following section we have synthesized the data from case studies of the six firms we studied in particular depth, into a *six*-step model that describes the factors that influenced how resources were allocated across competing proposals to develop new sustaining vs. disruptive technology in these firms. The struggle of Seagate Technology, the industry's dominant maker of 5.25-inch drives, to successfully commercialize the disruptive 3.5-inch drive, is recounted here to illustrate each of the steps in the model. Short excerpts from a fuller report of other case histories (Christensen, 1992a) are also presented to illustrate what happened in specific companies at each point in the process. Table 6.3 describes how the findings from each of the case studies support, or do not support, the principal propositions in the model. In Yin's (1989) terms, the high degree of literal and theoretical replication shown in Table 6.3, and the extent of "pattern matching" across case studies where more than one firm encountered the same technological change, lend high degrees of reliability and external validity to the model.[9]

A MODEL OF THE RESOURCE-ALLOCATION PROCESS IN ESTABLISHED FIRMS FACED WITH DISRUPTIVE CHANGE

1. Although entrants were the leaders in *commercializing* disruptive technology, it did not start out that way: the first engineers to develop the disruptive architectures generally did so while employed by a leading established firm, using bootlegged resources. Their work was rarely initiated by senior management.

Table 6.3. Support of Key Elements of the Model Found in Each of Six In-Depth Case Studies

Companies Studied	Prototypes of disruptive architecture drive developed internally, well before widespread industry adoption (model step 1)	Marketers show early prototypes to lead customers of prior architecture; they reject product; marketing issues pessimistic forecast (model step 2)	Project to commercialize disruptive product is shelved; company aggressively pursues sustaining innovations (model step 3)	New firms are established to commercialize disruptive architecture; they find new markets, where product's attributes are valued (model step 4)	Entrant firms which initially sold product only in new market improve performance faster than initial market requires, enabling them to attack established markets (model step 5)	In response to entrants' attack, established firms belatedly introduce disruptive product. Sales are largely to existing customers, cannibalizing sales of prior architecture products. (model step 6)
Quantum Corp.	L	L	L, T	L, T	L	L, T
Conner Peripherals	L		L	L	L	
Miniscribe		L		L	L	L
Seagate Technology	L	L	L	L	L	L
Micropolis	T	L	L, T	L, T	L	T
Control Data	L	L	L, T	L, T	L	L, T

Note: An "L" in the matrix indicates that this step was a clear, explicit element in that firm's case history—in Yin's (1989) terms, a "literal replication." Where "T" is shown, the firm avoided the fate described in the model by explicitly recognizing the factors in the model, and dealing with them in the manner described in the final section of this paper. These constitute what Yin calls "theoretical replications" of the model. Where no "L" or "T" is shown, that step was not a clear or prominent part of the firm's encounter with the disruptive technology being studied. Some firms studied confronted only one disruptive architecture. Miniscribe, for example, started making 5.25-inch drives generally in the pattern indicated by our model and was subsequently driven from the industry. Other firms, such as Quantum and Control Data, confronted a series of disruptive innovations and dealt with some of them differently than they did with others, as described in the last section of the paper. In such instances, an "L" and a "T" are entered in the matrix. As Yin points out, when multiple case studies are used to support a multi-element model, as in this study, each cell in a matrix such as this constitutes an independent "observation." Hence, the model is supported in 32 of the 36 observations.

While architecturally innovative, these designs almost always employed off-the-shelf components. For example, engineers at Seagate Technology, the leading 5.25-inch drive maker, were the second in the industry to develop working prototype 3.5-inch models, in 1985. They made over 80 prototype models before the issue of formal project approval was raised with senior management. The same thing happened earlier at Control Data, the dominant 14-inch drive maker. Its engineers had designed working 8-inch drives internally, nearly 2 years before they appeared in the market.

2. The marketing organization then used its habitual procedure for testing the market appeal of new drives, by showing prototypes to leading customers of the existing product line, asking them to evaluate the new models.[10] Again drawing on the Seagate case, marketers tested the new 3.5-inch drives with IBM and other makers of XT and AT-class desktop personal computers—even though the drives, as shown in Fig-

ure 6.2 above, had significantly less capacity than the mainstream desktop market demanded.

These customers showed little interest in the disruptive drives, because they did not address their need for higher performance within the established architectural framework. As Figure 6.2 shows, the established customers needed new drives that would take them *along* their existing performance trajectory. As a consequence, the marketing managers were unwilling to support the disruptive technology and offered pessimistic sales forecasts.

Generally, because the disruptive drives were targeted at emerging markets, initial forecasts of sales were small. In addition, because such products were simpler and offered lower performance, forecast profit margins were also lower than established firms had come to require. Financial analysts in established firms, therefore, joined their marketing colleagues in opposing the disruptive programs. As a result, in the ensuing allocation process resources were explicitly withdrawn, and the disruptive projects were slowly starved.

For example, when Seagate's main customer, IBM's PC division, rejected Seagate's 3.5-inch prototypes for insufficient capacity, sales forecasts were cut and senior managers shelved the program—just as 3.5-inch drives were becoming firmly established in laptops. "We needed a new model," recalled a former Seagate manager, "which could become the next ST412 (a very successful product generating $300 million sales annually in the desktop market that was near the end of its life cycle). Our forecasts for the 3.5-inch drive were under $50 million because the laptop market was just emerging—and the 3.5-inch product just didn't fit the bill." And earlier, when engineers at Control Data, the leading 14-inch drive maker, developed its initial 8-inch drives, its customers were looking for an average of 300 MB per computer, whereas CDC's earliest 8-inch drives offered less than 60 MB. The 8-inch project was given low priority, and engineers assigned to its development kept getting pulled off to work on problems with 14-inch drives being designed for more important customers. Similar problems plagued the belated launches of Quantum's and Micropolis's 5.25-inch products.

3. In response to the needs of current customers, the marketing managers threw impetus behind alternative *sustaining* projects, such as incorporating better heads or developing new recording codes. These would give their customers what they wanted, could be targeted at large markets, and generate the sales and profits required to maintain growth. Although they generally involved greater development expense, such sustaining investments appeared *far* less risky than investments in the disruptive technology, because the customers were there. The rationality of Seagate's decision to shelve the 3.5-inch drive in 1985–86, for example, is stark. Its view downmarket (in terms of Figure 6.2) was at a $50 million total market forecast for 3.5-inch drives in 1987. What gross margins it could achieve in that market were uncertain, but its manufacturing executives predicted that costs per megabyte in 3.5-inch drives would be much higher than in 5.25-inch products. Seagate's view upmarket was quite different. Volumes in 5.25-inch drives with capacities of 60–100 MB were forecast to be $500 million in size by 1987. And companies serving the 60–100 MB market

were earning gross margins of 35–40 percent, whereas Seagate's margins in its high-volume 20 MB drives were between 25 and 30 percent. It simply did not make sense for Seagate to put resources behind the 3.5-inch drive, when competing proposals to move up-market to develop its ST251 line of drives were also actively being evaluated.

After Seagate executives shelved the 3.5-inch project, it began introducing new 5.25-inch models at a dramatically accelerating rate. In the years 1985, 1986, and 1987, the numbers of new models it introduced each year as a percentage of the total number of its models on the market in the prior year were 57, 78, and 115 percent, respectively. And during the same period, Seagate incorporated complex and sophisticated new component technologies such as thin-film disks, voice coil actuators, RLL codes, and embedded, SCSI interfaces. In each of our other case studies as well, the established firms introduced new models in their established architectures employing an array of new component technologies at an accelerating rate, after the new architectures began to be sold. The clear motivation of the established firms in doing this was to win the competitive wars against each other, rather than to prepare for an attack by entrants from below.

4. New companies, usually including members of the frustrated engineering teams from established firms, were formed to exploit the disruptive product architecture. For example, the founders of the leading 3.5-inch drive maker, Conner Peripherals, were disaffected employees from Seagate and Miniscribe, the two largest 5.25-inch manufacturers. The founders of 8-inch drive maker Micropolis came from Pertec, a 14-inch manufacturer; and the founders of Shugart and Quantum defected from Memorex.[11] The start-ups were as unsuccessful as their former employers in interesting established computer makers in the disruptive architecture. Consequently, they had to find *new* customers. The applications that emerged in this very uncertain, probing process were the minicomputer, the desktop personal computer, and the laptop (see Figure 6.2). These are obvious markets for hard drives in retrospect. But at the time, whether these would become significant markets for disk drives was highly uncertain. Micropolis was founded before the market for desk-side minicomputers and word processors, in which its products came to be used, emerged. Seagate was founded 2 years before IBM introduced its PC, when personal computers were simple toys for hobbyists. And Conner Peripherals got its start before Compaq knew the portable computer market had potential. The founders of these firms sold their products without a clear marketing strategy, essentially to whomever would buy them. Out of what was largely a trial-and-error approach to the market, the ultimately dominant applications for their products emerged.

5. Once the start-ups had found an operating base in new markets, they found that by adopting sustaining improvements in new component technologies,[12] they could increase the capacity of their drives at a faster rate than was required by their new market. As shown in Figure 6.2, they blazed trajectories of 50 percent annual improvement, fixing their sights on the large, established computer markets immediately above them on the performance scale. As noted above, the established firms' views downmarket, and the entrant firms' views upmarket, were asymmetrical. In contrast to the unattractive margins and market size the established firms saw when eyeing the new markets for simpler drives as they were emerging, the entrants tended to view the potential volumes and margins in the upscale, high-performance markets above them as highly attractive. Customers in these established markets eventually embraced the new architectures they had rejected earlier, because once their needs for capacity and speed were met, the new drives' smaller size and architectural simplicity made them cheaper, faster, and more reliable than the older architectures. For example, Seagate, which started in the desktop personal computer market, subsequently invaded and came to dominate the minicomputer, engineering workstation, and mainframe computer markets for disk drives. Seagate, in turn was driven from the desktop personal computer market for disk drives by Conner and Quantum, the pioneering manufacturers of 3.5-inch drives.

6. When the smaller models began to invade established market segments, the drive makers that had initially controlled those markets took their prototypes off the shelf (where they had been put in step 3), and defensively introduced them to defend their customer base in their own market.[13] By this time, of course, the new architecture had shed its disruptive character, and had become fully performance competitive with the larger drives in the established markets. Although some established manufacturers were able to defend their market positions through belated introduction of the new architecture, many found that the entrant firms had developed insurmountable advantages in manufacturing cost and design experience, and they eventually withdrew from the market. For those established manufacturers that did succeed in introducing the new architectures, survival was the only reward. None of the firms we studied was ever able to win a significant share of the new market whose emergence had been enabled by the new architecture; the new drives simply cannibalized sales of older, larger-architecture products with existing customers. For example, as of 1991 almost none of Seagate's 3.5-inch drives had been sold to portable/laptop manufacturers: its 3.5-inch customers still were desktop computer manufacturers, and many of its 3.5-inch drives continued to be shipped with frames permitting them to be mounted in XT and AT-class computers that had been designed to accommodate 5.25-inch drives. Control Data, the 14-inch leader, never captured even a 1 percent share of the minicomputer market. It introduced its 8-inch drives nearly 3 years after the pioneering start-ups did, and nearly all of its drives were sold to its existing mainframe customers. Miniscribe, Quantum, and Micropolis all had the same cannibalistic experience when they belatedly introduced disruptive-technology drives. They failed to capture a significant share of the new market, and at best succeeded in defending a portion of their prior business.

There are curious asymmetries in the ex post risks and rewards associated with sustaining and disruptive innovations. Many of the sustaining innovations (such as thin-film heads, thin-film disks, and the 14-inch Winchester architecture) were *extremely* expensive and risky from a *technological* point of view. Yet because they addressed well-understood needs of known customers, perceived market risk was low; impetus coalesced; and resources were allocated with only prudent hesitation. Yet, although these innovations clearly helped the innovators retain their customers, there is no evidence from the industry's history that any firm was able to gain observable market share by virtue of such technology leadership.[14]

On the other hand, disruptive innovations were technologically straightforward: several established firms had already developed them by the time formal resource allocation decisions were made. But these were viewed as extremely risky, because the markets were not "there." The most successful of the entrants that accepted the risks of creating new markets for disruptive innovations generated billions in revenues upon foundations of architectural technology that cost at most a few million dollars to put into place.

We argue that although differences in luck, resource endowments, managerial competence, and bureaucratic agility matter, the patterns of technology leadership displayed by established and entrant firms in the disk drive industry accurately reflect differences in the fully informed, rational *ex ante* perceptions of risks and rewards held by managers in the two types of firms. In each of the companies studied, a key task of senior managers was to decide which of the many product and technology development programs continually being proposed to them should receive a formal allocation of resources. The criteria used in these decisions were essentially the total return perceived in each project, adjusted by the perceived riskiness of the project, as these data were presented to them by mid-level managers. Projects targeted at the known needs of big customers in established markets consistently won the rational debates over resource allocation. Sophisticated systems for planning and compensation ensured that this would be the case.[15]

The contrast between the innovative behavior of some *individuals* in the firm, vs. the manner in which the firm's *processes* allocated resources across competing projects, is an important feature of this model.[16] In the cases studied, the pioneering engineers in established firms that developed disruptive-architecture drives were innovative not just in technology, but in their view of the market. They intuitively perceived opportunities for a very different disk drive. But organizational processes allocated resources based on rational assessments of data about returns and risks. Information provided by innovating engineers was at best hypothetical: without existing customers, they could only guess at the size of the market, the profitability of products, and required product performance. In contrast, current customers could articulate features, performance, and quantities they would purchase with *much* less ambiguity. Because of these differences in information clarity, firms were led toward particular sorts of innovations—many of which were

extremely challenging and risky—and away from others. In the firms studied here, the issue does not seem so much to be innovativeness per se, as it is what *type* of innovation the firms' processes could facilitate.

In light of this research, the popular slogan, "Stay close to your customers" (which is supported by the research of von Hippel, 1988, and others), appears not always to be robust advice. One instead might expect customers to lead their suppliers toward sustaining innovations, and to provide no leadership—or even to explicitly *mis*lead—in instances of disruptive technology change. Henderson (1993) saw similar potential danger for being held captive by customers in her study of photolithographic aligner equipment manufacturers.

We close our discussion of the model with a final note. Neglect of disruptive technologies proved damaging to established drive makers because the trajectory of performance improvement that the technology *provided* was steeper than the improvement trajectory *demanded* in individual markets (see Figure 6.2). The mismatch in these trajectories provided pathways for the firms that entered new markets eventually to become performance competitive in established markets as well. If the trajectories were parallel, we would expect disruptive technologies to be deployed in new markets and to stay there; each successive market would constitute a relatively stable niche market out of which technologies and firms would not migrate.

THE LINKAGE BETWEEN MODELS OF RESOURCE DEPENDENCE AND RESOURCE ALLOCATION

We mentioned at the outset that a contribution of this paper is that it establishes a linkage between the school of thought known as *resource dependence* (Pfeffer and Salancik, 1978) and the models of the resource allocation process proposed by Bower (1970) and Burgelman (1983a, 1983b). Our findings support many of the conclusions of the resource dependence theorists, who contend that a firm's scope for strategic change is strongly bounded by the interests of external entities (customers, in this study) who provide the resources the firm needs to survive. We show that the mechanism through which customers wield this power is the process in which impetus coalesces behind investments in sustaining technologies, directing resources to innovations that address current customers' needs.

But although our findings lend support to the theory of resource dependence, they decidedly do not support a contention that managers are powerless to change the strategies of their companies in directions that are inconsistent with the needs of their customers as resource providers (Pfeffer and Salancik, 1978: 263–265).[17] The evidence from this study is that managers can, in fact, change strategy—but that they can successfully do so only if their actions are consistent with, rather than in counteraction to, the principle of resource dependence. In the disk drive industry's history, three established firms achieved a measure of commercial success in disruptive technologies. Two did so by spinning out organizations that were completely independent, in terms of customer relationships, from the mainstream groups. The third launched the disruptive technology with extreme managerial effort, from within the mainstream organization. This paper closes by summarizing these case histories and their implications for theory.

Distinct Organizational Units for Small Drives at Control Data

Control Data (CDC) was the dominant manufacturer of 14-inch disk pack and Winchester drives sold into the OEM market between 1975 and 1982: its market share fluctuated between 55 and 62 percent. When the 8-inch architecture emerged in the late 1970s, CDC missed it by 3 years. It never captured more than 3–4 percent of the 8-inch market, and those 8-inch drives that it did sell, were sold almost exclusively to its established customer base of mainframe computer manufacturers. The reason given by those interviewed in this study was that engineers and marketers kept getting pulled off the 8-inch program to resolve problems in the launch of next-generation 14-inch products for CDC's mainstream customers.

CDC also launched its first 5.25-inch model 2 years after Seagate's pioneering product appeared in 1980. This time, however, CDC located its 5.25-inch effort in Oklahoma City—according to one manager, "not to escape CDC's Minneapolis engineering culture, but to isolate the (5.25-inch product) group from the company's mainstream customers. We needed an organization that could get excited about a $50,000 order. In Minneapolis (which derived nearly $1 billion from the sale of 14-inch drives in the mainframe market) you needed a million-dollar order just to turn anyone's head." Although it was late and never reascended to its position of dominance, CDC's foray into 5.25-inch drives was profitable, and at times it commanded a 20 percent share of higher-capacity 5.25-inch drives.

Having learned from its experience in Oklahoma City, when CDC decided to attack the 3.5-inch market it set up yet another organization in Simi Valley, California. This group shipped its first products in mid-1988, about 18 months behind Conner Peripherals, and enjoyed modest commercial success. The creation of these stand-alone organizations was CDC's way of handling the "strategic forcing" and "strategic context determination" challenges described by Burgelman (1983b, 1984).

Quantum Corporation and the 3.5-Inch Hardcard

Quantum Corporation, a leading maker of 8-inch drives sold in the minicomputer market, introduced its first 5.25-inch product 3 years after those drives had first appeared in the market. As the 5.25-inch pioneers began to invade the minicomputer market from below, for all of the reasons described above, Quantum launched a 5.25-inch product and was temporarily successful in defending some of its existing customers by selling its 5.25-inch drive to them. But it never sold a single drive in the desktop PC market, and its overall sales began to sag. In 1984 a group of Quantum engineers saw a market for a thin 3.5-inch drive plugged into an expansion slot in IBM XT- and AT-class desktop computers—drives that would be sold to end-users, rather than OEM computer manufacturers. Quantum financed and retained 80 percent ownership of this spin-off venture, called Plus Development Corporation, and set the company up in different facilities. Plus was extremely successful. As sales of Quantum's line of 8-inch drives began to evaporate in the mid-1980s, they were offset by Plus's growing "Hardcard" revenues. By 1987, sales of 8- and 5.25-inch products had largely evaporated. Quantum purchased the 20 percent of Plus it did not own; essentially closed down the old corporation, and installed Plus's executives in Quantum's most senior positions. They then reconfigured Plus's 3.5-inch products to appeal to desktop computer makers such as Apple, just as the capacity vector for 3.5-inch drives was invading the desktop, as shown in Figure 6.2. By 1994 the new Quantum had become the largest unit-volume producer of disk drives in the world. Quantum's spin-out of the Hardcard effort and its subsequent strategic reorientation appears to be an example of the processes of strategy change described in Burgelman (1991).

Micropolis: Transition Through Managerial Force

Managers at Micropolis Corporation, also an 8-inch drive maker, employed a very different approach in which senior management initiated a disruptive program within the mainstream organization that made 8-inch drives. As early as 1982, Micropolis's founder and CEO, Stuart Mabon, intuitively saw the trends mapped in Figure 6.2 and decided the firm needed to become primarily a maker of 5.25-inch drives. While initially hoping to keep adequate resources focused on the 8-inch line that Micropolis could straddle both markets,[18] he assigned the company's premier engineers to the 5.25-inch program. Mabon recalls that it took "100% of his time and energy for 18 months" to keep adequate resources focused on the 5.25-inch program, because the organization's own mechanisms allocated resources to where the customers were: 8-inch

drives. By 1984 Micropolis had failed to keep pace with competition in the minicomputer market for disk drives, and withdrew its remaining 8-inch models. With Herculean effort, however, it did succeed in its 5.25-inch programs. Figure 6.3 shows why this was necessary: in the transition, Micropolis assumed a position on a very different technological trajectory (Dosi, 1982). In the process it had to walk away from every one of its major customers, and replace the lost revenues with sales of the new product line to an entirely different group of desktop computer makers. Mabon remembers the experience as the most exhausting of his life. Micropolis aborted a 1989 attempt to launch its first 3.5-inch drive and as of 1992 the company still had not introduced a 3.5-inch product.

Table 6.4 arrays the experiences of the six companies we studied in depth, as they addressed disruptive technologies from within their mainstream organization, and through independent organizations. Companies are classed as having been successful in this table if their market share in the new market enabled by the disruptive disk drive technology was at least 25 percent of its percentage share in the prior, established market in which it was dominant. Hence, Control Data, whose share of the 14-inch mainframe computer disk drive market often exceeded 60 percent, was classed as a failure in its attempt to sell 8-inch drives, because its share of minicomputer disk drives never exceeded 3 percent.

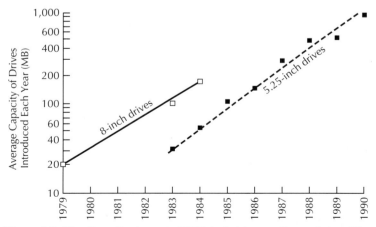

Figure 6.3. The disruptive impact of 5.25-inch drives on the market position of Micropolis Corp.

Table 6.4. The Success and Failure of Companies Addressing Disruptive Technologies Through Mainstream vs. Independent Organizations

	Commercialized from within an independent organization	Commercialized from within the mainstream organization
Succeeded	Control Data 5.25-inch (L) Control Data 3.5-inch (L) Quantum 3.5-inch (L) *Maxtor 3.5-inch (L)*	Micropolis 5.25-inch (T)
Failed		Control Data 8-inch (L) Quantum 5.25-inch (L) Miniscribe 3.5-inch (L) Seagate 3.5-inch (L) Micropolis 3.5-inch (L) *Memorex 8-inch (L)* *Memorex 5.25-inch (L)* *Priam 5.25-inch (L)* *Century Data 8-inch (L)* *Ampex 8-inch (L)* *Ampex 5.25-inch (L)*

Its share of 5.25-inch drives sold to the desktop workstation market, however, reached 20 percent, and it was therefore classed as a success in that effort. An organization was defined as being independent from the mainstream if it was geographically separated; was held accountable for full profit and loss; and included within it all of the functional units of a typical company: sales and marketing, manufacturing, finance, human resources, engineering, and so on.

In addition to the six firms studied in depth, Table 6.4 lists other firms, shown in *italic type,* whose histories were researched through public sources and a more limited number of personal interviews. The "L" and "T" shown next to each company in the table, as in Table 6.3, denotes whether that firm's experience lends literal or theoretical support (Yin, 1989) to the proposition that managers can effect a strategy change despite resource dependence, by creating independent organizations that depend exclusively upon resources in the targeted market. Micropolis's transition from 8- to 5.25-inch drives is classed as a theoretical replication, because of the enormous managerial effort that was required to counteract the force of resource dependence in that transition.[19] Note that in every instance except Micropolis's 5.25-inch entry, firms that *fought* the

forces of resource dependence by attempting to commercialize disruptive technology from within their mainstream organizations failed, as measured by *Disk/Trend* data. And the firms that *accounted for* the forces of resource dependence by spinning out independent organizations succeeded.

Note in Table 6.4 that there do not seem to be strong firm or managerial effects, compared to the organizational effect. Control Data, Quantum, and Micropolis encountered multiple disruptive technologies; and *the same general managers sat atop these organizations across each of these transitions.* What seems to have distinguished these firms' successful from failed attempts to commercialize these disruptive technologies was not the talent of the managers per se, but whether the managers created organizationally distinct units to accomplish the task—where the forces of resource dependence could work in their favor, rather than against them. The successful cases cited here are the only ones in the industry's history in which a leading incumbent stayed atop its market when faced with disruptive technological change—and as a result, the number of data points in the top half of the matrix is limited. But these findings do suggest that, while the forces of resource dependence act as strong constraints on managerial discretion, managers can in fact manipulate those constraints effectively in order to achieve strategic change.

CONCLUSIONS

This study highlights an important issue for managers and scholars who strive to understand the reasons why strong, capably managed firms stumble when faced with particular types of technological change. While many scholars see the issue primarily as an issue of *technological competence,* we assert that at a deeper level it may an issue of *investment.* We have observed that when competence was lacking, but impetus from customers to develop that competence was sufficiently strong, established firms successfully led their industries in developing the competencies required for sustaining technological change. Importantly, because sustaining technologies address the interests of established firms' existing customers, we saw that technological change could be achieved without strategy change.

Conversely, when technological competence existed, but impetus from customers was lacking, we saw consistently that firms were unable to commercialize what they already could do. This is because disruptive technologies initially tend to be saleable only in different markets whose economic and financial characteristics render them unattractive to established firms. Addressing these technologies therefore requires a change in strategy in order to attack a very different market. In the end, it appears that although the stumbles of these established firms are *associated* with technological change, the key issue appears to be firms' disabilities in changing strategy, not technology.

Our model is not presented as the path every firm follows when faced with disruptive technology. We believe, however, that it may contribute several insights for scholars interested in the factors that affect strategic change in firms. First, it notes that the allocation of resources to some product development and commercialization programs, and the denial of resources to others, is a key event or decision in the implementation of strategy. The model highlights the process by which impetus and consequent resources may be denied to technological opportunities that do not contribute to the needs of prominent customers. These findings suggest a causal relationship might exist between resource allocation processes, as modeled by Bower (1970) and Burgelman (1983a, 1983b), and the phenomenon of resource dependence (Pfeffer and Salancik, 1978). Our findings suggest that despite the powerful forces of resource dependence, however, managers can, in fact, wield considerable power, and wield it effectively, in changing the strategic course of their firms in directions other than those in which its resource providers are pulling it. By understanding the processes that link customers' needs, impetus, and resource allocation, managers can align efforts to commercialize disruptive technology (which entails a change in strategy) with the forces of resource dependence. This involves managing disruptive technology in a manner that is out of the organizational and strategic context of mainstream organizations—where of necessity, incentives and resource allocation processes are designed to nourish sustaining innovations that address current customers' needs. In this way, the model and these case studies illustrate the mechanisms through which autonomous and induced strategic behavior (Burgelman, 1983a) can affect, or fail to affect, a company's course.

Much additional research must be done. Efforts to explore the external validity and usefulness of the model through studies of sustaining and disruptive technological change in other industries has begun (Rosenbloom and Christensen, 1995), but much more is required. In addition, we hope that future researchers can develop clearer models for managerial action and strategic change in the face of disruptive technology change that are consistent with the principles of resource dependence and the processes of resource allocation.

ACKNOWLEDGMENTS

We gratefully acknowledge the financial support of the Harvard Business School Division of Research in conducting the research for this paper, and thank the editors of *Disk/Trend Report* for sharing their industry data with us. We are indebted to Professors Robert Burgelman of Stanford University, Rebecca Henderson of the Massachusetts Institute of Technology,

David Garvin and several of our other colleagues at the Harvard Business School, as well as the anonymous referees, for invaluable suggestions for improving earlier versions of this paper. Any remaining deficiencies are our sole responsibility.

APPENDIX 1: A BRIEF PRIMER ON HOW DISK DRIVES WORK

Rigid disk drives are comprised of one or more rotating disks—polished aluminum platters coated with magnetic material—mounted on a central spindle. Data are recorded and read on concentric tracks on the surfaces of these disks. Read/write heads—one each for the top and bottom surfaces of each disk on the spindle—are aerodynamically designed to fly a few millionths of an inch over the surface of the disk. They generally rest on the disk's surface when the drive is at rest; "take off" as the drive begins to spin; and "land" again when the disks stop. The heads are positioned over the proper track on the disk by an actuator motor, which moves the heads across the tracks in a fashion similar to the arm on a phonograph. The head is essentially a tiny electromagnet which, when current flows in one direction, orients the polarity of the magnetic domain on the disk's surface immediately beneath it. When the direction of current through the electromagnet reverses, its polarity changes. This induces an opposite switch of the polarity of the adjacent domain on the disk's surface as the disk spins beneath the head. In this manner, data are written in binary code on the disk. To read data, changes in magnetic field on the disk as it spins beneath the head are used to induce changes in the direction of current—essentially the reverse process of writing. Disk drives also include electronic circuitry enabling computers to control and communicate with the drive.

As in other magnetic recording products, *areal recording density* (measured in megabits per square inch of disk surface area, or mbpsi) was the pervasive measure of product performance in the disk drive industry. Historically, areal density in the industry has increased at a steady 35 percent annual rate. A drive's total capacity is the product of the available square inches on the top and bottom surfaces of the disks mounted on the spindle of the drive, multiplied by its areal recording density. Historically, the capacity of drives in a giv-

en product architecture has increased at about 50 percent annually. The difference between the 35 percent increase in areal density and the 50 percent increase in total capacity has come from mechanical engineering innovations, which enable manufacturers to squeeze additional disks and heads into a given size of drive.

APPENDIX 2: CALCULATION OF THE TRAJECTORIES MAPPED IN FIGURE 6.2

The trajectories mapped in Figure 6.2 were calculated as follows. Data on the capacity provided with computers in the mainframe, minicomputer, desktop personal computer, and portable computer classes were obtained from *Data Sources,* an annual publication that lists the technical specifications of all computer models available from each computer manufacturer. Where particular models were available with different features and configurations, the manufacturer provided *Data Sources* with a "typical" system configuration, with defined RAM capacity, performance specifications of peripheral equipment (including disk drives), list price, and year of introduction. In instances where a given computer model was offered for sale over a sequence of years, the hard disk capacity provided in the typical configuration generally increased. *Data Sources* divides computers into mainframe, mini/midrange, desktop personal, portable and laptop, and notebook computers. For each class of computers, all models available for sale in each year were ranked by price, and the hard disk capacity provided with the median-priced model was identified, for each year. The best-fit line through the resultant time series for each class of computer is plotted as the solid lines in Figure 6.2. These single solid lines are drawn in Figure 6.2 for expository simplification, to indicate the trend in typical machines. In reality, of course, there is a wide band around these lines. The leading and trailing edges of performance—the highest and lowest capacities offered with the most and least expensive computers—were substantially higher and lower, respectively, than the typical values mapped in Figure 6.2.

The dotted lines in Figure 6.2 represent the best-fit line through the unweighted average capacity of all disk drives introduced for sale in each given architecture, for each year. These data were taken from *Disk/Trend Report.* Again, for expository simplification, only this average line is shown. There was a wide band of capacities introduced for sale in each year, so that the highest-capacity drive introduced in each year was substantially above the average shown. Stated another way, a distinction must be made between the full range of products available for purchase, and those in typical systems of use. The upper and lower bands around the median and average trajectories in Figure 6.2 are generally parallel to the lines shown.

Because higher-capacity drives were available than the capacities offered with the median-priced systems, we state in the text that the solid-line trajectories in Figure 6.2 represent the capacities "demanded" in each market. In other words, the capacity per machine was not constrained by technological availability. Rather, it represents a *choice* for hard disk capacity, made by computer users, given the prevailing cost.

NOTES

1. Evidence supporting this conclusion is provided below. In making this statement, we contest the conclusions of scholars such as Tushman and Anderson (1986), who have argued that incumbent firms are most threatened by attacking entrants when the innovation in question destroys, or does not build upon, the competence of the firm. We observe that established firms, though often at great cost, have led their industries in developing critical competence-destroying technologies, when the new technology was needed to meet existing customers' demands.

2. *Disk/Trend Report* identified 133 firms that participated in the disk drive industry in the period studied. The search of *Electronic Business* magazine yielded information on one additional firm, Peach Tree Technology, that never generated revenues and somehow had escaped detection by the *Disk/Trend* editors.

3. Table 3 (which refers to Yin, 1989: 35–37) describes this pattern-matching.

4. The examples of technology change presented in Figures 6.1 and 6.2 in this paper introduce some ambiguity to the unqualified term "discontinuity," as it has been used by Dosi (1982). Tushman and Anderson (1986), and others. The innovations in head and disk technology described in the left graph of Figure 6.1 represent *positive discontinuities* in an established technological trajectory, while the development of trajectory-disrupting technologies charted in Figure 6.2 represent *negative* discontinuities. As will be shown below, established firms seemed quite capable of leading the industry over positive discontinuities. The negative ones were the points at which es-

tablished firms generally lost their positions of industry leadership.

5. These trajectories represent the disk capacity *demanded* in each market because in each instance, greater disk capacity could have been supplied to users by the computer manufacturers, had the market demanded additional capacity at the cost for which it could be purchased at the time.

6. The parallel impact of sustaining innovations across these architectural generations results from the fact that the same sustaining technologies, in the form of componentry, were available simultaneously to manufacturers of each generation of disk drives (Christensen, 1992b).

7. Note that the statistics shown in Table 6.2 are not a sample—they represent the entire population of firms in each of the years shown offering models incorporating the technologies in question. For that reason, tests of statistical significance are not relevant in this case.

8. We believe this insight—that attacking firms have an advantage in disruptive innovations but not in sustaining ones—clarifies but is not in conflict with Foster's (1986) assertions about the attacker's advantage. The historical examples Foster uses to substantiate his theory generally seem to have been disruptive innovations.

9. For readers who are unfamiliar with the work of scholars such as Yin (1989) and Campbell and Stanley (1966) on research methodology, a *literal* replication of a model occurs when an outcome happens as the model would predict. A *theoretical* replication of the model occurs when a different outcome happens than what would have been predicted by the model, but where this outcome can be explained by elements in the model. In the instance here, the success of entrants and the failure of established forms at points of disruptive technology change are directly predicted by the model, and would be classed as literal replications. Instances where an established firm succeeded in the face of disruptive technological change because it acted in a way that dealt with the factors in the model that typically precipitated failure, would be classed as *theoretical* replications of the model. Several of these instances occurred in the industry's history, as explained later in this paper.

10. This is consistent with Burgelman's observation that one of the greatest difficulties encountered by corporate entrepreneurs was finding the right "beta test site," where products could be interactively developed and refined with customers. Generally, the entrée to the customer was provided by the salesman who sold the firm's established product lines. This helped the firm develop new products for established markets, but did not help it identify new applications for its new technology (Burgelman and Sayles, 1986: 76–80). Professor Rebecca Henderson pointed out to us that this tendency always to take new technologies to mainstream customers reflects a rather narrow *marketing* competence—that although these issues tend to be framed by many scholars as issues of technological competence, a firm's disabilities in finding new markets for new technologies may be its most serious innovative handicap.

11. Ultimately, nearly all North American manufacturers of disk drives can trace their founders' genealogy to IBM's San Jose division, which developed and manufactured its magnetic recording products (Christensen, 1993).

12. In general, these component technologies were developed within the largest of the established firms that dominated the markets above these entrants, in terms of the technology and market trajectories mapped in Figure 6.2.

13. Note that at this point, because the disruptive innovation invading below had become fully performance competitive with the established technology, the innovation had essentially acquired the character of a sustaining innovation—it gave customers what they needed.

14. Christensen (1992b) shows that there was no discernible first-mover advantage associated with trajectory-sustaining innovations to firms in the disk drive industry. In contrast, there were *very* powerful first-mover advantages to leaders in trajectory-disruptive innovations that fostered the creation of new markets.

15. It is interesting that 20 years after Bower's (1970) study of resource allocation, we see in leading-edge systems for planning and compensation the same bias against risk taking. Morris and Ferguson's description of how IBM allowed Microsoft to gain control of PC operating system standards is centered on the role of mainframe producers in IBM's resource allocation process. In a 1990 interview with one of the authors, one of the most successful innovators in IBM history recounted how time and again he was forced to battle the controlling influence of middle-management's commitment to serve commercial mainframe customers.

16. We are indebted to Professor Robert Burgelman for his comments on this issue. He has also noted, given the sequence of events we observed—where engineers inside the established firms began pursuing the disruptive product opportunity before the start-up entrants did—that timing matters a lot. It may be that when individuals in the established firms were pressing their ideas internally, they were too far ahead of the market. In the year or two that it took them to leave their employers, create new firms, and create new products, the nascent markets may have become more ready to accept the new drives.

17. In Chapter 10 of Pfeffer and Salancik's (1978) book, for example, they assert that the manager's most valuable role is symbolic, and they cite a hypothetical example. When external forces induce hard times in a company, managers can usefully be fired—not because bringing in a new manager will make any difference to the performance of the organization, but because of the symbolic content of that action. It creates the *feeling* in the organization that something is being done to address this problem, even though it will have no effect. The evidence from these case studies does not support this assertion about the ability of managers to change the course of their organizations. *As long as managers act in a manner consistent with the forces of resource dependence,* it appears that they can, indeed, wield significant power.

18. The failure of Micropolis to maintain simultaneous competitive commitments to its established technology while adequately nurturing the 5.25-inch technology is consistent with the technological histories recounted in Utterback (1994). Utterback found historically that firms that attempted to develop radically new technology almost always tried simultaneously to maintain their commitments to the old; and that they almost always failed.

19. The success or failure of these other firms at each point of disruptive technology change was unambiguously determinable from *Disk/Trend Report* data. Similarly, whether these firms managed the launch of disruptive technology products from within their mainstream organization, or through an organizationally separate unit, was a matter of public record and general industry knowledge. Hence, there were no subjective judgments involved in constructing Table 6.4.

REFERENCES

Bower, J. (1970). *Managing the Resource Allocation Process.* Irwin, Homewood, IL.

Burgelman, R. (1983a). "A model of the interaction of strategic behavior, corporate context, and the concept of strategy," *Academy of Management Review,* **3**(1), pp. 61–69.

Burgelman, R. (1983b). "A process model of internal corporate venturing in the diversified major firm," *Administrative Science Quarterly,* **28,** pp. 223–244.

Burgelman, R. (1984). "Designs for corporate entrepreneurship in established firms," *California Management Review,* **26,** Spring, pp. 154–166.

Burgelman, R. (1991). "Intraorganizational ecology of strategy-making and organizational adaptation: Theory and field research," *Organization Science,* **2,** pp. 239–262.

Burgelman, R. and L. Sayles (1986). *Inside Corporate Innovation.* Free Press, New York.

Campbell, D. T. and J. C. Stanley (1966). *Experimental and Quasi-Experimental Designs for Research.* Houghton Mifflin, Boston, MA.

Christensen, C. M. (1992a). "The innovator's challenge: Understanding the influence of market demand on processes of technology development in the rigid disk drive industry." Unpublished DBA dissertation. Graduate School of Business Administration, Harvard University.

Christensen, C. M. (1992b). "Exploring the limits of the technology S-curve," *Production and Operations Management,* **1,** pp. 334–366.

Christensen, C. M. (1993). "The rigid disk drive industry: A history of commercial and technological turbulence," *Business History Review,* **67,** pp. 531–588.

Christensen, C. M. and R. S. Rosenbloom (1995). "Explaining the attacker's advantage: Technological paradigms, organizational dynamics, and the value network," *Research Policy,* **24,** pp. 233–257.

Cooper, A. and D. Schendel (February 1976). "Strategic responses to technological threats," *Business Horizons,* **19,** pp. 61–69.

Data Sources: The Comprehensive Guide to the Information Processing Industry (annual). Ziff-Davis Publishing, New York.

Disk/Trend Report (annual). Disk/Trend, Inc., Mountain View, CA.

Dosi, G. (1982). "Technological paradigms and technological trajectories," *Research Policy,* **11,** pp. 147–162.

Foster, R. J. (1986). *Innovation: The Attacker's Advantage.* Summit Books, New York.

Henderson, R. M. (1993). "Keeping too close to your customers," working paper, Sloan School of Management, Massachusetts Institute of Technology.

Henderson, R. M. and K. B. Clark (1990). "Architectural innovation: The reconfiguration of existing systems and the failure of established firms," *Administrative Science Quarterly,* **35,** pp. 9–30.

Pfeffer, J. and G. R. Salancik (1978). *The External Control of Organizations: A Resource Dependence Perspective.* Harper & Row, New York.

Rosenbloom, R. S. and C. M. Christensen (1995). "Technological discontinuities, organizational capabilities, and strategic commitments," *Industrial and Corporate Change,* **4,** pp. 655–685.

Tushman, M. L. and P. Anderson (1986). "Technological discontinuities and organizational environments," *Administrative Science Quarterly,* **31,** pp. 439–465.

Utterback, J. (1994). *Mastering the Dynamics of Innovation.* Harvard Business School Press, Boston, MA.

von Hippel, E. (1988). *The Sources of Innovation.* Oxford University Press, New York.

Yin, R. K. (1989). *Case Study Research: Design and Methods.* Sage, Newbury Park, CA.

7

Architectural Innovation

The Reconfiguration of Existing Product Technologies and the Failure of Established Firms

REBECCA M. HENDERSON
KIM B. CLARK

This paper demonstrates that the traditional categorization of innovation as either incremental or radical is incomplete and potentially misleading and does not account for the sometimes disastrous effects on industry incumbents of seemingly minor improvements in technological products. We examine such innovations more closely and, distinguishing between the components of a product and the ways they are integrated into the system that is the product "architecture," define them as innovations that change the architecture of a product without changing its components. We show that architectural innovations destroy the usefulness of the architectural knowledge of established firms, and that since architectural knowledge tends to become embedded in the structure and information-processing procedures of established organizations, this destruction is difficult for firms to recognize and hard to correct. Architectural innovation therefore presents established organizations with subtle challenges that may have significant competitive implications. We illustrate the concept's explanatory force through an empirical study of the semiconductor photolithographic alignment equipment industry, which has experienced a number of architectural innovations.

The distinction between refining and improving an existing design and introducing a new concept that departs in a significant way from past practice is one of the central notions in the existing literature on technical innovation (Mansfield, 1968; Moch and Morse, 1977; Freeman, 1982). Incremental innovation introduces relatively minor changes to the existing product, exploits the potential of the established design, and often reinforces the dominance of established firms (Nelson and Winter, 1982; Ettlie, Bridges, and O'Keefe, 1984; Dewar and Dutton, 1986; Tushman and Anderson, 1986). Although it draws from no dramatically new science, it often calls for considerable skill and ingenuity and, over time, has very significant economic consequences (Hollander, 1965). Radical innovation, in contrast, is based on a different set of engineering and scientific principles and often opens up whole new markets and potential applications (Dess and Beard, 1984; Ettlie, Bridges, and O'Keefe, 1984; Dewar and Dutton, 1986). Radical innovation often creates great difficulties for established firms (Cooper and Schendel, 1976; Daft,

Reprinted from "Architectural Innovation: The Reconfiguration of Existing Product Technologies and the Failure of Existing Firms," by Rebecca M. Henderson and Kim B. Clark, published in *Administrative Science Quarterly,* Vol. 35, No. 1, by permission of *Administrative Science Quarterly,* Vol. 35, No. 1. Copyright © 1990 by the Johnson Graduate School of Management, Cornell University.

1982; Rothwell, 1986; Tushman and Anderson, 1986) and can be the basis for the successful entry of new firms or even the redefinition of an industry.

Radical and incremental innovations have such different competitive consequences because they require quite different organizational capabilities. Organizational capabilities are difficult to create and costly to adjust (Nelson and Winter, 1982; Hannan and Freeman, 1984). Incremental innovation reinforces the capabilities of established organizations, while radical innovation forces them to ask a new set of questions, to draw on new technical and commercial skills, and to employ new problem-solving approaches (Burns and Stalker, 1966; Hage, 1980; Ettlie, Bridges, and O'Keefe, 1984; Tushman and Anderson, 1986).

The distinction between radical and incremental innovation has produced important insights, but it is fundamentally incomplete. There is growing evidence that there are numerous technical innovations that involve apparently modest changes to the existing technology but that have quite dramatic competitive consequences (Clark, 1987). The case of Xerox and small copiers and the case of RCA and the American radio receiver market are two examples.

Xerox, the pioneer of plain-paper copiers, was confronted in the mid-1970s with competitors offering copiers that were much smaller and more reliable than the traditional product. The new products required little new scientific or engineering knowledge, but despite the fact that Xerox had invented the core technologies and had enormous experience in the industry, it took the company almost eight years of missteps and false starts to introduce a competitive product into the market. In that time Xerox lost half of its market share and suffered serious financial problems (Clark, 1987).

In the mid-1950s engineers at RCA's corporate research and development center developed a prototype of a portable, transistorized radio receiver. The new product used technology in which RCA was accomplished (transistors, radio circuits, speakers, tuning devices), but RCA saw little reason to pursue such an apparently inferior technology. In contrast, Sony, a small, relatively new company, used the small transistorized radio to gain entry into the U.S. market. Even after Sony's success was apparent, RCA remained a follower in the market as Sony introduced successive models with improved sound quality and FM capability. The irony of the situation was not lost on the R&D

engineers: for many years Sony's radios were produced with technology licensed from RCA, yet RCA had great difficulty matching Sony's product in the marketplace (Clark, 1987).

Existing models that rely on the simple distinction between radical and incremental innovation provide little insight into the reasons why such apparently minor or straightforward innovations should have such consequences. In this paper, we develop and apply a model that grew out of research in the automotive, machine tool, and ceramics industries that helps to explain how minor innovations can have great competitive consequences.

CONCEPTUAL FRAMEWORK

Component and Architectural Knowledge

In this paper, we focus on the problem of product development, taking as the unit of analysis a manufactured product sold to an end user and designed, engineered, and manufactured by a single product-development organization. We define innovations that change the way in which the components of a product are linked together, while leaving the core design concepts (and thus the basic knowledge underlying the components) untouched, as "architectural" innovation.[1] This is the kind of innovation that confronted Xerox and RCA. It destroys the usefulness of a firm's architectural knowledge but preserves the usefulness of its knowledge about the product's components.

This distinction between the product as a whole—the system—and the product in its parts—the components—has a long history in the design literature (Marples, 1961; Alexander, 1964). For example, a room fan's major components include the blade, the motor that drives it, the blade guard, the control system, and the mechanical housing. The overall architecture of the product lays out how the components will work together. Taken together, a fan's architecture and its components create a system for moving air in a room.

A component is defined here as a physically distinct portion of the product that embodies a core design concept (Clark, 1985) and performs a well-defined function. In the fan, a particular motor is a component of the design that delivers power to turn the fan. There are several design concepts one could use to deliver power. The choice of one of them—the decision to use an electric motor, for example, establishes a core concept of the design. The actual component—the electric motor—is then a physical implementation of this design concept.

The distinction between the product as a system and the product as a set of components underscores the idea that successful product development requires two types of knowledge. First, it requires component knowledge, or knowledge about each of the core design concepts and the way in which they are implemented in a particular component. Second, it requires architectural knowledge or knowledge about the ways in which the components are integrated and linked together into a coherent whole. The distinction between architectural and component knowledge, or between the components themselves and the links between them, is a source of insight into the ways in which innovations differ from each other.

Types of Technological Change

The notion that there are different kinds of innovation, with different competitive effects, has been an important theme in the literature on technological innovation since Schumpeter (1942). Following Schumpeter's emphasis on creative destruction, the literature has characterized different kinds of innovations in terms of their impact on the established capabilities of the firm. This idea is used in Figure 7.1, which classifies innovations along two dimensions. The horizontal dimension captures an innovation's impact on components, while the vertical captures its impact on the linkages between components.[2] There are, of course, other ways to characterize different kinds of innovation. But given the focus here on innovation and the development of new products, the framework outlined in Figure 7.1 is useful because it focuses on the impact of an innovation on the usefulness of the existing architectural and component knowledge of the firm.

Framed in this way, radical and incremental innovation are extreme points along both dimensions. Radical innovation establishes a new dominant design and, hence, a new set of core design concepts embodied in components that are linked together in a new architecture. Incremental innovation refines and extends an established design. Improvement occurs in individual components, but the underlying core design concepts, and the links between them, remain the same.

Figure 7.1 shows two further types of innovation:

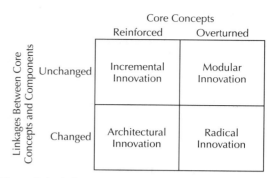

Figure 7.1. A framework for defining innovation.

innovation that changes only the core design concepts of a technology and innovation that changes only the relationships between them. The former is a modular innovation, such as the replacement of analog with digital telephones. To the degree that one can simply replace an analog dialing device with a digital one, it is an innovation that changes a core design concept without changing the product's architecture. Our concern, however, is with the last type of innovation shown in the matrix: innovation that changes a product's architecture but leaves the components, and the core design concepts that they embody, unchanged.

The essence of an architectural innovation is the reconfiguration of an established system to link together existing components in a new way. This does not mean that the components themselves are untouched by architectural innovation. Architectural innovation is often triggered by a change in a component—perhaps size or some other subsidiary parameter of its design—that creates new interactions and new linkages with other components in the established product. The important point is that the core design concept behind each component—and the associated scientific and engineering knowledge—remain the same.

We can illustrate the application of this framework with the example of the room air fan. If the established technology is that of large, electrically powered fans, mounted in the ceiling, with the motor hidden from view and insulated to dampen the noise, improvements in blade design or in the power of the motor would be incremental innovations. A move to central air conditioning would be a radical innovation. New components associated with compressors, refrigerants, and their associated controls would add whole new technical disciplines and new interrelationships. For the maker of large, ceiling-mounted room fans, however, the introduction of a portable fan would be an architectural innovation. While the primary components would be largely the same (e.g., blade, motor, control system), the architecture of the product would be quite different. There would be significant changes in the interactions between components. The smaller size and the co-location of the motor and the blade in the room would focus attention on new types of interaction between the motor size, the blade dimensions, and the amount of air that the fan could circulate, while shrinking the size of the apparatus would probably introduce new interactions between the performance of the blade and the weight of the housing.

The distinctions between radical, incremental, and architectural innovations are matters of degree. The intention here is not to defend the boundaries of a particular definition, particularly since there are several other dimensions on which it may be useful to define radical and incremental innovation. The use of the term architectural innovation is designed to draw attention to innovations that use many existing core design concepts in a new architecture and that therefore have a more significant impact on the relationships between components than on the technologies of the components themselves. The matrix in Figure 7.1 is designed to suggest that a given innovation may be less radical or more architectural, not to suggest that the world can be neatly divided into four quadrants.

These distinctions are important because they give us insight into why established firms often have a surprising degree of difficulty in adapting to architectural innovation. Incremental innovation tends to reinforce the competitive positions of established firms, since it builds on their core competencies (Abernathy and Clark, 1985) or is "competence enhancing" (Tushman and Anderson, 1986). In the terms of the framework developed here, it builds on the existing architectural and component knowledge of an organization. In contrast, radical innovation creates unmistakable challenges for established firms, since it destroys the usefulness of their existing capabilities. In our terms, it destroys the usefulness of both architectural and component knowledge (Cooper and Schendel, 1976; Daft, 1982; Tushman and Anderson, 1986).

Architectural innovation presents established firms with a more subtle challenge. Much of what the firm knows is useful and needs to be applied in the new product, but some of what it knows is not only not useful but may actually handicap the firm. Recognizing what is useful and what is not, and acquiring and applying new knowledge when necessary, may be quite difficult for an established firm because of the way knowledge—particularly architectural knowledge—is organized and managed.

The Evolution of Component and Architectural Knowledge

Two concepts are important to understanding the ways in which component and architectural knowledge are managed inside an organization. The first is that of a dominant design. Work by Abernathy and Utterback (1978), Rosenberg (1982), Clark (1985), and Sahal (1986) and evidence from studies of several industries show that product technologies do not emerge fully developed at the outset of their commercial lives (Mansfield, 1977). Technical evolution is usually characterized by periods of great experimentation followed by the acceptance of a dominant design. The second concept is that organizations build knowledge and capability around the recurrent tasks that they perform (Cyert and March, 1963; Nelson and Winter, 1982). Thus one cannot understand the development of an organization's innovative capability or of its knowledge without understanding the way in which they are shaped by the organization's experience with an evolving technology.

The emergence of a new technology is usually a period of considerable confusion. There is little agreement about what the major subsystems of the product should be or how they should be put together. There is a great deal of experimentation (Burns and Stalker, 1966; Clark, 1985). For example, in the early days of the automobile industry, cars were built with gasoline, electric, or steam engines, with steering wheels or tillers, and with wooden or metal bodies (Abernathy, 1978).

These periods of experimentation are brought to an end by the emergence of a dominant design (Abernathy and Utterback, 1978; Sahal, 1986). A dominant design is characterized both by a set of core design concepts that correspond to the major functions performed by the product (Marples, 1961; Alexander, 1964; Clark, 1985) and that are embodied in components and by a product architecture that defines the ways in which these components are integrated (Clark, 1985; Sahal, 1986). It is equivalent to the general acceptance of a particular product architecture and is characteristic of technical evolution in a very wide range of industries (Clark, 1985). A dominant design often emerges in response to the opportunity to obtain economies of scale or to take advantage of externalities (David, 1985; Arthur, 1988). For example, the dominant design for the car encompassed not only the fact that it used a gasoline engine to provide motive force but also that it was connected to the wheels through a transmission and a drive train and was mounted on a frame rather than on the axles. A dominant design incorporates a range of basic choices about the design that are not revisited in every subsequent design. Once the dominant automobile design had been accepted, engineers did not reevaluate the decision to use a gasoline engine each time they developed a new design. Once any dominant design is established, the initial set of components is refined and elaborated, and progress takes the shape of improvements in the components within the framework of a stable architecture.

This evolutionary process has profound implications for the types of knowledge that an organization developing a new product requires, since an organization's knowledge and its information-processing capabilities are shaped by the nature of the tasks and the competitive environment that it faces (Lawrence and Lorsch, 1967; Galbraith, 1973).[3]

In the early stages of a technology's history, before the emergence of a dominant design, organizations competing to design successful products experiment with many different technologies. Since success in the market turns on the synthesis of unfamiliar technologies in creative new designs, organizations must actively develop both knowledge about alternate components and knowledge of how these components can be integrated. With the emergence of a dominant design, which signals the general acceptance of a single architecture, firms cease to invest in learning about alternative configurations of the established set of components. New component knowledge becomes more valuable to a firm than new architectural knowledge because competition between designs revolves around refinements in particular components. Successful organizations therefore switch their limited attention from learning a little about many different possible designs to learning a great deal about the dominant design.

Once gasoline-powered cars had emerged as the technology of choice, competitive pressures in the industry strongly encouraged organizations to learn more about gasoline-fired engines. Pursuing refinements in steam- or electric-powered cars became much less attractive. The focus of active problem solving becomes the elaboration and refinement of knowledge about existing components within a framework of stable architectural knowledge (Dosi, 1982; Clark, 1985).

Since in an industry characterized by a dominant design, architectural knowledge is stable, it tends to become embedded in the practices and procedures of the organization. Several authors have noted the importance of various institutional devices like frameworks and routines in completing recurring tasks in an organization (Galbraith, 1973; Nelson and Winter, 1982; Daft and Weick, 1984). The focus in this paper, however, is on the role of communication channels, information filters, and problem-solving strategies in managing architectural knowledge.

CHANNELS, FILTERS, AND STRATEGIES

An organization's communication channels, both those that are implicit in its formal organization (A reports to B) and those that are informal ("I always call Fred because he knows about X"), develop around those interactions within the organization that are critical to its task (Galbraith, 1973; Arrow, 1974). These are also the interactions that are critical to effective design. They are the relationships around which the organization builds architectural knowledge. Thus an organization's communication channels will come to embody its architectural knowledge of the linkages between components that are critical to effective design. For example, as a dominant design for room fans emerges, an effective organization in the industry will organize itself around its conception of the product's primary components, since these are the key subtasks of the organization's design problem (Mintzberg, 1979; von Hippel, 1990). The organization may create a fan-blade group, a motor group, and so on. The communication channels that are created between these groups will reflect the organization's knowledge of the critical interactions between them. The fact that those working on the motor and the fan blade report to the same supervisor and meet weekly is an embodiment of the organization's architectural knowledge about the relationship between the motor and the fan blade.

The information filters of an organization also embody its architectural knowledge. An organization is constantly barraged with information. As the task that it faces stabilizes and becomes less ambiguous, the organization develops filters that allow it to identify immediately what is most crucial in its information stream (Arrow, 1974; Daft and Weick, 1984). The emergence of a dominant design and its gradual elaboration molds the organization's filters so that they come to embody parts of its knowledge of the key relationships between the components of the technology. For instance, the relationships between the designers of motors and controllers for a room fan are likely to change over time as they are able to express the nature of the critical interaction between the motor and the controller in an increasingly precise way that allows them to ignore irrelevant information. The controller designers may discover that they need to know a great deal about the torque and power of the motor but almost nothing about the materials from which it is made. They will create information filters that reflect this knowledge.

As a product evolves, information filters and communication channels develop and help engineers to work efficiently, but the evolution of the product also means that engineers face recurring kinds of problems. Over time, engineers acquire a store of knowledge about solutions to the specific kinds of problems that have arisen in previous projects. When confronted with such a problem, the engineer does not reexamine all possible alternatives but, rather, focuses first on those that he or she has found to be helpful in solving previous problems. In effect, an organization's problem-solving strategies summarize what it has learned about fruitful ways to solve problems in its immediate environment (March and Simon, 1958; Lyles and Mitroff, 1980; Nelson and Winter, 1982). Designers may use strategies of this sort in solving problems within components, but problem-solving strategies also reflect architectural knowledge, since they are likely to express part of an organization's knowledge about the component linkages that are crucial to the solution of routine problems. An organization designing fans might learn over time that the most effective way to design a quieter fan is to focus on the interactions between the motor and the housing.

The strategies designers use, their channels for communication, and their information filters emerge in an organization to help it cope with complexity. They are efficient precisely because they do not have to be actively created each time a need for them arises. Further, as they become familiar and effective, using them becomes natural. Like riding a bicycle, using a strategy, working in a channel, or employing a filter does not require detailed analysis and conscious, deliberate execution. Thus the operation of channels, filters, and strategies may become implicit in the organization.

Since architectural knowledge is stable once a dominant design has been accepted, it can be encoded in these forms and thus becomes implicit. Organizations that are actively engaged in incremental innovation, which occurs within the context of stable architectural knowledge, are thus likely to manage much of their architectural knowledge implicitly by embedding it in their communication channels, information filters, and problem-solving strategies. Component knowledge, in contrast, is more likely to be managed explicitly because it is a constant source of incremental innovation.

Problems Created by Architectural Innovation

Differences in the way in which architectural and component knowledge are managed within an experienced organization give us insight into why architectural innovation often creates problems for established firms. These problems have two sources. First, established organizations require significant time (and resources) to identify a particular innovation as architectural, since architectural innovation can often initially be accommodated within old frameworks. Radical innovation tends to be obviously radical—the need for new modes of learning and new skills becomes quickly apparent. But information that might warn the organization that a particular innovation is architectural may be screened out by the information filters and communication channels that embody old architectural knowledge. Since radical innovation changes the core design concepts of the product, it is immediately obvious that knowledge about how the old components interact with each other is obsolete. The introduction of new linkages, however, is much harder to spot. Since the core concepts of the design remain untouched, the organization may mistakenly believe that it understands the new technology. In the case of the fan company, the motor and the fan-blade designers will continue to talk to each other. The fact that they may be talking about the wrong things may only become apparent after there are significant failures or unexpected problems with the design.

The development of the jet aircraft industry provides an example of the impact of unexpected architectural innovation. The jet engine initially appeared to have important but straightforward implications for airframe technology. Established firms in the industry understood that they would need to develop jet engine expertise but failed to understand the ways in which its introduction would change the interactions between the engine and the rest of the plane in complex and subtle ways (Miller and Sawyers, 1968; Gardiner, 1986). This failure was one of the factors that led to Boeing's rise to leadership in the industry.

This effect is analogous to the tendency of individuals to continue to rely on beliefs about the world that a rational evaluation of new information should lead them to discard (Kahneman, Slovic, and Tversky, 1982). Researchers have commented extensively on the ways in which organizations facing threats may continue to rely on their old frameworks—or in our terms on their old architectural knowledge—and hence misunderstand the nature of a threat. They shoehorn the bad news, or the unexpected new information, back into the patterns with which they are familiar (Lyles and Mitroff, 1980; Dutton and Jackson, 1987; Jackson and Dutton, 1988).

Once an organization has recognized the nature of an architectural innovation, it faces a second major source of problems: the need to build and to apply new architectural knowledge effectively. Simply recognizing that a new technology is architectural in character does not give an established organization the architectural knowledge that it needs. It must first switch to a new mode of learning and then invest time and resources in learning about the new architecture (Louis and Sutton, 1989). It is handicapped in its attempts to do this, both by the difficulty all organizations experience in switching from one mode of learning to another and by the fact that it must build new architectural knowledge in a context in which some of its old architectural knowledge may be relevant.

An established organization setting out to build new architectural knowledge must change its orientation from one of refinement within a stable architecture to one of active search for new solutions within a constantly changing context. As long as the dominant design remains stable, an organization can segment and specialize its knowledge and rely on standard operating procedures to design and develop products. Architectural innovation, in contrast, places a premium on exploration in design and the assimilation of new knowledge. Many organizations encounter difficulties in their attempts to make this type of transition (Argyris and Schön, 1978; Weick, 1979; Hedberg, 1981; Louis and Sutton, 1989). New entrants, with smaller commitments to older ways of learning about the environment and organizing their knowledge, often find it easier to build the organizational flexibility that abandoning old architectural knowledge and building new requires.

Once an organization has succeeded in reorientating itself, the building of new architectural knowledge still takes time and resources. This learning may be quite subtle and difficult. New entrants to the industry must also build the architectural knowledge necessary to exploit an architectural innovation, but since they have no existing assets, they can optimize their organization and information-processing structures to exploit the potential of a new design. Established firms are faced with an awkward problem. Because their architectural knowledge is embedded in channels, filters, and strategies, the discovery process and the process of creating new information (and rooting out the old) usually takes time. The organization may be tempted to modify the channels, filters, and strategies that already exist rather than to incur the significant fixed costs and considerable organizational friction required to build new sets from scratch (Arrow, 1974). But it may be difficult to identify precisely which filters, channels, and problem-solving strategies need to be modified, and the attempt to build a new product with old (albeit modified) organizational tools can create significant problems.

The problems created by an architectural innovation are evident in the introduction of high-strength-low-alloy (HSLA) steel in automobile bodies in the 1970s. The new materials allowed body panels to be thinner and lighter but opened up a whole new set of interactions that were not contained in existing channels and strategies. One automaker's body-engineering group, using traditional methods, designed an HSLA hood for the engine compartment. The hoods, however, resonated and oscillated with engine vibrations during testing. On further investigation, it became apparent that the traditional methods for designing hoods worked just fine with traditional materials, although no one knew quite why. The knowledge embedded in established problem-solving strategies and communication channels was sufficient to achieve effective designs with established materials, but the new material created new interactions and required the engineers to build new knowledge about them.

Architectural innovation may thus have very significant competitive implications. Established organizations may invest heavily in the new innovation, interpreting it as an incremental extension of the existing technology or underestimating its impact on their embedded architectural knowledge. But new entrants to the industry may exploit its potential much more effectively, since they are not handicapped by a legacy of embedded and partially irrelevant architectural knowledge.

We explore the validity of our framework through a brief summary of the competitive and technical history of the semiconductor photolithographic alignment equipment industry. Photolithographic aligners are sophisticated pieces of capital equipment used in the manufacture of integrated circuits. Their performance has improved dramatically over the last twenty-five years, and although the core technologies have changed only marginally since the technique was first invented, the industry has been characterized by great turbulence. Changes in market leadership have been frequent, the entry of new firms has occurred throughout the industry's history, and incumbents have often suffered sharp declines in market share following the introduction of equipment incorporating seemingly minor innovation. We believe that these events are explained by the intrusion of architectural innovation into the industry, and we use three episodes in the industry's history—particularly Canon's introduction of the proximity aligner and Kasper's response to it—to illustrate this idea in detail.

INNOVATION IN PHOTOLITHOGRAPHIC ALIGNMENT EQUIPMENT

Data

The data were collected during a two-year, field-based study of the photolithographic alignment equipment industry. The study was initially designed to serve as

an exploration of the validity of the concept of architectural innovation, a concept originally developed by one of the authors during the course of his experience with the automobile and ceramics industry (Clark, 1987).

The core of the data is a panel data set consisting of research and development costs and sales revenue by product for every product development project conducted between 1962, when work on the first commercial product began, and 1986. This data is supplemented by a detailed managerial and technical history of each project. The data were collected through research in both primary and secondary sources. The secondary sources, including trade journals, scientific journals, and consulting reports, were used to identify the companies that had been active in the industry and the products that they had introduced and to build up a preliminary picture of the industry's technical history.

Data were then collected about each product-development project by contacting directly at least one of the members of the product-development team and requesting an interview. Interviews were conducted over a fourteen-month period, from March 1987 to May 1988. During the course of the research, over a hundred people were interviewed. As far as possible, the interviewees included the senior design engineer for each project and a senior marketing executive from each firm. Other industry observers and participants, including chief executives, university scientists, skilled design engineers, and service managers were also interviewed. Interview data were supplemented whenever possible through the use of internal firm records. The majority of the interviews were semistructured and lasted about two hours. Respondents were asked to describe the technical, commercial, and managerial history of the product-development projects with which they were familiar and to discuss the technical and commercial success of the products that grew out of them.

In order to validate the data that were collected during this process, a brief history of product development for each equipment vendor was circulated to all the individuals who had been interviewed and to others who knew a firm's history well, and the accuracy of this account was discussed over the telephone in supplementary interviews. The same validation procedure was followed in the construction of the technical history of the industry. A technical history was constructed using interview data, published product literature, and the scientific press. This history was circulated to key individuals who had a detailed knowledge of the technical history of the industry, who corrected it as appropriate.

We chose to study the semiconductor photolithographic alignment equipment industry for two reasons. The first is that it is very different from the industries in which our framework was first formulated, since it is characterized by much smaller firms and a much faster rate of technological innovation. The second is that it provides several examples of the impact of architectural innovation on the competitive position of established firms. Photolithographic equipment has been shaken by four waves of architectural innovation, each of which resulted in a new entrant capturing the leadership of the industry. In order to ground the discussion of architectural innovation we provide a brief description of photolithographic technology.

The Technology

Photolithographic aligners are used to manufacture solid-state semiconductor devices. The production of semiconductors requires the transfer of small, intricate patterns to the surface of a wafer of semiconductor material such as silicon, and this process of transfer is known as lithography. The surface of the wafer is coated with a light-sensitive chemical, or "resist." The pattern that is to be transferred to the wafer surface is drawn onto a mask and the mask is used to block light as it falls onto the resist, so that only those portions of the resist defined by the mask are exposed to light. The light chemically transforms the resist so that it can be stripped away. The resulting pattern is then used as the basis for either the deposition of material onto the wafer surface or for the etching of the existing material on the surface of the wafer. The process may be repeated as many as twenty times during the manufacture of a semiconductor device, and each layer must be located precisely with respect to the previous layer (Watts and Einspruch, 1987). Figure 7.2 gives a very simplified representation of this complex process.

A photolithographic aligner is used to position the mask relative to the wafer, to hold the two in place during exposure, and to expose the resist. Figure 7.3 shows a schematic diagram of a contact aligner, the first generation of alignment equipment developed. Improvement in alignment technology has meant im-

STEPS

1. Expose Resist

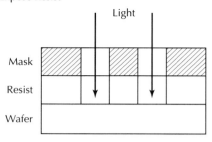

2. Develop Resist

3. Deposit Material

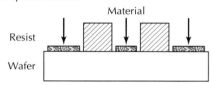

4. Remove Remaining Resist

Figure 7.2. Schematic representation of the lithographic process.

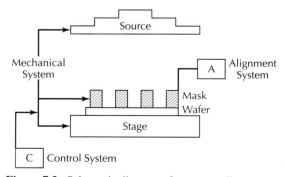

Figure 7.3. Schematic diagram of a contact aligner.

provement in minimum feature size, the size of the smallest pattern that can be produced on the wafer surface, yield, the percentage of wafers successfully processed, and throughput, the number of wafers the aligner can handle in a given time.

Contact aligners were the first photolithographic aligners to be used commercially. They use the mask's shadow to transfer the mask pattern to the wafer surface. The mask and the wafer are held in contact with each other, and light shining through the gaps in the mask falls onto the wafer surface. Contact aligners are simple and quick to use, but the need to bring the mask and the wafer into direct contact can damage the mask or contaminate the wafer. The first proximity aligner was introduced in 1973 to solve these problems.

In a proximity aligner the mask is held a small distance away from (in proximity to) the wafer surface, as shown in the simplified drawing in Figure 7.4. The separation of the mask and the wafer means that they are less likely to be damaged during exposure, but since the mask and wafer are separated from each other, light coming through the mask spreads out before it reaches the resist, and the mask's shadow is less well defined than it is in the case of a contact aligner. As a result, users switching to proximity aligners traded off some minimum feature size capability for increased yield.

The basic set of core design concepts that underlie optical photolithography—the use of a visible light source to transmit the image of the mask to the wafer, a lens or other device to focus the image of the mask on the wafer, an alignment system that uses visible light, and a mechanical system that holds the mask and the wafer in place—have remained unchanged since the technology was first developed, although aligner performance has improved dramatically. The minimum-feature-size capability of the first aligners was about fifteen to twenty microns. Modern aligners are sometimes specified to have minimum feature sizes of less than half a micron.

Radical alternatives, making use of quite different core concepts, have been explored in the laboratory but have yet to be widely introduced into full-scale production. Aligners using x-rays and ion beams as sources have been developed, as have direct-write electron beam aligners, in which a focused beam of electrons is used to write directly on the wafer (Chang et al., 1977; Brown, Venkatesan, and Wagner, 1981; Burggraaf, 1983). These technologies are clearly radical. They rely not only on quite different core concepts for the source, but they also use quite different mask, alignment, and lens technologies.

A constant stream of incremental innovation has been critical to optical photolithography's continuing success. The technology of each component has been significantly improved. Modern light sources are significantly more powerful and more uniform, and modern alignment systems are much more accurate. In addition, the technology has seen four waves of architectural innovation: the move from contact to proximity alignment, from proximity to scanning projection alignment, and from scanners to first- and then second-generation "steppers." Table 7.1 summarizes the changes in the technology introduced by each generation. In each case the core technologies of optical lithography remained largely untouched, and much of the technical knowledge gained in building a previous generation could be transferred to the next. Yet, in each case, the industry leader was unable to make the transition.

Table 7.2 shows share of deflated cumulative sales, 1962–1986, by generation of equipment for the leading firms. The first commercially successful aligner was introduced by Kulicke and Soffa in 1965. They were extremely successful and held nearly 100 percent of the (very small) market for the next nine years, but by 1974 Cobilt and Kasper had replaced them. In 1974 Perkin-Elmer entered the market with the scanning projection aligner and rapidly became the largest firm in the industry. GCA, in turn, replaced Perkin-Elmer through its introduction of the stepper, only to be

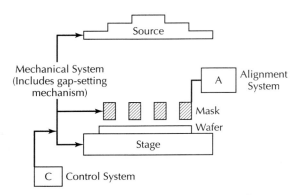

Figure 7.4. Schematic diagram of a proximity aligner.

Table 7.1. A Summary of Architectural Innovation in Photolithographic Alignment Technology

Equipment	Major Changes	
	Technology	Critical relationships between components
Proximity aligner	Mask and wafer separated during exposure.	Accuracy and stability of gap is a function of links between gap-setting mechanism and other components.
Scanning projection	Image of mask projected onto wafer by scanning reflective optics.	Interactions between lens and other components is critical to successful performance.
First-generation stepper	Image of mask projected through refractive lens. Image "stepped" across wafer.	Relationship between lens field size and source energy becomes significant determinant of throughput. Depth of focus characteristics—driven by relationship between source wavelength and lens numerical aperture—become critical. Interactions between stage and alignment system are critical.
Second-generation stepper	Introduction of "site-by-site" alignment, larger 5× lenses.	Throughput now driven by calibration and stepper stability. Relationship between lens and mechanical system becomes crucial means of controlling distortion.

Source: Field interviews, internal firm records (Henderson, 1988).

Table 7.2. Share of Deflated Cumulative Sales (%) 1962–1986, by Generation, for the Leading Optical Photolithographic Alignment Equipment Manufacturers*

Firm	Alignment Equipment				
	Contact	Proximity	Scanners	Step and repeat (1)	Step and repeat (2)
Cobilt	44		<1		
Kasper	17	8		7	
Canon		67	21	9	
Perkin-Elmer			78	10	<1
GCA				55	12
Nikon					70
Total	61	75	99+	81	82+

*This measure is distorted by the fact that all of these products are still being sold. For second-generation step and repeat aligners this problem is particularly severe, since in 1986 this equipment was still in the early stages of its life cycle.
Source: Internal firm records, Dataquest, VLSI Research Inc.

supplanted by Nikon, which introduced the second-generation stepper.

In nearly every case, the established firm invested heavily in the next generation of equipment, only to meet with very little success. Our analysis of the industry's history suggests that a reliance on architectural knowledge derived from experience with the previous generation blinded the incumbent firms to critical aspects of the new technology. They thus underestimated its potential or built equipment that was

markedly inferior to the equipment introduced by entrants.

The Kasper Saga

The case of Kasper Instruments and its response to Canon's introduction of the proximity printer illustrates some of the problems encountered by established firms. Kasper Instruments was founded in 1968 and by 1973 was a small but profitable firm supplying approximately half of the market for contact aligners.

In 1973 Kasper introduced the first contact aligner to be equipped with proximity capability. Although nearly half of all the aligners that the firm sold from 1974 onward had this capability, Kasper aligners were only rarely used in proximity mode, and sales declined steadily until the company left the industry in 1981. The widespread use of proximity aligners only occurred with the introduction and general adoption of Canon's proximity aligner in the late 1970s.

The introduction of the proximity aligner is clearly not a radical advance. The conceptual change involved was minor, and most proximity aligners can also be used as contact aligners. However, in a proximity aligner, a quite different set of relationships between components is critical to successful performance. The introduction of the proximity aligner was thus an architectural innovation. In particular, in a proximity aligner, the relationships between the gap-setting mechanism and the other components of the aligner are significantly different.

In both contact and proximity aligners, the mask and the wafer surface must be parallel to each other during exposure if the quality of the final image on the wafer is to be adequate. This is relatively straightforward in a contact aligner, since the mask and the wafer are in direct contact with each other during exposure. The gap-setting mechanism is used only to separate the mask and the wafer during alignment. Its stability and accuracy have very little impact on the aligner's performance. In a proximity aligner, however, the accuracy and precision of the gap-setting mechanism are critical to the aligner's performance. The gap between the mask and the wafer must be precise and consistent across the mask and wafer surfaces if the aligner is to perform well. Thus, the gap-setting mechanism must locate the mask at exactly the right point above the wafer by dead reckoning and must then ensure that the mask is held exactly parallel to the wafer. Since the accuracy and stability of the mechanism is as much a function of the way in which it is integrated with the other components as it is of its own design, the relationships between the gap-setting mechanism and the other components of the aligner must change if the aligner is to perform well. Thus, the successful design of a proximity aligner requires both the acquisition of some new component knowledge—how to build a more accurate and more stable gap-setting mechanism—and the acquisition of new architectural knowledge.

Kasper's failure to understand the challenge posed by the proximity aligner is especially puzzling given its established position in the market and its depth of experience in photolithography. There were several highly skilled and imaginative designers at Kasper during the early 1970s. The group designed a steady stream of contact aligners, each incorporating significant incremental improvements. From 1968 to 1973, the minimum-feature-size capability of its contact aligners improved from fifteen to five microns.

But Kasper's very success in designing contact aligners was a major contributor to its inability to design a proximity aligner that could perform as successfully as Canon's. Canon's aligner was superficially very similar to Kasper's. It incorporated the same components and performed the same functions, but it performed them much more effectively because it incorporated a much more sophisticated understanding of the technical interrelationships that are fundamental to successful proximity alignment. Kasper failed to develop the particular component knowledge that would have enabled it to match Canon's design. More importantly, the architectural knowledge that Kasper had developed through its experience with the contact aligner had the effect of focusing its attention away from the new problems whose solution was critical to the design of a successful proximity aligner.

Kasper conceived of the proximity aligner as a modified contact aligner. Like the incremental improvements to the contact aligner before it, design of the proximity aligner was managed as a routine extension to the product line. The gapsetting mechanism that was used in the contact aligner to align the mask and wafer with each other was slightly modified, and the new aligner was offered on the market. As a result, Kasper's proximity aligner did not perform well. The gap-setting mechanism was not sufficiently accurate or stable to ensure adequate performance, and the aligner was rarely used in its proximity mode. Kasper's failure to understand the obsolescence of its architectural knowledge is demonstrated graphically by two incidents.

The first is the firm's interpretation of early complaints about the accuracy of its gap-setting mechanism. In proximity alignment, misalignment of the mask and the wafer can be caused both by inaccuracies or instability in the gap-setting mechanism and by distortions introduced during processing. Kasper attributed many of the problems that users of its proximity equipment were experiencing to processing error, since it believed that processing error had been the primary source of problems with its contact aligner. The firm "knew" that its gap-setting mechanism was entirely adequate, and, as a result, devoted very little time to improving its performance. In retrospect, this may seem like a wanton misuse of information, but it represented no more than a continued reliance on an information filter that had served the firm well historically.

The second illustration is provided by Kasper's response to Canon's initial introduction of a proximity aligner. The Canon aligner was evaluated by a team at Kasper and pronounced to be a copy of a Kasper machine. Kasper evaluated it against the criteria that it used for evaluating its own aligners—criteria that had been developed during its experience with contact aligners. The technical features that made Canon's aligner a significant advance, particularly the redesigned gap mechanism, were not observed because they were not considered important. The Canon aligner was pronounced to be "merely a copy" of the Kasper aligner.

Kasper's subsequent commercial failure was triggered by several factors. The company had problems designing an automatic alignment system of sufficient accuracy and in managing a high-volume manufacturing facility. It also suffered through several rapid changes of top management during the late 1970s. But the obsolescence of architectural knowledge brought about by the introduction of architectural innovation was a critical factor in its decline.

Kasper's failure stemmed primarily from failures of recognition: the knowledge that it had developed through its experience with the contact aligner made it difficult for the company to understand the ways in which Canon's proximity aligner was superior to its own. Similar problems with recognition show up in all four episodes of architectural innovation in the industry's history. The case of Perkin-Elmer and stepper technology is a case in point. By the late 1970s Perkin-Elmer had achieved market leadership with its scanning projection aligners, but the company failed to maintain that leadership when stepper technology came to dominate the industry in the early 1980s. When evaluating the two technologies, Perkin-Elmer engineers accurately forecast the progress of individual components in the two systems but failed to see how new interactions in component development—including better resist systems and improvements in lens design—would give stepper technology a decisive advantage.

GCA, the company that took leadership from Perkin-Elmer, was itself supplanted by Nikon, which introduced a second-generation stepper. Part of the problem for GCA was recognition, but much of its failure to master the new stepper technology lay in problems in implementation. Echoing Kasper, GCA first pronounced the Nikon stepper a "copy" of the GCA design. Even after GCA had fully recognized the threat posed by the second-generation stepper, its historical experience handicapped the company in its attempts to develop a competitive machine. GCA's engineers were organized by component, and cross-department communication channels were all structured around the architecture of the first-generation system. While GCA engineers were able to push the limits of the component technology, they had great difficulty understanding what Nikon had done to achieve its superior performance.

Nikon had changed aspects of the design—particularly the ways in which the optical system was integrated with the rest of the aligner—of which GCA's engineers had only limited understanding. Moreover, because these changes dealt with component interactions, there were few engineers responsible for developing this understanding. As a result, GCA's second-generation machines did not deliver the kind of performance that the market demanded. Like Kasper and Perkin-Elmer before them, GCA's sales languished, and they lost market leadership. In all three cases, other factors also played a role in the firm's dramatic loss of market share, but a failure to respond effectively to architectural innovation was of critical importance.

DISCUSSION AND CONCLUSIONS

We have assumed that organizations are boundedly rational and, hence, that their knowledge and information-processing structure come to mirror the internal structure of the product they are designing. This is clearly an approximation. It would be interesting to explore the ways in which the formulation of architectural and component knowledge are affected by factors such as the firm's history and culture. Similarly, we have assumed that architectural knowledge embedded in routines and channels becomes inert and hard to change. Future research designed to investigate information filters, problem-solving strategies and communication channels in more detail could explore the extent to which this can be avoided.

The ideas developed here could also be linked to those of authors such as Abernathy and Clark (1985), who have drawn a distinction between innovation that challenges the technical capabilities of an organization and innovation that challenges the organization's knowledge of the market and of customer needs. Research could also examine the extent to which these insights are applicable to problems of process innovation and process development.

The empirical side of this paper could also be developed. While the idea of architectural innovation provides intriguing insights into the evolution of semiconductor photolithographic alignment equipment, further research could explore the extent to which it is a useful tool for understanding the impact of innovation in other industries.

The concept of architectural innovation and the related concepts of component and architectural knowledge have a number of important implications. These ideas not only give us a richer characterization of different types of innovation, but they open up new areas in understanding the connections between innovation and organizational capability. The paper suggests, for example, that we need to deepen our understanding of the traditional distinction between innovation that enhances and innovation that destroys competence within the firm, since the essence of architectural innovation is that it both enhances and destroys competence, often in subtle ways.

An architectural innovation's effect depends in a direct way on the nature of organizational learning. This paper not only underscores the role of organizational learning in innovation but suggests a new perspective on the problem. Given the evolutionary character of development and the prevalence of dominant designs, there appears to be a tendency for active learning among engineers to focus on improvements in performance within a stable product architecture. In

this context, learning means learning about components and the core concepts that underlie them. Given the way knowledge tends to be organized within the firm, learning about changes in the architecture of the product is unlikely to occur naturally. Learning about changes in architecture—about new interactions across components (and often across functional boundaries)—may therefore require explicit management and attention. But it may also be that learning about new architectures requires a different kind of organization and people with different skills. An organization that is structured to learn quickly and effectively about new component technology may be ineffective in learning about changes in product architecture. What drives effective learning about new architectures and how learning about components may be related to it are issues worth much further research.

These ideas also provide an intriguing perspective from which to understand the current fashion for cross-functional teams and more open organizational environments. These mechanisms may be responses to a perception of the danger of allowing architectural knowledge to become embedded within tacit or informal linkages.

To the degree that other tasks performed by organizations can also be described as a series of interlinked components within a relatively stable framework, the idea of architectural innovation yields insights into problems that reach beyond product development and design. To the degree that manufacturing, marketing, and finance rely on communication channels, information filters, and problem-solving strategies to integrate their work together, architectural innovation at the firm level may also be a significant issue.

Finally, an understanding of architectural innovation would be useful to discussions of the effect of technology on competitive strategy. Since architectural innovation has the potential to offer firms the opportunity to gain significant advantage over well-entrenched, dominant firms, we might expect less-entrenched competitor firms to search actively for opportunities to introduce changes in product architecture in an industry. The evidence developed here and in other studies suggests that architectural innovation is quite prevalent. As an interpretive lens, architectural innovation may therefore prove quite useful in understanding technically based rivalry in a variety of industries.

ACKNOWLEDGMENTS

This research was supported by the Division of Research, Harvard Business School. Their support is gratefully acknowledged. We would like to thank Dataquest and VLSI Research Inc for generous permission to use their published data, the staffs at Canon, GCA. Nikon, Perkin Elmer, and Ultratech, and all those individuals involved with photolithographic alignment technology who gave so generously of their time. We would also like to thank the editors of this journal and three anonymous reviewers who gave us many helpful comments. Any errors or omissions remain entirely our responsibility.

NOTES

1. In earlier drafts of this paper we referred to this type of innovation as "generational." We are indebted to Professor Michael Tushman for his suggestion of the term architectural.

2. We are indebted to one of the anonymous *ASQ* reviewers for the suggestion that we use this matrix.

3. For simplicity, we will assume here that organizations can be assumed to act as boundedly rational entities, in the tradition of Arrow (1974) and Nelson and Winter (1982).

REFERENCES

Abernathy, William J. 1978. *The Productivity Dilemma: Roadblock to Innovation in the Automobile Industry.* Baltimore: Johns Hopkins University Press.

Abernathy, William J., and Kim Clark. 1985. "Innovation: Mapping the winds of creative destruction." *Research Policy,* 14: 3–22.

Abernathy, William J., and James Utterback. 1978. "Patterns of industrial innovation." *Technology Review,* June-July: 40–47.

Alexander, Christopher. 1964. *Notes on the Synthesis of Form.* Cambridge, MA: Harvard University Press.

Argyris, Chris, and Donald Schön. 1978. *Organizational Learning.* Reading, MA: Addison-Wesley.

Arrow, Kenneth. 1974. *The Limits of Organization.* New York: Norton.

Arthur, Brian. 1988. "Competing technologies: An overview." In Giovanni Dosi et al. (eds.), *Technical Change and Economic Theory:* 590–607. New York: Columbia University Press.

Brown, William L., T. Venkatesan, and A. Wagner. 1981. "Ion beam lithography." *Solid State Technology,* August: 60–67.

Burggraaf, Pieter. 1983. "X-Ray lithography: Optical's heir." *Semiconductor International,* September: 60–67.

Burns, Tom, and George Stalker. 1966. *The Management of Innovation.* London: Tavistock.

Change, T. H. P., M. Hatzakis, A. D. Wilson, and A. N. Broers. 1977. "Electron-beam lithography draws a finer line." *Electronics,* May: 89–98.

Clark, Kim B. 1985. "The interaction of design hierarchies and market concepts in technological evolution." *Research Policy,* 14: 235–251.

———. 1987. "Managing technology in international competition: The case of product development in response to foreign entry." In Michael Spence and Heather Hazard (eds.), *International Competitiveness:* 27–74. Cambridge, MA: Ballinger.

Cooper, Arnold C., and Dan Schendel. 1976. "Strategic response to technological threats." *Business Horizons,* 19: 61–69.

Cyert, Richard M., and James G. March. 1963. *A Behavioral Theory of the Firm.* Englewood Cliffs, NJ: Prentice-Hall.

Daft, Richard L. 1982. "Bureaucratic versus nonbureaucratic structure and the process of innovation and change." In Samuel B. Bacharach (ed.), *Research in the Sociology of Organizations,* 1:129–166. Greenwich, CT: JAI Press.

Daft, Richard L., and Karl E. Weick. 1984. "Towards a model of organizations as interpretation systems." *Academy of Management Review,* 9: 284–295.

David, Paul A. 1985. "Clio and the economics of QWERTY." *American Economic Review,* 75: 332–337.

Dess, Gregory G., and Donald Beard. 1984. "Dimensions of organizational task environments." *Administrative Science Quarterly,* 29: 52–73.

Dewar, Robert D., and Jane E. Dutton. 1986. "The adoption of radical and incremental innovations: An empirical analysis." *Management Science,* 32: 1422–1433.

Dosi, Giovanni. 1982. "Technological paradigms and technological trajectories: A suggested interpretation of the determinants and directions of technical change." *Research Policy,* 11: 147–162.

Dutton, Jane E., and Susan E. Jackson. 1987. "Categorizing strategic issues: Links to organizational action." *Academy of Management Review,* 12: 76–90.

Ettlie, John E., William P. Bridges, and Robert D.

O'Keefe. 1984. "Organizational strategy and structural differences for radical vs. incremental innovation." *Management Science,* 30: 682–695.

Freeman, Christopher. 1982. *The Economics of Industrial Innovation,* 2d ed. Cambridge, MA: MIT Press.

Galbraith, Jay. 1973. *Designing Complex Organizations.* Reading, MA: Addison-Wesley.

Gardiner, J. P. 1986. "Design trajectories for airplanes and automobiles during the past fifty years." In Christopher Freeman (ed.), *Design, Innovation and Long Cycles in Economic Development:* 121–141. London: Francis Pinter.

Hage, Jerald. 1980. *Theories of Organization.* New York: Wiley Interscience.

Hannan, Michael T., and John Freeman. 1984. "Structural inertia and organizational change." *American Sociological Review,* 49: 149–164.

Hedberg, Bo L. T. 1981. "How organizations learn and unlearn." In P. C. Nystrom and W. H. Starbuck (eds.), *Handbook of Organizational Design,* 1: 3–27. New York: Oxford University Press.

Henderson, Rebecca M. 1988. "The failure of established firms in the face of technical change: A study of photolithographic alignment equipment." Unpublished Ph.D. dissertation, Harvard University.

Hollander, Samuel. 1965. *The Sources of Increased Efficiency: A Study of Du Pont Rayon Plants.* Cambridge, MA: MIT Press.

Jackson, Susan E., and Jane E. Dutton. 1988. "Discerning threats and opportunities." *Administrative Science Quarterly,* 33: 370–387.

Kahneman, David, Paul Slovic, and Amos. Tversky. 1982. *Judgement Under Uncertainty: Heuristics and Biases.* Cambridge: Cambridge University Press.

Lawrence, Paul R., and Jay W. Lorsch. 1967. *Organization and Environment: Managing Differentiation and Integration.* Homewood, IL: Irwin.

Louis, Meryl R., and Robert I. Sutton. 1989. "Switching cognitive gears: From habits of mind to active thinking." Working Paper School of Industrial Engineering, Stanford University.

Lyles, Majorie A., and Ian I. Mitroff. 1980. "Organizational problem formulation: An empirical study." *Administrative Science Quarterly,* 25: 102–119.

Mansfield, Edwin. 1968. *Industrial Research and Technical Innovation.* New York: Norton.

———. 1977 *The Production and Application of New Industrial Technology.* New York: Norton.

March, James G., and Herbert A. Simon. 1958. *Organizations.* New York: Wiley.

Marples, David L. 1961. "The decisions of engineering design." *IEEE Transactions on Engineering Management,* EM.8 (June): 55–71.

Miller, Ronald, and David Sawyers. 1968. The *Technical Development of Modern Aviation.* New York: Praeger.

Mintzberg, Henry. 1979. *The Structuring of Organizations.* Englewood Cliffs, NJ: Prentice-Hall.

Moch, Michael, and Edward V. Morse. 1977. "Size, centralization and organizational adoption of innovations." *American Sociological Review,* 42: 716–725.

Nelson, Richard, and Sidney Winter. 1982. *An Evolutionary Theory of Economic Change.* Cambridge, MA: Harvard University Press.

Rosenberg, Nathan. 1982. *Inside the Black Box: Technology and Economics.* Cambridge: Cambridge University Press.

Rothwell, Roy. 1986. "The role of small firms in the emergence of new technologies." In Christopher Freeman (ed.), *Design, Innovation and Long Cycles in Economic Development:* 231–248. London: Francis Pinter.

Sahal, Devendra. 1986 "Technological guideposts and innovation avenues." *Research Policy,* 14: 61–82.

Schumpeter, Joseph A. 1942. *Capitalism, Socialism and Democracy.* Cambridge, MA: Harvard University Press.

Tushman, Michael L., and Philip Anderson. 1986. "Technological discontinuities and organizational environments." *Administrative Science Quarterly,* 31: 439–465.

von Hippel, Eric. 1990. "Task partitioning: An innovation process variable." *Research Policy* (in press).

Watts, Roderick K., and Norman G. Einspruch (eds.) 1987. *Lithography for VLSI, VLSI Electronics—Microstructure Science.* New York: Academic Press.

Weick, Karl E. 1979. "Cognitive processes in organizations." In B. M. Staw and L. L. Cummings (eds.), *Research in Organizational Behavior,* 1: 41–47. Greenwich, CT: JAI Press.

8

The Dynamics of Standing Still

Firestone Tire & Rubber and the Radial Revolution

DONALD N. SULL

Business historians have illuminated how first movers in many emerging industries secure an enduring leadership position, but have devoted less attention to the processes by which industry leaders relinquish their dominance. This paper examines why rubber industry leader Firestone Tire & Rubber failed to respond effectively to new technology and foreign competition. The author argues that Firestone did not respond by doing nothing, but rather accelerated activities that had contributed to its past success. Firestone's response was constrained by managers' existing strategic frames and values, and the company's processes and long-standing relationships with customers and employees.

Alfred Chandler's research provides a compelling theoretical model and extensive empirical support for the rise of large industrial enterprises in American business.[1] Corporations which invested early in mass production and marketing, according to Chandler, achieved economies of scale and scope that secured their early lead against subsequent challengers. Chandler has noted, however, that occasionally these first movers relinquish their initial lead, often under pressure from technological discontinuities or aggressive foreign competition.[2] The dynamics by which market leaders lose their position is less well understood than the process of establishing a first-mover's advantage, and offers a productive domain for historical research.

The U.S. tire industry provides a striking example of market dominance lost in the face of aggressive foreign competition and technological change. The five largest firms established their market leadership by the early 1930s, and continued to dominate the domestic market nearly half a century later.[3] After French tire manufacturer Michelin introduced the radial tire into the U.S. market in the late 1960s, however, most of the U.S. tire makers suffered costly setbacks while trying to close the technology gap with Michelin and lost significant market share.[4] Each of the five largest companies was the target of at least one hostile takeover bid, and by 1988 only Goodyear remained an independent tire company.[5] In the span of three years, Firestone, Uniroyal, B. F. Goodrich and General Tire—each a household name for half a century—had all been acquired by foreign firms.

Although the tire industry leaders fumbled the transition to the radial tire, it was not because they failed to see the new technology coming. Domestic rival B. F. Goodrich had introduced radial tires into the U.S. market before Michelin, and demonstrated their superior performance in terms of longer wear, lower cost, and enhanced safety.[6] European consumers and automobile manufacturers had rapidly adopted radials

Reprinted with permission from *Business History Review,* Vol. 73, Donald N. Sull, "The Dynamics of Standing Still: Firestone Tire & Rubber and the Radial Revolution," pp. 430–464, copyright © 1999 by The President and Fellows of Harvard College.

in each of the countries where Michelin had introduced them in the decade prior to its U.S. market entry. The major American tire producers all had subsidiaries in Europe, and had witnessed first-hand consumers' rapid switch to the new technology.[7] In the early 1970s, Michelin completed a large radial tire factory in Canada and Japan's Bridgestone began exporting radial tires to the United States. With credible foreign suppliers in place, Detroit's automobile manufacturers—which together purchased 30 percent of all tires—demanded in 1972 that their American suppliers provide radial tires or lose market share to foreign competitors.[8] Thus, by 1973 the rapid adoption of radials was both inevitable and predictable, and tire makers in fact accurately forecasted rapid inroads by the new technology.

In the decades prior to the advent of radial tires, Firestone Tire & Rubber was viewed by some observers as the best managed U.S. tire company.[9] Despite its historical leadership, however, Firestone made the same mistakes as its tire industry peers in responding to Michelin's invasion, and generally exaggerated these gestures with disastrous results. Firestone's crash investment in radials contributed to quality problems with the Firestone 500 radial tire, which resulted in one of the largest product recalls in history, and delays in closing bias tire plants brought the company closer to bankruptcy than any of its beleaguered competitors.[10] While Goodyear survived as one of the global tire leaders in the radial era, Firestone relinquished its independence to Japanese competitor Bridgestone. Firestone's historical excellence and disastrous response to global competition and technological innovation posed a paradox for industry observers: Why had the industry's best managed company turned in the worst performance in a weak field?

Closer analysis reveals that Firestone failed not despite, but because of its historical success. In the years immediately following World War II, Firestone had honed a competitive formula that focused attention on its domestic rivals and large customers, refined processes to design and make tires, forged a dense set of relationships with customers and employees that secured their continued loyalty, and reinforced a strong set of corporate values. While this competitive formula enabled Firestone to succeed in the booming tire market of the 1960s, it constrained the company's ability to respond to the changes brought about by the advent of the radial tire.[11]

THE DAYS OF WINE AND ROSES

The 1960s were a go-go decade for the U.S. tire industry, and Firestone got more than its fair share of the action. Unit demand for tires increased an average 5.5 percent between 1960 and 1969, and Firestone's growth outpaced the industry as a whole and the company doubled its revenues over the course of the decade.[12] Firestone met this growing demand by investing heavily in new production capacity, building five new factories between 1960 and 1969, which constituted one-quarter of all new tire plants built in the U.S. during this period.[13] The company also invested upstream by building four components facilities producing tire textiles and synthetic rubber, and downstream by acquiring or erecting over 500 company-owned retail tire outlets.[14] Tire stocks were Wall Street darlings, and Firestone's 62 percent increase in stock price easily outpaced the S&P index.[15] At the end of 1969, Chairman Raymond C. Firestone reflected on the preceding decade with pride and looked forward with optimism, observing "we are confident that the progress made in all areas of our operations during the past year and the past decade has given us a solid foundation for future growth. As we enter the new decade we believe our Company is on the threshold of one of the greatest growth periods in our history."[16]

Firestone's success was no accident. The company exemplified several of the management nostrums accepted as best practice in the 1960s and later codified into principles by Peters and Waterman in their best-selling book *In Search of Excellence*.[17] Throughout the 1950s and 1960s, Firestone "stuck to the knitting" and maintained a clear strategic focus on its core tire market, which accounted for more than 80 percent of revenues between 1945 and 1972.[18] While many large corporations pursued diversification during the takeover wave of the 1960s, Firestone remained unfashionably focussed in the tire industry and extended its scope only into closely related businesses such as steel wheels for trucks.[19]

Firestone's top managers closely tracked and frequently discussed the strategic initiatives and tactical

Table 8.1. Comparative Financial Performance of Major U.S. Tire Manufacturers: Average 1968–1974

	Total Corporation		Domestic Tire		
	Sales ($ million)	Pretax Return on Sales (%)	Sales ($ million)	Tire Sales as Percentage of Total	Pretax Return on Sales (%)
Goodyear	4,003	7.7	2,146	53.6	8.0
Firestone	2,770	8.6	1,395	50.4	7.1
Uniroyal	1,829	3.8	736	40.2	0.0
B. F. Goodrich	1,468	4.7	553	37.7	2.1
General	1,210	7.7	472	39.0	8.2

Source: Business Strategy Study, B. F. Goodrich corporate archives, dated 23 February 1976.

moves of their four leading rivals—i.e., Goodyear, Uniroyal, B. F. Goodrich and General Tire (see Table 8.1 for comparative financial performance of the five largest U.S. tire manufacturers). Their discussions were informed by detailed management information systems that reported on rivals' technical innovations and patents, new product introductions, marketing initiatives and pricing.[20] The company's Economic Department benchmarked Firestone's financial performance and share of key customer's purchases against the other four industry majors, thereby stoking rivalry for higher market share and profits relative to its peers.[21] Thus, Firestone's strategic worldview was reinforced by management information systems that provided a laser-like focus on the core tire business and the company's traditional rivals.

Firestone's focus on its four major competitors was intensified by long-standing rivalry and geographic proximity. Although hundreds of entrepreneurs entered the tire industry at the turn of the century, "murderous" price wars and "insane" competition triggered a shakeout in the tire sector which consolidated the leadership of first-movers U.S. Rubber (renamed Uniroyal in 1964), Goodyear, B. F. Goodrich and Firestone, each of which was among America's hundred largest industrial enterprises by 1917.[22] When General Tire emerged as a strong fifth competitor by the end of the Second World War, a competitive structure emerged which endured for decades to follow. Four of the five companies that emerged as tire industry leaders had their headquarters in Akron, and by 1926 approximately 60 percent of all American tire production took place within the city limits, earning Akron

the nickname "Rubber City."[23] A host of institutions sprouted to support the burgeoning tire industry, including Buchtel College, which offered the first course in rubber chemistry in 1909, the United Rubber Workers, established in 1935, and the *Akron Beacon Journal*. The *Akron Beacon* was the flagship paper of the Knight family's newspaper empire, and provided in-depth coverage of the tire industry beginning in 1903 when Charles Knight acquired the paper.[24] Perhaps the most influential institution in Akron had nothing to do with tires and rubber directly. The Portage Country Club provided the social setting where successive generations of executives from Goodyear, Firestone, B. F. Goodrich, and General Tire would congregate to "talk tires" over a snifter of brandy and a good cigar.[25]

Peters and Waterman characterize the best companies as not only focused on their competitors, but also having a "bias for action" which they define as "a preference for doing something—anything—rather than sending a question through cycles and cycles of analyses and committee reports."[26] Firestone's processes for designing new products, manufacturing tires, and allocating capital all enabled rapid action. Throughout the 1950s and 1960s Firestone produced a steady stream of new products, increasing the total number of individual tire types sold from 4,000 to 6,700 between 1968 and 1972 alone.[27] Firestone's thousand person Research and Development Department had honed a process for modifying the basic bias tire design through cosmetic changes, such as raised white letters and alternative tread shapes and sizes, that differentiated the product without disrupting well-established manufacturing routines.[28] Thus, when Goodyear introduced its first belted bias tire in November 1967, Firestone was able to quickly follow suit and bring its own version of the belted tire to market within a few months.[29]

Firestone's capital investment process also allowed the company to rapidly translate customer demand into capacity additions. Like other successful companies during the 1960s, Firestone had in place a bottom-up capital budgeting process that excelled in adding new production capacity in response to growing demand.[30] In this process, front-line marketing and sales employees identified opportunities to sell more tires to the automobile manufacturers or dealers, and worked with manufacturing managers to translate these opportunities into concrete proposals for investment in new capacity. Middle managers then selected the most promising proposals from the many they saw, and championed the chosen few before Firestone's Executive Committee.[31] This committee met weekly, and rapidly approved nearly all the proposals it considered.[32] In the late 1960s, for example, the Executive Committee rejected or reduced under 10 percent of all proposals it reviewed, approving big ticket expenditures as quickly as smaller items.[33] In this bottom up process, each level in the hierarchy relied on the level below them to weed out unattractive proposals and add momentum to promising alternatives, and their confidence was premised on the superior information their subordinates possessed as well as their strong incentives to pick winners.[34] Like its new product development, Firestone's bottom-up capital budgeting process allowed the company to rapidly invest in building new production capacity to seize share in the booming tire market.

Firestone's relationships with Ford and its loyal dealers exemplified the principle of "staying close to your customer." Six decades after Firestone tires were placed on the Model T, Firestone remained the dominant supplier to the Ford Motor Company accounting for nearly one-half of Ford tires.[35] The ties that bound the two companies were knotted more tightly when Harvey's granddaughter married William Clay Ford, Henry's grandson and the largest shareholder in Ford Motors. Firestone managers carefully monitored and jealously guarded their company's market share at Ford and the other Detroit automobile manufacturers. Firestone also supported the company's largest dealers

with a number of services, including cooperative advertising, technical assistance and financing to win their loyalty and stimulate their growth, and even provided personal financing to help loyal dealers suffering financial difficulties.[36] Firestone's close relationships with its end customers and dealers kept management abreast of emerging market trends and gave the company an edge in protecting and expanding its market share.

Firestone managers also placed great emphasis on a set of core values, embodied in the idea of "family loyalty," which top managers repeatedly underscored in their public and private statements.[37] The emphasis on family values may have stemmed, in part, from the enduring role played by the founding Firestone family in the company's operations. In the late 1960s, the Firestone family owned approximately 25 percent of the firm, and Raymond C. Firestone, one of the founder's five sons, served as the Chairman of the Board, along with his brothers Leonard and Harvey, Jr., who also sat on the Board. Kimball C. Firestone took his father's seat when Leonard resigned in 1974 ensuring the Firestone family a continued say in how the firm was run.[38] The company's process for recruiting and promoting professional managers also reinforced their corporate loyalty, and ensured a steady stream of executives steeped in the company's values. In the early 1970s all of Firestone's top management team had spent their entire career with the company, two-thirds were Akron born and bred, and one-third followed in their fathers' footsteps as Firestone executives.[39] Tire industry insiders referred to these managers as "gum dipped," a reference to a manufacturing process in which cloth strips were dipped in rubber and took on a uniform shape.[40]

Firestone's family values were manifest concretely in local buildings and institutions bearing the Firestone family name, many of which stemmed from the early days of the industry. Fueled by explosive growth in tire production, Akron grew faster than any other U.S. city between 1910 and 1920, with the population tripling in a decade.[41] The population explosion severely taxed the city's housing, and in some of Akron's boom years the number of residents exceeded the total number of beds, let alone housing units.[42] Harvey Firestone responded to housing shortages in 1915 by dipping into the corporate coffers to underwrite the design and construction of Firestone Park, a

1,000 home development providing affordable housing for employees.[43] The Firestone family and corporation generously funded local charities, and the Firestone name graced a high school, park, school of nursing, music conservatory, and an eight lane highway in Akron.

The Firestone Country Club epitomized the company's family values for many people.[44] In contrast to the exclusive Portage Country Club, the Firestone Country Club was open to all employees based on tenure with the company rather than rank in the corporate hierarchy, and provided a social setting where employees across levels of the company socialized together. Richard Riley, who joined the company in 1939, and rose to the rank of president in 1971, regularly golfed with Firestone employees at the Firestone Country Club.[45] These actions by managers inspired reciprocal loyalty from Firestone employees, who felt "a tremendous sense of family loyalty to the company," according to former Firestone President Lee Brodeur, and which led them to "dedicate their lives to the company way beyond the call of duty."[46]

The corporate values also influenced how executives managed the company on a daily basis. Like other leading companies at the time, Firestone implicitly promised employees a job for life.[47] Top-level executives took a genuine interest in the employees' well-being and devoted considerable discussion to issues such as a physical exercise program for plant workers and a mandatory seat belt policy designated to prevent traffic injuries among workers.[48] To promote corporate citizenship, Firestone executives set an example of civic leadership and strongly encouraged other managers to serve on charitable and civic boards, and also carefully monitored United Way contributions to ensure that Firestone led in contributions in every community where the company operated.[49]

Thus, in the 1950s and 1960s, Firestone owed its success in large part to managers who exemplified best management practices. The company had a clear strategic focus, strong relationships with key customers and employees, product design, and capital budgeting processes that facilitated rapid action, all of which were supported by a strongly held set of corporate values. And Firestone's competitive formula served the company well in the decades immediately following the Second World War.

BUSINESS AS USUAL

By the mid-1960s, however, U.S. tire companies began to feel the first tremors of the competitive earthquake that would ultimately reshape the industry. In 1966, Michelin struck a deal with Sears to manufacture radial tires for sale under the "Allstate" label and within four years Sears was selling one million units per year.[50] In the mid-1960s, B. F. Goodrich embraced radial technology as a means to win market share from its larger rivals, and the company introduced the first American made radial in the mid-1960s and supported the launch with the "Radial Age" advertising campaign in 1968.[51] The August 1968 *Consumer Reports* awarded its top two spots to radials and documented the new technology's longer life, increased safety, handling and economy relative to even top of the line bias tires.[52]

While radials produced a boon to consumers, this widespread acceptance would prove a bane for incumbent U.S. tire makers. Radials' longer life would decrease unit demand in the profitable replacement market provide an opening for foreign producers and smaller players like B. F. Goodrich to seize market share. Shifting to the new technology would also require an enormous investment by incumbent players to upgrade their existing production capacity.[53] Industry leader Goodyear acted quickly to deflate radials' progress, and in 1967 introduced the belted bias tire, an extension of the existing bias technology.[54] Goodyear aggressively promoted the bias belted tire, claimed that it conferred significant performance improvements and launched an advertising campaign questioning the benefits of radials. Firestone, Uniroyal, and General Tire quickly followed Goodyear's lead and introduced their own belted bias tires, and the new tire design rapidly gained share in the U.S. market (see Figure 8.1).

Although radials represented a sharp break with existing tire technology, tire industry managers interpreted the new technology in terms of their pre-existing strategic worldview. Many Firestone managers saw the thrust and parry between Goodrich and Goodyear as the latest battle between two traditional foes in which the smaller player tried to win market share through innovation, while the industry leader continued by marketing an upgraded version of the ex-

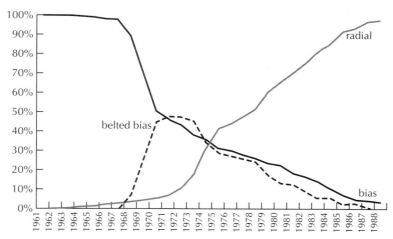

Figure 8.1. Percentage of tires shipped by construction type: 1961–1989. (*Sources:* Rubber Manufacturers Association, "Tire Shipments by Construction," *Tire Industry Facts* (Akron, Ohio, 1990); Firestone Tire & Rubber Company, "Sales Forecasts," Corporate Archives (Akron, Ohio, 1980).)

isting technology.[55] Firestone executives expected the new tire to fuel the next spurt of industry growth, much as earlier product extensions had in previous years.[56]

Just as Firestone's managers could easily interpret Goodyear's introduction of belted bias technology using their traditional strategic framework, the existing processes enabled the company to respond rapidly to the new product. After Goodyear introduced its first belted bias tire in 1967, Firestone's Research and Development group responded with a matching product in a matter of months and provided a second generation belted bias tire within a year.[57] Belted bias tires could be manufactured with minor modifications of existing production equipment, and Firestone increased its capital spending in tires in 1968 and 1969, retooling its factories to accommodate belted bias production.[58] The records of Firestone's board meetings demonstrate no systematic evaluation of the decision to invest in the belted bias transition, but rather reveal a pattern of incremental investments approved individually. Although Firestone encountered some production glitches in refining the new process, overall the transition from bias to belted bias tires proceeded smoothly.[59] Former Firestone President Lee Brodeur, recalls that the transition to belted bias entailed "a

certain amount of development and improvement, but nothing major. It was pretty much business as usual."[60]

Firestone's investment in radials, it appears, also followed the pattern of business as usual. When the automakers switched to radials in the fall of 1972, Firestone's bottom-up capital budgeting process functioned flawlessly, quickly converting Ford and General Motors's demands into concrete commitments to radial production capacity. In a November 1972 Executive Committee meeting, Manufacturing Vice President Mario DiFederico informed his colleagues that marketing managers had already made commitments to supply Ford and General Motors with 433,000 radial tires per month by the following summer and wanted to promise additional tires if capacity was on stream.[61] DiFederico argued that the quickest way to ramp up the additional capacity would be to convert existing factories, but that this "quick fix" would prove insufficient in the long term and that Firestone would need to build a dedicated radial factory. The Committee, according to the minutes, "instructed Mr. DiFederico to proceed immediately to place orders for the long lead time equipment and bring the formal request to the Committee as soon as possible," thus preapproving the required capital spending without benefit of formal review or even in-depth discussion.

The Executive Committee reconvened one month later to review the formal request for $90 million to build a new radial factory, and an additional $56 million to convert existing plants to radial production and build radial inventories.[62] Following the informal authorization granted a month earlier, the Committee treated the request's approval as a fait accompli, and the discussion focused on implementation details, such as optimal plant location, rather than the fundamental soundness of investing so heavily in radials.[63] The strategic question as to "whether Management wants to invest the substantial capital to provide the additional capacity that will be required" was buried in a footnote on the ninth page of a forty-nine page presentation. This investment in radial tires for Firestone's North American business was the first of many, and in the subsequent seven years Firestone invested an average of $60 million of capital expenditure in excess of depreciation per year.[64]

In this December meeting, Firestone managers also decided to manufacture radials using modified bias tire equipment.[65] This decision allowed Firestone to rapidly ramp up its radial production capacity to narrow the gap with Michelin and meet automakers' requirements. Within two years of its introduction, the company's flagship Firestone 500 Steel Belt was the most recognized brand in the industry.[66] While the decision to leverage existing manufacturing processes allowed rapid market penetration, it also contributed to quality problems with the tire's steel cords which failed to adhere properly to the rest of the tire.[67] Although other companies also experienced quality problems with their radials, Firestones' were the most severe, and the company came under heavy pressure from consumer groups and the National Highway Safety Administration. In 1978, the company agreed to a voluntary recall of 8.7 million Firestone 500 tires at a cost of $150 million after taxes—an action that constituted the largest consumer recall in U.S. history.[68]

Firestone's move into radials was not only consistent with the company's standard operating procedures for developing products and allocating capital, but also enhanced its relationships with established customers and employees. Ford and General Motors provided the initial impetus for radials when they demanded the new tires, and Firestone marketing managers responded by giving their core customers exactly what they wanted. It is important to note that no attempt was made to justify the investment for automakers on economic grounds. The projected return on the investment to serve Detroit was 6.5 percent, which fell below the investment hurdle rate of 8 to 10 percent used to evaluate other investments at the time, and was well below the 28 percent average return on investments the company enjoyed outside its North American Tire business.[69] Even this low return was optimistic, moreover, since Firestone had actually lost money on its sales to automakers (even before deducting any corporate overheads) in three of the preceding four years, for a cumulative loss of $12.7 million.[70] While the radial investment served the interests of long-standing customers, it could hardly be expected to earn an acceptable return.

The investment in radials also supported Firestone's relationships with employees and host communities. In his 1976 annual address to shareholders, Firestone Chairman and CEO Richard Riley justified his company's heavy investment in terms of creating jobs instead of creating value for owners:

> The replacement and building of plants is what enables companies to continue to provide jobs . . . jobs that will eventually dry up unless companies invest . . . and when this happens, it will not be something abstract that we may call "The World of Business" or "The Corporation" that will be harmed. It will be companies, and people, and families.[71]

The desire to protect current employees' interests also helps explain why managers chose to build most of their radial capacity by converting existing factories rather than building greenfield facilities, despite the economic advantages that the latter offered over the former.[72]

NO EXIT

While investment served the interests of employees in the converted factories, it jeopardized jobs in the bias plants left behind. The arithmetic of radials was simple: The new tires lasted twice as long as existing bias design, and consumers would therefore buy replacement tires with approximately one-half the frequency. Since the existing factories could be converted to produce approximately the same number of radials as bias tires, the tire industry's heavy investment in radial production capacity necessarily resulted in excess capacity to produce bias tires. Symptoms of bias overcapacity appeared soon after Firestone's investment in radials, as capacity utilization dropped below the break-even level. Operating profits on bias tires slipped to $1 per unit and internal analysis revealed that certain bias plants were losing up to $10 million per year.[73] Despite the underutilization and resulting losses, Firestone managers closed only a single plant in the seven years following their large plunge into radial tires.

Although Firestone's three outside directors constituted a minority on the company's eleven person board, they repeatedly took management to task for shrinking profits in the core tire business, discussed deterioration in the company's stock price and credit rating, and urged management to develop a long-term financial plan.[74] Outside board members also requested profit and loss statements for individual bias plants to identify candidates for closure but had not received the requested information after a year and a half, at which point they apparently gave up asking.[75] Willard Butcher, the president of Firestone's lead banker Chase-Manhattan, repeatedly urged management to close unneeded bias factories, and finally vented his frustration in a 1978 board meeting:[76]

The investment made in North America in the last few years meant that the radial tire had been given to motoring public for nothing, because the old bias tire capacity was still in place and the radial tire capacity had been added at enormous expense to it.[77]

Thus, it was both obvious that bias capacity reductions were necessary and clear that Firestone management was resisting these actions.

Failure to close bias factories can be partially explained by managers' instinctive strategic framing of tires as a growth industry, which it had in fact been for the preceding decades. In six of his seven annual addresses to Firestone shareholders between 1972 and 1979, Riley stressed growth as the company's primary objective.[78] Firestone management planned to achieve this growth by adding more radial capacity, entering new segments of the tire business such as radial truck tires, stepping up new tire development and diversifying into closely related fields.[79] Even Riley, however, questioned Firestone's ability to achieve the growth that he himself forecast. After presenting the company's five year plan in early 1978, Riley told the Board "I have to confess that all of us, even after reviewing, dissecting and challenging this plan . . . feel somewhat uncomfortable when we see the Corporate totals [i.e., aggregate growth projections] I have presented this morning."[80] Riley apparently suffered cognitive dissonance when his view of tires as a growth business clashed with the realities of the market in the wake of radial tires.

Firestone's bottom-up capital budgeting process, which promoted investment so smoothly, unfortunately stalled in reverse and therefore hindered the company from closing unnecessary factories. Existing customers had no incentive to advocate capacity reductions that would decrease their bargaining power, nor were middle managers likely to promote plant closures that jeopardized their jobs and communities. John Nevin, the outsider who joined Firestone from Zenith in 1980, later recalled that the managers of the factories would think "oh my god, its my wife and my kids that need the income . . . so we never had situations where the Decatur plant volunteered to be shut down because it was good for the company."[81] Instead of proposing plant closure, middle managers presented proposals for capacity additions and upgrades to improve their operations.[82]

Absent bottom-up pressure, the onus for disinvestment fell squarely on the lap of Firestone's top management. Yet they conspicuously failed to advocate plant closure. Their failure cannot be attributed to ignorance of the problem, since they experienced constant and growing pressure from outside board members to close bias plants. Nor can their reluctance be attributed to insufficient financial incentives for managers to improve profits. Richard Riley owned 70,000 shares of Firestone stock, which constituted the majority of his personal net worth, and personally lost over $1 million through the deterioration in Firestone's stock price during his tenure.[83]

Reluctance to harm the interests of employees and host communities offers a more persuasive explanation of Firestone managers' delays in plant closure. In his addresses to increasingly restive investors, Riley explicitly referred to employees and communities in addition to owners and customers as part of "the worldwide Firestone family," asserted the commonality of all stakeholders interests, and requested "shareholders' patience while management tried to increase profits without harming employees or communities."[84] This concern for employees was illustrated in how Firestone proceeded in closing the one plant it did shutter in 1978. Although the Akron 2 factory had been losing money for years before radial adoption further depressed its profits, management decided to gradually phase out production over several years through a hiring freeze and planned retirements, and prided themselves on closing the plant without any layoffs.[85] The physical building also defied quick demolition, and the Eslich Wrecking company required two years to demolish the building, twice the time normally required to destroy a comparable building.[86] One former Firestone Vice President recalled that "Riley just lingered and lingered trying to hold on to the employees, he knew them, their kids, he had golfed with them for years and years."[87]

Although the motives for delaying exit may have been admirable, the financial results were disastrous. Operating profits in Firestone's North American Tire Operations deteriorated rapidly as bias losses first negated and then exceeded profits from radial tires (Figure 8.2). These losses, coupled with the large cost to cover the Firestone 500 recall and the investment in radial capacity resulted in a cash deficit of over $700 million between 1973 and 1979.[88] Firestone covered this shortfall by doubling long-term debt from a 1972 level of $635 million (30 percent of entity value) to $1,294 million in 1979 (70 percent of entity value).[89] Banks refused to lend money to Firestone after credit rating agencies downgraded the companies debt four times between 1977 and 1979, after which time Firestone resorted to off balance sheet financing through its Credit Card subsidiary.[90] In late 1979, a year in which Firestone's plants had operated at 59 percent of rated capacity and the company's domestic tire business had consumed over $200 million in cash, Riley told the board that "he saw no plant closures on the immediate horizon."[91]

By 1979, Firestone's situation had grown acute. *Fortune* reported that "in a shrinking U.S. market, Firestone rented warehouses and crammed them with Brobdingnagian inventories of unsaleable products."[92] Over 700 irate investors thronged to the company's 1979 shareholders' meeting, where one dissident investor proposed firing top management, liquidating the company, and distributing the proceeds to sharehold-

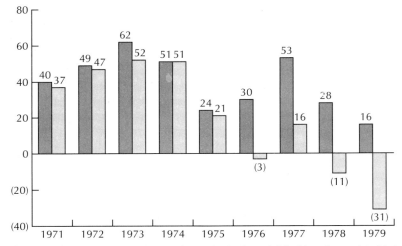

Figure 8.2. Firestone's North American Tire budgeted (black) and actual (white) pretax profits ($ millions): 1971–1979. (*Note:* Budgeted and actual profits exclude extraordinary charges for the Firestone 500 tire recall. *Source:* Firestone Tire & Rubber Company, "Internal Financial Reports," Corporate Archives (Akron, Ohio, 1972–1980).)

ers.[93] When Firestone's fifty-seven-year-old President retired in July 1979 for "personal reasons," the three outside members of the board formed a search committee to find his replacement outside the firm. In November of that year, the board elected John J. Nevin—the former CEO of Zenith—as the first outside president in Firestone's seventy-nine-year history.[94]

NEW BROOM SWEEPS CLEAN

Three months after joining the company, John Nevin announced that he would close five of seventeen North American tire plants, which were then operating at 50 percent of capacity, cut inventories from 16.7 million tires in 1979 to 9.7 million in 1981, and slash the number of different tires produced from 7,300 to 2,600.[95] In addition to restructuring Firestone's North American Tire operations, Nevin also terminated or sold several overseas tire subsidiaries and nontire businesses. These actions resulted in a sharp reduction in revenues, and 24,000 workers (22 percent of employees in 1979) leaving the payroll. Although some considered Nevin's actions "brutal," one tire industry analyst concluded that "Nevin did exactly what the board had hired him to do . . . rescue the company from the brink of financial disaster."[96]

The operational and financial results of Nevin's actions were dramatic. After these steps, Firestone's remaining tire facilities ran at 91 percent of capacity, North American operating profit increased from a $31 million loss in 1979 to a profit of $85 million in 1981, and debt was pared to 29 percent of book equity in 1981 from its peak of 70 percent the previous year.[97] Firestone's average annual return to shareholders in Nevin's first two years was 41 percent, easily outperforming both the rest of the tire industry at 32 percent and the S&P index return of 14 percent. A consultant to Firestone observed "that Nevin did more in five weeks than had been done in the previous fifty years."[98]

What Nevin needed to do was pretty obvious, and one adviser noted that "you could almost outline the restructuring on a piece of paper . . . the company had overcapacity and it was pretty simple to figure out which plants were worst."[99] The specific steps Nevin took in restructuring Firestone, however, provide insights into the sources of inertia. When Nevin arrived at Firestone, he found the incumbent management team "a bunch of clones" who all viewed the world in the same way, an observation that he shared with a reporter from a national business magazine.[100] Nevin quickly proceeded to hire outside managers who brought a fresh perspective on the tire business, and by 1983 only five of twenty-five corporate officers remained from 1979.[101] The influx of outside managers rankled many Firestone veterans, who resented having to "humiliate themselves and take advice from these young Harvard Business School people who think they know everything."[102] Nevin, in contrast, believed that some of the outsiders were not aggressive enough. He replaced Firestone's CFO three times in as many years, leading the wife of one Firestone executive to quip "John, I hope you're not planning to make this an annual event."[103] Nevin also raised the number of outsiders on Firestone's board from 4 of 10 when he joined, to 7 of 12 two years later.[104]

To drive necessary plant closure, Nevin initially circumvented Firestone's bottom-up capital budgeting process. Nevin bypassed the traditional channels within Firestone in gathering data, and instead engaged an outside consulting firm to gather market information. He personally met with Firestone's top 100 managers, over 100 salespeople, all three automotive companies, and over 200 dealers and store managers in his first four months on the job.[105] To analyze the data and evaluate alternatives, Nevin relied on a team of six hand picked executives whom he forbade to discuss their work with anyone else in the company.[106] Although previous investment and disinvestment proposals had always gone through the Executive Committee before moving to the Board, Nevin took his initial restructuring proposal directly to the Board without consulting anyone but Riley, whom he informed of his recommendations the night before the March 1980 board meeting.[107] "We were shocked," recalls Board member Lee Brodeur. "He made one big move and bango we closed five plants."[108] In the months that followed his initial restructuring proposal, Nevin repeatedly bypassed the Executive Committee and brought recommendations to close or sell operations directly to the Board.[109]

After initially circumventing Firestone's bottom-up investment process, Nevin later dismantled it altogether. In his first board meeting as CEO, Nevin stripped the Executive Committee of responsibility for "new plants, major expansions, acquisitions, new business ventures, and major capital expenditures." He also mandated that the six-member committee include three outside directors, although it had historically consisted solely of insiders. Nevin also dissolved the Appropriations Committee of line managers that screened capital requests at the behest of the Executive Committee.[110] Six months later Nevin assumed the Chair of the Executive Committee, and decreased its membership to himself, one other inside manager, and three outside board members, thereby seizing what little influence the Executive Committee still had.[111]

Nevin also took steps to dissolve historical relationships with customers and employees. Private brand customers had grown accustomed to Firestone bearing the costs of short production runs, warehousing, and carrying large inventories and were shocked when Nevin stated that Firestone would only sell tires with a 15 percent return on investment, and proceeded to slash the least profitable 60 percent of the private brand business.[112] While sharply curtailing the private brand business, the new CEO maintained relationships with automakers, primarily to maintain the company's attractiveness as an acquisition for a foreign tire maker trying to enter the U.S. market.[113]

Firestone's relationships with employees were shattered through repeated layoffs and management's new policy of pitting one plant against another to ensure their survival.[114] While sympathetic to veteran managers' concern for their employees, Nevin also realized that this loyalty had driven Firestone to the brink of bankruptcy, and wanted to replace the implicit contract of loyalty in exchange for life-time employment with a new deal that emphasized pay for performance. "Philosophically," Nevin later recalled, "I believe very strongly that executives should get rewarded in some direct relationship to shareholder value."[115] Nevin fundamentally restructured Firestone's incentive structure to reflect this change in values. Nevin granted stock options extensively at all levels in the organization, and instituted performance-based bonuses for top executives which could reach 25 to 50 percent of their base pay if the company and their divisions met or exceeded budget.[116]

Nevin also took a series of actions that had tremendous symbolic impact in signaling the break with Firestone's traditional values. He kept his distance from the Akron tire elite, maintaining his house in Chicago and renting a small apartment in Akron, well outside the five block radius where most top tire executives lived.[117] He later moved corporate head-quarters to Chicago, in part to distance the company's top executives from its Akron past.[118] In what was perhaps the most symbolic break with the past, however, Nevin sold off the Firestone Country Club in 1981, ending a decades old tradition, and inspiring a flurry of hostile press in Akron.[119]

THE REALLY HARD PART

"John J. Nevin has completed the tough, nasty part of the job of turning Firestone Tire & Rubber Co. around," *The Wall Street Journal* reported in late 1981. "Now comes the really hard part."[120] During his first two years, Nevin had improved Firestone's operations by mainly closing money-losing operations, but by 1982 most of the obvious restructuring was behind him. Firestone needed to improve ongoing performance despite low growth in tire demand, a surge in imports, and large investment demands from OE customers. In this Nevin failed. Firestone's core tire business fell $230 million short of projected operating profits in 1985, and provided a return on assets of minus 2 percent.[121]

The company continued to liquidate significant portions of its portfolio, and in June 1981 Nevin presented the board with a strategy to sell all divisions except for domestic passenger tires and the company controlled retail outlets.[122] The biggest shock to many managers came when Nevin decided to dispose of Firestone's Seat Belt, Automotive Foam Rubber, and Truck Wheel businesses, although they all enjoyed returns on equity ranging from 15 percent to 50 percent, were first or second in their respective markets, and offered significant growth opportunities.[123] Veteran executives were also shocked that Nevin insisted on investing heavily in expanding Firestone's owned retail operations, which earned returns on assets that averaged 3 percent despite favorable transfer prices.[124]

Ironically, it appears that the very steps Nevin took to break Firestone's inertia gave rise to a set of processes and strategic frames that locked the restructured organization into a new pattern of continuous restructuring and hindered efforts to grow profitably. After eviscerating Firestone's bottom-up capital budgeting process, Nevin imposed a top-down procedure in which he dominated the company's allocation of capital, presenting his proposals directly to the board and unilaterally rejecting capital requests if he was dissatisfied with the underlying assumptions or analysis.[125]

"Nevin made all the decisions as to who got capital," former Vice President Roy Gilbert recalled, "he invested in a few businesses, others got shut down, but he called the shots."[126]

This top-down process left the company's capital budgeting process very susceptible to the strategic frames of one man at the top of the organization. Early in his tenure, Nevin adopted a view which one of his colleagues characterized, "if it doesn't relate to rubber, I'm going to sell it" and this led to Firestone's rapid divestment of nontire businesses.[127] Although company veterans realized the potential for profitable growth some of these businesses offered, the top-down process failed to capture their knowledge. Based on his experience at Zenith, Nevin saw growth in tire retailing where incumbent managers saw only headaches. Only two months after joining the company, Nevin informed the board "I concluded long ago that a first-rate retailing organization is an absolute requisite for the success of any consumer product manufacturer."[128] Although the stores barely managed to break even, Nevin continued to invest in the business without applying the same level of analytical scrutiny he brought to bear on other divisions, leading one senior manager to conclude that "John loved the stores . . . he was completely irrational on the subject."[129] The top-down investment process lacked the checks and balances required to temper some of Nevin's enthusiasm.

After an initial surge in 1980 and 1981, Firestone's returns to shareholders of 9.3 percent in the subsequent seven years lagged both the tire industry returns of 15.9 percent and the S&P of 15.1 percent.[130] Despite continuous restructuring, Firestone attracted the attention of two corporate raiders in 1982, when both the Loews Corporation and Carl Icahn made unsolicited takeover bids for the company.[131] In March 1988 the Japanese tire maker Bridgestone offered $80 per share for Firestone, a 167 percent premium over the stock's 1987 closing price, trumping a lower offer made weeks earlier by Italian tire maker Pirelli. John Nevin was very pleased with the Bridgestone merger:

> Of all the decisions I've made in my recent tire career, this is the first one I would call a "win-win" situation—because it benefits shareholders, employees, customers, and all of the areas where we have operations.[132]

Thus the Firestone Tire & Rubber Company ceased to exist as an independent entity eighty-seven years after its founding.

WE'RE THE OTHER GUYS, REMEMBER

Although ultimately ineffective, Firestone's response to radial tires was eminently understandable. In rising to industry leadership Firestone forged a strategic worldview, set of processes, relationships and corporate values which enabled its initial success. The company later refined this winning formula to defend its leadership position. When faced with the discontinuity in technology posed by radial tires, Firestone managers responded not by doing things differently but by doing more of what had worked in the past. Over time a gap emerged between the actions necessary to succeed in the market and Firestone's established activities. By 1979 the gap had grown to a chasm and the company was poised on the brink of bankruptcy. Once the situation had reached a crisis, the Board of Directors looked outside for a president unencumbered by Firestone's administrative heritage to restructure the company.

John Nevin did the job the board had hired him to do, and within a few months he radically changed every aspect of Firestone's competitive formula. He brought in other managers from outside the industry who saw the world differently, he re-engineered Firestone's capital budgeting process, he severed long-standing relationships with employees, customers, and host communities and replaced Firestone's "family values" with a pay-for-performance ethic. In the late 1970s, Firestone resembled a person who ignored increasingly severe chest pains and persisted in unhealthy habits until a major heart attack required radical surgery. Nevin saved his patient, but the radical surgery sapped Firestone's long-term health and impaired its ability to thrive in the future.

In broad strokes the Firestone story represents an archetypal pattern of how successful companies respond to major changes in their competitive environment. Companies tend to persist in well worn behaviors until deteriorating performance triggers a crisis and an outsider comes in who changes all elements of the firm's winning formula simultaneously. This pattern is consistent with prominent examples of restructuring such as Tom Graham at U.S. Steel, George Fisher at Kodak, Ann Iverson at Laura Ashley, or "Chainsaw" Al Dunlap at Scott Paper.

This pattern not only describes many well known restructurings, but also bears out the predictions of a prominent theory of strategic change. Punctuated equilibrium theory postulates that organizations have "deep structures," consisting of components like Firestone's strategic frames, processes, relationships, and values.[133] Because these components are interdependent and mutually reinforce one another, they resist piecemeal change. This deep structure, as a result, locks organizations into long periods of stability when none of the pieces change fundamentally. If performance deteriorates, however, managers (generally outsiders) lead revolutionary change by completely dismantling the deep structure and replacing it with a new one. This pattern gives rise to the name "punctuated equilibrium."

Given the strong theoretical predictions and conspicuous empirical examples, one might expect that Firestone's rivals followed the same pattern in response to radial technology. B. F. Goodrich, however, provides a fascinating counterexample to the predictions of punctuated equilibrium theory. In an attempt to distinguish their brand from Goodyear's, B. F. Goodrich launched an advertising campaign in the 1960s with the tag line "we're the other guys, remember."[134] The slogan could as easily describe the company's response to radials which differed from that of the other four tire majors at every turn.[135] While the other leading U.S. tire firms neglected radial tires in the 1960s, Goodrich broke ranks with its traditional rivals and introduced the first U.S. manufactured radial tire in 1966, and supported the product launch with its "Radial Age" advertising campaign in 1968. B. F. Goodrich's management hoped to win share from its larger competitors by introducing the new technology before they did.[136]

B. F. Goodrich's management bet heavily on radials but lost that bet when none of its competitors followed suit. Led by Goodyear, BFG's competitors took steps to thwart Goodrich's radial initiative by refusing to act as second suppliers to the auto companies, aggressively promoting the belted-bias as an alternative technology and—in Goodyear's case—outspending Goodrich four-to-one in a television advertising campaign casting doubts on radials' benefits.[137] When Goodrich's bet failed to pay off, the company's poor performance attracted the unwanted attention of Ben Heineman, who launched a hostile takeover bid in January of 1969.[138] Goodrich CEO Ward Keener forceful-

ly defended the company's independence, and erected a series of barriers to prevent Heineman or any other raider from gaining control by placing 9 percent of BFG equity in friendly hands, arranging a Congressional hearing, and lodging an objection with the Securities and Exchange Commission. Goodrich's defenses appeared insurmountable, and after a brief siege, Heineman retreated.

Thus, Goodrich's crisis passed, leaving the company better fortified against external threats in the future. Rather than breathe a sigh of relief and return to business as usual once this crisis had passed, however, Keener decided that drastic actions were required to improve the company's financial performance. To increase profits in the tire business, B. F. Goodrich's top management decided to explore options to merge with another tire maker.[139] Since the Justice Department would probably oppose further concentration of the tire industry through the merger of the tire domestic competitors, Keener approached Michelin and initiated secret discussions, which ultimately collapsed when Michelin officials demanded they lead any joint-venture, even in B. F. Goodrich's core North American market.[140] Keener's subsequent efforts to reverse Goodrich's declining fortunes met with little success.

By 1970, Keener recognized that he was not the right man to lead the radical restructuring BFG required.[141] Keener recommended that the board look outside the firm for his replacement, but was surprised by the enthusiasm with which the directors embraced his advice. In 1971 the board abruptly replaced Keener—prior to his scheduled retirement—with O. Pendleton "Pen" Thomas, a highly regarded executive from the Atlantic Richfield Oil Company. Thomas tapped outside managers to assemble his team, and by 1972 the majority of Goodrich's top managers came from outside the company, and none of the top seven were Akron natives.[142]

At first glance, B. F. Goodrich's response bears a striking similarity to Firestone's: a crisis motivates the board to bring in an outside leader to clean house. Goodrich's response differed, however, in the magnitude of the crisis that provoked the executive change as well as the timing of the restructuring. Both of these differences had profound implications for how B. F. Goodrich responded to the radial revolution. While Firestone's directors delayed radical steps until the company was nearly bankrupt, the B. F. Goodrich's

Board acted when the company's position in 1971 was still relatively strong. While the low profitability that had attracted Heineman persisted, BFG's balance sheet was still sturdy, and the company was well fortified against hostile takeover bids in the wake of Heineman's unsuccessful raid. While Firestone's Board failed to act decisively until the company suffered the corporate equivalent of a major heart attack, B. F. Goodrich's directors took drastic steps after surviving the first bouts of angina. By acting before Goodrich's financial and strategic situation deteriorated severely, Goodrich's Board gave the newly appointed CEO the luxury of time which Nevin lacked.

Thomas used his time well. He quickly divested several unprofitable businesses outside the core tire operations. While Thomas and his team continued to invest in tires, they carefully monitored the resulting returns. A 1977 postcompletion study of major capital investments revealed that eight major projects to increase radial capacity had delivered only one-third of the projected sales increase and just one-tenth of the forecasted incremental profits.[143] By the late 1970s, Thomas and his management team codified their growing misgivings about the tire business into an explicit strategy to milk their tire division and to reduce capital spending to the bare minimum necessary to maintain the business as an attractive acquisition for another tire company.[144] Thomas and his team had decided that when it came to tires, it was better to quit than fight—a conclusion that Nevin would reach several years later.

Thomas' early recognition that going it alone in the tire industry was not an attractive option for B. F. Goodrich allowed the company to avoid many of the costly investments that sapped its rivals of their financial vitality. Alone among the major American tire makers, Goodrich avoided the large investment necessary to build a new factory dedicated to radial production. While other tire companies continued to fight tooth and nail for share in the unprofitable OEM market, B. F. Goodrich focused on the more attractive replacement market. In January of 1981, B. F. Goodrich took the dramatic step of abandoning the OEM market altogether, although the company had served Detroit since 1896 and sales to automakers still accounted for 10 percent of total revenues.[145] B. F. Goodrich was also the most aggressive company in exiting from redundant bias tire production. Goodrich drew first blood among the Big Five when it closed two bias

plants in 1975, two years before any other major tire manufacturer did so.[146]

The steps taken by B. F. Goodrich managers paid off. Between 1971 and 1981, Goodrich rose from the least profitable to the most profitable tire company in the industry.[147] In 1986, the company merged its tire operations with those of Uniroyal, and two years later sold their 50 percent stake in the merged Uniroyal Goodrich Tire Company. Thus, BFG management finally achieved their goal of exiting tires to focus on more promising lines of business.

CONCLUSION

This study of Firestone Tire & Rubber's response to foreign competition and new technology yields intriguing insights into how industry leaders respond to changes in their competitive environment. Faced with obvious technical innovations or aggressive new entrants, incumbent leaders are often accused of inertia, and sometimes compared to the proverbial deer frozen in the headlights of an oncoming automobile. Firestone, however, clearly did not react to radials by doing nothing: The company rapidly developed a belted bias tire to meet Goodyear's offering and invested heavily in radial production capacity once Detroit's automobile producers switched to radials. While inertia is often equated with inaction, the term can also refer to the tendency of a moving object to persist in an established trajectory in the face of outside force. I define the term "active inertia" to describe an organization's tendency to persist in the activities that contributed to its past success despite even the most dramatic changes in its competitive environment.[148] Faced with new technology and aggressive foreign competition, Firestone responded with active inertia rather than inaction.

Firestone's active inertia raises the questions of what forces lock established competitors into historical responses. This paper identifies established strategic frames, processes, relationships, and values as the key structural elements that channeled Firestone's response to radial tires into well-worn grooves. Firestone managers looked to Akron for competitors, to Detroit for customers, and to the future for growth, but these strategic frames blinded them to the hard realities of the radial age. Firestone's processes for developing new products and allocating capital were well suited to incremental product extensions in a growing market, but inappropriate for adopting discontinuous product technology and closing redundant plants. The values embodied in the notion of the "Firestone Family" were manifest in deep relationships with customers and employees, were instrumental in growing the company, but became chains that bound Firestone managers to the past when the environment changed dramatically.

The active inertia framework builds on an influential stream of research analyzing how firms' investment processes influence their response to technological changes. Carliss Baldwin and Kim Clark argue that capital budgeting processes developed and honed by large American firms after the Second World War enabled these companies to conduct sophisticated analyses of investment proposals whose benefits were easy to quantify, but their processes hindered them from evaluating investments that defied quantification.[149] Because investments in capabilities were difficult to quantify, large firms systematically underinvested in the integration capabilities critical to their long-term success. In a series of influential publications, Clayton Christensen has demonstrated that the resource allocation process within established firms systematically favors existing customers at the expense of potential future customers.[150]

The Firestone history reaffirms the central role that companies' investment processes play in channeling their response to new technologies. This paper contributes two insights to previous research on the investment process. First, the Firestone history highlights the importance of the capital budgeting process not only in shaping investments in new technology, but also in influencing the timing of exit from old technology. Firestone's delays in closing unnecessary bias factories resulted in cumulative pretax losses in excess of $350 million in the 1970s, compared to the company's total market capitalization of $500 million when Nevin became CEO.[151] Second, the Firestone history also demonstrates that a bottom-up investment process well suited to investments for traditional customers can stall in reverse and fail to promote necessary disinvestment from old technologies.

Christensen argues that a company's resource allocation process is influenced by its relationships with established customers, and ties to Ford clearly influenced Firestone's willingness to invest in radial tech-

nology despite the poor financial returns.[152] The Firestone history suggests that the investment process is also deeply intertwined with a company's strategic frames, relationships with employees, and corporate values. Firestone's continued investment in tires resulted in part from managers' mindset that tires was a growth market, just as it had been for the preceding decades. Firestone managers' relationship with employees slowed the process of closing redundant bias plants. The incumbent managers who first faced the radial threat in the 1960s and 1970s were deeply steeped in the company's "family values," which increased the difficulty of closing factories even when the economic case for doing so was compelling.

Firestone's story is deeply intertwined with the history of Akron, and can therefore contribute to the current discussion on industrial clusters. Michael Porter defines industrial clusters as "critical masses-in-one place of unusual competitive success in particular fields," and along with other economists argues that geographic co-location increases firms' productivity and innovativeness by concentrating specialized resources in a condensed area, by facilitating knowledge transfer and heightening competition among firms within a cluster.[153] The conspicuous vibrancy of firms in Silicon Valley, Hollywood, and Wall Street provide compelling evidence to support these economists' arguments.

Akron's tire industry was one of America's most dynamic and technically exciting industrial clusters at the turn of the century. In the 1920s the rubber industry was the second most research intensive industry in the United States, measured by the ratio of research workers as a percentage of total employees, and this research increased both product design and productivity.[154] Improvements in tire design dramatically improved tire wear in the industry's first three decades, as the average tire service life increased from 2,000 miles in 1908 to 22,000 miles by 1932.[155] Labor productivity increased from an average of thirty tires per man-hour in 1914 to 160 tires per man-hour in 1935, the greatest percentage rise in labor productivity of any American industry over that time period.[156] In the wake of the radial revolution, however, three of Akron's four tire leaders were relegated to the ash-heap of history. Nor was the tire story an isolated example. Once vibrant clusters centered around steel in Pittsburgh, automobiles in Detroit, minicomputers in

Boston, watches in Geneva, and cutlery in Sheffield, and all suffered similar fates.

Elsewhere, I present a framework of how industrial clusters evolve over time to help explain how once vibrant clusters lose their dynamism.[157] In the early stages of an industry, according to this model, industrial clusters attract entrepreneurs because they provide ready access to specialized resources, including labor, funding, and knowledge necessary to form a new venture. At the turn of the century, Akron provided the aspiring tire magnate a large pool of skilled tire workers and engineers, specialized equipment manufacturers, and with Buchtel College a center of expertise in rubber chemistry. Because executives in an industrial cluster closely monitor local rivals, quickly imitate best practices, and rapidly hear the latest industry gossip, they may be better positioned to thrive than firms outside the cluster in an industry's turbulent early days. Over time, however, the firms within a cluster may converge on a similar mode of competition—"how we do things around here." This shared way of doing things is reinforced by the dense interweaving of social and professional networks within the cluster. Executives in Akron's tire industry all read the *Akron Beacon Journal,* lived in the same five block radius, and socialized at the same country club. Sanctified by precedent and reaffirmed by competitors following the same rules, the established way of doing things within an industrial cluster can assume a taken-for-granted character and become institutionalized.[158] Faced with an exogenous shock that challenges every aspect of their modus operandi, firms within clusters struggle to adapt.

The Firestone history also highlights the difficulties of assigning industries to broad categories based on technological intensity. In his review of U.S. industrial enterprises since the Second World War, Chandler classifies industries into three categories—i.e., "high-tech," "stable-tech," and "low-tech"—based on their level of R&D intensity. Chandler uses his taxonomy to draw inferences about firms' mode of competition based on their level of technical intensity.[159] While the simple categories that Chandler proposes illuminate broad trends in the economy as a whole, they can also obscure important characteristics of individual firms and industries. Chandler classifies the tire industry (S.I.C. 30) as a "stable-tech" sector, where "the final product has historically remained much the same. Here

competition . . . is based more on the improvement of the existing product and processes, on better marketing and distribution, and on better relations with suppliers and the work force."[160]

One can imagine that most tire industry executives in the late 1960s would have heartily agreed with Chandler's description of their industry, and therein lies the danger. Firestone's managers were blindsided by the magnitude of change wrought by radial technology, at least in past, because they framed their industry as stable and immune to major shifts in technology. The mistaken assumption of industrial stability may also help explain why American steel producers were so slow in coming to terms with mini-mill technology, and Detroit's tardiness in responding to the fuel-efficient cars manufactured by Japanese competitors.

The findings from the Firestone case study also suggest a possibility to extend life-cycle theories of industry evolution. In a series of theoretical and empirical studies, Steven Klepper has examined the evolution of industry structure in new sectors.[161] Klepper argues that nascent industries pass through three stages—i.e., an early growth phase during which many new competitors enter, a "shakeout" period when many firms exit in a short period of time, and a maturity phase characterized by limited entry and gradual attrition of incumbents. The industrial restructuring triggered by the adoption of radial tires raises the intriguing possibility that mature industries may be vulnerable to a second "shakeout" precipitated by major changes in technology (e.g., tires, minicomputers), consumer preferences (e.g., tobacco), or regulation (e.g., airlines, telecommunications). Shocks arising outside the industry's traditional boundaries may prove particularly vexing.

Chandler has provided a parsimonious theory and compelling evidence that during the Second Industrial Revolution those firms that invested earliest to build economies of scale and scope secured defensible positions for decades to come. The importance of these first-mover advantages ranks among the most powerful and best-established insights from the historical analysis of business. Firestone was an archetypal first mover and secured a leading position in the tire industry through the first three-quarters of the century. Yet the very formula which enabled its initial success hindered its subsequent ability to adapt to major changes in this competitive environment. When faced with major changes that could trigger a second shakeout, established companies are often constrained by their legacy and may suffer from a first-mover's disadvantage

The decline and fall of great institutions has intrigued historians from Herodotus and Thucydides through Gibbon, Spengler, and Toynbee. The increasing pace of technical innovation and global competition have placed great pressure on many of the corporate empires which have dominated their industries since the Second Industrial Revolution. The Firestone case study revisits the enduring theme of how success breeds failure in a modern business setting, and despite its modest scope aspires to shed some light on the dynamics of standing still.

ACKNOWLEDGMENTS

I gratefully acknowledge the cooperation of the Firestone Tire & Rubber Company, the United Rubber Workers, the Akron Public Library, B. F. Goodrich, and the University of Akron Historical Documents Department for full and open access to their internal archives. Research support from the Division of Research at Harvard Business School is gratefully acknowledged. I also thank Richard Tedlow for demonstrating the power of historical analysis as a lens to illuminate the dynamics of strategy. I thank three anonymous referees for their insightful and constructive comments.

NOTES

1. Alfred D. Chandler, Jr., *The Visible Hand: The Managerial Revolution in American Business* (Cambridge, Mass., 1977); Chandler, "The Emergence of Managerial Capitalism," *Business History Review* 58 (Winter 1984): 473–503; Chandler, *Scale and Scope: The Dynamics of Industrial Capitalism* (Cambridge, Mass., 1990).

2. Chandler, "The Competitive Performance of U.S. Industrial Enterprises since the Second World War," *Business History Review* 68 (Spring 1994): 1–72.

3. Michael French, "Structural Change and Competition in the United States Tire Industry, 1920–1937," *Business History Review* 60 (Spring 1986): 28–54. French, *The U. S. Tire Industry: A History* (Boston, Mass., 1990); French, "Structure, Personality, and Business Strategy in the U.S. Tire Industry: The Seiberling Rubber Company, 1922–1964," *Business History Review* 67 (Summer 1993): 246–275.

4. Donald N. Sull, Richard S. Tedlow, and Richard

S. Rosenbloom, "Managerial Commitments and Technological Change in the U.S. Tire Industry," *Industrial and Corporate Change* 6 (March 1997): 461–500.

5. John J. Nevin, "The Bridgestone/Firestone Story," *California Management Review* (Summer 1990): 114–132.

6. Mansel G. Blackford and K. Austin Kerr, *BF Goodrich: Tradition and Transformation 1870–1995* (Columbus, Ohio, 1996), chap. 8.

7. David Harkleroad, "Pneumatiques Michelin II" *INSEAD Case Study* (1978).

8. Daniel-Guy Denoual, "The Diffusion of Innovations: An Institutional Approach" (Ph.D. diss., Harvard Business School, 1990).

9. Value Line, *Firestone Analysis* (11 July 1975): 161.

10. Steve Love and David Giffels, *Wheels of Fortune: The Story of Rubber in Akron* (Akron, Ohio, 1998): 153; Dekkers L. Davidson, "Managing Product Safety: The Case of the Firestone 500," Harvard Business School, Case 9-383-130 (1983).

11. For a fuller discussion of why successful companies fail to adapt to changes in their competitive environment, see Donald N. Sull, "Why Good Companies Go Bad," *Harvard Business Review* (July–August 1999).

12. *Firestone Tire Rubber Company Annual Reports* (1960–1969); Tire Business, *U.S. Tire Industry Profile* (19 November 1990): 8–9.

13. United Rubber Workers, *Report on the Structure of the Tire Industry* (1980), United Rubber Workers Archives, Akron, Ohio.

14. *Firestone Tire & Rubber Company Annual Reports* (1960–1969).

15. Center for Research in Security Prices, *CRSP Stock Files,* (Chicago, 1996).

16. *Firestone Tire & Rubber Company Annual Report* (1969): 3.

17. Thomas J. Peters and Robert H. Waterman, *In Search of Excellence* (New York, 1982).

18. *Firestone Tire & Rubber Company Annual Report* (various years).

19. D. J. Ravenscraft and F. M. Scherer, *Mergers, Selloffs and Economic Efficiency* (Washington, D.C., 1987); Firestone Tire & Rubber Company, *Internal Financial Reports* (various years). All Firestone internal documents cited in this article are located in the Firestone Archives, Akron, Ohio.

20. *Minutes of the Executive Committee Meeting* (various years).

21. Firestone Tire & Rubber Company Economic Department, *Rubber Industry Handbook* (various years).

22. On entrepreneurs in the tire industry, see John Dick, "The Effect of Technological Innovations on the Structure of the Tire Industry" (master's thesis, University of Akron, 1979); Dick estimates the peak number of competitors at 178 in 1920, while Klepper and Simons

use *Thomas' Register of American Manufacturers* and estimate the peak number producers at 274 in 1922 in Steven Klepper and Kenneth L. Simons, "Technological Extinctions of Industrial Firms: An Inquiry into their Nature and Causes," *Industrial and Corporate Change* 6:2 (March 1997). The "murderous" price wars are described in the *American Economic Review,* a journal not normally noted for its hyperbole. See Lloyd Reynolds, "Competition in the Rubber Tire Industry," *American Economic Review* (October 1938): 459. On the ranking of American industrial companies, see Chandler, *Scale and Scope,* appendix A.

23. Charles A. Jeszeck, "Plant Dispersion and Collective Bargaining in the Rubber Tire Industry" (Ph.D. diss., University of California, Berkeley, 1982), 32.

24. Love and Giffels, *Wheels of Fortune,* 300–303; United Rubber Workers, *A Brief History of the United Rubber Workers.* Akron, Ohio: United Rubber Workers internal document.

25. Love and Giffels, *Wheels of Fortune,* 314.

26. Peters and Waterman, *In Search of Excellence,* front page.

27. Donald N. Sull, "Organizational Adaptation and Inertia in a Declining Market: A Study of the U.S. Tire Industry" (Ph.D. diss., Harvard Business School, 1996), 105. Firestone was not alone in developing this stream of new products and its competitors also barraged customers with a series of new products, see French, *The U.S. Tire Industry,* 94.

28. Sarah C. Benioff, "The Tire Industry, 1973," Harvard Business School, Case 9-391-008 (1990): 16.

29. Love and Giffels, *Wheels of Fortune,* 146; *Firestone Tire & Rubber Company Annual Report* (1969): 17.

30. The seminal theoretical and empirical research on intrafirm resource allocation processes was conducted by Joseph L. Bower, *Managing the Resource Allocation Process* (Boston, 1970). The resource allocation process in Firestone is documented in Sull, "Organizational Adaptation and Inertia," 96–106.

31. The Board of Directors generally accepted most recommendations of the Executive Committee without discussion for three reasons. First, the members of the Executive Committee constituted a majority of the Board. Second, Raymond C. Firestone chaired both the Executive Committee and the Board of Directors through 1973. Finally, the Board was dominated by insiders, with the first outside board member without close ties to the Firestone family elected in 1972.

32. *Report of Appropriations* (various years). These documents were kept for every capital investment proposal brought before the Executive Committee, and detailed the department originating the proposal, a description of the proposal, the date of first proposal, the amount requested, and the committee's ultimate disposition. Taken together, these reports constitute a paper trail for analyzing capital budgeting by proposal over time within Firestone.

33. There is no evidence that the Committee scrutinized big-ticket projects while rubber-stamping smaller requests. In the late 1960s, the median value of approved projects was approximately $500,000 while the median value of cancelled projects was less than one-half of that amount.

34. Descriptions of Firestone's internal capital budgeting process are drawn from interviews with former Firestone presidents: Lee Brodeur, interview with author, tape recording, Akron, Ohio, 11–13 August 1994 and Mario DiFederico, interview with author, tape recording, Akron, Ohio, 10 May 1995. Both men had served as Firestone's president.

35. J. S. Dick, "How Technological Changes Have Affected the Tire Industry's Structure," *Elastomerics* (November 1980): 43.

36. R. Reiff, "Firestone's Lost Harvey's Touch," *Akron Beacon Journal,* 3 December 1978.

37. *Remarks of the CEO to Annual Stockholders' Meeting* (various years).

38. *Proxy Statement* (1976): 2–7.

39. Sull et al., "Managerial Commitments," table 1.

40. Harry Millis, interview with author, 21 July 1994. Millis was a leading tire industry analyst.

41. J. D. Gaffey, *The Productivity of Labor in the Rubber Tire Industry* (New York, 1938): 161–2.

42. Love and Giffels, *Wheels of Fortune,* 47.

43. Ibid., chap. 5.

44. John Nevin, interview with author, tape recording, Akron, Ohio, 21 September 1994; Lee Brodeur interview; Love & Giffels, *Wheels of Fortune.*

45. Tom Reese (former Firestone Vice President of Sales), interview with author, tape recording, Cleveland, Ohio, 19 July 1994; and Paul Vatter (member of Firestone's Board of Directors during the late 1970s and early 1980s), interview with author, tape recording, Boston, Mass., 22 July 1994.

46. Brodeur interview.

47. Brodeur interview; Nevin interview; DiFederico interview. R. Reiff, "Surviving the Shakedown: Three Firestone Plants Provide Contrasts in Survival," *Akron Beacon Journal,* 21 January 1980.

48. *Minutes of the Board of Directors' Meetings* (21 September 1976 and 13 October 1976).

49. *Minutes of the Board of Directors' Meetings* (13 December 1977). The company would go to great lengths to protect its employees, and paid $3 million to ransom a middle manager kidnapped by Argentinean terrorists in 1973.

50. Michael van der Poel, "Michelin III: The United States," unnumbered INSEAD case (1982).

51. Blackford and Kerr, *B. F. Goodrich,* 276.

52. Consumer Reports, "Tires," *Consumer Reports,* (August 1968): 404–409.

53. Sull et al., "Managerial Commitments."

54. Maurice O'Reilly, *The Goodyear Story* (Elmsford, NY, 1981): 156–159. French, *The U.S. Tire Industry,* 94.

55. Millis interview; Brodeur interview.

56. *Firestone Tire & Rubber Company Annual Report,* (1969): 3–5.

57. Love and Giffels, *Wheels of Fortune,* 146; *Firestone Tire & Rubber Company Annual Report,* (1969): 17.

58. D. Daryl Wyckoff, "Firestone Tire and Rubber Company," Harvard Business School, Case 9-684-044 (1984); French, *The U.S. Tire Industry,* 101; Jeszeck, "Plant Dispersion," 64–65.

59. Value Line, *Tire & Rubber Industry,* (17 October 1969).

60. Brodeur interview.

61. *Minutes of the Executive Committee Meeting* (3 November 1972).

62. *Minutes of the Executive Committee Meeting* (6 December 1972).

63. DiFederico interview.

64. Sull, "Organizational Adaptation and Inertia," 111, table 4.

65. Wyckoff, "Firestone," 3; Davidson, "Managing Product Safety," 4.

66. Love and Giffels, *Wheels of Fortune,* 150.

67. Ibid., 150–151.

68. Ibid., 152.

69. Sull, "Organizational Adaptation and Inertia," 111.

70. *Internal Financial Reports* (1968–1972).

71. *Remarks of CEO to Annual Stockholders' Meeting* (1972).

72. *Minutes of the Executive Committee Meeting* (6 December 1972).

73. *Minutes of the Board of Directors' Meetings* (21 March 1978 and 13 March 1980).

74. On deteriorating profits, see *Minutes of the Board of Directors' Meeting* (23 March 1976); on stock price and credit rating, see *Minutes of the Board of Directors' Meetings* (25 May 1976 and 16 November 1976); and on need for financial plan, see *Minutes of the Board of Directors' Meeting* (21 August 1979).

75. *Minutes of the Board of Directors' Meetings* (20 June 1978 and 14 November 1978); *Minutes of the Board of Directors' Meeting* (16 October 1979).

76. *Minutes of the Board of Directors' Meetings* (21 June 1977, 23 August 1977, 21 March 1978, 13 November 1979).

77. *Minutes of the Board of Directors' Meeting* (21 March 1978).

78. *Transcript of Chairman's Remarks to the Annual Stockholders Meeting* (1973–1979).

79. *Minutes of the Board of Directors' Meeting* (21 February 1978).

80. Ibid. Other top managers agreed. North American Tire Operations President Frank LePage told the oth-er members of the Executive Committee "that he was not spending enough money to keep the Domestic Tire business healthy, and yet he had difficulty in promising a satisfactory rate of return on the money actually being spent because of the nature of the market." *Minutes of the Executive Committee Meeting* (16 March 1979).

81. Nevin interview.

82. Roy Gilbert (former Vice President who worked closely with Nevin), interview with author, tape recording, Fairlawn, Ohio, 10 August 1994.

83. *Proxy statements* (various years). Riley owned over three times as many shares as his successor John Nevin when the latter led Firestone's restructuring. *Employment Agreement between John Nevin and Firestone* (1 December 1979).

84. *Transcript of Chairman's Remarks to the Annual Stockholders Meeting* (9 February 1980); ibid. (21 January 1978).

85. *Minutes of the Executive Committee Meeting* (7 March 1971); Nevin interview.

86. Love and Giffels, *Wheels of Fortune,* 194–196.

87. Reece interview.

88. Sull, "Organizational Adaptation and Inertia," 110–111.

89. Ibid., 111. Entity value is defined as the sum of a corporation's total market capitalization and long term obligations.

90. *The Wall Street Journal,* 22 September 1977, 8 December 1977, 11 September 1978, 27 September 1978; on Credit Card subsidy, Nevin interview.

91. *Minutes of the Board of Directors' Meeting* (13 November 1979).

92. "Less Means More at Firestone," *Fortune,* 20 October 1980, 116.

93. Doug Oplinger, "Firestone Stockholders Get Say," *Akron Beacon Journal,* 28 January 1979; James Toms, "Firestone Stockholders Want More," *Akron Beacon Journal,* 30 January 1979.

94. *Minutes of the Board of Directors' Meeting* (13 November 1979).

95. Nevin, "The Bridgestone/Firestone Story," 114–132.

96. Zachary Schiller and Marc Frons, "John Nevin Rescued Firestone," *Business Week,* 11 May 1987, 96.

97. Ibid.

98. Managing Director of Management Consulting Firm, interview with author, tape recording, Boston, Mass., 19 September 1994. This consultant, who consented to an interview under the condition of anonymity, had worked closely with John Nevin.

99. Ibid.

100. Nevin interview; Brodeur interview.

101. Robert W. Ackerman, "Firestone, Inc.," Harvard Business School, Case 9-388-127 (1988): 13.

102. Brodeur interview.

103. Nevin interview.

104. *Proxy statements* (1979–1982).

105. *Transcript of John Nevin's Remarks to the Annual Stockholder's Meeting* (9 February 1980).

106. Nevin interview.

107. Ibid.

108. Brodeur interview.

109. *Minutes of the Board of Directors' Meetings* (16 September 1980, 21 October 1980, 17 March 1981, 16 June 1981).

110. *Minutes of the Board of Directors' Meeting* (19 August 1980).

111. *Minutes of the Board of Directors' Meeting* (28 February 1981).

112. Reese interview.

113. Nevin interview.

114. Ibid. See also "Surviving the Shakedown: Three Firestone Plants Provide Contrasts in Survival," *Akron Beacon Journal*, 21 January 1980.

115. Nevin interview.

116. For general discussion of traditional and revised management incentives see Nevin, Brodeur, and Gilbert interviews.

117. Nevin interview; Love and Giffels, *The Wheels of Fortune*, 261.

118. Nevin interview.

119. Love and Giffels, *The Wheels of Fortune*, 261.

120. "Retread Time: Firestone Chief Tries to Raise Its Earnings, Gird for Diversification," *The Wall Street Journal*, 11 August 1981.

121. Ackerman, "Firestone, Inc.," 10.

122. *Minutes of the Board of Directors' Meeting* (16 June 1981); Ackerman, "Firestone, Inc.," 8.

123. Ackerman, "Firestone, Inc.," 9; Brodeur interview; Reese interview; Managing Director of Consulting Firm interview. Brodeur estimated that the combined revenues of these three former Firestone divisions exceeded $2 billion, which would have increased Firestone's corporate sales in 1987 by over 50 percent.

124. Ackerman, "Firestone Inc.," 9.

125. *Minutes of the Board of Directors' Meeting* (28 February 1981); Nevin interview.

126. Gilbert interview. See also Brodeur inter-view.

127. Reese interview. See also Brodeur and DiFederico interviews.

128. *Transcript of John Nevin's Remarks to the Annual Stockholder's Meeting* (9 February 1980): 2.

129. Gilbert interview. Other interviewees made the same point, see Consultant and DiFederico interviews.

130. Sull, "Organizational Adaptation and Inertia."

131. Nevin, "The Bridgestone/Firestone Story." The Firestone board adopted a poison pill provision in 1986, which suggests that management feared the possibility of another takeover threat. Investor Responsibility Research Center, *Directory of Antitakeover Defenses* (Washington, D.C., 1987).

132. Ackerman, "Firestone, Inc.," 19.

133. For the clearest expositions of punctuated equilibrium theory see Michael Tushman and Elaine Romanelli, "Organizational Evolution: A Metamorphasis Model of Convergence and Reorientation," in *Research in Organizational Behavior*, edited by L. L. Cummings, and B. M. Staw 7 (1985): 171–222 and C. J. Gersick, "Revolutionary Change Theories: A Multilevel Exploration of the Punctuated Equilibrium Paradigm," *Academy of Management Review* 16 (1991): 10–36.

134. Blackford & Kerr, *B. F. Goodrich*, 317.

135. Sull et al., "Managerial Commitments," 491–494.

136. Blackford & Kerr, *B. F. Goodrich*, 276.

137. Ibid., 277–278. Love & Giffels, *Wheels of Fortune*, 146.

138. Blackford & Kerr, *B. F. Goodrich*, 290–292.

139. Ibid., 278–279.

140. Ibid.

141. Ibid., 296–297.

142. Sull et al., "Managerial Commitments," 492.

143. Ibid., table 7.

144. Blackford & Kerr, *B. F. Goodrich*, 309–310.

145. Blackford & Kerr, *B. F. Goodrich*, 363.

146. Sull et al., "Managerial Commitments," table 5.

147. "Pumping Up Morale in the Tire Business," *Industry Week* (24 August 1981).

148. Sull, "Why Good Companies Go Bad."

149. Carliss Y. Baldwin and Kim B. Clark, "Capital-Budgeting Systems and Capabilities Investments in U.S. Companies After the Second World War," *Business History Review* 68 (Spring 1994): 73–109.

150. Clayton M. Christensen, *The Innovator's Dilemma: When New Technologies Cause Great Firms to Fail* (Boston, 1997) and Clayton M. Christensen, "The Rigid Disk Drive Industry, 1956–1990: A History of Commercial and Technological Turbulence," *Business History Review* 67 (Winter 1993): 531–588.

151. Sull, "Organizational Adaptation and Inertia," 98.

152. Christensen, *The Innovator's Dilemma*, 42–48.

153. Michael E. Porter, "Clusters and the New Economics of Competition," *Harvard Business Review* (November–December 1998): 78. For the seminal work industrial clusters see Alfred Marshall, *Principles of Economics* (London, 1922). Alfred Marshall, *Industry and Trade* (New York, 1923). More recent work includes Brian Arthur, "Industry location and the importance of history," CEPR paper no. 43, Stanford University (1986) and David Krugman, *Geography and Trade* (Cambridge, Mass., 1991).

154. For information on research intensive industries, see Chandler, *Scale and Scope*, 108.

155. Jeszeck, "Plant Dispersion," 396.

156. Steven Klepper and Kenneth L. Simons, "Technological Extinctions of Industrial Firms: An Inquiry into their Nature and Causes," *Industrial and Cor-*

porate Change 6:2 (March 1997): 411. Chandler, *Scale and Scope,* 108.

157. Donald N. Sull, "Industrial Clusters and Organizational Inertia: An Institutional Perspective," *London Business School Working Paper* (1999).

158. L. G. Zucker, "The Role of Institutionalization in Cultural Persistence," *American Sociological Review* 42 (1977): 726–743.

159. Alfred D. Chandler, Jr., "The Competitive Performance of U.S. Industrial Enterprises Since the Second World War," *Business History Review* 68 (Spring 1994): 1–72.

160. Ibid., 24–5.

161. See Steven Klepper and Elizabeth Graddy, "The Evolution of New Industries and the Determinants of Market Structure," *RAND Journal of Economics* 21:1 (Spring 1990): 27–44. Klepper and Simons, "Technological Extinctions," 379–460.

9

The Panda's Thumb of Technology

STEPHEN JAY GOULD

The brief story of Jephthah and his daughter (Judg. 11:30–40) is, to my mind and heart, the saddest of all biblical tragedies. Jephthah makes an intemperate vow, yet all must abide by its consequences. He promises that if God grants him victory in a forthcoming battle, he will sacrifice by fire the first living thing that passes through his gate to greet him upon his return. Expecting (I suppose) a dog or a goat, he returns victorious to find his daughter, and only child, waiting to greet him "with timbrels and with dances."

Handel's last oratorio, *Jephtha,* treats this tale with great power (although his librettist couldn't bear the weight of the original and gave the story a happy ending, with angelic intervention to spare Jephthah's daughter at the price of her lifelong chastity). At the end of part 2, while all still think that the terrible vow must be fulfilled, the chorus sings one of Handel's wonderful "philosophical" choruses. It begins with a frank account of the tragic circumstance:

How dark, O Lord, are thy decrees! . . .
No certain bliss, no solid peace,
We mortals know on earth below.

Yet the last two lines, in a curious about-face, proclaim (with magnificent musical solidity as well):

Yet on this maxim still obey:
WHATEVER IS, IS RIGHT.

This odd reversal, from frank acknowledgment to unreasonable acceptance, reflects one of the greatest

biases ("hopes" I like to call them) that human thought imposes upon a world indifferent to our suffering. Humans are pattern-seeking animals. We must find cause and meaning in all events (quite apart from the probable reality that the universe both doesn't care much about us and often operates in a random manner). I call this bias "adaptationism"—the notion that everything must fit, must have a purpose, and in the strongest version, must be for the best.

The final line of Handel's chorus is, of course, a quote from Alexander Pope, the last statement of the first epistle of his *Essay on Man,* published just thirteen years before Handel's oratorio. Pope's text contains (in heroic couplets to boot) the most striking paean I know to the bias of adaptationism. In my favorite lines, Pope chastises those people who may be unsatisfied with the senses that nature bestowed upon us. We may wish for more acute vision, hearing, or smell, but consider the consequences.

If nature thunder'd in his op'ning ears
And stunn'd him with the music of the spheres
How would he wish that Heav'n had left him still
The whisp'ring zephyr, and the purling rill!

And my favorite couplet, on olfaction:

Or, quick effluvia darting thro' the brain,
Die of a rose in aromatic pain.

What we have is best for us—whatever is, is right.

By 1859, most educated people were prepared to

Reprinted with permission from *Natural History,* January 1987, Stephen Jay Gould, "The Panda's Thumb of Technology," pp. 14–23. Copyright © 1987 by Natural History Magazine, Inc.

accept evolution as the reason behind similarities and differences among organisms—thus accounting for Darwin's rapid conquest of the intellectual world. But they were decidedly not ready to acknowledge the radical implications of Darwin's proposed mechanism of change, natural selection, thus explaining the brouhaha that the *Origin of Species* provoked—and still elicits (at least before our courts and school boards).

Darwin's world is full of "terrible truths," two in particular. First, when things do fit and make sense (good design of organisms, harmony of ecosystems), they did not arise because the laws of nature entail such order as a primary effect. They are, rather, only epiphenomena, side consequences of the basic causal process at work in natural populations—the purely "selfish" struggle among organisms for personal reproductive success. Second the complex and curious pathways of history guarantee that most organisms and ecosystems cannot be designed optimally. Indeed, to make the statement even stronger, imperfections are the primary proofs that evolution has occurred, since optimal designs erase all signposts of history.

This principle of imperfection has been the main theme of these essays for several years. I call it the panda principle to honor my favorite example, the panda's false thumb, subject of an old essay (*Natural History,* November 1978) that reemerged as the title to one of my books. Pandas are the herbivorous descendants of carnivorous bears. Their true anatomical thumbs were, long ago during ancestral days of meat eating, irrevocably committed to the limited motion appropriate for this mode of life and universally evolved by mammalian Carnivora. When adaptation to a diet of bamboo required more flexibility in manipulation, pandas could not redesign their thumbs but had to make do with a makeshift substitute—an enlarged radial sesamoid bone of the wrist, the panda's false thumb. The sesamoid thumb is a clumsy, suboptimal structure, but it works. Pathways of history (commitment of the true thumb to other roles during an irreversible past) impose such jury-rigged solutions upon all creatures. History inheres in the imperfections of living organisms—thus we know that they had a different past, converted by evolution to their current state.

We can accept this argument for organisms (we know, after all, about our own appendixes and aching backs). But is the panda principle more pervasive? Is it a general statement about all historical systems? Will it

apply, for example, to the products of technology? We might deem it irrelevant to the manufactured objects of human ingenuity—and for good reason. After all, constraints of genealogy do not apply to steel, glass, and plastic. The panda cannot shuck its digits (and can only build its future upon this inherited ground plan), but we can abandon gas lamps for electricity and horse carriages for motor cars. Consider, for example, the difference between organic architecture and human buildings. Complex organic structures cannot be reevolved following their loss; no snake will redevelop front legs. But the apostles of so-called postmodern architecture, in reaction to the sterility of so many glass-box buildings of the international style, have juggled together all the classical forms of history in a cascading effort to rediscover the virtues of ornamentation. Thus, Philip Johnson could place a broken pediment atop a New York skyscraper and raise a medieval castle of plate glass in downtown Pittsburgh. Organisms cannot recruit the virtues of their lost pasts.

Yet I am not so sure that technology is exempt from the panda principle of history, for I am now sitting face to face with the best example of its application. Indeed, I am in most intimate (and striking) contact with this object—the typewriter keyboard.

I could type before I could write. My father was a court stenographer, and my mother is a typist. I learned proper eight-finger touch-typing when I was about nine years old and still endowed with small hands and weak, tiny pinky fingers. I was thus, from the first, in a particularly good position to appreciate the irrationality of the distribution of letters on the standard keyboard, called QWERTY by all aficionados in honor of the first six letters on the top letter row.

Clearly, QWERTY makes no sense (beyond the whiz and joy of typing QWERTY itself). More than 70 percent of English words can be typed with the letters DHIATENSOR, and these should be on the most accessible second, or home, row—as they were in a failed competitor to QWERTY introduced as early as 1893. But in QWERTY, the most common English letter, E, requires a reach to the top row, as do the vowels U, I, and O (with O struck by the weak fourth finger), while A remains in the home row but must be typed with the weakest finger of all (at least for the dexterous majority of right handers)—the left pinky. (How I struggled with this as a boy. I just couldn't depress that key. I once tried to type the Declaration of

Independence and ended up with: th t ll men re cre ted equ l.)

As a dramatic illustration of this irrationality, consider the keyboard of an ancient Smith-Corona upright, identical with the one (my Dad's original) that I use to type these essays (a magnificent machine—no breakdown in twenty years and a fluidity of motion unmatched by any manual typewriter since). After more than half a century of use, some of the most commonly struck keys have been worn right through the surface into the soft pad below (they weren't solid plastic in those days). Note that E, A, and S are worn in this way—and note also that all three are either not in the home row or are struck with the weak fourth and pinky fingers in QWERTY.

This claim is not just a conjecture based on idiosyncratic personal experience. Evidence clearly shows that QWERTY is drastically suboptimal. Competitors have abounded since the early days of typewriting, but none has supplanted or even dented the universal dominance of QWERTY for English typewriters. The best-known alternative, DSK, for Dvorak Simplified Keyboard, was introduced in 1932. Since then, virtually all records for speed typing have been held by DSK, not QWERTY, typists. During the 1940s, the U.S. Navy, ever mindful of efficiency, found that the increased speed of DSK would amortize the cost of retraining typists within ten days of full employment. (Mr. Dvorak was not Anton of the *New World Symphony*, but August, a professor of education at the University of Washington, who died disappointed in 1975. Dvorak was a disciple of Frank B. Gilbreth, pioneer of time and motion studies in industrial management.)

Since I have a special interest in typewriters (my affection for them dates to those childhood days of splendor in the grass and glory in the flower), I have wanted to write such an essay for years. But I never had the data I needed until Paul A. David, Coe Professor of American Economic History at Stanford University, kindly sent me his fascinating article, "Understanding the Economics of QWERTY: The Necessity of History" (in *Economic History and the Modern Economist*, edited by W. N. Parker. New York: Basil Blackwell Inc., 1986, pp. 30–49). Virtually all the non-idiosyncratic data in this essay come from David's work, and I thank him for this opportunity to satiate an old desire.

The puzzle of QWERTY's dominance resides in two separate questions: Why did QWERTY ever arise in the first place? And why has QWERTY survived in the face of superior competitors?

My answers to these questions will invoke analogies to principles of evolutionary theory. Let me, then, state some ground rules for such a questionable enterprise. I am convinced that comparisons between biological evolution and human cultural or technological change have done vastly more harm than good—and examples abound of this most common of all intellectual traps. Biological evolution is a bad analogue for cultural change because the two systems are so very different for three major reasons that could hardly be more fundamental.

First, cultural evolution can be faster by orders of magnitude than biological change at its maximal Darwinian rate—and questions of timing are of the essence in evolutionary arguments. Second, cultural evolution is direct and Lamarckian in form: the achievements of one generation are passed by education and publication directly to descendants, thus producing the great potential speed of cultural change. Biological evolution is indirect and Darwinian, as favorable traits do not descend to the next generation unless, by good fortune, they arise as products of genetic change. Third, the basic topologies of biological and cultural change are completely different. Biological evolution is a system of constant divergence without any subsequent joining of branches. Lineages, once distinct, are separate forever. In human history, transmission across lineages is, perhaps, the major source of cultural change. Europeans learned about corn and potatoes from Native Americans and gave them smallpox in return.

So, when I compare the panda's thumb with a typewriter keyboard, I am not attempting to derive or explain technological change by biological principles. Rather, I ask if both systems might not record common, deeper principles of organization. Biological evolution is powered by natural selection, cultural evolution by a different set of principles that I understand but dimly. But both are systems of historical change. There must be (perhaps I now only show my own bias for intelligibility in our complex world) more general principles of structure underlying all systems that proceed through history—and I rather suspect that the panda principle of imperfection might reside among them.

My main point, in other words, is not that type-writers are like biological evolution (for such an argument would fall right into the nonsense of false analogy), but that both keyboards and the panda's thumb, as products of history, must be subject to some regularities governing the nature of temporal connections. As scientists, we must believe that general principles underlie structurally related systems that proceed by different overt rules. The proper unity lies, not in false applications of these overt rules (like natural selection) to alien domains (like technological change), but in seeking the more general rules of structure and change themselves.

THE ORIGIN OF QWERTY

True randomness has limited power to intrude itself into the forms of organisms. Small and unimportant changes, unrelated to the working integrity of a complex creature, may drift in and out of populations by a process akin to throwing dice. But intricate structures, involving the coordination of many separate parts, must arise for an active reason—since the bounds of mathematical probability for fortuitous association are soon exceeded as the number of working parts grows.

But if complex structures must arise for a reason, history may soon overtake the original purpose—and what was once a sensible solution becomes an oddity or imperfection in the altered context of a new future. Thus, the panda's true thumb permanently lost its ability to manipulate objects when carnivorous ancestors found a better use for this digit in the limited motions appropriate for creatures that run and claw. This altered thumb then becomes a constraint imposed by past history upon the panda's ability to adapt in an optimal way to its new context of herbivory. The panda's thumb, in short, becomes an emblem of its different past, a sign of history.

Similarly, QWERTY had an eminently sensible rationale in the early technology of typewriting but soon became a constraint upon faster typing as advances in construction erased the reason for QWERTY's origin. The key (pardon the pun) to QWERTY's origin lies in another historical vestige easily visible on the second row of letters. Note the sequence: DFGHJKL—a good stretch of the alphabet in order,

with the vowels E and I removed. The original concept must have simply arrayed the letters in alphabetical order. Why were the two most common letters of this sequence removed from the most accessible home row? And why were other letters dispersed to odd positions?

Those who remember the foibles of manual typewriters (or, if as hidebound as yours truly, still use them) know that excessive speed or unevenness of stroke may cause two or more keys to jam near the striking point. You also know that if you don't reach in and pull the keys apart, any subsequent stroke will produce a repetition of the key leading the jam—as any key subsequently struck will hit the back of the jammed keys and drive them closer to the striking point.

These problems were magnified in the crude technology of early machines—and too much speed became a hazard rather than a blessing, as key jams canceled the benefits of celerity. Thus, in the great human traditions of tinkering and pragmatism, keys were moved around to find a proper balance between speed and jamming. In other words—and here comes the epitome of the tale in a phrase—QWERTY arose in order to slow down the maximal speed of typing and prevent jamming of keys. Common letters were either allotted to weak fingers or dispersed to positions requiring a long stretch from the home row.

This basic story has gotten around, thanks to short takes in *Time* and other popular magazines, but the details are enlightening, and few people have the story straight. I have asked nine typists who knew this outline of QWERTY's origin and all (plus me for an even ten) had the same misconception. The old machines that imposed QWERTY were, we thought, of modern design—with keys in front typing a visible line on paper rolled around a platen. This leads to a minor puzzle: key jams may be a pain in the butt, but you see them right away and can easily reach in and pull them apart. So why QWERTY?

As David points out, the prototype of QWERTY, a machine invented by C. L. Sholes in the 1860s, was quite different in form from modern typewriters. It had a flat paper carriage and did not roll paper right around the platen. Keys struck the paper invisibly from beneath, not patently from the front as in all modern typewriters. You could not view what you were typing unless you stopped to raise the carriage and inspect your product. Keys jammed frequently, but you could not see (and often did not feel) the aggregation. Thus, you might type a whole page of deathless prose and emerge only with a long string of E's.

Sholes filed for a patent in 1867 and spent the next six years in trial-and-error efforts to improve his machine. QWERTY emerged from this period of tinkering and compromise. As another added wrinkle (and fine illustration of history's odd quirks), R joined the top row as a last-minute entry, and for a somewhat capricious motive according to one common tale—for salesmen could then impress potential buyers by smooth and rapid production of the brand name TYPE WRITER, all on one row. (Although I wonder how many sales were lost when TYPE EEEEEE appeared after a jam!)

THE SURVIVAL OF QWERTY

We can all accept this story of QWERTY's origin, but why did it persist after the introduction of the modern platen roller and frontstroke key? (The first typewriter with a fully visible printing point was introduced in 1890). In fact, the situation is even more puzzling. I though that alternatives to keystroke typing only became available with the IBM electric ball, but none other than Thomas Edison filed a patent for an electric print-wheel machine as early as 1872, and L. S. Crandall marketed a writing machine without typebars in 1879. (Crandall arranged his type on a cylindrical sleeve and made the sleeve revolve to the required letter before striking the printing point.)

The 1880s were boom years for the fledgling typewriter industry, a period when a hundred flowers bloomed and a hundred schools of thought contended. Alternatives to QWERTY were touted by several companies, and both the variety of printing designs (several without typebars) and the improvement of keystroke typewriters completely removed the original rationale for QWERTY. Yet during the 1890s, more and more companies made the switch to QWERTY, which became an industry standard by the early years of our century. And QWERTY has held on stubbornly, through the introduction of the IBM Selectric and the Hollerith punch card machine to that ultimate example of its nonnecessity, the microcomputer terminal (Apple does offer a Dvorak option with the touch of a button but emblazons QWERTY on its keyboard and reports little use of this high-speed alternative).

To understand the survival (and domination to this day) of drastically suboptimal QWERTY, we must recognize two other commonplaces of history, as applicable to life in geological time as to technology over decades—contingency and incumbency. We call a historical event—the rise of mammals or the dominance of QWERTY—contingent when it occurs as the chancy result of a long string of unpredictable antecedents, rather than as a necessary outcome of nature's laws. Such contingent events often depend crucially upon choices from a distant past that seemed tiny and trivial at the time. Minor perturbations early in the game can nudge a process into a new pathway, with cascading consequences that produce an outcome vastly different from any alternative.

Incumbency also reinforces the stability of a pathway once the little quirks of early flexibility push a sequence into a firm channel. Suboptimal politicians often prevail nearly forever once they gain office and grab the reins of privilege, patronage, and visibility. Mammals waited 100 million years to become the dominant animals on land and only got a chance because dinosaurs succumbed during a mass extinction. If every typist in the world stopped using QWERTY tomorrow and began to learn Dvorak, we would all be winners, but who will bell the cat or start the ball rolling? (Choose your cliché, for they all record this evident truth.) Stasis is the norm for complex systems; change, when it happens at all, is usually rapid and episodic.

QWERTY's fortunate and improbable ascent to incumbency occurred by a concatenation of circumstances, each indecisive in itself, but all probably necessary for the eventual outcome. Remington had marketed the Sholes machine with its QWERTY keyboard, but this early tie with a major firm did not secure QWERTY's victory. Competition was tough, and no lead meant much with such small numbers in an expanding market. David estimates that only 5,000 or so QWERTY machines existed at the beginning of the 1880s.

The push to incumbency was complex and multifaceted, dependent more upon the software of teachers and promoters than upon the hardware of improving machines. Most early typists used idiosyncratic hunt-and-peck, few-fingered methods. In 1882, Ms. Longley, founder of the Shorthand and Typewriter Institute in Cincinnati, developed and began to teach the eight-finger typing that professionals use today. She happened to teach with a QWERTY keyboard, although many competing arrangements would have served her purposes as well. She also published a do-it-yourself pamphlet that was widely used. At the same time, Remington began to set up schools for typewriting using (of course) its QWERTY standard. The QWERTY ball was rolling but this head start did not guarantee a place at the summit. Many other schools taught rival methods on different machines and might have gained an edge.

Then a crucial event in 1888 probably added the decisive increment to QWERTY's small advantage. Longley was challenged to prove the superiority of her eight-finger method by Louis Taub, another Cincinnati typing teacher, who worked with four fingers on a rival non-QWERTY keyboard with six rows, no shift action, and (therefore) separate keys for upper and lower case letters. As her champion, Longley engaged Frank E. McGurrin, an experienced QWERTY typist who had given himself a decisive advantage that, apparently, no one had thought of before. He had memorized the QWERTY keyboard and could therefore operate his machine as all competent typists do today—by what we now call touch-typing. McGurrin trounced Taub in a well-advertised and well-reported public competition.

In public perception, and (more importantly) in the eyes of those who ran typing schools and published typing manuals, QWERTY had proved its superiority. But no such victory had really occurred. The tie of McGurrin to QWERTY was fortuitous and a good break for Longley and for Remington. We shall never know why McGurrin won, but reasons quite independent of QWERTY cry out for recognition: touch-typing over hunt-and-peck, eight fingers over four fingers, the three-row letter board with a shift key versus the six-row board with two separate keys for each letter. An array of competitions that would have tested QWERTY were never held—QWERTY versus other arrangements of letters with both contestants using eight-finger touch-typing on a three-row keyboard or McGurrin's method of eight-finger touch-typing on a non-QWERTY three-row keyboard versus Taub's procedure to see whether the QWERTY arrangement (as I doubt) or McGurrin's method (as I suspect) had secured his success.

In any case, the QWERTY steamroller now gained crucial momentum and prevailed early in our century. As touch-typing by QWERTY became the norm in America's typing schools, rival manufacturers (especially in a rapidly expanding market) could adapt their machines more easily than people could change their habits—and the industry settled upon the wrong standard.

If Sholes had not gained his tie to Remington, if the first man who decided to memorize a keyboard had used a non-QWERTY design, if McGurrin had a bellyache or drank too much the night before, if Longley had not been so zealous, if a hundred other perfectly possible things had happened, then I might be typing this essay with more speed and much greater economy of finger motion.

But why fret over lost optimality. History always works this way. If Montcalm had won a battle on the Plains of Abraham, perhaps I would be typing *en français.* If a portion of the African jungles had not dried to savannas, I might still be an ape up a tree. If some comets had not struck the earth (if they did) some 60 million years ago, dinosaurs might still rule the land, and all mammals would be rat-sized creatures scurrying about in the dark corners of their world. If *Pikaia,* the only chordate of the Burgess Shale, had not survived the great sorting out of body plans after the Cambrian explosion, mammals might not exist at all. If multicellular creatures had never evolved after five-sixths of life's history had yielded nothing more complicated than an algal mat, the sun might explode a few billion years hence with no multicellular witness to the earth's destruction.

Compared with these weighty possibilities, my indenture to QWERTY seems a small price indeed for the rewards of history. For if history were not so maddening quirky, we would not be here to enjoy it. Streamlined optimality contains no seeds for change. We need our odd little world, where QWERTY rules and the quick brown fox jumps over the lazy dog.[1]

NOTE

1. I must close with a pedantic note, lest nonaficionados be utterly perplexed by this ending. This quirky juxtaposition of uncongenial carnivores is said to be the shortest English sentence that contains all twenty-six letters. It is, as such, *de rigueur* in all manuals that teach typing.

10

The Art of Standards Wars

CARL SHAPIRO
HAL R. VARIAN

Standards wars—battles for market dominance between incompatible technologies—are a fixture of the information age. Based on our study of historical standards wars, we have identified several generic strategies, along with a number of winning tactics, to help companies fighting today's—and tomorrow's—battles.

There is no doubt about the significance of standards battles in today's economy. Public attention is currently focused on the Browser War between Microsoft and Netscape (oops, America Online). Even as Judge Jackson evaluates the legality of Microsoft's tactics in the Browser War, the Audio and Video Streaming Battle is heating up between Microsoft and RealNetworks over software to deliver audio and video over the Internet. The 56k Modem War of 1997 pitted 3Com against Rockwell and Lucent. Microsoft's Word and Excel have vanquished WordPerfect and Lotus 1-2-3 respectively. Most everyone remembers the Video-Cassette Recorder Duel of the 1980s, in which Matsushita's VHS format triumphed over Sony's Betamax format. However, few recall how Philips's digital compact cassette and Sony's minidisk format both flopped in the early 1990s. This year, it's DVD versus Divx in the battle to replace both VCRs and CDs.

Virtually every high-tech company has some role to play in these battles, perhaps as a primary combatant, more likely as a member of a coalition or alliance supporting one side, and certainly as a customer seeking to pick a winner when adopting new technology. The outcome of a standards war can determine the very survival of the companies involved. How do you win one?

HISTORICAL EXAMPLES

Happily, companies heading off to fight a standards war do not have to reinvent the wheel. The fact is, standards wars are *not* unique to the information age. Unlike technology, the economics underlying such battles changes little, if at all, over time. We begin with three instructive standards battles of old. From these and many more historical episodes we have distilled the battle manual for standards wars that follows.

North vs. South in Railroad Gauges[1]

As railroads began to be built in the early 19th century, tracks of varying widths (gauges) were employed in the United States. By 1860, seven different gauges were in use in America. Just over half of the total mileage was of the $4'8^1/2''$ standard. The next most popular was the $5'$ gauge concentrated in the South. Despite clear benefits, railroad gauge standardization faced three major obstacles: it was costly to change the width of existing tracks; each group wanted the others to make the move; and workers whose livelihoods depended upon the incompatibilities resisted the proposed changes, in fact to the point of rioting. Nonetheless, standardization was gradually achieved between 1860 and 1890. How?

Copyright © 1999 by The Regents of the University of California. Reprinted from the *California Management Review*, Vol. 41, No. 2. By permission of The Regents.

The Westward expansion provided part of the answer. The big eastern railroads wanted to move western grain to the East, and pushed for new lines to the West to be at standard gauge. Since the majority of the Eastbound traffic terminated on their lines, they got their way. The Civil War played a role, too. The Union military had pressing needs for efficient East-West transportation, giving further impetus for new western lines to be built at standard gauge. In 1862, when Congress specified the standard gauge for the transcontinental railroads, the Southern states had seceded, leaving no one to push for the 5' gauge. After the war, the Southern railroads found themselves increasingly in the minority. For the next twenty years, they relied upon various imperfect interconnections with the North and West: cars with a sliding wheel base, hoists to lift cars from one wheel base to another, and, most commonly, building a third rail.

Southern railroad interests finally threw in the towel and adopted the standard gauge in 1886. On two days during the Spring of 1886, the gauges were changed, converting 5' gauge into the now-standard $4'8^1/_2''$ gauge on more than 11,000 miles of track in the South to match the Northern standard—a belated victory for the North.

Many of the lessons from this experience are very relevant today:

- Incompatibilities can arise almost by accident, yet persist for many years.
- Network markets tend to tip toward the leading player, unless the other players coordinate to act quickly and decisively.
- Seceding from the standard-setting process can leave you in a weak market position in the future.
- A large buyer (in this case the U.S. government) can have more influence than suppliers in tipping the balance.
- Those left with the less popular technology will find a way to cut their losses, either by employing adapters or by writing off existing assets and joining the bandwagon.

Edison vs. Westinghouse in Electric Power: The Battle of the Systems[2]

Another classic 19th century standards battle concerned the distribution of electricity. Thomas Edison promoted a direct current (DC) system of electrical power generation and distribution. Edison was the pioneer in building power systems, beginning in New York City in 1882. Edison's direct current system was challenged by the alternating current (AC) technology developed and deployed in the U.S. by George Westinghouse.

Thus was joined the "Battle of the Systems." Each technology had pros and cons. Direct current had, for practical purposes relating to voltage drop, a one-mile limit between the generating station and the user, but was more efficient at generating power. Direct current had also had two significant commercial advantages: a head start and Edison's imprimatur.

Unlike railroads, however, standardization was less of an imperative in electricity. Indeed, the two technologies initially did not compete directly, but were deployed in regions suited to their relative strengths. DC was most attractive in densely populated urban areas, while AC made inroads in small towns. Nonetheless, a battle royal ensued in the 1887–1892 period, a struggle that was by no means confined to competition in the marketplace, but rather extended to the courtroom, the political arena, public relations, and academia. We can learn much today from the tactics followed by the rival camps.

The Edison group moved first with infringement actions against the Westinghouse forces, which forced Westinghouse to invent around Edison patents, including patents involving the Edison lamp. Edison also went to great lengths to convince the public that the AC system was unsafe, going so far as to patent the electric chair. Edison first demonstrated the electric chair using alternating current to electrocute a large dog, and then persuaded the State of New York to execute condemned criminals "by administration of an alternating current." The Edison group even used the term "to Westinghouse" to refer to electrocution by alternating current.

Ultimately, three factors ended the Battle of the Systems. First and foremost, advances in polyphase AC made it increasingly clear that AC was the superior alternative. Second, the rotary converter introduced in 1892 allowed existing DC stations to be integrated into AC systems, facilitating a graceful retreat for DC. Third, by 1890 Edison had sold his interests, leading to the formation of the General Electric Company in 1892, which was no longer a DC-only manufacturing entity.[3] By 1893, both General Electric and Westinghouse were offering AC systems and the battle was over.

The battle between Edison and Westinghouse illustrates several key aspects of strategy in standards wars:

- Edison fought hard to convince consumers that DC was safer, in no small part because consumer expectations can easily become self-fulfilling in standards battles.

- Technologies can seek well-suited niches if the forces toward standardization are not overwhelming.

- Ongoing innovation (here, polyphase AC) can lead to victory in a standards war.

- A first-mover advantage (of DC) can be overcome by a superior technology (of AC), if the performance advantage is sufficient and users are not overly entrenched.

- Adapters can be the salvation of the losing technology and can help to ultimately defuse a standards war.

RCA vs. CBS in Color Television[4]

Our third historical example is considerably more recent: the adoption of color television in the United States fifty years ago. Television is perhaps the biggest bandwagon of them all. Some 99% of American homes have at least one television, making TV sets more ubiquitous than telephones or flush toilets.

We begin our story with the inauguration of commercial black-and-white television transmission in the United States on July 1, 1941. At that time, RCA—the owner of NBC and a leading manufacturer of black-and-white sets—was a powerful force in the radio and television world. However, the future of television was clearly to be color, which had first been demonstrated in America by Bell Labs in 1929.

Throughout the 1940s, CBS, the leading television network, was pushing for the adoption of the mechanical color television system it was developing. During this time RCA was busy selling black-and-white sets, improving its technology, and, under the legendary leadership of David Sarnoff, working on its own all-electronic color television system. As the CBS system took the lead in performance, RCA urged the

FCC to wait for an electronic system. A major obstacle for the CBS system was that it was not backward-compatible: color sets of the CBS-type would not be able to receive existing black-and-white broadcasts without a special attachment.

Despite this drawback, the FCC adopted the CBS system in October 1950, after a test between the two color systems. The RCA system was just not ready. As David Sarnoff himself said, "The monkeys were green, the bananas were blue, and everyone had a good laugh." This was a political triumph of major proportions for CBS.

The market outcome was another story. RCA and Sarnoff refused to throw in the towel. To the contrary, they re-doubled their efforts, on three fronts. First, RCA continued to criticize the CBS system in an attempt to slow its adoption. Second, RCA intensified its efforts to place black-and-white sets and thus build up an installed base of users whose equipment would be incompatible with the CBS technology. "Every set we get out there makes it that much tougher on CBS," said Sarnoff at the time. Third, Sarnoff intensified RCA's research and development on its color television system, with around-the-clock teams working in the lab.

CBS was poorly placed to take advantage of its political victory. To begin with, CBS had no manufacturing capability at the time, and had not readied a manufacturing ally to move promptly into production. As a result, the official premier of CBS color broadcasting, on June 25, 1951, featuring Ed Sullivan among others, was largely invisible, only seen at special studio parties. There were about 12 million TV sets in America at the time, but only a few dozen could receive CBS color. Luck, of a sort, entered into the picture, too. With the onset of the Korean War, the U.S. government said that the materials needed for production of color sets were critical instead for the war effort and ordered a suspension of the manufacture of color sets.

By the time the ban was modified in June 1952, the RCA system was ready for prime time. A consensus in support of the RCA system had formed at the National Television Systems Committee (NTSC). This became known as the NTSC system, despite the fact that RCA owned most of the hundreds of patents controlling it. This re-labeling was a face-saving device for the FCC, which could be seen to be following the industry consortium rather than RCA. In March 1953,

Frank Stanton, the President of CBS, raised the white flag, noting that with 23 million black and white sets in place in American homes, compatibility was rather important. In December 1953, the FCC officially reversed its 1950 decision.

However, yet again, political victory did not lead so easily to success in the market. In 1954, Sarnoff predicted that RCA would sell 75,000 sets. In fact, only 5,000 sets were purchased, perhaps because few customers were willing to pay $1,000 for the $12^{1}/_{2}''$ color set rather than $300 for a 21" black-and-white set. With hindsight, this does not seem surprising, especially since color sets would offer little added value until broadcasters invested in color capability and color programming became widespread. All this takes time. The chicken-and-egg problem had to be settled before the NBC peacock could prevail.

As it turned out, NBC and CBS affiliates invested in color transmission equipment quite quickly: 106 of 158 stations in the top 40 cities had the ability to transmit color programs by 1957. This was of little import to viewers, since the networks were far slower in offering color programming. By 1965, NBC offered 4,000 hours of color, but CBS still showed only 800 color hours, and ABC 600. The upshot: by 1963, only about 3% of TV households had color sets, which remained three to five times as expensive as black-and-white sets.

As brilliant as Sarnoff and RCA had been in getting their technology established as the standard, they, like CBS, were unable to put into place all the necessary components of the system to obtain profitability during the 1950s. As a result, by 1959, RCA had spent $130 million to develop color TV with no profit to show for it. The missing pieces were the creation and distribution of the programming itself: content. Then, as now, a "killer app" was needed to get households to invest in color television sets. The killer app of 1960 was "Walt Disney's Wonderful World of Color," which Sarnoff obtained from ABC in 1960. RCA's first operating profit from color television sales came in 1960, and RCA started selling picture tubes to Zenith and others. The rest is history: color sets got better and cheaper, and the NBC peacock became famous.

We can all learn a great deal from this episode, ancient though it is by Internet time.

- Adoption of a new technology can be painfully slow if the price/performance ratio is unattractive and if it requires adoption by a number of different players.[5]

- First-mover advantages need not be decisive, even in markets strongly subject to tipping.

- Victory in a standards war often requires building an alliance.

- A dominant position in one generation of technology (such as RCA enjoyed in the sale of black-and-white sets) does not necessarily translate into dominance in the next generation of technology.

WAR OR PEACE?

Standards wars are especially bitter—and especially crucial to business success—in markets with strong *network effects* that cause consumers to play high value on compatibility.[6] We do not consider it a coincidence that there is a single worldwide standard for fax machines and for modems (for which compatibility is crucial), while multiple formats persist for cellular telephones and digital television (for which compatibility across regions is far less important).

We do not mean to suggest that every new information technology must endure a standards war. Take the compact disk (CD) technology, for instance. Sony and Philips pooled together and openly licensed their CD patents as a means to establish their new CD technology. While CDs were completely incompatible with the existing audio technologies of phonographs, cassette players, and reel-to-reel tapes, Sony and Philips were not in a battle with another new technology. They "merely" had to convince consumers to take a leap and invest in a CD player and compact disks.

What is distinct about standards wars is that there are *two* firms, or more commonly alliances, vying for dominance. In some cases, one of the combatants may be an incumbent that controls a significant base of customers who use an older technology, as when Nintendo battled Sony in the video game market in the mid-1990s. Nintendo had a large installed base from the previous generation when both companies introduced 64-bit systems. In other instances, both sides may be starting from scratch, as in the battle between Sony and Matsushita in videotape machines as well as in the browser war between Netscape and Microsoft.

Standards wars can end in: a *truce,* as happened

in 56k modems and color television where a common standard was ultimately adopted; a *duopoly,* as we see in video games today with Nintendo and Sony battling toe-to-toe; or a *fight to the death,* as with railroad gauges, AC versus DC electric power, and videotape players. True fight-to-the-death standards wars are unique to markets with powerful positive feedback based on strong network effects. Thus, traditional principles of strategy, while helpful, need to be supplemented to account for the peculiar economics of networks.

Before entering into a standards battle, would-be combatants are well advised to consider a peaceful solution.[7] Unlike many other aspects of competition, where coordination among rivals would be branded as illegal collusion, declaring an early truce in a standards war can benefit *consumers* as well as vendors, and thus pass antitrust muster.[8]

Even bitter enemies such as Microsoft and Netscape have repeatedly been able to cooperate to establish standards when compatibility is crucial for market growth. First, when it appeared that a battle might ensue over standards for protecting privacy on the Internet, Microsoft announced its support for Netscape's *Open Profiling Standard,* which subsequently became part of the *Platform for Privacy Preferences* being developed by the Word Wide Web Consortium. Second, Microsoft and Netscape were able to reach agreement on standards for viewing 3-D images over the Internet. In August 1997, they decided to support compatible versions of *Virtual Reality Modeling Language,* a 3-D viewing technology, in their browsers. Again, Microsoft was pragmatic rather than proud, adopting a language invented at Silicon Graphics. Third, Microsoft and Netscape teamed up (along with Visa and MasterCard as well as IBM) to support the *Secure Electronic Transactions* standard for protecting the security of electronic payments by encrypting credit card numbers sent to online merchants. Cooperative standard-setting often takes place through the auspices of formal standard-setting organizations such as the American National Standards Institute or the International Telecommunications Union.[9]

We must note, however, the clear analogy between technology battles and military battles: the more costly a battle is to both sides, the greater are the pressures to negotiate a truce; and one's strength in battle is an overriding consideration when meeting to conduct truce talks. Whether you are planning to negotiate a product standard or fight to the death, you will benefit from understanding the art (read: economics and strategy) of standards wars.

CLASSIFICATION OF STANDARDS WARS

Not all standards wars are alike. Standards battles come in three distinct flavors. The starting point for strategy in a standards battle is to understand which type of war you are fighting. The critical distinguishing feature of the battle is the magnitude of the switching costs, or more generally the adoption costs, for each rival technology. We classify standards wars depending on how compatible each player's proposed new technology is with the current technology.

When a company or alliance introduces new technology that is *compatible* with the old, we say that they have adopted an "Evolution" strategy. Evolutionary strategies are based on offering superior performance with minimal consumer switching or adoption costs. The NTSC color television system selected by the FCC in 1953 was evolutionary: NTSC signals could be received by black-and-white sets, and the new color sets could receive black-and-white signals, making adoption of color far easier for both television stations and households. In contrast, the CBS system that the FCC had first endorsed in 1950 was not backward compatible.

When a company or alliance introduces new technology that is *incompatible* with the old, we say that they have adopted a "Revolution" strategy. Revolutionary strategies are based on offering such compelling performance that consumers are willing to incur significant switching or adoption costs.

If both your technology and your rival's technology are compatible with the older, established technology, but incompatible with each other we say the battle is one of "Rival Evolutions." Competition between DVD and Divx (both of which will play CDs), the 56k modem battle (both types communicate with slower modems), and competition between various flavors of Unix (which can run programs written for older versions of plain vanilla Unix) all fit this pattern.

If your technology offers backward compatibility and your rival's does not, we have "Evolution versus Revolution." The "Evolution versus Revolution" war is a contest between the backward compatibility of Evolution and the superior performance of Revolution. Evolution versus Revolution includes the important case of an upstart fighting against an established technology that is offering compatible upgrades. The struggle in the late 1980s between Ashton Tate's dBase IV and Paradox in the market for desktop database software fit this pattern. (The mirror image of this occurs if your rival offers backward compatibility but you do not: "Revolution versus Evolution.")

Finally, if neither technology is backward compatible we have "Rival Revolutions." The contest between Nintendo 64 and the Sony Playstation, and the historical example of AC versus DC in electrical systems, follow this pattern.

These four types of standards battles are described in Figure 10.1.

KEY ASSETS IN NETWORK MARKETS

In our view, successful strategy generally must harness a firm's resources in a manner that harmonizes with the underlying competitive environment. In a standards battle, the competitive environment is usefully characterized by locating the battle in Figure 10.1. What about the firms' resources?

Your ability to successfully wage a standards war depends on your ownership of seven key assets:

- control over an installed base of users;
- intellectual property rights;
- ability to innovate;
- first-mover advantages;
- manufacturing capabilities;
- strength in complements; and
- brand name and reputation.

What these assets have in common in that they place you in a potentially unique position to contribute to the adoption of a new technology. If you own these assets, your value-added to other players is high. Some assets, however, such as the ability to innovate or manufacturing capabilities, may even be more valuable in peace than in war. No one asset is decisive. For example, control over an older generation of technology does not necessarily confer the ability to pick the next gen-

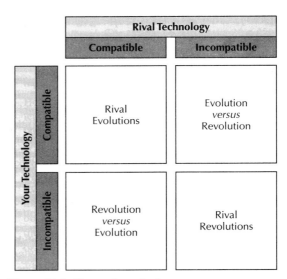

Figure 10.1. Types of standards wars.

eration. Sony and Philips controlled CDs but could not move unilaterally into DVDs. Atari had a huge installed base of first-generation video games in 1983, but Nintendo's superior technology and hot new games caught Atari flat-footed. The early leader in modems, Hayes, tried to buck the crowd when modems operating at 9,600 kbps were introduced, and ended up in Chapter 11.

Don't forget that *customers* as well as technology suppliers can control key assets, too. A big customer is automatically in "control" of at least part of the installed base. America Online recognized this in the recent 56k modem standards battle. Content providers played a key role in the DVD standards battle. IBM was pivotal in moving the industry from $5^{1}/_{4}''$ diskettes to $3^{1}/_{2}''$ disks. Most recently, TCI has not been shy about flexing its muscle in the battle over the technology used in TV set-top boxes.

Control over an Installed Base of Customers

An incumbent firm, like Microsoft, that has a large base of loyal or locked-in customers is uniquely placed to pursue an Evolution strategy offering backward compatibility. Control over an installed base can be used to block cooperative standard setting and force a standards war. Control can also be used to block rivals from offering compatible products, thus forcing them to play the more risky Revolution strategy.

Intellectual Property Rights

Firms with patents and copyrights controlling valuable new technology or interfaces are clearly in a strong position. Qualcomm's primary asset in the digital wireless telephone battle was its patent portfolio. The core assets of Sony and Philips in the CD and DVD areas were their respective patents. Usually, patents are stronger than copyrights, but computer software copyrights that can be used to block compatibility can be highly valuable. This is why Lotus fought Borland all the way to the Supreme Court to try to block Borland's use of the Lotus command structure (see below), and why Microsoft watched the trial intently to protect Excel's ability to read macros originally written for Lotus 1-2-3.

Ability to Innovate

Beyond your existing intellectual property, the ability to make proprietary extensions in the future puts you in a strong position today. In the color TV battle, NBC's R&D capabilities were crucial after the FCC initially adopted the CBS color system. NBC's engineers quickly developed a color system that was compatible with the existing black-and-white sets, a system which the FCC then accepted. Hewlett-Packard's engineering skills are legendary in Silicon Valley; it is often in their interest to compromise on standards since they can out-engineer their competition once the standard has been defined, even if they have to play some initial catch up.

First-Mover Advantages

If you already have done a lot of product development work and are further down the learning curve than the competition, you are in a strong position. Netscape obtained stunning market capitalization based on a their ability to bring new technology to market quickly. RealNetworks currently has a big lead on Microsoft in audio and video streaming.

Manufacturing Capabilities

If you are a low-cost producer, due to either scale economies or manufacturing competence, you are in a strong position. Cost advantages can help you survive a standards war, or capture share competing to sell a standardized product. Compaq and Dell both have pushed hard on driving down their manufacturing costs, which gives them a strong competitive advantage in the PC market. Rockwell has lower costs than its competitors in making chipsets for modems. HP has long been a team player in Silicon Valley, welcoming standards because of their engineering and manufacturing skills. These companies benefit from open standards, which emphasize the importance of efficient production.

Strength in Complements

If you produce a product that is a significant complement for the market in question, you will be strongly motivated to get the bandwagon rolling. This, too, puts you in a natural leadership position, since acceptance of the new technology will stimulate sales of the other products you produce. This force is stronger, the larger are your gross margins on your established products. Intel's thirst to sell more CPUs has been a key driver in their efforts to promote new standards for other PC components, including interfaces between motherboards and CPUs, busses, chipsets, and graphics controllers.

Reputation and Brand Name

A brand-name premium in any large market is highly valuable. But reputation and brand name are especially valuable in network markets, where expectations are pivotal. It's not enough to have the best product; you have to convince consumers that you will win. Previous victories and a recognized name count for a lot in this battle. Microsoft, HP, Intel, Sony, and Sun each have powerful reputations in their respective domains, giving them instant credibility.[10]

PREEMPTION

Preemption is one of two crucial marketplace tactics that arise over and over again in standards battles. The logic of preemption is straightforward: build an early lead, so positive feedback works for you and against your rival. The same principle applies in markets with strong learning-by-doing: the first firm to gain significant experience will have lower costs and can pull even further ahead. Either way, the trick is to exploit positive feedback. With learning-by-doing, the positive feedback is through lower costs. With network externalities, the positive feedback comes on the demand side; the leader offers a more valuable product or service.

One way to preempt is simply to be first to market. Product development and design skills can be critical to gaining a first-mover advantage. But watch out: early introduction also can entail compromises in quality and a greater risk of bugs, either of which can doom your product. This was the fate of the color television system promoted by CBS and of Japan's HDTV system. The race belongs to the swift, but speed must come from superior product design, not by marketing an inferior system.

In addition to launching your product early, you need to be aggressive early on to build an installed base of customers. Find the "pioneers" (a.k.a. gadget freaks) who are most keen to try new technology and sign them up swiftly. Pricing below cost (i.e., *penetration pricing*) is a common tactic to build an installed base. Discounting to attract large, visible, or influential customers is virtually unavoidable in a standards war.

In some cases, especially for software with a zero marginal cost, you can go beyond free samples and actually *pay* people to take your product. As we see it, there is nothing special about zero as a price, as long as you have multiple revenue streams to recover costs. Some cable television programmers pay cable operators to distribute their programming, knowing that a larger audience will augment their advertising revenues. In the same fashion, Netscape is prepared to give away its browser for free, or even pay OEMs (original equipment manufacturers) to load it on new machines, in order to increase the usage of Navigator and thus direct more traffic to the Netscape Website.

The big danger with negative prices is that someone will accept payment for "using" your product and then not really use it. This problem is easily solved in the cable television context, because programmers simply insist that cable operators actually carry their programming once they are paid to do so. Likewise, Netscape can check that an OEM loads Navigator (in a specified way) on new machines, and can conduct surveys to see just how the OEM configuration affects usage of Navigator.[11]

Before you go overboard giving your product away, or paying customers to take it, you need to ask three questions. First, if you pay someone to take your product, will they really use it and generate network externalities for other, paying customers? Second, how much is it really worth to you to build up your installed

base? Where is the offsetting revenue stream, and when will it arrive? Third, are you fooling yourself? Beware the well-known "Winner's Curse": the tendency of the most optimistic participant to win in a bidding war, only to find that they were overly optimistic and other bidders were more realistic.

Penetration pricing may be difficult to implement if you are building a coalition around an "open" standard. The sponsor of a proprietary standard can hope to recoup the losses incurred during penetration pricing once it controls an established technology. Without a sponsor, no single supplier will be willing to make the necessary investments to preempt using penetration pricing. For precisely this reason, penetration pricing can be particularly effective when used by a company with a proprietary system against a rival touting its openness.

Another implication is that the player in a standards battle with the largest profit streams from related products stands to win the war. We have seen this with smart cards in Europe. They were introduced with a single application—public telephone service—but soon were expanded to other transactions involving small purchases. Eventually, many more applications such as identification and authentication will be introduced. Visa, MasterCard, and American Express are already jockeying for position in the smart card wars. Whichever player can figure out the most effective way to generate multiple revenue streams from an installed base of smart card holders will be able to bid most aggressively, but still profitably, to build up the largest base of customers.

EXPECTATIONS MANAGEMENT

The second key tactic in standards wars is the management of expectations. Expectations are a major factor in consumer decisions about whether or not to purchase a new technology, so make sure that you do your best to manage those expectations. Just as incumbents will try to knock down the viability of new technologies that emerge, so will those very entrants strive to establish credibility.

Vaporware is a classic tactic aimed at influencing expectations: announce an upcoming product so as to freeze your rival's sales. In the 1994 antitrust case brought by the Justice Department against Microsoft, Judge Sporkin cited vaporware as one reason why he found the proposed consent decree insufficient. In an earlier era, IBM was accused of the same tactic. Of course, drawing the line between "predatory product pre-announcements" and simply being late bringing a product to market is not so easy to draw, especially in the delay-prone software market. Look at what happened to Lotus in spreadsheets and Ashton-Tate and database software. After both of these companies repeatedly missed launch dates, industry wags said they should be merged and use the stock ticker symbol "LATE." We must note with some irony that Microsoft's stock took a 5.3% nosedive in late 1997 after Microsoft announced a delay in the launch of Windows 98 from the first to the second quarter of 1998.

The most direct way to manage expectations is by assembling allies and by making grand claims about your product's current or future popularity. Sun has been highly visible in gathering allies in support of Java, including taking out full-page advertisements listing the companies in the Java coalition. Indicative of how important expectations management is in markets with strong network externalities, WordPerfect even filed a court complaint against Microsoft to block Microsoft from claiming that its word processing software was the most popular in the world. Barnes & Noble did the same thing to Amazon, arguing that their claim to being the "world's largest bookstore" was misleading.

ONCE YOU'VE WON

Moving on from war to the spoils of victory, let's consider how best to proceed once you have actually *won* a standards war. Probably you made some concessions to achieve victory, such as promises of openness or deals with various allies. Of course, you have to live with those, but there is still a great deal of room for strategy. In today's high-tech world, the battle never really ends. So, take a deep breath and be ready to keep moving.

Staying on Your Guard
Technology marches forward. You have to keep looking out for the next generation of technology, which can come from unexpected directions. Microsoft, with all its foresight and savvy, has had to scurry to deal with the Internet phenomenon and try to defuse any threat to its core business.

You may be especially vulnerable if you were victorious in one generation of technology through a preemption strategy. Going early usually means making technical compromises, which gives that much more room for others to execute an incompatible Revolution strategy against you. Apple pioneered the market for personal digital assistants, but U.S. Robotics perfected the idea with their Palm Pilot. If your rivals attract the power users, your market position and the value of your network may begin to erode.

The hazards of moving early and then lacking flexibility can be seen in the case of the French Minitel system. Back in the 1980s, the French were world leaders in on-line transactions with the extensive Minitel computer network, which was sponsored and controlled by France Telecom. Before the Internet was widely known, much less used, million of French subscribers used the Minitel system to obtain information and conduct secure online transactions. Today, Minitel boasts more than 35 million French subscribers and 25,000 vendors. One reason Minitel has attracted so many suppliers is that users pay a fee to France Telecom each time they visit a commercial site, and a portion of these fees are passed along to vendors. Needless to say, this is quite a different business model than we see on the Web.

Now, however, the Minitel systems is seen as inflexible, and France is lagging behind in moving onto the Internet. Just as companies that invested in dedicated word processing systems in the 1970s were slow to move to more generalized personal computers in the 1980s, the French have been slow to invest in equipment that can access the Internet. Only about 3% of the French population uses the Internet, far short of the estimated 20% in the U.S. and 9% is the U.K. and Germany. Roughly 15% of French companies have a Web site, versus nearly 35% of U.S. businesses. Only in August 1997 did the French government admit that the Internet, not Minitel, was the way of the future rather than an instrument of American cultural imperialism. France Telecom is now in the planning stages to introduce next-generation Minitel terminals that will access the Internet as well as Minitel.

What is the lesson here? The French sluggishness to move to the Internet stems from two causes that are present in many other settings. First, France Telecom and the vendors had an incentive to preserve the revenue streams they were earning from Minitel. This is understandable, but it should be recognized as a choice to harvest an installed base, with adverse implications for the future. Milking the installed base is sometimes the right thing to do, but make this a calculated choice, not a default decision. Second, moving to the Internet presents substantial collective switching costs—and less incremental value—to French consumers in contrast with, say, American consumers. Precisely because Minitel was a success, it reduced the attractiveness of the Internet.

The strategic implication is that you need a migration path or road map for your technology. If you cannot improve your technology with time, while offering substantial compatibility with older versions, you will be overtaken sooner or later. Rigidity is death, unless you build a really big installed base, and even this will fade eventually without improvements.

Offer Customers a Migration Path

To fend off challenges from upstarts, you need to make it hard for rivals to execute a revolution strategy. The key is to anticipate the next generation of technology and co-opt it. Look in all directions for the next threat and take advantage of the fact that consumers will not switch to a new incompatibility technology unless it offers a marked improvement in performance. Microsoft has been the master of this strategy with its "Embrace and Extend" philosophy of anticipating or imitating improvements and incorporating them into its flagship products.[12] Avoid being frozen in place by your own success. If you cater too closely to your installed base by emphasizing backward compatibility, you open the door to a Revolution strategy by an upstart. This is precisely what happened to Ashton-Tate in databases, allowing Borland and later Microsoft to offer far superior performance with their Paradox and FoxPro products. Your product road map has to offer your customers a smooth migration path to ever-improving technology, and it must stay close to, if not on, the cutting edge.

One way to avoid being dragged down by the need to retain compatibility is to give older members of your installed base free or inexpensive upgrades to a recent but not current version of your product. This is worth doing for many reasons: users of much older versions have revealed that they do not need the latest bells and whistles and thus are less likely to actually buy the latest version; the free "partial" upgrade can restore some lost customer loyalty; you can save on

support costs by avoiding "version-creep"; and you can avoid being hamstrung in designing your latest products by a customer-relations need to maintain compatibility with older and older versions. To compromise the performance of your latest version in the name of compatibility with ancient versions presents an opening for a rival to build an installed base among more demanding users. Happily, this "lagged upgrade" approach is easier and easier with distribution so cheap over the Internet.

Microsoft did a good job with this problem with migration to Windows 95. Politely put, Windows 95 is a kludge, with all sorts of special workarounds to allow DOS programs to execute in the Windows environment, thereby maintaining compatibility with customers' earlier programs. Microsoft's plan with Windows 98 is to move the consumer version of Windows closer to the professional version, Windows NT, eventually ending up with only one product, or at least only one user interface.

Commoditize Complementary Products

Once you've won, you want to keep your network alive and healthy. This means that you've got to attend not only to your own products, but to the products produced by your complementors as well. Your goal should be to retain your franchise as the market leader, but have a vibrant and competitive market for complements to your product.

This can be tricky. Apple has flipped back and forth on its developer relations over the years. First they wanted to just be in the computer business, and let others develop applications. Then they established a subsidiary, Claris, to do applications development. When this soured relations with other developers they spun Claris off. And so it went—a back-and-forth dance.

Microsoft faced the same problem, but with a somewhat different strategy. If an applications developer became successful, Microsoft just bought them (or tried to—Microsoft's intended purchase of Intuit was blocked by the Department of Justice). Nowadays a lot of new business plans in the software industry have the same structure: "Produce product, capture emerging market, be bought by Microsoft."

Our view is that you should try to maintain a competitive market in complementary products and avoid the temptation to meddle. Enter into these markets only if integration of your core product with adjacent products adds value to consumers, or if you can inject significant additional competition to keep prices low. If you are truly successful, like Intel, you will need to spur innovation in complementary products to continue to grow, both by capturing revenues from new complementary products and by stimulating demand for your core product.

Competing Against Your Own Installed Base

You may need to improve performance just to compete against your installed base, even without an external threat. How can you continue to grow when your information product or technology starts to reach market saturation? One answer is to drive innovation ever faster. Intel is pushing to improve hardware performance of complementary products (such as graphics chips and chipsets) and helping develop applications that crave processing power so as to drive the hardware upgrade cycle. Competition with one's own installed base is not a new problem for companies selling durable goods. The stiffest competition faced by Steinway in selling pianos is from used Steinways.

One way to grow even after you have a large installed base is to start discounting as a means of attracting the remaining customers who have demonstrated (by waiting) that they have a relatively low willingness-to-pay for your product. This is a good instinct, but be careful. First, discounting established products is at odds with a penetration pricing strategy to win a standards war. Second, if you regularly discount products once they are well established, consumers may learn to wait for the discounts. The key question: Can you expand the market and not spoil your margins for traditional customers?

Economists have long recognized this as the "durable-goods monopoly" problem. Ronald Coase, recent winner of the Nobel Prize in Economics, wrote 35 years ago about the temptation of a company selling a durable product to offer lower and lower prices to expand the market once many consumers already purchased the durable good. He conjectured that consumers would come to anticipate these price reductions and hold off buying until prices fall. Since then, economists have studied a variety of strategies designed to prevent the resulting erosion of profits. The problem raised by Coase is especially severe for highly durable products such as information and software.

One of the prescriptions for solving the durable-goods monopoly problem is to *rent* your product rather than sell it. This will not work for a microprocessor or a printer, but rapid technological change can achieve the same end. If a product becomes obsolete in two or three years, used versions won't pose much of a threat to new sales down the line. This is a great spur for companies like Intel to rush ahead as fast as possible increasing the speed of their microprocessors. The same is true on the software side, where even vendors who are dominant in their category (such as Autodesk in computer-aided design) are forced to improve their programs to generate a steady stream of revenues.

Protecting Your Position

A variety of defensive tactics can help secure your position. This is where antitrust limits come in most sharply, however, since it is illegal to "maintain a monopoly" by anticompetitive means.

One tactic is to offer ongoing attractive terms to important complementors. For example, Nintendo worked aggressively to attract developers of hit games and used its popularity to gain very strong distribution. This tactic can, however, cross the legal line if you insist that your suppliers, or distributors, deal with you to the exclusion of your rivals. For example, FTD, the floral network, under pressure from the Justice Department, had to cancel its program giving discounts to florists who used FTD exclusively. Since FTD had the lion's share of the floral delivery network business, this quasi-exclusivity provision was seen as protecting FTD's near-monopoly position. Ticketmaster was subjected to an extensive investigation for adopting exclusivity provisions in its contracts with stadiums, concert halls, and other venues. The Justice Department in 1994 attacked Microsoft's contracts with OEMs for having an effect similar to that of exclusive licenses.

A less controversial way to protect your position is to take steps to avoid being held up by others who claim that your product infringes their patents or copyrights. Obviously, there is no risk-free way to do this. However, it makes a great deal of sense to ask those seeking access to your network to agree not to bring the whole network down in an infringement action. Microsoft took steps along these lines when it launched Windows 95, including a provision in the Windows 95 license for OEMs that prevented Microsoft licensees from attempting to use certain software patents to block Microsoft from shipping Windows 95. Intel regularly asks companies taking licenses to its open specifications to agree to offer royalty-free licenses to other participants for any patents that would block the specified technology. This "two-sided openness" strategy prevents ex post hold-up problems and helps safely launch a new specification.

Leveraging Your Installed Base

Once you have a strong installed base, basic principles of competitive strategy dictate that you seek to leverage into adjacent product spaces, exploiting the key assets that give you a unique ability to create value for consumers in those spaces. In some cases, control over an interface can be used to extend leadership from one side of the interface to the other.

But don't get carried away. You may be better off encouraging healthy competition in complementary products, which stimulates demand for your core product, rather than trying to dominate adjacent spaces. Acquisitions of companies selling neighboring products should be driven by true synergies of bringing both products into the same company, not simply by a desire to expand your empire. Again, legal limits on both "leveraging" and on vertical acquisitions can come into play. For example, the FTC forced Time Warner to agree to carry a rival news channel on its cable systems when Time Warner acquired CNN in its merger with Turner.

Geographic expansion is yet another way to leverage your installed base. This is true for traditional goods and services, but with a new twist for network products: when expanding the geographic scope of your network, make sure your installed base in one region becomes a competitive advantage in another region. But careful: don't build a two-way bridge to another region where you face an even stronger rival; in that case, more troops will come across the bridge attacking you than you can send to gain new territory.

Geographic effects were powerful in the FCC auctions of spectrum space for PCS services, the successor to the older cellular telephone technology. If you provide Personal Digital Assistance (PDA) wireless services in Minneapolis, you have a big advantage if you also provide such services in St. Paul. The market leader in one town would therefore be willing to outbid rivals in neighboring locations. In the PCS

auctions, bidders allegedly "signaled" their most-preferred territories by encoding them into their bids as an attempt to avoid a mutually unprofitable bidding war. The Department of Justice is investigating these complaints. Our point is not to offer bidding strategy, but to remind you that geographic expansion of a network can be highly profitable. Network growth generates new customers and offers more value to existing customers at the same time.

Staying a Leader

How can you secure a competitive advantage for yourself short of maintaining direct control over the technology, e.g., through patent or copyright protection? Even without direct control over the installed base or ownership of key patents, you may be able to make the other factors work for you, while garnering enough external support to set the standards you want.

If you have a good development team, you can build a bandwagon using an "openness" approach of ceding current control over the technology (e.g., through licenses at low or nominal royalties) while keeping tight control over improvements and extensions. If you know better than others how the technology is likely to evolve, you can use this informational advantage to preserve important future rights without losing the support of your allies. IBM chose to open up the PC, but then they lost control because they did not see what the key assets would be in the future. Besides the now-obvious ones (the design of the operating system and manufacturing of the underlying microprocessor), consider the example of interface standards between the PC and the monitor. During the 1980s, IBM set the first four standards: the Monochrome Graphics Adapters (MGA), the Color Graphics Adapter (CGA), the Enhanced Graphics Adapter (EGA), and the Video Graphics Adapter (VGA), the last in 1987. But by the time of the VGA, IBM was losing control, and the standard started to splinter with the Super VGA around 1988. Soon, with the arrival of the VESA interface, standard-setting passed out of IBM's hands altogether. By anticipating advances in the resolution of monitors, IBM could have done more to preserve its power to set these interface standards, without jeopardizing the initial launch of the PC.

Developing proprietary extensions is a valuable tactic to recapture at least partial control over your own technology. You may not be able to exert strong control at the outset, but you may gain some control later if you launch a technology that takes off and you can be first to market with valuable improvements and extensions.

One difficulty with such an approach is that your new technology may be *too* successful. If the demand for your product grows too fast, many of your resources may end up being devoted to meeting current demand rather than investing in R&D for the future. This happened to Cisco. All of their energies were devoted to the next generation of networking gear, leaving them little time for long-run research. If you are lucky enough to be in Cisco's position, do what they did: use all the profits you are making to identify and purchase firms that are producing the next-generation products. As Cisco's CEO, John Chambers, puts it: "We don't do research—we buy research!"

Allow complementors, and even rivals, to participate in developing standards, but under *your* terms. Clones are fine, so long as you set the terms under which they can operate. Don't flip-flop in your policies, as Apple did with its clone manufacturers: stay open, but make sure that you charge enough for access to your network (e.g., in the form of licensing fees) that your bottom line does not suffer when rivals displace your own sales. Build the opportunity costs of lost sales into your access prices or licensing fees.

REAR-GUARD ACTIONS

What happens if you fall behind? Can you ever recover?

That depends upon what you mean by "recover." Usually it is not possible to wrest leadership from another technology that is equally good and more established, unless your rival slips up badly. However, if the network externalities are not crushing, you may be able to protect a niche in the market. And you can always position yourself to make a run at leadership in the next generation of technology.

Atari, Nintendo, Sega, and Sony present a good example. Atari was dominant in 8-bit systems, Nintendo in 16-bit systems, Sega made inroads by being first-to-market with 32-bit systems, and Sony is giving Nintendo a run for their money in 64-bit systems. Losing one round does not mean you should give up, especially if backward compatibility is not paramount.

This leaves a set of tricky issues of how to manage your customers if you have done poorly in one round of the competition. Stranding even a small installed base of customers can have lasting reputational effects. IBM was concerned about this when they dropped the PC Jr. in the mid-1980s. Apart from consumer goodwill, retaining a presence in the market can be vital to keeping up customer relations and brand identity, even if you have little prospect of making major sales until you introduce a new generation of products. Apple faces this problem with their new operating system, Rhapsody. How do they maintain compatibility with their loyal followers while still building a path to what they hope will be a dramatic improvement in the operating environment?

Adapters and Interconnection

A tried and true tactic when falling behind is to add an adapter, or to somehow interconnect with the larger network. This can be a sign of weakness, but one worth bearing if the enhanced network externalities of plugging into a far larger network are substantial. We touched on this in our discussion of how to negotiate a truce; if you are negotiating from weakness, you may simply seek the right to interconnect with the larger network.

The first question to ask is whether you even have the right to build an adapter. Sometimes the large network can keep you out. Atari lacked the intellectual property rights to include an adapter in their machines to play Nintendo cartridges, because of Nintendo's lock-out chip. In other cases, you may be able to break down the door, or at least try. The dominant ATM network in Canada, Interac, was compelled to let nonmember banks interconnect. In the telephone area, the FCC is implementing elaborate rules that will allow competitive local exchange carriers to interconnect with the incumbent monopoly telephone networks.

The most famous legal case of a less-popular network product maneuvering to achieve compatibility is the battle between Borland and Lotus in spread-sheets. To promote its QuattroPro spreadsheet as an alternative to the dominant spreadsheet of the day, Lotus 1-2-3, Borland not only made sure than QuattroPro could import Lotus files, but copied part of the menu structure used by Lotus. Lotus sued Borland for copyright infringement. The case went all the way to the Supreme Court; the vote was deadlocked so Borland prevailed based on its victory in the First Circuit Court of Appeals. This case highlights the presence of legal uncertainty over what degree of imitation is permissible; the courts are still working out the limits on how patents and copyrights can be used in network industries.

There are many diverse examples of "adapters." Conversion of data from another program is a type of adapter. Translators and emulators can serve the same function when more complex code is involved. Converters can be one-way or two-way, with very different strategic implications. Think about WordPerfect and Microsoft Word today. WordPerfect is small and unlikely to gain much share, so they benefit from two-way compatibility. Consumers will be more willing to buy or upgrade WordPerfect if they can import files in Word format and export files in a format that is readable by users of Word. So far, Word will import files in WordPerfect format, but if Microsoft ever eliminates this feature of Word, WordPerfect should attempt to offer an export capability that preserves as much information as possible.

The biggest problem with adapters, when they are technically and legally possible, is performance degradation. Early hopes that improved processing power would make emulation easy have proven false. Tasks become more complex.

Digital's efforts with its Alpha microprocessor illustrate some of the ways in which less popular technologies seek compatibility. The Alpha chip has been consistently faster than the fastest Intel chips on the market. Digital sells systems with Alpha chips into the server market, a far smaller market than the desktop and workstation markets. And Digital's systems are far more expensive than systems using Intel chips. As a result, despite its technical superiority, the Alpha sold only 300,000 chips in 1996 compared to 65 million sold by Intel. This leaves Digital in the frustrating position of having a superior product but suffering from a small network. Recognizing that Alpha is in a precarious position, Digital has been looking for ways to interconnect with the Intel (virtual) network. Digital offers an emulator to let its Alpha chip run like an Intel architecture chip, but most of the performance advantages that Alpha offers are neutralized by the emulator. Hoping to improve the performance of systems using the Alpha chip, Digital and Microsoft announced in January 1998 an enhanced Alliance for Enterprise Computing, under which Windows NT server-based products will be released concurrently for Alpha- and Intel-based systems. Digital also has secured a commitment from Microsoft that Microsoft will cooperate to provide source-code compatibility between Alpha- and Intel-based systems for Windows NT application developers, making it far easier for them to develop applications to run on Alpha-based systems in native mode.

Adapters and converters among software programs are also highly imperfect. Converting files from WordStar to WordPerfect, and now from WordPerfect to Word, is notoriously buggy. Whatever the example, consumers are rightly wary of translators and emulators, in part because of raw performance concerns and in part because of lurking concerns over just how compatible the conversion really is: consider the problems that users have faced with Intel to Motorola architectures, of dBase to Paradox databases.

Apple offers a good example of a company that responded to eroding market share by adding adapters. Apple put in disk drives that could read floppy disks formatted on DOS and Windows machines in the mideighties. In 1993, Apple introduced a machine that included an Intel 486 chip and could run DOS and Windows software along with Macintosh software. But Apple's case also exposes the deep tension underlying an adapter strategy: the adapter adds (some) value, but undermines confidence in the smaller network itself.

Finally, be careful about the large network changing interface specifications to avoid compatibility. IBM was accused of this in mainframe computers. Indeed, we suggested this very tactic in the section above on strategies for winners, so long as the new specifications are truly superior, not merely an attempt to exclude competitors.

Survival Pricing

The marginal cost of producing information goods is close to zero. This means that you can cut your price very low and still cover (incremental) costs. Hence, when you find yourself falling behind in a network industry, it is tempting to cut price in order to spur sales, a tactic we call *survival pricing*.

However, the temptation should be resisted. Survival pricing is unlikely to work. It shows weakness, and it is hard to find examples where it made much difference. Computer Associates gave away "Simply Money" (for a $6.95 shipping and handling fee), but this didn't matter. Simply Money still did not take off in its battle against Quicken and Money. On the other hand, Computer Associates got the name and vital statistics of each buyer, which was worth something in the mail list market, so it wasn't a total loss. IBM offered OS/2 for as little as $50, but look where it got them. Borland priced QuattroPro very aggressively when squeezed between Lotus1-2-3 and Microsoft Excel back in 1993.

The problem is that the purchase price of software is minor in comparison with the costs of deployment, training, and support. Corporate purchasers, and even individual consumers, were much more worried about picking the winner of the spreadsheet wars than they were in whether their spreadsheet cost $49.95 or $99.95. At the time of the cut-throat pricing, Borland was a distant third in the spreadsheet market. Lotus and Microsoft both said they would not respond to the low price. Frank Ingari, Lotus's vice president for marketing, dismissed Borland as a "fringe player" and said the $49 price was a "last gasp move."

Survival pricing—cutting your price after the tide has moved against you—should be distinguished from penetration pricing, which is offering a low price to invade another market. Borland used penetration pricing very cleverly in the early 1980s with its Turbo Pascal product. Microsoft, along with other compiler companies, ignored Turbo Pascal, much to their dismay later on.

Legal Approaches

If all else fails, sue. No, really. If the dominant firm has promised to be open and has reneged on that promise, you should attack its bait-and-switch approach. The Supreme Court in the landmark *Kodak* case opened the door to antitrust attacks along these lines, and many companies have taken up the invitation. The key is that a company may be found to be a "monopolist" over its own installed base of users, even if it faces strong competition to attract such users in the first place. Although the economics behind the *Kodak* case are murky and muddled, it can offer a valuable lever to gain compatibility or interconnection with a dominant firm.

CONCLUSIONS AND LESSONS

Before you can craft standards strategy, you first need to understand what type of standards war you are waging. The single most important factor to track is the compatibility between the dueling new technologies and established products. Standards wars come in three types: Rival Evolutions, Rival Revolutions, and Revolution versus Evolution.

Strength in the standards game is determined by ownership of seven critical assets:

- control of an installed base
- intellectual property rights
- ability to innovate
- first-mover advantages
- manufacturing abilities
- presence in complementary products
- brand name and reputation

Our main lessons for strategy and tactics, drawn from dozens of standards wars over the past century and more, are these:

- *Before you go to war, assemble allies.* You'll need the support of consumers, suppliers of complements, and even your competitors. Not even the strongest companies can afford to go it alone in a standards war.

- *Preemption is a critical tactic during a standards war.* Rapid design cycles, early deals with pivotal customers, and penetration pricing are the building blocks of a preemption strategy.

- *Managing consumer expectations is crucial in network markets.* Your goal is to convince customers—and your complementors—that you will emerge as the victor. Such expectations can easily become a self-fulfilling prophecy when network effects are strong. To manage expectations you should engage in aggressive marketing, make early announcements of new products, assemble allies, and make visible commitments to your technology.

- *When you've won your war, don't rest easy.* Cater to your own installed base and avoid complacency. Don't let the desire for backward compatibility hobble your ability to improve your product; doing so will leave you open to an entrant offering less compatibility but superior performance. Commoditize complementary products to make your systems more attractive for consumers.

- *If you fall behind, avoid survival pricing; it just signals weakness.* A better tactic is to establish a compelling performance advantage, or to interconnect with the prevailing standard using converters and adapters.

ACKNOWLEDGMENTS

Prepared for the *California Management Review*. This material is adapted from our book, *Information Rules: A Strategic Guide to the Network Economy* (Harvard Business School Press, Boston, MA, 1998). We are indebted to our colleagues Joseph Farrell and Michael L. Katz who have greatly contributed over the past 15 years to our understanding of these issues.

NOTES

1. For a lengthy discussion of railroad gauge standardization, see Amy Friedlander, *Emerging Infrastructure: The Growth of Railroads* (Reston, VA: Corporation for National Research Initiatives, 1995).

2. For further details on the Battle of the Systems, see Julie Ann Bunn and Paul David, "The Economics of Gateway Technologies and Network Evolution: Lessons from Electricity Supply History," *Information Economics and Policy,* 3/2 (1988).

3. In this context, Edison's efforts can be seen as an attempt to prevent or delay tipping toward AC, perhaps to obtain the most money in selling his DC interests.

4. A very nice recounting of the color television story can be found in David Fisher and Marshall Fisher, "The Color War," *Invention & Technology,* 3/3 (1997). See, also, Joseph Farrell and Carl Shapiro, "Standard Setting in High-Definition Television," *Brookings Papers on Economic Activity: Microeconomics* (1992).

5. For color TV to truly offer value to viewers, it was not enough to get set manufacturers and networks to agree on a standard; they had to produce sets that performed well at a reasonable cost, they had to create compelling content, and they had to induce broadcasters to invest in transmission gear. The technology was just not ready for the mass market in 1953, much less 1950. Interestingly, the Europeans, by waiting another decade before the adoption of PAL and SECAM, ended up with a better system. The same leapfrogging is now taking place in re-

verse: the digital HDTV system being adopted in the U.S. is superior to the system selected years before by the Japanese.

6. For a fuller discussion of positive feedback, network effects, and network externalities, see Chapter 7 of Carl Shapiro and Hal R. Varian, *Information Rules: A Strategic Guide to the Network Economy* (Boston, MA: Harvard Business School Press, 1998). See, also, Michael Katz and Carl Shapiro, "Systems Competition and Network Effects," *Journal of Economic Perspectives,* 8/2 (1994); Brian Arthur, *Increasing Returns and Path Dependence in the Economy* (Ann Arbor, MI: University of Michigan Press, 1994).

7. We recognize, indeed emphasize, that building an alliance of customers, suppliers, and complementors to support one technology over another in a standards battle can be the single most important tactic in such a struggle. We explore alliances and cooperative strategies to achieve compatibility separately in Chapter 8 of *Information Rules* [Shapiro and Varian, op. cit.]. See, also, David B. Yoffie, "Competing in the Age of Digital Convergence," *California Management Review,* 38/4 (1996).

8. For a discussion of the antitrust treatment of standards, see the Federal Trade Commission Staff Report, *Competition Policy in the New High-Tech, Global Marketplace,* Chapter 9, "Networks and Standards"; Joel Klein, "Cross-Licensing and Antitrust Law," 1997, available at www.usdoj.gov/atr/public/speeches/1123.htm; Carl Shapiro, "Antitrust in Network Industries," 1996, available at www.usdoj.gov/atr/public/speeches/shapir. mar; Carl Shapiro, "Setting Compatibility Standards: Cooperation or Collusion?" Working Paper, University of California, Berkeley, 1998.

9. We cannot explore cooperation and compatibility tactics in any depth here. We discuss tactics for participation in formal standard setting in Chapter 8 of *Information Rules* [Shapiro and Varian, op. cit.].

10. Even these companies have had losers, too, such as Microsoft's Bob, Intel's original Celeron chip, and Sun's 386 platform. Credibility and brand name recognition without allies and a sound product are not enough.

11. Manufacturers do the same thing when they pay "slotting allowances" to supermarkets for shelf space by checking that their products are actually displayed where they are supposed to be displayed.

12. Indeed, the strategy has been so successful that some have amended the name to "Embrace, Extend, and Eliminate."

11

Managing in an Age of Modularity

CARLISS Y. BALDWIN
KIM B. CLARK

In the nineteenth century, railroads fundamentally altered the competitive landscape of business. By providing fast and cheap transportation, they forced previously protected regional companies into battles with distant rivals. The railroad companies also devised management practices to deal with their own complexity and high fixed costs that deeply influenced the second wave of industrialization at the turn of the century.

Today the computer industry is in a similar leading position. Not only have computer companies transformed a wide range of markets by introducing cheap and fast information processing, but they have also led the way toward a new industry structure that makes the best use of these processing abilities. At the heart of their remarkable advance is modularity—building a complex product or process from smaller subsystems that can be designed independently yet function together as a whole. Through the widespread adoption of modular designs, the computer industry has dramatically increased its rate of innovation. Indeed, it is modularity, more than speedy processing and communication or any other technology, that is responsible for the heightened pace of change that managers in the computer industry now face. And strategies based on modularity are the best way to deal with that change.

Many industries have long had a degree of modularity in their production processes. But a growing number of them are now poised to extend modularity to the design stage. Although they may have difficulty taking modularity as far as the computer industry has,

managers in many industries stand to learn much about ways to employ this new approach from the experiences of their counterparts in computers.

A SOLUTION TO GROWING COMPLEXITY

The popular and business presses have made much of the awesome power of computer technology. Storage capacities and processing speeds have skyrocketed while costs have remained the same or have fallen. These improvements have depended on enormous growth in the complexity of the product. The modern computer is a bewildering array of elements working in concert, evolving rapidly in precise and elaborate ways.

Modularity has enabled companies to handle this increasingly complex technology. By breaking up a product into subsystems, or *modules,* designers, producers, and users have gained enormous flexibility. Different companies can take responsibility for separate modules and be confident that a reliable product will arise from their collective efforts.

The first modular computer, the System/360, which IBM announced in 1964, effectively illustrates this approach. The designs of previous models from IBM and other mainframe manufacturers were unique; each had its own operating system, processor, peripherals, and application software. Every time a manufacturer introduced a new computer system to take advan-

Reprinted by permission of *Harvard Business Review.* From "Managing in an Age of Modularity," by Carliss Y. Baldwin and Kim B. Clark, September 1997. Copyright © 1997 by the Harvard Business School Publishing Corporation; all rights reserved.

tage of improved technology, it had to develop software and components specifically for that system while continuing to maintain those for the previous systems. When end users switched to new machines, they had to rewrite all their existing programs, and they ran the risk of losing critical data if software conversions were botched. As a result, many customers were reluctant to lease or purchase new equipment.

The developers of the System/360 attacked that problem head-on. They conceived of a family of computers that would include machines of different sizes suitable for different applications, all of which would use the same instruction set and could share peripherals. To achieve this compatibility, they applied the principle of *modularity in design:* that is, the System/360's designers divided the designs of the processors and peripherals into *visible* and *hidden* information. IBM set up a Central Processor Control Office, which established and enforced the visible overall design rules that determined how the different modules of the machine would work together. The dozens of design teams scattered around the world had to adhere absolutely to these rules. But each team had full control over the hidden elements of design in its module—those elements that had no effect on other modules. (See the box "A Guide to Modularity.")

When IBM employed this approach and also made the new systems compatible with existing software (by adding "emulator" modules), the result was a huge commercial and financial success for the company and its customers. Many of IBM's mainframe rivals were forced to abandon the market or seek niches focused on customers with highly specialized needs. But modularity also undermined IBM's dominance in the long run, as new companies produced their own so-called plug-compatible modules—printers, terminals, memory, software, and eventually even the central processing units themselves—that were compatible with, and could plug right into, the IBM machines. By following IBM's design rules but specializing in a particular area, an upstart company could often produce a module that was better than the ones IBM was making internally. Ultimately, the dynamic, innovative industry that has grown up around these modules developed entirely new kinds of computer systems that have taken away most of the mainframe's market share.

The fact that different companies (and different units of IBM) were working independently on mod-

ules enormously boosted the rate of innovation. By concentrating on a single module, each unit or company could push deeper into its workings. Having many companies focus on the design of a given module fostered numerous, parallel experiments. The module designers were free to try out a wide range of approaches as long as they obeyed the *design rules* ensuring that the modules would fit together. For an industry like computers, in which technological uncertainty is high and the best way to proceed is often unknown, the more experiments and the more flexibility each designer has to develop and test the experimental modules, the faster the industry is able to arrive at improved versions.

This freedom to experiment with product design is what distinguishes modular suppliers from ordinary subcontractors. For example, a team of disk drive designers has to obey the overall requirements of a personal computer, such as data transmission protocols, specifications for the size and shape of hardware, and standards for interfaces, to be sure that the module will function within the system as a whole. But otherwise, team members can design the disk drive in the way they think works best. The decisions they make need not be communicated to designers of other modules or even to the system's architects, the creators of the visible design rules. Rival disk-drive designers, by the same token, can experiment with completely different engineering approaches for their versions of the module as long as they, too, obey the visible design rules.[1]

MODULARITY OUTSIDE THE COMPUTER INDUSTRY

As a principle of production, modularity has a long history. Manufacturers have been using it for a century or more because it has always been easier to make complicated products by dividing the manufacturing process into modules or *cells.* Carmakers, for example, routinely manufacture the components of an automobile at different sites and then bring them together for final assembly. They can do so because they have precisely and completely specified the design of each part. In this context, the engineering design of a part (its dimensions and tolerances) serves as the visible information in the manufacturing system, allowing a complicated process to be split up among many factories and even outsourced to other suppliers. Those suppliers may experiment with production processes or logistics, but, unlike in the computer industry, they have historically had little or no input into the design of the components.

Modularity is comparatively rare not only in the actual design of products but also in their use. *Modularity in use* allows consumers to mix and match elements to come up with a final product that suits their tastes and needs. For example, to make a bed, consumers often buy bed frames, mattresses, pillows, linens, and covers from different manufacturers and even different retailers. They all fit together because the different manufacturers put out these goods according to standard sizes. Modularity in use can spur innovation in design: the manufacturers can independently experiment with new products and concepts, such as futon mattresses or fabric blends, and find ready consumer acceptance as long as their modules fit the standard dimensions.

If modularity brings so many advantages, why aren't all products (and processes) fully modular? It turns out that modular systems are much more difficult to design than comparable interconnected systems. The designers of modular systems must know a great deal about the inner workings of the overall product or process in order to develop the visible design rules necessary to make the modules function as a whole. They have to specify those rules in advance. And while designs at the modular level are proceeding independently, it may seem that all is going well; problems with incomplete or imperfect modularization tend to appear only when the modules come together and work poorly as an integrated whole.

IBM discovered that problem with the System/360, which took far more resources to develop than expected. In fact, had the developers initially realized the difficulties of ensuring modular integration, they might never have pursued the approach at all because they also underestimated the System/360's market value. Customers wanted it so much that their willingness to pay amply justified IBM's increased costs.

We have now entered a period of great advances in modularity. Breakthroughs in materials science and other fields have made it easier to obtain the deep product knowledge necessary to specify the design rules. For example, engineers now understand how metal reacts under force well enough to ensure modular coher-

A Guide to Modularity

Modularity is a strategy for organizing complex products and processes efficiently. A *modular* system is composed of units (or modules) that are designed independently but still function as an integrated whole. Designers achieve modularity by partitioning information into *visible design rules* and *hidden design parameters*. Modularity is beneficial only if the partition is precise, unambiguous, and complete.

The visible design rules (also called *visible information*) are decisions that affect subsequent design decisions. Ideally, the visible design rules are established early in a design process and communicated broadly to those involved. Visible design rules fall into three categories:

- An *architecture,* which specifies what modules will be part of the system and what their functions will be.
- *Interfaces* that describe in detail how the modules will interact, including how they will fit together, connect, and communicate.
- *Standards* for testing a module's conformity to the design rules (can module X function in the system?) and for measuring one module's performance relative to another (how good is module X versus module Y?).

Practitioners sometimes lump all three elements of the visible information together and call them all simply "the architecture," "the interfaces," or "the standards."

The hidden design parameters (also called *hidden information*) are decisions that do not affect the design beyond the local module. Hidden elements can be chosen late and changed often and do not have to be communicated to anyone beyond the module design team.

ence in body design and metal-forming processes for cars and big appliances. And improvements in computing, of course, have dramatically decreased the cost of capturing, processing, and storing that knowledge, reducing the cost of designing and testing different modules as well. Concurrent improvements in financial markets and innovative contractual arrangements are helping small companies find resources and form alliances to try out experiments and market new products or modules. In some industries, such as telecommunications and electric utilities, deregulation is freeing companies to divide the market along modular lines.

In automobile manufacturing, the big assemblers have been moving away from the tightly centralized design system that they have relied on for much of this century. Under intense pressure to reduce costs, accelerate the pace of innovation, and improve quality, automotive designers and engineers are now looking for ways to parcel out the design of their complex electromechanical system.

The first step has been to redefine the cells in the production processes. When managers at Mercedes-Benz planned their new sport-utility assembly plant in Alabama, for example, they realized that the complexities of the vehicle would require the plant to control a network of hundreds of suppliers according to an intricate schedule and to keep substantial inventory as a buffer against unexpected developments. Instead of trying to manage the supply system directly as a whole, they structured it into a smaller set of large production modules. The entire driver's cockpit, for example—including air bags, heating and air-conditioning systems, the instrument cluster, the steering column, and the wiring harness—is a separate module produced at a nearby plant owned by Delphi Automotive Systems, a unit of General Motors Corporation. Delphi is wholly responsible for producing the cockpit module according to certain specifications and scheduling requirements, so it can form its own network of dozens of suppliers for this module. Mercedes' specifications and the scheduling information become the visible information that module suppliers use to coordinate and control the network of parts suppliers and to build the modules required for final production.

Volkswagen has taken this approach even further in its new truck factory in Resende, Brazil. The company provides the factory where all modules are built and the trucks are assembled, but the independent suppliers obtain their own materials and hire their own workforces to build the separate modules. Volkswagen does not "make" the car, in the sense of producing or assembling it. But it does establish the architecture of

the production process and the interfaces between cells, it sets the standards for quality that each supplier must meet, and it tests the modules and the trucks as they proceed from stage to stage.

So far, this shift in supplier responsibilities differs little from the numerous changes in supplychain management that many industries are going through. By delegating the manufacturing process to many separate suppliers, each one of which adds value, the assembler gains flexibility and cuts costs. That amounts to a refinement of the pattern of modularity already established in production. Eventually, though, strategists at Mercedes and other automakers expect the newly strengthened module makers to take on most of the design responsibility as well—and that is the point at which modularity will pay off the most. As modularity becomes an established way of doing business, competition among module suppliers will intensify. Assemblers will look for the best-performing or lowest cost modules, spurring these increasingly sophisticated and independent suppliers into a race for innovation similar to the one already happening with computer modules. Computer-assisted design will facilitate this new wave of experimentation.

Some automotive suppliers are already moving in that direction by consolidating their industry around particular modules. Lear Seating Corporation, Magna International, and Johnson Controls have been buying related suppliers, each attempting to become the worldwide leader in the production of entire car interiors. The big car manufacturers are indirectly encouraging this process by asking their suppliers to participate in the design of modules. Indeed, GM recently gave Magna total responsibility for overseeing development for the interior of the next-generation Cadillac Catera.

In addition to products, a wide range of services are also being modularized—most notably in the financial services industry, where the process is far along. Nothing is easier to modularize than stocks and other securities. Financial services are purely intangible, having no hard surfaces, no difficult shapes, no electrical pins or wires, and no complex computer code. Because the science of finance is sophisticated and highly developed, these services are relatively easy to define, analyze, and split apart. The design rules for financial transactions arise from centuries-old traditions of bookkeeping combined with modern legal and industry standards and the conventions of the securities exchanges.

As a result, providers need not take responsibility for all aspects of delivering their financial services. The tasks of managing a portfolio of securities, for example—selecting assets, conducting trades, keeping records, transferring ownership, reporting status and sending out statements, and performing custody services—can be readily broken apart and seamlessly performed by separate suppliers. Some major institutions have opted to specialize in one such area: Boston's State Street Bank in custody services, for example.

Other institutions, while modularizing their products, still seek to own and control those modules, as IBM tried to control the System/360. For example, Fidelity, the big, mass-market provider of money management services, has traditionally kept most aspects of its operations in-house. However, under pressure to reduce costs, it recently broke with that practice, announcing that Bankers Trust Company would manage $11 billion worth of stock index funds on its behalf. Index funds are a low-margin business whose performance is easily measured. Under the new arrangement, Bankers Trust's index-fund management services have become a hidden module in Fidelity's overall portfolio offerings, much as Volkswagen's suppliers operate as hidden modules in the Resende factory system.

The other result of the intrinsic modularity of financial instruments has been an enormous boost in innovation. By combining advanced scientific methods with high-speed computers, for example, designers can split up securities into smaller units that can then be reconfigured into derivative financial products. Such innovations have made global financial markets more fluid so that capital now flows easily even between countries with very different financial practices.

COMPETING IN A MODULAR ENVIRONMENT

Modularity does more than accelerate the pace of change or heighten competitive pressures. It also transforms relations among companies. Module designers rapidly move in and out of joint ventures, technology alliances, subcontracts, employment agreements, and financial arrangements as they compete in a relentless race to innovate. In such markets, revenue and profits are far more dispersed than they would be in traditional industries. Even such companies as Intel and Microsoft, which have substantial market power by virtue of their control over key subsets of visible information, account for less of the total market value of all computer companies than industry leaders typically do.

Being part of a shifting modular cluster of hundreds of companies in a constantly innovating industry is different from being one of a few dominant companies in a stable industry. No strategy or sequence of moves will always work; as in chess, a good move depends on the layout of the board, the pieces one controls, and the skill and resources of one's opponent. Nevertheless, the dual structure of a modular marketplace requires managers to choose carefully from two main strategies. A company can compete as an architect, creating the visible information, or design rules, for a product made up of modules. Or it can compete as a designer of modules that conform to the architecture, interfaces, and test protocols of others. Both strategies require companies to understand products at a deep level and be able to predict how modules will evolve, but they differ in a number of important ways.

For an architect, advantage comes from attracting module designers to its design rules by convincing them that this architecture will prevail in the marketplace. For the module maker, advantage comes from mastering the hidden information of the design and from superior execution in bringing its module to market. As opportunities emerge, the module maker must move quickly to fill a need and then move elsewhere or reach new levels of performance as the market becomes crowded.

Following the example of Intel and Microsoft, it is tempting to say that companies should aim to control the visible design rules by developing proprietary architectures and leave the mundane details of hidden modules to others. And it is true that the position of architect is powerful and can be very profitable. But a challenger can rely on modularity to mix and match its own capabilities with those of others and do an end-run around an architect.

That is what happened in the workstation market in the 1980s. Both of the leading companies, Apollo Computer and Sun Microsystems, relied heavily on other companies for the design and production of most of the modules that formed their workstations. But

How Palm Computing Became an Architect

In 1992, Jeff Hawkins founded Palm Computing to develop and market a handheld computing device for the consumer market. Having already created the basic software for handwriting recognition, he intended to concentrate on refining that software and developing related applications for this new market. His plan was to rely on partners for the basic architecture, hardware, operating system software, and marketing. Venture capitalists funded Palm's own development. The handwriting recognition software became the key hidden module around which a consortium of companies formed to produce the complete product.

Sales of the first generation of products from both the consortium and its rivals, however, were poor, and Palm's partners had little interest in pursuing the next generation. Convinced that capitalizing on Palm's ability to connect the device directly to a PC would unlock the potential for sales, Hawkins and his chief executive, Donna Dubinsky, decided to shift course. If they couldn't get partners to develop the new concept, they would handle it themselves—at least the visible parts, which included the device's interface protocols and its operating system. Palm would have to become an architect, taking control of both the visible information and the hidden information in the handwriting recognition module. But to do so, Hawkins and Dubinsky needed a partner with deeper pockets than any venture capital firm would provide.

None of the companies in Palm's previous consortium was willing to help. Palm spread its net as far as U.S. Robotics, the largest maker of modems. U.S. Robotics was so taken with the concept for and development of Palm's product that it bought the company. With that backing, Palm was able to take the product into full production and get the marketing muscle it needed. The result was the Pilot, or what Palm calls a Personal Connected Organizer, which has been a tremendous success in the marketplace. Palm remains in control of the operating system and the handwriting recognition software in the Pilot but relies on other designers for hardware and for links to software that runs on PCs.

Palm's strategy with the Pilot worked as Hawkins and Dubinsky had intended. In order for its architecture to be accepted by customers and outside developers, Palm had to create a compelling concept that other module makers would accept, with attractive features and pricing, and bring the device to market quickly. Hawkins's initial strategy—to be a hidden module producer while partners delivered the architecture—might have worked with a more familiar product, but the handheld-computer market was too unformed for it to work in that context. So, when the other members of the consortium balked in the second round of the design process, Palm had to take the lead role in developing both the proof of concept and a complete set of accessible design rules for the system as a whole.

We are grateful to Myra Hart for sharing with us her ongoing research on Palm. She describes the company in detail in her cases "Palm Computing, Inc. (A)," HBS case no. 396245, and "Palm Pilot 1995," HBS case, forthcoming.

Apollo's founders, who emphasized high performance in their product, designed a proprietary architecture based on their own operating and network management systems. Although some modules, such as the microprocessor, were bought off the shelf, much of the hardware was designed in-house. The various parts of the design were highly interdependent, which Apollo's designers believed was necessary to achieve high levels of performance in the final product.

Sun's founders, by contrast, emphasized low costs and rapid time to market. They relied on a simplified, nonproprietary architecture built with off-the-shelf hardware and software, including the widely available UNIX operating system. Because its module makers did not have to design special modules to fit into its system, Sun was free of the investments in software and hardware design Apollo required and could bring products to market quickly while keeping capital costs low. To make up for the performance penalty incurred by using generic modules, Sun developed two proprietary, hidden hardware modules to link the microprocessor efficiently to the workstation's internal memory.

In terms of sheer performance, observers judged Apollo's workstation to be slightly better, but Sun had the cost advantage. Sun's reliance on other module makers proved superior in other respects as well. Many end users relied on the UNIX operating system in other networks or applications and preferred a workstation that ran on UNIX rather than one that used a more proprietary operating system. Taking advantage of its edge in capital productivity, Sun opted for an aggressive strategy of rapid growth and product improvement.

Soon, Apollo found itself short of capital and its products' performance fell further and further behind Sun's. The flexibility and leanness Sun gained through its nonproprietary approach overcame the performance advantages Apollo had been enjoying through its proprietary strategy. Sun could offer customers an excellent product at an attractive price, earn superb margins, and employ much less capital in the process.

However, Sun's design gave it no enduring competitive edge. Because Sun controlled only the two hidden modules in the workstation, it could not lock its customers into its own proprietary operating system or network protocols. Sun did develop original ideas about how to combine existing modules into an effective system, but any competitor could do the same since the architecture—the visible information behind the workstation design—was easy to copy and could not be patented.

Indeed, minicomputer makers saw that workstations would threaten their business and engineering markets, and they soon offered rival products, while personal computer makers (whose designs were already extremely modular) saw an opportunity to move into a higher-margin niche. To protect itself, Sun shifted gears and sought greater control over the visible information in its own system. Sun hoped to use equity financing from AT&T, which controlled UNIX, to gain a favored role in designing future versions of the operating system. If Sun could control the evolution of UNIX, it could bring the next generation of workstations to market faster than its rivals could. But the minicomputer makers, which licensed UNIX for their existing systems, immediately saw the threat posed by the Sun-AT&T alliance, and they forced AT&T to back away from Sun. The workstation market remained wide open, and when Sun stumbled in bringing out a new generation of workstations, rivals gained ground with their own offerings. The race was on—and it continues.

NEEDED: KNOWLEDGEABLE LEADERS

Because modularity boosts the rate of innovation, it shrinks the time business leaders have to respond to competitors' moves. We may laugh about the concept of an "Internet year," but it's no joke. As more and more industries pursue modularity, their general managers, like those in the computer industry, will have to cope with higher rates of innovation and swifter change.

As a rule, managers will have to become much more attuned to all sorts of developments in the design of products, both inside and outside their own companies. It won't be enough to know what their direct competitors are doing—innovations in other modules and in the overall product architecture, as well as shifting alliances elsewhere in the industry, may spell trouble or present opportunities. Success in the marketplace will depend on mapping a much larger competitive terrain and linking one's own capabilities and options with those emerging elsewhere, possibly in companies very different from one's own.

Those capabilities and options involve not only product technologies but also financial resources and the skills of employees. Managers engaged with modular design efforts must be adept at forging new financial relationships and employment contracts, and they must enter into innovative technology ventures and alliances. Harvard Business School professor Howard Stevenson has described entrepreneurship as "the pursuit of opportunity beyond the resources currently controlled," and that's a good framework for thinking about modular leadership at even the biggest companies. (See the boxes "How Palm Computing Became an Architect" and "How Quantum Mines Hidden Knowledge.")

At the same time that modularity boosts the rate of innovation, it also heightens the degree of uncertainty in the design process. There is no way for managers to know which of many experimental approaches will win out in the marketplace. To prepare for sudden and

How Quantum Mines Hidden Knowledge

Quantum Corporation began in 1980 as a maker of 8-inch disk storage drives for the minicomputer market. After the company fell behind as the industry shifted to 5.25-inch drives, a team led by Stephen M. Berkley and Dave Brown rescued it with an aggressive strategy, applying their storage expertise to developing a 3.5-inch add-on drive for the personal computer market. The product worked, but competing in this sector required higher volumes and tighter tolerances than Quantum was used to. Instead of trying to meet those demands internally, Berkley and Brown decided to keep the company focused on technology and to form an alliance with Matsushita-Kotobuki Electronics Industries (MKE), a division of the Matsushita Group, to handle the high-volume, high-precision manufacturing. With the new alliance in place, Quantum and MKE worked to develop tightly integrated design capabilities that spanned the two companies. The products resulting from those processes allowed Quantum to compete successfully in the market for drives installed as original equipment in personal computers.

Quantum has maintained a high rate of product innovation by exploiting modularity in the design of its own products and in its own organization. Separate, small teams work on the design and the production of each submodule, and the company's leaders have developed an unusually clear operating framework within which to coordinate the efforts of the teams while still freeing them to innovate effectively.

In addition to focusing on technology, the company has survived in the intensely competitive disk-drive industry by paying close attention to the companies that assemble personal computers. Quantum has become the preferred supplier for many of the assemblers because its careful attention to developments in the visible information for disk drives has enabled its drives to fit seamlessly into the assemblers' systems. Quantum's general managers have a deep reservoir of knowledge about both storage technology and the players in the sector, which helps them map the landscape, anticipating which segments of the computer market are set to go into decline and where emerging opportunities will arise. Early on, they saw the implications of the Internet and corporate intranets, and with help from a timely purchase of Digital Equipment Corporation's stagnating storage business, they had a head start in meeting the voracious demand for storage capacity that has been created by burgeoning networks. Despite what some observers might see as a weak position (because the company must depend on the visible information that other companies give out) Quantum has prospered, recently reporting strong profits and gains in stock price.

We are grateful to Steven Wheelwright and Clayton Christensen for sharing with us their ongoing research on Quantum. They describe the company in more detail in their case "Quantum Corp.: Business and Product Teams" HBS case no. 692023.

dramatic changes in markets, therefore, managers need to be able to choose from an often complex array of technologies, skills, and financial options. Creating, watching, and nurturing a portfolio of such options will become more important than the pursuit of static efficiency per se.

To compete in a world of modularity, leaders must also redesign their internal organizations. In order to create superior modules, they need the flexibility to move quickly to market and make use of rapidly changing technologies, but they must also ensure that the modules conform to the architecture. The answer to this dilemma is modularity within the organization.

Just as modularity in design boosts innovation in products by freeing designers to experiment, so managers can speed up development cycles for individual modules by splitting the work among independent teams, each pursuing a different submodule or different path to improvement.

Employing a modular approach to design complicates the task of managers who want to stabilize the manufacturing process or control inventories because it expands the range of possible product varieties. But the approach also allows engineers to create families of parts that share common characteristics and thus can all be made in the same way, using, for example, changes in machine settings that are well understood. Moreover, the growing power of information technology is giving managers more precise and timely information about sales and distribution channels, thus enhancing the efficiency of a modular production system.

For those organizational processes to succeed, however, the output of the various decentralized teams (including the designers at partner companies) must be tightly integrated. As with a product, the key to integration in the organization is the visible information. This is where leadership is critical. Despite what many observers of leadership are now saying, the heads of these companies must do more than provide a vision or goals for the decentralized development teams. They must also delineate and communicate a detailed operating framework within which each of the teams must work.

Such a framework begins by articulating the strategy and plans for the product line's evolution into which the work of the development teams needs to fit over time. But the framework also has to extend into the work of the teams themselves. It must, for example, establish principles for matching appropriate types of teams to each type of project. It must specify the size of the teams and make clear what roles senior management, the core design team, and support groups should play in carrying out the project's work. Finally, the framework must define processes by which progress will be measured and products released to the market. The framework may also address values that should guide the teams in their work (such as leading by example). Like the visible information in a modular product, this organizational framework establishes an overall structure within which teams can operate, provides ways for different teams and other groups to interact, and defines standards for testing the merit of the teams' work. Without careful direction, the teams would find it easy to pursue initiatives that may have individual merit but stray from the company's defining concepts.

Just like a modular product that lacks good interfaces between modules, an organization built around decentralized teams that fail to function according to a clear and effective framework will suffer from miscues and delays. Fast changing and dynamic markets—like those for computers—are unforgiving. The well-publicized problems of many computer companies have often been rooted in inadequate coordination of their development teams as they created new products.

Less obvious, but equally important, are the problems that arise when teams fail to communicate the hidden information—the knowledge they develop about module technology—with the rest of the organization. That lack of communication, we have found, causes organizations to commit the same costly mistakes over and over again.

To take full advantage of modularity, companies need highly skilled, independent-minded employees eager to innovate. These designers and engineers do not respond to tight controls; many reject traditional forms of management and will seek employment elsewhere rather than submit to them. Such employees do, however, respond to informed leadership—to managers who can make reasoned arguments that will persuade employees to hold fast to the central operating framework. Managers must learn how to allow members of the organization the independence to probe and experiment while directing them to stay on the right overall course. The best analogy may be in biology, where complex organisms have been able to evolve into an astonishing variety of forms only by obeying immutable rules of development.

A century ago, the railroads showed managers how to control enormous organizations and masses of capital. In the world fashioned by computers, managers will control less and will need to know more. As modularity drives the evolution of much of the economy, general managers' greatest challenge will be to gain an intimate understanding of the knowledge behind their products. Technology can't be a black box to them because their ability to position the company, respond to market changes, and guide internal innovation depends on this knowledge. Leaders cannot manage knowledge at a distance merely by hiring knowledgeable people and giving them adequate resources. They need to be closely involved in shaping and directing the way knowledge is created and used. Details about the inner workings of products may seem to be merely technical engineering matters, but in the context of intense competition and fast changing technology, the success of whole strategies may hinge on such seemingly minor details.

NOTE

1. Practical knowledge of modularity has come largely from the computer industry. The term *architecture* was first used in connection with computers by the de-

signers of the System/360: Gene M. Amdahl, Gerrit A. Blaauw, and Frederick P. Brooks, Jr., in "Architecture of the IBM System/360," *IBM Journal of Research and Development,* April 1964, p. 86. The scientific field of computer architecture was established by C. Gordon Bell and Allen Newell in *Computer Structures: Readings and Examples* (New York: McGraw-Hill, 1971). The principle of *information hiding* was first put forward in 1972 by David L. Parnas in "A Technique for Software Module Specification with Examples," *Communications of the ACM,* May 1972, p. 330. The term *design rules* was first used by Carver Mead and Lynn Conway in *Introduction to VLSI Systems* (Reading, Massachusetts: Addison-Wesley, 1980). Sun's architectural innovations, described in the text, were based on the work of John L. Hennessy and David A. Patterson, later summarized in their text *Computer Architecture: A Quantitative Approach* (San Mateo, California: Morgan Kaufman Publishers, 1990).

REFERENCES

For more information on modular product design, see Steven D. Eppinger, Daniel E. Whitney, Robert P. Smith, and David Gebala, "A Model-Based Method for Organizing Tasks in Product Development," *Research in Engineering Design 6,* 1994. For more about modular processes, see James L. Nevins and Daniel E. Whitney, *Concurrent Design of Products and Processes* (New York: McGraw-Hill, 1989). For more information on the design of financial securities and the global financial system, see Robert C. Merton and Zvi Bodie, "A Conceptual Framework for Analyzing the Financial Environment" and "Financial Infrastructure and Public Policy: A Functional Perspective," in *The Global Financial System: A Functional Perspective,* (Boston, Massachusetts: Harvard Business School Press, 1995).

For descriptions of how companies compete in industries using modular products, see Richard N. Langlois and Paul L. Robertson, "Networks and Innovation in a Modular System: Lessons from the Microcomputer and Stereo Component Industries," *Research Policy.* August 1992, Charles R. Morris and Charles H. Ferguson, "How Architecture Wins Technology Wars," HBR March–April 1993, Raghu Garud and Arun Kumaraswamy, "Changing Competitive Dynamics in Network Industries: An Exploration of Sun Microsystems' Open Systems Strategy," *Strategic Management Journal,* July 1993, p. 351, and Clayton M. Christensen and Richard S. Rosenbloom, "Explaining the Attacker's Advantage: Technological Paradigms, Organizational Dynamics, and the Value Network," *Research Policy,* March 1995, p. 233.

12

Nobody Ever Gets Credit for Fixing Problems That Never Happened

Creating and Sustaining Process Improvement

NELSON P. REPENNING
JOHN D. STERMAN

How much would your organization pay to develop manufacturing capability equal to Toyota's? How much would a world-class, six-sigma quality program be worth to your company? How about Harley-Davidson's ability to tap into the hearts and minds of its customers or Dell's ability to manage its supply chain? Most firms are working aggressively to develop these and similar capabilities through process improvement. The combined expenditure of U.S. companies on management consultants and training in 1997 was over $100 billion, and a sizable fraction went toward efforts to develop operational capabilities matching those of the best firms in business. Whether it's an advanced manufacturing system or the ability to respond quickly to changing customer needs, the drive toward improvement has become a way of life in corporations today. There is only one problem. Despite these vast expenditures, and notwithstanding dramatic successes in a few companies, few efforts to implement such programs actually produce significant results.

Consider, for example, Total Quality Management (TQM). In the 1980s, spurred by the success of many Japanese firms, TQM was all the rage among U.S. firms. Consultants and business school faculty preached its virtues and managers made pilgrimages to companies with award-winning quality programs. By the mid-1990s, however, TQM was considered passé. Academics had moved on to other issues, TQM received rare mention in the popular business press, and articles that did mention it usually did so in a negative context. TQM had all the earmarks of a management fad: An initial burst of enthusiasm, a flurry of activity, and then a steady decline as it was replaced by newer innovations such as re-engineering. It would be easy to conclude that TQM's underlying value was minimal.

However, when one looks at the experience a little more carefully, a different picture emerges. A number of careful studies have now demonstrated that companies making a serious commitment to the disciplines and methods associated with TQM outperform their competitors.[1] There is now little doubt that when used properly, TQM produces significant value to both organizations and their customers. Yet paradoxically, it remains little used. A recent study found that fewer than 10% of the *Fortune 1000* had well-developed TQM programs; and, in another study, TQM fell from the third most commonly used business tool in 1993 to 14th in 1999.[2] The situation is similar for a wide range of other administrative and technological innovations.[3] Techniques touted as today's "core competencies" all

Copyright © 2001 by The Regents of the University of California. Reprinted from the *California Management Review*, Vol. 43, No. 4. By permission of The Regents.

too often become tomorrow's failed programs. Once an effort has failed, there is an almost irresistible temptation to label it a fad or "flavor of the month." However, digging a little deeper shows that many such techniques have useful content. It should come as little surprise then that many currently popular innovations are little more than old ideas with new acronyms. The core disciplines associated with statistical process control and variance reduction become six-sigma; what was once called a quality circle is now a high-performance work team.

Thus, today's managers face a paradox. On the one hand, the number of tools and techniques available to improve performance is growing rapidly. Further, with advances in information technology and the ever-growing legions of management consultants, it is easier than ever to learn about these techniques and to learn who else is using them. On the other hand, there has been little improvement in the ability of organizations to incorporate these innovations in their everyday activities. The ability to *identify* and *learn about* new improvement methods no longer presents a significant barrier to most managers. Instead, successfully *implementing* these innovations presents the biggest challenge. Put more simply, you can't *buy* a turnkey six-sigma quality program. It must be developed from within.

To learn how firms can overcome this "improvement paradox," we have, over the past decade, studied process improvement and learning programs, focusing on the dynamics of implementation and organizational change. We conducted over a dozen in-depth case studies in industries including telecommunications, semiconductors, chemicals, oil, automobiles, and recreational products.[4] We gathered data through observations, extensive interviews with participants, archival records, and quantitative metrics. We complemented our field research with the development of a series of models capturing the dynamics of implementation and improvement.[5] Using system dynamics as the basis for understanding implementation has yielded a number of insights into the improvement paradox. In at least some cases, these insights have proven instrumental in helping firms benefit from the potential provided by available improvement tools and techniques.

Most importantly, our research suggests that the inability of most organizations to reap the full benefit of these innovations has little to do with the specific improvement tool they select. Instead, the problem has its roots in how the introduction of a new improvement program interacts with the physical, economic, social, and psychological structures in which implementation takes place. In other words, it's not just a tool problem, any more than it's a human resources problem or a leadership problem. Instead it is a systemic problem, one that is created by the interaction of tools, equipment, workers, and managers.

THE STRUCTURE OF IMPROVEMENT

We present the lessons that have emerged from our study in the form of a causal loop diagram. Our model provides both a useful framework for thinking about the challenges associated with implementing improvement programs and practical suggestions to increase the chances that your next such effort will succeed. While the theory reported here initially emerged from the study of two improvement initiatives in a major automaker,[6] the resulting model is quite general and can be applied to a range of situations. We have observed these dynamics in almost every organization we have studied.

Figure 12.1 begins with the basic "physics" underlying process improvement. The actual performance of any process depends on two factors: the amount of *Time Spent Working* and the *Capability* of the process used to do that work. For example, in manufacturing, net usable output is given by the product of labor hours per day and productivity (usable units per labor hour).

The performance of any process can be increased by dedicating additional effort to either work or improvement. However, the two activities do not produce equivalent results. Time spent on improving the capability of a process typically yields the more enduring change. For example, boosting the workweek 20% might increase output 20%, but only for the duration of the overtime. Gains in process capability, however, boost the output generated by every subsequent hour of effort. Similarly, overtime devoted to reworking defective products can boost net usable output, but only as long as the overtime is continued, while eliminating the root causes of those defects permanently reduces the need for rework. We capture this persistence by representing *Capability* as a stock (denoted by a rec-

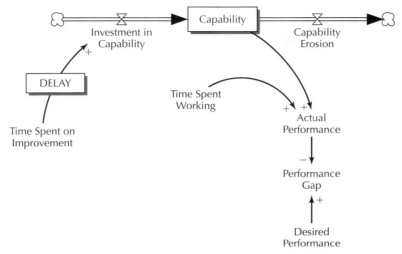

Figure 12.1. The "Physics" of improvement. Arrows indicate the direction of causality. Signs ("+" or "–") at arrowheads indicate the polarity of relationships: a "+" means that an increase in the independent variable causes the dependent variable to increase, all else being equal (a decrease causes a decrease); similarly, a "–" indicates that an increase in the independent variable causes the dependent variable to decrease (a decrease causes an increase). For more details, see J. Sterman, *Business Dynamics: Systems Thinking and Modeling for a Complex World* (New York: Irwin/McGraw-Hill, 2000).

tangle), that is, as an asset that accumulates improvements over time. Specifically, *Time Spent on Improvement* increases the flow of *Investments in Capability* that augments process capability.

While it often yields the more permanent gain, time spent on improvement does not immediately improve performance. It takes time to uncover the root causes of process problems and then to discover, test, and implement solutions, shown in the diagram as a delay between improvement activities and the resulting change in process capability. Moreover, no improvement in capability lasts forever. Machines wear, processes go out of control without regular attention, designs become obsolete, and procedures become outdated. Thus, we also show an outflow from the stock capturing the inevitable decline of any capability that is not regularly maintained. The lag in enhancing capability depends on the technical and organizational complexity of the process. Studies show that the delay in improving relatively simple processes such as the yield of machines in a job shop is on the order of a few

months, while the delay in improving highly complex processes such as product development can be several years or more.[7] Similarly, the lifetime of improvements in capability will be shorter in organizations with high rates of change in products and people.

Besides the physical and institutional structures that determine performance, Figure 12.1 also shows the goal for process throughput set by senior managers (labeled *Desired Performance*). The goal could be the number of products demanded by customers each day, the rate at which claims need to be processed by an insurance company, or the number of new products the firm seeks to launch this quarter. People compare that goal to their actual performance to determine the *Performance Gap*. Not surprisingly, in the organizations we studied it was rare to find a process performing above expectations. Instead, managers, workers, and engineers usually faced high and rising demands, sometimes despite downsizing and cuts in resources. They were constantly searching for ways to improve and close the performance gap. Since most organizations are reluctant to increase plant and equipment or hire more staff, managers hoping to close a performance gap have only two basic options.

First, they can try to increase the amount of time people actually spend working. Figure 12.2 shows this option, which forms a *balancing* feedback, the *Work Harder* loop B1. The process represented by this loop works as follows: Managers facing a performance gap are under pressure to increase performance. They pressure people to spend more time and energy doing work. An increase in the time spent working increases the performance of the process and closes the performance gap. This structure is called a balancing feedback loop because it constantly works to balance desired and actual performance.

Pressure to Do Work includes, most obviously, direct measures such as telling people to work faster or put in overtime, setting more aggressive targets for throughput, and imposing more severe penalties for missing those targets. Pressure also includes more subtle actions designed to extract greater effort from employees. These include the frequency with which performance is reviewed, the detail with which the reviews are conducted, and the seniority of those doing the reviewing. At one company we studied, it was not unusual for senior vice-presidents to review the performance of individual machines on the factory floor. Not

surprisingly, such attention sent a strong message to all involved: keep the machines busy at all costs. Similarly, a project manager we interviewed recalled that when a subsystem for which he was responsible fell behind schedule, his boss required him to call in every *hour* with a status report until the prototype met its specifications.

A second option to close a performance gap is to improve the capability of the process. In Figure 12.3 we represent this option as another balancing feedback process, the *Work Smarter* loop B2. Here, managers respond to a performance shortfall by increasing the pressure on people to improve capability. They may launch improvement programs, encourage people to experiment with new ideas, and invest in training. If successful, these investments will, with time, yield improvements in process capability, boost throughput, and close the performance gap. Of course, everyone knows that it is better to work smarter than to work harder: An hour spent working produces an extra hour's worth of output, while an hour spent on improvement may improve the productivity of every subsequent hour dedicated to production. Yet, despite its obvious and documented benefits, working smarter does have limitations. First, as shown in the diagram, there is often a substantial delay between investing in improvement activities and reaping the benefits. Further, the

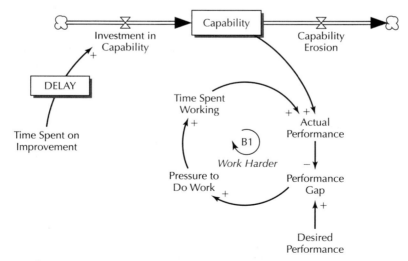

Figure 12.2. The *Work Harder* balancing loop. The loop identifier, B1, indicates a negative (balancing) feedback. See J. Sterman, op. cit.

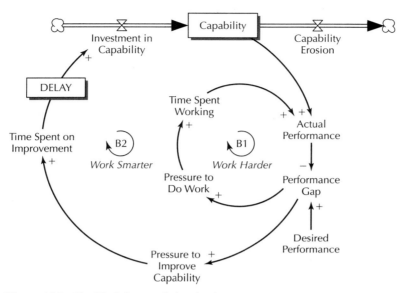

Figure 12.3. The *Work Smarter* balancing loop.

greater the complexity of the process, the longer it takes to improve.[8] Second, investments in capability can be risky. Improvement efforts don't always find the root cause of defects, new tools sometimes don't produce the desired gains, and experiments often fail. While investments in capability might eventually yield large and enduring improvements in productivity, they do little to solve the problems managers face *right now.*

Thus, it is not surprising that managers frequently use the *Work Harder* loop to both accommodate variations in daily workload and solve pressing problems created by unexpected breakdowns or defects. When a manufacturing line serving an important customer goes down, a manager is unlikely to react by sending the work team to training in reliability improvement. Instead, that manager is going to get the line running and push for overtime until the shipment is out the door. Of course when the line is back running and the product has been shipped, the manager should return attention to the improvement activities that will prevent future breakdowns, and make up for the improvement time that was lost during the crunch. However, it doesn't usually happen. Instead, what we repeatedly observe, and what is more difficult to understand, are organizations in which working harder is not merely a means to deal with isolated incidents, but is instead standard op-

erating procedure. Rather than using the *Work Harder* loop to occasionally offset daily variations in workload, managers, supervisors, and workers all come to rely constantly on working harder to hit their targets and, consequently, never find the time to invest in improvement activities. What starts as a temporary emphasis on working harder quickly becomes routine.

The Reinvestment Loop

To understand why, it is helpful to consider how working smarter and working harder are connected. The most important interconnection arises because organizations rarely have excess resources. Increasing the pressure to do work leads people to spend less time on non-work-related activities like breaks and to put in overtime (that is, they use the *Work Harder* loop). For knowledge workers such overtime is often unpaid and spills into nights and weekends, stealing time from family and community activities. There are, however, obvious limits to long hours. After a while there is simply no more time. If the performance gap continues to rise, workers have no choice but to reduce the time they spend on improvement as they strive to meet their ever-increasing objectives. Figure 12.4 adds the connection between pressure to do work and the amount of time spent on improvement.

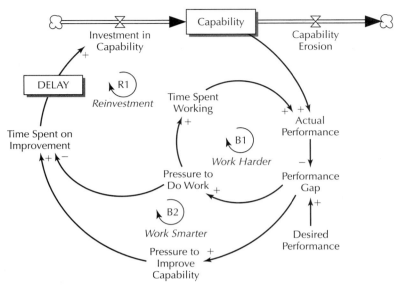

Figure 12.4. The *Reinvestment* reinforcing loop. The loop identifier, R1, indicates a positive (reinforcing) feedback. See J. Sterman, op. cit.

The additional link creates the *Reinvestment* loop. Unlike those described so far, the *Reinvestment* loop is a positive feedback that tends to reinforce whichever behavior currently dominates. An organization that successfully improves its process capability will experience rising performance. As the performance gap falls, workers have even more time to devote to improvement, creating a virtuous cycle of improved capability and increasing attention to improvement. Conversely, if managers respond to a throughput gap by increasing work pressure, employees increase the amount of time spent working and cut the time spent on improvement. Capability begins to decay. As capability erodes, the performance gap grows still more, forcing a further shift towards working harder and away from improvement. Here the reinvestment loop operates as a vicious cycle, driving the organization to ever-higher degrees of work pressure and minimal levels of process capability. Not surprisingly, such a vicious cycle quickly drives out meaningful improvement activity. Here, for example, is the way a manager in an electronics assembly plant explained the persistent failure of the organization to engage in process improvement:

Supervisors never had time to make improvements or do preventative maintenance on their lines . . .

they had to spend all their time just trying to keep the line going, but this meant it was always in a state of flux, which, in turn, caused them to want to hold lots of protective inventory, because everything was so unpredictable. A quality problem might not be discovered until we had produced a pile of defective parts. This of course meant we didn't have time to figure out why the problem happened in the first place, since we were now really behind our production schedule. It was a kind of snowball effect that just kept getting worse.

Shortcuts and the Capability Trap

The *Reinvestment* loop means a temporary emphasis on one option at the expense of the other is likely to be reinforced and eventually become permanent. Organizations that invest in improvement will experience increasing capability and find that they have more time to allocate to working smarter and less need for heroic efforts to solve problems by working harder. In the successful initiatives we studied, leadership often worked to strengthen the reinvestment process by explicitly allocating the resources freed up by productivity gains to further improvement. Unfortunately, however, these initiatives were the exception rather than the rule. In most of the organizations in our study the

Reinvestment loop worked as a vicious cycle and prevented improvement programs from getting off the ground. Even when improvement programs yielded initial results, cost and schedule pressures soon tempted many organizations into downsizing or higher performance goals that drained resources away from improvement, weakening the *Reinvestment* loop and causing capability to stall or even fall.[9]

Understanding why the *Reinvestment* loop typically worked in the downward, vicious direction rather than the upward, virtuous direction requires that we add a final link to the model (see Figure 12.5). As discussed above, cutting investments in maintenance and improvement in favor of working harder erodes process capability and hurts performance. However, capability does not drop right away. It takes time for process integrity to depreciate. In the meantime, the decision to skimp on improvement—skipping improvement team meetings, neglecting to take machines down for scheduled maintenance, or ignoring documentation requirements—boosts the time available to get work done right now. We capture this interconnection by adding a negative link between *Time Spent on Improvement* and *Time Spent Working*. When the performance gap rises and managers resort to increased work pressure, overworked people cut back improvement activity to free still more time for production.

The performance gap falls, closing a third feedback that works to balance desired and actual performance. We label this the *Shortcuts* loop (B3) to capture the idea that increased throughput comes at the cost of departing from standard routines and processes, cutting corners, and reducing the time spent on learning and improvement.

Shortcuts are tempting because there is often a substantial delay between cutting corners and the consequent decline in capability. For example, supervisors who defer preventive maintenance often experience a "grace period" in which they reap the benefits of increased output (by avoiding scheduled downtime) and save on maintenance costs. Only later, as equipment ages and wears do they begin to experience lower yields and lower uptimes (see section 4). Similarly, a software engineer who forgoes documentation in favor of completing a project on time incurs few immediate costs; only later, when she returns to fix bugs discovered in testing does she feel the full impact of a decision made weeks or months earlier.[10] Thus, the *Shortcuts* loop is effective in closing the throughput gap only because capability does not change immediately when the time dedicated to learning and improvement declines.

To illustrate these dynamics, Figure 12.6 shows two simulations of the model in which we show how a

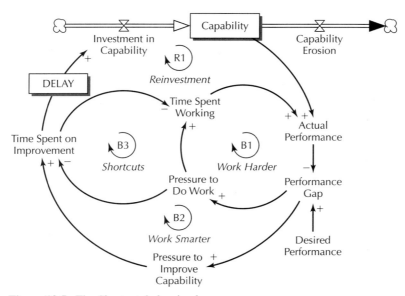

Figure 12.5. The *Shortcuts* balancing loop.

SYSTEM RESPONSE TO

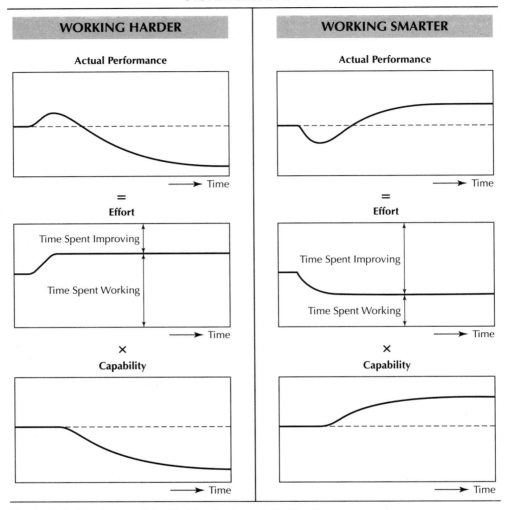

Figure 12.6. Simulations of the *Working Harder* and *Working Smarter* strategies.

hypothetical process reacts to working harder versus working smarter. Both simulations begin in the same equilibrium state. The first simulation shows the response to an increased emphasis on working harder. As more effort is dedicated to work, gross throughput immediately rises. Time spent improving falls immediately, but capability does not. Performance therefore rises. The benefit of working harder is, however, short-lived. With less time devoted to improvement, capability gradually erodes, eventually more than offsetting the increased time spent working. Working harder creates a

"better-before-worse" situation. Conversely, as seen in the second simulation, increasing the time spent on improvement reduces output in the short run. Eventually, however, capability rises more than enough to offset the drop in work effort and performance is permanently higher, a "worse-before-better" dynamic.

The interaction between the balancing *Shortcuts* loop and the reinforcing *Reinvestment* loop creates a phenomenon we call the *Capability Trap* and helps explain why organizations often find themselves stuck in a vicious cycle of declining capability. Managers and workers in need of an immediate performance boost can get it by skimping on improvement and maintenance. However, capability eventually declines, causing the *Reinvestment* loop to work as a vicious cycle. Managers who rely on working harder and shortcuts to meet immediate throughput needs soon find the process falling short of its objectives, requiring a further shift toward working harder and away from improvement. To see the *Capability Trap* in action, consider how a manufacturing supervisor in an auto company explained the inability of her organization to make a commitment to regular improvement activities:

> In the minds of the [operations team leaders] they had to hit their pack counts. This meant if you were having a bad day and your yield had fallen . . . you had to run like crazy to hit your target. You could say, "you are making 20% garbage, stop the line and fix the problem," and they would say, "I can't hit my pack count without running like crazy." They could never get ahead of the game.

By keeping the line going rather than stopping to fix the problem, these team leaders relied on the *Shortcuts* loop to hit their throughput objectives. However, by "running like crazy" they also caused the *Reinvestment* loop to operate as a vicious cycle, driving the line to a minimal level of capability and forcing them to run ever faster.

The *Capability Trap* is not limited to manufacturing—we have observed it in firms ranging from financial services to construction. For example, the *Capability Trap* prevented a product development organization we studied from developing new processes that would have increased productivity. Like many firms, they sought to create an engineering library or "bookshelf" of reusable designs and software. However, as described by an engineering manager,

> An engineer might not take the time to document her steps or put the results of a simulation on the bookshelf and because of that she saved engineering time and did her project more efficiently. But in the long run it prevented us from being able to deploy the reusability concepts that we were looking for.

Just as machine operators and supervisors in the first example faced a basic trade-off between producing and improving, development engineers were forced to trade off getting their assigned tasks done against documenting what they learned so that others might benefit. Engineers could make more rapid progress toward their objectives by taking shortcuts and ignoring the bookshelf, but doing so prevented them from initiating the self-reinforcing *Reinvestment* loop that would have led to improved process capability.

THE PERSISTENCE OF THE CAPABILITY TRAP

Because working harder and taking shortcuts produce more immediate gains and help solve today's problems, managers unaware of the inherent "better-before-worse" trade-off are likely to choose them over working smarter. Unfortunately, these temporary gains come at the expense of the long-run health of the process. By pressuring people to work harder, managers often unwittingly force their organizations into the *Capability Trap* where ever-increasing levels of effort are required to maintain performance. Of course, this phenomenon is not limited to large organizations. Many readers will recognize this dynamic in different aspects of their personal lives. In situations ranging from learning how to use a new software package to committing to a new exercise program, we often fail to do the things that will improve our long-run productivity and well-being due to the short-run stresses of other obligations.

A question naturally arising at this point is: "Wouldn't managers eventually figure this out?" While it is understandable that, on occasion, people get caught in the *Capability Trap,* wouldn't they eventually realize the true source of their problems and rebalance their efforts between working harder and working smarter? Unfortunately, the data suggest that overcoming the *Capability Trap* is rare. Managers often do not realize how deeply they are trapped in it. Instead, the lessons that people learn when caught in the *Capability Trap* often lead to actions that make the situation worse.

Faulty Attributions

Suppose you are a manager faced with inadequate performance. Your operation is not meeting its objectives and you have to do something about it. As we have outlined so far, you have two basic choices: get people to work harder or get them to work smarter. To decide, you have to make a judgment about the cause of the low performance. If you believe the system is under-performing due to low capability, then you should focus on working smarter. If, on the other hand, you think that your workers or engineers are a little lazy, undisciplined, or just shirking, you need to get them to work harder.

How do you decide? Research suggests that people generally assume that cause and effect are closely related in time and space: To explain a puzzling event, we look for another recent, nearby event that might have triggered it. People also tend to assume each event has a single cause, underestimate time delays, and fail to account for feedback processes. How do these causal attributions play out in a work setting? Consider a manager observing a machine operator who is producing an unusually high number of defects. The manager is likely to assume that the worker is at fault: The worker is close in space and time to the production of defects, and other operators have lower defect rates. The true cause, however, may be distant in space and time from the defects it creates. Perhaps the defect is actually the result of an inadequate maintenance procedure or the poor quality of the training program. In this case, the delay between the true cause and the defective output is long, variable, and often unobservable. As a result, managers are likely to conclude that the cause of low throughput is inadequate worker effort or insufficient discipline, rather than features of the process. The attribution of a problem to the characteristics—and character flaws—of individuals in a system rather than to the system in which they find themselves is so pervasive that psychologists call it the "fundamental attribution error."[11]

Suppose managers conclude that people, not the process, are the source of low performance. Having made such an attribution it makes sense to increase production pressure. As discussed above, an increase in production pressure has two effects. Worker effort immediately rises, closing the performance gap as the manager intended. However, workers are now less able to achieve their objectives by increasing the time they spend working. To continue to hit their ever-increasing targets, they eventually resort to shortcuts, cutting the time spent on improvement. However, as highlighted above, the *Shortcuts* loop, while having the desired effect in the short run, yields a long-run side effect. With less effort dedicated to improvement, capability begins

to decline. Performance falls, offsetting the initial gains. By continually increasing throughput objectives in the pursuit of better performance, managers who mistakenly attribute low performance to the attitudes and dispositions of their workforce inadvertently force the system into the *Capability Trap*.

Superstitious Learning

The bias toward blaming people rather than the system in which those people are embedded means managers are prone to push their organizations into the *Capability Trap*. As workers spend more and more of their time on throughput and cut back on fundamental improvement, shouldn't managers realize that the true cause of sub-standard performance is low process capability rather than unmotivated workers? Unfortunately, in many situations managers learn the opposite lesson.

Managers cannot observe all the activities of the workers. Hence, after they apply production pressure, they cannot easily determine how much of the resulting rise in throughput is due to increased work effort (the *Work Harder* loop) and how much to cutting back on training, improvement, or maintenance (the *Shortcuts* loop). For example, suppose there is a performance gap requiring an additional six hours of productive effort per person per week. Managers, believing employees are simply not working hard enough, increase production pressure. Workers buckle down, cutting back on breaks, web-surfing, and other nonproductive time. Suppose these responses yield only two hours per person per week. To close the remaining throughput gap, workers resort to shortcuts and gradually reduce the time they spend on process improvement, training, and experimentation until they free the needed four hours per week. Managers observe that throughput rises by the equivalent of six hours of productive effort.

Because managers do not fully observe the reduction in training, experimentation, and improvement effort (they fail to account for the *Shortcuts* loop), they overestimate the impact of their get-tough policy, in our example by as much as a factor of three. The feedback managers receive does not correct the error. To the contrary, managers quickly learn that boosting production pressure *works*—throughput rose when they turned up the pressure. The gains resulting from production pressure provide powerful evidence confirming their suspicions that workers were not giving their full effort.

We call this syndrome the *Self-Confirming Attribution Error:* Once managers decide that the workforce is the source of their difficulties, they take actions that provide convincing and immediate evidence confirming this erroneous attribution. The cycle of self-confirming attributions drives the organization to higher levels of production pressure and fewer resources dedicated to process improvement. Far more importantly, however, it gradually changes the mental models of the managers by providing them with increasingly compelling evidence that the source of low throughput can be found in the poor attitudes and weak character of the workforce. Recall the project manager discussed above who was required to provide hourly status reports on a balky prototype. Soon afterward the problem was solved, confirming the boss's belief that he had acted appropriately, indeed had decisively taken charge of the situation, even though the team was already working around the clock and his interference drained precious time from their efforts to solve the problem.

More subtly, the long-run effects of production pressure also reinforce managers' belief that workers are the problem. The delay between increased production pressure and increased throughput (via the *Work Harder* and *Shortcuts* loops) is short, and the connection between work effort and output is unambiguous. In contrast, the erosion of process capability caused by production pressure is delayed, gradual, and diffuse. It is distant in time and space from its cause. Managers are unlikely to attribute the cause of a throughput gap to the pressure they placed on workers months or even years before. Instead, they are likely to conclude that the workers have once again slacked off, requiring another increase in production pressure.

Workers often unwittingly conspire in strengthening the managers' attributions. Faced with intense production pressure, people are naturally reluctant to tell supervisors they can't meet all their objectives. The more effectively workers cover up the shortcuts they take to meet their throughput targets, the less aware managers will be of the long-run costs of production pressure. Unaware that improvement activity, maintenance, and problem solving have been cut, throughput appears to rise without requiring any sacrifices, reinforcing management's attribution that the workers really were not working hard enough. When managers

eventually discover these shortcuts, their view of workers as untrustworthy is confirmed. Managers are then, as they see it, *forced* to monitor worker effort even more closely (e.g., more frequent status reports, stiffer penalties for missing targets, software for monitoring key-stroke rates of data entry operators). What starts as an erroneous attribution about the skills, effort, and character of the workers becomes true. Managers' worst fears are realized as a consequence of their own actions.

Consistent with our theory, we are not attributing these dynamics to unskilled, inexperienced, or ill-intentioned managers. Rather, the structure of the system inadvertently leads even many talented and dedicated managers into the *Capability Trap,* while at the same time providing compelling evidence that the sources of their difficulties lie in factors beyond their control, such as lazy workers, a "difficult" union, faulty machinery, or fickle customers. Managers are unlikely to escape the *Capability Trap* because they rarely realize they are in it. Instead, as capability stagnates despite repeated attempts at improvement, they slowly, perhaps reluctantly, but with increasing conviction, come to believe that their problems lie in the attitudes and character of the people that work for them. Having made such an attribution, the actions they take, while rational from their perspective, make the situation worse.

How Superstitious Learning Thwarts Improvement Programs

What happens when an organization stuck in the *Capability Trap* attempts to implement an improvement program? Performance is low and work pressure intense. In such environments, improvement programs add to the workload—the organization is so far behind that it cannot afford to cut back throughput. Indeed, in many organizations, management imposes aggressive stretch objectives for both throughput and improvement in the belief that aggressive goals are needed to shake things up and motivate people. In one firm we studied, the general manager laid out his goals for improving the product development process by saying:

> We need a development process that is fast, is the best in the industry, and it needs to increase throughput by 50% in two years. And everyone must adhere to the same process.

At the same time, they launched many new development projects in anticipation of the expected productivity gains. Viewed through the lens of management's mental model these decisions were entirely rational. However, that mental model, conditioned by the self-confirming attribution error dynamics discussed above, led them to the erroneous belief that the delay between improvement effort and results was short and that their engineers were underutilized, undisciplined, unmotivated, and unwilling to adhere to the specified process.

The company spent millions and invested countless person-hours to create a new product development process. The new process included better technical tools, such as improved CAD/CAE/CAM systems, but also increased monitoring, including a structured stage-gate review process and mandated use of project management software. While there were some pockets of success, in most cases the effort had little impact. The leaders of the change effort often attributed its failure to the engineers' lack of discipline:

> Engineers—by trade, definition, and training—want to forever tweak things. It's a Wild West culture. (Manager A)

> We went through a period where we had so little discipline that we really had the "process du jour." Get the job done and how you did it was up to you. (Manager B)

> A lot of the engineers felt that [the new process] was no value-add and that they should have spent all their time doing engineering and not filling out project worksheets. It's brushed off as bureaucratic. (Manager A)

> It was fair to say that a lot of engineers viewed this as a neat way to get some fancy tools and to hell with process. (Manager C)

Yet, when we asked engineers why the effort failed, we got a different story:

> We never had time to take the courses and get the equipment we needed to really make this stuff work. . . . It was really exhausting trying to learn how to use the tools and do the design at the same time. (Engineer A)

> People had to do their normal work as well as [use the new project management system]. There just

weren't enough hours in the day, and the work wasn't going to wait. (Engineer B)

> Under this system . . . the new workload was all increase. . . . In some cases your workload could have doubled. (Engineer C)

> How did we catch up? We stayed late. Most of the team was working from 7:00 A.M. to 8:00 P.M. and on weekends. A lot of people worked right through the Christmas vacation. (Engineer D)

> The new process is a good one. Someday I'd like to work on a project that actually uses it. (Engineer E)

While managers felt the engineers had little interest in following the process, engineers became increasingly frustrated with leaders they felt had no understanding of what was really required to develop new products. Faced with the double bind of hitting aggressive performance targets and equally aggressive improvement targets, they were forced to cut corners while still appearing to follow the process. As one engineer remarked,

> In many ways we worked around the [new] system. Good, bad, or indifferent that's what happened. We had a due date and we did whatever it took to hit it.

As management discovers the engineers' shortcuts and workarounds, their view that the engineers can't be trusted is confirmed, and they are forced to step up their monitoring. Faced with similar difficulties in its effort to implement a new product development process, a different firm even created a cadre of "compliance managers" whose sole job was to enforce adherence to their new development process.

Workers in such organizations quickly learn to hide problems from others. In all of the organizations we studied, engineers routinely neglected to reveal the existence of serious design issues for fear of retribution from managers. In one firm, the motto of the development engineers was "never reveal you have a problem until you also have the solution." In another, engineers called the weekly progress review meetings the "liars' club"—each participant overstated the progress of his subsystem and hid known defects from others in the hope that others would be discovered first, giving them time to catch up.[12] The consequence is long delays in the discovery of needed rework, greatly increasing costs, delaying launch, and, often, compromising quality.

The *Capability Trap* goes beyond low capability and high work pressure. Eventually it gets embedded in deeper structures, including incentives and corporate culture. As organizations grow more dependent on firefighting and working harder to solve problems caused by low process capability, they reward and promote those who, through heroic efforts, manage to save troubled projects or keep the line running. Consequently, most organizations reward last-minute problem solving over the learning, training, and improvement activities that prevent such crises in the first place. As an engineer at an auto company told us, "Nobody ever gets credit for fixing problems that never happened." Over time, senior management will increasingly consist of these war heroes, who are likely to groom and favor other can-do people like themselves. As described by a project leader we interviewed,

> Our [company] culture rewards the heroes. Frankly, that's how I got where I've gotten. I've delivered programs under duress and difficult situations and the reward that comes with that is that you are recognized as someone that can deliver. Those are the opportunities for advancement.

Thus incentives and culture not only reinforce the tendency toward short-run thinking and working harder, but also are themselves shaped by that very short-term focus and work-harder mentality, creating another reinforcing feedback that intensifies the capability trap.[13]

An organization suffering from the self-confirming attribution error is poorly positioned to escape the *Capability Trap*. Improvement programs add stress to the organization, triggering greater work pressure that prevents people from investing in improvement, and encourages shortcuts. In such organizations many improvement programs never get off the ground. If, despite the work pressure, people do succeed in allocating more time to improvement, the result is a short-term drop in performance as time spent working falls before the investments in improvement bear fruit. Observing that performance is not improving, managers conclude the particular improvement method is not working and abandon it. Since the need to improve remains, they search for another, more promising tool, only to find it too suffers a similar fate. The result is

growing cynicism among employees about "flavor of the month" programs.

More insidiously, these dynamics strengthen stereotypes and conflicts that not only hurt organizational performance but damage society. Consider, for example, how a senior manager explained why the product development improvement effort he ran had failed:

> Program management and the disciplines associated with it continue to be a problem in my opinion in most western cultures. The people that are particularly rigorous and disciplined, the Japanese and the Germans, tend to be so by cultural norms. I can't tell you if it's hereditary or society or where it is they get it but the best engineers are those that tend to be the most disciplined, not as individual contributors but as team-based engineers. So there's a strong push back from the western type of engineer for much of this.

There is no mention of the structural features of the system or the pressure, felt throughout the organization, to deliver ambitious projects on time. Instead, this manager blames the failure on the undisciplined character of "Western" engineers. Such attributions, here generalized to entire national groups, and invoking a disturbing racial and ethnic subtext, are typical of the fundamental attribution error. As these attributions are shared and repeated they become institutionalized. They become part of the corporate culture, and, as suggested by the quote above, can strengthen pernicious stereotypes and prejudices in society at large.

OVERCOMING THE CAPABILITY TRAP

So what can be done? The most important implication of our analysis is that our experiences often teach us exactly the wrong lessons about how to maintain and improve the long-term health of the systems in which we work and live. Successful improvement must include a significant shift in the mental models of those both leading and participating in an improvement effort. This insight was captured succinctly by one manager in a successful improvement effort:

> There are two theories. One says, 'there's a problem, let's fix it.' The other says "we have a problem, someone is screwing up, let's go beat them

up." To make improvement, we could no longer embrace the second theory, we had to use the first.

Once the cycle of self-confirming attributions is broken, any number of process improvement tools and methods can help improve capability. Without this shift, new tools and techniques, no matter how great their potential, are unlikely to succeed.

Breaking the cycle of self-confirming attributions is not easy, but it can be done. The following are examples from two organizations that overcame these difficulties and introduced successful improvement efforts.[14]

DuPont

In 1991, an in-house benchmarking study documented a gap between DuPont's maintenance record and those of the best performing companies in the chemicals industry. The benchmarking study revealed an apparent paradox: DuPont spent more on maintenance than industry leaders but got less for it. DuPont had the highest number of maintenance employees per dollar of plant value, yet its mechanics worked more overtime. Spare parts inventories were excessive, yet they relied heavily on costly expedited procurement of critical components. Overall, DuPont spent 10%–30% more on maintenance per dollar of plant value than the industry leaders, while overall plant uptime was some 10%–15% lower.

An experienced manager, Winston Ledet, and a team charged with improving maintenance operations, developed a system dynamics model of these issues. The modeling process involved extensive hands-on workshops in which the team, assisted by an experienced modeler, discussed, tested, and changed the model as they identified areas needing improvement. Using the model as a laboratory to design and test different policies, the team gradually developed an appreciation for the *Capability Trap* and the paradox of high maintenance costs and low reliability.

To see how the *Capability Trap* arose in the chemicals industry, imagine the effects of cost cuts on maintenance, such as those beginning with the oil crisis of 1973 and subsequent recession. In chemical plants, when critical equipment breaks down, it must be fixed. Hence maintenance managers required to reduce costs must cut preventive maintenance, training,

and investments in equipment upgrades. The drop in planned maintenance eventually causes breakdowns to increase, forcing management to reassign more mechanics from planned maintenance to repair work. Breakdowns then rise even more. As uptime falls, operators find it harder to meet demand and become less willing to take equipment down for scheduled maintenance, leading to more breakdowns and still lower uptime. More breakdowns simultaneously constrain revenue (by lowering production) and increase costs (due to overtime, expedited parts procurement, the nonroutine and often hazardous nature of outages, collateral damage, and so forth). More subtly, lower uptime erodes a plant's ability to meet its delivery commitments. As it develops a reputation for poor delivery reliability, business volume and margins fall further. The plant slowly slides into the *Capability Trap,* with high breakdowns, low uptime, and high costs.

Policy analysis showed that escaping the *Capability Trap* necessarily meant performance would deteriorate before it could improve: While continuing to repair breakdowns, the organization has to invest additional resources in planned maintenance, training and part quality, raising costs. Most importantly, increasing planned maintenance *reduces* uptime in the short run because operable equipment must be taken off-line for the planned maintenance to be done. Only later, as the *Reinvestment* loop begins to work in the virtuous direction, does the breakdown rate drop. Fewer unplanned breakdowns give mechanics more time for planned maintenance. As maintenance expenses drop the savings can be reinvested in training, parts quality, reliability engineering, planning and scheduling systems, and other activities that further reduce breakdowns. For example, upgrading to a more durable pump seal improves reliability, allowing maintenance intervals to be lengthened and inventories of replacement seals to be cut. Higher uptime also yields more revenue and provides additional resources for still more improvement. All the positive feedbacks that once acted as vicious cycles dragging reliability down become virtuous cycles, progressively and cumulatively boosting uptime and cutting costs.

Now the challenge facing the team was implementation. They knew nothing could happen without the willing participation of thousands of people, from the lowest-grade hourly mechanic to regional vice presidents. They also realized that their views had changed because they had participated in the modeling process. Somehow they had to facilitate a similar learning process throughout the plants.

The team converted the maintenance model into an interactive role-playing simulation they called the Manufacturing Game.[15] The game is closely based on the model and realistically captures the time delays, costs, and other parameters characterizing typical plants. They embedded the game in an interactive workshop designed to create an environment for learning that addressed emotional as well as cognitive issues. The process at DuPont's Washington Works complex in Parkersburg, West Virginia, was typical:

> The team was initiated with a two-day learning lab . . . learning the concepts of defect elimination and experiencing the Manufacturing Game. . . . The material is presented in the form of lectures, skits and participative exercises in an off-site environment. Posters and music are used. The atmosphere is much different than routine plant meetings or training, to open up their thinking. . . . Through interactive exercises, the team develops their personal aspirations for improving the area where they have chosen to work. . . . [Then] they . . . develop an action plan to immediately start working.[16]

Despite its many simplifications, the game quickly becomes in many ways a real plant with real emotions and conflicts among players. Initialized with high breakdowns and low uptime, the people playing the role of operations managers face intense pressure to keep equipment running and often rebuff attempts to increase planned maintenance, just as in the real world. Players who stick with the prevailing cost-minimization, work-harder, reactive maintenance policies can keep costs low for a while. However, as defects accumulate, uptime slowly sinks while costs rise. Teams who follow a planned maintenance strategy first find costs rise while uptime falls. Soon, however, costs begin to fall and uptime rises. The game allows people to experience the worse-before-better dynamic in a few hours instead of a few months. For many, the game was the first time in their careers they experienced the possibility that improvement was actually possible.

The game and learning laboratory proved popular. However, playing it once was not enough. The team found that they had to run several workshops for a given plant before a critical mass emerged to lead action teams and put proactive maintenance policies into practice. Individual plants needed the capability to run the game so their own people, with their site-specific experience and legitimacy, could run it on demand. By the end of 1992, some 1,200 people had participated in the workshop, and more than 50 facilitators had been certified.

At plants that implemented the program by the end of 1993, the mean time between failure (MTBF) for pumps (the focus of the program) rose by an average of 12% each time cumulative operating experience doubled. Direct maintenance costs fell an average of 20%. In 23 comparable plants not implementing the program the learning rate averaged just 5% and costs were *up* an average of 7%. Washington Works boosted production capability 20%, improved customer service 90%, and cut delivery lead time by 50%, all with minimal capital investment and a drop in maintenance costs. For the company as a whole, conservative estimates exceed $350 million/year in avoided maintenance costs alone.

However, success creates its own challenges. One issue related to the persistence of the cost-saving mentality. A member of the modeling team commented, "As soon as you get the problems down, people will be taken away from the effort and the problems will go back up." In fact, mandated corporate cost-cutting programs did cause significant downsizing throughout the entire company, weakening the reinvestment feedback and limiting their ability to expand the program. Winston Ledet took early retirement and began working with other companies interested in the game and learning lab. These firms include other chemicals manufacturers along with firms in the energy, automotive, and high-tech sectors.

British Petroleum

One of the organizations Ledet worked with after leaving DuPont was British Petroleum's refinery in Lima, Ohio. Founded in 1886 by John D. Rockefeller, and once "Queen of the Fleet," the refinery engaged in cost cutting during the 1980s that triggered the vicious cycle of increasing breakdowns, higher maintenance costs, and less planned maintenance, pushing it into the *Capability Trap*. By the early 1990s, Lima lagged well behind other U.S. refineries. BP began to think about selling or closing the facility.

In 1994, the Lima facility introduced the maintenance learning lab and other system dynamics tools. It was not a top management intervention: The original champions were an equipment specialist, a maintenance training supervisor, and an engineer. Successful pilot projects led to favorable word of mouth; eventually 80% of all employees participated in the program. Soon dozens of improvement teams were in place. During the first six months, maintenance costs ballooned by 30%. Having experienced it in the game, management was prepared for the worse-before-better dynamic, and focused on the improvements generated by the action teams.

In January 1996, BP announced that it intended to sell the Lima refinery and stepped up its cost cutting and downsizing. A few months later BP stunned the employees by announcing that it could not find a buyer at a satisfactory price and would therefore close the refinery. The announcement was a deep blow to the workers and the community. One of the most important businesses in the community, the refinery employed 450 people and pumped more than $60 million per year into Lima's depressed economy. Some employees became discouraged and questioned the value of the learning lab and improvement program. A few transferred to other BP facilities or left altogether. Winston Ledet described what happened next:

> For those who decided to stay with the ship, a new spirit emerged. They realized that they needed a future in Lima and should take responsibility for creating that future. The first step was to ensure that the exit of many experienced people did not throw them back in the reactive mode. . . . It actually created a clearer focus for the people who remained. They were all there because they had chosen to be there.

Soon the impact of the new maintenance policies and attitudes was clearly visible (Table 12.1).

These dramatic improvements did not go unnoticed. On July 2, 1998, the banner headline of the *Lima News* announced "Oil Refinery Rescued." Clark USA, a privately held *Fortune 500* company with refining and distribution interests, agreed to buy the Lima refinery for $215 million and keep it operating.

The DuPont and BP cases illustrate the power of a shift in mental models. The model, game, and workshop do not teach anyone how to maintain equipment.

Table 12.1. Improvement at the Lima Refinery

- Pump MTBF up from 12 to 58 months (failures down from more than 640 in 1991 to 131 in 1998). Direct savings: $1.8 million/year.
- Hydrocarbon flare-off down from 1.5% to 0.35%, saving $0.27/barrel and improving environmental quality.
- On-line analyzer uptime improved from 75% and not trusted to 97% and trusted, permitting real-time optimization of product flow. Savings: $0.10–0.12/barrel.
- Safety incidents and lost hours cut by a factor of 4.
- Thirty-four production records set.
- Cash margin improved by $0.77 per barrel of oil processed.
- Total new value created: $43 million/year. Total cost: $320,000/year. Ratio: 143:1.
- Learning initiative under way for other BP facilities around the world.

Source: Paul Monus, "Proactive Manufacturing at BP's Lima Oil Refinery," presented at National Petroleum Refiners Association Maintenance Conference, May 20–23, 1997, New Orleans; J. Griffith, D. Kuenzli, and P. Monus, "Proactive Manufacturing: Accelerating Step Change Breakthroughs in Performance," NPRA Maintenance Conference, MC-98-92, 1998; Paul Monus, personal communication.

For example, a BP team reduced butane flare-off to zero, saving $1.5 million/year and reducing pollution. The effort took two weeks and cost $5,000, a return on investment of 30,000%/year. Members of the team had known about the problem and how to solve it for eight years. They already had all the engineering know-how they needed, and most of the equipment and materials were already on site. What had stopped them from solving the problem long ago? The only barrier was the mental model that there were no resources or time for improvement, that these problems were outside their control, and that they could never make a difference.

The modeling process and the resulting game were effective because they eliminated many of the impediments to learning in the real system. Dynamics such as the progressive slide into the *Capability Trap* that normally play out over years or even decades could be experienced in just a few hours. Unlike the real world, people could take different roles: A mechanic playing the role of plant manager might find himself with low uptime and then cut preventive maintenance to avoid equipment takedowns and cut costs. Seeing people from different functions and backgrounds enacting the same behaviors helped break the vicious cycle of self-confirming attribution errors and blame. The systems thinking process enabled people to experience for themselves the long-term, organization-wide consequences of their actions. They discovered how to use initial successes to create resources for further improvement and how to survive the short-run drop in performance. They saw how small actions could snowball into major gains. Most importantly, they learned that they could, after all, make a difference.

ACKNOWLEDGMENTS

Work reported here was supported by the MIT Center for Innovation in Product Development under NSF Cooperative Agreement Number EEC-9529140. For more information on the research program that generated this article, visit http://web.mit.edu/nelsonr/www/.

NOTES

1. See G. Easton and S. Jarrell, "The Effects of Total Quality Management on Corporate Performance: An Empirical Investigation," *Journal of Business,* 2 (1998): 253–307; K. Hendricks and V.R. Singhal, "Quality Awards and the Market Value of the Firm: An Empirical Investigation," *Management Science,* 43/3 (1996): 415–436.

2. See Easton and Jarrell, op. cit.; Darrell Rigby, "Management Tools and Techniques: A Survey," *California Management Review,* 43/2 (Winter 2001): 139–159.

3. See J. Pfeffer and R. Sutton, *The Knowing-Doing Gap* (Boston, MA: Harvard Business School Press, 2000); K. Klein and J. Sorra, "The Challenge of Innovation Implementation," *Academy of Management Review,* 4 (1996): 1055–1080.

4. Published summaries can be found in J. Sterman, N. Repenning, and F. Kofman "Unanticipated Side Effects of Successful Quality Programs: Exploring a Paradox of Organizational Improvement," *Management Science,* 43/4 (1997): 503–521; N. Repenning and J. Sterman, "Getting Quality the Old Fashion: Self-Confirming Attributions in the Dynamics of Process Improvement," in R. B. Cole and R. Scott, eds., *Improving Theory and Research on Quality Enhancement in Organizations* (Thousand Oaks, CA: Sage, 2000), pp. 201–235; E. Keating and R. Oliva, "A Dynamic Theory of Sustaining Process Improvement Teams in Product Development," in M. Beyerlein and D. Johnson, eds., *Advances in Interdisciplinary Studies of Teams* (Greenwich, CT: JAI Press, 2000); R. Oliva, S. Rockart, and J. Sterman, "Managing Multiple Improvement Efforts: Lessons from a Semiconductor

Manufacturing Site," in D. Fedor and S. Ghosh, eds., *Advances in the Management of Organizational Quality* (Greenwich, CT: JAI Press, 1998), pp. 1–55; J. Carroll, J. Sterman, and A. Markus, "Playing the Maintenance Game: How Mental Models Drive Organization Decisions," in R. Stern and J. Halpern, eds., *Debating Rationality: Nonrational Elements of Organizational Decision Making* (Ithaca, NY: ILR Press, 1997).

5. For formal models of implementation see Sterman, Repenning, and Kofman op. cit.; N. Repenning, "Drive Out Fear (Unless You Can Drive It In): The Role of Agency and Job Security in Process Improvement Efforts," *Management Science,* 46/11 (2000): 1385–1396; N. Repenning, "A Dynamic Model of Resource Allocation in Multi-Project Research and Development Systems," *System Dynamics Review,* 16/3 (2000): 173–212; N. Repenning, "A Simulation Based-Approach to Understanding the Dynamics of Innovation Implementation," *Organization Science* (forthcoming).

6. Repenning and Sterman (2000), op. cit.

7. See A. Schneiderman, "Setting Quality Goals," *Quality Progress* (April 1988), pp. 55–57; J. Sterman, N. Repenning, and F. Kofman, op. cit.

8. Schneiderman, op. cit.

9. For an example, see Sterman, Repenning, and Kofman, op. cit.

10. The dynamics of project management and software development have been treated extensively in system dynamics. See, for example, T. Abdel-Hamid, "The Economics of Software Quality Assurance: A Simulation-Based Case Study," *MIS Quarterly,* 3 (1997): 395–411; D. Ford and J. D. Sterman "Dynamic Modeling of Product Development Processes," *System Dynamics Review,* 14 (1998): 31–68.

11. For an excellent summary of attribution theory, see S. Plous, *The Psychology of Judgment and Decision Making* (New York: McGraw-Hill, 1993).

12. See also George Roth and Art Kleiner, *Car Launch* (New York: Oxford University Press, 2000).

13. See N. Repenning et al., "Past the Tipping Point: The Persistence of Fire-Fighting in Product Development," published in this issue [*California Management Review,* 43/4 (Summer 2001)].

14. These cases are discussed in depth in J. Sterman, *Business Dynamics: Systems Thinking and Modeling for a Complex World* (New York: Irwin/McGraw-Hill, 2000), chapter 2.

15. See Winston Ledet, "Engaging the Entire Organization: Key to Improving Reliability," *Oil and Gas Journal,* 97/21 (1999): 54–57.

16. R. Tewksbury and R. Steward, "Improved Production Capability Program at DuPont's Washington Works," Proceedings of the 1997 Society for Maintenance and Reliability annual conference.

13

Tailoring Process Management to Situational Requirements

Beyond the Control and Exploration Dichotomy

KATHLEEN M. SUTCLIFFE
SIM B. SITKIN
LARRY D. BROWNING

Scholars have recently distinguished two fundamentally different types of process improvement approaches that are reflected in two parallel but independent streams of research on organizational effectiveness and change. The first stream emphasizes the need for continuous improvement and efficiency, focusing on customer-responsive, highly reliable processes for the delivery of products and services (e.g., quality management methods, business process reengineering). The second stream emphasizes anticipating disjunctive change requirements, focusing on the need to adopt flexible, "boundaryless," learning-oriented processes. Taken together, the streams capture two simultaneous and opposing pressures for organizational evolution.

The dominant (perhaps even exclusive) assumption in this work has been that the two approaches reflected in the two research streams are antithetical and that organizations can be most effective by striking a balance between the two (March, 1995). As March (1995) observes, this dilemma is

> well known to students of rational choice (where it is represented by the problem of balancing search

and action), by students of evolution (where it is represented by the problem of balancing variation and selection), and by students of institutional change (where it is represented by the problem of balancing change and stability). (p. 432)

Yet even with such an acknowledgment of the need to consider reliability and learning simultaneously, there has been no conceptual framework proposed to begin to systematically examine this phenomenon. Several questions critical to developing such a framework remain unarticulated and, thus, unaddressed: What is meant by "balance"? Is balancing the only way to think about the two approaches? What tensions exist between the two that can help to clarify whether there are some conditions for which balancing is not the best solution? What are the implications of these tensions for organization design and management? Articulating a conceptual framework to begin to answer these questions is the goal of this chapter. Specifically, in this chapter, we conceptualize process management in a less bifurcated way than has been the case in the literature to date by integrating past theory and recent empirical research.

Kathleen M. Sutcliffe, Sim B. Sitkin, and Larry D. Browning, in Robert E. Cole and W. Richard Scott (eds.), *The Quality Movement and Organization Theory,* pp. 315–330, copyright © 2001 by Sage Publications, Inc. Reprinted by permission of Sage Publications, Inc.

DISTINGUISHING PROCESS REQUIREMENTS

The need for dramatically improved reliability (e.g., the capacity to produce collective outcomes of a certain minimum quality repeatedly) has driven the recent scholarly interest in process improvement methods, such as quality management (e.g., Dean and Bowen, 1994) and high-reliability organizations (e.g., Weick and Roberts, 1993). Goals associated with increased reliability are the reduction of unwanted variance and the desire to improve existing capabilities and technologies. Concurrent with rising demands for reliability, scholars have noted how the world confronting organizations is increasingly characterized as discontinuous, uncertain, and chaotic (D'Aveni, 1994; Nonaka and Takeuchi, 1995). These scholars argue that uncertain conditions favor organizations that are flexible and can adapt quickly to changing conditions. Therefore, organizations are faced with simultaneous demands to become both more reliable and more adaptable. To understand these dual (and perhaps competing) pressures and their effect on organizational processes, there has been a rising interest in studying how organizations can respond predictably to the demands of an unpredictable world. Researchers have begun to examine how organizations become more adept at ensuring reliability while learning and innovating concerning products, services, and administrative structures and processes.

The implications of this changing competitive landscape have led to a similar set of ideas being proposed almost simultaneously by several groups of scholars. These researchers have argued that the essence of process management (e.g., quality management and related change efforts) involves dual core goals—reliability and learning—and that distinct types of processes (i.e., control-oriented and exploration-oriented) are related to each of those goals. For example, issues of process management and how they relate to the distinctions just outlined can be found in our own work (Sitkin, 1992; Sitkin, Sutcliffe, and Schroeder, 1994; Sutcliffe, Sitkin, and Browning, 1997), as well as in the work of March (March, 1991, 1995) and his colleagues (e.g., Levinthal and March, 1993; March, Sproull, & Tamuz, 1991; Tamuz, 1987, 1994), Eisenhardt (1993) and her colleagues (e.g., Brown & Eisenhardt, 1995; Eisenhardt and Tabrizi, 1995), and others (e.g., Henderson and Clark, 1990; Sterman, Repenning, and Kofman, 1997).

Most prior work in this area has suggested that these fundamentally distinct goals (reliability and learning) are antithetical in that the pursuit of one is presumed to preclude the pursuit of the other. Much of the organizational literature still suggests that organizations face a choice: to compete by being highly reliable in exploiting that which they already know and are known for, or to compete by being a leader in exploring new, breakthrough technologies or systems. By focusing on *either* the enhanced delivery of product, service, and/or performance reliability *or* the enhancement of organizational learning capacity, these approaches at best implicitly assume that the pursuit of reliability or learning is a trade-off.

There is a growing recognition by scholars and practitioners that we need to move beyond framing this choice in either/or terms. A few analyses have recognized that not only can these dual goals coexist but also that the processes associated with each of these goals is present to some extent in all organizational settings. Pushing this argument further, it has been proposed that the simultaneous consideration of the dual goals is associated with increased effectiveness in that competitive conditions will require the simultaneous pursuit of two metaprocesses—reliability-focused control processes and learning-focused exploration processes—or, at a minimum, will favor those organizations that are able to master the apparent inconsistency suggested by their simultaneous pursuit (March, 1995; Sitkin, 1992; Sutcliffe et al., 1997). Thus, this argument goes, organizational survival will increasingly hinge on the capacity to balance control-based performance reliability and exploration-based resilience.

Although a recognition of the need for balance has been reflected in past work, the purpose of this chapter is to begin to go beyond this recognition by identifying the alternative logics underlying different kinds of balance—thus setting the stage for additional in-depth work on the issue in the future. In the next section, we review the evolution of organizational process models, showing the underlying logics of models that view processes in singular or binary terms. We also propose a third type of model that reflects the simultaneous presence and interaction of control and exploration approaches, in what is referred to here as a "dual" approach. After introducing the notion of dual process models, the third section of the chapter answers the question, What does it mean in a concrete sense for organizations to balance or integrate the use of control-oriented and exploration-oriented approaches? We draw together theory and data to explore in more detail the conditions under which control and exploration involve zero-sum trade-offs, are orthogonally related, or are synergistic and result in mutually greater gains, and we also discuss the implications of this conceptualization for future research on organizational process management.

EVOLUTION OF ORGANIZATIONAL PROCESS MODELS

Work on organizational processes has been scant compared with other forms of organizational study. Most macro-organizational research over the past 20 years has been dominated by a focus on structure and function, rather than process. One reason for this is that processes tend to be harder to perceive than structures such as departments, functions, or tasks. Specifically, organizational processes have tended to be unnoticed and unnamed in the literature because our attention has been focused on individual departments and their goals rather than on sets of interrelated work activities that cross formal boundaries and involve a variety of organizational members.

It is useful to focus on organizational process when discussing organizations and their future adaptability because it allows us to concern ourselves with the specific managerial and employee action sets that might be associated with differing conditions. More specifically, it allows us to distinguish between processes concerned with the improvement of existing production processes and stable value chains (reliability-enhancing processes) and processes concerned with defining or redefining real or potential value chains (innovation/learning-enhancing processes). Attempts to classify organizational processes are made more difficult because the available database is inadequate. Nevertheless, researchers during the past 30 years have proposed several classification schemes to describe organizational processes. For example, March and his colleagues (e.g., Cyert and March, 1963; March and Simon, 1958) distinguish between problem-driven and slack-driven search processes; Quinn (1980) distinguishes between synoptic and incremental strategic decision-making processes; Burns and Stalker (1961)

contrast mechanistic and organic organizational processes; and Ouchi (1977, 1979, 1981) describes input, behavioral, and output control processes.

The recent classification of organizational processes into the dual categories noted above (i.e., control vs. exploration) grew out of the growing interest in adaptive processes and organizational learning. However, this typology is not entirely without precedent because it mirrors one of the central and enduring paradoxes in organization theory concerning the trade-off between efficiency and flexibility (Thompson, 1967). Organization theorists have argued that bureaucracy enhances efficiency but impedes flexibility, the implication being that organizations cannot achieve both. We discuss the distinctions between control and exploration below before moving on to a more in-depth discussion of the relationships between the two.

There are two key distinctions between control and exploration. First, control emphasizes systematically clarifying that which is shared or convergent, whereas exploration emphasizes systematically discovering that which is unforeseen and divergent. Second, control stresses the clear, the articulated, and the specific. In contrast, exploration stresses the emergent, the suggestive, and the general.

In a recent review of process management perspectives and implications for organizational design, Denison (1997) builds a hierarchical framework that distinguishes three fundamental organizational process modalities. Denison's framework is helpful in terms of translating reliability-focused control and resilience-focused exploration goals into types of actions available to organizational managers and other members. Specifically, Denison distinguishes the need to *design* a facilitating infrastructure, *manage* the interaction among units and individuals, and *implement* the designs through practices that accomplish the work to be done. By parsing the processes into three modes—designing, managing, and implementing—Denison's scheme helps to clarify how actions taken in pursuit of control or exploration can be distinguished.

Designing for control involves the pursuit of reliability by articulating clear, specific, shared understandings that will govern activities. If reliability is to be achieved, it is crucial that goals not be divergent, responsibilities not be fuzzy, and criteria to be met in products or services be unequivocal. The designer's role in control-oriented processes is to be sure that goals and responsibilities are clear and shared; schedules and criteria for performance are specific and understood; and that any general understandings about the purpose, tasks, or roles are as concrete as possible. Design for exploration, in contrast, emphasizes the opposite: distinct and independently defined goals, fuzzy expectations, and performance criteria carried out by independent operating units.

Managing for control and exploration exhibit equally distinctive practices. Given a well-defined set of goals, plans, and performance expectations, a control orientation stresses tightly coupled action plans and close coordination across operating units and individuals. Because the thrust of control-oriented processes is to more carefully hone in on established targets, systems and procedures to reduce needless variation are an essential part of managing for control. In contrast, the pursuit of the fuzzier goals and emergent expectations associated with an exploration orientation fosters the use of parallel processes and the development of innovative ideas (Bendor, 1985; Cohen, March, and Olsen, 1972). The management of exploration processes, in other words, involves the active generation of greater variance as the only route to discovery and capacity building (Sitkin, 1992).

Implementing refers to doing work in a way that supports the underlying goals for which a process is being used. The implementation practices that support control include conforming to work, product, and service specifications—and even tightening those specifications as a result of experience. Research on learning curves illustrates this approach (Epple, Argote, and Devadas, 1991). In contrast, when practices are implemented that support exploration, these efforts involve challenging accepted standards and specifications rather than conforming to them, and looking for new and novel opportunities rather than avoiding or minimizing risky activities.

But the question still remains, how are control and exploration linked? Table 13.1 distinguishes three models for thinking about the relationship between control-oriented and exploration-oriented organizational processes. The models can be distinguished along several dimensions: their primary goal, the relationship between goals, and the strategic and management challenges posed by the implementation of that model. In the following paragraphs, we discuss each model in terms of these dimensions.

Singular Organizational Process Model

The "singular" model has dominated until quite recently in that almost all of the literature and much

Table 13.1. The Evolution of Organizational Process Models

	Singular	Binary	Dual
Control focus	• Increase reliability and predictability • Exploit existing capabilities • Conformity	• Increase reliability and predictability • Exploit existing capabilities • Conformity	• Increase reliability and predictability • Exploit existing capabilities • Conformity
Exploration focus	NOT RECOGNIZED	• Increase resilience and flexibility • Explore new capabilities • Risk-taking	• Increase resilience and flexibility • Explore new capabilities • Risk-taking
Relationship between control and exploration	None because there is no exploration focus to consider	Both apply to different circumstances and thus are unrelated	Balance must be struck between the two because both are relevant to varying degrees under different circumstances
Strategic challenge	Simplification of mission	Recognition of contingent missions	Acknowledgment of simultaneous pursuit of dual missions
Management challenge	Implementation of solutions	Differentiation of solutions	Identification of distributive solution

practice concerning quality management and other process improvement methods have reflected a singular, monolithic view. Dating back to the early 20th-century scientific management movement, this approach has emphasized the achievement of control by stressing the importance of variance reduction, whether that logic was applied to formal procedures, norms, practices, personnel, or other features of organizations. This conceptualization of organizational processes typically ignores the possibility that significant contingency factors may be relevant to whatever processes are being proposed.

As Sitkin et al. (1994) describe, much of the TQM movement in the United States has adopted this singular stance, suggesting that the tenets and practices of quality management are universally applicable (but see Cole, Chapter 4, this volume, concerning how this attribute of the American TQM movement may not apply to Japanese quality management efforts). This is illustrated in some of our earlier research on the forcing of a singular, control-oriented model of TQM on a basic research laboratory, in which efforts to achieve zero-defect research was described by employees as "quality through conformity" (Sitkin and Stickel, 1996).

The implications of this approach for management practice are twofold. First, the organization's strategy is likely to reflect a clear, focused emphasis on reliability by reducing unwanted, unanticipated, and unexplainable variance in performance and by focusing attention on meeting stated milestones and achievement targets. Once clarified, the key strategic challenge is to simply articulate the mission so that it is applicable and implementable throughout the organization. Given the assumption of a clear, singular, strategic goal, the critical managerial challenge is to carry out that goal through disciplined implementation. Proponents of this approach are likely to stress the importance of clear and comprehensive measures and motivational procedures, all keyed tightly to the core, unified strategic goal. If there is a central theme in this work, it concerns the value of high levels of control through standard routines and procedures to achieve the goal of high reliability.

Binary Organizational Process Model

A central distinction in organization theory is made between situations described as certain, analyzable, routine, and predictable and those situations described as uncertain, unanalyzable, nonroutine, and unpredictable. For example, Thompson (1967) discusses the much more complex and open-ended coordination requirements needed when action interdependencies cannot be specified a priori. Williamson (1975) describes the difficulties associated with contractually specifying transaction expectations under uncertain conditions. Scholars from a wide variety of disciplinary perspectives have long recognized that technical transformation processes that are well understood present organizational members with a fundamentally different challenge than do processes that are poorly understood (Perrow, 1967). An implication of this distinction is that whereas more certain activities can be accomplished through the use of systematic, routine, rational, bureaucratic procedures, uncertain conditions require a more flexible, experimental, and improvisational approach.

We drew on this distinction in our theorizing about the quality management perspective, its practices, and related outcomes by developing a binary model of quality management. Most process management programs had been advocated as universally applicable to all organizational activities with virtually no attention to the nature of situational or task uncertainty. Thus, we proposed a binary model as an alternative to the standard singular models that dominated to that point. Our thinking was based on the familiar contingency theory notion that problematic outcomes may result when organizational systems are poorly attuned to contextual requirements. This led to the hypothesis that highly uncertain conditions would require an alternative to standard process management practices (i.e., standard quality control practices) and also to the hypothesis that matching process management techniques to situational requirements would enhance their effectiveness. In our contingency-based model, we suggested that rational cybernetic control approaches (e.g., engineering approaches) fit best in highly certain situations, whereas experiential, learning-oriented, improvisational approaches fit best in highly uncertain situations. The central point is that taking situational uncertainty into account and tailoring process methods to the nature of uncertain situations allows for a more accurate and quicker diagnosis of the problems, as well as more effective problem resolution through the use of situationally appropriate quality practices.

The hypothesized benefits of control-oriented process management practices in routine/certain situations is relatively straightforward, and there are numerous empirical examples of improved process accuracy (e.g., reduced error rates), process efficiency (e.g., reduced costs), and process cycle time (e.g., reduced time to complete a process) (Hackman and Wageman, 1995). In contrast, there is little or no empirical support for the idea that traditional process management practices lead to improvements under less certain, nonroutine situations. In fact, it has been generally accepted in organization theory that highly uncertain organic situations lack structure, and that process management is futile under such conditions (e.g., Burns and Stalker, 1961). Contrary to this received wisdom, in our earlier work, we proposed that actively implementing *appropriate* process management can be helpful in carrying out work in uncertain and nonroutine conditions and that this idea had been missed in mainstream process management thinking.

We explored how process management practices could be designed and tailored to uncertain situations to enhance performance and pointed out that there are at least two benefits of using process management tactics in uncertain situations. First, process management tactics may help people cope with unclear and changing environments because such practices help to more rapidly build intuition and flexibility (Sitkin, 1992; Weick, 1984, 1985). Second, process management tactics may simultaneously "provid[e] enough structure so that people will create sensemaking, avoid procrastination, and be confident enough to act in these highly uncertain situations, which easily lead to paralyzing anxiety and conflict" (Eisenhardt and Tabrizi, 1995, p. 88).

Dual Organizational Process Model

Neither the singular nor the binary model examines the relationship between the two types of process. The two either do not recognize that two distinct processes exist (singular model) or merely distinguish them in a traditional contingent choice sense (binary model). The third type of model shown in Table 13.1, the dual process model, reflects that organizations cannot typically focus on only one type of goal (as a simple contingency) but that they must do both simultaneously to remain adaptable under differing conditions. As Stacey (1992) observed,

When you look at the world or organizing through new lens, you do not see "either/or" choices. Instead you see "both/and" choices. Successful organizations—that is, continually innovative organizations—cannot choose between tight, formal control systems and structures on one hand and loose, informal processes that provoke learning on the other . . . they must do both at the same time. (p. 19)

The nature of the situation and the nature of the relationship between the control-oriented and exploration-oriented processes is crucial in determining the effectiveness of organizational adaptation efforts. Even when earlier binary models recognized both the control and exploration approaches, standard assumptions about their relationship (e.g., that they were negatively related in a zero sum trade-off) sidestepped the need to deal with their relationship. Thus, the recognition and awareness of both types of processes is not sufficient; rather, this approach stresses how the decision of how to balance the two approaches necessarily involves considering potential trade-offs in resource and attention allocation. However, this issue has never been addressed explicitly or analyzed systematically in the organizational process literature. In the next section, we outline the basic contours of a framework for examining the various forms that the relationship between control and exploration can take, and the implications of those relational forms for managerial actions and organizational effectiveness.

BALANCING CONTROL AND EXPLORATION IN ORGANIZATIONS

Although some previous work has acknowledged the need for balance, none has actually explored the nature of that balance or the tensions and impediments that balancing dual processes poses for organizations and their members. Although one potential implication of using the term "balance" is to suggest equality between the two types of processes, that is not how we use the term here. Instead, our use of the notion of balancing focuses on the need to actively consider both types of process and to determine what an appropriate balance should be, contingent upon situational conditions. We wish to highlight that balancing is active and lies along a continuum. Furthermore, understanding the nature of balancing requires that we specify distinct ways that the two processes might be related to each other.

Past work has tended to only look at balancing these processes in terms of trade-offs, and calls for balance have typically taken a singular form by suggesting that the more one turns attention to learning-enhancing exploration, the more that concern comes at the expense of a focus on reliability-enhancing control (and vice versa). However, this general logic reflects just one of the three potential types of relationships (antithetical) that we describe below.

Table 13.2 shows the characteristics associated with each of three logical alternatives in how the two processes can be related to each other. The first explores conditions under which they are negatively associated ("antithetical"), the second explores conditions under which they are unrelated ("orthogonal"), and the third explores conditions under which they are positively related ("synergistic"). The antithetical perspective assumes that process choices occupy a fixed attention/resource space, and that the choice to pursue control or exploration is a zero-sum game. The orthogonal perspective reflects the notion that there are conditions in which the two types of processes might be pursued independently of each other, draw on different and noncompeting resource pools, and thus be viewed as orthogonal contributors to an organization. The synergistic model refers to conditions under which the effective pursuit of reliability and learning are mutually supportive, such that doing one better simultaneously enhances the ability to do the other.

As we examine each of these three models below, we structure our discussion around three key points.

First, we discuss the logic underlying the relationship between control-oriented and exploration-oriented processes. Second, we illustrate how that relationship can be manifested by drawing upon case study data gathered as part of a longitudinal field study of 10 organizations cited as having exemplary quality management programs. Third, we raise several challenges posed by each model.

The Antithetical Perspective on Balancing Processes

Scholars who have recognized that balance is needed commonly hold the view that the relationship between control and exploration is antithetical. That is, the two processes are presumed to exist in a kind of zero-sum world in which one pursues the novel at the expense of ensuring reliable improvement, and pursues incremental improvement by sacrificing a willingness to innovate. The following quotation from March (1995) illustrates:

> A system that specializes in [control] will discover itself becoming better and better at an increasingly obsolescent technology. A system that specializes in exploration will never realize the advantages of its discoveries. . . . Exploration and [control] are linked in an enduring symbiosis. . . . Each interferes with the other . . . [and] organizations persistently fail to maintain an effective balance between the two. (pp. 432–433)

In an earlier examination of this issue, the distinction between small wins (Weick, 1984) and small losses (Sitkin, 1992) stressed how the pursuit of one re-

Table 13.2. Clarifying the Control/Exploration Relationship

	Relationship Between Control and Exploration	
	Antithetical (Negative)	Orthogonal (Independent)
Description of relationship	Zero-sum game with negative feedback loops, in which each approach can be increased only by decreasing attention or resources devoted to the other.	The two approaches coexist independently of each other, with no feedback loops. Increased attention to learning in one part of the organization does not detract from the emphasis on control in another part of the organization.
Strategic challenge	Balanced choice	Understanding and respecting differences
Management challenge	Identification of distributive solution	Protection of nonequivalent solutions

duced the capacity to pursue the other. As routines and systems become more focused on amplifying and developing a single strength, several things can result: Flexibility decreases, myopia increases, and exploratory learning and adaptation are curtailed (Miller, 1993)—a potentially problematic combination under conditions such as environmental decline, turbulence, uncertainty, or complexity. Illustrating this point, simulation studies have demonstrated that enhancing reliability under conditions of uncertainty or rapid change can put fast-learning firms at a disadvantage by foreclosing opportunities to discover other good alternatives (Levinthal and March, 1981; March, 1988, 1995).

Although the presumption has been that the pursuit of one process inevitably takes place at the expense of the other, in our research, we found that this presumed pattern was not always observed. If the logic underlying the antithetical model is that control and exploration processes involve a trade-off in attention or other resources, then firms facing antithetical situations could either recognize them as such and act appropriately for a zero-sum choice or they could mistakenly think about the situation as involving orthogonal or synergistic relations and, thus, take a course of action inappropriate for the situational attributes. In our research, we found examples of each of these possible courses of action.

The first example concerns a semiconductor equipment manufacturer that faced dramatically increased demand for its products from customers who preferred to get products on time with defects rather than receiving higher-quality products late or in smaller quantities. This firm had been engaged in a significant learning-oriented effort to enhance its production capabilities, focusing not just on capacity and reliability but also on broader exploration capabilities. When confronted with the demands for sheer production volume, it recognized the unavoidable trade-off for managerial attention, staffing, and facility expansion—and chose to abandon its exploratory efforts in the short-term. Company executives told us that they assumed that they would be able to resume exploratory activities when future industry shifts occurred without hampering their long-term viability. Thus, they recognized the situation as fundamentally antithetical and chose to "re-balance" control and exploration by investing all of their resources in control. They could have chosen otherwise and kept some level of exploratory efforts

going, if they had determined that their competitors threatened to be better prepared for the next competitive wave in their industry.

The second example, drawn from a premier hotel chain, concerns the successful transformation of front desk operations at one of its properties. This property, already noted as excellent on nearly all quality indicators and also known as a leading innovator in the chain, developed new arrangements to enhance its quality services and to build the property's organizational capacity for continued learning. In effect, it wanted to pursue synergistic process improvements by melding its reliability focus with its effort to increase individual and subunit learning. To achieve this goal, it implemented self-managing teams throughout the property. Its front desk operation was exemplary among all of the subunits measured across a variety of indicators. Yet success began to have untoward effects, as front desk staff received promotions, were transferred to other units (sometimes to gain broader experience and other times to facilitate transfer of learning from the front desk operation to other hotel subunits), or used success as an opportunity to move on to other personal or professional pursuits. As turnover increased, front desk performance declined (it moved from first place to last place on most performance measures).

Our analysis suggests that the basis for reliability rested in the focused attention and shared knowledge of the front desk team members. The organization failed to realize that the pursuit of learning came at the expense of control. Key leaders anticipated that promotions and transfers would benefit individual employees, other units, and the property as a whole but did not realize that these resource reallocations undermined the single-minded reliability focus that had been the underpinning of the front desk's initial success. Even one transfer would have hurt the operation's reliability but not so much as to be noticeable. However, high levels of turnover pushed to the forefront the degree to which its pursuit of learning in this case involved a direct zero-sum trade-off with its pursuit of control-oriented reliability.

The trade-offs associated with the antithetical condition arise because inadequate resources are available to carry out both processes effectively. The examples cited above suggest that in an ideal world it is desirable to pursue both control and exploration processes. However, when managerial attention, employee knowledge, time to expand human and physical capacity, and other resources are limited, difficult choices have to be made. Thus, a key condition under which antithetical relationships emerge is when control and exploration processes do not need to be actively intertwined, but where they do draw upon common underlying—and limited—resource pools.

Failures of the antithetical approach provide rich fodder for post hoc critiques, which may explain why salient examples of zero-sum trade-offs have been so often alluded to in the past. Antithetical relations have often been associated with negative outcomes; however, in the case of the semiconductor equipment manufacturer, it was the timely recognition and strategic response to an antithetical situation that led to positive outcomes (at least in the short term).

The issues associated with trade-offs between control and exploration raise important implications for researchers (and managers as well). One key issue involves simply recognizing when control and learning are competing for limited resources. In the two cases cited, the key differentiating factor was the extent to which key leaders were able to discern important nuances in the situation they faced. The ability to perceive strategic situations clearly and accurately (Sutcliffe, 1994) may play an important role in appropriately tailoring resource use to the more complex and subtle demands of dual process requirements. Thus, when the two processes are in opposition, the key strategic choice is to determine the most appropriate distribution of critical resources between the pursuit of reliability goals and learning goals.

Second, creatively identifying distributive options and matching them to the politics and cultural norms of the situation are critical managerial skills. For example, as the language of empowerment becomes widely accepted, it can become more difficult to acknowledge those situations where it does not fit, unless leaders can offer other, more culturally acceptable frames for these tough choices. Justice researchers have studied what are referred to as "distributive outcome" situations and have found that acknowledging the validity of opposing claims, treating both losers and winners with respect, and helping to put the tough choices into a broader strategic context can be critically important in gaining acceptance of decisions made under antithetical conditions. Like the distributive situations described by justice researchers, when in antithetical conditions, impression management skills become especially important.

The Orthogonal Perspective on Balancing Processes

The conceptualization of control and exploration processes as orthogonal rests on the assumption of slack resources that permit attention and resources devoted to one type of process not to come at the expense of the other. Much like divisions operating in a pooled interdependence arrangement (Thompson, 1967), where operations and outcomes associated with one do not substantially affect the functioning or outcomes of the other, the two processes may draw on the same resource base but do not need to interact to do so. The distinction between orthogonal and antithetical process relationships hinges on the degree to which pooled interdependency is coupled with resource scarcity or munificence. When resources are scarce, one must make trade-offs in who gets to use the limited resources, and thus antithetical relations arise because resource use by one precludes use by the other. In contrast, when resources are ample, such trade-offs do not need to be made, and the two processes can coexist without interaction or interference.

Even though most past work on control and learning processes has either ignored the balance issue or focused on the antithetical form, there are several streams of related research that can inform an analysis of the orthogonal condition. Perhaps most prominent is the large body of work that has examined the multidivisional organizational form to describe the conditions under which organizations will create quasi-independent operating units or divisions. Whether units are differentiated based on products, geography, or other reasons, the two key factors identified in this work are that the processes used require no coordination, and that there are sufficient resources to accommodate some inefficiencies associated with cross-divisional duplication. These same conditions apply to orthogonal relations between processes.

Several other streams of work are also relevant to our understanding of orthogonal processes. Daft's (1982) notion of "dual core" organizations is also parallel to the orthogonal model's emphasis on the independence of distinct organizational goals and processes. A similar set of ideas is reflected in work on "preservative" acquisitions (Haspeslagh and Jemison, 1991), in which firms recognize the need to keep a newly acquired subsidiary separate because its value comes from its unique processes and perspective, which could be lost if the previously independent organizations fully merged their operations.

Orthogonal relations can be handled either by structurally partitioning control and learning-oriented activities (e.g., by creating a separate R&D laboratory) or by developing the capability to carry out both types of processes and using switching rules to handle the transitions between them. Our first example illustrates how switching rules can enable a work unit to achieve reliability while also pursuing organizational learning. In a high-technology manufacturing company, several cross-functional product development teams designed a process they referred to as "shelf technology" production. Their routine work focused on the design of new products to meet specific internal and external customer needs. However, when opportunities arose to develop new designs that went beyond customer requirements, these design teams recognized that the situation could be constructively seen as an opportunity to decouple their customer request-driven efforts from their creation of new product features unrelated to current customer needs. Teams did both kinds of design work but switched their goals and the processes used to achieve them depending upon whether they needed to meet specifications and time lines or "simply" create a preliminary technology or feature to the point where it could be retrieved at a later date. What permitted their creation of shelf technologies was the availability of adequate resources to continue to reliably meet current customer demands, while also allowing teams to explore.

In the second example, a heavy equipment maintenance unit of an educational institution faced the problem of how to proactively handle an expected increase in workload. The popularity of participatory management, self-managed teams, and empowerment seduced the organization's management to adopt a synergistic approach when its previously orthogonal approach was better suited to the situation. The unit was reorganized into a self-managing team, and employees were required to explore new mechanisms to work with external stakeholders while also maintaining timely and reliable service—all while workloads increased and personnel levels stayed the same. The idea was that direct contact with external stakeholders, extensive intragroup interaction, and increased exploration of new ways of organizing their work would improve not only their control over routine tasks but also their exploration and adoption of new ideas and processes. They tried simultaneously to operate a high throughput repair production line and to create a learning organization. The unit's performance declined quickly and dramatically in both reliability and learning terms because members' skills, interests, and task demands were ill-suited to the synergistic approach they had been encouraged to adopt. Service to key customers declined, and team members became so confused and defensive that learning all but ceased. Although the team members had been informed that they could expand their resource base as needed to continue to perform their critical function, they never acted as though these resources were available to them. Virtually all team members reported that the old system seemed very well-suited to the task and was very effective. Unfortunately, they came to blame each other and management for the performance problems rather than ever being able to clearly point to the inappropriate situational diagnosis and linking of orthogonal processes as the root source of their difficulties.

The logic underlying the orthogonal model is that control and exploration processes do not involve any interdependencies and thus do not imply the need for trade-offs. Acting appropriately under orthogonal conditions can take two forms. At a minimum, it involves ensuring that the two distinct processes are understood for what they are and respected for those differences and that sufficient resources are available to allow them to operate independently and distinctly. This may be accomplished by structural partitioning or process switching. If the firm is to gain learning insights across the two distinct processes, it also requires cross-process linkages that permit the diffusion of information and insight without forcing conformity. Thus, the strategic challenge for organizations is to appropriately recognize distinct process capabilities and needs and how those distinctions link to organizational reliability and learning goals. The managerial challenge in such arrangements is to promote a respect for the range of differences implied by distinct processes—because these are often accompanied by different cultures, structures, and personnel—and to ensure that linkages are put in place that transfer critical learning without permitting the desire for hegemony to override the interest in tapping the potential benefits of diversity.

The Synergistic Perspective on Balancing Processes

For the synergistic perspective, greater control and greater exploration are mutually reinforcing in that each process facilitates and contributes to the effectiveness of the other. Table 13.2 portrays the synergistic view as a systems perspective, conceptualizing the relationship in terms of joint optimization across both processes for both the short- and long-term. Whereas both the antithetical and the orthogonal views focus on the core differences between control and exploration and recognize their low level of interdependence, a synergistic view stresses their complementarities and interdependencies.

Brown's (1991) description of "research that reinvents the corporation" at Xerox Corporation highlights how the joining of short-term production problems and long-term, futuristic research can serve to benefit both of these functions by creating a shared sense of pioneering ideas—solutions that simultaneously serve immediate product development problems while also unearthing long-term research problems in fundamentally new ways. A strikingly similar example can be seen in the argument, used by several leading business schools, that engaging leading scholars in teaching and work with organizations in the field serves to fill a unique role by identifying problems and solutions that would not be otherwise apparent to either the scholar or the practitioner. Both Xerox and the universities are using a synergistic logic.

A question to be asked is, How can synergy be achieved? As noted throughout this chapter, reliability and its accompanying performance enhancements are important in the short-term and are often an effective strategy under conditions of stability. But under conditions of change, resilience is typically more important than reliability. However, reliability and resilience are mutually reinforcing. According to *Webster's Third New International Dictionary,* resilience is defined as (a) the capability of a strained body to withstand a shock without permanent deformation or rupture or (b) an act of springing back. Effective coping and adaptability in the long-term rest on the resilience of an organization, its units, and its members.

Research suggests that resilience in individuals is enhanced by experiences that allow for the exercise of judgment, discretion, and imagination; by the ability to make and recover from mistakes; and by observing role models who demonstrate these behaviors (Kobasa, 1979; Sternberg and Kolligian, 1990). The attributes of exploratory processes coupled with control processes are likely to instantiate the conditions necessary to bring about resilience. Control processes often hinge on the co-location of decision-making authority with those who are most likely to have the relevant and specific knowledge necessary to make a decision and resolve a problem (Wruck and Jensen, 1994). At the same time, control hinges on individual training, experience, and the development of specialized knowledge. As individuals gain control over key task behaviors and exercise discretion in performing those behaviors, they develop a sense of competence. As a sense of competence increases, individuals are better able to respond effectively in unfamiliar or challenging situations, and effective action subsequently reinforces a sense of competence. Resilience is an outcome of the self-reinforcing nature of this cycle.

The process underlying resilience at the team and organizational levels is similar and is facilitated as these units come to better understand their collective capabilities, competencies, and identities. Researchers increasingly acknowledge that collective beliefs can have a very positive effect on performance (Wood and Bandura, 1989). In particular, collective beliefs about the efficacy of the group and beliefs about the group's capacity for action (response repertoires) (Sutcliffe and Bunderson, 1996; Weick, 1988) may be particularly important for cultivating resilience and for achieving the synergies associated with control and exploratory processes in the long-term.

The basis for this line of thinking is derived from the idea that it takes a complex sensing system to register and regulate complexity (Weick, 1979). Specially trained, multifunctional teams may develop better sensing and coping capabilities—especially when they perceive that they have the ability to act (Westrum, 1991). As the capabilities for action increase, work groups that perceive many possibilities for action may be better able to grasp variations in their environments. The more an entity sees in any situation, the greater the likelihood that it will see specific changes that need to be made. Jointly believing that a work group has capacity and that this capacity makes a difference reduces defensive perception; allows the members to see more; and, as they see more, increases the likelihood that they will see where they can intervene to make a difference. Exploratory processes coupled with control processes build resilience and also enhance longer term capabilities through their effect on registering and handling dynamic and complex decision environments and through their effect on motivation and persistence in handling obstacles and adversities.

Two cases from our data illustrate how to build synergistic capacity and the problems associated with the missed opportunity for synergy. Our first example is drawn from a highly regarded high-technology manufacturing company that was trying to achieve control over complex manufacturing processes while also trying to develop new products and processes. In its fast-moving, highly competitive sector, it was essential that new ideas be leveraged whenever possible to enhance both productivity and innovation. As an advanced practitioner of quality management, this firm was quite skilled at taking even the newest learning breakthroughs and routinizing them to gain maximum benefit. One example of this involved its adaptation of Failure Mode Effects Analysis (FMEA) techniques. In particular, its use of FMEA involved gathering broad, in-house expertise in a single room and applying an especially rigorous analytical process to new product design and launch. Using this approach to product analysis, it created a profile of opportunities and threats as well as a broader range of possible futures. By combining selective elements from its dual arsenals of reliability-enhancing and learning-enhancing tools, it created a process by which both goals could be simultaneously and more effectively achieved. First, it was able to draw on deep knowledge about routine problems in innovative ways by combining routine knowledge from different experts in nonroutine ways. Second, it built the future learning capacities of both the individuals involved and the organization as a whole by creating previously unrecognized knowledge linkages and action repertoires. Finally, these techniques were used to anticipate and resolve specific product problems in a way that enhanced the reliability of product design and process engineering.

The second example illustrates the problems associated with the missed opportunity for synergy. In an office equipment company, efforts to bring the discipline of quality management were applied to training

world-class scientists in a basic research laboratory. The company's renowned quality program had led to a strong belief by corporate leaders in the importance of enhancing reliability and control throughout the organization, including the research labs. Historical culture clashes between the laboratory and the corporation's central office had led to a mutual distrust and win-lose approach typical of the antithetical approach. Because both sides (central office trainers and laboratory research scientists) came to the training prepared for a battle, the disruption that followed was surprising only in its intensity (Sitkin and Stickel, 1996). What appeared to be a classical antithetical situation later emerged more clearly as a missed opportunity for synergism. Specifically, it later became clear that the training focused on terminology and analytic techniques that allowed scientists and business managers to communicate more effectively about shared ideas and opportunities. The training program design, once adapted to foster synergism, began to help scientists to see business unit input as an opportunity for novel ideas or problems. In parallel, business unit managers who once saw science as a tax on their profitability began to see the value of more rigorous, data-based decision making and analysis. The situation was potentially synergistic from the outset, but because it was initially viewed in purely antithetical terms, it took nearly 10 years before training could be effectively offered to the laboratory and before scientists and business unit managers could work together constructively.

There is little research examining the competencies, investments, and performance trade-offs of trying to balance the pursuit of both types of processes. However, some recent empirical research is consistent with the essence of the synergistic argument, bolstering the contention that each of the approaches to balance presents a viable option and should be examined and compared more systematically. The strategic challenge in synergistic conditions is to generate insight into the interdependencies associated with the simultaneous relevance of high reliability and highly effective learning, often associated with fast-moving, highly complex situations. For managers facing synergistic conditions, the creation of truly integrative solutions that limit the rejection of one or another process is the crucial but difficult challenge.

Recently, researchers have found that an integrated control/exploration approach to innovation-enhancing processes may be critical for fast and flexible adaptation (Cardinal, 1995; Eisenhardt and Tabrizi, 1995; Henderson and Clark, 1990; Simon, 1995). That is, the acquisition of skills and accomplishments in each domain (control and exploration) appears—at least under some conditions—to enhance the likelihood of succeeding in the other domain. More generally, the resilience of organizations and their members for withstanding change and ambiguity appears to be facilitated by the simple pursuit and balancing of the two overarching processes and associated practices. Thus, firms may need to pursue reliability while simultaneously paying attention to the development of new competencies (i.e., innovation-enhancing processes) if they are to remain viable over both the short and long term.

ACKNOWLEDGMENTS

The authors gratefully acknowledge support from the National Science Foundation (Grant Nos. SBR-94-96229 and SBR-94-20461) and the U.S. Air Force (Grant No. USAF-F49642-97-P-0083) for the program of research on which this text is based. Portions of this text were previously presented at the ORSA/TIMS meeting in Detroit, October 1994.

REFERENCES

Bendor, J. B. (1985). *Parallel systems.* Berkeley: University of California Press.

Brown, J. S. (1991). Research that reinvents the corporation. *Harvard Business Review, 69,* 102–111.

Brown, S. L., and Eisenhardt, K. M. (1995). Product development: Past research, present findings, and future directions. *Academy of Management Review, 20,* 343–378.

Burns, T., and Stalker, G. M. (1961). *The management of innovation.* London: Tavistock.

Cardinal, L. B. (1995). *Technological innovation in the pharmaceutical industry: Managing research and development using input, behavior, and output controls.* Working paper.

Cohen, M. D., March, J. G., and Olsen, J. P. (1972). A garbage can model of organizational choice. *Administrative Science Quarterly, 17,* 1–25.

Cyert, R. M., and March, J. G. (1963). *A behavioral theory of the firm.* Englewood Cliffs, NJ: Prentice Hall.

D'Aveni, R. A. (1994). *Hypercompetition: Managing the dynamics of strategic maneuvering.* New York: Free Press.

Daft, R. L. (1982). Bureaucratic vs. nonbureaucratic structure and the process of innovation and change. In S. Bacharach (Ed.), *Research in the sociology of organizations* (Vol. 1, pp. 129–166). Greenwich, CT: JAI.

Dean, J. W., and Bowen, D. E. (1994). Management theory and total quality: Improving research and practice through theory development. *Academy of Management Review, 19,* 392–418.

Denison, D. R. (1997). Toward a process-based theory of organizational design: Can organizations be designed around value chains and networks? In J. Walsh and A. Huff (Eds.), *Advances in strategic management* (Vol. 14, pp. 1–44). Greenwich, CT: JAI.

Eisenhardt, K. M. (1993). High reliability organizations meet high velocity environments: Common dilemmas in nuclear power plants. In K. H. Roberts (Ed.), *New challenges to understanding organizations* (pp. 117–136). New York: Macmillan.

Eisenhardt, K. M., and Tabrizi, B. N. (1995). Accelerating adaptive processes: Product innovation in the global computer industry. *Administrative Science Quarterly, 40,* 84–110.

Epple, D. E., Argote, L., and Devadas, R. (1991). Organizational learning curves: A method for investigating intra-plant transfer of knowledge acquired through learning by doing. *Organization Science, 2,* 58–70.

Hackman, J. R., and Wageman, R. (1995). Total quality management: Empirical, conceptual, and practical issues. *Administrative Science Quarterly, 40,* 309–342.

Haspeslagh, P., and Jemison, D. (1991). *Managing acquisitions.* New York: Free Press.

Henderson, R. M., and Clark, K. B. (1990). Architectural innovation: The reconfiguration of existing product technologies and the failure of established firms. *Administrative Science Quarterly, 35,* 9–30.

Kobasa, S. C. (1979). Stressful life events, personality, and health: An inquiry into hardiness. *Personality and Social Psychology, 37,* 1–11.

Levinthal, D., and March, J. G. (1981). A model of adaptive organizational search. *Journal of Economic Behavior and Organization, 2,* 307–333.

Levinthal, D. A., and March, J. G. (1993). The myopia of learning. *Strategic Management Journal, 14,* 95–112.

March, J. G. (1988). *Decisions and organizations.* New York: Basil Blackwell.

March, J. G. (1991). Exploration and exploitation in organizational learning. *Organization Science, 2,* 71–87.

March, J. G. (1995). The future, disposable organizations, and the rigidities of imagination. *Organization, 2,* 427–440.

March, J. G., and Simon, H. A. (1958). *Organizations.* New York: Wiley.

March, J. G., Sproull, L. S., and Tamuz, M. (1991). Learning from samples of one or fewer. *Organization Science, 2,* 1–13.

Miller, D. (1993). The architecture of simplicity. *Academy of Management Review, 18,* 116–138.

Nonaka, I., and Takeuchi, H. (1995). *The knowledge-creating company.* New York: Oxford University Press.

Ouchi, W. G. (1977). The relationship between organizational structure and organizational control. *Administrative Science Quarterly, 22,* 95–113.

Ouchi, W. G. (1979). A conceptual framework for the design of organizational control mechanisms. *Management Science, 25,* 833–848.

Ouchi, W. G. (1981). Markets, bureaucracies, and clans. *Administrative Science Quarterly, 25,* 129–141.

Perrow, C. (1967). A framework for the comparative analysis of organizations. *American Sociological Review, 32,* 194–208.

Quinn, J. B. (1980). *Strategies for change: Logical incrementalism.* Homewood, IL: Irwin-Dorsey.

Simon, R. (1995). *Levers of control.* Boston: Harvard Business School Press.

Sitkin, S. B. (1992). Learning through failure: The strategy of small losses. In B. M. Staw & L. L. Cummings (Eds.), *Research in organizational behavior* (Vol. 14, pp. 231–266). Greenwich, CT: JAI.

Sitkin, S. B., and Stickel, D. (1996). The road to hell: The dynamics of distrust in an era of quality. In R. M. Kramer and T. R. Tyler (Eds.), *Trust in organizations: Frontiers of theory and research* (pp. 196–215). Thousand Oaks, CA: Sage.

Sitkin, S. B., Sutcliffe, K. M., and Schroeder, R. G. (1994). Distinguishing control from learning in total quality management: A contingency perspective. *Academy of Management Review, 19,* 537–564.

Stacey, R. D. (1992). *Managing the unknowable: Strategic boundaries between order and chaos in organizations.* San Francisco: Jossey-Bass.

Sterman, J. D., Repenning, N. P., and Kofman, F. (1997). Unanticipated side effects of successful quality programs: Exploring a paradox of organizational improvement. *Management Science, 43,* 503–521.

Sternberg, R. J., and Kolligian, J. (1990). *Competence considered.* New Haven, CT: Yale University Press.

Sutcliffe, K. M. (1994). What executives notice: Accurate perceptions in top management teams. *Academy of Management Journal, 7,* 1360–1378.

Sutcliffe, K. M., and Bunderson, J. S. (1996, August). *Competence learned: Developmental processes in organizational teams.* Paper presented at the annual meeting of the Academy of Management, Cincinnati, OH.

Sutcliffe, K. M., Sitkin, S. B., and Browning, L. D. (1997). Perspectives on process management: Implications of research on 21st century organizations. In C. Cooper & S. Jackson (Eds.), *Handbook of organizational behavior* (pp. 207–229). Chichester, UK: Wiley.

Tamuz, M. (1987). The impact of computer surveillance on air safety reporting. *Columbia Journal of World Business, 22*(1), 69–77.

Tamuz, M. (1994). Developing organizational safety information systems for monitoring potential dangers. In G. E. Apostolakis and T. S. Win (Eds.), *Proceedings of PSAM II* (Vol. 2, Section 71, pp. 7–12). Los Angeles: University of California Press.

Thompson, J. D. (1967). *Organizations in action.* New York: McGraw-Hill.

Weick, K. E. (1979). *The social psychology of organizing* (2nd ed.). Reading, MA: Addison-Wesley.

Weick, K. E. (1984). Small wins: Redefining the scale of social problems. *American Psychologist, 39*(1), 40–49.

Weick, K. E. (1985). A stress analysis of future battlefields. In J. G. Hunt and J. D. Blair (Eds.), *Leadership on the future battlefield* (pp. 32–46). McLean, VA: Pergamon.

Weick, K. E. (1988). Enacted sensemaking in crisis situations. *Journal of Management Studies, 25,* 305–317.

Weick, K. E., and Roberts, K. (1993). Collective mind in organizations: Heedful interrelating on flight decks. *Administrative Science Quarterly, 38,* 357–381.

Westrum, R. (1991). *Technologies and society: The shaping of people and things.* Belmont, CA: Wadsworth.

Williamson, O. E. (1975). *Markets and hierarchies.* New York: Free Press.

Wood, R., and Bandura, A. (1989). Social cognitive theory of organizational management. *Academy of Management Review, 14,* 361–384.

Wruck, K., and Jensen, M. (1994). Science, specific knowledge, and total quality management. *Journal of Accounting and Economics, 18,* 247–287.

SECTION III

ORGANIZATIONAL ARCHITECTURES AND MANAGING INNOVATION

Innovation streams create significant organizational challenges. To excel in both incremental and nonincremental innovation, to create innovation streams, requires that a given organization be able to continue to exploit existing capabilities even as it explores new domains. This section focuses on building organizational architectures that can execute a firm's innovation strategy more swiftly than its competitors. We focus on managers as organizational architects, architects with a considerable set of materials and tools to use in building organizational capabilities. Our organizational model focuses on members of a managerial team designing their unit's hardware as well as software in service of its strategy. Tushman and O'Reilly articulate the section's core model, which focuses on building organizational capabilities that are rooted in tasks and associated work processes, human resource competencies, organizational arrangements, and organizational culture. For a given strategy, congruence, or fit, between these components is associated with organizational effectiveness. Or a unit's performance gaps are rooted in the lack of congruence among existing organizational components or from a mismatch between the unit's strategy and its context. The rest of the articles in this section add depth to the different components of the congruence model. Collins and Porras suggest that organizational capabilities are in service of the unit's strategy and vision and that an important role of the leader is to infuse the organization with value. Katz discusses the challenges of managing professionals and managing professionals over time, whereas Flynn and Chatman emphasize the important role of creating cultures that enhance innovation. Pfeffer describes another aspect of organizational culture—power and organizational politics. He discusses how to diagnose and shape political dynamics to execute innovation and change. Sutton describes the fundamentally different cultures, organizational designs, and competencies associated with incremental versus more discontinuous innovation. Tushman and O'Reilly introduce the notion of an ambidextrous organizational design. Ambidextrous organizational forms help firms simultaneously manage incremental and more discontinuous innovation. Finally, Leonard-Barton looks at the downside of congruence, fit, and building core capabilities. She argues that building these highly interrelated capabilities drives short-term effectiveness but also longer-term organizational rigidities.

14

Managerial Problem Solving

A Congruence Approach

MICHAEL L. TUSHMAN
CHARLES O'REILLY III

Kurt Huber is a lean, intense manager with a doctorate in chemistry and 18 years of experience managing within Ciba-Geigy. In 1993, he was transferred as head of Ciba's U.K. chemical plant to general manager of its plant in Grenzach, Germany. The Grenzach plant was a large facility located on the Rhine River bordering Switzerland. Originally established in 1898, it was one of Ciba's oldest plants, a traditional chemical manufacturing site with a long-service, highly skilled work force; formal union-management relations; a seven-level formal hierarchy; a functional structure; and rigid work rules. The facility had four separate production lines and manufactured a variety of chemical compounds for Ciba's industrial divisions. It was also one of the Chemical Division's least competitive plants, with labor costs 20 percent above comparable European facilities and four times more costly than wages paid by emerging competitors in Mexico, China, and India. Reflecting these cost problems were a loss in market share, as well as a lack of new products. Worse, since chemical production facilities are expensive, they need to run at full volume. Yet, as volume dropped, the already costly facility became even less competitive. Huber's assignment was to either fix the plant or close it.

Huber had spearheaded other successful turn-arounds but had serious doubts about Grenzach. "There were too many problems and too many possible causes. I knew that addressing one or two of them wouldn't work. I didn't think a standard turnaround effort would succeed." The sheer magnitude of the problems was almost overwhelming. Huber knew that he had only one shot at fixing Grenzach. The head of the Chemicals Division made it clear that he had 24 months or 1,500 people would lose their jobs, including Huber.

To solve this problem, Huber needed a method that would quickly and accurately identify the root causes of Grenzach's problems. Once critical performance or opportunity gaps are identified, managers like Kurt Huber can rapidly diagnose the causes of these gaps and, in turn, take action to close them. To help managers like Huber perform this diagnosis, we introduce a congruence-based problem-solving approach that is straight-forward, easy to use, and supported by an extensive body of research and practice.[1] Our approach does not require outside consultants or sophisticated technology. This method has been used by managers, from CEOs to first-level managers, around the world. It suggests that the alignment, or congruence, between strategy and four organizational building blocks—critical tasks and work flows, formal

Reprinted by permission of Harvard Business School Press. From *Winning Through Innovation,* by Michael L. Tushman and Charles O'Reilly III, pp. 57–77. Copyright © 2002 by the Harvard Business School Publishing Corporation; all rights reserved.

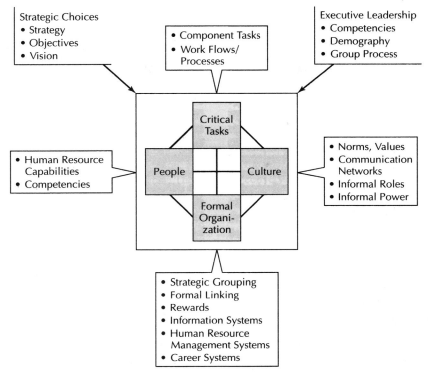

Figure 14.1. Organizational architecture: a congruence model of organizations (adapted from Nadler and Tushman, 1992).

organizational arrangements, people, and culture—drives today's success. Incongruence, a lack of alignment, or inconsistencies among these elements is almost always at the root of today's performance gaps (see Figure 14.1).[2]

The reason this systematic approach is important is simple: Unless managers and their teams clearly understand the roots of today's performance gaps or those barriers to achieving strategic opportunities, their attempts to solve these problems or realize the opportunities are likely to be incomplete or cause other unanticipated problems. We illustrate this problem-solving approach with the cases of three managers in three different countries and in three different industries: Kurt Huber, head of the Grenzach plant of Ciba-Geigy, C. K. Chow, CEO of BOC's Industrial Gases business headquartered outside of London, and John

Torrance, vice president of R&D at Medtek, a clinical diagnostic instrument firm located in New York.

A PROCESS FOR ORGANIZATIONAL PROBLEM SOLVING

First we outline the five steps needed to use the model and complete a congruence analysis. Each step is simple and straightforward. Although we focus on managers who have used this approach, we encourage readers to apply it to their own performance or opportunity gaps. At the end of this chapter there is a practical guide that shows in greater detail how a congruence analysis may be done. This will be useful for gaining a greater understanding of organizational data gathering and in doing a careful diagnosis of your own

Steps:

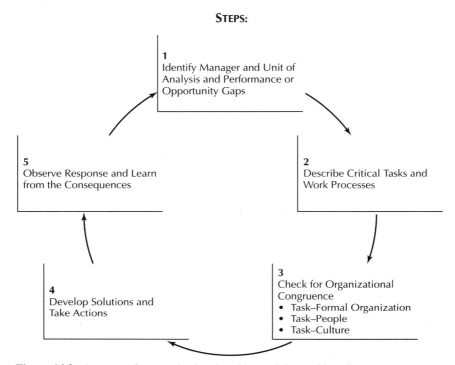

Figure 14.2. A process for organizational problem solving and learning.

issues. Here we offer a quick overview of this prob-lem-solving process to illustrate the power of this five-step approach (see Figure 14.2).

Step I: Identify the Unit's Crucial Performance or Opportunity Gaps

A diagnosis begins with a manager and his or her team defining the performance gaps facing their unit or or-ganization. It is important in doing this to identify those problems or opportunities that lie at least poten-tially within control of the unit and avoid defining gaps too broadly or in a way that cedes responsibility to a higher level manager. The person doing the diagnosis needs to "own" the gap. At BOC Gases, for example, Chow and his team identified lack of innovation and customer responsiveness as the key performance gaps. For John Torrance at Medtek, the gap centered on a failure to produce new products and turnover among key scientists.

Kurt Huber, faced with the challenge of fixing or closing Grenzach, gathered his senior team at an off-

site meeting to reach consensus on the critical perfor-mance gaps they needed to address. To help focus its efforts, Huber began by asking each member of the team to prepare an obituary (*Nachruf*) describing how and when they believed Grenzach would fail. The re-sults were sobering. All the managers predicted that if left unchecked, the plant would fail within the next several years. One common cause of death was identi-fied as "a lack of agreement and focus among manage-ment about problems." Motivated by this insight, the team identified a list of problems, including:

- Loss of market share and shrinking margins
- Lack of new products
- Slow introduction of new products
- Loss of sales
- Cost of goods sold too high

After discussion, Huber and his team decided that the most critical issue to be resolved was "Loss of market share and shrinking margins." Having taken this first step, they turned to diagnosing the root causes of the gap.

Step 2: Describe Critical Tasks and Work Processes

With clarity about vision and strategy, managers can then describe the critical tasks necessary to implement the strategy. What are the concrete tasks necessary to accomplish the objectives and add value from the customer's perspective? In describing these, also consider how much interdependence or integration is needed among the critical tasks. The amount of required integration is a critical determinant of the skills, structure, and culture required for successful execution of strategy. . . . For instance, at Medtek, Torrance realized that if he were to be successful at developing innovative new products, his laboratory would have to be world-class in chemical and hydraulic technologies and be able to link these technologies to manufacturing and marketing requirements. For Chow at BOC, a critical task identified for delivering customized service to global customers was close integration across geographically dispersed organizations. With the Grenzach team's goal of reducing costs, the critical tasks were to maintain the functional excellence within the plant as well as to increase integration across the functional areas.

Step 3: Check for Organizational Congruence

Once the critical tasks and work processes have been defined, the alignment or congruence of the three other major organizational building blocks (formal organization structure and systems, people, and the culture or informal organization) can be examined to ensure that these elements are supporting the attainment of the critical tasks. The key diagnostic questions for assessing congruence are: Given the critical tasks and work flows that must be accomplished, how aligned or congruent are the current formal organizational arrangements (e.g., structure, systems, rewards), culture (e.g., norms, values, informal communication networks), and people (e.g., individual competencies, motives)? Do these organizational building blocks fit with task requirements? Do they fit with each other?

This diagnosis requires only that a manager or team carefully and systematically describe each component of the model and consider its alignment with the critical tasks and work processes. The goal is to describe these, preferably on paper or flip chart, to see whether the current organization is aligned with the critical tasks required to meet the strategic challenges. To the extent that these components fit with each other, the organization is likely to be successful in the short run. On the other hand, if the components are incongruent with the critical tasks or with each other, these inconsistencies are likely to be at the root of today's performance gaps. . . . To briefly illustrate this process, consider the diagnoses that Chow and Huber completed at BOC and Grenzach shown in Figures 14.3a and 14.3b and 14.4. (Solid lines indicate congruent relationships; dotted lines indicate incongruent relationships.)

ALIGNING THE FORMAL ORGANIZATION

To ensure that the formal organization and critical tasks are aligned, ask the following diagnostic question: Given the critical tasks and processes needed to execute the strategy, does the current structure facilitate the accomplishment of both the component tasks and their required integration? For example, as shown in Figure 14.3b, Chow and his team identified as a key inconsistency the misfit of their current geographic structure with the critical task of global integration. While BOC's strategic goal was to provide service to global customers, its structure promoted fierce geographic loyalties and offered no way to link these geographic units together. At Grenzach (Figure 14.4), Huber and his team noted that the seven-level hierarchy and formal structure were inconsistent with speed and were associated with higher costs of coordination and supervision. Further, the rigid job specifications resulted in overstaffing and slow response times.

Several related questions to ask when checking the alignment of the formal organization are: Do the formal linking mechanisms facilitate task integration? Do the existing measurement, control, and career systems track the outcomes important for the execution of the critical tasks and work flows? and Given task demands, are the right things being rewarded (e.g., compensation, recognition, and promotion)? At BOC, the financial reporting system was geographically based and did not permit worldwide reporting by customer. At Grenzach, promotions historically had been based on rigid compliance with procedures. Risk taking and

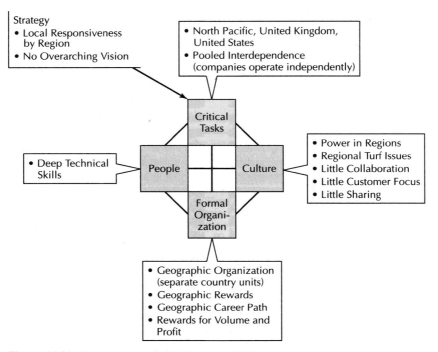

Figure 14.3a. Congruence at BOC Gases pre-1993.

boundary spanning were frowned on. In both instances, it was clear that the formal organization was not aligned with critical tasks.

ALIGNING HUMAN RESOURCES

In addition to checking for the congruence of the formal organization and critical tasks, managers also need to verify that their human resources are aligned with the critical tasks; that is, to ensure that people have the right skill sets and are motivated and committed to accomplish critical tasks. Here several diagnostic questions can be asked: Given the critical tasks, do people have the required competencies to perform them? Are there additional skills or incentives that are needed? Can employees be trained in these new skills or do we need to bring in new people?

For example, at BOC middle managers had deep engineering skills but were weak in marketing and the collaborative skills needed to operate a global matrix. A similar incongruency was discovered at Grenzach. With the firm's emphasis on narrow technical skills, it was apparent to the Grenzach team that people

throughout the plant would need help in working across boundaries. Further, Huber's team observed that the greatest danger resided among managers who lacked the skills needed to manage in a flatter, less top-down organization. Both teams also realized that there was a further inconsistency between the reward system and the new skills required. Unless the formal and informal reward systems were changed, they realized that there would be little incentive for people to acquire the needed new competencies or to excel at them.

ALIGNING THE CULTURE

Finally, there is the difficult issue of ensuring congruence between the unit's or organization's culture and the required critical tasks. Does the existing culture energize the accomplishment of the critical tasks? Do the informal communication network and informal distribution of power help get the work done? Are there existing aspects of the current culture that may hinder the execution of these tasks? ... [T]his is a critical and much overlooked factor in the management of innovation.

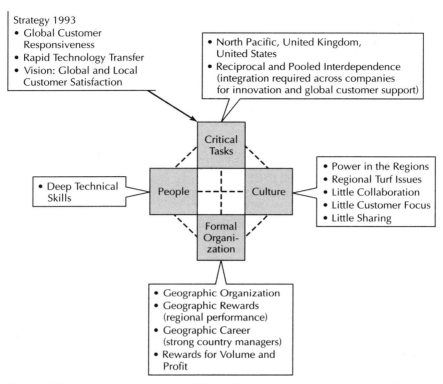

Figure 14.3b. Lack of congruence in 1993 at BOC is caused by new strategy, vision, and critical tasks.

For instance, at Grenzach the culture diagnosis identified as central norms a reluctance to take ownership and a reliance on being told what to do rather than a willingness to take action. Huber and his team knew immediately that these norms would never encourage the initiative and responsiveness required by a flatter and cross-functional organization. Unless these norms were changed, neither the cost savings from a leaner organization nor the bottom-up innovation required would occur. At BOC, the current culture of noncooperation across geographies was misaligned with the critical tasks and the new formal organizational arrangements.

This short overview illustrates how the alignment of strategy, critical tasks, and the basic organizational building blocks of the formal organization (structure, systems, and rewards), people (competencies and motivation), and the culture (norms, values, informal communication, and power) is associated with short-term success. A lack of fit among these elements is the cause of performance gaps (assuming the strategy chosen is appropriate) and may require managers and their teams to realign their formal structures, people, and culture with their new critical tasks. Ironically, it is usually the case that the misalignments result from past organizational strengths that, if not modified, can become a future liability.

Step 4: Develop Solutions and Take Corrective Actions

Once core inconsistencies are identified, managers can then take targeted action to bring the system back into alignment. The greater the number of inconsistencies among the organizational building blocks, the more substantial the interventions must be. For instance, a change in only one or two components, such as a new reward system or a shift in culture to reflect a new competitive demand, can usually be managed as incre-

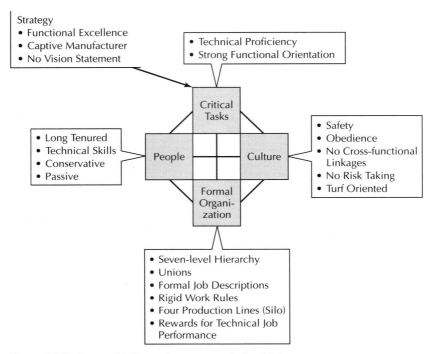

Figure 14.4. Grenzach's internal congruence before Huber.

mental change. Systemwide lack of congruence, re-quiring changes in three or more of the organizational building blocks, demands discontinuous organization-al change.

For instance, at Grenzach, Huber and his team determined that to survive they would have to change their critical tasks (technical proficiency and increased integration). Chow and his team at BOC came to a similar conclusion. To help them focus their efforts, both managers and their teams developed revised con-gruence models that reflected the needed realignment (see Figures 14.5 and 14.6). Realigning Grenzach re-quired simultaneous changes in human resources (new skills, gradual downsizing), formal organizational arrangements (from seven levels to three with new structures, systems, and rewards), and a radically dif-ferent culture (from security, stability, technology, and tradition to teamwork, initiative, flexibility, openness, and customer orientation). The discontinuous change effort took a year and a massive amount of energy and involvement of Huber and his team. After the initial resistance, the results are gratifying. Today, a new

Grenzach plant has emerged with a competitive cost structure, new products, lower accident and absen-teeism rates, and the ability to compete in global markets.

A similar discontinuous change has occurred at BOC Gases. Based on their diagnosis, Chow and his team have implemented a new global matrix struc-ture supported by a new measurement and control sys-tem; changed the culture to promote collaboration, cross-boundary communication, and a customer fo-cus; and brought in new marketing skills. These systemwide changes are bearing fruit. By 1996, BOC Gases was winning new gas supply contracts, leading innovation, and running more efficiently. For managers in both organizations, the process was the same: Identify the performance gaps; determine the critical tasks needed to achieve strategic objec-tives; assess the congruence among tasks, people, the formal organization, and culture; and, depending on the diagnosis, take actions targeted to bring these inconsistencies into alignment with the critical tasks.

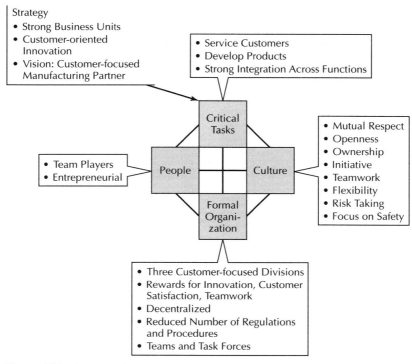

Figure 14.5. Congruencies required by Grenzach's new strategy and vision.

Step 5: Observe the Response and Learn from the Consequences

Since any action is likely to be incomplete, it is improbable that all performance gaps will be reduced. The diagnosis and actions will typically reveal other problems. But managers and their teams can learn from these situations and reinitiate the process. The idea is to continually refine and readjust the internal congruence of the unit, not to determine the optimal solution for all problems. At Grenzach, for instance, Huber has recently reinitiated the culture change process and changed the structure and rewards systems to make the plant even more entrepreneurial. At BOC, the inevitable difficulties in operating in a matrix organization have caused Chow and his team to iterate their diagnosis and to refine their operations further. Unlike the old Peters and Waterman exhortation, "Ready, fire, aim," managers at Grenzach and BOC have used a rapid, diagnostically driven process to continuously aim and fire.

ASSESSING CONGRUENCE

Organizational diagnoses are made to understand the causes of today's performance gaps or to anticipate what might cause problems in the future. Managers begin by first gathering data and describing the four organizational building blocks. Once this is done, the fit among them can be evaluated by determining the degree to which the needs, demands, goals, and structure of each component are aligned with the others. For example, is the reward system congruent with the culture? Are the skills of the people consistent with the career paths offered? Does the structure of the unit facilitate accomplishment of the critical tasks? See Table 14.1 for a full set of congruence relationships.

Internal fit is associated with short-term organizational performance. A lack of congruence between components, drives performance shortfalls and is a root cause of today's problems. Since these root causes

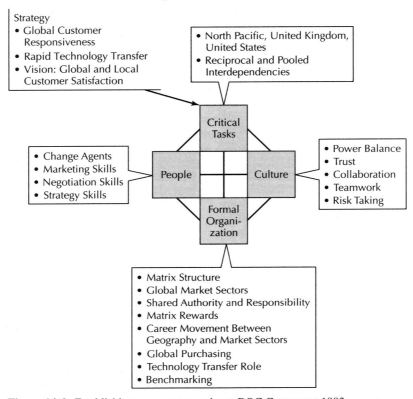

Figure 14.6. Establishing new congruencies at BOC Gases post-1993.

can be anywhere in the system, managers need to be systematic in their diagnosis. Rather than solving the problem, an incomplete diagnosis or partial fix may lead to further problems. While each congruence relationship is important . . . , the three relating to aligning (or realigning) organizational components to get the unit's critical tasks accomplished are particularly crucial. These three alignments are:

1. *Task-People.* To what extent do the skills, abilities, and motives of today's human resources fit with task requirements? For example, at BOC, Chow's new strategy and tasks demanded deep marketing competencies. Yet an audit of Chow's current marketing skills indicated real weaknesses not only within Chow's team but also within the larger organization. If this task-human resource inconsistency is not addressed, BOC's ability to execute its new strategy will be stunted.

2. *Task-Formal Organization.* To what extent do organizational arrangements fit with task requirements? For example, at Medtek, Torrance's laboratory was functionally organized but the new tasks emphasized developing new products, which required strong integration across functions. Unless formal linking mechanisms are developed, this task-structure inconsistency will impede the innovation critical to Medtek's survival.

3. *Task-Culture.* To what extent does the unit's culture fit with task requirements? At Grenzach, almost a hundred years of tradition emphasized technical excellence and formal authority. But the new task requirements demand speed, teamwork, and initiative. If left unaddressed, the old culture would drag down Huber's efforts to save the plant, regardless of how the organization is structured. This culture-task inconsistency was a major cause of the performance gap at Grenzach.

Table 14.1. Congruence Among Organizational Building Blocks

Fit	Issues
People/Formal Organization	How are individual needs met by the organizational arrangements? Are individuals motivated to accomplish critical tasks?
	Do individuals have clear perceptions of organizational structures?
People/Critical Tasks	Do individuals have the skills and abilities to meet task demands? How are individual needs met by the task?
People/Culture	How are individual needs met by the informal organization?
Critical Tasks/Formal Organization	Are formal organizational arrangements adequate to meet the demands of the task? Do they motivate behavior that is consistent with task demands?
Critical Tasks/Culture	Does the culture facilitate task performance? Does it help meet the demands of the task?
Formal Organization/Culture	Are the goals, rewards, and structures of the culture consistent with those of the formal organization?

Organizational diagnoses pivot on the critical tasks and work processes. Once these are specified, managers can use the congruence model to diagnose the current degree of fit between their current organization and that needed to successfully execute their strategy. The basic principle of our approach is: Today's effectiveness is enhanced the greater the total degree of congruence among different organizational components. The lack of congruence among organizational buildings blocks are the causes of today's performance or opportunity gaps.

Once critical problems or opportunities and their root causes are identified, the focus is not on searching for the single "right" answer, but on a process by which managers can determine which of several possibly correct answers might work for them. For a particular manager with a particular context and performance gaps, there are almost always a number of right answers. The correct ones are those that deal with the specific inconsistencies identified in the diagnoses. For example, at BOC Gases, Chow and his team discovered that the current structures, systems, cultures, and marketing capabilities were inconsistent with their aspirations for effective technology transfer and satisfied global customers. This diagnosis led, in turn, to several possible systemwide changes at BOC. Chow and his team evaluated the relative costs and benefits of the various options and decided on a global matrix as their structural intervention.

While our method does not provide optimal answers, it does offer a rigorous process for initiating targeted actions based on systematic analysis. No intervention will ever be perfect. Our approach simply asks

managers to quickly gather data, take targeted action, and learn from their actions. As Percy Barnevik of ABB is fond of saying, "Nothing is worse than procrastination. . . . It's better to make decisions quickly and be right seven out of ten times than to waste time trying to achieve the perfect solution."[3] In articulating the management principles for ABB, Barnevik notes that to stick one's neck out and do the right thing is obviously best. But he says that second best is to take action, make a mistake, and learn from your actions. To take no action is the only unacceptable behavior for ABB managers. We agree. It is better to get an approximately correct solution quickly than an optimal solution slowly. Organizational learning is about finding good-enough solutions to important problems or opportunities and making error-correcting adjustments to get better and better; learning, especially in a rapidly changing world, is not about always finding the precise answer.

USING THE CONGRUENCE MODEL

We have helped and observed hundreds of managers using the congruence model. The guide at the end of this chapter reflects our experience and provides greater detail on doing a diagnosis. Based on the experiences of these managers, a number of suggestions for using the congruence model as a tool for managerial problem solving have been offered. They reflect common problems that managers have encountered and their suggestions for how to avoid these difficulties. The following rules of thumb are designed to alert managers to possible pitfalls before using the congruence model and ensure greater success from its use:

1. Be clear about the unit of analysis; that is, who owns the problem. What is controllable and what isn't? Managers in different positions may have different problems and develop different diagnoses to the same performance gaps. The first step in organizational diagnosis is to clarify who the manager is and to identify performance or opportunity gaps from that perspective. This sounds trivial but it is easy for a manager to define a problem from the boss's or CEO's perspective with the result that many solutions are not implementable because they exceed the specific manager's control.

2. To the extent that the strategy or vision is wrong, no amount of diagnosis and root cause analysis will help. Organizations exist to accomplish strategic goals. If the strategy emphasizes the wrong product or service, to the wrong market, with the wrong technology and bad timing, no amount of organizational problem solving can help. Tight alignment with the wrong strategy ensures quick failure.

3. Comprehensive diagnoses are necessary. Since success depends on the alignment of the four organizational building blocks, it is critical that any diagnosis consider all of them. Focusing on one or two, as is customary in reengineering or TQM efforts, may miss the need to align other components. For instance, a common failure in reengineering efforts is that managers ignore the informal organization with the result that cultural inertia and political resistance wreck the process.

4. The type of change required depends on the number of inconsistencies discovered. If a diagnosis reveals incongruencies between only one or two organizational building blocks, incremental change is possible. If, however, the diagnosis shows inconsistencies among three or more building blocks (e.g., new critical tasks require changes in people, formal arrangements, and culture), discontinuous change is needed. ... [T]his has important ramifications for how a manager thinks about and initiates change.

5. For any diagnosis, there may be many possible interventions. As such, there is no single best solu-

tion. Rather, the question is what set or combination of components needs to be changed to achieve congruence? Different managers may choose to intervene in different ways. What is important is that any intervention deal with the inconsistencies identified in the diagnosis and drive greater congruence among the building blocks.

6. Our approach focuses on problem definition and root cause analyses from a particular manager's position. Sometimes, a diagnosis shows that the root causes of the performance gap are beyond the control of the focal manager. In these circumstances, the manager needs the skills to manage his or her boss, peers, customers, or others outside the unit. If the manager lacks these influence skills outside his or her area or has no leverage, all the diagnostic work will yield is an insightful but frustrated manager.

7. The congruence approach emphasizes gathering data prior to taking action. Although logical, our experience suggests that this is often an unnatural act for many managers. In the press of day-to-day business, managers often lack the time to be systematic. There is a bias toward immediate, decisive action. We urge managers to step back and gather data prior to intervening—to be systematic in their diagnoses.[4] This is not paralysis through analysis but data-driven problem solving. Both Chow and Huber completed their initial diagnoses over two-day periods, not months of analysis. Their diagnoses led, in turn, to systematic interventions over 12–18 month periods.

8. Successful problem solving is a function of both what managers do (i.e., the actions they take) and how they do it (i.e., their execution). Effective managers do the right thing and do it well. Knowing what to do is half the solution. Being able to implement the needed changes is equally as important. Great ideas executed poorly are as bad as poor ideas executed flawlessly. . . .

9. This disciplined problem-solving approach and learning from one's actions is associated with greater effectiveness over time. Different managers may develop different diagnoses for the same problem. Further, the same diagnosis can spawn multiple possible interventions. Rather than focusing on the correct intervention to solve a particular prob-

lem, our approach asks managers to focus on the process by which they attack the problem. All managers will make mistakes in both diagnoses and action. Excellent managers are not paralyzed by studying problems, or by making mistakes, rather, they are able to learn by doing.[5]

Although managers may know that organizational hardware and software must fit task requirements, they are often most familiar and comfortable with the vertical axis of our model—the organization's technical systems.

NOTES

1. This chapter builds on Nadler and Tushman, 1980, 1992, 1997.

2. See also other approaches to the notion of fit or congruence, including Davis and Lawrence, 1977; Galbraith, 1973; Gresov, 1989; Miles and Snow, 1994; Miller, 1986 and 1993; and Peters and Waterman, 1983.

3. See Taylor, 1991.

4. This mode of problem solving is consistent with the work on TQM and organizational learning. See, for example, Cohen and Sproul, 1996; Huber, 1991; Kano, 1993; Kolesar, 1993; Levitt and March, 1988; Nonaka, 1993; Senge, 1990; and Walton, 1986.

5. See also Argyris and Schon, 1978; and Weick, 1979.

REFERENCES

Argyris, C., and D. Schon. 1978. *Organizational Learning*. Reading, Mass.: Addison-Wesley.

Cohen, M., and L. Sproul, eds. 1996. *Organizational Learning*. London: Sage.

Davis, S., and P. Lawrence. 1977. *Matrix*. Reading, Mass.: Addison-Wesley.

Galbraith, J. 1973. *Designing Complex Organizations*. Reading, Mass.: Addison-Wesley.

Gresov, C. 1989. "Exploring Fit and Misfit with Multiple Contingencies." *Administrative Science Quarterly* 34: 431–453.

Huber, G. 1991. "Organization Learning: Contributing Processes and the Literature." *Organization Science* 2: 88–115.

Kano, N. 1993. "A Perspective on Quality Activities in American Firms." *California Management Review* (Spring): 12–30.

Kolesar, P. J. 1993. "Vision Values Milestones: Paul O'Neill Starts Total Quality at Alcoa." *California Management Review* 35(3): 133–165.

Levitt, B., and J. March. 1988. "Organization Learning." *American Review of Sociology* 14: 319–340.

Miles, R., and C. Snow. 1994. *Fit, Failure, and the Hall of Fame*. New York: Free Press.

Miller, D. 1986. "Configurations of Strategy and Structure: Towards a Synthesis." *Strategic Management Journal* 7: 233–249.

Miller, D. 1993. "The Architecture of Simplicity." *Academy of Management Review* 18: 116–138.

Nadler, D., and M. Tushman. 1980. "A Model for Diagnosing Organization Behavior." *Organization Dynamics* (Spring): 148–163.

Nadler, D., and M. Tushman. 1992. "Designing Organizations That Have Good Fit." In *Organization Architecture,* edited by D. Nadler. San Francisco: Jossey-Bass.

Nadler, D., and M. Tushman. 1997. *Competing by Design: The Power of Organizational Architectures*. New York: Oxford University Press.

Nonaka, I. 1993. *The Knowledge Creating Company*. New York: Oxford University Press.

Peters, T., and R. Waterman. 1983. *In Search of Excellence*. New York: Free Press.

Senge, P. 1990. *The Fifth Discipline*. New York: Doubleday.

Taylor, W. 1991. "The Logic of Global Business: An Interview with ABB's Percy Barnevik." *Harvard Business Review* (March–April): 91–105.

Walton, M. 1986. *The Deming Method*. New York: Dodd Mead.

Weick, K. 1979. *The Social Psychology of Organizing*. Reading, Mass.: Addison-Wesley.

15

Building Your Company's Vision

JIM COLLINS
JERRY I. PORRAS

**We shall not cease from exploration
And the end of all our exploring
Will be to arrive where we started
And know the place for the first time.**

T. S. ELIOT, *FOUR QUARTETS*

Companies that enjoy enduring success have core values and a core purpose that remain fixed while their business strategies and practices endlessly adapt to a changing world. The dynamic of preserving the core while stimulating progress is the reason that companies such as Hewlett-Packard, 3M, Johnson & Johnson, Procter & Gamble, Merck, Sony, Motorola, and Nordstrom became elite institutions able to renew themselves and achieve superior long-term performance. Hewlett-Packard employees have long known that radical change in operating practices, cultural norms, and business strategies does not mean losing the spirit of the HP Way—the company's core principles. Johnson & Johnson continually questions its structure and revamps its processes while preserving the ideals embodied in its credo. In 1996, 3M sold off several of its large mature businesses—a dramatic move that surprised the business press—to refocus on its enduring core purpose of solving unsolved problems innovatively. We studied companies such as these in our research for *Built to Last: Successful Habits of Visionary Companies* and found that they have outper-

formed the general stock market by a factor of 12 since 1925.

Truly great companies understand the difference between what should never change and what should be open for change, between what is genuinely sacred and what is not. This rare ability to manage continuity and change—requiring a consciously practiced discipline—is closely linked to the ability to develop a vision. Vision provides guidance about what core to preserve and what future to stimulate progress toward. But *vision* has become one of the most overused and least understood words in the language, conjuring up different images for different people: of deeply held values, outstanding achievement, societal bonds, exhilarating goals, motivating forces, or raisons d'être. We recommend a conceptual framework to define vision, add clarity and rigor to the vague and fuzzy concepts swirling around that trendy term, and give practical guidance for articulating a coherent vision within an organization. It is a prescriptive framework rooted in six years of research and refined and tested by our ongoing work with executives from a great variety of organizations around the world.

A well-conceived vision consists of two major components: *core ideology* and *envisioned future*. (See Figure 15.1.) Core ideology, the yin in our scheme, defines what we stand for and why we exist. Yin is unchanging and complements yang, the envisioned future. The envisioned future is what we aspire to

Copyright © 1996 by Jim Collins and Jerry I. Porras. Reprinted by permission of the authors. More of Jim Collins' work can be found at www.jimcollins.com.

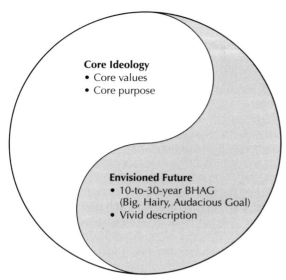

Figure 15.1. Articulating a vision.

become, to achieve, to create—something that will require significant change and progress to attain.

CORE IDEOLOGY

Core ideology defines the enduring character of an organization—a consistent identity that transcends product or market life cycles, technological breakthroughs, management fads, and individual leaders. In fact, the most lasting and significant contribution of those who build visionary companies is the core ideology. As Bill Hewlett said about his longtime friend and business partner David Packard upon Packard's death not long ago, "As far as the company is concerned, the greatest thing he left behind him was a code of ethics known as the HP Way." HP's core ideology, which has guided the company since its inception more than 50 years ago, includes a deep respect for the individual, a dedication to affordable quality and reliability, a commitment to community responsibility (Packard himself bequeathed his $4.3 billion of Hewlett-Packard stock to a charitable foundation), and a view that the company exists to make technical contributions for the advancement and welfare of humanity. Company builders such as David Packard, Masaru Ibuka of Sony, George Merck of Merck, William McKnight of 3M,

and Paul Galvin of Motorola understood that it is more important to know who you are than where you are going, for where you are going will change as the world around you changes. Leaders die, products become obsolete, markets change, new technologies emerge, and management fads come and go, but core ideology in a great company endures as a source of guidance and inspiration.

Core ideology provides the glue that holds an organization together as it grows, decentralizes, diversifies, expands globally, and develops workplace diversity. Think of it as analogous to the principles of Judaism that held the Jewish people together for centuries without a homeland, even as they spread throughout the Diaspora. Or think of the truths held to be self-evident in the Declaration of Independence, or the enduring ideals and principles of the scientific community that bond scientists from every nationality together in the common purpose of advancing human knowledge. Any effective vision must embody the core ideology of the organization, which in turn consists of two distinct parts: core values, a system of guiding principles and tenets; and core purpose, the organization's most fundamental reason for existence.

Core Values

Core values are the essential and enduring tenets of an organization. A small set of timeless guiding principles, core values require no external justification; they have *intrinsic* value and importance to those inside the organization. The Walt Disney Company's core values of imagination and wholesomeness stem not from market requirements but from the founder's inner belief that imagination and wholesomeness should be nurtured for their own sake. William Procter and James Gamble didn't instill in P&G's culture a focus on product excellence merely as a strategy for success but as an almost religious tenet. And that value has been passed down for more than 15 decades by P&G people. Service to the customer—even to the point of subservience—is a way of life at Nordstrom that traces its roots back to 1901, eight decades before customer service programs became stylish. For Bill Hewlett and David Packard, respect for the individual was first and foremost a deep personal value; they didn't get it from a book or hear it from a management guru. And Ralph S. Larsen, CEO of Johnson & Johnson, puts it this way: "The core values embodied in our credo might be a competitive advantage, but that is not *why* we have them. We have them because they define for us what we stand for, and we would hold them even if they became a competitive *dis*advantage in certain situations."

The point is that a great company decides for itself what values it holds to be core, largely independent of the current environment, competitive requirements, or management fads. Clearly, then, there is no universally right set of core values. A company need not have as its core value customer service (Sony doesn't) or respect for the individual (Disney doesn't) or quality (Wal-Mart Stores doesn't) or market focus (HP doesn't) or teamwork (Nordstrom doesn't). A company might have operating practices and business strategies around those qualities without having them at the essence of its being. Furthermore, great companies need not have likable or humanistic core values,

although many do. The key is not *what* core values an organization has but that it has core values at all.

Companies tend to have only a few core values, usually between three and five. In fact, we found that none of the visionary companies we studied in our book had more than five: most had only three or four. (See the box "Core Values Are a Company's Essential Tenets.") And, indeed, we should expect that. Only a few values can be truly *core*—that is, so fundamental and deeply held that they will change seldom, if ever.

To identify the core values of your own organization, push with relentless honesty to define what values are truly central. If you articulate more than five or six, chances are that you are confusing core values (which do not change) with operating practices, business strategies, or cultural norms (which should be open to change). Remember, the values must stand the test of time. After you've drafted a preliminary list of the core

---

Core Values Are a Company's Essential Tenets

MERCK

- Corporate social responsibility
- Unequivocal excellence in all aspects of the company
- Science-based innovation
- Honesty and integrity
- Profit, but profit from work that benefits humanity

NORDSTROM

- Service to the customer above all else
- Hard work and individual productivity
- Never being satisfied
- Excellence in reputation, being part of something special

PHILIP MORRIS

- The right to freedom of choice
- Winning—beating others in a good fight

- Encouraging individual initiative
- Opportunity based on merit; no one is entitled to anything
- Hard work and continuous self-improvement

SONY

- Elevation of the Japanese culture and national status
- Being a pioneer—not following others; doing the impossible
- Encouraging individual ability and creativity

WALT DISNEY

- No cynicism
- Nurturing and promulgation of "wholesome American values"
- Creativity, dreams, and imagination
- Fanatical attention to consistency and detail
- Preservation and control of the Disney magic

values, ask about each one, If the circumstances changed and *penalized* us for holding this core value, would we still keep it? If you can't honestly answer yes, then the value is not core and should be dropped from consideration.

A high-technology company wondered whether it should put quality on its list of core values. The CEO asked, "Suppose in ten years quality doesn't make a hoot of difference in our markets. Suppose the only thing that matters is sheer speed and horsepower but not quality. Would we still want to put quality on our list of core values?" The members of the management team looked around at one another and finally said no. Quality stayed in the *strategy* of the company, and quality-improvement programs remained in place as a mechanism for stimulating progress; but quality did not make the list of core values.

The same group of executives then wrestled with leading-edge innovation as a core value. The CEO asked, "Would we keep innovation on the list as a core value, no matter how the world around us changed?" This time, the management team gave a resounding yes. The managers' outlook might be summarized as, "We always want to do leading-edge innovation. That's who we are. It's really important to us and always will be. No matter what. And if our current markets don't value it, we will find markets that do." Leading-edge innovation went on the list and will stay there. A company should not change its core values in response to market changes; rather, it should change markets, if necessary, to remain true to its core values.

Who should be involved in articulating the core values varies with the size, age, and geographic dispersion of the company, but in many situations we have recommended what we call a *Mars Group*. It works like this: Imagine that you've been asked to re-create the very best attributes of your organization on another planet but you have seats on the rocket ship for only five to seven people. Whom should you send? Most likely, you'll choose the people who have a gut-level understanding of your core values, the highest level of credibility with their peers, and the highest levels of competence. We'll often ask people brought together to work on core values to nominate a Mars Group of five to seven individuals (not necessarily all from the assembled group). Invariably, they end up selecting highly credible representatives who do a super job of articulating the core values precisely because they are

exemplars of those values—a representative slice of the company's genetic code.

Even global organizations composed of people from widely diverse cultures can identify a set of shared core values. The secret is to work from the individual to the organization. People involved in articulating the core values need to answer several questions: What core values do you personally bring to your work? (These should be so fundamental that you would hold them regardless of whether or not they were rewarded.) What would you tell your children are the core values that you hold at work and that you hope *they* will hold when they become working adults? If you awoke tomorrow morning with enough money to retire for the rest of your life, would you continue to live those core values? Can you envision them being as valid for you 100 years from now as they are today? Would you want to hold those core values, even if at some point one or more of them became a competitive *dis*advantage? If you were to start a new organization tomorrow in a different line of work, what core values would you build into the new organization regardless of its industry? The last three questions are particularly important because they make the crucial distinction between enduring core values that should not change and practices and strategies that should be changing all the time.

Core Purpose

Core purpose, the second part of core ideology, is the organization's reason for being. An effective purpose reflects people's idealistic motivations for doing the company's work. It doesn't just describe the organization's output or target customers; it captures the soul of the organization. (See the box "Core Purpose Is a Company's Reason for Being.") Purpose, as illustrated by a speech David Packard gave to HP employees in 1960, gets at the deeper reasons for an organization's existence beyond just making money. Packard said,

I want to discuss why a company exists in the first place. In other words, why are we here? I think many people assume, wrongly, that a company exists simply to make money. While this is an important result of a company's existence, we have to go deeper and find the real reasons for our being. As we investigate this, we inevitably come to the conclusion that a group of people get together and exist as

Core Purpose Is a Company's Reason for Being

3M: To solve unsolved problems innovatively

Cargill: To improve the standard of living around the world

Fannie Mae: To strengthen the social fabric by continually democratizing home ownership

Hewlett-Packard: To make technical contributions for the advancement and welfare of humanity

Lost Arrow Corporation: To be a role model and a tool for social change

Pacific Theatres: To provide a place for people to flourish and to enhance the community

Mary Kay Cosmetics: To give unlimited opportunity to women

McKinsey & Company: To help leading corporations and governments be more successful

Merck: To preserve and improve human life

Nike: To experience the emotion of competition, winning, and crushing competitors.

Sony: To experience the joy of advancing and applying technology for the benefit of the public

Telecare Corporation: To help people with mental impairments realize their full potential

Wal-Mart: To give ordinary folk the chance to buy the same things as rich people

Walt Disney: To make people happy

---

an institution that we call a company so they are able to accomplish something collectively that they could not accomplish separately—they make a contribution to society, a phrase which sounds trite but is fundamental. . . . You can look around [in the general business world and] see people who are interested in money and nothing else, but the underlying drives come largely from a desire to do something else: to make a product, to give a service—generally to do something which is of value.[1]

Purpose (which should last at least 100 years) should not be confused with specific goals or business strategies (which should change many times in 100 years). Whereas you might achieve a goal or complete a strategy, you cannot fulfill a purpose; it is like a guiding star on the horizon—forever pursued but never reached. Yet although purpose itself does not change, it does inspire change. The very fact that purpose can never be fully realized means that an organization can never stop stimulating change and progress.

In identifying purpose, some companies make the mistake of simply describing their current product lines or customer segments. We do not consider the following statement to reflect an effective purpose: "We exist to fulfill our government charter and participate in the secondary mortgage market by packaging mortgages into investment securities." The statement is merely descriptive. A far more effective statement of

purpose would be that expressed by the executives of the Federal National Mortgage Association, Fannie Mae: "To strengthen the social fabric by continually democratizing home ownership." The secondary mortgage market as we know it might not even exist in 100 years, but strengthening the social fabric by continually democratizing home ownership can be an enduring purpose, no matter how much the world changes. Guided and inspired by this purpose, Fannie Mae launched in the early 1990s a series of bold initiatives, including a program to develop new systems for reducing mortgage underwriting costs by 40% in five years; programs to eliminate discrimination in the lending process (backed by $5 billion in underwriting experiments); and an audacious goal to provide, by the year 2000, $1 trillion targeted at 10 million families that had traditionally been shut out of home ownership—minorities, immigrants, and low-income groups.

Similarly, 3M defines its purpose not in terms of adhesives and abrasives but as the perpetual quest to solve unsolved problems innovatively—a purpose that is always leading 3M into new fields. McKinsey & Company's purpose is not to do management consulting but to help corporations and governments be more successful: in 100 years, it might involve methods other than consulting. Hewlett-Packard doesn't exist to make electronic test and measurement equipment but to make technical contributions that improve people's lives—a purpose that has led the company far afield from its origins in electronic instruments. Imagine if Walt Disney had conceived of his company's purpose as to make cartoons, rather than to make people happy; we probably wouldn't have Mickey Mouse, Disneyland, EPCOT Center, or the Anaheim Mighty Ducks Hockey Team.

One powerful method for getting at purpose is the *five whys.* Start with the descriptive statement We make X products or We deliver X services, and then ask, Why is that important? five times. After a few whys, you'll find that you're getting down to the fundamental purpose of the organization.

We used this method to deepen and enrich a discussion about purpose when we worked with a certain market-research company. The executive team first met for several hours and generated the following statement of purpose for their organization: To provide the best market-research data available. We then asked the following question: Why is it important to provide the best market-research data available? After some discussion, the executives answered in a way that reflected a deeper sense of their organization's purpose: To provide the best market-research data available so that our customers will understand their markets better than they could otherwise. A further discussion let team members realize that their sense of self-worth came not just from helping customers understand their markets better but also from making a *contribution* to their customers' success. This introspection eventually led the company to identify its purpose as: To contribute to our customers' success by helping them understand their markets. With this purpose in mind, the company now frames its product decisions not with the question Will it sell? but with the question Will it make a contribution to our customers' success?

The five whys can help companies in any industry frame their work in a more meaningful way. An asphalt and gravel company might begin by saying, We make gravel and asphalt products. After a few whys, it could conclude that making asphalt and gravel is important because the quality of the infrastructure plays a vital role in people's safety and experience; because driving on a pitted road is annoying and dangerous; because 747s cannot land safely on runways built with poor workmanship or inferior concrete; because buildings with substandard materials weaken with time and crumble in earthquakes. From such introspection may emerge this purpose: To make people's lives better by improving the quality of man-made structures. With a sense of purpose very much along those lines, Granite Rock Company of Watsonville, California, won the Malcolm Baldrige National Quality Award—not an easy feat for a small rock quarry and asphalt company. And Granite Rock has gone on to be one of the most progressive and exciting companies we've encountered in *any* industry.

Notice that none of the core purposes fall into the category "maximize shareholder wealth." A primary role of core purpose is to guide and inspire. Maximizing shareholder wealth does not inspire people at all levels of an organization, and it provides precious little guidance. Maximizing shareholder wealth is the standard off-the-shelf purpose for those organizations that have not yet identified their true core purpose. It is a substitute—and a weak one at that.

When people in great organizations talk about their achievements, they say very little about earnings per share. Motorola people talk about impressive quality improvements and the effect of the products they create on the world. Hewlett-Packard people talk about their technical contributions to the marketplace. Nordstrom people talk about heroic customer service and remarkable individual performance by star salespeople. When a Boeing engineer talks about launching an exciting and revolutionary new aircraft, she does not say, "I put my heart and soul into this project because it would add 37 cents to our earnings per share."

One way to get at the purpose that lies beyond merely maximizing shareholder wealth is to play the "Random Corporate Serial Killer" game. It works like this: Suppose you could sell the company to someone who would pay a price that everyone inside and outside the company agrees is more than fair (even with a very generous set of assumptions about the expected future cash flows of the company). Suppose further that this buyer would guarantee stable employment for all employees at the same pay scale after the purchase but with no guarantee that those jobs would be in the same industry. Finally, suppose the buyer plans to kill the company after the purchase—its products or services would be discontinued, its operations would be shut down, its brand names would be shelved forever, and so on. The company would utterly and completely cease to exist. Would you accept the offer? Why or why not? What would be lost if the company ceased to exist? Why is it important that the company continue to exist? We've found this exercise to be very powerful for helping hard-nosed financially focused executives reflect on their organization's deeper reasons for being.

Another approach is to ask each member of the Mars Group, How could we frame the purpose of this organization so that if you woke up tomorrow morning with enough money in the bank to retire, you would nevertheless keep working here? What deeper sense of purpose would motivate you to continue to dedicate your precious creative energies to this company's efforts?

As they move into the twenty-first century, companies will need to draw on the full creative energy and talent of their people. But why should people give full measure? As Peter Drucker has pointed out, the best and most dedicated people are ultimately volunteers, for they have the opportunity to do something else with their lives. Confronted with an increasingly mobile society, cynicism about corporate life, and an expanding entrepreneurial segment of the economy, companies more than ever need to have a clear understanding of their purpose in order to make work meaningful and thereby attract, motivate, and retain outstanding people.

DISCOVERING CORE IDEOLOGY

You do not create or set core ideology. You *discover* core ideology. You do not deduce it by looking at the external environment. You understand it by looking inside. Ideology has to be authentic. You cannot fake it. Discovering core ideology is not an intellectual exercise. Do not ask, What core values should we hold? Ask instead, What core values do we truly and passionately hold? You should not confuse values that you think the organization ought to have—but does not—with authentic core values. To do so would create cynicism throughout the organization. ("Who're they trying to kid? We all know that isn't a core value around here!") Aspirations are more appropriate as part of your envisioned future or as part of your strategy, not as part of the core ideology. However, authentic core values that have weakened over time can be considered a legitimate part of the core ideology—as long as you acknowledge to the organization that you must work hard to revive them.

Also be clear that the role of core ideology is to guide and inspire, not to differentiate. Two companies can have the same core values or purpose. Many companies could have the purpose to make technical contributions, but few live it as passionately as Hewlett-Packard. Many companies could have the purpose to preserve and improve human life, but few hold it as deeply as Merck. Many companies could have the core value of heroic customer service, but few create as intense a culture around that value as Nordstrom. Many companies could have the core value of innovation, but few create the powerful alignment mechanisms that stimulate the innovation we see at 3M. The authenticity, the discipline, and the consistency with which the ideology is lived—not the content of the ideology—differentiate visionary companies from the rest of the pack.

Core ideology needs to be meaningful and inspirational only to people inside the organization; it need not be exciting to outsiders. Why not? Because it is the people inside the organization who need to commit to the organizational ideology over the long term. Core ideology can also play a role in determining who *is* inside and who is not. A clear and well-articulated ideology attracts to the company people whose personal values are compatible with the company's core values; conversely, it repels those whose personal values are incompatible. You cannot impose new core values or purpose on people. Nor are core values and purpose things people can buy into. Executives often ask, How do we get people to share our core ideology? You don't. You can't. Instead, find people who are predisposed to share your core values and purpose; attract and retain those people; and let those who do not share your core values go elsewhere. Indeed, the very process of articulating core ideology may cause some people to leave when they realize that they are not personally compatible with the organization's core. Welcome that outcome. It is certainly desirable to retain within the core ideology a diversity of people and viewpoints. People who share the same core values and purpose do not necessarily all think or look the same.

Don't confuse core ideology itself with core-ideology statements. A company can have a very strong core ideology without a formal statement. For example, Nike has not (to our knowledge) formally articulated a statement of its core purpose. Yet, according to our observations, Nike has a powerful core purpose that permeates the entire organization: to experience the emotion of competition, winning, and crushing competitors. Nike has a campus that seems more like a shrine to the competitive spirit than a corporate office complex. Giant photos of Nike heroes cover the walls, bronze plaques of Nike athletes hang along the Nike Walk of Fame, statues of Nike athletes stand alongside the running track that rings the campus, and buildings honor champions such as Olympic marathoner Joan Benoit, basketball superstar Michael Jordan, and tennis pro John McEnroe. Nike people who do not feel stimulated by the competitive spirit and the urge to be ferocious simply do not last long in the culture. Even the company's name reflects a sense of competition: Nike is the Greek goddess of victory. Thus, although Nike has not formally articulated its purpose, it clearly has a strong one.

Identifying core values and purpose is therefore not an exercise in wordsmithery. Indeed, an organization will generate a variety of statements over time to describe the core ideology. In Hewlett-Packard's archives, we found more than half a dozen distinct versions of the HP Way, drafted by David Packard between 1956 and 1972. All versions stated the same principles, but the words used varied depending on the era and the circumstances. Similarly, Sony's core ideology has been stated many different ways over the company's history. At its founding, Masaru Ibuka described two key elements of Sony's ideology: "We shall welcome technical difficulties and focus on highly sophisticated technical products that have great usefulness for society regardless of the quantity involved; we shall place our main emphasis on ability, performance, and personal character so that each individual can show the best in ability and skill."[2] Four decades later, this same concept appeared in a statement of core ideology called Sony Pioneer Spirit: "Sony is a pioneer and never intends to follow others. Through progress, Sony wants to serve the whole world. It shall be always a seeker of the unknown. . . . Sony has a principle of respecting and encouraging one's ability . . . and always tries to bring out the best in a person. This is the vital force of Sony."[3] Same core values, different words.

You should therefore focus on getting the content right—on capturing the essence of the core values and purpose. The point is not to create a perfect statement but to gain a deep understanding of your organization's core values and purpose, which can then be expressed in a multitude of ways. In fact, we often suggest that once the core has been identified, managers should generate their own statements of the core values and purpose to share with their groups.

Finally, don't confuse core ideology with the concept of core competence. Core competence is a strategic concept that defines your organization's capabilities—what you are particularly good at—whereas core ideology captures what you stand for and why you exist. Core competencies should be well aligned with a company's core ideology and are often rooted in it, but they are not the same thing. For example, Sony has a core competence of miniaturization—a strength that can be strategically applied to a wide array of products and markets. But it does not have a core *ideology* of miniaturization. Sony might not even have miniaturization as part of its strategy in 100 years, but to remain a great company, it will still have the same core values described in the Sony Pioneer Spirit and the same fundamental reason for being—namely, to advance technology for the benefit of the general public. In a visionary company like Sony, core competencies change over the decades, whereas core ideology does not.

Once you are clear about the core ideology, you should feel free to change absolutely *anything* that is not part of it. From then on, whenever someone says something should not change because "it's part of our culture" or "we've always done it that way" or any such excuse, mention this simple rule: If it's not core, it's up for change. The strong version of the rule is, *If it's not core, change it!* Articulating core ideology is just a starting point, however. You also must determine what type of progress you want to stimulate.

ENVISIONED FUTURE

The second primary component of the vision framework is *envisioned future*. It consists of two parts: a 10-to-30-year audacious goal plus vivid descriptions of what it will be like to achieve the goal. We recognize that the phrase *envisioned future* is somewhat paradoxical. On the one hand, it conveys concreteness—something visible, vivid, and real. On the other hand, it involves a time yet unrealized—with its dreams, hopes, and aspirations.

Vision-Level BHAG

We found in our research that visionary companies often use bold missions—or what we prefer to call *BHAGs* (pronounced BEE-hags and shorthand for Big, Hairy, Audacious Goals—as a powerful way to stimulate progress. All companies have goals. But there is a difference between merely having a goal and becoming committed to a huge, daunting challenge—such as climbing Mount Everest. A true BHAG is clear and compelling, serves as a unifying focal point of effort, and acts as a catalyst for team spirit. It has a clear finish line, so the organization can know when it has achieved the goal; people like to shoot for finish lines. A BHAG engages people—it reaches out and grabs them. It is tangible, energizing, highly focused. People get it right away; it takes little or no explanation. For example, NASA's 1960s moon mission didn't need a committee of wordsmiths to spend endless hours turning the goal into a verbose, impossible-to-remember mission statement. The goal itself was so easy to grasp—so compelling in its own right—that it could be said 100 different ways yet be easily understood by everyone. Most corporate statements we've seen do little to spur forward movement because they do not contain the powerful mechanism of a BHAG.

Although organizations may have many BHAGs at different levels operating at the same time, vision requires a special type of BHAG—a vision-level BHAG that applies to the entire organization and requires 10 to 30 years of effort to complete. Setting the BHAG that far into the future requires thinking beyond the current capabilities of the organization and the current environment. Indeed, inventing such a goal forces an executive team to be visionary, rather than just strategic or tactical. A BHAG should not be a sure bet—it will have perhaps only a 50% to 70% probability of success—but the organization must believe that it can reach the goal anyway. A BHAG should require extraordinary effort and perhaps a little luck. We have helped companies create a vision-level BHAG by advising them to think in terms of four broad categories: target BHAGs, common-enemy BHAGs, role-model BHAGs, and internal-transformation BHAGs. (See the box "Big, Hairy, Audacious Goals Aid Long-Term Vision.")

Vivid Description

In addition to vision-level BHAGs, an envisioned future needs what we call *vivid description*—that is, a vi-

brant, engaging, and specific description of what it will be like to achieve the BHAG. Think of it as translating the vision from words into pictures, of creating an image that people can carry around in their heads. It is a question of painting a picture with your words. Picture painting is essential for making the 10-to-30-year BHAG tangible in people's minds.

For example, Henry Ford brought to life the goal of democratizing the automobile with this vivid description: "I will build a motor car for the great multitude. . . . It will be so low in price that no man making a good salary will be unable to own one and enjoy with his family the blessing of hours of pleasure in God's great open spaces. . . . When I'm through, everybody will be able to afford one, and everyone will have one. The horse will have disappeared from our highways, the automobile will be taken for granted . . . [and we will] give a large number of men employment at good wages."

The components-support division of a computer-products company had a general manager who was able to describe vividly the goal of becoming one of the most sought-after divisions in the company: "We will be respected and admired by our peers. . . . Our solutions will be actively sought by the end-product divisions, who will achieve significant product 'hits' in the marketplace largely because of our technical contribution. . . . We will have pride in ourselves. . . . The best up-and-coming people in the company will seek to work in our division. . . . People will give unsolicited feedback that they love what they are doing. . . . [Our own] people will walk on the balls of their feet. . . . [They] will willingly work hard because they want to. . . . Both employees and customers will feel that our division has contributed to their life in a positive way."

In the 1930s, Merck had the BHAG to transform itself from a chemical manufacturer into one of the preeminent drug-making companies in the world with a research capability to rival any major university. In describing this envisioned future, George Merck said at the opening of Merck's research facility in 1933, "We believe that research work carried on with patience and persistence will bring to industry and commerce new life; and we have faith that in this new laboratory, with the tools we have supplied, science will be advanced, knowledge increased, and human life win ever a greater freedom from suffering and disease. . . . We pledge our every aid that this enterprise shall merit the faith we have in it. Let your light so shine—

Big, Hairy, Audacious Goals Aid Long-Term Vision

TARGET BHAGS CAN BE QUANTITATIVE OR QUALITATIVE

- Become a $125 billion company by the year 2000 (Wal-Mart, 1990)
- Democratize the automobile (Ford Motor Company, early 1900s)
- Become the company most known for changing the worldwide poor-quality image of Japanese products (Sony, early 1950s)
- Become the most powerful, the most serviceable, the most far-reaching world financial institution that has ever been (City Bank, predecessor to Citicorp, 1915)
- Become the dominant player in commercial aircraft and bring the world into the jet age (Boeing, 1950)

COMMON-ENEMY BHAGS INVOLVE DAVID-VERSUS-GOLIATH THINKING

- Knock off RJR as the number one tobacco company in the world (Philip Morris, 1950s)
- Crush Adidas (Nike, 1960s)
- *Yamaha wo tsubusu!* We will destroy Yamaha! (Honda, 1970s)

ROLE-MODEL BHAGS SUIT UP-AND-COMING ORGANIZATIONS

- Become the Nike of the cycling industry (Giro Sport Design, 1986)
- Become as respected in 20 years as Hewlett-Packard is today (Watkins-Johnson, 1996)
- Become the Harvard of the West (Stanford University, 1940s)

INTERNAL-TRANSFORMATION BHAGS SUIT LARGE, ESTABLISHED ORGANIZATIONS

- Become number one or number two in every market we serve and revolutionize this company to have the strengths of a big company combined with the leanness and agility of a small company (General Electric Company, 1980s)
- Transform this company from a defense contractor into the best diversified high-technology company in the world (Rockwell, 1995)
- Transform this division from a poorly respected internal products supplier to one of the most respected, exciting, and sought-after divisions in the company (Components Support Division of a computer products company, 1989)

that those who seek the Truth, that those who toil that this world may be a better place to live in, that those who hold aloft that torch of science and knowledge through these social and economic dark ages, shall take new courage and feel their hands supported."

Passion, emotion, and conviction are essential parts of the vivid description. Some managers are uncomfortable expressing emotion about their dreams, but that's what motivates others. Churchill understood that when he described the BHAG facing Great Britain in 1940. He did not just say, "Beat Hitler." He said, "Hitler knows he will have to break us on this island or lose the war. If we can stand up to him, all Europe may be free, and the life of the world may move forward into broad, sunlit uplands. But if we fail, the whole world, including the United States, including all we have known and cared for, will sink into the abyss of a new Dark Age, made more sinister and perhaps more protracted by the lights of perverted science. Let us therefore brace ourselves to our duties and so bear ourselves that if the British Empire and its Commonwealth last for a thousand years, men will still say, 'This was their finest hour.' "

A Few Key Points

Don't confuse core ideology and envisioned future. In particular, don't confuse core purpose and BHAGs. Managers often exchange one for the other, mixing the two together or failing to articulate both as distinct items. Core purpose—not some specific goal—is the reason why the organization exists. A BHAG is a clearly articulated goal. Core purpose can never be completed, whereas the BHAG is reachable in 10 to 30 years. Think of the core purpose as the star on the horizon to be chased forever; the BHAG is the mountain to be climbed. Once you have reached its summit, you move on to other mountains.

Identifying core ideology is a discovery process, but setting the envisioned future is a creative process. We find that executives often have a great deal of difficulty coming up with an exciting BHAG. They want to analyze their way into the future. We have found, therefore, that some executives make more progress by starting first with the vivid description and backing from there into the BHAG. This approach involves starting with questions such as, We're sitting here in 20 years; what would we love to see? What should this company look like? What should it feel like to employees? What should it have achieved? If someone writes an article for a major business magazine about this company in 20 years, what will it say? One biotechnology company we worked with had trouble envisioning its future. Said one member of the executive team, "Every time we come up with something for the entire company, it is just too generic to be exciting—something banal like 'advance biotechnology worldwide.'" Asked to paint a picture of the company in 20 years, the executives mentioned such things as "on the cover of *Business Week* as a model success story . . . the *Fortune* most admired top-ten list . . . the best science and business graduates want to work here . . . people on airplanes rave about one of our products to seatmates . . . 20 consecutive years of profitable growth . . . an entrepreneurial culture that has spawned half a dozen new divisions from within . . . management gurus use us as an example of excellent management and progressive thinking," and so on. From this, they were able to set the goal of becoming as well respected as Merck or as Johnson & Johnson in biotechnology.

It makes no sense to analyze whether an envisioned future is the right one. With a creation—and the task is creation of a future, not prediction—there can be no right answer. Did Beethoven create the right Ninth Symphony? Did Shakespeare create the right *Hamlet?* We can't answer these questions; they're nonsense. The envisioned future involves such essential questions as Does it get our juices flowing? Do we find it stimulating? Does it spur forward momentum? Does it get people going? The envisioned future should be so exciting in its own right that it would continue to keep the organization motivated even if the leaders who set the goal disappeared. City Bank, the predecessor of Citicorp, had the BHAG "to become the most powerful, the most serviceable, the most far-reaching world financial institution that has ever been"—a goal that generated excitement through multiple generations until it was achieved. Similarly, the NASA moon mission continued to galvanize people even though President John F. Kennedy (the leader associated with setting the goal) died years before its completion.

To create an effective envisioned future requires a certain level of unreasonable confidence and commitment. Keep in mind that a BHAG is not just a goal; it is a Big, Hairy, Audacious Goal. It's not reasonable for a small regional bank to set the goal of becoming "the most powerful, the most serviceable, the most far-reaching world financial institution that has ever been," as City Bank did in 1915. It's not a tepid claim that "we will democratize the automobile," as Henry Ford said. It was almost laughable for Philip Morris—as the sixth-place player with 9% market share in the 1950s—to take on the goal of defeating Goliath R.J. Reynolds Tobacco Company and becoming number one. It was hardly modest for Sony, as a small, cash-strapped venture, to proclaim the goal of changing the poor-quality image of Japanese products around the world. (See the box "Putting It All Together: Sony in the 1950s.") Of course, it's not only the audacity of the goal but also the level of commitment to the goal that counts. Boeing didn't just envision a future dominated by its commercial jets; it bet the company on the 707 and, later, on the 747. Nike's people didn't just talk about the idea of crushing Adidas; they went on a crusade to fulfill the dream. Indeed, the envisioned future should produce a bit of the "gulp factor": when it dawns on people what it will take to achieve the goal, there should be an almost audible gulp.

But what about failure to realize the envisioned future? In our research, we found that the visionary companies displayed a remarkable ability to achieve even their most audacious goals. Ford did democratize the automobile; Citicorp did become the most far-reaching bank in the world; Philip Morris did rise from sixth to first and beat R.J. Reynolds worldwide; Boeing did become the dominant commercial aircraft company; and it looks like Wal-Mart will achieve its $125 billion goal, even with out Sam Walton. In contrast, the comparison companies in our research fre-

Putting It All Together: Sony in the 1950s

CORE IDEOLOGY

Core Values

- Elevation of the Japanese culture and national status
- Being a pioneer—not following others, doing the impossible
- Encouraging individual ability and creativity

Purpose

To experience the sheer joy of innovation and the application of technology for the benefit and pleasure of the general public

ENVISIONED FUTURE

BHAG

Become the company most known for changing the worldwide poor-quality image of Japanese products

Vivid Description

We will create products that become pervasive around the world. . . . We will be the first Japanese company to go into the U.S. market and distribute directly. . . . We will succeed with innovations that U.S. companies have failed at—such as the transistor radio. . . . Fifty years from now, our brand name will be as well known as any in the world . . . and will signify innovation and quality that rival the most innovative companies anywhere. . . . "Made in Japan" will mean something fine, not something shoddy.

---

quently did not achieve their BHAGs, if they set them at all. The difference does not lie in setting easier goals: the visionary companies tended to have even more audacious ambitions. The difference does not lie in charismatic, visionary leadership: the visionary companies often achieved their BHAGs without such larger-than-life leaders at the helm. Nor does the difference lie in better strategy: the visionary companies often realized their goals more by an organic process of "let's try a lot of stuff and keep what works" than by well-laid strategic plans. Rather, their success lies in building the strength of their organization as their primary way of creating the future.

Why did Merck become the preeminent drugmaker in the world? Because Merck's architects built the best pharmaceutical research and development organization in the world. Why did Boeing become the dominant commercial aircraft company in the world? Because of its superb engineering and marketing organization, which had the ability to make projects like the 747 a reality. When asked to name the most important decisions that have contributed to the growth and success of Hewlett-Packard, David Packard answered entirely in terms of decisions to build the strength of the organization and its people.

Finally, in thinking about the envisioned future, beware of the We've Arrived Syndrome—a complacent lethargy that arises once an organization has achieved one BHAG and fails to replace it with another. NASA suffered from that syndrome after the successful moon landings. After you've landed on the moon, what do you do for an encore? Ford suffered from the syndrome when, after it succeeded in democratizing the automobile, it failed to set a new goal of equal significance and gave General Motors the opportunity to jump ahead in the 1930s. Apple Computer suffered from the syndrome after achieving the goal of creating a computer that nontechies could use. Start-up companies frequently suffer from the We've Arrived Syndrome after going public or after reaching a stage in which survival no longer seems in question. An envisioned future helps an organization only as long as it hasn't yet been achieved. In our work with companies, we frequently hear executives say, "It's just not as exciting around here as it used to be; we seem to have lost our momentum." Usually, that kind of remark signals that the organization has climbed one mountain and not yet picked a new one to climb.

Many executives thrash about with mission statements and vision statements. Unfortunately, most of those statements turn out to be a muddled stew of values, goals, purposes, philosophies, beliefs, aspirations, norms, strategies, practices, and descriptions. They are usually a boring, confusing, structurally unsound stream of words that evoke the response "True, but who cares?" Even more problematic, seldom do these statements have a direct link to the fundamental dynamic of visionary companies: preserve the core and stimulate progress. That dynamic, not vision or mission statements, is the primary engine of enduring companies. Vision simply provides the context for bringing this dynamic to life. Building a visionary company requires 1% vision and 99% alignment. When you have superb alignment, a visitor could drop in from outer space and infer your vision from the operations and activities of the company without ever reading it on paper or meeting a single senior executive.

Creating alignment may be your most important work. But the first step will always be to recast your vision or mission into an effective context for building a visionary company. If you do it right, you shouldn't have to do it again for at least a decade.

NOTES

1. David Packard, speech given to Hewlett-Packard's training group on March 8, 1960; courtesy of Hewlett-Packard Archives.

2. See Nick Lyons, *The Sony Vision* (New York: Crown Publishers, 1976). We also used a translation by our Japanese student Tsuneto Ikeda.

3. Akio Morita, *Made in Japan* (New York: E. P. Dutton, 1986), p. 147.

16

Managing Professional Careers

The Influence of Job Longevity and Group Age

RALPH KATZ

Any serious consideration of organizational careers must eventually explore the dynamics through which the concerns, abilities, and experiences of individual employees combine and mesh with the demands and requirements of their employing work environments. How do employees' motivational needs for security, equitable rewards, and opportunities for advancement and self-development, for example, interact with the needs of organizations for ensured growth, profitability, and innovativeness? More important, how should they interact so that both prescription sets are filled satisfactorily?

Further complexity is added to this "matching" process with the realization that interactions between individuals and organizations are not temporally invariant but can shift significantly throughout workers' jobs, careers, and life cycles. As employees pass from one phase in their work lives to the next, different concerns and issues are emphasized; and the particular perspectives that result produce different behavioral and attitudinal combinations within their job settings. Over time, therefore, employees are continuously revising and adjusting their perspectives toward their organizations and their roles in them. And it is the perspective that one has formulated at a particular point in time that gives meaning and direction to one's work and professional career.

Because the effectiveness of any given group of professional employees ultimately depends on the combined actions and performances of its membership, we need to analyze more precisely the different kinds of concerns and behaviors that seem to preoccupy and characterize employees as they enter their work environments and proceed through respective jobs, project groups, and organizational career paths. Clearly, a better understanding of the changes taking place over time will help clarify the accommodation processes between organizations and individuals so that eventual motivational and performance problems can be dealt with more quickly and satisfactorily.

A MODEL OF JOB LONGEVITY

Based on some findings on how job satisfaction and performance relate to certain task dimensions of job challenge, Katz (1980) has developed a general theory for describing how employees' perspectives unfold and change as they proceed through their own discrete sequences of job situations. In particular, a three-transitional stage model of job longevity has been proposed to illustrate how certain kinds of concerns might change in importance according to the actual length of time an employee has been working in a given job position. Generally speaking, each time an employee is assigned to a new job position within an or-

From *Managing Strategic Innovation and Change: A Collection of Readings,* 1st edition, edited by Michael L. Tushman and Philip Anderson. Copyright © 1997 by Oxford University Press, Inc. Used by permission of Oxford University Press, Inc.

ganization, either as a recent recruit or through transfer or promotion, the individual enters a relatively brief but nevertheless important "socialization" period. With increasing familiarity about his or her new job environment, however, the employee soon passes from socialization into the "innovation" stage, which, in turn, slowly shifts into a "stabilization" state as the individual gradually adapts to extensive job longevity (i.e., as the employee continues to work in the same overall job context for an extended period of time). Figure 16.1 summarizes the sequential nature of these three stages by comparing some of the different kinds of issues affecting employees as they cycle through their various job positions.[1]

Socialization

As outlined under the initial socialization stage, employees entering new job positions are concerned primarily with reality construction, building more realistic understandings of their unfamiliar social and task environments. In formulating their new perspectives, they are busily absorbed with problems of establishing and clarifying their own situational roles and identities and with learning all the attitudes and behaviors that are appropriate and expected within their new job settings. Estranged from their previous work environ-

ments and supporting relationships, newcomers must construct situational definitions that allow them to understand and interpret the myriad of experiences associated with their new organizational memberships. They need, for example, to learn the customary norms of behavior, decipher how reward systems actually operate, discover supervisory expectations, and more generally learn how to function meaningfully within their multiple group contexts (Schein, 1978). Through information communicated by their new "significant others," newcomers learn to develop perceptions of their own roles and skills that are both supported within their new surroundings and which permit them to organize their activities and interactions in a meaningful fashion. As pointed out by Hughes (1958) in his discussion of "reality shock," when new employees suddenly discover that their somewhat "overglorified" work-related expectations are neither realistic nor mutually shared by their boss or co-workers, they are likely to feel disenchanted and will experience considerable pressure to either redefine more compatible expectations or terminate from their work settings.

The importance of such a "breaking-in" period has long been recognized in discussions of how social processes affect recent organizational hires trying to make sense out of their newfound work experiences.

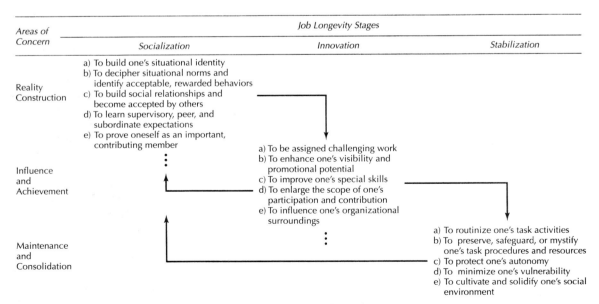

Figure 16.1. Examples of special issues during each stage of job longevity.

What is also important to recognize is that veteran employees must also relocate or "socialize" themselves following their displacements into new job positions within their same organizations (Wheeler, 1966). Just as organizational newcomers have to define and interpret their new territorial domains, veteran employees must also restructure and reformulate perceptions regarding their new social and task realities.[2] As they assume new organizational positions and enter important new relationships, veterans must learn to integrate their new perceptions and experiences with prior organizational knowledge in order to develop fresh situational perspectives, including perceptions about their own self-images and their images of other organizational members.

Such perceptual revisions are typically necessary simply because work groups and other organizational subunits are often highly differentiated with respect to their idiosyncratic sets of norms, beliefs, perceptions, time perspectives, shared language schemes, goal orientations, and so on (Lawrence and Lorsch, 1967). As communications and interactions within an organizational subunit continue to take place or intensify, it is likely that a more common set of understandings about the subunit and its environment will develop through informational social influence. Such shared meanings and awarenesses not only provide the subunit's members with a sense of belonging and identity but will also demarcate the subunit from other organizational entities (Pfeffer, 1981). Consequently, as one shifts job positions and moves within the organization, one is likely to encounter and become part of a new set of groups with their correspondingly different belief systems and perspectives about themselves, their operations, and their operating environments. It is in this initial socialization period, therefore, that organizational employees, and newcomers in particular, learn not only the technical requirements of their new job assignments but also the interpersonal behaviors and social attitudes that are acceptable and necessary for becoming a true contributing member.

Since employees in the midst of socialization are strongly motivated to reduce ambiguity by creating out of their somewhat vague and unfamiliar surroundings, it becomes clear why a number of researchers have discovered organizational newcomers being especially concerned with psychological safety and security and with clarifying their new situational identities (Kahn et al., 1964; Hall and Nougaim, 1968). In a similar vein, Schein (1971) suggests that to become accepted and to prove one's competence represent two major problems that newcomers and veterans must face before they can function comfortably within their new job positions. It is these kinds of concerns that help to explain why Katz (1978a) discovered that during the initial months of their new job positions, employees are not completely ready to respond positively to all the challenging characteristics of their new task assignments. Instead, they appear most responsive to job features that provide a sense of personal acceptance and importance as well as a sense of proficiency through feedback and individual guidance.[3] As illustrations of just how influential such communication and feedback processes can be during socialization, the studies of professionals' careers by Lee (1992) and Katz and Tushman (1983) have shown very strong relationships between employees' communication networks and their subsequent degree of turnover and level of performance. In fact, Katz and Tushman reported that young engineers and scientists who left their organization over the 5-year interval in which the research study took place, had had more than four to five times less work-related interaction with their immediate supervisors and department heads during socialization as those engineers and scientists who still remained during this 5-year period.

How long this initial socialization period lasts probably depends on how long it takes employees to feel accepted and competent within their new work environments. Not only is the length of such a time period greatly influenced by the abilities, needs, and prior experiences of individual workers and influenced as well by the clarity and usefulness of the interpersonal interactions that take place, but it also probably differs significantly across occupations. Based on the retrospective answers of his hospital employee sample, for example, Feldman (1977) reports that on the average, accounting clerks, registered nurses, and engineering tradesmen reporting feeling accepted after one, two, and four months, respectively, although they did not feel completely competent until after three, six, and eight months, respectively. Generally speaking, one might posit that the length of one's initial socialization period varies positively with the level of complexity within one's job and occupational requirements, ranging perhaps from as little as a month or two on very routine, programmed-type jobs to as much as a year or more on very skilled, unprogrammed-type jobs, as in the engineering and scientific professions. With respect to engineering, for example, it is generally recognized that a substantial socialization period is often required before engineers can fully contribute within their new organizational settings, using their particular knowledge and technical specialties. Thus, even though one might have received an excellent education in mechanical engineering principles at a university or college, one must still figure out from working and interacting with others in the setting how to be an effective mechanical engineer at Westinghouse, DuPont, or Procter and Gamble.[4]

Innovation

With time, interaction, and increasing familiarity, employees soon discover how to function appropriately in their jobs and to feel sufficiently secure in their perceptions of their workplace. Individual energies can now be devoted more toward task performance and accomplishment instead of being expended on learning the previously unfamiliar social knowledge and skills necessary to make sense out of one's work-related activities and interactions. As a result, employees become increasingly capable of acting in a more responsive, innovative, and undistracted manner.

The movement from socialization to the innovation stage of job longevity implies that employees no longer require much assistance in deciphering their new job and organizational surroundings. Having adequately constructed their own understandings of their situations during the socialization period, employees are now freer to participate within their own conceptions of organizational reality. They are now able to divert their attention from an initial emphasis on psychological safety and acceptance to concerns for achievement and influence. Thus, what becomes progressively more pertinent to employees as they proceed from socialization to the innovation stage are the opportunities to participate and grow within their job settings in a very meaningful and responsible manner.

The idea of having to achieve some reasonable level of psychological safety and security in order to be fully responsive to challenges in the work setting is very consistent with Kuhn's (1963) concept of "creative tensions." According to Kuhn it is likely that only

when conditions of *both* stability and challenge are present can the creative tensions between them generate considerable innovative behavior. Growth theorists such as Maslow (1962) and Rogers (1961) have similarly argued that the presence of psychological safety is one of the chief prerequisites for self-direction and individual responsiveness. For psychological safety to occur, however, individuals must be able to understand and attach sufficient meaning to the vast array of events, interactions, and information flows involving them throughout their workdays. Of particular importance to growth theorists is the idea that employees must be able to expect positive results to flow from their individual actions. Such a precondition implies that employees must have developed sufficient knowledge about their new job situations in order for there to be enough predictability for them to take appropriate kinds of actions.[5]

A similar point of view is taken by Staw (1977) when he argues that if employees truly expect to improve their overall job situations, they must first learn to predict their most relevant set of behavioral-outcome contingencies before they try to influence or increase their control over them. One must first construct a reasonably valid perspective about such contingencies before one can sensibly strive to manage them for increasingly more favorable outcomes. In short, there must be sufficient awareness of one's environment, sufficient acceptance and competence within one's setting, and sufficient openness to new ideas and experiences in order for employees to be fully responsive to the "richness" of their job demands.

Stabilization

As employees continue to work in their same overall job settings for a considerable length of time, without any serious disruption or displacement, they may gradually proceed from innovation to stabilization in the sense of shifting from being highly involved in and receptive to their job demands to becoming progressively unresponsive. For the most part, responsive individuals prefer to work at jobs they find stimulating and challenging and in which they can self-develop and grow. With such kinds of work-related activities and opportunities, they are likely to inject greater effort and involvement into their tasks, which, in turn, will be reflected in their performances (Hackman and

Oldham, 1975; Katz, 1978b). It seems reasonable to assume, however, that in time even the most challenging job assignments and responsibilities can appear less exciting and more habitual to jobholders who have successfully mastered and become increasingly accustomed to their everyday task requirements. With prolonged job longevity and stability, therefore, it is likely that employees' perceptions of their present conditions and of their future possibilities will become increasingly impoverished. They may begin essentially to question the value of what they are doing and where it may lead. If employees cannot maintain, redefine, or expand their jobs for continual challenge and growth, the substance and meaning of their work begins to deteriorate. Enthusiasm wanes, for what was once challenging and exciting may no longer hold much interest at all.

At the same time, it is also important to mention that if an individual is able to increase or even maintain his or her own sense of task challenge and excitement on a given job for an extended period of time, then instead of moving toward stabilization, the process might be the reverse (i.e., continued growth and innovation). As before, the extent to which an individual can maintain his or her responsiveness on a particular job strongly depends on the complexity of the underlying tasks as well as on the individual's own capabilities, needs, and prior experiences. With respect to individual differences, for example, Katz's (1978b) findings suggest that employees with high growth needs are able to respond to the challenging aspects of their new jobs sooner than employees with low growth needs. At the same time, however, high-order-need employees might not retain their responsiveness for as long a job period as employees with low-growth-need strength.

It should also be emphasized that in addition to job longevity, many other contextual factors can affect a person's situational perspective strongly enough to influence the level of job interest as one continues to work in a given job position over a long period of time. New technological developments, rapid growth and expansion, the sudden appearance of external threats, or strong competitive pressures could all help sustain or even enhance an individual's involvement in his or her job-related activities. On the other hand, having to work closely with a group of unresponsive peers might

shorten an individual's responsive period on that particular job rather dramatically. Clearly, the reactions of individuals are not only influenced by psychological predispositions and personality characteristics but also by individuals' definitions of and interactions with their overall situational settings (Homans, 1961; Salancik and Pfeffer, 1978).

Generally speaking, however, as tasks become progressively less stimulating to employees with extended job longevity, they can either leave the setting or remain and adapt to their present job situations (Argyris, 1957). In moving from innovation to stabilization, it is suggested that employees who continue to work in their same overall job situations for long periods of time gradually succeed in adapting to such steadfast employment by becoming increasingly indifferent and unresponsive to the challenging task features of their job assignments (Katz, 1978a). In the process of adaptation, they may also redefine what they consider to be important, most likely by placing relatively less value on intrinsic kinds of work issues. The findings of Kopelman (1977) and Hall and Schneider (1973) suggest, for example, that when individuals perceive their opportunities for intrinsic-type satisfactions and challenges to be diminishing, they begin to match such developments by placing less value on such types of expectations. And as employees come to care less about the intrinsic nature of the actual work they do, the greater their relative concern for certain contextual features, such as salary, benefits, vacations, friendly co-workers, and compatible supervision.

The passage from innovation to stabilization is not meant to suggest that job satisfaction necessarily declines with long-term job longevity. On the contrary, it is likely that in the process of adaptation, employees' expectations have become adequately satisfied as they continue to perform their familiar duties in their normally acceptable fashions. If aspirations are defined as a function of the disparity between desired and expected (Kiesler, 1978), then as long as what individuals desire is reasonably greater than what they can presently expect to attain, there will be energy for change and achievement. On the other hand, when employees arrive at a stage where their chances for future growth and challenges in their jobs are perceived to be remote, then as they adapt, it is likely that existing situations will become accepted as the desired and aspirations for growth and change will have been reduced. As a result, the more employees come to accept their present circumstances, the stronger the tendency to keep the existing work environment fairly stable. Career interests and aspirations become markedly constricted, for in a sense, adapted employees simply prefer to enjoy rather than try to add to their present job accomplishments.

Uncertainty and Motivation

Underpinning the descriptive changes represented by the stabilization stage is the basic idea that over time individuals try to organize their work lives in a manner that reduces the amount of stress they must face and which is also low in uncertainty (Pfeffer, 1980; Staw, 1977). Weick (1969) also relies on this perspective when he contends that employees seek to "enact" their environments by directing their activities toward the establishment of a workable level of certainty and clarity. In general, one can argue that employees strive to bring their work activities into a state of equilibrium where they are more capable of predicting events and of avoiding potential conflicts.[6]

Given such developmental trends, it seems reasonable that with considerable job longevity most employees have been able to build a work pattern that is familiar and comfortable, a pattern in which routine and precedent play a relatively large part. According to Weick (1969), as employees establish certain structures of interlocked behaviors and relationships, these patterns will in time become relatively stable simply because they provide certainty and predictability to these interlinked employees. It is further argued that as individuals adapt to their long-term job tenure and become progressively less responsive to their actual task demands, they will come to rely more on their established modes of conduct to complete their everyday job requirements. Most likely, adapted employees feel safe and comfortable in such stability, for its keeps them feeling secure and confident in what they do, yet requires little additional vigilance or effort. In adapting to extended job longevity, therefore, employees become increasingly content and ensconced in their customary ways of doing things, in their comfortable routines and interactions, and in their familiar sets of task demands and responsibilities.

If change or uncertainty is seen by individuals in the stabilization period as particularly disruptive, then the preservation of familiar routines and patterns of be-

havior is likely to be of prime concern. Given such a disposition, adapted employees are probably less receptive toward any change or toward any information that might threaten to disturb their developing sense of complacency. Rather than striving to enlarge the scope of their job demands, they may be more concerned with maintaining their comfortable work environments by protecting themselves from sources of possible interference, from activities requiring new kinds of attention, or form situations that might reveal their shortcomings. Adapted employees, for example, might seek to reduce uncertainty in their day-to-day supervisory dealings perhaps by solidifying their attractiveness through ingratiating kinds of behavior (Wortman and Linsenmeier, 1977) or perhaps by isolating themselves from such supervisory contacts (Pelz and Andrews, 1966). Or they might seek to reduce uncertainty by trying to safeguard their personal allocations of resources and rewards through the use of standardized practices and policies. Whatever the specific behaviors that eventually emerge in a given setting, it is likely that employees who have become unresponsive to the challenging features of their assigned tasks will strongly resist events threatening to introduce uncertainty into their work environments.

One of the best examples of the effects of such long-term stability can still be found in Chinoy's (1955) classic interviews of automobile factory workers. Chinoy discovered that although almost 80% of the workers had wanted to leave their present jobs at one time or another, very few could actually bring themselves to leave. Most of the workers were simply unwilling to give up the predictability and comfortableness of their presently familiar routines and cultivated relationships for the uncertainties of a new job position. Individuals do not resist change in and of itself. What individuals resist is the uncertainty provoked by change. For as long as employees are able to process information that allows them to reduce the uncertainties surrounding the changes, their apprehensions and concerns become progressively diminished.

SITUATIONAL VERSUS INDIVIDUAL CONTROL OF INTERPRETATION

In presenting this three-stage model of job longevity, I have tried to describe some of the major concerns affecting employees as they enter and adapt to their particular job positions. Of course, the extent to which any specific individual is affected by these issues depends on the particular perceptual outlook that has been developed over time through job-related activities and through role-making processes with other individuals, including supervisors, subordinates, and peers (Weick, 1969; Graen, 1976). Employees, as a result, learn to cope with their particular job and organizational environments through their interpretations of relevant work experiences as well as their expectations and hopes of the future. To varying degrees, then, situational perspectives are derivatives of both retrospective and prospective processes, in that they are built and shaped through knowledge of past events and future anticipations.

One of the more important aspects of the socialization process, however, is that the information and knowledge previously gathered by employees from their former settings are no longer sufficient or necessarily appropriate for interpreting or understanding their new organizational domains. Newcomers, for instance, have had only limited contact within their new institutional surroundings from which to construct their perceptual views. Similarly, the extent to which veterans who are assuming new job positions can rely on their past organizational experiences and perspectives to function effectively within their new work settings can also be rather limited, depending of course on their degrees of displacement.

Essentially, individuals in the midst of socialization are trying to navigate their way through new and unfamiliar territories without the aid of adequate or even accurate perceptual maps. During this initial period, therefore, they are typically more malleable and more susceptible to change (Schein, 1968). In a sense, they are working under conditions of high "situational control" in that they must depend on other individuals within their new situations to help them define and interpret the numerous activities taking place around them. The greater their unfamiliarity or displacement within their new organizational areas, the more they must rely on their situations to provide the necessary information and interactions by which they can eventually construct their own perspectives and reestablish new situational identities. And it is precisely this external need or "situational dependency" that enables these individuals to be more easily influenced during

their socialization processes through social interactions (Salancik and Pfeffer, 1978; Katz, 1980).

As employees become increasingly cognizant of their overall job surroundings, however, they also become increasingly capable of relying on their own perceptions for interpreting events and executing their everyday task requirements. In moving from socialization into the innovation or stabilization stage, employees have succeeded in building a sufficiently robust situational perspective, thereby freeing themselves to operate more self-sufficiently within their familiar work settings. They are now working under conditions of less "situational" but more "individual" control, in the sense that they are now better equipped to determine for themselves the importance and meaning of the various events and information flows surrounding them. Having established their own social and task supports, their own perceptual outlooks, and their own situational identities, they become less easily changed and less easily manipulated. As pointed out by Schein (1973), when individuals no longer have to balance their situational perspectives against the views of significant others within their settings, they become less susceptible to change and situational influences. Thus, movement through the three stages of job longevity can also be characterized, as shown in Figure 16.2, by relative shifts to more individual and less situational control of interpretation.

As the locus of "control of interpretation" shifts with increasing job longevity and individuals continue to stabilize their situational definitions, other impor-

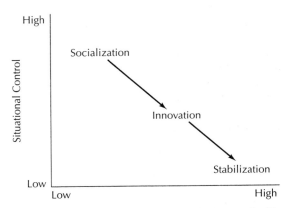

Figure 16.2. Situational versus individual control of interpretation along the job-longevity continuum.

tant behavioral tendencies can also materialize. In particular, strong biases can develop in the way individuals select and interpret information, in their cognitive abilities to generate new options and strategies creatively, and in their willingness to innovate or implement alternative courses of action. Table 16.1 outlines in more detail some of the specific possibilities within each of these three general areas. Furthermore, it is the capacity either to prevent or overcome these kinds of tendencies that is so important to the long-term success of organizations; for, over time, each of these trends could lead to less effective performance and decision-making outcomes.

Problem-Solving Processes

It has been argued throughout this paper that as employees gradually adapt to prolonged periods of job longevity, they may become less receptive toward any change or innovation threatening to disrupt significantly their comfortable and predictable work practices and patterns of behavior. Individuals, instead, are more likely to develop reliable and effective routine responses (i.e., standard operating procedures) for dealing with their frequently encountered tasks in order to ensure predictability, coordination, and economical information processing. As a result, there may develop over time increasing rigidity in one's problem-solving activities—a kind of functional fixedness that reduces the individual's capacity for flexibility and openness to change. Responses and decisions are made in their fixed, normal patterns while novel situations requiring

Table 16.1. Representative Trends Associated with Long-Term Job Longevity

Problem-solving processes
  Increased rigidity
  Increased commitment to established practices and
    procedures
  Increased mainlining of strategies
Information processes
  Increased insulation from critical areas
  Increased selective exposure
  Increased selective perception
Cognitive processes
  Increased reliance on own experiences and expertise
  Increased narrowing of cognitive abilities
  Increased homophyly

responses that do not fit such established molds are either ignored or forced into these molds. New or changing situations either trigger responses of old situations or trigger no responses at all. It becomes, essentially, a work world characterized by phrases such as, "business as usual," or "we've never done that before," or "we're not in that business," etc.

Furthermore, as individuals continue to work by their well-established problem-solving strategies and procedures, the more committed they may become to such existing methods. Commitment is a function of time, and the longer individuals are called upon to follow and justify their problem-solving approaches and decisions, the more ingrained they are likely to become. Drawing from his work on decision making, Allison (1971) strongly warns that increasing reliance on regularized practices and procedures can become highly resistant to change, since such functions become increasingly grounded in the norms and basic attitudes of the organizational unit and in the operating styles of its members. Bion (1961) and Argyris (1969) even suggest that it may be impossible for individuals to break out of fixed patterns of activity and interpersonal behavior without sufficiently strong outside interference or help.

With extended job tenure, then, problem-solving activities can become increasingly guided by consideration of methods and programs that have worked in the past. Moreover, in accumulating this experience and knowledge, alternative ideas and approaches were probably considered and discarded. With such refutations, however, commitments to the present courses of action can become even stronger—often to the extent that these competing alternatives are never reconsidered.[7] In fact, individuals can become overly preoccupied with the survival of their particular approaches, protecting them against fresh approaches or negative evaluations. Much of their energy becomes directed toward "mainlining their strategies," that is, making sure their specific solution approaches are selected and followed. Research by Janis and Mann (1977) and Staw (1980) has demonstrated very convincingly just how strongly committed individuals can become to their problem-solving approaches and decisions, even in the face of adverse information, especially if they feel personally responsible for such strategies. And under these kinds of conditions, professional knowledge workers are more likely to come to tough meetings, not with open-mindedness and problem-solving information, but with preconceived solutions based on filtered information.

Information Processes

One of the potential consequences of developing this kind of "status-quo" perspective with respect to problem-solving activity is that employees may also become increasingly insulated from outside sources of relevant information and important new ideas. As individuals become more protective of and committed to their current work habits, the extent to which they are willing or even feel they need to expose themselves to new or alternative ideas, solution strategies, or constructive criticisms becomes progressively less and less. Rather than becoming more vigilant about events taking place outside their immediate work settings, they become increasingly complacent about external environmental changes and new technological developments. Studies, such as those of D'Aveni (1994) and Miller (1990), have convincingly shown just how important it is to pay attention to outside sources of information if organizations truly hope to survive under the pressures of long-term competition.

In addition to this possible decay in the amount of external contact and interaction, there may also be an increasing tendency for individuals to communicate only with those whose ideas are in accord with their current interests, needs, or existing attitudes. Such a tendency is referred to as selective exposure. Generally speaking, there is always the tendency for individuals to communicate with those who are most like themselves (Rogers and Shoemaker, 1971). With increasing adaptation to long-term job longevity and stability, however, this tendency is likely to become even stronger. Thus, selective exposure may increasingly enable these individuals to avoid information and messages that might be in conflict with their current practices and dispositions.

One should also recognize, of course, that under these kinds of circumstances, any outside contact or environmental information that does become processed by these long-tenured individuals might not be viewed in the most open and unbiased fashion. Janis and Mann (1977), for example, discuss at great length the many kinds of cognitive defenses and distortions commonly used by individuals in processing outside information in order to support, maintain, or protect certain decisional policies and strategies. Such defenses are often used to argue against any disquieting information and evidence in order to maintain self-esteem, commitment, and involvement. In particular, selective perception is the tendency to interpret information and communication messages in terms favorable to one's existing attitudes and beliefs. And it is this combination of increasing insulation, selective exposure, and selective perception that can be so powerful in keeping critical information and important new ideas and innovations from being registered.

Cognitive Processes

As individuals become more comfortable and secure in their long-tenured work environments, their desire to seek out and actively internalize new knowledge and new developments may begin to deteriorate. Not only may they become increasingly isolated from outside sources of information, but their willingness to accept or pay adequate attention to the advice and ideas of fellow experts may become less and less. Unlike the socialization period in which individuals are usually very attentive to sources of expertise and influence within their new job settings, individuals in the stabilization stage have probably become significantly less receptive to such information sources. They may prefer, instead, to rely on their own accumulated experience and wisdom and consequently are more apt to dismiss the approaches, advice, or critical comments of others. As a result, adapted employees may be especially defensive with regard to critical evaluations and feedback messages, whether they stem from sources of outside expertise or from internal supervision. Long-tenured veteran employees, for example, would not regard "constructive" performance appraisals with nearly as much enthusiasm as newcomers who might welcome such discussions in order to calibrate more accurately their organizational career paths and contributions.

It should also not be surprising that with increasing job stability one is more likely to become increasingly specialized, that is, moving from broadly defined capabilities and solution approaches to more narrowly defined interests and specialties. Without new challenges and opportunities, the diversity of skills and of ideas generated are likely to become narrower and narrower. And as individuals welcome information from fewer sources and are exposed to fewer alternative points of view, the more constricted their cognitive abilities can become. This often results in a more restricted perspective of one's situation, coupled with a more limited set of coping responses—all of which affect creativity. Such a restricted outlook can also be very detrimental to the organization's overall effectiveness, for it could lead at times to the screening out of some vitally important environmental and competitive information cues.

Homophyly refers to the degree to which interacting individuals are similar with respect to certain attributes, such as beliefs, values, education, and social status (Rogers and Shoemaker, 1971). Not only is there a strong tendency for individuals to communicate with those who are most like themselves, but it is also likely that continued interaction can lead to greater homophyly in knowledge, beliefs, and problem-solving behaviors and perceptions (Burke and Bennis, 1961; Pfeffer, 1980). The venerable proverb "birds of a feather flock together" makes a great deal of sense, but it may be just as sensible to say that "when birds flock together, they become more of a feather." Accordingly, as individuals stabilize their work settings and patterns of communication, a greater degree of homophyly is likely to have emerged between these individuals and those with whom they have been interacting over the long tenure period. And any increase in homophyly could lead in turn to further stability in the communications of the more homophilous pairs, thereby increasing their insulation from heterophilous others. Thus, it is possible for the various trends to feed on each other. For as previously discussed, although individuals may be able to coordinate and communicate with similar partners more easily and economically, such homogeneous interactions can also yield less creative and innovative outcomes (Pelz and Andrews, 1966).

Longevity and Performance

These problem-solving, informational, and cognitive tendencies, of course, can be very serious in their consequences, perhaps even fatal. Much depends, however, on the nature of the work being performed and on the extent to which such trends actually transpire. The performances of individuals working on fairly routine, simple tasks in a rather stable organizational environ-

ment, for example, may not suffer as a result of these trends, for their own knowledge, experiences, and abilities become sufficient. Maintaining or improving on one's routine behaviors is all that is required—at least for as long as there are no changes and no new developments. However, as individuals function in a more rapidly changing environment and work on more complex tasks requiring greater levels of change, creativity, and informational vigilance, the effects of these long-term longevity trends are likely to become significantly more dysfunctional.

GROUP AGE

The degree to which any of these previously described trends actually materializes for any given individual depends, of course, on the overall situational context. Individuals' perceptions and responses do not take place in a social vacuum but develop over time as they continue to interact with various aspects of their job and organizational surroundings (Crozier, 1964; Katz and Van Maanen, 1977). And in any job setting one of the most powerful factors affecting individual perspectives is the nature of the particular group or project team in which one is a functioning member (Schein, 1978, Katz and Kahn, 1978).

Ever since the well-known Western Electric Studies (Cass and Zimmer, 1975), much of our research in the social sciences has been directed toward learning just how strong group associations can be in influencing individual member behaviors, motivations, and attitudes (Asch, 1956; Shaw, 1971; Katz, 1977). From the diffusion of new innovations (Robertson, 1971) to the changing of meat consumption patterns, to less desirable but more plentiful cuts such as liver (Lewin, 1965), to the implementation of job enrichment (Hackman, 1978), group processes and effects have been extremely critical to more successful outcomes. The impact of groups on individual responses is substantial, if not pervasive, simply because groups mediate most of the stimuli to which their individual members are subjected while fulfilling their everday task and organizational requirements. Accordingly, whether individuals experiencing long-term job longevity enter the stabilization period and become subjected to the tendencies previously described may strongly depend on the particular reinforcements, pressures, and behavioral norms encountered within their immediate project or work groups (Likert, 1967; Weick, 1969).

Generally speaking, as members of a project group continue to work together over an extended period of time and gain experience with one another, their patterns of activities are likely to become more stable, with individual role assignments becoming more well-defined and resistant to change (Bales, 1955; Porter et al., 1975). Emergence of the various problem-solving, informational, and cognitive trends, therefore, may be more a function of the average length of time the group members have worked together (i.e., group age or group longevity) rather than varying according to the particular job longevity of any single individual. A project group, then, might either exacerbate or ameliorate the various trends (e.g., insulation from outside developments and expertise), just as previous studies have shown how groups can enforce or amplify certain standards and norms of individual behavior (e.g., Seashore, 1954; Stoner, 1968). Thus, it may be misleading to investigate the responses and reactions of organizational individuals as if they functioned as independent entities; rather, it may be more insightful to examine the distribution of responses as a function of different project teams, especially when project teams are characterized by relatively high levels of group stability as measured by group age.

To investigate such a possibility, Professor Tom Allen and I conducted a field study in a large chemical company to investigate the effects of group age on the group's overall project performance, where group age was measured by the average length of time the project or group members had worked together. A comparative analysis of some sixty R&D project teams within this organization revealed a very strong curvilinear relationship between group age and project performance, the lower performing project groups either having worked together for less than a year or they had been working together for at least four years.

Further analyses suggested that this curvilinear relationship may be the result of two component forces, as shown in Figure 16.3. One component term rises rapidly with mean group tenure, showing the positive effects of "team-building." Group members develop better understanding of each other's capabilities, contributions, working styles, etc. and such improvements in communication and working relationships result in higher levels of group performance. At the same

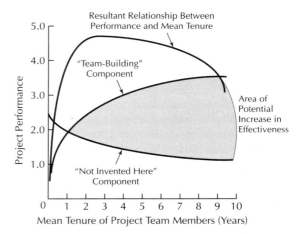

Figure 16.3. The relationship between mean tenure project and performance analyzed into its components.

time, however, a decay component term sets in, resulting in part from the previously described problem-solving, communication, and cognitive processes that become established, reinforced, and habitual as individuals reduce uncertainty together within their stabilized group setting. Katz and Allen describe this decay component as the well-recognized Not Invented Here (N.I.H.) syndrome. Between these two component curves lies the area for potentially influencing a project's performance. Managers need to balance the advantages of team-building by also making sure that over time they take those steps necessary to counter the negative effects of N.I.H.

CONCLUSIONS

What is suggested by this discussion of job and group longevities is that employee perspectives and behaviors, and their subsequent effects on performance, might be significantly managed through staffing and career decisions. One could argue, for example, that the energizing and destabilizing function of new team members can be very important in preventing a project group from developing some of the tendencies previously described for long-tenured individuals, including insulation from key communication areas. The benefit of new team members is that they may have a relative advantage in generating fresh ideas and approaches. With their active participation, existing group members might consider more carefully ideas and alternatives they might have otherwise ignored or dismissed. In short, project newcomers can represent a novelty-enhancing condition, challenging and improving the scope of existing methods and accumulated knowledge.[8]

The longevity framework also seems to suggest that periodic job mobility or rotation might help prevent employees from moving into a stabilization stage. As long as the socialization period is positively negotiated, employees can simply cycle from one innovation period into another.[9] Put simply, movements into new positions may be necessary to keep individuals stimulated, flexible, and vigilant with respect to their work environments. Within a single job assignment, the person may eventually reach the limit to which new and exciting challenges are possible or even welcomed. At that point, a new job position may be necessary. To maintain adaptability and to keep employees responsive, what might be needed are career histories containing sequences of job positions involving new challenges and requiring new skills (Kaufman, 1974). As pointed out by Schein (1968), continued growth and development often come from adaptations to new or changing work environments requiring individuals to give up familiar and stable work patterns in favor of developing new ones.

As important as job mobility is, it is probably just as important to determine whether individuals and project groups can circumvent the effects of longevity without new assignments or rejuvenation from new project members. Rotations and promotions are not always possible, especially when there is little organizational growth. As a result, we need to learn considerably more about the effects of increasing job and group longevities. Just how deterministic are the trends? Can long-tenured individuals and project teams remain high-performing, and if so, how can it be accomplished?

In a general sense, then, we need to learn how to detect the many kinds of changes that either have taken place or are likely to take place within a group as its team membership ages. Furthermore, we need to learn if project groups can keep themselves energized and innovative over long periods of group longevity, or whether certain kinds of organizational structures and managerial practices are needed to keep a project team effective and high-performing as it ages.

In response to this issue, a more extensive study in twelve different organizations involving over 300

R&D project teams has been undertaken by Katz and Allen. Within this overall sample of project groups, approximately fifty of the groups had been working together for more than four years. More importantly, a large number of these long-tenured groups were still judged to have very high levels of group performance. The research question, of course, is how have these particular long-tenured groups managed to circumvent the N.I.H. problem and maintain their high levels of performance. Although the data are still being processed, preliminary analyses seem to indicate that the nature of the project's supervision may be the most important factor differentiating the more effective long-tenured teams from those less effective. In particular, engineers belonging to the high-performing, long-tenured groups perceived their project supervisors to be superior in dealing with conflicts between groups and individuals, in obtaining necessary resources for project members, in setting project goals, and in monitoring the activities and progress of project members toward these goals. Furthermore, in performing these supervisory functions, the more effective project managers of long-tenured groups were not very participative in their approaches, instead, they were extremely demanding of their teams, challenging them to perform in new ways and directions. In fact, the most participative managers (as viewed by project members) were significantly less effective in managing teams with high group longevity. Our study also revealed that not all managers may be able to gain the creative performances out of long-term technical groups. Typically, the managers of the higher performing long-term groups had been with their teams less than 3 years and had come to this assignment with a strong history of prior managerial success. It was not their first managerial experience! To the contrary, most were well-respected technical managers who had "made things happen" and who had developed strong power bases and strong levels of senior managerial support within their R&D units or divisions. It was this combination of technical credibility and managerial respect and power that enabled these managers to be effective with their long-term stabilized R&D project teams.

What these and other initial findings seem to indicate is that in managing long-tenured groups, project managers who have the appropriate credibility and experience should place less emphasis on participative decision making and empowerment and place more emphasis on direction and control. As long as members of long-tenured groups are unresponsive to the challenges in their tasks, participative management will only be related to job satisfaction—not project performance.

In a broader context, we need to learn how to manage workers, professionals, and project teams as they enter and proceed through different stages of longevity. Clearly, different kinds of managerial styles and behaviors may be more appropriate at different stages of longevity. Delegative or participative management, for example, may be very effective when individuals are vigilant and highly responsive to their work demands, but such supervisory activities may prove less successful when employees are unresponsive to their job environments, as in the stabilization stage. Furthermore, as perspectives and responsiveness shift over time, the actions required of the managerial role will also vary. Managers may be effective, then, to the extent they are able to recognize and cover such changing conditions. Thus, it may be the ability to manage change—the ability to diagnose and manage between socialization and stabilization—that we need to learn so much more if we truly hope to provide careers that keep employees responsive and also keep organizations effective.

NOTES

1. For a more extensive discussion of the job-longevity model, see Katz (1980). In the current presentation, the term "stabilization" is used in place of "adaptation" since individuals are in effect adapting to their job situations in all three stages, albeit in systematically different ways.

2. The extent to which a veteran employee actually undergoes socialization depends on how displaced the veteran becomes in undertaking his or her new job assignment. Generally speaking, the more displaced veterans are from their previously familiar task requirements and interpersonal associations, the more intense the socialization experience.

3. After comparing the socialization reactions of veterans and newcomers, Katz (1978a) suggests that newcomers may be especially responsive to interactional issues involving personal acceptance and "getting on board," whereas veterans may be particularly concerned with reestablishing their sense of competency in their newly acquired task assignments.

4. One of the factors contributing to the importance of this socialization period lies in the realization that engineering strategies and solutions within organizations are often not defined in very generalizeable terms but are peculiar to their specific settings (Allen, 1977; Katz and Tushman, 1979). As a result, R&D project groups in different organizations may face similar problems yet may define their solution approaches and parameters very differently. And it is precisely because technical problems are typically expressed in such "localized" terms that engineers must learn how to contribute effectively within their new project groups.

5. It is also interesting to note that in discussing his career-anchor framework, Schein (1978) points out that career anchors seem to represent a stable concept around which individuals are able to organize experiences and direct activities. Furthermore, it appears from Schein's research that it is within this area of stability that individuals are most likely to self-develop and grow.

6. There are, of course, alternative arguments, such as in activation theory (Scott, 1966), suggesting that people do in fact seek uncertainty, novelty, or change. The argument here, however, is that as individuals adapt and become increasingly indifferent to the task challenges of their jobs, it is considerably more likely that they will strive to reduce uncertainty and maintain predictability rather than the reverse.

7. As shown by Allen's (1966) research on parallel project efforts, such reevaluations can be very important in reaching more successful outcomes.

8. As discussed by Katz and Allen (1981), the socialization process of individuals can greatly affect the extent to which newcomers may be willing to try to innovate on existing "widsoms."

9. A discussion on effectively managing the socialization process is beyond the scope of this paper. The reader is referred to the descriptive theory presented in Schein (1968), Kotter (1973), Hall (1976), Katz (1980), and Wanous (1980).

REFERENCES

Allen, T. J. "Studies of the problem-solving processes in engineering designs." *IEEE Transactions in Engineering Management,* 1966, *13,* 72–83.

Allen, T. J. *Managing the Flow of Technology.* Cambridge, Mass.: M.I.T. Press, 1977.

Allison, G. T. *Essence of Decision: Explaining the Cuban Missile Crisis.* Boston: Little, Brown, 1971.

Argyris, C. *Personality and Organization.* New York: Harper Torch Books, 1957.

Argyris, C. "The incompleteness of social psychological theory: examples from small group, cognitive consistency and attribution research." *American Psychologist,* 1969, *24,* 893–908.

Asch, S. E. "Studies of independence and conformity: a minority of one against a unanimous majority." *Psychological Monographs,* 1956, *70.*

Bales, R. F. "Adaptive and integrative changes as sources of strain in social systems." In A. P. Hare, E. F. Borgatta, and R. F. Bales, eds., *Small Groups: Studies in Social Interaction.* New York: Knopf, 1955, pp. 127–31.

Bion, W. R. *Experiences in Groups.* New York: Basic Books, 1961.

Burke, R. L., and Bennis, W. G. "Changes in perception of self and others during human relations training." *Human Relations,* 1961, *14,* 165–82.

Cass, E. L., and Zimmer, F. G. *Man and Work in Society.* New York: Van Nostrand Reinhold, 1975.

Chinoy, E. *Automobile Workers and the American Dream.* Garden City, N.Y.: Doubleday, 1955.

Crozier, M. *The Bureaucratic Phenomenon.* Chicago: University of Chicago Press, 1964.

D'Aveni, R. A. *Hypercompetition.* New York: Free Press, 1994.

Dewhirst, H., Avery, R., and Brown, E. "Satisfaction and performance in research and development tasks as related to information accessibility." *IEEE Transactions on Engineering Management,* 1978, *25,* 58–63.

Dubin, S. S. *Professional Obsolescence.* Lexington, Mass.: Lexington Books, D. C. Heath, 1972.

Feldman, D. "The role of initiation activities in socialization." *Human Relations,* 1977, *30,* 977–90.

Graen, G. "Role-making processes within complex organizations." In M. D. Dunnette, ed., *Handbook of Industrial and Organizational Psychology,* Chicago: Rand McNally, 1976.

Hackman, J. R. "The design of self managing work groups." In B. King, S. Streufert, and F. Fielder, eds., *Managerial Control and Organizational Democracy.* New York: Wiley, 1978.

Hackman, J. R., and Oldham, G. R. "Development of the job diagnostic survey." *Journal of Applied Psychology,* 1975, *60,* 159–70.

Hall, D. T. *Careers in Organizations.* Pacific Palisades, Calif.: Goodyear, 1976.

Hall, D. T., and Nougaim, K. E. "An examination of Maslow's need hierarchy in an organizational setting." *Organizational Behavior and Human Performance,* 1968, *3,* 12–35.

Hall, D. T., and Schneider, B. *Organizational Climates and Careers.* New York: Seminar Press, 1973.

Homans, C. C. *Social Behavior: Its Elementary Forms.* New York: Harcourt, Brace and World, 1961.

Hughes, E. C. *Men and Their Work.* Glencoe, Ill.: Free Press, 1958.

Janis, I. L., and Mann, L. *Decision Making.* New York: Free Press, 1977.

Kahn, R. L., Wolfe, D. M., Quinn, R. P., Snock, J. D., and Rosenthal, R. A. *Organizational Stress: Studies on Role Conflict and Ambiguity.* New York: Wiley, 1964.

Katz, D., and Kahn, R. L. *The Social Psychology of Organizations.* New York: Wiley, 1978.

Katz, R. "The influence of group conflict on leadership effectiveness." *Organizational Behavior and Human Performance,* 1977, *20,* 265–86.

Katz, R. "Job longevity as a situational factor in job satisfaction." *Administrative Science Quarterly,* 1978a, *10,* 204–23.

Katz, R., "The influence of job longevity on employee reactions to task characteristics." *Human Relations,* 1978b, *31,* 703–25.

Katz, R. "Time and work: toward an integrative perspective." In B. Staw and L. L. Cummings, eds., *Research in Organizational Behavior,* Vol. 2. Greenwich, Conn.: JAI Press, 1980, 81–127.

Katz, R., and Allen, T. "Investigating the not-invented-here syndrome." In A. Pearson, ed., *Industrial R&D Strategy and Management,* London: Basil Blackwell Press, 1981.

Katz, R., and Tushman, M. "Communication patterns, project performance and task characteristics: an empirical evaluation and integration in an R&D setting." *Organizational Behavior and Human Performance,* 1979, *23,* 139–62.

Katz, R., and Tushman, M. "A longitudinal study of the effects of boundary spanning supervision in turnover and promotion in Research and Development." *Academy of Management Journal,* 1983, *26,* 437–56.

Katz, R., and Van Maanen, J. "The loci of work satisfaction: job, interaction, and policy." *Human Relations,* 1977, *30,* 469–86.

Kaufman, H. G. *Obsolescence of Professional Career Development.* New York: AMACOM, 1974.

Kiesler, S. *Interpersonal Processes in Groups and Organizations.* Arlington Heights, Ill.: AHM Publishers, 1978.

Kopelman, R. E. "Psychological stages of careers in engineering: an expectancy theory taxonomy." *Journal of Vocational Behavior,* 1977, *10,* 270–86.

Kotter, J. "The psychological contract: managing the joining-up process." *California Management Review,* 1973, *15,* 91–99.

Kuhn, T. S. *The Structure of Scientific Revolutions.* Chicago: University of Chicago Press, 1963.

Lawrence, P. R., and Lorsch, J. W. *Organizational and Environment.* Boston: Harvard Business School, 1967.

Lee, D. "The effects of socialization on performance." Unpublished Working Paper Manuscript, Suffolk University, 1992.

Lewin, K. "Group decision and social change." in H. Proshansky and B. Seidenberg, eds., *Basic Studies in Social Psychology.* New York: Holt, Rinehart, and Winston, 1965, pp. 423–36.

Likert, R. *The Human Organization*. New York: McGraw-Hill, 1967.

Maslow, A. *Toward a Psychology of Being*. Princeton, N.J.: D. Van Nostrand, 1962.

Menzel, H. "Information needs and uses in science and technology." In C. Cuadra, ed., *Annual Review of Information Science and Technology*, New York: Wiley, 1965.

Miller, D. *The Icarus Paradox*. New York: Harper Collins, 1990.

Pélz, D. C., and Andrews, F. M. *Scientists in Organizations*. New York: Wiley, 1966.

Pfeffer, J. "Management as symbolic action: the creation and maintenance of organizational paradigms." In L. L. Cummings and B. Staw, eds., *Research in Organizational Behavior*, Vol. 3. Greenwich, Conn.: JAI Press, 1981.

Porter, L. W., Lawler, E. E., and Hackman, J. R. *Behavior in Organizations*. New York: McGraw-Hill, 1975.

Robertson, T. S. *Innovative Behavior and Communications*. New York: Holt, Rinehart, and Winston, 1971.

Rogers, C. R. *On Becoming a Person*. Boston: Houghton-Mifflin, 1961.

Rogers, E. M., and Shoemaker, F. F. *Communication of Innovations: A Crosscultural Approach*. New York: Free Press, 1971.

Salancik, G. R., and Pfeffer, J. "A social information processing approach to job attitudes and task design." *Administrative Science Quarterly*, 1978, *23*, 224–53.

Schein, E. H. "Organizational socialization and the profession of management." *Industrial Management Review*, 1968, *9*, 1–15.

Schein, E. H. "The individual, the organization, and the career: a conceptual scheme." *Journal of Applied Behavioral Science*, 1971, *7*, 401–26.

Schein, E. H. "Personal change though interpersonal relationships." In W. G. Bennis, D. E. Berlew, E. H. Schein, and F. I. Steele, eds., *Interpersonal Dynamics: Essays and Readings on Human Interaction*, Homewood, Ill.: Dorsey Press, 1973.

Schein, E. H. *Career Dynamics*. Reading, Mass.: Addison-Wesley, 1978.

Scott, W. E., "Activation theory and task design." *Organizational Behavior and Human Performance*, 1966, *1*, 3–30.

Seashore, S. F. "Group cohesiveness in the industrial work group." Ann Arbor, Mich.: Survey Research Center, University of Michigan, 1954.

Shaw, M. E. *Group Dynamics: The Psychology of Small Group Behavior*. New York: McGraw-Hill, 1971.

Staw, B. "Motivation in organizations: toward synthesis and redirection." In B. Staw and G. R. Salancik, eds., *New Directions in Organizational Behavior*, Chicago: St. Clair Press, 1977.

Staw, B. "Rationality and justification in organizational life." In B. Staw and L. L. Cummings, eds., *Research in Organizational Behavior*, Vol. 2. Greenwich, Conn.: JAI Press, 1980, pp. 45–80.

Stoner, J. A. "Risky and cautious shifts in group decisions: the influence of widely held values." *Journal of Experimental Social Psychology*, 1968, *4*, 442–59.

Tushman, M., and Katz, R. "External communication and project performance: an investigation into the role of gatekeepers." *Management Science*, 1980, *26*, 1071–1085.

Wanous, J. *Organizational Entry*. Reading, Mass.: Addison-Wesley, 1980.

Weick, K. E., *The Social Psychology of Organizing*. Reading, Mass.: Addison-Wesley, 1969.

Wheeler, S. "The structure of formerly organized socialization settings." In O. G. Brim and S. Wheeler, eds., *Socialization after Childhood: Two Essays*. New York: Wiley, 1966.

Wortman, C. B., and Linsenmeier, J. "Interpersonal attraction and techniques of ingratiation in organizational settings." In B. Staw and G. R. Salancik, eds., *New Directions in Organizational Behavior*. Chicago: St. Clair Press, 1977.

17

Strong Cultures and Innovation

Oxymoron or Opportunity?

FRANCIS J. FLYNN
JENNIFER A. CHATMAN

INTRODUCTION

Organizational scholars and managers agree that innovation is a critical determinant of organizational survival and success due, in part, to a rapidly changing and increasingly competitive business environment. As Amabile (1997, p. 40) stated, "[i]nnovation is absolutely vital for long-term corporate success . . . [N]o firm that continues to deliver the same products and services in the same way can long survive. By contrast, firms that prepare for the future by implementing new ideas oriented toward this changing world are likely to thrive." Despite the growing number of studies focusing on innovation, however, our understanding of how organizations cultivate innovation remains limited (Tushman and O'Reilly, 1997).

Case studies of exemplary organizations reveal a set of dimensions associated with innovation success (e.g., Kanter et al., 1997; Robinson and Stern, 1997; Zell, 1997). For example, 3M has created well over 50,000 products (usually over 100 major new products a year) and consistently obtains 30% of its revenue from products developed within the past 4 years (Nicholson, 1998). This constant stream of product innovations has kept 3M in the upper echelon of Fortune 500 firms for several decades and made it one of "America's most admired corporations" (O'Reilly, 1997, p. 60). But, how are 3M consistently and successfully innovative? The people they employed over the years have changed, and many organizations have replicated specific aspects of their structure without ever achieving similar results.

One factor that may have contributed to 3M's sustained innovation success is their strong organizational culture. By emphasizing norms that support the generation and implementation of creative ideas, 3M's culture transcended specific management practices and allowed 3M to be consistently innovative over a long period. To promote creativity, 3M advanced a supportive "value system" that encouraged organizational members to develop original and useful products (Peters and Waterman, 1982). And, the cohesion found among 3M's product development teams was seen as instrumental to implementing these creative ideas as successful product launches. In contrast, the notion that a strong, cohesive culture could be an essential component of innovation in organizations is often viewed with skepticism among academics. Many believe that strong cultures induce uniformity (e.g., Nemeth and Staw, 1989); in their view, ambiguity is needed to promote the behavioral variation essential for creativity in organizations (e.g., Nemeth, 1997).

Reprinted from the *International Handbook of Organizational Culture and Climate,* Cary L. Cooper, Sue Cartwright, and P. Christopher Earley (eds.), "Strong Cultures and Innovation: Oxymoron or Opportunity?," by Francis J. Flynn and Jennifer A. Chatman. Copyright © 2001 by John Wiley & Sons Limited. Reproduced by permission of John Wiley & Sons Limited, West Sussex, UK.

This presents organizational researchers with an intriguing paradox: cultural strength purportedly limits individual creativity, yet creativity may be even better directed, in terms of producing and implementing more relevant and better ideas, in a strong culture that emphasizes particular innovation-enhancing norms.

At the heart of this apparent paradox lies a limited consideration of culture and its effects on creativity and innovation in organizations. In particular, the distinction between culture content and culture strength has been blurred, which, in turn, has clouded the relationship between organizational culture and innovation. Our goal in this chapter is to clarify the impact of culture, particularly in terms of its content and strength, on an organization's ability to innovate.

Focusing on the organization as the level of analysis, we begin our discussion by briefly reviewing and integrating notions of organizational innovation and culture. We find that past research supports a relationship between emphasizing norms that foster creativity and implementation and successful organizational innovation. We then attempt to resolve some of the conflicting evaluations of the culture—innovation relationship by distinguishing between the concepts of culture strength and content. We also examine the purported constraints that group cohesion imposes on the relationship between culture and innovation by pressuring group members to conform to particular norms. Further, we suggest ways that various content-specific norms, particularly those focusing on individualism or collectivism, may be better suited for different stages of the innovation process. Throughout our discussion, we present a set of propositions to help guide future research exploring the relationship between organizational culture and innovation. We conclude by arguing that the apparent paradox between strong organizational culture and innovation results from an overly simplistic view of conformity and culture strength and content.

DEFINING INNOVATION

Enhancing the creative performance of employees is a critical task for organizations interested in promoting innovation (e.g., Amabile, 1988; Kanter, 1988; Shalley, 1995; Staw, 1990). "When employees perform creatively, they suggest novel and useful products, ideas,

or procedures that provide an organization with raw material for subsequent development and implementation" (Oldham and Cummings, 1996, p. 607). However, creativity is not a sufficient condition for innovation. Instead, the term innovation typically refers to the successful implementation of creative ideas. Following Caldwell and O'Reilly (1995), we define innovation as the combination of two processes: (1) creativity, or the generation of new ideas; and (2) implementation, or the actual introduction of the change. For the purpose of our discussion, we assume that creativity and implementation are distinct, sequential stages in the innovation process, although we recognize that the two stages may overlap substantially.

INNOVATION IN ORGANIZATIONS

Innovation research has focused on identifying the determinants of creative potential at the individual level (e.g., Amabile, 1996) or the structural correlates of innovation at the organizational level (e.g., Cummings, 1965; Kanter, 1988; Thompson, 1965). Less attention has been given to groups of individuals that are charged with developing innovations, yet groups are increasingly responsible for innovation in organizations (e.g., Ancona and Caldwell, 1998). Leavitt (1975) suggested that groups, not individuals, should be the building blocks of organizations partly because they hold greater creative potential, and Hackman (1987) argued that groups may yield more creative products because they benefit from diverse members' interactions. As such, any discussion of organizational innovation should recognize that much of the innovation process occurs within work team environments.

Past research has identified several determinants of group creativity, including leadership, longevity, cohesiveness, heterogeneity, structure, size, communication patterns and resource availability (e.g., King and Anderson, 1990; Payne, 1990). A critical, yet less obvious source of influence on innovation are group norms. West (1990) identified four norms that increased the quantity and quality of group innovations: (1) vision; (2) participative safety; (3) task orientation; and (4) support for innovation. Caldwell and O'Reilly (1995) identified a similar set of cultural norms that focused on (1) support for risk taking, (2) tolerance of mistakes, (3) teamwork, and (4) speed of action.

Cultural norms can be a powerful means of stimulating innovation by attaching social approval to activities that facilitate innovation. Past research has found that norms are central to characterizing how work is conducted at the organizational and group levels (e.g., Chatman and Barsade, 1995; Earley, 1993) and may influence group creativity (e.g., Chatman et al., 1998). Thus, successful innovation may depend on the unique cultural norms that groups develop and the extent to which the group's cultural orientation aligns with, and is supported by, the organization's overall orientation (Amabile et al., 1996). In contrast to creativity research, innovation research has rarely focused on the underlying psychological processes that cause people and groups to develop innovative products and processes. Exploring the link between organizational culture, as it is manifest in norms, and innovation may provide insight into these psychological processes.

THE RELATIONSHIP BETWEEN CULTURE AND INNOVATION

Though researchers disagree about how to conceptualize and measure organizational culture, it can be understood as a "system of shared values (that define what is important) and norms that define appropriate attitudes and behaviors for organizational members (how to feel and behave)" (O'Reilly and Chatman, 1996, p. 166). As a system of social control, organizational culture can influence members' focus of attention, behavior, and commitment. Through members' clarity about organizational objectives and their willingness to work toward these objectives, culture influences the attainment of valued organizational goals by enhancing an organization's ability to execute its strategy (e.g., Tushman and O'Reilly, 1997). Two primary concerns become relevant using this conceptualization: (1) the extent to which members agree and care about values and norms (culture strength); and (2) the extent to which these norms and values differ across settings (culture content). Further, by conceptualizing culture in terms of observable norms and values that characterize a group or organization, researchers can develop quantitative measurement schemes that allow for the psychometric assessment of core attitudes and behaviors culled from self-reports or observations

(e.g., Denison and Mishra, 1995; Enz, 1988; O'Reilly et al., 1991; Rousseau, 1990).

Although researchers and practitioners generally agree that culture influences organizational performance, surprisingly few studies have actually tested this relationship. Denison and Mishra (1995) showed evidence that certain aspects of organizational culture are linked to growth and profitability. Both Gordon and DiTomaso (1992) and Kotter and Heskett (1992) found that firms emphasizing adaptability and change in their cultures were more likely to perform well over time, though the specific reasons for this relationship are unclear. Sorensen (1999) recently reanalyzed the Kotter and Heskett (1992) data and found that organizations with strong cultures performed more consistently over time only when industry volatility was low. Organizational learning may explain this effect. Strong culture firms may be unable to engage in exploration learning, or to discover alternative routines, technologies, and purposes that would be necessary in a volatile industry (Sorensen, 1999, p. 10).

The observation by Sorensen (1999) suggests that, depending on certain conditions, the presence of a strong culture may hinder innovation, yet improve organizational performance in other ways. Many researchers would agree that strong cultures can be detrimental, claiming that strength of agreement, in any form, effectively stunts innovation. Nemeth and Staw (1989), for example, have argued that as cohesion among group (or organizational) members intensifies, groups tolerate less deviation. Purportedly, it is this deviation from group culture, which we conceptualize as agreed upon norms and values, that furnishes the potential for innovation in organizations (Nemeth, 1997). If people are free to express any ideas they wish without fear of reprisal from other members of their group, more creative solutions will be generated.

In support of this argument, Nemeth and Staw (1989) reviewed several studies of conformity in the face of ambiguity, most of which were drawn from the classic Asch (1955) and Milgram (1974) experiments. Here, the presence of strong norms served to enforce a dominant perspective among group members. In an environment where such strong norms are in place, dissenters who may provide alternative perspectives will refrain from voicing their opinions for fear of rejection or ostracism. Instead, according to Nemeth and Staw (1989), many will choose to adopt the dominant perspective or at least affirm it in the presence of their peers. This tendency may be exacerbated in organizations, where "one of the most significant psychological tendencies is a strain toward uniformity, a tendency for people to agree on some issue or to conform to some behavioral pattern" (Nemeth and Staw, 1989, p. 175).

Although the above argument makes intuitive sense, it is not exactly clear whether and how agreement limits innovation in organizations. For example, what if the norm that members of an organization expect adherence to is divergent thinking? In an analysis of IDEO, a successful product design firm, Sutton and Hargadon (1996) described how having norms that encouraged people to express "wild ideas" during brainstorming sessions enhanced the innovation process. "Facilitators and participants discourage criticism, even negative facial expression, but often nod, smile, and say 'wow' and 'cool' in response to an idea" (Sutton and Hargadon, 1996, p. 694). Brain-storming norms were strongly enforced in that those who did not conform to the norm to "be outrageous" tended to occupy lower positions of status in the organization.

Like psychologists, organizational sociologists disagree about whether strong cultures may inhibit innovation in organizations. On the one hand, Burns and Stalker (1961) posited that organizations with strong, organic structures were better suited for innovation than were those with mechanistic structures. To accomplish their objectives, organic structures rely on informal sources of control, such as organizational culture, whereas mechanistic structures rely on rules, procedures, and rigidities of formal hierarchy. On the other hand, March (1991) developed a simulation model that compared the ability of strong and weak culture firms to facilitate "exploitation" and "exploration" forms of learning. Tests of this model showed that strong culture organizations learned less from their environments and engaged in less exploration activity. March (1991) attributed this diminished capacity for exploration learning to the rapid socialization rates and resistance to alternative perspectives that characterized strong culture firms.

Finally, some scholars have asserted that organizations with strong cultures may limit their potential for innovation through selection processes. The Schneider (1987) Attraction Selection Attrition (ASA) model suggests that job candidates are more likely to apply to and join firms that they believe hold similar values to their own. If a firm has an easily identifiable culture, which is to say a strong culture, then an efficient self-selection process will probably ensue, assuming that applicants possess some self-insight. Efficient self-selection among potential entrants will increase the level of employee homogeneity in strong culture firms that may subsequently limit their potential for creativity, and in turn, innovation (e.g., Hoffman, 1959). The claim that homogeneity engendered by the selection process limits creativity is dubious, however, because the selection process can also deliberately favor innovation. Firms that value creativity as part of their organizational culture will likely attract highly creative applicants, which, in turn, should enhance their innovative potential. But, rather than debate whether homogeneity caused by efficient selection processes is problematic, it would be more useful to examine whether cultural strength truly hinders organizational innovation. A reasonable first step in this direction would be to clarify our understanding of culture strength and content, two concepts that are closely linked but often misconstrued in innovation research.

DISTINGUISHING BETWEEN CULTURE STRENGTH AND CULTURE CONTENT, OR CONFORMITY AND UNIFORMITY: A KEY TO THE ORGANIZATIONAL CULTURE–INNOVATION RELATIONSHIP

Are culture and innovation opposing forces in organizations? Answering this question depends, in part, on how culture strength is conceptualized. A strong culture can be understood as one in which cohesion exists about values and behavioral norms, and such norms are consistently and rigorously enforced by all members (e.g., O'Reilly and Chatman, 1996). Here, norms are viewed as legitimate, socially shared standards against which the appropriateness of behavior can be evaluated (Birenbaum and Sagarin, 1976). Cultural norms influence how members perceive and interact with one another, approach decisions, and solve problems. Although the mere existence of norms suggests that there is some *conformity* among organizational or group members, it does not necessarily suggest that there is also *uniformity* among these members. Conformity entails bringing different peoples' interests into agreement, correspondence, or harmony. Uniformity, on the other hand, implies that a group of people is not simply in harmony, but identical to one another in terms of interests, attitudes, and behaviors. This distinction may seem unnecessarily detailed, but it is more than just a semantic clarification.

Norm strength in a group or organization reflects the extent to which members conform to those norms, but not necessarily the extent to which members behave uniformly. Two examples may help illustrate this point. First, a group norm that induces conformity but not uniformity is the understanding that "we agree to disagree." Such a norm can be found in many organizations (e.g., Sutton and Hargadon, 1996; Wetlaufer, 2000) and can be quite effective in achieving efficiency gains in decision making. For example, some organizations use the nominal group technique, in which decision alternatives are ranked by the number of votes from group members, and all members agree to endorse whichever decision alternative receives the most votes (e.g., Henrich and Greene, 1991). Second, cultural values can be characterized by strong norms that foster conformity, but not uniformity. In particular, individualistic cultures tend to value the unique contributions made by each member and the pursuit of individual interests above group interests (Triandis, 1995). Yet, individualistic norms may be strongly enforced, just as collectivistic norms are, if norm strength is defined in terms of agreement and not content. In a recent study of group norms, Chatman and Flynn (2000) found that individualistic and collectivistic groups did not differ significantly in terms of norm strength, which was defined as the extent to which norms were "widely shared" and "strongly held" and measured at three separate times during each group's lifespan. Thus, norm strength and content are independent forces.

There is also confusion about the influence of culture content, which refers to the exact behaviors or attitudes that are valued in a particular culture, on innovation. Some scholars believe that the very presence of shared norms in organizations constrains innovation, regardless of their content (e.g., Nemeth and Staw, 1989). But, the content of norms and the behaviors they support vary widely in organizations. For example, some organizations may have strong norms emphasizing dress (e.g., Pratt and Rafaeli, 1997) whereas other norms may emphasize where people should sit in meetings (e.g., Puffer, 1999) or when they should ar-

rive (e.g., Sutton and Hargadon, 1996). Likewise, some norms emphasize similar thinking among team members, whereas other norms may emphasize divergent thinking (e.g., Sutton and Hargadon, 1996). Members of innovative firms may share the expectation that they will become technical leaders in their industries—which helps to legitimize divergent activity and increase the firm's tolerance for failure (Kanter, 1988).

Perhaps one reason that the concepts of culture content and strength have been blurred is that organizations known to have strong cultures have been compared to controlling and manipulative cults (O'Reilly and Chatman, 1996). In cults, of course, there is no tolerance for non-conformity, only strict adherence to a single set of attitudes, behaviors, and beliefs—that are, unfortunately, frequently dysfunctional and deviant (e.g., Festinger et al., 1964; Galanter, 1989). Japanese firms have often been likened to cults because their employees tend to demonstrate an unusually high level of commitment, bordering on blind allegiance (Lincoln and Kalleberg, 1990). Strong cultures in Japanese firms are established and maintained through the use of company songs, rigorous training programs, exercise sessions, mottoes, uniforms, and sports competitions (Clark, 1979). Similar approaches have been adopted and highly publicized in some U.S. firms, such as Mary Kay Cosmetics (Biggart, 1989), Southwest Airlines (Freiberg et al., 1998), and McDonalds (Kroc, 1977). Each of these organizations has a strong culture, yet the organizational values they emphasize, including unanimity and uniformity, differ from those emphasized by other organizations with equally strong cultures.

Although not as sensationalistic, many firms challenge the link between conformity and uniformity, or culture strength and content. At 3M, for example, organizational norms encourage, reward, and recognize innovative employees and treat their inevitable mistakes as learning experiences, instead of reason for punishment (Nicholson, 1998). Employees at Hewlett-Packard (HP) strongly agree about the norms of the firm, but the norms emphasize individual freedom and autonomy to accomplish work goals (Cole, 1999). To demonstrate its commitment to individual freedom, HP often provides informal rewards, such as the legendary "Medal of Defiance," to employees for instances of useful dissent. Thus, HP's organizational culture is considered strong because of the high level of agreement among employees about "how things are done around here," not because employees work in a synchronous, lock-step pattern of uniformity (Packard, 1995). The manner in which United Hospitals Inc. (UHI), a multi-health-care corporation in the Philadelphia area, developed its corporate culture demonstrates the potential balance between strong culture and differences of opinion. In employee orientations at UHI, time is devoted to discussing "constructive dissent"— the act of making a positive recommendation for change that could result in a negative reaction by a manager (Markowich and Farber, 1989).

Firms with strong cultures can still demonstrate a risk-taking attitude and a high tolerance for conflict. At Coca-Cola, evidence of risk-taking norms can be found in employee meetings, internal publications, and human resource practices (Allen, 1994). The corporate giant even celebrated the 10th anniversary of the launch of New Coke, a notorious failure. According to one executive, "We celebrated the failure because it led to fundamental learning and showed that its okay to fail" (Dutton, 1996, p. 45). At Honda, employees have found a way to harness the benefits of contention and dissent (Pascale, 1993). Takeo Fujisawa, one of Honda's co-founders, observed that when his Japanese employees engaged in a heated discussion, it created a particular "wai-ga-ya-wai-ga-ya" sound. Fujisawa liked the sound and helped institutionalize "Waigaya" discussion sessions, in which rank is irrelevant and dissent is welcomed. American employees at Honda's Marysville, Ohio, plant have become accustomed to the Waigaya concept. When an employee or manager is holding back from expressing an opinion during a meeting, he can suggest having a Waigaya session.

At Disney, a company that develops at least two new products a week, from rides at their theme parks, to TV shows and movies, to CD-ROMs and Little Mermaid makeup kits, Michael Eisner encourages a culture based on supportive conflict (Wetlaufer, 2000, p. 116). This includes the use of a "gong show" in which people pitching new animation film ideas are subjected to the possibility of being "gonged" if their ideas are not considered viable. In addition, the animation department holds marathon development meetings designed to force creative ideas out and then edit them without status differences interfering.

In summary, a strong culture can be a powerful

form of social control because it provides agreed-upon standards that members may use to assess the appropriateness of their own and others' actions or beliefs. But, it would be incorrect to assume that strong, cohesive organizational cultures induce identical or uniform patterns of thought and behavior among members. As the preceding examples suggest, cohesive organizational cultures can emphasize divergent thinking because *cohesion relates to the strength of group norms rather than their content.* In addition to the anecdotal examples provided above, we examine psychological research on cohesion and the implications for innovation to gain further insight into the relationship between culture and innovation.

A CLOSER LOOK AT THE EFFECTS OF GROUP COHESION ON INNOVATION

Cohesion and Creativity

Group cohesion has been defined as "the degree to which members of the group are attracted to each other" (Shaw, 1981, p. 213), "the resultant of all forces acting on all members to remain in the group" (Cartwright, 1968, p. 74), and "the total field of forces that act on members to remain in the group" (Festinger et al., 1950, p. 164). Thus, cohesion specifically focuses on members' interest in maintaining membership, or the attractiveness of a group to its members (Goodman et al., 1987). This appeal of maintaining group membership may result in a higher level of normative agreement among members.

Research on groups has identified several negative consequences stemming from group cohesion that may hinder creativity in organizations. Janis (1982) found that groupthink, which is a pattern of faulty decision making that occurs when like-minded people reinforce one another's tendencies to interpret events and information in similar ways, might be a consequence of group cohesion and homogeneity. Members of homogeneous groups, which tend to be highly cohesive, often fail to provide sufficient criticism of other members' ideas and possible alternatives (e.g., Hogg and Hains, 1998). Further, they tend to share only common information with one another (e.g., Gruenfeld et al., 1996) and resist differentiating themselves in order to maintain their relationship with others in the group.

Adopting certain roles, such as a "devil's advocate," can reduce the likelihood of groupthink occurring, even in highly cohesive groups (Janis, 1982). A devil's advocate can be anyone in the group who is willing to argue against a cause or position in order to determine its validity. Research has found that groups using a devil's advocate approach produce higher quality decisions than do groups using a consensual approach (e.g., Schweiger et al., 1986). Having a devil's advocate does not suggest the presence of weak norms, but it may reflect conformity about the value of voicing dissent to improve the group's outcomes. The behavior produced emphasizes a lack of cohesion, in the form of disagreement about task content, as a tactic for enhancing the group product. Realistically then, groupthink only poses a significant threat to performance within groups that do not anticipate its effects and respond appropriately by designing approaches to increase task conflict.

The "risky shift" phenomenon, in which groups tend to make riskier decisions than do individuals, is another negative consequence of group cohesion (e.g., Moscovici and Lecuyer, 1972). Individuals often experience deindividuation in groups (Diener, 1980), and thus are less threatened by and feel less accountable for the negative outcomes of group decisions. Researchers have assumed that risky shifts negatively influence group decision making (Stoner, 1968). Interestingly, the willingness to take risks is considered a positive determinant of creativity (Amabile, 1988) and, in turn, innovation. As individuals, organizational members may be more risk averse due to the personal costs of taking risks and benefits of being critical of risky ideas (e.g., Amabile, 1983). But, in groups, otherwise risk averse individuals may be more willing to consider potentially worthwhile risks. Thus, the risky shift phenomenon may be useful, as long as rationality is not sacrificed in terms of the degree or type of risk adopted. Further research is needed to test the extent to which the risky shift effect inhibits or enhances innovation in groups and organizations.

Escalation of commitment, or the tendency to invest additional time, money, or effort into what are essentially bad decisions or losing courses of action (Staw, 1976), may also influence the link between culture and innovation. Researchers have speculated that escalation of commitment causes decision making groups to retain unsuccessful or outdated ideas rather than adopt new, innovative ideas (e.g., King and An-

derson, 1990). Group cohesion may contribute to members' tendencies to escalate their commitment to outdated ideas or processes because, given their interest in maintaining membership in the group, they may be reluctant to raise opposing views and, instead, support continuing down a flawed path (e.g., Gruenfeld et al., 1996; Janis, 1982). As mentioned earlier, developing a bifurcated decision procedure, providing some support for failure, and having an individual who is not invested in the initial decision offer constructive criticism may diminish the potential for irrational group decision making (e.g., Bazerman et al., 1984; Staw and Ross, 1987). Thus, some of the potentially harmful effects of cohesion can be anticipated and addressed through group or organizational design.

Critics who question the potential benefit of a strong culture on innovation argue that cohesion limits organizational members' willingness to deviate from norms (e.g., Nemeth and Staw, 1989). For example, the classic study of group influence by Asch (1955) has been cited as a clear example of how conformity in the face of pressure from fellow group members can result in uniformity of opinion. In the original Asch experiments, subjects were asked to evaluate whether two lines differed in length, usually after hearing a number of incorrect evaluations offered by confederates. Subjects tended to agree with the confederates' preceding evaluations, even when it was obvious they were wrong.

There are two problems with using the Asch experiments as evidence of the negative effects of social cohesion on innovation. First, subjects in the Asch studies generally had no prior relationship with one another, and thus it is likely that they had no sense of group cohesion. If they were a cohesive group, the study's results might have been different. Although it may sound counterintuitive, group cohesion might actually *increase* group members' willingness to deviate from some norms because cohesion provides members with a comfortable level of psychological safety that allows them to engage in divergent thinking and risk-taking behavior (Nystrom, 1979). As Nystrom (1979, p. 45) explained, when cohesiveness is high, a person recognizes "that he is not alone responsible for possible failures, which is reassuring." Such a high level of trust among members is invaluable because members must be willing to share information, particularly divergent information, in order to achieve optimal group performance (Nemeth, 1992). Second, because no explicit norms were established in these experimental settings *ex ante,* subjects utilized their knowledge about existing norms of social interaction, which emphasize adherence to the majority perspective. However, organizations are unique social settings; as such, common social norms do not always apply within them (Spataro, 2000). Indeed, it is plausible that organizations may develop specific norms that run counter to societal norms (e.g., Galanter, 1989). Therefore, researchers cannot assume that group cohesion inhibits innovation without studying norms as they exist in real organizational groups.

The assumption that norms promoting social cohesion will, in turn, discourage creativity is troublesome. In truth, there are many norms associated with cohesiveness that are necessary to promote creativity. For example, a norm mandating that organizational members share information will not only increase interaction and cohesion, but also expose members to diverse perspectives (e.g., Nemeth, 1992). And, past research suggests that a norm to entertain any brainstorming idea, no matter how wild and outrageous, is necessary in fostering creativity and is more likely to be found in highly cohesive groups within organizations (e.g., Sutton and Hargadon, 1996).

Nemeth (1997) argued that with each incidence of dissent, which is a position or idea that differs from the dominant one, creativity would increase linearly. "One must feel free to 'deviate' from expectations, to question shared ways of viewing things, in order to evidence creativity" (Nemeth, 1997, p. 60). Of course, this may be true only if norms allow for such disagreements to emerge in a productive manner. We concur that dissenting opinion can be useful in generating creative ideas, but dissenting opinions are often discounted for a variety of reasons that are unrelated to the quality of the opinion. In particular, ideas emanating from dissent for the sake of dissent or due to political conflict are not likely to be acknowledged. Rather, norms that foster greater tolerance of intellectual debate are more likely to engender creative ideas (e.g., Sutton and Hargadon, 1996).

We suggest that certain strong norms can facilitate the generation and expression of creative ideas. Strong norms that reward information sharing, particularly unique pieces of information, and emphasize greater tolerance for intellectual debate should reduce inhibitions and encourage divergent thinking (e.g., Stasser and Stewart, 1992). Further, norms that require organizational members to build upon others' ideas rather than limit their attention to their own ideas are vital to creativity (Sutton and Hargadon, 1996). Without a combination of diverse perspectives, groups charged with generating creative ideas may adopt the best individual idea rather than utilize their combined potential (Chatman et al., 1998). Taken together, this suggests the following proposition:

Proposition 1. Members of organizations that strongly agree and care about norms that encourage the expression of creative ideas (e.g., brainstorming, uncensored idea generation) will generate more creative ideas than those who agree less and/or care less about such norms.

Cohesion and Implementation

Our discussion thus far has focused on the creative component of innovation. To understand how organizational culture influences innovation, however, it is important to also consider how creative ideas are implemented, that is, whether a new idea becomes a reality (Caldwell and O'Reilly, 1995). Although many claim that innovation is hampered by social cohesion, few would disagree with the notion that cohesion is necessary to implement creative ideas. Keller (1986) found that cohesion among members of R&D teams, whose primary role is to identify and develop new products, predicted their performance. Further, cohesiveness and participation predicted the quality and number of innovations produced (Anderson and West, 1998). And, innovative organizations were characterized by teamwork, effective (e.g., frequent, clear) communication, and interdepartmental cooperation, factors akin to social cohesion (Pillinger and West, 1995).

Researchers have outlined at least three advantages of social cohesion and informal control yielded by strong cultures as opposed to the formal control provided by hierarchical structures (Ebers, 1995; Kunda, 1992; O'Reilly and Chatman, 1996): (1) clearer direction for employees under ambiguous circumstances; (2) decreased need for monitoring and surveillance due to increased internalization of organizational objectives; and (3) increased satisfaction and decreased reactance despite the reduced individual freedom imposed by social control. The first of these advantages, providing direction when employees are faced with uncertainty, may be particularly important to implement innovations. The implementation of a creative idea is, by definition, a novel experience, and therefore, the confidence to take action in the face of ambiguity is essential to success. Kanter (1988) described the implementation of an innovation as an ambiguous process requiring extraordinary commitment, conviction, and enthusiasm by "champions," who attempt to manage the disruptive pattern of the innovation process and guide members' efforts in the desired direction. But, the need for champions can be reduced if organizations have developed cohesive norms supporting the innovation process. Just as unproven firms benefit from associations with others (e.g., Podolny, 1993), developing a coalition of supporters for an unproven innovative idea may provide a signaling function that facilitates its implementation. In other words, even if the quality of the idea itself is not readily apparent, the strength of group consensus may be compelling to skeptics.

Although cohesion among organizational members is likely to be associated with higher levels of agreement, it is possible that such agreement is variegated, applying to some processes but not others. For example, members of a cohesive organization may agree about their general approach to performing tasks, but lack agreement about specific methods to adopt in specific situations. Cohesive organizations may be innovative if they possess a high level of *process agreement* (e.g., Jehn, 1995) in order to complete tasks successfully and efficiently, but not *intellectual agreement,* which refers to the similarity of ideas and opinions they contribute that may limit their potential for creative thinking. The willingness to yield to others during the implementation stage may be one outcome of social cohesion. Past research found that when members' mental images of how a task should be approached and completed concurred, task accomplishment proceeded with relatively little conflict and uncertainty (Bettenhausen and Murnighan, 1991, p. 21). Thus, social cohesion, here conceptualized in terms of shared norms, can facilitate implementation for the very reason that it, allegedly, inhibits creativity.

We suggest that certain strong norms can facilitate the implementation of creative ideas. In particular, emphasizing task-oriented norms that focus on members' cooperation may determine the success of the implementation process (Abbey and Dickson, 1983). Norms that encourage adherence to an organizationally universal plan of action and preset deadlines should be more efficient for organizations striving to use innovation as a competitive advantage. By emphasizing a uniform approach to the work process during the implementation stage, organizations will be better equipped to deliver creative ideas quickly, as we suggest in the following proposition:

> **Proposition 2.** Members of organizations that both agree and care more about the value of task-oriented norms (e.g., being decisive, meeting deadlines) will be more likely to implement creative ideas successfully than will members of organizations that agree and/or care less about task-oriented norms.

To summarize, past theory and research on innovation suggests an interesting paradox: strong cultural norms may limit individual creativity, yet organizations require cohesion to implement creative ideas. How can organizations reconcile this inherent conflict? We propose that this paradoxical relationship between cohesion and innovation can be resolved by recognizing that normative agreement does not necessarily stifle creativity. Rather, it is the content (what is regulated) of group norms that determine innovation success. In the next section, we focus on a specific dimension of cultural norms, individualism—collectivism, and explain how each end of the continuum may be linked to different stages of the innovation process.

THE ROLE OF INDIVIDUALISTIC AND COLLECTIVISTIC NORMS IN THE INNOVATION PROCESS

In our discussion of the relationship between organizational culture and innovation, we have proposed two critical ideas about the nature of norms. First, though norms are a powerful means of social control, they do not necessarily restrict and constrain members' abilities to be creative, and indeed, we have suggested that agreement on certain norms may lead to more, rather than less, innovation. Second, norms are often misconstrued as rigid rules of behavior that apply inflexibly in all social situations. However, as socially constructed standards, norms, and behavior emanating from norms, can be adjusted according to the mandate of their adherents. This second point is most critical in reconciling the culture—innovation paradox. Because norms are socially shared standards, organizational members should be able to emphasize different norms depending on whether the immediate objective is to generate creative ideas or implement them.

Two implicit assumptions found in the literature on norms may weaken this argument. One assumption is that every group, or organization, promotes a single set of norms, which is applicable in all situations. But, realistically, different norms may emerge or diminish at different times during the duration of a project (e.g., Chatman and Flynn, 2000; Gersick, 1988; Jehn and Mannix, 1998). For example, norms supporting team meeting attendance or the full participation of all team members may not exist early on in a project's lifespan because the pressure to complete the task is minimal. However, as the task deadline approaches, norms for meeting attendance and full participation by members may change, such that members are expected to attend and participate in all team meetings and decisions. Similarly, different norms may exist during the creativity stage of innovation than during the implementation stage. For example, norms may encourage members to offer novel, even outrageous, alternatives during the creativity stage, but disapprove of these suggestions during the implementation stage (e.g., Caldwell and O'Reilly, 1995).

Another problematic assumption is that cultural norms simply emerge—they cannot be intentionally constructed. Indeed, norms can be constructed, although perhaps more easily among groups of neophytes than members who share tenure and familiarity (Levine and Moreland, 1990). In a laboratory study, Chatman and her colleagues (Chatman and Barsade, 1995; Chatman et al., 1998) manipulated whether teams held collectivistic or individualistic norms simply by changing a few words and hypothetical compensation schemes in the materials presented to subjects the night before an experiment. Participants' behaviors were significantly affected by these seemingly minor differences. At IDEO, Sutton and Hargadon (1996) reported that brainstorming norms were simply posted on the wall to indoctrinate newcomers and remind existing members about how they should behave in all brainstorming sessions.

Given that norms can be established easily and may change according to the mandate of their adherents, researchers should focus on identifying which norms may be more appropriate for each stage of the innovation process. Some norms would obviously foster creativity (e.g., rewarding creative thinking, willingness to take risks), but there are also more subtle and pervasive norms that may influence members' willingness to both express and implement creative ideas. In particular, the concept of individualism–collectivism, which refers to the conceptualization of the self as either independent or interdependent in relation to others, can be used to describe how members of organizations interact with one another (e.g., Chatman et al., 1998; Earley, 1989, 1993). We propose that the overarching cultural dimension of individualism–collectivism may infuse the norms found in organizations, which, in turn, set the context for innovation.

Individualism and Collectivism

Individualism can be defined as a social pattern that consists of loosely linked individuals who view themselves as independent of collectives, are primarily motivated by their own preferences, needs, rights, and the contracts they have established with others, give priority to their personal goals over the goals of others, and emphasize rational analyses of the advantages and disadvantages of associating with others (Triandis, 1995). The concept of individualism could be misconstrued as weak culture, but, in our view, individualism is a particular dimension of culture in which the self is defined as independent and autonomous from collectives. It represents the content of a culture and not its strength. Organizations seeking innovation may find it desirable to emphasize individualistic norms because they encourage members to pursue individual aspirations and allow members to confront and challenge one another without fear of reprisal (Triandis, 1995).

This is not to suggest that the complementary concept of collectivism is unsuitable for organizations seeking innovation. Collectivism can be referred to as a social pattern consisting of closely linked individuals who see themselves as parts of a collective (e.g., family, coworkers, tribe, nation), are primarily motivated by the norms of, and duties imposed by, the collective, are willing to give priority to the goals of the collective over their own personal goals, and emphasize their connectedness to members of the collective (Triandis,

1995). A collectivistic orientation may help foster innovation in organizations by focusing members' attention on superordinate goals. For example, organizations increasingly use cross-functional teams, in part, to enhance the potential for product and process innovation (Shapiro, 1992). These functionally diverse teams can be difficult to manage because members' interests and points of view vary. A collectivistic orientation, emphasizing innovation as a collective goal over varying individual goals, increases the likelihood that such diverse teams will produce innovative outcomes (Chatman et al., 1998).

Past discussions of organizational or group creativity have often overlooked the benefits of keeping members' attention focused on a common goal. Rather, researchers have concentrated on the fundamental importance of dissent in enhancing creativity (e.g., Nemeth, 1997). But, without a shared schema that orients members toward a common goal, dissent could eventually lead to unproductive chaos. Dissent, or divergent thinking, can still be emphasized in collectivistic organizational cultures, so long as it is viewed as being useful in achieving the superordinate goal of innovation. Even in strong, collectivistic cultures, dissenting ideas will not necessarily be viewed as defiant. Instead, members will tend to accept ideas that are consistent with their collective values and reject ideas that challenge those values. If the collective value is dissent for the sake of creativity, then dissent will be welcomed and encouraged.

Some critics may argue that an individualistic emphasis is more appropriate when the goal is innovation because it will encourage the individual motivation and autonomy necessary to be creative. However, an organization with an individualistic orientation may be less likely to capitalize on its potential synergy and members may be less willing to both discount their own ideas and endorse their peers' superior ideas. Conversely, members of organizations emphasizing collectivistic norms and cooperation (Wagner, 1995) will be more likely to support an idea selected by the majority of members and agree upon an approach to its implementation (Erez, 1992). Thus, we propose that emphasizing collectivism will be more likely to result in the generation and implementation of innovative ideas than will emphasizing individualism. However, we add one critical caveat—that, when emphasizing collectivism, the goal would need to shift from divergent thinking during the creativity stage to consensus thinking during the implementation stage. This suggests the following propositions:

Proposition 3. Organizations emphasizing collectivistic norms and divergent thinking will perform better during the creativity stage (e.g., generating more ideas) of innovation than will organizations emphasizing only one or the other, or neither, or both at a low level.

Proposition 4. Organizations emphasizing collectivistic norms and non-divergent thinking will perform better during the implementation stage (e.g., speed of getting the product or service out the door) of innovation than will organizations emphasizing only one or the other, or neither, or both at a low level.

Vertical and Horizontal Varieties of Individualism–Collectivism

Researchers have suggested that individualism and collectivism exist in horizontal and vertical forms (e.g. Triandis, 1996). In some cultures, hierarchy is most important, and in-group authorities regulate the behavior of in-group members (Vertical). In other cultures, social behavior is more egalitarian; that is, each member is treated as an equal (Horizontal). The vertical and horizontal varieties of individualism and collectivism may also be germane to the process of innovation. We have already suggested that emphasizing collectivism will contribute to organizational innovation so long as norms emphasize divergent thinking during the creativity stage and non-divergent thinking during the implementation stage. But, the extent to which a collectivistic group or organization is able to engender divergent thinking during the creativity stage may depend on the strength of its egalitarian emphasis, that is, the extent to which the horizontal form of collectivism exists. If members believe they are among peers, they will be less likely to censor their opinions than if they were in the presence of members with hierarchical authority over them. For example, an Israeli kibbutz is considered a highly collectivistic group, but because of their egalitarian emphasis, members welcome and even encourage intellectual arguments. Conversely, a collectivistic group or organization may be better able to promote non-divergent thinking during the implementation stage if norms support an authoritarian (vertical) social structure, such that lower status members deferred to higher ranking leaders. This suggests the following proposition:

> **Proposition 5.** Collectivistic organizations that emphasize the horizontal form of collectivism during the creativity stage and the vertical form during the implementation stage will produce more and higher quality innovations.

Radical and Routine Innovation as an Organizational Goal

Organizational goals must also be considered when constructing norms to foster innovation. Organizations may have different objectives that depend on their unique combination of strategy, resources, and existing market conditions (Nord and Tucker, 1987). For example, different types of behavior are needed to successfully complete radical, compared to routine, innovations (Zaltman et al., 1973). Further, past research has found that a country's national culture influences the organizational cultures of home country firms (e.g., Hofstede, 1991; Hofstede et al., 1990). Debate exists about whether American companies, which tend to be more individualistic, are better suited to develop radical innovations and whether Japanese firms, which tend to be more collectivistic, are better suited to develop routine innovations (e.g., Botkin, 1986). Because collectivistic norms demand adherence to a uniform approach to the work process, such norms yield greater efficiency, an essential component of routine innovation (Chatman and Flynn, 2000). Conversely, an individualistic orientation may be more appropriate if the goal is radical innovation because these firms are more likely to engage in "exploration learning," which is required in radical innovation (March, 1991).

These arguments imply that collectivistic organizations may be better suited to develop routine innovations and individualistic organizations may be better suited to develop radical innovations. However, we propose that a collectivistic orientation is better suited to generate both radical and routine forms of innovation in organizations. Although organizations in collectivistic countries may choose to develop routine innovations as a competitive strategy, it is not necessarily the case that the same organizations would be incapable of developing radical innovations if that were their explicit goal. Granted, adherence to a common goal will facilitate the implementation process, which is of paramount importance in routine innovation. But, collectivism also promotes the smooth flow of communication, which increases the sharing of knowledge, ideas, and information that enhances radical innovation (Erez, 1992). Therefore, whether the desired product is radical or routine, if members focus on innovation *as an organizational goal,* then synergy will be enhanced without inhibiting creativity, suggesting the following proposition:

> **Proposition 6.** Organizations with a collectivistic orientation will be more likely to develop successful radical and routine innovations than will organizations with an individualistic orientation.

Heterogeneity and Individualism–Collectivism

Nystrom (1979) attempted to resolve the culture–innovation paradox by suggesting that member composition be altered according to the current stage of the innovation process. Early on, loosely joined heterogeneous groups should be constructed to facilitate the creative process, but as the creative idea becomes more clearly formulated, groups should be more cohesive and homogenous in order to facilitate implementation. Although intuitively appealing, the problem with this suggestion is the coordination difficulties it presents. It is doubtful that such a structural transition could be achieved in practice because any given group, or organization, may be involved in the introduction of several innovations at the same time, all at different stages in the process (King and Anderson, 1990). And, specific technical suggestions may be too great for more than one work team to grasp. Finally, the "implementation team" may lose the benefits of members' commitment generated by having had input into the task early on (Kanter, 1988).

The role of heterogeneity in enhancing innovation is complex. Cognitive and experiential diversity may add to the perspectives generated within an organization and facilitate clarifying, organizing, and combining novel approaches to accomplishing work goals (Jehn et al., 1999; Thomas and Ely, 1996). However, heterogeneous work groups tend to be less socially integrated and experience more communication problems, more conflict, and higher turnover rates than do homogeneous groups (Jackson et al., 1991; O'Reilly et al., 1989; Zenger and Lawrence, 1989). Further, employees who are more different from their coworkers report feeling more uncomfortable and less attached to their employing organization (Tsui et al., 1992). Thus, highly diverse organizations may have a more difficult time implementing creative ideas.

Decreasing the salience of members' individual differences and increasing the extent to which their organizational identity is salient can increase members' commitment and contributions to work goals (e.g., Chatman et al., 1998). With a collectivistic orientation that emphasizes group membership over other salient categories (such as demography or functional background), groups can retain the benefits of increased heterogeneity in, for example, past experience, while still maintaining sufficient cohesion necessary for effective implementation (Chatman and Flynn, 2000). This suggests the following proposition:

> **Proposition 7.** Organizations employing members who are more heterogeneous will produce significantly more and higher quality innovations when they emphasize collectivistic versus individualistic norms, while organizations employing members who are more homogeneous will produce similarly moderate innovation regardless of whether their culture emphasizes individualistic or collectivistic norms.

Patterns of Interpersonal Conflict and Individualism–Collectivism

Research that demonstrates the advantages of a collectivistic orientation on work team behavior (e.g., Wagner, 1995) suggests that collectivistic groups suffer from conflict less than do individualistic groups (e.g., Chatman et al., 1998). But, all groups and organizations, even those that are collectivistic, develop clear patterns of interpersonal conflict. The usefulness of such conflict, particularly how it helps or hinders innovation, may depend on its form and timing. For example, Jehn and Mannix (1998) showed that groups performed more effectively when task conflict was moderately high during the middle of the project, and process and relationship conflict were relatively constant at moderate and low levels, respectively, throughout the entire project. Certain types of conflict may be more appropriate for specific stages of innovation. Teams with higher levels of task conflict will produce

more creative products, but, as argued previously, task conflict will be less desirable during the implementation stage. Relationship and process conflict, which are detrimental to group performance (e.g., Jehn, 1997), may be less desirable in both the creativity and implementation stages of innovation.

We argue that more beneficial patterns of conflict will emerge when collectivistic norms are emphasized. In an organization characterized by a collectivistic culture, relationship conflict would likely be minimized throughout the innovation process because collectivism promotes harmonious relationships among team members whereas an individualistic culture does not (Triandis, 1995). Process conflict should also be minimized given that members of collectivistic cultures adopt a uniform approach to task accomplishment (Earley, 1994). And, if collectivistic organizations succeed in promoting divergent thinking during the creativity stage and non-divergent thinking during the implementation stage, then task conflict will occur when it can contribute most, during the creativity stage.

> **Proposition 8.** Organizations emphasizing collectivistic norms that also emphasize divergent thinking during the creativity stage and non-divergent thinking during the implementation stage will experience more beneficial conflict (task conflict) during the creativity stage, and less detrimental conflict (process and relational) throughout the project's duration.

To better understand the relationship between organizational culture and innovation, we focused on distinguishing between culture content and culture strength, two concepts that are fundamental to the culture–innovation relationship. Our primary conclusion from this discussion is that organizational culture will be more likely to contribute to the innovation process when members strongly agree and care about norms that emphasize divergent thinking when creativity is desired and non-divergent thinking when implementation is the goal. A number of additional complexities influence this relationship, however, and should be considered in future research. In particular, organizations are made up of an array of norms (e.g., Chatman, 1991; O'Reilly et al., 1991). Thus, the entire profile of norms that characterizes an organization's culture must be considered, rather than simply examining the extent to which, for example, individualism or collectivism is emphasized. Second, researchers need to examine how formal incentives may reward innovation and behaviors leading to innovation, although it is not completely clear whether such incentives will enhance, by demonstrating the organization's commitment to innovation, or diminish member's intrinsic motivation to be creative (Amabile, 1996). Finally, various exogenous conditions, such as the pace and accessibility of external technological developments and the availability of capable employees in the labor pool, will affect the relationship between organizational culture and innovation.

CONCLUSION

We have argued that the relationship between culture and innovation is more complex than described in past research, which has proposed that normative agreement hinders innovation, particularly its creative component (e.g., Nemeth and Staw, 1989). Rather, the impact of culture strength on innovation depends on the nature of agreement more than its mere existence. If members collectively exhibit a higher level of agreement about the manner in which creative ideas should be generated, such as developing a brainstorming process, rather than what creative ideas should look like, greater creativity may emerge (e.g., Sutton and Hargadon, 1996). Further, research suggests that cohesion, which is derived from normative agreement, should facilitate the implementation process (e.g., Anderson and West, 1998; Keller, 1986). Although some argue that organizations cannot maintain these two seemingly conflicting sets of norms, we suggest that organizational norms emerge from the situational demands at hand, not just from members' attributes (e.g., West and Anderson, 1996). Thus, when the nature of an organization's task changes, norms can change accordingly.

The extant innovation literature lacks an agreed upon theoretical model that explains the conditions under which innovation is most likely to occur. To date, most attempts to model the characteristics contributing to innovation have focused on one component of innovation or another, either creativity or implementation, rather than considering the complete innovation process. Future research might reconcile this problem by focusing on the role that organizational culture plays in the innovation process. While some research shows that strong norms, or higher levels of cohesiveness, may lead to less creativity, simple generalizations from these findings may be incorrect. Instead, agreement and intensity about certain configurations of norms may enhance, rather than hinder, both the creativity and implementation components of the innovation process. Specifically, promoting horizontal (egalitarian) collectivism during the creativity stage will encourage the divergent thinking necessary to engender creativity and promoting vertical (authoritarian) collectivism during the implementation stage will encourage the non-divergent thinking necessary to facilitate implementation. By focusing on the collective goal of innovation throughout the entire process, organizations may achieve this duality and capitalize on their creative potential, which is derived from member heterogeneity and interpersonal conflict.

Our objective in this chapter has been to increase the salience of the distinction between conformity and uniformity in order to clarify the relationship between organizational culture and innovation. We argued that strong organizational cultures increase conformity among members through various selection and socialization practices that have been described by organizational culture researchers (e.g., O'Reilly and Chatman, 1996). These practices increase group cohesion, and ultimately, members' willingness to conform to organizational norms. But, conformity of this sort is not necessarily a detriment to innovation because, we argue, it can be distinguished from the content of the cultural norms emphasized. That is, cultures can emphasize conformity, in the form of adherence to shared norms, without dictating that members' behavior be identical to one another, or uniform. Though it might be more difficult to establish creativity enhancing norms in cohesive groups, it is still unclear why, and to what extent, this is true. Given the potential advantages of cohesion in facilitating the implementation of innovation that we have outlined here, future research should explore ways in which cohesion *could* also engender creativity.

We, therefore, propose that the culture–innovation paradox is not a paradox at all. Instead, the paradox misnomer stems from a conceptual misunderstanding about culture strength and content, two concepts that are clearly unique, but are often blurred in the innovation literature. Organizations can strike a balance between creativity and social control by developing cultural norms that foster the divergence and uniqueness necessary for the creative process to occur and still maintain the cohesion among members necessary to develop and implement creative ideas. Adherence to such norms will likely reduce the political and ego-based conflict that might exist among members who fail to trust and cooperate with one another and will be less likely to result in uniform attitudes, ideas, and behavior. Members may be highly committed to and intensely value non-conformity such that they encourage the contribution of divergent ideas and challenges to existing routines. Thus, the presence of strong organizational norms, depending on their orientation, may promote the attitudes and behaviors that are critical to organizational innovation.

REFERENCES

Abbey, A. and Dickson, J. W. (1983) R&D work climate and innovation in semiconductors. *Academy of Management Journal,* 26(2): 362–368.

Agrell, A. and Gustafson, R. (1994) The Team Climate Inventory (TCI) and group innovation: a psychometric test on a Swedish sample of work groups. *Journal of Occupational & Organizational Psychology,* 67(2): 143–151.

Allen, F. (1994) *Secret Formula: How Brilliant Marketing and Relentless Salesmanship Made Coca-Cola the Best-Known Product in the World.* New York: HarperBusiness.

Amabile, T. M. (1983) *The Social Psychology of Creativity.* New York: Springer-Verlag.

Amabile, T. M. (1988) A model of creativity and innovation in organizations. In B. Staw and L. Cummings (Eds), *Research in Organizational Behavior,* pp. 123–167. Greenwich, CT: JAI Press.

Amabile, T. M. (1996) *Creativity in Context: Update to "The Social Psychology of Creativity."* Boulder, CO: Westview Press.

Amabile, T. M. (1997) Motivating creativity in organizations: on doing what you love and loving what you do. *California Management Review,* 40(1): 39–58.

Amabile, T. M., Conti, R., Coon, H., Lazenby, J., et al. (1996) Assessing the work environment for creativity. *Academy of Management Journal,* 39(5): 1154–1184.

Ancona, D. and Caldwell, D. (1998) Rethinking team composition from the outside in. In M. Neale, B. Mannix, and D. Gruenfeld (Eds), *Research on Groups and Teams,* Vol. 1. Greenwich, CT: JAI Press.

Anderson, N. R. and West, M. A. (1998) Measuring climate for work group innovation: development and validation of the Team Climate Inventory. *Journal of Organizational Behavior,* 19(3): 235–258.

Asch, S. (1955) Opinions and social pressure. *Scientific American,* 193(5): 31–35.

Bazerman, M. H., Giuliano, T., and Appelman, A. (1984) Escalation of commitment in individual and group decision making. *Organizational Behavior & Human Decision Processes,* 33: 87–98.

Bettenhausen, K. L. and Murnighan, J. K. (1991) The development of an intragroup norm and the effects of interpersonal and structural challenges. *Administrative Science Quarterly,* 36: 20–35.

Biggart, N. W. (1989) *Charismatic Capitalism: Direct Selling Organizations in America.* Chicago, IL: University of Chicago Press.

Birenbaum, A. and Sagarin, E. (1976) *Norms and Human Behavior.* New York: Praeger.

Botkin, J. (1986) Transforming creativity into innovation: processes, prospects, and problems. In R. Kuhn (Ed), *Frontiers in Creative and Innovative Management,* pp. 25–40. Cambridge, MA: Ballinger.

Burns, T. and Stalker, G. M. (1961) *The Management of Innovation.* London: Tavistock.

Caldwell, D. F. and O'Reilly, C. A. (1995) Norms supporting innovation in groups: an exploratory analysis. Paper presented at the 54th Annual Meetings of the Academy of Management.

Cartwright, D. (1968). The nature of group cohesiveness. In D. Cartwright and A. Zander (Eds), *Group Dynamics,* 3rd Ed., pp. 91–109. New York: Harper & Row.

Chatman, J. A. (1991) Matching people and organizations: selection and socialization in public accounting firms. *Administrative Science Quarterly,* 36(3): 459–484.

Chatman, J. A. and Barsade, S. (1995) Personality, organizational culture, and cooperation: evidence from a business simulation. *Administrative Science Quarterly,* 40: 423–443.

Chatman, J. A. and Flynn, F. J. (2000) The influence of demographic composition on the emergence and consequences of cooperative norms in work teams. *Academy of Management Journal* (in press).

Chatman, J. A., Polzer, J., Barsade, S., and Neale, M. (1998) Being different yet feeling similar: the influence of demographic composition and organizational culture on work processes and outcomes. *Administrative Science Quarterly,* 41: 423.

Clark, R. (1979) *The Japanese Company.* New Haven, CT: Yale University Press.

Cole, R. E. (1999) *Managing Quality Fads: How American Business Learned to Play the Quality Game.* New York: Oxford University Press.

Cummings, L. L. (1965) Organizational climates for creativity. *Academy of Management Journal,* 3: 220–227.

Denison, D. R. and Mishra, A. K. (1995) Toward a theory of organizational culture and effectiveness. *Organization Science,* 6(2): 204–223.

Diener, E. (1980) Deindividuation: the absence of self-awareness and self-regulation in group members. In P. Paulus (Ed), *Psychology of Group Influence,* pp. 209–242. Hillsdale, NJ: Erlbaum.

Dutton, G. (1996) Enhancing creativity. *Management Review,* 85(11): 44–46.

Earley, C. P. (1989) Social loafing and collectivism: a comparison of the United States and the People's Republic of China. *Administrative Science Quarterly,* 34: 565–581.

Earley, C. P. (1994) Self or group? Cultural effects of training on self-efficacy and performance. *Administrative Science Quarterly,* 39(1): 89–117.

Ebers, M. (1995) The framing of organizational cultures. *Research in the Sociology of Organizations,* Vol. 13, pp. 129–170. Greenwich, CT: JAI Press.

Enz, C. (1988) The role of value congruity in intraorganizational power. *Administrative Science Quarterly,* 33: 284–304.

Erez, M. (1992) Interpersonal communication systems in organisations, and their relationship to cultural values, productivity, and innovation: the case of Japanese Corporations. *Applied Psychology: an International Review,* 41(1): 43–64.

Festinger, L., Schachter, S. and Back, K. (1950) *Social Pressures in Informal Groups.* New York: Harper & Row.

Festinger, L., Riecken, H. W., and Schachter, S. (1964) *When Prophecy Fails: a Social and Psychological Study of a Modern Group that Predicted the Destruction of the World.* New York: Harper Torchbooks.

Freiberg, K., Freiberg, J., and Peters, T. (1998) *Nuts!: Southwest Airlines' Crazy Recipe for Business and Personal Success.* New York: Bantam Doubleday.

Galanter, M. (1989) *Cults: Faith, Healing, and Coercion.* New York: Oxford University Press.

Gersick, C. J. G. (1988) Time and transition in work teams: toward a new model of group development. *Academy of Management Journal,* 41: 9–41.

Goodman, P., Ravlin, E., and Schminke, M. (1987) Understanding groups in organizations. In L. L. Cummings and B. Staw (Eds.), *Research in Organizational Behavior,* pp. 121–173. Greenwich, CT: JAI Press.

Gordon, G. G. and DiTomaso, N. (1992) Predicting corporate performance from corporate culture. *Journal of Management Studies,* 29(6): 783–798.

Gruenfeld, D. H., Mannix, E. A., Williams, K. Y., and

Neale, M. A. (1996) Group composition and decision making: how member familiarity and information distribution affect process and performance. *Organizational Behavior & Human Decision Processes,* 67(1): 1–15.

Hackman, J. R. (1987) The design of work teams. In J. Lorsch (Ed.), *Handbook of Organizational Behavior,* pp. 315–342. Englewood Cliffs, NJ: Prentice-Hall.

Henrich, T. R. and Greene, T. J. (1991) Using the nominal group technique to elicit roadblocks to an MRP II: implementation. *Computers & Industrial Engineering,* 21(1–4): 335–338.

Hoffman, L. R. (1959) Homogeneity of member personality and its effect on group problem-solving. *Journal of Abnormal & Social Psychology,* 58: 27–32.

Hofstede, G. (1991) *Cultures and Organizations.* New York: McGraw-Hill.

Hofstede, G., Neuijen, B., Ohayv, D., and Sanders, G. (1990) Measuring organizational cultures: a qualitative and quantitative study across twenty cases. *Administrative Science Quarterly,* 35(2): 286–316.

Hogg, M. A. and Hains, S. C. (1998) Friendship and group identification: a new look at the role of cohesiveness in groupthink. *European Journal of Social Psychology,* 28(3): 323–341.

Jackson, S., Brett, J., Sessa, V., Cooper, D., Julin, J., and Peyronnin, K. (1991) Some differences make a difference: individual dissimilarity and group heterogeneity as correlates of recruitment, promotions, and turnover. *Journal of Applied Psychology,* 76: 675–689.

Janis, I. L. (1982) *Groupthink,* 2nd Ed. Boston, MA: Houghton-Mifflin.

Jehn, K. A. (1995) A multimethod examination of the benefits and detriments of intragroup conflict. *Administrative Science Quarterly,* 40(2): 256–282.

Jehn, K. A. (1997) A qualitative analysis of conflict types and dimensions in organizational groups. *Administrative Science Quarterly,* 42(3): 530–557.

Jehn, K. A. and Mannix, E. (1998) The dynamic nature of conflict: a longitudinal study of intragroup conflict and group performance. Working paper, The Wharton School, University of Pennsylvania, Philadelphia, PA.

Jehn, K. A., Northcraft, G. B., and Neale, M. A. (1999) Why differences make a difference: a field study of diversity, conflict, and performance in workgroups. *Administrative Science Quarterly,* 44(4): 741–763.

Kanter, R. M. (1988) When a thousand flowers bloom: structural, collective, and social conditions for innovation in organization. In B. Staw and L. Cummings (Eds.), *Research in Organizational Behavior,* Vol. 10, pp. 169–211. Greenwich, CT: JAI Press.

Kanter, R. M., Kao, J., and Wiersema, F. (1997) *Innova-*

tion: *Breakthrough Ideas at 3M, DuPont, GE, Pfizer, and Rubbermaid.* New York: HarperBusiness.

Keller, R. T. (1986) Predictors of the performance of project groups in R&D organizations. *Academy of Management Journal,* 29(4): 715–726.

King, N. and Anderson, N. (1990) Innovation in working groups. In M. West and J. Farr (Eds.), *Innovation and Creativity at Work: Psychological and Organizational Strategies,* pp. 81–100. Chichester: Wiley.

Kotter, J. P. and Heskett, J. L. (1992) *Corporate Culture and Performance.* New York: Free Press.

Kroc, R. (1977) *Grinding It Out: the Making of McDonald's.* Chicago, IL: H. Regnery.

Kunda, G. (1992) *Engineering Culture: Control and Commitment in a High-Tech Corporation.* Philadelphia, PA: Temple University Press.

Leavitt, H. (1975) Suppose we took groups seriously. In E. Cass and F. Zimmer (Eds.), *Man and Work in Society.* New York: Van Nostrand Reinhold.

Levine, J. M. and Moreland, R. L. (1990) Progress in small group research. *Annual Review of Psychology,* 41: 585–634.

Lincoln, J. R. and Kalleberg, A. L. (1990) *Culture, Control, and Commitment: a Study of Work Organization and Work Attitudes in the United States and Japan.* New York: Cambridge University Press.

March, J. G. (1991) Exploration and exploitation in organizational learning. *Organization Science,* 3: 71–87.

Markowich, M. M. and Farber, J. A. (1989) If your employees were the customers. *Personnel Administrator,* 34(9): 70–73, 101.

Milgram, S. (1974) *Obedience to Authority; an Experimental View,* 1st Ed. New York: Harper & Row.

Moscovici, S. and Lecuyer, R. (1972) Studies in group decision: social space, patterns of communication and group consensus. *European Journal of Social Psychology,* 2(3): 221–244.

Nemeth, C. J. (1992) Minority dissent as a stimulant to group performance. In S. Worchel, W. Wood, and J. Simpson (Eds.), *Group Process and Productivity.* London: Sage.

Nemeth, C. J. (1997) Managing innovation: when less is more. *California Management Review,* 40(1): 59–74.

Nemeth, C. J. and Staw, B. M. (1989) The tradeoffs of social control and innovation in groups and organizations. In L. Berkowitz (Ed.), *Advances in Experimental Social Psychology,* pp. 175–210. San Diego, CA: Academic Press.

Nicholson, G. C. (1998) Keeping innovation alive. *Research-Technology Management,* 41(3): 34–40.

Nord, W. R. and Tucker, S. (1987) *Implementing Routine and Radical Innovations.* Lexington, MA: Lexington Books.

Nystrom, H. (1979) *Creativity and Innovation.* New York: Wiley.

Oldham, G. R. and Cummings, A. (1996) Employee creativity: personal and contextual factors at work. *Academy of Management Journal,* 39(3): 607–634.

O'Reilly, B. (1997) The secrets of America's most admired corporations: new ideas, new products. *Fortune,* 135(4): 60–64.

O'Reilly, C. A. and Chatman, J. A. (1996) Culture as social control: corporations, cults, and commitment. In B. Staw and L. Cummings (Eds.), *Research in Organizational Behavior,* Vol. 18, pp. 157–200. Greenwich, CT: JAI Press.

O'Reilly, C. A., Caldwell, D. F., and Barnett, W. P. (1989) Work group demography, social integration, and turnover. *Administrative Science Quarterly,* 34: 21–37.

O'Reilly, C. A., Chatman, J. A., and Caldwell, D. F. (1991) People and organizational culture: a profile comparison approach to assessing person-organization fit. *Academy of Management Journal,* 34(3): 487–516.

Packard, D. (1995) *The HP Way: How Bill Hewlett and I Built Our Company.* New York: HarperBusiness.

Pascale, R. T. (1993) The benefit of a clash of opinions. *Personnel Management,* 25(10): 38–41.

Payne, R. L. (1990) The effectiveness of research teams. In M. West and J. Farr (Eds.), *Innovation and Creativity at Work: Psychological and Organizational Strategies,* pp. 101–122. Chichester: Wiley.

Peters, T. J. and Waterman Jr., R. H. (1982) *In Search of Excellence: Lessons From America's Best-Run Companies,* 1st Ed. New York: Harper & Row.

Pillinger, T. and West, M. A. (1995) *Innovation in UK Manufacturing: Findings From a Survey Within Small and Medium Sized Manufacturing Companies.* Sheffield: Institute of Work Psychology, University of Sheffield.

Podolny, J. (1993) A status-based model of market competition. *American Journal of Sociology,* 98: 829–872.

Pratt, M. G. and Rafaeli, A. (1997) Organizational dress as a symbol of multilayered social identities. *Academy of Management Journal,* 40(4): 862–898.

Puffer, S. M. (1999) CompUSA's CEO James Halpin on technology, rewards, and commitment. *Academy of Management Executive,* 13(2): 29–36.

Robinson, A. G. and Stern, S. (1997) *Corporate Creativity: How Innovation and Improvement Actually Happen.* San Francisco, CA: Berrett-Koehler.

Rousseau, D. M. (1990) Normative beliefs in fund-raising organizations: linking culture to organizational performance and individual responses. *Group & Organization Studies,* 15(4): 448–460.

Schneider, B. (1987) The people make the place. *Personnel Psychology,* 40(3): 437–453.

Schweiger, D. M., Sandberg, W. R., and Ragen, J. W. (1986) Group approaches for improving strategic decision making: a comparative analysis of dialectical inquiry, devil's advocacy, and consensus. *Academy of Management Journal,* 29: 51–71.

Shalley, C. E. (1995) Effects of coaction, expected evaluation, and goal setting on creativity and productivity. *Academy of Management Journal,* 38(2): 483–503.

Shapiro, B. (1992) Functional integration: getting all the troops to work together. In J. Gabarro (Ed.), *Managing People and Organizations.* Boston, MA: Harvard Business School Press.

Shaw, M. E. (1981) *Group Dynamics:* the Psychology of Small Group Behavior, 3rd Ed. New York: McGraw-Hill.

Sorensen, J. (1999) The strength of corporate culture and the reliability of firm performance. Working paper, University of Chicago, Graduate School of Business, Chicago, IL.

Spataro, S. (2000) Not all differences are the same: the role of status in predicting reactions to demographic diversity in organizations. Dissertation, University of California, Berkeley, CA.

Stasser, G. and Stewart, D. (1992) Discovery of hidden profiles by decision-making groups: solving a problem versus making a judgment. *Journal of Personality and Social Psychology,* 63: 426–434.

Staw, B. M. (1976) Knee-deep in the Big Muddy: a study of escalating commitment to a chosen course of action. *Organizational Behavior & Human Decision Processes,* 16(1): 27–44.

Staw, B. M. (1990) An evolutionary approach to creativity and innovation. In M. West and J. Farr (Eds.), *Innovation and Creativity at Work: Psychological and Organizational Strategies,* pp. 287–308. Chichester: Wiley.

Staw, B. M. and Ross, J. (1987) Behavior in escalation situations: antecedents, prototypes, and solutions. In L. Cummings and B. Staw (Eds.), *Research in Organizational Behavior,* Vol. 9, pp. 39–78. Greenwich, CT: JAI Press.

Stoner, J. A. F. (1968) Risky and cautious shifts in group decisions: the influence of widely held values. *Journal of Experimental Social Psychology,* 4: 442–459.

Sutton, R. I. and Hargadon, A. (1996) Brainstorming groups in context: effectiveness in a product design firm. *Administrative Science Quarterly,* 41(4): 685–718.

Thomas, D. A. and Ely, R. J. (1996) Making differences matter: a new paradigm for managing diversity. *Harvard Business Review,* 74: 79–90.

Thompson, V. A. (1965) Bureaucracy and innovation. *Administrative Science Quarterly,* 1: 1–20.

Triandis, H. C. (1995) *Individualism and Collectivism.* Boulder, CO: Westview Press.

Triandis, H. C. (1996) The psychological measurement of cultural syndromes. *American Psychologist,* 51: 407–415.

Tsui, A. S., Egan, T. D., and O'Reilly, C. (1992) Being different: relational demography and organizational attachment. *Administrative Science Quarterly,* 37: 549–579.

Tushman, M. and O'Reilly, C. A. (1997) *Winning Through Innovation: a Practical Guide to Leading Organizational Change and Renewal.* Boston, MA: Harvard Business School Press.

Wagner, J. A. (1995) Studies of individualism-collectivism: effects on cooperation in-groups. *Academy of Management Journal,* 38: 152–172.

West, M. A. (1990) The social psychology of innovation in groups. In M. West and J. Farr (Eds.), *Innovation and Creativity at Work: Psychological and Organizational Strategies,* pp. 309–333. Chichester: Wiley.

West, M. A. and Anderson, N. R. (1996) Innovation in top management teams. *Journal of Applied Psychology,* 81(6): 680–693.

Wetlaufer, S. (2000) Common sense and conflict: an interview with Disney's Michael Eisner. *Harvard Business Review,* 78(1): 114–124.

Zaltman, G., Duncan, R., and Holbeck, J. (1973) *Innovations and Organizations.* New York: Wiley.

Zell, D. (1997) *Changing by Design: Organizational Innovation at Hewlett-Packard.* Ithaca, NY: ILR Press.

Zenger, T. R. and Lawrence, B. S. (1989) Organizational demography: the differential effects of age and tenure distributions on technical communication. *Academy of Management Journal,* 32: 353–376.

18

Understanding Power in Organizations

JEFFREY PFEFFER

Norton Long, a political scientist, wrote, "People will readily admit that governments are organizations. The converse—that organizations are governments—is equally true but rarely considered."[1] But organizations, particularly large ones, are like governments in that they are fundamentally political entities. To understand them, one needs to understand organizational politics, just as to understand governments, one needs to understand governmental politics.

Ours is an era in which people tend to shy away from this task. As I browse through bookstores, I am struck by the incursion of "New Age" thinking, even in the business sections. New Age can be defined, I suppose, in many ways, but what strikes me about it are two elements: (1) a self-absorption and self-focus, which looks toward the individual in isolation; and (2) a belief that conflict is largely the result of misunderstanding, and if people only had more communication, more tolerance, and more patience, many (or all) social problems would disappear. These themes appear in books on topics ranging from making marriages work to making organizations work. A focus on individual self-actualization is useful, but a focus on sheer self-reliance is not likely to encourage one to try to get things done with and through other people—to be a manager or a leader. "Excellence can be achieved in a solitary field without the need to exercise leadership."[2] In this sense, John Gardner's (former secretary of HEW and the founder of Common Cause) concerns about community are part and parcel of a set of concerns about organizations and getting things accomplished in them.[3] One can be quite content, quite happy, quite fulfilled as an organizational hermit, but one's influence is limited and the potential to accomplish great things, which requires interdependent action, is almost extinguished.

If we are suspicious of the politics of large organizations, we may conclude that smaller organizations are a better alternative. There is, in fact, evidence that the average size of establishments in the United States is decreasing. This is not just because we have become more of a service economy and less of a manufacturing economy; even within manufacturing, the average size of establishments and firms is shrinking. The largest corporations have shed thousands, indeed hundreds of thousands of employees—not only middle managers, but also production workers, staff of all kinds, and employees who performed tasks that are now contracted out. Managers and employees who were stymied by the struggles over power and influence that emerge from interdependence and differences in point of view have moved to a world of smaller, simpler organizations, with less internal interdependence and less internal diversity, which are, as a consequence, less political. Of course, such structural changes only increase interdependence among organizations, even as they decrease interdependence and conflict within these organizations.

I see in this movement a parallel to what I have seen in the management of our human resources.

Reprinted with permission of Harvard Business School Press. From *Managing with Power: Politics and Influences in Organizations,* by Jeffrey Pfeffer. Copyright © 1993 by the Harvard Business School Publishing Corporation; all rights reserved. Adapted in *California Management Review* 34, no. 2 (1992): 29–50.

Many corporations today solve their personnel problems by getting rid of the personnel. The rationale seems to be that if we can't effectively manage and motivate employees, then let's turn the task over to another organization. We can use leased employees or contract workers, or workers from temporary help agencies, and let those organizations solve our problems of turnover, compensation, selection, and training.

It is an appealing solution, consistent with the emphasis on the individual, which has always been strong in U.S. culture, and which has grown in recent years. How can we trust large organizations when they have broken compacts of long-term employment? Better to seek security and certainty within oneself, in one's own competencies and abilities, and in the control of one's own activities.

There is, however, one problem with this approach to dealing with organizational power and influence. It is not clear that by ignoring the social realities of power and influence we can make them go away, or that by trying to build simpler, less interdependent social structures we succeed in building organizations that are more effective or that have greater survival value. Although it is certainly true that large organizations sometimes disappear,[4] it is also true that smaller organizations disappear at a much higher rate and have much worse survival properties. By trying to ignore issues of power and influence in organizations, we lose our chance to understand these critical social processes and to train managers to cope with them.

By pretending that power and influence don't exist, or at least shouldn't exist, we contribute to what I and some others (such as John Gardner) see as the major problem facing many corporations today, particularly in the United States—the almost trained or produced incapacity of anyone except the highest-level managers to take action and get things accomplished. As I teach in corporate executive programs, and as I compare experiences with colleagues who do likewise, I hear the same story over and over again. In these programs ideas are presented to fairly senior executives, who then work in groups on the implications of these ideas for their firms. There is real strength in the experience and knowledge of these executives, and they often come up with insightful recommendations and ideas for improving their organizations. Perhaps they discover the wide differences in effectiveness that exist

in different units and share suggestions about how to improve performance. Perhaps they come to understand more comprehensively the markets and technologies of their organizations, and develop strategies for both internally oriented and externally oriented changes to enhance effectiveness. It really doesn't matter, because the most frequently heard comment at such sessions is, "My boss should be here." And when they go back to their offices, after the stimulation of the week, few managers have either the ability or the determination to engineer the changes they discussed with such insight.

I recall talking to a store manager for a large supermarket chain with a significant share of the northern California grocery market. He managed a store that did in excess of $20 million in sales annually, which by the standards of the average organization makes him a manager with quite a bit of responsibility—or so one would think. In this organization, however, as in many others, the responsibilities of middle-level managers are strictly limited. A question arose as to whether the store should participate in putting its name on a monument sign for the shopping center in which the store was located. The cost was about $8,000 (slightly less than four hour's sales in that store). An analysis was done, showing how many additional shoppers would need to be attracted to pay back this small investment, and what percentage this was of the traffic count passing by the center. The store manager wanted the sign. But, of course, he could not spend even this much money without the approval of his superiors. It was the president of the northern California division who decided, after a long meeting, that the expenditure was not necessary.

There are many lessons that one might learn from this example. It could be seen as the result of a plague of excessive centralization, or as an instance of a human resource management policy that certainly was more "top down" than "bottom up." But what was particularly interesting was the response of the manager—who, by the way, is held accountable for this store's profits even as he is given almost no discretion to do anything about them. When I asked him about the decision, he said, "Well, I guess that's why the folks at headquarters get the big money; they must know something we don't." Was he going to push for his idea, his very modest proposal? Of course no, he said. One gets along by just biding one's time, going along with whatever directives come down from the upper management.

I have seen this situation repeated in various forms over and over again. I talk to senior executives who claim their organizations take no initiative, and to high-level managers who say they can't or won't engage in efforts to change the corporations they work for, even when they know such changes are important, if not essential, to the success and survival of these organizations. There are politics involved in innovation and change. And unless and until we are willing to come to terms with organizational power and influence, and admit that the skills of getting things done are as important as the skills of figuring out what to do, our organizations will fall further and further behind. The problems is, in most cases, not an absence of insight or organizational intelligence. Instead the problem is one of passivity, a phenomenon that John Gardner analyzed in the following way:

> In this country—and in most other democracies—power has such a bad name that many good people persuade themselves they want nothing to do with it. The ethical and spiritual apprehensions are understandable. But one cannot abjure power. Power, as we are now speaking of it . . . is simply the capacity to bring about certain intended consequences in the behavior of others. . . . In our democratic society we make grants of power to people for specified purposes. If for ideological or temperamental reasons they refuse to exercise the power granted, we must turn to others. . . . To say a leader is preoccupied with power is like saying that a tennis player is preoccupied with making shots his opponent cannot return. Of course leaders are preoccupied with power! The significant questions are: What means do they use to gain it? How do they exercise it? To what ends do they exercise it?[5]

If leadership involves skill at developing and exercising power and influence as well as the will to do so, then perhaps one of the causes of the so-called leadership crisis in organizations in the United States is just this attempt to sidestep issues of power. This diagnosis is consistent with the arguments made by Warren Bennis and his colleagues, who have studied leaders and written on leadership. For instance, Bennis and Nanus noted that one of the major problems facing organizations today is not that too many people exercise too much power, but rather the opposite:

> These days power is conspicuous by its absence. Powerlessness in the face of crisis. Powerlessness in the face of complexity. . . . power has been sabotaged. . . . institutions have been rigid, slothful, or mercurial.[6]

They go on to comment on the importance of power as a concept for understanding leadership and as a tool that allows organizations to function productively and effectively:

> However, there is something missing . . . POWER, the basic energy to initiate and sustain action translating intention into reality, the quality without which leaders cannot lead. . . . power is at once the most necessary and the most distrusted element exigent to human progress. . . . power is the basic energy needed to initiate and sustain action or, to put it another way, the capacity to translate intention into reality and sustain it.[7]

Such observations about power are not merely the province of theorists. Political leaders, too, confirm that the willingness to build and wield power is a prerequisite for success in public life. In this consideration of power and leadership, Richard Nixon offered some observations that are consistent with the theme of this article:

> Power is the opportunity to build, to create, to nudge history in a different direction. There are few satisfactions to match it for those who care about such things. But it is not happiness. Those who seek happiness will not acquire power and would not use it well if they did acquire it.
>
> A whimsical observer once commented that those who love laws and sausages should not watch either being made.
>
> By the same token, we honor leaders for what they achieve, but we often prefer to close our eyes to the way they achieve it. . . .
>
> In the real world, politics is compromise and democracy is politics. Anyone who would be a statesman has to be a successful politician first. Also, a leader has to deal with people and nations as they are, not as they should be. As a result, the qualities required for leadership are not necessarily

those that we would want our children to emulate—unless we wanted them to be leaders.

In evaluating a leader, the key question about his behavioral traits is not whether they are attractive or unattractive, but whether they are useful.[8]

OUR AMBIVALENCE ABOUT POWER

That we are ambivalent about power is undeniable. Rosabeth Kanter, noting that power was critical for effective managerial behavior, nevertheless wrote, "Power is America's last dirty word. It is easier to talk about money—and much easier to talk about sex—than it is to talk about power."[9] Gandz and Murray did a survey of 428 managers whose responses nicely illustrate the ambivalence about power in organizations.[10] Some items from their survey, along with the percentage of respondents reporting strong or moderate agreement, are reproduced in Table 18.1. The concepts of power and organizational politics are related; most authors, myself included, define organizational politics as the exercise or use of power, with power being defined as a potential force. Note that more than 90% of the respondents said that the experience of workplace politics is common in most organizations, 89% said that successful executives must be good politicians, and 76% said that the higher one progresses in an organization, the more political things become. Yet 55% of these same respondents said that politics were detrimental to efficiency, and almost half said that top management should try to get rid of politics within organizations. It is as if we know that power and politics exist, and we even grudgingly admit that they are necessary to individual success, but we nevertheless don't like them.

This ambivalence toward, if not outright disdain for, the development and use of power in organizations stems from more than one source. First, there is the issue of ends and means—we often don't like to consider the methods that are necessary to get things accomplished, as one of the earlier quotes from Richard Nixon suggests. We are also ambivalent about ends and means because the same strategies and processes that may produce outcomes we desire can also be used to produce results that we consider undesirable. Second, some fundamental lessons we learn in school really hinder our appreciation of power and influence. Finally, in a related point, the perspective from which we judge organizational decisions often does not do justice to the realities of the social world.

Table 18.1. Managers' Feelings About Workplace Politics

Statement	Percentage Expressing Strong or Moderate Agreement
The existence of workplace politics is common to most organizations	93.2
Successful executives must be good politicians	89.0
The higher you go in organizations, the more political the climate becomes	76.2
Powerful executives don't act politically	15.7
You have to be political to get ahead in organizations	69.8
Top management should try to get rid of politics within the organization	48.6
Politics help organizations function effectively	42.1
Organizations free of politics are happier than those where there are a lot of politics	59.1
Politics in organizations are detrimental to efficiency	55.1

Source: Jeffrey Gandz and Victor V. Murray, "The Experience of Workplace Politics," *Academy of Management Journal,* 23 (1980).

Ends and Means

On Saturday, September 25, 1976, an elaborate testimonial dinner was held in San Francisco for a man whose only public office was as a commissioner on the San Francisco Housing Authority board. The guest list was impressive—the mayor, George Moscone; Lieutenant Governor Mervyn Dymally, at that time the highest-ranking Afro-American in elected politics; District Attorney Joe Freitas; Democratic Assemblyman Willie Brown, probably the most powerful and feared individual in California politics; Republican State Senator Milton Marks; San Francisco Supervisor Robert Mendelsohn; the city editor of the morning newspaper; prominent attorneys—in short, both Democrats and Republicans, a veritable who's who of the northern California political establishment. The man they were there to honor had recently met personally with the president's wife, Rosalynn Carter. Yet when the world heard more of this guest of honor, some two years later, it was to be with shock and horror at what happened in a jungle in Guyana. The person being honored that night in September 1976—who had worked his way into the circles of power in San Francisco using some of the very same strategies and tactics described in this article—was none other than Jim Jones.[11]

There is no doubt that power and influence can be acquired and exercised for evil purposes. Of course, most medicines can kill if taken in the wrong amount, thousands die each year in automobile accidents, and nuclear power can either provide energy or mass destruction. We do not abandon chemicals, cars, or even atomic power because of the dangers associated with them; instead we consider danger an incentive to get training and information that will help us to use these forces productively. Yet few people are willing to approach the potential risks and advantages of power with the same pragmatism. People prefer to avoid discussions of power, apparently on the assumption that "If we don't think about it, it won't exist." I take a different view. John Jacobs, now a political editor for the *San Francisco Examiner*, co-authored a book on Jim Jones and gave me a copy of it in 1985. His view, and mine, was that tragedies such as Jonestown could be prevented, not by ignoring the processes of power and influence, but rather by being so well schooled in them that one could recognize their use and take countermeasures, if necessary—and by developing a well-honed set of moral values.

The means to any end are merely mechanisms for accomplishing something. The something can be grand, grotesque, or, for most of us, I suspect, somewhere in between. The end may not always justify the means, but neither should it automatically be used to discredit the means. Power and political processes in organizations can be used to accomplish great things. They are not always used in this fashion, but that does not mean we should reject them out of hand. It is interesting that when we use power ourselves, we see it as a good force and wish we had more. When others use it against us, particularly when it is used to thwart our goals or ambitions, we see it as an evil. A more sophisticated and realistic view would see it for what it is— an important social process that is often required to get things accomplished in interdependent systems.

Most of us consider Abraham Lincoln to have been a great president. We tend to idealize his accomplishments: he preserved the Union, ended slavery, and delivered the memorable Gettysburg Address. It is easy to forget that he was also a politician and a pragmatist—for instance, the Emancipation Proclamation freed the slaves in the Confederacy, but not in border states that remained within the Union, whose support he needed. Lincoln also took a number of actions that far overstepped his constitutional powers. Indeed, Andrew Johnson was impeached for continuing many of the actions that Lincoln had begun. Lincoln once explained how he justified breaking the laws he had sworn to uphold:

> My oath to preserve the Constitution imposed on me the duty of preserving by every indispensable means that government, that nation, of which the Constitution was the organic law. Was it possible to lose the nation and yet preserve the Constitution? . . . I felt that measures, otherwise unconstitutional, might become lawful by becoming indispensable to the preservation . . . of the nation.[12]

Lessons to Be Unlearned

Our ambivalence about power also comes from lessons we learn in school. The first lesson is that life is a matter of individual effort, ability, and achievement. After all, in school, if you have mastered the intricacies of cost accounting, or calculus, or electrical engineering, and the people sitting on either side of you haven't, their failure will not affect your performance—unless, that is, you had intended to copy from their papers. In the classroom setting, interdependence is minimized. It is you versus the material, and as long as you have mastered the material, you have achieved what is expected. Cooperation may even be considered cheating.

Such is not the case in organizations. If you know your organization's strategy but your colleagues do not, you will have difficulty accomplishing anything. The private knowledge and private skill that are so useful in the classroom are insufficient in organizations. Individual success in organizations is quite frequently a matter of working with and through other people, and organizational success is often a function of how successfully individuals can coordinate their activities. Most situations in organizations resemble football more than golf, which is why companies often scan résumés to find not only evidence of individual achievement but also signs that the person is skilled at working as part of a team. In achieving success in organizations, "power transforms individual interests into coordinated activities that accomplish valuable ends."[13]

The second lesson we learn in school, which may be even more difficult to unlearn, is that there are right and wrong answers. We are taught how to solve problems, and for each problem, that there is a right answer, or at least one approach that is more correct than another. The right answer is, of course, what the instructor says it is, or what is in the back of the book, or what is hidden away in the instructor's manual. Life appears as a series of "eureka" problems, so-called because once you are shown the correct approach or answer, it is immediately self-evident that the answer is, in fact, correct.

This emphasis on the potential of intellectual analysis to provide the right answer—the truth—is often, although not invariably, misplaced. Commenting on his education in politics, Henry Kissinger wrote, "Before I served as a consultant to Kennedy, I had believed, like most academics, that the process of decision-making was largely intellectual and all one had to do was to walk into the President's office and convince him of the correctness of one's view. This perspective I soon realized is as dangerously immature as it is widely held."[14] Kissinger noted that the easy decisions, the ones with right and wrong answers that can be readily discerned by analysis, never reached the president, but rather were resolved at lower levels.

In the world in which we all live, things are seldom clearcut or obvious. Not only do we lack a book or an instructor to provide quick feedback on the quality of our approach, but the problems we face often have multiple dimensions—which yield multiple methods of evaluation. The consequences of our decisions are often known only long after the fact, and even then with some ambiguity.

AN ALTERNATIVE PERSPECTIVE ON DECISION MAKING

Let me offer an alternative way of thinking about the decision-making process. There are three important things to remember about decisions. First, a decision by itself changes nothing. You can decide to launch a new product, hire a job candidate, build a new plant, change your performance evaluation system, and so forth, but the decision will not put itself into effect. As a prosaic personal example, recall how many times you or your friends "decided" to quit smoking, to get more exercise, to relax more, to eat healthier foods, or to lose weight. Such resolutions often fizzle before producing any results. Thus, in addition to knowledge of decision science, we need to know something about "implementation science."

Second, at the moment a decision is made, we cannot possibly know whether it is good or bad. Decision quality, when measured by results, can only be known as the consequences of the decision become known. We must wait for the decision to be implemented and for its consequences to become clear.

The third, and perhaps most important, observation is that we almost invariably spend more time living with the consequences of our decisions than we do in making them. It may be an organizational decision, such as whether to acquire a company, change the compensation system, fight a union-organizing campaign; or a personal decision, such as where to go to school, which job to choose, what subject to major in, or whom to marry. In either case, it is likely that the effects of the decision will be with us longer than it took us to make the decision, regardless of how much time and effort we invested. Indeed, this simple point has led several social psychologists to describe people as rationalizing (as contrasted with rational) animals.[15] The match between our attitudes and our behavior, for instance, often derives from our adjusting our attitudes after the fact to conform to our past actions and their consequences.[16]

If decisions by themselves change nothing; if, at the time a decision is made, we cannot know its consequences; and if we spend, in any event, more time living with our decisions than we do in making them, then it seems evident that the emphasis in much management training and practice has been misplaced. Rather than spending inordinate amounts of time and effort in the decision-making process, it would seem at least as useful to spend time implementing decisions and dealing with their ramifications. In this sense, good managers are not only good analytic decision makers; more important, they are skilled in managing the consequences of their decisions. "Few successful leaders spend much time fretting about decisions once they are past. . . . The only way he can give adequate attention to the decisions he has to make tomorrow is to put those of yesterday firmly behind him."[17]

There are numerous examples that illustrate this point. Consider, for instance, the acquisition of Fairchild Semiconductor by Schlumberger, an oil service company.[18] The theory behind the merger was potentially sound—to apply Fairchild's skills in electronics to the oil service business. Schlumberger wanted, for example, to develop more sophisticated exploration devices and to add electronics to oil servicing and drilling equipment. Unfortunately, the merger produced none of the expected synergies:

> When Schlumberger tried to manage Fairchild the same way it had managed its other business units, it created many difficulties. . . . resources were not made available to R&D with the consequence of losing technical edge which Fairchild once had. Creative . . . technical people left the organization and the company was unable to put technical teams together to pursue new technological advancement.[19]

A study of 31 acquisitions found that "problems will eventually emerge after acquisitions that could not have been anticipated. . . . both synergy and problems must be actively managed."[20] Moreover, firms that see acquisitions as a quick way of capturing some financial benefits are often insensitive to the amount of time and effort that is required to implement the merger and to produce superior performance after it occurs. Emphasis on the choice of a merger partner and the terms of the deal can divert focus away from the importance of the activities that occur once the merger is completed.

Or, consider the decision to launch a new product. Whether that decision produces profits or losses is often not simply a matter of the choices made at the time of the launch. It also depends on the implementation of those choices, as well as on subsequent decisions such as redesigning the product, changing the channels of distribution, adjusting prices, and so forth. Yet what we often observe in organizations is that once a decision is made, more effort is expended in assigning credit or blame than in working to improve the results of the decision.

I can think of no example that illustrates my argument as clearly as the story of how Honda entered the American market, first with motorcycles, and later, of course, with automobiles and lawn mowers. Honda established an American subsidiary in 1959, and between 1960 and 1965, Honda's sales in the United States went from $500,000 to $77 million. By 1966, Honda's share of the U.S. motorcycle market was 63%,[21] starting from zero just seven years before. Honda's share was almost six times that of its closest competitors, Yamaha and Suzuki, and Harley-Davidson's share had fallen to 4%. Pascale showed that this extraordinary success was largely the result of "miscalculation, serendipity, and organizational learning," not of the rational process of planning and foresight often emphasized in our efforts to be successful.[22]

Sochiro Honda himself was more interested in racing and engine design than in building a business, but his partner, Takeo Fujisawa, managed to convince him to turn his talent to designing a safe, inexpensive motorcycle to be driven with one hand and used for package delivery in Japan. The motorcycle was an immediate success in Japan. How and why did Honda decide to enter the export market and sell to the United States? Kihachiro Kawashima, eventually president of American Honda, reported to Pascale:

> In truth, we had no strategy other than the idea of seeing if we could sell something in the United States. It was a new frontier . . . and it fit the "success against all odds" culture that Mr. Honda had cultivated. I reported my impressions . . . including the seat-of-the-pants target of trying, over several years, to attain a 10 percent share of U.S. imports. . . . We did not discuss profits or deadlines for breakeven.[23]

Money was authorized for the venture, but the Ministry of Finance approved a currency allocation of only $250,000, of which less than half was in cash and the rest in parts and motorcycle inventory. The initial attempt to sell motorcycles in Los Angeles was disastrous. Distances in the United States are much greater than in Japan, and the motor cycles were driven farther and faster than their design permitted. Engine failures were common, particularly on the larger bikes.

The company had initially focused its sales efforts on the larger, 250cc and 350cc bikes, and had not even tried to sell the 50cc Supercub, believing it was too small to have any market acceptance:

> We used the Honda 50s . . . to ride around Los Angles on errands. They attracted a lot of attention. One day we had a call from a Sears buyer. . . . we took note of Sears' interest. But we still hesitated to

push the 50cc bikes out of fear they might harm our image in a heavily macho market. But when the larger bikes started breaking, we had no choice. We let the 50cc bikes move. And surprisingly, the retailers who wanted to sell them weren't motorcycle dealers, they were sporting goods stores.[24]

Honda's "you meet the nicest people on a Honda" advertising campaign was designed as a class project by a student at UCLA, and was at first resisted by Honda. Honda's distribution strategy—sporting goods and bicycle shops rather than motorcycle dealers—was made *for* them, not *by* them. And its success with the smaller motorbike was almost totally unanticipated. It occurred through a combination of circumstances: the use of the motorbike by Honda employees, who couldn't afford anything fancier; the positive response from people who saw the bike; and the failure of Honda's larger bikes in the American market.

Honda did not use decision analysis and strategic planning. In fact, it is difficult to see that Honda made any decisions at all, at least in terms of developing alternatives and weighing options against an assessment of goals and the state of the market. Honda succeeded by being flexible, by learning and adapting, and by working to have decisions turn out right, once those decisions had been made. Having arrived with the wrong product for a market they did not understand, Honda spent little time trying to find a scapegoat for the company's predicament; rather, Honda personnel worked vigorously to change the situation to their benefit, being creative as well as opportunistic in the process.

The point is that decisions in the world of organizations are not like decisions made in school. There, once you have written down an answer and turned in the test, the game is over. This is not the case in organizational life. The important actions may not be the original choices, but rather what happens subsequently, and what actions are taken to make things work out. This is a significant point because it means that we need to be somewhat less concerned about the quality of the decision at the time we make it (which, after all, we can't really know anyway), and more concerned with adapting our new decisions and actions to the information we learn as events unfold. Just as Honda emerged as a leader in many American markets more by accident and trial-and-error learning than by design,

it is critical that organizational members develop the fortitude to continue when confronted by adversity, and the insight about how to turn situations around. The most important skill may be managing the consequences of decisions. And, in organizations in which it is often difficult to take any action, the critical ability may be the capacity to have things implemented.

WAYS OF GETTING THINGS DONE

Why is implementation difficult in so many organizations, and why does it appear that the ability to get decisions implemented is becoming increasingly rare? One way of thinking about this issue, and of examining the role of power and influence in the implementation process, is to consider some possible ways of getting things done.

One way of getting things to happen is through hierarchical authority. Many people think power is merely the exercise of formal authority, but it is considerably more than that, as we will see. Everyone who works in an organization has seen the exercise of hierarchical authority. Those at higher levels have the power to hire and fire, to measure and reward behavior, and to provide direction to those who are under their aegis. Hierarchical direction is usually seen as legitimate, because the variation in formal authority comes to be taken for granted as a part of organizational life. Thus the phrase, "the boss wants . . ." or "the president wants . . ." is seldom questioned or challenged. Who can forget Marine Lieutenant Colonel Oliver North testifying, during the Iran-contra hearings, about his willingness to stand on his head in a corner if that was what his commander-in-chief wanted, or maintaining that he never once disobeyed the orders of his superiors?

There are three problems with hierarchy as a way of getting things done. First, and perhaps not so important, is that it is badly out of fashion. In an era of rising education and the democratization of all decision processes, in an era in which participative management is advocated in numerous places,[25] and particularly in a country in which incidents such as the Vietnam War and Watergate have led many people to mistrust the institutions of authority, implementation by order or command is problematic. Readers who are parents need only reflect on the difference in parental authority between the current period and the 1950s to see what I mean. How many times have you been able to get your children to do something simply on the basis of your authority as a parent?

A second, more serious problem with authority derives from the fact that virtually all of us work in positions in which, in order to accomplish our job and objectives, we need the cooperation of others who do not fall within our direct chain of command. We depend, in other words, on people outside our purview of authority, whom we could not command, reward, or punish even if we wanted to. Perhaps, as a line manager in a product division, we need the cooperation of people in human resources for hiring, people in finance for evaluating new product opportunities, people in distribution and sales for getting the product sold and delivered, and people in market research for determining product features and marketing and pricing strategy. Even the authority of a chief executive is not absolute, since there are groups outside the focal organization that control the ability to get things done. To sell overseas airline routes to other domestic airlines requires the cooperation of the Transportation and Justice Departments, as well as the acquiescence of foreign governments. To market a drug or medical device requires the approval of the Food and Drug Administration; to export products overseas, one may need both financing and export licenses. The hierarchical authority of all executives and administrators is limited, and for most of us, it is quite limited compared to the scope of what we need in order to do our jobs effectively.

There is a third problem with implementation accomplished solely or primarily through hierarchical authority: what happens if the person at the apex of the pyramid, the one whose orders are being followed, is incorrect? When authority is vested in a single individual, the organization can face grave difficulties if that person's insight or leadership begins to fail. This was precisely what happened at E. F. Hutton, where Robert Fomon, the chief executive officer, ruled the firm through a rigid hierarchy of centralized power:

> Fomon's strength as a leader was also his weakness. As he put his stamp on the firm, he did so more as monarch than as a chief executive. . . . Fomon surrounded himself with . . . cronies and yes men who would become the managers and directors of E.F. Hutton and who would insulate him from the real world.[26]

Because Fomon was such a successful builder of his own hierarchical authority, no one in the firm challenged him to see the new realities that Hutton, and every other securities firm, faced in the 1980s.[27] Consequently, when the brokerage industry changed, Hutton did not, and it eventually ceased to exist as an independent entity.

Another way of getting things done is by developing a strongly shared vision or organizational culture. If people share a common set of goals, a common perspective on what to do and how to accomplish it, and a common vocabulary that allows them to coordinate their behavior, then command and hierarchical authority are of much less importance. People will be able to work cooperatively without waiting for orders from the upper levels of the company. Managing through a shared vision and with a strong organizational culture has been a very popular prescription for organizations.[28] A number of articles and books tell how to build commitment and shared vision and how to socialize individuals, particularly at the time of entry, so that they share a language, values, and premises about what needs to be done and how to do it.[29]

Without denying the efficacy and importance of vision and culture, it is important to recognize that implementation accomplished through them can have problems. First, building a shared conception of the world takes time and effort. There are instances when the organization is in crisis or confronts situations in which there is simply not sufficient time to develop shared premises about how to respond. For this very reason, the military services rely not only on techniques that build loyalty and esprit de corps,[30] but also on a hierarchical chain of command and a tradition of obeying orders.

Second, there is the problem of how, in a strong culture, new ideas that are inconsistent with that culture can penetrate. A strong culture really constitutes an organizational paradigm, which prescribes how to look at things, what are appropriate methods and techniques for solving problems, and what are the important issues and problems.[31] In fields of science, a well-developed paradigm provides guidance as to what needs to be taught and in what order, how to do research, what are appropriate methodologies, what are the most pressing research questions, and how to train new students.[32] A well-developed paradigm, or a strong culture, is overturned only with great difficulty, even if it fails to account for data or to lead to new discoveries.[33] In a similar fashion, an organizational paradigm provides a way of thinking about and investigating the world, which reduces uncertainty and provides for effective collective action, but which also overlooks or ignores some lines of inquiry. It is easy for a strong culture to produce groupthink, a pressure to conform to the dominant view.[34] A vision focuses attention, but in that focus, things are often left out.

An organization that had difficulties, as well as great success, because of its strong, almost evangelical culture is Apple Computer. Apple was founded and initially largely populated by counterculture computer hackers, whose vision was a computer-based form of power to the people—one computer for each person. IBM had maintained its market share through its close relations with centralized data processing departments. IBM was the safe choice—the saying was, no one ever got fired for buying IBM. The Apple II was successful by making an end run around the corporate data processing manager and selling directly to the end-user, but "by the end of '82 it was beginning to seem like a good idea to have a single corporate strategy for personal computers, and the obvious person to coordinate that strategy was the data processing manager."[35] Moreover, computers were increasingly being tied into networks; issues of data sharing and compatibility were critical in organizations that planned to buy personal computers by the thousands. Companies wanted a set of computers that could run common software, to save on software purchasing as well as training and programming expenses. Its initial vision of "one person-one machine," made it difficult for Apple to see the need for compatibility, and as a consequence:

> The Apple II wouldn't run software for the IBM PC; the PC wouldn't run software for Lisa, Lisa wouldn't run software for the Apple II; and none of them would run software for the Macintosh. . . . Thanks largely to Steve [Jobs], Apple had an entire family of computers none of which talked to one another.[36]

Apple's strong culture and common vision also helped cause the failure of the Apple III as a new product. The vision was not only of "one person-one machine," but also of a machine that anyone could design, modify, and improve. Operating systems stood between the user and the machine, and so the Apple culture denigrated operating systems: The problem with an operating system, from the hobbyist point of view, was that it made it more difficult to reach down inside the computer and show off your skills; it formed a barrier between the user and the machine. Personal computers meant power to the people, and operating systems took some of that power away. . . . It wasn't a design issue; it was a threat to the inalienable rights of a free people.[37]

Apple III had an operating system known as SOS for Sophisticated Operating System, which was actually quite similar to the system Microsoft had developed for IBM's personal computer—MS DOS (Microsoft Disk Operating System), except it was even better in some respects. Yet Apple was too wary of operating systems to try to make its system *the* standard, or even *a* standard, in personal computing. As a result the company lost out on a number of important commercial opportunities. The very zeal and fervor that made working for Apple like a religious crusade and produced extraordinary levels of commitment from the work force made it difficult for the company to be either cognizant of or responsive to shifts in the marketplace for personal computers.

There is a third process of implementation in organizations—namely, the use of power and influence. With power and influence the emphasis is on method rather than structure. It is possible to wield power and influence without necessarily having or using formal authority. Nor is it necessary to rely on a strong organizational culture and the homogeneity that this often implies. Of course, the process of implementation through power and influence is not without problems of its own. What is important is to see power and influence as one of a set of ways of getting things done—not the only way, but an important way.

From the preceding discussion we can see that implementation is becoming more difficult because: (1) changing social norms and greater interdependence within organizations have made traditional, formal authority less effective than it once was, and (2) developing a common vision is increasingly difficult in organizations composed of heterogeneous members—heterogeneous in terms of race and ethnicity, gender, and even language and culture. At the same time, our ambivalence about power, and the fact that training in its use is far from widespread, mean that members of organizations are often unable to supplement their formal authority with the "unofficial" processes of power and influence. As a result their organizations suffer, and promising projects fail to get off the ground. This is why learning how to manage with power is so important.

THE MANAGEMENT PROCESS: A POWER PERSPECTIVE

From the perspective of power and influence, the process of implementation involves a set of steps, which are outlined below.

- Decide what your goals are, what you are trying to accomplish.
- Diagnose patterns of dependence and interdependence; what individuals are influential and important in your achieving your goal?
- What are their points of view likely to be? How will they feel about what you are trying to do?
- What are their power bases? Which of them is more influential in the decision?
- What are your bases of power and influence? What bases of influence can you develop, to gain more control over the situation?
- Which of the various strategies and tactics for exercising power seem most appropriate and are likely to be effective, given the situation you confront?
- Based on the above, choose a course of action to get something done.

The first step is to decide on your goals. It is, for instance, easier to drive from Albany, New York, to Austin, Texas, if you know your destination than if you just get in your car in Albany and drive randomly. Although this point is apparently obvious it is something that is often overlooked in a business context. How many times have you attended meetings or conferences or talked to someone on the telephone without a clear idea of what you were trying to accomplish? Our calendars are filled with appointments, and other interactions occur unexpectedly in the course of our day. If we don't have some clear goals, and if we don't know

what our primary objectives are, it is not very likely that we are going to achieve them. One of the themes Tom Peters developed early in his writing was the importance of consistency in purpose. Having the calendars, knowing the language, what gets measured, and what gets talked about—all focus on what the organization is trying to achieve.[38] It is the same with individuals; to the extent that each interaction, in each meeting, in each conference, is oriented toward the same objective, the achievement of that objective is more likely.

Once you have a goal in mind, it is necessary to diagnose who is important in getting your goal accomplished. You must determine the patterns of dependence and interdependence among these people and find out how they are likely to feel about what you are trying to do. As part of this diagnosis, you also need to know how events are likely to unfold, and to estimate the role of power and influence in the process. In getting things accomplished, it is critical to have a sense of the game being played, the players, and what their positions are. One can get badly injured playing football in a basketball uniform, or not knowing the offense from the defense. I have seen, all too often, otherwise intelligent and successful managers have problems because they did not recognize the political nature of the situation, or because they were blindsided by someone whose position and strength they had not anticipated.

Once you have a clear vision of the game, it is important to ascertain the power bases of the other players, as well as your own potential and actual sources of power. In this way you can determine your relative strength, along with the strength of other players. Understanding the sources of power is critical in diagnosing what is going to happen in an organization, as well as in preparing yourself to take action.

Finally, you will want to consider carefully the various strategies, or, to use a less grand term, the tactics that are available to you, as well as those that may be used by others involved in the process. These tactics help in using power and influence effectively, and can also help in countering the use of power by others.

Power is defined here as the potential ability to influence behavior, to change the course of events, to overcome resistance, and to get people to do things that they would not otherwise do.[39] Politics and influence are the processes, the actions, the behaviors through which this potential power is utilized and realized.

WHAT DOES IT MEAN, TO MANAGE WITH POWER?

First, it means recognizing that in almost every organization, there are varying interests. This suggests that one of the first things we need to do is to diagnose the political landscape and figure out what the relevant interests are, and what important political subdivisions characterize the organization. It is essential that we do not assume that everyone necessarily is going to be our friend, or agree with us, or even that preferences are uniformly distributed. There are clusters of interests within organizations, and we need to understand where these are and to whom they belong.

Next, it means figuring out what point of view these various individuals and subunits have on issues of concern to us. It also means understanding why they have the perspective that they do. It is all too easy to assume that those with a different perspective are somehow not as smart as we are, not as informed, not as perceptive. If that is our belief, we are likely to do several things, each of which is disastrous. First, we may act contemptuously toward those who disagree with us—after all, if they aren't as competent or as insightful as we are, why should we take them seriously? It is rarely difficult to get along with those who resemble us in character and opinions. The real secret of success in organizations is the ability to get those who differ from us, and whom we don't necessarily like, to do what needs to be done. Second, if we think people are misinformed, we are likely try to "inform" them, or to try to convince them with facts and analysis. Sometimes this will work, but often it will not, for their disagreement may not be based on a lack of information; it may, instead, arise from a different perspective on what our information means. Diagnosing the point of view of interest groups as well as the basis for their positions will assist us in negotiating with them in predicting their response to various initiatives.

Third, managing with power means understanding that to get things done, you need power—more power than those whose opposition you must overcome—and thus it is imperative to understand where power comes from and how these sources of power can be developed. We are sometimes reluctant to think very purposefully or strategically about acquiring and using power. We are prone to believe that if we do our best, work hard, be nice, and so forth, things will work out for the best. I don't mean to imply that one should not, in general, work hard, try to make good decisions, and be nice, but that these and similar platitudes are often not very useful in helping us get things accomplished in our organizations. We need to understand power and try to get it. We must be willing to do things to build our sources of power, or else we will be less effective than we might wish to be.

Fourth, managing with power means understanding the strategies and tactics through which power is developed and used in organizations, including the importance of timing, the use of structure, the social psychology of commitment and other forms of interpersonal influence. If nothing else, such an understanding will help us become astute observers of the behavior of others. The more we understand power and its manifestations, the better will be our clinical skills. More fundamentally, we need to understand strategies and tactics of using power so that we can consider the range of approaches available to us, and use what is likely to be effective. Again, as in the case of building sources of power, we often try not to think about these things, and we avoid being strategic or purposeful about employing our power. This is a mis take. Although we may have various qualms, there will be others who do not. Knowledge without power is of remarkably little use. And power without the skill to employ it effectively is likely to be wasted.

Managing with power means more than knowing the ideas discussed in this article. It means being, like Henry Ford, willing to do something with that knowledge. It requires political savvy to get things done, and the willingness to force the issue. For years in the United States, there had been demonstrations and protests, court decisions and legislative proposals attempting to end the widespread discrimination against minority Americans in employment, housing, and public accommodations. The passage of civil rights legislation was a top priority for President Kennedy, but although he had charisma, he lacked the knowledge of political tactics, and possibly the will to use some of the more forceful ones, to get his legislation passed. In the hands of someone who knew power and influence inside out, in spite of the opposition of Southern congressmen and senators, the legislation would be passed quickly.

In March 1965, the United States was wracked by violent reactions to civil rights marches in the South. People were killed and injured as segregationists attacked demonstrators, with little or no intervention by the local law enforcement agencies. There were demonstrators across from the White House holding a vigil as Lyndon Johnson left to address a joint session of Congress. This was the same Lyndon Johnson who, in 1948, had opposed federal antilynching legislation, arguing that it was a matter properly left to the states. This was the same Lyndon Johnson who, as a young congressional secretary and then congressman, had talked conservative to conservatives, liberal to liberals, and was said by many to have stood for nothing. This was the same Lyndon Johnson who in eight years in the House of Representatives had introduced not one piece of significant legislation and had done almost nothing to speak out on issues of national importance. This was the same Lyndon Johnson who, instead, had used some of his efforts while in the House to enrich himself by influencing colleagues at the Federal Communications Commission to help him obtain a radio station in Austin, Texas, and then to change the operating license so the station would become immensely profitable and valuable. This was the same Lyndon Johnson who, in 1968, having misled the American people, would decide not to run for reelection because of his association with both the Vietnam War and a fundamental distrust of the presidency. On that night Johnson was to make vigorous use of his power and his political skill to help the civil rights movement:

> With almost the first words of his speech, the audience . . . knew that Lyndon Johnson intended to take the cause of civil rights further than it had ever gone before. . . . He would submit a new civil rights bill . . . and it would be far stronger than the bills of the past. . . . "their cause must be our cause, too," Lyndon Johnson said. "Because it is not just Negroes, but really it is all of us, who must over-

come the crippling legacy of bigotry and injustice. . . . And we shall overcome."[40]

As he left the chamber after making his speech, Johnson sought out the 76-year-old chairman of the House Judiciary Committee, Emmanuel Celler:

> "Manny," he said, "I want you to start hearings tonight."
> "Mr. President," Cellar protested, "I can't push that committee or it might get out of hand. I am scheduling hearings for next week.
> . . . Johnson's eyes narrowed, and his face turned harder. His right hand was still shaking Celler's, but the left hand was up, and a finger was out, pointing, jabbing.
> "Start them *this* week, Manny," he said. "And hold night sessions, too."[41]

Getting things done requires power. The problem is that we would prefer to see the world as a kind of grand morality play, with the good guys, and the bad ones easily identified. Obtaining power is not always an attractive process, nor is its use. And it somehow disturbs our sense of symmetry that a man who was as sleazy, to use a term of my students, as Lyndon Johnson was in some respects, was also the individual who almost single-handedly passed more civil rights legislation in less time with greater effect than anyone else in U.S. history. We are troubled by the issue of means and ends. We are perplexed by the fact that "bad" people sometimes do great and wonderful things, and that "good" people sometimes do "bad" things, or often, nothing at all. Every day, managers in public and private organizations acquire and use power to get things done. Some of these things may be, in retrospect, mistakes, although often that depends heavily on your point of view. Any reader who always does the correct thing that pleases everyone should immediately contact me—we will get very wealthy together. Mistakes and opposition are inevitable. What is not inevitable is passivity, not trying, not seeking to accomplish things.

In many domains of activity we have become so obsessed with not upsetting anybody, and with not making mistakes, that we settle for doing nothing. Rather than rebuild San Francisco's highways, possibly in the wrong place, maybe even in the wrong way, we do nothing, and the city erodes economically without adequate transportation. Rather than possibly being wrong about a new product, such as the personal computer, we study it and analyze it, and lose market opportunities. Analysis and forethought are, obviously, fine. What is not so fine is paralysis or inaction, which arises because we have little skill in overcoming the opposition that inevitably accompanies change, and little interest in doing so.

Theodore Roosevelt, making a speech at the Sorbonne in 1910, perhaps said it best:

> It is not the critic who counts; not the man who points out how the strong man stumbles, or where the doer of deeds could have done them better. The credit belongs to the man who is actually in the arena, whose face is marred by dust and sweat and blood; who strives valiantly; who errs, and comes short again and again; because there is not effort without error and shortcoming; but who does actually strive to do the deeds; who knows the great enthusiasms, the great devotions; who spends himself in a worthy cause, who at the best knows in the end the triumphs of high achievement and who at the worst, if he fails, at least fails while daring greatly, so that his place shall never be with those cold and timid souls who know neither victory or defeat.[42]

It is easy and often comfortable to feel powerless—to say, "I don't know what to do, I don't have the power to get it done, and besides, I can't really stomach the struggle that may be involved." It is easy, and now quite common, to say, when confronted with some mistakes in your organization, "It's not really my responsibility, I can't do anything about it anyway, and if the company wants to do that, well that's why the senior executives get the big money—it's their responsibility." Such a response excuses us from trying to do things; in not trying to overcome opposition, we will make fewer enemies and are less likely to embarrass ourselves. It is, however, a prescription for both organizational and personal failure. This is why power and influence are not the organization's last dirty secret, but the secret of success for both individuals and their organizations. Innovation and change in almost any arena requires the skill to develop power, and the willingness to employ it to get things accomplished.

Or, in the words of a local radio newscaster, "If you don't like the news, go out and make some of your own."

REFERENCES

1. Norton E. Long, "The Administrative Organization as a Political System," in S. Mailick and E. H. Van Ness, eds., *Concepts and Issues in Administrative Behavior* (Englewood Cliffs, NJ: Prentice-Hall, 1962), p. 110.
2. Richard M. Nixon, *Leaders* (New York, NY: Warner Books, 1982), p. 5.
3. John W. Gardner, *On Leadership* (New York, NY: Free Press, 1990).
4. Michael T. Hannan and John Freeman, *Organizational Ecology* (Cambridge, MA: Harvard University Press, 1989).
5. Gardner, op. cit., pp. 55–57.
6. Warren Bennis and Burt Nanus, *Leaders: The Strategies for Taking Charge* (New York, NY: Harper and Row, 1985), p. 6.
7. Ibid., pp. 15–17.
8. Nixon, op. cit., p. 324.
9. Rosabeth Moss Kanter, "Power Failure in Management Circuits," *Harvard Business Review, 57* (July/August 1979): 65.
10. Jeffrey Gandz and Victor V. Murray, "The Experience of Workplace Politics," *Academy of Management Journal, 23* (1980): 237–251.
11. Tim Reiterman with John Jacobs, *Raven: The Untold Story of the Rev. Jim Jones and His People* (New York, NY: E. P. Dutton, 1982), pp. 305–307.
12. Nixon, op cit., p. 326.
13. Abraham Zaleznick and Manfred F. R. Kets de Vries, *Power and the Corporate Mind* (Boston, MA: Houghton Mifflin, 1975), p. 109.
14. Henry Kissinger, *The White House Years* (Boston, MA: Little Brown, 1979), p. 39.
15. Elliot Aronson, *The Social Animal* (San Francisco, CA: W. H. Freeman, 1972), chapter 4; Barry M. Staw, "Rationality and Justification in Organizational Life," *Research in Organizational Behavior,* B. M. Staw and L. L. Cummings, eds. (Greenwich, CT: JAI Press, 1980), vol. 2, pp. 45–80; Gerald R. Salancik, "Commitment and the Control of Organizational Behavior and Belief," *New Directions in Organizational Behavior,* Barry M. Staw and Gerald R. Salancik, eds. (Chicago, IL: St. Clair Press, 1977), pp. 1–54.
16. Leon Festinger, *A Theory of Cognitive Dissonance* (Stanford, CA: Stanford University Press, 1957).
17. Nixon, op. cit., p. 329.

18. Alok K. Chakrabarti, "Organizational Factors in Post-Acquisition Performance," *IEEE Transactions on Engineering Management, 37* (1990): pp. 259–268.

19. Ibid., p. 259.

20. Ibid., p. 266.

21. D. Purkayastha, "Note on the Motorcycle Industry—1975," #578-210, Harvard Business School, 1981.

22. Richard T. Pascale, "Perspectives on Strategy: The Real Story Behind Honda's Success," *California Management Review, 26* (1984): 51.

23. Ibid., p. 54.

24. Ibid., p. 55.

25. William A. Pasmore, *Designing Effective Organizations: The Sociological Systems Perspective* (New York, NY: John Wiley, 1988); David L. Bradford and Allan R. Cohen, *Managing for Excellence* (New York, NY: John Wiley, 1984).

26. Mark Stevens, *Sudden Death: The Rise and Fall of E. F. Hutton* (New York, NY: Penguin, 1989), p. 98.

27. Ibid., p. 121.

28. Thomas J. Peters and Robert H. Waterman, Jr., *In Search of Excellence* (New York, NY: Harper and Row, 1982); Terrence Deal and Allan A. Kennedy, *Corporate Cultures* (Reading, MA: Addison-Wesley, 1982); Stanley Davis, *Managing Corporate Culture* (Cambridge, MA: Ballinger, 1984).

29. Richard T. Pascale, "The Paradox of 'Corporate Culture': Reconciling Ourselves to Socialization," *California Management Review, 26* (1985): 26–41; Charles O'Reilly, "Corporations, Culture, and Commitment: Motivation and Social Control in Organizations," *California Management Review, 31* (1989): 9–25.

30. Sanford M. Dornbusch, "The Military Academy as an Assimilating Institution," *Social Forces, 33* (1955): 316–321.

31. Richard Harvey Brown, "Bureaucracy as Praxis: Toward a Political Phenomenology of Formal Organizations," *Administrative Science Quarterly, 23* (1978): 365–382.

32. Janice Lodahl and Gerald Gordon, "The Structure of Scientific Fields and the Functioning of University Graduate Departments," *American Sociological Review, 37* (1972): 57–72.

33. Thomas S. Kuhn, *The Structure of Scientific Revolutions,* 2d ed. (Chicago, IL: University of Chicago Press, 1970).

34. Irving L. Janis, *Victims of Groupthink* (Boston, MA: Houghton Mifflin, 1972).

35. Frank Rose, *West of Eden: The End of Innocence at Apple Computer* (New York, NY: Viking Penguin, 1989), p. 81.

36. Ibid., p. 85.

37. Ibid., p. 97.

38. Thomas J. Peters, "Symbols, Patterns, and Settings: An Optimistic Case for Getting Things Done," *Organizational Dynamics, 7* (1978): 3–23.

39. Jeffrey Pfeffer, *Power in Organizations* (Marshfield, MA: Pitman Publishing, 1981); Kanter, op. cit.; Richard M. Emerson, "Power-Dependence Relations," *American Sociological Review 27* (1962): 31–41.

40. Robert A. Caro, *Means of Ascent: The Years of Lyndon Johnson* (New York, NY: Alfred A. Knopf, 1990), pp. xix–xx.

41. Ibid., p. xxi.

42. Nixon, op. cit., p. 345.

19

The Weird Rules of Creativity

ROBERT I. SUTTON

For the past decade at least, the holy grail for companies has been innovation. Managers have gone after it with all the zeal their training has instilled in them. They've focused on identifying the optimal incentives and inputs to the creative process, on bringing customers' and other important perspectives to bear, on investing in ideas according to their odds of success, and on slashing the percentage of losers. There's only one problem: None of that works very well.

What does foster creativity doesn't look at all like rational management to most experienced executives. The practices go beyond counterintuitive; they seem downright weird. For example, you might reasonably expect that creativity would flourish in a fun, low-stress workplace, where conflict is held in check and managers keep a close watch on how money is spent and people use their time. You'd be wrong. After studying creative companies and teams for more than a decade, I've found them to be remarkably inefficient and often terribly annoying places to work, where "managing by getting out of the way" is often the best approach of all.

Managing for creativity, I've discovered, means taking most of what we know about management and standing it on its head. It means placing bets on ideas without much heed to their projected ROI. It means ignoring what has worked before. It means taking perfectly happy people and goading them into fights among themselves. Good creativity management means hiring the candidate you have a gut feeling

against. And as for those people who stick their fingers in their ears and chant, "I'm not listening, I'm not listening," when customers are making suggestions? It means praising and promoting them.

In this article, I advocate several ideas about managing creativity that are clearly odd but just as clearly effective. One set of ideas relates to hiring, another to management, and a third to risk and randomness. All of them have solid grounding in academic research. And here's what's really weird. I've actually found numerous companies and teams that use these ideas with great results.

WHY THESE WEIRD IDEAS WORK

The practices in this article succeed by increasing the range of a company's knowledge, by causing people to see old problems in new ways, and by helping companies break from the past. Decades of research show that these three conditions produce the richest soil for creative work. So why do ideas for promoting them seem so strange to managers?

It's because as important as innovation is to most companies, it isn't—and never will be—their primary activity. Quite the contrary, companies are overwhelmingly focused—and correctly so—on the more routine work of making money *right now* from tried-and-true products, services, and business models. The practices that are well suited for cashing in on old, proven ways

Reprinted by permission of *Harvard Business Review*. From "The Weird Rules of Creativity," by Robert I. Sutton, September 2001. Copyright © 2001 by the Harvard Business School Publishing Corporation; all rights reserved.

are drastically different from those needed for innovation. Consider the contrast between how Disney organizes the work of cast members at its theme parks and that of "imagineers" at its research and development facility in Burbank, California. The job titles are revealing metaphors for the two kinds of work. Cast members in theme parks follow well-defined scripts; whether they are playing the role of Cinderella or Goofy, acting as guides on the Jungle Cruise, or sweeping the streets, precise guidelines are enforced to ensure that they stay in character. This is Disney's routine work. In contrast, Disney Imagineering is a place where people are expected to keep trying different things. Imagineers come to work each day to dream up wild ideas about new things a guest might experience. The best practices for imagineers can't be choreographed in the same detail as those of cast members. After all, the management problem is to expand the possibilities of what an imagineer might do, not to constrain them.

The right balance of what organizational theorist James March has termed exploitation of proven knowledge versus exploration of new possibilities varies across industries. But even in companies that are much ballyhooed for innovation, only a small percentage of effort is usually devoted to generating and testing new products and services. This comparative rarity helps explain why practices that support innovation may seem odd and provoke discomfort and why managers hesitate to use them even when they should. Study after study shows that, independent of other factors, the more often people are exposed to something, the more positive they feel about it; rare and unfamiliar things provoke negative evaluations. This "mere exposure effect" has been found, as Stanford psychologist Robert Zajonc writes, for "geometric figures, random polygons, Chinese and Japanese ideographs, photographs of faces, numbers, letters of the alphabet, letters of one's own name, random sequences of tone, food, odors, flavors, colors, actual persons, stimuli that were initially liked and initially disliked stimuli." People are unaware of the effect and routinely deny it is happening, but still it persists.

Little wonder, then, that the best ideas for promoting and sustaining creativity seem strange, even wrong, to most managers. As we'll see, managing for innovation often means shifting your traditional, rational approaches to hiring, management, and risk 180 degrees.

IT STARTS WITH HIRING

The difference begins with hiring. What rational manager would intentionally hire someone who would be slow to learn the company culture or who would make coworkers feel uncomfortable? Who would waste a hire on a candidate whose skills the company doesn't even need? Or bring in a person without previous experience in solving the type of problem at hand? Yet these are all sound approaches for building companies that embrace innovation as a way of life.

Let's begin with those "slow learners." Most companies, of course, screen job candidates to pick out the fast learners—those gregarious people with social graces who can figure out quickly how to do things "the right way." But companies and teams that do innovative work need at least some members who are slow to learn how things are "supposed to be done." Otherwise, each newcomer will soon become a perfect imitation of everyone else in the company, and there won't be any new ideas around to develop and test.

Research in personality psychology suggests that people with certain traits are best able to avoid, ignore, or reject "the heat of the herd," as futurist George Gilder puts it. These include people who have high self-esteem and those who psychologist Mark Snyder calls "low self-monitors"—people who are especially insensitive to subtle, and even not so subtle, hints from others about how to act. For better or worse, low self-monitors are relatively unfettered by social norms. These mavericks and misfits can drive bosses and coworkers crazy, but they increase the range of what is thought, noticed, said, and done in a company. High self-monitors are likely to be yes-men and women; they can't stop themselves from telling others what they think they want to hear. Low self-monitors can't stop themselves from saying and doing what they think is right because they don't notice—or don't care about—pressures to follow the herd. People with high self-esteem think and act independently as well; confident people continue to believe in their ideas despite rejection and criticism.

The Xerox researcher who invented the laser printer, Gary Starkweather, is a great example of someone who succeeded because he felt compelled to do what he felt was right and had enough self-confidence to reject the organizational code. As Michael Hiltzik recounts in his book *Dealers of Light-*

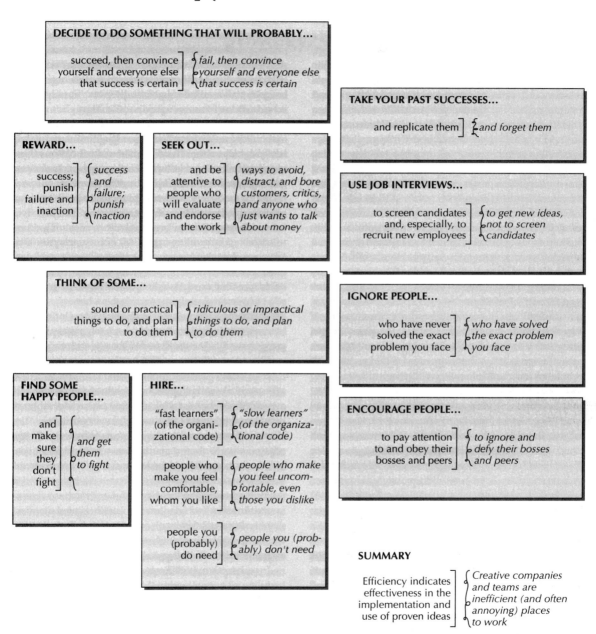

Figure 19.1. Weird ideas for managing creativity. What makes for effective management practice can look very different, depending on whether the aim is to exploit already-proven ideas or explore new ones. In researching my book, *Weird Ideas That Work,* I uncovered ideas for managing creativity and innovation—nearly all 180 degrees different from standard management practice.

ning, Starkweather was hired in 1968 as an optics researcher by Xerox's main technical laboratory in Webster, New York. He kept insisting that the then new "technology of lasers could be used to 'paint' an image onto a xerographic drum with greater speed and precision than ordinary white light." The traditional "white light" researchers at the Webster lab repeatedly dismissed lasers as impractical and too expensive. Starkweather responded by doing one experiment after another that answered nearly every objection raised by his superiors and peers. When Starkweather's manager still tried to stop his research, he was confident enough to complain to a senior manager at Xerox about how "laboratory dogma" was ruining both a good idea and his career. He was then transferred to the new Xerox PARC research facility in Palo Alto, California; by 1974, he had developed his ideas into a commercially feasible product. When it was finally launched in 1977, the 9700 printer became one of Xerox's best-selling products.

Hiring people who make you uncomfortable, even those you don't like, is another way to find a few useful misfits who will ignore and reject the organizational code, increasing the variety in what people think, say, and do. A senior executive in a toy company once told me that her managers kept hiring people who pretended to "think like us" during job interviews but showed their true colors after being hired by pointing out how bad the company's products were. The behavior, in her words, "makes us hate them"—but, she admitted, some of those complainers were crucial to her company's success because they kept coming up with great ideas for new toys ("probably just to spite us"). Of course, the next step, which I recommended to her, is to intentionally hire people that she and others in the company dislike.

Another way to spark creativity is to hire people with skills you don't think you need. If this sounds ridiculous, consider that the practice is not uncommon among product design companies, which live or die on innovation. This attitude led IDEO to hire Craig Syverson because he seemed to have a lot of "cool" skills in areas like computers and the arts. When IDEO's managers offered him a position, they weren't quite sure what the job would entail or if they needed his skills at all. Syverson experimented with several jobs, but soon focused on video production work even though, at

first, there was no demand for custom videos from IDEO clients. As IDEO's focus expanded, however, from designing products to designing user and customer experiences, Syverson's ability to capture how people use different products became a crucial—and profitable—service to clients.

Design Continuum is another product design company that brings in new ideas by hiring people with varied, even offbeat, backgrounds. It has hired engineers who moonlight or have worked as sculptors, carpenters, and rock musicians. The company likes to hire people such as Roy Thompson, who started out writing graffiti on the streets and subways of Brooklyn, and David Cohen, who worked as an aircraft mechanic. These diverse experiences give the company a broad palette of ideas to try in new ways and places.

If I were running a company that depended on innovation, I would go even further to import fresh knowledge: I would hire some people who had never tried to solve problems like the ones I was addressing. In the creative process, ignorance is bliss, especially in the early stages. People who don't know how things are "supposed to be" aren't blinded by preconceptions.

The easiest way to guarantee such naïveté is to hire novices, as Jane Goodall's ground-breaking research on chimpanzees shows. When anthropologist Louis Leakey offered Goodall the opportunity to do two years of intensive observations of these apes in Africa, Goodall hesitated to take the job because she had no scientific training. Leakey insisted that not only was university training unnecessary, it had serious drawbacks. Goodall explains in her book *In the Shadow of Man,* "He wanted someone with a mind uncluttered and unbiased by theory who would make the study for no other reason than a real desire for knowledge." Ultimately, Goodall and Leakey both believed that if she had not been ignorant of existing theories, she never would have been able to observe and explain so many new chimp behaviors.

Dyson Appliances, maker of the hottest-selling vacuum cleaner in the United Kingdom, takes much the same approach to hiring. Dyson's Dual Cyclone has a powerful and groundbreaking vacuum technology and requires no bag. The machine has a striking colorful design and see-through chamber that lets you view the cyclone inside as it spins at nearly 1,000 miles per hour. Founder and CEO James Dyson believes that one reason his company invents successful products is that it employs graduates straight from universities. He writes, "They are unsullied. They have not been strapped into a suit and taught to think by a company with nothing on its mind but short-term profit and early retirement."

Naïveté can also come in the form of people who are experts in some other area, which allows them to see—and perhaps solve—problems from a new perspective. This approach was used during the early days of Ballard Power Systems, whose innovative fuel cell technology might just replace the internal combustion engine. As Tom Koppell describes in his book *Powering the Future,* founder and then CEO Geoffrey Ballard hired a young chemistry professor named Keith Prater in 1974 to work on batteries the company was developing. Prater warned Ballard that he had no experience in batteries. "That's fine," said Ballard, "I don't want someone who knows batteries. They know what won't work. I want someone who is bright and creative and willing to try things that others might not try." And indeed, Prater played a key role in developing innovative batteries during the company's early days, and later, in making breakthroughs in fuel cells for powering buses and cars.

MANAGING FOR CREATIVE SPARKS

Once you've got your talent in the door, the next order of business is to do something with it. Again, my ideas will seem strange to people who believe that the best ways for managing routine tasks are equally well suited to innovative work, but they are supported by theory and practice. If it's creativity you want, you should encourage people to ignore and defy superiors and peers—and while you're at it, get them to fight among themselves. You should reassign people who have settled into productive grooves in their jobs. And you should start rewarding failure, not just success; reserve punishment only for inaction.

People who do what they think is right—rather than what they are told or what they anticipate their superiors want—can drive their bosses crazy and get their companies in deep trouble. But they also force companies to try ideas that some boss or powerful group may have rejected as a waste of time or money.

3M's former CEO William McKnight, for example, once ordered a young employee named Richard Drew to abandon a project he was working on, insisting it would never work. Drew disregarded the order and went on to invent masking tape, one of 3M's breakthrough products. Drew's perseverance also laid the foundation for 3M's defining product, Scotch tape.

Similarly, in *The HP Way,* David Packard brags about an employee who defied a direct order from him. "Some years ago," he writes, "at an HP laboratory in Colorado Springs devoted to oscilloscope technology, one of our bright, energetic engineers, Chuck House, was advised to abandon a display monitor he was developing. Instead he embarked on a vacation to California—stopping along the way to show potential customers a prototype." House was convinced he was on to something, so he persisted with the project, even persuading his R&D manager to rush the monitor into production. The resulting $35 million in revenue proved he was right. Packard continues: "Some years later, at a gathering of HP engineers, I presented Chuck with a medal for 'extraordinary contempt and defiance beyond the normal call of engineering duty.'"

I've never seen an organization with guidelines such as, "Ignore your boss if you think he or she is wrong." If you work in a place that actually enforces a rule like this, please contact me immediately. I have, however, found companies where managers provide vague encouragement for employees to work on what they want and don't demand to know the details. This "don't ask, don't tell" policy is made explicit at 3M, where technical people are expected to allocate up to 15% of their time to projects of their own choosing. The same attitude and similar practices are seen at Corning's Sullivan Park R&D lab, which churns out hundreds of kinds of experimental glass each year. Scientists there are required to spend 10% of their time on "Friday afternoon experiments" to develop "slightly crazy ideas." This policy not only allows scientists to work on pet projects that bosses don't know about but also frees them to work on pet projects that superiors have discontinued. For instance, an entire genomics-technology business is being built on an idea that was officially killed by the head of research but was pursued in Friday afternoon experiments.

In fact, creative work must be sheltered from the cold light of day, especially when ideas are incomplete and untested. William Coyne, former vice president of R&D at 3M, remarked in a speech at Motorola University, "After you plant a seed in the ground, you don't dig it up every week to see how it is doing." In an age of customer centricity, this may border on the heretical. But if you want to develop new products and services, I urge you to keep your creative people away from your biggest customers—and for that matter from critics and anyone whose primary concern is money.

Doing so helps creativity blossom. Psychological research shows that people are especially hesitant to try new things in front of "evaluative others" like critics and bosses. The virtues of doing innovative work in isolation are well documented. Tracy Kidder's Pulitzer Prize-winning book, *The Soul of a New Machine,* describes an engineering team that was sequestered in the basement offices of Data General. Kidder shows how the resulting lack of attention helped the "MicroKids" on this "Eagle Team" do a better and faster job of designing a minicomputer. Kiyoshi Kawashima, former president of Honda, used a similar approach in 1978. He was concerned that Honda was losing its vitality because senior managers couldn't understand what kinds of cars young people wanted. Kawashima assembled the youngest members of his staff (average age 27) to design a car that would appeal to younger customers and promised that senior managers would not interfere with the team's operation. The result was the hot-selling Honda City Car. Few companies, it seems, are able to innovate without shielding teams from the mainstream.

At the same time, a company shouldn't let a team get too cozy. One of my most well-supported ideas for man aging creativity is that you should find some happy people and then get them to fight. Mind you, I'm not talking about provoking personality conflicts or relationship issues; battles between people who despise one another squelch innovation. The fights you need to cause are all about ideas. Bob Taylor, a psychologist turned research administrator, first encouraged this kind of conflict among the computer scientists from various universities he funded while at the U.S. Department of Defense's Advanced Research Projects Agency (ARPA) in the 1960s and later at Xerox PARC in the 1970s. These scientists and engineers, perhaps more than any others, are responsible for the technologies that made the computer revolution possible, in-

cluding the personal computer, the Internet, and the laser printer. The computer scientists Taylor funded through ARPA met at an annual series of research conferences, as retold by Michael Hiltzik:

> The daily discussions unfolded in a pattern that remained peculiar to Taylor's management style throughout his career. Each participant got an hour or so to describe his work. Then he would be thrown to the mercy of the assembled court like a flank steak to a pack of ravenous wolves. "I got them to argue with each other," Taylor recalled with unashamed glee. . . . "These were people who cared about their work. . . . If there were technical weak spots, they would almost always surface under these conditions. It was very, very healthy."

Enhancing innovation also has to do with how performance is rewarded. This, too, entails a dramatic departure from the management practices ingrained in most companies. Rather than rewarding success and punishing failure, companies should reward both.

Again, I must distinguish between what is right for routine work and what is right for creative work. When known procedures are used by well-trained people, failure does signal improper training, weak motivation, or poor leadership. But applying this standard to innovative work stifles intelligent risks. Every bit of solid theory and evidence demonstrates that it is impossible to generate a few good ideas without also generating a lot of bad ideas. Former Time Warner chairman Steve Ross had a philosophy that people who didn't make enough mistakes should be fired. That's an anomaly, though. Few companies tolerate failure, let alone reward it.

If you want a creative organization, inaction is the worst kind of failure—and the only kind that deserves to be punished. Researcher Dean Keith Simonton provides strong evidence from multiple studies that creativity results from action. Renowned geniuses like Picasso, da Vinci, and physicist Richard Feynman didn't succeed at a higher rate than their peers. They simply produced more, which meant that they had far more successes *and failures* than their unheralded colleagues. In every occupation Simonton studied, from composers, artists, and poets to inventors and scientists, the story is the same: Creativity is a function of the quantity of work produced. These findings mean that measuring whether people are doing something—

Growing Up Is Hard to Do

The relative age of a company is no guide to its creativity level; start-ups are as vulnerable as established companies. Consider what happened at Lotus Development in the mid-1980s. Lotus, now part of IBM, was founded in 1982 by Mitchell Kapor and Jonathan Sachs to bring to market their "killer app," Lotus 1-2-3. In just two years, sales grew from $53 million to $156 million, which led to an urgent need for experienced professional managers. McKinsey consultant James Manzi was brought in as president in 1984 and became CEO in 1985. Manzi built enormously profitable marketing and sales operations, modeling them after those of *Fortune* 500 companies.

But Lotus started having trouble developing successful new products. Part of the problem was that management techniques suitable only for managing routine work were being used throughout the company. By 1985 or so, around the time the company had grown to more than 1,000 employees, many original members felt that they no longer fit in. Most of the new hires were MBAs cut from the "big-company cloth," many having worked for such organizations as Coca-Cola and Procter & Gamble.

In 1985, Kapor (then chairman of the board) and Freada Klein (then head of organizational development and training) tried an experiment. With Kapor's approval, Klein pulled together the résumés of the first 40 people to join the company. She disguised the names and put them into the applicant pool. Some of these people had the right technical and managerial skills for the jobs they applied for, but they also had done a lot of "wacko and risky things." They had been community organizers, clinical psychologists, and transcendental meditation teachers (Kapor included); several had lived at an ashram.

Not one of the applicants was called for an interview. Kapor and Klein viewed this as a sign that Lotus was unwittingly screening out innovative people. They seem to have been correct. Lotus Notes, the only hit product invented by the company after Lotus 1-2-3, was developed 20 miles from headquarters so as Klein puts it, "the team could work unfettered by the narrow Lotus culture." Lotus did need a great marketing and sales organization to cash in on its innovative ideas. The narrowness that came along with these changes, however, was a double-edged sword.

---

or nothing—is one of the ways to assess the performance of people who do creative work. Companies should demote, transfer, and even fire those who spend day after day talking about and planning what they are going to do but never do anything.

SOME IDEAS ABOUT RISK AND RANDOMNESS

One of the main reasons for rewarding both success and failure is that most managers, analysts, and other so-called experts (like everyone else) do a poor job of judging new ideas and predicting which ones will succeed. Organizations use all sorts of methods, such as "gates" in the product development process, to try to improve their odds of success. But there is little evidence that such practices actually reduce the propor-

tion of flops. As James March writes, "Unfortunately, the difference between visionary genius and delusional madness is much clearer in history books than in experience."

Yet there is one simple, proven, and powerful thing you can do to increase the likelihood that a risky project will succeed: Commit to it wholeheartedly. Forget the slim odds; simply convince yourself and everyone else that, with determination and persistence, the project is destined to be a triumph.

More than 500 academic studies confirm the power of positive thinking. As the famous sociologist Robert Merton explained it:

The self-fulfilling prophecy is, in the beginning, a *false* definition of the situation evoking a new behavior which makes the originally false conception come *true*. The specious validity of the self-fulfilling prophecy perpetuates a reign of error. For the prophet will cite the actual course of events as proof that he was right from the very beginning. Such are the perversities of social logic.

Henry Ford put it more succinctly: "If you think you can, or if you think you can't, you are right."

Successful heretics tend to be confident and persistent. They believe deeply in what they are doing and are skilled at convincing everyone around them that they are right. Apple confounder (and, once again, CEO) Steve Jobs does this with his widely touted "reality distortion field." Insiders recount how he casts a spell on those around him, convincing them that the success of an idea, project, or person is virtually certain. Aircraft designer and former test pilot Burt Rutan managed to do this with the team developing the Voyager, which became the first airplane to fly nonstop around the world without refueling. Numerous "experts" predicted that the Voyager was doomed to fail, just as they predicted that other experimental aircraft designed by Rutan wouldn't work. Rutan told his engineers, "Confidence in nonsense is required." This suggests that, if you can't decide which new projects or ideas to bet on based on their objective merits, pick those that will be developed by the most committed and persuasive heretics.

If predictions about which new ideas will succeed are so hard to make, and commitment to an idea, any idea, is one of the only surefire ways to increase the odds of success, does this mean that companies might as well use a random process to generate possibilities to explore? Actually, yes. Random selection is one of the best ways to ensure that new ideas will not be biased by knowledge of past successes. I got this idea from Karl Weick of the University of Michigan, who has described the ritual used by Naskapi Indians to determine where to hunt game. They placed the shoulder bone of a caribou over a fire until it cracked—then read the cracks as a map. Weick asserts that the ritual was effective because plans for future hunts were not shaped by the results of past hunts. It kept the Naskapis from mindlessly returning to—and depleting—territory they had covered before.

The same logic is used by some companies to generate ideas about different paths they might take. Reactivity, a software company I advise, holds regular brainstorming sessions where employees talk about ideas for new technologies, products, and companies. After holding a few of these sessions, software designers Jeremy Henrickson, Graham Miller, and Bill Walker were becoming concerned that the ideas discussed were getting too narrow. So they invented a random selection process: Attendees at the sessions were given index cards and told to jot down on each a technology (one stack of cards) or an industry (a second stack). The stacks were then used to create random pairings of technologies to industries, and the group brainstormed for five minutes on the possibilities of each pair. Some seemed hopeless—how much could XML programming, for instance, reshape the funeral industry? But others—an idea about dynamic risk management in the shipping industry, for instance—seemed well worth researching in more detail. Most important, Miller reports, it "helped get us out of the rut we were in."

Companies that want to avoid getting stuck in a rut should be especially wary of opinions from customers who use their current products or services, and from the marketing and sales people who represent their views. Michael Eisner, CEO of Disney, put it this way in an interview in the January–February 2000 issue of *Harvard Business Review:* "Most audience—or customer—research is useless." Just because everyone loved *Titanic,* he argued, doesn't mean they want another movie "about a love affair and a sinking ship." Most of the mainframe computer users that IBM surveyed in the 1970s couldn't imagine why they would ever want a small computer on their desks. And Bob Metcalfe, the founder of 3Com, wrote in MIT's *Technology Review* that the financial success of 3Com's Etherlink, a high-speed way to connect computers, happened because he ignored reports from salespeople that customers were clamoring for a slight improvement in a popular product.

A CONSTANT, CONSTRUCTIVE CONTEST

My aim here is not to convince your company to discard every routine it uses and devote all efforts to inventing new ways of thinking and acting. On the contrary, doing routine work with proven methods is the right thing to do most of the time. It is wise to manage most organizations as if the future will be a perfect imitation of the past: Hospitals want surgical residents to perform operations exactly as their experienced mentors do. Airlines want new pilots to fly 747s just like the experienced pilots who came before them did. McDonald's wants each new trainee to make Big Macs just the way they have always been made. Tried and true wins out over new and improved most of the time.

But if part of your mission is to explore new possibilities, then your goal must be to build a culture that supports constant mindfulness and experimentation. It isn't sufficient to generate new ideas now and then. Your company—or more likely a part of it—needs to be a place that generates and tests many disparate ideas. It should be an arena, a constant and constructive contest, where the best ideas win.

Will these ideas for innovation ever look anything but weird to the majority of managers? Probably not, because most companies will always devote more time, people, and money to exploiting old ideas than to exploring new ones. Exposure effects being what they are, managing for creativity will always require a conscious effort. However, if you read "Dilbert" or have friends in the arts, you know that exposure effects cut both ways. To people who spend their days doing creative work, the way that most companies are managed seems just as weird.

20

The Ambidextrous Organization
Managing Evolutionary and Revolutionary Change

MICHAEL L. TUSHMAN
CHARLES O'REILLY III

All managers face problems in overcoming inertia and implementing innovation and change. But why is this problem such an enduring one? Organizations are filled with sensible people and usually led by smart managers. Why is anything but incremental change often so difficult for the most successful organizations? And why are the patterns of success and failure so prevalent across industries and over time? To remain successful over long periods, managers and organizations must be ambidextrous—able to implement both incremental and revolutionary change.

PATTERNS IN ORGANIZATION EVOLUTION

Across industries there is a pattern in which success often precedes failure. But industry-level studies aren't very helpful for illustrating what actually went wrong. Why are managers sometimes ineffective in making the transition from strength to strength? To understand this we need to look inside firms and understand the forces impinging on management as they wrestle with managing innovation and change. To do this, let's examine the history of two firms, RCA semiconductors and Seiko watches, as they dealt with the syndrome of success followed by failure.

The stark reality of the challenge of discontinuous change can be seen in Table 20.1. This is a listing of the leading semiconductor firms over a forty-year period. In the mid-1950s, vacuum tubes represented roughly a $700 million market. At this time, the leading firms in the then state-of-the-art technology of vacuum tubes included great technology companies such as RCA, Sylvania, Raytheon, and Westinghouse. Yet between 1955 and 1995, there was almost a complete turnover in industry leadership. With the advent of the transistor, a major technological discontinuity, we see the beginnings of a remarkable shakeout. By 1965, new firms such as Motorola and Texas Instruments had become important players while Sylvania and RCA had begun to fade. Over the next 20 years still other upstart companies like Intel, Toshiba, and Hitachi became the new leaders while Sylvania and RCA exited the product class.

Why should this pattern emerge? Is it that managers and technologists in 1955 in firms like Westinghouse, RCA, and Sylvania didn't understand the technology? This seems implausible. In fact, many vacuum tube producers did enter the transistor market, suggesting that they not only understood the technology, but saw it as important. RCA was initially successful at making the transition. While from the outside it appeared that they had committed themselves to transistors, the inside picture was very different.

Copyright © 1996 by The Regents of the University of California. Reprinted from the *California Management Review,* Vol. 38, No. 4. By permission of The Regents.

Table 20.1. Semiconductor Industry, 1955–95

	1955 (Vacuum Tubes)	1955 (Transistors)	1965 (Semiconductors)	1975 (Integrated Circuits)	1982 (VLSI)	1995 (Submicron)
1.	RCA	Hughes	TI	TI	Motorola	Intel
2.	Sylvania	Transitron	Fairchild	Fairchild	TI	NEC
3.	General Electric	Philco	Motorola	National	NEC	Toshiba
4.	Raytheon	Sylvania	GI	Intel	Hitachi	Hitachi
5.	Westinghouse	TI	GE	Motorola	National	Motorola
6.	Amperex	GE	RCA	Rockwell	Toshiba	Samsung
7.	National Video	RCA	Sprague	GI	Intel	TI
8.	Rawland	Westinghouse	Philco	RCA	Philips	Fujitsu
9.	Eimac	Motorola	Transitron	Philips	Fujitsu	Mitsubishi
10.	Lansdale	Clevite	Raytheon	AMD	Fairchild	Philips

Source: Adapted from R. Foster, *Innovation: The Attacker's Advantage* (New York, NY: Summit Books, 1986).

Within RCA, there were bitter disputes about whether the company should enter the transistor business and cannibalize their profitable tube business. On one side, there were reasonable arguments that the transistor business was new and the profits uncertain. Others, without knowing whether transistors would be successful, felt that it was too risky not to pursue the new technology. But even if RCA were to enter the solid-state business, there were thorny issues about how to organize it within the company. How could they manage both technologies? Should the solid-state division report to the head of the electronics group, a person steeped in vacuum tube expertise?

With its great wealth of marketing, financial, and technological resources, RCA decided to enter the business. Historically, it is common for successful firms to experiment with new technologies.[1] Xerox, for example, developed user-interface and software technologies, yet left it to Apple and Microsoft to implement them. Western Union developed the technology for telephony and allowed American Bell (AT&T) to capture the benefits. Almost all relatively wealthy firms can afford to explore new technologies. Like many firms before them, RCA management recognized the problems of trying to play two different technological games but were ultimately unable to resolve them. In the absence of a clear strategy and the cultural differences required to compete in both markets, RCA failed.

In his study of this industry, Richard Foster (then a Director at McKinsey & Company) notes, "Of the 10 leaders in vacuum tubes in 1955 only two were left in 1975. There were three variants of error in these case histories. First is the decision not to invest in the new technology. The second is to invest but picking the wrong technology. The third variant is cultural. Companies failed because of their inability to play two games at once: To be both effective defenders of what quickly became old technologies and effective attackers with new technologies."[2] Senior managers in these firms fell victim to their previous success and their inability to play two games simultaneously. New firms, like Intel and Motorola, were not saddled with this internal conflict and inertia. As they grew, they were able to re-create themselves, while other firms remained trapped.

In contrast to RCA, consider Hattori-Seiko's watch business. While Seiko was the dominant Japanese watch producer in the 1960s, they were a small player in global markets (see Table 20.2). Bolstered by an aspiration to be a global leader in the watch business, and informed by internal experimentation between alternative oscillation technologies (quartz, mechanical, and turning fork), Seiko's senior management team made a bold bet. In the mid-1960s, Seiko transformed itself from being merely a mechanical watch firm into being both a quartz and mechanical watch company. This move into low-cost, high-quality watches triggered wholesale change within Seiko and, in turn, within the world-wide watch industry. As transistors replaced vacuum tubes (to RCA's chagrin), quartz movement watches replaced mechanical watch-

Table 20.2. Employment in the Swiss Watch Industry, 1955–85

Year	No. of Firms	No. of Employees
1955	2300	70,000
1965	1900	84,000
1970	1600	89,000
1975	1200	63,000
1980	900	47,000
1985	600	32,000

es. Even though the Swiss had invented both the quartz and tuning fork movements, at this juncture in history they moved to reinvest in mechanical movements. As Seiko and other Japanese firms prospered, the Swiss watch industry drastically suffered. By 1980, SSIH, the largest Swiss watch firm, was less than half the size of Seiko. Eventually, SSIH and Asuag, the two largest Swiss firms, went bankrupt. It would not be until after these firms were taken over by the Swiss banks and transformed by Nicholas Hayek that the Swiss would move to recapture the watch market.

The real test of leadership, then, is to be able to compete successfully by both increasing the alignment or fit among strategy, structure, culture, and processes, while simultaneously preparing for the inevitable revolutions required by discontinuous environmental change. This requires organizational and management skills to compete in a mature market (where cost, efficiency, and incremental innovation are key) *and* to develop new products and services (where radical innovation, speed, and flexibility are critical). A focus on either one of these skill sets is conceptually easy. Unfortunately, focusing on only one guarantees short-term success but long-term failure. Managers need to be able to do both at the same time, that is, they need to be ambidextrous. Juggling provides a metaphor. A juggler who is very good at manipulating a single ball is not interesting. It is only when the juggler can handle multiple balls at one time that his or her skill is respected.

These short examples are only two illustrations of the pattern by which organizations evolve: periods of incremental change punctuated by discontinuous or revolutionary change. Long-term success is marked by increasing alignment among strategy, structure, people, and culture through incremental or evolutionary change punctuated by discontinuous or revolutionary change that requires the simultaneous shift in strategy, structure, people, and culture. These discontinuous changes are almost always driven either by organizational performance problems or by major shifts in the organization's environment, such as technological or competitive shifts. Where those less successful firms (e.g., SSIH, RCA) react to environmental jolts, those more successful firms proactively initiate innovations that reshape their market (e.g., Seiko).[3]

WHAT'S HAPPENING? UNDERSTANDING PATTERNS OF ORGANIZATIONAL EVOLUTION

These patterns in organization evolution are not unique. Almost all successful organizations evolve through relatively long periods of incremental change punctuated by environmental shifts and revolutionary change. These discontinuities may be driven by technology, competitors, regulatory events, or significant changes in economic and political conditions. For example, deregulation in the financial services and airline industries led to waves of mergers and failures as firms scrambled to reorient themselves to the new competitive environment. Major political changes in Eastern Europe and South Africa have had a similar impact. The combination of the European Union and the emergence of global competition in the automobile and electronics industries has shifted the basis of competition in these markets. Technological change in microprocessors has altered the face of the computer industry.

The sobering fact is that the cliché about the increasing pace of change seems to be true. Sooner or later, discontinuities upset the congruence that has been a part of the organization's success. Unless their competitive environment remains stable—an increasingly unlikely condition in today's world—firms must confront revolutionary change. The underlying cause of this pattern can be found in an unlikely place: evolutionary biology.

Innovation Patterns Over Time

For many years, biological evolutionary theory proposed that the process of adaptation occurred gradually over long time periods. The process was assumed to be one of variation, selection, and retention. Variations occurred naturally within species across generations. Those variations that were most adapted to the environment would, over time, enable a species to survive and reproduce. This form would be selected in that it endured while less adaptable forms reproduced less productively and would diminish over time. For instance, if the world became colder and snowier, animals who were whiter and had heavier coats would be advantaged and more likely to survive. As climatic changes affected vegetation, those species with longer necks or stronger beaks might do better. In this way, variation led to adaptation and fitness, which was subsequently retained across generations. In this early view, the environment changed gradually and species adapted slowly to these changes. There is ample evidence that this view has validity.

But this perspective missed a crucial question: What happened if the environment was characterized, not by gradual change, but periodic discontinuities? What about rapid changes in temperature, or dramatic shifts in the availability of food? Under these conditions, a reliance on gradual change was a one-way ticket to extinction. Instead of slow change, discontinuities required a different version of Darwinian theory—that of punctuated equilibria in which long periods of gradual change were interrupted periodically by massive discontinuities. What then? Under these conditions, survival or selection goes to those species with the characteristics needed to exploit the new environment. Evolution progresses through long periods of incremental change punctuated by brief periods of revolutionary or discontinuous change.

So it seems to be with organizations. An entire subfield of research on organizations has demonstrated many similarities between populations of insects and animals and populations of organizations. This field, known as "organizational ecology," has successfully applied models of population ecology to the study of sets of organizations in areas as diverse as wineries, newspapers, automobiles, biotech companies, and restaurants.[4] The results confirm that populations of organizations are subject to ecological pressures in which they evolve through periods of incremental adaptation punctuated by discontinuities. Variations in organizational strategy and form are more or less suitable for different environmental conditions. Those organizations and managers who are most able to adapt

to a given market or competitive environment will prosper. Over time, the fittest survive—until there is a major discontinuity. At that point, managers of firms are faced with the challenge of reconstituting their organizations to adjust to the new environment. Managers who try to adapt to discontinuities through incremental adjustment are unlikely to succeed. The processes of variation, selection, and retention that winnow the fittest of animal populations seem to apply to organizations as well.

To understand how this dynamic affects organizations, we need to consider two fundamental ideas; how organizations grow and evolve, and how discontinuities affect this process. Armed with this understanding, we can then show how managers can cope with evolutionary and revolutionary change.

Organizational Growth and Evolution

There is a pattern that describes organizational growth. All organizations evolve following the familiar S-curve shown in Figure 20.1. For instance, consider the history of Apple Computer and how it grew. In its inception, Apple was not so much an organization as a small group of people trying to design, produce, and sell a new product, the personal computer. With success, came the beginnings of a formal organization, assigned roles and responsibilities, some rudimentary systems for accounting and payroll, and a culture based on the shared expectations among employees about innovation, commitment, and speed. Success at this stage was seen in terms of congruence among the strategy, structure, people, and culture. Those who fit the Apple values and subscribed to the cultural norms stayed. Those who found the Jobs and Wozniak vision too cultish left. This early structure was aligned with the strategy and the critical tasks needed to implement it. Success flowed not only from having a new product with desirable features, but also from the ability of the organization to design, manufacture, market, and distribute the new PC. The systems in place tracked those outcomes and processes that were important for the implementation of a single product strategy. Congruence among the elements of the organization is a key to high performance across industries.

As the firm continued its successful growth, several inexorable changes occurred. First, it got larger. As this occurred, more structure and systems were added. Although this trend toward professionalization

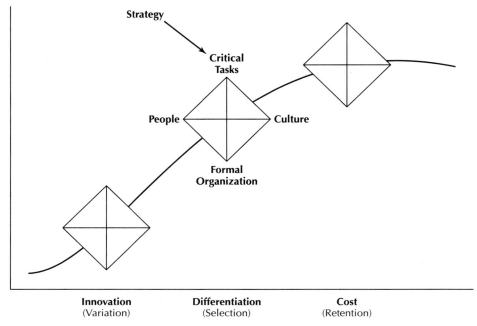

Figure 20.1. Punctuated equilibrium and organizational evolution. Over time, the fit among business unit strategy, structure, skills, and culture evolve to reflect changing markets and technology. When these changes occur, managers need to realign their units to reflect their new strategic challenges.

was resisted by Jobs (who referred to professional managers as "bozos"), the new structures and procedures were required for efficiency and control. Without them, chaos would have reigned. As Apple got older, new norms were developed about what was important and acceptable and what would not be tolerated. The culture changed to reflect the new challenges. Success at Apple and at other firms is based on learning what works and what doesn't.

Inevitably, even Apple's strategy had to change. What used to be a single-product firm (selling the Apple PC and then its successor, the Apple II) now sold a broader range of products in increasingly competitive markets. Instead of a focused strategy, the emphasis shifted to a market-wide emphasis. Not only was Apple selling to personal computer users, but also to the educational and industrial markets. This strategic shift required further adjustment to the structure, people, culture, and critical tasks. What worked in a smaller, more focused firm was no longer adequate for the larger, more differentiated Apple. Success at this phase of evolution required management's ability to realign the

organization to insure congruence with the strategy. The well-publicized ouster of Steve Jobs by Apple's board of directors reflected the board's judgment that John Sculley had the skills necessary to lead a larger, more diversified company. Jobs's approach was fine for a smaller, more focused firm but inappropriate for the challenges Apple faced in the mid-1980s.

Over an even longer period of success, there are inevitably more changes—sometimes driven by technology, sometimes by competition, customers, or regulation, sometimes by new strategies and ways of competing. As the product class matures, the basis of competition shifts. While in the early stages of a product class, competition is based on product variation, in the later stages competition shifts to features, efficiency, and cost. In the evolution of Apple, this can be seen as the IBM PC and the clones emerged. The Windows operating system loosened the grip Apple had maintained on the easy-to-use graphical interface and triggered a battle between three incompatible operating systems—the Mac, IBM's OS/2, and Microsoft Windows. Once Windows became the industry standard in operating systems, the basis of competition shifted to cost, quality and efficiency. Faced with these realities, Apple managers once again had to re-balance the congruence among strategy, structure, people, and culture. Success comes from being able to out do the competition in this new environment. So the board of directors replaced Sculley as CEO in 1994 with Michael Spindler, who was seen as having the operational skills needed to run the company in a mature market. Spindler's task was to emphasize the efficiencies and lower margins required in today's markets and reshape Apple to compete in this new market. With Apple's performance stagnant, its board chose a turnaround expert, Gil Amelio, to finish what Spindler could not do.

Notice how Apple evolved over a 20-year period. Incremental or evolutionary change was punctuated by discontinuous or revolutionary change as the firm moved through the three stages of growth in the product class; innovation, differentiation, and maturity. Each of these stages required different competencies, strategies, structures, cultures, and leadership skills. These changes are what drives performance. But while absolutely necessary for short-term success, incremental change is not sufficient for long-term success. It is not by chance that Steve Jobs was successful at Apple until the market became more differentiated and demanded the skills of John Sculley. Nor is it surprising that, as the industry consolidated and competition emphasized costs, operations-oriented managers such as Michael Spindler and, in turn, Gil Amelio were selected to reorient Apple.

To succeed over the long haul, firms have to periodically reorient themselves by adopting new strategies and structures that are necessary to accommodate changing environmental conditions. These shifts often occur through discontinuous changes—simultaneous shifts in strategy, structures, skills, and culture. If an environment is stable and changes only gradually, as is the case in industries such as cement, it is possible for an organization to evolve slowly through continuous incremental change. But, many managers have learned (to their stockholders' chagrin) that slow evolutionary change in a fast-changing world is, as it was for the dinosaurs, a path to the boneyard.

Technology Cycles

Although organizational growth by itself can lead to a periodic need for discontinuous change, there is another more fundamental process occurring that results in punctuated change. This is a pervasive phenomenon that occurs across industries and is not widely appreciated by managers. Yet it is critical to understanding when and why revolutionary change is necessary: This is the dynamic of product, service, and process innovation, dominant designs, and substitution events which together make up technology cycles. Figure 20.2 shows the general outline of this process.[5]

In any product or service class (e.g., microprocessors, automobiles, baby diapers, cash management accounts) there is a common pattern of competition that describes the development of the class over time. As shown in Figure 20.2, technology cycles begin with a proliferation of innovation in products or services as the new product or service gains acceptance. Think, for example, of the introduction of VCRs. Initially, only a few customers bought them. Over time, as demand increased, there was increasing competition between Beta and VHS. At some point, a design emerged that became the standard preferred by customers (i.e., VHS). Once this occurred, the basis of competition shifted to price and features, not basic product or service design. The emergence of this *dominant design* transforms competition in the product class.[6] Once it is clear that a dominant design has emerged, the basis of competition shifts to process innovation, driving down costs, and adding features. Instead of competing through product or service innovation, successful strategies now emphasize compatibility with the standard and productivity improvement. This competition continues until there is a major new product, service, or process substitution event and the technology cycle kicks off again as the basis of competition shifts back again to product or service variation (e.g., CDs replacing audiotapes). As technology cycles evolve, bases of competition shift within the market. As organizations change their strategies, they must also realign their organizations to accomplish the new strategic objectives. This usually requires a revolutionary change.

A short illustration from the development of the automobile will help show how dramatic these changes can be for organizations. At the turn of the century, bicycles and horse-driven carriages were threatened by the "horseless carriage," soon to be called the automobile. Early in this new product class there was substantial competition among alternative technologies. For instance, there were several competing alternative energy sources—steam, battery, and internal combustion engines. There were also different

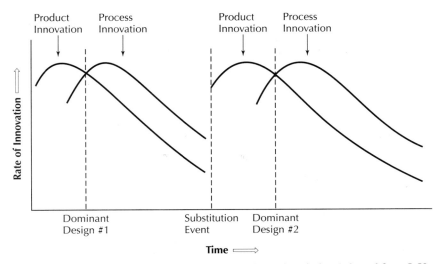

Figure 20.2. Two invisible forces: technology cycles and evolution (adapted from J. Ut-terback, *Mastering the Dynamics of Innovation,* Boston, MA: Harvard Business School Press, 1994).

steering mechanisms and arrangements for passenger compartments. In a fairly short period of time, however, there emerged a consensus that certain features were to be standard—that is, a dominant design emerged. This consisted of an internal combustion engine, steering wheel on the left (in the U.S.), brake pedal on the right, and clutch on the left (this dominant design was epitomized in the Ford Model T). Once this standard emerged, the basis of competition shifted from variations in what an automobile looked like and how it was powered to features and cost. The new competitive arena emphasized lower prices and differentiated market segments, not product variation. The imperative for managers was to change their strategies and organizations to compete in this market. Those that were unable to manage this transition failed. Similar patterns can be seen in almost all product classes (e.g., computers, telephones, fast foods, retail stores).

With a little imagination, it is easy to feel what the managerial challenges are in this environment. Holding aside the pressures of growth and success, managers must continually readjust their strategies and realign their organizations to reflect the underlying dynamics of technological change in their markets. These changes are not driven by fad or fashion but reflect the imperatives of fundamental change in the technology. This dynamic is a powerful cause of punctuated equi-

libria and can demand revolutionary rather than incremental change. This pattern occurs across industries as diverse as computers and cement, the only issue is the frequency with which these cycles repeat themselves. Faced with a discontinuity, the option of incremental change is not likely to be viable. The danger is that, facing a discontinuous change, firms that have been successful may suffer from life-threatening inertia—inertia that results from the very congruence that made the firm successful in the first place.

THE SUCCESS SYNDROME: CONGRUENCE AS A MANAGERIAL TRAP

Managers, as architects of their organizations, are responsible for designing their units in ways that best fit their strategic challenges. Internal congruence among strategy, structure, culture, and people drives short-term performance.[7] Between 1915 and 1960, General Radio had a strategy of high-quality, high-priced electronic equipment with a loose functional structure, strong internal promotion practices, and engineering dominance in decision making. All these things worked together to provide a highly congruent system and, in turn, a highly successful organization. However, the strategy and organizational congruence that made General Radio a success for 50 years became, in the face of major competitive and technological change, a recipe for failure in the 1960s. It was only after a revolutionary change that included a new strategy and simultaneous shifts in structure, people, and culture that the new company, renamed GenRad, was able to compete again against the likes of Hewlett-Packard and Textronix.[8]

Successful companies learn what works well and incorporate this into their operations. This is what organizational learning is about; using feedback from the market to continually refine the organization to get better and better at accomplishing its mission. A lack of congruence (or internal inconsistency in strategy, structure, culture, and people) is usually associated with a firm's current performance problems. Further, since the fit between strategy, structure, people, and processes is never perfect, achieving congruence is an ongoing process requiring continuous improvement and incremental change. With evolutionary change, managers are able to incrementally alter their organizations. Given that these changes are comparatively small, the incongruence injected by the change is controllable. The process of making incremental changes is well known and the uncertainty created for people affected by such changes is within tolerable limits. The overall system adapts, but it is not transformed.

When done effectively, evolutionary change of this sort is a crucial part of short-term success. But there is a dark side to this success. As we described with Apple, success resulted in the company becoming larger and older. Older, larger firms develop structural and cultural inertia—the organizational equivalent of high cholesterol. Figure 20.3 shows the paradox of success. As companies grow, they develop structures and systems to handle the increased complexity of the

work. These structures and systems are interlinked so that proposed changes become more difficult, more costly, and require more time to implement, especially if they are more than small, incremental modifications. This results in *structural inertia*—a resistance to change rooted in the size, complexity, and interdependence in the organization's structures, systems, procedures, and processes.

Quite different and significantly more pervasive than structural inertia is the *cultural inertia* that comes from age and success. As organizations get older, part of their learning is embedded in the shared expectations about how things are to be done. These are sometimes seen in the informal norms, values, social networks and in myths, stories, and heroes that have evolved over time. The more successful an organization has been, the more institutionalized or ingrained these norms, values, and lessons become. The more institutionalized these norms, values, and stories are, the greater the cultural inertia—the greater the organizational complacency and arrogance. In relatively stable environments, the firm's culture is a critical component of its success. Culture is an effective way of controlling and coordinating people without elaborate and rigid formal control systems. Yet, when confronted with discontinuous change, the very culture that fostered success can quickly become a significant barrier to change. When Lou Gerstner took over as CEO at IBM, he recognized that simply crafting a new strategy was not the solution to IBM's predicament. In his view, "Fixing the culture is the most critical—and the most difficult—part of a corporate transformation."[9] Cultural inertia, because it is so ephemeral and difficult to attack directly, is a key reason managers often fail to successfully introduce revolutionary change—even when they know that it is needed.

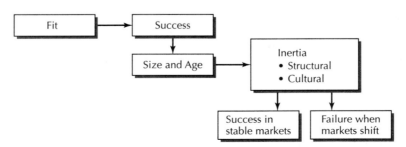

Figure 20.3. The success syndrome.

THE PARADOX OF CULTURE

The paradox of culture in helping or hindering companies as they compete can be seen in many ways. Consider, for example, the list of companies shown in Table 20.3. These are firms about which there have recently been stories in the business press and in which the culture of the firm was seen as a part of the organization's success or failure. What is notable about this list is its diversity. The importance of organizational culture transcends country, industry, and firm size. Whether they are electronics giant Samsung, a Hong Kong bank, U.S. conglomerate Allied Signal, a high-tech firm such as Applied Materials or a low-tech company such as Nordstrom, or car manufacturers Nissan, Rover, or General Motors, culture appears to be a critical factor in the performance of the company. The language used in describing the importance of culture is often similar. Yukata Kume, President of Nissan, observed: "The most challenging task I faced when I became president five years ago was to reform the corporate culture . . . I decided that the major reason for our suffering or business predicament lay within Nissan itself."[10] Jack Welch at GE commented on the future demands on organizations: "In the nineties the heroes, the winners, will be entire companies that have developed cultures that instead of fearing the pace of change, relish it."[11]

While news articles about successes and failures are not proof of anything, they offer an interesting window on the concerns of practicing managers and savvy journalists. Whether the issue is can Nike successfully export its "Just do it" culture to help drive global growth, or can Nokia, a Finnish maker of mobile phones, shed its stodgy culture in time to compete in the fast-moving telecommunications market, the managerial challenges are similar: How can managers diagnose and actively shape organizational cultures to both execute today's strategies and create the capabilities to innovate for tomorrow's competitive demands? To help focus and frame the crucial issue of managing culture, let's reflect on a few examples in which organizational culture helped firms succeed or was a significant part of their problem in adapting to new circumstances.

Here's the Good News

First, consider the remarkable transformation of British Airways. In 1981, British Airways lost almost $1 billion. Their customers often referred to the airline's initials "BA" as standing for "Bloody Awful." Ask any frequent flyer for his or her experiences on

Table 20.3. Firms Recently Mentioned in the Business Press: Culture as a Factor in Success or Difficulty

Hewlett-Packard	British Airways	Federal Express
Oki Electric	Kodak	Sears
Johnson & Johnson	Allied Signal	Deutsche Bank
General Electric	Home Depot	Pepsico
Silicon Graphics	McKinsey	Philips
Motorola	Royal Dutch/Shell	Bausch & Lomb
Levi Strauss	Southwest Airlines	Applied Materials
Microsoft	PPG	General Motors
Samsung	Nike	Wal-Mart
Siemens	Saturn	Boeing
Nordstrom	IBM	Nissan
Procter & Gamble	Tenneco	Rover
Coca Cola	Broken Hill Proprietary	Ford
Lucky-Goldstar	Goldman, Sachs	NUMMI
SBC Warburg	Westinghouse	United Airlines
Apple	Bear Stearns	British Petroleum
Swiss Bank Corp	Rubbermaid	Unilever
Nokia	Matsushita	Salomon
Intel	Chrysler	Rubbermaid
Aetna	Medtronics	Kao

BA during this period and horror stories will emerge. Even the employees were embarrassed. One employee acknowledged that "I remember going to parties in the late 1970s, and if you wanted to have a civilized conversation, you didn't actually say that you worked for British Airways, because it got you talking about people's last travel experience, which was usually an unpleasant one."[12] When the announcement was made by the British government that the firm was to be privatized, the *Financial Times* newspaper sniffed that it might be that some investors would buy the stock, but only because "every market has a few masochists."

A scant five years later, however, BA's profits were the highest in the industry, 94 percent of its employees bought stock in 1987 when the firm went public, and passengers were making statements like the following: "I can't tell you how my memory of British Airways as a company and the experience I had 10 years ago contrasts with today. The improvement in service is truly remarkable." What accounts for this turnaround? The answer is largely to be found in the cultural revolution engineered by top management, Lord King, and Sir Colin Marshall.

After deciding that they were in the service business rather than the transportation business, British Airways put virtually it's entire 37,000 person work force through a two-day culture change program entitled "Putting People First." Almost all of the 1,400 managers went through a five-day version entitled "Managing People First" (MPF). On the surface this program is not conceptually unique. What separates MPF from most management training sessions is its magnitude, the consistency with which it was applied, and the support of top management. Colin Marshall, the Chief Executive Officer, has called it the "single most important program now in operation" at BA and has addressed almost all of the 64 MPF classes.[13]

The emphasis on the culture change effort at BA was on instilling the new culture, establishing an evaluation scheme that measured not only what managers did but how they did it, and a compensation program with bonuses up to 20 percent based on how managers behave. Managers at BA appreciate that any airline can load passengers on a plane and fly them across the Atlantic. BA understands that they are in the service business and any competitive advantage has to be in the service they offer customers. As Bob Nelson, head of the program noted, "The issue with customer service is

that you can train monkeys to smile and make eye-contact, but what the hell do you do when you get a nonstandard requirement?"[14]

With essentially the same workforce, flying largely the same routes, and using the same technology, British Airways has become one of the world's leading airlines. Its competitive advantage is not in strategy or technology but in a culture shared throughout the organization that provides a level of service that competitors have found difficult to imitate. The lesson that we need to explore is how senior managers were successful in managing the culture to provide competitive advantage. What was it that they did that their competitors have been unable to do?

Similar success stories abound. Consider a phenomenon in the retail clothing industry, Nordstrom. While firms like Federated, Macy's, and Carter-Hawley-Hale have wrestled with bankruptcy, Nordstrom has grown from 36 stores and 9,000 employees in 1983 to 76 stores and over 35,000 employees by 1995, with average sales per square foot double the industry average. What accounts for Nordstrom's competitive advantage? A close reading of the strategy literature will quickly suggest that it is not the usual factors such as barriers to entry, power over suppliers and customers, or lack of industry rivalry. The retail industry is quite competitive and buyers and suppliers move easily from one firm to another. It isn't location, merchandise, appearance of the stores, or even the piano in the lobby. Each of these is easily imitable. Rather, as anyone who has shopped Nordstrom knows, it is the remarkable service that Nordstrom provides that differentiates it from its competitors. To deliver this service, Nordstrom relies not on the extensive formal controls manifest in policies, procedures, and close supervision, but rather on its culture, which is characterized by a set of norms and values that provide for a *social* control system. This social control system is used to coordinate activities in the face of the need for change and allows Nordstrom to meet the nonstandard requirements that are the true test of service.

Here's the Bad News

Until now we have told happy stories, ones in which managers have successfully used organizational culture to provide competitive advantage. But there are equally unhappy stories to tell as well; ones in which the culture of the firm is sometimes linked to failure.

And, as suggested earlier, the paradox is often that it is the culture associated with the earlier success of the firm that becomes a part of its downfall. Think briefly about two icons of American business success and the difficulties they currently face: IBM and Sears. (While we use IBM and Sears, the phenomenon is worldwide.)

Between 1990 and 1993, IBM lost a total of $14 billion, with an $8.1 billion loss in 1993 alone. How could this happen? Certainly the computer business is a complex one. IBM was and is a very large firm, which complicates the decision-making process. Nevertheless, numerous presumably smart people were employed specifically to anticipate changes and insure that the firm was prepared to meet them. How, then, can we account for this failure, a failure that has cost almost 200,000 people their jobs and shareholders a loss of billions of dollars? It would be wrong to underestimate the complex difficulties in managing a firm of IBM's size. Certainly the answer must include aspects of strategy, organizational design, technology, and people.

However, perhaps the most important part of the answer to this question, and certainly a part of any solution, is in the culture of IBM; a culture characterized by an inward focus, extensive procedures for resolving issues through consensus and "push back," an arrogance bred by previous success, and a sense of entitlement that guaranteed jobs without a reciprocal quid pro quo by some employees. This culture—masquerading under the old IBM basic beliefs in excellence, customer satisfaction, and respect for the individual—was manifest in norms that led to a preoccupation with internal procedures rather than understanding the reality of the changing market. In his letter to the shareholders in the 1993 Annual Report, CEO Lou Gerstner states, "We have been too bureaucratic and too preoccupied with our own view of the world." He sees as one of his toughest and most critical tasks to change this entrenched and patriarchical culture into one characterized by a sense of urgency. Without this shift, he believes IBM will continue to squander its talent and technology.

While occurring in a very different industrial context, a similar drama is playing out at Sears, the great American retailer. Again, the picture is a complicated one and it would be wrong to oversimplify it. The broad outlines of the problem are, however, easily vis-

ible. Until 1991, Sears was the largest retailer in the U.S. with over 800 stores and 500,000 employees, including over 6,000 at headquarters in the Sears Tower in Chicago. For decades it was the family department store for America, a place where one could buy everything from clothes to tools to kitchen appliances. However, by the mid-1980s, trouble had begun to surface. Market share had fallen 15 percent from its high in the 70s, the stock price had dropped by 40 percent since Edward Brennan had become CEO in 1985, and chronic high costs hindered Sears from matching the prices of competitors such as Wal-Mart, K-Mart, Circuit City, the Home Depot, and other low-cost specialty stores.[15]

Under Brennan's leadership, Sears made a number of strategic changes in attempts to halt the slide. Yet the execution of the strategy was dismal. Observers and analysts attributed the failure to Brennan's inability to revamp the old Sears culture that, as one respected analyst noted, was a "culture . . . rooted in a long tradition of dominating the retailing industry. . . . But this success bred in Sears executives an arrogance and an internal focus that was almost xenophobic." Another observed that "the main problem with Sears is that its managers and executives are 'Sears-ized'—so indoctrinated in the lore of past glories and so entrenched in an overwhelming bureaucracy that they cannot change easily."[16] The old Sears culture, like the old IBM culture, was a product of their success: proud, inward-looking, and resistant to change.

The lesson is a simple one: organizational culture is a key to both short-term success *and,* unless managed correctly, long-term failure. Culture can provide competitive advantage, but as we have seen, it can also create obstacles to the innovation and change necessary to be successful. In the face of significant changes in technology, regulation, or competition, great managers understand this dynamic and effectively manage *both* the short-term demands for increasing congruence and bolstering today's culture *and* the periodic need to transform their organization and re-create their unit's culture. These organizational transformations involve fundamental shifts in the firm's structure and systems as well as in its culture and competencies. Where change in structure and systems is relatively simple, change in culture is not. The issue of actively managing organization cultures that can handle both incremental and discontinuous change is perhaps the most demanding aspect in the management of strategic innovation and change.

AMBIDEXTROUS ORGANIZATIONS: MASTERING EVOLUTIONARY AND REVOLUTIONARY CHANGE

The dilemma confronting managers and organizations is clear. In the short run they must constantly increase the fit or alignment of strategy, structure, and culture. This is the world of evolutionary change. But this is not enough for sustained success. In the long run, managers may be required to destroy the very alignment that has made their organizations successful. For managers, this means operating part of the time in a world characterized by periods of relatively stability and incremental innovation, and part of the time in a world characterized by revolutionary change. These contrasting managerial demands require that managers periodically destroy what has been created in order to reconstruct a new organization better suited for the next wave of competition or technology.[17]

Ambidextrous organizations are needed if the success paradox is to be overcome. The ability to simultaneously pursue both incremental and discontinuous innovation and change results from hosting multiple contradictory structures, processes, and cultures within the same firm. There are good examples of companies and managers who have succeeded in balancing these tensions. To illustrate more concretely how firms can do this, consider three successful ambidextrous organizations, Hewlett-Packard, Johnson & Johnson, and ABB (Asea Brown Boveri). Each of these has been able to compete in mature market segments through incremental innovation and in emerging markets and technologies through discontinuous innovation. Each has been successful at winning by engaging in both evolutionary and revolutionary change.

At one level they are very different companies. HP competes in markets like instruments, computers, and networks. J&J is in consumer products, pharmaceuticals, and professional medical products ranging from sutures to endoscopic surgical equipment. ABB sells power plants, electrical transmission equipment, transportation systems, and environmental controls. Yet each of them has been able to be periodically renew itself and to produce streams of innovation. HP has gone from an instrument company to a minicomputer firm to a personal computer and network company. J&J has moved from consumer products to pharmaceuticals. ABB transformed itself from a slow heavy engineering company based primarily in Sweden and Switzerland to an aggressive global competitor with major investments in Eastern Europe and the Far East. In spite of their differences, each has been ambidextrous in similar ways.

Organizational Architectures

Although the combined size of these three companies represents over 350,000 employees, each has found a common way to remain small by emphasizing autonomous groups. For instance, J&J has over 165 separate operating companies that scramble relentlessly for new products and markets. ABB relies on over 5,000 profit centers with an average of 50 people in each. These centers operate like small businesses. HP has over 50 separate divisions and a policy of splitting divisions whenever a unit gets larger than a thousand or so people. The logic in these organizations is to keep units small and autonomous so that employees feel a sense of ownership and are responsible for their own results. This encourages a culture of autonomy and risk taking that could not exist in a large, centralized organization. In the words of Ralph Larsen, CEO of J&J, this approach "provides a sense of ownership and responsibility for a business you simply cannot get any other way."[18]

But the reliance on small, autonomous units are not gained at the expense of firm size or speed in execution. These companies also retain the benefits of size, especially in marketing and manufacturing. ABB continually reevaluates where it locates its worldwide manufacturing sites. J&J uses its brand name and marketing might to leverage new products and technologies. HP uses its relationships with retailers developed from its printer business to market and distribute its new personal computer line. But these firms accomplish this without the top-heavy staffs found at other firms. Barnevik reduced ABB's hierarchy to four levels and a headquarters staff of 150 and purposely keeps the structure fluid. At J&J headquarters, there are roughly a thousand people, but no strategic planning is done by corporate. The role of the center is to set the vision and review the performance of the 165 operating companies. At HP, the former CEO, John Young, recognized in the early 1990s that the more centralized structure that HP had adopted in the 1980s to coordinate their mini-computer business had resulted in a suffocating bureaucracy that was no longer appropriate. He wiped it out, flattening the hierarchy and dramatically reducing the role of the center.

In these companies, size is used to leverage economies of scale and scope, not to become a checker and controller that slows the organization down. The focus is on keeping decisions as close to the customer or the technology as possible. The role of headquarters is to facilitate operations and make them go faster and better. Staff have only the expertise that the field wants and needs. Reward systems are designed to be appropriate to the nature of the business unit and emphasize results and risk taking. Barnevik characterizes this as his 7–3 formula; better to make decisions quickly and be right seven out of ten times than waste time trying to find a perfect solution. At J&J this is expressed as a tolerance for certain types of failure; a tolerance that extends to congratulating managers who take informed risks, even if they fail. There is a delicate balance among size, autonomy, teamwork, and speed which these ambidextrous organizations are able to engineer. An important part of the solution is massive decentralization of decision making, but with consistency attained through individual accountability, information sharing, and strong financial control. But why doesn't this result in fragmentation and a loss of synergy? The answer is found in the use of social control.

Multiple Cultures

A second commonality across these firms is their reliance on strong social controls.[19] They are simultaneously tight and loose. They are tight in that the corporate culture in each is broadly shared and emphasizes norms critical for innovation such as openness, autonomy, initiative, and risk taking. The culture is loose in that the manner in which these common values are expressed varies according to the type of innovation required. At HP, managers value the openness and consensus needed to develop new technologies. Yet, when implementation is critical, managers recognize that this consensus can be fatal. One senior manager in charge of bringing out a new work station prominently posted a sign saying, "This is not a democracy." At J&J, the emphasis on autonomy allows managers to

routinely go against the wishes of senior management, sometimes with big successes and sometimes with failures. Yet, in the changing hospital supply sector of their business, managers recognized that the cherished J&J autonomy was stopping these companies from coordinating the service demanded by their hospital customers. So, in this part of J&J, a decision was made to take away some of the autonomy and centralize services. CEO Larsen refers to this as J&J companies having common standards but unique personalities.

A common overall culture is the glue that holds these companies together. The key in these firms is a reliance on a strong, widely shared corporate culture to promote integration across the company and to encourage identification and sharing of information and resources—something that would never occur without shared values. The culture also provides consistency and promotes trust and predictability. Whether it is the Credo at J&J, the HP Way, or ABB's Policy Bible, these norms and values provide the glue that keeps these organizations together. Yet, at the same time, individual units entertain widely varying subcultures appropriate to their particular businesses. For example, although the HP Way is visible in all HP units worldwide, there are distinct differences between the new video server unit and an old line instrument division. What constitutes risk taking at a mature division is different than the risk taking emphasized at a unit struggling with a brand new technology. At J&J, the Credo's emphasis on customers and employees can be seen as easily in the Philippines as in corporate headquarters in New Brunswick, New Jersey. But the operating culture in the Tylenol division is distinctly more conservative than the culture in a new medical products company.

This tight-loose aspect of the culture is crucial for ambidextrous organizations. It is supported by a common vision and by supportive leaders who both encourage the culture and know enough to allow appropriate variations to occur across business units. These companies promote both local autonomy and risk taking and ensure local responsibility and accountability through strong, consistent financial control systems. Managers aren't second-guessed by headquarters. Strategy flows from the bottom up. Thus, at HP the $7 billion printer business emerged not because of strategic foresight and planning at HP's headquarters, but rather due to the entrepreneurial flair of a small group of managers who had the freedom to pursue what was believed to be a small market. The same approach allows J&J and ABB to enter small niche markets or develop unproven technologies without the burdens of a centralized bureaucratic control system. On the other hand, in return for the autonomy they are granted, there are strong expectations of performance. Managers who don't deliver are replaced.

Ambidextrous Managers

Managing units that pursue widely different strategies and that have varied structures and cultures is a juggling act not all managers are comfortable with. At ABB, this role is described as "preaching and persuading." At HP, managers are low-key, modest, team players who have learned how to manage this tension over their long tenures with the company. At HP, they also lead by persuasion. "As CEO my job is to encourage people to work together, to experiment, to try things, but I can't order them to do it," says Lew Platt.[20] Larsen at J&J echoes this theme, emphasizing the need for lower level managers to come up with solutions and encouraging reasonable failures. Larsen claims that the role is one of a symphony conductor rather than a general.

One of the explanations for this special ability is the relatively long tenure managers have in these organizations and the continual reinforcement of the social control system. Often, these leaders are low-keyed but embody the culture and act as visible symbols of it. As a group the senior team continually reinforces the core values of autonomy, teamwork, initiative, accountability, and innovation. They ensure that the organization avoids becoming arrogant and remains willing to learn from its competitors. Observers of all three of these companies have commented on their modesty or humility in constantly striving to renew themselves. Rather than becoming complacent, these organizations are guided by leaders who venerate the past but are willing to change continuously to meet the future.

The bottom line is that ambidextrous organizations learn by the same mechanism that sometimes kills successful firms: variation, selection, and retention. They promote variation through strong efforts to decentralize, to eliminate bureaucracy, to encourage individual autonomy and accountability, and to experi-

ment and take risks. This promotes wide variations in products, technologies, and markets. It is what allows the managers of an old HP instrument division to push their technology and establish a new division dedicated to video servers. These firms also select "winners" in markets and technologies by staying close to their customers, by being quick to respond to market signals, and by having clear mechanisms to "kill" products and projects. This selection process allowed the development of computer printers at HP to move from a venture that was begun without formal approval to the point where it now accounts for almost 40% of HP's profits. Finally, technologies, products, markets, and even senior managers are retained by the market, not by a remote, inwardly focused central staff many hierarchical levels removed from real customers. The corporate vision provides the compass by which senior managers can make decisions about which of the many alternative businesses and technologies to invest in, but the market is the ultimate arbiter of the winners and losers. Just as success or failure in the marketplace is Darwinian, so too is the method by which ambidextrous organizations learn. They have figured out how to harness this power within their companies and organize and manage accordingly.

SUMMARY

Managers must be prepared to cannibalize their own business at times of industry transitions. While this is easy in concept, these organizational transitions are quite difficult in practice. Success brings with it inertia and dynamic conservatism. Four hundred years ago, Niccolo Machiavelli noted, "There is no more delicate matter to take in hand, nor more dangerous to conduct, nor more doubtful in its success, than to be a leader in the introduction of changes. For he who innovates will have for enemies all those who are well off under the old order of things, and only lukewarm supporters in those who might be better off under the new."[21]

While there are clear benefits to proactive change, only a small minority of farsighted firms initiate discontinuous change before a performance decline. Part of this stems from the risks of proactive change. One reason for RCA's failure to compete in the solid-state market or for SSIH's inability to compete in quartz movements came from the divisive internal disputes over the risks of sacrificing a certain revenue stream from vacuum tubes and mechanical watches for the uncertain profits from transistors and quartz watches. However, great managers are willing to take this step. Andy Grove of Intel puts it succinctly, "There is at least one point in the history of any company when you have to change dramatically to rise to the next performance level. Miss the moment and you start to decline."[22]

NOTES

1. A. Cooper and C. Smith, "How Established Firms Respond to Threatening Technologies," *Academy of Management Executive,* 16/2 (1992): 92–120.

2. R. Foster, *Innovation: The Attacker's Advantage* (New York, NY: Summit Books, 1986), p. 134.

3. B. Virany, M. Tushman, and E. Romanelli, "Executive Succession and Organization Outcomes in Turbulent Environments," *Organization Science,* 3 (1992): 72–92; E. Romanelli and M. Tushman, "Organization Transformation as Punctuated Equilibrium," *Academy of Management Journal,* 37 (1994): 1141–1166; M. Tushman and L. Rosenkopf, "On the Organizational Determinants of Technological Change: Towards a Sociology of Technological Evolution," in B. Staw and L. Cummings, eds., *Research in Organization Behavior,* Vol. 14 (Greenwich, CT: JAI Press, 1992); D. Miller, "The Architecture of Simplicity," *Academy of Management Review,* 18 (1993): 116–138; A. Meyer, G. Brooks, and J. Goes, "Environmental Jolts and Industry Revolutions," *Strategic Management Journal,* 6 (1990): 48–76.

4. There is an extensive literature studying organizations using models from population ecology. A number of excellent reviews of this approach are available in M. Hannan and G. Carroll, *Dynamics of Organizational Populations* (New York, NY: Oxford University Press, 1992); G. Carroll and M. Hannan, eds., *Organizations in Industry: Strategy, Structure and Selection* (New York, NY: Oxford University Press, 1995); and J. Baum and J. Singh, eds., *Evolutionary Dynamics of Organizations* (New York, NY: Oxford University Press, 1994).

5. M. Tushman and L. Rosenkopf, "On the Organizational Determinants of Technological Change: Towards a Sociology of Technological Evolution," in B. Staw and L. Cummings, *Research in Organization Behavior,* Vol. 14 (Greenwich, CT: JAI Press, 1992); M. Tushman and P. Anderson, "Technological Discontinuities and Organization Environments," *Administrative Science Quarterly,* 31 (1986): 439–465; W. Abernathy and K. Clark, "Innovation: Maping the Winds of Creative Destruction," *Re-*

search Policy, 1985, pp. 3–22; J. Wade, "Dynamics of Organizational Communities and Technological Bandwagons," *Strategic Management Journal,* 16 (1995): 111–133; J. Baum and H. Korn, "Dominant Designs and Population Dynamics in Telecommunications Services," *Social Science Research,* 24 (1995): 97–135.

6. For a more complete treatment of this subject, see J. Utterback, *Mastering the Dynamics of Innovation* (Boston, MA: Harvard Business School Press, 1994). See also R. Burgelman and A. Grove, "Strategic Dissonance," *California Management Review,* 38/2 (Winter 1996): 8–28.

7. D. Nadler and M. Tushman, *Competing by Design* (New York, NY: Oxford University Press, 1997); D. Nadler and M. Tushman, "Beyond Charismatic Leaders: Leadership and Organization Change," *California Management Review* (Winter 1990): 77–90.

8. See M. Tushman, W. Newman, and E. Romanelli, "Convergence and Upheaval: Managing the Unsteady Pace of Organizational Evolution," *California Management Review,* 29/1 (Fall 1986): 29–44.

9. L. Hays, "Gerstner Is Struggling as He Tries to Change Ingrained IBM Culture," *Wall Street Journal,* May 13, 1994.

10. J. Kotter and N. Rothbard, "Cultural Change at Nissan Motors," *Harvard Business School Case,* #9-491-079, July 28, 1993.

11. "Today's Leaders Look to Tomorrow," *Fortune,* March 26, 1990, p. 31.

12. J. Leahey, "Changing the Culture at British Airways," *Harvard Business School Case,* #9-491-009, 1990.

13. L. Bruce, "British Airways Jolts Staff with a Cultural Revolution," *International Management,* March 7, 1987, pp. 36–38.

14. Ibid.

15. See, for example, D. Katz, *The Big Store: Inside the Crisis and Revolution at Sears* (New York, NY: Viking, 1987); S. Caminiti, "Sears' Need: More Speed," *Fortune,* July 15, 1991, pp. 88–90.

16. S. Strom, "Further Prescriptions for the Convalescent Sears," *New York Times,* October 10, 1992.

17. D. Hurst, *Crisis and Renewal* (Boston, MA: Harvard Business School Press, 1995); R. Burgelman, "Intraorganizational Ecology of Strategy Making and Organizational Adaptation," *Organizational Science,* 2/3 (1991): 239–262; K. Eisenhardt and B. Tabrizi, "Acceleration Adaptive Processes," *Administrative Science Quarterly,* 40/1 (1995): 84–110; J. Morone, *Winning in High Tech Markets* (Boston, MA: Harvard Business School Press, 1993); M. Iansiti and K. Clark, "Integration and Dynamic Capability," *Industry and Corporation Change,* 3/3 (1994): 557–606; D. Leonard-Barton, *Wellsprings of Knowledge* (Boston, MA: Harvard Business School Press, 1995).

18. J. Weber, "A Big Company that Works," *Business Week,* May 4, 1992, p. 125.

19. See C. O'Reilly, "Corporations, Culture, and Commitment: Motivation and Social Control in Organizations," *California Management Review,* 31/4 (Summer 1989): 9–25; or C. O'Reilly and J. Chatman, "Culture as Social Control: Corporations, Cults, and Commitment," in B. Staw and L. Cummings, eds., *Research in Organizational Behavior,* Vol. 18 (Greenwich, CT: JAI Press, 1996).

20. A. Deutschman, "How H-P Continues to Grow and Grow," *Fortune,* May 2, 1994, p. 100.

21. N. Machiavelli, *The Prince,* translated by L.P.S. de Alvarez (Dallas, TX: University of Dallas Press, 1974).

22. S. Sherman, "Andy Grove: How Intel Makes Spending Pay Off," *Fortune,* February 22, 1993, p. 58.

Core Capabilities and Core Rigidities

A Paradox in Managing New Product Development

DOROTHY LEONARD-BARTON

INTRODUCTION

Debate about the nature and strategic importance of firms' distinctive capabilities has been heightened by the recent assertion that Japanese firms understand, nurture and exploit their core competencies better than their U.S.-based competitors (Prahalad and Hamel, 1990). This paper explores the interaction of such capabilities with a critical strategic activity: the development of new products and processes. In responding to environmental and market changes, development projects become the focal point for tension between innovation and the status quo—microcosms of the paradoxical organizational struggle to maintain, yet renew or replace core capabilities.

In this paper, I first examine the history of core capabilities, briefly review relevant literature, and describe a field-based study providing illustrative data. The paper then turns to a deeper description of the nature of core capabilities and detailed evidence about their symbiotic relationship with development projects. However, evidence from the field suggests the need to enhance emerging theory by examining the way that capabilities inhibit as well as enable development, and these arguments are next presented. The paper concludes with a discussion of the project/capabilities interaction as a paradox faced by project managers, observed management tactics, and the po-

tential of product/process development projects to stimulate change.

THE HISTORY OF CORE CAPABILITIES

Capabilities are considered *core* if they differentiate a company strategically. The concept is not new. Various authors have called them distinctive competences (Snow and Hrebiniak, 1980; Hitt and Ireland, 1985), core or organizational competencies (Prahalad and Hamel, 1990; Hayes Wheelwright, and Clark, 1988), firm-specific competence (Pavitt, 1991), resource deployments (Hofer and Schende, 1978), and invisible assets (Itami, with Roehl, 1987). Their strategic significance has been discussed for decades, stimulated by such research as Rumelt's (1974) discovery that of nine diversification strategies, the two that were built on an existing skill or resource base in the firm were associated with the highest performance. Mitchell's (1989) observation that industry-specific capabilities increased the likelihood a firm could exploit a new technology within that industry, has confirmed the early work. Therefore some authors suggest that effective competition is based less on strategic leaps than on incremental innovation that exploits carefully developed capabilities (Hayes, 1985; Quinn, 1980).

On the other hand, institutionalized capabilities

Reprinted from *Strategic Management Journal*, Vol. 13, Dorothy Leonard-Barton, "Core Capabilities and Core Rigidities: A Paradox in Managing New Product Development," pp. 111–125, copyright © 1992. Reproduced by permission of John Wiley & Sons Limited.

may lead to "incumbent inertia" (Lieberman and Montgomery, 1988) in the face of environmental changes. Technological discontinuities can enhance or destroy existing competencies within an industry (Tushman and Anderson, 1986). Such shifts in the external environment resonate within the organization, so that even "seemingly minor" innovations can undermine the usefulness of deeply embedded knowledge (Henderson and Clark, 1990). In fact, all innovation necessarily requires some degree of "creative destruction" (Schumpeter, 1942).

Thus at any given point in a corporation's history, core capabilities are evolving, and corporate survival depends upon successfully managing that evolution. New product and process development projects are obvious, visible arenas for conflict between the need for innovation and retention of important capabilities. Managers of such projects face a paradox: core capabilities *simultaneously* enhance and inhibit development.[1] Development projects reveal friction between technology strategy and current corporate practices; they also spearhead potential new strategic directions (Burgelman 1991). However, most studies of industrial innovation focus on the new product project as a self-contained unit of analysis, and address such issues as project staffing or structure (Souder, 1987; Leonard-

Barton, 1988a; Clark and Fujimoto, 1991, Chapter 9).[2] Therefore there is little research-based knowledge on managing the interface between the project and the organization, and the interaction between development and capabilities in particular. Observing core capabilities through the lens of the project places under a magnifying glass one aspect of the "part-whole" problem of innovation management, which Van de Ven singles out as "[p]erhaps the most significant structural problem in managing complex organizations today . . ." (1986:598).

Recent field research on 20 new product and process development projects provided an opportunity to explore and conceptually model the relationship between development practices and a firm's core capabilities. As described in the Appendix, four extensive case studies in each of five companies (Ford, Chaparral Steel, Hewlett Packard, and two anonymous companies, Electronics and Chemicals) were conducted by joint teams of academics and practitioners.[3] (Table 21.1). Before describing the interactions observed in the field, I first define core capabilities.

Dimensions of Core Capabilities

Writers often assume that descriptors of core capabilities such as "unique," "distinctive," "difficult to imi-

Table 21.1. Description of Projects Studied

Company	Product/Process Description
Ford Motor Company	FX15 Compressor for automobile air-conditioning systems EN53 New full-sized car built on carryover platform MN12 All new car platform including a novel supercharged engine FN9 Luxury automobile built on carryover platform with major suspension system modifications
Chaparral Steel	Horizontal Caster New caster used to produce higher grades steel Pulpit Controls Furnace control mechanism upgrade from analog to digital Microtuff 10 New special bar quality alloy steel Arc Saw Electric arc saw for squaring ends of steel beams
Hewlett-Packard Company	Deskjet Low-cost personal computer and office printer using new technology Hornet Low-cost spectrum analyzer HP 150 Terminal/PC linked to high-end computer Logic Analyzer Digital logic analyzer
Chemicals	Special use camera Large format printer for converting digital input to continuous images New polymer used in film 21st century "factory of the future"
Electronics	New RISC/UNIX workstation Local area network linking multiple computer networks Software architecture for desktop publishing High-density storage disk drive

tate," or "superior to competition" render the term self-explanatory, especially if reference is also made to "resource deployment" or "skills." A few authors include activities such as "collective learning" and explain how competence is and is not cultivated (Prahalad and Hamel, 1990). Teece, Pisano, and Shuen provide one of the clearest definitions: ("a set of differentiated skills, complementary assets, and routines that provide the basis for a firm's competitive capacities and sustainable advantage in a particular business") (1990:28).

In this article, I adopt a knowledge-based view of the firm and define a core capability as the knowledge set that distinguishes and provides a competitive advantage. There are four dimensions to this knowledge set. Its content is embodied in (1) employee *knowledge and skills* and embedded in (2) *technical systems*. The processes of knowledge creation and control are guided by (3) *managerial systems*. The fourth dimension is (4) the *values and norms* associated with the various types of embodied and embedded knowledge and with the processes of knowledge creation and control. In managerial literature, this fourth dimension is usually separated from the others or ignored.[4] However, understanding it is crucial to managing both new product/process development and core capabilities.

The first dimension, knowledge and skills embodied in people, is the one most often associated with core capabilities (Teece et al., 1990) and the one most obviously relevant to new product development. This knowledge/skills dimension encompasses both firm-specific techniques and scientific understanding. The second, knowledge embedded in technical systems, results from years of accumulating, codifying, and structuring the tacit knowledge in peoples' heads. Such physical production or information systems represent compilations of knowledge, usually derived from multiple individual sources; therefore the whole technical system is greater than the sum of its parts. This knowledge constitutes both information (e.g., a data base of product tests conducted over decades) and procedures (e.g., proprietary design rules). The third dimension, managerial systems, represents formal and informal ways of creating knowledge (e.g., through sabbaticals, apprenticeship programs or networks with partners) and of controlling knowledge (e.g., incentive systems and reporting structures).

Infused through these three dimensions is the fourth: the value assigned within the company to the content and structure of knowledge (e.g., chemical engineering vs. marketing expertise; "open systems" software vs. proprietary systems), means of collecting knowledge (e.g., formal degrees v. experience) and controlling knowledge (e.g., individual empowerment vs. management hierarchies). Even physical systems embody values. For instance, organizations that have a strong tradition of individual vs. centralized control over information prefer an architecture (software and hardware) that allows much autonomy at each network node. Such "debatable, overt, espoused values" (Schein, 1984:4) are one "manifestation" of the corporate culture (Schein, 1986:7).[5]

Core capabilities are "institutionalized" (Zucker, 1977). That is, they are part of the organization's taken-for-granted reality, which is an accretion of decisions made over time and events in corporate history (Kimberly, 1987; Tucker, Singh, and Meinhard, 1990; Pettigrew, 1979). The technology embodied in technical systems and skills usually traces its roots back to the firm's first products. Managerial systems evolve over time in response to employees' evolving interpretation of their organizational roles (Giddens, 1984) and to the need to reward particular actions. Values bear the "imprint" of company founders and early leaders (Kimberly, 1987). All four dimensions of core capabilities reflect accumulated behaviors and beliefs based on early corporate successes. One advantage of core capabilities lies in this unique heritage, which is not easily imitated by would-be competitors.

Thus a core capability is an interrelated, interdependent knowledge system. See Figure 21.1. The four dimensions may be represented in very different proportions in various capabilities. For instance, the information and procedures embedded in technical systems such as computer programs are relatively more important to credit card companies than to engineering consulting firms, since these latter firms likely rely more on the knowledge base embodied in individual employees (the skills dimension).[6]

Interaction of Development Projects and Core Capabilities: Managing the Paradox

The interaction between development projects and capabilities lasts over a period of months or years and differs according to how completely aligned are the values, skills, and managerial and technical systems required by the project with those currently prevalent

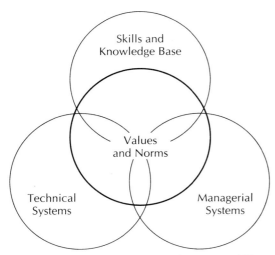

Figure 21.1. The four dimensions of a core capability.

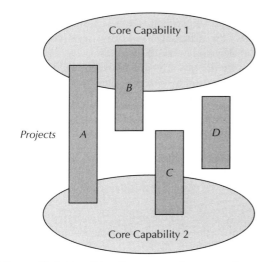

Figure 21.2. Possible alignments of new product and process development projects with current core capabilities at a point in time.

in the firm (see Figure 21.2). Companies in the study described above identified a selected, highly traditional, and strongly held capability and then one project at each extreme of alignment: highly congruent vs. not at all (Table 21.2). Degree of congruence does not necessarily reflect project size, or technical or market novelty. Chaparral's horizontal caster and Ford's new luxury

car, for instance, were neither incremental enhancements nor small undertakings. Nor did incongruent projects necessarily involve "radical" innovations by market or technological measures. Electronic's new workstation used readily available, "state-of-the-shelf" components. Rather, unaligned projects were nontraditional for the organization along several dimensions of the selected core capability.

For instance, Chemicals' project developing a new polymer used in film drew heavily on traditional values, skills, and systems. In this company, film designers represent the top five percent of all engineers. All projects associated with film are high status, and highly proprietary technical systems have evolved to produce it. In contrast, the printer project was nontraditional. The key technical systems, for instance, were hardware rather than chemical or polymer and required mechanical engineering and software skills. Similarly, whereas the spectrum analyzer project at Hewlett Packard built on traditional capabilities in designing measurement equipment, the 150 terminal as a personal computer departed from conventional strengths. The 150 was originally conceived as a terminal for the HP3000, an industrial computer already on the market and as a terminal, was closely aligned with traditional capabilities. The attempt to transform the 150 into a personal computer was not very successful because different technical and marketing capabilities were required. Moreover, the greater system complexity represented by a stand-alone computer (e.g., the need for disk drives) required very untraditional cross-divisional cooperation.

Similar observations could be made about the other projects featured in Table 21.2. Chaparral's horizontal caster pushed the traditional science of molds to new heights, whereas the arc saw required capabilities that turned out to be unavailable. The local area networks project at Electronics grew directly out of networking expertise, whereas the new RISC/UNIX workstation challenged dominant and proprietary software/hardware architecture. At Ford, the three car projects derived to varying degrees from traditional strengths—especially the new luxury car. However, the air-conditioner compressor had never been built in-house before. Since all new product development departs somewhat from current capabilities, project misalignment is a matter of degree. However, as discussed later, it is also a matter of kind. That is, the type as well

Table 21.2. Relationship of Selected Projects with a Very Traditional Core Capability in Each Company Studied

Company Name	Traditional Core Capability	Degree of Alignment	
		Very High	Very Low
Ford Motor Co.	Total vehicle architecture	Luxury car built on carryover platform (FN9)	Compressor for air-conditioner system (FX15)
Chaparral Steel	Science of casting molds	Horizontal caster	Electric arc saw
Hewlett Packard	Measurement technology	Low-cost spectrum analyzer	150 terminal/personal computer
Chemicals	Silver halide technology	New polymer for film	Factory of the future
Electronics	Networking	Local area network link	Stand-alone workstation

as the number of capability dimensions challenged by a new project determines the intensity of the interaction and the project's potential to stimulate change.

THE UP SIDE: CAPABILITIES ENHANCE DEVELOPMENT

In all projects studied, deep stores of knowledge embodied in people and embedded in technical systems were accessed; all projects were aided by managerial systems that created and controlled knowledge flows, and by prevalent values and norms. That is, whether the projects were aligned or not with the prominent core capability identified by the company, *some* dimensions of that capability favored the project. However, the closer the alignment of project and core knowledge set, the stronger the enabling influence.

In order to understand the dynamic interaction of project with capabilities, it is helpful to tease apart the dimensions of capabilities and put each dimension separately under the microscope. However, we must remember that these dimensions are interrelated; each is supported by the other three. Values in particular permeate the other dimensions of a core capability.

Skills/Knowledge Dimension

EXCELLENCE IN THE DOMINANT DISCIPLINE
One of the most necessary elements in a core capability is excellence in the technical and professional skills and knowledge base underlying major products. The professional elite in these companies earn their status by demonstrating remarkable skills. They expect to

"achieve the impossible"—and it is often asked of them. Thus managers of development projects that draw upon core capabilities have rich resources. In numerous cases, seemingly intractable technical problems were solved through engineering excellence. For instance, although engineers working on the thin film media project at Electronics had little or no prior experience with this particular form of storage technology, (because the company had always used ferrite-based media) they were able to *invent* their way out of difficulties. Before this project was over, the geographically dispersed team had invented new media, new heads to read the data off the thin film media, as well as the software and hardware to run a customized assembly and test line for the new storage device.

PERVASIVE TECHNICAL LITERACY
Besides attracting a cadre of superbly qualified people to work in the dominant discipline, time-honored core capabilities create a reservoir of complementary skills and interests outside the projects, composed of technically skilled people who help shape new products with skilled criticism. In the Electronics Software Applications project, the developers enlisted employees through computer networks to field test emerging products. After trying out the software sent them electronically, employees submitted all reactions to a computerized "Notes" file. This internal field testing thus took advantage of both willing, technically able employees and also a computer system set up for easy world-wide networking. Similarly, Electronics Workstation developers recruited an internal "wrecking crew" to evaluate their new product. Employees who found the most "bugs" in the prototype workstations

were rewarded by getting to keep them. At Chemicals, developers tested the special purpose camera by loading down an engineer going on a weekend trip with film, so that he could try out various features for them. In these companies, internal testing is so commonplace that it is taken for granted as a logical step in new product/process creation. However, it represents a significant advantage over competitors trying to enter the same market without access to such technically sophisticated personnel. Internal "field testers" not only typify users but can translate their reactions into technical enhancements; such swift feedback helps development teams hit market windows.

The Technical Systems Dimension

Just as pervasive technical literacy among employees can constitute a corporate resource, so do the systems, procedures and tools that are artifacts left behind by talented individuals, embodying many of their skills in a readily accessible form. Project members tap into this embedded knowledge, which can provide an advantage over competitors in timing, accuracy, or amount of available detail. At Ford Motor Company, the capability to model reliability testing derives in part from proprietary software tools that simulate extremely complex interactions. In the full-sized car project, models simulating noise in the car body allowed engineers to identify nonobvious root causes, some originating from interaction among physically separated components. For instance, a noise apparently located in the floor panel could be traced instead to the acoustical interaction of sound waves reverberating between roof and floor. Such simulations cut development time as well as costs. They both build on and enhance the engineers' skills.

The Management Systems Dimension

Managerial systems constitute part of a core capability when they incorporate unusual blends of skills and/or foster beneficial behaviors not observed in competitive firms. Incentive systems encouraging innovative activities are critical components of some core capabilities, as are unusual educational systems. In Chaparral Steel, all employees are shareholders. This rewards system interacts with development projects in that employees feel that every project is an effort to improve a process they own. "I feel like this

company partly belongs to me," explains a millwright. Consequently, even operators and maintenance personnel are tenacious innovation champions. The furnace controls upgrade (incorporating a switch from analog to digital) was initiated by a maintenance person, who persevered against opposition from his nominal superiors. Chaparral Steel also has a unique apprenticeship program for the entire production staff, involving both classroom education and on-the-job training. Classes are taught by mill foremen on a rotating basis. The combination of mill-specific information and general education (including such unusual offerings as interpersonal skills for furnace operators) would be difficult to imitate, if only because of the diversity of abilities required of these foremen. They know what to teach from having experienced problems on the floor, and they must live on the factory floor with what they have taught. This managerial system, tightly integrating technical theory and practice, is reflected in every development project undertaken in the company (Leonard-Barton, 1991).

Values Dimension

The values assigned to knowledge creation and content, constantly reinforced by corporate leaders and embedded in management practices, affect all the development projects in a line of business. Two subdimensions of values are especially critical: the degree to which project members are empowered and the status assigned various disciplines on the project team.

EMPOWERMENT OF PROJECT MEMBERS

Empowerment is the belief in the potential of every individual to contribute meaningfully to the task at hand and the relinquishment by organizational authority figures to that individual of responsibility for that contribution. In HP, "Electronics," and Chaparral, the assumption is that empowered employees will create multiple potential futures for the corporation and these options will be selected and exercised as needed. The future of the corporation thus rests on the ability of such individuals to create new businesses by championing new products and processes. Since strategy in these companies is "pattern in action" or "emergent" rather than "deliberate" (Mintzberg, 1990), empowerment is an especially important element of their core capabilities, and project members initiating new capabilities were exhilarated by the challenges they had created. The Hewlett Packard printer and the Electronics storage teams actually felt that they had turned the course of their mammoth corporate ship a critical degree or two.

HIGH STATUS FOR THE DOMINANT DISCIPLINE
A business generally recognized for certain core capabilities attracts, holds, and motivates talented people who value the knowledge base underlying that capability and join up for the challenges, the camaraderie with competent peers, the status associated with the skills of the dominant discipline or function. Each company displays a cultural bias toward the technical base in which the corporation has its historical roots. For Chemicals, that base is chemistry and chemical engineering; for Hewlett Packard and Electronics, it is electronics/computer engineering and operating systems software. A history of high status for the dominant discipline enables the corporation and the projects to attract the very top talent. Top chemical engineers can aspire to become the professional elites constituting the five percent of engineers who design premier film products at Chemicals. At Hewlett Packard and Electronics, design engineers are the professional elite.

A natural outgrowth of the prominence of a particular knowledge base is its influence over the development process. In many firms, a reinforcing cycle of values and managerial systems lends power and authority to the design engineer. That is, design engineers have high status because the new products that are directly evaluated by the market originate in design engineering; in contrast, the expertise of manufacturing engineers is expended on projects less directly tied to the bottom line and more difficult to evaluate. The established, well-paid career path for product designers attracts top engineering talent, who tend to perform well. The success (of failure) of new products is attributed almost entirely to these strong performers, whose high visibility and status constantly reinforce the dominance of their discipline.

As the above discussion suggests, projects derive enormous support from core capabilities. In fact, such capabilities continually spawn new products and processes because so much creative power is focused on identifying new opportunities to apply the accumulated knowledge base. However, these same capabilities can also prove dysfunctional for product and process development.

THE DOWN SIDE: CORE RIGIDITIES INHIBIT DEVELOPMENT

Even in projects that eventually succeed, problems often surface as product launch approaches. In response to gaps between product specifications and market information, or problems in manufacture, project managers face unpalatable choices. They can cycle back to prior phases in the design process (Leonard-Barton, 1988a), revisiting previous decisions higher up the design hierarchy (Clark, 1985), but almost certainly at the cost of schedule slippage. Or they may ship an inadequate product. Some such problems are idiosyncratic to the particular project, unlikely to occur again in the same form and hence not easily predicted. Others, however, occur repeatedly in multiple projects. These recurring shortfalls in the process are often traceable to the gap between current environmental requirements and a corporation's core capabilities. Values, skills, managerial systems, and technical systems that served the company well in the past and may still be wholly appropriate for some projects or parts of projects, are experienced by others as core rigidities—inappropriate sets of knowledge. Core rigidities are the flip side of core capabilities. They are not neutral; these deeply embedded knowledge sets actively create problems. While core rigidities are more problematic for projects that are deliberately designed to create new, nontraditional capabilities, rigidities can affect all projects—even those that are reasonably congruent with current core capabilities.

Skills and Knowledge Dimension

LESS STRENGTH IN NONDOMINANT DISCIPLINES
Any corporation's resources are limited. Emphasizing one discipline heavily naturally makes the company somewhat less attractive for top people in a nondominant one. A skilled marketing person knows that she will represent a minority discipline in an engineering-driven firm. Similarly, engineers graduating from top U.S. schools generally regard manufacturing in fabri-

cation industries less attractive than engineering design (see Hayes et al., 1988) not only because of noncompetitive salaries, but because of a lower level of expertise among potential colleagues.

In each of the nonaligned and hence more difficult projects (Table 21.2), specific nontraditional types of knowledge were missing. Chaparral Steel's electric arc saw project required understanding electromagnetic fields for a variety of alloys—a very different knowledge set than the usual metallurgical expertise required in casting. The Hewlett Packard 150 project suffered from a lack of knowledge about personal computer design and manufacture. The company has a long history of successful instrument development based on "next-bench" design, meaning the engineering designers based their decisions on the needs and skills of their colleagues on the bench next to them. However, such engineers are not representative of personal computer users. Therefore traditional sources of information and design feedback were not applicable for the 150 project. Similarly, the new workstation project of Electronics met with less than optimal market acceptance because the traditional focus on producing a "hot box," i.e., excellent hardware, resulted in correspondingly less attention to developing software applications. The knowledge relevant to traditional hardware development flows through well-worn channels, but much less knowledge exists about creating application software. Therefore, the first few working prototypes of the UNIX/RISC workstation were shipped to customers rather than to third-party software developers. While this practice had worked well to stimulate interest in the company's well-established lines of hardware, for which much software is available, it was less appropriate for the new hardware, which could not be used and evaluated without software.

Technical Systems Dimension

Physical systems can embody rigidities also, since the skills and processes captured in software or hardware become easily outdated. New product designers do not always know how many such systems they are affecting. For example, in the RISC/UNIX workstation project at Electronics, the new software base posed an extreme challenge to manufacturing because hundreds of diagnostic and test systems in the factory were based on the corporate proprietary software. The impact of

this incompatibility had been underestimated, given the very tight 8-month product delivery targets.

Management Systems Dimension

Management systems can grow just as intractable as physical ones—perhaps more so, because one cannot just plug in a new career path when a new project requires strong leadership in a hithertofore underutilized role. Highly skilled people are understandably reluctant to apply their abilities to project tasks that are undervalued, lest that negative assessment of the importance of the task contaminate perceptions of their personal abilities. In several companies, the project manager's role is not a strong one—partly because there is no associated career path. The road to the top lies through individual technical contribution. Thus a hardware engineer in one project considered his contribution as an engineering manager to be much more important than his simultaneous role as project manager, which he said was "not my real job." His perception of the relative unimportance of project leadership not only weakened the power of the role in that specific project but reinforced the view held by some that problem-solving in project management requires less intelligence than technical problem-solving.

Values Dimension

Core rigidities hampered innovation in the development projects especially along the values dimension. Of course, certain generic types of corporate cultures encourage innovation more than others (Burns and Stalker, 1961; Chakravarthy, 1982). While not disagreeing with that observation, the point here is a different one: the very same values, norms and attitudes that support a core capability and thus enable development can also constrain it.

EMPOWERMENT AS ENTITLEMENT

A potential down side to empowerment observed is that individuals construe their empowerment as a psychological contract with the corporation, and yet the boundaries of their responsibility and freedom are not always clear. Because they undertake heroic tasks for the corporation, they expect rewards, recognition and freedom to act. When the contract goes sour, either because they exceed the boundaries of personal freedom that the corporation can tolerate, or their project is technically successful but fails in other ways, or their ideas are rejected, or their self-sacrifice results in too little recognition, they experience the contract as abrogated and often leave the company—sometimes with a deep sense of betrayal.

Engineers in projects that fall toward the "incongruity" end of the spectrum speak of "betting their [corporate identification] badges," on the outcome, and of having "their backs to the cliff" as ways of expressing their sense of personal risk. One engineering project manager describes "going into the tunnel," meaning the development period, from which the team emerges only when the job is done. "You either do it or you don't. . . . You don't have any other life." Such entrapreneurs seem to enjoy the stress—as long as their psychological contract with the company remains intact. In this case the manager believed her contract included enormous freedom from corporate interference with her management style. When corporate management imposed certain restrictions, she perceived her contract as abrogated, and left the company just 2 months before product launch, depriving the project of continuity in the vision she had articulated for an entire stream of products.

Empowerment as a value and practice greatly aids in projects, therefore, until it conflicts with the greater corporate good. Because development requires enormous initiative and yet great discipline in fulfilling corporate missions, the management challenge is to channel empowered individual energy towards corporate aims—without destroying creativity or losing good people.

LOWER STATUS FOR NONDOMINANT DISCIPLINES

When new product development requires developing or drawing upon technical skills traditionally less well respected in the company, history can have an inhibiting effect. Even if multiple subcultures exist, with differing levels of maturity, the older and historically more important ones, as noted above, tend to be more prestigious. For instance, at Chemicals, the culture values the chemical engineers and related scientists as somehow "more advanced" than mechanical engineers and manufacturing engineers. Therefore, projects involving polymers or film are perceived as more prestigious than equipment projects. The other companies displayed similar, very clear perceptions about what disciplines and what kinds of projects are high status.

The lower status of nondominant disciplines was manifested in pervasive but subtle negatively reinforcing cycles that constrained their potential for contributions to new product development and therefore limited the cross-functional integration so necessary to innovation (Pavitt, 1991). Four of these unacknowledged but critical manifestations are: who travels to whom, self-fulfilling expectations, unequal credibility and wrong language.[7]

One seemingly minor yet important indication of status affecting product/process development is that lower status individuals usually travel to the physical location of the higher. Manufacturing engineers were far more likely to go to the engineering design sites than vice versa, whether for one-day visits, or temporary or permanent postings. Not only does such one-way travel reinforce manufacturing's lower status, but it slows critical learning by design engineers, reinforcing their isolation from the factory floor. The exception to the rule, when design engineers traveled to the manufacturing site, aided cross-functional coordination by fostering more effective personal relationships. Such trips also educated the design engineers about some of the rationale behind design for manufacture (Whitney, 1988). A design engineer in one project returned to alter designs after seeing "what [manufacturing] is up against" when he visited the factory floor.

Expectations about the status of people and roles can be dangerously self-fulfilling. As dozens of controlled experiments manipulating unconscious interpersonal expectations have demonstrated, biases can have a "Pygmalion effect": person A's expectations about the behavior of person B affect B's actual performance—for better or worse (Rosenthal and Rubin, 1978). In the engineering-driven companies studied, the expectation that marketing could not aid product definition was ensured fulfillment by expectations of low quality input, which undermined marketers' confidence. In the Electronics Local Area Network project, the marketing people discovered early on that users would want certain very important features in the LAN. However, they lacked the experience to evaluate that information and self-confidence to push for inclusion of the features. Not until that same information was gathered directly from customers by two experienced consulting engineers who presented it strongly was it acted upon. Precious time was lost as the schedule was slipped four months to incorporate the "new" customer information. Similarly, in the Hewlett Packard printer project, marketing personnel conducted studies in shopping malls to discover potential customers' reactions to prototypes. When marketing reported need for 21 important changes, the product designers enacted only five. In the next mall studies, the design engineers went along. Hearing from the future customers' own lips the same information rejected before, the product developers returned to the bench and made the other 16 changes. The point is certainly not that marketing always has better information than engineering. Rather history has conferred higher expectations and greater credibility upon the dominant function, whereas other disciplines start at a disadvantage in the development process.

Even if nondominant disciplines are granted a hearing in team meetings, their input may be discounted if not presented in the language favored by the dominant function. Customer service representatives in the Electronics LAN project were unable to convince engineering to design the computer boards for field repair as opposed to replacing the whole system in the field with a new box and conducting repairs back at the service center, because they were unable to present their argument in cost-based figures. Engineering assumed that an argument not presented as compelling financial data was useless.

Thus, nondominant roles and disciplines on the development team are kept in their place through a self-reinforcing cycle of norms, attitudes, and skill sets. In an engineering-dominated company, the cycle for marketing and manufacturing is: low status on the development team, reinforced by the appointment of either young, less experienced members or else one experienced person, whose time is splintered across far too many teams. Since little money is invested in these roles, little contribution is expected from the people holding them. Such individuals act without confidence, and so do not influence product design much—thus reinforcing their low status on the team.

THE INTERACTION OF PRODUCT/PROCESS DEVELOPMENT PROJECTS WITH CORE RIGIDITIES

The severity of the paradox faced by project managers because of the dual nature of core capabilities depends upon both (1) the number and (2) the types of dimensions comprising a core rigidity. The more dimensions represented, the greater the misalignment potentially experienced between project and capability. For example, the Arc Saw project at Chaparral Steel was misaligned with the core metallurgical capability mostly along two dimensions: technical systems (not originally designed to accommodate an arc saw), and more importantly, the skills and knowledge-base dimension. In contrast, the Factory-of-the-Future project at Chemicals challenged all four dimensions of the traditional core capability. Not only were current proprietary technical systems inadequate, but existing managerial systems did not provide any way to develop the cross-functional skills needed. Moreover, the values placed on potential knowledge creation and control varied wildly among the several sponsoring groups, rendering a common vision unattainable.

The four dimensions vary in ease of change. From technical to managerial systems, skills and then values, the dimensions are increasingly less tangible, less visible, and less explicitly codified. The technical systems dimension is relatively easy to alter for many reasons, among them the probability that such systems are local to particular departments. Managerial systems usually have greater organizational scope (Leonard-Barton, 1988b), i.e., reach across more subunits than technical systems, requiring acceptance by more people. The skills and knowledge content dimension is even less amenable to change because skills are built over time and many remain tacit, i.e., uncodified and in employees' heads (see von Hippel, 1990). However, the value embodied in a core capability is the dimension least susceptible to change; values are most closely bound to culture, and culture is hard to alter in the short term (Zucker, 1977), if it can be changed at all (Barney, 1986).

Effects of the Paradox on Projects

Over time, some core capabilities are replaced because their dysfunctional side has begun to inhibit too many projects. However, that substitution or renewal will not occur within the lifetime of a single project. Therefore, project managers cannot wait for time to resolve the paradox they face (Quinn and Cameron, 1988). In the projects observed in this study, managers handled the paradox in one of four ways: (1) abandonment; (2) recidivism, i.e., return to core capabilities; (3) reorientation; and (4) isolation. The arc saw and factory-of-the-future projects were abandoned, as the managers found no way to resolve the problems. The HP150 personal computer exemplifies recidivism. The end product was strongly derivative of traditional HP capabilities in that it resembled a terminal and was more successful as one than as a personal computer. The special-use camera project was reoriented. Started in the film division, the stronghold of the firm's most traditional core capability, the project languished. Relocated to the equipment division, where the traditional corporate capability was less strongly ensconced and other capabilities were valued, the project was well accepted. The tactic of isolation, employed in several projects to varying degrees, has often been invoked in the case of new ventures (Burgelman, 1983). Both the workstation project at Electronics and the HP Deskjet project were separated physically and psychologically from the rest of the corporation, the former without upper management's blessing. These project managers encouraged their teams by promoting the group as hardy pioneers fighting corporate rigidities.

Effects of the Paradox on Core Capabilities

Although capabilities are not usually dramatically altered by a single project, projects do pave the way for organizational change by highlighting core rigidities and introducing new capabilities. Of the companies studied, Chaparral Steel made the most consistent use of development projects as agents of renewal and organization-wide learning. Through activities such as benchmarking against best-in-the-world capabilities, Chaparral managers use projects as occasions for challenging current knowledge and for modeling alternative new capabilities. For instance, personnel from vice presidents to operators spent months in Japan learning about horizontal casting and in the case of the new specialty alloy, the company convened its own academic conference in order to push the bounds of current capabilities.

In other companies, negative cycles reinforcing the lower status of manufacturing or marketing were broken—to the benefit of both project and corporation. In the workstation project at Electronics, the manufacturing engineers on the project team eventually demonstrated so much knowledge that design engineers who had barely listened to 20 percent of their comments at the start of the project, gave a fair hearing to 80 percent, thereby allowing manufacturing to influence design. In the deskjet printer project at Hewlett Packard, managers recognized that inequality between design and manufacturing always created unnecessary delays. The Vancouver division thus sought to raise the status of manufacturing engineering skills by creating a manufacturing engineering group within R&D and then, once it was well established, moving it to manufacturing. A rotation plan between manufacturing and R&D was developed to help neutralize the traditional status differences; engineers who left research to work in manufacturing or vice versa were guaranteed a "return ticket." These changes interrupted the negative reinforcing cycle, signaling a change in status for manufacturing and attracting better talent to the position. This same project introduced HP to wholly unfamiliar market research techniques such as getting customer reactions to prototypes in shopping malls.

As these examples indicate, even within their 1–8 year lifetime, the projects studied served as small departures from tradition in organizations providing a "foundation in experience" to inspire eventual large changes (Kanter, 1983). Such changes can be *precipitated* by the introduction of new capabilities along any of the four dimensions. However, for a capability to become *core,* all four dimensions must be addressed. A core capability is an interconnected set of knowledge collections—a tightly coupled system. This concept is akin to Pfeffer's definition of a paradigm, which he cautions is not just a view of the world but "embodies procedures for inquiring about the world and categories into which these observations are collected. Thus, he warns, "paradigms have within them an internal consistency that makes evolutionary change of adaptation nearly impossible" (1982:228). While he is thinking of the whole organization, the caution might apply as well to core capabilities. Thus, new technical systems provide no inimitable advantage if not accompanied by new skills. New skills atrophy or flee the corporation if the technical systems are inadequate, and/or if the managerial systems such as training are incompatible. New values will not take root if associated behaviors are not rewarded. Therefore, when the development process encounters rigidities, projects can be managed consciously as the "generative" actions characteristic of learning organizations (Senge, 1990) only if the multidimensional nature of core capabilities is fully appreciated.

CONCLUSION

This paper proposes a new focus of inquiry about technological innovation, enlarging the boundaries of "middle range" project management theory to include interactions with development of capabilities, and hence with strategy. Because core capabilities are a collection of knowledge sets, they are distributed and are being constantly enhanced from multiple sources. However, at the same time that they enable innovation, they hinder it. Therefore in their interaction with the development process, they cannot be managed as a single good (or bad) entity.[8] They are not easy to change because they include a pervasive dimension of values, and as Weick (1979:151) points out, "managers unwittingly collude" to avoid actions that challenge accepted modes of behavior.

Yet technology-based organizations have no choice but to challenge their current paradigms. The swift-moving environment in which they function makes it critical that the "old fit be consciously disturbed." (Chakravarthy, 1982:42). Itami points out that "The time to search out and develop a new core resource is when the current core is working well" (1987:54)—a point that is echoed by Foster (1982). Development projects provide opportunities for creating the "requisite variety" for innovation (Van de Ven, 1986:600; Kanter, 1986). As micro-level social systems, they create conflict with the macro system and hence a managerial paradox. Quinn and Cameron argue that recognizing and managing paradox is a powerful lever for change: "Having multiple frameworks available . . . is probably the single most powerful attribute of self-renewing . . . organizations" (1988:302).

Thus project managers who constructively "discredit" (Weick, 1979) the systems, skills, or values traditionally revered by companies may cause a complete redefinition of core capabilities or initiate new ones. They can consciously manage projects for continuous organizational renewal. As numerous authors have noted (Clark and Fujimoto, 1991; Hayes et al., 1988; Pavitt, 1991), the need for this kind of emphasis on organizational learning over immediate output alone is a critical element of competition.

ACKNOWLEDGMENTS

The author is grateful to colleagues Kim Clark, Richard Hackman, and Steven Wheelwright as well as members of the research team and two anonymous reviewers for comments on earlier drafts of this paper, to the Division of Research at Harvard Business School for financial support, and to the companies that served as research sites.

A full report on the research on which this paper is based will be available in Kent Bowen, Kim Clark, Chuck Holoway, and Steven Wheelwright, *Vision and Capability: High Performance Product Development in the 1990s,* Oxford University Press, New York.

APPENDIX: METHODOLOGY

Structure of Research Teams
Four universities (Harvard, MIT, Stanford, and Purdue) participated in the "Manufacturing Visions" project. Each research team was composed of at least one engineering and one management professor plus one or two designated company employees. The research was organized into a matrix, with each research team having primary responsibility for one company and also one or more specific research "themes" across sites and companies. Some themes were identified in the research protocol; others (such as the capabilities/project interaction) emerged from initial data analysis. In data collection and analysis, the internal company and outside researchers served as important checks on each other— the company insiders on the generalizability of company observations from four cases and the academics on the generalizability of findings across companies.

Data-Gathering
Using a common research protocol, the teams developed case histories by interviewing development team members, including representatives from all functional groups who had taken active part and project staff members. These in-person interviews, conducted at multiple sites across the U.S., each lasted 1–3 hours.

Interviewers toured the manufacturing plants and design laboratories and conducted follow-up interview sessions as necessary to ensure comparable information across all cases. The data-gathering procedures thus adhered to those advocated by Huber and Power (1985) to increase reliability of retrospective accounts (e.g., interviews conducted in tandem, motivated informants selected from different organizational levels, all responses probed extensively). In addition, the interviewers' disparate backgrounds guarded against the dominance of one research bias, and much archival evidence was collected. I personally interviewed in 3 of the 5 companies.

Data Analysis

Notes compiled by each team were exchanged across a computer network and joint sessions were held every several months to discuss and analyze data. Company-specific and theme-specific reports were circulated, first among team members and then among all research teams to check on accuracy. Team members "tested" the data against their own notes and observations and reacted by refuting, confirming or refining it. There were four within-team iterations and an additional three iterations with the larger research group. Thus observations were subjected to numerous sets of "thought trials" (Weick, 1989).

Each team also presented interim reports to the host companies. These presentations offered the opportunity to check data for accuracy, obtain reactions to preliminary conclusions, fill in missing data and determine that observations drawn from a limited number of projects were in fact representative of common practice in the company. The examples of traditional core capabilities presented in Table 21.2 were provided by the companies as consensus judgments, usually involving others besides the company team members. While the 20 projects vary in the degree of success attributed to them by the companies, only two were clear failures. The others all succeeded in some ways (e.g., met a demanding schedule) but fell short in others (e.g., held market leadership for only a brief period).

NOTES

1. According to Quinn and Cameron, "(t)he key characteristic in paradox is the simultaneous presence of contradictory, even mutually exclusive elements" (1988:2).

2. Exceptions are historical cases about a developing technical innovation in an industry (see, for example, Rosenbloom and Cusumano, 1987).

3. Other members of the data-collection team on which I served are Kent Bowen, Douglas Braithwaite, William Hanson, Gil Preuss, and Michael Titelbaum. They contributed to the development of the ideas presented herein through discussion and reactions to early drafts of this paper.

4. Barney (1986) is a partial exception in that it poses organizational culture as a competitive advantage.

5. Schein distinguishes between these surface values and "preconscious" and "invisible" "basic assumptions" about the nature of reality (1984:4).

6. Each core capability draws upon only *some* of a company's skill and knowledge base, systems, and values. Not only do some skills, systems, and norms lie outside the domain of a particular core capability, but some may lie outside *all* core capabilities, as neither unique nor distinctly advantageous. For instance, although every company has personnel and pay systems, they may not constitute an important dimension of any core capability.

7. Such cycles, or "vicious circles" as psychiatry has labeled them, resemble the examples of self-fulfilling prophecies cited by Weick (1979: 159–164).

8. This observation is akin to Gidden's argument that structure is always both constraining and enabling (1984:25).

REFERENCES

Barney, J. B. "Organizational culture: Can it be a source of sustained competitive advantage?" *Academy of Management Review,* 11(3), 1986, pp. 656–665.

Burgelman, R. "A process model of internal corporate venturing in the diversified major firms," *Administrative Science Quarterly,* 28, 1983, pp. 223–244.

Burgelman, R. "Intraorganizational ecology of strategy making and organizational adaptation: Theory and field research," *Organization Science* 2(3), 1991, pp. 239–262.

Burns, T. and G. M. Stalker. *The Management of Innovation,* Tavistock, London, 1961.

Chakravarthy, B. S. "Adaptation: A promising metaphor for strategic management," *Academy of Management Review,* 7(1), 1982, pp. 35–44.

Clark, K. "The interaction of design hierarchies and market concepts in technological evolution," *Research Policy,* 14, 1985, pp. 235–251.

Clark, K. and T. Fujimoto. *Product Development Perfor-*

mance, Harvard Business School Press, Boston, MA 1991.

Foster, R. "A call for vision in managing technology," *Business Week,* May 24, 1982, pp. 24–33.

Giddens, A. *The Constitution of Society: Outline of the Theory of Structuration.* Polity Press, Cambridge, UK, 1984.

Hayes, R. H. "Strategic planning—forward in reverse?" *Harvard Business Review,* November–December 1985, pp. 111–119 (Reprint #85607).

Hayes, R. H., S. C. Wheelwright and K. B. Clark. *Dynamic Manufacturing: Creating the Learning Organization,* Free Press, New York, 1988.

Henderson, R. and K. B. Clark. "Architectural innovation: The reconfiguration of existing product technologies and the failure of established firms," *Administrative Science Quarterly,* 35, 1990, pp. 9–30.

Hitt, M. and R. D. Ireland. "Corporate distinctive competence, strategy, industry and performance," *Strategic Management Journal,* 6, 1985, pp. 273–293.

Hofer, C. W. and D. Schendel. *Strategy Formulation: Analytical Concepts.* West Publishing, St. Paul, MN, 1978.

Huber, G. and D. J. Power. "Retrospective reports of strategic-level managers: Guidelines for increasing their accuracy," *Strategic Management Journal,* 6(2), 1985, pp. 171–180.

Itami, H. with T. Roehl. *Mobilizing Invisible Assets,* Harvard University Press, Cambridge, MA, 1987.

Kanter, R. M. *The Change Masters.* Simon and Schuster, New York, 1983.

Kanter, R. M. "When a thousand flowers bloom: Structural, collective and social conditions for innovation in organizations," Harvard Business School Working Paper # 87-018, 1986.

Kimberly, J. R. "The study of organization: Toward a biographical perspective." In J. W. Lorsch (ed.), *Handbook of Organizational Behavior,* Prentice-Hall, Englewood Cliffs, NJ, 1987, pp. 223–237.

Leonard-Barton, D. "Implementation as mutual adaptation of technology and organization," *Research Policy,* 17, 1988a, pp. 251–267.

Leonard-Barton, D. "Implementation characteristics in organizational innovations," *Communication Research,* 15(5), October 1988b, pp. 603–631.

Leonard-Barton, D. "The factory as a learning laboratory," Harvard Business School Working Paper # 92-023, 1991.

Lieberman, M. and D. B. Montgomery. "First-mover advantages," *Strategic Management Journal,* 9, Summer 1988, pp. 41–58.

Mintzberg, H. "Strategy formation: Schools of thought." In J. W. Fredrickson (ed.), *Perspectives on Strategic Management,* Harper & Row, New York, 1990.

Mitchell, W. "Whether and when? Probability and timing of incumbents' entry into emerging industrial subfields," *Administrative Science Quarterly,* 34, 1989, pp. 208–230.

Pavitt, K. "Key characteristics of the large innovating firm," *British Journal of Management,* 2, 1991, pp. 41–50.

Pettigrew, A. "On studying organizational cultures," *Administrative Science Quarterly,* 24, 1979, pp. 570–581.

Pfeffer, J. *Organizations and Organization Theory,* Ballinger Publishing, Cambridge, MA, 1982.

Prahalad, C. K. and G. Hamel. "The core competence of the corporation," *Harvard Business Review,* 68(3), 1990, pp. 79–91 (Reprint #90311).

Quinn, J. B. *Strategies for Change: Logical Incrementalism,* Richard D. Irwin, Homewood, IL, 1980.

Quinn, R. and K. Cameron. "Organizational paradox and transformation." In R. Quinn and K. Cameron (eds.), *P-aradox and Transformation,* Cambridge, MA, Ballinger Publishing, 1988.

Rosenbloom, R. and M. Cusumano. "Technological pioneering and competitive advantage: The birth of the VCR industry," *California Management Review,* 29(4), 1987, pp. 51–76.

Rosenthal, R. and D. Rubin. "Interpersonal expectancy effects: The first 345 studies," *The Behavioral and Brain Sciences,* 3, 1978, pp. 377–415.

Rumelt, R. P. *Strategy, Structure and Economic Performance,* Harvard Business School Classics, Harvard Business School Press, Boston, MA, 1974 and 1986.

Schein, E. "Coming to a new awareness of organizational culture," *Sloan Management Review,* Winter, 1984, pp. 3–16.

Schein, E. *Organizational Culture and Leadership,* Jossey-Bass, San Francisco, CA, 1986.

Schumpeter, J. *Capitalism, Socialism, and Democracy,* Harper, New York, 1942.

Senge, P. "The leader's new work: Building a learning organization," *Sloan Management Review,* 32(1), 1990, pp. 7–23. (Reprint #3211).

Snow, C. C. and L. G. Hrebiniak. "Strategy, distinctive competence, and organizational performance," *Administrative Science Quarterly,* 25, 1980, pp. 317–335.

Souder, W. E. *Managing New Product Innovations,* Lexington Books, Lexington, MA, 1987.

Teece, D. J., G. Pisano and A. Shuen. "Firm capabilities, resources and the concept of strategy," Consortium on Competitiveness and Cooperation Working Paper # 90–9, University of California at Berkeley, Center for Research in Management, Berkeley, CA, 1990.

Tucker, D., J. Singh and A. Meinhard. "Founding characteristics, imprinting and organizational change." In J. V. Singh (ed.), *Organizational Evolution: New Directions,* Sage Publications, Newbury Park, CA, 1990.

Tushman, M. L. and P. Anderson. "Technological discontinuities and organizational environments," *Administrative Science Quarterly,* 31, 1986, pp. 439–465.

Van de Ven, A. "Central problems in management of innovations," *Management Science,* 32(5), 1986, pp. 590–607.

von Hippel, E. "The impact of 'Sticky Data' on innovation and problem-solving," Sloan Management School, Working Paper # 3147-90-BPS, 1990.

Weick, K. E. "Theory construction as disciplined imagination," *Academy of Management Review,* 14(4), 1989, pp. 516–531.

Weick, K. E. *The Social Psychology of Organizing,* Random House, New York, 1979.

Whitney, D. "Manufacturing by design," *Harvard Business Review,* 66(4), 1988, pp. 83–91.

Zucker, L. G. "The role of institutionalization in cultural persistence," *American Sociological Review,* 42, 1977, pp. 726–743.

SECTION IV

INNOVATION AND BUSINESS STRATEGY

History is replete with examples of firms that pioneered innovations, only to watch rivals capture most of the profits. A new product, process, or service will not succeed in the marketplace simply because it is "better" on some dimensions. To realize superior returns, the innovator must be able to differentiate itself from imitators. Otherwise, it will assume all the costs and burdens of exploration only to see margins tumble as cheaper or slightly improved copies of its original breakthrough proliferate. Creating and sustaining valuable, differentiated positions is the domain of business strategy.

Innovation strategies must take into account the shifting landscape caused by fast-changing customer preferences and competitors' adjustments. Technological superiority alone may not generate growth, particularly if an innovator takes today's value drivers for granted. Changing the terms of engagement by offering new customer value propositions will often produce better results than playing the game by today's rules. Choosing one's innovation path with an eye toward alternative growth scenarios is equally important. In a dynamic environment, new products and services often succeed or fail for unforeseen reasons. It is impossible to specify in a plan how markets and rivals will react to an innovation, but it is possible to manage a portfolio of projects to maximize its option value.

Teece, Pisano, and Shuen address the problem of sustaining differentiation by introducing the idea of "dynamic capabilities." They build on the resource-based view of the firm, which suggests that competitive advantage springs from core competences: distinctive assets, processes, and know-how that are difficult to imitate. In fast-changing environments, they contend, competitive advantage stems from being able to integrate, build, and reconfigure existing competences. Developing a superior capacity for creating and rearranging routines is the key task of strategic management under such conditions. Kim and Mauborgne place the idea of value innovation at the heart of strategic thinking. In their view, competitive advantage does not stem from assessing what competitors do and doing it better. Rather, successful innovators render competition irrelevant by providing buyers with a significant increase in value, priced to reach the mass of buyers. The authors pose five questions that contrast the conventional logic with this strategic orientation and highlight the importance of motivating knowledge workers to make value innovation happen. MacMillan and McGrath set forth a portfolio approach to planning research and development projects. They recommend assessing market and technical uncertainty and then allocating resources among three types of option-creating initiatives, balancing new platforms with enhancements to existing ones. By translating high-level strategic positions into concrete innovation projects in this fashion, they suggest, a firm can implement new products and services rapidly while maintaining the flexibility needed to adjust to unexpected events.

22

Dynamic Capabilities and Strategic Management

DAVID J. TEECE
GARY PISANO
AMY SHUEN

The dynamic capabilities framework analyzes the sources and methods of wealth creation and capture by private enterprise firms operating in environments of rapid technological change. The competitive advantage of firms is seen as resting on distinctive processes (ways of coordinating and combining), shaped by the firm's (specific) asset positions (such as the firm's portfolio of difficult-to-trade knowledge assets and complementary assets), and the evolution path(s) it has adopted or inherited. The importance of path dependencies is amplified where conditions of increasing returns exist. Whether and how a firm's competitive advantage is eroded depends on the stability of market demand, and the ease of replicability (expanding internally) and imitatability (replication by competitors). If correct, the framework suggests that private wealth creation in regimes of rapid technological change depends in large measure on honing internal technological, organizational, and managerial processes inside the firm. In short, identifying new opportunities and organizing effectively and efficiently to embrace them are generally more fundamental to private wealth creation than is strategizing, if by strategizing one means engaging in business conduct that keeps competitors off balance, raises rival's costs, and excludes new entrants.

INTRODUCTION

The fundamental question in the field of strategic management is how firms achieve and sustain competitive advantage.[1] We confront this question here by developing the dynamic capabilities approach, which endeavors to analyze the sources of wealth creation and capture by firms. The development of this framework flows from a recognition by the authors that strategic theory is replete with analyses of firm-level strategies for sustaining and safeguarding extant competitive advantage, but has performed less well with respect to assisting in the understanding of how and why certain firms build competitive advantage in regimes of rapid change. Our approach is especially relevant in a Schumpeterian world of innovation-based competition, price/performance rivalry, increasing returns, and the "creative destruction" of existing competences. The approach endeavors to explain firm-level success and failure. We are interested in both building a better theory of firm performance, as well as informing managerial practice.

In order to position our analysis in a manner that displays similarities and differences with existing approaches, we begin by briefly reviewing accepted frameworks for strategic management. We endeavor to expose implicit assumptions, and identify competitive circumstances where each paradigm might display some relative advantage as both a useful descriptive

Reprinted from *Strategic Management Journal*, Vol. 18, David J. Teece, Gary Pisano, and Amy Shuen, "Dynamic Capabilities and Strategic Management," pp. 509–533, copyright © 1997. Reproduced by permission of John Wiley & Sons Limited.

and normative theory of competitive strategy. While numerous theories have been advanced over the past two decades about the sources of competitive advantage, many cluster around just a few loosely structured frameworks or paradigms. In this paper we attempt to identify three existing paradigms and describe aspects of an emerging new paradigm that we label dynamic capabilities.

The dominant paradigm in the field during the 1980s was the competitive forces approach developed by Porter (1980). This approach, rooted in the structure–conduct–performance paradigm of industrial organization (Mason, 1949; Bain, 1959), emphasizes the actions a firm can take to create defensible positions against competitive forces. A second approach, referred to as a strategic conflict approach (e.g., Shapiro, 1989), is closely related to the first in its focus on product market imperfections, entry deterrence, and strategic interaction. The strategic conflict approach uses the tools of game theory and thus implicitly views competitive outcomes as a function of the effectiveness with which firms keep their rivals off balance through strategic investments, pricing strategies, signaling, and the control of information. Both the competitive forces and the strategic conflict approaches appear to share the view that rents flow from privileged product market positions.

Another distinct class of approaches emphasizes building competitive advantage through capturing entrepreneurial rents stemming from fundamental firm-level efficiency advantages. These approaches have their roots in a much older discussion of corporate strengths and weaknesses; they have taken on new life as evidence suggests that firms build enduring advantages only through efficiency and effectiveness, and as developments in organizational economics and the study of technological and organizational change become applied to strategy questions. One strand of this literature, often referred to as the "resource-based perspective," emphasizes firm-specific capabilities and assets and the existence of isolating mechanisms as the fundamental determinants of firm performance (Penrose, 1959; Rumelt, 1984; Teece, 1984; Wernerfelt, 1984).[2] This perspective recognizes but does not attempt to explain the nature of the isolating mechanisms that enable entrepreneurial rents and competitive advantage to be sustained.

Another component of the efficiency-based approach is developed in this paper. Rudimentary efforts are made to identify the dimensions of firm-specific capabilities that can be sources of advantage, and to explain how combinations of competences and resources can be developed, deployed, and protected. We refer to this as the "dynamic capabilities" approach in order to stress exploiting existing internal and external firm-specific competences to address changing environments. Elements of the approach can be found in Schumpeter (1942), Penrose (1959), Nelson and Winter (1982), Prahalad and Hamel (1990), Teece (1976, 1986a, 1986b, 1988), and in Hayes, Wheelwright, and Clark (1988). Because this approach emphasizes the development of management capabilities, and difficult to-imitate combinations of organizational, functional and technological skills, it integrates and draws upon research in such areas as the management of R&D, product and process development, technology transfer, intellectual property, manufacturing, human resources, and organizational learning. Because these fields are often viewed as outside the traditional boundaries of strategy, much of this research has not been incorporated into existing economic approaches to strategy issues. As a result, dynamic capabilities can be seen as an emerging and potentially integrative approach to understanding the newer sources of competitive advantage.

We suggest that the dynamic capabilities approach is promising both in terms of future research potential and as an aid to management endeavoring to gain competitive advantage in increasingly demanding environments. To illustrate the essential elements of the dynamic capabilities approach, the sections that follow compare and contrast this approach to other models of strategy. Each section highlights the strategic insights provided by each approach as well as the different competitive circumstances in which it might be most appropriate. Needless to say, these approaches are in many ways complementary and a full understanding of firm-level, competitive advantage requires an appreciation of all four approaches and more.

MODELS OF STRATEGY EMPHASIZING THE EXPLOITATION OF MARKET POWER

Competitive Forces

The dominant paradigm in strategy at least during the 1980s was the competitive forces approach. Pioneered by Porter (1980), the competitive forces approach views the essence of competitive strategy formulation as "relating a company to its environment . . . [T]he key aspect of the firm's environment is the industry or industries in which it competes." Industry structure strongly influences the competitive rules of the game as well as the strategies potentially available to firms.

In the competitive forces model, five industry-level forces—entry barriers, threat of substitution, bargaining power of buyers, bargaining power of suppliers, and rivalry among industry incumbents—determine the inherent profit potential of an industry or subsegment of an industry. The approach can be used to help the firm find a position in an industry from which it can best defend itself against competitive forces or influence them in its favor (Porter, 1980: 4).

This "five-forces" framework provides a systematic way of thinking about how competitive forces work at the industry level and how these forces determine the profitability of different industries and industry segments. The competitive forces framework also contains a number of underlying assumptions about the sources of competition and the nature of the strategy process. To facilitate comparisons with other approaches, we highlight several distinctive characteristics of the framework.

Economic rents in the competitive forces framework are monopoly rents (Teece, 1984). Firms in an industry earn rents when they are somehow able to impede the competitive forces (in either factor markets or product markets) which tend to drive economic returns to zero. Available strategies are described in Porter (1980). Competitive strategies are often aimed at altering the firm's position in the industry vis-à-vis competitors and suppliers. Industry structure plays a central role in determining and limiting strategic action.

Some industries or subsectors of industries become more "attractive" because they have structural impediments to competitive forces (e.g., entry barriers) that allow firms better opportunities for creating sustainable competitive advantages. Rents are created largely at the industry or subsector level rather than at the firm level. While there is some recognition given to firm-specific assets, differences among firms relate primarily to scale. This approach to strategy reflects its incubation inside the field of industrial organization and in particular the industrial structure school of Mason and Bain[3] (Teece, 1984).

Strategic Conflict

The publication of Carl Shapiro's 1989 article, confidently titled "The Theory of Business Strategy," announced the emergence of a new approach to business strategy, if not strategic management. This approach utilizes the tools of game theory to analyze the nature of competitive interaction between rival firms. The main thrust of work in this tradition is to reveal how a firm can influence the behavior and actions of rival firms and thus the market environment.[4] Examples of such moves are investment in capacity (Dixit, 1980), R&D (Gilbert and Newberry, 1982), and advertising (Schmalensee, 1983). To be effective, these strategic moves require irreversible commitments.[5] The moves in question will have no effect if they can be costlessly undone. A key idea is that by manipulating the market environment, a firm may be able to increase its profits.

This literature, together with the contestability literature (Baumol, Panzar, and Willig, 1982), has led to a greater appreciation of the role of sunk costs, as opposed to fixed costs, in determining competitive outcomes. Strategic moves can also be designed to influence rivals' behavior through signaling. Strategic signaling has been examined in a number of contexts, including predatory pricing (Kreps and Wilson, 1982a, 1982b) and limit pricing (Milgrom and Roberts, 1982a, 1982b). More recent treatments have emphasized the role of commitment and reputation (e.g., Ghemawat, 1991) and the benefits of firms simultaneously pursuing competition and cooperation[6] (Brandenburger and Nalebuff, 1995, 1996).

In many instances, game theory formalizes long-standing intuitive arguments about various types of business behavior (e.g., predatory pricing, patent races), though in some instances it has induced a substantial change in the conventional wisdom. But by rationalizing observed behavior by reference to suitably designed games, in explaining everything these models also explain nothing, as they do not generate testable predictions (Sutton, 1992). Many specific game-theoretic models admit multiple equilibrium, and a wide range of choice exists as to the design of the appropriate game form to be used. Unfortunately, the results often depend on the precise specification chosen. The equilibrium in models of strategic behavior crucially depends on what one rival believes another rival will do in a particular situation. Thus the qualitative features of the results may depend on the way price competition is modeled (e.g., Bertrand or Cournot) or on the presence or absence of strategic asymmetries such as first-mover advantages. The analysis of strategic moves using game theory can be thought of as "dynamic" in the sense that multiperiod analyses can be pursued both intuitively and formally. However, we use the term "dynamic" in this paper in a different sense, referring to situations where there is rapid change in technology and market forces, and "feedback" effects on firms.[7]

We have a particular view of the contexts in which the strategic conflict literature is relevant to strategic management. Firms that have a tremendous cost or other competitive advantage vis-à-vis their rivals ought not be transfixed by the moves and countermoves of their rivals. Their competitive fortunes will swing more on total demand conditions, not on how competitors deploy and redeploy their competitive assets. Put differently, when there are gross symmetries in competitive advantage between firms, the results of game-theoretic analysis are likely to be obvious and uninteresting. The stronger competitor will generally advance, even if disadvantaged by certain information asymmetries. To be sure, incumbent firms can be undone by new entrants with a dramatic cost advantage, but no "gaming" will overturn that outcome. On the other hand, if firms' competitive positions are more delicately balanced, as with Coke and Pepsi, and United Airlines and American Airlines, then strategic conflict is of interest to competitive outcomes. Needless to say, there are many such circumstances, but they are rare in industries where there is rapid technological change and fast-shifting market circumstances.

In short, where competitors do not have deep-seated competitive advantages, the moves and countermoves of competitors can often be usefully formulated in game-theoretic terms. However, we doubt that game theory can comprehensively illuminate how Chrysler should compete against Toyota and Honda, or how United Airlines can best respond to Southwest Airlines since Southwest's advantage is built on organizational attributes which United cannot readily replicate.[8] Indeed, the entrepreneurial side of strategy—how significant new rent streams are created and protected—is largely ignored by the game-theoretic approach.[9] Accordingly, we find that the approach, while important, is most relevant when competitors are closely matched[10] and the population of relevant competitors

and the identity of their strategic alternatives can be readily ascertained. Nevertheless, coupled with other approaches it can sometimes yield powerful insights.

However, this research has an orientation that we are concerned about in terms of the implicit framing of strategic issues. Rents, from a game-theoretic perspective, are ultimately a result of managers' intellectual ability to "play the game." The adage of the strategist steeped in this approach is "do unto others before they do unto you." We worry that fascination with strategic moves and Machiavellian tricks will distract managers from seeking to build more enduring sources of competitive advantage. The approach unfortunately ignores competition as a process involving the development, accumulation, combination, and protection of unique skills and capabilities. Since strategic interactions are what receive focal attention, the impression one might receive from this literature is that success in the marketplace is the result of sophisticated plays and counterplays, when this is generally not the case at all.[11]

In what follows, we suggest that building a dynamic view of the business enterprise—something missing from the two approaches we have so far identified—enhances the probability of establishing an acceptable descriptive theory of strategy that can assist practitioners in the building of long-run advantage and competitive flexibility. Below, we discuss first the resource-based perspective and then an extension we call the dynamic capabilities approach.

MODELS OF STRATEGY EMPHASIZING EFFICIENCY

Resource-Based Perspective

The resource-based approach sees firms with superior systems and structures being profitable not because they engage in strategic investments that may deter entry and raise prices above long-run costs, but because they have markedly lower costs, or offer markedly higher quality or product performance. This approach focuses on the rents accruing to the owners of scarce firm-specific resources rather than the economic profits from product market positioning.[12] Competitive advantage lies 'upstream' of product markets and rests on the firm's idiosyncratic and difficult-to-imitate resources.[13]

One can find the resources approach suggested by the earlier preanalytic strategy literature. A leading text of the 1960s (Learned et al., 1969) noted that "the capability of an organization is its demonstrated and potential ability to accomplish against the opposition of circumstance or competition, whatever it sets out to do. Every organization has actual and potential strengths and weaknesses; it is important to try to determine what they are and to distinguish one from the other." Thus what a firm can do is not just a function of the opportunities it confronts; it also depends on what resources the organization can muster.

Learned et al. proposed that the real key to a company's success or even to its future development lies in its ability to find or create "a competence that is truly distinctive."[14] This literature also recognized the constraints on firm behavior and, in particular, noted that one should not assume that management "can rise to any occasion." These insights do appear to keenly anticipate the resource-based approach that has since emerged, but they did not provide a theory or systematic framework for analyzing business strategies. Indeed, Andrews (1987: 46) noted that "much of what is intuitive in this process is yet to be identified." Unfortunately, the academic literature on capabilities stalled for a couple of decades.

New impetus has been given to the resource-based approach by recent theoretical developments in organizational economics and in the theory of strategy, as well as by a growing body of anecdotal and empirical literature[15] that highlights the importance of firm-specific factors in explaining firm performance. Cool and Schendel (1988) have shown that there are systematic and significant performance differences among firms which belong to the same strategic group within the U.S. pharmaceutical industry. Rumelt (1991) has shown that intraindustry differences in profits are greater than interindustry differences in profits, strongly suggesting the importance of firm-specific factors and the relative unimportance of industry effects.[16] Jacobsen (1988) and Hansen and Wernerfelt (1989) made similar findings.

A comparison of the resource-based approach and the competitive forces approach (discussed earlier in the paper) in terms of their implications for the strategy process is revealing. From the first perspective, an entry decision looks roughly as follows: (1) pick an industry (based on its "structural attractiveness"); (2) choose an entry strategy based on conjectures about competitors' rational strategies; (3) if not already possessed, acquire or otherwise obtain the requisite assets to compete in the market. From this perspective, the process of identifying and developing the requisite assets is not particularly problematic. The process involves nothing more than choosing rationally among a well-defined set of investment alternatives. If assets are not already owned, they can be bought. The resource-based perspective is strongly at odds with this conceptualization.

From the resource-based perspective, firms are heterogeneous with respect to their resources/capabilities/endowments. Further, resource endowments are "sticky": at least in the short run, firms are to some degree stuck with what they have and may have to live with what they lack.[17] This stickiness arises for three reasons. First, business development is viewed as an extremely complex process.[18] Quite simply, firms lack the organizational capacity to develop new competences quickly (Dierickx and Cool, 1989). Secondly, some assets are simply not readily tradeable, for example, tacit know-how (Teece, 1976, 1980) and reputation (Dierickx and Cool, 1989). Thus, resource endowments cannot equilibrate through factor input markets. Finally, even when an asset can be purchased, firms may stand to gain little by doing so. As Barney (1986) points out, unless a firm is lucky, possesses superior information, or both, the price it pays in a competitive factor market will fully capitalize the rents from the asset.

Given that in the resources perspective firms possess heterogeneous and sticky resource bundles, the entry decision process suggested by this approach is as follows: (1) identify your firm's unique resources; (2) decide in which markets those resources can earn the highest rents; and (3) decide whether the rents from those assets are most effectively utilized by (a) integrating into related market(s), (b) selling the relevant intermediate output to related firms, or (c) selling the assets themselves to a firm in related businesses (Teece, 1980, 1982).

The resource-based perspective puts both vertical integration and diversification into a new strategic light. Both can be viewed as ways of capturing rents on scarce, firm-specific assets whose services are difficult to sell in intermediate markets (Penrose, 1959; Williamson, 1975; Teece, 1980, 1982, 1986a, 1986b; Wernerfelt, 1984). Empirical work on the relationship between performance and diversification by Werner-felt and Montgomery (1988) provides evidence for this proposition. It is evident that the resource-based per-spective focuses on strategies for exploiting existing firm-specific assets.

However, the resource-based perspective also invites consideration of managerial strategies for developing new capabilities (Wernerfelt, 1984). Indeed, if control over scarce resources is the source of economic profits, then it follows that such issues as skill acquisition, the management of knowledge and know-how (Shuen, 1994), and learning become fundamental strategic issues. It is in this second dimension, encompassing skill acquisition, learning, and accumulation of organizational and intangible or "invisible" assets (Itami and Roehl, 1987), that we believe lies the greatest potential for contributions to strategy.

The Dynamic Capabilities Approach: Overview

The global competitive battles in high-technology industries such as semiconductors, information services, and software have demonstrated the need for an expanded paradigm to understand how competitive advantage is achieved. Well-known companies like IBM, Texas Instruments, Philips, and others appear to have followed a "resource-based strategy" of accumulating valuable technology assets, often guarded by an aggressive intellectual property stance. However, this strategy is often not enough to support a significant competitive advantage. Winners in the global marketplace have been firms that can demonstrate timely responsiveness and rapid and flexible product innovation, coupled with the management capability to effectively coordinate and redeploy internal and external competences. Not surprisingly, industry observers have remarked that companies can accumulate a large stock of valuable technology assets and still not have many useful capabilities.

We refer to this ability to achieve new forms of competitive advantage as "dynamic capabilities" to emphasize two key aspects that were not the main focus of attention in previous strategy perspectives. The term "dynamic" refers to the capacity to renew competences so as to achieve congruence with the changing business environment; certain innovative responses are required when time-to-market and timing are critical, the rate of technological change is rapid, and the nature of future competition and markets difficult to determine. The term "capabilities" emphasizes the key role of strategic management in appropriately adapting, integrating, and reconfiguring internal and external organizational skills, resources, and functional competences to match the requirements of a changing environment.

One aspect of the strategic problem facing an innovating firm in a world of Schumpeterian competition is to identify difficult-to-imitate internal and external competences most likely to support valuable products and services. Thus, as argued by Dierickx and Cool (1989), choices about how much to spend (invest) on different possible areas are central to the firm's strategy. However, choices about domains of competence are influenced by past choices. At any given point in time, firms must follow a certain trajectory or path of competence development. This path not only defines what choices are open to the firm today, but it also puts bounds around what its internal repertoire is likely to be in the future. Thus, firms, at various points in time, make long-term, quasi-irreversible commitments to certain domains of competence.[19]

The notion that competitive advantage requires both the exploitation of existing internal and external firm-specific capabilities and developing new ones is partially developed in Penrose (1959), Teece (1982), and Wernerfelt (1984). However, only recently have researchers begun to focus on the specifics of how some organizations first develop firm-specific capabilities and how they renew competences to respond to shifts in the business environment.[20] These issues are intimately tied to the firm's business processes, market positions, and expansion paths. Several writers have recently offered insights and evidence on how firms can develop their capability to adapt and even capitalize on rapidly changing environments.[21] The dynamic capabilities approach seeks to provide a coherent framework which can both integrate existing conceptual and empirical knowledge, and facilitate prescription. In doing so, it builds upon the theoretical foundations provided by Schumpeter (1934), Penrose (1959), Williamson (1975, 1985), Barney (1986), Nelson and Winter (1982), Teece (1988), and Teece et al. (1994).

TOWARD A DYNAMIC CAPABILITIES FRAMEWORK

Terminology

In order to facilitate theory development and intellectual dialogue, some acceptable definitions are desirable. We propose the following.

FACTORS OF PRODUCTION

These are "undifferentiated" inputs available in disaggregate form in factor markets. By undifferentiated we mean that they lack a firm-specific component. Land, unskilled labor, and capital are typical examples. Some factors may be available for the taking, such as public knowledge. In the language of Arrow, such resources must be "nonfugitive."[22] Property rights are usually well defined for factors of production.

RESOURCES[23]

Resources are firm-specific assets that are difficult if not impossible to imitate. Trade secrets and certain specialized production facilities and engineering experience are examples. Such assets are difficult to transfer among firms because of transactions costs and transfer costs, and because the assets may contain tacit knowledge.

ORGANIZATIONAL ROUTINES/COMPETENCES

When firm-specific assets are assembled in integrated clusters spanning individuals and groups so that they enable distinctive activities to be performed, these activities constitute organizational routines and processes. Examples include quality, miniaturization, and systems integration. Such competences are typically viable across multiple product lines, and may extend outside the firm to embrace alliance partners.

CORE COMPETENCES

We define those competences that define a firm's fundamental business as core. Core competences must accordingly be derived by looking across the range of a firm's (and its competitors) products and services.[24] The value of core competences can be enhanced by combination with the appropriate complementary assets. The degree to which a core competence is distinctive depends on how well endowed the firm is relative to its competitors, and on how difficult it is for competitors to replicate its competences.

DYNAMIC CAPABILITIES

We define dynamic capabilities as the firm's ability to integrate, build, and reconfigure internal and external competences to address rapidly changing environments. Dynamic capabilities thus reflect an organization's ability to achieve new and innovative forms of competitive advantage given path dependencies and market positions (Leonard-Barton, 1992).

PRODUCTS

End products are the final goods and services produced by the firm based on utilizing the competences that it possesses. The performance (price, quality, etc.) of a firm's products relative to its competitors at any point in time will depend upon its competences (which over time depend on its capabilities).

Markets and Strategic Capabilities

Different approaches to strategy view sources of wealth creation and the essence of the strategic problem faced by firms differently. The competitive forces framework sees the strategic problem in terms of industry structure, entry deterrence, and positioning; game-theoretic models view the strategic problem as one of interaction between rivals with certain expectations about how each other will behave;[25] resource-based perspectives have focused on the exploitation of firm-specific assets. Each approach asks different, often complementary questions. A key step in building a conceptual framework related to dynamic capabilities is to identify the foundations upon which distinctive and difficult-to-replicate advantages can be built, maintained, and enhanced.

A useful way to vector in on the strategic elements of the business enterprise is first to identify what is not strategic. To be strategic, a capability must be honed to a user need[26] (so there is a source of revenues), unique (so that the products/services produced can be priced without too much regard to competition) and difficult to replicate (so profits will not be competed away). Accordingly, any assets or entity which are homogeneous and can be bought and sold at an established price cannot be all that strategic (Barney, 1986). What is it, then, about firms which undergirds competitive advantage?

To answer this, one must first make some fundamental distinctions between markets and internal organization (firms). The essence of the firm, as Coase

(1937) pointed out, is that it displaces market organization. It does so in the main because inside the firms one can organize certain types of economic activity in ways one cannot using markets. This is not only because of transaction costs, as Williamson (1975, 1985) emphasized, but also because there are many types of arrangements where injecting high-powered (market like) incentives might well be quite destructive of cooperative activity and learning.[27] Inside an organization, exchange cannot take place in the same manner that it can outside an organization, not just because it might be destructive to provide high-powered individual incentives, but because it is difficult if not impossible to tightly calibrate individual contribution to a joint effort. Hence, contrary to Arrow's (1969) view of firms as quasi markets, and the task of management to inject markets into firms, we recognize the inherent limits and possible counterproductive results of attempting to fashion firms into simply clusters of internal markets. In particular, learning and internal technology transfer may well be jeopardized.

Indeed, what is distinctive about firms is that they are domains for organizing activity in a nonmarket-like fashion. Accordingly, as we discuss what is distinctive about firms, we stress competences/capabilities which are ways of organizing and getting things done which cannot be accomplished merely by using the price system to coordinate activity.[28] The very essence of most capabilities/competences is that they cannot be readily assembled through markets (Teece, 1982, 1986a; Zander and Kogut, 1995). If the ability to assemble competences using markets is what is meant by the firm as a nexus of contracts (Fama, 1980), then we unequivocally state that the firm about which we theorize cannot be usefully modeled as a nexus of contracts. By "contract" we are referring to a transaction undergirded by a legal agreement, or some other arrangement which clearly spells out rights, rewards, and responsibilities. Moreover, the firm as a nexus of contracts suggests a series of bilateral contracts orchestrated by a coordinator. Our view of the firm is that the organization takes place in a more multilateral fashion, with patterns of behavior and learning being orchestrated in a much more decentralized fashion, but with a viable headquarters operation.

The key point, however, is that the properties of internal organization cannot be replicated by a portfolio of business units amalgamated just through formal contracts as many distinctive elements of internal organization simply cannot be replicated in the market.[29] That is, entrepreneurial activity cannot lead to the immediate replication of unique organizational skills through simply entering a market and piecing the parts together overnight. Replication takes time, and the replication of best practice may be illusive. Indeed, firm capabilities need to be understood not in terms of balance sheet items, but mainly in terms of the organizational structures and managerial processes which support productive activity. By construction, the firm's balance sheet contains items that can be valued, at least at original market prices (cost). It is necessarily the case, therefore, that the balance sheet is a poor shadow of a firm's distinctive competences.[30] That which is distinctive cannot be bought and sold short of buying the firm itself, or one or more of its subunits.

There are many dimensions of the business firm that must be understood if one is to grasp firm-level distinctive competences/capabilities. In this paper we merely identify several classes of factors that will help determine a firm's distinctive competence and dynamic capabilities. We organize these in three categories: processes, positions, and paths. The essence of competences and capabilities is embedded in organizational processes of one kind or another. But the content of these processes and the opportunities they afford for developing competitive advantage at any point in time are shaped significantly by the assets the firm possesses (internal and market) and by the evolutionary path it has adopted/inherited. Hence organizational processes, shaped by the firm's asset positions and molded by its evolutionary and co-evolutionary paths, explain the essence of the firm's dynamic capabilities and its competitive advantage.

Processes, Positions, and Paths

We thus advance the argument that the competitive advantage of firms lies with its managerial and organizational processes, shaped by its (specific) asset position, and the paths available to it.[31] By managerial and organizational processes, we refer to the way things are done in the firm, or what might be referred to as its routines, or patterns of current practice and learning. By position we refer to its current specific endowments of technology, intellectual property, complementary assets, customer base, and its external relations with suppliers and complementors. By paths we refer to the strategic alternatives available to the firm, and the presence or absence of increasing returns and attendant path dependencies.

Our focus throughout is on asset structures for which no ready market exists, as these are the only assets of strategic interest. A final section focuses on replication and imitation, as it is these phenomena which determine how readily a competence or capability can be cloned by competitors, and therefore distinctiveness of its competences and the durability of its advantage.

The firm's processes and positions collectively encompass its competences and capabilities. A hierarchy of competences/capabilities ought to be recognized, as some competences may be on the factory floor, some in the R&D labs, some in the executive suites, and some in the way everything is integrated. A difficult-to-replicate or difficult-to-imitate competence was defined earlier as a distinctive competence. As indicated, the key feature of distinctive competence is that there is not a market for it, except possibly through the market for business units. Hence competences and capabilities are intriguing assets as they typically must be built because they cannot be bought.

Organizational and Managerial Processes

Organizational processes have three roles: coordination/integration (a static concept); learning (a dynamic concept); and reconfiguration (a transformational concept). We discuss each in turn.

Coordination/integration. While the price system supposedly coordinates the economy,[32] managers coordinate or integrate activity inside the firm. How efficiently and effectively internal coordination or integration is achieved is very important (Aoki, 1990).[33] Likewise for external coordination.[34] Increasingly, strategic advantage requires the integration of external activities and technologies. The growing literature on strategic alliances, the virtual corporation, and buyer-supplier relations and technology collaboration evidences the importance of external integration and sourcing.

There is some field-based empirical research that provides support for the notion that the way production is organized by management inside the firm is the source of differences in firms' competence in various domains. For example, Garvin's (1988) study of 18 room air-conditioning plants reveals that quality performance was not related to either capital investment or the degree of automation of the facilities. Instead, quality performance was driven by special organizational routines. These included routines for gathering and processing information, for linking customer experiences with engineering design choices, and for coordinating factories and component suppliers.[35] The work of Clark and Fujimoto (1991) on project development in the automobile industry also illustrates the role played by coordinative routines. Their study reveals a significant degree of variation in how different firms coordinate the various activities required to bring a new model from concept to market. These differences in coordinative routines and capabilities seem to have a significant impact on such performance variables as development cost, development lead times, and quality. Furthermore, Clark and Fujimoto tended to find significant firm-level differences in coordination routines and these differences seemed to have persisted for a long time. This suggests that routines related to coordination are firm-specific in nature.

Also, the notion that competence/capability is embedded in distinct ways of coordinating and combining helps to explain how and why seemingly minor technological changes can have devastating impacts on incumbent firms' abilities to compete in a market. Henderson and Clark (1990), for example, have shown that incumbents in the photolithographic equipment industry were sequentially devasted by seemingly minor innovations that, nevertheless, had major impacts on how systems had to be configured. They attribute these difficulties to the fact that systems-level or "architectural" innovations often require new routines to integrate and coordinate engineering tasks. These findings and others suggest that productive systems display high interdependency, and that it may not be possible to change one level without changing others. This appears to be true with respect to the "lean production" model (Womack et al., 1991) which has now transformed the Taylor or Ford model of manufacturing organization in the automobile industry.[36] Lean production requires distinctive shop floor practices and processes as well as distinctive higher-order managerial processes. Put differently, organizational processes often display high levels of coherence, and when they do, replication may be difficult because it requires systemic changes throughout the organization and also among interorganizational linkages, which might be very hard to effectuate. Put differently, partial imitation or replication of a successful model may yield zero benefits.[37]

The notion that there is a certain rationality or coherence to processes and systems is not quite the same concept as corporate culture, as we understand the latter. Corporate culture refers to the values and beliefs that employees hold; culture can be a de facto governance system as it mediates the behavior of individuals and economizes on more formal administrative methods. Rationality or coherence notions are more akin to the Nelson and Winter (1982) notion of organizational routines. However, the routines concept is a little too amorphous to properly capture the congruence amongst processes and between processes and incentives that we have in mind. Consider a professional service organization like an accounting firm. If it is to have relatively high-powered incentives that reward individual performance, then it must build organizational processes that channel individual behavior; if it has weak or low-powered incentives, it must find symbolic ways to recognize the high performers, and it must use alternative methods to build effort and enthusiasm. What one may think of as styles of organization in fact contain necessary, not discretionary, elements to achieve performance.

Recognizing the congruences and complementarities among processes, and between processes and incentives, is critical to the understanding of organizational capabilities. In particular, they can help us explain why architectural and radical innovations are so often introduced into an industry by new entrants. The incumbents develop distinctive organizational processes that cannot support the new technology, despite certain overt similarities between the old and the new. The frequent failure of incumbents to introduce new technologies can thus be seen as a consequence of the mismatch that so often exists between the set of organizational processes needed to support the conventional product/service and the requirements of the new. Radical organizational reengineering will usually be required to support the new product, which may well do better embedded in a separate subsidiary where a new set of coherent organizational processes can be fashioned.[38]

Learning. Perhaps even more important than integration is learning. Learning is a process by which repetition and experimentation enable tasks to be performed better and quicker. It also enables new production opportunities to be identified.[39] In the context of the firm, if not more generally, learning has several key characteristics. First, learning involves organizational as well as individual skills.[40] While individual skills are of relevance, their value depends upon their employment, in particular organizational settings. Learning processes are intrinsically social and collective and occur not only through the imitation and emulation of individuals, as with teacher–student or master–apprentice, but also because of joint contributions to the understanding of complex problems.[41] Learning requires common codes of communication and coordinated search procedures. Second, the organizational knowledge generated by such activity resides in new patterns of activity, in "routines," or a new logic of organization. As indicated earlier, routines are patterns of interactions that represent successful solutions to particular problems. These patterns of interaction are resident in group behavior, though certain subroutines may be resident in individual behavior. The concept of dynamic capabilities as a coordinative management process opens the door to the potential for interorganizational learning. Researchers (Doz and Shuen, 1990; Mody, 1993) have pointed out that collaborations and partnerships can be a vehicle for new organizational learning, helping firms to recognize dysfunctional routines, and preventing strategic blindspots.

Reconfiguration and transformation. In rapidly changing environments, there is obviously value in the ability to sense the need to reconfigure the firm's asset structure, and to accomplish the necessary internal and external transformation (Amit and Schoemaker, 1993; Langlois, 1994). This requires constant surveillance of markets and technologies and the willingness to adopt best practice. In this regard, benchmarking is of considerable value as an organized process for accomplishing such ends (Camp, 1989). In dynamic environments, narcissistic organizations are likely to be impaired. The capacity to reconfigure and transform is itself a learned organizational skill. The more frequently practiced, the easier accomplished.

Change is costly and so firms must develop processes to minimize low pay-off change. The ability to calibrate the requirements for change and to effectuate the necessary adjustments would appear to depend on the ability to scan the environment, to evaluate markets and competitors, and to quickly accomplish reconfiguration and transformation ahead of competition. Decentralization and local autonomy assist these processes. Firms that have honed these capabilities are sometimes referred to as "high-flex."

POSITIONS

The strategic posture of a firm is determined not only by its learning processes and by the coherence of its internal and external processes and incentives, but also by its specific assets. By specific assets we mean, for example, its specialized plant and equipment. These include its difficult-to-trade knowledge assets and assets complementary to them, as well as its reputational and relational assets. Such assets determine its competitive advantage at any point in time. We identify several illustrative classes.

Technological assets. While there is an emerging market for know-how (Teece, 1981), much technology does not enter it. This is either because the firm is unwilling to sell it[42] or because of difficulties in transacting in the market for know-how (Teece, 1980). A firm's technological assets may or may not be protected by the standard instruments of intellectual property law. Either way, the ownership protection and utilization of technological assets are clearly key differentiators among firms. Likewise for complementary assets.

Complementary assets. Technological innovations require the use of certain related assets to produce and deliver new products and services. Prior commercialization activities require and enable firms to build such complementarities (Teece, 1986b). Such capabilities and assets, while necessary for the firm's established activities, may have other uses as well. These assets typically lie downstream. New products and processes either can enhance or destroy the value of such assets (Tushman, Newman, and Romanelli, 1986). Thus the development of computers enhanced the value of IBM's direct sales force in office products, while disk brakes rendered useless much of the auto industry's investment in drum brakes.

Financial assets. In the short run, a firm's cash position and degree of leverage may have strategic implications. While there is nothing more fungible than cash, it cannot always be raised from external markets without the dissemination of considerable information to potential investors. Accordingly, what a firm can do in short order is often a function of its balance sheet. In the longer run, that ought not be so, as cash flow ought be more determinative.

Reputational assets. Firms, like individuals, have reputations. Reputations often summarize a good deal of information about firms and shape the responses of customers, suppliers, and competitors. It is sometimes difficult to disentangle reputation from the firm's current asset and market position. However, in our view, reputational assets are best viewed as an intangible asset that enables firms to achieve various goals in the market. Its main value is external, since what is critical about reputation is that it is a kind of summary statistic about the firm's current assets and position, and its likely future behavior. Because there is generally a strong asymmetry between what is known inside the firm and what is known externally, reputations may sometimes be more salient than the true state of affairs, in the sense that external actors must respond to what they know rather than what is knowable.

Structural assets. The formal and informal structure of organizations and their external linkages have an important bearing on the rate and direction of innovation, and how competences and capabilities co-evolve (Argyres, 1995; Teece, 1996). The degree of hierarchy and the level of vertical and lateral integration are elements of firm-specific structure. Distinctive governance modes can be recognized (e.g., multiproduct, integrated firms; high "flex" firms; virtual corporations; conglomerates), and these modes support different types of innovation to a greater or lesser degree. For instance, virtual structures work well when innovation is autonomous; integrated structures work better for systemic innovations.

Institutional assets. Environments cannot be defined in terms of markets alone. While public policies are usually recognized as important in constraining what firms can do, there is a tendency, particularly by economists, to see these as acting through markets or through incentives. However, institutions themselves are a critical element of the business environment. Regulatory systems, as well as intellectual property regimes, tort laws, and antitrust laws, are also part of the environment. So is the system of higher education and national culture. There are significant national differences here, which is just one of the reasons geographic location matters (Nelson, 1994). Such assets may not be entirely firm specific; firms of different national and regional origin may have quite different institutional assets to call upon because their institutional/policy settings are so different.

Market (structure) assets. Product market position matters, but it is often not at all determinative of the fundamental position of the enterprise in its external environment. Part of the problem lies in defining the market in which a firm competes in a way that gives economic meaning. More importantly, market position in regimes of rapid technological change is often extremely fragile. This is in part because time moves on a different clock in such environments.[43] Moreover, the link between market share and innovation has long been broken, if it ever existed (Teece, 1996). All of this is to suggest that product market position, while important, is too often overplayed. Strategy should be formulated with regard to the more fundamental aspects of firm performance, which we believe are rooted in competences and capabilities and shaped by positions and paths.

Organizational boundaries. An important dimension of "position" is the location of a firm's boundaries. Put differently, the degree of integration (vertical, lateral, and horizontal) is of quite some significance. Boundaries are not only significant with respect to the technological and complementary assets contained within, but also with respect to the nature of the coordination that can be achieved internally as compared to through markets. When specific assets or poorly protected intellectual capital are at issue, pure market arrangements expose the parties to recontracting hazards or appropriability hazards. In such circumstances, hierarchical control structures may work better than pure arms-length contracts.[44]

PATHS

Path dependencies. Where a firm can go is a function of its current position and the paths ahead. Its current position is often shaped by the path it has traveled. In standard economics textbooks, firms have an infinite range of technologies from which they can choose and markets they can occupy. Changes in product or factor prices will be responded to instantaneously, with technologies moving in and out according to value maximization criteria. Only in the short run are irreversibilities recognized. Fixed costs—such as equipment and overheads—cause firms to price below fully amortized costs but never constrain future investment choices. "Bygones are bygones." Path dependencies are simply not recognized. This is a major limitation of microeconomic theory.

The notion of path dependencies recognizes that "history matters." Bygones are rarely bygones, despite the predictions of rational actor theory. Thus a firm's previous investments and its repertoire of routines (its "history") constrain its future behavior.[45] This follows because learning tends to be local. That is, opportunities for learning will be "close in" to previous activities and thus will be transaction and production specific (Teece, 1988). This is because learning is often a process of trial, feedback, and evaluation. If too many parameters are changed simultaneously, the ability of firms to conduct meaningful natural quasi experiments is attenuated. If many aspects of a firm's learning environment change simultaneously, the ability to ascertain cause–effect relationships is confounded because cognitive structures will not be formed and rates of learning diminish as a result. One implication is that many investments are much longer term than is commonly thought.

The importance of path dependencies is amplified where conditions of increasing returns to adoption exist. This is a demand-side phenomenon, and it tends to make technologies and products embodying those technologies more attractive the more they are adopted. Attractiveness flows from the greater adoption of the product amongst users, which in turn enables them to become more developed and hence more useful. Increasing returns to adoption has many sources including network externalities (Katz and Shapiro, 1985), the presence of complementary assets (Teece, 1986b) and supporting infrastructure (Nelson, 1996), learning by using (Rosenberg, 1982), and scale economies in production and distribution. Competition between and among technologies is shaped by increasing returns. Early leads won by good luck or special circumstances

(Arthur, 1983) can become amplified by increasing returns. This is not to suggest that first movers necessarily win. Because increasing returns have multiple sources, the prior positioning of firms can affect their capacity to exploit increasing returns. Thus, in Mitchell's (1989) study of medical diagnostic imaging, firms already controlling the relevant complementary assets could in theory start last and finish first.

In the presence of increasing returns, firms can compete passively, or they may compete strategically through technology-sponsoring activities.[46] The first type of competition is not unlike biological competition amongst species, although it can be sharpened by managerial activities that enhance the performance of products and processes. The reality is that companies with the best products will not always win, as chance events may cause "lock-in" on inferior technologies (Arthur, 1983) and may even in special cases generate switching costs for consumers. However, while switching costs may favor the incumbent, in regimes of rapid technological change switching costs can become quickly swamped by switching benefits. Put differently, new products employing different standards often appear with alacrity in market environments experiencing rapid technological change, and incumbents can be readily challenged by superior products and services that yield switching benefits. Thus the degree to which switching costs cause "lock-in" is a function of factors such as user learning, rapidity of technological change, and the amount of ferment in the competitive environment.

Technological opportunities. The concept of path dependencies is given forward meaning through the consideration of an industry's technological opportunities. It is well recognized that how far and how fast a particular area of industrial activity can proceed is in part due to the technological opportunities that lie before it. Such opportunities are usually a lagged function of foment and diversity in basic science, and the rapidity with which new scientific breakthroughs are being made.

However, technological opportunities may not be completely exogenous to industry, not only because some firms have the capacity to engage in or at least support basic research, but also because technological opportunities are often fed by innovative activity itself. Moreover, the recognition of such opportunities is af-

fected by the organizational structures that link the institutions engaging in basic research (primarily the university) to the business enterprise. Hence, the existence of technological opportunities can be quite firm specific.

Important for our purposes is the rate and direction in which relevant scientific frontiers are being rolled back. Firms engaging in R&D may find the path dead ahead closed off, though breakthroughs in related areas may be sufficiently close to be attractive. Likewise, if the path dead ahead is extremely attractive, there may be no incentive for firms to shift the allocation of resources away from traditional pursuits. The depth and width of technological opportunities in the neighborhood of a firm's prior research activities thus are likely to impact a firm's options with respect to both the amount and level of R&D activity that it can justify. In addition, a firm's past experience conditions the alternatives management is able to perceive. Thus, not only do firms in the same industry face "menus" with different costs associated with particular technological choices, they also are looking at menus containing different choices.[47]

Assessment

The essence of a firm's competence and dynamic capabilities is presented here as being resident in the firm's organizational processes, that are in turn shaped by the firm's assets (positions) and its evolutionary path. Its evolutionary path, despite managerial hubris that might suggest otherwise, is often rather narrow.[48] What the firm can do and where it can go are thus rather constrained by its positions and paths. Its competitors are likewise constrained. Rents (profits) thus tend to flow not just from the asset structure of the firm and, as we shall see, the degree of its imitability, but also by the firm's ability to reconfigure and transform.

The parameters we have identified for determining performance are quite different from those in the standard textbook theory of the firm, and in the competitive forces and strategic conflict approaches to the firm and to strategy.[49] Moreover, the agency theoretic view of the firm as a nexus of contracts would put no weight on processes, positions, and paths. While agency approaches to the firm may recognize that opportunism and shirking may limit what a firm can do, they do not recognize the opportunities and constraints imposed by processes, positions, and paths.

Moreover, the firm in our conceptualization is much more than the sum of its parts—or a team tied together by contracts.[50] Indeed, to some extent individuals can be moved in and out of organizations and, so long as the internal processes and structures remain in place, performance will not necessarily be impaired. A shift in the environment is a far more serious threat to the firm than is the loss of key individuals, as individuals can be replaced more readily than organizations can be transformed. Furthermore, the dynamic capabilities view of the firm would suggest that the behavior and performance of particular firms may be quite hard to replicate, even if its coherence and rationality are observable. This matter and related issues involving replication and imitation are taken up in the section that follows.

Replicability and Imitatability of Organizational Processes and Positions

Thus far, we have argued that the competences and capabilities (and hence competitive advantage) of a firm rest fundamentally on processes, shaped by positions and paths. However, competences can provide competitive advantage and generate rents only if they are based on a collection of routines, skills, and complementary assets that are difficult to imitate.[51] A particular set of routines can lose their value if they support a competence which no longer matters in the marketplace, or if they can be readily replicated or emulated by competitors. Imitation occurs when firms discover and simply copy a firm's organizational routines and procedures. Emulation occurs when firms discover alternative ways of achieving the same functionality.[52]

REPLICATION

To understand imitation, one must first understand replication. Replication involves transferring or redeploying competences from one concrete economic setting to another. Since productive knowledge is embodied, this cannot be accomplished by simply transmitting information. Only in those instances where all relevant knowledge is fully codified and understood can replication be collapsed into a simple problem of information transfer. Too often, the contextual dependence of original performance is poorly appreciated, so unless firms have replicated their systems of productive knowledge on many prior occasions, the act of replication is likely to be difficult (Teece, 1976).

Indeed, replication and transfer are often impossible absent the transfer of people, though this can be minimized if investments are made to convert tacit knowledge to codified knowledge. Often, however, this is simply not possible.

In short, competences and capabilities, and the routines upon which they rest, are normally rather difficult to replicate.[53] Even understanding what all the relevant routines are that support a particular competence may not be transparent. Indeed, Lippman and Rumelt (1992) have argued that some sources of competitive advantage are so complex that the firm itself, let alone its competitors, does not understand them.[54] As Nelson and Winter (1982) and Teece (1982) have explained, many organizational routines are quite tacit in nature. Imitation can also be hindered by the fact few routines are "stand-alone;" coherence may require that a change in one set of routines in one part of the firm (e.g., production) requires changes in some other part (e.g., R&D).

Some routines and competences seem to be attributable to local or regional forces that shape firms' capabilities at early stages in their lives. Porter (1990), for example, shows that differences in local product markets, local factor markets, and institutions play an important role in shaping competitive capabilities. Differences also exist within populations of firms from the same country. Various studies of the automobile industry, for example, show that not all Japanese automobile companies are top performers in terms of quality, productivity, or product development (see, for example, Clark and Fujimoto, 1991). The role of firm-specific history has been highlighted as a critical factor explaining such firm-level (as opposed to regional or national-level) differences (Nelson and Winter, 1982). Replication in a different context may thus be rather difficult.

At least two types of strategic value flow from replication. One is the ability to support geographic and product line expansion. To the extent that the capabilities in question are relevant to customer needs elsewhere, replication can confer value.[55] Another is that the ability to replicate also indicates that the firm has the foundations in place for learning and improvement. Considerable empirical evidence supports the notion that the understanding of processes, both in production and in management, is the key to process improvement. In short, an organization cannot improve that which it does not understand. Deep process under-standing is often required to accomplish codification. Indeed, if knowledge is highly tacit, it indicates that underlying structures are not well understood, which limits learning because scientific and engineering principles cannot be as systematically applied.[56] Instead, learning is confined to proceeding through trial and error, and the leverage that might otherwise come from the application of scientific theory is denied.

IMITATION

Imitation is simply replication performed by a competitor. If self-replication is difficult, imitation is likely to be harder. In competitive markets, it is the ease of imitation that determines the sustainability of competitive advantage. Easy imitation implies the rapid dissipation of rents.

Factors that make replication difficult also make imitation difficult. Thus, the more tacit the firm's productive knowledge, the harder it is to replicate by the firm itself or its competitors. When the tacit component is high, imitation may well be impossible, absent the hiring away of key individuals and the transfers of key organization processes.

However, another set of barriers impedes imitation of certain capabilities in advanced industrial countries. This is the system of intellectual property rights, such as patents, trade secrets, and trademarks, and even trade dress.[57] Intellectual property protection is of increasing importance in the United States, as since 1982 the legal system has adopted a more pro-patent posture. Similar trends are evident outside the United States. Besides the patent system, several other factors cause there to be a difference between replication costs and imitation costs. The observability of the technology or the organization is one such important factor. Whereas vistas into product technology can be obtained through strategies such as reverse engineering, this is not the case for process technology, as a firm need not expose its process technology to the outside in order to benefit from it.[58] Firms with product technology, on the other hand, confront the unfortunate circumstances that they must expose what they have got in order to profit from the technology. Secrets are thus more protectable if there is no need to expose them in contexts where competitors can learn about them.

One should not, however, overestimate the overall importance of intellectual property protection; yet it presents a formidable imitation barrier in certain particular contexts. Intellectual property protection is not uniform across products, processes, and technologies, and is best thought of as islands in a sea of open competition. If one is not able to place the fruits of one's investment, ingenuity, or creativity on one or more of the islands, then one indeed is at sea.

We use the term appropriability regimes to describe the ease of imitation. Appropriability is a function both of the ease of replication and the efficacy of intellectual property rights as a barrier to imitation. Appropriability is strong when a technology is both inherently difficult to replicate and the intellectual property system provides legal barriers to imitation. When it is inherently easy to replicate and intellectual property protection is either unavailable or ineffectual, then appropriability is weak. Intermediate conditions also exist.

CONCLUSION

The four paradigms discussed above are quite different, though the first two have much in common with each other (strategizing) as do the last two (economizing). But are these paradigms complementary or competitive? According to some authors, "the resource perspective complements the industry analysis framework" (Amit and Schoemaker, 1993: 35). While this is undoubtedly true, we think that in several important respects the perspectives are also competitive. While this should be recognized, it is not to suggest that there is only one framework that has value. Indeed, complex problems are likely to benefit from insights obtained from all of the paradigms we have identified plus more. The trick is to work out which frameworks are appropriate for the problem at hand. Slavish adherence to one class to the neglect of all others is likely to generate strategic blindspots. The tools themselves then generate strategic vulnerability. We now explore these issues further. Table 22.1 summarizes some similarities and differences.

Efficiency vs. Market Power

The competitive forces and strategic conflict approaches generally see profits as stemming from strategizing—that is, from limitations on competition which firms achieve through raising rivals' costs and exclu-

Table 22.1. Paradigms of Strategy: Salient Characteristics

Paradigm	Intellectual roots	Representative authors addressing strategic management questions	Nature of rents	Rationality assumptions of managers	Fundamental units of analysis	Short-run capacity for strategic reorientation	Role of industrial structure	Focal concern
(1) Attenuating competitive forces	Mason, Bain	Porter (1980)	Chamberlinean	Rational	Industries, firms, products	High	Exogenous	Structural conditions and competitor positioning
(2) Strategic conflict	Machiavelli, Schelling, Cournot, Nash, Harsanyi, Shapiro	Ghemawat (1986) Shapiro (1989) Brandenburger and Nalebuff (1995)	Chamberlinean	Hyper-rational	Firms, products	Often infinite	Endogenous	Strategic interactions
(3) Resource-based perspectives	Penrose, Selznick, Christensen, Andrews	Rumelt (1984) Chandler (1966) Wernerfelt (1984) Teece (1980, 1982)	Ricardian	Rational	Resources	Low	Endogenous	Asset fungibility
(4) Dynamic capabilities perspective	Schumpeter, Nelson, Winter, Teece	Dosi, Teece, and Winter (1989) Prahalad and Hamel (1990) Hayes and Wheelwright (1984) Dierickx and Cool (1989) Porter (1990)	Schumpeterian	Rational	Processes, positions, paths	Low	Endogenous	Asset accumulation, replicability and inimitability

sionary behavior (Teece, 1984). The competitive forces approach in particular leads one to see concentrated industries as being attractive—market positions can be shielded behind entry barriers, and rivals costs can be raised. It also suggests that the sources of competitive advantage lie at the level of the industry, or possibly groups within an industry. In text book presentations, there is almost no attention at all devoted to discovering, creating, and commercializing new sources of value.

The dynamic capabilities and resources approaches clearly have a different orientation. They see competitive advantage stemming from high-performance routines operating "inside the firm," shaped by processes and positions. Path dependencies (including increasing returns) and technological opportunities mark the road ahead. Because of imperfect factor markets, or more precisely the nontradability of "soft" assets like values, culture, and organizational experience, distinctive competences and capabilities generally cannot be acquired; they must be built. This sometimes takes years—possibly decades. In some cases, as when the competence is protected by patents, replication by a competitor is ineffectual as a means to access the technology. The capabilities approach accordingly sees definite limits on strategic options, at least in the short run. Competitive success occurs in part because of policies pursued and experience and efficiency obtained in earlier periods.

Competitive success can undoubtedly flow from both strategizing and economizing,[59] but along with Williamson (1991) we believe that "economizing is more fundamental than strategizing . . . or put differently, that economy is the best strategy."[60] Indeed, we suggest that, except in special circumstances, too much "strategizing" can lead firms to underinvest in core competences and neglect dynamic capabilities, and thus harm long-term competitiveness.

Normative Implications

The field of strategic management is avowedly normative. It seeks to guide those aspects of general management that have material effects on the survival and success of the business enterprise. Unless these various approaches differ in terms of the framework and heuristics they offer management, then the discourse we have gone through is of limited immediate value. In this paper, we have already alluded to the fact that

the capabilities approach tends to steer managers toward creating distinctive and difficult-to-imitate advantages and avoiding games with customers and competitors. We now survey possible differences, recognizing that the paradigms are still in their infancy and cannot confidently support strong normative conclusions.

UNIT OF ANALYSIS AND ANALYTIC FOCUS

Because in the capabilities and the resources framework business opportunities flow from a firm's unique processes, strategy analysis must be situational.[61] This is also true with the strategic conflict approach. There is no algorithm for creating wealth for the entire industry. Prescriptions they apply to industries or groups of firms at best suggest overall direction, and may indicate errors to be avoided. In contrast, the competitive forces approach is not particularly firm specific; it is industry and group specific.

STRATEGIC CHANGE

The competitive forces and the strategic conflict approach, since they pay little attention to skills, know-how, and path dependency, tend to see strategic choice occurring with relative facility. The capabilies approach sees value augmenting strategic change as being difficult and costly. Moreover, it can generally only occur incrementally. Capabilities cannot easily be bought; they must be built. From the capabilities perspective, strategy involves choosing among and committing to long-term paths or trajectories of competence development.

In this regard, we speculate that the dominance of competitive forces and the strategic conflict approaches in the United States may have something to do with observed differences in strategic approaches adopted by some U.S. and some foreign firms. Hayes (1985) has noted that American companies tend to favor "strategic leaps" while, in contrast, Japanese and German companies tend to favor incremental, but rapid, improvements.

ENTRY STRATEGIES

Here the resources and the capabilities approaches suggest that entry decisions must be made with reference to the competences and capabilities which new entrants have, relative to the competition. Whereas the other approaches tell you little about where to look to find likely entrants, the capabilities approach identifies likely entrants. Relatedly, whereas the entry deterrence approach suggests an unconstrained search for new business opportunities, the capabilities approach suggests that such opportunities lie close in to one's existing business. As Richard Rumelt has explained it in conversation, "the capabilities approach suggests that if a firm looks inside itself, and at its market environment, sooner or later it will find a business opportunity."

Entry Timing

Whereas the strategic conflict approach tells little abut where to look to find likely entrants, the resources and the capabilities approach identifies likely entrants and their timing of entry. Brittain and Freeman (1980) using population ecology methodologies argued that an organization is quick to expand when there is a significant overlap between its core capabilities and those needed to survive in a new market. Recent research (Mitchell, 1989) showed that the more industry-specialized assets or capabilities a firm possesses, the more likely it is to enter an emerging technical subfield in its industry, following a technological discontinuity. Additionally, the interaction between specialized assets such as firm-specific capabilities and rivalry had the greatest influence on entry timing.

Diversification

Related diversification—that is, diversification that builds upon or extends existing capabilities—is about the only form of diversification that a resources/capabilities framework is likely to view as meritorious (Rumelt, 1974; Teece, 1980, 1982; Teece et al., 1994). Such diversification will be justifiable when the firms' traditional markets decline.[62] The strategic conflict approach is likely to be a little more permissive; acquisitions that raise rivals' costs or enable firms to effectuate exclusive arrangements are likely to be seen as efficacious in certain circumstances.

Focus and Specialization

Focus needs to be defined in terms of distinctive competences or capability, not products. Products are the manifestation of competences, as competences can be molded into a variety of products. Product market specialization and decentralization configured around

product markets may cause firms to neglect the development of core competences and dynamic capabilities, to the extent to which competences require accessing assets across divisions.

The capabilities approach places emphasis on the internal processes that a firm utilizes, as well as how they are deployed and how they will evolve. The approach has the benefit of indicating that competitive advantage is not just a function of how one plays the game; it is also a function of the "assets" one has to play with, and how these assets can be deployed and redeployed in a changing market.

Future Directions

We have merely sketched an outline for a dynamic capabilities approach. Further theoretical work is needed to tighten the framework, and empirical research is critical to helping us understand how firms get to be good, how they sometimes stay that way, why and how they improve, and why they sometimes decline.[63] Researchers in the field of strategy need to join forces with researchers in the fields of innovation, manufacturing, and organizational behavior and business history if they are to unlock the riddles that lie behind corporate as well as national competitive advantage. There could hardly be a more ambitious research agenda in the social sciences today.

ACKNOWLEDGMENTS

Research for this paper was aided by support from the Alfred P. Sloan Foundation through the Consortium on Competitiveness and Cooperation at the University of California, Berkeley. The authors are grateful for helpful comments from two anonymous referees, as well as from Raffi Amit, Jay Barney, Joseph Bower, Henry Chesbrough, Giovanni Dosi, Sumantra Goshal, Pankaj Ghemawat, Connie Helfat, Rebecca Henderson, Dan Levinthal, Richard Nelson, Margie Peteraf, Richard Rosenbloom, Richard Rumelt, Carl Shapiro, Oliver Williamson, and Sidney Winter. Useful feedback was obtained from workshops at the Haas School of Business, the Wharton School, the Kellogg School (Northwestern), the Harvard Business School, and the International Institute of Applied Systems Analysis (IIASA) in Vienna, the London School of Economics, and the London Business School.

NOTES

1. For a review of the fundamental questions in the field of strategy, see Rumelt, Schendel, and Teece (1994).

2. Of these authors, Rumelt may have been the first to self-consciously apply a resource perspective to the field of strategy. Rumelt (1984: 561) notes that the strategic firm "is characterized by a bundle of linked and idiosyncratic resources and resource conversion activities." Similarly, Teece (1984: 95) notes: "Successful firms possess one or more forms of intangible assets, such as technological or managerial know-how. Over time, these assets may expand beyond the point of profitable reinvestment in a firm's traditional market. Accordingly, the firm may consider deploying its intangible assets in different product or geographical markets, where the expected returns are higher, if efficient transfer modes exist." Wernerfelt (1984) was early to recognize that this approach was at odds with product market approaches and might constitute a distinct paradigm of strategy.

3. In competitive environments characterized by sustainable and stable mobility and structural barriers, these forces may become the determinants of industry-level profitability. However, competitive advantage is more complex to ascertain in environments of rapid technological change where specific assets owned by heterogeneous firms can be expected to play a larger role in explaining rents.

4. The market environment is all factors that influence market outcomes (prices, quantities, profits) including the beliefs of customers and of rivals, the number of potential technologies employed, and the costs or speed with which a rival can enter the industry.

5. For an excellent discussion of committed competition in multiple contexts, see Ghemawat (1991).

6. Competition and cooperation have also been analyzed outside of this tradition. See, for example, Teece (1992) and Link, Teece, and Finan (1996).

7. Accordingly, both approaches are dynamic, but in very different senses.

8. Thus even in the air transport industry game-theoretic formulations by no means capture all the relevant dimensions of competitive rivalry. United Airlines's and United Express's difficulties in competing with Southwest Airlines because of United's inability to fully replicate Southwest's operation capabilities is documented in Gittel (1995).

9. Important exceptions can be found in Brandenburger and Nalebuff (1996) such as their emphasis on the role of complements. However, these insights do not flow uniquely from game theory and can be found in the organizational economics literature (e.g., Teece, 1986a, 1986b; de Figueiredo and Teece, 1996).

10. When closely matched in an aggregate sense, they may nevertheless display asymmetries which game theorists can analyze.

11. The strategic conflict literature also tends to focus practitioners on product market positioning rather than on developing the unique assets which make possible superior product market positions (Dierickx and Cool, 1989).

12. In the language of economics, rents flow from unique firm-specific assets that cannot readily be replicated, rather than from tactics which deter entry and keep competitors off balance. In short, rents are Ricardian.

13. Teece (1982: 46) saw the firm as having "a variety of end products which it can produce with its organizational technology."

14. Elsewhere Andrews (1987: 47) defined a distinctive competence as what an organization can do particularly well.

15. Studies of the automobile and other industries displayed differences in organization which often underlay differences among firms. See, for example, Womack, Jones, and Roos (1991), Hayes and Clark (1985), Barney, Spender, and Reve (1994), Clark and Fujimoto (1991), Henderson and Cockburn (1994), Nelson (1991), Levinthal and Myatt (1994).

16. Using FTC line of business data, Rumelt showed that stable industry effects account for only 8 percent of the variance in business unit returns. Furthermore, only about 40 percent of the dispersion in industry returns is due to stable industry effects.

17. In this regard, this approach has much in common with recent work on organizational ecology (e.g., Freeman and Boeker, 1984) and also on commitment (Ghemawat, 1991: 17–25).

18. Capability development, however, is not really analyzed.

19. Deciding, under significant uncertainty about future states of the world, which long-term paths to commit to and when to change paths is the central strategic problem confronting the firm. In this regard, the work of Ghemawat (1991) is highly germane to the dynamic capabilities approach to strategy.

20. See, for example, Iansiti and Clark (1994) and Henderson (1994).

21. See Hayes et al. (1988), Prahalad and Hamel (1990), Dierickx and Cool (1989), Chandler (1990), and Teece (1993).

22. Arrow (1996) defines fugitive resources as ones that can move cheaply amongst individuals and firms.

23. We do not like the term 'resource' and believe it is misleading. We prefer to use the term firm-specific asset. We use it here to try and maintain links to the literature on the resource-based approach which we believe is important.

24. Thus Eastman Kodak's core competence might be considered imaging, IBM's might be considered integrated data processing and service, and Motorola's untethered communications.

25. In sequential move games, each player looks

ahead and anticipates his rival's future responses in order to reason back and decide action, i.e., look forward, reason backward.

26. Needless to say, users need not be the current customers of the enterprise. Thus a capability can be the basis for diversification into new product markets.

27. Indeed, the essence of internal organization is that it is a domain of unleveraged or low-powered incentives. By unleveraged we mean that rewards are determined at the group or organization level, not primarily at the individual level, in an effort to encourage team behavior, not individual behavior.

28. We see the problem of market contracting as a matter of coordination as much as we see it a problem of opportunism in the fact of contractual hazards. In this sense, we are consonant with both Richardson (1960) and Williamson (1975, 1985).

29. As we note in Teece et al. (1994), the conglomerate offers few if any efficiencies because there is little provided by the conglomerate form that shareholders cannot obtain for themselves simply by holding a diversified portfolio of stocks.

30. Owners' equity may reflect, in part, certain historic capabilities. Recently, some scholars have begun to attempt to measure organizational capability using financial statement data. See Baldwin and Clark (1991) and Lev and Sougiannis (1992).

31. We are implicitly saying that fixed assets, like plant and equipment which can be purchased off-the-shelf by all industry participants, cannot be the source of a firm's competitive advantage. Inasmuch as financial balance sheets typically reflect such assets, we point out that the assets that matter for competitive advantage are rarely reflected in the balance sheet, while those that do not are.

32. The coordinative properties of markets depend on prices being "sufficient" upon which to base resource allocation decisions.

33. Indeed, Ronald Coase, author of the pathbreaking 1937 article. "The nature of the firm," which focused on the costs of organizational coordination inside the firm as compared to across the market, half a century later has identified as critical the understanding of "why the costs of organizing particular activities differs among firms" (Coase, 1988: 47). We argue that a firm's distinctive ability needs to be understood as a reflection of distinctive organizational or coordinative capabilities. This form of integration (i.e., inside business units) is different from the integration between business units; they could be viable on a stand-alone basis (external integration). For a useful taxonomy, see Iansiti and Clark (1994).

34. Shuen (1994) examines the gains and hazards of the technology make-vs.-buy decision and supplier codevelopment.

35. Garvin (1994) provides a typology of organizational processes.

36. Fujimoto (1994: 18–20) describes key elements as they existed in the Japanese auto industry as follows: "The typical volume production system of effective Japanese makers of the 1980s (e.g., Toyota) consists of various intertwined elements that might lead to competitive advantages. Just-in-Time (JIT), Jidoka (automatic defect detection and machine stop), Total Quality Control (TQC), and continuous improvement (Kaizen) are often pointed out as its core subsystems. The elements of such a system include inventory reduction mechanisms by Kanban system; levelization of production volume and product mix (heijunka); reduction of 'muda' (non-value adding activities), 'mura' (uneven pace of production) and 'muri' (excessive workload); production plans based on dealers' order volume (genyo seisan); reduction of die set-up time and lot size in stamping operation; mixed model assembly; piece-by-piece transfer of parts between machines (ikko-nagashi); flexible task assignment for volume changes and productivity improvement (shojinka); multi-task job assignment along the process flow (takotei-mochi); U-shape machine layout that facilitates flexible and multiple task assignment, on-the-spot inspection by direct workers (tsukurikomi); fool-proof prevention of defects (poka-yoke); real-time feedback of production troubles (andon); assembly line stop cord; emphasis on cleanliness, order, and discipline on the shop floor (5-S); frequent revision of standard operating procedures by supervisors; quality control circles; standardized tools for quality improvement (e.g., 7 tools for QC, QC story); worker involvement in preventive maintenance (Total Productive Maintenance); low cost automation or semi-automation with just-enough functions); reduction of process steps for saving of tools and dies, and so on. The human-resource management factors that back up the above elements include stable employment of core workers (with temporary workers in the periphery); long-term training of multi-skilled (multitask) workers; wage system based in part on skill accumulation; internal promotion to shop floor supervisors; cooperative relationships with labor unions; inclusion of production supervisors in union members; generally egalitarian policies for corporate welfare, communication, and worker motivation. Parts procurement policies are also pointed out often as a source of the competitive advantage."

37. For a theoretical argument along these lines, see Milgrom and Roberts (1990).

38. See Abernathy and Clark (1985).

39. For a useful review and contribution, see Levitt and March (1988).

40. Levinthal and March, 1993. Mahoney (1992) and Mahoney and Pandian (1995) suggest that both resources and mental models are intertwined in firm-level learning.

41. There is a large literature on learning, although only a small fraction of it deals with organizational learning. Relevant contributors include Levitt and March (1988), Argyris and Schon (1978), Levinthal and March

(1981), Nelson and Winter (1982), and Leonard-Barton (1995).

42. Managers often evoke the "crown jewels" metaphor. That is, if the technology is released, the kingdom will be lost.

43. For instance, an Internet year might well be thought of as equivalent to 10 years on many industry clocks, because as much change occurs in the Internet business in a year that occurs in say the auto industry in a decade.

44. Williamson (1996: 102–103) has observed, failures of coordination may arise because "parties that bear a long term bilateral dependency relationship to one another must recognize that incomplete contracts require gap filling and sometimes get out of alignment. Although it is always in the collective interest of autonomous parties to fill gaps, correct errors, and affect efficient realignments, it is also the case that the distribution of the resulting gains is indeterminate. Self-interested bargaining predictably obtains. Such bargaining is itself costly. The main costs, however, are that transactions are maladapted to the environment during the bargaining interval. Also, the prospect of ex post bargaining invites exante prepositioning of an inefficient kind."

45. For further development, see Bercovitz, de Figueiredo, and Teece (1996).

46. Because of huge uncertainties, it may be extremely difficult to determine viable strategies early on. Since the rules of the game and the identity of the players will be revealed only after the market has begun to evolve, the payoff is likely to lie with building and maintaining organizational capabilities that support flexibility. For example, Microsoft's recent about-face and vigorous pursuit of Internet business once the Netscape phenomenon became apparent is impressive, not so much because it perceived the need to change strategy, but because of its organizational capacity to effectuate a strategic shift.

47. This is a critical element in Nelson and Winter's (1982) view of firms and technical change.

48. We also recognize that the processes, positions, and paths of customers also matter. See our discussion above on increasing returns, including customer learning and network externalities.

49. In both the firm is still largely a black box. Certainly, little or no attention is given to processes, positions, and paths.

50. See Alchian and Demsetz (1972).

51. We call such competences distinctive. See also Dierickx and Cool (1989) for a discussion of the characteristics of assets which make them a source of rents.

52. There is ample evidence that a given type of competence (e.g., quality) can be supported by different routines and combinations of skills. For example, the Garvin (1988) and Clark and Fujimoto (1991) studies both indicate that there was no one "formula" for achieving either high quality or high product development performance.

53. See Szulanski's (1995) discussion of the intrafirm transfer of best practice. He quotes a senior vice president of Xerox as saying "you can see a high performance factory or office, but it just doesn't spread. I don't know why." Szulanski also discusses the role of benchmarking in facilitating the transfer of best practice.

54. If so, it is our belief that the firm's advantage is likely to fade, as luck does run out.

55. Needless to say, there are many examples of firms replicating their capabilities inappropriately by applying extant routines to circumstances where they may not be applicable, e.g., Nestle's transfer of developed-country marketing methods for infant formula to the Third World (Hartley, 1989). A key strategic need is for firms to screen capabilities for their applicability to new environments.

56. Different approaches to learning are required, depending on the depth of knowledge. Where knowledge is less articulated and structured, trial and error and learning-by-doing are necessary, whereas in mature environments where the underlying engineering science is better understood, organizations can undertake more deductive approaches or what Pisano (1994) refers to as "learning-before-doing."

57. Trade dress refers to the "look and feel" of a retail establishment, e.g., the distinctive marketing and presentation style of The Nature Company.

58. An interesting but important exception to this can be found in second sourcing. In the microprocessor business, until the introduction of the 386 chip, Intel and most other merchant semi producers were encouraged by large customers like IBM to provide second sources, i.e., to license and share their proprietary process technology with competitors like AMD and NEC. The microprocessor developers did so to assure customers that they had sufficient manufacturing capability to meet demand at all times.

59. Phillips (1971) and Demsetz (1974) also made the case that market concentration resulted from the competitive success of more efficient firms, and not from entry barriers and restrictive practices.

60. We concur with Williamson that economizing and strategizing are not mutually exclusive. Strategic ploys can be used to disguise inefficiencies and to promote economizing outcomes, as with pricing with reference to learning curve costs. Our view of economizing is perhaps more expansive than Williamson's as it embraces more than efficient contract design and the minimization of transactions costs. We also address production and organizational economies, and the distinctive ways that things are accomplished inside the business enterprise.

61. On this point, the strategic conflict and the resources and capabilities are congruent. However, the aspects of "situation" that matter are dramatically different, as described earlier in this paper.

62. Cantwell shows that the technological competence of firms persists over time, gradually evolving through firm-specific learning. He shows that technological diversification has been greater for chemicals and pharmaceuticals than for electrical and electronic-related fields., and he offers as an explanation the greater straight-ahead opportunities in electrical and electronic fields than in chemicals and pharmaceuticals. See Cantwell (1993).

63. For a gallant start, see Miyazaki (1995) and McGrath et al. (1996). Chandler's (1990) work on scale and scope, summarized in Teece (1993), provides some historical support for the capabilities approach. Other relevant studies can be found in a special issue of *Industrial and Corporate Change* 3(3), 1994, that was devoted to dynamic capabilities.

REFERENCES

Abernathy, W. J. and K. Clark (1985). "Innovation: Mapping the winds of creative destruction," *Research Policy,* **14,** pp. 3–22.

Alchian, A. A. and H. Demsetz (1972). "Production, information costs, and economic organization," *American Economic Review,* **62,** pp. 777–795.

Amit, R. and P. Schoemaker (1993). "Strategic assets and organizational rent," *Strategic Management Journal* **14**(1), pp. 33–46.

Andrews, K. (1987). *The Concept of Corporate Strategy* (3rd ed.). Dow Jones-Irwin, Homewood, IL.

Aoki, M. (1990). "The participatory generation of information rents and the theory of the firm." In M. Aoki, B. Gustafsson, and O. E. Williamson (eds.), *The Firm as a Nexus of Treaties.* Sage, London, pp. 26–52.

Argyres, N. (1995). "Technology strategy, governance structure and interdivisional coordination," *Journal of Economic Behavior and Organization,* **28,** pp. 337–358.

Argyris, C. and D. Schon (1978). *Organizational Learning.* Addison-Wesley, Reading, MA.

Arrow, K. (1969). "The organization of economic activity: Issues pertinent to the choice of market vs. non-market allocation." In *The Analysis and Evaluation of Public Expenditures: The PPB System, 1.* U.S. Joint Economic Committee, 91st Session. U.S. Government Printing Office, Washington, DC, pp. 59–73.

Arrow, K. (1996) "Technical information and industrial structure', *Industrial and Corporate Change,"* **5**(2), pp. 645–652.

Arthur, W. B. (1983). "Competing technologies and lock-in by historical events: The dynamics of allocation under increasing returns," working paper WP-83-90, International Institute for Applied Systems Analysis, Laxenburg, Austria.

Bain, J. S. (1959). *Industrial Organization.* Wiley, New York.

Baldwin, C. and K. Clark (1991). "Capabilities and capital investment: New perspectives on capital budgeting," Harvard Business School working paper #92-004.

Barney, J. B. (1986). "Strategic factor markets: Expectations, luck, and business strategy," *Management Science* **32**(10), pp. 1231–1241.

Barney, J. B., J.-C. Spender, and T. Reve (1994). *Crafoord Lectures,* Vol. 6. Chartwell-Bratt, Bromley, U.K. and Lund University Press, Lund, Sweden.

Baumol, W., J. Panzar, and R. Willig (1982). *Contestable Markets and the Theory of Industry Structure.* Harcourt Brace Jovanovich, New York.

Bercovitz, J. E. L., J. M. de Figueiredo, and D. J. Teece (1996). "Firm capabilities and managerial decision-making: A theory of innovation biases." In R. Garud, P. Nayyar and Z. Shapira (eds), *Innovation: Oversights and Foresights.* Cambridge University Press, Cambridge, U.K. pp. 233–259.

Brandenburger, A. M. and B. J. Nalebuff (1996). *Coopetition.* Doubleday, New York.

Brandenburger, A. M. and B. J. Nalebuff (1995). "The right game: Use game theory to shape strategy," *Harvard Business Review,* **73**(4), pp. 57–71.

Brittain, J. and J. Freeman (1980). "Organizational proliferation and density-dependent selection." In J. R. Kimberly and R. Miles (eds.), *The Organizational Life Cycle.* Jossey-Bass, San Francisco, CA, pp. 291–338.

Camp, R. (1989). *Benchmarking: The Search for Industry Best practices that Lead to Superior Performance.* Quality Press, Milwaukee, WI.

Cantwell, J. (1993). "Corporate technological specialization in international industries." In M. Casson and J. Creedy (eds.), *Industrial Concentration and Economic Inequality.* Edward Elgar, Aldershot, pp. 216–232.

Chandler, A. D., Jr. (1966). *Strategy and Structure.* Doubleday, Anchor Books Edition, New York.

Chandler, A. D., Jr. (1990). *Scale and Scope: The Dynamics of Industrial Competition.* Harvard University Press, Cambridge, MA.

Clark, K. and T. Fujimoto (1991). *Product Development Performance: Strategy, Organization and Management in the World Auto Industries.* Harvard Business School Press, Cambridge, MA.

Coase, R. (1937). "The nature of the firm," *Economica,* **4,** pp. 386–405.

Coase, R. (1988). "Lecture on the Nature of the Firm, III,"

Journal of Law, Economics and Organization, **4,** pp. 33–47.

Cool, K. and D. Schendel (1988). "Performance differences among strategic group members," *Strategic Management Journal,* **9**(3), pp. 207–223.

de Figueiredo, J. M. and D. J. Teece (1996). "Mitigating procurement hazards in the context of innovation," *Industrial and Corporate Change,* **5**(2), pp. 537–559.

Demsetz, H. (1974). "Two systems of belief about monopoly." In H. Goldschmid, M. Mann, and J. F. Weston (eds.), *Industrial Concentration: The New Learning.* Little, Brown, Boston, MA, pp. 161–184.

Dierickx, I. and K. Cool (1989). "Asset stock accumulation and sustainability of competitive advantage," *Management Science,* **35**(12), pp. 1504–1511.

Dixit, A. (1980). "The role of investment in entry deterrence," *Economic Journal,* **90,** pp. 95–106.

Dosi, G., D. J. Teece, and S. Winter (1989). "Toward a theory of corporate coherence: Preliminary remarks," unpublished paper, Center for Research in Management, University of California at Berkeley.

Doz, Y. and A. Shuen (1990). "From intent to outcome: A process framework for partnerships," INSEAD working paper.

Fama, E. F. (1980). "Agency problems and the theory of the firm," *Journal of Political Economy,* **88,** pp. 288–307.

Freeman, J. and W. Boeker (1984). "The ecological analysis of business strategy." In G. Carroll and D. Vogel (eds.), *Strategy and Organization.* Pitman, Boston, MA, pp. 64–77.

Fujimoto, T. (1994). "Reinterpreting the resource-capability view of the firm: A case of the development-production systems of the Japanese automakers," draft working paper, Faculty of Economics, University of Tokyo.

Garvin, D. (1988). *Managing Quality.* Free Press, New York.

Garvin, D. (1994). "The processes of organization and management," Harvard Business School working paper #94-084.

Ghemawat, P. (1986). "Sustainable advantage," *Harvard Business Review,* **64**(5), pp. 53–58.

Ghemawat, P. (1991). *Commitment: The Dynamics of Strategy.* Free Press, New York.

Gilbert, R. J. and D. M. G. Newberry (1982). "Preemptive patenting and the persistence of monopoly," *American Economic Review,* **72,** pp. 514–526.

Gittell, J. H. (1995). "Cross functional coordination, control and human resource systems: Evidence from the airline industry," unpublished Ph.D. thesis, Massachusetts Institute of Technology.

Hansen, G. S. and B. Wernerfelt (1989). "Determinants of firm performance: The relative importance of eco-nomic and organizational factors," *Strategic Management Journal,* **10**(5), pp. 399–411.

Hartley, R. F. (1989). *Marketing Mistakes.* Wiley, New York.

Hayes, R. (1985). "Strategic planning: Forward in reverse," *Harvard Business Review,* **63**(6), pp. 111–119.

Hayes, R. and K. Clark (1985). "Exploring the sources of productivity differences at the factory level." In K. Clark, R. H. Hayes and C. Lorenz (eds.), *The Uneasy Alliance: Managing the Productivity-Technology Dilemma.* Harvard Business School Press, Boston, MA, pp. 151–188.

Hayes, R. and S. Wheelwright (1984). *Restoring Our Competitive Edge: Competing Through Manufacturing.* Wiley, New York.

Hayes, R., S. Wheelwright, and K. Clark (1988). *Dynamic Manufacturing: Creating the Learning Organization.* Free Press, New York.

Henderson, R. M. (1994). "The evolution of integrative capability: Innovation in cardiovascular drug discovery," *Industrial and Corporate Change,* **3**(3), pp. 607–630.

Henderson, R. M. and K. B. Clark (1990). "Architectural innovation: The reconfiguration of existing product technologies and the failure of established firms," *Administrative Science Quarterly,* **35,** pp. 9–30.

Henderson, R. M. and I. Cockburn (1994). "Measuring competence? Exploring firm effects in pharmaceutical research," *Strategic Management Journal,* Summer Special Issue, **15,** pp. 63–84.

Iansiti, M. and K. B. Clark (1994). "Integration and dynamic capability: Evidence from product development in automobiles and mainframe computers," *Industrial and Corporate Change,* **3**(3), pp. 557–605.

Itami, H. and T. W. Roehl (1987). *Mobilizing Invisible Assets.* Harvard University Press, Cambridge, MA.

Jacobsen, R. (1988). "The persistence of abnormal returns," *Strategic Management Journal,* **9**(5), pp. 415–430.

Katz, M. and C. Shapiro (1985). "Network externalities, competition and compatibility," *American Economic Review,* **75,** pp. 424–440.

Kreps, D. M. and R. Wilson (1982a). "Sequential equilibria," *Econometrica,* **50,** pp. 863–894.

Kreps, D. M. and R. Wilson (1982b). "Reputation and imperfect information," *Journal of Economic Theory,* **27,** pp. 253–279.

Langlois, R. (1994). "Cognition and capabilities: Opportunities seized and missed in the history of the computer industry," working paper, University of Connecticut. Presented at the conference on Technological Oversights and Foresights, Stern School of Business, New York University, 11–12 March 1994.

Learned, E., C. Christensen, K. Andrews, and W. Guth (1969). *Business Policy: Text and Cases.* Irwin, Homewood, IL.

Leonard-Barton, D. (1992). "Core capabilities and core rigidities: A paradox in managing new product development," *Strategic Management Journal,* Summer Special Issue, **13,** pp. 111–125.

Leonard-Barton, D. (1995). *Wellsprings of Knowledge.* Harvard Business School Press, Boston, MA.

Lev, B. and T. Sougiannis (1992). "The capitalization, amortization and value-relevance of R&D," unpublished manuscript, University of California, Berkeley, and University of Illinois, Urbana-Champaign.

Levinthal, D. and J. March (1981). "A model of adaptive organizational search," *Journal of Economic Behavior and Organization,* **2,** pp. 307–333.

Levinthal, D. A. and J. G. March (1993). "The myopia of learning," *Strategic Management Journal,* Winter Special Issue, **14,** pp. 95–112.

Levinthal, D. and J. Myatt (1994). "Co-evolution of capabilities and industry: The evolution of mutual fund processing," *Strategic Management Journal,* Winter Special Issue, **15,** pp. 45–62.

Levitt, B. and J. March (1988). "Organizational learning," *Annual Review of Sociology,* **14,** pp. 319–340.

Link, A. N., D. J. Teece, and W. F. Finan (October 1996). "Estimating the benefits from collaboration: The Case of SEMATECH," *Review of Industrial Organization,* **11,** pp. 737–751.

Lippman, S. A. and R. P. Rumelt (1992) "Demand uncertainty and investment in industry-specific capital," *Industrial and Corporate Change,* **1**(1), pp. 235–262.

Mahoney, J. (1995). "The management of resources and the resources of management," *Journal of Business Research,* **33**(2), pp. 91–101.

Mahoney, J. T. and J. R. Pandian (1992). "The resource-based view within the conversation of strategic management," *Strategic Management Journal,* **13**(5), pp. 363–380.

Mason, E. (1949). "The current state of the monopoly problem in the U.S.," *Harvard Law Review,* **62,** pp. 1265–1285.

McGrath, R. G., M-H. Tsai, S. Venkataraman, and I. C. MacMillan (1996). "Innovation, competitive advantage and rent: A model and test," *Management Science,* **42**(3), pp. 389–403.

Milgrom, P. and J. Roberts (1982a). "Limit pricing and entry under incomplete information: An equilibrium analysis," *Econometrica,* **50,** pp. 443–459.

Milgrom, P. and J. Roberts (1982b). "Predation, reputation and entry deterrence," *Journal of Economic Theory,* **27,** pp. 280–312.

Milgrom, P. and J. Roberts (1990). "The economics of modern manufacturing: Technology, strategy, and organization," *American Economic Review,* **80**(3), pp. 511–528.

Mitchell, W. (1989). "Whether and when? Probability and timing of incumbents' entry into emerging industrial subfields," *Administrative Science Quarterly,* **34,** pp. 208–230.

Miyazaki, K. (1995). *Building Competences in the Firm: Lessons from Japanese and European Optoelectronics.* St. Martins Press, New York.

Mody, A. (1993). "Learning through alliances," *Journal of Economic Behavior and Organization,* **20**(2), pp. 151–170.

Nelson, R. R. (1991). "Why do firms differ, and how does it matter?" *Strategic Management Journal,* Winter Special Issue, **12,** pp. 61–74.

Nelson, R. R. (1994). "The co-evolution of technology, industrial structure, and supporting institutions," *Industrial and Corporate Change,* **3**(1), pp. 47–63.

Nelson, R. (1996). "The evolution of competitive or comparative advantage: A preliminary report on a study," WP-96-21, International Institute for Applied Systems Analysis, Laxemberg, Austria.

Nelson, R. and S. Winter (1982). *An Evolutionary Theory of Economic Change.* Harvard University Press, Cambridge, MA.

Penrose, E. (1959). *The Theory of the Growth of the Firm.* Basil Blackwell, London.

Phillips, A. C. (1971). *Technology and Market Structure.* Lexington Books, Toronto.

Pisano, G. (1994). "Knowledge integration and the locus of learning: An empirical analysis of process development," *Strategic Management Journal,* Winter Special Issue, **15,** pp. 85–100.

Porter, M. E. (1980). *Competitive Strategy.* Free Press, New York.

Porter, M. E. (1990). *The Competitive Advantage of Nations.* Free Press, New York.

Prahalad, C. K. and G. Hamel (1990). "The core competence of the corporation," *Harvard Business Review,* **68**(3), pp. 79–91.

Richardson, G. B. H. (1960, 1990). *Information and Investment.* Oxford University Press, New York.

Rosenberg, N. (1982). *Inside the Black Box: Technology and Economics.* Cambridge University Press, Cambridge, MA

Rumelt, R. P. (1974). *Strategy, Structure, and Economic Performance.* Harvard University Press, Cambridge. MA.

Rumelt, R. P. (1984). "Towards a strategic theory of the firm." In R. B. Lamb (ed.), *Competitive Strategic Management.* Prentice-Hall, Englewood Cliffs, NJ, pp. 556–570.

Rumelt, R. P. (1991). "How much does industry matter?" *Strategic Management Journal,* **12**(3), pp. 167–185.

Rumelt, R. P., D. Schendel, and D. Teece (1994). *Funda-*

mental Issues in Strategy. Harvard Business School Press, Cambridge, MA.

Schmalensee, R. (1983). "Advertising and entry deterrence: An exploratory model," *Journal of Political Economy,* **91**(4), pp. 636–653.

Schumpeter, J. A. (1934). *Theory of Economic Development.* Harvard University Press, Cambridge, MA.

Schumpeter, J. A. (1942). *Capitalism, Socialism, and Democracy.* Harper, New York.

Shapiro, C. (1989). "The theory of business strategy," *RAND Journal of Economics,* **20**(1), pp. 125–137.

Shuen, A. (1994). "Technology sourcing and learning strategies in the semiconductor industry," unpublished Ph.D. dissertation, University of California, Berkeley.

Sutton, J. (1992). "Implementing game theoretical models in industrial economies," In A. Del Monte (ed.), *Recent Developments in the Theory of Industrial Organization.* University of Michigan Press, Ann Arbor, MI, pp. 19–33.

Szulanski, G. (1995). "Unpacking stickiness: An empirical investigation of the barriers to transfer best practice inside the firm," *Academy of Management Journal,* Best Papers Proceedings, pp. 437–441.

Teece, D. J. (1976). *The Multinational Corporation and the Resource Cost of International Technology Transfer.* Ballinger, Cambridge, MA.

Teece, D. J. (1980). "Economics of scope and the scope of the enterprise," *Journal of Economic Behavior and Organization,* **1**, pp. 223–247.

Teece, D. J. (1981). "The market for know-how and the efficient international transfer of technology," *Annals of the Academy of Political and Social Science,* **458**, pp. 81–96.

Teece, D. J. (1982). "Towards an economic theory of the multiproduct firm," *Journal of Economic Behavior and Organization,* **3**, pp. 39–63.

Teece, D. J. (1984). "Economic analysis and strategic management," *California Management Review,* 26(3), pp. 87–110.

Teece, D. J. (1986a). "Transactions cost economics and the multinational enterprise," *Journal of Economic Behavior and Organization,* **7**, pp. 21–45.

Teece, D. J. (1986b). "Profiting from technological innovation," *Research Policy,* **15**(6), pp. 285–305.

Teece, D. J. 1988. "Technological change and the nature of the firm." In G. Dosi, C. Freeman, R. Nelson, G.

Silverberg, and L. Soete (eds.), *Technical Change and Economic Theory.* Pinter Publishers, New York, pp. 256–281.

Teece, D. J. (1992). "Competition, cooperation, and innovation: Organizational arrangements for regimes of rapid technological progress," *Journal of Economic Behavior and Organization,* **18**(1), pp. 1–25.

Teece, D. J. (1993). "The dynamics of industrial capitalism: Perspectives on Alfred Chandler's *Scale and Scope* (1990)," *Journal of Economic Literature,* **31**(1), pp. 199–225.

Teece, D. J. (1996). "Firm organization, industrial structure, and technological innovation," *Journal of Economic Behavior and Organization,* **31**, pp. 193–224.

Teece, D. J. and G. Pisano (1994). "The dynamic capabilities of firms: An introduction," *Industrial and Corporate Change,* **3**(3), pp. 537–556.

Teece, D. J., R. Rumelt, G. Dosi, and S. Winter (1994). "Understanding corporate coherence: Theory and evidence," *Journal of Economic Behavior and Organization,* **23**, pp. 1–30.

Tushman, M. L., W. H. Newman, and E. Romanelli (1986). "Convergence and upheaval: Managing the unsteady pace of organizational evolution," *California Management Review,* **29**(1), pp. 29–44.

Wernerfelt, B. (1984). "A resource-based view of the firm," *Strategic Management Journal,* **5**(2), pp. 171–180.

Wernerfelt, B. and C. Montgomery (1988). "Tobin's Q and the importance of focus in firm performance," *American Economic Review,* **78**(1), pp. 246–250.

Williamson, O. E. (1975). *Markets and Hierarchies.* Free Press, New York.

Williamson, O. E. (1985). *The Economic Institutions of Capitalism.* Free Press, New York.

Williamson, O. E. (1991). "Strategizing, economizing, and economic organization," *Strategic Management Journal,* Winter Special Issue, **12**, pp. 75–94.

Williamson, O. E. (1996). *The Mechanisms of Governance.* Oxford University Press, New York.

Womack, J., D. Jones, and D. Roos (1991). *The Machine that Changed the World.* Harper-Perennial, New York.

Zander, U. and B. Kogut (1995). "Knowledge and the speed of the transfer and imitation of organizational capabilities: An empirical test," *Organization Science,* **6**(1), pp. 76–92.

23

Strategy, Value Innovation, and the Knowledge Economy

W. CHAN KIM
RENÉE MAUBORGNE

For the past twenty years, competition has occupied the center of strategic thinking. Indeed, one hardly speaks of strategy without drawing on the vocabulary of competition—competitive strategy, competitive benchmarking, competitive advantages, outperforming the competition. In fact, most strategic prescriptions merely redefine the ways companies build advantages over the competition. This has been the strategic objective of many firms, and, in itself, nothing is wrong with this objective. After all, a company needs some advantages over the competition to sustain itself in the marketplace. When asked to build competitive advantage, however managers typically assess what competitors do and strive to do it better. Their strategic thinking thus regresses toward the competition. After expending tremendous effort, companies often achieve no more than incremental improvement—imitation, not innovation.[1]

Consider what happened in the microwave oven and VCR industries. As a result of competitive benchmarking, product offerings were nearly mirror images of each other and, from the customer's perspective, they were overdesigned and overpriced. Most buyers had no use for most of the features and found them confusing and irritating. These companies may have outdone one another, but they missed an opportunity to capture the mass market by offering microwaves and VCRs that were easy to use at accessible prices.

Another classic example is the battle of IBM versus Compaq in the PC market. In 1983, when Compaq launched its IBM-compatible machines with technologically superb quality at a 15 percent lower price than IBM's, it rapidly won the mass of PC buyers. Once roused by Compaq's success, IBM started a race to beat Compaq; Compaq likewise focused on beating IBM. Trying to outperform one another in sophisticated feature enhancements, neither company foresaw the emergence of the low-end PC market in which user-friendliness and low price—not the latest technology—were keys to success. Both companies created a line of overly designed and overpriced PCs, and both companies missed the emerging low-end market. When IBM walked off the cliff in the late 1980s, Compaq was following closely.

These cases illustrate that strategy driven by the competition usually has three latent, unintended effects:[2]

- *Imitative, not innovative, approaches to the market.* Companies often accept what competitors are doing and simply strive to do it better.

- *Companies act reactively.* Time and talent are un-

Reprinted from "Strategy, Value Innovation, and the Knowledge Economy," by W. Chan Kim and Renée Mauborgne, *MIT Sloan Management Review,* Spring 1999, pp. 41–54, by permission of the publisher. Copyright © 1999 by Massachusetts Institute of Technology. All rights reserved.

consciously absorbed in responding to daily competitive moves, rather than creating growth opportunities.

- *A company's understanding of emerging mass markets and changing customer demands becomes hazy.*

Over the past decade, we have studied companies of sustained high growth and profits vis-à-vis their less successful competitors. Regardless of size, years of operation, industry conditions, and country of origin, the strategy these companies pursue is what we call *value innovation*.[3] Value innovation is quite different from building layers of competitive advantages and is not about striving to outperform the competition. Nor is value innovation about segmenting the market and accommodating customers' individual needs and differences. Value innovation makes the competition irrelevant by offering fundamentally new and superior buyer value in existing markets and by enabling a quantum leap in buyer value to create new markets. (For details of our research process, see the box "Researching the Roots of Profitable Growth.")

Take, for example, Callaway Golf, the U.S. golf club manufacturer, which in 1991 launched its "Big Bertha" golf club. The product rapidly rose to dominate the market, wresting market share from its rivals and expanding the total golf club market. Despite intense competition, Callaway did not focus on its competitors. Rival golf clubs looked alike and featured sophisticated enhancements, a result of attentive benchmarking of the competitors' products. In the meantime, Callaway pondered the "country club" markets of golf and tennis. Many people play tennis because they find the task of hitting a little golf ball with a little golf club head too daunting. Recognizing a business opportunity, Callaway made a golf club with a larger head that made playing golf less difficult and more fun. The result: not only were new players drawn into the market, but Callaway captured an overwhelming share of existing players as well.

Similar examples of value innovation arise in diverse industries. Consider Enron in energy, CNN in news broadcasting, Wal-Mart in discount retailing, Compaq in computers (after its turnaround), Kinepolis in cinema, IKEA in home products retail, Charles Schwab & Co. in investment and brokerage account management, Home Depot in home improvement retail, SAP in business application software, Barnes & Noble in book retailing, Southwest Airlines in short-haul air travel, and others. Their steady growth and high profits are not a consequence of daring young organizational members, of being a small entrepreneurial start-up, of being in attractive industries, or of making big commitments in the latest technology. Instead, the superperforming companies that we studied are united in their pursuit of innovation outside a conventional context. That is, they do not pursue innovation as technology, but as value. The companies cited above created quantum leaps in some aspect of value; many have nothing to do with new technology. This is why we call these companies value innovators.[4]

Many high achievers excel despite bad industry conditions. Instead of falling victim to industry conditions, these value innovators focus on creating opportunities in their fields. They ask, "How can we offer buyers greater value that will result in soaring profitable growth irrespective of industry or competitive conditions?" Because they question everything about a particular industry and their competitors, they explore a far wider range of strategic options than other companies. This broadens their creative scope, allowing them to find opportunities where other companies can see only constraints imposed by external conditions.[5]

To achieve sustained profitable growth, companies must break out of the competitive and imitative trap. Rather than striving to match or outperform the competition, companies must cultivate value innovation. Emphasis on value places the buyer, not the competition, at the center of strategic thinking; emphasis on innovation pushes managers to go beyond incremental improvements to totally new ways of doing things.

Consider a recent study of the profitable growth consequences of more than a hundred new business launches.[6] We found that while 86 percent of these business launches were "me too" businesses or businesses with value improvements over the competition, they generated only 62 percent of total revenues and 39 percent of total profits. In contrast, the remaining 14 percent of the business launches—those that were

Researching the Roots of Profitable Growth

Almost a decade ago, we researched the growth problems of a particular company. Our interviews with the company's managers revealed a typical story. They were suffering from bad industry conditions—stagnant growth, overcapacity, and intense competition. They could do little about these factors, so they were trying to create some advantages over the competition by improving their products, services, and cost structure. Nevertheless, their performance was not improving greatly because the competition was also moving forward.

Not long after, we studied another company with a record of sustained profitable growth despite bad industry conditions. Managers of this company told us a different story. To them, bad industry conditions were excuses for tired executives. The competition was not the reference point for their strategy because they were striving to go far beyond the competition. They were searching for new ideas that could grab the market by providing exceptional value for customers.

As we pondered these two companies, we became interested in further developing and testing our initial observations on firm growth. Since a company's profits must support its growth to be sustainable, we targeted companies with sustained high growth in both revenues and profits. Through our professional and personal network, we systematically identified national and global growth champions from many industries and built strategic, organizational, and performance profiles of them. During this process, we also identified their less successful competitors. We targeted companies in more than thirty industries; their diversity ranges from hotel, cinema, retailing, airline, energy, computer, broadcasting, home construction, automobile, to steel manufacturing. We then interviewed managers from profitable high-growth companies and those from their less suc-

cessful competitors. We also spoke with investment and private research group analysts, who track these companies regularly, to gain further insight into their strategic approaches.

We first examined whether industry or corporate characteristics could explain the distinction between these two groups. Are certain industry or corporate characteristics common to companies with high profitable growth, distinguishing them from their less successful competitors? We failed to find any systematic differences. Robust profitable growth was achieved by small and large companies, by young and old managers, by companies in high-and low-growth industries, by new entrants and established incumbents, by private and public companies, and by companies of diverse national origins.

Next, we decided to explore our original insights on possible divergent approaches to strategy. We analyzed the content of managers' remarks about their strategic approach to the market. We analyzed comments from interviews, speeches to analysts or shareholders, and statements gleaned from print media to find examples of implicit and explicit strategic thinking. To further validate our analyses, major business launches (as manifestations of strategic thinking) were reviewed for consistency with management statements and real actions in the marketplace. As we searched for convergence within each group and divergence across the two groups, we found that the focus of corporate strategy differed. Less successful companies were racing to beat the competition, highly successful companies did not use the competition as their strategic reference. Rather than building advantages over their competitors, companies with high profitable growth aimed to make competition irrelevant by providing buyers with a quantum leap in value. We have come to call their way of strategic thinking *value innovation*.

value innovations—generated 38 percent of total revenues and a whopping 61 percent of total profits. The performance of value innovators far exceeds that of companies focusing on matching or beating their competitors. Companies pursuing value innovation are on the rise. Value innovation fuels small companies to grow profitably and regenerates the fortunes of big companies.

SHIFTING THE BASIS OF STRATEGY

Why has competition been the key building block of strategy in theory and practice? Think of the competitive penetration of Japanese companies into U.S. industries that awakened U.S. companies to the reality of global competition. After a period of denial, U.S. companies vigorously responded, making competition the centerpiece of their strategic thinking. Concurrently, under the strong influence of old economics—especially in the form of industrial organization—academics were comfortable with competition-based strategy too.[7] In neoclassical economics, firms and innovations are treated as "black boxes." What firms do is determined by market conditions because market conditions are assumed to be beyond the influence of individual companies.[8] In such a setting, innovations are random events exogenous to firms. If market conditions and innovations are treated as given sets of the external environment, a firm strategically chooses a distinctive cost or differentiation position that best fits with its internal systems and capabilities to counter the competition in that particular environment. In such a situation, innovation is not endogenous to its system, so cost and product performance are seen as trade-offs.

Competition-based strategy, however, has waning power in today's economy in which, in many industries, supply exceeds demand. Competing for a share of contracting markets is a marginal and "second best" strategy. Such a zero-sum strategy is cutthroat and does not create new wealth. A "first best" strategy in today's economy stimulates the demand side of the economy. It expands existing markets and creates new markets.[9] Such a non-zero-sum strategy generates new wealth and has high payoffs. In regard to profitable growth, creating shareholder value, and generating new jobs and wealth for society, companies pursuing the first-best strategy through value innovation far outperform companies following the second-best strategy. In our studies, we see this happening in the business world today.

During the past two decades, for example, we have seen a rapid change in the *Fortune* 500 list—both in rankings and those who qualify for the list; some 60 percent have disappeared from the list. Value innovators are now among the most rapidly growing companies. In less than forty years, a value innovator like Wal-Mart, for example, has become the world's eighth largest company in revenues and the world's second largest employer (825,000 people).

Shareholder value and wealth created by value innovators are equally compelling. The market value of SAP, for example, exceeds that of 150-year-old Siemens; Microsoft's market value towers over the combined values of General Motors and Ford. In 1995, with $6 billion in revenues and $7 billion in assets, the market value of Microsoft was 1.5 times that of GM with $168 billion in revenues and $217 billion in assets.

Why do value innovators such as SAP have such high market valuations despite their much smaller physical and fiscal assets? What do investors value in these companies that is not reflected on their balance sheets? As far as the market is concerned, their high stock of *knowledge* portends tremendous wealth-creating potential despite their much smaller sizes. In creating wealth, knowledge is increasingly taking a front seat to the traditional factors of production, that is, physical and fiscal assets.[10] The gap between a company's market value and its tangible asset value is widening; the key variable explaining this gap is a firm's stock of knowledge. Unlike land, labor, and capital—the economist's traditional, finite factors of production—knowledge and ideas are infinite economic goods that can generate increasing returns through their systematic use, as SAP and Nintendo prove.

What we observe in the real world of business is consistent with the theory of new economics. New economics proposes endogenous growth theory, in which growth and innovation come from within a system.[11] While its unit of analysis is primarily the nation-state, the principal argument in endogenous growth theory is applicable to the firm. The theory informs us of the arrival of the knowledge economy and argues that innovations are no longer exogenous and can be created with the ideas and knowledge within a system.

In a world in which industry conditions no longer dictate corporate well-being because companies can transcend these conditions through the systematic pursuit of innovation, a firm need not compete for a share of given demand—it can create new demand. Moreover, low cost and differentiation do not have to be an either-or choice because innovation can be a sustainable strategy.[12] In fact, to innovate in this knowledge economy, companies employing the first best strategy often pursue low cost and differentiation simultaneously. Indeed, our field observations support the prediction of new growth theory. Rising companies, small or large, that have achieved sustained high growth and profits are those that have pursued value innovation. Their strategic focus was not on outcompeting within given industry conditions, but on creating fundamentally new and superior value, making their competitors irrelevant. They went beyond competing in existing markets to expanding the demand side of the economy.

VALUE AND INNOVATION

Value innovation places equal emphasis on *value* and *innovation*. Value without innovation tends to focus on improving the buyer's net benefit or value creation on an incremental scale. Innovation without value can be too strategic or wild (by betting on a company's long-term industry foresight) or too technology-driven or futuristic (shooting far beyond what buyers are ready to accept). Value innovation anchors innovation with buyer value. Hence, value innovation is not the same as *value creation*. Value creation as a concept of strategy is too broad because no boundary condition specifies the direction a company should follow to bring about successful strategic actions. Value creation on an incremental scale, for example, still creates some value but is not sufficient for high performance.

Value innovation also differs from *technology innovation*. As previously mentioned, technology innovation is not a requisite for value innovation; value innovation can occur with or without new technology. Moreover, technology innovation does not necessarily produce value innovation. For example, although Ampex innovated video recording technology in the 1950s, the company failed to convert this new technology into a value innovation cheap enough for mass buyers. As a result, later value innovators, such as Sony and JVC, profited greatly by unlocking the mass market at almost 1 percent of Ampex's initial price. Value innovators are not necessarily first entrants to

their markets in technological terms. In this sense, they are not necessarily technology pioneers, but they are value pioneers.

Value innovation links innovation to what the mass of buyers value. To value innovate, companies must ask two questions: (1) Are we offering customers radically superior value? (2) Is our price level accessible to the mass of buyers in our target market? High-growth companies understand that offering a new and superior product or service at a price that most buyers cannot afford is like laying an egg that other companies will hatch. (See Figure 23.1 for the relationships among value creation, value innovation, and technology innovation.)

While technology innovators such as Ampex failed to capture profits for themselves, their technological discoveries often benefited the overall economy because later value innovators eventually use these technological discoveries successfully. In light of this, the distinction between technology innovation and value innovation may not be relevant to economists whose main concern is a theory of growth at the macro level. Such a distinction, however, is important to those whose interest is in building a theory of firm growth. Who will capture the profit is a pertinent and critical issue to individual firms.

Many innovation and creativity studies have focused on improving or redefining solutions to problems with technology as a central component of the discussions. Researchers attempted to explain how an organization develops technological solutions to customers' problems.[13] Because technologies are seen as solutions to problems, most innovation studies have been solution driven.[14] Unlike technology innovation, value innovation focuses on redefining the problems

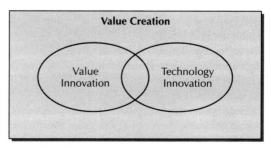

Figure 23.1. Relationships among value creation, value innovation, and technology innovation.

themselves. This is how value innovation makes the competition irrelevant. By redefining the problem an industry focuses on, a value innovator shifts the performance criteria that matter to customers. This creates new market space. To redefine customers' problems, market insights are needed to discover existing but "hidden" demand or to create totally new demand. Value innovation is a consequence of such market insights gained from creative strategic thinking.[15]

Callaway Golf, for example, created its Big Bertha golf club after redefining the consumer's need, that is, a desire to hit the ball more easily. Rivals focused on offering better solutions to hitting the ball farther—some were cost leaders and some were differentiators in solving this particular problem. By addressing a redefined problem, Big Bertha expanded the total market by attracting new customers who had not previously played golf. The company gained this market insight by thinking in terms of alternative industries—golf versus tennis—as opposed to thinking in terms of its industry competitors. Its main strategic question was why people choose tennis over golf in the country club market; Callaway Golf did not concentrate on how to outperform other golf club manufacturers by offering a better solution to the conventional goal of hitting the ball farther.

The concept of value innovation is consistent with the Schumpeterian notion of "creative destruction" in the sense that it is about creating fundamentally new and superior value, hence making existing things and ways of doing things irrelevant.[16] But whereas the entrepreneur is the major input in creating Schumpeterian innovation, knowledge and ideas are the major inputs for value innovation. Whether an executive or a factory worker, anyone can have a good idea; value innovation can occur in any organization and at any time in a sustainable manner with the proper process. In contrast, the realization of Schumpeterian innovation is subject to the availability of entrepreneurs who are in short supply. Hence, while an understanding of entrepreneurship and the entrepreneur as an economic hero are critical to Schumpeterian innovation, it is not with value innovation.

Unlike the old economics in which monopoly power is the enemy of economic development, both new growth theory and Schumpeter argue for the importance of the innovators' monopoly profits to bolster future discovery that stimulates economic growth.[17]

They argue that monopolies must be tolerated to a degree. Value innovators in the new knowledge economy, however, act quite differently from the typical monopolists portrayed in economics.

MARKET DYNAMICS OF VALUE INNOVATION

Consider Enron, the Houston-based energy company. Enron's roots are traceable to one of the oldest, capital-intensive commodity industries in the world—gas and utilities. Yet, for three consecutive years, *Fortune* has ranked Enron the most innovative company in the United States. During the past fifteen years, Enron has struck upon repeated value innovations, lowering the cost of gas and electricity to customers by as much as 40 percent to 50 percent. Enron did so while dramatically reducing its own cost structure by, for example, creating the first national spot market for gas in which commodity swaps, future contracts, and other complex derivatives effectively stripped the risk and volatility out of gas prices. Today, Enron has as many traders, analysts, and scientists—including a rocket scientist from the former Soviet Union—employed at Enron's headquarters as gas and pipeline personnel. Enron exemplifies the transition from the production to the knowledge economy. The proportion and value of knowledge to land, labor, and capital—even in this most basic industry—are rising dramatically. Think also of IKEA in furniture, Starbucks in coffee, Wal-Mart in discount retail, or Borders and Barnes & Noble in bookstores—all are offering buyers fundamentally new and superior value in traditional businesses through innovative ideas and knowledge.

The transition from a production to a knowledge economy has two new consequences. First, it creates the potential for increasing returns.[18] This is easy to understand in the software industry in which, for example, producing the first copy of the Windows 95 operating system cost Microsoft millions, whereas subsequent copies involved no more than the near trivial cost of a diskette. In capital-intensive businesses such as Enron's, after paying the fixed cost of developing sophisticated risk management financial tools, the company can apply the tools to infinite transactions at insignificant marginal cost. Second, it creates the potential for free-riding. This relates to the nonrival and partially excludable nature of knowledge, a discussion of which follows.[19]

The use of a *rival good* by one firm precludes its use by another. So, for example, Nobel Prize-winning scientists employed by IBM cannot simultaneously be employed by another company. Nor can scrap steel consumed by Nucor be simultaneously consumed for production by other minimill steel makers. In contrast, the use of a *nonrival good* by one firm does not limit its use by another. Ideas fall into this category. So, for example, when Virgin Atlantic Airways launched its "Upper Class" value innovation—a new concept in business class travel that essentially combined the huge seats and leg room of traditional first class with the price of business class tickets—other airlines could apply this idea to their own business class service without limiting Virgin's ability to use it. This makes competitive imitation not only possible but less costly, as the cost and risk of developing the innovative idea is borne by the value innovator, not the follower. This challenge is exacerbated when the notion of *excludability* is considered.

Excludability is a function of both the nature of the good and the legal system. A good is excludable if the company can prevent others from using it due to, for example, limited access or patent protection. So, for example, Intel can exclude other microprocessor chipmakers from using its manufacturing facilities through property ownership laws. Starbucks Coffee can prevent coffee chain start-ups from using its coffee beans by refusing to sell to would-be copycats, that is, by strategically limiting access. However, Starbucks cannot exclude others from walking into any store, studying its layout, atmosphere, and product range, and mimicking the chic coffee bar concept in which exotic coffee is sold by the cup in elite locations. The highest value-added element of Starbuck's formula is not excludable. Once ideas are "out there," knowledge naturally spills over to other firms. This lack of excludability reinforces the risk of free-riding.

Of course, were it possible to get a patent and formal legal protection for innovative ideas, the risk of free-riding would be considerably lower. Pharmaceutical companies, for example, have long enjoyed the benefit of formal patent protection to prevent the free-riding of other drug companies on their scientific discoveries for a specified time. But, how do you patent a radically superior concept for a coffee store such as

Starbucks, which has tremendous value but in itself consists of no new technological discoveries? It is the arrangement of the items that adds fundamentally new value, that is, the way they are combined, not the items themselves. While collectively this represents a new, creative, and explosive concept, little about the Starbuck's concept is scientifically new and, hence, patentable and excludable. Starbucks, like The Body Shop, Home Depot, Schwab, Virgin Atlantic Airways, Amazon.com, Borders, and Barnes & Noble, is not about patentable technology innovation, but value innovation.

Even value innovations in software run the risk of free-riding. Although computer software companies can obtain copyrights to prohibit others from copying program code, the look, feel, and functionality of software is not patentable.[20] Thus, any successful program can be copied. Competing firms need only write their own code; the software functionality, the structure of the internal programming components, and the software's look and feel can be imitated, as Netscape painfully learned. The same can be said for Wal-Mart's valuable inventory replenishment system. In other words, the ideas that contain the real value are usually not excludable or only partially so.

The question is how best to maximize profits from value innovation ideas that have the potential for both increasing returns and free-riding. Should value innovators follow the conventional practice of technology innovators: set high prices, limit access, initially engage in price skimming to earn a premium on the innovation, and only later focus on lowering price and costs to retain market share and discourage imitators?

In a world of nonrival and nonexcludable goods that are imbued with the potential of economies of scale, learning, and increasing returns, the importance of volume, price, and cost grows in unprecedented ways. From the outset, the aim is to capture the mass of buyers and expand the size of the market by offering radically superior value at price points accessible to a mass market. This means that value innovators should not follow conventional practices for maximizing profits. First, by charging a high premium and restricting supply, unmet demand combined with a high price ceiling is a huge incentive for others to free-ride to undercut the price of the innovator and capture the market. Second, high prices and limited volume that create an image of exclusivity and uniqueness do not allow the innovator to exploit either economies of scale and learning or the potential for increasing returns. This undermines the innate profit advantage of knowledge-intensive goods.

In our studies, we observed successful value innovators using a distinctly different market approach from that of conventional monopolists. Their approach has two components:

- *Strategic pricing for demand creation.* Strategic pricing leads to high volume and rapidly establishes a powerful brand reputation.

- *Target costing for profit creation.* Target costing leads to attractive profit margins and a cost structure that is hard for potential followers to match.

Consider how Nicholas Hayek, the chairman of SMH, used this new market approach with the launch of the Swatch, a value innovation that revived the Swiss watch industry. The Swatch transformed the wristwatch from a functional item used to tell time to a mass-market fashion accessory. The company innovated the concept of a watch by combining mechanical punctuality with creative designs that conveyed a powerful emotional message.

To profit from this value innovation, Hayek set up a project team to determine the strategic price for the Swatch. At the time, cheap (about $75), high-precision quartz watches from Japan and Hong Kong were capturing the mass market. To entice these customers and to quickly build a strong brand name, SMH aggressively set the Swatch's price at $40, a price at which customers could buy several Swatches as fashion accessories. The low price left no profit margin for Japanese or Hong Kong-based companies to copy Swatch and undercut its price. Directed to sell the Swatch for that price and not a penny more, the SMH project team had worked backwards to arrive at the target cost, which involved determining the margin SMH needed to support marketing and services. On this basis, the project team then devised a suitable production system. SMH was compelled to innovate the design of the Swatch's mechanics, production, and assembly, which produced an unbeatable cost structure in the worldwide watch industry.

How can a value innovator like Swatch sustain its profitable growth over time? Value innovation radically increases the appeal of a good, shifting the demand

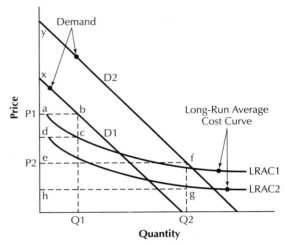

Figure 23.2. Market dynamics of value innovation.

curve from D1 to D2 (see Figure 23.2). However, recognizing the nonrival and only partial excludable nature of its innovative good, the value innovator strategically prices the product from the outset to capture the mass of buyers in the expanded market, in the case of Swatch shifting the price from P1 to P2. This increases the quantity sold from Q1 to Q2 and builds strong brand recognition for unprecedented value. The value innovator, however, engages in target costing to simultaneously reduce the long-run average cost curve from LRAC1 to LRAC2 to expand its ability to profit and to discourage free-riding and imitation. Hence, buyers receive a quantum leap in value, shifting the consumer surplus from *axb* to *eyf*. And the value innovator earns a leap in profit and growth, shifting the profit zone from *abcd* to *efgh*. The rapid brand recognition built by the value innovator as a result of the unprecedented value offered in the marketplace combined with the simultaneous drive to lower costs makes the competition near to irrelevant and hard to catch up as economies of scale, learning, and increasing returns kick in. Hence, the emergence of the new phenomena such as category killers and winner-take-most markets where companies earn dominant positions while customers simultaneously come out big winners.

While value innovators do not always exercise low strategic pricing as Swatch did, attracting a mass of buyers is, in many respects, at odds with the tactics of conventional monopolists.[21] In the production economy, firms with dominant market positions have been associated with two social welfare loss activities. First, to maximize their profits, companies set high prices, which prohibited the mass of customers who, though desiring the product, could not afford it. Second, lacking viable competition, firms with monopolistic positions did not focus on efficiency and hence consumed more of society's resources.

However, in the knowledge economy, innovative companies engage less in the exorbitant price skimming common in the production economy. The focus shifts from restricting output at a high price to creating new aggregate demand through a leap in value and introduction at an accessible price. This creates a strong incentive to reduce costs to the lowest possible level. Perhaps this explains why the antitrust actions against Microsoft proceed slowly despite its dominant market position. Microsoft is not acting as a monopolist in the traditional sense; customers are winning, and innovation in its industry has not slowed but is accelerating as others strive to capture the powerful profitable growth consequences of being a market leader in the knowledge economy.

SHIFTING STRATEGY FOCUS

The underlying foundation of business is shifting in unprecedented ways. Consider the emergence of the Internet, the rise of multimedia, the speed of globalization, and the advent of the euro. The rate of change seems to increase as new knowledge, idea creation, and global diffusion accelerate. This new reality requires new strategic responses. Companies that continue to focus on the competition, on leveraging and extending their current capabilities, and on retaining and extending their existing customers are off the mark.[22] As has been argued, the competition provides a sticky starting point for strategic thinking. A focus on matching and beating the competition leads to reactive, incremental, and often imitative strategic moves—not what is needed in a knowledge economy. The irony of competition is this: intense competition makes innovation indispensable, but an obsessive focus on the competition makes innovation difficult to attain.

At the same time, thinking beyond a company's boundaries is necessary. Since the field of strategy emerged, its focus has been on building and leveraging a company's strengths. The basic argument here is that firms possess unique resources, reputation, and skills—capabilities that should be nurtured and leveraged to guide their strategic decisions. Extended and refined over time, this basic argument persists in theory and practice. An inwardly driven focus on capabilities within a company, however, significantly limits a company's opportunity horizon and introduces resistance to change if the market is evolving away from a company's forte.[23] As we enter an era of the modular society in which networks become more prevalent, companies can increasingly pursue strategic relations with other firms to capture emerging opportunities on the basis of their respective strengths.

The central quest of a value innovator's strategic mind-set is to create radically new and superior value. The conventional focus on retaining and better satisfying existing customers tends to promote hesitancy to challenge the status quo for fear of losing or dissatisfying existing customers.[24] However, companies must focus on capturing the mass of buyers, even if that means losing some existing customers. Value innovators monitor existing customers but, more importantly, follow noncustomers closely because they provide deep insights into trends and changes.

After radically superior value is discovered, value innovators deploy capabilities that exist both inside and outside their companies to actualize an opportunity. Value innovators often have a network of partners that provide complementary assets, capabilities, products, and services.

The strategic responses of value innovators illustrate how the three basic building blocks of strategy—competition, customers, and corporate capabilities—must shift to thrive in this rapidly changing knowledge economy (see Figure 23.3).

SMH's innovative Swatch idea did not originate with the competition. The company did not have a core competency in mass-market watches, in plastic molding, or in contemporary design. At the time of the Swatch introduction, the young mass-market customers were not SMH customers. What did SMH have in its favor? Hayek had a relentless desire to offer buyers radically superior value, an idea (to create a watch exuding joie de vivre), and the insight to create, buy, or borrow the expertise needed to produce the watches. Likewise, SAP possessed no core competencies or distinctive resources. At the time of its founding more

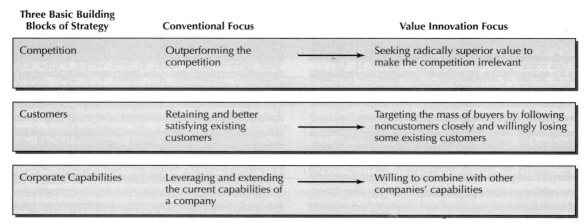

Three Basic Building Blocks of Strategy	Conventional Focus	Value Innovation Focus
Competition	Outperforming the competition	→	Seeking radically superior value to make the competition irrelevant
Customers	Retaining and better satisfying existing customers	→	Targeting the mass of buyers by following noncustomers closely and willingly losing some existing customers
Corporate Capabilities	Leveraging and extending the current capabilities of a company	→	Willing to combine with other companies' capabilities

Figure 23.3. Shifting strategy focus.

than twenty-five years ago, SAP did not own computers to use in writing its software. Yet, SAP not only created its first value innovation, R/2 business application software for the mainframe environment, but repeatedly launched value innovations, including R/3, client-server business application software. As Hasso Plattner, SAP cofounder, put it: "The only resource we had was our brains and the idea of how to build powerful software." Later SAP leveraged the resources and capabilities of others, including Andersen Consulting, which served as SAP's marketing and implementation arm; Oracle, which supplied the necessary sophisticated database; and IBM, which supplied hardware. SAP has continuously renewed its customer base by moving aggressively from mainframe users, to client-server users, and to midsized and small companies to capitalize on emerging market opportunities. "Noncustomers often offer the greatest insights into where the market is moving and what we should be doing fundamentally differently," remarked Plattner. "We never look at what the competition is doing." As a result, SAP is the global leader in business application software.

MAKING VALUE INNOVATION HAPPEN

To make value innovation happen, top management must clearly communicate the company's commitment to value innovation as the key strategy component by articulating its underlying logic.[25] The aim is to drive out of the organization conventional competition-

based thinking that usually leads to only incremental market improvements. The CEO and his or her top management team play a critical role in initiating this change.[26] Through strategic retreats, corporate communications, and by continuously challenging proposed strategic plans on the basis of value innovation, staff members will gradually orient themselves toward the principles of value innovation.[27] Five key questions, which contrast conventional competition-based logic with that of value innovation, can serve as a guide to reframing strategic thinking toward the new mind-set (see Table 23.1).

What type of organization best unlocks the ideas and creativity of its employees to achieve this end? In our studies, two structural characteristics are common to value innovation companies:

- *Small autonomous units or teams focusing on a common business or product goal* rather than organization on the basis of function, region, or channel type.[28] Although top managers must clearly specify that the strategic goal is to value innovate (as opposed to benchmarking the competition), teams must freely explore how to achieve these objectives. Some degree of freedom heightens a sense of ownership among team members, promotes creativity, and ensures that individual expertise is fully exploited.[29]

- *Team members of diverse backgrounds and perspectives.* This seems most conducive to higher levels of creativity.[30]

Table 23.1. Five Key Questions to Reframe Strategic Thinking

	Conventional Logic	Value Innovation Logic
Question 1	Does your company allow industry conditions to dictate the realm of what is possible, probable, and profitable?	Does your company challenge the inevitability of industry conditions?
Question 2	Does your company focus on outpacing the competition?	Does your company focus on dominating the market by introducing a major advance in buyer value?
Question 3	Does management start by considering current assets and capabilities?	Does management consider starting anew?
Question 4	Does your company focus on customer segmentation, customization, and retention?	Does your company search for key value commodities that can unlock the mass market even if some existing customers will be lost?
Question 5	Does your company strive to improve the products and services of your industry?	Does your company think in terms of a total customer solution even if this pushes beyond the industry's traditional offerings?

When putting value innovation strategies into action, structural conditions create only the *potential* for individuals to share their best ideas and knowledge. To *actualize* this potential, a company must cultivate a corporate culture conducive to willing collaboration.

How to promote voluntary cooperation among organizational members is critical to value innovation efforts. An organization must supply and create knowledge and ideas effectively, because these are the primary inputs for value innovation. Unlike traditional production factors, such as land, labor, and capital, knowledge and ideas are intangible assets locked in the human mind. Even in ideal organizational conditions, creating and sharing knowledge—intangible activities—cannot be supervised or forced; they happen only when individuals cooperate voluntarily.

The distinction between compulsory and voluntary cooperation is worth noting. Compulsory cooperation is in accordance with organizational rules, regulations, and acceptable standards, whereas voluntary cooperation goes beyond the call of duty: individuals exert effort, energy, and initiative to the best of their abilities on behalf of the organization.[31] Companies can mandate compulsory cooperation by using organizational force; voluntary cooperation is not achievable without trust and commitment that can only be cultivated purposefully. Compulsory cooperation alone cannot effectively supply and generate the knowledge required to formulate value innovation plans.[32]

Voluntary cooperation is also essential because effectively executing planned value innovation usually involves major changes in how a company functions.

This often requires behavioral changes. The collaborative initiative and spontaneity that is characteristic of voluntary cooperation are key to adapting to change.

As we studied successes and failures in this area, one central theme repeatedly emerged whether we were working with senior executives or shop floor employees: individuals are most likely to share ideas and cooperate voluntarily when the company acknowledges their intellectual and emotional worth. Individuals are gratified when the company solicits and thoughtfully considers their ideas and shares opinions with them. Recognizing individuals as human beings worthy of respect regardless of hierarchical level rather than "labor," "personnel," or "human resources" engenders loyalty and willingness to collaborate for the welfare of the company.

We found that exercising *fair process*—fairness in the process of making and executing decisions—is a powerful way to recognize people's intellectual and emotional worth.[33] Fair process brings forth trust and commitment, whereas treatment perceived as unfair elicits idea hoarding and foot dragging. The three bedrock principles of fair process are: (1) *engaging* people in decisions that affect them, (2) *explaining* final decisions, and (3) *establishing clear expectations* of actions and deliverables. Fair process is a key organizational practice for effectively conceiving and executing any strategy, but is particularly efficacious when companies wish to break from the status quo to value innovate.

Consider the recent successes of Compaq Computer. In 1991, Compaq saw tremendous opportunity in the low-end PC market. Because its existing production systems and logistics had neither the cost dynamics nor distribution reach to capture this burgeoning market, Compaq swiftly reinvented itself to serve the low-end PC market. In several months, for example, the company moved from 3,000 value-added resellers to more than 30,000 dealers, including mass-market merchandisers like Wal-Mart and Circuit City. In six years, its sales increased from $3 billion to $25 billion, and it is the world's top-ranked desktop computer maker, sporting a world-class line of portables, servers, and workstations. Compaq Chairman Eckhard Pfeiffer clearly articulated and never wavered from his intention to value innovate. Beyond autonomous teams populated with diversity, use of fair process methods defined a working mode that built trust and voluntary cooperation around the corporation's strategic goal.

Fair process and value innovation create a positively reinforcing cycle (see Figure 23.4). Each success in implementing a general value innovation strategy based on fair process strengthens group cohesiveness and people's belief in the process, which perpetuates the collaborative and creative modes inherent to value innovation.

Most companies strive to deliver *fair outcomes* without distinguishing this concept from fair process.

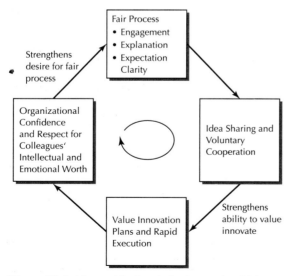

Figure 23.4. The positively reinforcing cycle of fair process.

Delivering fair outcomes ensures that individuals receive power, resources, or material rewards in exchange for compulsory cooperation.[34] To induce knowledge creation and voluntary cooperation between individuals, however, companies must go beyond fair outcome to fair process.

People possessing knowledge are the key resource of companies pursuing value innovation; this cherished resource is independent and mobile. Today's knowledge economy traffics actively in this key resource. As a result, companies must meet fair outcome expectations *and* fair process expectations to produce fulfilling work environments. This is how many successful value innovation companies, such as SAP, retain their talented employees. In an industry notorious for its lack of employee loyalty, the annual staff turnover rate of SAP, for example, is 4 percent—about half the industry average.

VALUE INNOVATION AS STRATEGY

In the coming decade, what is the key strategic agenda for corporate giants like Microsoft, Intel, Compaq, Enron, SAP, Procter & Gamble, Johnson & Johnson, Motorola, Chrysler, SMH, 3M, Sony, Toyota, and Samsung? For example, Procter & Gamble's strategic goal for the next decade is to double its $35 billion business through assertive efforts to achieve business breakthroughs. As we participated in, heard, and read about their management training, strategic planning discussions, and executive retreats, we unfailingly noted that all these companies aspire to attain breakthroughs in their markets.

We believe that value innovation is the essence of strategy in the knowledge economy. It must be supported by the proper tactics to prolong and maximize an innovation's profit-making potential, distancing it from emulators. After a value innovation is created, business line extensions and continuous improvements can maximize profits before another value innovation is launched. However, these business and operational improvements are not strategies; they are tactics.[35] Value innovation as strategy creates a pattern of punctuated equilibrium, in which bursts of value innovation that reshape the industrial landscape are interspersed with periods of improvements, geographic and product line extensions, and consolidation.

In some industrial and regional sectors of the

economy, however, many companies will still be successful on the basis of competition-driven strategy without spurts of value innovation. We predict that these dormant sectors of the economy will increasingly dwindle as value innovation and its globalization penetrates farther into the economy. Nevertheless, other successful strategies exist. Along with value innovators, cost leaders and differentiators can achieve profitable growth. In markets where value innovation occurs, however, the space for success of cost leaders and differentiators narrows as value innovators occupy the core of markets by attracting the mass of buyers. For example, since Wal-Mart has grown to dominate the discount retail market by capturing its core, successful cost leaders and differentiators in this market are those pursuing a rock-bottom pricing strategy (Dollar General, Family Dollar, Dollar Tree) or targeting high-end segments (specialty stores). As value innovation further penetrates into markets, strategies of cost leadership and differentiation are likely to succeed best at the low end (cost leaders) and the high end (differentiators). As happened in discount retailing, cost leaders and differentiators may become peripheral players relative to value innovators that emerge to capture the core of expanded markets. It is important to note here that value innovators do capture the core of the market not at the direct expense of other market players since they expand the market by creating new demand.

NOTES

1. W. C. Kim and R. Mauborgne, "When Competitive Advantage Is Neither," *Wall Street Journal,* 21 April 1997a, p. 22.

2. W. C. Kim and R. Mauborgne, "On the Inside Track," *Financial-Times,* 7 April 1997b, p. 10.

3. W. C. Kim and R. Mauborgne, "Value Innovation: The Strategic Logic of High Growth," *Harvard Business Review,* volume 75, January–February 1997c, pp. 102–112.

4. W. C. Kim and R. Mauborgne, "Opportunity Beckons," *Financial Times,* 18 August 1997d, p. 8.

5. W. C. Kim and R. Mauborgne, "How to Leapfrog the Competition," *Wall Street Journal Europe,* 6 March 1997e, p. 10.

6. Kim and Mauborgne (1997c).

7. R. P. Rumelt, D. Schendel, and D. J. Teece, "Strategic Management and Economics," *Strategic Management Journal,* volume 12, Winter 1991, pp. 5–29.

8. R. R. Nelson, "Why Do Firms Differ, and How

Does It Matter?" *Strategic Management Journal,* volume 12, Winter 1991, pp. 61–74.

9. For a discussion on the importance and patterns of creating new markets, see W. C. Kim and R. Mauborgne, "Creating New Market Space," *Harvard Business Review,* volume 77, January–February 1999, pp. 83–93; also see G. Hamel and C. K. Prahalad, *Competing for the Future* (Boston: Harvard Business School Press, 1994).

10. W. C. Kim and R. Mauborgne, "Value Knowledge or Pay the Price," *Wall Street Journal Europe,* 29 January 1998a, p. 6; and T. A. Stewart, *Intellectual Capital* (New York: Currency/Doubleday, 1997).

11. P. Romer, "Endogenous Technological Change," *Journal of Political Economy,* volume 98, October 1990, pp. S71–S102; P. M. Romer, "The Origins of Endogenous Growth," *Journal of Economic Perspectives,* volume 8, Winter 1994, pp. 3–22; and G. M. Grossman and E. Helpman, *Innovation and Growth* (Cambridge, Massachusetts: MIT Press, 1995).

12. C. W. L. Hill, "Differentiation Versus Low Cost or Differentiation and Low Cost," *Academy of Management Review,* volume 13, July 1988, pp. 401–412. Hill argues that low cost and differentiation do not have to be an either-or choice.

13. For the most recent research on this, see A. Hargadon and R. Sutton, "Technology Brokering and Innovation in a Product Development Firm," *Administrative Science Quarterly,* volume 42, December 1997, pp. 716–749.

14. For an excellent discussion on this, see E. M. Rogers, *Diffusion of Innovations* (New York: Free Press, 1995).

15. For more discussion on this, see Kim and Mauborgne (1999).

16. For a discussion of "creative destruction," see J. A. Schumpeter, *The Theory of Economic Development* (Cambridge, Massachusetts: Harvard University Press, 1934).

17. For discussion of the importance of innovators' monopoly profits, see Schumpeter (1934); Romer (1990); and W. B. Arthur, "Increasing Returns and the New World of Business," *Harvard Business Review,* volume 74, July–August 1996, pp. 100–109.

18. P. Romer, "Increasing Returns and Long-Run Growth," *Journal of Political Economy,* volume 94, October 1986, pp. 1002–1037; and Arthur (1996).

19. K. J. Arrow, "Economic Welfare and the Allocation of Resources for Inventions," in R. R. Nelson, ed., *The Rate and Direction of Inventive Activity* (Princeton, New Jersey: Princeton University Press, 1962), pp. 609–626; and Romer (1990). It is worth noting that both Arrow and Romer limited their discussions of nonrival and nonexcludable goods to technological innovations as is the tradition of economics. When the concept of innovation is redefined as value innovation, which is more relevant at the microeconomic firm level, the importance of the nonrival and nonexcludable notion is even more striking. This is because technological innovation often has a greater excludable component due to the possibility and relative ease of obtaining patent protection.

20. For a brilliant discussion of this issue, see L. C. Thurow, "Needed: A New System of Intellectual Property Rights," *Harvard Business Review,* volume 75, September–October 1997, pp. 94–103.

21. The extent to which the idea behind a value innovation is nonexcludable affects the strategic price set by the value innovator. As we have argued, while innovative ideas and processes are usually nonexcludable or only partially so, some value innovators have patentable ideas that are excludable for a given time. In these cases, value innovators may be inclined to price their product the same or higher than rivals' products and services. However, recognizing the powerful economies of scale, learning, and increasing returns that come with high volumes of knowledge-intensive goods, the strategic price will still be set from the outset with an aim to capture the mass of buyers. In the United Kingdom, Dyson Appliances, for example, created a value innovation in vacuum cleaners with its launch of the Dyson Dual Cyclone, which eliminated vacuum cleaner bags and the hassle of replacing bags for the life of the vacuum. In doing so, Dyson also increased the suction power of its vacuum cleaner dramatically over the industry average. Given the radically superior value of its product and the fact that its value innovation was patentable, Dyson strategically set its price relatively high while still capturing the mass of buyers. Although the vacuum cleaner was priced higher than the competition, it was a leap in value and within the economic reach of the mass of buyers. In this instance, Dyson did not use the conventional monopolist's practice of restricting supply by establishing a high price.

22. W. C. Kim and R. Mauborgne, "A Corporate Future Built with New Blocks," *New York Times,* 29 March 1998b, Section 3, p. 14.

23. For thought-provoking discussions on the implications of a focus on a company's current capabilities, see M. E. Porter, "Towards a Dynamic Theory of Strategy," *Strategic Management Journal,* volume 12, Winter 1991, pp. 95–117; and M. L. Tushman and P. Anderson, "Technological Discontinuities and Organizational Environments," *Administrative Science Quarterly,* volume 31, September 1986, pp. 439–465.

24. That a focus on current customers can be detrimental to a firm's long-run viability is also discussed in J. L. Bower and C. M. Christensen, "Disruptive Technologies: Catching the Wave," *Harvard Business Review,* volume 73, January–February 1995, pp. 43–53.

25. For a more thorough discussion on this, see Kim and Mauborgne (1997c).

26. The critical importance of top management setting clear expectations is highlighted in the works of Kanter and Amabile. See R. M. Kanter, "When a Thousand Flowers Bloom: Structural, Collective, and Social Conditions for Innovation in Organizations," in P. S. Myers, ed., *Knowledge Management and Organization Design* (Boston: Butterworth-Heinemann, 1996), pp. 169–211; and T. M. Amabile, "A Model of Creativity and Innovation in Organizations," in *Research in Organizational Behavior* (Greenwich, Connecticut: JAI Press, 1988), pp. 123–167.

27. This is consistent with the work of Amabile (1988), who argues that the most important elements of motivating innovation are concise and compelling articulation of the value of innovation, orientation away from the status quo, and activating an offensive leadership strategy aimed at the future, rather than simply trying to protect an organization's past.

28. Kanter (1996) also argues for the importance of smaller units organized around common business objectives as a catalyst for innovative thinking in organizations.

29. The important work on creativity conducted by Amabile clearly establishes the importance of autonomy in achieving strategic goals to foster creativity. See T. M. Amabile, "How to Kill Creativity," *Harvard Business Review,* volume 76, September–October 1998, pp. 76–87.

30. The need for diversity or cross-disciplinary contact to spark innovation is also well articulated in the excellent works of Kanter (1996); and Amabile (1998).

31. The roots of our distinction between voluntary and compulsory cooperation originate with: P. Blau and W. R. Scott, *Formal Organizations* (San Francisco: Chandler Publishing Company, 1962); and O. E. Williamson, *Markets and Hierarchies* (New York: Free Press, 1975).

32. Kim and Mauborgne (1998a); and W. C. Kim and R. Mauborgne, "Building Trust," *Financial Times,* 9 January 1998c, p. 25.

33. W. C. Kim and R. Mauborgne, "Fair Process: Managing in the Knowledge Economy," *Harvard Business Review,* volume 75, July–August 1997, pp. 65–75; W. C. Kim and R. Mauborgne, "Procedural Justice, Strategic Decision Making and the Knowledge Economy," *Strategic Management Journal,* volume 19, April 1998, pp. 323–338; and W. C. Kim and R. Mauborgne, "A Procedural Justice Model of Strategic Decision Making: Strategy Content Implications," *Organization Science,* volume 19, January–February 1995, pp. 44–61.

34. W. C. Kim and R. Mauborgne, "Procedural Justice and Managers' In-role and Extra-role Behavior," *Management Science,* volume 42, April 1996, pp. 499–515.

35. For an excellent discussion of how strategy differs from operational improvements, see M. E. Porter, "What Is Strategy?" *Harvard Business Review,* volume 74, November–December 1996, pp. 61–78.

24

Crafting R&D Project Portfolios

IAN C. MACMILLAN
RITA GUNTHER MCGRATH

OVERVIEW: Uncertain, but promising, R&D projects should be treated as one of three types of real options, depending on their degree of technical and market uncertainty. Positioning options are designed to preserve a company's future right to compete in a highly uncertain technological arena. Scouting options are used to create information about customer needs and market conditions. Stepping-stone options provide a technological path forward for an organization's long-run technology strategy, while containing cost and risk as new knowledge is created. Corporations rarely distinguish between such options and product launches or line extensions, with the result that they are managed and valued inappropriately. The guidelines provided here can not only help determine the right category for individual R&D projects, but also enable designing a portfolio of projects that is consistent with a firm's technology strategy.

Readers of *Research • Technology Management* are by now familiar with the argument that highly uncertain technology projects are better assessed by using options logic than by more conventional approaches, such as deriving their net present value (1, 2, 3). R&D projects can be viewed as the technological analogy of a financial options contract if they meet certain conditions. Provided that they represent a limited downside investment that gives a company a privileged position to create a commercial product at some point in the future, projects can have substantial potential value under uncertainty. This is so even if it isn't quite clear what that future asset is going to deliver in terms of profits or revenues at the time of the original investment.

Because so much of the value of highly uncertain projects lies in the future, it is hard to know when, or whether, they are going to pay off. This creates enormous stresses in the resource allocation process for most companies. Given finite resources, how can R&D managers choose between projects that have a near-term and quantifiable outcome and projects whose returns are hard to estimate and far-off in time? Particularly when resources are stretched thin, it is common for companies to focus too much on extending their existing technological bases, thus under-investing in the future.

It is also not unusual for all projects to be treated as though they were substantially the same, even when they have different levels and types of uncertainty and serve different strategic purposes. Such useful tools as stage-gate management processes don't really help resolve the fundamental question of what the whole portfolio of projects should look like for a given company.

Reprinted by permission of Harvard Business School Press. From *The Entrepreneurial Mindset*, by Rita Gunther McGrath and Ian C. MacMillan, adapted from Chapter 8. Copyright © 2000 by the Harvard Business School Publishing Corporation; all rights reserved. (As appeared in *Research • Technology Management*, Sept.–Oct. 2002, pp. 48–59.)

MARKET AND TECHNOLOGICAL UNCERTAINTY

An important distinction that is seldom explicitly made with respect to R&D options is that their purpose and nature are not the same. Some options are taken out to preserve a company's opportunity to compete in some future and still unclear technological arena. Because these essentially position the company to make further moves, we call them positioning options. They are quite different from options in which one invests in order to learn about the market by probing or offering prototypes to potential early adopters (4). We call such options scouting options, because they help a company scout out potential opportunities. A final category of options are highly uncertain on both market and technological dimensions, but have the potential to open entirely new classes of opportunity for the firm. We call these options stepping-stone options because they represent steps toward a highly uncertain future. As their name suggests, when properly managed, they are contained investments that systematically build both market insight and technical competence to move a company forward without exposure to potentially catastrophic downside risks.

In highly unpredictable situations, smart companies have learned that the best way to make sure they are able to respond effectively to future challenges is to deploy patterns of options. Rather than making a single big bet on one means of access to an attractive opportunity, they have found that it makes more sense to fund a number of small ventures intended to capture market opportunity in different ways. Thus, established firms such as Intel and Microsoft might take multiple equity positions in startups pursuing similar solutions, research consortia supported by multiple firms might explore various alternative solutions, and joint ventures entered into by a wide variety of players might employ technology-sharing arrangements. Just as you might think of your company as a portfolio of businesses, there is a lot to be said for thinking of the initiatives you are pursuing within a given business as a portfolio of options.

This brings us to a point of departure for making the assessment of what your own R&D portfolio should look like. First, we develop a simple categorization scheme for the three kinds of options (and also

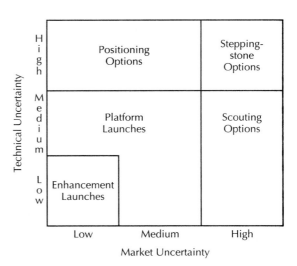

Figure 24.1. There are five types of R&D projects, depending on the degree of technical and market uncertainty.

for less uncertain investments in enhancements and major platform launches). This categorization scheme is depicted in Figure 24.1, which provides a simplified structure for depicting your entire R&D portfolio at any given point in time. To map the portfolio, you next need to categorize all the projects you are currently working on into the five different types depicted in Figure 24.1. To do this, you need to assess the nature of the uncertainties faced in each project.

Is the issue one of determining whether the technology will work in the field, whether it will scale, whether complementary technologies will be ready in time or what the standards will be? These are issues of high technical uncertainty. Notice that they are very different questions than trying to figure out what need the technology really addresses, who will buy it at what price and in what frequency, and how best to get to that customer. These issues reflect market uncertainty.

A simple way to estimate the level of market uncertainty is to use the questionnaire in Table 24.1. Ideally, a multifunctional group comprising R&D, engineering, operations, marketing and sales would venture their opinions on those responses for which they are qualified. Discussing major differences between the responses of different team members helps

Table 24.1. Evaluating Market Uncertainty

How certain is YOUR TEAM of the following?
Score on scale of 1 (certain) to 7 (highly uncertain).*

Market demand for future products using the fruits of the project
Total future revenues from these products
The stability of the revenue stream generated
Extent to which you will be able to obtain needed support from
　distributors and suppliers
Extent to which premium pricing can be expected
Extent to which premium pricing can be sustained
The speed with which products will be accepted in the market
The speed with which products will be approved by necessary
　regulatory bodies
Who the major competitors will be
The probability that competitors will rapidly imitate us
The probability of other technologies matching our offerings
The probability of having our technology blocked by others
Whether the technology has the potential to be licensed
Degree to which we will have to constantly change designs
The degree to which parallel technologies will be needed
Whether such parallel technologies will be available in time
Degree to which technical specifications will be required in the
　industry
Degree to which technical specifications will be standardized in
　the industry
The probability of profits being disrupted by third-party
　intervention (governments, distribution channels, labor
　unions, etc.)

*Do not answer where you do not know.

Table 24.2. Evaluating Technical Uncertainty

How certain is YOUR MANAGEMENT TEAM
of the following?
Score on scale of 1 (certain) to 7 (highly uncertain).*

The time it will take to complete development
The type of skills needed for development
The availability of necessary skills
The cost of staffing those skills
The type of equipment needed for development
The availability of equipment needed
The cost of equipment that is needed
The systems needed for development
The availability of systems needed
The cost of systems needed
The raw materials that will be needed
The availability of needed raw materials
The cost of raw materials
Total costs of development
The infrastructure that needs to be created
Our ability to access necessary complementary technologies
The cost of access to needed complementary technologies
The technology barriers we will face
Our ability to overcome technology barriers we will face
The cost to overcome technology barriers
The required level of product quality
Required levels of support and service
How much production capacity will be needed
The commitment level of senior management

*Do not answer where you do not know.

highlight important information known to some but not others.

For each project, calculate the average of your scores and then assign each average according to the rule below:

Average less than 3: Low market uncertainty

Average between 3 and 5: Medium market uncertainty

Average 5 or more: High market uncertainty

Next comes the assessment of technical uncertainty. Different issues, same idea: Ask yourselves how certain you are about each of the issues listed in Table 24.2.

As before, input from multiple functions is more valuable, and once again, people should not reply to sections that don't apply or that they don't know.

As before, for each project, calculate the average of your scores and assign each average according to the rule below:

Average less than 3: Low technical uncertainty

Average between 3 and 5: Medium technical uncertainty

Average 5 or more: High technical uncertainty

These procedures are deliberately a little rough-and-ready because, in highly uncertain situations, you need an inexpensive, quick means of structuring the decisions you need to make. We have found simple tools such as those we recommend here to be far superior to more elegant ones that serve mostly to take up shelf space in an untouched binder. With scores in hand, you are now ready to categorize each of your projects into one of five types: positioning options, scouting options, stepping stone options, launches, or enhancements.

POSITIONING OPTIONS

Positioning options represent cases in which the level of technical uncertainty is high but you have some confidence that you know which markets and segments you eventually want to serve. Your uncertainty may stem from a lack of knowledge with respect to the feasibility of a major technical development step, from the lack of confidence that a particular technology trajectory is feasible, the lack of confidence as to which of several alternative technology trajectories to follow, the lack of a dominant design or standard, or from issues such as the regulatory acceptability of certain technologies. Because the major uncertainties have to do with alternative technological solutions, the idea is to take a minimal number of positions to hedge against making a single wrong bet, thus containing the damage done if any one position does not work out.

Positioning projects are most appropriate under two conditions. First is when you are uncertain what the trajectory of development of a technology is likely to be, so you make small "initiating" projects that you use to uncover that trajectory. Second is when there are several competing technologies that could satisfy a predictably high-potential market demand, but it is not yet clear which technology will dominate. You can't afford to pursue all technologies aggressively—this would be too expensive, yet you cannot afford to end up losing the market by betting on the wrong technology.

Consider mobile telephony in the United States. As of this writing, there are four or more different communication standards and massive uncertainty about which will ultimately become *the* standard. The plausible scenarios include: (1) a lock-in on one of the three standards, (2) preservation of the current multistandard system, and (3) the emergence of some new standard or way of communicating that makes the current mobile concept obsolete. Given such uncertainty, a sensible route for an R&D program to take might be to make modest investments that will prepare the firm for pursuing any of the three scenarios. We see this, of course, in practice, as telecom companies engage in a vast array of mergers, acquisitions of smaller firms and

joint ventures and alliances with larger firms while also aggressively lobbying regulatory agencies and making investments in the development of standards.

The two reasons to select a positioning option are therefore to generate knowledge that tells you whether a particular technology trajectory is possible and/or to buy time, flexibility and capability to pursue the best course of action once it becomes clear.

Ideally, positioning options are low-cost probes of alternative technological directions, such as experimental programs to probe the potential to develop a new technology. If pursuing several alternatives starts to look expensive, it may be possible to lay off the risk via cross-licensing or technology access deals, joint ventures for commercialization of new technologies, or joint marketing agreements. Of course, if money is no object, one can be a lot more aggressive in staking out positioning options. AT&T for instance, has spent billions of dollars on capturing attractive positions, acquiring cable companies such as Tele-Communications and MediaOne in 1998/1999, entering joint venture agreements with British Telecom and Japan Telecom, and setting up deals with Microsoft for set-top box software. Whatever happens in the telecommunications industry, AT&T is likely to have some options in its portfolio that will position it to participate. The box "Guidelines for Managing Your Options" provides guidelines for managing positioning option projects.

SCOUTING OPTIONS

Scouting options are used when you are confident you can develop the technology but you are not sure which combination of attributes the market will eventually prefer. The core questions you seek to answer with scouting projects concern how future markets will be segmented and what would be the way to develop technology applications for these emerging segments. The guiding principle is to get some prototype offering into the hands of customers in order to get feedback on their reactions to its features.

Scouting options allow you to explore new terrain from your current technology base, gathering information on its most attractive application. Scouting options differ from positioning options in that they extend your evolving technologies into application arenas that could allow you to capture significant market opportunities. The primary reason for selecting a scouting option is to learn.

It can not be stressed enough that these options should be consciously managed as scouts—that is, they are meant to be *small* investments made without expecting an immediate payoff. You use them to learn, to gather information. The idea is to send out your scouts using the smallest possible fixed investment or sunk cost and to then redirect your efforts after you find the most promising path.

Scouting is an area in which large companies often make mistakes that small entrepreneurial companies avoid, simply because the large firms have more money to spend. Redirection becomes much more difficult when you load yourself down with heavy fixed costs or massive sunk investment. Even fabulously well-researched and technically brilliant new products can disappoint in the marketplace. Not investing enough in scouting has been deadly for many technology-push kinds of ventures, such as the original launch of the Iridium world phone concept, which consumed over $7 billion to produce clunky, expensive phones that businesspeople could not use indoors.

It is crucial not to assume that you know what the customer wants. Your team of scientists and engineers should be encouraged to go out and actually talk to, and observe, the customers using the current products or prototypes before deciding on the direction of development of applications.

STEPPING-STONE OPTIONS

Stepping-stone options commence with small exploratory forays into less challenging market niches and use the experience gained there as stepping-stones to build technologies in increasingly challenging and attractive market arenas discovered as you go. Investments in stepping-stones are thus made as a series of deliberately staged and sequenced real options.

Managing such investments calls for the kind of discipline used by venture capitalists, in which funding decisions are made only when key milestones are reached and a great many assumptions have been tested. As each milestone is reached, you have the opportunity to stop further development or to sell, trade, license, or otherwise attempt to gain some returns on

investments in technological and market development to that point. The idea is to keep each successive round of investment to an absolute minimum, to reassess the project frequently, and to be willing to redirect it.

With stepping-stone options, the organization has a lot of learning to do on both market and technical dimensions. You should not necessarily expect to make profits from these early forays. They are your sacrificial products, and you need to prepare yourself for the fact that they are unlikely to be successful right off the bat. The idea is to follow Silicon Valley's famous principle for learning: "Fail fast, fail cheap, try again."

The primary difference between stepping-stone and scouting options is that scouting options involve technology that your R&D people are confident can be developed. Stepping-stone options focus on the creation of a new technological competence base in what seem to be irresistibly attractive opportunities. As this competence base develops, the new skills are used to progressively enter specialized sub-fields or new niche markets. This is done deliberately to develop experience and generate cash flow, sometimes with no intention of remaining in the early markets once the competence is sufficiently well developed. In this way, you can make deliberately parsimonious resource allocations designed to pursue carefully selected and increasingly challenging opportunities, with the objective of developing a new competence along an increasingly sophisticated trajectory and deploying it in unfolding markets.

The Sanyo Corporation, for example, used this approach to pursue the solar cell business. When energy conversion from light to electricity was in its early stages and hugely inefficient, instead of investing to crack high-level applications like solar panels for factory heating, Sanyo initially invested in low-end applications for known niche markets in which conversion efficiency was irrelevant. For instance, by focusing on light cells for wrist watches and calculators, the company generated modest cash flows while resolving considerable technical uncertainty with respect to cell construction and conversion efficiency. This created an initial technological competence which, as it evolves, is taking Sanyo along a trajectory of increasing technical sophistication in higher-end applications of light-to-energy conversion.

In a similar vein, 3M's movement into its optical business did not start with a massive launch into high-

Guidelines for Managing Your Options

MANAGING POSITIONING OPTIONS

1. Identify the major problems that the proposed technology could solve.

2. Develop the major scenarios that would make a positioning investment worthwhile, looking at the number and scale of the major problems that will be solved by the solution that the proposed project will enable. Build a convincing argument to show why taking one or more positioning options is called for.

3. Identify the full array of possible technological solutions that have potential to provide solutions to the problems.

4. Identify all the alternative technological bases that need to be covered in case the proposed positioning play does not work out.

5. Assess whether these other bases can be covered by taking options with other players—by means of alliances, joint ventures, cross-licensing agreements.

6. Make sure that you are not over-investing in this position—be sure you are covering alternative positions.

7. Using a planning approach along the lines of stage-gating, clearly identify what technical results need to be accomplished and what data you will use to track results.

8. Identify which data will be tracked to monitor the progress of competing technical solutions. Put in place a rigorous intelligence system to capture, interpret and make decisions based on these data.

9. Specify clearly which data you will use to let the option expire by discontinuing. This is critical—projects that are not accomplishing target outcomes or are losing out to competing technologies must be shut down so as to deploy resources, particularly talent, to other projects.

10. Make sure that a system is in place to ensure

that information from steps 7, 8, and 9 is delivered in a timely way to a person with authority to decide whether to continue the option(s) or to let them expire by discontinuing one or more.

11. This person must be in a position to make an objective decision to continue or shut down—it is very difficult for the person in charge of an option to discontinue it.

MANAGING SCOUTING OPTIONS

1. Identify as many applications as you can of the technology.

2. Use these to identify possible major markets and assemble small experimental probes deliberately designed to capture data about the market's reaction to the product.

3. Insist on design parsimony—spend as little as possible to gather specific information about the reaction of the scouted market.

4. Specify a clear business model—what the value added of the technology will be that will generate revenues and drive profits.

5. Specify how you will be using the scouting option to test the validity of the business model.

6. Ruthlessly reject proposals that suggest you develop the whole business to determine whether there is market demand or where no business model is proposed. The initial business model is seldom the final one, but the option needs to continuously test both the initial and evolving models for validity.

7. Specify the major assumptions about the market and the business model and decide where you can test the assumptions during the scouting option.

8. Ensure that you have plans to scout in markets that are different from your current segments

and that you are scouting not only for lead users but for the mass market as well.

9. As soon as responses are garnered from lead users, push them hard to establish why they adopted the offering so as to tease out where the real applications are.

10. Identify which data will be tracked to monitor the progress of competing technical solutions. Put in place a rigorous intelligence system to capture, interpret, and make decisions based on these data.

11. Specify clearly which data you will use to let the option expire by discontinuing. This is critical—projects that are not delivering target outcomes, or are losing out to competing technologies, must be shut down so as to deploy resources, particularly talent, to other projects.

12. Make sure that a system is in place to ensure that information from steps 7, 9, 10, and 11 is delivered in a timely way to a person with the authority to decide whether to continue the option(s) or to let them expire by discontinuing one or more.

13. This person must be in a position to make an objective decision to continue or shut down—it is very difficult for the person in charge of an option to discontinue it.

MANAGING STEPPING-STONE OPTIONS

1. Identify several early possible applications of the technology that do not challenge the technology too much.

2. Use these to identify a possible early, non-demanding market—even a small market—that will genuinely benefit from what you are proposing to offer.

3. Assemble small experimental probes deliberately designed to (a) capture data about the market's reaction to the product and (b) learn how to apply capability of the technology.

4. Insist on design parsimony—spend as little as

possible to gather specific information about the useful features of the technology and the reaction of the experimental market.

5. Develop a program whereby you stage and sequence the project in a way that redirects the program toward unfolding opportunities.

6. Develop clear metrics that, rather than measure revenues and profits, initially measure learning progress. This is done by specifying at each stage which assumptions about markets and the technologies capabilities will be tested.

7. Ensure that rather than conventional measures of success, evidence of learning is used to assess progress.

8. At each stage, assess what has been learned, then design the next stage by selecting a more challenging technology requirement for a larger, more demanding market.

9. Define, and be alert for, indicators that a major opportunity is opening up.

10. Identify which data will be tracked to monitor the progress of competing technical solutions. Put in place a rigorous intelligence system to capture, interpret and make decisions based on these data.

11. Specify clearly which data you will use to let the option expire by discontinuing. This is critical—projects that are not accomplishing target outcomes or are losing out to competing technologies must be shut down so as to deploy resources, particularly talent, to other projects.

12. Make sure that a system is in place to ensure that information from steps 7, 8, and 9 is delivered in a timely way to a person with authority to decide on whether to continue the option(s) or let them expire by discontinuing one or more.

13. This person must be in a position to make an objective decision to continue or shut down—it is very difficult for the person in charge of an option to discontinue it.

end optical applications. Instead, 3M started by using a simple technology for building "louvers" in glass that prevented light from penetrating at certain angles. This was tested first in applications like protecting valuable paintings from direct sunlight, to securing computer screens from nearby viewers. As new small markets were penetrated, the technology skills improved and diversified, and bigger and bigger markets were uncovered, so that today the optical products business is a major contributor to both growth and profits.

One point that bears mention: to the extent that you fix early on a particular design or feature set, you are limiting your future flexibility. Try, if you can, to pursue new designs and applications in a modular way, so that as new information comes in you can change your design plans. "Guidelines for Managing Your Options" contains guidelines for managing a stepping-stone venture.

LAUNCHES

Options are unnecessary when the R&D project is not saddled with high uncertainty—with moderate to low uncertainties, it makes more sense to undertake an outright launch. Intel, for instance, would have been crazy to use any strategy other than an outright launch for each next-generation chip for the bulk of its x86-to-Pentium lines. Why? Because for these products, the company's uncertainty with respect to market demand was low (Intel is a dominant player, people wanted those speedy processors, and manufacturers wanted to put them in the next generation PC's). Also, technical uncertainty was moderate as well.

In fact, there are as many examples of situations in which a launch is the preferred alternative to a more cautious options strategy. Cases in point include Gillette's longtime strategy in selling razors (always be the first to market with the most sophisticated shaving technology), most pharmaceutical companies' market entry for approved new drugs, and Texas Instruments' plunge into all manner of digital signal processing applications.

We categorize launches into two types: enhancements and platform launches. Enhancements represent improvements in existing products and services and are basically incremental improvements on an existing business model where both technical and market un-

certainty are low. Enhancements make existing offerings better, cheaper, easier to use, or improve them in some other way. On the other hand, platform launches are moderately uncertain and require more substantial investments. These are launches that are intended to create a substantial new base of business or basis of competitiveness for the firm.

Following Wheelwright and Clark (5), some launches create new product or service platforms from which you can build a substantial future business. The primary goal of a platform launch is to establish your company in a strong technological position with a target market that you think will respond favorably to what you have to offer. It is worthwhile, as you are doing the R&D work associated with platform launches, to think through what follow-on and enhancement launches may need to come later. To the extent that you can develop your technology in such a way that customers have a natural path to either migrate to your next-generation product or to buy a greater variety of products from you, growth prospects for the project will be better.

Platform launches provide the basis for next-generation advantages and are therefore critical to the company's medium-term competitiveness.

Enhancements represent R&D projects based on highly certain technology and directed to well-known markets, and that are critical for continuing support from those customers who are delivering the majority of the firm's current cash flows. These development projects basically enhance or deliver variations on an existing platform—and continuously improve your company's current offering relative to competitors. These critical projects are often not regarded as "sexy" enough by the R&D people and consequently can be seriously neglected unless management applies pressure to include them in the portfolio.

ASSEMBLING A STRATEGIC R&D PORTFOLIO

Trading off between shorter-term but surer, and longer-term and uncertain projects is always problematic for the R&D leader. A second common complaint is that project ideas come one at a time, and unpredictably, while budgets and plans are assembled all at once at specific time points. This can, over time, create a lack of alignment between both the strategy of the company and its available resources. All too often, the R&D group finds that it is totally over-committed in terms of projects, without a clear sense of what its priorities should be.

We suggest that one way to try to create alignment between budgets, strategies, available resources, and projects is to use the simple portfolio depicted in Figure 24.1 to take strategic control of the flow of projects. The core concept is to let your strategy and available resources guide your choice of how much emphasis to put on each of the categories. There is no cookbook for how best to do this. In general, though, you want to craft a project portfolio that suits the strategic environments in which you will have to compete. Thus, if you are in a fast-moving, highly uncertain industry, you will want to weight the proportion of resources in your portfolio more heavily toward options. If you are in a relatively stable or capital-intensive industry, you should probably be investing a greater percentage of project resources in platforms. Thus, it makes perfect sense for companies like Intel and Hewlett-Packard to invest substantially in options, such as equity investments in small entrepreneurial companies with interesting technology. It makes equally good sense for a company like Boeing to place its emphasis on platforms, such as its successful introduction of the 777 line of aircraft.

An approach that we have found powerful is to look at the pace of technology change and the nature of R&D in your business and then decide what you consider to be a competitive mix of projects by allocating different, strategically decided, proportions of your resources to each type of R&D project. We show an example in Figure 24.2.

Here is the key point: After you have determined the mix of projects you need to support your strategy and how many projects you can support, similar projects compete *only* against other similar projects, and *only* for the percentage budget and staff allocated to that category of project. Let's say that you have decided to allocate 15 percent of your available resources to positioning projects. Any new candidate for acquiring resources that is a positioning project should compete *only* against all the other positioning projects for those 15 percent of resources, and not compete against any other type of project. In other words it should not compete at all against other kinds of options or against launches or enhancements. This ensures that you will

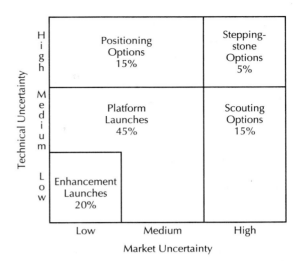

Figure 24.2. A strategic R&D portfolio showing the proportion of resources allocated to each type of project.

pick only the very best positioning projects for your portfolio. More importantly, it gets you out of the constant tug of war between projects intended to produce short-term results, and projects that you know are important for the long term.

The strategic choice is thus how many of your resources you will put into each category. Within a category, the best projects should compete against one another for consideration.

Allocating resources is a process that in our experience most companies undertake with a fair amount of iteration. A fruitful place to start is by getting a handle on what the portfolio of projects (and ongoing businesses) looks like for you at the moment. Next, you need to determine whether you have the financial and human resource capacity to handle your existing portfolio of businesses and those new initiatives you wish to start. If you are out of capacity, you have two choices: find more resources, or cut back on what you are doing.

As part of this process, you will need to also assess (at least roughly) not only what mix of project types are needed to support your strategy but also how many you are realistically able to undertake. Most companies, for instance, would be hard pressed to start many platform launches simultaneously—they are terribly draining for the organization.

The first step in sorting out what your ideal portfolio should look like is thus figuring out what your actual portfolio looks like today. Because everything new you want to do will add to the work people are already doing, you need to look both at your portfolio of new ideas and at the portfolio of work already in the pipeline. In our experience, most firms chase many more projects and ideas than they can execute successfully.

BUILDING THE PORTFOLIO

To show how this works, we illustrate the process with a project we worked on for a medical devices manufacturer. We began by listing all the projects currently under way in the company. We then worked with the senior executive team to categorize them into the five portfolio categories (positioning option, scouting option, stepping-stone option, platform launch, or enhancement). Next, we estimated the effort (roughly in full-time, equivalent person-months) that would be required to bring each project to the next budget period, at which stage the portfolio would be re-evaluated. This gave us a picture of where the company was spending its energy today. On top of this, we loaded in all the new initiatives the senior executive team indicated they were considering undertaking within the next two years, and what resources it would take to get to the next budget period. Finally, we mapped the results onto a chart similar to Figure 24.1.

We show the results in Figure 24.3. Each circle in the figure represents a project. The size of the circle represents the (roughly) estimated revenue benefits expected, and the number in the circle represents the number of person-months currently budgeted for on-going projects in the next year. Blank circles represent projects that were on the list, but to which no resources had been allocated at the time we did the mapping. The idea was to try to get everything that was or could be consuming R&D time and energy mapped in a way that allowed people to identify the totality of what was going on.

This visualization exercise was a revelation. After comparing demand for man-hours with available scientist/engineer resources, it became crystal clear that the company was pursuing many more projects than people thought it was or should. In particular, by trying to engage in many highly demanding platform launch-

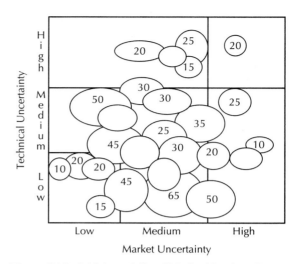

Figure 24.3. Initial portfolio of Medical Devices Corporation.

es at the same time, the company was unlikely to do justice to its portfolio of options. Time and talent needed for options investments were being siphoned away to shorter-term platform launches. Furthermore, enhancements to satisfy the firm's customers were simply not being allocated the necessary resources because many of these were still on the drawing board and competing for the same scarce design and engineering talent as the major platform launches. (This happens often—scientists are more interested in the "hot" platform projects than the simple enhancements.)

In short, the company was doing both too much and too little. The results of over-commitment to large platform programs meant that project deadlines perpetually slipped, promises of enhancements to key customers were often broken, and people were beginning to feel burned out.

It is not unusual for the usual process through which companies take on projects to lead them to discover later that they lack the resources to do justice to everything on their plates. In particular, when managers have not clearly thought through which projects will be needed to support their needs to either build new platforms or learn through options, the different kinds of projects compete with each other and confusion results. It is also typical of companies that have not matched their strategy to available resources. A far wiser approach is to pursue a few well-run projects than to chase a grab-bag of forever-behind-schedule and over-budget initiatives.

If you do a similar exercise, you will now be able to determine whether there is any rhyme or reason to the projects that you currently have on the drawing board.

The next thing we did was to decide what the appropriate percentage of resources should be for each project category. Our medical devices client, after considering the pressure from current customers for enhancements and the paucity of options that it was pursuing, decided to reallocate its resources. The company put several major platform launches on hold for later development, and reassigned staff and budget to more enhancements (which require relatively less resources), and to an increased number of options. After considerable, and sometimes heated discussion, our medical devices client redrew its original portfolio to reflect the projects in Figure 24.4.

The goal of this piece of the opportunity selection process is to ensure that the key people available are not hopelessly overloaded with projects. Part of the challenge is to match desired effort with your carrying capacity for projects. Though part of the puzzle is obviously capital budget allocations, most companies seem to have a much higher awareness of the rules by which capital and assets are allocated than they do about how skilled people should be spending their time. R&D managers and CTOs need to focus on the allocation of skills and talents they will need to cope with the demands of current businesses, to run successful launches, and to manage options.

If you are willing to begin with some educated guesses as to how people are going to allocate their time, the process of figuring out how much your organization can handle is pretty straightforward. Start by making rough estimates of the number of different kinds of people who will be needed to work on the projects you have identified in your version of Figure 24.4 in the course of the next year, as shown in Table 24.3 We like to break it up in six-month chunks but you may prefer shorter or longer periods. There is no need for precision; you need only estimate in broad terms to see the scope of the human resource challenge that you face. This table allows you to map out how many, and what kind of staff you will need to do everything you want to do within the timeframe specified.

The next step is to consider how many and what kind of skilled people you already have. If your business is anything like our exemplar firm, or indeed like most of the companies we have worked with, you will find that the projects you have committed to complete represent well over 100 percent of your carrying capacity. This can have surprising effects on the length of time each project takes to complete. For instance, imagine a project that will take a skilled software developer six months to complete. The lead time to completion if this person is working full-time on the project is six months. Divide this person's time between four projects, however, and most of the time, three out of the four are not getting any attention and the lead time to completion of all four projects is two years! Delays like this can be deadly in a world where speed matters.

In the process of planning and then allocating your human resource needs, it is important not to overload. Putting together a table like Table 24.4 will help you begin to flesh out realistic allocations of time for people to pursue new ventures and to conduct their current, ongoing business. We strongly recommend that no more than 90 percent of an employee's time be pre-allocated. The built-in slack allows for contingencies and breathing space for creativity as well as for the networking that is the heart's blood of entrepreneurial organizations.

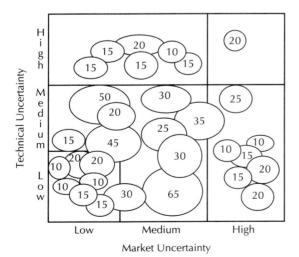

Figure 24.4. Revised portfolio of Medical Devices Corporation.

Table 24.3. Estimating Approximate R&D Human Resource Demand

Key Contribution	Project 1: January–June	Project 1: July–December	Project 1: Total	Project 2: January–June	Project 2: July–December	Etc.	All Projects January–December
Development staff	1	1	2	1	—	—	5
Engineering staff	1	2	3	2	1	—	6
Software staff	—	1	1	2	2	—	6
Marketing staff	—	1	1	—	2	—	4
And so on . . .							

Table 24.4. How You Might Depict Key R&D Human Resource Allocations

	Functional Contribution	% Time on Current Business	% Time on Project 1	% Time on Project 2	And So On . . .	% Total Time (Maximum 90%)
Person 1	Development	0	90	0		90
Person 2	Development	0	0	80		80
Person 3	Engineering	60	20	10		90
Person 4	Marketing	70	20	0		90
Person 5	Marketing	75	0	15		90
And so on . . .						

It may seem trivial to account for employee time to this degree, but it is absolutely vital, particularly if you plan to take on a number of projects with different time demands, different levels of uncertainty, and different requirements from the people you are working with. This much being said, don't get trapped into micro-allocating people's time. Allocating manmonths is sufficient for most projects of any strategic significance. Regularly reviewing a chart like this can also clear up a lot of misunderstandings. Absent information about how many other projects colleagues are working on, it is easy to misinterpret absences or exhaustion as a lack of commitment.

After you have made a realistic assessment of the human resources required for each project, you can further adjust your portfolio of opportunities to accommodate this assessment. The effort to group projects by type really pays off here. You have already given some thought as to what an ideal portfolio of projects would look like for your firm. Now you can be specific about the number of each kind of project you want and have the resources to pursue.

In the company we were advising, we suggested that managers cut back the number of projects in their portfolio mix to include only one stepping-stone proj-

ect, the nine most important platform launches, eight enhancement launches, six positioning options, and seven low-budget scouting options. This project load did not exceed the capacity of the organization. At the same time, it accommodated the firm's need to generate growth through platform launches, to meet the enhancement needs of current customers, and to support a number of positioning options that would allow it to react swiftly should technology suddenly shift in certain arenas.

We did not suggest that they completely kill off other good projects. Most of those could be deferred without undue damage, so they were kept in an "opportunity register" for future use should resources or opportunity emerge. You can also consider spinning off projects you don't have the capacity to handle, either through joint venture or other mechanisms (such as licensing).

Making comparisons within each category of launch or option allows you to make project tradeoffs without having to worry about trading off between the different categories—that is a separate decision that gets made when you determine how many projects you want in each category. This can be a big relief, as it is common corporate practice to put people in the position of having to choose between an essential enhancement launch (a short-term goal) and a stepping-stone that is thought to be crucial to the firm's future viability (a long-term goal). Using the categories, and your target number of projects within each category, you can compare launches to launches and scouts to scouts and pursue only those ventures that are really attractive.

You must also make a realistic assessment of what else is going on in your corporate environment. If your company is in the midst of a major reorganization, merger, business crisis, or other significant change, the amount of time and attention people will have for new initiatives will be limited.

TAKING ACTION

The action steps that follow are meant to get you started on the concepts and processes discussed in this article. Feel free to elaborate in a way that works for your company.

1. For each R&D project in your portfolio, assess the market and technical uncertainty using the questions in Tables 24.1 and 24.2.

2. Decide on what proportion of your resources you will allocate to each of the different kinds of initiatives you might want to take: positioning options, scouting options, stepping-stone options, platform launches, and enhancement launches, along the lines of Figure 24.2. The greater the uncertainty and amount of change in your arenas, the more resources you should allocate to options as a proportion of your overall portfolio (think of this as your initial rule of thumb—you can adjust it later as warranted by experience).

3. Assign each R&D project to one of the portfolio categories. You can use your scores from Tables 24.1 and 24.2 to do the allocations. Estimate the number of man-months to the next budget period

for each of them. Chart the projects in a format similar to that in Figure 24.3.

4. Determine the carrying capacity of your organization for new initiatives and older ones, using the technique demonstrated in Table 24.3.

5. If you have more projects than capacity, consider which should be postponed or dropped. Your objective is to manage your portfolio of projects so that they fall within the carrying capacity of your organization. Compare projects within a category to other projects within that category (for instance, launches to launches).

6. Assign specific responsibilities to specific people and make a record of them in a figure like Figure 24.4, so there will be no future confusion as to who is supposed to do what.

7. Make it a point to regularly review capacity, the portfolio of opportunities, and the match of people to projects.

REFERENCES

1. Mitchell, George R. and Hamilton, William F. "Managing R&D as a Strategic Option. *Research • Technology Management,* May–June 1988, pp. 15–22.
2. McGrath, Rita Gunther and MacMillan, Ian C. "Assessing Technology Projects Using Real Options Reasoning." *Research • Technology Management,* July–August 2000, pp. 35–49.
3. Morris, Peter A, Elizabeth Olmsted Teisberg, and A. Lawrence Kolbe. "When Choosing R&D Projects, Go with Long Shots." *Research • Technology Management,* January–February 1991, pp. 35–40.
4. Lynn, G. S., J. G. Morone and A. S. Paulson. "Marketing and DisContinuous Innovation: The Probe and Learn Process." In M. Tushman and P. Anderson (Eds) *Managing Strategic Innovation and Change.* New York: Oxford University Press, pp. 353–375, 1997.
5. Wheelwright, S. C. and Clark, K. B. "Creating Project Plans to Focus Product Development. *Harvard Business Review.* March–April 1992, pp. 70–82.

SECTION V

KNOWLEDGE, LEARNING, AND INTELLECTUAL CAPITAL

As opposed to pure imitators, innovators create new products or services by extending their existing knowledge base. Because they are moving beyond the bounds of existing practice, innovators, by definition, must learn as they go, and the more effectively they learn, the greater the opportunity they have to develop distinctive competences that are difficult for imitators to copy. Knowledge and learning are key strategic levers because knowledge development is cumulative. For example, in learning mathematics, one cannot understand algebra without learning arithmetic first, and one cannot understand calculus without a sound foundation in algebra. Commercial knowledge is similar, whether or not it is highly technical: what one already knows determines what one is ready to learn next.

Because knowledge cumulates in this fashion, innovators must carefully consider the path along which a firm's intellectual capital grows, even as they strive to maximize their ability to learn. Inevitably, a knowledge base becomes too large for anyone to master, so individuals and organizational subunits must specialize. At this point, transferring and recombining existing knowledge becomes at least as important as adding new knowledge. Managing the growth and transfer of knowledge is especially important when know-how is tacit. One learns such skills by working with those who already possess them; they cannot be reduced to a written recipe. Consequently, knowledge management is often more of an organizational challenge than a technical one—helping people learn from one another matters more than building an advanced information technology infrastructure.

More and more of the value created in a modern economy is the product of information and insight. Software is a paradigmatic case. The software sector is one of the richest and fastest-growing sectors, and increasingly, software and databases underpin value creation in other industries. Software is essentially pure thought, and the price that customers pay for it reflects the enormous value of intellectual capital. The cost of the chemicals in an ethical drug or the materials in a semiconductor is trivial—the margins for such products reflect the great value of the intellectual capital that goes into them. Even in so-called low-technology sectors, the intellect and knowledge that turn products and services into solutions are a tremendous source of value. For example, McDonald's sells meat and potatoes like other restaurants; knowing how to run a franchise efficiently in a way that creates loyal customers generates extraordinary profits.

Section V builds on the strategic concepts introduced in Section IV by introducing a set of frameworks for creating competitive advantage through knowledge and learning.

Von Krogh, Nonaka, and Aben define a knowledge strategy as the employment of knowledge processes to an existing or new domain in order to achieve strategic goals. They discuss four strategies that are based on applying knowledge creation or knowledge transfer processes to existing or new domains and describe the critical success factors for each, drawing on a rich case example from Unilever. Kim then describes how Hyundai built up the "absorptive capacity" it needed to acquire, assimilate, and improve imported technologies to catch up with foreign automobile manufacturers. Next, Powell discusses how biotechnology and pharmaceutical firms form collaborative networks and organize to learn from their partners. Finally, Seely Brown and Duguid show how Xerox created a set of "communities of practice" that organized the creation and transfer of know-how through decentralized, informal structures with their own rules and procedures.

25

Making the Most of Your Company's Knowledge

A Strategic Framework

GEORG VON KROGH
IKUJIRO NONAKA
MANFRED ABEN

This paper develops a framework of four strategies for managing knowledge. Companies can leverage their knowledge throughout the organization, expand their knowledge further based on existing expertise, appropriate knowledge from partners and other organizations, and develop completely new expertise by probing new technologies or markets. The two core processes of knowledge creation and transfer are central to the execution of these strategies, as is the company's domains of knowledge. The framework is based on conceptualization about knowledge management practices at Unilever, a multinational fast-moving consumer goods company.

INTRODUCTION

In the knowledge economy a key source of sustainable competitive advantage and superior profitability within an industry is how a company creates and shares its knowledge.[1] The strategic management field is currently developing new concepts and tools for guiding managers in their efforts to ride the waves of the knowledge economy. At the heart of this development are fundamentally new mental maps that give credence to the nature of knowledge. Currently strategic planners, for example, know perfectly well how to analyze the strengths and weakness of a company's tangible resources, as well as how to match these with opportunities and threats in the environment. They know how to use these analyses for capital resource allocation, for calculating discounted cash-flow from investments in tangible assets; but do they know equally well how to analyze knowledge and allocate resources accordingly to knowledge activities? A number of issues remain open, but one needs to be addressed first: what strategic alternatives are available with respect to knowledge? It is very likely that strategic management in the knowledge economy will be quite different from the one we have grown used to over the past decades.[2] In this paper, we develop a framework for knowledge strategy, based on observing knowledge management practices at Unilever, one of the world's largest fast-moving consumer goods companies. Unilever has been particularly active in knowledge management for the past 10 years and has achieved measurable results from these activities, such as a faster rate of innovation, increased efficiency in manufacturing and supply chain, and an acceleration of rolling out best practices.

For some time now, Unilever managers have been convinced about the role of knowledge as a key differ-

Reprinted from *Long Range Planning,* Vol. 34, Georg von Krogh, Ikujiro Nonaka, and Manfred Aben, "Making the Most of Your Company's Knowledge: A Strategic Framework," pp. 421–439. Copyright © 2001, with permission from Elsevier.

entiator, and investment in innovation is substantial. Unilever's Corporate Purpose states: "We will bring our wealth of knowledge and international expertise to the service of local consumers. . . ." But, as the company has become more focused, and bottom-line improvements are bearing fruit, it is becoming increasingly important to ensure that the investments in knowledge contribute truly to top-line growth and profitability. In Unilever's Culinary Category, the management and development of knowledge and creativity are seen as a strategic priority and approached as such through a new way of strategizing for knowledge and innovation.[3]

DEVELOPING YOUR COMPANY'S "KNOWLEDGE DOMAIN"

In order to get a better grasp of the term "knowledge domain," let us go directly to our case. Unilever is an Anglo-Dutch consumer goods company with corporate centers in London and Rotterdam. With annual sales of about $48 billion, Unilever is one of the world's largest consumer products companies. It produces and markets a wide range of foods, home and personal care products, including well-known brands such as Lipton, Ragu, Flora, I Can't Believe It's Not Butter, Breyers, Omo, All, Calvin Klein Cosmetics, Elizabeth Arden, and Dove. With a global presence, Unilever employs almost 290,000 people. About 2 percent of annual turnover is invested in basic research and product innovations, leading to the filing of more than 400 patent applications annually. In several product areas Unilever has advanced and diverse methods for developing knowledge strategies, for creating and transferring knowledge.

Knowledge creation and transfer have been key to the development of the Culinary Category—which was formed in 1996 and covers products such as meal sauces, cold sauces, and cooking ingredients. A Knowledge Initiative has been in place within this category since December 1996. In order to capture what the company knows and does not know in various functional and product areas, *Knowledge Workshops* have been organized to bring together key experts and practitioners from around the world. In a facilitated and structured way, learning and understanding are discussed and captured. Among the key results are a

shared vocabulary and terminology, the initiation of a *Community of Practice (CoP)*,[4] and the identification of knowledge gaps. This CoP has a core group consisting of the participants of the workshop (usually 10 to 12 members) and is expanded by the inclusion of other people in the same line of practice. The Knowledge Workshops define the Knowledge Domain to which the CoP participants contribute, for instance, the manufacture of meal sauces around the world. A knowledge domain consists of relevant data, information, articulated knowledge, such as handbooks, manuals or presentations, and a list of key people and groups with tacit knowledge based on long-term work experiences. The purpose of these communities is to act as custodian for the Knowledge Domain, nurturing the sharing and creation of practices and knowledge that are key to the achievement of both company and personal objectives.

The portfolio of CoPs and knowledge domains is determined by their importance to the effectiveness of business operations, and whether the knowledge typically is tacit and bound to a smaller group of professional experts. For example, in sauce manufacturing the calibration of equipment, the layout of a production process, the reduction of downtime, etc., are all intimately linked to work experience of professionals operating locally. The purpose of the community is to ensure that the professionals collaborate across plants, geographical boundaries, and sometimes also functional boundaries. Such CoPs have already led to a number of significant benefits in Unilever, ranging from improved investment decisions, rollout of best practices, and collaborative innovation across plants and firm boundaries. A senior business stakeholder champions each CoP. This ensures delivery to the business targets and appropriate visibility of the CoP's efforts and impact.

The knowledge workshop and the CoP also typically identify what is termed "knowledge gaps." A technical or marketing problem might have been identified, but the knowledge on how to solve the problem is not available. In those cases, sub-groups among CoP participants are charged with the task of collecting data, information, and creating knowledge around how to solve the problem based on their existing work practices. This increases the depth of knowledge in the domain. In some cases, other professionals from Unilever must be invited to join the CoP on a short- to medium-term basis to help solve the problem. These newcomers bring new work experiences, explicit procedures, information, and data to the party. This enlarges the *scope* of knowledge in the domain.

On the company side, once the knowledge domain has been identified, together with the key participants, manufacturing plant managers from around the world can contact domain leaders with technical queries ranging from a change in color or taste of a meal sauce to an assessment of a new manufacturing technology. In Unilever, the knowledge domain appoints a "domain leader." This is not necessarily the most highly recognized expert in the field, but a "primus inter pares" that coordinates and integrates the work of the people contributing to the domain. Normally these participants also select their domain leader. The domain leader may in turn contact his domain members via e-mail, fax, or telephone or call for a face-to-face meeting. Based on the discussions among the experts, the domain leaders can return to the plant manager with possible answers to the queries.

On the personal side, members of the community of practice learn, pick up small and large tricks of improving their own local manufacturing practice, and jointly develop a more refined language for analyzing the manufacturing process. They can also test out ideas and concepts on a group of peers before starting to implement these in their local organization. Normally, because the benefit to each of the participants of membership is direct and valuable, sharing knowledge within a knowledge domain is not necessarily considered to be a problem.

In general a company has several such knowledge domains at its disposal, and you have a choice in focusing on existing and new knowledge domains. First, you can decide to let knowledge develop from the existing knowledge domain,[5] that is, increase the depth and/or scope of the knowledge. Second, you can decide to create a new knowledge domain, that is, create new data, new information and new tacit and explicit knowledge at the individual and collective levels, e.g., new CoPs, with loose connections to existing knowledge domains. This domain in turn can develop in depth and scope.

In the literature on knowledge management, we can distinguish two core knowledge processes: knowledge creation and knowledge transfer.[6] The target of a process for knowledge creation is to enhance the potential of creating innovations. According to Ikujiro Nonaka and others, such knowledge creation processes typically take place in five steps in a group of limited size (most authors recommend between 5 and 15).[7] First, knowledge domain members start by creating collective tacit knowledge by jointly experiencing new work processes, tasks, technological characteristics, use of technologies, customer sites, etc. This is not an easy process. Members of the knowledge domain must spend considerable time together, discuss and reflect upon their experiences, observe how their colleagues solve tasks and interact with technologies, explain and give sense to their own actions. In the next phase, the team attempts to make these collective experiences explicit, through agreeing on proper, just, and accurate descriptions of their experiences. These descriptions in turn are used in a brainstorming fashion to develop new product and service concepts based on their experiences.[8] In the third step, this concept then becomes subject to scrutiny. It is matched against market data, consumer trends, and technological requirements such as the process data, cost of manufacturing the finished product, strategies, goals, and so forth. In this step, customers and suppliers might even be invited to give their views on the concept. A concept that successfully passes through this phase is transformed into a prototype process, product, or service. Here, various design tools are at work, such as activity-based costing, computer-aided manufacturing and design systems, workflow maps, process descriptions, historical production data, and so forth. While these four steps typically cover the major steps of knowledge creation, the fully fledged process goes further by integrating the newly created knowledge in existing manufacturing, marketing and sales. An important issue of knowledge creation is to enhance the pace of innovation and to reduce the time span to commercial success in the market. Key factors here are, for example, leadership experiences in project management,[9] an available and easily accessible database of individualized customer preferences,[10] or someone who mobilizes knowledge creation and coordinates various knowledge creation initiatives in the company.[11]

Whereas the knowledge creation process typically happens in communities of practice or other small-sized groups, your company should benefit from such knowledge on a larger scale. Here it is key to remember that knowledge transfer is a mechanism to be used selectively: not everybody in the company needs to know everything at all times. Specialization secures the development of a knowledge domain, but occasionally other domains and functions have needs to be fulfilled. That is, knowledge domains, functions, departments, and business units should have the possibility to leverage knowledge through transfer processes.[12] To accelerate such processes in your company, three conditions should be satisfied.[13] First, the parties are aware of the opportunity to exchange the knowledge. Second, the parties involved expect the knowledge transfer to prove worthwhile for both parties. Third, the parties must be motivated to pursue the knowledge transfer—they must be interested in applying the knowledge transferred into their own activities to realize the benefits of the transfer. A typical knowledge transfer then starts with the identification of knowledge to be transferred, in which the potential benefits of the transfer are signaled to the receiving partner or to the sending partner.[14] A typical example in Unilever is the Category World Conferences, where global strategies and available knowledge and tools for implementing these strategies are transferred to key local company operatives. At the Culinary World Conference, for instance, tools for understanding consumers were shared to support market entry and business growth. Clear linkage between the corporate strategy and local strategies is provided during these conferences. Next, the receiver assesses the value of knowledge for local use, and the sender assesses the potential loss or gain. The next step covers packaging and dispatching of knowledge in such a way as to enhance the receiver's potential to act. Local training and instructions complement data and information, in order to make knowledge useable. The last step includes adaptation, in which the transferred knowledge is integrated with the local knowledge.

Knowledge transfer with external partners is also important. Strategic partnerships provide mutual access to other companies' knowledge.[15] Research and training agreements with universities and other research institutions provide companies with access to recent research knowledge.[16] In terms of learning from the outside, concrete learning targets are needed for the relationship. This has been shown to improve a company's ability to appropriate and integrate new knowledge rapidly from the partners. Furthermore, attention has to be paid to the management of knowledge flow, wanted and unwanted, between the firms, as well as the ability to absorb the new knowledge effectively.[17]

FORMULATING YOUR COMPANY'S KNOWLEDGE STRATEGIES

The term "Knowledge Strategy" denotes the employment of knowledge processes to an existing or new knowledge domain in order to achieve strategic goals (see Appendix A). First, this definition entails a process focus rather than a contents focus, and it assumes that knowledge is dynamic rather than static. Second, our view assumes that knowledge domains are starting points rather than end states. Imagine that you are setting out for a city unknown to you (i.e., you have no knowledge of the city except for its location on the map). However, you know your starting point; the city in which you live, your car, your gas, your map, the music you take along for entertainment, and so on. The map is the strategy. It shows you the routes to your destination. At the same time, you have goals to satisfy, such as timing, the fuel you will use, a safe journey, and so forth. The contents of the knowledge domain will gradually change as you drive through the unknown terrain. Third, our definition assumes that the processes that you apply to a knowledge domain impact the way that domain will change, in order to reach a strategic goal, for example of innovating, enhancing efficiency, and better managing risk. The core-processes of creation and transfer dominate the evolution of the domain. The strategist's choice is to strike a balance between existing and new knowledge domains, and the core-knowledge processes, and the firm's goals. Therefore, we fourthly assume that strategy means choice and that the firm should allocate resources to knowledge domains and processes. Striking a balance between developing existing or new knowledge domains is difficult and must be pursued with care. There are strong trade-offs between pushing the outside of the envelope in a new science area and improving the logistics in a warehouse. Some initial thinking should guide your resource allocation. If your industry is stable and mature, and few technological developments are under way, more emphasis could be given to maintain and refine existing knowledge than building new knowledge. Perhaps partnering with other firms within the industry provides important new sources of insight and experience. When established industries are exposed to actual and potential substitutes (e.g., internet distribution of music for the packaged media industry), new knowledge about technologies and actions need to be rapidly supported. You will need to build the firm's capacity at absorbing these technologies and information, but this in turn is difficult unless you commit substantial resources.[18] If your already operate in an emerging industry, such as biotechnology, media, or financial services, your commitment to building new knowledge should be higher than if your industry is stable. Research and development budgets compared with those of your competitors might be an indicator of how much you spend on developing new knowledge domains, but really, these measures are only tentative and rough. You need to examine activities and spending patterns in various functional areas throughout the firm in order to identify the level of activity on knowledge creation and transfer. Look for things such as technology investments, profiles of new hires, job rotation and turnover of employees, training budgets, managerial career patterns, partnership with firms and other organizations, collaborations across functions, departments, countries, and business units. You might also want to keep in mind that most industries are either exposed to substitutes in one form or the other or subject to major transformation (e.g., telecommunications). Hence an over-reliance on what you know might be dangerous in the long run.

In order to help your resource allocation you can distinguish four generic knowledge strategies: leveraging, expanding, appropriating, and probing (Figure 25.1).

		Knowledge Process	
		Transfer	Creation
Knowledge Domain	Existing	Leveraging Strategy	Expanding Strategy
	New	Appropriating Strategy	Probing Strategy

Figure 25.1. Four knowledge strategies.

The Leveraging Strategy

This strategy sets out from existing knowledge domains and focuses on transferring that knowledge throughout the organization. In terms of strategic goal contributions, the leveraging strategy can first be orientated toward achieving efficiency in operations as well as reducing risks in operations. The strategy ensures that the company internally transfers existing knowledge from various knowledge domains, for example, in areas such as product development, manufacturing, marketing and sales, human resources, purchasing, finance, and so forth. Efficiency increase results from local adaptation of cost-effective processes and services invented and developed elsewhere. Furthermore, knowledge transfer is essential to the consolidation of activities, as well as the standardization of tasks. An internal benchmarking program is a useful tool to achieve awareness of the potential transfer opportunities, highlighting the benefits of a possible transfer and providing some motivation to locally appropriate knowledge. The benchmarking program reveals differences in local practices and their performance effects.[19]

For Unilever, the Knowledge Workshops and Communities of Practice are an important means to leverage knowledge domains in the Culinary Category. The knowledge captured during the workshops is refined and shared by a larger community of experts and practitioners. Each of the CoP members will bring back results from their work in the community to their respective country or functional organization. In this way, experience and good proven practice are shared and applied across the world very rapidly. For example, one area where knowledge was captured in knowledge workshops was in the construction of manufacturing sites for meal sauces. Thanks to knowledge leveraging strategies, documentation and handbooks have become available and recognized professionals identified and asked to work on new construction sites, Unilever has been able to reduce the time for designing, planning, and commissioning the construction of a new plant by approximately 50 percent.

In innovation-oriented Knowledge Workshops, knowledge is shared across disciplines, including successes and failures, which allows for faster innovation. By sharing knowledge in this way, building upon trust between the participants, the risk of repeat mistakes and "reinventing the wheel" is significantly reduced, and creativity and entrepreneurship are nurtured. One of the first examples of this was a debriefing of a large innovation project. The project, which focused on the development of a new product technology, started mid-1995 and officially ended at the end of 1998 when it was clear that the product innovation target would not be met due to technical difficulties and changing market realities. Typically, when projects stop without meeting the targets, all involved tend to move on quickly to new projects and challenges, often without properly recording the lessons learned. It is crucial that a firm learns from both successes and failures. Moreover, although a project can be terminated because targets have not been achieved, this does not imply failure or that no valuable learning has taken place, which could well be applied in other projects. The project management team therefore decided to organize a debriefing on the project to capture and secure the learning of the project in a structured way and to be able to disseminate the captured knowledge to other research or application projects. Most of the team members from the project were present during the debriefing. Independently, a new Culinary project on dressings had been proposed, which could take up most of the learning. Therefore, two delegates from the new project were present at the debriefing. This exercise is now known in Unilever as "Knowledge Debrief."

Two types of learnings were captured during the Knowledge Debrief: *technical* learning in each of the science and application areas involved and *process* learnings that related to the way the project and the team functioned and how prospective failure could have been determined earlier. Both these types are crucial for continuous improvement. The *process learnings* were captured during individual interviews with the participants prior to the meeting, focusing on the five worst and the five best things that the participants felt happened during the project. The results of these interviews were grouped and discussed plenary at the start of the workshop. The *technical learnings* were captured by focusing on key product attributes such as taste, aroma, and texture in relation to the consumer attributes that were set at the beginning of the project. All recommendations, both technical and process related, were prioritized and turned into actions, timings, and responsibilities and were followed up successfully. Senior management was present at the start and end of the workshop to reinforce the message that terminated projects constitute a benefit to the company (indicating the willingness to take risks) as long as lessons are learned and failure is not repeated.

Information and communication technologies (ICT) also play an important role in leveraging knowledge across domains in the company. For example community software (such as community platforms, e-groups, or Geocrawler) allow organizational members to form but also to organize and maintain their community interaction across geographical boundaries and time zones at very low cost. Coupled with database software, or web-technology with search engines, ICT also helps to create a repository that allows parties to become aware of the opportunity to exchange the knowledge. Such repositories of knowledge, say of manufacturing handbooks or software development tools, can be coupled with "chat groups" where people can enter tips and hints on how, where, and when to use the available material. Hence, the parties can judge whether the knowledge transfer proves worthwhile. Seeing that the knowledge has turned out to be valuable on one comparable site or part of the organization, these chat groups can also motivate individuals within the organization to pursue the transfer and apply the knowledge locally.[20]

The leveraging strategy also affects the ability to manage risk. Sharing existing knowledge within or between knowledge domains throughout the organization will reduce the risk of overtaxing resources. Locally, members of the organization can increase the scope and the depth of their knowledge to accomplish tasks successfully. They gain access to new data and information, they acquire new tools and procedures to solve new tasks, win new insights, and so forth. By sharing existing knowledge on competitors and regulatory environments, the organization will become increasingly aware of competitors' moves and possible policy changes that could affect the performance of the company.

A good example of risk reduction in Unilever has been the development of a Knowledge-Based System for Microbiological Design Approval (MiDAS). MiDAS incorporates a wealth of knowledge and experience of specialists in Unilever about microbiological safety in product and process design. The system allows a process or product developer to enter a product and process design and obtain an immediate assessment of the microbiological safety of the proposed

Table 25.1. The Leveraging Strategy Impacts on Strategic Goals

Efficiency	Share knowledge in the organization, e.g., on manufacturing, product development, marketing, sales
Innovation	Share knowledge between domains to improve innovation processes
Managing Risk	Share knowledge to reduce risk of overtaxing resources
	Share knowledge on competitors and regulatory environment

product. Previously, the developers would have to actually make the product and send a sample to the central laboratory. It would take quite some time to get such feedback, modify the product, and repeat the approval process. The experts were not available at the right time and place and were overwhelmed by "trivial" product clearance work, allowing them little time for innovation. The product developers on the other hand, were tempted to take more risks by not officially clearing slight modifications, increasing the risk of contamination and subsequent market impact. The MiDAS system does not give final clearance, but it allows quick prototype development. In the vast majority of product and process systems suggested, the central department offers a quick clearance.

Table 25.1 summarizes the major impact on the leveraging strategy on the business goals of efficiency, innovation, and better risk management.

The Expansion Strategy

This strategy proceeds from the existing knowledge domain of the organization and targets knowledge creation by drawing on existing data, information, and knowledge. The emphasis is on increasing the scope and depth of knowledge by refining what is known and by bringing in additional expertise relevant for knowledge creation. Some of this expertise could come from partner firms, or partner firms could provide data, information, and knowledge in order to fuel the knowledge-creation process. The process occurs in various knowledge-creating groups throughout a company, and the aim here is to utilize an existing knowledge domain. This can be achieved for example by combining new and existing explicit knowledge, by creating new product and service concepts based on tacit knowledge, or by socializing members around certain prob-

lems, tasks, and work processes. Research and development as well as market research are key activities to facilitate expansion of the domain. However, since the knowledge domain can be centerd on practices, data, information, experience relevant to any business operation or business process, the expansion strategy should be conceived of more broadly. Knowledge creation happens in a research laboratory, but it can be equally powerful and important in manufacturing or accounting. Some of the same ideas hold that we spoke about above: a group shares some insights and experiences, they attempt to reflect systematically on what they have learned, and bring out concepts that in turn are up for scrutiny.

This strategy affects strategic goals in three ways. Better understanding of key processes, such as bottlenecks in manufacturing or product-development, can allow for substantial cost reduction. In Unilever, a common flavor language is used as a tool to facilitate general communication in terms of flavors, independent of regional and cultural differences, background and experience of the user. In the absence of a common flavor language, people would speak and describe flavors in hedonistic rather than objective terms. Unilever had extensive expertise in this area, mainly in its Research Labs, but the common flavor language and associated training have made this knowledge more widely accessible, generating many local opportunities for improvement, innovation, and rollout.

Second, the strategy helps to achieve innovations. Existing consumer data, customer focus groups, information about new technologies, new manufacturing procedures, etc., will be combined by the group in new ways to create incremental innovations, such as variants of existing products or the launch of an existing product in a new market. During the Knowledge Workshops in the Culinary Category, *Knowledge Gaps* are identified in the Knowledge Domain. Understanding where there are significant gaps in strategically important knowledge ensures that the R&D program of the Culinary Category is focused, and progress can be better monitored. Knowledge gaps indicate to knowledge domain members where they need to seek new insights, invest their time and energy.

Third, creating new knowledge based on existing knowledge domains will also enhance your ability to manage risk, primarily by leveraging, thus reducing the hazard of overtaxing knowledge and resources.

Table 25.2. The Expanding Strategy Impacts on Strategic Goals

Efficiency	Expanding on knowledge related to existing processes
Innovation	Creating new process and product innovations from existing knowledge domain
Managing Risk	Developing knowledge domains to reduce the risk of overtaxing resources
	Developing knowledge domains to reduce the exposure to the risk of deterioration
	Developing knowledge domains on the regulatory and competitive environment

The expansion strategy focuses on new knowledge that enables members of the organization to build up competence and skills locally. This in turn could make the company less exposed to the risk of gradual deterioration of the value of historical technical knowledge. Creating new knowledge, increasing depth and scope of knowledge on competitors and the regulatory environment can also help to reduce risks associated with policy changes and competitors' actions.

Table 25.2 summarizes the major impact of the expansion strategy on the business goals of efficiency, innovation, and better risk management.

The Appropriation Strategy

This strategy is predominantly an externally orientated strategy. Here, the key challenge is to build up a new knowledge domain by transfer of knowledge from external sources. The difference between appropriation strategy and the last strategy is that here a knowledge domain does not pre-exist within the firm. Appropriation can occur by means of acquisitions or strategic partnerships with selected companies, research institutions, universities, or other external organizations. The appropriation strategy can help to achieve operational efficiencies. In pursuit of appropriation strategies, Unilever is actively developing partnerships and alliances with academia, societal groups, and corporate parties. Examples include the Marine Stewardship Council, established by Unilever and the World Wildlife Fund to ensure sustainable fishery. One of the challenges for large food companies today is to ensure that raw material supply is kept at a level where the resources can renew themselves. The Marine Stewardship Council makes good business sense: Unilever is

the world's largest fish processor, and a significant part of its business relies on understanding how to ensure a sufficient supply of fish. By working closely together with this now independent body, Unilever has built up significant understanding of sustainable fisheries and its impact on consumer products and supply chains. Prior to this collaboration, knowledge on sustainable fisheries in Unilever was fragmented and scattered broadly through the organization.

The appropriation strategy also helps to attain innovation goals. Innovation with a partner is a common strategy for companies. The partner company provides market, manufacturing, and product knowledge that can provide a unique platform for building up new knowledge, products, and services internally. The appropriation strategy can be translated into concrete learning targets for the company. A new group must be given the responsibility for building up the new knowledge domain, but with a focus not so much on creating knowledge within the firm, but building the domain by capturing and transferring knowledge from partners. The learning targets guide the group's acquisition of new knowledge, and when the targets are clearly formulated, the likelihood of effectively appropriating the new knowledge is higher.[21] For example, the recent alliances with Microsoft, America Online, NetGrocer, and WomenOnline ensure the development and exploitation of understanding on how to interact with consumers through new online channels. Bringing together Unilever's fast marketing expertise, from which partners can benefit greatly, with leading-edge technology capability allows the development of a new knowledge domain on e-business and business-to-consumer solutions. This new knowledge domain will be of high strategic importance in the future. In the area of basic research, collaborations with leading academic groups, and in some cases the installation of top institutes with universities are ways in which Unilever secures leading-edge science that delivers radical innovations. For instance, the Unilever Centre for Molecular Informatics, established with Cambridge University, develops theory and tools to derive knowledge from vast amounts of molecular data. Progress in high throughput data screening is already providing Unilever with the ability to speed up product testing and hence innovation.

The appropriation strategy also helps to manage risk. By capturing new knowledge from the external

Table 25.3. The Appropriating Strategy Impacts on Strategic Goals

Efficiency	Transferring new knowledge from partners, e.g., in manufacturing, sales, marketing, and product development
Innovation	Transferring new knowledge from partners for future innovation
Managing Risk	Transferring new knowledge from partners to reduce the risk of overtaxing resources
	Transferring new knowledge from partners to reduce exposure to the risk of deteriorating knowledge domain
	Transferring new knowledge on the regulatory environment and competitors

environment, rather than developing it in-house, the risk of overtaxing resources decreases.[22] In addition, the risk of a deterioration in the value of knowledge can be better managed. Companies that develop a web of partnerships, for example, focused on alternative technologies serving the same basic customer needs, can more effectively monitor emerging technology developments.[23] The appropriation strategy can also be aimed at gaining new knowledge about the competitive environment. Strategic alliances with existing or potential competitors might provide new knowledge about their strategies, technologies, and personnel resources, thereby enhancing the internal capability to predict their future strategic moves.

Table 25.3 summarizes the major impact of the appropriation strategy on the business goals of efficiency, innovation, and better risk management.

The Probing Strategy

This strategy gives one or several teams the responsibility to build up a new knowledge domain from scratch. Here knowledge creation is somehow different compared with the case of the expansion strategy. First of all, for an existing knowledge domain, key professionals have already been identified, and second, there is knowledge available where you can judge the relevance for further expansion of the domain. For example, entries in the knowledge repository (for example, a database with software development tools) coupled with results from chat groups give you a rough indication of whether or not what you have is good enough to build upon.

The probing strategy requires a different approach. Here you must identify participants with an interest in doing something new within the company, and these individuals in turn need to build their own community around a loose idea or vision of a future knowledge domain. In some ways, these individuals become "corporate revolutionaries" who create knowledge that in turn can become imperative to the long-term performance and survival of your firm.[24] Further, gathering or developing new relevant data sets, creating new information, and new tacit and explicit, individual and social knowledge, are important parts of probing. This strategy has a twofold impact on strategic goals. First, it may contribute to achieving innovations. Radical innovations, beyond mere variants of existing products or technologies employed by competitors, will result from new data, insights, models, concepts, and technologies. It can also help the company see business processes and tasks in a new light, and thereby have some impact on the efficiency goals. Creating new knowledge in a new knowledge domain will always be risky, because it potentially overtaxes the existing resources of the company, and dramatically exposes the company to risks of competitor retaliation[25] and it might break a necessary coherence between the new knowledge and the existing scope of business the firm is engaged in. However, the probing strategy, reduces exposure to knowledge deterioration risks because it allows a more balanced portfolio of existing knowledge (enabling the company to act on current business opportunities), alongside new knowledge (enabling the company to exploit future business opportunities).

In order to break with existing patterns of thinking and established routines, the company can often benefit from executing something unconventional. For example, "indwelling" in the lives of consumers and customers. At the heart of Unilever's corporate purpose is the ambition to be a truly multilocal multinational company understanding and anticipating the everyday needs of people everywhere and meeting these with branded products and services. To achieve such a deep consumer understanding, Unilever market researchers and marketers are immersed in the lifestyle, habits, and attitudes of the consumer. The company employs a variety of methods and approaches to get at this tacit knowledge and this method-kit becomes a focal point in the development of the new consumer knowledge domains. In these domains, immersion by product developers and marketers gives

Table 25.4. The Probing Strategy Impacts on Strategic Goals

Efficiency	Creating new knowledge that can improve business process
Innovation	Creating new knowledge for radical product and process innovation and better adaptation
Managing Risk	Reducing exposure to the risk of existing knowledge domain deterioration

radically new insights into tacit consumer knowledge, which sometimes changes the definition of a whole market segment. Knowledge creation here often happens at the premises of customers and consumers. Insights into lifestyles, norms, the use of technology, strong and weak social ties, habit reinforcing and weakening behavior, life-changing experiences, and so on lead to dramatically new segmentation forms and bring out entirely new areas of knowledge that Unilever's marketers perfect, both within the Culinary Category and in other categories.

Table 25.4 summarizes the major impact of the appropriation strategy on the business goals of innovation, and better risk management.

FINAL THOUGHTS: TAKE A PROACTIVE APPROACH TO COMPANY KNOWLEDGE

In this paper, we have addressed some fundamental questions concerning strategic management in the knowledge economy. We began by urging managers to obtain an overview of knowledge in the company, not as a loosely coupled cluster of experts, but as vibrant domains where experts create and share knowledge on a continuous basis. Once such knowledge domains have been identified and "mapped," managers can start to think about further development, primarily through knowledge creation and transfer between and within knowledge domains. Knowledge strategy is the allocation of resources to knowledge creation and transfer for the sake of developing existing and new knowledge domains. The four strategies we developed in this paper are leveraging existing knowledge throughout the company; expanding on existing knowledge within the company; appropriating new knowledge from outside the company to build up a new knowledge domain; and finally, probing new

knowledge within the company. If you want to make the most out of your company's knowledge, we believe knowledge strategy formulation and choice need to be tightly coupled with other strategizing activities within the company because the development of a knowledge-based advantage requires adequate attention and resource allocation paralleling the development of other types of company advantages. A company benefits from taking a proactive approach to its knowledge and expertise, rather than just letting knowledge drift and evolve at the periphery of management's attention. In this sense, strategizing in the knowledge economy is about moving away from "driving ahead by looking in the rear-view mirror" to "driving ahead by knowing what is around the corner."

The cost of Knowledge Creation is high, as it is difficult to predict results from creativity. However, in light of the increasing pressure to innovate and with high employee mobility, managing the effectiveness of knowledge creation is becoming crucial for business success. One way of managing these costs is to provide structure and tools that will stimulate *focused creativity*. In Unilever, this is to some extent achieved through creativity workshops and tools, and through innovation management. But in particular, multidisciplinary and international teams are critical to manage knowledge creation effectiveness and efficiency. In Unilever, the term "liberating rigor" is used to stress the importance of standardizing and simplifying where it is possible. This release the creative energy to those areas where it really brings value to consumers.

The Unilever experience should inspire other firms to adopt the knowledge strategy framework. As firms base more and more of their business on the uniqueness and novelty of their knowledge base, an economic approach to knowledge will become inevitable for the future prosperity and survivability of most business organizations. Thinking in terms of knowledge domains guides managers in both their goal setting and resource allocation. Sharing a language that outlines strategies and courses of action will be instrumental to the follow-up on the development of knowledge in the firm. However, while this economic perspective is highly appealing, one should never forget that knowledge is inherently fluid, social, and evolving through practice. Eventually, to get the knowledge domains to work as vibrant, energetic, creative, social arenas, managers need to enable rather than control knowledge creation and transfer processes.

APPENDIX A: SOME NOTES ON THE METHOD OF THIS STUDY

Our method has been a case study of knowledge management practices and approaches in Unilever, and the study's goal was to provide a new perspective on knowledge strategy. Unilever was selected because of access as well as its interesting and novel management approaches.[26] The company also has relatively long experience in knowledge management activities, dating back more than 10 years, which have evolved to a strategic level. This makes Unilever a critical case for studying knowledge strategy, rather than other more operational aspects of knowledge management. Our research proceeded in two stages, first through preliminary reporting of the knowledge management initiative in the Culinary Category, and second an in-depth study of knowledge management comprising a wider scope in the firm. We do not claim to report a full overview of knowledge management approaches within such a diverse, innovative, and geographically dispersed company, but in both stages we chose data where contributions were made to the strategies (constructs). We used multiple sources of evidence, including documents (e.g., internal and external reports on Unilever's knowledge management approaches, such as a comprehensive report on innovation management and one on communities of practice), archival records on projects that have used knowledge management, interviews with experts from the company who have been involved in knowledge management initiatives in a functional or project-based role, and participant observation from knowledge workshops and training programs related to knowledge management and innovation. Two research reports on manufacturing communities of practice in the Culinary category, as well as the history of an innovation project resulted from the first phase of the research. These were used for internal discussions in the company in order to ensure a fit with the propositions, data, outline of the case history, and the conclusions drawn by the researchers. These reports confirmed a strong overlap between managers' own perceptions of the knowledge domains and knowledge management initiatives, and the researchers' attempt to "bracket" and capture those experiences. The reports are available from the first and third authors.

A key issue in qualitative strategy research is to have a sufficiently long period of interaction between the firm and the researchers, where more than two years is considered necessary for generating empirical insights into change processes and new management approaches.[27] Knowledge management introduction and implementation often involves considerable change for the company in question.[28] The data collection in Unilever lasted for almost three years of intimate work with the firm. Another key issue is enhancing construct validity:[29] making concepts adequately capture important organizational events, processes, decisions, and actions. Beyond reporting back to Unilever and discussing the two research reports with a select group of managers, we tried to improve such validity by co-authoring the article with a senior manager. Having had an active role in knowledge management at Unilever's corporate level for the past five years, the manager also reported on his personal experiences through this writing. The strategic constructs in our framework are gradually becoming increasingly used terminology within Unilever, and they were based on development work with the company.

ACKNOWLEDGMENTS

The authors wish to thank Charles Baden-Fuller, two LRP reviewers, Mark Macus, Simon Grand, Michael Cusumano, Ian Ritchie, and Wouter de Vries for their helpful comments.

NOTES

1. See, for instance, *The New Economy: A Primer.* Research report, Cambridge Technology Partners, Cambridge, MA (1999) and M. Boisot *Knowledge Assets: Securing Competitive Advantage in the Knowledge Economy,* Oxford University Press, New York (1998).

2. J. Sampler, Redefining industry structure for the information age, *Strategic Management Journal* **19,** 343–356 (1998).

3. N. W. A. FitzGerald, Value from the centre in G. W. Dauphinais, G. Means, and C. Price (eds.), *Wisdom of the CEO,* pp. 25–31. Wiley, New York (1999).

4. E. Wenger, *Communities of Practice,* Cambridge University Press, Cambridge (1998).

5. Please note that existing base knowledge means that we use the existing base as a starting point for developing the knowledge domain. This is to remain consistent with the view that knowledge truly is in flow.

6. See, for example, T. Davenport and L. Prusak, *Working Knowledge,* Harvard Business School Press,

Cambridge, MA (1998). A good overview of contemporary efforts can be found in R. L. Ruggles, 9th ed.) *Knowledge Management Tools,* 9th ed., Butterworth-Heinemann, Boston, MA (1997). A good companion piece with a higher level of detail on knowledge management tools is V. Allee, *The Knowledge Evolution: Expanding Organizational Intelligence,* Butterworth-Heinemann, Boston, MA (1997).

7. The five-stage process is explained further in I. Nonaka and H. Takeuchi, *The Knowledge Creating Company,* Oxford University Press, New York (1995); G. von Krogh, K. Ichijo, and I. Nonaka, *Enabling Knowledge Creation: How to Unlock the Mystery of Tacit Knowledge and Unleash the Power of Innovation,* Oxford University Press, New York (2000); and I. Nonaka, A dynamic theory of organizational knowledge creation, *Organization Science* **5,** 337–351 (1994). See also I. Tuomi, *Corporate Knowledge: Theory and Practice of Intelligent Organizations,* Metaxis, Helsinki (1999), and D. Leonard and S. Sensiper, The role of tacit knowledge in group innovation, *California Management Review* **40**(3), 112–132 (1998).

8. Leonard and Sensiper (1998) (see Note 7).

9. D. Leonard, *Wellsprings of Knowledge,* Harvard Business School Press, Boston, MA (1995).

10. Fortune, The Customized, digitized, have-it-your-way economy, *Fortune* (28 September), 68–78 (1998).

11. von Krogh et al. (2000) (see Note 7).

12. See also R. M. Grant, Towards a knowledge-based theory of the firm, *Strategic Management Journal* **17**(2S), 109–123 (1996); and R. M. Grant, Prospering in dynamically-competitive environments: organizational capability as knowledge integration, *Organization Science* **7,** 375–388 (1996).

13. J. E. Nahapiet and S. Ghoshal, Social capital, intellectual capital, and the organisational advantage, *Academy of Management Review* **2,** 242–266 (1998). An important companion piece discussing individual motives for knowledge transfer is M. Osterloh and B. Fre, Knowledge sharing and motivation, *Organization Science* (forthcoming).

14. Here Davenport and Prusak (1998) (see Note 6) talk about "sellers" and "buyers" of knowledge and the need to create market conditions in which sellers and buyers are known to each other.

15. An early contribution to this argument was J. L. Badaracco, *The Knowledge Link: How Firms Compete Through Strategic Alliances,* Harvard Business School Press, Boston, MA (1991). See also T. Khanna, R. Gulati, and N. Nohria, The dynamics of learning alliances: competition, cooperation, and relative scope, *Strategic Management Journal* **19,** 193–210 (1998); A. C. Inkpen and A. Dinur, Knowledge management processes and international joint ventures, *Organization Science* **9,** 454–468 (1998).

16. W. Powell, Learning from collaboration: knowledge networks in the biotechnology and pharmaceutical industries, *California Management Review* **40**(Spring), 228–241 (1998).

17. G. Hamel, Competition for competence and interpartner learning within international alliances, *Strategic Management Journal* **12,** 83–103 (1991).

18. W. Cohen and D. Levinthal, Absorptive capacity: a new perspective on learning and innovation, *Administrative Science Quarterly* **35,** 128–152 (1990).

19. C. O'Dell and J. Grayson, If only we knew what we know: Identification and transfer of internal best practices, *California Management Review* **40**(Spring), 154–174 (1998).

20. Seeing that knowledge works elsewhere and having knowledge appraised and approved by people you trust might be a powerful motivator to undertake knowledge transfer. See G. Szulanski, Exploring internal stickiness: impediments to the transfer of best practice within the firm, *Strategic Management Journal* **17**(1S), 17–44 (1996).

21. Hamel (1991) (see Reference 17).

22. D. Teece, Capturing value from knowledge assets: the new economy, markets for know-how, and intangible assets, *California Management Review* **40**(Spring), 55–79 (1998).

23. T. Gonard and T. Durand, Public research/industry relationships: efficiency conditions, *International Business Review* **3,** 469–490 (1994).

24. G. Hamel *Leading the Revolution,* Harvard Business School Press, Cambridge, MA (2000). In some emerging industries, like biotechnology, such the intensity of probing significantly impacts a firm's market value compared to more mature industries where knowledge is more settled [D. M. DeCarolis and D. L. Dees, The impact of stocks and flows of organizational knowledge on firm performance: An empirical investigation of the biotechnology industry, *Strategic Management Journal* **20,** 953–968 (1999)].

25. See, for example, R. Rummelt, Toward a strategic theory of the firm, in R. Lamb (ed.), *Competitive Strategic Management,* pp. 137–158, Prentice-Hall, Englewood Cliffs, NJ (1984).

26. R. K. Yin, *Case Study Research: Design and Methods,* Sage, Newbury Park (1984).

27. S. Ghoshal and C. A. Bartlett, Linking organizational context and managerial action: the dimensions of quality of management, *Strategic Management Journal* **15,** 91–112 (1995).

28. A. K. Gupta and V. Govindarajan, Knowledge management's social dimension: lessons from Nucor Steel, *Sloan Management Review* **42,** 71–80 (2000).

29. T. Hedrick, L. Bickman, and D. J. Rog, *Applied Research Design: A Practical Guide,* Sage, Newbury Park (1993).

26

Crisis Construction and Organizational Learning

Capability Building in Catching-Up at Hyundai Motor

LINSU KIM

ABSTRACT: **Effective organizational learning requires high absorptive capacity, which has two major elements: prior knowledge base and intensity of effort. Hyundai Motor Company, the most dynamic automobile producer in developing countries, pursued a strategy of independence in developing absorptive capacity. In its process of advancing from one phase to the next through the preparation for and acquisition, assimilation, and improvement of foreign technologies, Hyundai acquired migratory knowledge to expand its prior knowledge base and proactively constructed crises as a strategic means of intensifying its learning effort. Unlike externally evoked crises, proactively constructed internal crises present a clear performance gap, shift learning orientation from imitation to innovation, and increase the intensity of effort in organizational learning. Such crisis construction is an evocative and galvanizing device in the personal repertoires of proactive top managers. A similar process of opportunistic learning is also evident in other industries in Korea.**

Organizational learning and innovation have become crucially important subjects in management. Research on these subjects, however, is concentrated mainly in advanced countries (e.g., Argyris and Schon 1978, Dodgson 1993, Nonaka and Takeuchi 1995, Utterback 1994, von Hippel 1988). Despite the fact that many developing countries have made significant progress in industrial, educational, and technological development, research on learning, capability building, and innovation in those countries is scanty (e.g., Fransman and King 1984, Kim 1997, Kim and Kim 1985). Models that capture organizational learning and technological change in developing countries are essential to understand the dynamic process of capability building in catching-up in such countries and to extend the theories developed in advanced countries.

Understanding the catching-up process is also relevant and important to firms in advanced countries. Not all firms can be pioneers of novel breakthroughs, even in those countries. Most firms must invest in second-hand learning to remain competitive. Nevertheless, much less attention is paid to the imitative catching-up process than to the innovative pioneering process. For instance, ABI/Inform, a computerized business database, lists a total of 9,006 articles on the subject of innovation but only 145 on imitation (Schnaars 1994).

A crisis is usually regarded as an unpopular, largely negative phenomenon in management. It can, however, be an appropriate metaphor for strategic and technological transformation. Several observers postu-

Reprinted by permission, Linsu Kim, "Crisis Construction and Organizational Learning: Capability Building in Catching-up at Hyundai Motor," *Organization Science,* Vol. 9, No. 4, July–August 1998. Copyright © 1998 by the Institute for Operations Research and the Management Sciences (INFORMS).

late that constructing and then resolving organizational crises can be an effective means of opportunistic learning (e.g., Nonaka 1988, Pitt 1990, Schon 1967, Weick 1988), but no one has clearly linked the construct variable to corresponding empirical evidence.

The purpose of this article is to develop a model of organizational learning in an imitative catching-up process, and at the same time a model of crisis construction and organizational learning, by empirically analyzing the history of technological transformation at the Hyundai Motor Company (hereinafter Hyundai), the most dynamic automaker in developing countries, as a case in point.

Despite the prediction that none of South Korea's automakers will survive the global shakeout of the 1990s, having been driven out or relegated to niche markets dependent on alliances with leading foreign car producers (*Far Eastern Economic Review* 1992), Hyundai is determined to become a leading automaker on its own. Unlike most other automobile companies in developing countries, Hyundai followed an explicit policy of maintaining full ownership of all of its 45 subsidiaries, entering the auto industry in 1967 as a latecomer without foreign equity participation. Hyundai has progressed remarkably since then.

In quantitative terms, Hyundai increased its production more than tenfold every decade, from 614 cars in 1968, to 7,009 in 1973, to 103,888 in 1983, and to 1,134,611 in 1994, rapidly surpassing other automakers in Korea, and steadily ascending from being the sixteenth-largest producer in the world in 1991 to being the thirteenth-largest in 1994. Hyundai is now the largest automobile producer in a developing country. It produced its one-millionth car in January 1986, taking 18 years to reach that level of production in contrast to 29 years for Toyota and 43 years for Mazda (Hyun and Lee 1989).

In qualitative terms, Hyundai began assembling a Ford compact car on a knockdown basis in 1967. It rapidly assimilated foreign technology and developed sufficient capability to unveil its own designs, Accent and Avante, in 1994 and 1995, respectively. The company thus eliminated the royalty payment on the foreign license and was able to export production and design technology abroad.

Hyundai's rapid surge raises several research questions: (1) How did Hyundai acquire the technological capability to transform itself so expeditiously from imitative "learning by doing" to innovative "learning by research"? (2) How does learning in the catching-up process in a developing country differ from learning in the pioneering process in advanced countries? (3) Why is crisis construction an effective mechanism for organizational learning? (4) Can Hyundai's learning model be emulated by other catching-up firms? (5) What are the implications of Hyundai's model for future research? The following section briefly reviews theories related to organizational learning and knowledge creation. Then Hyundai is analyzed as a case in point to illustrate how the Korean firm has expedited organizational learning and to answer the research questions.

CRISES AND ORGANIZATIONAL LEARNING

Organizational learning, whether to imitate or to innovate, takes place at two levels: the individual and organizational. The prime actors in the process of organizational learning are individuals within the firm. Organizational learning is not, however, the simple sum of individual learning (Hedberg 1981); rather, it is the process whereby knowledge is created, is distributed across the organization, is communicated among organization members, has consensual validity, and is integrated into the strategy and management of the organization (Duncan and Weiss 1978). Individual learning is therefore an indispensable condition for organizational learning but cannot be the sufficient condition. Organizations learn only when individual insights and skills become embodied in organizational routines, practices, and beliefs (Attewell 1992). Only effective organizations can translate individual learning into organizational learning (Hedberg 1980, Kim 1993, Shrivastava 1983).

Absorptive Capacity
Organizational learning is a function of an organization's absorptive capacity. Absorptive capacity requires learning capability and develops problem-solving skills. Learning capability is the capacity to assimilate knowledge (for imitation), whereas problem-solving skills represent a capacity to create new knowledge (for innovation).

Absorptive capacity has two important elements, prior knowledge base and intensity of effort (Cohen and Levinthal 1990). Prior knowledge base consists of individual units of knowledge available within the organization. Accumulated prior knowledge increases the ability to make sense of and to assimilate and use new knowledge. Relevant prior knowledge base comprises basic skills and general knowledge in the case of developing countries, but includes the most recent scientific and technological knowledge in the case of industrially advanced countries. Hence, prior knowledge base should be assessed in relation to task difficulty (Kim 1995).

Intensity of effort represents the amount of energy expended by organizational members to solve problems. Exposure of a firm to relevant external knowledge is insufficient unless an effort is made to internalize it. Learning how to solve problems is usually accomplished through many practice trials involving related problems (Harlow 1959). Hence, considerable time and effort must be directed to learning how to solve problems before complex problems can be addressed. Such effort intensifies interaction among organizational members, thus facilitating knowledge conversion and creation at the organizational level.

As shown in Figure 26.1, prior knowledge base and intensity of effort in the organization constitute a 2×2 matrix that indicates the level of absorptive capacity. When both are high (quadrant 1), absorptive capacity is high; when both are low (quadrant 4), absorptive capacity is low. Organizations with high prior knowledge in relation to task difficulty and low intensity of effort (quadrant 2) will gradually lose their absorptive capacity, moving rapidly down to quadrant 4, because their prior knowledge base will become obso-

lete as task-related technology moves along its trajectory. In contrast, organizations with low prior knowledge in relation to task difficulty and high intensity of effort (quadrant 3) will be able to acquire absorptive capacity, moving progressively to quadrant 1, as repeated efforts to learn and solve problems elevate the level of relevant prior knowledge (Kim 1995).

Knowledge and Learning

Many social scientists have attempted to delineate knowledge dimensions (Garud and Nayyar 1994, Kogut and Zander 1992, Polanyi 1966, Rogers 1983, Winter 1987). Polanyi's two dimensions, explicit and tacit, are the most widely accepted. Explicit knowledge is knowledge that is codified and transmittable in formal, systematic language. It therefore can be acquired in the form of books, technical specifications, and designs, or as embodied in machines. Tacit knowledge, in contrast, is so deeply rooted in the human mind and body that it is difficult to codify and communicate and can be expressed only through action, commitment, and involvement in a specific context. Tacit knowledge can be acquired only through experience such as observation, imitation, and practice.

Tacit knowledge is the core of a firm's prior knowledge base. The firm may have some proprietary explicit knowledge such as firm-specific blueprints and standard operating procedures. However, they are useful only when tacit knowledge enables its members to utilize them. Much of the knowledge that underlies the effective performance of an organization is tacit knowledge embodied in its members (Howells 1996, Nelson and Winter 1982).

Organizational learning takes place primarily through the dynamic process of four modes of conversion between the two dimensions of knowledge within the organization (Nonaka 1994, Nonaka and Takeuchi 1995). Tacit-to-tacit conversion (socialization) takes place when tacit knowledge within one individual is shared with another through training, whereas explicit-to-explicit conversion (combination) takes place when an individual combines discrete pieces of explicit knowledge into a new whole. Tacit-to-explicit conversion (externalization) takes place when an individual is able to articulate the foundations of his or her tacit knowledge, whereas explicit-to-tacit conversion (internalization) takes place when new explicit knowledge is shared throughout the firm and other members begin to

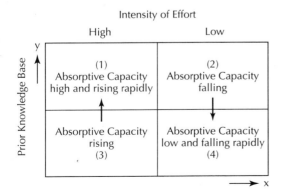

Figure 26.1. Dynamics of absorptive capacity.

use it to broaden, extend, and reframe their own tacit knowledge.

Figure 26.2 depicts the dynamic process of organizational learning in the catching-up process. It shows that prior knowledge base and intensity of effort affect the dynamics of knowledge conversion through a spiral process that starts at the individual level and moves up to the organizational level. Organizational learning tends to become faster and larger in scale as more actors in and around the firm with adequate prior knowledge intensify their efforts to convert knowledge within and between themselves. The outcome of knowledge conversion and creation feeds back to the prior knowledge base to increase its level.

In addition, migratory knowledge significantly affects the building of the prior knowledge base in the catching-up process (Badaracco 1991). Books, technical specifications, designs, and physical equipment transfer explicit knowledge, whereas the migration of individuals from one organization or country to another transfers tacit knowledge, elevating the level of the prior knowledge base.

Learning Systems

All organizations are learning systems. They learn as they develop, produce, and market products. All learning systems have a specific learning orientation reflecting the values and practices that determine what is learned and where. Learning orientation determines the way organizations acquire, share, and utilize knowledge. It might emphasize knowledge source, product-process focus, documentation mode, dissemination mode, learning focus, value-chain focus, or skill development focus (Nevis et al. 1995). In the catching-up process, as shown in Figure 26.2, different learning focus (duplicative imitation, creative imitation, or innovation) requires a different level of prior knowledge and a different degree of the intensity of effort. Learning orientation affects the spiral process of knowledge conversion.

Organizational factors (intention, autonomy, fluctuation and creative chaos, redundancy, requisite variety, and leadership) affect formal and informal processes and structures that facilitate organizational learning (Nonaka 1994, Nonaka and Takeuchi 1995). Redundancy and requisite variety reflect the characteristics of units of knowledge available in the organization. Redundancy in information and experience

facilitates "learning by intrusion" from different perspectives, whereas requisite variety advances the knowledge creation spiral by matching the variety and complexity of the environment. Intention and autonomy shape the knowledge frame that provides the ability to link units of knowledge and their priorities. Intention defines an organization's goals and fosters its employees' commitment, providing direction for the intensity of effort, and autonomy provides an environment in which a self-organizing team is able to function creatively. Fluctuation and creative chaos shape knowledge dynamics that foster the ability to manage the dynamic process in which individual units of knowledge are combined and transformed. Entrepreneurial leadership is also an important factor that creates organizational conditions conducive to learning.

As shown in Figure 26.2, the organizational factors also affect the spiral process of knowledge conversion and crisis construction. In addition, sociocultural factors influence the formation of work ethics. Vogel (1991) provides a seminal discussion of how cultural and situational factors formed work ethics in Korea and three other East Asian countries. What is most notable in Korean organizations is crises constructed proactively by top managers, which serve to intensify effort.

Crises and Learning

Cumulative or linear learning along the current trajectory can take place under normal circumstances. Discontinuous or nonlinear learning, however, takes place normally when a firm perceives a crisis and deploys strategy to resolve the critical situation (Meyers 1990). Organizations tend to engage in major changes mainly after they have been confronted with crises (Miller and Friesen 1984, Tushman et al. 1985). In such cases, the firm must invest heavily in the acquisition of new tacit and explicit knowledge as well as in knowledge conversion activities to overcome the crisis in the shortest possible time. The term "crisis" is expressed in Chinese using two characters (weiji, 危機), the first meaning "danger" and the second "opportunity." Some firms manage to turn a crisis into an opportunity by transforming absorptive capacity in a discontinuous way to reap tremendous growth through enhanced competitiveness. A crisis may be creative in that sense; otherwise, it is apt to become destructive.

Crises may stem from external sources. They may

be evoked naturally when the firm loses its competitive standing in the market and in technology. Literature abounds on market and technology-evoked crises (e.g., Abernathy 1978, Cooper and Schendel 1976, De Greene 1982, Meyers 1990, Miller and Friesen 1984, Shrivastava 1988, Tushman and Anderson 1986, Utterback and Kim 1985). A crisis may also be generated deliberately by an external principal. In developing countries, particularly where the state orchestrates industrialization, the government could impose a crisis by setting challenging goals for firms in a strategically designated industry. An external change generates a crisis for top managers but not necessarily for organizational members at the lower echelon.

Top managers can construct a crisis internally, either in response to or in the absence of an external crisis. A constructed crisis (Pitt 1990) may be set up deliberately at either the corporate level (corporate crisis) or the suborganization level (team crisis). Crises constructed at Hyundai are primarily team crises. Team crises may be more frequent and easier to manage than corporate crises, because they may have more focused and clearer goals. The shared sense of the internally constructed crisis among organizational members intensifies their efforts to expedite learning, elevating the absorptive capacity of the organization (see Figure 26.2). An organization with effective learning may frequently evoke constructed crises and institutionalize the process and structure to make discontinuous learning possible and turn crises into opportunities.

A case study was conducted to assess the impact of crisis construction on discontinuous learning in the catching-up process. It illustrates how the two elements of absorptive capacity, migratory knowledge, the four modes of knowledge conversion, organizational factors, externally evoked and internally constructed crises, and learning orientation affect organizational learning in a Korean firm.

RESEARCH METHODOLOGY

Stage 1
In 1984, an analysis was done to compare independent Hyundai and dependent Daewoo, a company engaged in a joint venture with General Motors. Company records, plant observations, and interviews with executives were used in the research (see Amsden and Kim 1989).

Stage 2
Subsequently, indepth case studies of Hyundai's technological learning were done almost once every two years. Again, information was obtained from Hyun-

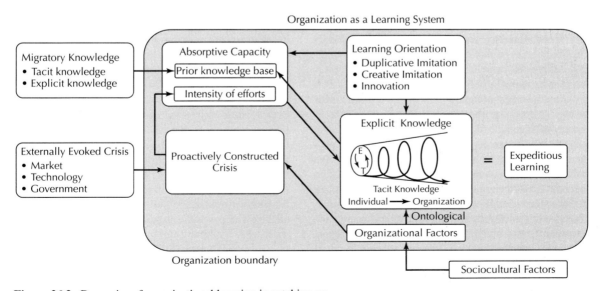

Figure 26.2. Dynamics of organizational learning in catching-up.

dai's company records, plant tours, and interviews with executives in manufacturing and R&D.

Stage 3

Hyundai published a well-documented history book (1,130 pages) in 1992 (see Hyundai Motor Company 1992), which provided rich historical information about the 1960s and 1970s and helped to verify and enrich case writeups of Hyundai's transformation in the 1980s and 1990s. It was supplemented with more recent records and interviews.

Stage 4

The case writeup covering 1967 to 1995 was completed in 1995. It was thoroughly reviewed by a senior engineer at Hyundai and an independent industry analyst.

ORGANIZATIONAL LEARNING IN CATCHING-UP AT HYUNDAI

Phase 1: Assimilation of Assembly Operations

Lacking experience in automobile production at the outset, Hyundai formed a taskforce in 1967. By drawing some team members from its construction division who had strong project management and engineering background, and recruiting some from other auto producers who had production experience, Hyundai ensured requisite variety in taskforce experience and knowledge. The recruited engineers brought in migratory knowledge that raised Hyundai's level of tacit knowledge related to automobile production.

In 1968 Hyundai entered into an Overseas Assembler Agreement with Ford, whereby Hyundai was to assemble Ford compact cars on a semi-knocked-down (SKD) basis. Ford transferred "packaged" technology to Hyundai with a set of explicit knowledge, such as blueprints, technical specifications, and production manuals. The agreement also included the training of Hyundai engineers at Ford sites and the dispatch of 10 Ford engineers to Hyundai to help translate the transferred explicit knowledge into tacit knowledge and to transfer to Hyundai Ford's tacit knowledge on procurement planning, procurement coordination, production engineering, process engineering, production management, welding, painting, after-service, and marketing. Also, Hyundai's suppliers sent their engi-

neers to set up equipment and train Hyundai technicians. The most competent engineers trained by Ford were assigned to production and production engineering departments. In other words, the agreement with Ford gave Hyundai valuable migratory knowledge with which to upgrade its tacit and explicit knowledge related to auto assembly, moving the company up along the y-axis (toward a higher prior knowledge level) in Figure 1. Migratory knowledge alone is not sufficient, however. It must be reinvented by its user (Rice and Rogers 1980) through learning by doing (Arrow 1962) or learning by using (Rosenberg 1982).

At the same time, Hyundai constructed a crisis by setting an ambitious goal to complete plant construction in the shortest possible time to minimize lead time of production. Its engineers, technicians, and construction workers lived together in a makeshift structure on the plant site and worked 16 hours a day, seven days a week. The crisis generated intense interactions among the members, intensifying knowledge conversion in a spiral manner at the individual, group, and organizational levels and thus moving Hyundai leftward along the x-axis (toward higher intensity of effort) in Figure 26.1. Consequently, with high prior knowledge and high intensity of effort (quadrant 1), Hyundai achieved the shortest time (six months) between groundbreaking and first commercial production among the 118 Ford assembly plants around the world.

Hyundai also created a crisis for its production members by setting an ambitious goal to acquire a production capability in the shortest possible time. While plant construction was underway, production teams rehearsed production operations by disassembling and reassembling two passenger cars, a bus, and a truck over and over to routinize the production procedures, internalizing transferred explicit knowledge (production manuals) into tacit knowledge. When the plant was completed, workers had sufficient tacit knowledge to assemble cars with minimum trial and error. At the outset, technical emphasis was largely on the mastery of production capability to meet Ford's technical specifications. Rapid assimilation of production capability enabled the assembly production to evolve gradually from SKD toward a complete-knocked-down (CKD) operation. In short, in the first phase Hyundai expedited organizational learning by constructing an internal crisis in the absence of an external crisis.

Phase 2: Development of a "Korean" Car Under License

The second major jump in technological learning at Hyundai came in the mid-1970s, when the government imposed a crisis by making a radical policy change requiring the automobile industry to shift from assembly production of foreign cars on a CKD basis to the development of locally designed "Korean" cars. Policy implementation to develop "Korean" subcompact cars was highly centralized by the government, with the nation's president as the chief policymaker and the Ministry of Trade and Industry as a coordinating and implementing agency. In 1973, the government formulated The Long-Term Plan for Promotion of the Automobile Industry and ordered four automobile companies to submit detailed plans to develop Korean cars. Progress reports had to be briefed to the president regularly. The government's plan was very specific. For instance, the indigenous model had to be original, smaller than 1,500 cc in engine size with a local content ratio of at least 95%, less than $2,000 in production cost, and introduced in the market by 1975. The government also specified that production capacity per plant should be more than 50,000 units per year, at a time when the total annual passenger car production in the nation was a mere 12,751 units. To foster growth of the industry, the government established seven principles to promote indigenous subcompact model development. They included, among other things, protection of the local market from new entrants and from new foreign knockdown imports, a significant tax reduction, promotion of vertical integration leading to new business opportunities, preferential financing, tax concessions, and an administrative decree to guarantee a large market share for the indigenous model. Thus the crisis gave Hyundai an opportunity to expand its car business into the subcompact market under government protection.

In 1973 Hyundai submitted its masterplan for a new plant with a capacity of 80,000 "Korean" cars. Its actual production in that year was 5,426 cars. The plan represented a drastic departure from the past strategy of merely assembling foreign cars. It required the development of a highly successful "Korean" subcompact car that could be exported in substantial volume and simultaneously increase local market share enough to absorb the proposed production capacity. The plan posed a major constructed crisis for Hyundai engineers.

Although it lacked absorptive capacity, Hyundai decided to obtain foreign technologies from many different sources in an "unpackaged" form to maintain independence from foreign multinationals. However, the company had the clear goal of assimilating the imported foreign technology as rapidly as possible. Prior knowledge accumulated from mere assembly of largely foreign parts and components was inadequate for the new task. As the first step, Hyundai organized a project team and had its members master literature related to the various aspects of auto design and manufacture, thus accumulating new tacit knowledge converted from explicit literature-knowledge to enhance its prior knowledge level.

Hyundai approached 26 firms in five countries to acquire different technologies: 10 firms in Japan and Italy for car design, 4 firms in Japan and the United States for stamping shop equipment, 5 firms in the United Kingdom and Germany for casting and forging plants, 2 firms in Japan and the United Kingdom for engines, and 5 U.S. and U.K. firms for an integrated parts/components plant. The foreign companies gave Hyundai engineers observation tours not only of their own sites but also of the leading automobile manufacturing plants that were using the suppliers' technology, enabling Hyundai engineers to relate knowledge converted from literature to actual physical operations. Through that process, Hyundai engineers gained significant insight to large-scale, modern automobile manufacturing systems. Hyundai then entered into a licensing agreement with Italdesign for body styling and design, and with Mitsubishi for gasoline engine, transmission, and rear axle designs, as well as casting technology. Engineers were sent to those technology suppliers for training.

Hyundai acquired more foreign technologies from a greater variety of sources than its competitors in Korea. Up to 1985, Hyundai had signed 54 licenses with foreign suppliers in contrast to 22 for Daewoo, 14 for Kia, and 9 for Ssangyong. Licensing sources included Japan (22), the United Kingdom (14), the United States (5), Italy (5), Germany (3), and others (5). Mitsubishi accounted for only half of the Japanese licenses, reflecting Hyundai's independence in acquiring foreign technologies (Hyun and Lee 1989).

How Hyundai assimilated style design technology is illustrative. Hyundai formed a team of five design engineers, had them study literature related to auto styling, and sent them to Italy to participate closely with Italdesign engineers in the design process. Hyundai gave the team the ambitious goal of assimilating all the styling technology from Italdesign so that they could undertake subsequent style designs on their own. For one and a half years, the engineers lived together in an apartment near Italdesign, kept a record of what they were learning during the day, and had group reviews every evening. Such intensive interaction among the team members resulted in a very rapid spiral process of knowledge conversion within the team, significantly expanding Hyundai's tacit and explicit knowledge in styling. The team engineers later became the core of the style design department at Hyundai.

Although many engineers at Hyundai acquired necessary knowledge related to specific technologies, the company did not have experienced engineers who could put the knowledge together. To minimize trial and error, Hyundai hired for a three-year period (1974–1977) a former managing director of British Leyland as its vice president and six other British technical experts for the successful development of its first indigenous model, further increasing the prior tacit knowledge level of the firm. The technical experts, as the chief engineers of the chassis design, body design, development and testing, die and tooling, body production, and commercial vehicle design departments, played crucial roles in helping Hyundai engineers convert explicit knowledge supplied by licensors into tacit knowledge and integrate specific tacit knowledge into a workable system. After the British engineers left, Hyundai used moonlighting Japanese engineers to troubleshoot problems.

Hyundai developed its first indigenous model, Pony, with a 90% domestic content in 1975, making Korea the second nation in Asia to have its own domestic automobile. Hyundai quickly improved the car's quality over the years. It exported 62,592 cars to Europe, the Middle East, and Asia, accounting for 67% of Korea's total auto exports in 1976–1980 and 97% in 1983–1986. Pony accounted for 98% of Hyundai's exports during those periods. The company's local market share in passenger cars also increased, from 19.2% in 1970, to 59.4% in 1976, to 73.9% in 1979.

CRISIS CONSTRUCTION AND SHIFT OF LEARNING ORIENTATION

A constructed crisis speeded plant construction and expedited the assimilation of production technology. However, the continuing assembly operation (first vertical line in Figure 26.3) had a low performance goal and hence required little effort, leading to boredom and limited learning (point A in Figure 26.3), to a point where efforts had some property of decreasing return. The vertical direction of each succeeding phase has the same problem of decreasing returns on efforts.

Crisis construction shifted learning orientations (horizontal directions in Figure 26.3). The second constructed crisis shifted learning orientation from duplicative assembly of Ford cars on a CKD basis to the development of a "Korean car," moving to point (C). It provided a new learning frontier and increased return on effort. Because changing learning paths requires a huge amount of human psychological energy, top managers had to construct crises. Hyundai has continuously shifted its learning path—from a duplicative imitation-oriented one, to a more creative imitation-oriented one, to an innovation-oriented one—and in the process has accelerated its learning in a stepwise pattern, as shown in Figure 26.3.

Another important point is that Hyundai could not enter at point (B) from the beginning because of its insufficient prior knowledge base. Point (B) required too high a performance goal, given the company's prior knowledge base, and in turn too much efforts. Effort alone cannot expedite learning. It must be matched with the necessary prior knowledge to elevate absorptive capacity. Prior knowledge gained in the assembly of foreign cars provided a platform for the development of a Korean car.

LEARNING PROCESS IN CATCHING UP

A joint venture with a leading automobile firm is apt to lead to a passive attitude on the part of the recipient in the learning process, as technical assistance is always available from the parent company and the performance of the transferred technology is guaranteed by the supplier. In contrast, Hyundai pursued an independence strategy. It unpackaged technology transfer and independently took the responsibility of organizing imported technologies and components from multiple sources into a workable mass production system. That

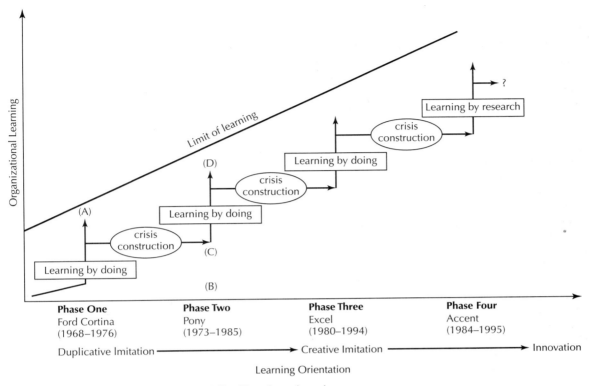

Figure 26.3. Crisis construction and the shift of learning orientation.

approach entailed a major risk because Hyundai would have to take total blame, not the foreign suppliers, if technology failed. However, it forced and motivated Hyundai engineers to assimilate foreign technologies as rapidly as possible throughout the process.

Each of Hyundai's learning phases apparently was associated with four stages: preparation, acquisition, assimilation, and improvement/application, leading to the rapid import substitution of personnel, engineering, and research in each phase (see Table 26.1).

At the outset of each learning jump, Hyundai took *preparatory* measures to acquire the migratory knowledge needed to elevate to its prior knowledge base. Those measures included poaching of experienced personnel from outside, extensive literature search, observation of technology in operation, and temporary hiring of foreign engineers. Experienced personnel from other firms or from abroad significantly raised the tacit knowledge base not only by the knowledge

embodied in them, but also through knowledge socialization (from poached personnel to Hyundai personnel) prior to investment. The poached personnel constituted the core of Hyundai's taskforce team.

Such an elevated prior knowledge base, albeit insufficient, enabled the team members to comprehend and internalize advanced explicit knowledge in literature. The team members were then sent abroad to observe facilities in operation in advanced countries, which gave them the opportunity to relate their knowledge from literature to actual physical settings in operation, further advancing the prior knowledge base. Whenever its tacit knowledge base was judged to be insufficient, Hyundai hired foreign engineers to augment its personnel.

The tacit knowledge base developed during the preparation phase helped Hyundai identify sources of foreign technology, strengthened its bargaining power in negotiations with foreign suppliers, and enabled it to

Table 26.1. Spiral Process of Organizational Learning in Catching-Up[a]

	Phase 1	Phase 2	Phase 3	Phase 4
Cars produced	Ford Cortina	Pony	Excel	Accent
Technology mastered	Assembly technology	Initial design technology	Deepening design technology	Own design technology
Time period	1967–1976	1973–1985	1980–1994	1984–1995
Learning Stages				
Preparation	Poaching experienced personnel, literature review, observation tours	Literature review, observation tour, hiring foreign expatriates	Literature review, observation tour	Poaching scientists, literature review
Acquisition	Packaged technology transfer, hiring foreign expatriates	Unpackaged technology transfer	Unpackaged technology transfer	Acquisition by research, overseas R&D, hiring foreign expatriates
Assimilation	Learning by doing	Learning by doing	Learning by doing	Learning by research
Improvement/Application	Learning by doing	Learning by doing	Learning by doing	Learning by research

[a]A constructed crisis facilitated expeditious learning at each phase. Prior knowledge base developed at the end of each phase provided a platform for the succeeding phase.

acquire foreign technology on favorable terms. Foreign firms supplied both explicit (blueprints, technical specifications, equipment, manuals, etc.) and tacit knowledge (training and OJT supervised by foreign expatriates), but it was the prior knowledge base and intensity of effort at Hyundai that made the foreign technology transfer effective. Hyundai first relied on "packaged" technology transfer but rapidly unpackaged it as it developed the capability to substitute increasing portions of foreign input. Through preparing for and acquiring foreign technologies, Hyundai significantly increased its prior knowledge base.

Hyundai then intensified its in-house efforts to expedite the *assimilation* of imported foreign technologies. The assimilation of know-how took place largely through "learning by doing" and "learning by using" in production. The assimilation of imported technologies led to incremental *improvement* of the imported technologies and their *application* to other areas. The sense of crisis intensified knowledge conversion at the individual level, and the shared sense of crisis heightened knowledge conversion at the organizational level through intense interaction among members.

After the first cycle of preparation to improvement/application in assembling Ford cars, Hyundai repeated a similar cycle in developing the Pony. Phases 3 and 4 also went through such a cycle. The mastery of one cycle provided the platform for starting the next

cycle (Kim and Kogut 1995). Such repetition of similar cycles made up the spiral process of learning in catching-up.

Phase 3: Development of an Advanced Car Under Limited License

The third major jump in Hyundai's acquisition of absorptive capacity came in the early 1980s after the second oil crisis. In the face of losses due to rising gasoline prices and falling car sales, Hyundai decided to make a major investment to develop the next generation FF (front engine, front wheel drive) car to sell in the North American market, attempting once again to turn a crisis into an opportunity. The proposed production capacity was 300,000 units per year at a time when Hyundai was producing 57,054 passenger cars and the total number of cars produced in Korea was a mere 85,693 units. Hyundai was using only 32% of its production capacity (150,000 units). It was determined to turn the domestic-market-oriented automobile business into a largely export-oriented one. In response to the external oil crisis, Hyundai once again constructed a major internal crisis. The objective was to acquire the absorptive capacity needed to develop the next generation car and triple the production capacity.

Hyundai approached several major car producers—Volkswagen, Ford, Renault, and Alfa Romeo—for FF technology as a way to diversify its technology sources. However, all those companies demanded equity and management participation and viewed Hyundai as a local assembly subsidiary of their FF cars. Hyundai eventually approached Mitsubishi again. In 1981, Mitsubishi agreed to license engine, transaxle, chassis, and emission control technology to Hyundai. In return, Hyundai gave a 10% equity share to Mitsubishi without the latter's management participation. Not only did Hyundai retain all managerial control, but also reserved the right to import parts and technology from Mitsubishi's competitors and to compete directly in Mitsubishi's own markets. Hyundai sourced body styling from Italdesign and constant velocity joint technology from British GKN and Japanese NTN.

With the background of developing and manufacturing the Pony since 1976, Hyundai had a sufficient prior knowledge base to assimilate FF car design and manufacturing without foreign engineering assistance. However, technological learning was important in three areas. The first was the manufacture of a car to meet the most stringent safety and environmental requirements of the United States. The second was the adoption of the computer-aided-design and computer-aided manufacturing (CAD/CAM) systems, the adoption of the assembly line control (ALC) system, and the development of transfer machines, which would lead to full computerization from design to manufacturing and parts/components handling and thus lay a crucially important foundation for Hyundai's development of cars on its own. The third was the construction of a proving ground, which would complete the infrastructure necessary for the next stage of strategy.

In the case of CAD/CAM systems, Hyundai organized a project team in March 1979 to develop a long-term plan to computerize design and manufacture. The project team collected literature and catalogs on CAD/CAM and spent the next 14 months internalizing explicit literature-knowledge into tacit knowledge. Using knowledge gained from literature, the team purchased an advanced computer system and a graphic plotter and undertook an in-depth study of Mitsubishi's operational CAD/CAM system. The team expanded to include two or three representatives from each department that would be affected by the CAD/CAM system, "socializing" tacit knowledge gained by the original members to new members. During the next 19 months, the expanded team determined the scope of CAD/CAM application and undertook an

in-depth study of available alternative software packages. Hyundai selected the Catia package developed by French Dasso Aerospace in May 1982 and conducted preparatory work for almost 36 months before implementing the system.

Hyundai completed the FF plant in February 1985, tripling its production capacity from 150,000 units to 450,000 units per year. Its FF Excel passed both emission and safety tests and began being exported to the U.S. market in February 1986. Hyundai sold 168,882 Excels in 10 months during 1986, over 60% more than its ambitious goal, turning its loss to profit. With the sale of 263,610 in 1987, Excels became the best-selling import car of the year in the United States, overtaking Nissan Centra, Honda Civic, Subaru DL/GL, and Toyota Corolla.

Phase 4: Becoming Independent

The fourth jump in technological learning took place in September 1994, when the fiercely independent Hyundai unveiled Accent, the first subcompact car designed on its own (its predecessors had been based on Mitsubishi designs). It was benchmarked on the Toyota Tercel for performance and the Chrysler Neon for cost (Fortune 1995).

Although Hyundai was successful in manufacturing a subcompact FF car (Excel) and selling it in the North American market during the mid 1980s, it soon faced a technological dilemma. Mitsubishi, its major source of important technology for the FF car, and other foreign suppliers were unwilling to share their latest technology. Hyundai, however, lacked the absorptive capacity to keep upgrading its car quality to match that of its competitors in the North American market. Consequently, like Japanese export cars in the 1970s, Hyundai's Excel ended at the bottom of the *Consumer Reports* ranking, which greatly tarnished its image in the U.S. market. That experience prompted Hyundai to develop an extensive R&D network, not only in Korea but also abroad, to expand its absorptive capacity.

Hyundai's R&D efforts date back to 1978, when it established a primitive R&D center, primarily for facelifting current compact and subcompact cars. Efforts to develop its own capability, however, began to take shape in 1984 when Hyundai established the Advanced Engineering and Research Institute to develop its own engines and transmissions, the Passenger Vehicle R&D Center, the Commercial Vehicle R&D Center, and the Manufacturing Technology R&D Center. Hyundai also established joint R&D laboratories with local universities. In addition, in 1986 the Hyundai American Technical Center, Inc. (HATCI) opened in Ann Arbor, Michigan, and the Hyundai Styling Studio opened in Los Angeles to conduct R&D on cars for the U.S. market. Hyundai set up a technical center in Frankfurt to monitor technological developments in Europe and to design and engineer new cars for the European market. It opened an R&D center in Japan as the initial step toward entering that market in 1997.

The number of research engineers at Hyundai has increased, as shown in Table 26.2, from 197 in 1975 to 3,418 in 1990 and 3,890 in 1994, accounting for nearly 10% of the company's total employment; almost half of the engineers hold postgraduate engineering degrees. Hyundai recruited many Korean-American engineers from U.S. universities, some with experience at General Motors and Chrysler. For example, all but a few of the 35 senior research engineers with Ph.D. degrees at its Advanced Engineering and Research Institute are U.S. trained. Hyundai also invested heavily in continued training of its engineers. The number of R&D scientists and engineers sent abroad for training, ranging from short-term training and observation to long-term graduate degree programs increased from 74 in 1982 to 351 by 1986. R&D investment also increased sharply, from 1.1 billion Korean won ($2.2 million) in 1975 to 400 billion won ($501.3 million) by 1994. R&D expenditures were 1.8% of Hyundai sales in 1982 and 4.4% in 1994, almost 60% higher than those of its domestic competitors such as Daewoo and Kia.

The development of its alpha engine illustrates how Hyundai became independent of Mitsubishi, which licensed Hyundai "old" engines but refused to share its state-of-the-art ones. As Hyundai lacked ex-

perience in designing even a carburetor engine, let alone an electronically controlled one, its decision to develop a state-of-the-art engine was another example of major crisis in technological learning. In 1984, Hyundai organized a taskforce with a vision of developing such an engine. However, none of the team members had any experience in engine design, and no car with an electronically controlled engine was available locally from which Hyundai engineers could learn.

The taskforce was divided into several teams to do research on (1) hydrodynamics, thermodynamics, fuel engineering, emission control, and lubrication; (2) kinetics and dynamics related to engine and car design and CAD; (3) vibration and noise; (4) new ceramics; (5) electronics and control systems; and (6) manufacturing control and CAM. More than 300 R&D personnel had received training overseas before the engine project was officially launched in 1984. Those team members collected all available English and Japanese language literature on engines and transmissions and mastered the literature to raise their prior knowledge level. Hyundai then entered into an agreement with British Ricardo Engineering, which provided initial assistance in technical training for engine design. Hyundai next hired two Korean experts who had gotten engine development experience at General Motors and Chrysler, respectively, after earning their doctoral degrees at American universities. Hyundai also hired an engineer from Ricardo for a three-year period beginning in 1985 (Hyun 1995).

Despite the training and consulting services by Ricardo and the three experts, Hyundai engineers underwent 14 months of trial and error before the first prototype was made. However, the engine block broke into pieces in its first test. New prototype engines were made almost every week, only to be broken again and

Table 26.2. R&D Investment at Hyundai[a]

	1975	1978	1982	1984	1986	1988	1990	1992	1994
Sales[b]	30	216	430	669	1906	3411	4656	6079	9052
R&D[b]	1.1	5.4	7.9	22.7	79.5	116.0	190.4	248.8	400.0
R&D as % of sales	3.5	2.5	1.8	3.4	4.2	3.4	4.1	4.1	4.4
Number of researchers	197	381	725	1298	2247	2459	3418	3192	3890

[a]Hyundai Motor Company.
[b]Unit: billion won.

again. No one on the team could figure out why the prototypes broke down during the test runs, and even Hyundai managers began to doubt the company's capability to develop a competitive engine. The team had to scrap 11 more broken prototypes before 1 survived the test. There were 288 engine design changes, 156 changes in 1986 alone (Hyun 1995). Ninety-seven test engines had to be made before Hyundai refined its NA (natural aspiration) and TC (turbo charge) engines, 53 more engines for durability improvement, 88 more for developing a car, 26 more for developing its transmission, and 60 more for other testing, totaling 324 test engines, as well as more than 200 transmissions and 150 vehicles before Hyundai perfected them in 1992.

Hyundai's alpha engine outperformed comparable Japanese ones. Hyundai's NA engine, for example, took 11.1 seconds to reach 100 km/h, whereas Honda CRX 3V took 11.30 seconds. Hyundai also outperformed Honda in fuel efficiency: 20.2 km/l versus 19.4 km/l for a four-gear manual transmission. The successful experience of developing the alpha engines (1.3 and 1.5 liters) led to the development of beta engines (1.6, 1.8, and 2.0 liters), making Hyundai completely independent of foreign license in engines for midsize, compact, and subcompact cars. Hyundai's new 1.8-liter, 16-valve, double overhead camshaft engine (DOHC), for instance, takes only nine seconds to reach 100 km/h, outperforming a similar model of Japan's Toyota (HMC 1992). With the two engines and its own transmissions, Hyundai reduced royalty payments for compact and subcompact cars to zero.

As a result of continuous R&D efforts, Hyundai achieved the largest domestic market share in 1995: its Accent is the best selling subcompact; the Avante is the best selling compact; the Sonata II is the best selling mid-size car; and the Grandeur is the best selling full-size car in Korea. Hyundai also bounced back in its exports, particularly in new markets, from 225,393 units in 1990 to 392,239 in 1994. Hyundai is still behind the high-class Japanese and U.S. manufacturers, but the quality gap has definitely narrowed. The company's aim is to match Japanese quality but at a more competitive price. Hyundai has also become an important technology exporter to Thailand, Egypt, Zimbabwe, the Philippines, Malaysia, and other countries. It even exported a style design to Mitsubishi. Further, Hyundai is betting billions of dollars on a "green" car breakthrough. It plans to spend more than $5 billion on

R&D from 1995 to 2000, lifting its R&D spending from 4.4% of sales in 1994 to 7.0% by 2000.

Behind the process of expeditious learning are Chung Ju-Yung, chairman of the Hyundai Group, and Chung Se-Young, his brother and chairman of Hyundai Motor. The group chairman is known as the most far-sighted and boldest risk-taking entrepreneur in Korea (see Kirk 1994). The history of his construction and shipbuilding divisions is also repeated with constructed crises and their successful transformation into creative learning (see Amsden 1989, Amsden and Kim 1985). He managed ongoing dialogues with task-force leaders and their members. He visited sites regularly and maintained daily telephone contact with task-force leaders to check the work in progress.

SUMMARY AND DISCUSSION

Hyundai has transformed itself from a mere assembler of Ford models to a designer and exporter of its own cars and engines in less than three decades. Unlike firms in other developing countries, Hyundai has pursued a strategy of independence in developing technological capability. Its advancement from one phase to the next through the preparation for and acquisition, assimilation, and improvement of foreign technology appears to have been a spiral process. Migratory knowledge gave rise to prior knowledge base, and constructed crises intensified efforts, leading to expeditious organizational learning. The Hyundai case illustrates not only the process of expeditious learning, but also several idiosyncratic characteristics of organizational learning in catching-up.

First, catching-up firms, particularly those in developing countries, reverse the sequence of research, development and engineering (RD&E) of the advanced countries. Hyundai first acquired a production capability from its eight-year (1968–1976) experience in the assembly of Ford models. It then focused on the acquisition of an engineering capability, sequencing from subcompact to compact, to medium-size, to large cars. The number of years between steps steadily decreased: seven years (1976–1983) between subcompact and compact, five years (1983–1988) between compact and medium-size, and four years (1988–1992) between medium-size and large cars. It is logical for an inexperienced company in a catching-up country to sequence from a subcompact model, as its competitive edge depends more on price than quality in comparison with larger models. On the basis of production and engineering capability, Hyundai launched the development of its own cars. Again, Hyundai sequenced from subcompact (1994) to compact (1995), requiring only one year between the two. Hyundai is now doing serious research to break through in its "green" car project.

A similar process is evident in other industries in Korea. A series of studies covering more than 200 firms in different industries (Kim 1997) has shown that industries in Korea reversed the sequence of RD&E. They started with engineering (E) for products and processes imported from abroad in the 1960s and 1970s, then progressively evolved into the position of undertaking substantial development (D) in the 1980s. Research (R) became critical only in the 1990s.

Hyundai also reversed the sequence of technology trajectory of the advanced countries. Assembly technology from Ford in 1967 and technologies imported from various sources to produce the Pony in the mid-1970s were all mature technologies of advanced countries. Assimilating and improving those technologies through learning by doing enabled Hyundai to challenge more advanced technologies related to FF cars. Core technologies were again imported from advanced countries. The mastery of the FF technologies provided a platform for Hyundai's development of its state-of-the-art engines.

Second, migratory knowledge gives rise to a prior knowledge base. For catching-up firms, relevant knowledge is available elsewhere in various forms. The acquisition of prior knowledge through literature review and poaching of new personnel may be very effective for identifying and acquiring technology available elsewhere and facilitating learning in the subsequent phases. Particularly, mobile experienced personnel have been a major source of new tacit knowledge at Korean firms, as well as a major source of technology diffusion in many industries within Korea. The role of migratory knowledge and the government in the Hyundai case indicates the importance of institutions and interorganizational relations in organizational learning and innovation (Lundvall 1992). However, in-house efforts are indispensable to reinvent the transferred knowledge, particularly in the absence of mediating institutions that provide technology services (Attewell 1992).

Third, crises were constructed proactively rather than reactively. The first two crises (i.e., to expedite the assimilation of assembly production and to develop a "Korean car") were constructed proactively in the absence of external crises, and the third crisis (to develop an FF car and triple production capacity for the U.S. market) was constructed in response to the externally evoked oil crisis. However, the external crisis served only as a trigger. Hyundai's internally constructed crisis was not designed to return Hyundai to its pre-oil-crisis position, but rather to transform Hyundai from a small automaker focusing primarily on the domestic market into an international contender challenging the most sophisticated U.S. market. It was proactive for long-term growth, rather than reactive to an externally evoked crisis for short-term survival. The fourth constructed crisis (to develop its own cars) was also proactive. The taskforce to develop Hyundai's own engines and transmissions was formed in 1984, four years before the company faced a market crisis in the United States, and most critical R&D problems were solved by 1986, two years before the market crisis. In other words, all the crises Hyundai constructed internally were proactive and at the suborganization level.

Why is an internally constructed proactive crisis, particularly at the suborganization level, more effective for organizational learning than an externally evoked crisis as a reactive means to respond to an external change? An evoked crisis creates a performance gap, a major discrepancy between how the organization performs now and how it ought to perform to survive. However, the phenomenon of crisis denial may occur: refusal to recognize that the crisis is real. It sometimes stems from different perceptions and interpretations of environmental changes among people involved and sometimes from active resistance to maintain the status quo or inertia in adhering to current norms and past practice. Consequently, the organization facing an evoked crisis must exert a significant portion of its energy to educate management coalition and organizational members to agree that there is a crisis, mitigate resistance to change, and unlearn past practices. Different perceptions of crises and diverse opinions on prescriptions also make it difficult for an organization facing an evoked crisis to direct its energy toward effective learning.

In contrast, constructed crises present a clear gap between the current performance and the performance needed in the future. Further, the top managers can manipulate the performance gap in constructed crises so as to make them creative rather than destructive. Constructed crises are an antidote to inertia. They generate intense pressure to create mandates for change (Meyers 1990), enabling the management coalition to reach consensus on organizational goals. Given unambiguous goals to close a performance gap, mandates for change, and determination of the management coalition, constructed crises also prompt members to accept organizational goals.

Crisis construction can be used as a strategic means to shift learning orientation. Hyundai used constructed crises to shift its learning from duplicative-imitation-oriented, to a more creative-imitation-oriented, and finally to innovation-oriented, continuously expanding the learning frontier to increase the return on effort. Because changing learning paths requires an enormous amount of psychological energy, entrepreneurial top managers had to construct crises.

Constructed crises also increase the intensity of effort at the individual and organizational levels in the search for alternative courses of action, and hence are creative rather than destructive (Kim 1997). Mandates for change generate volume of effort, whereas goal consensus and identification provide direction of effort, clearly focusing effort on expeditious learning for growth. The goal focus and high intensity of efforts to resolve crises not only prompt members to search actively for information on new ways to respond to them and to expedite knowledge conversion and accumulation at the individual level, but also intensify interaction among members, giving rise to knowledge conversion and accumulation at the organizational level.

Finally, past successes in transforming crises into creative learning evoke the self-confidence that leads to further risk-taking by crisis construction (March and Shapira 1987). A cycle from crisis construction to successful resolution to self-confidence and back to crisis construction characterizes Hyundai's history in accumulating an absorptive capacity.

Is Hyundai's learning model evident in other industries in Korea? A similar learning process is used, albeit to a different degree, in other Korean industries. For example, Korean firms in electronics (Kim 1980, 1997), shipbuilding (Amsden 1989, Amsden and Kim 1985), steel (Amsden 1989, Amsden and Kim 1985), machinery (Amsden and Kim 1986), and semiconductors (Kim 1997) have undergone a similar process of crisis construction and expeditious learning in

catching-up. Crisis construction and expeditious learning are widespread in Korean manufacturing.

Hyundai is the most outstanding company in constructing crises proactively for opportunistic learning, mainly because it has the most entrepreneurial and boldest risk-taking top managers. In addition, the top and middle managers have been trained largely in the crisis construction and transformational process in Hyundai's project-based construction and shipbuilding companies. Those managers maintained ongoing dialogue during the process of crisis management, which created a "can-do" culture at Hyundai. Pitt (1990) concludes that crisis construction is an evocative and galvanizing device in the personal repertoires of proactive top managers, who think synthetically rather than analytically and are prophetic and single-minded.

Can Hyundai also use crisis construction for pioneering? Learning goals may be more specific and clearer in catching-up than in pioneering. The catching-up company can use crisis construction to achieve goal identification and consensus and to generate enormous energy from organizational members in searching for and converting knowledge at the individual and organizational levels. Relevant knowledge is readily available in various forms. The catching-up company can acquire prior knowledge through literature review, poaching of personnel, observation tours, and technology licensing. In contrast, the pioneering company must work with a strategic ambiguity that provides only broad direction (Nonaka 1988) and it has difficulty identifying external sources of relevant knowledge. Consequently, learning in pioneering may be creative but not necessarily expeditious.

Can catching-up firms in other countries emulate Hyundai's learning model? The answer is yes and no. They can improve the effectiveness of organizational learning by emulating the learning process illustrated in Figure 26.2 and 26.3 and the learning cycles listed in Table 26.1. But they may lack some of Hyundai's implicit advantages, such as well-developed human resources with the trait of being hardworking and cushions provided by the government and subsidiaries.

First, the availability of well-trained human resources cannot be easily matched by firms in other countries. According to a United Nations report, Korea is one of the only four developing countries that made a double jump from low level to medium level and from medium level to high level in terms of the human development index between 1960 and 1992. It had the largest absolute increase and the highest score among those four countries in 1992 (United Nations Development Programme 1994). The number of scientists and engineers per 10,000 population is the highest among the developing countries and closer to that of France and the United Kingdom, at least in quantity (Ministry of Science and Technology, Korea 1994). Human resource development requires a long-term investment.

Second, the Koreans' habit of hard work and their long working hours cannot be easily emulated by firms in other countries. Such cultural traits stem from several factors. Korea's land area is scarcely bigger than New Jersey in the United States or Hungary. It is crossed by mountains, and a relatively small portion of the land is arable for its population of more than 44 million people. In population density, Korea trails only Bangladesh and Taiwan. The cramped conditions and severely cold winters appear to have forced Koreans to work hard and long to survive in an unfavorable environment. Additionally, the older generation has been motivated by the memory of deprivation and hard times under Japanese occupation and the destructive Korean War. An obsession to "beat Japan" to settle old scores and national economic competition with North Korea are also major forces motivating Koreans (Porter 1990). Such cultural and situational factors cannot be duplicated in other countries.

Third, government strategy and support, as well as cushions provided by cash-cow subsidiaries within the diversified Hyundai Group, enabled its automobile division to have a long-term focus and to take risks. For companies using equity market financing or operating in a single business, such long-term thinking and risk-taking may be difficult.

In conclusion, the Hyundai case leads to several speculative propositions to explore in the future. (1) A proactively constructed crisis is a more effective strategic means of shifting learning orientation and facilitating organizational learning than a reactively evoked crisis. (2) Entrepreneurial owners are more likely to construct and resolve crises than employed managers, particularly when they have governmental and interorganizational support for a long-term view. (3) A visionary entrepreneur, energetic teams, and effective dialogues between them are needed to turn constructed crises into expeditious learning. (4) Crisis construction and its transformation into expeditious learning may be easier to implement in catching-up than in pioneering. (5) Catching-up firms in both developing and advanced countries can elevate their prior knowledge base significantly by tapping migratory knowledge. (6) Catching-up firms in the developing countries reverse the sequence of technology trajectory of the advanced countries, entering first into the mature stage of technology and progressing gradually toward increasingly sophisticated technologies. (7) Catching-up firms in the developing countries sequence the process of capability building from production to engineering and innovation, reversing the direction of research, development and engineering (RD&E) common in the advanced countries. (8) For catching-up firms in developing countries, a strategy of independence is more difficult to manage but more effective in organizational learning than is joint venture with firms from advanced countries.

ACKNOWLEDGMENT

The author acknowledges the thorough and constructive comments from four anonymous reviewers, one of whom gave creative ideas underlying Figures 26.2 and 26.3. The case study underlying this article is based on Chapter 5 of the author's book, *Imitation to Innovation: The Dynamics of Korea's Technological Learning,* Boston, MA: Harvard Business School Press, 1997.

REFERENCES

Abernathy, William J. (1978), *Productivity Dilemma,* Baltimore: Johns Hopkins University Press.

Amsden, Alice H. (1989), *Asia's Next Giant: South Korea and Late Industrialization,* New York: Oxford University Press.

Amsden, Alice H. and Linsu Kim (1985), "The Acquisition of Technological Capability in Korean Industries," World Bank, mimeograph (available from the authors upon request).

Amsden, Alice H. and Linsu Kim (1986), "Technological Perspective on the General Machinery Industry in the Republic of Korea," in Martin Fransman (Ed.), *Machinery and Economic Development,* London: Macmillan Press, 93–123.

Amsden, Alice H. and Linsu Kim (1989), "Comparative Analysis of Local and Transnational Corporations in the Korean Automobile Industry," in DongKi Kim and Linsu Kim (Eds.), *Management Behind Indus-*

trialization: Readings in Korean Business, Seoul: Korea University Press, 579–596.

Argyris, Chris and Donald A. Schon (1978), Organizational Learning: A Theory of Action Perspective, Reading, MA: Addison-Wesley.

Arrow, Kenneth (1962), "Economic Implications of Learning by Doing," Review of Economic Studies, 29, 166–170.

Attewell, Paul (1992), "Technology Diffusion and Organizational Learning: The Case of Business Computing," Organization Science, 3, 1, 1–19.

Badaracco, Joseph L. Jr. (1991), The Knowledge Link: How Firms Compete Through Strategic Alliances, Boston: Harvard Business School Press.

Cohen, Wesley M. and Daniel A. Levinthal (1990), "Absorptive Capacity: A New Perspective on Learning and Innovation," Administrative Science Quarterly, 35, 128–152.

Cooper, Arnold C. and Dan E. Schendel (1976), "Strategic Responses to Technological Threats," Business Horizons, 19, 61–69.

De Greene, K. B. (1982), The Adaptive Organization: Anticipation and Management of Crisis, New York: Wiley.

Dodgson, Mark (1993), "Organizational Learning: A Review of Some Literature," Organization Studies, 14, 3, 375–394.

Duncan, Robert B. and Andrew Weiss (1978), "Organizational Learning: Implications for Organizational Design" in B. Staw (Ed.), Research in Organizational Behavior, 1, 75–123.

Far Eastern Economic Review (FEER) (1992), "An Industry in Suspension," August 13, 25.

Fransman, Martin and Kenneth King (Eds.) (1984), Technological Capability in the Third World, London: Macmillan.

Fortune (1995) "Korea's Automakers Take on the World (Again)," March 6, 77.

Garud, R. and P. R. Nayyar (1994), "Transformative Capacity: Continual Structuring by Intertemporal Technology Transfer," Strategic Management Journal, 14, 365–385.

Harlow, H. F. (1959), "Learning Set and Error Factor Theory," in S. Koch (Ed.), Psychology: A Study of Science, New York: McGraw-Hill, 492–537.

Hedberg, Bo (1981), "How Organizations Learn and Unlearn," in P. C. Nystrom and W. H. Starbuck (Eds.), Handbook of Organizational Design, Vol. 1: Adapting Organizations to Their Environments, New York: Oxford University Press, 3–26.

Howells, Jeremy (1996), "Tacit Knowledge, Innovation and Technology Transfer," Technology Analysis and Strategic Management, 8, 2, 91–106.

Hyun, Young-Suk (1995), "The Road to Self-Reliance: New Product Development of Hyundai Motor Company" paper presented at International Motor Vehicle Program Annual Sponsors Meeting, Toronto, June 4–7, 1995 (available from the author upon request).

Hyun, Young-Suk and Jinjoo Lee (1989), "Can Hyundai Go It Alone?" Long Range Planning, 22, 2, 63–69.

Hyundai Motor Company (HMC) (1992), Hyundai Jadongcha Sa (The History of Hyundai Motor) Seoul: Hyundai Motor Company, 1111.

Kim, Daniel H. (1993), "The Link Between Individual and Organizational Learning," Sloan Management Review, 35, 1, 37–50.

Kim, Dong-Jae and Bruce Kogut (1995), "Technological Platforms and Diversification" Organization Science, 7, 3, 283–301.

Kim, Linsu (1980), "Stages of Development of Industrial Technology in a Less Developed Country: A Model," Research Policy, 9, 3, 254–277.

Kim, Linsu (1995), "Absorptive Capacity and Industrial Growth: A Conceptual Framework and Korea's Experience," in Bon-Ho Koo and Dwight Perkins (Eds.), Social Capability and Long-Term Economic Growth, London: St. Martins, 266–287.

Kim, Linsu (1997), Imitation to Innovation: The Dynamics of Korea's Technological Learning, Boston: Harvard Business School Press.

Kim, Linsu and Youngbae Kim (1985), "Innovation in a Newly Industrializing Country: A Multiple Discriminant Analysis," Management Science, 31, 3, 312–322.

Kirk, Donald (1994), Korean Dynasty: Hyundai and Chung Ju Yung, Armonk, NY: M. E. Sharpe.

Kogut, Bruce and Udor Zander (1992), "Knowledge of the Firm and the Replication of Technology," Organization Science, 3, 383–397.

Lundvall, Bengt-Ake (Ed.) (1992), National Systems of Innovation—Towards a Theory of Innovation and Interactive Learning, London: Printer Publishers.

March, James G. and Z. Shapira (1987), "Managerial Perspectives on Risk and Risk Taking," Management Science, 33, 1404–1418.

Meyers, Patricia W. (1990), "Non-linear Learning in Large Technological Firms: Period Four Implies Chaos," Research Policy, 19, 97–115.

Miller, Danny and Peter H. Friesen (1984), Organization: A Quantum View, Englewood Cliffs, NJ: Prentice-Hall.

Ministry of Science and Technology, Korea (MOST) (1994), 1994 Report on the Survey of Research and Development in Science and Technology, Seoul: MOST, 75.

Nelson, Richard R. and Sidney G. Winter (1982), An Evolutionary Theory of Economic Change, Cambridge, MA: Harvard University Press, 134.

Nevis, Edwin C., Anthony J. DiBella, and Janet M. Gould (1995), "Understanding Organizations as Learning Systems," *Sloan Management Review,* Winter, 73–85.

Nonaka, Ikujiro (1988), "Creating Organizational Order Out of Chaos: Self-Renewal in Japanese Firms," *California Management Review,* 30, 3, 57–73.

Nonaka, Ikujiro (1994), "A Dynamic Theory of Organizational Knowledge Creation," *Organization Science* 5, 1, 14–37.

Nonaka, Ikujiro and Hirotaka Takeuchi (1995), *The Knowledge-Creating Company,* New York: Oxford University Press.

Pitt, Martyn (1990), "Crisis Modes of Strategic Transformation: A New Metaphor for Managing Technological Innovation," in R. Loveridge and M. Pitt (Eds.), *The Strategic Management of Technological Innovation,* Chichester, England: Wiley, 253–272.

Polanyi, M. (1966), *The Tacit Dimension,* London: Routledge and Kegan Paul.

Porter, Michael E. (1990), *The Competitive Advantage of Nations,* New York: The Free Press.

Rice, Ronald and Everett Rogers (1980), "Reinvention in the Innovation Process," *Knowledge: Creation, Diffusion, Utilization,* 1, 4, 499–514.

Rogers, Everett M. (1983), *Diffusion of Innovation,* New York: Free Press.

Rosenberg, Nathan (1982), *Inside the Black Box: Technology and Economics,* Cambridge, UK: Cambridge University Press.

Schnaars, Steven P. (1994), *Managing Imitation Strategies,* New York: Free Press.

Schon, Donald A. (1967) *Technology and Change: The New Heraclitus,* Oxford, UK: Pergamon.

Shrivastava, Paul (1983), "A Typology of Organizational Learning Systems," *Journal of Management Studies,* 20, 1–28.

Shrivastava, Paul (1988), "Industrial Crisis Management:

Learning from Organizational Failures," *Journal of Management Studies,* 25, 4, 283–284.

Tushman, Michael L. and Philip A. Anderson (1986), "Technological Discontinuities and Organizational Environment," *Administrative Science Quarterly,* 31, 439–456.

Tushman, Michael L., B. Virany, and E. Romanelli (1985), "Executive Succession Strategic Reorientations and Organizational Evolution," *Technology in Society,* 7, 297–314.

United Nations Development Programme (UNDP) (1994), *Human Resource Development Report, 1994,* New York: Oxford University Press.

Utterback, James M. (1994), *Mastering the Dynamics of Innovation: How Companies Can Seize Opportunities in the Face of Technological Change,* Boston: Harvard Business School Press.

Utterback, James M. and William J. Abernathy (1975), "A Dynamic Model of Process and Product Innovation," *Omega,* 3, 6, 639–656.

Utterback, James M. and Linsu Kim (1985), "Invasion of Stable Business by Radical Innovation," in Paul R. Kleindorfer (Ed.), *Management of Productivity and Technology in Manufacturing,* New York: Plenum Press, 113–151.

Vogel, Ezra F. (1991), *The Four Little Dragons: The Spread of Industrialization in East Asia,* Cambridge, MA: Harvard University Press.

von Hippel, Eric (1988), *The Sources of Innovation,* New York: Oxford University Press.

Weick, Karl (1988), "Enacted Sensemaking in Crisis Situations," *Journal of Management Studies,* 25, 4, 305–317.

Winter, Sidney G. (1987), "Knowledge and Competence as Strategic Assets," in David Teece (Ed.), *The Competitive Challenge—Strategies for Industrial Innovation and Renewal,* Cambridge, MA: Ballinger, 159–184.

27

Learning from Collaboration

Knowledge and Networks in the Biotechnology and Pharmaceutical Industries

WALTER W. POWELL

In a number of technologically advanced industries, a new logic of organizing is developing. Rather than viewing firms as vehicles for processing information, making decisions, and solving problems, the core capabilities of organizations are based increasingly on knowledge-seeking and knowledgecreation. In technologically intensive fields, where there are large gains from innovation and steep losses from obsolescence, competition is best regarded as a learning race. The ability to learn about new opportunities requires participation in them, thus a wide range of interorganizational linkages is critical to knowledge diffusion, learning, and technology development. These connections may be formal contractual relationships, as in a research and development partnerships or a joint venture, or informal, involving participation in technical communities. Both mechanisms are highly salient for the transfer of knowledge and are reinforcing. Yet even though the awareness of the importance of both external sources of knowledge and external participation has grown, we know much less about how knowledge is generated, transferred, and acted upon in these new contexts.

THE TWIN FACES OF COLLABORATION

By a variety of accounts, the number and scope of interorganizational collaborations have grown rapidly in many industries, most notably in the field of biotechnology.[1] In the world of practice, this heightened interest is captured in discussions of the "virtual firm," and evidenced in all manner of cooperative relationships that join two or more organizations in some form of common undertaking.[2] In the world of theory, research on various forms of collaboration has two principle foci: on the transaction and the mutual exchange of rights and on the relationship and the mechanisms through which information flows and mutual adjustments take place. Typically, the more exchange-oriented analysis treats collaboration as a variant of the make or buy decision and analyzes key features of the transaction: how it is negotiated and which party retains what control rights.[3] Thus, it matters a great deal whether common assets are being pooled or different resources traded, what stage of development a project is at, and whether some form of ownership is involved.[4] This strand of research, based primarily in the fields of industrial organization economics and business strategy, focuses more on the contractual mechanisms for coordinating interorganizational relations.

The second line of inquiry, stemming more from sociology and organization theory, adopts a processual focus, analyzing whether features of the task require continuous communication and organization learning, and the extent to which the collaboration is embedded

Copyright © 1998 by The Regents of the University of California. Reprinted from the *California Management Review,* Vol. 40, No. 3. By permission of The Regents.

in multiple, ongoing relationships.[5] This approach focuses on the relational capability of organizations, how and when organizations are able to combine their existing competencies with the abilities of others. These capabilities are not viewed as static, but rather emerge and deepen over time as firms both develop existing relationships and explore new ones.

These two perspectives are, at times, viewed as competing explanations, but since they involve different units of analysis—the transaction and the relationship, respectively—they need not be. Key structural features of an industry may determine the relative weight that contractual and processual elements play in interorganizational collaborations.[6] Large-scale reliance on interorganizational linkages reflects a fundamental and pervasive concern with access to knowledge. In the rapidly-developing field of biotechnology, the knowledge base is both complex and expanding and the sources of expertise are widely dispersed. When uncertainty is high, organizations interact more, not less, with external parties in order to access both knowledge and resources. Hence, the locus of innovation is found in networks of learning, rather than in individual firms. How contracts are structured is not unimportant; in fact, getting the intellectual property rights specified clearly is critical. But focusing too closely on the transactional details of an exchange risks missing the boat as the larger field rides the waves of rapid technological change. Moreover, current work on contractual aspects of collaboration between biotech and pharmaceutical firms suggests that as the relationships unfold, many of the specific covenants contained in contracts are not invoked.[7] In short, process matters, and firms differ in their ability to do relational contracting.

In several key respects, arguments about the learning and strategic aspects of collaboration converge to produce new questions about the pivotal role of learning and interfirm relationships in rapidly developing industries. Firms in technologically intensive fields rely on collaborative relationships to access, survey, and exploit emerging technological opportunities. As the structure of an industry becomes shaped by interorganizational relations, the nature of competition is altered, but the direction of change is very much open. First, collaboration raises entry barriers. To the extent that the capabilities of organizations are based in part on the qualities or capabilities of those with whom they are allied, collaboration increases the price of admission to a field. If parties act either opportunistically or restrictively, collaborating only with a narrow range of partners whose behavior they can influence, then collaboration can exclude admission to many. But if the participants interact broadly and engage in mutual learning with the organizations they are affiliated with, the effects of collaboration are expansive, mobilizing resources throughout a field, with collaboration serving as an inclusive entry pass. Second, interfirm cooperation accelerates the rate of technological innovation. In our earlier work, we demonstrated a ladder effect, in which firms with experienced partners competed more effectively in high-speed learning races.[8] Rather than seeking to monopolize the returns from innovative activity and forming exclusive partnerships with only a narrow set of organizations, successful firms positioned themselves as the hubs at the center of overlapping networks, stimulating rewarding research collaborations among the various organizations to which they are aligned, and profiting from having multiple projects in various stages of development.

Third, reliance on collaboration has potentially transformative effects on all participants. Those positioned in a network of external relations adopt more administrative innovations, and do so earlier.[9] The presence of a dense network of collaborative ties may even alter participants' perceptions of competition. Inside a densely connected field, organizations must adjust to a novel perspective in which it is no longer necessary to have exclusive, proprietary ownership of an asset in order to extract value from it. Moreover, since a competitor on one project may become a partner on another, the playing field resembles less a horse race and more a rugby match, in which players frequently change their uniforms.[10] Seen from this perspective, decisions that were initially framed as strategic have cumulative consequences that alter the economic calculus, while choices motivated by learning and experimentation remake the institutional landscape.

Finally, collaboration may itself become a dimension of competition. As firms turn to outside parties for a variety of resources, they develop a network profile, or portfolio of ties to specific partners for certain activities. Thus, for example, an emerging biotech company may have a research grant from a branch of the National Institutes of Health, a research collaboration with a leading university, licensing agreements with other universities or nonprofit research institutes, clinical studies underway with a research hospital, and sales or distribution arrangements with a large pharmaceutical corporation. Others may have only one such relationship, or may hook up with the same partners for different activities, or with disparate partners for similar activities, or have complex relationships involving multiple activities with each partner. Analytically, each combination of partnership and business activity represents a distinct collaborative relationship. A firm's portfolio of collaborations is both a resource and a signal to markets, as well as to other potential partners, of the quality of the firm's activities and products. Whether firms in a field are constrained to a narrow set of relationships or have broad options in determining their portfolios has profound consequences for competition. To draw on the language of political sociology, heterogeneity and interdependence are greater spurs to collective action than homogeneity and discipline.[11] If the members on an industry are constrained in their choice of partners to a small set of potential partners, competition is increased, but within a narrow sphere. The effect is like a tournament, in which the "winners" receive exclusive sponsorship in order to compete against each other in ever-fiercer rounds. On the other hand, if there is a broad and growing set of nonexclusive partners, then the participants will evince heterogeneous collaborations, and the avenues of rivalry are widened.

In sum, regardless of whether collaboration is driven by strategic motives, such as filling in missing pieces of the value chain, or by learning considerations to gain access to new knowledge, or by embeddedness in a community of practice, connectivity to an interorganizational network and competence at managing collaborations have become key drivers of a new logic of organizing. This view of organizations and networks as vehicles for producing, synthesizing, and distributing ideas recognizes that the success of firms is increasingly linked to the depth of their ties to organizations in diverse fields. Learning in these circumstances is a complex, multi-level process, involving learning from and with partners under conditions of uncertainty, learning about partners' behavior and developing routines and norms that can mitigate the risks of opportunism, and learning how to distribute newly acquired knowledge across different projects and functions. But learning is also closely linked to the conditions under which knowledge is gained, and in this sense the motives that drive collaboration can shape what can be learned. Much sophisticated technical knowledge is tacit in character—an indissoluble mix of design, process, and expertise. Such information is not easily transferred by license or purchase. Passive recipients of new knowledge are less likely to fully appreciate its value or be able to respond rapidly. In fields such as biotechnology, firms must have the ability to absorb knowledge.[12] In short, internal capability and external collaborations are complementary. Internal capability is indispensable in evaluating ideas or skills developed externally, while collaboration with outside parties provides access to news and resources that cannot be generated internally. A network serves as the locus of innovation in many high-tech fields because it provides timely access to knowledge and resources that are otherwise unavailable, while also testing internal expertise and learning capabilities.

THE NETWORK STRUCTURE OF THE BIOTECHNOLOGY FIELD

The science underlying the field of biotechnology had its origins in discoveries made in university laboratories in the early 1970s. These promising breakthroughs were initially exploited by science-based start-up firms (DBFs, or dedicated biotechnology firms, in industry parlance) founded in the mid to late 1970s. The year 1980 marked a sea change with the U.S. Supreme Court ruling in the *Diamond vs. Chakrabaty* case that genetically engineered life forms were patentable. And Genentech, which along with Cetus was the most visible biotech company, had its initial public offering, drawing astonishing interest on Wall Street. Over the next two decades, hundreds of DBFs have been founded, mostly in the U.S. but more recently in Canada, Australia, Britain, and Europe.

The initial research—most notably Herbert Boyer and Stanley Cohen's discovery of recombinant DNA methods and Georges Köhler and Cesar Milstein's cell infusion technology that creates monoclonal antibodies—drew primarily on molecular biology and immunology. The early discoveries were so path-breaking that they had a kind of natural excludability, that is, without interaction with those involved in the research, the knowledge was slow to transfer. But what was considered a radical innovation then has changed considerably as the science diffused rapidly. Genetic engineering, monoclonal antibodies, polymerase chain reaction amplification, and gene sequencing are now part of the standard toolkit of microbiology graduate students. To stay on top of the field, one has to be at the forefront of knowledge-seeking and technology development. Moreover, many new areas of science have become inextricably involved, ranging from genetics, biochemistry, cell biology, general medicine, computer science, to even physics and optical sciences. Modern biotechnology, then, is not a discipline or an industry per se, but a set of technologies relevant to a wide range of disciplines and industries.

The commercial potential of biotechnology appealed to many scientists and entrepreneurs even at its embryonic stage. In the early years, the principal efforts were directed at making existing proteins in new ways, then the field evolved to use the new methods to make new proteins, and now today the race is on to design entirely new medicines. The firms that translated the science into feasible technologies and new medical products faced a host of challenges. Alongside the usual difficulties of start-up firms, the DBFs needed huge amounts of capital to fund costly research, assistance in managing themselves and in conducting clinical trials, and eventually experience with the regulatory approval process, manufacturing, marketing, distribution, and sales. In time, established pharmaceutical firms were attracted to the field, initially allying with DBFs in research partnerships and in providing a set of organizational capabilities that DBFs were lacking. Eventually, the considerable promise of biotechnology led nearly every established pharmaceutical corporation to develop, to varying degrees of success, both in-house capacity in the new science and a portfolio of collaborations with DBFs.

Thus the field is not only multi-disciplinary, it is multi-institutional as well. In addition to research universities and both start-up and established firms, government agencies, nonprofit research institutes, and leading research hospitals have played key roles in conducting and funding research, while venture capitalists and law firms have played essential parts as talent scouts, advisers, consultants, and financiers. Two factors are highly salient. One, all the necessary skills and organizational capabilities needed to compete in biotechnology are not readily found under a single roof.

Two, in fields such as biotech, where knowledge is advancing rapidly and the sources of knowledge are widely dispersed, organizations enter into a wide array of alliances to gain access to different competencies and knowledge. Progress with the technology goes hand-in-hand with the evolution of the industry and its supporting institutions. The science, the organizations, and the associated institutions' practices are co-evolving. Universities are more attentive to the commercial development of research, DBFs are active participants in basic science inquiry, and pharmaceuticals more keyed into developments at DBFs and universities.

Nevertheless, organizations vary in their abilities to access knowledge and skills located beyond their boundaries. Organizations develop very different profiles of collaboration, turning to partners for divergent combinations of skills, funding, experience, access, and status. Biotech firms have not supplanted pharmaceutical companies, and large pharmaceuticals have not absorbed the biotechnology field. Nor has the basic science component of the industry receded in its importance. Consequently, DBFs, research universities, pharmaceutical companies, research institutions, and leading medical centers are continually seeking partners who can help them stay abreast of, or in front of, this fast-moving field. But organizations vary considerably in their approaches to collaboration. Put differently, some organizations reap more from the network seeds they sow than do others. Despite the efforts of nearly every DBF to strengthen its collaborative capacity, not all of them cultivate similar profiles of relationships, nor are all able to harvest their networks to comparable advantage. Similarly, not every pharmaceutical firm is positioned comparably to exploit the latest breakthroughs in genomics, gene therapy, and a host of other novel methodologies for drug discovery. A key challenge, then, for both small biotechnology firms and large global pharmaceutical corporations is in learning from collaborations with external parties, and in constructing a portfolio of collaborators that provides access to both the emerging science and technology and the necessary organizational capabilities.

COLLABORATIVE PORTFOLIOS

The various key participants in the biotechnology and pharmaceutical industries pursue different avenues of collaboration. A cursory study of the portfolios of key firms reveals distinctive mixes of alliances for different business functions. For example, in biotech, Amgen, a Los Angeles-based firm founded in 1980, is often regarded as a bellwether for the industry. Amgen has extensive R&D and marketing collaborations with numerous small biotech companies, among them ARRIS, Envirogen, Glycomex, Guilford, Interneuron, Regeneron, and Zynaxis. These are relationships based on a division of labor in which the smaller firm develops promising technology with Amgen's financial and scientific assistance, and Amgen will market the eventual product. Amgen also holds several key licensing agreements with Sloan-Kettering Hospital (for a cell growth factor), the Ontario Cancer Institute (for knockout mice), and Rockefeller University (for an obesity gene). In contrast, Cambridge-based Biogen, founded in 1978 but with only 750 employees, adopted a strategy of licensing its initial research discoveries to such established firms as Abbott, Lilly, Pharmacia Upjohn, Merck, Organon Teknika, and Schering Plough. By 1996, Biogen's royalty stream had grown to $150 million annually. Biogen also outsourced the costly and time-consuming task of analyzing clinical trial data on its medicines in development to contract research organizations, but monitored the work with in-house experts.[13] Chiron, the largest biotech with more than 7500 employees, and 9 subsidiaries, is also partially owned by Novartis (49.9%) and Johnson and Johnson (4.6%). Chiron, founded in 1981, has the most extensive array of collaborations of any biotech with numerous R&D ties with smaller biotechs and universities, licensing agreements with large pharmaceutical and animal health companies, partnerships with larger biotechs, and manufacturing and marketing alliances with other large firms as well. Indeed, in a January, 1997 news release, Chiron reported that it now has more than 1,400 (informal) agreements with universities and research institutions and 64 (formal) collaborations with other companies. "This network is a core strength of Chiron," the release proclaims.

These different collaborative profiles reflect, in important respects, the mixed motives of strategy and exigency in the early years of building a company. Amgen works with younger, early-stage biotechs, but eschews close affiliations with many established pharmaceuticals. Biogen licensed out some of its initial research discoveries, and the substantial royalties it takes

in now fund the development, sales, and distribution of Avonex, its successful drug for multiple sclerosis. Chiron has a spider-webbed universe of affiliations with basic scientists in universities, and it maintains ongoing ties with diverse biotechs and health-care companies. The partial "parent" owner, Novartis of Switzerland, appears to use Chiron as its window into this rapidly developing field.

Similarly, in the pharmaceutical industry, divergent approaches to collaboration are pursued. By the accounting of Recombinant Capital, a San Francisco company that tracks high tech, the big pharmaceutical firms poured $4.5 billion into deals with biotech companies in 1996.[14] Their aim is to capitalize on promising technology and the skills of the nimbler small companies in doing more rapid development. But dominant firms pursue these aims in quite different ways. Industry giant Merck, for example, spreads its search efforts globally, working with research institutes in France, Canada, China, Japan, Costa Rica, and the United States, while pursuing research partnerships with but a few biotechs such as Affymetrix and Transcell to access new technologies. In addition, Merck has innumerable licensing agreements, as well as arrangements to do manufacturing, marketing, and sales for smaller companies. Eli Lilly, another big pharmaceutical player, but about two-thirds the size of Merck, has both more focused and more extensive collaborations. Pursuing a strategy of "discovery without walls," Lilly has several dozen research alliances with a wide variety of U.S. biotech firms, ranging from new startups to more established companies. In addition to these extensive external discovery efforts, Lilly also has licensing and joint sales and distribution agreements with biotechs, but the clear emphasis has been on the research side. The Swiss firm Hoffman LaRoche, one of the largest firms in the industry, has an even more focused approach, owning 66% of the stock in the U.S. biotech firm Genentech, in addition to multiple research, development, and marketing collaborations with Genentech. Roche counts Amgen, Affymetrix, and several other biotechs as partners also, but it utilizes Genentech as its primary talent scout to stay abreast of the field.

At a more micro level, however, these collaborative profiles have their origins in myriad small decisions, stemming from different purposes and initiated by different parties. At one of the larger U.S. pharmaceutical firms, I was involved in a multi-year internal executive development program. During this time, I had regular contact with senior managers on the science side, in the finance and strategy groups, and those in charge of the different therapeutic product lines. I used our conversations to informally trace the origins of the more than twenty R&D partnerships the firm has with various small biotechs. In following these different "stories," it became apparent that collaborations emerged from very different routes. Some were brought forward by business development staff who had "found" young biotechs in financial trouble and in need of cash. Thus, promising technology could be "had" inexpensively. In other circumstances, however, breakthrough technologies triggered great interest throughout the pharmaceutical industry, and all the major players were part of the gold rush, bidding for the new discovery. In still other cases, long-standing personal ties among scientists, sometimes forged decades earlier at universities, led to formal collaborations. Other partnerships were driven by a pressing need to fill out a product portfolio or to replenish the product pipeline in a particular therapeutic category. And still other connections literally fell into their laps, as biotech firms approached the company with proposals that proved viable.

I use these examples of very different starting points not to suggest that the process of deciding which parties to collaborate with is random or haphazard, but to illustrate that there are, especially in a larger company, multiple inputs and opportunities and many decision makers involved. Except in the smallest companies, the same people rarely review all the relevant information and make decisions about whom to ally with and under what terms and for what period of time. Nor should such decisions necessarily be made by the same people or units. But what is necessary is the ability to negotiate two hurdles, the first leaping from information to knowledge, and the second jumping from individual-level learning and expertise to organizational-level learning and routines. In any technology-intensive field, information is abundant and accumulates rapidly. Long ago, Herbert Simon alerted us to the fact that, increasingly, attention is the scarcest commodity in organizations. As firms embark on different combinations of formal and informal collaborations and divergent mixes of external sourcing and internal production, the parties who are most closely

involved with outsiders develop skills at relational contracting: How much of an agreement needs to be specified in a contract? How much should rest on a handshake or good faith? What role should the "entangling strings" of friendship or reputation play? What kinds of milestones or interventions are needed to insure a project stays on course?[15] In short, knowledge of how to collaborate means that information is filtered by a specific context and an ongoing relationship, by experience and reflection, and by interpretation. When multiple participants are involved, and their availability varies, making knowledgeable decisions is a challenge.

But even more daunting is moving from individual learning (which is embodied in experienced personnel) to organization-level learning (in which the skills of relational contracting become embedded in organizational routines and procedures) without rendering those competencies lifeless and inert. As an illustration, Richard Di Marchi, Vice President for Endocrine Research at Eli Lilly and Company, remarks that one of the bigger challenges his company faces in managing research partnerships with small firms is in not treating them as "one-offs," that is, independent relationships pursued separately. On the other hand, it is ineffective to force all decisions about collaboration to go forward only after the decision has been vetted by a key committee, composed of staff from different business functions. Such a move can result in a needless delay, which is fatal in a fast-moving field, and can also dampen initiative. Another side-effect of formalizing the approval process is to force external relationships underground, into subterranean linkages, as savvy managers opt to pursue relationships without risking going through the rigamarole of formal approval. But covert efforts may run the risk that key intellectual property or process issues are not aired at the outset. The challenge, then, is to develop routines for cooperation that are widely shared, that apply across decisions, and allow for lessons to be transferred from project to project. In the biotechnology and pharmaceutical fields, firms vary enormously in their capacity to learn across projects.

LEARNING HOW AND WHAT TO LEARN

My claim that learning from collaboration is both a function of access to knowledge and possession of capabilities for utilizing and building on such knowledge is not a claim that individuals and organizations are exceedingly calculating or far-sighted. In making the argument that knowledge facilitates the acquisition of more knowledge, I am building on research that stresses that skills are embedded in the exercise of routines. The development of these routines is a key feature in explaining the variability of organizations' capacity for learning. Only by building these skills can knowledge be transferred from one project to another, from one unit to another, in a manner that allows insights gained from one set of experiences to shape subsequent activities.

Most firms in biotech and pharmaceuticals have key individuals who function as network managers, "marriage counselors," and honest brokers. These individuals provide the glue that sustains relationships between parties who have ample opportunities to question one another's intentions or efforts. The participants in a collaboration often learn at very different speeds, prompting one side to wonder if it is benefiting equally. Moreover, the wealthier party is sometimes regarded as a "sugar daddy," present only to write checks. So there are numerous situations where monitoring and interventions are needed to maintain balance in a collaboration. A critical task for the participants enmeshed in a web of many such relationships is to take lessons learned on one project and make them systemic, that is, portable across multiple relationships.

Finding solutions to the problem of learning how to learn is critical for both small and large firms. Biotech companies have created organizational capabilities well out of proportion to their relatively small size by building on relationships with external parties to gain access to resources, knowledge, and skills to support every organizational function from R&D to distribution. And given the huge sums that pharmaceuticals are pouring into biotech, these large firms have had to find methods to harmonize and coordinate their far-flung partnerships. The steps involved range widely, and it is probably too early to pronounce some efforts most efficacious. Clearly not all firms maneuver with equal ease, have comparable access, or utilize high-quality partners with similar results. But some methods do hold promise for facilitating learning.

An enormous amount of information and knowledge resides in the minds and electronic mail of key people, but this material is rarely organized in a fash-

ion that allows for its transmission to others. Some firms build repositories, where contracts, milestone agreements, working papers, publications, press releases, and overheads are stored. These data banks are primarily useful for novices and new hires. A few firms have set up discussion databases in which archival material and reports are enlivened with notes and chatroom-like interactions about lessons learned. These more active sources, where key participants record their experiences as well as respond to others, are potentially quite valuable. Nevertheless they have, according to some informants, a somewhat sterile feel to them, like critiquing others' critiques of a performance, rather than engaging the performance itself. And, to many people, there simply is not sufficient time to join in these discussions. They are too busy with the press of daily activities.

Informal seminars on lessons learned from a partnership, particularly when staff from multiple functions are involved, are a good way to transmit experience across projects. Only limited effort needs to be made to organize such presentations, so they have the advantage of freshness and a hands-on feel. Nevertheless, these seminars, unless performed on a more or less regular basis, are much more valuable in a smaller company than a larger one because the information diffuses more extensively. I have not personally encountered any case where participants from both sides of a collaboration made a joint presentation, although almost every time I suggest such an approach. I am met with a comment, "That would be interesting!" Talking about failures, shortcomings, and rough spots in a relationship would be equally as valuable as discussions of successes and lessons learned. But I have rarely seen presentations where such difficulties are openly discussed. To be sure, these conversations are often pursued, heatedly, but off-stage, again the closed nature of the discussion inhibits the transfer of information. Moreover, problematic points are often dismissed as idiosyncratic to a particular party and not felt to be generalizable. While there is, of course, truth to such claims, a large part of building a reputation as a preferred partner is learning how to broker unexpected disputes.

Many biotech and pharmaceutical firms turn to multi-functional teams to supervise collaborative activities, building on the popular idea of the heavyweight teams used in product development efforts. The more thoughtful teams opt to disseminate their discussions either through electronic posting of minutes of their meetings or by having different participants act as scribes to send out short summaries of meetings.

In all these activities, there is a persistent tension between those activities done informally and on an ad hoc basis and those efforts that are more formalized and structured. Clearly, there are tradeoffs with both approaches. The insight appreciated by only a minority of the firms that we have had contact with is that developing routines for the transmission of information and experience does not necessarily entail formalization. Information can be conveyed routinely through informal means. While formal repositories and powerful task forces can be useful, they are too often not a forum in which outside input is allowed. Building routines for regular contact without formalization allows for the possibility that participants not only contribute ideas, they will take lessons learned and spread them in unexpected and unobtrusive ways.

CONCLUSION

In innovation-driven fields, firms are engaged in learning races. These contests proceed on parallel tracks, one involving learning *from* collaborations, the other concerns learning *how* to collaborate. Both contests require the development of skills to facilitate the transfer of information and knowledge and their subsequent deployment in other situations. In some respects, the task of learning from outside parties is more difficult. But perhaps because of the importance of the task and/or its considerable expense, organizations in the biotechnology and pharmaceutical fields are rapidly developing the capability to collaborate with a diverse array of partners to speed the timely development of new medicines. Much less refined is the more mundane but difficult and vital task of transferring information and knowledge obtained from external parties throughout the organization. This is done in order that subsequent actions are informed by, and strategic thinking based on, these experiences. A variety of efforts at learning are underway, ranging from electronic discussions to data depositories to seminars to regular meetings of heavyweight teams. All these activities reflect efforts to see that information becomes more widely diffused, and that with reflection and interpretation, becomes "thickened" into knowledge. But developing routines for knowledge dissemination is always a double-edged sword: informal mechanisms may preclude wide dissemination, while formal procedures can inhibit learning. The challenge is to develop regular venues for the informal transmission of information, such that the process itself becomes tied to knowledge seeking and creation.

ACKNOWLEDGMENTS

This article draws on collaborative research done with colleague Ken Koput, and with our graduate research assistants Jason Owen-Smith and Laurel Smith-Doerr. The financial support of the National Science Foundation (NSF grant #9710729) is greatly appreciated.

NOTES

1. See data presented in National Science Board, *Science and Technology Indicators—1996* (Washington, D.C.: U.S. Government Printing Office, 1996).

2. A good discussion is found in H. Chesbrough and D. J. Teece, "When Is Virtual Virtuous: Organizing for Innovation," *Harvard Business Review,* 74/1 (January/February 1996): 65–73.

3. See O. Williamson, "Comparative Economic Organization," *Administrative Science Quarterly,* 36 (1996): 269–296; O. Hart, *Firms, Contracts, and Financial Structure* (New York, NY: Oxford University Press, 1995).

4. Representative examples include Paul Joskow, "Contract Duration and RelationSpecific Investments," *American Economic Review,* 77 (1987): 168–195; Gary Pisano and P. Y. Mang, "Collaborative Product Development and the Market for KnowHow," *Research on Technological Innovation, Management, and Policy,* 5 (1993): 109–136; Phillipe Aghion and Jean Tirole, "On the Management of Innovation," *Quarterly Journal of Economics,* 109 (1994): 361–379.

5. See, for example, Mark Granovetter, "Economic Action and Social Structure: The Problem of Embeddedness," *American Journal of Sociology,* 91 (1985): 481–510; Charles Sabel, "Learning by Monitoring," in N. Smelser and R. Swedberg, eds., *Handbook of Economic Sociology* (Princeton, NJ: Princeton University Press, 1994), pp. 137–165; Brian Uzzi, "The Sources and Consequences of Embeddedness for the Economic Performance of Organizations," *American Sociological Review,* 61 (1996): 624–648.

6. Walter W. Powell, Kenneth Koput, and Laurel

Smith-Doerr, "Interorganizational Collaboration and the Locus of Innovation: Networks of Learning in Biotechnology," *Administrative Science Quarterly,* 41 (1996): 116–145; Peter Grindley and David Teece, "Managing Intellectual Capital: Licensing and Cross-Licensing in Semiconductors and Electronics," *California Management Review,* 38/2 (Winter 1997): 8–41.

7. Josh Lerner and Robert P. Merges, "The Control of Strategic Alliances: An Empirical Analysis of Biotechnology Collaborations," unpublished manuscript, Harvard Business School.

8. Powell et al., op. cit.

9. On the diffusion of matrix management, see L. R. Burns and D. R. Wholey, "Adoption and Abandonment of Matrix Management Programs," *Academy of Management Journal,* 36 (1993): 106–138; on the spread of the "poison pill," see G. Davis, "Agents Without Principles?" *Administrative Science Quarterly,* 36 (1991): 583–613; on the multidivisional form, see D. Palmer, P. D. Jennings, and X. Zhan, "Late Adoption of the Multidivisional Form by Large U.S. Corporations," *Administrative Science Quarterly,* 38 (1993): 100–131; on the diffusion of total quality management, see J. D. Westphal, R. Gulati, and S. Shortell, "Customization or Conformity," *Administrative Science Quarterly,* 42 (1997): 366–394.

10. Walter W. Powell and Laurel Smith-Doerr, "Networks and Economic Life," in N. Smelser and R. Swedberg, eds., *Handbook of Economic Sociology* (Princeton, NJ: Princeton University Press, 1994), pp. 368–402; Richard S. Rosenbloom and Williams J. Spencer, "The Transformation of Industrial Research," *Issues in Science and Technology,* 12/3 (1996): 68–74.

11. For introductions to the political sociology literature, see Gerald Maxwell and Pamela Oliver, *The Critical Mass in Collective Action* (Cambridge: Cambridge University Press, 1993); Sidney Tarrow, *Power in Movement: Social Movements, Collective Action, and Politics* (Cambridge: Cambridge University Press, 1994).

12. This argument draws freely on Cohen and Levinthal's ideas about absorptive capacity, Nelson and Winter's work on developing routines for learning, and Brown and Duguid's ideas on situated learning. See Wesley Cohen and Daniel Levinthal, "Absorptive Capacity: A New Perspective on Learning and Innovation," *Administrative Science Quarterly,* 35 (1990): 128–152; Richard Nelson and Sidney Winter, *An Evolutionary Theory of Economic Change* (Cambridge, MA: Harvard University Press, 1982); John Seeley Brown and Paul Duguid, "Organizational Learning and Communities-of-Practice," *Organization Science,* 2 (1991): 40–57.

13. Lawrence M. Fisher, "Biogen's Triumph against the Odds," *Strategy and Business,* 8 (3rd Quarter 1997): 55–63.

14. See Erick Schonfield, "Merck vs. the Biotech Industry: Which One Is More Potent?" *Fortune,* March 31, 1997, pp. 161–162.

15. See Ian Macneil, "Relational Contracting: What We Do and Do Not Know," *Wisconsin Law Review,* 3 (1985): 483–526.

28

Organizing Knowledge

JOHN SEELY BROWN
PAUL DUGUID

The firm, taken for granted in the conventional economy, appears to have a doubtful future in the information economy. The new technologies that are helping to define this new economy are simultaneously battering the venerable institutions of the old economy—the press, broadcast media, universities, even governments and nations are all under threat. Enthusiasts suggest that no formal organization need or should come between the empowered individual and Marshall McLuhan's amorphous "global village." So it's not surprising to hear that cyberspace has served notice on the firm that its future, at best, may only be virtual.

Many such predictions favor a "transaction cost" view of the firm. Transaction costs are portrayed as the glue that holds an organization together, and many of these are thought to derive from inefficiencies in communication. Thus, it is easy to conclude that the new communications technologies might drive transaction costs so low that hierarchical firms will dissolve into markets of self-organizing individuals.[1]

Recently, however, through the work of Ikujiro Nonaka and others, a "knowledge-based" view of the firm has risen to counter the transaction-cost approach. Knowledge-based arguments suggest that organizational knowledge provides a synergistic advantage not replicable in the marketplace. Thus its knowledge, not its transaction costs, holds an organization together.[2] The knowledge-based view provides vital insight into why firms exist (and will continue to exist) and thus why organizing knowledge is a critical part of what firms do.

While knowledge is often thought to be the property of individuals, a great deal of knowledge is both produced and held collectively. Such knowledge is readily generated when people work together in the tightly knit groups known as "communities of practice."[3] As such work and such communities are a common feature of organizations, organizational knowledge is inevitably heavily social in character. Because of its social origin, this sort of knowledge is not frictionless. Beyond communities, locally developed knowledge is difficult to organize. The hard work of organizing knowledge is a critical aspect of what firms and other organizations do.

There are those who see the organization as primarily the unintended consequence of individuals acting in isolation and who believe that an organization's central challenge is to discover knowledge. Once found, such arguments tend to assume, knowledge should travel easily. However, organizations are often replete with knowledge (and also deeply embedded in larger fields or "ecologies" of knowledge). The critical challenge, from this perspective, is to make this knowledge cohere.[4]

It is easy to assume that knowledge-based arguments apply only to what are recognized as "knowledge" firms. These are firms (in software or biotechnology, for example) whose market value far outstrips

Copyright © 1998 by The Regents of the University of California. Reprinted from the *California Management Review,* Vol. 40, No. 3. By permission of The Regents.

their conventional assets and rests instead on intellectual capital. The transaction-cost view, it might seem, still applies to every other form of organization. This, however, is not the case. All firms are in essence knowledge organizations. Their ability to outperform the marketplace rests on the continuous generation and synthesis of collective, organizational knowledge.[5] For all organizations, the cultivation of this knowledge—often an implicit, unreflecting cultivation—is the essence of developing a core competency to maintain the organization and resist its dissolution.

The organizational knowledge that constitutes "core competency" is more than "know-what," explicit knowledge which may be shared by several. A core competency requires the more elusive "know-how"—the particular ability to put know-what into practice.[6] While these two work together, they circulate separately. Know-what circulates with relative ease. Consequently, of course, it is often hard to protect. (Hence the current crisis in intellectual property laws.) Know-how, by contrast, embedded in work practice (usually *collective* work practice) is sui generis and thus relatively easy to protect.[7] Conversely, however, it can be hard to spread, coordinate, benchmark, or change.

The recent vogue for knowledge management must encompass not simply protecting intellectual property in canonical knowledge organizations, but fostering this more complex form of organizational capital. In practice, this sort of fostering is very much what good managers do, but as knowledge production becomes more critical, they will need to do it more reflectively.

ENDS OF ORGANIZATION

Self-Organizing Systems

Disintermediation, demassification, and disaggregation have become the watchwords of cyberspace. New technologies are apparently breaking collectives down into individual units. (Indeed, it sometimes seems that the only large aggregates needed for the "third wave" will be very long words.) Any form of coherence and coordination beyond the individual, it is predicted, will be the effect of self-organizing systems.[8]

Undoubtedly, in the hands of prominent economists like Kenneth Arrow or Friedrich Hayek, analysis of self-organizing "catallaxies" has helped reveal the

very real limits of formal organization.[9] In particular, they have helped show the folly of planning economies or ignoring markets. They do not, however, necessarily reject planning or nonmarket behavior on a more local scale. Nor do they prove, as some would have us believe, that deliberate organization is somehow vicious, unnatural, and anti-market. As Hayek himself noted, within spontaneous catallaxies, goal-oriented organizational planning is important.

Curiously, many who argue for self organization often sound less like economists than entomologists: bees, ants, and termites (as well as bats and other small mammals) provide much of the self-organizing case. In a related vein, others draw examples from "artificial life," whose systems are themselves usually modeled on insect- and animal-like behavior.[10] While these provide forceful models, it's important to notice their limits. Humans and insects show many intriguing similarities, but these should not mask some important differences.

In particular, most champions of complex adaptive systems, particularly those of artificial life, overlook the importance to human behavior of deliberate social organization. It is well known that humans distinguish themselves from most other life forms by the increasingly sophisticated technologies they design. It is less often noted that they also distinguish themselves by designing sophisticated social institutions. To pursue the analogies from entomology or artificial life much further, we would need to know what might happen if bugs decided to form a committee or pass a law or artificial agents organized a strike or joined a firm.

Ants moving across a beach, for example, do exhibit elaborate, collective patterns that emerge as each individual adjusts to the environment. In this way, they reflect important aspects of human behavior—of, for example, the uncoordinated synchronicity of sunbathers on the same beach seeking the sun or trying to keep the blown sand out of their sandwiches. But, unlike the sunbathers, ants don't construct coastal highways to reach the beach; or beachfront supermarkets to provide food; or farms to supply the supermarket; or coastal commissions to limit highway building, supermarkets, and farming; or supreme courts to rule on the infringement on constitutionally protected private property rights of coastal commissions; or, indeed, constitutions or property rights at all.

Thus, while ants easily fall victim to diminishing

provisions of their local ecology, humans do not. By organizing collectively, people have learned to produce more food out of the same areas of land, to extend known energy resources and search for new ones, to establish new regions for human endeavor, and to design the very technologies that are now paradoxically invoked as the end of organization. In all such cases, organization has helped to foster and focus humanity's most valuable resource: its infinitely renewable knowledge base.[11]

But perhaps most significantly of all, humanity has relied on organization not merely to harness advantage, but to ward off disasters produced by the downside of self-organizing behavior. For example, establishing and continually adjusting socially acknowledged property rights have limited the "tragedy of the commons." Establishing certain trading regulations has prevented markets from spontaneously imploding. Such institutional constraints help channel self-organizing behavior and knowledge production in productive rather than destructive directions. This ability may be one of humanity's greatest assets.

It is easy to cite the undeniable power of spontaneous organization as a way to damn formal organization. However, it makes no more sense to demonize institutions than it does to demonize self-organizing systems. Rather, each must be deployed to restrain the other's worst excesses. That challenge is profoundly difficult, facing as it must the complex, reflexive feedback loops that social institutions create. These make human organization quite different from that of other species (and consequently make social sciences different from natural sciences).

Institutions and Technology

If institutions are endemic to human society, then it seems a mistake to set them in opposition to technologies or economies as some of the cybergurus do. Indeed, a glance back to the last great period of technological innovation suggests the importance of institutions. The end of the nineteenth century gave us the telegraph, the train, the car, the telephone, the airplane, the cinema, and much more. Yet it has been argued that the incredible creative energies of the nineteenth century are evident less in industry, engineering, or the arts than in the new kinds of social institutions that developed (among which are the limited liability corporation, the research university, and the union).[12] Moreover, Nobel economist Douglass North suggests that it

was the absence of suitable institutions that caused the century-long lag between the dawn of industrial revolution and the late-nineteenth century's dramatic technological and economic expansion. Similarly, business historian Alfred Chandler claims that half of this expansion resulted from organizational, not technological innovation.[13]

So, while the changing economy may indeed be suffering from the drag of "second wave" institutions, as Alvin Toffler suggests, it doesn't necessarily follow (as Toffler's wired disciples often seem to think) that therefore the third wave will not need institutions at all. One clue to today's "productivity paradox" (which notes that the increasing investment in new technology is not yet showing up in increased national productivity) may well be that society is still struggling to develop third-wave institutions adequate for a new economy.[14]

If nothing else, these examples suggest a complex relationship between organizations and technologies which crude juxtaposition of new technologies and old institutions oversimplifies. It is often pointed out that the arrival of printing technology in the West profoundly destabilized the Catholic church, the dominant institution of its day. But even here, the direction was not simply against institutions. Printing allowed other institutions, the university in particular (and, in some arguments, the modern state) to flourish. And today, while communications technologies have dispersed power and control in some sectors, leading to disaggregation and empowerment, in others they have clearly led to centralization and concentration. Francis Fukuyama points, for instance, to the extraordinary success of firms like Wal-Mart and Benetton, both of which have used technology to centralize decision making and disempower their peripheries. In other sectors (communication in particular) the trend has also been towards concentration.

More generally, the relationship between improving technologies and shrinking organizations has not been linear. The telegraph, typewriter, and telephone—which launched the communications revolution—allowed the growth and spread of the giant firms of industrial capitalism as well as the proliferation of small businesses.[15] Similarly, today the emergence of small, adaptable firms may not point in any simple way to market disaggregation. Research into small firms and start-ups highlights the concept of the "embedded firm."[16] These arguments indicate that many important relations between firms, let alone *within* firms, are not ultimately self-organizing, market relations. Increasingly, they reflect complex interorganizational networks. Even where interfirm relations are extremely competitive, cross-sector cooperation and agreements are often highly significant. In the cutthroat world of silicon chip manufacture, for example, firms continuously cross-license one another's patents and even engage in joint research through SEMATECH, a supraorganizational body. The classic antithesis between hierarchy (the firm) and market—even when hedged with the notion of "hybrids"—seems inadequate to describe what is going on. To understand them, we need better insight into what organizations do, and how knowledge plays an important part.

ORGANIZATIONAL ADVANTAGE

The firm has a future because it provides an important means of knowledge generation. In particular, it gives rise to types of knowledge not supported in a marketplace of individuals linked only by market relations. It also plays an important role in the development and circulation of complex knowledge in society—circulation that is too readily assumed to be friction free.

Know-How and the Community of Practice

Knowledge is usually thought of as the possession of individuals. Something people carry around in their heads and pass between each other. Know-what is to a significant degree like this. Know-how is different.

Know-how embraces the ability to put know-what into practice. It is a disposition, brought out in practice. Thus, know-how is critical in making knowledge actionable and operational. A valuable manager, for example, is not simply one who knows in the abstract how to act in certain circumstances, but who in practice can recognize the circumstances and acts appropriately when they come along. That disposition only reveals itself when those circumstances occur.

Such dispositional knowledge is not only revealed in practice. It is also created out of practice. That is, know-how is to a great extent the product of experience and the tacit insights experience provides. A friend and lawyer once told us that law school—with its research, writing, and moot courts—prepared her for almost everything she encountered in her work. It did not, however, prepare her for what she did most: answer the phone. That ability—the ability to deal in

real time with critical situations, demanding clients, and irrevocable commitments, putting the knowledge she had acquired in school to effective use in practice—she was only able to acquire in practice itself. Her own and her colleagues' ongoing practice has created an invaluable reservoir of dispositional knowledge, which she calls on (and improves) all the time.

Experience at work creates its own knowledge. And as most work is a collective, cooperative venture, so most dispositional knowledge is intriguingly collective—less held by individuals than shared by work groups. This view of knowledge as a social property stands at odds with the pervasive ideas of knowledge as individual. Yet synergistic potential of certain people working in unison—a Gilbert and Sullivan, a Merchant and Ivory, a Young and Rice, or a Pippin and Jordan—is widely acknowledged. In less-exalted work places, too, the ability of certain groups to outstrip their individual potential when working together is a common feature.

Shared know-how can turn up quite unexpectedly. Julian Orr, a colleague at Xerox, studied the firm's "Tech Reps," the technicians who service machines on site. These technicians work most of the time in relative isolation, alone at a customer's office. And they carry with them extensive documentation about the machines they work with. They would seem to be the last people to have collective dispositional knowledge. Yet Orr revealed that despite the individualist character of their work and the large geographical areas they often have to cover, Tech Reps take great pains to spend time with one another at lunch or over coffee. Here they continuously swap "war stories" about malfunctioning machines that outstripped the documentation. In the process of telling and analyzing such stories, the reps both feed into and draw on the group's collective knowledge.[17]

Orr describes an extraordinary scene in which one technician brought in another to help tackle a machine that had defied all standard diagnostic procedures. Like two jazz players involved in an extended, improvisational riff, they spent an afternoon picking up each other's half-finished sentences and partial insights while taking turns to run the machine and watch it crash until finally and indivisibly they reached a coherent account of why the machine didn't work. They tested the theory. It proved right. And the machine was fixed.

This case and Orr's study as a whole suggest that,

even for apparently individual workers armed with extensive know-what, collective know-how can be highly significant. More generally it supports the notion that collective practice leads to forms of collective knowledge, shared sensemaking, and distributed understanding that doesn't reduce to the content of individual heads.

A group across which such know-how and sensemaking are shared—the group which needs to work together for its dispositional know-how to be put into practice—has been called a "community of practice." In the course of their ongoing practice, the members of such a group will develop into a de facto community. (Often, the community, like the knowledge, is implicit. Communities of practice do not necessarily think of themselves as a community in the conventional sense. Equally, conventional communities are not necessarily communities of practice.) Through practice, a community of practice develops a shared understanding of what it does, of how to do it, and how it relates to other communities and their practices—in all, a "world view." This changing understanding comprises the community's collective knowledge base. The processes of developing the knowledge and the community are significantly interdependent: the practice develops the understanding, which can reciprocally change the practice and extend the community. In this context, knowledge and practice are intricately involved. (For a related argument, see Nonaka's celebrated "Knowledge Creation Spiral.")[18]

This picture of knowledge embedded in practice and communities does not dismiss the idea of personal, private knowledge. What people have by virtue of membership in a community of practice, however, is not so much personal, modular knowledge as shared, partial knowledge.[19] Individual and collective knowledge in this context bear on one another much like the parts of individual performers to a complete musical score, the lines of each actor to a movie script, or the roles of team members to the overall performance of a team and a game. Each player may know his or her part. But on its own, that part doesn't make much sense. Alone it is significantly incomplete: it requires the ensemble to make sense of it.[20]

Communities of Practice and Organizations

If in many situations, work and knowledge do not readily decompose into the possession of individuals but remain stubbornly group properties, then markets themselves do not readily reduce to homo economicus, the idealized individual. Nonmarket organization (the community of practice) may be a salient factor of market activity.

Does this suggest that, if nonmarket organization is needed at all, it is only at the level of community of practice? that everything else can be done in the market? On the contrary, most formal organizations are not single communities of practice, but, rather, hybrid groups of overlapping and interdependent communities. Such hybrid collectives represent another level in the complex process of knowledge creation. Intercommunal relationships allow the organization to develop collective, coherent, synergistic organizational knowledge out of the potentially separate, independent contributions of the individual communities. The outcome is what we think of as organizational knowledge, embracing not just organizational know-what but also organizational know-how.

Cross-community organization is important because it helps to overcome some of the problems communities of practice create for themselves. For instance, as Dorothy Leonard-Barton points out, isolated communities can get stuck in ruts, turning core competencies into core rigidities. When they do, they need external stimuli to propel them forward.[21]

Communities of practice, while powerful sources of knowledge, can easily be blinkered by the limitations of their own world view. In a study of technological innovation, for example, Raghu Garud and Michael A. Rappa show how even the most sophisticated of knowledge workers can fail to recognize quite damning evidence.[22] New knowledge often requires new forms of evaluation, and when the two are produced together, knowledge, belief, and evaluation may only reinforce one another, while evaluation independent of that belief appears irrelevant.

Garud and Rappa's study explores this self-deluding/self-reinforcing social behavior in highly technological communities, where counterevidence is usually assumed to be easily capable of overwhelming belief. Obviously, such problematic interdependence between belief and evaluation is even more likely in areas where what counts as evidence is less clear cut and where beliefs, hunches, predictions, and intimations are all there is to go on—which, of course, is the case in most areas of human behavior.

Markets offer one very powerful way to punish self-deluding/self-reinforcing behavior or core rigidities once these have set in.[23] Such punishment tends, however, to be severe, drastic, and reserved for organizations as a whole. Organizations present an alternative antidote, which works more readily at the community level and is both more incremental and less destructive. By yoking diverse communities—with different belief systems and distinct evaluative practices—together into cohesive hybrids, organizations as a whole challenge the limits of each community's belief. This process generates knowledge through what Hirshhorn calls the "productive tension" or Leonard-Barton "creative abrasion," forcing particular communities beyond their own limits and their own evaluative criteria.[24]

Thus while markets punish those who produce bad ideas (or fail to produce at all), organizations work to produce beneficial knowledge out of social (rather than market) relations. The productive side of organizational tension, drawing on the experience of people throughout an organization, produces knowledge that requires systemic, not individual explanation. It adds value to the organization as a whole (and redeems those otherwise intractable battles between designers and engineers, sales and marketing, or accounting and almost any other division).

As most people know from experience, cross-divisional synthesis is itself an achievement. But organizations must reach beyond synthesis to synergy. In so doing, they both draw on and continuously create their unique organizational know-how—their ability to do what their competitors cannot. For this they must produce true, coherent organizational knowledge (which is quite distinct from an organization's knowledge—the scattered, uncoordinated insights of each individual in its community of practice). Organizations that fail to achieve this particular synthesis are most likely to fall prey to market alternatives.

DIVISIONS OF LABOR AND DIVISIONS OF KNOWLEDGE

Search and Retrieval

In many ways the relationship between communities of practice and organizations presents an parallel to that between individuals and communities of practice.

Yet there are important differences in the way knowledge moves in each relationship.

Organizing knowledge across hybrid communities is the essential activity of organizational management. It is also difficult, though why is not often appreciated. Certainly, most managers will acknowledge that getting knowledge to move around organizations can be difficult. In general, however, such problems are reduced to issues of information flow. If, as the saying goes, organizations don't always know what they know, the solution is seen to lie primarily in better techniques for search and retrieval. Given the opportunity, information appears to flow readily. Hence the belief that technology, which can shift information efficiently, can render organizations, which shift it inefficiently, obsolete. A great deal of hope (and money) is thus being placed on the value of Intranets. Intranets are indeed valuable, but social knowledge suggests that there is more to consider both with regards to search and retrieval.

The distribution of knowledge in an organization, or in society as a whole, reflects the social division of labor. As Adam Smith insightfully explained, the division of labor is a great source of dynamism and efficiency. Specialized groups are capable of producing highly specialized knowledge. The tasks undertaken by communities of practice develop particular, local, and highly specialized knowledge within the community.

From the organizational standpoint, however, this knowledge is as divided as the labor that produced it. Moreover, what separates divided knowledge is not only its explicit content but the implicit shared practices and know-how that help produce it. In particular, as Garud and Rappa's example suggests, communities develop their own distinct criteria for what counts as evidence and what provides "warrants"—the endorsements for knowledge that encourage people to rely on it and hence make it actionable. (Warrants are particularly important in situations in which people confront increasing amounts of information, ideas, and beliefs; warrants show people what to attend to and what to avoid.) The locally embedded nature of these practices and warrants can make knowledge extremely "sticky," to use Eric von Hippel's apt term.[25]

If the division of labor produces the division of knowledge, then it would seem reasonable to conclude that the market, used to coordinate the division of labor, would serve to coordinate the division of knowledge. But markets work best with commodities, and this "sticky" knowledge isn't easily commodified. Within communities, producing, warranting, and propagating knowledge are almost indivisible. Between communities, as these get teased apart, division becomes prominent and problematic. Hence, the knowledge produced doesn't readily turn into something with exchange value or use value elsewhere. It takes organizational work to develop local knowledge for broader use. Development of knowledge in the organization is a process somewhat analogous to the way a film production company takes a story idea and, stage by stage, develops it into a movie.

Thus, ideas of "retrieving" locally developed knowledge for use elsewhere doesn't address the whole issue. Furthermore, organizations, while they may help get beyond "retrieval," present problems with the antecedent problem of search.

Organizational Blindness

Organizations, as economists have long realized, offer an alternative to markets. Instead of synchronizing goods and labor through markets, they do it through hierarchy. This allows them to overcome some of the stickiness arising from the indivisibility of know-how and practice. Nonetheless, in the organization of knowledge, hierarchical relations unfortunately introduce their own weaknesses. Hierarchical divisions of labor often distinguish thinkers from doers, mental from manual labor, strategy (the knowledge required at the top of a hierarchy) from tactics (the knowledge used at the bottom). Above all, a mental–manual division predisposes organizations to ignore a central asset, the value of the know-how created throughout all its parts.

For example, the Xerox service technicians develop highly insightful knowledge about the situated use (and misuse) of the complex machines they service. As such machines encounter a wide range of locations (some hot, some cold, some dry, some humid) and an inexhaustible range of uses (and abuses), the possible combinations make it impossible to calculate and anticipate all behaviors and problems that might arise. Knowledge about these only emerges in practice. Yet mental–manual divisions tend to make this knowledge invisible to the organization as a whole.

In an analysis of the importance (and anomalous

position) of technologists in the modern work place, Stephen Barley has argued forcefully that the knowledge potential in the practice of such front-line employees must eventually force organizations to reconsider the division of labor and the possible loci of knowledge production. As Henry Chesebrough and David Teece point out, "some competencies may be on the factory floor, some in the R&D labs, some in the executive suits." The key to organizational knowledge is to weave it all together. Successful organizational synthesis of knowledge requires discovering knowledge as it emerges in practice. That can't be done if when and where to look are predetermined ex ante.[26]

BEYOND SEARCH AND RETRIEVAL

Within and Between

Bringing this knowledge into view is only a first step, however. Restricted search paths alone are not the problem, significant though these may be. Organizations that set out to identify useful knowledge often underestimate the challenge of making that knowledge useful elsewhere. Robert Cole's study of Hewlett-Packard's approach to quality, for example, shows how the firm successfully pursued "best practices" throughout the corporation. The search, however, assumed that, once these practices were identified, the knowledge (and practice) would spread to where it was needed. In the end, HP was quite successful in identifying the practices. It was not, however, so successful in moving them.[27]

Some knowledge moves quite easily. People assume that it is explicit knowledge that moves easily and tacit knowledge that moves with difficulty.[28] It is, rather, socially embedded knowledge that "sticks," because it is deeply rooted in practice. Within communities, practice helps to generate knowledge and evince collective know-how. The warranting mechanisms—the standards of judgment whereby people distinguish what is worthwhile and valid from what is not—inhere in the knowledge. Consequently, trying to move the knowledge without the practice involves moving the know-what without the know-how.

Due to its social origins, knowledge moves differently *within* communities than it does *between* them. Within communities, knowledge is continuously embedded in practice and thus circulates easily. Members of a community implicitly share a sense of what practice is and what the standards for judgment are, and this supports the spread of knowledge. Without this sharing, the community disintegrates.

Between communities, however, where by definition practice is no longer shared, the know-how, know-what, and warrants embedded in practice must separate out for knowledge to circulate. These divisions becomes prominent and problematic. Different communities of practice have different standards, different ideas of what is significant, different priorities, and different evaluating criteria. What looks like a best practice in California may not turn out to be the best practice in Singapore (as HP found out).

The divisions between communities tend to encourage local innovation, as Adam Smith recognized, but they also encourage isolation. Anyone who has spent some time on a university campus knows how knowledge-based boundaries can isolate highly productive communities from one another. That it is very hard to get sociologists and mathematicians to learn from one another is obvious. What is sometimes less clear is that biochemists can't always share insights with chemists, economic historians with historians, economists with the business school, and so forth. Different precepts and different attitudes, shaped by practice, make interchange between quite similar subjects remarkably difficult, and thus they invisibly pressure disciplines to work among themselves rather than to engage in cross-disciplinary research. Over time, disciplines increasingly divide rather than combine.

On the campus, however, work across different communities has been relatively unimportant. In the past, few have expected a campus as a whole to produce synthesized, collective insight. Physicists work on physics problems; historians on history problems; and except when they come to blows over the history of physics the two, like most other departments, lead predominantly independent lives.

Firms, by contrast, cannot afford to work this way. When they get to the point they are so loosely connected that there is no synthesis or synergy of what is produced in their various communities—when, as Teece and colleagues argue, there is no "coherence"—then a firm has indeed lost its edge over the market. The firm then needs either to work towards synergy or divest until it achieves coherence.[29] Indeed, firms are valuable exactly to the extent that, unlike universities,

they make communities of practice that expand their vision and achieve collective coherence. Consequently, the problematic *between* relationship is a critical organizational feature—and one that demands significant organizational investment.

It is a mistake to equate knowledge and information and to assume that difficulties can be overcome with information technologies. New knowledge is continuously being produced and developed in the different communities of practice throughout an organization. The challenge occurs in evaluating it and moving it. New knowledge is not capable of the sorts of friction-free movement usually attributed to information. Moreover, because moving knowledge between communities and synthesizing it takes a great deal of work, deciding what to invest time and effort in as well as determining what to act upon is a critical task for management.

STICKINESS AND LEAKINESS

The "leakiness" of knowledge out of—and into—organizations, however, presents an interesting contrast to its internal stickiness.[30] Knowledge often travels more easily between organizations than it does within them. For while the division of labor erects boundaries within firms, it also produces extended communities that lie across the external boundaries of firms. Moving knowledge among groups with similar practices and overlapping memberships can thus sometimes be relatively easy compared to the difficulty of moving it among heterogeneous groups within a firm. Similar practice in a common field can allow ideas to flow. Indeed, it's often harder to stop ideas spreading than to spread them.

A study of interorganizational work by Kristen Kreiner and Majken Schultz suggests that the tendency of knowledge to spread easily reflects not suitable technology, but suitable social contexts. They show how many of the disciplinary links between business and academia are informal. They argue that the informal relations between firms and universities are more extensive and probably more significant than the formal ones. Informal relations dominate simply because they are easier, building on established social links. Formal interfirm relations, by contrast, can require tricky intrafirm negotiations between quite diverse communities (senior management, lawyers, and so forth).

Studies of biotechnology support this view. A study by Walter Powell reveals biotechnologists working extensively across the boundaries of organizations. Some articles in this field have more than one hundred authors from different (and different types of) institutions.[31] Their extensive collaboration undoubtedly relies on communications technologies. But these are available to researchers in other fields where such collaboration does not occur. Biotechnology is distinct in that being a relatively young, emerging field, its researchers are significantly linked through personal connections. The field is not as tight as a local community of practice, but nonetheless relations are dense enough and practices sufficiently similar to help knowledge spread. While a field is small and relatively unfragmented, practitioners have a lot in common: their training, their institutional backgrounds, their interests, and in particular the warrants with which they evaluate what is important from what is not.[32]

People connected this way can rely on complex networks of overlapping communities, common backgrounds, and personal relationships to help evaluate and propagate knowledge. In such conditions, practices are fairly similar and consequently the barriers *between* different groups are relatively low.[33] In such knowledge ecologies, knowledge that is sticky within organizations can become remarkably fluid outside of them, causing great difficulties for the intellectual property side of knowledge management. The challenge of plugging these leaks is significant. But cutting off the outflow can also cut off the inflow of knowledge. Living in a knowledge ecology is a reciprocal process, with organizations feeding into each other.

TOWARD AN ARCHITECTURE FOR ORGANIZATIONAL KNOWLEDGE

The way ecologies spread knowledge helps point to some of the ways that organizations can help to propagate knowledge internally and develop an enabling architecture for organizational knowledge. Social strategies for promoting the spread of knowledge between communities can be described in terms of "translation," "brokering," and "boundary objects"—terms developed by the sociologists Susan Leigh Star and James Griesemer.[34]

Translators

Organizational translators are individuals who can frame the interests of one community in terms of another community's perspective. The role of translator can be quite complex and the translator must be sufficiently knowledgeable about the work of both communities to be able to translate. The powerful position of translator requires trust, since translation is rarely entirely innocent (translators may favor the interests of one group over another deliberately or inadvertently). Yet, participants must be able to rely on translators to carry negotiations in both directions, making them mutually intelligible to the communities involved. The difficulty of doing this makes translators extremely valuable and extremely difficult to find. External mediators and consultants are often called in to provide such translation.

Knowledge Brokers

The role of in-firm brokers, in contrast to that of translators, involves participation rather than mediation. They are a feature of overlapping communities, whereas translators work among mutually exclusive ones. In an analysis of the diffusion of knowledge across networks, sociologist Mark Granovetter noted that overlaps are hard to develop in communities with very strong internal ties. These tend to preclude external links. Thus Granovetter argued for the "strength of weak ties," suggesting that it was often people loosely linked to several communities who facilitated the flow of knowledge among them.[35]

As almost all communities within an organization overlap, those who participate in the practices of several communities may in theory broker knowledge between them. Trust is less of a tendentious issue than with translation. Brokers who truly participate in both worlds, unlike translators, are subject to the consequences of messages they carry, whatever the direction.

Boundary Objects

Boundary objects are another way to forge coordinating links among communities, bringing them, intentionally or unintentionally, into negotiation. Boundary objects are objects of interest to each community involved but viewed or used differently by each of them. These can be physical objects, technologies, or techniques shared by the communities. Through them, a community can come to understand what is common and what is distinct about another community, its practices, and its world view. Boundary objects not only help to clarify the attitudes of other communities, they can also make a community's own presuppositions apparent to itself, encouraging reflection and "second-loop" learning.[36]

Contracts are a classic example of boundary objects. They develop as different groups converge, through negotiation, on an agreed meaning that has significance for both. Documents more generally play a similar role, and forms and lists that pass between and coordinate different communities make significant boundary objects. Plans and blueprints are another form of boundary object. Architectural plans, for instance, define a common boundary among architects, contractors, engineers, city planners, cost estimators, suppliers and clients. Severally and collectively these groups negotiate their different interests, priorities, and practices around the compelling need to share an interpretation of these important documents.

To help produce intercommunal negotiation, organizations can seed the border between communities with boundary objects. The idea-fomenting metaphors that Nonaka describes draw some of their power by being boundary objects.[37] They work within groups to spark ideas. Once a group has found one metaphor particularly powerful, that metaphor may also serve to foster understanding between groups.

Business Processes as Boundary Objects: Enabling and Coercive

Business processes can play a similar role. Ideally, processes should allow groups, through negotiation, to align themselves with one another and with the organization as a whole. Business processes can enable productive cross-boundary relations as different groups within an organization negotiate and propagate a shared interpretation. In the right circumstances, the interlocking practices that result from such negotiations should cohere both with one another and with the overall strategy of the company. The processes provide some structure, the negotiations provide room for improvisation and accommodation, and the two together can result in coordinated, loosely coupled, but systemic behavior.[38]

Many business processes, however, attempt not to support negotiation but to pre-empt it, trying to impose compliance and conformity through what Geoffrey Bowker and Susan Leigh Star call "frozen negotiation."

Here Paul Adler and Bryan Borys's discussion of "enabling" and "coercive" bureaucracies suggests the importance of enabling and coercive business processes. The first produces fruitful intercommunal relations and, in the best case, widespread strategic alignment; the second is more likely to produce rigid organizations with strong central control but little adaptability.[39]

TECHNOLOGY ISSUES

As noted earlier, the ease or difficulty of moving knowledge is a reflection of its social context. Technologies inevitably have an enormous role to play, but they play it only to the extent that they respond to the social context. The desire to disaggregate, disintermediate, and demassify, however, is more likely to produce socially unresponsive behavior.

A good deal of new technology attends primarily to individuals and the explicit information that passes between them. To support the flow of knowledge, within or between communities and organizations, this focus must expand to encompass communities and the full richness of communication. Successful devices such as the telephone and the fax, like the book and newspaper before them, spread rapidly not simply because they carried information to individuals, but because they were easily embedded in communities.

Supporting the Informal

One important issue for technology involves the way the local informality found within communities differs from levels of explicitness and formality often demanded between communities—much as the slang and informal language people use among immediate colleagues differ from the formal language of presentations or contracts. The demands for formality demanded by technologies can disrupt more productive informal relations. For instance, in many situations, asking for explicit permission changes social dynamics quite dramatically—and receiving a direct rejection can change them even further. Consequently, people negotiate many permissions tacitly. A great deal of trust grows up around the ability to work with this sort of implicit negotiation. Direct requests and insistence of rights and duties do not work well.

Technologies thus have to include different degrees of formality and trust.[40] The range will become apparent as different types of "trusted systems" being to emerge. At one end are systems that more or less eliminate the need for social trust. They simply prevent people from behaving in ways other than those explicitly negotiated ahead of time and constrained by the technology. Everything must be agreed (and paid for, usually) ex ante. For high-security demands, such technologies will be increasingly important. People are glad they can trust bank machines and Internet software servers. But if new technologies ask people to negotiate all their social interrelations like their banking relations, they will leave little room for the informal, the tacit, and the socially embedded—which is where know-how lies and important work gets done.

This choice between formality and informality will have repercussions in the design of complex technologies. But it also has repercussions in the implementation of such things as corporate intranets and mail systems. Increasingly, workplaces seek to control the sorts of interactions and exchanges these are used for. Yet these systems in many ways replace the coffee pot and the water cooler as the site of informal but highly important knowledge diffusion. Limiting their informality is likely to limit their importance.

Reach and Reciprocity

As continual chatter about the global information network reminds us, information technology has extensive reach. Markets supported by this technological reach spread further and further daily. However, it is a mistake to conclude that knowledge networks, which require a social context, will spread in the same fashion. Technology to support the spread of new knowledge needs to be able to deal not with the *reach* involved in delivery so much as with the *reciprocity* inherent in shared practice. The ability to support complex, multi-directional, implicit negotiation will become increasingly important.

The Internet provides an interesting example of the way people retrofit information technology to enhance its social capacities. It was designed primarily so that computers could exchange electronic information and computer users could exchange files. Early in its development, though, some insightful programmers at Bolt Beranek and Newman piggy-backed e-mail on the protocol for transferring files. This highly social medium superimposed on the fetch-and-deliver infrastructure planted the seed that would transform this scientific network into the social network

that has flourished so dramatically in the last few years. E-mail still accounts for the bulk of Internet traffic. Similarly, the World Wide Web has been the most recent and dramatic example that further accelerated the social use of the technology. Its designer, Tim Berners-Lee, a programmer at the CERN laboratories in Switzerland, saw that the Internet was much more interesting if used not simply for exchanging information between individuals, but to support "collaborators . . . in a common project." That social imperative, quite as much as the technology, has driven the Web's extraordinary evolution.[41]

Interactivity, Participation, Learning

One of the Net's greatest assets is that it is interactive and thus has the potential reciprocity to foster knowledge and learning. On campuses, conventional classes now regularly increase not so much reach as reciprocity by using Web pages and listserves (communal mailing lists) to do this. Similarly, well-designed corporate intranets, which supplement more conventional communication, do the same. In particular, these help present and circulate boundary objects. New forms of multicasting, such as the "M-Bone" or Multi-Cast Backbone, offer yet denser prospects for such interaction.[42]

When simply combined with reach, interactivity is often merely burdensome. To cultivate true reciprocity (rather than babble), people often find it necessary to introduce limits on the reach. Listserves now increasingly restrict participation, Web sites demand passwords, and intranets erect firewalls. Imposing limits, however, can prove disadvantageous.

Reciprocity is a feature of what Jean Lave and Etienne Wenger (who developed the notion of "communities of practice") refer to as "legitimate peripheral participation."[43] People learn by taking up a position on the periphery of skilled practice and being allowed (hence the importance of legitimacy) to move slowly from the periphery into the community and the practice involved. New communications technologies provide intriguing forms of peripherality. They allow newcomers to "lurk" on the side of interactions in which they are not taking part and of communities of which they are not members. Students, for example, lurk on the sides of exchanges among graduate students and faculty. Novices oversee the Net traffic among experts. Lave and Wenger also showed, however, how vibrant training programs die once newcomers are cut off from such experienced practice. Closing lists to lurkers can have the same results. Consequently, the negotiation of access, of reach, and of reciprocity in such circumstances needs to remain a complex socio-technological challenge and not simply a technological one.

The rewards of reciprocity are high. Technologies that can recognize and to some extent parse how relations *within* communities (where reciprocity is inevitable) differ from those *between* communities (where reciprocity must be cultivated) may actually help to extend reach between communities without disrupting reciprocity within. Understand the challenges of the *between* relation should be a significant issue for new design—of both technologies and organizations.

Technology that supports not merely the diffusion of know-what, but the development of know-how and that allows for knowledge to be shared rather than marketed. Curiously, this highlights a pervasive trajectory in the development of communications software, where explicit design strategies for exchanging information are repeatedly subverted by users who press for a social network.

CONCLUSION: DIALECTICAL THINKING

The propagandists of cyberspace have a tendency to speak in terms of discontinuity. The new, they always insist, will simply sweep away the old, so they confidently predict that hypertext will replace the book. (Here they might do well to pay attention to *The New York Times's* confident prediction in the 1930s that the typewriter would replace the pencil. The pencil seems to have won that particular struggle.) Or, as in the issue at stake here, the prediction is that communications technology will sweep away the firm.

Undoubtedly, the present technological revolution will sweep many familiar aspects of life away. Nonetheless, sometimes it is useful to think in terms of "both/and" rather than simply "either/or." This seems particularly true when considering the effect of heterogeneous categories on one another, such as the effects of technologies on institutions.

Instead of thinking of individuals vs. institutions, or markets vs. firms, or start-ups vs. large corporations, it may be more instructive to think of how the two are interlaced. From this perspective, it does not seem as though disintermediation, demassification, and disaggregation are the only watchwords of the future. Community, practice, organization, network, and above all organizational knowledge and distributed know-how are equally important.

ACKNOWLEDGMENTS

The authors are grateful for help generously provided by Robert Cole, Susan Haviland, Richard Kade. Johan de Kleer, Bruce Kogut, Kristina Lee, Teresa da Silva Lopes, Ikujiro Nonaka, J.-C. Spender, Sim Sitkin, Participants in the First Berkeley Knowledge Forum, September 1997.

NOTES

1. The classic statement on transaction costs is R. H. Coase, "The Nature of the Firm," *Economica* (1937), pp. 386–405. For more recent explorations, see, for example, Oliver Williamson and Sidney G. Winter, eds., *The Nature of the Firm: Origins, Evolution, and Development* (New York, NY: Oxford University Press, 1993). For relations between technology and transaction costs, see, for example, Thomas W. Malone JoAnne Yates, and Robert Benjamin, "Electronic Markets and Electronic Hierarchies," *Communications of the ACM* (1987), pp. 484–497 or Claudio U. Ciborra, *Teams, Markets, and Systems: Business Innovation and Information Technology* (New York, NY: Cambridge University Press, 1993). For variants of arguments about "the fading boundaries of the firm," see vol. 152 of *Journal of Institutional and Theoretical Economics* (1966). It is interesting to note that Williamson has retreated a little from the totalizing view of transaction costs reflected in many of these works and acknowledged the "complementary perspectives" that an understanding of "embeddedness" contributes. See Oliver Williamson, "*Transaction Cost Economics: How It Works; Where It is Headed,*" Business and Public Policy Working Paper, BPP 67, University of California, Institute of Management, Innovation, and Organization, Berkeley, CA, October 1997.

2. See, for example, Ikujiro Nonaka and Hiotaka Takeuchi, *The Knowledge-Creating Company: How Japanese Companies Create the Dynamics of Innovation* (New York, NY: Oxford University Press, 1995); Bruce Kogut and Udo Zander, "What Firms Do? Coordination, Identity, and Learning," *Organization Science,* 7/5 (1996): 502–518; R. M. Grant, "Toward a Knowledge-Based Theory of the Firm," *Strategic Management Jour-*

nal, 17 (1996): 109–122; J.-C. Spender, "Making Knowledge the Basis of a Dynamic Theory of the Firm," *Strategic Management Journal,* 17 (1966): 45–62; Dorothy Leonard-Barton, *Wellsprings of Knowledge: Building and Sustaining the Sources of Innovation* (Cambridge, MA: Harvard Business School Press, 1995). For a dissenting voice, see Nicolai J. Foss, "Knowledge-Based Approaches to the Theory of the Firm: Some Critical Comments," *Organization Science,* 7/5 (1996): 470–476. It might be argued that knowledge production simply imposes another transaction cost, so the knowledge-based view is merely part of the transaction cost argument. We argue, however, that some important knowledge is only produced through social, nonmarket relations. Thus the transaction cost for individuals in market relations would be infinite. To embrace infinite transaction costs as part of the transaction cost argument trivializes the very important contribution of transaction cost analysis to understanding organizations.

3. For "communities of practice," see Jean Lave and Etienne Wenger, *Situated Learning: Legitimate Peripheral Participation* (New York, NY: Cambridge University Press, 1993); John Seely Brown and Paul Duguid, "Organizational Learning and Communities of Practice: Towards a Unified View of Working, Learning, and Innovation," *Organization Science,* 2 (1991): 40–57.

4. It might be possible to reach such a conclusion from Mark Casson, *Information and Organization: A New Perspective on the Theory of the Firm* (Oxford: Clarendon Press, 1997). It is important, however, not to elide information, Casson's main topic, and knowledge, though we do not expand on this problem here. See John Seely Brown and Paul Duguid, "The Knowledge Continuum," in preparation.

5. See, for example, Leonard-Barton's portrayal of the "learning organization" and her example of Chaparral Steel. Leonard-Barton, op. cit.

6. The distinction between know-what and know-how and the notion of "dispositional knowledge" comes from Gilbert Ryle, *The Concept of Mind* (London: Hutchinson, 1954). Know-how may appear to be little more than so-called "physical" skills, such as catching a ball or riding a bicycle. It is much more, however. For any student to "know" Newton's second law in any meaningful way requires having the skill to deploy the law in an analysis of colliding objects. This sort of knowledge, a disposition as well as a possession, emerges when called upon. It is evident, for instance, in such complex skills as talking, writing, and thinking or in negotiating with clients, overseeing employees, controlling production processes, developing strategy, conducting scientific experiments, fixing complex machines, cooking a meal, or writing computer programs. For the importance of dispositional knowledge, see S. Noam Cook and John Seely Brown, "Bridging Epistemologies: The Generative Dance

between Organizational Knowledge and Organizational Knowing," *Organization Science* (forthcoming).

7. As the CEO of Chaparral Steel told Leonard-Barton, "He can tour competitors through the plant, show them almost 'everything and we will be giving away nothing because they can't take it home with them.'" Leonard-Barton, op. cit., p. 7.

8. See, for example, George Gilder, *Life After Television* (New York, NY: W. W. Norton, 1994) for disintermediation; Alvin Toffler, *The Third Wave* (New York, NY: Morrow, 1980) for demassification; Nicholas Negroponte, *Being Digital* (New York, NY: Alfred A. Knopf, 1996) for disaggregation.

9. Friedrich Hayek, *The Fatal Conceit: The Errors of Socialism* (Chicago, IL: University of Chicago Press, 1988). See, also, Friedrich Hayek, "The Use of Knowledge in Society," *American Economic Review,* 35 (September 1945): 519–530); Kenneth J. Arrow, *The Limits of Organization* (New York, NY: W.W. Norton, 1974).

10. See, for example, Kevin Kelly, *Out of Control: The New Biology of Machines, Social Systems, and the Economic World* (New York, NY: Addison-Wesley, 1994) for bees; Andy Clark, *Being There: Putting Brain, Body, and World Together Again* (Cambridge, MA: MIT Press, 1997) for termites; Richard Dawkins, *The Blind Watchmaker* (New York, NY: W. W. Norton, 1986) and Sherry Turkle, *Life On the Screen: Identity in the Age of the Internet* (New York, NY: Simon & Schuster, 1996) for artificial life.

11. See Douglass C. North, *Structure and Change in Economic History* (New York, NY: W. W. Norton, 1981).

12. Raymond Williams, *The Long Revolution* (New York, NY: Columbia University Press, 1961).

13. Douglass C. North, *Institutions, Institutional Change, and Economic Performance* (New York, NY: Cambridge University Press, 1990); Alfred D. Chandler, *The Visible Hand: The Managerial Revolution in American Business* (Cambridge, MA: Harvard University Press, 1977).

14. Though for a qualified view of this argument, see Daniel E. Sichel, *The Computer Revolution: An Economic Perspective* (Washington, DC: Brookings Institutions Press, 1997).

15. Francis Fukuyama, "Social Networks and Digital Networks," in preparation. For an analysis of the complex relationship between communications technology and institutions see the classic study Harold Innis, *The Bias of Communication* (Toronto: University of Toronto Press, 1951).

16. See Mark Granovetter, "Economic Action and Social Structure: The Problem of Embeddedness," *American Journal of Sociology,* 91 (1985): 481–510; Gordon Walker, Bruce Kogut, and Weijian Shan, "Social Capital, Structural Holes and the Formation of an Industry Network," *Organization Science,* 8 (1997): 109–112; Martin Kenney and Urs von Burg, "Bringing Technology Back In: Explaining the Divergence between Silicon Valley and Route 128," in preparation; AnnaLee Saxenian, *Regional Advantage: Culture and Competition in Silicon Valley and Route 128* (Cambridge, MA: Harvard University Press, 1996); Gernot Grabher, *The Embedded Firm: On the Socioeconomics of Industrial Networks* (London: Routledge, 1993).

17. Julian E. Orr, *Talking About Machines: An Ethnography of a Modern Job* (Ithaca, NY: ILR Press, 1996).

18. Nonaka and Takeuchi, op. cit., p. 72; Ikujiro Nonaka and Noboru Konno, "The Concept of '*Ba*': Building a Foundation for Knowledge Creation," *California Management Review,* 40/3 (Spring 1998).

19. For views of personal knowledge, see M. Polanyi, *The Tacit Dimension: The Terry Lectures.* (Garden City, NJ: Doubleday, 1966); Ludwig Wittgenstein, *Philosophical Investigations,* G.E.M. Anscombe, trans. (New York, NY: Macmillan, 1953); David Bloor, *Wittgenstein: A Social Theory of Knowledge* (New York, NY: Columbia University Press, 1983); Thomas Nagel, *The Last Word* (New York, NY: New York University Press, 1997).

20. For a discussion of collective sensemaking, see Karl Weick, *Sensemaking in Organizations* (Beverly Hills, CA: Sage Books, 1995); Karl Weick and K. Roberts, "Collective Mind in Organizations," *Administrative Science Quarterly,* 38/3 (September 1993): 357–381.

21. Leonard-Barton, op. cit., especially chapter 2.

22. Raghu Garud and Michael A. Rappa, "A Socio-Cognitive Model of Technology Evolution: The Case of Cochlear Implants," *Organization Science,* 5 (1994): 344–362.

23. Garud and Rappa argue that in such cases, markets are actually quite inefficient means to challenge the interdependence of belief and evaluation—in part because markets, too, rely on evaluations provided by the blinkered technologies. Garud and Rappa, op. cit., p. 358.

24. Larry Hirschhorn, *Reworking Authority: Leading and Following in the Post-Modern Organization* (Cambridge, MA: MIT Press, 1997); Leonard-Barton attributes "creative abrasion" to Gerald Hirshberg of Nissan Design International. Leonard-Barton, op. cit., p. 63. See also Karl Jaspers, *The Idea of the University,* H. Reiche and T. Vanderschmidt, trans. (Boston, MA: Beacon Press, 1959) for the notion of "creative tension."

25. Eric Von Hippel, "'Sticky Information' and the Locus of Problem Solving: Implications for Innovation," *Management Science,* 40 (1994): 429–439.

26. Stephen R. Barley, "Technicians in the Workplace: Ethnographic Evidence for Bringing Work into Organization Studies," *Administrative Science Quarterly,* 41 (1966): 401–444; Henry W. Chesbrough and David J. Teece, "When is Virtual Virtuous? Organizing for Innovation." *Harvard Business Review,* 74/1 (1996): 65–73.

27. Robert Cole, *The Quest for Quality Improvement: How American Business Met the Challenge* (New York, NY: Oxford University Press, forthcoming).

28. Polanyi, op. cit.

29. David Teece, Richard Rumelt, Giovanni Dosi, and Sidney Winter, "Understanding Corporate Coherence: Theory and Evidence," *Journal of Economic Behavior and Organization,* 23/1 (1994): 1–30.

30. For the notion of leakiness, see R. M. Grant and J.-C. Spender. "Knowledge and the Firm: Overview," *Strategic Management Journal,* 17 (1996): 5–9.

31. Walter W. Powell, "Inter-Organizational Collaboration in the Biotechnology Industry." *Journal of Institutional and Theoretical Economics,* 152 (1996): 197–215; Kristen Kreiner and Majken Schultz, "Informal Collaboration in R&D: The Formation of Networks across Organizations," *Organization Science,* 14 (1993): 189–209.

32. To some degree, such fields resemble "social worlds." See Anselm Strauss, "A Social World Perspective," *Studies in Symbolic Interaction,* 1 (1978): 119–128.

33. See John Seely Brown and Paul Duguid, "The Knowledge Continuum," in preparation.

34. Susan Leigh Star and James R. Griesemer, "Institutional Ecology, 'Translations' and Boundary Objects: Amateurs and Professionals in Berkeley's Museum of Vertebrate Zoology, 1907–39," *Social Studies of Science,* 19 (1989): 387–420.

35. Mark Granovetter, "The Strength of Weak Ties," *American Journal of Sociology* (1976), pp. 1360–1380; Granovetter's argument presupposes that for knowledge to spread, groups cannot simply be related as isolated individuals connected by market; they (and, indeed, markets) must be embedded in complex social systems. This argument appears more forcefully in his critique of transaction costs cited above.

36. Chris Argyris and Donald Schön, *Organizational Learning* (Reading, MA: AddisonWesley, 1978).

37. Ikujiro Nonaka, "The Knowledge Creating Company," *Harvard Business Review.* 69/6 (November/December 1991): 96–104.

38. For the notion of "loosely coupled" systems, see Karl E. Weick, "Organizational Culture as a Source of High Reliability," *California Management Review,* 29/2 (Winter 1987): 112–127; J. Douglas Orton and Karl E. Weick, "Loosely Coupled Systems: A Reconceptualization," *Academy of Management Review,* 15/2 (April 1990): 203–223.

39. Geoffrey Bowker and Susan Leigh Star, "Knowledge and Infrastructure in International Information Management: Problems of Classification and Coding," in Lisa Bud-Frierman, ed., *Information Acumen: The Understanding and Use of Knowledge in Modern Business* (London: Routledge, 1994), pp. 187–213; Paul

Adler and Bryan Borys, "Two Types of Bureaucracy: Enabling and Coercive," *Administrative Science Quarterly,* 41 (1996): 61–89.

40. For an insightful view of the interplay between the formal and the informal in the creation of trust, see Sim B. Sitkin, "On the Positive Effect of Legalization on Trust," *Research on Negotiation in Organizations* (1995), pp. 185–217.

41. Tim Berners Lee, "The World Wide Web: Past, Present, and Future, [available online]: http://www.w3.org/People/Berners-Lee/1996/ppf.html

42. See John Seely Brown and Paul Duguid, "The University in the Digital Age," *Change,* 28 (1996): 10–15; John Seely Brown and Paul Duguid, "The Social Life of Documents," *Release 1.0* (October 1995), pp. 1–12.

43. Lave and Wenger, op. cit.

SECTION VI

MANAGING LINKAGES

Organizations of any size grow through the division of labor. People and business units specialize, mastering a limited number of routines and a defined knowledge base. The pursuit of efficiency often leads to more and more specialization, until an organization consists of so many intricately interconnected parts that change becomes difficult. As noted in Section V, innovation is often driven by transferring ideas and practices from one setting to another and recombining them in new ways. Bringing a new product, service, or process to market therefore requires coordination and cooperation that transcend boundaries within a company and between companies. Specialization and the division of labor cannot be abolished altogether. Rather, innovators must devise effective linkages that overcome the tendency of focused specialists to overlook the bigger picture and resist requests for cooperation that are viewed as distracting or obstructive.

Typically, innovation projects are executed by cross-functional teams. Integrating such groups across functions is the theme of Clark and Wheelwright's discussion of "heavyweight" teams. Clark and Wheelwright describe four types of team structure and highlight the challenges involved in managing such teams. In a similar vein, Ancona and Caldwell argue that developing a product with support throughout an organization requires managing across traditional functional and hierarchical boundaries. They identify three activity sets that groups use to manage their boundaries and show that effective groups actively engage in two of them, drawing out implications for how to select and reward teams.

Linking separate business units within an organization is a theme introduced by Nadler and Tushman, who describe the organizational architectures and behaviors needed to make linkages effective. Eisenhardt and Galunic adopt a different perspective, maintaining that the best way to promote effective collaboration is to allow business unit managers to choose their own links in a decentralized fashion, so the enterprise as a whole forms a shifting web of collaborative relationships. Such a system works, they suggest, when business unit heads come together frequently as a multibusiness team. Eisenhardt and Galunic decry collaboration for its own sake and contend that stale links should be eliminated and competition among business units for the same customers should be permitted. Birkinshaw describes in greater detail how to manage competition among business units, and he prescribes strategies for managing competition between different technologies within an enterprise. He proposes a set of rules for governing interunit competition and for deciding when to merge competing entities or close one down.

We then turn to managing linkages between organizations. Hargadon and Sutton provide a rich description of IDEO, a product design firm that innovates by acting as a technology broker. With clients in forty industries, it creates new products through original combinations of existing knowledge from different sectors. The authors describe the set of organizational routines that IDEO uses to generate breakthroughs by exploiting its central position in a diverse interorganizational network. Handfield, Ragatz, Petersen, and Moncz-ka focus on a different kind of cross-organizational linking in their discussion of how to involve suppliers in product, process, and service development. They set forth a model for assessing suppliers' capabilities and identifying which suppliers to integrate into the new product development cycle. Chesbrough and Socolof examine a third type of interorganizational linkage: the corporate venture. They describe Lucent's New Ventures Group, a mechanism for commercializing technologies developed within Bell Laboratories more rapidly by spinning off small, agile startups. The challenge such a corporate venturing arm faces is linking the startups with the parent to exploit the advantages of both.

29

Organizing and Leading "Heavyweight" Development Teams

KIM B. CLARK
STEVEN C. WHEELWRIGHT

Effective product and process development requires the integration of specialized capabilities. Integrating is difficult in most circumstances, but is particularly challenging in large, mature firms with strong functional groups, extensive specialization, large numbers of people, and multiple, ongoing operating pressures. In such firms, development projects are the exception rather than the primary focus of attention. Even for people working on development projects, years of experience and the established systems—covering everything from career paths to performance evaluation, and from reporting relationships to breadth of job definitions—create both physical and organizational distance from other people in the organization. The functions themselves are organized in a way that creates further complications: the marketing organization is based on product families and market segments; engineering around functional disciplines and technical focus; and manufacturing on a mix between functional and product market structures. The result is that in large, mature firms, organizing and leading an effective development effort is a major undertaking. This is especially true for organizations whose traditionally stable markets and competitive environments are threatened by new entrants, new technologies, and rapidly changing customer demands.

This article zeros in on one type of team structure—"heavyweight" project teams—that seems particularly promising in today's fast-paced world yet is strikingly absent in many mature companies. Our research shows that when managed effectively, heavyweight teams offer improved communication, stronger identification with and commitment to a project, and a focus on cross-functional problem solving. Our research also reveals, however, that these teams are not so easily managed and contain unique issues and challenges.

Heavyweight project teams are one of four types of team structures. We begin by describing each of them briefly. We then explore heavyweight teams in detail, compare them with the alternative forms, and point out specific challenges and their solutions in managing the heavyweight team organization. We conclude with an example of the changes necessary in individual behavior for heavyweight teams to be effective. Although heavyweight teams are a different way of organizing, they are more than a new structure; they represent a fundamentally different way of working. To the extent that both the team members and the surrounding organization reorganize that phenomenon, the heavyweight team begins to realize its full potential.

Reprinted with the permission of The Free Press, a Division of Simon & Schuster Adult Publishing Group, from *Revolutionizing Product Development: Quantum Leaps to Speed, Efficiency and Quality,* by Steven C. Wheelwright and Kim B. Clark. Copyright © 1992 by Steven C. Wheelwright and Kim B. Clark.

TYPES OF DEVELOPMENT PROJECT TEAMS

Figure 29.1 illustrates the four dominant team structures we have observed in our studies of development projects: functional, lightweight, heavyweight, and autonomous (or tiger). These forms are described below, along with their associated project leadership roles, strengths, and weaknesses. Heavyweight teams are examined in detail in the subsequent section.

Functional Team Structure

In the traditional functional organization found in larger, more mature firms, people are grouped principally by discipline, each working under the direction of a specialized subfunction manager and a senior functional manager. The different subfunctions and functions coordinate ideas through detailed specifications all parties agree to at the outset, and through occasional meetings where issues that cut across groups are dis-

1. Functional Team Structure

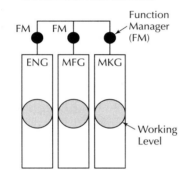

2. Lightweight Team Structure

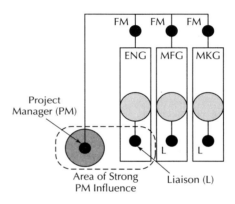

3. Heavyweight Team Structure

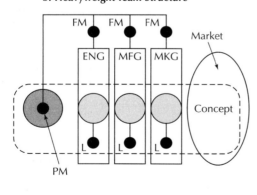

4. Autonomous Team Structure

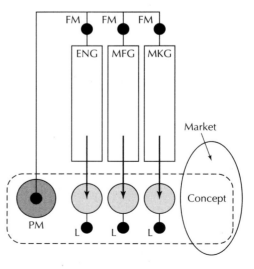

Figure 29.1. Types of development teams.

cussed. Over time, primary responsibility for the project passes sequentially—although often not smoothly—from one function to the next, a transfer frequently termed "throwing it over the wall."

The functional team structure has several advantages and associated disadvantages. One strength is that those managers who control the project's resources also control task performance in their functional area; thus, responsibility and authority are usually aligned. However, tasks must be subdivided at the project's outset, i.e., the entire development process is decomposed into separable, somewhat independent activities. But on most development efforts, not all required tasks are known at the outset, nor can they all be easily and realistically subdivided. Coordination and integration can suffer as a result.

Another major strength of this approach is that, because most career paths are functional in nature until a general management level is reached, the work done on a project is judged, evaluated, and rewarded by the same subfunction and functional managers who make the decisions about career paths. The associated disadvantage is that individual contributions to a development project tend to be judged largely independently of overall project success. The traditional tenet cited is that individuals cannot be evaluated fairly on outcomes over which they have little or no control. But as a practical matter, that often means that no one directly involved in the details of the project is responsible for the results finally achieved.

Finally, the functional project organization brings specialized expertise to bear on the key technical issues. The same person or small group of people may be responsible for the design of a particular component or subsystem over a wide range of development efforts. Thus the functions and subfunctions capture the benefits of prior experience and become the keepers of the organization's depth of knowledge while ensuring that it is systematically applied over time and across projects. The disadvantage is that every development project differs in its objective and performance requirements, and it is unlikely that specialists developing a single component will do so very differently on one project than on another. The "best" component or subsystem is defined by technical parameters in the areas of their expertise rather than by overall system characteristics or specific customer requirements dic-

tated by the unique market the development effort aims for.

Lightweight Team Structure

Like the functional structure, those assigned to the lightweight team reside physically in their functional areas, but each functional organization designates a liaison person to "represent" it on a project coordinating committee. These liaison representatives work with a "lightweight project manager," usually a design engineer or product marketing manager, who coordinates different functions' activities. This approach usually figures as an add-on to a traditional functional organization, with the functional liaison person having that role added to his or her other duties. The overall coordination assignment of lightweight project manager, however, tends not to be present in the traditional functional team structure.

The project manager is a "lightweight" in two important respects. First, he or she is generally a middle- or junior-level person who, despite considerable expertise, usually has little status or influence in the organization. Such people have spent a handful of years in a function, and this assignment is seen as a "broadening experience," a chance for them to move out of that function. Second, although they are responsible for informing and coordinating the activities of the functional organizations, the key resources (including engineers on the project) remain under the control of their respective functional managers. The lightweight project manager does not have power to reassign people or reallocate resources, and instead confirms schedules, updates time lines, and expedites across groups. Typically, such project leaders spend no more than 25% of their time on a single project.

The primary strengths and weaknesses of the lightweight project team are those of the functional project structure. But now at least one person over the course of the project looks across functions and seeks to ensure that individual tasks—especially those on the critical path—get done in a timely fashion and that everyone is kept aware of potential cross-functional issues and what is going on elsewhere on this particular project.

Thus, improved communication and coordination are what an organization expects when moving from a functional to a lightweight team structure. Yet, because power still resides with the subfunction and functional managers, hopes for improved efficiency, speed, and project quality are seldom realized. Moreover, lightweight project leaders find themselves tolerated at best, and often ignored and even preempted. This can easily become a "no-win" situation for the individual thus assigned.

Heavyweight Team Structure

In contrast to the lightweight setup, the heavyweight project manager has direct access to and responsibility for the work of all those involved in the project. Such leaders are "heavyweights" in two respects. First, they are senior managers within the organization; they may even outrank the functional managers. Hence, in addition to having expertise and experience, they also wield significant organizational clout. Second, heavyweight leaders have primary influence over the people working on the development effort and supervise their work directly through key functional people on the core teams. Often, the core group of people are dedicated and physically co-located with the heavyweight project leader. However, the longer-term career development of individual contributors continues to rest not with the project leader—although that heavyweight leaders makes significant input to individual performance evaluations—but with the functional manager, because members are not assigned to a project team on a permanent basis.

The heavyweight team structure has a number of advantages and strengths, along with associated weaknesses. Because this team structure is observed much less frequently in practice and yet seems to have tremendous potential for a wide range of organizations, it will be discussed in detail in the next section.

Autonomous Team Structure

With the autonomous team structure, often called the "tiger team," individuals from the different functional areas are formally assigned, dedicated, and co-located to the project team. The project leader, a "heavyweight" in the organization, is given full control over the resources contributed by the different functional groups. Furthermore, that project leader becomes the sole evaluator of the contribution made by individual team members.

In essence, the autonomous team is given a "clean sheet of paper"; it is not required to follow existing organizational practices and procedures, but allowed to create its own. This includes establishing incentives and rewards as well as norms for behavior. However, the team will be held fully accountable for the final results of the project: success or failure is its responsibility and no one else's.

The fundamental strength of the autonomous team structure is focus. Everything the individual team members and team leader do is concentrated on making the project successful. Thus, tiger teams can excel at rapid, efficient new product and new process development. They handle cross-functional integration in a particularly effective manner, possibly because they attract and select team participants much more freely than the other project structures.

Tiger teams, however, take little or nothing as "given"; they are likely to expand the bounds of their project definition and tackle redesign of the entire product, its components, and subassemblies, rather than looking for opportunities to utilize existing materials, designs, and organizational relationships. Their solution may be unique, making it more difficult to fold the resulting product and process—and, in many cases, the team members themselves—back into the traditional organization upon project completion. As a consequence, tiger teams often become the birthplace of new business units, or they experience unusually high turnover following project completion.

Senior managers often become nervous at the prospects of a tiger team because they are asked to delegate much more responsibility and control to the team and its project leader than under any of the other organization structures. Unless clear guidelines have been established in advance, it is extremely difficult during the project for senior managers to make midcourse corrections or exercise substantial influence without destroying the team. More than one team has "gotten away" from senior management and created major problems.

THE HEAVYWEIGHT TEAM STRUCTURE

The best way to begin understanding the potential of heavyweight teams is to consider an example of their success, in this case, Motorola's experience in developing its Bandit line of pagers.

The Bandit Pager Heavyweight Team

This development team within the Motorola Communications Sector was given a project charter to develop an automated, on-shore, profitable production operation for its high-volume Bravo pager line. (This is the belt-worn pager that Motorola sold from the mid-1980s into the early 1990s.) The core team consisted of a heavyweight project leader and a handful of dedicated and co-located individuals, who represented industrial engineering, robotics, process engineering, procurement, and product design/CIM. The need for these functions was dictated by the Bandit platform automation project and its focus on manufacturing technology with a minimal change in product technology. In addition, human resource and accounting/finance representatives were part of the core team. The human resource person was particularly active early on as subteam positions were defined and jobs posted throughout Motorola's Communications Sector, and played an important subsequent role in training and development of operating support people. The accounting/finance person was invaluable in "costing out" different options and performing detailed analyses of options and choices identified during the course of the project.

An eighth member of the core team was a Hewlett Packard employee. Hewlett Packard was chosen as the vendor for the "software backplane," providing an HP 3000 computer and the integrated software communication network that linked individual automated workstations, downloaded controls and instructions during production operations, and captured quality and other operating performance data. Because HP support was vital to the project's success, it was felt essential they be represented on the core team.

The core team was housed in a corner of the Motorola Telecommunications engineering/manufacturing facility. The team chose to enclose in glass the area where the automated production line was to be set up so that others in the factory could track the progress, offer suggestions, and adopt the lessons learned from it in their own production and engineering environments. The team called their project Bandit to indicate a willingness to "take" ideas from literally anywhere.

The heavyweight project leader, Scott Shamlin, who was described by team members as "a crusader," "a renegade," and "a workaholic," became the champion for the Bandit effort. A hands-on manager who played a major role in stimulating and facilitating communication across functions, he helped to articulate a vision of the Bandit line and to infuse it into the detailed work of the project team. His goal was to make sure the new manufacturing process worked for the pager line, but would provide real insight for many other production lines in Motorola's Communications Sector.

The Bandit core team started by creating a contract book that established the blueprint and work plan for the team's efforts and its performance expectations; all core team members and senior management signed on to the document. Initially, the team's executive sponsor—although not formally identified as such—was George Fisher, the Sector Executive. He made the original investment proposal to the Board of Directors and was an early champion and supporter, as well as direct supervisor in selecting the project leader and helping get the team underway. Subsequently, the vice president and general manager of the Paging Products division filled the role of executive sponsor.

Throughout the project, the heavyweight team took responsibility for the substance of its work, the means by which it was accomplished, and its results. The project was completed in 18 months as per the contract book, which represented about half the time of a normal project of such magnitude. Further, the automated production operation was up and running with process tolerances of five stigma (i.e., the degree of precision achieved by the manufacturing processes) at the end of 18 months. Ongoing production verified that the cost objectives (substantially reduced direct costs and improved profit margins) had indeed been met, and product reliability was even higher than the standards already achieved on the off-shore versions of the Bravo product. Finally, a variety of lessons were successfully transferred to other parts of the Sector's operations, and additional heavyweight teams have proven the viability and robustness of the approach in Motorola's business and further refined its effectiveness throughout the corporation.

The Challenge of Heavyweight Teams

Motorola's experience underscores heavyweight teams' potential power, but it also makes clear that creating an effective heavyweight team capability is more than merely selecting a leader and forming a team. By their very nature—being product (or process) focused, and needing strong, independent leadership, broad skills and cross-functional perspective, and clear missions—heavyweight teams may conflict with the functional organization and raise questions about senior management's influence and control. And even the advantages of the team approach bring with them potential disadvantages that may hurt development performance if not recognized, and averted.

Take, for example, the advantages of ownership and commitment, one of the most striking advantages of the heavyweight team. Identifying with the product and creating a sense of esprit de corps motivate core team members to extend themselves and do what needs to be done to help the team succeed. But such teams sometimes expand the definition of their role and the scope of the project, and they get carried away with themselves and their abilities. We have seen heavyweight teams turn into autonomous tiger teams and go off on a tangent because senior executives gave insufficient direction and the bounds of the team were only vaguely specified at the outset. And even if the team stays focused, the rest of the organization may see themselves as "second class." Although the core team may not make that distinction explicit, it happens because the team has responsibilities and authority beyond those commonly given to functional team members. Thus, such projects inadvertently can become the "haves" and other, smaller projects the "have-nots" with regard to key resources and management attention.

Support activities are particularly vulnerable to an excess of ownership and commitment. Often the heavyweight team will want the same control over secondary support activities as it has over the primary tasks performed by dedicated team members. When waiting for prototypes to be constructed, analytical tests to be performed, or quality assurance procedures to be conducted, the team's natural response is to "demand" top priority from the support organization or to be allowed to go outside and subcontract to independent groups. While these may sometimes be the appropriate choices, senior management should establish make-buy guidelines and clear priorities applicable to all projects—perhaps changing service levels provided by support groups (rather than maintaining the traditional emphasis on resource utilization)—or have support groups provide capacity and advisory technical services but let team members do more of the actual task work in those support areas. Whatever actions the organization takes, the challenge is to achieve a balance between the needs of the individual project and the needs of the broader organization.

Another advantage the heavyweight team brings is the integration and integrity it provides through a system solution to a set of customer needs. Getting all of the components and subsystems to complement one another and to address effectively the fundamental requirements of the core customer segment can result in a winning platform product and/or process. The team achieves an effective system design by using generalist skills applied by broadly trained team members, with fewer-specialists and, on occasion, less depth in individual component solutions and technical problem solving.

The extent of these implications is aptly illustrated by the nature of the teams Clark and Fujimoto studied in the auto industry.[1] They found that for U.S. auto firms in the mid-1980s, typical platform projects—organized under a traditional functional or lightweight team structure—entailed full-time work for several months by approximately 1,500 engineers. In contrast, a handful of Japanese platform projects—carried out by heavyweight teams—utilized only 250 engineers working full-time for several months. The implications of 250 versus 1500 full-time equivalents (FTEs) with regard to breadth of tasks, degree of specialization, and need for coordination are significant and help explain the differences in project results as measured by product integrity, development cycle time, and engineering resource utilization.

But that lack of depth may disclose a disadvantage. Some individual components or subassemblies may not attain the same level of technical excellence they would under a more traditional functional team structure. For instance, generalists may develop a windshield wiper system that is complementary with and integrated into the total car system and its core concept. But they also may embed in their design some potential weaknesses or flaws that might have been caught by a functional team of specialists who had designed a long series of windshield wipers. To counter this potential disadvantage, many organizations order more testing of completed units to discover such possible flaws and have components and subassemblies reviewed by expert specialists. In some cases, the quality assurance function has expanded its role to make sure sufficient technical specialists review designs at appropriate points so that such weaknesses can be minimized.

Managing the Challenges of Heavyweight Teams

Problems with depth in technical solutions and allocations of support resources suggest the tension that exists between heavyweight teams and the functional groups where much of the work gets done. The problem with the teams exceeding their bounds reflects, in part, how teams manage themselves, in part, how boundaries are set, and, in part, the ongoing relationship between the team and senior management. Dealing with these issues requires mechanisms and practices that reinforce the team's basic thrust—ownership, focus, system architecture, integrity—and yet improve its ability to take advantage of the strengths of the supporting functional organization—technical depth, consistency across projects, senior management direction. We have grouped the mechanisms and problems into six categories of management action: the project charter, the contract, staffing, leadership, team responsibility, and the executive sponsor.

THE PROJECT CHARTER

A heavyweight project team needs a clear mission. A way to capture that mission concisely is in an explicit, measurable project charter that sets broad performance objectives and usually is articulated even before the core team is selected. Thus, joining the core team includes accepting the charter established by senior management. A typical charter for a heavyweight project would be the following:

> The resulting product will be selected and ramped by Company X during Quarter 4 of calendar year 1991, at a minimum of a 20% gross margin.

This charter is representative of an industrial products firm whose product goes into a system sold by its customers. Company X is the leading customer for a certain family of products, and this project is dedicated to developing the next generation platform offering in that family. If the heavyweight program results in that platform product being chosen by the leading customer in the segment by a certain date and at a certain gross margin, it will have demonstrated that the next generation platform is not only viable, but

likely to be very successful over the next three to five years. Industries and settings where such a charter might be found would include a microprocessor being developed for a new computer system, a diesel engine for the heavy equipment industry, or a certain type of slitting and folding piece of equipment for the newspaper printing press industry. Even in a medical diagnostics business with hundreds of customers, a goal of "capturing 30% of market purchases in the second 12 months during which the product is offered" sets a clear charter for the team.

THE CONTRACT BOOK

Whereas a charter lays out the mission in broad terms, the contract book defines, in detail, the basic plan to achieve the stated goal. A contract book is created as soon as the core team and heavyweight project leader have been designated and given the charter by senior management. Basically, the team develops its own detailed work plan for conducting the project, estimates the resources required, and outlines the results to be achieved and against which it is willing to be evaluated. (The table of contents of a typical heavyweight team contract book are shown in Table 29.1.) Such documents range from 25 to 100 pages, depending on the complexity of the project and level of detail desired by the team and senior management before proceeding. A common practice following negotiation and acceptance of this contract is for the individuals from the team and senior management to sign the contract book as an indication of their commitment to honor the plan and achieve those results.

The core team may take anywhere from a long week to a few months to create and complete the con-

Table 29.1. Heavyweight Team, Contract Book— Major Sections

Executive summary
Business plan and purposes
Development plan
    Schedule
    Materials
    Resources
Produce design plan
Quality plan
Manufacturing plan
Project deliverables
Performance measurement and incentives

tract book; Motorola, for example, after several years of experience, has decided that a maximum of seven days should be allowed for this activity. Having watched other heavyweight teams—particularly in organizations with no prior experience in using such a structure—take up to several months, we can appreciate why Motorola has nicknamed this the "blitz phase" and decided that the time allowed should be kept to a minimum.

STAFFING

As suggested in Figure 29.1, a heavyweight team includes a group of core cross-functional team members who are dedicated (and usually physically co-located) for the duration of the development effort. Typically there is one core team member from each primary function of the organization; for instance, in several electronics firms we have observed core teams consisting of six functional participants—design engineering, marketing, quality assurance, manufacturing, finance, and human resources. (Occasionally, design will be represented by two core team members, one each for hardware and software engineering.) Individually, core team members represent their functions and provide leadership for their function's inputs to the project. Collectively, they constitute a management team that works under the direction of the heavyweight project manager and takes responsibility for managing the overall development effort.

While other participants—especially from design engineering early on and manufacturing later on—may frequently be dedicated to a heavyweight team for several months, they usually are not made part of the core team though they may well be co-located and, over time, develop the same level of ownership and commitment to the project as core team members. The primary difference is that the core team manages the total project and the coordination and integration of individual functional efforts, whereas other dedicated team members work primarily within a single function or subfunction.

Whether these temporarily dedicated team members are actually part of the core team is an issue firms handle in different ways, but those with considerable experience tend to distinguish between core and other dedicated (and often co-located) team members. The difference is one of management responsibility for the core group that is not shared equally by the others.

Also, it is primarily the half a dozen members of the core group who will be dedicated throughout the project, with other contributors having a portion of their time reassigned before this heavyweight project is completed.

Whether physical colocation is essential is likewise questioned in such teams. We have seen it work both ways. Given the complexity of development projects, and especially the uncertainty and ambiguity often associated with those assigned to heavyweight teams, physical colocation is preferable to even the best of on-line communication approaches. Problems that arise in real time are much more likely to be addressed effectively with all of the functions represented and present than when they are separate and must either wait for a periodic meeting or use remote communication links to open up cross-functional discussions.

A final issue is whether an individual can be a core team member on more than one heavyweight team simultaneously. If the rule for a core team member is that 70% or more of their time must be spent on the heavyweight project, then the answer to this question is no. Frequently, however, a choice must be made between someone being on two core teams—for example, from the finance or human resource function—or putting a different individual on one of those teams who has neither the experience nor stature to be a full peer with the other core team members. Most experienced organizations we have seen opt to put the same person on two teams to ensure the peer relationship and level of contribution required, even though it means having one person on two teams and with two desks. They then work diligently to develop other people in the function so that multiple team assignments will not be necessary in the future.

Sometimes multiple assignments will also be justified on the basis that a function such as finance does not need a full-time person on a project. In most instances, however, a variety of potential value-adding tasks exist that are broader than finance's traditional contribution. A person largely dedicated to the core team will search for those opportunities and the project will be better because of it. The risk of allowing core team members to be assigned to multiple projects is that they are neither available when their inputs are most needed nor as committed to project success as their peers. They become secondary core team members, and the full potential of the heavyweight team structure fails to be realized.

PROJECT LEADERSHIP

Heavyweight teams require a distinctive style of leadership. A number of differences between lightweight and heavyweight project managers are highlighted in Figure 29.2. Three of those are particularly distinctive. First, a heavyweight leader managers, leads, and evaluates other members of the core team, and is also the person to whom the core team reports throughout the project's duration. Another characteristic is that rather than being either neutral or a facilitator with regard to problem solving and conflict resolution, these leaders see themselves as championing the basic concept around which the platform product and/or process is being shaped. They make sure that those who work on subtasks of the project understand that concept. Thus they play a central role in ensuring the system integrity of the final product and/or process.

Finally, the heavyweight project manager carries out his or her role in a very different fashion than the lightweight project manager. Most lightweights spend the bulk of their time working at a desk, with paper. They revise schedules, get frequent updates, and encourage people to meet previously agreed upon deadlines. The heavyweight project manager spends little time at a desk, is out talking to project contributors, and makes sure that decisions are made and implemented whenever and wherever needed. Some of the ways in which the heavyweight project manager achieves project results are highlighted by the five roles illustrated in Table 29.2 for a heavyweight project manager on a platform development project in the auto industry.

The *first role* of the heavyweight project man ager is to provide for the team a direct interpretation of the market and customer needs. This involves gathering market data directly from customers, dealers, and industry shows, as well as through systematic study and contact with the firm's marketing organization. A *second role* is to become a multilingual translator, not just taking marketing information to the various functions involved in the project, but being fluent in the language of each of those functions and making sure the translation and communication going on among the functions—particularly between customer needs and product specifications—are done effectively.

A *third role* is the direct engineering manager, orchestrating, directing, and coordinating the various engineering subfunctions. Given the size of many development programs and the number of types of engineering disciplines involved, the project manager must be able to work directly with each engineering subfunction on a day-to-day basis and ensure that their work will indeed integrate and support that of others,

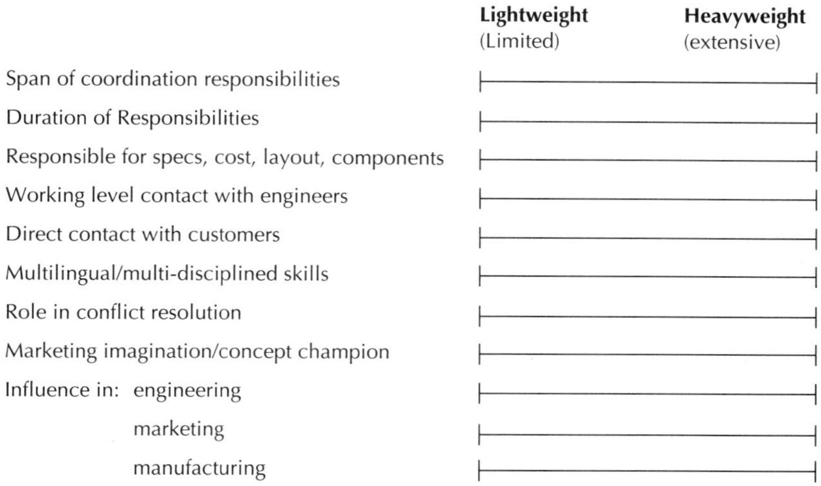

	Lightweight (Limited)	Heavyweight (extensive)
Span of coordination responsibilities	|———————————————|
Duration of Responsibilities	|———————————————|
Responsible for specs, cost, layout, components	|———————————————|
Working level contact with engineers	|———————————————|
Direct contact with customers	|———————————————|
Multilingual/multi-disciplined skills	|———————————————|
Role in conflict resolution	|———————————————|
Marketing imagination/concept champion	|———————————————|
Influence in: engineering	|———————————————|
marketing	|———————————————|
manufacturing	|———————————————|

Figure 29.2. Project manager profile.

Table 29.2. The Heavyweight Project Manager

Role	Description
Direct market interpreter	Firsthand information, dealer visits, auto shows, has own marketing budget, market study team, direct contact and discussions with customers
Multilingual translator	Fluency in language of customers, engineers, marketers, stylists; translator between customer experience/requirements and engineering specifications
"Direct" engineering manager	Direct contact, orchestra conductor, evangelist of conceptual integrity and coordinator of component development; direct eye-to-eye discussions with working level engineers; shows up in drafting room, looks over engineers' shoulders
Program manager "in motion"	Out of the office, not too many meetings, not too much paperwork, face-to-face communication, conflict resolution manager
Concept infuser	Concept guardian, confronts conflicts, not only reacts but implements own philosophy, ultimate decision maker, coordination of details and creation of harmony

so the chosen product concept can be effectively executed.

A *fourth role* is best described as staying in motion: out of the office conducting face-to-face sessions and highlighting and resolving potential conflicts as soon as possible. Part of this role entails energizing and pacing the overall effort and its key subparts. A *final role* is that of concept champion. Here the heavyweight project manager becomes the guardian of the concept and not only reacts and responds to the interests of others, but also sees that the choices made are consistent and in harmony with the basic concept. This requires a careful blend of communication and teaching skills so that individual contributors and their groups understand the core concept, and sufficient conflict resolution skills to ensure that any tough issues are addressed in a timely fashion.

It should be apparent from this description that heavyweight project managers earn the respect and right to carry out these roles based on prior experience, carefully developed skills, and status earned over time, rather than simply being designated "leader" by senior management. A qualified heavyweight project manager is a prerequisite to an effective heavyweight team structure.

TEAM MEMBER RESPONSIBILITIES

Heavyweight team members have responsibilities beyond their usual functional assignment. As illustrated in Table 29.3, these are of two primary types. Functional hat responsibilities are those accepted by the individual core team member as a representative of his or her function. For example, the core team member from

marketing is responsible for ensuring that appropriate marketing expertise is brought to the project, that a marketing perspective is provided on all key issues, that project sub-objectives dependent on the marketing function are met in a timely fashion, and that marketing issues that impact other functions are raised proactively within the team.

But each core team member also wears a team hat. In addition to representing a function, each member shares responsibility with the heavyweight project manager for the procedures followed by the team, and for the overall results that those procedures deliver. The core team is accountable for the success of the

Table 29.3. Responsibilities of Heavyweight Core Team Members

Functional Hat Accountabilities
Ensuring functional expertise on the project
Representing the functional perspective on the project
Ensuring that subobjectives are met that depend on their function
Ensuring that functional issues impacting the team are raised proactively within the team

Team Hat Accountabilities
Sharing responsibility for team results
Reconstituting tasks and content
Establishing reporting and other organizational relationships
Participating in monitoring and improving team performance
Sharing responsibility for ensuring effective team processes
Examining issues from an executive point of view (Answering the question, "Is this the appropriate business response for the company?")
Understanding, recognizing, and responsibly challenging the boundaries of the project and team process

project, and it can blame no one but itself if it fails to manage the project, execute the tasks, and deliver the performance agreed upon at the outset.

Finally, beyond being accountable for tasks in their own function, core team members are responsible for how those tasks are subdivided, organized, and accomplished. Unlike the traditional functional development structure, which takes as given the subdivision of tasks and the means by which those tasks will be conducted and completed, the core heavyweight team is given the power and responsibility to change the substance of those tasks to improve the performance of the project. Since this is a role that core team members do not play under a lightweight or functional team structure, it is often the most difficult for them to accept fully and learn to apply. It is essential, however, if the heavyweight team is to realize its full potential.

THE EXECUTIVE SPONSOR

With so much more accountability delegated to the project team, establishing effective relationships with senior management requires special mechanisms. Senior management needs to retain the ability to guide the project and its leader while empowering the team to lead and act, a responsibility usually taken by an executive sponsor—typically the vice president of engineering, marketing, or manufacturing for the business unit. This sponsor becomes the coach and mentor for the heavyweight project leader and core team, and seeks to maintain close, ongoing contact with the team's efforts. In addition, the executive sponsor serves as a liaison. If other members of senior management—including the functional heads—have concerns or inputs to voice, or need current information on project status, these are communicated through the executive sponsor. This reduces the number of mixed signals received by the team and clarifies for the organization the reporting and evaluation relationship between the team and senior management. It also encourages the executive sponsor to set appropriate limits and bounds on the team so that organizational surprises are avoided.

Often the executive sponsor and core team identify those areas where the team clearly has decision-making power and control, and they distinguish them from areas requiring review. An electronics firm that has used heavyweight teams for some time dedicates one meeting early on between the executive sponsor and the core team to generating a list of areas where the executive sponsor expects to provide oversight and be consulted; these areas are of great concern to the entire executive staff and team actions may well raise policy issues for the larger organization. In this firm, the executive staff wants to maintain some control over:

- resource commitment—head count, fixed costs, and major expenses outside the approved contract book plan;

- pricing for major customers and major accounts;

- potential slips in major milestone dates (the executive sponsor wants early warning and recovery plans);

- plans for transitioning from development project to operating status;

- thorough reviews at major milestones or every three months, whichever occurs sooner;

- review of incentive rewards that have company-wide implications for consistency and equity; and

- cross-project issues such as resource optimization, prioritization, and balance.

Identifying such areas at the outset can help the executive sponsor and the core team better carry out their assigned responsibilities. It also helps other executives feel more comfortable working through the executive sponsor, since they know these "boundary issues" have been articulated and are jointly understood.

THE NECESSITY OF FUNDAMENTAL CHANGE

Compared to a traditional functional organization, creating a team that is "heavy"—one with effective leadership, strong problem-solving skills and the ability to integrate across functions—requires basic changes in the way development works. But it also requires change in the fundamental behavior of engineers, designers, manufacturers, and marketers in their day-to-day work. An episode in a computer company with no previous experience with heavyweight teams illustrates the depth of change required to realize fully these teams' power.[2]

Two teams, A and B, were charged with development of a small computer system and had market introduction targets within the next 12 months. While each core team was co-located and held regular meetings, there was one overlapping core team member (from finance/accounting). Each team was charged with developing a new computer system for their individual target markets but by chance, both products were to use an identical, custom-designed microprocessor chip in addition to other unique and standard chips.

The challenge of changing behavior in creating an effective heavyweight team structure was highlighted when each team sent this identical, custom-designed chip—the "supercontroller"—to the vendor for pilot production. The vendor quoted a 20-week turnaround to both teams. At that time, the supercontroller chip was already on the critical path for Team B, with a planned turnaround of 11 weeks. Thus, every week saved on that chip would save one week in the overall project schedule, and Team B already suspected that it would be late in meeting its initial market introduction target date. When the 20-week vendor lead time issue first came up in a Team B meeting, Jim, the core team member from engineering, responded very much as he had on prior, functionally structured development efforts: because initial prototypes were engineering's responsibility, he reported that they were working on accelerating the delivery date, but that the vendor was a large company, with whom the computer manufacturer did substantial business, and known for its slowness. Suggestions from other core team members on how to accelerate the delivery were politely rebuffed, including one to have a senior executive contact their counterpart at the vendor. Jim knew the traditional approach to such issues and did not perceive a need, responsibility, or authority to alter it significantly.

For Team A, the original quote of 20-week turnaround still left a little slack, and thus initially the supercontroller chip was not on the critical path. Within a couple of weeks, however, it was, given other changes in the activities and schedule, and the issue was immediately raised at the team's weekly meeting. Fred, the core team member from manufacturing (who historically would not have been involved in an early engineering prototype), stated that he thought the turnaround time quoted was too long and that he would try to reduce it. At the next meeting, Fred brought some good news: through discussions with the vendor, he had been able to get a commitment that pulled in the delivery of the supercontroller chip by 11 weeks! Furthermore, Fred thought that the quote might be reduced even further by a phone call from one of the computer manufacturer's senior executives to a contact of his at the vendor.

Two days later, at a regular Team B meeting, the supercontroller chip again came up during the status review, and no change from the original schedule was identified. Since the finance person, Ann, served on both teams and had been present at Team A's meeting, she described Team A's success in reducing the cycle time. Jim responded that he was aware that Team A had made such efforts, but that the information was not correct, and the original 20-week delivery date still held. Furthermore, Jim indicated that Fred's efforts (from Team A) had caused some uncertainty and disruption internally, and in the future it was important that Team A not take such initiatives before coordinating with Team B. Jim stated that this was particularly true when an outside vendor was involved, and he closed the topic by saying that a meeting to clear up the situation would be held that afternoon with Fred from Team A and Team B's engineering and purchasing people.

The next afternoon, at his Team A meeting, Fred confirmed the accelerated delivery schedule for the supercontroller chip. Eleven weeks had indeed been clipped out of the schedule to the benefit of both Teams A and B. Subsequently, Jim confirmed the revised schedule would apply to his team as well, although he was displeased that Fred had abrogated "standard operating procedure" to achieve it. Curious about the differences in perspective, Ann decided to learn more about why Team A had identified an obstacle and removed it from its path, yet Team B had identified an identical obstacle and failed to move it at all.

As Fred pointed out, Jim was the engineering manager responsible for development of the supercontroller chip; he knew the chip's technical requirements, but had little experience dealing with chip vendors and their production processes. (He had long been a specialist.) Without that experience, he had a hard time pushing back against the vendor's "standard line." But Fred's manufacturing experience with several chip vendors enabled him to calibrate the vendor's dates against his best-case experience and understand what the vendor needed to do to meet a substantially earlier commitment.

Moreover, because Fred had bought into a clear team charter, whose path the delayed chip would block, and because he had relevant experience, it did not make sense to live with the vendor's initial commitment, and thus he sought to change it. In contrast, Jim—who had worked in the traditional functional organization for many years—saw vendor relations on a pilot build as part of his functional job, but did not believe that contravening standard practices to get the vendor to shorten the cycle time was his responsibility, within the range of his authority, or even in the best long-term interest of his function. He was more concerned with avoiding conflict and not roiling the water than with achieving the overarching goal of the team.

It is interesting to note that in Team B, engineering raised the issue, and, while unwilling to take aggressive steps to resolve it, also blocked others' attempts. In Team A, however, while the issue came up initially through engineering, Fred in manufacturing proactively went after it. In the case of Team B, getting a prototype chip returned from a vendor was still being treated as an "engineering responsibility," whereas in the case of Team A, it was treated as a "team responsibility." Since Fred was the person best qualified to attack that issue, he did so.

Both Team A and Team B had a charter, a contract, a co-located core team staffed with generalists, a project leader, articulated responsibilities, and an executive sponsor. Yet Jim's and Fred's understanding of what these things meant for them personally and for the team at the detailed, working level was quite different. While the teams had been through similar training and team startup processes, Jim apparently saw the new approach as a different organizational framework within which work would get done as before. In contrast, Fred seemed to see it as an opportunity to work in a different way—to take responsibility for reconfiguring tasks, drawing on new skills, and reallocating resources, where required, for getting the job done in the best way possible.

Although both teams were "heavyweight" in theory, Fred's team was much "heavier" in its operation and impact. Our research suggests that heaviness is not just a matter of structure and mechanism, but of attitudes and behavior. Firms that try to create heavyweight teams without making the deep changes needed to realize the power in the team's structure will find this team approach problematic. Those intent on using teams for platform projects and willing to make the basic changes we have discussed here, can enjoy substantial advantages of focus, integration, and effectiveness.

NOTES

1. See Kim B. Clark and Takahiro Fujimoto, *Product Development Performance* (Boston, MA: Harvard Business School Press, 1991).

2. Adapted from a description provided by Dr. Christopher Meyer, Strategic Alignment Group, Los Altos, CA.

30

Making Teamwork Work

Boundary Management in Product Development Teams

DEBORAH GLADSTEIN ANCONA
DAVID F. CALDWELL

The product team consisted of some of the best engineers in the company and had the support of top management. Members of the group worked long hours and quickly became a cohesive and motivated team. The team leader established common goal statements with manufacturing and marketing around product functionality, cost, and quality. About six months after the team began its work, coordination began to break down. Disputes between the team and the marketing and manufacturing functions became more frequent and were regularly elevated to top management for resolution. After months of delay, division management reorganized the team and replaced a number of members, including the team leader. While the product was ultimately successful, the delay of time in getting the product to market was extremely costly. The original manager of the team summarized his experiences by saying "I try to deal with things in a rational way, but that's not necessarily the way other groups operate around here. Many things that were planned for the product six, eight, ten months ago weren't ever really committed to by manufacturing."

Despite substantial resources, motivated and talented people, and even the ability to work together effectively, some teams fail because they are unable to develop a new product that meets the expectations of others in the organization. Developing a product that will be supported throughout the organization requires more than the use of concurrent engineering techniques or a cross-functional team. Rather, what is required is that a team learn to manage across traditional lines of function and authority. This paper summarizes an investigation of the activities product development teams undertake in managing relations with other groups and links the pattern of those activities to the teams' overall success.

Rapid changes in technology and markets are the reality for an increasing number of industries. Because of this, speed to market is critically important in determining whether or not a new product is successful. Perhaps the most common approach for responding to increasing technical complexity and need for speed is the use of a development team to design the product rather than assigning development to a single individual or even a small group of individuals from one function. Such teams have the potential of speeding development by improving interunit coordination, allowing for the use of a parallel as opposed to a sequential design process, and reducing delays due to the failure to include the necessary information from throughout the organization (Kazanjian, 1988; House and Price, 1991).

From *Managing Strategic Innovation and Change: A Collection of Readings,* 1st edition, edited by Michael L. Tushman and Philip Anderson. Copyright © 1997 by Oxford University Press, Inc. Used by permission of Oxford University Press, Inc.

However, if teams are to fulfill their promise of shortening the product development cycle, they must develop the ability to collect information and resources from a variety of sources—inside and outside the organization—and interact with others in the organization to negotiate deadlines and specifications, coordinate workflow, obtain support for the product idea, and smoothly transfer the product to those groups that will ultimately manufacture, sell, and service it.

A number of studies have shown the importance of communication across group boundaries in R&D laboratories and have identified some of the roles individuals play in communication. What much of this research has shown is that particular patterns of communication are related to the performance of technical teams. Allen (1971, 1984) showed that in successful R&D projects, some individuals serve as technological gatekeepers. These individuals provide an important link between other team members and the outside environment. Specifically, gatekeepers have broad connections to external, technical information sources and serve to refine that knowledge and direct it to other members of the team. These technological gatekeepers provide links between the team and the broad technical environment outside the organization. Tushman (1977, 1979) expanded on these ideas and identified two other boundary roles, organization liaisons and laboratory liaisons, who serve to link the team to the organization and other units in the R&D function through the same two-step process of collecting and reviewing outside information and then communicating it within the team. His work also showed that the fit between the team's communication networks and the demands of the project will be related to the team's performance.

A somewhat broader framework is described by Roberts and Fusfeld (1981). They argue that successfully completing technical projects requires five work roles: idea generating (developing an idea for a new product or procedure); championing (gaining formal management support for the new idea); project leading (coordinating the activities and people necessary to develop the idea into a product); gatekeeping (collecting outside information and channeling it into the team); and sponsoring (providing resources and support for the project). Roberts and Fusfeld hypothesize that the importance of these roles changes throughout the product development process and that if these roles are not filled, the team is not likely to be successful. Al-

though this classification covers a wide range of roles related to the product development process, two of them, championing and gatekeeping, directly address the importance of the group's interactions with outsiders.

Collectively, these studies clearly show the importance of bringing technical information into the group and of linking the product development team to others in the organization. The studies also describe the various roles individuals occupy in this process. However, these studies have not investigated the full range of activities these teams take in dealing with others. Developing an understanding of the things team members do to establish and maintain connections with others can do two things. First, it can clarify the specific actions that contribute to filling specific roles. Second, it may provide some direction as to what the team can do to both acquire the information necessary for successful innovation and build the necessary bridges with others in the organization to ensure that the work of the team is supported. Thus, the purpose of this paper is to explore a fuller set of activities product develop teams take in dealing with other groups and to investigate how those activities contribute to the success or failure of the team. Our goal is to identify the specific things that product development team members do to manage their relations with outside groups and determine whether or not engaging in these activities enhances team performance.

RESEARCH SETTING AND METHODS

An important goal of our research was to describe the types of things group members do when they interact with others outside the group, identify patterns among these activities, and determine how these activities are related to the overall performance of the team. To identify this set of activities, we interviewed thirty-eight experienced product development team managers. The duration of the interviews averaged three hours. In the interviews, we asked each individual to describe the activities that the manager and team members carried out with people outside the group boundary. Questions dealt with the timing, frequency, target, and purpose of interactions across the entire life of the product development process. Through a review of these interviews we tried to develop an inclusive set of the things team members do in dealing with others. Based on that, we identified twenty-four specific activities that represented the complete set of boundary actions the managers described.

The thirty-eight interviews provided a rich set of data about how teams deal with other groups; however, because our goal was to provide a more direct empirical test of the impact of boundary activities on team operations, we collected systematic data from a set of product development teams, unrelated to those described by the interviewees. Thus, the conclusions we report are drawn from a study of forty-five product development teams in five high-technology companies in the computer, analytic instrumentation, and photographic industries. Each team was responsible for developing a prototype product for manufacture and sale. For example, one team was developing a product to automate the sampling process used in liquid chromatography, and another was developing a device that combined photographic and computer imaging processes. To ensure some compatibility across the teams, all the projects represented new product development (a major extension to an existing product line or the start of a new product line) as opposed to either basic research or the enhancement of features of an existing product, and all had a time frame of between one and one-half and three years.

We collected data about each of the teams from three sources: (1) an interview with the team leader regarding the history and nature of the project; (2) interviews with division or corporate management regarding the performance of the teams; and (3) a questionnaire survey of all members of the team including the leader.

Surveys were completed by 409, or 89 percent, of the members of the product development teams. The survey contained sections regarding the frequency with which team members communicated with others and assessments of the team's group process. In addition, the survey asked each team member to report how responsible he or she was for engaging in each of the twenty-four boundary activities we identified through the interviews described earlier. Team members were also asked to rate their own performance.

Executives in each firm rated the teams' performance at two points in time. The first was when the teams were about halfway through their lives. The same executives rated the teams again, after they had completed their work. At both points in time, executives assessed the teams in terms of the effectiveness of their operations and their overall level of innovation.

The combination of surveys, interviews, and performance ratings allowed us to look systematically at how team members deal with others and determine whether or not the ways teams interacted with outside groups were related to assessments of performance.

PATTERNS OF BOUNDARY ACTIVITIES

The first issue we explored was the pattern of activities in which individuals engaged to manage the boundary of the group. Because the questionnaire asked individuals to rate their responsibility on twenty-four separate actions, we used a principal component analysis to identify the smaller set of dimensions or "themes" that underlie the specific actions. This analysis showed that the items relating to how team members dealt with others could be combined into three dimensions.

- *Ambassador*—One set of activities included those aimed at representing the team to others and protecting the team from outside interference. Examples of the actions making up this dimension included "Prevent outsiders from 'overloading' the team with too much information or too many requests" and "Persuade other individuals that the team's activities are important."

- *Task Coordination*—The second set of actions we identified were aimed at coordinating the team's efforts with others. Examples include discussing design problems with others, obtaining feedback about the team's progress, and coordinating and negotiating with other groups. Specific items included "Resolve design problems with other groups" and "Negotiate with others for delivery deadlines."

- *Scouting*—The third set of activities represented general scanning for ideas and information about the market, the competition, or the technology. In contrast to the other sets, these actions were less specifically focused and more directed to building a general awareness and knowledge base than addressing specific issues. Examples included "Find out what competing firms or groups are doing on similar projects" and "Collect technical information/ideas from individuals outside the team."

The nature of these activity sets represents the complexity of the boundary management tasks of technical teams. Scouting provides the team with the broad technical and market information that is necessary for product development. These activities are primarily lateral and involve investigating markets, technologies, and competition; in short, bringing a great deal of data into the team. Task Coordination represents the lateral connections across functions that are necessary to deliver a product that meets the expectations of other functional groups. Teams that excel at this activity bargain with other groups, trade services or essential resources, and get feedback from other groups. In contrast to the other activity sets, Ambassador activities are primarily, although not exclusively, vertical. That is, they are aimed at securing effective sponsorship for the team, ensuring that the team has necessary resources, aligning the new product to the strategic direction of the organization, and in general, creating a favorable impression of the team and its efforts.

BOUNDARY ACTIVITIES AND THE PRODUCT DEVELOPMENT TEAM

While it is useful to know the nature of the activities team members undertake to manage their relations with other groups, it is important to understand whether or not these activities are related to the performance of the team and how other factors may influence the way these activities are completed by teams. What follows are conclusions we have drawn from our research.

The Nature of External Activities Is Related to Teams' Performance

The ways teams managed their boundaries were strongly related to their performance. However, these relationships were not simple, rather they are dependent on both the frequency of specific activities and when performance is measured. The extent to which team members engaged Task Coordination activities was directly related to top management's evaluation of team performance; however, the relationship between the frequency of these activities and team success was much stronger when the evaluation was obtained *after* the team completed its work than if the evaluation was made while the team was still working. In other words,

the frequency that team members engaged in things such as problem solving with other groups was related to the ultimate success of the team's efforts but not to interim evaluations of the team's progress.

A surprising relationship existed between Scout activities and performance. Those teams with high levels of Scout activities were rated substantially lower in performance at all points in time than those teams who engaged in fewer of these activities. At first glance, these results seem contrary to previous work on teams and to common sense. Why would teams who spend a great deal of effort understanding technical and market trends have poorer performance than those that don't? In looking specifically at teams we followed, some never got beyond exploring possibilities and moving to exploiting a technology and market niche. That is, some teams were never able to commit to a particular design. Rather, any new information would lead the team to reconsider the decisions it had already made. While bringing general information into the group is critical, it seems that it cannot become an enduring pattern. In fact, our findings are consistent with the notion that scanning the environment for broad, competitive, technical, and market information is critical *before* the team begins to work, but potentially disruptive once the team has begun to make product decisions.

A different pattern emerged for the relationship between Ambassador activity and performance. Teams with high levels of Ambassador activity received very positive evaluations from executives during the team's operations. However, when performance was assessed after the project was completed, the relationship between these activities and the success of the team was much lower. It seems that teams that devoted a great deal of effort to "managing upward" were initially viewed as successful by top management—but the impact of these activities declined over time.

Combining these results suggests that there is a particular timeliness to boundary activities. Linking boundary activities to management's evaluation of teams' performance suggests that Scouting should be done very early, perhaps even before the full team has begun operations; Ambassador activities are most necessary early in the group's process; and Task Coordination is important throughout the life of the team. This sequence of activities is similar to relationships between the phase of a project and the importance of roles hypothesized by Roberts and Fusfeld (1982).

The way groups manage their boundaries is clearly related to how top management in the firm evaluates the group's performance. However, a different pattern occurs when individual team members are asked to assess the performance of their own teams. As part of the questionnaire, team members were asked to rate the performance of their teams and to evaluate the extent to which the team members had developed a good internal process for working with each other (e.g., defining goals, prioritizing work, etc.) and good interpersonal relationships (e.g., getting along with each other, sticking together, etc.). A number of factors are worth note. First, top management's ratings of the teams were essentially uncorrelated with the team's assessment of its own performance. Second, neither the internal process teams developed, nor interpersonal relations were related to management's ratings of performance but both were strongly related to the *teams' own* assessments of their performances. Thus, company executives and team members seemed to have different models of what led to high performance. Team members associated high levels of performance with effectiveness in working with one another while management's assessments were driven by how effective the team was in working with outsiders.

Neither Frequent Communications nor Cross-Functional Teams Are a Substitute for Effective Boundary Management

Our results show that how teams interact with outsiders is related to their performance. The next question is whether or not other factors may serve as substitutes for these activities. Two other factors may influence the extent to which teams are able to develop positive relations with other functional groups. The first of these is the frequency with which team members interact with outsiders. The second represents the question of how the team is formed. That is, is placing individuals who represent different functions on the team a replacement for good boundary management?

The frequency of communication between the team and outsiders was much less predictive of performance than the type of activities. The total amount of communication had a small positive relationship with initial assessments of performance—but none at all with the final evaluations of the teams' efforts. What this shows is that it is not simply the amount team members interact with others that influences performance; rather it is the nature of those interactions. In other words, frequent communication with outsiders is necessary but not sufficient to build the cross-functional relations necessary for successful new product introduction. What is required is careful attention to the lateral negotiations represented by the Task Coordination activities and those early Ambassador activities that both shape others' perceptions of the team and buffer the team from interference.

Although at first glance the lack of a relationship between frequency of communication and team performance may seem counterintuitive, our findings are very consistent with previous studies of research teams (Allen, 1984; Katz and Tushman, 1979). As studies of boundary spanning roles have shown, effective teams do not rely on extensive external communication by all members, but instead have individuals (gatekeepers or liaisons) who collect, interpret, and triage information from sources outside the team or organization.

A popular approach to facilitate coordination is to form product development teams of individuals who represent the functional areas necessary to not only design, but also to build and market and service the product. Although the conclusions we can draw must be somewhat tentative, the data from our teams show that simply using cross-functional teams is not the answer. In fact, among the teams we studied, there was very little difference in performance between those with individuals from many functions compared to those made up exclusively of engineers. What we did find was that teams made up of a diverse set of individuals had more frequent communication with outsiders, but that communication alone is not enough. Rather, external communication must be carefully managed to ensure that effective boundary tasks are accomplished. In addition, our results also showed that cross-functional teams had more difficulty in coordinating some aspects of their internal processes than did teams that were not so diverse.

What our research showed was that neither the frequency with which the team communicates with others nor the functional diversity of team, in and of themselves, were strongly related to team performance. Rather, if correctly managed, these factors may help provide some basis for helping the team effectively complete the Ambassador and Task Coordination activities that facilitate team performance.

The Importance of Boundary Management Is Independent of Most Characteristics of the Project

Although our sample of teams were all involved in the development of sophisticated products, there were substantial differences in the characteristics of the products. During the interviews with team leaders, we asked them to rate their projects in terms of: (1) the extent to which it used a "revolutionary" technology; (2) the experience of the company in developing similar products; (3) the degree of competition anticipated for the new product; (4) the extent to which resources were available to the product development team; and (5) the predictability of the market for the product. There were very few relationships between the characteristics of the product under development and the extent to which members of the product teams undertook the various boundary activities. Because all of our teams were developing products in high technology companies, there may be more similarities than differences among them. However, among teams of this type, specific characteristics of the product or environment had little effect on the extent to which individual team members felt responsible for Ambassador, Task Coordination, or Scout activities.

Related to this is the question of whether or not the nature of boundary activities change under the life of the project. Based on our data, the answer is partially "yes." Ambassador activities were highest among teams that were either beginning a project or were nearing project conclusion, that is, at the point where "ownership" of the new product was about to be transferred to others. These activities were lower among those teams in the middle of the process.

Finally, to what extent do individual characteristics relate to responsibility for boundary management activity? Not surprisingly, the answer is "somewhat." Team leaders and individuals who had experience in the marketing function were more likely to take on responsibilities for Ambassador activities than people without these characteristics. The lateral cooperation reflected in the Task Coordination activities is slightly more likely to be the responsibility of the team leader, employees who have been in the company a long time, and individuals with experience in the manufacturing function than of those who do not possess these characteristics. Individuals with experience in the market-ing function report that they assume more responsibility for Scout activities than individuals without that experience. In thinking about how individual characteristics affect the extent boundary management activities, what must be kept in mind is that personal characteristics we measured—assigned leadership role, tenure in the company, experience on other teams, and experience in functional areas—had relatively little effect on what individuals reported they were responsible for. At most, these characteristics explained about 20 percent of the variance in individual levels of these activities.

Teams Have Distinct Strategies for Performing Boundary Activities

Our results show that there are distinct activities in which team members engage in dealing with others and that the frequency of these activities is related to the performance of the team. What was clear from our initial interviews was that not all teams exhibited all of these activities. Rather, just as teams develop unique styles of working internally, teams seemed to develop distinct strategies for approaching their environment; some seemed to specialize in particular sets of activities, others were generalists, and others did not seem to engage in much activity at all. To empirically identify those strategies among the teams we surveyed, we used a type of factor analysis to "cluster" teams into groups based on the frequency of their use of the different boundary activities. We found that teams used one of four different strategies: Ambassadorial, Researchers, Isolationists, and Comprehensives. The Ambassadorial teams engaged in very low levels of Task Coordination and Scouting but high levels of Ambassador activity. Researchers displayed high levels of Scouting, moderate levels of Task Coordination, and low levels of Ambassador activities. Isolationists were low on all the boundary activities. The Comprehensives combined high levels of Ambassador activities and Task Coordination with a low level of Scouting. In our study, approximately an equal number of teams used each of the four strategies.

The Ambassadorial teams seemed to specialize in working "vertically," that is, they concentrated on developing and maintaining relations with upper management. Relative to teams using other strategies, they communicated less frequently with outsiders. In terms of performance, these teams were only moderately effective. During the course of their work, top management rated them relatively high, particularly in terms of meeting budgets and schedules. However, at the conclusion of the project, the outcomes of these teams were not highly rated.

The Researcher teams concentrated on acquiring broad technical and market information. Although they had relatively high levels of communication with outsiders, they devoted low effort toward cultivating relations with upper management or establishing links with other functional groups. The performance ratings of these teams were low, particularly in terms of meeting budgets and schedules. Much of the reason for this seemed to lay in the inability of these teams to commit to and follow through on a course of action. Perhaps because of their constant search for "new" information, the members of these teams reported difficulty in establishing goals and developing priorities.

The Isolationist teams attempted to be self-contained. Compared to other groups, they were low in their interactions with others. They generally reported that they worked well together, yet the evaluations they received from top management were very low. Of particular interest, the products these teams developed received very low ratings in terms of how innovative they were. This finding is one more piece of evidence that outside input, rather than simply the ability of a group of technologists to work together well, is necessary for innovation within an organization.

The highest performing teams combined high levels of Task Coordination and Ambassador activity. These Comprehensive teams were highly rated throughout the life of their projects. In addition, the products these groups developed were rated as much more innovative than those developed by teams using other strategies. Not surprisingly, these teams engaged in frequent communication with others. What is surprising is that these teams did not develop the same level of internal interaction and cohesiveness as did the less successful teams who used different strategies for dealing with others.

MANAGING THE TEAM'S BOUNDARY

The notion of managing beyond a team's borders is counterintuitive to many team managers. Most of our models of management suggest that team building be-

gins with setting goals and priorities and having team members get to know and trust one another. Little in these models suggests that what a team also needs to do early in its life is link team priorities to corporate objectives or get feedback from other groups. Even fewer models suggest that teams may need to work to actively shape the expectations others hold for the team and product. Thus, the first step in successfully carrying out boundary management is educating team members about its importance.

Simply building an awareness of the importance of boundary management is not enough. The team needs to be organized to take on these responsibilities. The team might begin by developing a list of those individuals or groups within the organization who have the information, expertise, or resources the team might need. Parallel lists could identify the concerns other groups might have and the issues that need to be successfully resolved to gain commitment from the other groups that will take over the product. With this as a start, teams may then be able to decide how to allocate the work of managing external relations. As our research shows, the overall level of the responsibility for Task Coordination and Ambassador activity are related to team performance, with Task Coordination most directly related to final evaluations of the groups' work and Ambassador activity related to earlier evaluations. This suggests that teams that begin to build bridges with other groups, before specific coordination problems arise, may have the greatest opportunity for long-term success. Along these same lines, teams may use this exercise to determine when particular types of boundary activity need to be curtailed. For example, too much Scout activity, particularly once the team has committed itself to specifications, may be counterproductive.

Effective boundary management places special demands on the team leader. Our research shows that team leaders take on a large amount of this responsibility, yet our results also show that nature of these relations is such that the team leader cannot do it alone. Thus, the team leader may need to monitor the entire web of relations between the team and outsiders and ensure that these important tasks are completed. This may mean that the leader does many of these activities himself or herself, particularly those up and down the hierarchy, and develops a plan to ensure that lateral activities are completed by those who have the relevant technical knowledge. At a less obvious level, our results present another set of challenges for the leader. We found that the performance of the team was at least partially dependent on its relations with others. Yet, team members' models of what leads to effective performance do not include these variables. The leader must look beyond the ability of the group to work together and get along with one another to develop benchmarks for team performance that reflect how effectively the team is in working with outsiders.

At a broader level, what must an organization do to make it more likely that teams will develop effective boundary management strategies? When we presented the results of our research to executives in the companies we studied, they identified a number of things they might do to improve the ability of groups to deal with others. Most of the ideas they generated had implications for how team members are chosen and rewarded.

Selection and Development

In addition to making assignments to teams based on technical skills and the ability to work as part of a group, an explicit criterion for team assignment should be boundary management. That is, does the team have individuals on it who can effectively deal with outsiders? Are there individuals assigned to the team who can perform the activities necessary to serve as a gatekeeper or liaison? Not all team members need to be skilled in these external activities, yet the team's effectiveness depends on having sufficient resources in this area. This implies that management ensure that teams have individuals who are skilled at both Ambassador and Task Coordination activities and are capable of managing and focusing Scouting. This may require providing the training and feedback to develop individuals that can take on these activities.

Part of this training may involve describing a more complete model of group effectiveness to team members. Cross-functional teams and those that focus on building effective relations with other groups are inherently difficult to manage. In fact, encouraging teams to spend time working with nonteam members is counter to what frequently is seen as necessary to build a smoothly operating group. In fact, among the teams we studied, those that had the *least* communication with outsiders became the most cohesive and rated their own performance higher than other groups. For a team manager, this is something of a paradox. Encouraging the groups to build effective relations with outsiders contributes to high performance but at the same time may reduce the cohesiveness and sense of accomplishment of the group. If team managers have an expanded model of what constitutes an effective group, they may be less likely to concentrate solely on what is going on within the group.

Reward Systems

If teams are to develop an external focus, systems for supporting that will have to be developed. Particularly important may be the reward and career development systems. If individuals are evaluated solely by their performance in a function or if product team members are accountable to a functional manager rather than a team manager, it will be difficult for individuals to take on unfamiliar responsibilities—especially when it takes them outside their own expertise. If an organization wants to encourage cross-functional work, it must reward it. This does not mean that functional skills can be ignored in evaluations; rather it means that if the product development process requires cooperation and problem solving across functional lines, individuals possessing those skills must be rewarded.

BEYOND PRODUCT DEVELOPMENT TEAMS

The importance of how teams manage their boundaries with other groups is not confined to product development. Rather, boundary management will become a critical factor for success in many organizations. Organizations are changing; the flat, flexible, networked, global organization is often team based. Teams in these organizations cannot work the ways they have in the past. Success depends on developing linkages with others in the organization to get work done. The teams that can best pull together the expertise of the firm and move their ideas and products quickly through the organization are those that will succeed.

NOTE

A more complete description of this research is reported in: Bridging the boundary: external activity and performance in organizational teams. *Administrative Science Quarterly,* 37, 4 (1992); and Demography and design: predictors of new product Team Performance. *Organization Science,* 3, 3 (1992).

REFERENCES

Allen, T. J. (1971). Communication networks in R&D laboratories. *R&D Management,* 1, 14–21.

Allen, T. J. (1984). *Managing the flow of technology: Technology transfer and the dissemination of technical information within the R&D organization.* Cambridge, MA: MIT Press.

House, C. H. and Price, R. L. (1991). The return map: Tracking product teams. *Harvard Business Review,* 69, 92–100.

Katz, R. and Tushman, M. (1979). Communication patterns, project performance, and task characteristics. *Organizational Behavior and Human Performance,* 23, 139–62.

Kazanjian, R. K. (1988). Relation of dominant problems to stages of growth in technology-based new ventures. *Academy of Management Journal,* 31, 257–79.

Roberts, E. and Fusfeld, A. (1981). Staffing the innovative technology-based organization. *Sloan Management Review,* 22(3), 19–34.

Roberts, E. and Fusfeld, A. (1982). Critical functions: Needed roles in the innovation process. In R. Katz (ed.), *Career issues in human resource management.* Englewood Cliffs, NJ: Prentice-Hall.

Tushman, M. (1977). Special boundary roles in the innovation process. *Administrative Science Quarterly,* 22, 587–605.

Tushman, M. (1979). Work characteristics and subunit communication structure: A contingency analysis. *Administrative Science Quarterly,* 24, 82–98.

31

Strategic Linking

DAVID A. NADLER
MICHAEL L. TUSHMAN

ABB (ASEA BROWN BOVERI)—A GLOBAL FEDERATION OF LOCAL BUSINESSES

ABB, the Zurich-based industrial giant that designs, produces, and sells electrical systems and equipment around the world, employs a complex organizational structure based on a series of strategic contradictions.

Formed in 1988 through the merger of Sweden's ASEA and Switzerland's Brown Boveri, ABB now does business in 140 countries. As the two companies were being merged, CEO Percy Barnevik envisioned a strategy that would exploit global economies of scale and the swift transfer of expertise while capitalizing on the deeply local roots of the hundreds of companies that made up the conglomerate. In other words, ABB wanted to be both big and small, both centralized and decentralized, both global and local.

Faced with that challenge, Barnevik assigned ten of the company's brightest people to a team he dubbed "The Manhattan Project" and gave them six weeks to design an entirely new organizational structure. The result: a complex matrix in which each of the 300 local companies is grouped within one of fifty business areas, which in turn are grouped into a dozen or so industry segments. In addition, for each country in which ABB operates, there is a manager who oversees areas such as governmental relations, labor-management issues, and staff development for all the ABB units within that country. Consequently, each company president reports to two bosses—a country manager and a business area manager. The president of ABB Combustion Engineering in Windsor, Connecticut, for example, reports both to the U.S. country manager and to the global manager of the Power Engineering Business Area (see Figure 31.1). The result is an organization that can act as a global powerhouse to amass resources, technological know-how, production innovations, and distribution networks to compete on a par with any major corporation even as it constantly emphasizes its deep connections to local markets and customers. The coordination of 210,000 employees, working in 300 companies and 5,000 profit centers in 140 countries, demonstrates the crucial role of linking mechanisms in turning a complex kaleidoscope of grouping patterns into a smoothly functioning organization. ABB also illustrates how successful such designs can be; with net income of $1.3 billion, ABB saw its stock price double between 1992 and 1996.

THE NEED FOR COORDINATION

Strategic grouping [Nadler and Tushman 1997, Chapter 5], by definition separates some jobs and individuals at the same time it brings others together. For example, if Percy Barnevik had decided to group ABB's companies exclusively by business area or by country, huge walls would have instantaneously gone up be-

From *Competing by Design: The Power of Organizational Architecture,* by David A. Nadler and Michael L. Tushman, pp. 89–115. Copyright © 1997 by Oxford University Press, Inc. Used by permission of Oxford University Press, Inc.

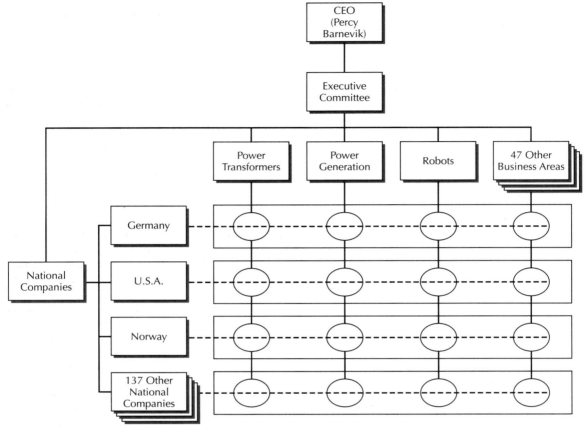

Figure 31.1. ABB (simplified structure).

tween operations with shared interests and responsibilities. If he'd chosen a geographic grouping, for instance, plants manufacturing similar products in Germany, Poland, and Muncie, Indiana, would have found it much more difficult to share staff and production technologies. If the grouping had been solely by business area, on the other hand, ABB companies in Norway or Portugal or any other country would have lacked the centralized leadership that has allowed them to deal efficiently with common issues such as tax policy, labor unions, and executive recruitment.

Strategic linking, in essence, involves the design of formal structures and processes to link related operations that have been separated by strategic grouping. Once the key decisions have been made about strategic grouping, the next step is to provide the necessary

mechanisms to coordinate work so that the company can work as an integrated enterprise.

While grouping decisions are driven by strategy considerations, the basis for linking decisions is rooted in the concept of *task interdependence*. Different degrees of task interdependence among groups call for different kinds of formal linking mechanisms; the objective is to design mechanisms that allow each group to receive from other groups the information it needs to perform its work and achieve its objectives. Linkages that are incapable of providing the necessary flow of information inevitably result in poor coordination; those that are more extensive and elaborate than necessary prove costly and hinder the flow of information. The key is to figure out which mechanisms are essential, without going overboard. In this chapter, we discuss different variations of work interdependence, present a range of formal linking mechanisms, and offer an approach to making linking decisions. We conclude by looking at ways in which the informal organization enhances coordination throughout the organization (see Figure 31.2), supplementing the formal linking mechanisms.

VARIETIES OF WORK INTERDEPENDENCE

Linking, like grouping, involves several sets of considerations. For the organization designer, the problem is to select the right set of linking mechanisms to deal with: (1) work flows between distinct yet interdependent units, (2) the need for disciplinary or staff-based professionals to have contact across the company, and (3) work flows associated with emergencies or temporary, short-term goals.

The conceptual thread running through work flow, disciplinary linkages, and work requirements under crisis conditions is *work-related interdependence.* Managers choose linking mechanisms to deal with this source of uncertainty. The greater the task interdependence, the greater the need for coordination and joint problem solving. The higher the degree of interdependence, the more complex the formal linkage devices must be to handle work-related uncertainty. On the other hand, groups that are only minimally interdependent have relatively little need for coordination and joint problem solving and therefore need fairly simple formal linking devices.

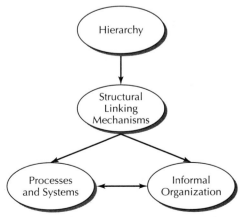

Figure 31.2. A range of formal linking mechanisms.

Consider branch banks located throughout a city. Each branch's operations are largely independent of the others, except to the extent that they share advertising and marketing resources. Similarly, business units within a diversified company with completely different product/market niches are also essentially independent of each other except for those corporate resources, such as staff and technology, that are shared among divisions. Both examples illustrate *pooled interdependence,* characterized by relatively independent units of the same organization that share certain scarce resources. In these situations, there is only a limited need for coordination and linking mechanisms (see Figure 31.3).

Now think about the back office operation of bank, where checks move through a progression of departments before exiting the bank. This is an example of *sequential interdependence;* each work unit must interact closely with those that immediately precede and follow it in the orderly sequence of performing a particular work process. Sequentially interdependent units must deal with a greater degree and variety of problem-solving and coordination requirements than is required for units that have pooled interdependence. Groups with sequential interdependence require close coordination and timing so that work flows remain smooth and uninterrupted; each unit in the work flow is dependent upon the units back upstream.

If you consider our Technicon case [Nadler and Tushman 1997, Chapter 3], the marketing division was heavily reliant on both R&D and Production for the development of new laboratory testing products. Each functional area had to be in close contact with the others to ensure the synthesis of market, technological, and production considerations. Similarly, in an advertising agency, the media, creative, and account services areas must work closely in the development of ad campaigns for their clients. These are examples of *reciprocal interdependence,* in which each group must work with all the others to create a common product or service (see Figure 31.3). Reciprocal interdependence imposes substantial coordination and problem-solving requirements between units; no single unit can accomplish its task without the active contributions of every other unit.

Pooled, sequential, and reciprocal interdependence represent progressively higher degrees of work-related interdependence. Reciprocal interdependence

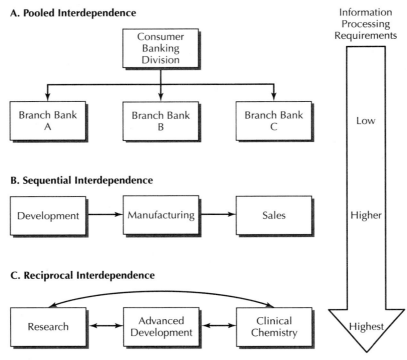

Figure 31.3. Forms of interdependence.

imposes greater coordination costs and complexity than does sequential interdependence, which, in turn, requires greater coordination than pooled interdependence.

Beyond normal work flows, organizations sometimes experience situations characterized by abnormally high degrees of task interdependence; these include emergencies, crises, short-term projects, and one-time efforts aimed at resolving important problems that require participation from throughout the organization. These are situations in which units that normally pool their resources suddenly have to work together with much closer coordination. Going back to our branch banks, for example, if a power blackout were to hit one part of town, branch banks in the unaffected areas would have to work together to deal with the emergency. Temporary alterations in interdependence frequently occur when product divisions that share similar technologies or knowledge bases are asked to join forces on a particular corporate venture

that requires the combination of their resources and particular skills.

Finally, quite apart from work flow considerations, professionals must maintain contacts across organization boundaries. If grouped only with others of the same discipline, they run the risk of becoming overly specialized; if cut off from professional colleagues, they may lose touch with current developments in their respective fields. The greater the rate of change in the particular discipline, the greater the need for interdependence.

Whether driven by work flows, crises, or professionally anchored need for collaboration, these differing degrees of work-related interdependence impose different information processing requirements. Those units that have pooled interdependence (or in which the rate of change of the underlying knowledge base is low) have fewer coordination demands and information-processing requirements than do units that have reciprocal interdependence. The designer's challenge is to choose the appropriate set of linking mechanisms to deal with the information-processing requirements that arise from work-related interdependence.

Finally, just as strategic grouping is relevant at multiple levels of analysis, so too is the assessment of work-related interdependence. At Technicon, not only was there reciprocal interdependence among the functional areas, but within R&D, each discipline was reciprocally interdependent in new-product-development efforts. Just as grouping patterns may vary from one level of the organization to another, and from one division to another, so too may the patterns of work-related interdependence vary throughout the enterprise. More and more companies are developing linking patterns that extend beyond the traditional outer boundaries of the company to reflect heightened interdependence with customers, suppliers, and partners. . . .

STRATEGIC LINKING: A RANGE OF ALTERNATIVES

Various types of formal mechanisms can be used to link and coordinate the efforts of organizational groups. Our objective is to choose those structural linking mechanisms that provide adequate information flows, procedures, and structures to deal with the information requirements imposed by work-related interdependence. The various options can be assessed in terms of their ability to handle information flows and complex problem-solving requirements.

The most obvious form of structural linking is the *hierarchy*—the formal distribution of power and authority. The hierarchy of authority follows directly from grouping decisions. In a divisional structure, for example, functional managers report to their respective divisional general managers, who, in turn, report to the company president. Coordination and linking between managers at the same level can be accomplished via their common boss, who channels information, controls the type and quantity of information that moves among groups, and adjudicates conflicts. If you think about it, that's precisely the function served by the hierarchical structure of ABB, our opening case. The combination of country managers and business area managers provides for linkages—coordination of joint projects, sharing of pooled resources, and contin-

ual flow of information—across functional and geographic boundaries.

The formal hierarchy is the simplest and one of the most pervasive formal linking mechanisms. Focused, sustained, and consistent behavior by the manager can both direct and set the stage for the effective coordination between organizational groups. And yet, hierarchy is a limited linking mechanisms. Uncertainty about external conditions, special projects, joint operations, occasional crises—any and all of the shifting conditions that can rearrange the interdependence of units with an organization can easily overload an individual manager. When that happens, other devices must be used to complement the manager's role as a linking mechanism. These include:

- *Liaison roles.* Situations involving two or more groups in intensive problem-solving situations often require the assignment of specific people to work together in liaison roles. They serve as sources of information and expertise and as contacts and advisers on work involving their respective groups. In essence, they serve as information conduits deep within the organization. Although people in liaison roles are responsible for enhanced coordination and information flows between units, they rarely have the authority to impose their decisions on others. The liaison role is not usually a full-time responsibility but rather is done in conjunction with other activities (see Figure 31.4).

- *Cross-unit groups.* Another device used frequently to coordinate the work of multiple units is the cross-unit group. These are groups designed to focus on particular clients, products, markets, or problems. Representatives from each related work group are pulled together, either permanently or on an ad hoc

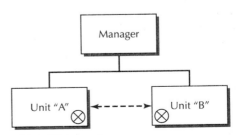

Figure 31.4. Liaison roles.

basis, to pool their expertise and to coordinate their efforts. In contrast with liaison roles, cross-unit groups provide a more extensive forum for coordinating, exchanging information, and resolving conflict among work units. Although these task forces, teams, or groups may be created only when needed, it often makes sense to design them into the formal structure if it's apparent that cross-unit projects will be common. In a medical center, for example, a permanent group with representatives of each of the major divisions of the complex might be responsible for establishing and adjusting guidelines and processes that affect work flows across divisions (see Figure 31.5).

- *Integrator roles.* In situations that require decisions involving several groups, informal teams and liaison roles might not be sufficient. No single individual may feel accountable for collective performance. The manager responsible for the various groups may lack the time or the expertise to adjudicate differences. Faced with the need for swift problem-solving and a general management perspective, organiza-

tions sometimes assign an individual to act as an integrator. The person in this role is responsible for taking a general management point of view in helping multiple-work groups accomplish a joint task, such as a specific product or project (see Figure 31.6).

Product, brand, geographic, and account managers all are examples of formal integrator roles; their purpose is to identify someone who will share a general management perspective with other, specialized managers who bring to the table essential expertise but relatively narrow concerns. Integrators have the formal responsibility of achieving coordination across the organization. While they report to senior management, they usually lack the formal authority to direct their functional and/or disciplinary colleagues. Because of this dotted-line relationship to members of their team, integrators must rely on expertise, interpersonal competence, and team and conflict-resolution skills to shape the efforts of sometimes recalcitrant team members.

It's essential for integrators to acquire the functional or disciplinary resources necessary to accomplish their work. When there are several projects, accounts, or products, each is competing with the others for scarce resources. Consider the Technicon research lab [Nadler and Tushman 1997, Chapter 3]. Each project manager was left to his or her own devices to scavenge help from each of the divisions within the lab; all were competing for some of the same people, while the division heads were reluctant to part with any staff at all. In such situations, to increase the power of the special projects integrators

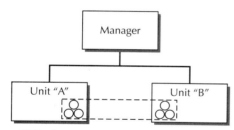

Figure 31.5. Cross-unit groups.

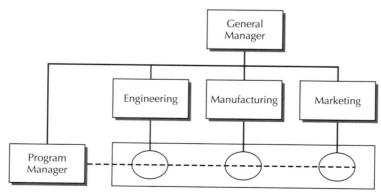

Figure 31.6. Integrators (project, brand, program, account managers).

and to coordinate resources, organizations sometimes create departments specifically to oversee product development (see Figure 31.7).

These structures are common in functional or geographic organizations that must also focus on developing specific products. In these situations, the product side of the organization has its own senior manager, who reports along the same line as the functional managers. This senior manager formally represents the product side of the organization at senior levels and assists in resource allocation across projects. However, the functional organization still reports to its functional supervisors and has a dotted-line relationship with the project/product manager. Consider how this might have worked in the Technicon lab; the project managers, who continued to complain of their inability to deal with the resistance of lab division managers might have had more success if they had been reporting to a product development manager who reported directly to the lab director.

While we've focused on integrator roles in the realm of product development, the role is, in fact, quite common and applicable in numerous situations. Regardless of the nature of the organization in which it is used, the purpose of the role is to offset the coun-terproductive consequences of strategic grouping and to achieve coordination and real-time problem solving at lower levels of complex organizations.

- *Matrix structures.* As we've already seen in the cases of Xerox, SMH, and ABB, corporate strategies frequently require equal attention to multiple priorities: products and functions, for instance, or markets and technical expertise. Whenever strategy requires simultaneous emphasis on several dimensions—product, market, and geography, for example—or when numerous operations are positioned in permanent relationships involving intense degrees of interdependence, normal integrator roles lack the capacity to handle the enormous information-processing requirements. In these situations, what's called for is a matrix structure.

A matrix organization structurally improves coordination by balancing the power between competing aspects of the organization and by installing systems and roles designed to achieve multiple objectives simultaneously. For example, an R&D facility that wants to maximize both disciplinary competence and product focus might design a matrix structure, with directors of the different laboratories reporting to both disciplinary and product managers. The dotted-line relationship (seen in the integrator role) becomes

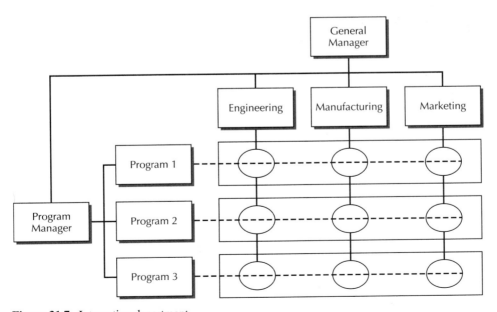

Figure 31.7. Integrating department.

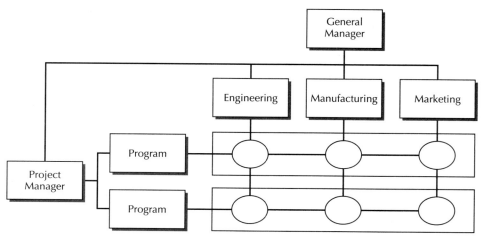

Figure 31.8. Matrix organization.

solid; key members of the laboratory have two bosses. In more concrete terms, that's exactly the way
ABB is set up: The president of each operating company has two bosses, a country manager and a business area manager.

   Figure 31.8 illustrates a classic matrix structure,
with two chains of command. On the right side are
the traditional functional departments: engineering,
manufacturing, and marketing. The organization still
benefits from the information exchange and control
provided by the grouping of people by function. On
the left is another chain of command, with a product
manager for each major new product coordinating
the activities of individuals across functional groups.
Thus, functional managers who supervise product-
related activities have two bosses—a functional boss
and a product boss. In this way, information is
processed both within and across functional groups
at the same time that product-related activities are
being coordinated.

   From every perspective, matrix structures are
complex. They require dual systems, roles, controls,
and rewards. Systems, structures, and processes must
be developed to handle both dimensions of the matrix. Furthermore, matrix managers must deal with
the difficulties of sharing a common subordinate,
while the common subordinate must face off against
two bosses.

   As shown in Figure 31.9, the general manager is

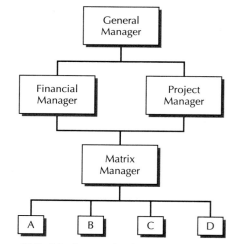

Figure 31.9. Matrix organization: another perspective.

the single boss, the point at which each side of the
matrix comes together. This individual must ensure
that each side of the matrix enjoys equal power and
influence; otherwise, the organization will revert to a
single-focus organization. Below the matrix manager
there is also a clear hierarchy; his or her subordinates
report to one boss. The matrix is most directly felt by
the matrix manager and the two matrix supervisors.
It is this relatively narrow slice of the organization
that really sees matrix systems, roles, procedures,

and processes. This set of four roles must constantly balance the pressures and conflicts in a structure that attempts to work several strategic directions at once.

In the case of ABB, only 500 or so of the 210,000 employees actually find themselves in matrix roles, with two bosses. But for each of them, the challenge of handling continuous ambiguity is considerable. Those managers, says CEO Percy Barnevik, "must have the self-confidence not to become paralyzed if they receive conflicting signals, and the integrity not to play one boss off against the other" (Taylor 1991).

While the matrix structure is the most complex and conducive to conflict of the major linking mechanisms, it is, at the same time, the only structure designed to maximize several strategically important considerations at once. Given its complexity and its inherent instability, a matrix structure should be reserved for situations in which no other linking alternative is workable.

MAKING STRUCTURAL LINKING DECISIONS

There are a number of basic criteria for comparing alternative linking mechanisms: cost and resource utilization; dependence on the informal organization; and inherent capacity for processing information (see Figure 31.10). The key to effective decisions about linking mechanisms is to choose the formal structures that are most consistent with the work-related interdependence of the groups to be linked. As we stated earlier, overly complex mechanisms are expensive and inefficient; arrangements that are too simple for the work at hand just won't get the job done.

In general terms, major forms of structural linking mechanisms can be assessed on the basis of these dimensions:

1. The *cost, in terms of both money and resources,* associated with each mechanism differs greatly. The formal hierarchy and liaison roles require sustained attention to coordination by only a few key individuals; matrix structures, on the other hand, require dual structures, systems, and procedures. Matrix structures also require time, energy, and effort devoted to committees and teams that attend to both axes of the matrix. The more people, systems, and procedures that are involved, the more costly the linking mechanism.

2. Formal linking mechanisms also differ in their *dependence on the informal organization.* Whereas the hierarchy and some liaison roles rest firmly on the formal organization, cross-group units, integrator roles, and matrix structures depend to a great degree on a healthy informal organization. Those more complex linking mechanisms actually create conflict within the organization; accordingly, they succeed best in situations where a resilient informal operating environment can handle the ambiguity and the conflict inherent in intense relationships of interdependence. Indeed, matrix structures work only in organizations whose values, beliefs, and practices allow for open conflict resolution, constant collaboration, and ambiguous relationships. Thus, the more complex the formal linking mechanism, the greater the dependence on the informal system.

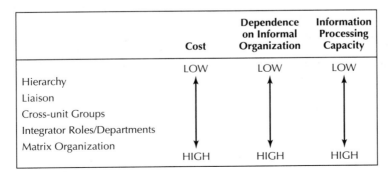

Figure 31.10. Consequences of structural linking mechanisms.

3. The *information-processing capacities* of the various linking mechanisms vary significantly. The hierarchy and the liaisons forms are limited by capacity of the individuals involved to collect, process, and channel information. These simple linking mechanisms deal well with simple interdependence but cannot deal with substantial uncertainty or complex work interdependence. Liaison roles, for example, can relay only limited amounts of information; while they can identify issues that require coordination, their capacity to resolve conflicts is limited. Integrator roles, task forces, cross-unit groups, and matrix structures not only can identify the issues to be handled but can also involve the right number of people from various units to coordinate and complete a job. These more complex mechanisms push decision making deep into the system and take advantage of a great many more resources and perspectives. They allow for multiple points of view and real-time problem solving and error correction.

As is the case with grouping, decisions about linking must be made at every level of the organization. Because managers at each level are dealing with different degrees of work interdependence and different information-processing requirements, each will face different choices about linking mechanisms. For example, the sequential interdependence at the corporate level can be handled by a senior team or committee; more complex linking mechanisms are required to deal with reciprocal interdependence within the division.

Structural linking is an important managerial tool. Whereas a single form of strategic grouping is selected for each level of the organization, there may be a host of structural linking mechanisms within a single unit. At Technicon's R&D facility, for example, structural linking might be accomplished via a matrix organization throughout the laboratory. Furthermore, special task forces might be set up to deal with the impact of new technologies on the organization; a top team might be convened to deal with a new competitive threat; and informal committees might be established to share expertise across disciplines within the laboratory. Linking, then, can be a powerful and flexible tool to deal with the different coordination requirements that exist within all organizations.

Finally, as work interdependence shifts over time, so too should the choice of linking mechanisms. These mechanisms need not be permanent; indeed, one of their advantages is that they can be created to deal specifically with an immediate problem—the rapid development and introduction of a new product, the formulation of a response to an immediate competitive threat, or the resolution of problems involving a specific customer or supplier. At Ford, for example, a special Skunk Works was created in 1989 for the express purpose of redesigning—and, in truth, rescuing—the Mustang. Engineers and production specialists from throughout the Ford empire were drafted to work exclusively on the project, which lasted until the first new Mustang rolled off the assembly line in 1993. At that point, the team was disbanded, although the Skunk Works concept had proven to be so effective that Ford decided to use it again to focus cross-unit resources intensively on other problems (Ingrassia and White 1994).

LINKING THROUGH PROCESSES AND SYSTEMS

Up to this point, we've discussed linking mechanisms largely in terms of the formal roles and structures that constitute the hierarchy of any organization or work group. But designers of organizations have become increasingly aware in recent years that *processes* and *systems* also play a vital role in coordinating activity and in enabling people to link their efforts into productive work. In this context, we use the term "processes" to describe sequences of collaborative efforts by groups and individuals, at various organizational levels and frequently across structural boundaries, performed in the pursuit of a common objective. The term "systems" refers to mechanisms that use human or physical technology to enable people and groups to perform the work required by a particular process.

Although processes and systems seem somewhat nebulous in contrast with formal hierarchical structures, they are gaining growing attention as potentially powerful sources of linking in coordination. In practice, processes and systems often complement formal hierarchical roles and structures. In some cases—and to a limited extent—processes and systems can even take the place of traditional hierarchies.

Because the focus on processes is a relatively recent phenomenon, there is still considerable discussion and a wide range of views on how to approach them from the perspective of organization design. In general, however, we believe that organization processes can be classified in three broad categories:

1. *Strategic management processes.* These are processes involved in shaping, directing, and controlling activity at the enterprise level. Strategic planning, general management, resource allocation, and operational reviews all fall into this category. These are processes that link and coordinate activities by creating overall plans, providing the resources and direction that allow units to mesh their activities in accordance with the plan, and then assessing the degree to which the units have met their goals. These are basically control processes that set direction and provide the information necessary for assessment and error correction.

2. *Business management processes.* These processes coordinate work flow—the movement of products, services, and resources through the organization and across grouping boundaries—in order to create an offering of value to the customer. More and more organizations are coming to perceive product development, for example, as a cross-unit process rather than as the exclusive domain of a single department where scientists and engineers work in a vacuum to dream up new products divorced from any timely insights into market trends or customer needs. Increasingly, product development is being seen as a continuous feedback loop, with sales, marketing, and service people working closely with the units that design, produce and distribute goods and services; it is a multidimensional process that draws on the skills, experience, and information of numerous people from a wide range of functions and disciplines. The design of product development, order fulfillment, and customer management as coordinated processes, rather than as isolated departments, represents a fundamentally new way of thinking about how organizations should be architected.

3. *Support management processes.* These include activities such as human resources, public relations, and information management, which provide the policies and practices that enable the organization to conduct its operations in an orderly way and in keeping with its articulated standards and values.

It's important to note that each set of processes has an associated set of systems—communications systems, production systems, systems for staff selection and training. Processes and systems are inherently wed; generally speaking, processes are incapable of functioning without the requisite systems. A budget-planning and control process, for example, is worthless without an appropriate business information system capable of identifying, gathering, processing, and reporting the necessary data. At each level, the smooth integration of processes and systems plays a large role in determining the organization's capacity to coordinate work.

While the emergence of business processes as an important form of linking has attracted considerable attention . . . design leaders should also be paying close attention to the significant linking power inherent in support processes such as human resources, quality assurance, and information systems.

SUPPORT MANAGEMENT PROCESSES

Consider, for example, the strategic selection process at Xerox, first designed to identify candidates for top-management positions during the 1992 restructuring. In this process, a systematic determination of the skills and the personal characteristics required for leadership positions is made; these are then matched with profiles of prospective candidates. The employment of a company-wide process for selection and assessment, including a shared list of the most important criteria, not only links the business units through a shared understanding of leadership requirements; it also helps identify people in each unit who have the potential to take on important jobs in other parts of the company.

Reward systems, in particular, are among the most potent support processes for reinforcing linkages throughout the organization by motivating the required behavior. It's only human nature for each of us to pay close attention to the performance criteria on which we'll be evaluated and rewarded. Consequently, there has to be a high degree of consistency between linkage mechanisms and patterns of rewards; otherwise, the organization is sending conflicting signals, which can only result in confusion, frustration, and inadequate performance.

Consider, for example, an organization in which the manufacturing division is rewarded on the basis of gross margins, while the sales division is rewarded for volume. Clearly, sales will do everything possible to reduce the unit price in order to sell as much as possible. Every time it drops the price—and, as a result, the margin—the manufacturing group takes a beating. Manufacturing, on the other hand, may be cutting corners wherever possible to lower the unit cost—but in the process, it may be diminishing the product's quality or eliminating popular features that the sales force believes are important to customers. Driven by contradictory rewards systems, the two divisions end up working at cross-purposes. There is no set of structural linking mechanisms that can overcome such starkly conflicting reward patterns.

The Technicon research lab, despite its other problems, was making a creditable attempt to align its rewards systems with its linkage mechanisms. In the past, in keeping with its functional and activity-based grouping, scientists were rewarded solely on the basis of the technical quality of their research and of the recognition they'd won within the discipline. As the lab was reorganized with a team of project directors to focus attention on developing marketable products and processes, the incentive system was fundamentally changed; rewards were directly tied to product-related achievements.

Any bonus and incentive systems should incorporate these general principles:

- Incentives should clearly link performance to pay and should directly link performance to specific standards and objectives. If a team's objective is customer satisfaction, that should be the measure of performance, rather than volume or duration of service calls, which may bear little relation to whether the customer's needs were actually met.

- Rewards should relate directly to the nature of performance required at each level of the organization. At Corning, for example, in order to develop a true team perspective among top executives, the bonus plan for each member of the senior team is based largely on the entire company's success in meeting certain specific financial goals, such as stock price. But in other situations—fund managers in an invest-

ment firm, for example—it's more appropriate to base rewards on each person's individual performance.

- Rewards should be directly linked to objectives that are within the group's or individual's power to control. The manufacturing division we just mentioned had no control over margins, the basis of its incentives, as long as the sales division could unilaterally change prices to fuel volume sales.

- Incentive plans should match measurement periods for rewards to relevant performance periods; some goals can be assessed after three months, while it might not be practical to evaluate others in less than a year. Some incentive programs recognize that fact by containing both short- and long-term goals.

- Reward systems should be guided by the principle of equity, not equality.

From the standpoint of organizational architecture, designers need to step back, take a broad view, and appreciate the importance of processes at all three levels—strategic, business, and support. They need to examine these two issues:

1. To what extent will a new design affect existing processes? Some processes will continue to be valid, while others will become obsolete. Some processes may still be necessary but become unworkable in their present form.

2. In light of new grouping patterns introduced by redesign, what new processes will be needed to link those reconfigured groupings?

In short, as designers look at the new organization and the need for linkages, they need to think beyond traditional ideas of hierarchies and formal structures and fully explore the expanding role of processes in modern enterprises.

STAFF VERSUS LINE

Implicit in our discussion of processes is the obvious need for people to perform these vital management and support functions. But that's become something of a touchy subject in these times of downsizing, lean bureaucracies, and an overwhelming focus on concentrating resources in those areas that provide immediate value to the customer and add value directly to the bottom line.

Yet, the fact remains that no complex organization can function efficiently over an extended period of time without proper management, control, and support. The issue for designers is to figure out the extent to which those processes are required and then to manage the inherent conflict between staff and line positions. To be clear about our terms, *line* positions are jobs directly involved with the organization's core business processes—designing, producing, delivering, or selling the organization's offerings. *Staff,* on the other hand, refers to people and jobs assigned to management and support processes such as human resources, finance, planning, legal, and information services. Staff positions are essentially extensions of the management function, with the purpose of aiding in control and coordination.

The design of staff jobs always raises some fundamental problems. First, because these jobs, by definition, are not directly involved with producing or selling the company's offerings, they're generally viewed as unproductive overhead. Moreover, at a time when many companies are seeking the benefits of decentralization, staff jobs are seen as extensions of centralized planning and decision making. Indeed, staff jobs are often perceived as not just unproductive but as downright counterproductive.

That's an unfair generalization, although it's easy enough to understand the ongoing friction between line and staff managers. Particularly in large organizations, staff groups serve important functions. To begin with, as we've already seen, grouping promotes focus; without some staff groups, certain functions outside the realm of the core business, such as human resources, would inevitably become after-thoughts or even drop from sight altogether. Staff groups augment the ability of senior management to gather, process, and disseminate information; in a large corporation, it's just impossible for top executives to be everywhere and see everything. Third, staff groups monitor and coordinate policies among various units, ensuring consistency throughout the organization in areas such as personnel policies and financial reporting requirements. Finally, the pooling of expert resources in staff groups ought to provide economies of scale. Corporate human resource, planning, and research staff groups, for example, develop specialized expertise in their respective areas. They serve as resources for professionals working within the divisions and coordinate, link, and update their more local colleagues.

Those are the advantages of staff groups. On the other hand, the problems they present, in practice, are considerable. Some of the major ones are these:

1. *Proliferation and growth.* The seeds of staff groups, once planted in organizational soil, take root quickly and grow like crazy. After reaching maturity, they're tough to cut back and nearly impossible to wipe out; the work they do, by its very nature, never seems to be finished.

2. *Direct costs.* On one hand, staff groups do not directly contribute to output, nor do they generate revenue. But their payrolls can be staggering.

3. *Indirect costs.* In addition to salaries, expenses, clerical support, and facilities, support staffs impose substantial indirect costs. The most important are the time and effort line managers spend responding to requests, demands, and requirements imposed by staff. There's also the additional time required for making decisions whenever staff people get involved.

4. *Competition for power.* The often adversarial relationship between line and staff creates dysfunctional conflicts and power plays. The costs to the organization, both direct and indirect, can be immense.

5. *Internal management and motivation.* Staff groups frequently are hard to manage, difficult to motivate, and impossible to satisfy. Their work rarely lends itself to easy measurement or assessment, so rewards are tricky. Moreover, because of their role outside the core functions, they see their career opportunities as severely limited.

6. *Bureaucratization.* Staff groups, focused by definition on processes rather than outputs, can encourage bureaucratic cultures marked by increased costs, slower response times, and widespread frustration.

7. *Building defensive staffs.* The staff problem becomes truly critical when line managers create their own "defensive" staffs to ward off the attacks of the invading central staff. Like other staffs groups, the new ones contribute nothing to output or revenue, drive up costs, and immediately begin proliferating, thus continuing the perpetual life cycle of staff groups.

Given both the need for certain staff functions, plus the serious problems often associated with staff groups, the organization designer faces a delicate balancing act. The trick is to create staff groups capable of control and coordination without creating a bureaucratic monster that can reshape the very nature of the organization it was supposed to assist.

There are some specific techniques that effective organizations have used to prevent staff groups from manifesting some of their more dysfunctional characteristics. These include:

1. *Layering*—limiting the number of layers of staff groups by prohibiting redundant staffs at successive levels. Layering prevents excessive staff-to-staff interaction and speeds the movement of information through the hierarchy.

2. *Rotating*—limiting the number of career staff people and rotating line employees into staff assignments. This combines technical expertise with practical knowledge of the core business. It also alleviates internal management problems, minimizes conflict, and builds greater appreciation of various perspectives within the organization.

3. *Pruning*—periodically "pruning" staff groups by reassigning as many people as possible to line positions.

4. *Clarifying*—wherever possible, stipulating management processes and individual roles. The laws of organizational physics state that staff groups will expand to fill vacuums left by ambiguous processes (such as those for goal setting, decision making, and allocating resources). Clear boundaries limit their expansion and decrease opportunities for conflict.

5. *Managing*—articulating and demonstrating what you believe to be the proper role of staff groups. How managers spend their time—and who they spend it with—clearly conveys their true feelings about the respective roles of line and staff groups.

INFORMAL LINKING PROCESSES

Before leaving the topic of strategic linking, it's important to note that within most organizations there are powerful linking forces that lie beyond the scope of formal structures and processes. Although they are not an obvious element of the formal design process, they nevertheless are significant factors that managers need to take into consideration as they think about redesigning existing organizations. At the very least, managers should be looking for ways to provide for designs and roles that are consistent with—and that capitalize on—these informal processes.

The first informal process can be described as *socialization*. Each organization's culture—its values, beliefs, and behavioral norms—helps people understand how they're expected to act, even in the absence of formal structures and processes. Particularly in professional service firms—law firms, medical practices, accounting firms, for example—people tend to behave in accordance with a commonly shared code of conduct. That code is an integral part of the training people receive when they first enter the profession, and it is reinforced over the years through everyday practice.

Particularly in organizations with strong cultures, these universal codes of behavioral expectations play a powerful coordinating role that cuts across physical distances and jurisdictional boundaries. They provide a common language that facilitates collaboration, a frame of reference that helps guide decision making in ambiguous situations, and a set of expectations about how to deal with employees, peers, customers, and competitors.

A second source of linking lies in *informal relationships*. Particularly in large organizations with operating sites spread all over the country or around the globe, collaboration and decision making are infinitely easier if people have some relationship with the colleagues with whom they're dealing, rather than simply respond to a detached voice on the phone or an impersonal e-mail from a virtual stranger. That's why organizations such as ABB, among many others, go out of their way to provide periodic opportunities for managers from different countries and business groups to spend time together at training sessions and management conferences and in other settings where they can spend some time building the informal relationships that can prove invaluable down the road.

At the same time, informal relationships play an important linking role in practically every organization. In a classic situation [Nadler and Tushman 1997, Chapter 10], General Motors found out just how vital those relationships were in 1984 when it embarked on a massive restructuring that almost overnight disrupted thousands of relationships that had been built up over the years. Managers who would have in the past normally performed a certain job on the basis of a phone call from a colleague suddenly reverted to formal procedures and demanded half a dozen sign-offs from higher-ups before agreeing to the same request from a stranger (Keller 1989).

The third source of informal linking relates to what we call *emergent roles*. Over time, certain people, without being asked, tend to take on certain roles that serve important coordination functions. These roles, though nearly always informal, provide crucial linkages between various formal groups. They generally fall into four categories.

The first group can be described as *idea generators*. These are the people who, regardless of their job descriptions, have the inclination and the ability to synthesize creatively ideas and insights from different groups and disciplines. The second group includes the *champions,* those who take creative ideas—their own or someone else's—and bring them to fruition by selling the ideas, taking risks, and finding the necessary resources to pursue the "cause." The third group can be described as *gatekeepers* or *boundary spanners*. These are the people with an unusually global view of their industry or profession who effectively link their colleagues to important information outside the organization or business unit. Finally, there are the *sponsors,* the senior people within the organization who provide informal support, resources, and protection for unusual projects or ideas.

These critical linking functions can't be formalized; they can't be made part of the organization's official structure or systems. Indeed, turning them into formal jobs generally renders them ineffective. Their success relies on the skills and the interests of a small number of essential people; research suggests that no more than 15 percent of the employees within an organization actually perform these key functions.

While these informal roles can't be formalized, they can be encouraged and expanded. For example, one R&D director tried unsuccessfully to appoint gatekeepers. Having failed, she then identified people who were informally filling that role, gave them access to databases and an increased travel budget, and then found new ways to involve them in task forces with people throughout the organization. And she explicitly rewarded them for their successful efforts.

These informal roles can be critical. Without idea generators, the quality of interunit collaboration suffers. Without champions, joint efforts tend to fizzle on the launch pad. Without gatekeepers, both in-house and external expertise go to waste. And without senior sponsors, parochial resistance stymies collaborative projects.

These informal roles tend to evolve in organizations with particularly clear core values; their clarity and consistency give people both the guidance and the confidence to take on responsibilities beyond their specific job descriptions. When core values are murky, the informal organization tends to be chaotic, people hesitate to take on informal roles, and those who do assume them often become embroiled in conflict.

ABB REVISITED

ABB, as it has emerged over the years, illustrates practically every major form of structural linking mechanism. To begin with, its very structure—a complex matrix system—is, in essence, an organization-wide linking device. In that sense, ABB provides linkage through its hierarchy. Indeed, the linking extends even within the senior team; each of the dozen executive vice presidents has a variety of responsibilities; a single executive may supervise a corporate functional area, such as finance, oversee a large geographic area, and manage an industry segment involving four or five of the fifty business areas. It is a structure designed to maintain the close integration of 5,000 far-flung profit centers in a tight corporate office consisting of only 150 people.

Moreover, ABB links its operations at every opportunity—while still maintaining the essentially local nature of each operating company—by sharing technology, expertise, marketing strategies, and distribution networks. ABB companies around the world speak the same language, both literally and in terms of performance standards and strategic objectives. It is a constant balancing act—as Barnevik said—between big and small, global and local, centralized and decentralized. It is an amazingly complex pattern of linkages, a worldwide confederation of local companies.

While grouping decisions set the groundwork for organization design, the ensuing decisions about linking mechanisms are no less vital. They are essential to achieving the effective coordination of the various disparate units created by the grouping process.

Linking mechanisms can range from simple devices, such as liaison roles, to much more complex approaches, such as the matrix system we've described at ABB. Whatever their form, their function remains essentially the same: to provide whatever channels are necessary to let information flow freely among people and units separated by grouping. Those information-processing requirements will vary according to the information-sharing requirements that exist between each group. The challenge to managers is to design the appropriate pattern of linkages that will create the clearest channels of information with the minimum commitment of people, time, money, and other organizational resources.

REFERENCES

Our work on linking, managerial systems, and informal organizations builds on many others, including the following:

Brown, S., and K. Eisenhardt. "Product Development: Past Research and Present Findings." *Academy of Management Review* 20 (1995): 343–378.

Clark, K., and S. Wheelwright. "Organizing and Leading Heavyweight Development Teams." *California Management Review* (Spring 1992): 9–26.

Davis, S., and P. Lawrence. *Matrix.* Reading, Mass.: Addison-Wesley, 1977.

Eccles, R., and D. Crane. *Doing Deals: Investment Banks at Work.* Boston: Harvard Business School Press, 1988.

Galbraith, J. *Designing Complex Organizations.* Reading, Mass.: Addison-Wesley, 1973.

Hammer, M., and J. Champy. *Reengineering the Corporation.* New York: Harper, 1993.

Iansiti, M., and K. Clark. "Integration and Dynamic Capability." *Industry and Corporate Change* 5 (1994): 24–36.

Ingrassia, P., and White, J. B. *Comeback: The Fall and Rise of the American Automobile Industry.* New York: Simon & Schuster, 1994.

Katz, R. "Organizational Socialization." In R. Katz, ed., *Managing Professionals in Innovative Organizations.* New York: Harper, 1988.

Katz, R., M. Tushman, and T. Allen. "Dual Ladder Promotion in R & D." *Management Science* 41 (1995): 848–862.

Keller, M. *Rude Awakening: The Rise, Fall and Struggle for Recovery of General Motors.* New York: Harper/Collins, 1989.

Kerr, S. "On the Folly of Rewarding A, While Hoping for B." *Academy of Management Executive* 9 (1995): 7–14.

Lawler, E. *Pay and Organization Development.* Reading, Mass.: Addison-Wesley, 1981.

Lucas, H. The *T-Form Organization.* San Francisco: Jossey-Bass, 1996.

Nadler, D., and M. Tushman. *Competing by Design: The Power of Organizational Architecture.* New York: Oxford University Press, 1997.

Nohria, N., and R. Eccles. *Networks and Organizations: Structure, Form and Action.* Boston, Mass.: Harvard Business School Press, 1992.

Roberts, E., and A. Fusfeld. "Staffing the Innovative Technology-Based Organization." *Sloan Management Review* (1981): 19–34.

Sayles, L., and M. Chandler. *Managing Large Systems.* New York: Harper, 1971.

Taylor, W. "The Logic of Global Business: An Interview with ABB's Percy Barnevik." *Harvard Business Review* (March 1991): 91–104.

Van de Ven, A., A. Delbecq, and R. Koenig. "Determinants of Coordination Modes within Organizations." *American Sociological Review* 41 (1976): 322–337.

Wageman, R. "Interdependence and Group Effectiveness." *Administrative Science Quarterly* 40 (1995): 145–180.

32

Coevolving

At Last, a Way to Make Synergies Work

KATHLEEN M. EISENHARDT
D. CHARLES GALUNIC

The new rules of collaboration are counterintuitive: Let businesses decide whether to work together. Reward individual performance, not collaboration. And don't assume that more collaboration means more synergy.

Capturing cross-business synergies is at the heart of corporate strategy—indeed, the promise of synergy is a prime rationale for the existence of the multibusiness corporation. Yet synergies are notoriously challenging to capture. Shell's initial attempt to launch a common credit card across Europe failed. Allegis, United Airlines' bid to build synergies in related travel businesses like hotels and airlines, was dismantled. Amazon.com has yet to see significant synergies from its PlanetAll acquisition, which was supposed to drive additional sales by linking to people's Rolodex of family and friends. The truth is, for most corporations, the 1 + 1 = 3 arithmetic of cross-business synergies does not add up.

So how do the companies that actually achieve synergies do it? Their managers have mastered a corporate strategic process called *coevolving*. These managers routinely change the web of collaborative links—everything from information exchanges to shared assets to multibusiness strategies—among businesses. The result is a shifting web of relationships that exploits fresh opportunities for synergies and drops deteriorating ones.

The term *coevolution* originated in biology. It refers to successive changes among two or more ecologically interdependent but unique species such that their evolutionary trajectories become intertwined over time. As these species adapt to their environment, they also adapt to one another. The result is an ecosystem of partially interdependent species that adapt together. This interdependence is often symbiotic (each species helps the other), but it can also be commensalist (one species uses the other). Competitive interdependence can emerge as well: one species may drive out the other, or both species may evolve into distinct, noncompetitive niches. Interdependence can change, too, such as when external factors like the climate or geology shift.

A classic example of symbiotic coevolution is the acacia tree and the *pseudomyrmex* ant species. Ants need acacias for nectar and shelter. Acacias depend on the ants stinging to protect them from herbivores. Over time, the acacia has evolved to make it easy for the ants to hollow out thorns for shelter and to have access to its flowers. Similarly, the ants have evolved into a shape that makes it easier to enter the acacia flower.

Reprinted by permission of *Harvard Business Review*. From "Coevolving: At Last, a Way to Make Synergies Work," by Kathleen M. Eisenhardt and D. Charles Galunic, Jan.–Feb. 2000. Copyright © 2000 by the Harvard Business School Publishing Corporation; all rights reserved.

Together, the species are better off than they would be if they didn't collaborate.

Scholars from many disciplines have recognized that biological coevolution is just one kind of complex adaptive system. Recently, computer simulations have uncovered general laws of how these systems work, including social systems such as multicountry economies and multibusiness corporations. These laws reveal nonlinear effects such as leverage points with disproportionate impact on the entire system. They show how the number of connections can affect the agility of a system. And they indicate that complex adaptive systems are most effective when intelligence is decentralized. More generally, these laws are consistent with the notion that multibusiness corporations are coevolving ecosystems.

So what does all that mean for today's multibusiness companies? In essence, they need to take their cue from nature and approach cross-business synergies with a very different mind-set. Managers at coevolving companies assume that links among businesses are temporary. They think "Velcro organization." They also recognize that the number of connections—not just their content—matters. So they manage the tension between fewer links for agility and more links for efficiency. While traditional corporate managers plan collaborative strategy from the top, corporate executives in coevolving companies don't try to control or even predict it. They set the context and then let collaboration (and competition) emerge from business units. Incentives are different, too. Coevolving companies reward business units for individual performance, not for collaboration. Thus, collaboration occurs only when two business-unit managers both believe that a link makes sense for their respective businesses, not because collaboration per se is useful. Finally, managers in coevolving companies recognize the importance of business systems: frequent data-focused meetings among business-unit leaders, external metrics to gauge individual business performance, and incentives that favor self-interest. (See Table 32.1.)

Coevolving is a particularly crucial strategic process in new-economy corporations, where higher-velocity markets drive managers to keep individual businesses small enough to adapt but intense competition demands that they maintain economies of scope and rapid cross-business learning. Not surprisingly, many leading corporations with significant Internet businesses like Sun, Schwab, and Hewlett-Packard coevolve. Since even pre-IPO companies in the new economy often have multiple businesses, very young firms like eye-care specialist NovaMed coevolve as well. And finally, coevolving is crucial for knowledge-intensive corporations like consultancy Booz-Allen & Hamilton and product design firm IDEO, which constantly share learning throughout their organizations.

Our ideas about coevolving developed from a decade of research into successful corporate strategy in intensely competitive, fast-moving industries. Coevolution in natural ecosystems, we found, looks a lot like the collaborative webs within corporations that achieve significant multibusiness synergies. And both of these resemble the external ecosystems that link corporations together in webs of alliances. More generally, the disciplines of biology and complexity yield important insights into how superior corporate strategy—inside and outside the corporation—happens in dynamic markets.

Table 32.1. Traditional Collaboration Versus Coevolution

	Traditional Collaboration	Coevolution
Form of collaboration	Frozen links among static businesses	Shifting webs among evolving businesses
Objectives	Efficiency and economies of scope	Growth, agility, and economies of scope
Internal dynamics	Collaborate	Collaborate and compete
Focus	Content of collaboration	Content and number of collaborative links
Corporate role	Drive collaboration	Set collaborative context
Business role	Execute collaboration	Drive and execute collaboration
Incentive	Varied	Self-interest, based on individual business-unit performance
Business metrics	Performance against budget, the preceding year, or sister-business performance	Performance against competitors in growth, share, and profits

SHIFT COLLABORATIVE WEBS

In traditional corporations, the web of collaborations among businesses often freezes into fixed patterns. Business units share intangible resources such as brands physical resources such as manufacturing facilities, or organizational capabilities such as product development. Once the patterns are established, they're not revisited regularly. By contrast, managers in coevolving corporations frequently reconnect the links among businesses. Some links last a long time, others are much shorter. And while some links lead to predicted synergies, others open up unanticipated ones.

GE Capital is an example of a company that reconnects its collaborative webs. GE Capital was launched with collaborative links to GE's consumer businesses, such as refrigerators and dishwashers. As time went on, GE Capital gained enough scale and expertise to offer its financing services to GE's more sophisticated industrial products businesses like power plants and jet engines. The collaborative web shifted more toward these areas. The combination of products and innovative financing fed the growth of both GE Capital and the industrial products businesses. Eventually, GE Capital became its own web of interconnected businesses, like specialty insurance and credit card operations, by developing common acquisition procedures and sharing customers. As a result of that changing collaborative web, GE managers created synergistic growth beyond what static collaborations could have achieved.

Another company we'll call OfficeSys provides a detailed illustration of the types of collaborations that managers at coevolving companies use. Three years ago, OfficeSys was dominated by two large businesses: photocopiers and fax machines. For many years, those businesses had shared optical technologies and product components. As industry price cutting slashed margins, the managers of the two businesses combined their manufacturing and procurement activities. As a result, both were able to cut costs and compete more effectively in their markets. At about the same time in 1997, corporate executives at OfficeSys launched two new businesses around a revolutionary optical scanning technology that captures data for transfer to the Internet. These managers collaborated very informally by trading engineers back and forth in order to share scarce and costly talent. They also collaborated on developing a software protocol standard for data transmission among different Internet-connected devices.

But as is often the case in coevolving companies, the collaborative web evolved. When the two new businesses began to ship products, their managers ended the informal swapping of engineers. The managers of the fax business joined the software standard collaboration. The managers of all four businesses now have a joint advertising campaign to promote their collective brand.

The OfficeSys example is striking because of the variety of collaborations that took place. Some collaborations were major and long term, such as the joint development of common product components. Some were modest and transient, like the informal trading of engineers. Some were focused on creating revenue, like the software protocol initiative and brand building. Some drove down costs, like shared manufacturing. And they occurred all along the value chain, from R&D to marketing. Because of their coevolutionary efforts, OfficeSys's managers strengthened their businesses in the maturing photocopier and fax markets and grew their businesses in the emerging Internet appliances markets.

What drives managers to reconnect their collaborative webs? Sometimes it's changes in the market, pure and simple. For example, increased cost pressures forced managers at OfficeSys to expand manufacturing links between their mature businesses. Sometimes it's changes in the business units themselves. Managers pursue new directions, adjust to the changing business roles of sister divisions, or simply grow their businesses. Most commonly, it's a combination of the two.

NovaMed Eyecare Management, a fast-growing, successful health-care company, is an example of how changes made by an individual business unit can reverberate throughout the larger business group, affecting how other units relate to one another and how they all relate to the market. In 1995, NovaMed's eye-care medical practices throughout the United States were similar. The collaborative relationships among the practices focused on saving costs through common information systems, bulk purchasing, and shared staff.

The doctors in one practice, however, had particularly strong research skills, especially in refractive surgery. They decided to put those skills to use. As the doctors became the innovators and new laser technology for eye surgery was approved by the FDA, the pattern of collaboration shifted. Sharing resources to lower costs was still important, but the transmission of surgical innovations became far more crucial. That is, doctors at the research-driven practice pioneered new surgical procedures and then broadcast them throughout NovaMed.

In 1998, NovaMed launched a new kind of business, one that conducted clinical trials of surgical equipment and their related procedures for medical device companies. The doctors at the research-based practice worked closely with this new business, which strengthened their ability to pioneer leading-edge surgical techniques. Some of the more research-oriented doctors within the other practices also began collaborating with the clinical trials business. As a result, NovaMed was able to build the critical mass of participating doctors and patients necessary for meaningful clinical trials. Not surprisingly, the company has grown over 60% during the first half of 1999 compared with 1998, and it went through a successful IPO. More to the point, NovaMed's practices have moved much faster and with greater medical skill than competitors into refractive surgery, one of the hottest growth segments in health care.

BRING THE MARKET INSIDE

Managers at companies that follow the traditional rules for collaboration avoid internal competition on the grounds that it devastates teamwork, wastes resources, and cannibalizes existing products and businesses. By contrast, managers at coevolving companies let collaboration and competition coexist. E-businesses compete with their bricks-and-mortar counterparts, new technologies compete with established ones, and so on. While senior managers don't actively seek out competition, they don't discourage it if it occurs naturally as the result of alternative technologies, business models, distribution channels, and the like. Just as the distinction between friend and foe is blurring in the alliance webs outside the corporation, it is also blurring on the inside.

An exemplar of such thinking is Hewlett-Packard. For decades, the tension between competition and cooperation has helped HP thrive. A classic example involves the desk- and laser-jet printing technologies. Eventually the two businesses evolved into different market niches and became enormous businesses in their own right, but for several years they competed for the same customers. The company's managers knew they could not predict how the market would unfold, so they let the two compete until it became clear whether one would dominate or whether the businesses would diverge into viable market niches. Had the managers at HP squelched this competition by choosing one technology over the other, they would have lost out on a collective $15 billion business opportunity. Recently, that same kind of competition has emerged between HP's UNIX and NT computing businesses. Initially, UNIX was the primary business. Then NT looked to be the winner. Now with the rise of Linux and repeated NT delays, UNIX is resurgent. The result of such competition is that HP can win regardless of how the market unfolds.

Letting internal competition flourish is particularly important in the Internet world. Managers who think in terms of coevolution let Net businesses compete with established ones. A good example is Siebel Systems, a "best of breed" provider of enterprise software for sales and marketing. Siebel's managers didn't let the usual concerns about channel conflict keep them from quickly entering e-commerce. In fact, Siebel's new subsidiary, Sales.com, initially targeted the same customers as the existing business—major global corporations with complex selling requirements. Early on, the two diverged; Sales.com sold Web-hosted application products directly to individual salespeople in these corporations, and the traditional business concentrated on selling software for the entire sales force to senior executives. Sales.com's products turned out to be most appealing to small and mid-sized companies that found Web-hosting to be an attractive alternative to enterprise software resident on their own IT equipment. By letting competition unfold, Siebel managers figured out how to play the Internet game well before other ERP companies like PeopleSoft, while keeping their established business successful.

BALANCE THE NUMBER OF LINKS

Traditional corporations focus on picking the right collaborations. By contrast, coevolving companies recognize that the *number* of collaborative ties is often just as significant as the kinds of collaborations. They balance the tension between too many links that restrict adaptation and too few that miss important opportunities for synergies.

A terrific example is Vail Ski Resorts. When the group formed in a 1997 merger, the rationale was to gain extensive synergies by tightly linking the four member resorts—Vail, Breckenridge, Keystone, and Beaver Creek—with numerous collaborations, particularly branding under the Vail name. It was a classic, top-down plan to create synergies—with the usual subpar results. Vacationers wanted unique resort experiences, not four "would-be Vail" destinations. Once senior managers cut back on these connections, they could more freely adapt their resorts to their evolving markets. For example, Breckenridge's location next to a classic mining town has particular appeal for European skiers seeking a "Western" experience. Breckenridge's managers capitalized on this attraction by introducing unique features that appeal to these skiers, such as longer-stay vacation packages. Loosening the connections also allowed Vail Resorts' managers to figure out, over time, the right number of connections among the resorts. Today the resort group collaborates—by choice—in only a few high-payoff areas: supplies procurement, integrated information systems, and interchangeable lift ticketing.

As a general rule, more links among businesses make sense when markets are stable. In such circumstances, economies of scope dominate. Disney's approach to the Internet illustrates this principle. In general, Disney's businesses are highly connected. But the company's managers intentionally entered the volatile Internet world with businesses that were only weakly tied together. Their Infoseek business, in fact, was not even fully owned. Figuring that the old business models might not make sense, managers wanted plenty of freedom to evolve in and even shape whatever the emerging market spaces would be. They understood that agility—not control—matters in fast-moving markets. Yet now that the Internet markets are more crystallized, Disney's managers have aggressively linked their Internet plays with one another and other parts of Disney. Once again, economies of scope drive Disney's thinking. They bought the rest of Infoseek, combined it with other Internet businesses such as Disney Travel Online into a single business (Go.com), made their content Web sites accessible from a single portal (Go Network), and created new links to established

businesses like ESPN. Of course, the jury is still out on whether they connected too soon in the volatile I-world.

By contrast, when markets become dynamic and agility matters most, businesses need fewer connections in order to adapt. Consider the British Broadcasting Company. For years, the radio station, television broadcast, and television production businesses were tightly linked, even to the point of cross-subsidization. Radio, in particular, was viewed as the decidedly unglamorous cash cow. But, in one of the surprises of the Internet, radio's prospects have changed. Why? Many people shut off their televisions and turn on their radios for background entertainment while they surf the Web. So BBC has loosened the links among its businesses to let radio evolve more freely in the higher-velocity, less predictable Internet space.

UNCOVER THE HIGH-LEVERAGE LINKS

Especially in fast-paced markets, managers don't have time to oversee a lot of collaborative initiatives. So it's crucial to figure out what links are sensible, identify the high-payoff ones, and forget the rest. Typically, the highest-payoff links can be leverage points with disproportionate synergies.

A great example is the U.S. multichain retailer Dayton Hudson. There are only a few collaborative links between the rapidly growing Target chain and upscale retailers Marshall Field's and Dayton's. But senior managers have located a simple link that gives them a lot of leverage: regular exchange of fashion information. Target, in particular, has benefited. Its managers learn about fashion trends much sooner than competitors by paying attention to the upscale retailers, whose buyers spot trends early through their contacts with leading fashion designers. (For example, Target got wind of the recent "gray craze" from other Dayton Hudson managers and tailored its apparel and home furnishings accordingly.) This link helped Target managers to reposition the chain as "hip fashion at a low price" and achieve double-digit sales and profit growth that buried competitors like K-Mart and J.C. Penney. So does this success mean that Target should add more links? Absolutely not. In fact, for Target, more links such as common buyers might actually slow the retailer down, raise costs, and lower the syn-

Disney Versus Sony: Contrasting Cases in Patching and Coevolution

In the mid-1990s, Sony scored a box-office hit with *Men in Black,* while Disney had a similar box-office success with *The Lion King. Men in Black* grossed more money in its first weekend than almost any other film in history. For Sony, the $600 million box-office and video revenues were much of its success story. For Disney, those revenue sources were just the opening chapter. Disney's managers also released more than 150 kinds of *Lion King* merchandise (pencil cases, dolls, T-shirts, and so forth), turned the soundtrack into a musical sequel called *Rhythm of the Pride Lands,* and produced a video entitled *Simba's Pride.* The total take was approximately $3 billion. Disney also introduced *Lion King* themes at existing resorts and ultimately at its new Animal Kingdom theme park.

Most people understand the 1 + 1 = 3 arithmetic of Disney's collaboration, which funnels the same content into multiple media businesses. But few people recognize that Disney's managers use different collaborative patterns with different products. *Beauty and the Beast* became a play on Broadway, for example, whereas *Toy Story* was turned into a video game, and *The Little Mermaid* became a television show. Even fewer people understand that Disney's managers engage in many kinds of collaborative efforts that change over time. Managers of Disney World and the Big Red Boat cruise line collaborate on joint vacation packages to boost revenues for both businesses, for example. EuroDisney executives share knowledge about hotel management and ticket pricing

with other resort managers. ESPN managers work with the Internet businesses to share sports content and with the theme parks to launch ESPN restaurants. Touchstone Studios occasionally shares actors with animated films. Thus, Disney's managers have effectively patched together a changing quilt of entertainment businesses like theme parks, movie studios, retail stores, and broadcast networks. Simultaneously, they have created the corporate context (like synergy managers in each business, corporate Imagineers, and the Disney Dimensions program) that permits the coevolving mix of collaboration among these businesses.

By contrast, Sony's managers have not patched businesses such as theme parks, publishing, and retail outlets into their company, even though other entertainment companies have found that they're important for creating corporate synergies. They also have some businesses that on the surface seem synergistic but aren't. For example, Sony's Walkman products obviously depend on media content, but consumers are unlikely to listen to Sony-produced music just because they have a Walkman. Further, Sony's managers have been less effective in capturing the collaborative opportunities they do have because of long-distance relationships between business heads in Tokyo and New York. Not surprisingly, then, Disney has outperformed Sony in many one-on-one matchups like *The Lion King* versus *Men in Black*—and more generally in the creation of corporate value in the entertainment industry.

---

ergistic value of the businesses. In other words, fewer links—targeted at the right content—can, counterintuitively, create more synergies.

The exact location of these high-leverage links depends upon a company's resources, the relatedness of its businesses, and its strategic position. Take Cisco and Ascend, two competing stars of the turbulent networking industry. Given the pace and uncertainty of that industry, it makes sense for managers at both companies to focus on just a few collaborative areas. But because their circumstances are different, their man-

agers have chosen different links. Cisco has a huge market cap, which makes acquisitions relatively affordable. Managers have used that advantage brilliantly: they have developed a shared acquisition process—from target identification through due diligence to integration—that capitalizes on learning-curve effects of acquisitions throughout the corporation. Managers use this shared process to make frequent acquisitions that supplement in-house R&D and open up new product areas. In effect, Cisco's managers transfer R&D risk to venture capitalists and then scoop up the winners. Ascend, in comparison, was launched well after Cisco. When the company was young, its managers couldn't afford acquisitions to open up new product areas. But they needed to move very fast with a low profile to stay well ahead of Cisco. So Ascend's managers concentrated their cross-business collaborations on aggressively sharing software and other product components across businesses. This collaborative link preserved precious financial resources, accelerated time to market and, at least initially, kept Ascend off Cisco's radar screen.

LAY THE FOUNDATION

Understanding the essentials—frequently reconnect the relationships among businesses, blur collaboration and competition, manage the number of connections, and uncover high-leverage links—is crucial for companies that hope to coevolve. But it's not enough. There is an underlying foundation of structures and processes that managers must build if coevolution is to work.

Let Business Units Rule

A cornerstone of that foundation is letting heads of business units determine where and when to collaborate. If corporate managers take the lead, they often do not understand the nuances of the businesses. They naively see synergies that aren't there. They tend to overestimate the benefits of collaboration and underestimate its costs. Conversely, if junior managers take the lead, they lack the strategic perspective to pick the best opportunities. They may spot good opportunities for collaboration, but they rarely uncover the best ones. Thus, the most effective decision makers are those at the business-unit level, where strategic perspective meets operating savvy.

The locus of decision making at General Electric is a prime example. General managers of GE's businesses have regular meetings to search for cross-business synergies. These meetings typically include managers from related businesses where synergies could be expected. They engage in what is called "receiver-based communication." That is, they share information about their activities, and interested managers from other businesses (the "receivers") follow up as they see appropriate. Even though senior executives

may suggest areas of collaboration and individual business managers are expected to attend the meetings, nobody is forced to collaborate. Business general managers make the collaborative calls.

That doesn't mean that corporate-level managers have no role in cross-business collaboration. On the contrary, senior executives create the context in which that collaboration can happen. They act as "pollinators" of ideas as they travel among businesses. They stage modern-day bazaars that bring business-level managers together to talk and to perhaps find collaborative opportunities. They determine the lineup of businesses within the corporation by patching businesses against market opportunities so that effective collaboration can emerge. They ensure that each business is strong enough to be an attractive partner. They also foster a culture of information sharing by assigning synergy managers within individual business units. These executives may even suggest particular collaborations for individual businesses. But they don't force collaboration. (For more on the executive roles, see the box "Patching, Coevolving, and the New Corporate Strategy.")

Build the Multibusiness Team

Another cornerstone of coevolution is the multibusiness team—the group of business unit heads that orchestrates collaborations among their businesses. The key to making these teams work well is frequent group meetings. In the most successful coevolving companies, these meetings happen at least monthly and are "don't miss" events. The content of these meetings is a run-through of real-time internal operating numbers and external market statistics, as well as a qualitative discussion of shared interests such as competitors' moves, customer feedback, and technology developments. The meetings are fact-focused and pragmatic. Often managers discuss a specific strategic issue facing one or more of the businesses. Since travel can be a problem, effective teams rely a lot on videoconferences. They add fun to the mix, too Eli Lilly's managers, for example, organize some meetings in enticing locations like London, where they give executives time to shop, visit local pubs, or sightsee.

The most obvious effect of frequent meetings is that business heads become acquainted with opportunities for collaboration. But just as important, they weave the social fabric of familiarity and trust that

Patching, Coevolving, and the New Corporate Strategy

Traditional corporate strategy centers on establishing defensible strategic positions by setting corporate scope, acquiring or building assets, and weaving synergies among them. The result is sustained competitive advantage. Yet in high-velocity markets, strategic position can quickly erode. In these markets, the strategic *processes* by which managers reconfigure resources to build new strategic positions are more pivotal to corporate performance than any particular strategic position. The new corporate strategy focuses on these freshly defined corporate strategic processes.

One of these processes is patching. Patching is the frequent remapping of businesses to fit changing market opportunities. It involves combining, splitting, exiting, and transferring businesses within the corporation. (For more on the concept of patching, see Kathleen M. Eisenhardt and Shona L. Brown, "Patching: Restitching Business Portfolios in Dynamic Markets," HBR May–June 1999.) A second is coevolving.

With patching, corporate executives set the lineup of businesses within the corporation and keep it aligned with shifting markets. Their key skill is recognizing changing patterns in product and customer segments and in technology road maps. With coevolving, multibusiness teams (the heads of individual businesses working together) drive synergies by reconnecting the collaborative links among businesses as markets and businesses evolve. Their key skill is managing their own group dynamics.

While patching and coevolving are distinct corporate strategic processes, the two are often intertwined. For example, NovaMed's coevolution from purely cost-oriented collaboration among its different medical practices to innovation-oriented collaboration was enhanced when a new clinical-trials business was patched into the company. The new business strengthened the payoff from innovation-based synergies.

---

supports effective collaboration. (See the box "The Power of Multibusiness Teams.")

Consider Time Warner. Its managers are notoriously uncollaborative, and compared with other media giants, the corporation as a whole has not gained much synergistic value from its businesses. However, managers from the Turner Sports group, *Sports Illustrated* magazine, and the sports wing of HBO started meeting often. As a result, they have learned about one another's needs and resources. These meetings have led to several collaborative efforts, including the Turner Games boxing events. These were organized by Turner Sports, promoted and broadcast on HBO, and covered by *Sports Illustrated.*

A more subtle, albeit well-known, effect of these meetings is the emergence of roles. For example, at Vail Ski Resorts, their weekly meetings helped managers shape the business roles of their own ski areas in relation to one another. Vail's role, for example, has become the "capital of skiing," while Breckenridge evolved into the "Western" experience. Establishing very clear turf boundaries helped the managers of

those businesses communicate more clearly and collaborate more effectively by lowering political tension and clarifying opportunities. The result is that Vail Ski Resorts competes very successfully against competitors like Intrawest because of its distinctly focused ski experiences and effective synergies.

Finally, frequent meetings can lead to the emergence of a shared intuition. As managers regularly review the operating performances and markets of all the businesses together, they develop a common understanding—a gut sense—of the patterns shaping their industry. Because these meetings focus managers on factual data, their shared intuition remains tightly linked with shifting realities and helps multibusiness teams identify the best collaborations quickly.

But in certain situations (notably related businesses facing a small number of competitors), that shared intuition can deepen into a multibusiness strategy that goes beyond particular business roles to include coordinated pricing, technology and product road maps, and customer segmentation. This happened at a global computing company we'll call Cruising.

The Power of Multibusiness Teams

In traditional corporate strategy, the multibusiness team—the group of business-unit managers that oversees synergies among businesses—simply doesn't exist. And yet, it is an organizational requirement for coevolutionary companies. The team's primary job is to orchestrate the shifting collaborative web among the businesses. Most of the time, these managers represent their own businesses. But we have also observed that business-unit heads often temporarily assume functional perspectives. Those who have experience in engineering or marketing, for example, take on those perspectives, especially when the team is discussing multibusiness strategy. Members also take on other, equally distinctive roles—devil's advocate, conservative, innovator, to name a few—which can further enhance the team's effectiveness.

The multibusiness team is powerful because it can add significant value to the corporation beyond the sum of the businesses. Without the teams, individual business managers have difficulty finding collaborative links, developing the social relationships with other business heads that facilitate collaboration, and even conceptualizing a collective strategy. The multibusiness team can also create corporate value that the market cannot duplicate with a portfolio of investments. The market cannot reproduce either the deep understanding of collaborative possibilities that can exist among team members or the underlying social structure that enables effective collaborations over time. Of course, especially in very dynamic markets, many of the best collaborative links are outside the corporation. But even then, the market holds no advantage when multibusiness teams work well together and yet also focus on achieving individual business success.

The key to superior multibusiness teams is great group dynamics: fast decision making with plenty of conflict over content, but also with deep social bonds that limit interpersonal conflict. To create this group process, these teams rely on frequent meetings to build familiarity and trust, data-rich information to develop a shared intuition, and clear turf boundaries so that politicking is kept to a minimum.

The managers of Cruising's primary computing businesses instituted bimonthly meetings to track their turbulent industry. Over time, the different businesses developed distinct roles and a shared multibusiness strategy. For example, one business was in the fastest-growing, highest-margin segment of the industry. So it became the golden goose, and the company's overall strategy was to protect and grow this business. A second business took on the workhorse role. It was the largest business and sold the greatest number of products, so it contributed manufacturing volume and routines for many basic business processes. It also relayed information about low-end competitors attacking the golden goose from below. A third business competed in a small, high-margin segment of the industry. That business helped several other Cruising businesses to gain sales by promising delivery of these short-supply, high-quality products if the customer bought other products from Cruising. As a result of this multibusi-

ness strategy, Cruising became the industry's company to beat.

Get the Incentives Right

If coevolving requires multibusiness teams that can quickly identify and execute collaborative opportunities, then the incentives for business-unit heads must reward collaboration. Right? Wrong. Business-unit managers who coevolve their businesses are rewarded for self-interest, *not* for collaboration. That is, they are rewarded primarily for their individual business performance. That performance is measured externally against key competitors—not internally against planned, preceding year, or sister-business performance—with the metrics typically being a mix of growth, profit, and market share. The ultimate reward, as in professional sports, is being on the team. So, for example, the manager of a business in a very competitive market does not need to post the same numbers as a manager who competes with better strategic position. Both are expected to excel in their own markets. If they do, they are on the team and are well compensated. If not, they're off.

Rewarding self-interest works because it's simple. It turns the attention of business-unit managers to the most important thing they need to do—win in their own markets. By contrast, mixed incentives (some group, some individual) confuse and demotivate people. Self-interest works for another reason, too. It makes market realities, not friendship, the basis of collaboration. In particular, it banishes the "good people collaborate and bad people don't" thinking that

---

Seven Steps to Kick-Start Coevolution

1. Begin by establishing at least monthly, must-attend meetings among business heads that enable them to get to know one another and to see collaborative opportunities.

2. Keep the conversation focused on real-time information about operating basics to build intuition and business roles. Include one or two specific strategic issues within or across businesses.

3. Get rid of "good people collaborate, bad people don't" thinking by rewarding self-interested pursuit of individual business performance against rivals.

4. When collaborative opportunities arise, remember that many managers get stuck on their first idea. Instead, brainstorm to expand the range of possible collaborative tools—from simple information sharing to shared assets to strategy—and collaborative points along the value chain.

5. Realistically analyze the costs and benefits of the most promising options. Remember that benefits usually appear greater than they are.

6. Fine-tune as you go. Up-front analysis is never a substitute for real-time learning.

7. Avoid "collaboration creep." Take the time to cut stale links.

---

leads to ineffective collaboration. Finally, rewarding self-interest works because win-win collaborations usually create the biggest synergistic pie for the corporation, even when individual businesses get unequal slices. It's true that occasionally an opportunity that's great for the corporation is missed because it was not so good for the businesses—but in dynamic markets, worrying about the corporate optimum is just too slow.

Individual-based incentives run counter to the culture of companies that place a high value on collective behavior. But these companies pay a price. Take Mitsubishi. Mitsubishi outwardly has some of the infrastructure of coevolving companies, such as regular Friday lunch meetings for business-unit heads. The collectivist culture at Mitsubishi, however, has led to some ineffective collaborations. For example, *keiretsu* members purchased steel inside Mitsubishi even though better deals were available from outside suppliers. Similarly, fellow keiretsu member Kirin protected its premium beer business from internal competition and subsequently lost to outsider Asahi in key growth segments of the Japanese beer market.

Of course, even in the best coevolving companies, collaborative efforts may not happen when they should. Rather than switch to rewarding collaboration, coevolving executives look for alternatives: they improve information flow so that managers can see collaborative opportunities better; repatch closely aligned businesses together into larger business segments; or repair businesses that others may be avoiding because they are ineffective. What coevolving managers *don't* do is reward collaboration.

IS COEVOLVING RIGHT FOR YOUR COMPANY?

Capturing cross-business synergies is an essential part of corporate strategy. Yet many managers collaborate in too many areas or for too long, or they focus on the wrong opportunities. They forget that, especially in high-velocity markets, there's not a lot of time to collaborate. They neglect to update their collaborative links as businesses and markets emerge, grow, split, and combine. Of course, some managers simply ignore cross-business synergies, an approach that often beats poor collaboration. But it also defeats the point of the multibusiness corporation. Coevolving is a better alternative.

Coevolving is a subtle strategic process. In fact, it's a bit counterintuitive—build collaborative teams and yet reward self-interest, let competition flourish, don't worry too much about efficiency, collaborate less to gain more. Coevolving turns the corporation into an ecosystem with corporate strategy in the hands of business-unit managers. But it is precisely this oblique thinking that gives coevolving companies a competitive edge.

33

Strategies for Managing Internal Competition

JULIAN BIRKINSHAW

Internal competition evokes mixed feelings among most senior executives. When asked whether it is allowed within their firm, the gut reaction from executives is usually negative. It conjures up images of turf wars among departments. It is seen as indicative of an inability to define a clear strategic direction. Furthermore, it is often thought to result in massive duplication of effort and an insipid financial performance. Moreover, it is not hard to think of well-known cases to back up this argument. GEC, the British conglomerate, was built on a model of strict divisional autonomy and internal competition, which in the words of one former manager meant that "we duplicated development and then we cut each other's throats in front of the customer." The acrimonious divorce between Arthur Andersen and Andersen Consulting resulted in large part from their competing consulting operations.

However, many executives also recognize that there are important benefits to internal competition, as long as it is kept under control. Three primary benefits can be identified. First, internal competition creates flexibility. Rapid technological change can make even the most carefully constructed business plan meaningless. Rather than putting all their eggs in one basket, many companies today prefer to keep their options open. They will put R&D groups to work on different technologies, invest in different channels to market, and encourage several divisions to work with different approaches all because they do not know which path the future will take. Internal competition, carefully controlled, can provide the active experimentation and flexibility needed to keep up with such changes.

Second, internal competition challenges the status quo. Large firms typically become inertia-ridden over the years, victims of their own success. Customers and their needs are taken for granted. Management systems take on a life of their own. Practices and beliefs become ingrained. Such a system is hardly conducive to revolutionary new ideas. Typically such ideas are developed instead by small upstart firms or by frustrated employees who leave their inertia-ridden firm to sell their idea to someone else. Internal competition can provide an antidote for myopic thinking, essentially as a means of challenging the hidden assumptions that underlie a company's existing technologies or markets. For example, many R&D operations are set up in explicit competition to the mainstream business with great success—think of IBM's Personal Computer, Astra's blockbuster drug Losec, or Ericsson's mobile phone business.

Third, internal competition motivates greater effort. It is human nature for individuals to pull together and work harder when faced with a direct competitive threat. Often this competitive threat comes from outside—think, for example, of Apple Computer defining itself against the "evil empire" of IBM. However, competition can also be encouraged internally, through product shootouts and charter battles, and such approaches represent a strong motivational incentive to employees.

Copyright © 2001 by The Regents of the University of California. Reprinted from the *California Management Review*, Vol. 44, No. 1. By permission of The Regents.

These costs and benefits have to be carefully balanced against one another. Allow too little internal competition and you are likely missing out on any number of emerging markets and technologies. Allow too much and you will suffer the costs of duplication, strategic incoherence, and in-fighting. Senior executives need to get a better understanding of the costs and benefits of internal competition so that it can be used in a more judicious manner. Furthermore, they need to figure out a way of *managing* internal competition when it occurs.

This article is based on five years of detailed research in ten companies (see Appendix) and presents strategies for managing internal competition. Internal competition as described in this article refers to *parallel or overlapping activities inside the boundaries of the firm.*[1] The key point is that business units or project teams are competing for the rights to a particular technology or product charter and not just for access to financial resources. Thus, product shoot-outs between development teams and business units with overlapping product charters both represent cases of internal competition, whereas R&D operations may or may not be, depending on the extent of overlap with the mainstream business.

WHY DOES INTERNAL COMPETITION ARISE?

To make sense of how internal competition arises, it is useful to think about the process of strategy making in large firms. Essentially there are two parallel processes. One is a top-down (or "induced") process through which executives define strategic priorities and allocate resources.[2] The other is a bottom-up (or "autonomous") process though which strategic opportunities are identified by lower-level managers and brought forward for attention and funding. Most large firms today operate with a combination of these two processes. Senior executives have to define strategic priorities in order to create some coherence around strategy making, but at the same time they rely on individuals throughout the firm to bring to their attention ideas and opportunities for future market development. Some firms, such as Oracle and Intel, operate with a relatively powerful top-down strategic process. Others firms, such as Ericsson and 3M, have a more powerful bottom-up process.

Internal competition emerges in large part as a result of the tension between top-down and bottom-up processes.[3] Senior executives recognize that they need to encourage people lower down in the firm to bring their often competing ideas and projects forward as a means of keeping up to date with technology and market changes. At the same time, they know that there are significant drawbacks to internal competition, in terms of the simple costs of duplication and the ambiguity it can create around strategic direction. Thus, it is possible to think in terms of an *internal competition lifecycle.* It starts when two or more options are brought forward in parallel, and it ends when top executives select one of these options at the expense of the others. An episode of internal competition can therefore be very short—it can be stamped out as soon as it happens; or it can last for a very long time, such as when a financial services company allows an Internet bank to coexist alongside a traditional retail bank. The point is that every case of internal competition has to be evaluated on its own specific costs and benefits. As the flow diagram in Figure 33.1 shows, if the costs exceed the benefits, internal competition should be terminated and the activities in question consolidated. However, if the benefits outweigh the costs, then the competing entities should be allowed to coexist—at least for the time being.

Two key questions emerge from this framing. First, what criteria should be used to decide whether internal competition should be terminated or allowed to continue? Second, how do you manage the process—both in terms of the emergence of internal competition in the first place and in terms of evaluating it and shutting it down? To answer these questions, it is important to make a basic split between two different types of internal competition in large firms. The first is competition between technologies or product ideas, which takes place within the boundaries of the firm and typically as part of the product development process. The second is competition between business lines—between two or more businesses competing for the same customers.[4] Figure 33.2 illustrates these two forms. As shown, the most critical difference is the selection process by which the winner is chosen. In the first case, the competing technologies fight it out internally, with senior executives ultimately deciding the winner. In the second case, the business lines are competing in the marketplace and end customers make the

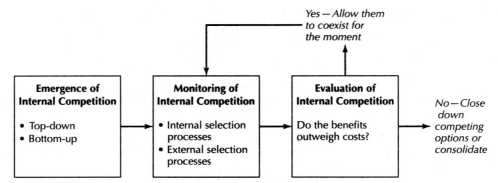

Figure 33.1. Managing the internal competition lifecycle.

1. Competition Between Technologies

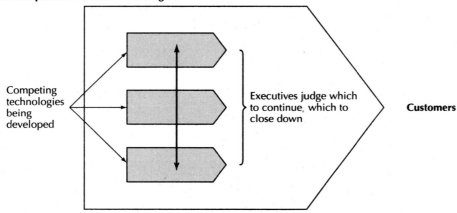

2. Competition Between Business Lines

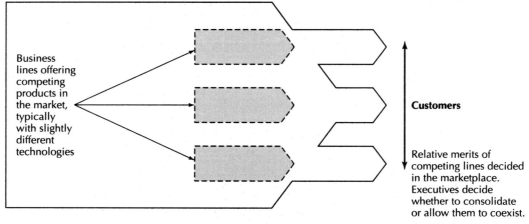

Figure 33.2. Two different forms of internal competition.

choice. However, there are also a number of other differences, and these have important implications for how the two forms are managed.

INTERNAL COMPETITION BETWEEN TECHNOLOGIES

The most common form of internal competition between technologies is when two or more divisions independently start developing very similar technologies. Consider the example of Hewlett-Packard's computer division. In 1988, a group vice president became aware of two divisions both developing an X Terminal workstation. One division located near Toronto had been aggressively developing a prototype X Terminal, despite a lack of prior expertise in this technology. A second division based in California had a strong background in terminal development but despite their stated intent to develop an X terminal, they had made little progress. As one Toronto executive noted, "They had a lot more credibility than us, but they had their plates full with the current business opportunity, so they did not come up with a credible business plan." In early 1989, the group vice president brought the two divisions together to review their progress and to assess their prospects for commercial success. It was clear at that point that the Toronto division was significantly ahead, so despite protestations from the California division that it was "their charter" by rights, Toronto was encouraged to continue. Ultimately Toronto came up with an X Terminal that proved to be a commercial success. The Californian division realized that they were too far behind in the X technology to catch up and shifted their development effort elsewhere. As one executive observed, "If they [California] had been doing their homework, this would never have happened. They started crying foul and complaining that Toronto was stealing their charter, but if they had been minding their business, this would not be an issue."

The other way that internal competition between technologies can occur is when it is *mandated* from above. In this situation, senior management's role is less about selecting between the competing alternatives and more about generating the options in the first place, putting in place a process by which a winner can be selected. For example, the copier development group in Fuji Xerox was working in the early 1990s on a next-generation color copier. The technology steering committee had fast-tracked technology B, a way of configuring the flow of paper through the copier. However, it had run into some technical problems, so they put together a new project team using technology A. The two technologies were developed in parallel, and a year later the steering committee undertook a review of the two technologies, getting input from the product group, salespeople, and even some customers. They eventually selected technology A as the one that would be incorporated in the new color copier. Technology B was continued with less funding and was eventually discontinued. The manager in charge of Technology B was given the job of incorporating Technology A into the copier to ensure that he did not become disillusioned by the failure of his technology. As this manager observed, "For me the process was very effective because the product was launched with no time loss and there was mutual consent over the final decision."

How do you decide if and when to put an end to internal competition of this sort? Table 33.1 provides a summary of the key criteria that emerged from the research. However, it should be recognized that this is a general list, and the challenge of prioritizing and trading the criteria off against each other is far from easy. A common scenario, which I refer to as "Sophie's Choice,"[5] is where there is a high level of technological or market uncertainty around the competing options, but the costs of duplication are becoming very high—for example, the investments made by telecom firms in the various 3G standards or the development of new pharmaceutical drugs. In such cases, the best approach is typically to keep options open by avoiding heavy investments until some uncertainties have been resolved. However, it is also possible to build relationships with external partners, to defray the cost of duplication through alliances or to buy in the critical technology if it is available.[6] These strategies have their own problems, as the Ericsson 3G example below shows, but they represent ways of resolving the almost inevitable tensions that arise.

In terms of managing the process, there are a number of important points to bear in mind.

Catch It Early

This applies only in cases where internal competition emerges in different parts of the company rather than when it is planned. However, it is absolutely essential

Table 33.1. Coexistence or Consolidation in Competing Technologies

	Question	Coexistence[a]	Consolidation[b]
Technological Uncertainty	Is it clear that one of the competing options is technologically superior or more certain to overcome technical obstacles?	No	Yes
Market Uncertainty	In your judgement, is one of the competing options clearly going to be more successful in the marketplace?	No	Yes
Costs of Duplication	Are the marginal costs of running two competing options in parallel prohibitively high?	No	Yes
Size of Market	Will the marketplace be big enough to support two different standards or two similar products?	Yes	No
Make or Buy	Is there an equally valid option to *buy* the technology in question rather than make it in-house?	No	Yes
Critical Mass	Will running two or more competing technologies in parallel spread you too thin in terms of the availability of qualified people?	No	Yes
Speed to Market	Is speed to market more critical to success than the cost of development?	Yes	No

[a]Allow internal competition to continue for the moment.
[b]Merge the competing options, or close all but one down.

to avoid the real nightmare scenario of near-identical products getting all the way to market before the company finds out. Consider the example of 3M's "self-check" library system. Back in 1989, Hilary Smith, a market development manager in 3M Canada, identified the possibility of a self-check system whereby patrons would check out their books themselves rather than giving them to the librarian. Having failed to get any interest in the product idea at corporate HQ, she pursued it anyway and put together a prototype using seed funding from the Canadian R&D budget. It was only when she presented the prototype at the annual American Library Association meeting that she discovered 3M Australia had developed a very similar product. Once they were aware of each other, Smith and the Australian team got together and ultimately came up with a very successful product that built on the best features of both prototypes. However, in retrospect it was clear that they should have become aware of each other's technology before the American Library Association meeting.

How can this sort of situation be avoided? A number of different systems were used by the companies involved in the research. ABB has a technology-based system called PIPE (project idea, planning and execution) in which R&D engineers place their project ideas at a very early stage to inform their colleagues around the world what they are doing and to get feedback from them. Ericsson operates with a very dispersed model in which it is accepted that internal competition

will emerge all the time.[7] However, the personal networks and lateral communication systems in the company are strong enough that cases of overlapping technologies or projects are quickly brought to the attention of senior managers. In one recent case, an executive was reviewing the company's prospective offerings in the Internet Protocol (IP) space and through his personal networks quickly identified *seven* competing technologies. Armed with this information, he was able to focus Ericsson's efforts toward a couple of them and redirect the work of the other five development groups. A third approach involved structuring the innovation process more formally. For example, Hewlett-Packard's Test and Measurement Organization (now spun off as Agilent) instituted an extra "tollgate" in the development process as a way of giving greater visibility to early-stage projects. This helped to avoid cases of internal competition going unnoticed in the early phases of technology development. Finally, all these companies made use of informal knowledge brokers—individuals who are well connected throughout the company and who are skilled at linking up people who need to talk to each other.

Bring the Competing Units Together

Regardless of whether internal competition is emergent or planned, it is important to bring the competing units together as soon as possible. In emergent cases, the key issue is to understand how the competing business units see the technology evolving, and what sort of market need they think it will serve. The value of competition of this sort is that the business units have different perspectives and different technologies, and this can be the source of new opportunities for the company. For example, one case in HP's Test and Measurement Organization led to three competing units coming together to discuss market potential in "Voice over IP" technology. In discussing their different views of the market, it became clear that the potential was far greater than each unit had realized individually. They were able to carve up the emerging market opportunity in such a way that each unit could continue to develop its products and also benefit from collaboration on certain aspects of the technology.

The other reason to bring competing units together is to alleviate the bitter rivalry that can sometimes emerge. One such case was an IT infrastructure company called Telstar that found itself running two competing middleware technology platforms. AX was a proprietary platform that had been used for years within Telstar. EX was a new, open standard that had first been used in the networking division and was now being pushed throughout the company. The competition between these two platforms came to a head when the new business unit had to choose one. As one manager commented, "there [were] very heated discussions. There was an almost religious passion among people on both sides as to which was the superior platform." After the discussions had ended in deadlock, top-level executives were brought in and they decided to choose in favor of EX, the open standard. However, they also placed the two warring teams in the same group in order build a common platform for future use. As one manager commented,

> This meant there were 50 people from each side working for the same boss, but with fundamentally different beliefs about which platform was superior. To this day, each group still claims their approach is the best. There are some shared features now, and the end user interface is basically the same. But ultimately one of them will have to be scrapped.

In this case, bringing the two units together was painful for the people involved, but was a necessary step for future technological developments in Telstar.

When internal competition is *mandated* by senior managers, bringing the two units together early on

serves the purpose of defining the "rules of engagement." As the Fuji Xerox example illustrated, this form of competition is typically undertaken to address a particular problem. The competing units have to understand the criteria against which they will be evaluated, the timing of the next review, and the extent to which they are allowed or expected to cooperate with one another. Pharmaceuticals companies typically do this very well in their research labs. While there is always a competitive element, the prevailing philosophy is that the competing units are working toward the same ultimate goal, and this makes it relatively easy for scientists to both collaborate and compete at the same time.

Accept Coexistence as a Possible Outcome

While the rule of thumb in this form of internal competition is that it should be resolved as quickly as possible, there may be cases where coexistence is the best outcome. Conceptually, the reason for this is that executive judgment cannot always substitute for real market data. Because of the level of technological uncertainty in many markets and the way that standards emerge, it can be very dangerous to make a premature decision on which technology to put the company's weight behind. Consider, for example, the dilemma facing Ericsson in the mid-1990s. The possibility of a high-bandwidth "third-generation" mobile system had begun to emerge, but as always there were competing standards—a new technology called WCDMA; a second technology developed by Qualcomm in the U.S. now known as CDMA-2000; and a way of upgrading the existing TDMA and GSM technologies called EDGE. What approach should Ericsson have taken? First, they made the obvious decision to work with WCDMA and EDGE. However, given the potentially enormous costs involved in commercializing both, they also started working with competitors, customers, and regulatory authorities to try to establish a single global standard, as well as negotiate with Qualcomm over patent disputes as to which one had the rights to CDMA technology. Unfortunately, it proved impossible for the various authorities to agree on a single standard, with the result that three different technologies ended up running in parallel. In other words, while Ericsson pushed very hard to consolidate the different technologies, they ultimately had to accept that they would coexist—at least in the medium term.

This example highlights the point made earlier about how to handle a Sophie's Choice scenario. First, keep the options open, by avoiding heavy investments until some uncertainties have been resolved. Second, seek strength in numbers, which in this case meant consortia of competing firms. Third, accept coexistence but only as a last resort. Betting on a single technology is always possible, but in the circumstances extremely risky.

Manage the Loser

There is a risk with internal competition that the individual or team whose technology is not taken forward will see themselves as the "loser" and will either lose motivation or leave the company. Many of the participating companies in the research took this issue very seriously. The preferred approach—as exemplified by HP, Ericsson, and others—was to manage the competition to avoid winners and losers. As one HP manager said, "There should not be a loser. You should be able to manage the situation so that everyone feels good about the outcome." HP does this through a process of "patching"—shifting charters between divisions and ensuring that even if a division loses one charter, it gains another. A similar process was observed in Ericsson. In one case, a piece of development work was transferred out from Stockholm to the losing development unit in Belgium to ensure that it stayed at capacity. However, it is worth bearing in mind that both HP and Ericsson benefit from being in fast-growing markets where there has always been enough work to go around.

If the problem could not be avoided completely, the other approach companies used was to find ways of keeping the losing party motivated. This was done by clarifying expectations in advance (e.g., that well-intentioned failure is a good thing) or by finding specific roles for the losing individuals to fulfil. For example, in the Fuji Xerox case referred to earlier, the head of the losing technology was put in charge of the winning technology as a way of demonstrating that the decision had not been a personal one.

INTERNAL COMPETITION BETWEEN BUSINESS LINES

The other major form of internal competition is between distinct lines of business. Because of the enormous costs of running business lines in parallel, this form of competition generally occurs with the full knowledge and permission of senior management. However, even though it is allowed to occur, it is still reviewed on a continuous basis; typically the internal competition lifecycle runs its complete course and the businesses in question are consolidated. Ericsson again provides an interesting example. When digital mobile telephony took off at the beginning of the 1990s, it rapidly became clear that there would be no global standard. Instead, three competing standards emerged— GSM in Europe, TDMA in North America, and PDC in Japan. For wireless infrastructure players such as Ericsson, this created a strategic dilemma: Should they try to develop infrastructure for all three standards (and, if so, how) or should they focus on one or two of them? Because of its strong international position, Ericsson decided that it had to offer all three standards. Rather than attempting to capitalize on the obvious commonalities across the standards, the company set up three separate business units that were acting in direct competition with one another. For example, in some South American countries (where two standards coexisted) the GSM and TDMA business units ended up offering competing products to the same wireless operator. The logic for this arrangement, in a nutshell, was that speed to market would be far more important than low-cost production, and this could be achieved best by giving each business unit complete freedom to develop its own software, source its own products, and build its own customer relationships. At the same time, Ericsson's strong corporate culture ensured that individuals in the three business units collaborated freely and openly with one another, sharing best practices and swapping ideas. The result was that Ericsson emerged as the undisputed global leader in second generation mobile infrastructure—and the only company with a strong position in all three standards.

The second-generation technology is now moving toward maturity and will soon be superseded by GPRS and 3G. Ericsson has therefore recognized that speed is now less important than efficient development, so changes are being made—development groups in the three divisions have been merged and the three business units are all being brought together so that commonalities across the technologies can be exploited. Essentially, top management has decided that internal competition should be phased out now that its benefits have been achieved.

Another example worth mentioning is Sony and their practice of launching dozens of products on a limited basis (e.g., different types of Walkman) and to use market feedback to decide which products they should subsequently launch on a global basis.[8] This approach makes sense because the cost of trial launches is moderate and the payoff in terms of market feedback is high. Again, however, the idea is that the competing business lines will exist only until top management has enough information to choose between them.

These examples illustrate the complete lifecycle of internal competition from establishment to coexistence to termination. However, many other cases are still in the coexistence phase and indeed may be for a very long time. For example, SEB, a large Stockholm-based bank, was one of the first banks to get into Internet banking. Back in 1995, its business development group, referred to internally as K2 (after the Himalayan mountain), was experimenting with a number of new ideas. One was to sell services over an emerging technology called the Internet. In the early stages of development this business was left within the K2 group, but when it was launched it was placed as a separate unit within the retail bank. The business was extremely successful as the first full-service Internet bank in Sweden with 100,000 customers after just one year, and despite the fact that there was some cannibalization of the retail bank it was left as a separate business unit. Today, it clearly coexists with the retail business on the basis that there are costs of duplication but they are more than outweighed by the benefits. For example, most customers now do their simple transactions such as bill payments and switching between accounts using the Internet bank, and they use the retail branch for investment and lending advice.

How should you decide whether to opt for consolidation or coexistence of competing business lines? Some of the criteria are exactly the same as with internal competition between technologies—market and technological uncertainty both favor coexistence, high costs of duplication favor consolidation, and the importance of speed to market lends support to a coexistence strategy. However, unlike in the previous list, the focus of attention here is more on the relationship between the two businesses in the marketplace. Three market-based factors emerged during the research:

- *Cannibalization*—Is one competing option cannibalizing a large portion of the sales of another? If yes, then consolidation is likely to make sense.

- *Market Heterogeneity*—Is the marketplace heterogeneous enough to support two or more similar solutions in different market segments? If yes, then coexistence is likely to be preferred.

- *Complementarities*—Are there benefits from having two or more competing options in the marketplace, such as cross-selling or brand-building opportunities? If yes, then coexistence is favored.

Competing business lines end up fighting it out in the marketplace with real customers, rather than for the attention and resources of top management, which means that competing businesses are both earning revenues as well as duplicating costs. The result is that competition among business lines is typically allowed to endure for far longer than competition between technologies.

As before, this list of criteria is no substitute for good judgment because trade-offs will almost always need to be made. For example, Ford has to evaluate the costs of cannibalization against the benefits of market coverage when it reviews its high-end brands Jaguar, Volvo, and Lincoln. Emap, the British magazines and radio group, has to decide whether the level of uncertainty in the Internet world justifies managing FHM.com as a separate business from the print version of *FHM Magazine*. WPP has to weigh the costs of running multiple advertising and PR agencies in parallel against the benefits that accrue from having focused and entrepreneurially minded units. Clearly, there are no simple ways of making these trade-offs, but the following points provide some general rules of thumb as to how the process should be managed.

Keep the Competing Businesses Apart at First

In contrast with competing technologies, the rule of thumb with competing business lines is to allow duplication while they develop their commercial offerings and bring them to market.[9] One reason for this is speed, as the Ericsson case showed. However, the more common reason is that this form of competition typically takes the form of a new and unproven business (e.g., Internet banking) challenging the traditional business (e.g., branch-based banking), so for the new business to have a chance of surviving it has to be given breathing space.[10] An example of this is R. R. Donnelley and Sons, the Chicago-based printing company.[11] In the early 1990s, digital printing had begun to emerge, but it was still seen as a niche business by the managers running the traditional printing presses. For this reason, Donnelley placed digital printing in a separate division called Global Software. Its boss, Rory Cowan, stated that he wanted to "create a new business and have it drip on the culture" and gradually change the perspective of people who had been brought up in the world of "big iron" presses. The same approach was also taken by most of the established retailers as they built Internet businesses, including Barnes and Noble and Wal-Mart.

Monitor the Level of Cannibalization

Cannibalization is the natural consequence of internal competition, so it cannot be avoided if parallel business units are allowed to coexist.[12] However, at the same time, it is important to gauge the level of cannibalization that you are experiencing on a continuous basis. Consider, for example, the British company Spirent, which is now a global leader in telecommunication testing equipment (along with Agilent). Spirent grew rapidly over the last four years through a series of acquisitions—Netcom Systems in California, Adtech in Hawaii, TAS in Massachusetts, and several smaller companies as well. The acquisitions were made as a way of building up critical mass in the fast-expanding telecom market, but inevitably there was some overlap in the product lines of the acquired companies, notably between Adtech and Netcom. Initially, top management did not intervene. They wanted to make sure the employees in the acquired companies stayed, and the market was growing fast enough that there was room for both product lines to coexist. Gradually, however, it became clear that there was considerable cannibalization in a couple of areas, which was creating some confusion in the minds of customers and some internal tensions as well. As a result, they decided to resolve the problem by creating a single global sales force to serve all the different business units, and they asked the business units heads to get together to resolve the duplication between their product lines.

Another example is SEB, the Swedish bank that has retail, Internet, and telephone banks operating in parallel. Again, their preferred approach is to monitor, rather than resolve, the cannibalization between these channels, primarily because they believe there are complementarities between them. Indeed, because it is so much cheaper to do routine transactions over the

Net, SEB encourages its customers to do so, which frees up the time of branch employees to do more value-added work. Careful attention is paid to the type and quantity of transactions that customers undertake using the three different channels and how these are changing over time.

Look for Opportunities to Integrate

While coexistence among the competing business lines can often be justified for several years, the ultimate objective is always to look for ways of integrating them. This does not necessarily mean complete integration, but it does imply that most of the duplicate activities should be eliminated and the potential synergies be sought out and delivered upon. The Ericsson case again provides a good example of how this works. Following the decision to put the three second-generation systems under a single business unit, there was a massive integration effort. For instance, the groups responsible for developing base stations in the old businesses began working together to produce a single base station that worked across all three standards. Equally, many established companies began by running their Internet businesses as stand-alone entities, but they realized they were missing out on potential complementarities and gradually moved the two businesses together. In the banking sector, for example, both Bank of Montreal and Bank One set up separate operating divisions (Mbanx and Wingspan.com), but they have since rolled these divisions back into their bricks-and-mortar counterparts to capitalize on synergies in their back-office activities.

Spirent provides a detailed example of *how* to manage the integration process. As noted earlier, top management asked the competing business units to get together to resolve the duplication in their product lines. However, as the executive responsible for the group explained,

> The two business units were not making progress, so I got them together, and told them to lock themselves away for a couple of days and sort it out. I have a basic belief in humanity. You come to work to do a good job. These guys wanted to resolve the problem, but it was down to me to put them in a position where it would happen. Essentially, I narrowed the pitch. I gave them deadlines to work to. So they got together, and they came out with a sol-

id proposal. Now they are working through the soft issues together.

This example underlines the point that internal competition is best resolved without external judges or arbitrators. The two business units were eventually able to divide their markets up so that each focused on its own core technology. However, by figuring this out for themselves, rather than having the solution imposed, they were far more likely to make it work—which was critical given the need for cooperation and technology sharing between them.

HOW MUCH INTERNAL COMPETITION DO YOU ALLOW?

The level of internal competition that is appropriate varies enormously from industry to industry. In pharmaceuticals, there is a lot of competition in early-stage discovery research, and virtually none in the development pipeline, simply because of the exorbitant cost of drug development once clinical trials have begun. In the fast-moving high-tech sector inhabited by companies such as HP, Ericsson, and Lucent, both forms of internal competition are very common. In scale-driven, low-margin industries such as chemicals, automobiles, and food products, neither form of internal competition is commonly seen.

However, despite the sector differences, the level of internal competition is highly specific to a particular company. Just compare, for example, the bottom-up driven strategy process in Ericsson with the more top-down driven process in rivals Alcatel and Siemens. The fact is that the level of internal competition is a function of the organizational systems in the company, including the way resources are allocated to projects and the attitude in the company towards risk-taking. It also comes down to specific incentive schemes. For example, in one fast-food company, top management challenged each region to come up with a new restaurant concept and promised to invest in what they considered to be the best three. This led, not surprisingly, to a great deal of competitive behavior as regions sought to out-do each other in developing the most innovative concept.[13] More broadly, the working environment inside 3M promotes individual initiative through a combination of the formal way that projects are managed and the informal culture that encourages individuals to bootleg resources and set time aside for developing new ideas. Internal competition is an unavoidable consequence of such an environment and 3M has proven itself to be consistently innovative as a result.

In terms of how such systems evolve, a case in point is Hewlett-Packard. For many years, HP had a highly decentralized structure and an entrepreneurial culture that was in many ways very similar to 3M's. Toward the late 1980s, however, there was a clear sense in the company that product development initiatives had gotten out of control. As a result, changes were made in 1990 to the funding mechanism so that all development work had to be aligned to existing divisions. This helped to reduce the level of internal competition between technologies, but there were still frequent cases of competition between businesses. More recently, CEO Carly Fiorina embarked on a major structural change that brought together HP's multitude of highly autonomous divisions into a much smaller number of business groups. The purpose of this structural change was to give the company greater focus, but one by-product will almost certainly be a reduction in the number of competing business ideas. Whether this turns out to be a good thing or a bad thing remains to be seen.

CONCLUSION

Internal competition will never be easy to manage. Even in companies that appear to manage it well, there are frequently voiced concerns that such competition is wasteful and should be stamped out—as the recent reorganizations in HP attest. Internal competition can be very damaging if it is allowed to propagate unchecked through the company. However, it can also be a very useful tool under certain conditions. The advice is to use it selectively and, equally important, to become much more aware of how it fits into the broader strategic agenda of the company.

APPENDIX

The Research

The research on which this article is based was undertaken as part of a broader research program called Capability Management in Network Organizations, a cooperative venture between the Institute of International Business at the Stockholm School of Economics and six Swedish firms (Askus, Ericsson, Pharmacia, Skandia, SEB, Volvo). See J. Birkinshaw and P. Hagstrom, *The Flexible Firm* (Oxford University Press, 2000), for some of the initial findings from this research.

The internal competition project that was part of this program began with a questionnaire survey, which was conducted to establish how common the phenomenon of internal competition was. The questionnaire was filled in by executives in just over 100 companies in Sweden and the UK. Most of these companies showed evidence of using competitive internal systems, including such things as "bottom-up processes

Table 33.2. Summary of Cases of Internal Competition Developed During Research

Case	Type of Internal Competition	How Established	How Managed
Ericsson, screenphone technology	Between technologies	Emergent—five competing projects	Groups brought together, a couple of projects selected to go forward
Ericsson, voice-over-IP opportunity	Between technologies	Emergent—seven competing projects	Review committee looked at them; after deliberation two were resourced, five were closed down
Ericsson, 2G Technologies	Between business lines	Mandated—corporate decision to create three separate units	Units coexisted for ten years; recently they have been merged to generate cost savings in a maturing industry
Ericsson, 3G Technologies	Between business lines	Mandated—corporate decision to create three separate units	Attempts to consolidate failed because no industry-wide standards could be agreed; currently coexisting
HP, X Terminal	Between technologies	Emergent—two competing projects	Brought together by senior management; one given the charter, one moved into a related technology
HP, voice over IP	Between technologies	Emergent—three competing projects	Brought together by senior management; market sufficiently large to allow them to coexist
HP, RTAP product	Between technologies	Emergent—two competing projects	Brought to attention of senior management: one given the charter because its development was more advanced
Spirent, core testing equipment	Between business lines	Two acquired businesses with overlapping products	Coexistence for two years; then senior management pushed the competing units to define distinct charters for themselves
Spirent, wireless testing equipment	Between business lines	Two acquired businesses with overlapping products	Similar to above, but company still in the process of dividing up responsibilities between the two units
Telstar, communications	Between technologies	Emergent, but with some knowledge from top management—two competing standards	Coexistence for a while; then two "warning" units forced into a single division to ensure consolidation
SEB, Internet bank	Between business lines	Mandated from above	Kept separate at first; gradually brought under control of retail bank with shared back office activities
Skandia, dial (a telephone insurance business)	Between business lines	Mandated from above	Deliberately kept entirely separate from the main insurance business, coexistence.
Fuji Xerox, printer driver	Between technologies	Mandated from above	Two projects run in parallel; winner chosen after a set period of time
Consecta, low-end consulting business	Between business lines	Mandated from above	Separate low-end business unit run in parallel; but cannibalization problems led to consolidation

for developing new products" and "marketlike processes for allocating activities between units." However, only 15% of the respondents acknowledged that the specific form of internal competition under discussion here (in terms of parallel or duplicate activities) occurred frequently in their company, and these were predominantly in the technology, media, and telecommunications industries. The second phase of research therefore focused on this set of companies. More than 60 semi-structured interviews were conducted in ten companies—ABB, Ericsson, Pharmacia, HP, Spirent, Xerox, SEB, Skandia, Volvo, and Telstar. The focus of the interviews was on identifying examples of internal competition, weighing up its costs and benefits, and describing the approaches companies used to manage the internal competition process. Fourteen individual cases of internal competition were drawn up as part of this process (see Table 33.2 for a summary of these cases).

ACKNOWLEDGMENTS

Thanks to George Yip, Sumantra Ghoshal, Kim Warren, Mats Lingblad, and seminar participants at London Business School for their comments on this research.

NOTES

1. For a more detailed discussion of the definition of internal competition, see J. M. Birkinshaw and M. Lingblad, "An Evolutionary Theory of Intra-Organizational Competition," London Business School working paper, 2001. Also M. Gaynor, "Competition Within the Firm," *Rand Journal of Economics,* 20/1 (1989): 59–76; A. W. Lerner, "There Is More than One Way to Be Redundant," *Administration and Society,* 18/3 (1987): 334–359.

2. Robert Burgelman, "A Model of the Interaction of Strategic Behavior, Corporate Context and the Concept of Strategy," *Academy of Management Review,* 8/1 (January 1983): 61–70.

3. There are also other important management processes that help to encourage (or suppress) internal competition—for example, zero-sum competitions or rewards for competitive behavior.

4. There is also a third type, namely, the competition between brands in the marketplace—a practice that Procter and Gamble, GM, and others have used very successfully. This is really a rather different phenomenon, though, because it is primarily about how best to segment the customer base and position the different brands to maximize coverage, rather than coping with technological or market uncertainty.

5. Sophie's Choice—in which you have to make a choice where no choice is possible. See the novel by William Styron.

6. The make-buy choice is not developed in the article, but is worth commenting on briefly. Many companies actively pursue both internal and external options when developing new technologies, essentially as a way of keeping their options open. Ultimately, the decision to pursue the internal development option comes down to a strategic analysis of whether that technology is core to the firm's competitiveness; but in the shorter term it can also facilitate more rapid time-to-market, and it can push internal development teams to try their hardest.

7. It is worth noting that all the detailed case studies in this article about Ericsson are concerned with the Mobile Systems business, which is still the world leader in infrastructure provision. Ericsson's problems have stemmed primarily from the handsets division.

8. This example was suggested by an anonymous reviewer.

9. This applies only on the basis that internal competition between technologies has been handled effectively. In other words, if two near-identical technologies end up finding their way to market, they should probably be consolidated, but really that problem should have been identified during the development process.

10. Clayton Christensen, *The Innovator's Dilemma* (Boston, MA: Harvard Business School Press, 1997).

11. This case is drawn from D.A Garvin, "R. R. Donnelley & Sons: The Digital Division," Harvard Business School case study, 9-396-154, 2000.

12. It is worth observing that the level of cannibalization in cases of internal competition is often overstated (particularly by the group whose products are being cannibalized). For example, some level of cannibalization may be needed to open up a new market segment; and there are enormous difficulties in quantifying the actual level of cannibalization. Executives need to be careful to consider the often-hidden benefits against the all-too-visible costs to get a balanced perspective.

13. Kim Warren at London Business School is to be thanked for providing this example.

34

Technology Brokering and Innovation in a Product Development Firm

ANDREW HARGADON
ROBERT I. SUTTON

We blend network and organizational memory perspectives in a model of technology brokering that explains how an organization develops innovative products. The model is grounded in observations, interviews, informal conversations, and archived data gathered during an ethnography of IDEO, a product design firm. This firm exploits its network position, working for clients in at least 40 industries, to gain knowledge of existing technological solutions in various industries. It acts as a technology broker by introducing these solutions where they are not known and, in the process, creates new products that are original combinations of existing knowledge from disparate industries. Designers exploit their access to a broad range of technological solutions with organizational routines for acquiring and storing this knowledge in the organization's memory and, by making analogies between current design problems and the past solutions they have seen, retrieving that knowledge to generate new solutions to design problems in other industries. We discuss the implications of this research for understanding the individual and organizational processes and norms underlying technology and knowledge transfer more generally.

Knowledge is imperfectly shared over time and across people, organizations, and industries. Ideas from one group might solve the problems of another, but only if connections between existing solutions and problems can be made across the boundaries between them. When such connections are made, existing ideas often appear new and creative as they change form, combining with other ideas to meet the needs of different users. These new combinations are objectively new concepts or objects because they are built from existing but previously unconnected ideas. This paper presents an ethnographic study of a product design firm that routinely creates new products by making such connections.

The role these connections can play in the innovation process is evident in inventions by Thomas Edison's laboratory. Edison and his colleagues used their knowledge of electromagnetic power from the telegraph industry, where they first worked, to transfer old ideas that were new to the lighting, telephone, phonograph, railway, and mining industries (Hughes, 1989; Millard, 1990). Edison's products often reflected blends of existing but previously unconnected ideas that his engineers picked up as they worked in these disparate industries. The phonograph blended old ideas from products that these engineers had devel-

Reprinted from "Technology Brokering and Innovation in a Product Development Firm," by Andrew Hargadon and Robert I. Sutton, published in *Administrative Science Quarterly,* Vol. 42, No. 4, by permission of *Administrative Science Quarterly,* Vol. 42, No. 4. Copyright © 1997 by the Johnson Graduate School of Management, Cornell University.

oped for the telegraph, telephone, and electric motor industries, as well as ideas developed by others that they had learned about while working in those industries. Edison's inventions were not wholly original. Like most creative acts and products, they were extensions and blends of existing knowledge (Merton, 1973). As Usher (1929; quoted in Petrovski, 1992: 44) argued, "invention finds its distinctive feature in the constructive assimilation of pre-existing elements into new syntheses, new patterns, or new configurations of behavior."

Social network theory suggests that Edison's laboratory could innovate routinely because it occupied a "structural hole" (Burt, 1992a, 1992b), a gap in the flow of information between subgroups in a larger network. For Edison, these gaps existed between industries where there was and was not knowledge about the newly emerging electromagnetic technologies. Actors filling these gaps are brokers who benefit by transferring resources from groups where they are plentiful to groups where they are dear (Marsden, 1982; Gould and Fernandez, 1989; Burt, 1992a; DiMaggio, 1992). Brokers have an advantage over competitors because "nonredundant contacts are linked only through the central player, [so brokers] are assured of being the first to see new opportunities created by the needs in one group that could be served by skills in another group" (Burt, 1992a: 70). Edison's laboratory acted as a broker of technological ideas because it had connections to many industries, rather than being central in one, and it linked industries that had few other ties (DiMaggio, 1992).

By highlighting the structure of resource flows across group boundaries, researchers have shown that brokers benefit from disparities in the level and value of particular knowledge held by different groups, but they have not explicated the process by which information is transformed or combined within these flows. Valuable solutions seldom arrive at the same time as the problems they solve, they seldom arrive to the people working on those problems, and they seldom arrive in forms that are readily recognizable or easily adaptable. Edison's laboratory did more than just transfer knowledge from groups where it was plentiful to groups where it was dear; this organization acquired such information, stored it, and retrieved it to create new combinations of old ideas. Walsh and Ungson (1991: 61) described these processes (i.e., acquisition,

retention, and retrieval) as routines supporting an organization's memory, which they defined as "stored information from an organization's history that can be brought to bear on present decisions." This perspective suggests that a technology broker depends on both its network position as a broker and on an organizational memory that allows it to acquire, retain, and retrieve new combinations of information obtained through such a position.

The notion that brokers transform and blend information is implicit in DiMaggio's (1992) description of how Professor Paul Sachs used his strong connections to the previously weakly connected worlds of museums, universities, and finance to help create New York's Museum of Modern Art. This notion is also implicit in writings on technology transfer (Rosenberg, 1982, 1994; Rogers, 1983), which recognize that existing technologies are often adapted and transformed before they become usable in a new field. But these writings do not focus on the role that individual actions and organizational routines play in recognizing, storing, blending, and transforming those technologies to make diffusion possible. Except for Attewell's (1992) description of how consultants facilitated the diffusion of a business computing technology, we don't know of any empirical or conceptual work that weaves together macro perspectives on external networks with micro perspectives on internal routines to describe the role of brokering in innovation.

This paper develops such an integrated perspective in a process theory of how one product design firm acts as a technology broker. Following Weick's (1992) approach to theory building, we develop a relatively full explanation of brokering in a small region, which is then used to guide general discussion about brokering in other settings. We use an ethnography of a product design consulting firm to develop a local theory of how this organization acts as a technology broker. This firm has designed products for several hundred different firms in over 40 industries, ranging from pagers to closet-size medical analysis products. The quantity of new product designs (the firm works on between 60 and 80 products at a time), together with the tangible nature of the mechanical solutions that usually make up those designs, allowed us to observe how this firm recognizes, blends, and transforms existing ideas into new and innovative combinations. By having strong connections to many industries but not being central in any one, the engineers in this firm have constant opportunities to learn about technologies from a broad range of industries. The firm exploits its network position with internal routines that help its designers create products for current clients that are new combinations of existing individual technologies that these designers have seen before. Many of these products reflect the transfer of ideas to industries where they have not been used before and the creation of combinations of ideas that no one in any industry has seen before.

METHODS

Research Setting

This ethnography was conducted at IDEO, the largest product design consulting firm in the United States.[1] IDEO was co-founded by the current CEO David Kelley in 1978. It employs over 125 designers who develop products for other companies. Headquarters are in Palo Alto, California, with smaller offices in Boston, Chicago, Grand Rapids, London, San Francisco, New York, and Tokyo. The bulk of IDEO's work is in mechanical engineering and industrial design. Mechanical engineers design products for physical performance and ease of manufacturing; industrial designers use artistic skills (with an appreciation of engineering) to design products that are attractive and easy to use. Our study focused on the 45 or so engineers in Palo Alto who do mechanical engineering and (to a lesser extent) electrical, software, and human factors engineering and on the 35 or so managers and staff who support their work. We follow our informants' usage and describe IDEO's engineers as "product designers" or "designers" most often, but we (and they) sometimes use "engineers." Most designers are 25 to 40 years old, male (about 80 percent), white (about 80 percent), and usually have a B.S. or an M.S. in engineering. Managers have a similar profile but tend to be older (35 to 50 years old). Support staff also have a profile similar to designers, but a higher proportion (approximately 50 percent) are women.

Clients typically hire IDEO to design part or all of a product that they would like to manufacture and sell but lack the expertise or staff levels to design. Clients range from *Fortune* 50 to start-up companies. IDEO usually charges clients for the time and materials required to design a product but occasionally works in exchange for a percentage of sales or profits from the finished product. Design projects last from a few weeks to three years, with an average of about a year. Results range from sketches of product concepts to crude working models, to complete new product designs. IDEO has contributed to the development of over 3,000 products. Widely known products include the original Apple computer mouse, a Microsoft computer mouse, Smith ski goggles, AT&T telephones, Oral-B toothbrushes, Crest toothpaste tubes, Steelcase furniture, Sega game controllers, Hewlett-Packard printers, rechargers for General Motors' electric vehicles, laptop computers for such firms as Apple Computers, Dell, and NEC, the Macintosh DuoDock, Regina vacuum cleaners, and a life-sized, functioning, mechanical killer whale used in the film *Free Willy.* Less widely known products include surgical skin staplers, a combination beach chair and cooler, a coin sorter, a blood platelet function analyzer, a toy guitar, and the Enorme telephone. IDEO is widely praised in the business press for its innovative designs; for instance, IDEO won more *Business Week* Design Excellence Awards in 1993, 1994, and 1995, and over the last decade, than any other product design firm.

Method

Each of the two authors spent six to eight hours per week doing an ethnographic study of IDEO from March 1994 through May 1995. Fieldwork continued at a less intensive level through February 1996, with at least one of us visiting IDEO each week. We wrote field notes after each visit or meeting. Each of us also visited IDEO at least once a month through December 1996, often to collect more evidence or to check the accuracy of facts that appear in papers about IDEO. Any visit to IDEO entailed unplanned conversations, because many engineers, support staff, and managers were curious about our research and because IDEO norms support friendly talk about the firm and the design process. The buildings where most design engineers work have a modified open-office plan, which further encourages informal talk. In addition, most IDEO buildings in Palo Alto (industrial design, administrative offices, two machine shops, and a joint venture with a large corporation) are on the same street and within a few blocks of one another, so many unplanned but enlightening conversations occurred as we walked between buildings.

We began this ethnography with a vague research question: How does IDEO innovate routinely? Although we often interacted with senior managers during these visits, our data collection focused on watching and talking to product designers and looking at and gathering the drawings and physical artifacts that resulted from their work. We adopted this focus because our primary aim was to understand how people do and experience innovative work, not how it is viewed by management or support staff. Following guidelines for inductive research, we were as descriptive as possible until major themes emerged from the data (Glaser and Strauss, 1967; Miles and Huberman, 1994). When a promising theme like technology brokering emerged, we focused data collection on it, read pertinent literature, and did preliminary analyses to decide if it was worth pursuing. Our interest in brokering was sparked in the winter of 1995 when we noticed that designers offered solutions to new problems by describing similar solutions they had seen in past products, a process they called "cross-pollination."[2] The evidence guiding our descriptions of and inferences about technology brokering at IDEO is divided into seven general categories:

1. *Tracking development projects.* Each of the two authors followed a development team as it designed a product. We met with team members about once every two weeks, attended design meetings, and were given sketches, reports, and videotapes. The first author followed a team for four months until it nearly finished designing a Regina vacuum cleaner. A new CEO stopped work on this prototype and other designs being done by and for Regina to reevaluate the firm's product strategy. About six months after we stopped tracking the team, Regina decided that IDEO should finish the design, and the product was completed, manufactured, and sold. The second author followed a team for six months while it worked on personal appliances. He followed this team until two prototypes and detailed drawings were completed. These completed designs were not manufactured and sold because the firm changed strategic direction after it was acquired by a larger corporation and the CEO stepped down.[3]

2. *Semistructured interviews with designers and managers.* We conducted 60 semistructured interviews;

37 were tape-recorded and transcribed; we took notes during others. We had multiple interviews with some informants, so approximately 35 people were interviewed. In initial interviews, we asked senior managers and designers general questions about IDEO's history, clients, competitors, structure, human resource practices, and work process. Subsequent interviews focused on themes like technology brokering that we wanted to learn about in detail.

3. *Informal discussions.* We had hundreds of informal conversations with managers, designers, and support staff, ranging from brief exchanges to long talks over lunch. We talked with almost every employee at the Palo Alto headquarters and had dozens of conversations with the CEO. We also had informal conversations with ten IDEO clients about the company. The content varied widely, with designers often gossiping about new clients, employees who had been hired or had left, the virtues or drawbacks of current IDEO prototypes, "cool" new technologies that they had seen or heard about, or why they loved or despised existing products, ranging from toy Slinkies to Harley-Davidson motorcycles. In addition, after we began asking questions about emerging themes, including technology brokering and brainstorming sessions, designers often approached us with comments, questions, stories, prototypes, and sketches that they believed would enhance our understanding of these topics. Conversations with clients were equally diverse, but at least three of them talked with us about technology brokering. For example, one client described how IDEO designers had introduced his organization to promising technical solutions that were new to that industry but were used widely elsewhere.

4. *Brainstorming sessions.* We observed 24 group brainstorming sessions in which products were designed, six in person and 18 on videotape. Each meeting was initiated by members of a design team. They invited IDEO designers who were not team members to generate possible design solutions for the project. IDEO brainstorms are scheduled meetings and are held in conference rooms. Five brainstorming rules are displayed in large letters in several locations in each room: (1) defer judgment; (2) build on the ideas of others; (3) one conversation at

a time; (4) stay focused on the topic, and (5) encourage wild ideas. IDEO's *Methodology Handbook,* which outlines IDEO's techniques for new designers, contains 11 pages of instructions about how to facilitate and participate in brainstorms. Designers who lead brainstorms are skilled and experienced facilitators; nearly all IDEO designers have extensive experience as participants in brainstorms.

The sessions we observed lasted between 45 minutes and two hours. The topics ranged widely: three about personal appliances, three about furniture, three about video cameras, two about surgical skin staplers, two about medical devices to aid healing, two about blood analyzers, two about laptop computers, two about personal communication, one about remote controls, one about ski goggles, one about vacuum cleaners, one about faucets, and one about a portable traffic control system. Typically, project engineers introduced the project and described a design problem they were facing, then the other engineers offered possible solutions, often in the form of solutions they had seen in other settings. Solutions were sometimes found in similar products that were brought to brainstorms (e.g., a designer suggested adapting a design solution for a new skin stapler that was already used in a competitor's product) or in products that were brought in from different industries (e.g., a designer showed how a gas engine from a model airplane could be used to power a skin stapler). Designers also described and sketched solutions on paper or on whiteboards in the room. The visible and vocal nature of these meetings offered us the opportunity to observe how new problems and existing solutions were shared among the designers.

We wrote field notes about each brainstorm and were given "brainstorming reports" for nine of the 24. These reports are prepared for the client by the brainstorm organizers; they summarize the ideas generated and develop promising ideas in greater depth. We also distributed a short survey about product design brainstorms at IDEO to engineers in the Palo Alto office. We distributed 45 surveys, and 37 were returned; 27 included written comments. This survey contained 40 closed-ended questions, but in this paper we only use written comments that designers made in response to a request for "any other comments about brainstorming at IDEO." See

Sutton and Hargadon (1996) for a more extensive discussion of brainstorming at IDEO.

5. *Other meetings.* We attended a session about how to handle a major client, a session with that client, a meeting with IDEO engineers who studied their firm's design process, and about twelve "Monday morning meetings." Most Mondays, CEO Kelley meets with the employees in Palo Alto who do or support "engineering design." They usually sit on the floor in a circle. Meetings start with Kelley talking about pressing, interesting, or funny events and then turn to new projects and progress on ongoing projects. "Show and tell" is next, in which designers display and describe new products, prototypes, materials, and methods. We also attended and participated in three meetings about IDEO's design process. The first and second of these were brainstorming sessions on how to describe and transfer IDEO's design process to other organizations. The third meeting focused on technology brokering; experienced designers talked about how and when they had combined their diverse technical knowledge to create new products and things they did to facilitate this process.

6. *Design team interviews.* We did retrospective interviews with four design teams, which were tape-recorded and transcribed. The products were a label-maker, a blood platelet analyzer, a mechanical killer whale, and a furniture system. Each was a large-scale project requiring multiple engineering disciplines. Designers brought prototypes and the final product to two of the interviews. We asked the group to describe how the project unfolded and the role that each member played. We asked them to describe the technical details of the project: the prominent technologies of the final design, how these were chosen, and how each team generated and explored alternative solutions throughout the project. Finally, we asked them to describe any interpersonal and political issues that arose during the project.

7. *Materials about the organization.* We gathered several dozen stories about IDEO from various sources, including *Fortune, Business Week, Wired, ID, Wall Street Journal,* and popular books. We viewed approximately fifteen television programs about IDEO first shown on outlets such as ABC,

CNN, BBC, PBS, and the Discovery Channel and explored a CD-ROM "tour" of IDEO. We gathered other materials produced by and about IDEO, including a *Methodology Handbook* for new engineers and sketches of prototypes. We also reviewed IDEO's collection of approximately 1,400 photographs of product sketches, prototypes, the design process (e.g., pictures of brainstorming sessions), and completed products.

A PROCESS MODEL OF TECHNOLOGY BROKERING

These qualitative data indicate that IDEO learns about potentially useful technologies by working for clients in multiple industries and finds opportunities to use that knowledge by incorporating it into new products for industries where there is little or no prior knowledge of these technologies. This design process results in the movement of technologies between industries, reflecting the technology transfer and diffusion that is recognized as fundamental to technological evolution (Rosenberg, 1982; Basalla, 1988; Hughes, 1989). Existing research has considered the social, economic, and political effects of this type of innovation, but little is known about the nuances of how such processes unfold within organizations.

Technology brokering at IDEO entails more than just transporting ideas between previously unconnected industries; it also means transforming, sometimes radically, those ideas to fit new environments and new combinations. An innovative product might contain several components that are new to the industry, blended with many old components that continue to fit the industry's needs. Brokering requires integrating these new and old technologies in ways that allow each to function well. For example, to develop the Cholestec Home Cholesterol Tester, IDEO designers combined a compact disk inject-eject mechanism, a simple software interface, and high-volume production design principles, each of which were relatively new ideas to the medical products industry, with sampling and testing components and chemical treatment technologies already used widely and fairly well understood in that industry. Designing the product required modifying both the compact disk inject-eject mechanism to fit the needs of the existing sampling technologies and modi-

fying the existing sampling technologies to fit the capabilities of the inject-eject mechanism. Many of IDEO's product designs are, like the home cholesterol tester, new combinations of existing components that reflect Weick's (1979a: 252) definition of creativity as "putting old things in new combinations and new things in old combinations."[4] This perspective on technology brokering began to develop when, early in our study, we noticed that many of IDEO's designs contained innovative features that engineers had seen in previous products. We created a list of IDEO-designed products that included features designers had adapted from previous products, prototypes, or other sources outside of the client's industry. We met with IDEO designers individually and in groups to add to and refine this list, which is shown in Table 34.1. It contains 30 examples of IDEO-designed products that are new combinations of old technologies taken from both inside and outside the client's industry. One example is a portable computer docking station designed for Apple Computer. It consists of traditional computer components that were combined with an insert and eject design adapted from video-cassette recorders and powered by an inexpensive motor found in toys.

Our data suggest that IDEO's ability to generate innovative products that are new combinations of existing technologies can be understood by considering both the organization's network position and the behaviors of its designers in exploiting that position. Figure 34.1 summarizes the relationship between network position and internal behaviors in a four-step model of technology brokering. *Access* (step 1) describes how IDEO fills a gap in the flow of information between industries and is able to see technological solutions in one area that are potentially valuable in others (Burt, 1992a, 1992b; DiMaggio, 1992). But the way these technologies become innovative solutions to current problems depends on how these potential solutions are shared within IDEO across designers and over time. The remaining three steps of the model describe the role of IDEO's organizational memory in turning technologies seen in past products into useful information for designing new ones (March and Simon, 1958; Huber, 1991; Walsh and Ungson, 1991).*Acquisition* (step 2) describes routines that IDEO's designers use to bring technological solutions into the organizational memory, where they are stored for possible use in future design projects. *Storage* (step 3) describes how

Table 34.1. IDEO-Designed Products That Incorporated Technological Solutions from Outside Industries

1. Water bottle: Combines existing body with leak-proof nozzle based on previous shampoo bottle design.
2. Blood analyzer: Combines existing analytic technologies with computer components: printer, keyboard, display, and circuit board.
3. Portable computer: Hinge design in portable computer display incorporates a bail mechanism found in typewriters.
4. Whale special effects: Mechanical whale combines hardware and software from the computer industry, hydraulics and robotics from designer's academic background, and latex skin and other existing special effects techniques.
5. Computer PCMCIA card adaptor: Eject mechanism combines nitinol (memory metal) from defense industry technology and existing circuit board and connector technologies.
6. Vacuum cleaner: Combines existing components with new complex plastic parts designed utilizing previous CAD experience.
7. Home cholesterol tester: Existing analytic components combined with CD inject/eject mechanism from consumer products.
8. Portable computer: Retracting foot design based on foot mechanism on slide projector.
9. Toy electric guitar: Incorporates toy industry materials and design with microprocessor technologies from previous computer projects.
10. Input device for kid's video games: Combines oversized trackball from previous computer input devices and existing toy industry components.
11. Cosmetics product: Incorporates flexible tubing from previous surgical product and vacuum technology from 2 previous vacuum cleaner projects.*
12. Bicycle helmet: Includes sailcloth strengthener from designer's sailing background as well as existing foam and shell components.*
13. Label maker: Existing label maker enhanced with interface design from computer projects and display screen, printer, input devices from computer projects.
14. Personal computer: New design for cooling computers based on design principles in ceiling fans.
15. Surgical skin stapler: Existing stapler combined with ideas from model airplane engines, office staplers, and other medical products.*
16. Original Apple mouse: Mouse design tracking mechanism adapted from giant trackball in video game machine.
17. Handheld computer: Hinge mechanism based on principles found in office binder clips.*
18. Personal computer: New computer door design based on idea from garage door via previous computer projects.
19. Tire pressure monitor and valve: Pressure gauge based on bellows mechanism found in stainless-steel fuel line product.
20. Desk lamp: Uses articulating ball-and-socket joint design taken from principles in human hip-bone sockets.
21. Portable computer docking station: Uses an eject mechanism based on ideas from video-cassette recorders, docking connectors from a previous computer docking project, and an inexpensive electric motor from toys.
22. Medical analysis product: Incorporates a solid-state fluid warmer found in portable coolers for automobiles.
23. Computer monitor: Existing monitor incorporates a clutch spring design based on idea of leaf-springs in automobile shocks.
24. Office chair spring: Seat spring combines existing seat spring components with design of rubber spring shocks used in tool and die industry.*
25. Electric car charger: Powered door opener uses gas piston from rear window of station wagon combined with electric charging components.*
26. Portable computer: Display fastened closed using bicycle spokes and existing display housing technologies.*
27. Waste paper collector: Take-up reel design based on ideas from continuous towel dispensers and typewriter printer ribbon cartridges.
28. Paper handling product: Paper tray mechanism combines parallel ruler designs in drafting boards with existing paper handling components.
29. Computer monitor: Concept for new mounting design based on "Monkey-on-a-tree" toy.
30. Slide printer: Motion control solution based on stainless steel, zero backlash motion control found in early disk-drive head designs.

*The early prototypes of these products used off-the-shelf components from these different industries in testing the performance of this technological solution in its new combination. Later designs became specific to the new product, but in the case of the bicycle spokes, a local wheel manufacturer actually became a supplier of production parts for a portable computer.

these solutions remain in memory until they are considered for use in future designs. Finally, *retrieval* (step 4) describes how designers retrieve some of these old technological solutions from the organizational memory in forms that fit the new combinations they are creating.

This process model presents access, acquisition, storage, and retrieval as linear and distinct phases. We use this model because it fits our data reasonably well and provides a simple and analytically useful way of summarizing these data. Nonetheless, the process was not always as neatly linear as the model implies and the steps could not always be cleanly distinguished. As Walsh and Ungson (1991: 82) recognize. "Because the

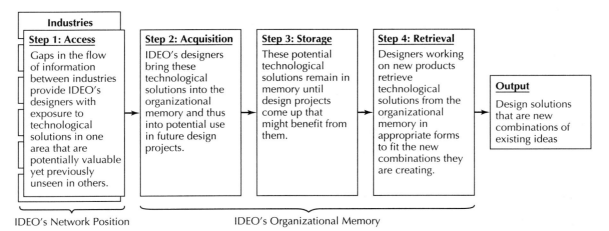

Figure 34.1. A process model of how innovation occurs through technology brokering.

acquisition, retention, and retrieval of memory is an ongoing process, it is difficult to pinpoint the exact boundaries between these processes."

We used an iterative process to develop the inferences about the process of innovation through technology brokering at IDEO that are summarized in Figure 34.1. Following Glaser and Strauss (1967) and Miles and Huberman (1994), a set of iterations usually began with a hunch inspired by the data or literature (e.g., an informant mentioned that the original idea for a water bottle valve came from another designer who had worked on a previous shampoo bottle project, which suggested that ideas from different industries provided IDEO with potentially valuable solutions in later projects). Then, to see if a hunch could be grounded, we compiled pertinent evidence from all seven data sources (e.g., we looked for evidence that IDEO's experience in a range of industries provided its engineers with useful ideas). These analyses led us to abandon, modify, or maintain each inference (e.g., we retained the inference that access to a range of industries was an important aspect of IDEO's innovation process). If the inference was retained, we summarized the grounding for it in a within-site display reflecting how strongly each inference could be grounded in each data source. We then wrote up our inferences about each retained consequence, weaving together conceptual arguments, additional evidence, and citations to pertinent literature. Table 34.2 presents the evidence that grounds our process model of technology brokering.

Access: IDEO's Network Position as Technology Broker

Brokers derive value by enabling the flow of resources between otherwise unconnected subgroups within a larger network (Marsden, 1982; Gould and Fernandez, 1989; Burt, 1992a; DiMaggio, 1992). Marsden (1982: 202) defined brokers as intermediate actors that "facilitate transactions between other actors lacking access to or trust in one another." Considerable network analytic research has shown the power that accrues to brokers. Fernandez and Gould (1994) showed that organizations occupying brokerage positions in the national health policy domain were more likely to have greater perceived influence. Padgett and Ansell (1993) explained the rise to power of the Medici family in fifteenth century Florence as the result of a network position spanning otherwise unconnected subgroups. Burt (1983, 1992a, 1992b) described how the value of connecting different subgroups depends on the relative lack of other ties between those subgroups. By restricting the flow of information between subgroups, this lack of ties creates disparities in the knowledge held by the different subgroups and enables brokers to profit by providing access for each subgroup to the ideas of the larger network. Such a disconnected network structure allows brokers to benefit because they "are well connected in several networks, rather than extremely central in just one" (DiMaggio, 1992: 130). When the ideas are technological solutions, brokers benefit by being well connected to a range of disparate industries

Table 34.2. Evidence Supporting the Process of Technology Brokering at IDEO*

Process	Tracking design teams	Semistructured interviews	Informal discussions
Access: Access to technological information in one area that is potentially valuable yet previously unseen in others	Sporadic evidence One design team was working on a vacuum cleaner design, the other on a product for personal cosmetics. Designers on each team had previously worked on medical products, computer projects, telephone headsets, and trackball devices.	Strong evidence Most designers interviewed stressed IDEO's range of clients and industries. Another designer mentioned that most of them had hobbies that cross-pollinated their designs. Ideas from model airplanes would work their way into portable computer designs.	Moderate evidence CEO talks about having clients in every industry: "you name an industry—Vacuum cleaners, washing machines, or pagers [and we've been there]."
Acquisition: IDEO's designers acquire technological solutions for possible use in later projects	Strong evidence "The best way to come up with ideas is first of all to go out and look at what's out there. So, look at the existing products, rip them apart . . . then it's looking for peripheral objects, toasters, blenders, and mixers." "We become as much of an expert [on the client's technologies] as we can in a short period of time."	Strong evidence "[The variety of industries and products] makes you more confident that you can use something you learned in this area and move from there." "[Clients] come in with a new technology and want to apply this technology and we have to come up to speed on that particular technology so the excitement of keeping up on the learning process is there."	Moderate evidence Designers talked about gaining "a big pile of tools" from their experiences in multiple industries, and how they collected many of them, when possible. One even described his "magic box of neat stuff" that stored all sorts of little interesting technologies like nitinol, velcro, high-strength alloys, etc., that he had acquired in his past projects and hoped to be able to use later.
Storage: Potential technological solutions remain in memory until design projects come up that might benefit from them	Strong evidence One designer kept a box of existing motors, hinges, joints, etc., that served as a "build-everything kit" from which he created prototypes for new projects. "[When you've developed knowledge about a particular field] there's no question that you're a resource."	Strong evidence The cubicles of individual designers were often filled with dozens of products they had worked on, models they had built, toys, and pictures of interesting products. "People know each other and they know who to ask. . . ." "The model is you become a real expert and you're recognized [around] the company as being an expert in that particular field."	Strong evidence Wandering around halls and offices we could see enormous collections of products, toys, and models. Designers would refer to people as experts in particular fields or technologies: one who knows about mechanisms, another about materials.
Retrieval: Designers working on new products retrieve old technological solutions from IDEO's memory in appropriate forms to fit the new combinations they are creating	Strong evidence In one case they took parts from a previous vacuum project and glued them into a new hair dryer of their own design to test the combination. "[You get help from other designers by] planting these seeds all over the place and . . . the wider you can plant it the more stuff that keeps coming in." "I just send an e-mail to 60 engineers . . . and one of them knows the answer and gets back to you within minutes. . . ."	Strong evidence "I especially love Japanese toys, but good toy design, because we bring them out in brainstormers and apply the ideas to skin staplers or mechanisms, whatever." "There's often things that people need help on, they put them on e-mail and there's almost always responses."	Moderate evidence Designer's talked about cross-pollination: they feel like they are bringing good ideas from one product to another. Many of the designers emphasized the importance of brainstorming, electronic mail, and informal sharing of ideas.

*Strong evidence = a dominant theme in this data source that is consistently supported; moderate evidence = a frequent, but not constant theme in this data source that is consistently supported; sporadic evidence = a theme that appears now and then in this data source and is consistently supported.

Other meetings	Design team interviews	Written material and videos	Observed brainstorms
Moderate evidence Current projects are discussed at each Monday meeting, including computers, fishing gear, keyboard supports, office systems, and bicycle wheels.	Moderate evidence Interviews were with design teams that had recently completed products in the medical industry, computer network communications, movie special effects, and a label maker for the typewriter industry.	Strong evidence Lists of clients show a range of industries. "Working with companies in such dissimilar industries as medical instruments, furniture, toys, and computers has given us a broad view of the latest technologies, materials, and components available."	Sporadic evidence Designers learn about new industries when clients or project leaders introduce technological problems in question and answer sessions lasting from 5 to 25 minutes at beginning of each brainstorming meeting.
Moderate evidence In the Monday meetings designers pass around parts they found that are good examples of manufacturing technologies, new products, or prototypes, for example, a co-injection molded plastic and rubber handle for a drill. These parts make their way around the room, and every designer looks at them, inside and out, with interest.	Moderate evidence One project team explained that "the first thing we do is, we [brought] a lot of different label printers, one of each, from Brother, from Casio and so forth [in an effort to learn about the industry]." "As always, there is the technical learning going on, so, that was the good part [about this project]."	Strong evidence "As consultants we need to quickly become experts in the client's product area. . . . We need to orient ourselves to the major pitfalls, alter natives, and opportunities." "The designers here become pretty flexible and fast on their feet, and they enjoy going from toy guitars, to microwave repeaters, to laptops, to anything."	Strong evidence One principal in the firm described a "technological awareness" that made IDEO's designers aware of many existing technologies and able to recall them later to solve particular design problems. As people brought in products and parts of products, all of the designers would begin to play with them and learn about them.
Moderate evidence In the Monday meetings designers learn about what others are doing as they pass around parts they found that are good examples of manufacturing technologies, new products, or prototypes. In addition, a large part of every meeting focuses on current projects, with each of the major project teams discussing what is going on and what they are doing or learning.	Sporadic evidence Designer would talk about buying and taking apart competitor's products. One team talked about the talents various designers brought to the project: manufacturing expertise or previous related experience in the design of medical disposables.	Strong evidence "Prototypes of all kinds of machines and in all stages of development literally litter the place." *Methodology Handbook* advises designers to "become an expert in the product area: learn everything that's out there." "Somebody is always running off to get something—a piece of hardware, a tool, a model, some materials, etc. . . ."	Moderate evidence One designer dumped on the table a box of 20 television remote controls from a previous project. The designers looked at these while generating ideas about a new "television navigation system." A designer put on the table pieces of IDEO-designed children's furniture to illustrate a particular material to use in a kitchen table design.
Sporadic evidence In Monday morning meetings, the evidence is mostly implicit: designers pass around examples from vendors or from interesting products to make everyone aware of these ideas. They also talk about the current status of their projects, including problems they are facing. Problems and solutions discussed in these meetings would often lead to later discussions one on one.	Sporadic evidence Designers mentioned holding brainstorming meetings to solve particular problems or bringing in outside consultants as experts in particular areas.	Strong evidence "It's valuable to get people to pull in bits of hardware, like having a bunch of squirrels going out and gathering things. You see these active minds making the connection." "When you get a lot of people thinking about the issues, you multiply the chances that somebody will come back with an idea or article that's pertinent."	Strong evidence "[The key to a good solution is to] get tons of related hardware in the brainstorm." A brainstorm report on "designing the future's TV remotes" lists 65 analogies to products or ideas. "Brainstormers are useful in getting detailed knowledge about your project out so it stimulates others to suggest solutions or offer leads that a simple e-mail message might not."

and enabling the flow of existing solutions between those that have such knowledge and those that do not.

Social network theory describes networks of individual or organizational actors and the relationships between them. Within these networks, subgroups bound sets of actors that "know one another, are aware of the same kinds of opportunities, have access to the same kinds of resources, and share the same kinds of perceptions" (Burt, 1983: 180). Another network perspective, actor network theory, has emerged from studies in the social construction of technology and presents networks as comprising not only actors but also the physical artifacts and concepts with which those actors relate (e.g., Callon, 1980; Latour, 1987; Law, 1987). The relationships of this more diverse network arrange physical artifacts, individuals, and concepts into complex organizational and technological systems. Just as organizations comprise networks of actors, products become "networks of juxtaposed components" (Law, 1987: 113). This expanded definition of network elements may more accurately reflect the technological environment that IDEO designers face, where information about existing solutions resides within the artifacts themselves, and brokers need not have close ties to other actors to access that information. For example, in one project we followed, designers learned as much about designing a new consumer product by studying the existing (and related) products as they did from talking to the client.

Subgroups in this expanded network, then, reflect relatively isolated sets of actors, technologies, and concepts. The boundaries between these subgroups can exist at many different levels, between individuals, organizations, or industries; we chose to draw them between industries because technologies most clearly emerge and evolve within particular industries yet may have potential value in other industries (Basalla, 1988; Hughes, 1989).[5] The transfer of potentially valuable technologies to other industries, when it occurs, can cause significant economic and competitive changes (Schumpeter, 1934; Rosenberg, 1982), but gaps in the flow of information across industry boundaries often prevent this diffusion. Organizations like IDEO, by occupying positions within multiple industries, may bridge these gaps.

IDEO's access to outside industries offers an advantage to clients who want new product innovations. IDEO's designers have generated part or all of over 3,000 new product designs for clients since its formation in 1978. They have worked most heavily in the personal computer, medical products, and office furniture industries and have also designed products for the toy, telephone, automotive, movie, ski, bicycle, printer, and video game markets. IDEO does not maintain a database of clients by industry, but our research indicates it has worked in over 40 industries. From these industries, IDEO's designers have typically seen a broader range of technologies than clients with experience in only one or a few industries. The network concept of range describes the extent to which an actor contacts a diversity of other actors and can be measured in two ways, as volume of contacts or as quality of contacts (Burt, 1983). Volume measures the total number of contacts an actor has; quality measures the extent to which an actor's contacts provide nonredundant information and support. The evidence summarized in table 2 suggests that IDEO's value as a technology broker depends not only on the number of clients and industries it works with (volume of contacts), but also on the technologies in those industries that are potentially valuable yet previously unknown in others (quality of contacts). IDEO's *Methodology Handbook* recognizes this value: "Working with companies in such dissimilar industries as medical instruments, furniture, toys, and computers has given us a broad view of the latest technologies, materials, and components available."

Access to dissimilar industries also describes Edison's laboratory in West Orange, which consulted to diverse clients. Millard (1990: 48) described Edison's simultaneous pursuit of electrical products for clients in multiple industries: "The extensive contract research carried out by the laboratory staff opened up new areas of investigation and offered valuable spillovers of information that Edison was waiting to exploit." Millard (1990: 68) cited an example of this spillover in Edison's work for different clients in sound recording and in telephones, both of which required technical knowledge about acoustics: "The experiments in reproducers [for recording] were paralleled by the continuing work on telephone transmitters and receivers; as usual he was hoping that one series of experiments might turn up some information useful in another." Millard (1990: 48) also implicitly recognized the value of such access when he described the purpose of Edison's laboratory: "to bring together flows of information at the right moment, providing the basic raw material for the invention factory."

Like Edison's laboratory, IDEO has access to dissimilar industries that enables it to generate new product innovations through technology brokering. In one case, a blood analyzer was originally designed to be controlled by a separate personal computer. IDEO's designers instead used their previous experience designing such computers to incorporate the necessary features—a circuit board, printer, keyboard, display screen, and software interface—into the product. The result was a new and more integrated blood analyzer that represented a relatively dramatic combination of existing solutions in computer and medical product technologies. Brokering also provides innovative solutions to more common design problems. For instance, when designers became aware that a portable computer display lacked the room necessary for traditional fasteners, they developed a solution using modified bicycle wheel spokes as fasteners. In both of these examples, IDEO's designers were able to bring together technologies from within and outside of their client's industry to generate innovative new products and solutions.

IDEO's *Methodology Handbook* recommends that designers "look for opportunities to expand IDEO's network and/or industry knowledge." This may be more easily done now that IDEO is relatively large and already well connected in a range of industries and thus has something to offer other clients. When IDEO was a small start-up company, access to disparate industries and technological knowledge was serendipitous. IDEO has its roots in the Silicon Valley and the computer industry, and one of the early IDEO employees described their original advantage: "At the time we were really naive, but our customer base, when we all just started, was just as naive. So, we knew just enough to be ahead of them and it worked pretty well. They were all electrical engineers and software guys. They didn't know anything about mechanical engineering or making things, and we knew just enough to be able to be useful to them." As the Silicon Valley and information technologies developed, IDEO was able to continue creating innovative products by designing the mechanical and electromechical components surrounding the new information technologies as they diffused to other industries. CEO David Kelley described this strategy as "being the high-technology

company to low-technology companies." And as IDEO's connections to different industries grew, designers gained experiences with many other technologies and have provided their clients in the computer industry with useful technologies, such as low-cost electric motors, new hinge designs, or new materials that were taken from these other industries.

Technology brokering is visible at the level of firms and industries, but it takes place through the actions of teams and people. IDEO's contact with different technologies comes through the individual engineers' contact with the industries where those technologies are used. For industries in which IDEO has multiple clients, such as the computer industry, many designers have worked with and understand the technologies involved. For industries in which fewer engineers have participated, such as surgical instruments, only a few might be familiar with the prevalent technologies. Designers also come into contact with potentially valuable solutions through the technical training and jobs they had before coming to IDEO and through their hobbies and personal backgrounds. IDEO has hired particular designers, in part, because of their past experience in and knowledge of medical products, manufacturing, and disk drives. In addition, IDEO hires designers for their knowledge and interest in areas outside of their work, such as toys, bicycles, model airplanes, sailing, sculpting, farming, woodworking, music, opera, cars, motorcycles, skiing, and mountain climbing. The broad knowledge and interests of IDEO's engineers result in access to design solutions beyond the solutions that IDEO is exposed to in its clients' industries.

Most social network analyses measure current social relations between actors. In contrast, because an engineer's knowledge of potential solutions represents past as well as ongoing relations, his or her network ties to a range of industries accumulate over time. As a result, each engineer has a distinct body of technological knowledge from working with IDEO clients, from past technical training and work experience, and from his or her personal interests and backgrounds. The role this diverse knowledge plays in creating new products is evident in a description of how one designer's personal background was the source of new solutions:

> Everybody seems to have a couple of kinds of interesting backgrounds. Fred—because he used to

build model airplanes—was very good at it. Model airplanes have all these swivel and control things, and he'd bring all this kind of technology to our prototypes: little brass tubes and all these little hinges. He knew all that was possible, and he would have a bunch of stuff in his garage and he'd bring that in and we'd make prototypes out of it. Other people are into a lot of stuff. The technology of bicycles, which is actually quite developed and refined, can be applied to so many things. People have a universal love of toys here and I think I'm the epitome of that. Toys have so many neat things to offer. They are high volume, mass production, often plastic, and very clever because they're so cheap. I especially love Japanese toys. We will bring 'em out in brainstormers and kind of apply the ideas to skin staplers or mechanisms, whatever.

At IDEO, designers view their community as a valuable clearinghouse for technological solutions that they have accumulated through years of access to dozens of industries. In their words, this community experience allows them to "cross-pollinate" their ideas between products and industries. A network perspective describes how IDEO is able to exploit this cross-pollination in its innovation process by describing the structural conditions that allow an actor linking otherwise disconnected domains to have access to ideas that are potentially valuable, but unknown, to others. Yet while this network perspective is necessary to explain the conditions that make technology brokering possible, it is not sufficient to explain how the innovation process occurs through brokering. Much of this creative process occurs within the firm. Solutions rarely come to the firm at the time they are needed, to the people who need them, or in the exact forms necessary to solve the problems designers face. To understand how designers at IDEO make connections between existing solutions and new problems over time and across people, we need to look within the firm at the routines that designers and teams use to create new products by learning of possible solutions, remembering them, and retrieving them in new forms that fit in new combinations.

Acquisition, Storage, and Retrieval: IDEO's Internal Routines for Technology Brokering

Technology brokering means that IDEO's designers solve current design problems by drawing on techno-

logical solutions they have seen in the past. This use of shared knowledge from past experiences is the focus of conceptual work on organizational memory (March and Simon, 1958; Huber, 1991; Walsh and Ungson, 1991), which refers to the means that organizations use to retain past stimulus-response information. Organizational memory becomes visible when individual members react to new demands by drawing on an organizational pool of prior responses to similar stimuli (Walsh and Ungson, 1991). Within the product development process, past stimulus-response information refers to past design problems and their technological solutions. The means by which IDEO retains these past solutions become visible in the routines its designers use to draw on this organizational pool of prior responses to solve current design problems.

There are conflicting perspectives on the role of organizational memory in innovative activities such as new product development. March (1972), Weick (1979b), and others have described its programmed responses as threats, because they increase the organization's potential for unconsciously or mistakenly invoking ingrained, but often inappropriate, behavior. Other scholars, sometimes the same scholars, have argued the opposite: that organizational memory supports organizational innovation (Cyert and March, 1963; Neustadt and May, 1986; Walsh and Dewar, 1987; Kantrow, 1987). By routinizing search activities in standard operating procedures, organizations can become more efficient at performing them. Organizational memory can also support innovation by retaining a broader range of potential responses, providing more options for organizational decision makers. March (1972: 427) asserted that "for most purposes, good memories make good choices." The tension between these two perspectives lies between the efficiency of "automatic retrieval processes" and the uncertainty that these processes will evoke responses that are "out of step with the [problems of the] present circumstances" (Walsh and Ungson, 1991: 73). Whether an organization's memory supports or undermines its ability to innovate depends on how well its past solutions—and routines for drawing on those alternatives—can be adapted to fit the problems of the present circumstances.

At IDEO, although the design problems change constantly, past knowledge remains valuable if designers can recognize similarities between old solutions and new problems. IDEO's network position provides its designers with access to a range of disparate industries. This vantage point enables designers to see a continuing stream of new problems to which their old solutions apply and a continuing stream of new (to IDEO) solutions that may be useful for future problems. IDEO's organizational memory provides the link between these solutions and problems, and thus between industries, by providing search routines for generating a range of alternative responses based on past experiences. IDEO's organizational memory can be described with the three fundamental processes presented by Walsh and Ungson (1991): acquisition, retention, and retrieval of information from the past.

ACQUISITION

Access to a wide range of industries has brought IDEO's designers into contact with a wide range of technological solutions; the acquisition process brings these solutions into the organizational memory for possible use in current and future designs (Walsh and Ungson, 1991). IDEO designers acquire these solutions by talking to and watching new clients and others in the industry, by reading about the industry, by looking at and taking apart products in and related to those in the industry, and, finally, by designing products for that industry.

Most projects at IDEO begin with clients describing their existing products and their desires for the new product. IDEO's *Methodology Handbook* says: "As consultants we need to quickly become experts in the client's product area. We want to acclimate ourselves to the market, the buzz words, the competition. We need to orient ourselves to the major pitfalls, alternatives, and opportunities." This expertise helps IDEO designers to understand and work with a client's existing technologies. This ongoing process of learning from clients started in IDEO's early days and remains part of all projects. A senior designer recalled:

We were learning as we went. If we didn't know how to do something we would never say to the customer, "we don't know how do that!" We would learn how to do it either on the job from people within the customer's company or just by going out and finding out about the stuff. Now, given our experience, there's probably very little about standard manufacturing processes that we don't know. But we still have the spark coming in because clients come in with a new technology and want to

apply it and we have to come up to speed on that particular technology. So the excitement of keeping up on the learning process is there and there's also the excitement that you get when you hire younger engineers who don't have the experience and they come up to speed very quickly on this mass of information.

IDEO's engineers keep "a mix of new technology coming in from the customer side" by actively searching for the potentially valuable technologies of new industries. Knowledge of these technologies resides in more than just the clients that approach IDEO, so designers also look to industry consultants, users, and suppliers as sources of existing knowledge. In one project we followed, the design team talked about how much they learned when they flew to Los Angeles to meet with an expert on the intricacies of the materials and physics involved in the project. On another project, designers hired an outside consultant, who they described as an "electromagnetic interference guru," to help them with the design of a new computer. A project to improve the 15-minute oil change offers a typical scenario:

Our approach was to understand what's going on, to understand and observe. So we talked to the president of the client company to see what is going on. The clients indoctrinated us into the new tune-up procedures. We talked to the head trainer, the woman who does training for all the trainers that are training the mechanics and that give demonstrative tune-ups. We talked about all the design methodology and guidelines for those types of products. We went to visit the training [center] and just watched and observed the entire process. We went to some shops, watched cars being worked on, talked to managers, looked in the back rooms. We went to training seminars. We just absorbed as much as we could as an objective outsider . . . they gave us all their tools and they gave us engine dummies, and so we were using the tools and doing all sorts of stuff. We were really getting familiar with what the tools were like to handle, just immersing yourself as much as you possibly can into the whole realm of it. We brought in a mechanic, we had him go through a tune-up as a group demo because we had a whole bunch of people who were going to be in the brainstorm. There were about 15 designers in the room.

The knowledge acquired during these broad industry searches was useful in this design project and may lead to innovative solutions in future projects.

IDEO engineers also acquire knowledge by studying an industry's existing products. As the quotes in Table 34.2 indicate, designers read industry trade magazines and product catalogs. They gather all available products in the field, use and sometimes abuse them, and take them apart to find out how they were designed. We saw this approach by a team that was designing a kitchen appliance. The project manager explained: "The best way to come up with ideas is first of all to go out and look at what's out there. So, look at the existing products, rip them apart, then look for peripheral objects, like toasters, blenders, and mixers. When you find technical problems you go out, look around [some more] and walk around ripping apart possibly relevant products." Designers on this project collected over 100 appliances from the client, stores, catalogs, and fellow designers to learn all they could about the nuances and possibilities of the technologies involved.

The primary goal of these learning activities is to design an innovative product that performs as well as, if not better than, what previously existed in the industry. While much of the knowledge acquired during these activities remains in the memories of IDEO's designers after a project is completed, the act of designing that new product is also an important step in bringing working knowledge of these new technologies into the organization. Rosenberg (1982) described this experience as "learning-by-using," and Cohen and Levinthal (1994) argued that it is critical to a firm's absorptive capacity, or ability to exploit emerging technologies. In creating new products, designers acquire intimate knowledge of the limitations and possibilities of technologies beyond what they might have learned by only talking about, looking at, or reading about those technologies. In addition, project teams will often develop alternative solutions throughout the project that, while not used in the final product, represent viable alternatives for subsequent projects. In one case, a sliding door covering a computer front panel was originally modeled after a garage door mechanism. The designer built a prototype, but that design was not ultimately chosen. Another project team was looking for a similar solution and borrowed the concept from the original prototype. Again it was not cho-

sen for the final design, but a third project team, years later, did use it and bring it to production.

To IDEO's designers, existing products serve as records of the technologies in an industry. By gathering together, studying, and ultimately designing such products while working on a specific project, designers acquire knowledge of these new technologies for use in both current and future projects. But they also constantly engage in less focused and often haphazard searches that, in addition to being fun, provide them with knowledge for future projects. These searches might be entertaining "field trips," like when designers went to an airplane junkyard to buy a DC-3 wing, to a "robot-wars" competition, and to the Barbie Hall of Fame: in each case they described the fun they had, as well as some "cool" design ideas they saw, to the rest of the company during "show and tell" at the Monday morning meeting. These searches also occur through more mundane acts, like collecting new materials, catalogs, or interesting products, or just taking a walk to the hardware store to look around, which might also yield "cool ideas" that are announced during "show and tell" or at least are mentioned during informal conversations. Designers also told us that they helped teach and grade design classes in local schools, partly because it was an opportunity to see new and interesting ideas.

STORAGE

Writings on organizational memory describe storage as how an organization puts away information until it is needed (March and Simon, 1958; Huber, 1991; Walsh and Ungson, 1991). At IDEO, the storage of technological knowledge became visible only as we observed the retrieval process in conversations, brainstorms, and other group problem-solving activities. From these observations, however, it was evident that much of the knowledge of potential solutions resides in the minds of the individual designers as products they had seen or used before, projects they had worked on, or technologies they had read, heard, or talked about. The evidence, summarized in table 2, indicates two types of routines at IDEO for storing potential technological solutions: routines for storing specific knowledge and routines for maintaining and refreshing that knowledge until it can be used.

Routines for storing specific technological knowledge at IDEO placed potential solutions in the memories of individual designers and in the objects and products that designers collected from their previous work. One designer grew up on a farm and, in two brainstorms we attended (one on a new faucet design and another on cleaning carpets), he offered potentially useful solutions based on technologies from tractors and combines. But designers do not consciously identify themselves with particular technological domains; this designer, for example, also offered many solutions that did not come from his farming background. Another designer talked about how his memory of design solutions was "one big pile of tools," and while "each industry has its own set of tools, I only remember the tools, not where they came from." Designers also keep written records of previous projects, such as brainstorming reports and part drawings. We went to one meeting about flexible tubing in which another designer (who was not in the meeting) overheard the discussion and interrupted. He had faced the same problem while on a project in another industry and offered an old brainstorming report that listed the potentially relevant solutions they had found.

Designers augment their individual memories and written materials by collecting, looking at, and talking about products or parts of products, which act as records of existing technologies. Designers stockpile old products and parts in their offices and hallways or hang them from the ceiling. Sometimes these are parts and prototypes of previous IDEO design efforts that act, as one designer described, like "congealed process—a three-dimensional snapshot of the ideas of a previous project." Sometimes they are toys, collections of products from industries IDEO has previously worked in, parts and assemblies collected from vendors, or objects that reflect designers' personal interests or quirks. The shelves in one designer's office held 23 battery-powered toy cars and robots, 13 different styles of plastic hotel keys collected during trips, a battery-less flashlight powered by squeezing the handle, an industrial pump, 11 prototypes of a portable computer, 14 prototypes of a computer docking station, six competitive computers in various stages of disassembly, 15 binders from past projects, a pile of disk drives, a collection of toothpaste tubes he had designed, a toy football with wings, a pair of ski goggles he had designed, four humorous plaques awarded for past projects (e.g., "under-the-gun" award for working under pressure), a Frisbee that flies under water, and

dozens of other products and parts. This designer was especially fond of toys and spent a lot of time telling us about how his toys contained useful ideas in the form of distinctive hinges, materials, molding features, or assembly requirements.

Designers routinely loaned these objects to one another for brainstorms and other parts of the design process. A group of designers took the notion of shared "cool stuff" a step further by filling several centrally located file cabinets with hundreds of "cool design inspirations." This "technology cabinet" was a collective rather than an individual good. It was started with "donations from several designers' private collections of cool stuff," and it soon became "cool" among a wider set of designers to add new "neat and strange things" and to tell other designers about what they added. One of the cabinet's self-appointed custodians told us, "every time you look in here, something new shows up." The contents include nitinol (a metal that predictably changes its shape in response to temperature changes), tiny fans and motors the size of a fingernail, magnetorheologic fluid (which changes viscosity when magnetized), samples of carbon fiber parts, an inflatable toy gorilla, and samples of flexible circuit boards, all or parts of which the designers hoped one day to use in their design projects. There are also metal cases in the cabinet so that designers can transport pertinent parts of the collection to meetings in IDEO and at client companies. There are also larger products on display, like the DC-3 airplane wing and an old Texaco gas pump placed next to a new electric vehicle charger that IDEO designed for Hughes/General Motors. A similarly diverse set of objects was evident in Edison's laboratory. Millard (1990: 15) quoted Edison as saying, "the most important part of an experimental laboratory is a big scrap heap," reflecting, Millard said, "his reliance on a well-stocked store-room and a collection of apparatus and equipment left over from previous experiments." Like Edison's equipment and apparatus, artifacts seem to lie around IDEO's offices as reminders of interesting and potentially useful technologies, patiently awaiting the appropriate problem.

The technological solutions in the minds, written records, and products of individual designers are valuable only when they can be retrieved easily for use in current projects. IDEO maintains these memories in ways that are easy to access. Displaying objects where other designers can see them makes ideas accessible, as do the constant conversations that IDEO designers have about who has what design knowledge. As the evidence in Table 34.2 indicates, designers informally "catalog" this knowledge about one another. Informants told us that, to be valued by one's peers, it was important to establish a reputation for having expertise that is distinctive within the community of IDEO designers. The *Methodology Handbook* is explicit in this advice: "become an expert in the product area: learn everything that's out there." IDEO designers act like "gatekeepers" (Allen, 1977) who bring knowledge from the outside world into organizations. Allen's gatekeepers represented a minority of the population, but most engineers at IDEO fill this role. Each designer acts as a technology broker within the internal network of IDEO designers, bringing the experiences of his or her unique background to bear on the problems faced by other designers and being rewarded for doing so with respect from peers, more responsibility, and more interesting work. For example, one designer who had worked in the medical industry was respected for her knowledge of technologies involving fluid transportation, such as pumps, tubing, or valves. When other designers believed that such technologies might offer potential solutions to problems they faced, they would try to involve her in their project. As a designer put it: "The model is you become a real expert and you're recognized around the company as being an expert in that particular field. You can specialize in some design area like materials or motions or whatever and at least be recognized in the company as being really good at that. So, people come to you with their questions." In addition, upper-level managers serve as quasi-librarians. By knowing who had worked previously on what projects, they could often direct designers to individuals with relevant knowledge. One informant described the value of an upper-level manager: "Peter was the best 'hub' of information; he is involved in all of the projects and knows what everyone is working on." This informal reference system equates individual designers with families of technological solutions. So beyond developing his or her own focused technical expertise, each designer develops broader knowledge about which designers have which technical knowledge. This broader knowledge grows in parallel with the retrieval process in brainstorming meetings and other social interactions like Monday morning meetings, informal lunches, and company

parties. Designers display their technical knowledge during these meetings and, in the process, teach others when it might (and might not) be useful to ask him or her for assistance. For example, we saw one brainstorming session lapse into a five-minute lecture by a designer on the mechanical properties of soap before the group started generating ideas again about carpet cleaning. In this way, the process of retrieval facilitates storage because it brings technical knowledge back to the surface, refreshes the memories of the individual designers, and reminds everyone else of what that designer knows.

RETRIEVAL

Retrieval describes those routines that support the application of stored information to an organization's present decisions (Walsh and Ungson, 1991). At IDEO, retrieval entails bringing stored knowledge of potentially valuable technological solutions to bear on the design problems of current projects. As the evidence in Table 34.2 indicates, IDEO designers retrieve technological solutions through analogic thinking and through established routines for sharing the problems of current design projects with other designers in the organization who have relevant and potentially valuable knowledge.

Technologies, in an abstract and conceptual form, carry the potential to address many different problems in many different industries. In most cases, however, designers at IDEO learn of possible technologies by seeing them in existing products, in specific forms intended to serve particular industries. To recognize the potential value of a product's technological components, the designers must abstract them from their specific, past implementation before adapting them to meet the needs of the current problem. One designer described the simplicity of the idea behind this difficult task: "If you take all the existing products or thoughts on existing products and gather them and then took the best part of each one and combined them, you'd have a better product. It is as simple as that." The way that IDEO's designers take all the existing products, recognize the best part of each one, and combine them is a critical aspect of the retrieval of potential solutions from IDEO's organizational memory. Neustadt and May (1986) argued that analogies play a critical role in organizational memory because they allow individuals to link past stimulus-response information to current stimuli. Similarly, Schon (1993) described the use of analogies, or "generative metaphors," in creative problem solving. In product design, creative problem solving draws on the organization's memory by making analogies between past technological solutions and current design problems. For example, a designer working on the hinge mechanism for the screen of a new portable computer might recognize the potential value of a hinge design that he or she had noticed holding together the wing of a plastic toy dragon. The retrieval process involves generating an analogy between this particular solution in its implementation as a toy's wing and the specific requirements of the new design problem, a portable computer.

Analogies allow product designers to see the portable computer screen momentarily as a toy dragon's wing, to view old technological solutions from a new frame of reference that allows them to recognize certain useful characteristics, such as material, design, or flexibility, and to ignore other less transferable features, such as shape, size, or original use. As a result, designers can recognize potential connections between technologies they have seen before and their current design problems. In one project, designers attempting to develop a spill-proof nozzle for a bicycle water bottle described how they recognized similarities between the problems of the water bottle design and a previous project designing a shampoo bottle that could hang upside down. In another, designers looking to power a door opener on an electric vehicle charger told us they recalled an analogous action in the pistons that open the rear window of a station wagon. In both of these examples, the ultimate solution built on the principles that were identified through these analogies, but not all analogies become part of the finished design. Designers will use analogies to generate a wide range of alternative solutions to choose from. One brainstorming session on "ways to deep-clean carpets" elicited analogies to tank treads, street sweepers, tractor combines, hair removal devices, shavers, whips, vibrating combs, squids, and Velcro (this last suggestion seems obligatory, and even humorously offered, in all brainstorms we attended). Another brainstorm, on designing a "portable kitchen counter," retrieved potential solutions by drawing analogies to jet fighter wings, plastic coolers, children's furniture, washing machines, bentwood chairs, surfboards, and skis. Elements on these lists may appear unrelated, but each analogy was used to turn aspects of existing technologies into potential so-

lutions for the problem at hand. Analogic thinking is critical to the brokering of potentially innovative solutions because it allows for acquisition and storage of technologies in their original implementations, but for retrieval in forms adapted to the needs of the current design problem.

To recognize the potential value of a technology and adapt it to disparate products, designers must be familiar enough with a technology to generate analogies appropriate for current designs. Thus, much of the retrieval process at IDEO entails bringing designers with knowledge of potentially relevant technologies into direct contact with the problems of a new design project. Brainstorming sessions are one of the most direct ways that such contact occurs. Brainstorms are face-to-face sessions for generating ideas (Osborn, 1957); design teams convene them intermittently throughout a project. Almost all IDEO designers participate in brainstorms, which typically include six to twelve designers who are targeted for their potentially relevant knowledge in a range of technologies or industries (Sutton and Hargadon, 1996). IDEO's *Methodology Handbook* tells project leaders: "Set up at least two major introductory brainstormers to get the best minds in the company, the collective consciousness of the office, working on your problem." And a designer described what people setting up brainstorming meetings should do:

> Look for others with related expertise that might see the idea from a different perspective. The most fruitful brainstorms in these types of areas are when at least one participant has a good deal of specific, available knowledge from a different area that is still very applicable. In these cases, the client is probably unaware of this new information, and we can transfer a lot of detailed, implementable solutions.

For one brainstorm, a designer picked participants with the mix of skills needed for designing ski goggles; some knew about foam materials and their design requirements, some knew clear plastics, some knew manufacturing, and some knew skiing. IDEO uses brainstorms throughout the development process, and these meetings often bring over half of IDEO's designers into contact with a particular project.

Designers create a visually rich environment in

brainstorms to help them make connections between existing product technologies and the design problems they currently face. Designers and brainstorm organizers typically bring in "tons of related hardware." One brainstorm was in a room filled with dozens of pieces from four or five vacuum cleaners plus another four assembled vacuum cleaners. A designer brought about twenty different television remote controls into another brainstorm. One designer described his preparation for brainstorms:

> When the brainstorm is on a tricky problem, I always set up what is called a crash cart. I get one of these roll-around carts and fill it with anything I can that is relevant and then some things that may not be even remotely relevant so that you have this big playpen full of stuff that's sitting on the table or it's sitting on the cart: information, devices, data. In this way, brainstorms are like a big open-book exam where you're allowed to bring stuff in.

Brainstorms are not the only arena where potential solutions are drawn from IDEO's organizational memory. Designers routinely ask for technical assistance at the company-wide Monday morning meetings (e.g., "Who knows about sheet metal fasteners?"). They use electronic mail to broadcast questions to the firm, for example, about fasteners, materials, adhesives. A designer explained: "There are often things that people need help on. They put them on e-mail and there's almost always responses. If you get a question and know the answer, you just take the time and answer it and that's part of the job description because you know you're going to get it back." Retrieval also occurs during informal conversations that follow meetings or e-mails, which are facilitated by IDEO's open office plan and (in Palo Alto) encounters that occur as designers walk between the seven IDEO buildings within a three-block radius. Informal conversations often occur between designers who are known to face specific technical challenges (who are expected to ask for help) and designers who are known to have pertinent expertise (who are expected to give help). A designer said:

> I think that people here feel really free about just throwing things out just in casual conversations in the halls. [You ask] "Oh, Lee, I got a problem,

maybe you have an answer for me." You stop and help if you've been into brainstormers on some of these things before, and so have some exposure to it, or hear about it at the Monday morning meeting and think about it, or if it's obvious what someone is doing. You stop and throw your ideas out.

Analogic thinking allows designers to take in specific implementations of technological solutions yet retrieve useful solutions for new problems that could not be predicted or that are, in form, distant from the technological solutions in IDEO's memory. The intimate knowledge required to enable such generative metaphors requires problem-solving arenas in which communication of complex problems and solutions are possible. IDEO's brainstorms, other scheduled meetings, e-mails, and informal conversations create such rich communications and allow the retrieval of specific technological solutions that often take far different forms than those in which they entered the organization's memory.

DISCUSSION

We blended network and organizational memory perspectives in a model of technology brokering that explains how one organization develops innovative products. This firm exploits its network position to gain knowledge of existing technological solutions in some industries that may be potentially valuable in others, but are rare or unknown. It acts as a technology broker by introducing these solutions to industries where they are not known, and, in the process, creates new products that are original combinations of existing knowledge from disparate industries. The organization's links to many industries provide its designers with access to a broader range of technological solutions than they would see working in a single industry. Designers acquire and store such solutions in the organization's memory. Then, by making analogies between new design problems and old solutions they have seen before, they retrieve such knowledge to generate new solutions to design problems in other industries.

Because the primary aim of this paper was to blend network and organizational memory perspectives in a model of technology brokering, we have devoted limited attention to explaining how IDEO encourages and supports employees to follow the internal routines that make such brokering possible. Our field study suggests that the organization's role is critical. The structure of the work, norms for collaboration, formal and informal reward systems, and employee selection processes may help explain why IDEO, and perhaps other organizations, have employees with the skill and motivation to carry out these routines.

Organizational Support for Technology Brokering

First, the structure of work at IDEO causes individual designers to face a continual flow of new problems requiring engineering solutions. This flow of new problems provides incentives for them to develop, and opportunities for them to exploit, a wide-ranging knowledge of potential solutions. IDEO's client base ensures that the organization will encounter a range of new problems and new solutions. Within the organization, however, the engineers also do not specialize in any single industry but, instead, often move to new industries after completing a single project in one industry. Engineers also often transfer on and off long-term projects to prevent "burn-out" and allow them to pursue interests in other areas. In a given year, an engineer may design portable computers, vacuum cleaners, medical products, and office furniture. One project manager described this lack of specialization: "As a designer you love variety and, not having to do the same thing for years on end, it keeps you fresh and it makes you more confident that you can use something you learned in this area and move from there." Work is also structured so that teams are formed and disbanded around individual projects and often pull in additional members for brainstorms or short bursts of effort. This movement between teams and projects not only provides designers with a wide range of experiences, it also provides them with exposure to the skills and backgrounds of their colleagues. So the constant flow of new problems, combined with the movement of engineers from team to team and industry to industry, creates opportunities for engineers to develop varied technological backgrounds and to learn about others' distinct knowledge and skills.

These varied backgrounds, and awareness of what others know, enables the engineers within IDEO to act as individual technology brokers by allowing them to draw on their own diverse technical knowledge to help others. Much of this benefit, however, depends on IDEO's strong norms for designers to share their disparate knowledge and help one another. We have proposed that these norms (and the associated values) can be summarized as an "attitude of wisdom" (Sutton and Hargadon, 1996). Building on Meacham's (1990) writing, people who have an attitude of wisdom are cooperative because they are neither too arrogant nor too insecure to ask others for help and because they treat what they know with humility and what others know with respect. Furthermore, wise people realize that they know things that others do not, so they constantly tell others what they know and offer others help and advice.

Newcomers at IDEO are taught the attitude of wisdom at IDEO and old-timers are reminded of it by the everyday interactions of the designers, interactions that are most visible in organizational routines such as brainstorming and Monday morning meetings. Brainstorms foster technology brokering at IDEO by pulling together groups of designers to work on an identified problem. Designers call these meetings to seek the help of other designers at IDEO who are not already involved in that project. In doing so, they demonstrate that they are neither too insecure nor too arrogant to ask for help, that they are treating what they know with humility and what others know with respect. One designer described brainstorms as "useful in getting detailed knowledge about your project out so it stimulates others to suggest solutions or offer leads." Another said, "The main reason I use brainstorms is to generate ideas that I know I wouldn't have on my own." The designers who attend brainstorming sessions do so because they believe they can contribute distinct technical solutions to the problem and because, if they don't help with others' projects, the favor will not be returned. This same sense of sharing was visible in the Monday morning meetings, when designers would announce problems they were working on (e.g., "Who knows about adhesives for sheet metal?") or would present potentially useful or interesting ideas they had recently seen (e.g., handing around an example of a co-molded plastic handle with rubber grip) during "show and tell." These interactions made visible the norms for asking for help, sharing knowledge, and giving help, which taught newcomers and reminded insiders how they were expected to behave at IDEO.

Third, IDEO's formal and informal reward systems provide substantial support for such collaboration. Top managers determine designers' pay and responsibility, and while they place weight on the number of hours billed, compensation decisions are based largely on informal reputation among fellow designers and formal peer reviews. A top manager described IDEO as a "peer-oriented meritocracy," so pay and status are closely related. A designer emphasized, "the only way to enhance your status in the organization is by earning the respect of your peers." Designers do earn respect from their peers through individual efforts that produced good designs, but a designer's reputation is based at least as much on using his or her skill to help others. A designer explained:

> People realize that the way to be respected and to get ahead is to be out there. It doesn't work just to be a grind on your project. I mean, you can do a great job on your project and meet all your goals, but I think the reward structure is set up in a way that if you don't participate in other stuff, that it's probably a little bit of a demerit. People don't know you as well so your capabilities aren't as well understood, you're not as likely to be invited on projects, you're not going to be in demand. So there's a benefit for spreading your knowledge and your skills around because you get to be seen by more people and so you become more desirable.

A designer's reputation among his or her peers is also enhanced by asking for help. Following the attitude of wisdom, people who don't ask for help are thought to be either too insecure or too arrogant, to lack humility about what they know and respect for what others at IDEO know. One engineer compared his experiences at IDEO to other engineering organizations: "Where I worked before, you just didn't ask for help. It was a sign of weakness. . . . [At IDEO] we don't have time to screw around. At the first hint I don't know something, I'll ask 'Does anyone know about this?' The whole thing here is you've got to leverage as much as possible. You ask for help. You are expected to ask for help here." There is especially low tolerance at IDEO for engineers who don't ask for help and then produce poor designs. One designer asserted that making mistakes was viewed as an expected and inevitable part of the design process. Failed or weak design efforts that represented the combined best efforts of a number of IDEO engineers were viewed as understandable. In contrast, designers who made mis-

takes but had not asked for help were not easily forgiven. Other designers sometimes reprimanded them for failing to follow IDEO's methodology, spread negative gossip about them, and, if they repeatedly failed to ask for help, shunned them by, for example, not inviting them to attend brainstorms or to work on interesting projects.

Fourth, as with performance evaluations, employee selection is done by (future) peers who look for new designers with the right technical knowledge and skill (including backgrounds that bring new design solutions into IDEO) and an inclination to follow IDEO's work practices and norms. A person is not hired unless at least ten designers express strong support for offering him or her a job. Furthermore, approximately 70 percent of IDEO's engineers are graduates of Stanford University's Design Division of the Mechanical Engineering Department. IDEO's CEO, David Kelley, is a tenured professor in the department and, along with at least ten other IDEO designers, teaches product design in this program. A senior designer and long-time lecturer described IDEO's relationship with Stanford: "I have twenty-five of my students here now. And Kelley, I'm sure, can count more like forty or fifty of the whole seventy. So we use, or have, a nice relationship with Stanford." David Kelley and many of IDEO's first employees graduated from this program, so there is much overlap between IDEO's and Stanford's design philosophy. As one designer and teacher put it, "We're not only following the philosophy of the Stanford product design program, we're setting the philosophy. It's not clear who's driving who now." As a result, IDEO engineers (and others) who teach these design courses socialize students in IDEO's design process and core norms. These IDEO engineers are also able to select newcomers from a pool of students whom they have observed working on design projects. Promising students often perform summer internships at IDEO. A senior designer said, "It's a great way to interview people. We just see these superstars coming through and they see us and they want to work here and we love to have them so we just grab them every year." In addition, the remaining 30 percent or so of IDEO engineers who did not attend the Stanford program usually first worked with IDEO engineers as clients or contract workers, so they learned about IDEO's work practices and core norms and were screened carefully by insiders before being offered jobs. The result is that IDEO's selection process not only screens potential new employees for pertinent technical skills and willingness to seek and offer help in the design process, it may also serve to instill such knowledge and beliefs in designers before they are hired.

These preliminary data from IDEO provide hints about means that other organizations may use to support and encourage employees to act in ways that support internal technology brokering routines, so as to establish and exploit individual ties to distinctive knowledge domains. By structuring work so that employees are exposed to a wide range of industries, individual employees become well versed in diverse, and perhaps otherwise disconnected, domains and the technologies within each. By constantly forming and disbanding teams, employees are exposed to the diverse knowledge held by their coworkers and learn who has what kinds of expertise within their organization. By developing and reinforcing strong norms for exchanging information and for asking for and giving help, employees will feel comfortable asking for help, will know the right people to ask for help, and those who are asked will feel compelled to help. By providing rewards for sharing information and helping others that are at least as great as the rewards for individual accomplishments, employees will cooperate rather than compete, or perhaps compete with one another over who shares the greatest amount of pertinent information and who is most helpful on others' projects. Finally, by screening employees for cultural fit as well as technical knowledge and skill, and by relying largely on what potential employees have shown they will do instead of what they say they can do, an organization is more likely to be composed of people who act, individually, as technology brokers and who help their coworkers do such brokering.

Directions for Future Research

Our effort to blend network and memory perspectives suggests that network theory might be developed further by devoting more attention to the transformation and combination of ideas and resources as they flow through network actors. The transformation and combination described in this paper occurs predominantly through individual actions within, and not between, such actors. Network theory describes the fragmented structure of knowledge across different domains and explains the value of people and organizations positioned as brokers in structural holes. But this perspective treats network actors largely as conduits that pass along unchanged ideas and resources to others. Little attention is devoted to if, how, or why those ideas and resources are transformed and combined into new solutions for other actors and subgroups.

IDEO, like Edison's laboratory, does more than just transfer technological information from groups where it is plentiful to groups where it is dear. IDEO acquires such information, stores it, changes it, and retrieves it to create new combinations of old things. Through this process, brokers create new value (and new knowledge) by adapting and recombining existing technological solutions in creating the specific forms of new products and processes that meet the needs of different markets. Network theory may be enhanced by future research that considers how brokers who span structural holes change the ideas and resources that they transfer and, additionally, how brokers' ability to add value to ideas and resources helps them maintain and further exploit their network position.

The purpose of an inductive study like the one reported here is to guide and inspire new ideas, not to validate existing ideas. The extent to which the local explanation of innovation summarized in figure 1 develops into a more general theory of technology brokering depends on how well it, or its descendants, explains innovation in other settings. One of the first questions for future work on technology brokering is whether or not this local model resembles innovation processes in other settings or is idiosyncratic to the firm that we studied. The extent to which our model generalizes to other organizations can only be determined by hypothesis-testing research in large, representative samples of other organizations involved in creative problem solving. A variety of existing cases suggest, however, that the process we observed at IDEO is much like that used in other organizations doing creative work.

Management consulting firms like McKinsey & Co. and Andersen Consulting profit by bringing to client organizations management techniques that clients were often not previously aware of but that have potential value to solve their current problems. For McKinsey, the result is reported to be a set of clients whose "demand for organizational knowledge and experience cuts across nearly every important client relationship regardless of industry" (Katzenbach and Smith, 1993: 98). Taking advantage of this position between clients and the knowledge these clients seek requires routines to acquire, store, and retrieve such knowledge in forms that their clients can use. To do so, McKinsey uses formal and informal mechanisms to store and retrieve potentially valuable knowledge. One example is their "Rapid Response Team," established to "respond to all requests for best current thinking and practice by providing access to both documents and experienced consultants" from across the company (Katzenbach and Smith, 1993: 98). Arthur Andersen similarly benefits from its ability to broker new solutions based on past experiences. The firm's promotional materials promise to "quickly produce innovative solutions" by drawing on a knowledge base that "abounds with breakthrough quantitative tools along with qualitative best practices compiled from client experiences and exhaustive research," and they promise to do so by using the formalized routines captured in their Global Best Practices approach (*Business Week*, 1996). As a result, these management consultants provide their clients with new solutions that are combinations of (what they believe to be) the best management techniques they have seen elsewhere.

Technology brokering may not be limited to consultants. The 3M Corporation is a large manufacturing firm that often finds new uses for existing technologies by adapting and introducing those technologies in new markets. The surface preparation technology known as "microreplication" that 3M originally developed for overhead projectors in 1964 has diffused and evolved to provide 3M with innovative products in electronics (magneto-optics), adhesives (smart adhesives), abrasives (structured surface abrasives), reflective materials (street signs and lane markers), illumination (light poles), film (liquid crystal display film), and lenses (low-profile overhead projectors) (Stewart, 1996). Our local model of technology brokering may offer insights into how organizations like McKinsey, Arthur Andersen, and 3M position themselves within a network of imperfectly shared technological knowledge and how they acquire, store, and retrieve past technologies for implementation in new designs for other industries.

Future research might also focus on specifying the environments in which technology brokering is likely to occur. Our perspective suggests that the primary feature of such environments will be a fragmentation in knowledge and communication between technological domains. When ideas exist in one domain that are potentially valuable in others, individuals and organizations can create innovative new concepts by acquiring, storing, and retrieving these ideas in new combinations and by transferring these combinations to new audiences. Technology brokering appears especially likely to occur when new technologies are developed that have potential value in a wide range of industries but such knowledge is not yet widely diffused. Examples include electromagnetic power at the turn of the century and information technologies in recent decades.

The general applicability of electric power meant that inventors like Edison could profit by finding problems in a wide range of industries that electric power could solve. In a similar, though less grand process, IDEO adapts information technologies for use in a range of industries that had previously lacked such knowledge. The historian Hughes (1989), in language reminiscent of March and Olsen's (1976) garbage can model of decision making, described the creative process used by independent inventors at the turn of the century as solutions in search of problems. The presence of technologies with potential value to a broad range of industries allowed organizations with knowledge of these existing "solutions" to create new products routinely by crossing industry boundaries in search of new problems. Elmer Sperry, a contemporary of Edison, whose firm pioneered the use of electric motors in gyrostabilizers and gyrocompasses, stated his rationale behind this strategy: "If I spend a lifetime on a dynamo [i.e., electric motor] I can probably make my little contribution toward increasing the efficiency of that machine six or seven percent. Now then, there are a whole lot of [industries] that need electricity, about four or five hundred percent, let me tackle one of those" (Hughes, 1989: 54). Theory about technology brokering might be advanced by considering how, given the nature of the technologies involved and the distribution of knowledge about them, environments facilitate or hamper innovation through brokering.

Our evidence from IDEO also suggests that internal routines are essential to organizations that exploit attachments to disparate industries. Organizations that face many different problems benefit from routines for acquiring, storing, and retrieving a broad range of technological knowledge when that knowledge will be useful in solving future problems. IDEO has clear ties to a wide range of industries, but other forms of organizations may hold similar network positions without sharing the same organizational forms. There may be alternative ways of organizing for technology brokering that reflect different environments and different strategies and result in different sets of internal routines. For instance, IDEO and other consulting firms continually explore the environment for new solutions while solving the specific problems of clients in a range of industries. Others, like Edison and Sperry, may innovate by specializing in a single, emerging technology and exploring the environment for possible applications of that one solution. Still other organizations may gain access to a range of industries through multiple divisions and share discoveries (and failures) in one industry that may have potential value in another. Large, multidivisional corporations, for example, have internalized access to the technologies and market needs of different industries. A division operating in one industry may broker potentially valuable technologies to other industries by sharing knowledge between divisions. Mueller (1975: 326) described the discovery by DuPont researchers of Duco lacquer, which reduced the drying time of automotive paint from days to hours. Seeking an improved photographic film, these researchers recognized in a failed experiment the potential for a new product in a wholly different industry. By adding pigments to a congealed and useless solution for photographic film, they created a vastly improved automotive lacquer. DuPont's access to such a broad range of industries and its internal routines for sharing problems and solutions turned a failed photographic film experiment into a highly successful automotive product. Organizations that have developed routines for technology brokering may be better able to take advantage of such serendipitous discoveries. Theory on technology brokering might be enhanced by considering the routines that such firms use to match potentially valuable technologies found in some parts of the organization with needs in other parts.

CONCLUSION

Our model of technology brokering suggests that innovation can and should be studied by considering both the social structure of technological knowledge and the internal routines of organizations able to exploit that structure. Innovation through brokering may generalize beyond technological innovations within the product development process. Scientists, artists, management consultants, and others involved in creative

problem-solving efforts often build innovative new ideas by recombining existing ideas. It is an old notion that innovations are built from existing works, but the image often remains of the lone genius inventing ideas from scratch. Technology brokering offers a perspective on innovation and innovators that recognizes the value not of invention but of inventive combination.

ACKNOWLEDGMENTS

We are grateful to Stephen Barley, Beth Bechky, Dennis Boyle, Kathleen Eisenhardt, Herminia Ibarra, Linda Johanson, Christine Oliver, David Owens, Marc Ventresca, and three anonymous reviewers for their contributions to this paper. We are also grateful for the support provided by the Center for the Advanced Study in the Behavioral Sciences, Hewlett-Packard, the Stanford Integrated Manufacturing Association, the National Science Foundation (SBR-9022192), and the Center for Innovation Management Studies at Lehigh University. We especially appreciate the time and effort that Paul Barsley, David Blakely, Gwen Books, Dennis Boyle, Sean Corcorran, Tony Fields, David Karshmer, David Kelley, Tom Kelley, Chris Kurjan, Bill Moggridge, Chuck Seiber, Larry Shubert, Peter Skillman, Roby Stancel, Rickson Sun, Scott Underwood, Don Westwood, Jim Yurchenko, and many others at IDEO Product Development devoted to this research.

NOTES

1. Sutton and Hargadon (1996) also used this ethnography as the basis for a paper on the effectiveness of brainstorming sessions. That paper contains additional information about the research setting for this ethnography and the methods used, as well as about IDEO's structure, work practices, norms, and values.

2. Various versions of this paper have been described to and read by IDEO designers and managers since our ethnography ended in March 1996. This conversation and reading has led some designers to adopt the term "technology brokering" as a synonym for "cross-pollination."

3. The technological details of the products and projects we observed at IDEO are critical to presenting a theory of technology brokering. For reasons of client confidentiality, however, we have had to disguise approximately 10 percent of these products. In doing so, we substituted products of similar technological complexity and confirmed these selections with the designers who were involved in the original projects.

4. This definition of creativity is not new. Schumpeter (1934: 65–66) described innovation as the "carrying out of new combinations," and Usher (1929: 11) described technological innovation as the "constructive assimilation of pre-existing elements into new syntheses." A decade earlier, Ogburn (1922; quoted in Basalla, 1988: 21) defined invention as "combining existing and known elements of culture in order to form a new element." And, even earlier, Ribot (1906; quoted in Torrance, 1988: 45), a psychologist studying creativity, maintained that creative thinking produced "unforeseen and novel combinations," but "in equal measure absurd combinations and very original inventions."

5. Evidence suggested that IDEO also brokered technological solutions between groups within client organizations (as one informant described, "we take your watch and tell you what time it is") and organizations within a single industry (though IDEO is careful to avoid intellectual property issues). We focused on brokering between industries, however, because conceptually and empirically it offers the clearest perspective on the process of technology brokering

REFERENCES

Allen, Thomas J. 1977. *Managing the Flow of Technology.* Cambridge, MA: MIT Press.

Attewell, Paul. 1992. "Technology diffusion and organizational learning: The case of business computing." *Organization Science,* 3: 1–19.

Basalla, George. 1988. *The Evolution of Technology.* New York: Cambridge University Press.

Burt, Ronald S. 1983. "Range." In R. S. Burt and M. J. Minor (eds.), *Applied Network Analysis: A Methodological Introduction:* 176–194. Beverly Hills, CA: Sage.

Burt, Ronald S. 1992a. "The social structure of competition." In N. Nohria and R. G. Eccles (eds.), *Networks and Organizations: Structure, Form, and Action:* 57–91. Boston: Harvard Business School Press.

Burt, Ronald S. 1992b. *Structural Holes: The Social Structure of Competition.* Cambridge, MA: Harvard University Press.

Business Week. 1996. Advertisement for Arthur Andersen and Co. February 26, p. 85.

Callon, Michel. 1980. "The state and technical innovation: A case study of the electric vehicle in France." *Research Policy,* 9: 358–376.

Cohen, Wesley M., and Daniel A. Levinthal. 1994. "Fortune favors the prepared firm." *Management Science,* 40: 227–251.

Cyert, Richard M., and James G. March. 1963. *A Behavioral Theory of the Firm.* Englewood Cliffs, NJ: Prentice-Hall.

DiMaggio, Paul. 1992. "Nadel's Paradox revisited: Relational and cultural aspects of organizational structure." In N. Nohria and R. G. Eccles (eds.), *Networks and Organizations: Structure, Form, and Action:* 118–142. Boston: Harvard Business School Press.

Fernandez, Roberto M., and Roger V. Gould. 1994. "A dilemma of state power: Brokerage and influence in the national health policy domain." *American Journal of Sociology,* 99: 1455–1491.

Glaser, Barney G., and Anselm L. Strauss. 1967. *The Discovery of Grounded Theory: Strategies for Qualitative Research.* New York: Aldine.

Gould, Roger V., and Roberto M. Fernandez. 1989. "Structures of mediation: A formal approach to brokerage in transaction networks." *Sociological Methodology,* 19: 89–126.

Huber, George P. 1991. "Organizational learning: The contributing processes and the literature." *Organization Science,* 2: 88–115.

Hughes, Thomas P. 1989. *American Genesis: A Century of Invention and Technological Enthusiasm.* New York: Penguin Books.

Kantrow, Alan M. 1987. *The Constraints of Corporate Tradition.* New York: Harper & Row.

Katzenbach, Jon R., and Douglas K. Smith. 1993. *The Wisdom of Teams: Creating the High-Performance Organization.* Boston: Harvard Business School Press.

Latour, Bruno. 1987. *Science in Action.* Cambridge, MA: Harvard University Press.

Law, John. 1987. "Technology and heterogenous engineering: The case of Portuguese expansion." In W. F. Bijker, T. P. Hughes, and T. Pinch (eds.), *The Social Construction of Technological Systems:* 111–134. Cambridge, MA: MIT Press.

March, James G. 1972. "Model bias in social action." *Review of Educational Research,* 44: 413–429.

March, James G., and Johan P. Olsen. 1976. *Ambiguity and Choice in Organizations.* Bergen, Norway: Universitetsforlaget.

March, James G., and Herbert A. Simon. 1958. *Organizations.* New York: Wiley.

Marsden, Peter V. 1982. "Brokerage behavior in restricted exchange networks." In P. V. Marsden and N. Lin (eds.), *Social Structure and Network Analysis:* 201–218. Beverly Hills, CA: Sage.

Meacham, John A. 1990. "The loss of wisdom." In R. J. Sternberg (ed.), *The Nature of Creativity:* 181–211. New York: Cambridge University Press.

Merton, Robert K. 1973. *The Sociology of Science: Theoretical and Empirical Investigations.* Chicago: University of Chicago Press.

Miles, Matthew B., and A. Michael Huberman. 1994. *Qualitative Data Analysis.* Thousand Oaks, CA: Sage.

Millard, Andre. 1990. *Edison and the Business of Innovation.* Baltimore: Johns Hopkins University Press.

Mueller, Willard F. 1975. "The origins of the basic inventions underlying DuPont's major product and process innovations, 1920 to 1950." In R. R. Nelson (ed.), *The Rate and Direction of Inventive Activity: Economic and Social Factors:* 323–358. Princeton: Princeton University Press.

Neustadt, Richard E., and Ernest R. May. 1986. *Thinking in Time: The Uses of History for Decision Makers.* New York: Free Press.

Ogburn, William F. 1922. *Social Change.* New York: B. W. Huebsch.

Osborn, Alex F. 1957. *Applied Imagination.* New York: Scribner.

Padgett, John F., and Christopher K. Ansell. 1993. "Robust action and the rise of the medici, 1400–1434." *American Journal of Sociology,* 98: 1259–1319.

Petrovski, Henry. 1992. *The Evolution of Useful Things.* New York: Knopf.

Ribot, T. 1906. *Essays on the Creative Imagination.* London: Routledge & Kegan Paul.

Rogers, E. M. 1983. *The Diffusion of Innovation,* 3rd ed. New York: Free Press.

Rosenberg, Nathan. 1982. *Inside the Black Box.* New York: Cambridge University Press.

Rosenberg, Nathan. 1994. *Exploring the Black Box: Technology, Economics, and History.* New York: Cambridge University Press.

Schon, Donald A. 1993. "Generative metaphor: A perspective on problem-setting in social policy." In A. Ortony (ed.), *Metaphor and Thought:* 137–163. Cambridge: Cambridge University Press.

Schumpeter, Joseph. 1934. *The Theory of Economic Development. Cambridge,* MA: Harvard University Press.

Sutton, Robert I., and Andrew B. Hargadon. 1996. "Brainstorming groups in context: Effectiveness in a product design firm." *Administrative Science Quarterly.* 41: 685–718.

Stewart, Thomas A. 1996. "3M fights back." *Fortune Magazine,* February 5: 94–99.

Torrance, E. P. 1988. "The nature of creativity as manifest in its testing." In R. J. Sternberg (ed.), *The Nature of Creativity:* 43–75. New York: Cambridge University Press.

Usher, Abbot Payton. 1929. *A History of Mechanical Inventions.* New York: McGraw-Hill.

Walsh, James P., and Robert D. Dewar. 1987. "Formalization and the organizational life cycle." *Journal of Management Studies,* 24: 216–231.

Walsh, James P., and Gerardo R. Ungson. 1991. "Organizational memory." *Academy of Management Review,* 16: 57–91.

Weick, Karl E. 1979a. *The Social Psychology of Organizing.* Reading. MA: Addison-Wesley.

Weick, Karl E. 1979b. "Cognitive processes in organizations." In B. M. Staw (ed.), *Research in Organizational Behavior,* 1: 41–74. Greenwich, CT: JAI Press.

Weick, Karl E. 1992. "Agenda setting in organizational behavior: A theory focused approach." *Journal of Management Inquiry,* 1: 171–182.

35

Involving Suppliers in New Product Development

ROBERT B. HANDFIELD
GARY L. RAGATZ
KENNETH J. PETERSEN
ROBERT M. MONCZKA

Within the last decade, the rapid rate of technological change, shortened product life cycles, and globalization of markets have resulted in renewed executive focus on new product development processes. In a competitive environment, suppliers are an increasingly important resource for manufacturers. Across all worldwide manufacturers, purchased materials account for over 50 percent of the cost of goods sold. In addition, suppliers have a large and direct impact on the cost, quality, technology, and time-to-market of new products. Effective integration of suppliers into the product value/supply chain will be a key factor for manufacturers in achieving the improvements necessary to remain competitive. As integration increases, joint resource dedication will follow. For instance, it is now commonplace for companies to dedicate engineers who learn the systems, procedures, and processes of suppliers in order to improve communication, reduce errors, and understand capabilities.[1] Many companies have recognized that involving suppliers in new product/process/service development efforts has the potential to provide significant results.[2] A number of reports in the popular press have highlighted the fact that supplier participation in product development projects can help reduce cost, reduce concept-to-customer development time, improve quality, and provide innovative technologies that can help capture market share. For instance, in developing its compact sedans (the Chrysler Cirrus and Dodge Stratus), Chrysler Corporation presourced 95 percent of the parts required for production. Chrysler used a team approach and chose the suppliers before the parts were even designed, which meant virtually eliminating traditional supplier bidding.[3] The results of this effort included significant reductions in cost, quality improvements, and innovative new designs. While such results typically go undisputed, there is mounting evidence that not all such efforts are successful.

Moreover, successful supplier integration involves a large number of variables. Questions that arise include tier structure, degree of responsibility for design, specific responsibilities in the requirement setting process, when to involve suppliers in the process, inter-company communication, intellectual property agreements, supplier membership on the project team, and alignment of organizational objectives with regard to outcomes. While the benefits of supplier integration appear to be obvious, successful supplier integration projects have special common characteristics. Specifically, successful supplier integration initiatives result in a *major change to the new product development process*. Further, the new process must be formally adapted by multiple functions within the organization to be successful. One of the most important activities in the

Copyright © 1999 by The Regents of the University of California. Reprinted from the *California Management Review*, Vol. 42, No. 1. By permission of The Regents.

new development process is understanding the focal suppliers' capabilities and design expertise, conducting a technology risk assessment, and weighing the risks against the probability of success.

This article presents a model of the product development process and the opportunities for supplier integration at various points of the process. This model is based on case studies of 17 manufacturing organizations and on results of a recent survey on supplier integration in 134 companies worldwide.

PRIOR RESEARCH

Several prior studies allude to the specific processes that occur when suppliers become involved in new product development. Kamath and Liker examine Japanese product development practices and identify a variety of roles that suppliers may play.[4] Littler, Leverick, and Bruce examined the key success factors for collaborative new product development efforts in 106 UK firms in which the collaborative partner could be a supplier, customer, or competitor.[5] They concluded that frequent inter-company communication, building trust, establishing partnership equity, ensuring that parties contribute as expected, and employing a product or collaboration champion increased the likelihood of success. There is evidence that the way firms organize their product development efforts has an impact on results. Larson and Gobeli found the project matrix and project team to be the most useful organizational structures for product development projects.[6] In their study of 108 cross-functional sourcing teams, Monczka and Trent identified a preliminary, yet strong link between formal supplier involvement and team performance, including teams responsible for new product development.[7] Smith and Reinertsen reached a similar conclusion, suggesting that "suppliers particularly need to be included as team members when the new product involves critical technologies in which the company is not expert."[8] Hartley, Meredith, McCutcheon, and Kamath found that the time of supplier involvement was significantly related to the perceived contribution to the new product design.[9]

A number of differences in supplier integration practices exist between companies in the U.S., Japan, and Europe. Clark[10] and Clark and Fujimoto[11] compared Japanese and U.S. manufacturers' use of suppliers in new product development and found that the contribution of suppliers to competitive advantage is especially critical in cases where R&D activities are shared. Several studies have also found that Japanese manufacturers made more extensive use of supplier involvement than American manufacturers.[12] A study by Liker, Kamath, Wasti, and Nagamachi found that the gaps between U.S. and Japanese automakers' use of supplier involvement in new product development has narrowed significantly.[13] However, the study found that Japanese automotive companies rely on target prices, performance monitoring, competition, and mutual dependence more than their U.S. counterparts to control suppliers entrusted with the design of complex auto systems. In general, all of these studies found performance improvement outcomes from supplier integration in the form of reduced cycle time, improved quality, greater technological improvements, and reduced costs.

A second body of literature emphasizes the importance of relationship development as a precursor to successful supplier involvement in new product development. Dyer and Ouchi suggest that the length of a buyer supplier relationship has a positive effect on product development efforts.[14] The supplier's existing knowledge of the buying firm's internal processes and objectives enables the supplier to plan for future product development efforts and to develop, in advance, the capabilities to meet those needs. Kanter argues that a well-developed ability to create and sustain fruitful collaborations can provide significant advantage, especially in new product development ventures.[15] This research further concludes that North American companies, more than others throughout the world, take a narrow, opportunistic view of relationships between buyers and sellers. Slade concurs that collaboration can create competitive advantage by saying that "the supplier relationship is only one of the many aspects of management that contribute to a company's performance. But ... the management of this relationship [is] of paramount importance to any company's success."[16] While the importance of supplier involvement is unarguable in these works, it is apparent that organizations still struggle with the fundamental changes to the new product development process that must occur to facilitate supplier integration. Some of the major questions that arise include:

- Which suppliers should be involved?
- Is the supplier able to meet our requirements?
- Is the supplier's technology roadmap aligned with our roadmap?
- Given the level of technical complexity, to what extent should the supplier be involved in the project?
- When exactly should the supplier be involved in the project?

SUPPLIER INTEGRATION APPROACHES

The possible forms of supplier integration can be framed within the context of the "generic" new product development process shown in Figure 35.1. The new product development process is a series of interdependent and often overlapping stages during which a new product (or process or service) is brought from the "idea" stage to readiness for full-scale production or service delivery. As the product concept moves through these stages, the idea is refined and evaluated for business and technical feasibility, the design is firmed up, prototyping and testing are done, the design is finalized, and preparations for full-scale operations (e.g., tooling, layout, personnel, equipment) are finalized. During this process, cost, performance, timing, quality, and other problems often crop up, which results in tradeoffs and changes in the design. The design may be modified numerous times before it is finalized.

In the first stage (idea generation), designers and marketing personnel consider the need for the product and typically tap customers for their ideas and input on what such a product/process/service might do, how much it might cost, and so on. Potential technologies may also be assessed at this point, especially if an existing supplier possesses an exciting new technology. In the second stage, the team may perform a business assessment of the product and also identify the technical solutions to the customer's requirements. In product and service design, tools such as Quality Function Deployment may be used to develop technical specifications that specifically address customer requirements. In the third stage of development, the product/process/service concept is effectively conceived, with performance specifications "frozen." In the case of product development, a preliminary prototype model may be created for purposes of concept definition. Next, the actual development process begins, wherein designers from both the supplying and buying organizations create blueprints and design specifications. A working prototype is created, which enables testing and verification of existing production systems. Finally, the product enters full-scale production and supplier volumes are ramped up.

Outside suppliers provide materials and services that constitute a majority of the cost of many new products. In addition, suppliers may provide innovative product or process technologies that are critical to the development effort. The supplier may have better information or greater expertise regarding these technologies than the buying company's design personnel. Supplier input and/or the active involvement of suppliers may be sought at any point in the development process (see Figure 35.1).

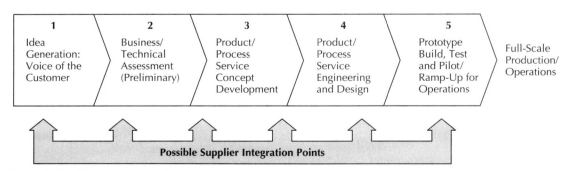

Figure 35.1. New product development process.

While the concept and design engineering phases of new product development incur a relatively small portion of the total product development costs, these two activities commit or "lock in" as much as 80 percent of the total cost of the product. Decisions made early in the design process have a significant impact on

---

The NSF/MSU Supplier Integration Research Project

This study was part of a larger project funded by the National Science Foundation and the Michigan State University Global Procurement and Supply Chain Electronic Benchmarking Network (GEBN). Members of the GEBN have agreed to participate in a series of benchmarking surveys conducted each year as part of a larger research initiative. Based on a preliminary model developed by Sussman and Dean[17] specifying methods of integrating internal cross-functional team members into new product development, the researchers carried out seventeen field studies in the U.S. and Japan to validate and verify the model. To further enhance the validity of the discussions, documentation of purchasing policies were obtained at each site when possible, as well as organization charts, product descriptions, marketing reports, and so on. Following each interview, the field notes were written up in typeface. The next step involved coding this data.[18] The transcribed field notes were reviewed several times by the researchers in order to code the events into their appropriate categories (consistent with an a priori conceptual model developed by Sussman and Dean) and to compare field notes taken during the same interview. In so doing, the events and processes observed at each site were classified according to the conceptual structure they described. The resulting process model of supplier integration is shown in Figure 35.2.

Concurrently, a survey was developed, which was pre-tested and reviewed by a team of industry experts and a team of academics from organizational behavior, marketing, operations management, and purchasing. An initial 2-page commitment letter and fax response form was mailed to approximately 3,000 companies in 18 countries around the world, and of these 225 indicated that they would be willing to participate.[19] Surveys were mailed to the 225 companies, and 134 responses were received. The responding companies represented a wide range of industry groups, including aerospace (12), automotive (24), chemicals (11), computers and electronics (19), consumer products (18), Industrial equipment (20), medical products and services (6), process industries (10), telecommunications (9), and government services (6). About 12.5 percent of the responses came from non-manufacturing organizations. The companies' 1996 sales (in U.S. dollars) ranged from $3 million to $160 billion with a median of $3.1 billion. A majority of the responses (68%) came from U.S. and Canadian companies. Just over 20 percent of the responses came from Western Europe, 7 percent from Asia/Australia, and 4 percent from South America.

A five-stage New Product Development model was presented in the survey as a reference point. The five stages precede full-scale production and include idea generation, preliminary business/technical assessment, product/process/service concept development, product/process/service design and development, and prototype build, test and production ramp up. The following definition of supplier integration into new product development was also included in the questionnaire to provide a solid base for response analysis.

"Supplier integration into new product/process/service development suggests that suppliers are providing information and directly participating in decision making for purchases used in the new product/process/service. This integration can occur at any point in the five stage new product/process/service development model."

The survey was divided into two major sections. The first section addressed questions related to the organization's overall strategy and experience with supplier integration. The second section asked the respondent to limit their responses to a single supplier integration experience. Both sets of responses were used to derive the results discussed in this study.

the resulting product quality, cycle time, and cost. As the development process continues, it becomes increasingly difficult and costly to make design changes. It is crucial then, for firms to bring to bear as much product, process, and technical expertise as possible early in the development process. In addition, compa-

nies whose development plans are well aligned with those of their key suppliers can shorten overall development time.

Based on a detailed analysis of our case studies, we developed a process model of supplier integration shown in Figure 35.2. This model was developed after

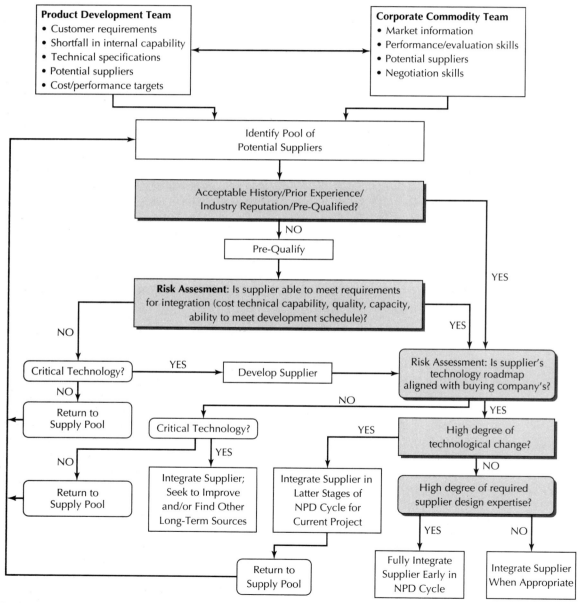

Figure 35.2. Process model for reaching consensus on suppliers to integrate into new product development project.

reviewing a number of companies' supplier integration processes and compiling their best practices into a generic process model. Additional insights into company practices at various stages of the model are provided in the form of summary statistics from our mail survey results.

Identifying Desired Supplier Capabilities and Potential Suppliers

In all the companies studied, the importance of the design/manufacturing decision is being subjected to a much more thorough analysis than in the past. An important initial decision involves a formal statement on the level of insourcing/outsourcing that will occur in core technology development. In reaching a consensus on difficult insourcing/outsourcing decisions, successful organizations have developed a *systematic process* for defining the level and types of product/process technologies to be outsourced. Whenever possible, companies are approaching the outsourcing decision from a systems perspective and are asking suppliers to increase their responsibility for subsystem integration. This was observed to be the case across a variety of products and processes, including chemical molecules, automobiles, installation and maintenance of new processes, and computer components.

The decision-making process begins at a high systemization level, where strategic core competencies in product and process design and manufacture are assessed (see Figure 35.3). At this level, the unit of analysis involves decisions regarding core technologies, system integration, and return on investment for resource allocations leading to internal technology development. Our study revealed a trend towards outsourcing commodity-like items and focusing internal efforts on added-value activities such as system integration. In all of the companies, this decision was made at higher levels in the organization and involved a strategic vision regarding the organization's future markets and technology roadmap in the next ten to twenty years.

Most of the supplier integration cases reported in our survey involved the supplier of either a customized product component or a product sub-assembly, sub-system, or system. Several cases also dealt with suppliers of materials, process technology, or capital equipment. A few cases dealt with suppliers of services or commodity-type components.

Once consensus is reached, executives formalize the insourcing/outsourcing technology strategy and communicate it to the divisions, who are then responsible for establishing current and future new product requirements. The process of cascading the decision to the next organizational decision-making level is achieved through a variety of means. One of the prevailing organizational structures to interpret and deploy technology strategies is the advanced technology group. These groups are typically located centrally and are assigned the task of identifying major new subsystem and component technologies required in new products. Another approach involves integration of suppliers into process development and start-up. Some companies use institutionalized "platform teams," responsible for new product development with suppliers on a permanent basis. Finally, other divisions employ a "letter of intent" that formally specifies the nature of the relationship. Note that the decision making at this stage is typically done by product development teams, which use the executive core competence vision as a guide.

The final insourcing/outsourcing decision-making hierarchy occurs at the component level, where decisions are typically made jointly by the product development and purchasing commodity teams (see Figure 35.3). Purchasing is responsible at this level for identifying leading suppliers within a commodity class and sharing this information with the commodity team. In some cases, however, the decision may be made independent of a commodity team.

After completing this initial stage of the strategic process, teams should have identified a vision statement regarding the company's internal core competencies, established a set of requirements for success in current and future new products, and have a general idea of the technology needs within these product groups. In addition, the company should have a general idea of the specific roles and responsibilities it wishes to place on suppliers that are selected for new product development. Product development and commodity teams should seek to formally specify these objectives in as much detail as possible. As shown in the next three stages in Figure 35.2, they become the primary criteria used in supplier selection, negotiation, alignment, and relationship management.

A number of case examples illustrate this process. At a major manufacturer of printers and faxes in Japan, the primary metric used to drive all supplier integra-

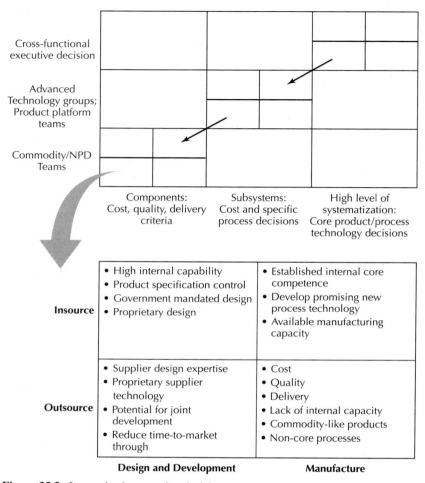

Figure 35.3. Insourcing/outsourcing decision.

tion projects is target cost. For example, a target cost for a fax machine was first developed based on marketing's input and was broken down into different categories of parts based on historical costs. The mechanical parts target cost was broken down into a target cost for all metal parts, of which about 90 percent were within the scope of the single metal parts supplier's production capability. This target cost was submitted to suppliers. Suppliers share their cost data with engineers, and provide information on labor, overhead, and material costs. To achieve the target cost, changes in processes and changes in materials are discussed first (avoiding the topic of profit margins). If the supplier still cannot meet the target cost, the company ini-

tiates negotiation of profit margins based on volume considerations.

Other considerations that may influence the decision to integrate suppliers include a lack of internal design capability and the need to develop a noncore technology. For example, a major electronics components manufacturer relies extensively on its suppliers to deliver state-of-the-art process technology that it cannot develop internally. The key strategy within this organization involves holding suppliers responsible for delivering, installing, servicing, and maintaining machine tools costing well over one million dollars each. Suppliers are responsible for process ramp-up and maintenance of equipment in wafer fabrication facilities. While the company is also involved in supplier integration into new product development, process integration represents a truly unique application in a non-traditional area. Suppliers are first fully responsible for the maintenance of these machine tools and the maintenance tasks are then gradually turned over to internal people. Each supplier is responsible for a single process, which is identically carried out at its three facilities in different parts of the world. The company emphasized the exact replication of processes across all of the facilities—this principle is emphasized throughout all of its business strategies. The principle refers to the fact that any time a specification or task is transferred between functions or suppliers, the other party is responsible for exactly reproducing the requirements.

In another case, a company's core competency is considered to be an overriding factor. A chemical manufacturer considered portions of molecules as building blocks in assessing supplier competence. The company's strategy was to accelerate the rate of new product development by focusing on fewer compounds annually and integrating suppliers who have proven capabilities and can perform multiple steps in the intermediate product process. Instead of asking suppliers to supply basic elements only, they are actively asking suppliers how to make the intermediate molecules with the final molecules in mind. This involved showing them a bigger picture (not just a small piece of the process), posing the question more broadly, and getting the supplier to perform a greater share of the process. Supplier integration was facilitated by having broader secrecy agreements to cover more issues as the supplier gains access to more pieces of the molecule puzzle. In some cases, the company even licensed parts of molecules from university research centers. The strategy driving this integration was to push increasingly higher up the compound chain, becoming more of an "assembler" of the final compound or molecule.

Supplier Risk Assessment

Once the product development/commodity team has reached consensus on the key objectives for integrating suppliers, a set of specific performance measures related to customers' needs and requirements should be used to reach a consensus on potential supplier capabilities and subsequent selection. Cost, quality, and delivery are, of course, relevant, but evaluating suppliers for potential integration into new product development should involve criteria beyond those used to evaluate ordinary material/service suppliers. Based on the experience of the companies studied, the following elements are likely to be important in considering new or existing suppliers for integration:

- *Targets*—Is the supplier capable of hitting affordable targets regarding cost, quality, and product performance/function (e.g., weight, size, speed)?
- *Timing*—Will the supplier be able to meet the product development schedule?
- *Ramp-Up*—Will the supplier be able to increase capacity and production fast enough to meet volume production requirements?
- *Innovation and Technical*—Does the supplier have the required engineering expertise and physical facilities to develop an adequate design, manufacture it, and solve problems when they occur?
- *Training*—Do the supplier's key personnel have the required training to start-up required processes and debug them?

All of the above criteria must be tied into the evaluation/measurement system in order to develop a comprehensive *risk assessment* that answers the following questions:

- What is the likelihood that this supplier has the ability to bring the product to market?
- How does this risk compare to other potential suppliers (if there are others)?
- At what point are we willing to reverse this decision if we proceed, and what are the criteria/measures for doing so?
- What is the contingency plan that takes effect in the event the supplier fails to perform?

It is no longer enough that a supplier be able to design and manufacture a prototype or start-up small volume production. Because of the intense competition and short product life cycles in many industries (such as electronics and computers), suppliers must also be able to meet product introduction deadlines *and* ramp-up their production volumes very quickly. Several of the companies we studied assessed these criteria through a variety of means.

A good example of a commodity team in action

involved a U.S. computer manufacturer team negotiation with a European supplier, who was selected after ten suppliers presented their design for a new project. The presentations were formally evaluated quantitatively by the commodity team. During the course of the selected supplier's presentation, the team found it could satisfy its requirements with an "off-the-shelf" chip set from the supplier. The team also visited selected supplier facilities, and the supplier deployed a dedicated engineering team over the course of the project. The commodity team also works in parallel with other commodity teams on the product development group. A key element in the structure of the teams in this company is that it is not a one-hundred percent engineering-led process, even though engineering has traditionally dominated decisions. The new vision is to retain a core set of knowledge to respond to end-customer needs and develop more interfaces with suppliers to identify which technologies can meet these requirements. The company cannot afford to be "shut out" of a new technology, so the group must constantly be transferring knowledge from a variety of sources, including customer requirements, after-market efforts (where new technologies often show up first), trade shows, competitive assessments, and alliances.

For another company (a U.S. computer manufacturer), the supplier's capacity and flexibility are critical issues, and the team will examine what kind of agreements the supplier has with their contract manufacturers and how they affect the supplier's ability to increase output quickly. The supplier must have upside flexibility requirements amounting to:

- 25 percent up in 4 weeks
- 50 percent up in 8 weeks
- 100 percent up in 12 weeks

A U.S. computer peripherals manufacturer faces the problem of having a very limited number of potential suppliers of several of its key components, worldwide. Because of the small number of suppliers, however, the company has done business with most of them and has experience with their capabilities. Supplier selection is based primarily on the supplier's capability to design and manufacture the product in large volumes to performance specifications within the required time.

At another U.S. computer company, in the first

stage of the new product development process (definition and planning), material support involves selection of a technology given the requirements of the product. Once this is complete, corporate materials can come up with a potential list of suppliers. If the supplier is new to the company, the supplier will first perform a self-assessment survey. Then the team will visit for several days and examines eight separate modules (including quality systems, control, reliability, financial analysis) and arrive at a performance score.

In our survey, respondents were asked to indicate the importance of various objectives related to integrating the supplier in this product development effort and also rate the impact that supplier integration had on achieving that objective. The objectives that emerged as most important to the companies are consistent with the competitive/strategic factors that are driving supplier integration (see Table 35.1). Further, the respondents believed that supplier integration had a positive impact on all of the objectives.

One other result is of interest. For the four objectives on which supplier integration had the least positive impact (financial risk, process technology, environmental regulations, and other government regulations), approximately ten percent of the respondents indicated that supplier integration actually had a negative effect on the objective. For the other objectives, no more than five percent of the respondents reported a negative impact. This suggests that in some cases, supplier integration efforts may not always result in successful outcomes.

In cases when the supplier's capabilities may not be up to desired levels, the product/commodity team has one of two options. If the technology is not critical to the product's functioning, a different supplier may be investigated. However, if there are limited numbers of suppliers available and the technology is critical to the product, than a more detailed technical assessment of the supplier may take place in an attempt to develop and improve the suppliers' capabilities early in the product development process.

Several of the companies carried out detailed assessments of the supplier's technical capabilities prior to selecting them for a new product development project. In most cases, both formal and informal approaches were required to develop a reliable assessment. A typical approach would start with a formal standard survey-type assessment, which would be augmented by informal assessments by internal engineer's assess-

Table 35.1. Company Objectives for Supplier Integration

Objective	Importance of Objective[a]	Effect of Supplier Integration on Achieving Objective[b]
Reduce design or development time	5.83	5.43
Reduce procured item cost	5.76	5.27
Improved procured item quality	5.70	5.49
Improve procured item reliability/durability	5.65	5.45
Reduce design and development cost	5.45	5.23
Access and improve product technology	5.27	5.20
Develop a long term supplier relationship	5.26	5.45
Improve product features	5.21	5.32
More effectively use human resources at my business unit and at the supplier	5.18	5.31
Improve customer service	5.02	4.98
Reduce technological risk	4.89	5.12
Reduce financial risk	4.78	4.83
Access and improve process technology	4.74	4.87
Improve my business unit's position as a preferred customer to the supplier	4.59	5.19
Comply with environmental regulations	3.88	4.61
Comply with other government regulations	3.77	4.64

a. 1 = "Totally Unimportant" to 7 = "Very Important."
b. 1 = "Strong Negative (Bad) Effect" to 7 = "Strong Positive (Good) Effect."

ments, based on face-to-face discussions with the supplier's technical personnel. The most detailed technical assessments considered both of these inputs, as informal discussions can often reveal problems that may not be obvious to an external uninformed party.

A good example of how this decision is made involved a component supplier who made lead frames and overmolding for a U.S. semiconductor manufacturer. Although the company had the capabilities internally, they chose to team up with the supplier to produce them after an insourcing/outsourcing decision was made by the product team (consisting of engineering, design, quality, marketing, and procurement). The outsourcing decision was made because the internal process could not meet the quality requirements (0–6 ppm required by the customer). After requiring the product and process FMEAs and control plans from the supplier and observing their capabilities, the supplier was selected. Next, the team was expanded to include the supplier to determine if they could meet the customer's requirements. Once it was established that they possessed the capability, the supplier became a full-time member of the team.

Suppliers involved early in a U.S. oil and chemical company's development efforts are evaluated using a number of criteria in a "Total Cost of Ownership" type of model that considers:

- reputation for meeting requirements
- cost/availability of raw materials
- difficulty of the process matched against the supplier's capability
- waste generated in the supplier's process
- number of steps required of the supplier
- environmental compliance
- technical competence

The choice of supplier is a decision made by the whole team, but not everyone on the team necessarily gets directly involved. A smaller group within the commercialization team may make a recommendation. Following the recommendation, the company audits the supplier's facilities for contamination, environmental compliance, quality, technical capability, cost, quality, and location—all of which are weighted (weights vary by commodity).

Assessing the Supplier's Technology Roadmap

After a detailed performance assessment has been carried out prior to selection, a second type of assessment must be carried out to ensure the long- and short-term alignment of the objectives and technology plans of the buying company and the supplier. To obtain maximum strategic benefit from the integration of the supplier, both parties must share objectives and have complementary future technology plans. This is most commonly described in terms of a convergence of the companies' technology "roadmaps," which describe the performance, cost, and technology characteristics of future products each company plans to develop/introduce over some specified time horizon.

The specific approaches companies use to assess and achieve alignment of technology roadmaps with suppliers varies considerably. Regardless of the specific approach, sharing information is one critical element of the process. A second important element is providing some incentive or motivation for suppliers to work at alignment with the buying company.

This is reflected in the importance of Supplier Selection Criteria for Supplier Integration (see Table 35.2). As shown in this table, the criteria for selecting suppliers for integration which are most critical include "soft" elements, such as product/process knowledge, production capability, trust, and design expertise. Prior to establishing the relationship, managers from both organizations should meet and engage in a frank discussion of the types of technologies that they intend to develop. As organizations seek to improve the technological capabilities of their supply base, they will need to first build stronger relationships with suppliers, which involve sharing future product plans and alignment of technology roadmaps. In turn, suppliers may need to adjust their technological plans to align them with those of major customers. As this exchange of information takes place, industry standards may be influenced. This will require an intimate understanding of not only current suppliers' capabilities, but a commitment and willingness to trust the other party.

At the same time, buying companies must maintain a competitive edge and be aware of potential new suppliers and technologies that emerge on the horizon. Organizations may need to create separate organizational groups within the business responsible for advanced technology development and expertise. These groups will need to continuously monitor competitors' products, processes, and supply bases and will need to suggest modifications to current sourcing strategies. In some cases, joint technology development with suppliers may yield substantive results, providing that appropriate targets can be set. This must occur on a global basis, scouring the world for the best suppliers. (As

Table 35.2. Supplier Selection Criteria for Supplier Integration

Objective	Mean Response[a]
Supplier's product/service knowledge/capability	6.07
Supplier's process knowledge/capability	6.00
Supplier's production quality capability/ certification	5.85
High level of trust between my business unit and the supplier	5.80
Supplier's design expertise	5.76
Supplier's willingness and ability to communicate effectively	5.65
Supplier's innovativeness	5.62
Supplier's flexibility to respond to design changes	5.60
Supplier's commitment to continuous improvement	5.42
Supplier's expertise in reducing/controlling cost	5.36
Supplier's flexibility to respond to requirements volume changes	5.35
Previous experience with supplier	5.34
Supplier's ability to quickly ramp-up to required output level	5.21
Supplier's ability to develop new technologies for *future* products	5.15
Supplier is fully certified by business unit	4.84
Supplier's goals are aligned with my business unit's goals	4.80
Supplier's culture is compatible with my business unit's culture	4.59
Supplier's use of concurrent development/ engineering practices	4.51
Supplier's use of JIT manufacturing and purchasing	3.92
Supplier's geographical proximity to my business unit	3.5

a. 1 = "Totally Unimportant" to 7 = "Very Important."

shown in Table 35.2, geographical proximity is one of the least important factors influencing the choice of supplier for integration).

Many companies attempt to manage and obtain the best technologies for application by developing a "bookshelf" of current and emerging technologies and suppliers of those technologies. These companies monitor the development of new technologies and, for those that appear to have promising applications, manage their introduction in new product applications so as to balance the benefits of "first mover" status with the risks of the technology. The objective is to maintain a selection of promising and accessible technologies and suppliers on the bookshelf, ready for use when the company wants to apply them in a new product application. The company must understand, influence, and possibly manage the development time of technologies so that they will be available when needed (see Figure 35.4).

At a U.S. electronics company we studied, the company's most successful supplier integration project was initiated by an engineer in the buying company. The engineer thought he saw synergies in the capabilities of his company and a supplier and began talking informally with a counterpart in the supplier company. This led to a high-level meeting between executives from the two companies. At this meeting, supplier executives shared technology plans and roadmaps, and they identified common research streams in a very broad category of materials. An executive consensus was reached regarding what the buying company wanted to work on to support the next product or product family. A "top four" list of projects was targeted directly to future product needs (both short-term and long-term.) This relationship has now become institutionalized, with the two companies meeting periodically to share their roadmaps and update the top-four project list.

Another Japanese computer company shares technology roadmaps with specific suppliers, based on non-disclosure agreements that are part of a broad general agreement with the supplier. Suppliers also share their technology roadmaps. Both parties may change their designs based on future roadmap directions. A chip supplier may include specific features for unique customers in what may become a future standard chip design. Only trusted suppliers who currently supply significant volumes are provided with general information on future products.

A different type of roadmap sharing is done by a Japanese electronics company which isn't sure where needed technology developments are most likely to occur. In select cases, internal development groups will share early information about future technology roadmaps with just about any global supplier who will listen in an attempt to ensure that the required technology will eventually be available. For instance, in one commodity, the manager has established a technology map with performance curves and expected target dates. The target area (known as the "sweet spot") is shared with multiple suppliers. Suppliers are told that if they can't hit the "sweet spot" by the target date, they won't get the business. This concept is somewhat different to conventional early involvement wisdom. Because of the volatility of this industry, the company

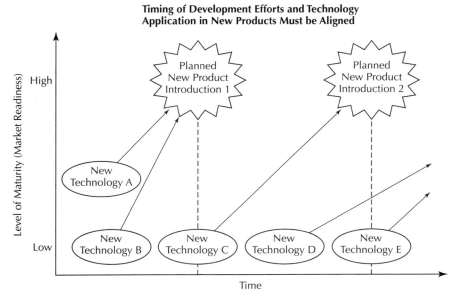

Figure 35.4. Managing product and technology development.

does not have the time or the need to form alliances and go through an early involvement program. Rather, the strategy is to make sure the technology is available by openly sharing technology roadmaps with any qualified supplier who will listen and moving the business around to take advantage of performance at the target price.

Assessing the Rate of Technological Change

Assuming that the buying company can establish that the supplier's technology roadmap is aligned with its own, another important factor to consider is the rate of change in product technology. The current rate of technological change is challenging many companies' capabilities, and they are seeking the help of suppliers with the development and application of critical but non-core technologies in their new products. For instance, the life cycle of some products such as computers is less than three months. One computer manufacturer in the U.S. mentioned that this is the single most important reason for integrating suppliers. Because of the need to quickly bring new products to market, this manufacturer actually skips the prototype stage and goes directly from development to full production.

Although supplier integration is a useful tool for managing the quick pace of technological change, it also represents a double-edged sword. If a particular technology is changing rapidly, then involving the supplier early has potential pitfalls. The buying company may become "locked into" a particular design or technology, release the product, and discover that the technology has now become obsolete or has been replaced by a technology with improved performance characteristics.

Across all of the companies, a large majority of the cases reported dealt with suppliers who were integrated into the development project starting in one of the first three stages of development (see Table 35.3).

Overall, there are two major factors that should be considered in deciding when to integrate the supplier into the product development process: the rate of change of the technology and the level of supplier expertise in the given technology. If the technology is undergoing a significant amount of technological change, it should be delayed in the product development cycle. Second, if a supplier's design expertise is significant and their technology experts can provide key insights

Table 35.3. Breakdown of Sample Integration Efforts by Stage at which Supplier Was First Integrated

Stage	Number (Percentage) of Responses
One: Idea generation	28 (23.1%)
Two: Preliminary business/technical assessment	27 (22.3%)
Three: Product/process/service concept development	45 (37.2%)
Four: Product/process/service development, engineering, design and/or creation	18 (14.9%)
Five: Prototype development build, test and pilot/ramp up for operations	3 (2.5%)

that are instrumental to crafting the new product, they should be included early on in the process (see Figure 35.5).

Our field studies suggest that certain types of suppliers are more likely to be integrated earlier. At a Japanese computer manufacturer, for instance, the extent of interaction that takes place between product development engineers and suppliers appears to depend on the volatility of the commodity technology. Suppliers of critical nonstandard commodities are involved much earlier in the product development initiative. These suppliers are involved in face-to-face discussions with engineers on a regular basis. On the other hand, suppliers of non-critical, standard items are not integrated until the final stages of the development cycle, and communication appears to occur more in the form of computerization (i.e., CAD is used with non-critical items such as PCBs, keyboards, and chassis). In general, face-to-face discussions are quicker and information can be exchanged more effectively. However, because suppliers are located within a day's travel to the operating divisions, co-location is often unnecessary.

At another U.S. electronics manufacturer, the level of involvement of the supplier may vary. To get a good quote, the supplier must be brought in early and sit in on the customer negotiation meeting. A supplier could be both an internal or an external party (i.e., fabricate both parts and processes.) The company typically relies on suppliers for their process technology, not their product technology (i.e., they are involved in

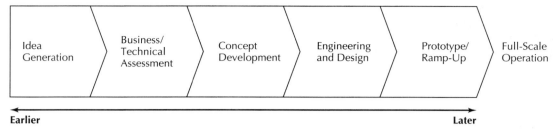

Figure 35.5. Integrate suppliers at different stages.

bringing in new processes that are not internal areas of expertise.) This was done because suppliers often understand the total design earlier and how they can influence the design. In this case, the functional specifications are defined and they work with the company to jointly ensure they are met.

One of the companies studied uses supplier-provided technologies extensively in its new products and has established an "Advanced Technology Group" that is charged with managing the development and adoption of new technologies for the company's products. The Advanced Technology Group monitors the supply market for new technologies and also takes a proactive role in developing technologies called for by the company's product line teams. This company has also implemented what it calls a "window of technology" process to help improve its access to new or developing technologies. The process provides a single point of contact in the company for a supplier who wants to propose a new technology or new product idea to the company. The supplier's idea gets a fair hearing, but the information is handled confidentially by the Advanced Technology Group, so the idea is protected. If the company is interested in the idea, it may commit to specific volume with the supplier or may work with the supplier to develop the technology further.

Another U.S. electronics company has an ongoing partnership with a supplier for development of new technologies that leverages the core competencies of each firm. Periodic meetings are held to discuss ideas for advanced technology development projects and to jointly select a set of future projects to pursue, based on such things as applications potential and resources required. The companies try to have a set number of projects underway at all times. At least one project is under way in each of three categories: "blue-sky" technologies, rapidly emerging technologies, and "maturing" technologies. As one project is completed—or terminated—the firms select a replacement from the queue.

In sharing roadmaps, it must be recognized that supplier involvement in new product development can have impacts, both positive and negative on technology risk/uncertainty:

Positive

- The supplier may have greater experience or expertise with the technology and, as a result, may have better information about where the technology can be successfully applied.

- Some (or all) of the technological risk may be taken on by the supplier.

- The buying firm may have some ability to influence the direction of the supplier's R&D efforts in order to match developing technologies with the buying firm's technology strategy.

- If a closer relationship between the buying company and the supplier develops as a result of supplier involvement, the supplier may be more willing to share information about its new/emerging technologies with the buying company.

Negative

- Involvement with a supplier may have a tendency to lock the buying company in to the supplier and its technologies. This makes initial selection of the supplier a more critical issue, as the buying company needs to anticipate whether the supplier will remain a technology leader.

- A supplier with "inside track" may not have as much incentive to innovate, slowing the pace of technological advancement. The buying company must find a way to make sure it is getting the supplier's best efforts.

One company has found that second tier raw material suppliers are often the technology leaders in its industry, rather than the first tier suppliers who process the raw material. Thus, the company is trying to get raw material suppliers involved in it development process. Often, to achieve this involvement, the company must make early commitment of its business. This is a risky proposition because some of the technologies are changing rapidly.

One U.S. company we studied uses a coding system to describe the maturity level of various technologies it is using or considering. Each is designated as a green, amber, or red dot technology:

- *Green dots*—well-known technologies that are internally developed and perfected
- *Amber dots*—not well known
- *Red dots*—brand new technology (high failure rates)

The company avoids using red dot technologies in new products, and tries to minimize the use of amber dot technologies.

CONCLUSIONS AND FUTURE PLANS FOR SUPPLIER INTEGRATION

The companies in our sample have a median of 6 years of experience integrating suppliers into new product development. They indicated that they expect to increase their use of supplier integration in the future and that they expect to involve suppliers *earlier* in the development process than they do now. Respondents were asked to characterize the success of the specific supplier integration effort as well as the success of the overall development project in which the supplier was involved. On average, the respondents considered both the supplier integration effort and the overall development project to have been fairly successful.

Results of the survey show that the responding companies achieved significant improvements in project results when suppliers participated, compared to similar new product development projects in which suppliers were *not* involved (see Table 35.4). These results reveal the potential benefits from involving suppliers in new product development efforts and demonstrate an important competitive advantage for companies that can manage this integration successfully.

Although this is not surprising, the results also indicated companies' level of satisfaction with their supplier integration efforts was quite varied. *Not all companies reported a high degree of satisfaction with the results of their supplier integration efforts.* Moreover, only 20 percent of the respondents agreed with the statement: "We are currently satisfied with the results of our supplier integration efforts." Over 45 percent disagreed with the above statement. Despite these mixed results, respondents are committed to supplier integration and their expectations for the future are that supplier integration will continue to be important. This

Table 35.4. Overall Performance Improvements Achieved Through Supplier Integration[a]

Performance Dimension	Median % Improvement	Range[b]
Purchased Material Cost ($n = 71$)[c]	15.0%	2.6%–50.0%
Purchased Material Quality ($n = 52$)	20.0%	2.0%–50.0%
Development Time ($n = 65$)	20.0%	5.0%–50.0%
Development Cost ($n = 54$)	15.0%	–1.0%–50.0%
Functionality/Features/Technology ($n = 53$)	10.0%	5.0%–50.0%
Product Manufacturing Cost ($n = 49$)	10.0%	0.0%–30.0%

a. Compared to similar projects in which a supplier was not integrated.

b. 80% of the companies' responses fall in this range—top and bottom 10% omitted.

c. Not all companies reported results on all dimensions.

is indicated by the fact that over 70 percent of respondents agreed with the statement: "Expectations about the results to be achieved from supplier integration with increase significantly." Together, these results seem to indicate that many companies realize the importance of supplier integration but have not yet discovered the means to successfully implement it. In some cases, they have not yet understood the root cause of "what went wrong" with their efforts.

This study clearly illustrates how a critical success factor in supplier integration projects is the level of knowledge regarding the supplier's capabilities. Not only must the project team understand the supplier's ability to meet cost, quality, and ramp-up goals, but they must also assess their technology roadmap, their level of design expertise, and the volatility of change within the particular technology being integrated. In this regard, the purchasing function will play an increasingly important role. We asked the respondents about their business unit's efforts to identify, develop, and maintain a "technologically capable" supply base for competitive advantage. By this we mean suppliers who have the technologies *currently needed* by the business unit for new products and who can be expected to have the emerging technologies that the business unit will need in the future. This is an area in which purchasing can play a major role. An indication of how important purchasing's knowledge of the supply base will be in the future is that 95.1 percent of the respondents said that developing and maintaining a technologically capable supply base is critically important to their business unit's competitive success. Only 43.9 percent of the respondents said that they currently have a more technologically capable supply base than their competitors.

The latter result is clearly a cause for concern. Clearly, organizations have not paid enough attention to technology trends and may be overlooking a significant element of supplier performance. In order to capture this information, purchasing managers will need to work closely with product development teams to create new supplier evaluation frameworks that go beyond the traditional dimensions of price, quality, delivery, and service.

As these strategies unfold, the role of purchasing managers will change dramatically. Purchasing managers must become dedicated "commodity experts" and develop specialized knowledge of product family

characteristics and trends. A greater focus will also be placed on relationship management and negotiation skills, particularly with regard to future technology development. Managers must have the ability to communicate effectively and will need to develop presentation and team leadership skills. Finally, managers will need to work more closely with design and technology experts in order to communicate to these parties the potential design contributions of leading-edge suppliers. Because of the complex nature of supplier integration strategies, a new breed of relationship manager will evolve, requiring a very different set of skills than in the past.

ACKNOWLEDGMENTS

This research was supported by the Global Procurement and Supply Chain Benchmarking Initiative in the Eli Broad Graduate School of Management at Michigan State University, and by the National Science Foundation under grant #SBR-9422407. A complete report on the results of this study can be found in the book *Product Development: Strategies for Supplier Integration,* by Monczka, Handfield, Ragatz, Scannell, and Frayer (Milwaukee, WI: American Society for Quality, 2000).

NOTES

1. B. Asanuma, "Manufacturer-Supplier Relationships in Japan and the Concept of Relation-Specific Skill," *Journal of the Japanese and International Economies,* 3 (1989): 1–30; J. H. Dyer, "Specialized Supplier Networks as a Source of Competitive Advantage: Evidence from the Auto Industry," *Strategic Management Journal,* 17/4 (April 1996): 271–292.

2. In the remainder of this article, the term "new product development" will refer to all efforts focused on creating either a new product, process, or service.

3. James Bennet, "Detroit Struggles to Learn Another Lesson from Japan," *The New York Times,* June 19, 1994, p. F5.

4. Rajan R. Kamath and Jeffrey K. Liker, "A Second Look at Japanese Product Development," *Harvard Business Review,* 72/6 (November/December 1994):155–170.

5. D. Littler, F. Leverick, and M. Bruce, "Factors Affecting the Process of Collaborative Product Development: A Study of UK Manufacturers of Information and

Communications Technology Products," *The Journal of Product Innovation Management,* 12/1 (January 1995): 16–23.

6. E. W. Larson and D. H. Gobeli, "Organizing for Development Projects," *Journal of Product Innovation Management,* 5/3 (September 1988): 180–190.

7. R. M. Monczka and R. J. Trent, *Purchasing and Sourcing Strategy: Trends and Implications* (Tempe, AZ: Center for Advanced Purchasing Studies, 1995).

8. P. G. Smith and D. G. Reinertsen, *Developing Products in Half the Time* (New York, NY: Van Nostrand, 1991).

9. J. L. Hartley, J. R. Meredith, D. McCutcheon, and R. R. Kamath, "Suppliers' Contributions to Product Development: An Exploratory Study," *IEEE Transactions on Engineering Management,* 44/3 (August 1997):258–267.

10. Kim B. Clark, "Project Scope and Project Performance: The Effect of Parts Strategy and Supplier Involvement on Product Development," *Management Science,* 35/10 (October 1989): 1247–1263.

11. Kim B. Clark and Takahiro Fujimoto, *Product Development Performance* (Boston, MA: Harvard University Press, 1991).

12. S. Helper, "Strategy and Irreversibility in Supplier Relations: The Case of the U.S. Automobile Industry," *Business History Review,* 65/4 (Winter 1991): 781–824; Asanuma, op. cit.; Dyer, op. cit.

13. J. K. Liker, R. R. Kamath, S. N. Wasti, and M. Nagamachi, "Supplier Involvement in Automotive Component Design: Are There Really Large U.S. Japan Differences?" *Research Policy,* 25/1 (January 1996): 59–89.

14. J. H. Dyer and W. G. Ouchi, "Japanese-Style Partnerships: Giving Companies a Competitive Edge," *Sloan Management Review,* 35/1 (Fall 1993): 51–63.

15. Rosabeth Moss Kanter, "Collaborative Advantage: The Art of Alliances," *Harvard Business Review,* 72/4 (July/August 1994): 96–108.

16. Bernard N. Slade, *Compressing the Product Development Cycle: From Research to Marketplace* (New York: NY: American Management Association, 1993).

17. G. Susman and J. Dean, *Development of a Model for Predicting Design for Manufacturability Effectiveness* (New York, NY: Oxford University Press, 1992).

18. M. B. Miles and A. M. Huberman, *Qualitative Data Analysis: A Sourcebook of New Methods* (Newbury Park, CA: Sage Publications, 1994).

19. Of the remaining 228 fax response forms that indicated they would not participate:

- 37 indicated that they do not participate in mail surveys
- 43 indicated that they do not integrate suppliers into new product/process/service development
- 24 indicated that they could not respond due to confidentiality issues
- 102 indicated that they lacked sufficient resources to complete the survey
- 22 indicated that they did not perceive any value-added in participating Given the nature of these responses, non-response bias does not appear to be a factor in the pooled sample of final responses we received. That is, the sample appears to be representative of companies who are actually implementing supplier integration strategies.

36

Creating New Ventures from Bell Labs Technologies

HENRY W. CHESBROUGH
STEPHEN J. SOCOLOF

OVERVIEW: Interest grows in the use of corporate venture capital as a way of unlocking the hidden potential of technologies which lie inside private central research labs and do not fit with established businesses. The experience of the New Ventures Group within Lucent Technologies illustrates both the challenges and the opportunities of using venture capital for these purposes. The challenge is to balance the forces of the venture capital model with those of an internal corporate development model. The New Ventures Group's experience to date suggests that balancing these forces is difficult but that there are rewards to the organization for doing so. These include the discovery of new sources of growth, the ability to leverage internal technology across multiple businesses, and the ability to stimulate cultural change within the organization.

Lucent Technologies began considering the use of corporate venture capital for three reasons. First, Lucent wanted to uncover new vehicles for increasing its growth. Second, it wanted to develop new mechanisms for leveraging its unparalleled technology base across multiple new business opportunities. Third, Lucent determined that it needed to increase the rate at which it commercialized its technologies, and it sought a cata-lyst to move technology out of the lab and into the market more rapidly.

The company began to investigate how it could accomplish these goals in the summer of 1996. It benefited from reviewing its own extensive experience with commercializing earlier technologies out of Bell Labs. It also conducted extensive external benchmarking activities to determine whether and how to utilize corporate money to finance new technology ventures. Some of this benchmarking activity involved discussion with other companies that had experience with this activity, including Intel, 3M, Raychem, Thermo-Electron, and Xerox. The planning staff also took the time for numerous discussions with the private venture capital community, including many of the leading VC partnerships, to understand how their approach to venture financing and commercializing new technologies worked. Sahlman provides an accessible overview of some of the key dimensions of the private venture capital model (*1*).

Lucent staff also reviewed the academic literature to learn about earlier attempts to utilize corporate venture structures to commercialize technology and foster the formation of new businesses. This corporate venturing literature illustrates the tension between strategic benefits to the corporation (which pulls a new venture group toward an internally focused, corporate development model) and maximizing the financial re-

Reprinted from *Research • Technology Management,* March–April 2000, Henry W. Chesbrough and Stephen J. Socolof, "Creating New Ventures from Bell Labs Technologies," pp. 13–17. Reprinted by permission of Industrial Research Institute, Inc.

turn from the new venture (which pulls the new venture group toward an externally focused, private venture capital model). We provide a brief review of this literature on the next page, while a more complete treatment can be found in (2).

Lucent concluded from its benchmarking activities that: (a) financing new technology ventures through corporate venture capital is hard; (b) there are more failures than successes; (c) some of the problems that firms encountered were due to structural problems; but (d) some of the problems were the result of how the programs were managed. Armed with this information, Lucent elected to proceed, and created the New Ventures Group (NVG) in 1997. We turn now to the structural problems facing the NVG, and shall then discuss how Lucent has chosen to manage its program.

CREATING THE PHANTOM WORLD

Lucent learned early that it needed to craft an operating model to blend the incentives, risk-taking, and speedy decision making of private venture capital with the deep technological resources and culture of Bell Laboratories. In trying to create this blend, it started with a culture that was steeped in technological capability, creativity and inventiveness. This culture had developed within a large and relatively stable business, and the key challenge for the NVG was to graft a more entrepreneurial spirit onto the culture of the organization. This required faster decisions, more individual risk taking, and greater individual identification with the business opportunities latent in the deep technical resources of the company.

To manage the cultural change process, the NVG consciously created what became known internally as "the phantom world." The phantom world did not exist outside of Lucent; it was a hybrid constructed out of a pure venture capital organization and a large technology-based company. It could be thought of as a "half-way house" that would enable people who were not ready or able to go outside for pure venture capital to develop their ideas further within Lucent.

By being sensitive to the cultural gaps that had to be bridged, and by being sensible about the right mix of risk and reward to offer, the phantom world created a launching pad for ideas to move out of Bell Labs into

markets outside of Lucent's traditional business channels. To date, Lucent NVG has deployed 12 ventures (8 external and 4 internal), and is investing over $80 million in capital per year. Most ventures have been in the Internet, networking, software, wireless, and digital broadcast spaces, which are of strategic interest to Lucent. While most investments have yet to achieve liquidity, those that have, have brought in an 80-percent return on invested capital.

CHOOSING THE STAFF

The people whom the NVG chose to launch new ventures proved vital. The NVG managers needed the founder of each venture to personally commit him or herself to the success of the venture, even as the NVG was making a financial commitment to the venture. This commitment included the founder's willingness to forego his or her annual bonus in return for shares in more risky "phantom stock" that would pay off only if the venture succeeded. Fringe benefits within the ventures were also usually less than those in Lucent overall, and founders needed to accept that as well. When some Lucent researchers realized the commitment involved, they chose to remain researchers. Others, though, were excited about the opportunity to become entrepreneurs and to carry their research out of the lab and into the market.

The phantom world also influences the type of person who can be brought in from outside to help launch new ventures from within Lucent. A pure entrepreneur with no experience operating within a larger company would likely be unable to function effectively in the phantom world. He or she might never have seen corporate overhead charges, annual operating plans, company-wide occupational safety and environmental regulations, or other corporate policy and personnel initiatives. The NVG has found that its most effective venture managers are those individuals who combine previous entrepreneurial experience with some years of experience working in large organizations. The Group now specifies this combination of experiences to its outside recruiters when it initiates a search for a new venture manager.

There is an opposing pull as well. Managers hired from outside of Lucent, and some internal Lucent researchers, seek a truly independent venture-capital-style arrangement. This involves substantial equity options, a commitment to achieving liquidity for that stock, and a desire to pursue financial success regardless of the cost or impact upon the parent company's business. An illustration of this is Xerox's XTV fund. XTV was structured to function as a "pure" venture capital fund in 1989, and it succeeded in earning attractive financial returns for Xerox. However, XTV pursued these returns without regard to its impact upon Xerox's culture as a whole, and the company decided to terminate the fund in 1996 (*3, 4*).

FINDING A MODEL

Lucent's culture is not yet ready for such a pure model. The NVG charter is to utilize its proprietary access to Bell Labs technology to aggressively invest in ventures that commercialize promising technologies from within Lucent. In fulfilling this charter, the NVG must work closely with Lucent's business groups, and, at times, prod those groups into acting faster. Over time, a more entrepreneurial culture is taking root with Lucent, and this is allowing the NVG to move more toward a venture capital model.

Lucent's Due Diligence on Earlier Corporate Venturing

Von Hippel conducted one of the first empirical examinations of new venture divisions (*5,6*). He found the most robust predictor of success was the extent to which the parent company had direct prior experience in the market for which the product from the new venture was intended. This was far more important then prior *technical* experience with the intended technology.

Fast found that new venture divisions (NVDs) were often viewed as threatening to established businesses in the parent firm, especially when they were successful financially (*7*). This threat arose from the ability of the new venture to compete for corporate resources (*8*). As the venture realized greater success, it required more resources and was better able to convince top management that it merited more resources.

Rind explored these conflicts further (*9*). If the new venture was serving a market already served by the parent firm, the parent might constrain the venture's marketing options to ensure that the new venture did not create conflict with the parent firm. Rind also identified the problem of the timing of the costs and benefits of managing new ventures. The costs required to manage a new venture successfully are incurred early in the venture's life under one NVD manager, while the benefits of those investments, if they were indeed realized, might arise later under another manager. This could create adverse incentives for new venture managers to avoid costly, risky decisions, because they would incur the costs of those decisions without necessarily receiving credit for their benefits in a later period.

Block and Ornati examined the compensation practices of firms when they established new venture divisions (*10*). They found that most of the companies using corporate venture programs do *not* compensate venture managers any differently from their other managers. In a telling remark, an unnamed CEO of a private venture capital firm admitted: "The only reason for our existence is the inability of corporations to provide the financial incentives which can be achieved in an independent startup" (p. 44).

An important book by Block and MacMillan reviewed the wealth of material on corporate venturing (*11*). They argued that, "On average, in terms of the percentage of successes and failures, [private] VCs probably do no better than corporations" (p. 27). They provide contextual advice on how to manage corporate ventures. Their view is that the question is not whether corporate venturing can be done successfully but that, "The real challenge involves *how* to do so" (p. 13).

—H. C. and S. S.

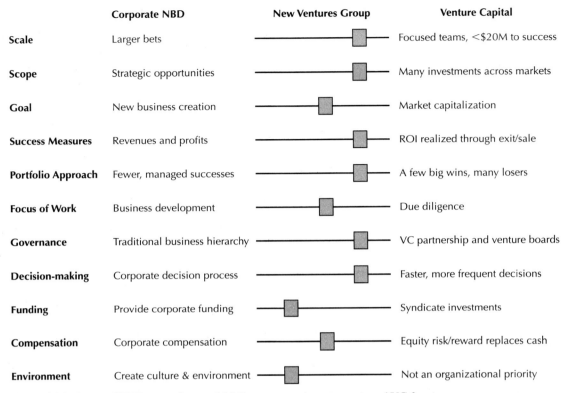

	Corporate NBD	New Ventures Group	Venture Capital
Scale	Larger bets		Focused teams, <$20M to success
Scope	Strategic opportunities		Many investments across markets
Goal	New business creation		Market capitalization
Success Measures	Revenues and profits		ROI realized through exit/sale
Portfolio Approach	Fewer, managed successes		A few big wins, many losers
Focus of Work	Business development		Due diligence
Governance	Traditional business hierarchy		VC partnership and venture boards
Decision-making	Corporate decision process		Faster, more frequent decisions
Funding	Provide corporate funding		Syndicate investments
Compensation	Corporate compensation		Equity risk/reward replaces cash
Environment	Create culture & environment		Not an organizational priority

Figure 36.1. Lucent NVG's operating model balances opposing corporate and VC forces.

As the NVG pursues its agenda, it must remain mindful of the Lucent culture and manage the balance of cultural forces. This balance is illustrated in Figure 36.1. The illustration shows a number of operating dimensions in which a pure internal business development model differs substantially from a pure venture capital model.

It is useful to describe the differences between each of the models in this illustration in order to understand how NVG attempts to accomplish its mission within the larger Lucent culture. The first dimension of the *Scale* of the investment shows that the corporate development model generally makes larger bets, while the venture model consciously limits the size of its individual investments. The *Scope* of investing also differs: The corporate model looks only for strategic opportunities, while the venture model seeks diversification by making investments in many, often

unrelated, spaces. The *Goal* of the corporate model is to create a new business, while the goal of the venture model is to achieve liquidity and financial return.

The *Funding* mechanisms also work differently; the corporate model supplies money on the annual budget cycle, and generally supplies all required funds, whereas the venture model provides funds in contingent stages, and usually brings in new investors at each stage to supply an objective external valuation of the company. *Success* is measured differently as well, with the corporate model looking at incremental annual revenue and profit while the venture model looks at its capitalized ROI at the time of exit. As a consequence, the corporate model yields fewer and larger investments and expects a high percentage of them to succeed, while the venture model expects the majority of its investments to fail, with the few winners returning enough money to earn high returns for the overall fund.

The internal operations of the models differ as well. The *Focus of Work* in the corporate model is one of business development, with extensive internal and external reviews conducted throughout the project. The venture capital approach is one of due diligence, with particular attention paid to the prior accomplishments of the people in the venture.

Governance differs, too, with the corporate model reporting into a hierarchical structure with multiple levels of oversight, review and potential reversals of policy. The venture model relies on the venture's board of directors—a single level of review, with no higher committee to reverse its decisions. Not surprisingly, decisions get made faster in the venture model.

Compensation also differs greatly between the models. The corporate model manages compensation in the context of the internal labor market, seeking equity across employees in "similar" positions of responsibility, while the venture model explicitly substitutes equity incentives for cash bonuses and makes no pretense of offering equity across other ventures or other companies.

Finally, the corporate model provides mechanisms to align its initiatives with the culture and environment of the company, while the venture model does not accord any importance to this dimension.

BALANCING THE OPPOSING FORCES

Figure 36.1 also shows where Lucent's New Ventures Group chose to place itself on these different dimensions when it began to make its investments. In some cases, the NVG attempted to emulate the venture model fairly closely, as shown when the square box is on the right-hand side of that dimension's scale. On the dimensions of *Scope* of investing, *Success Measures, Portfolio Approach, Governance,* and *Decision-making,* the NVG attempted to conduct its operations very much like a private venture firm. The average investment is small initially, and NVG attempted to make multiple investments to construct its initial portfolio. NVG also worked hard to insulate its ventures from having decisions reviewed, delayed and possibly overturned by executives in other parts of Lucent.

In other cases, the NVG chose to stay close to the corporate model, particularly on the *Environment* dimension. NVG is quite careful to fit in with the overall corporate culture, and makes many accommodations to be a "good citizen" within the Lucent community.

In still other cases, the NVG attempted to place itself between the models, such as with its goals, its funding mechanisms, and its compensation practices. NVG is consciously neither a business development program nor a venture capital program. Its funding, the compensation of its managers, and the incentives they receive, lie between those two approaches.

The NVG approach has evolved in the two years since it began operation. The Group has learned to invest more time and effort up-front in performing due diligence on prospective investments. To that end, its managers now specialize in specific investment areas, such as wireless communications and e-commerce, so that due diligence can be performed more rapidly. (The NVG consciously measures the time it takes to make decisions, and feels that it has reached a speed that is comparable to most venture firms.)

The NVG has also moved from seeking to supply all of the financing of its ventures to seeking to syndicate funding with outside venture firms. The composition of its boards has changed as a result, from knowledgeable technologists and consultants to partners of venture capital firms with a sizable financial stake in the venture. These outside board members add an important independent perspective, and often bring a network of useful contacts as well. Now that the venture model has gained credibility within Lucent, the NVG is shifting its focus away from many smaller investments to a few larger ones.

STRONGER CONNECTIONS

A final evolution has been to establish closer contacts with both lab researchers and managers within Bell Laboratories, and increasingly with business-unit managers within Lucent's ten business groups. These latter links have proven to be increasingly valuable to the NVG, both as a source of opportunities for new ventures as well as for learning about market trends and needs. These stronger connections with the external marketplace have sped up the NVG's due diligence process and improved its effectiveness in spotting important opportunities in a timely manner. They also increase the awareness of, and appreciation for, technical opportunities within Lucent's business groups. Ironically, NVG's early interest in technologies has caused some technologies to move directly into the business groups that might otherwise have been overlooked. This is one contribution NVG makes to Lucent that is not formally measured.

These closer contacts will probably continue, in part because certain ventures in the NVG portfolio may become strategic to the businesses within Lucent. In these instances, the NVG's return may be realized by a re-acquisition of the venture by a Lucent business. One Lucent NVG company, Elemedia, was re-acquired by Lucent in the summer of 1999. The price for this acquisition was set in part by the willingness of an outside company to acquire the venture. This acquisition provided another opportunity for the NVG to directly support the growth of Lucent's business— one of the three goals that led to the creation of the NVG. However, even as these linkages grow and deepen, the NVG will have to guard against being pulled back into the corporate business development model.

The challenge for the NVG's managers is to continue to monitor and manage the tension between these opposing corporate development and venture capital forces. If it can continue to do so, it promises to continue to engender greater entrepreneurship within Lucent and to expand its range of business models for technology commercialization of Bell Labs research.

REFERENCES

1. Sahlman, William. "The Structure and Governance of Venture Capital Organizations." *Journal of Financial Economics,* October 1990, pp. 473–524.
2. Chesbrough, Henry W. "Corporate Venturing in the Shadow of Private Venture Capital: A Review of the Academic Literature." Working Paper, Harvard Business School, 1999.
3. Lerner, Josh. "Xerox Technology Ventures: March 1995." Harvard Business School Case 9-295-127 (with Brian Hunt), 1995.
4. Lerner, Josh. "Xerox Technology Ventures: January 1997." Harvard Business School Case 9-298-109, 1997.
5. Von Hippel, Eric. "An Exploratory Study of Corporate Venturing—A New Product Innovation Strategy Used by Some Major Corporations," unpublished dissertation, Carnegie Mellon University, 1973.
6. Von Hippel, Eric. "Successful and Failing Internal Corporate Ventures: An Empirical Analysis." Industrial Marketing Management 6, pp. 163–174, 1977.
7. Fast, Norman. "The Rise and Fall of Corporate New Venture Divisions." UMI Research Press: Ann Arbor, MI, 1978.
8. Bower, Joseph. "Managing the Resource Allocation Process." Division of Research, Harvard Business School, 1970.
9. Rind, Kenneth. "The Role of Venture Capital in Corporate Development." *Strategic Management Journal* 2, pp. 169–180, 1981.
10. Block, Zenas, and Ornati, Oscar. "Compensating Corporate Venture Managers." *Journal of Business Venturing* 2, pp. 41–51, 1987.
11. Block, Zenas, and Macmillan, Ian. *Corporate Venturing: Creating New Businesses Within the Firm.* Harvard Business School Press, Cambridge, MA, 1993.

EXECUTIVE LEADERSHIP AND MANAGING INNOVATION AND CHANGE

Innovation is always disruptive. Innovation always challenges the firm's current organizational architecture and is often at odds with a firm's history. We close this book with a set of articles that focus on the fundamental nature of organizational changes associated with leading innovation streams, the role of leaders and their teams in executing organizational changes, and several examples of leadership, innovation, and managing change in very different industries. There is a debate on the nature of change associated with innovation and organizational evolution. Tushman, Newman, and Romanelli present a view that is anchored on punctuated or discontinuous change as necessary for organizations to evolve through innovation streams. In contrast, Eisenhardt and Brown present a view of organizational change that is rooted in rhythmic, paced, incremental change. Quite apart from the magnitude of the change effort, Nadler and Tushman present a well-tested set of ideas on managing organizational change, as well as a set of ideas on the benefits and costs of charismatic leadership. Finally, we close with two articles that bring together all the themes of *Managing Strategic Innovation and Change*. Burgelman discusses innovation streams at Intel and the role of senior leadership and organizational architectures in driving both induced and autonomous innovation. In contrast, Siggelkow's in-depth analysis of Liz Claiborne demonstrates the difficulties of sustained innovation as an industry evolves. The rise, fall, and renaissance of Liz Claiborne graphically illustrates how often successful organizations get trapped in their old ways of innovating and how powerful executive succession can be in driving innovation streams.

37

Convergence and Upheaval

Managing the Unsteady Pace of Organizational Evolution

MICHAEL L. TUSHMAN
WILLIAM H. NEWMAN
ELAINE ROMANELLI

A snug fit of external opportunity, company strategy, and internal structure is a hallmark of successful companies. The real test of executive leadership, however, is in maintaining this alignment in the face of changing competitive conditions.

Consider the Polaroid or Caterpillar corporations. Both firms virtually dominated their respective industries for decades, only to be caught off guard by major environmental changes. The same strategic and organizational factors which were so effective for decades became the seeds of complacency and organization decline.

Recent studies of companies over long periods show that the most successful firms maintain a workable equilibrium for several years (or decades), but are also able to initiate and carry out sharp, widespread changes (referred to here as reorientations) when their environments shift. Such upheaval may bring renewed vigor to the enterprise. Less successful firms, on the other hand, get stuck in a particular pattern. The leaders of these firms either do not see the need for reorientation or they are unable to carry through the necessary frame-breaking changes. While not all reorientations succeed, those organizations which do not initiate reorientations as environments shift underperform.

This article focuses on reasons why for long periods most companies make only incremental changes, and why they then need to make painful discontinuous, system-wide shifts. We are particularly concerned with the role of executive leadership in managing this pattern of convergence punctuated by upheaval.

Here are four examples of the convergence/upheaval pattern:

Founded in 1915 by a set of engineers from MIT the General Radio Company was established to produce highly innovative and high-quality (but expensive) electronic test equipment. Over the years, General Radio developed a consistent organization to accomplish its mission. It hired only the brightest young engineers, built a loose functional organization dominated by the engineering department, and developed a "General Radio culture" (for example, no conflict, management by consensus, slow growth). General Radio's strategy and associated structures, systems, and people were very successful. By World War II, General Radio was the largest test-equipment firm in the United States.

After World War II, however, increasing technology and cost-based competition began to erode General Radio's market share. While management made numerous incremental changes, General Ra-

Copyright © 1986 by The Regents of the University of California. Reprinted from the *California Management Review*, Vol. 29, No. 1. By permission of The Regents.

dio remained fundamentally the same organization. In the late 1960s, when CEO Don Sinclair initiated strategic changes, he left the firm's structure and systems intact. This effort at doing new things with established systems and procedures was less than successful. By 1972, the firm incurred its first loss.

In the face of this sustained performance decline, Bill Thurston (a long-time General Radio executive) was made President. Thurston initiated system-wide changes. General Radio adopted a more marketing-oriented strategy. Its product line was cut from 20 different lines to 3; much more emphasis was given to product-line management, sales, and marketing. Resources were diverted from engineering to revitalize sales, marketing, and production. During 1973, the firm moved to a matrix structure, increased its emphasis on controls and systems, and went outside for a set of executives to help Thurston run this revised General Radio. To perhaps more formally symbolize these changes and the sharp move away from the "old" General Radio, the firm's name was changed to GenRad. By 1984, GenRad's sales exploded to over $200 million (vs. $44 million in 1972).

After 60 years of convergent change around a constant strategy, Thurston and his colleagues (many new to the firm) made discontinuous system-wide changes in strategy, structure, people, and processes. While traumatic, these changes were implemented over a two-year period and led to a dramatic turnaround in GenRad's performance.

Prime Computer was founded in 1971 by a group of individuals who left Honeywell. Prime's initial strategy was to produce a high-quality/high-price minicomputer based on semiconductor memory. These founders built an engineering-dominated, loosely structured firm which sold to OEMs and through distributors. This configuration of strategy, structure, people, and processes was very successful. By 1974, Prime turned its first profit; by 1975, its sales were more than $11 million.

In the midst of this success, Prime's board of directors brought in Ken Fisher to reorient the organization. Fisher and a whole new group of executives hired from Honeywell initiated a set of discontinuous changes throughout Prime during 1975–1976. Prime now sold a full range of mini-

computers and computer systems to OEMs and end-users. To accomplish this shift in strategy, Prime adopted a more complex functional structure, with a marked increase in resources to sales and marketing. The shift in resources away from engineering was so great that Bill Poduska, Prime's head of engineering, left to form Apollo Computer. Between 1975–1981, Fisher and his colleagues consolidated and incrementally adapted structure, systems, and processes to better accomplish the new strategy. During this convergent period, Prime grew dramatically to over $260 million by 1981.

In 1981, again in the midst of this continuing sequence of increased volume and profits, Prime's board again initiated an upheaval. Fisher and his direct reports left Prime (some of whom founded Encore Computer), while Joe Henson and a set of executives from IBM initiated wholesale changes throughout the organization. The firm diversified into robotics, CAD/CAM, and office systems; adopted a divisional structure; developed a more market-driven orientation; and increased controls and systems. It remains to be seen how this "new" Prime will fare. Prime must be seen, then, not as a 14-year-old firm, but as three very different organizations, each of which was managed by a different set of executives. Unlike General Radio, Prime initiated these discontinuities during periods of great success.

The Operating Group at Citibank prior to 1970 had been a service-oriented function for the end-user areas of the bank. The Operating Group hired high school graduates who remained in the "back-office" for their entire careers. Structure, controls, and systems were loose, while the informal organization valued service, responsiveness to client needs, and slow, steady work habits. While these patterns were successful enough, increased demand and heightened customer expectations led to ever decreasing performance during the late 1960s.

In the face of severe performance decline, John Reed was promoted to head the Operating Group. Reed recruited several executives with production backgrounds, and with this new top team he initiated system-wide changes. Reed's vision was to transform the Operating Group from a *service*-oriented back office to a *factory* producing high-quality products. Consistent with this new mission, Reed and his colleagues initiated sweeping changes in strategy, structure, work flows, controls, and culture. These changes were initiated concurrently throughout the back office, with very little participation, over the course of a few months. While all the empirical performance measures improved substantially, these changes also generated substantial stress and anxiety within Reed's group.

For 20 years, Alpha Corporation was among the leaders in the industrial fastener industry. Its reliability, low cost, and good technical service were important strengths. However, as Alpha's segment of the industry matured, its profits declined. Belt-tightening helped but was not enough. Finally, a new CEO presided over a sweeping restructuring: cutting the product line, closing a plant, trimming overhead; then focusing on computer parts which call for very close tolerances, CAD/CAM tooling, and cooperation with customers on design efforts. After four rough years, Alpha appears to have found a new niche where convergence will again be warranted.

These four short examples illustrate periods of incremental change, or convergence, punctuated by discontinuous changes throughout the organization. Discontinuous or "frame-breaking" change involves simultaneous and sharp shifts in strategy, power, structure, and controls. Each example illustrates the role of executive leadership in initiating and implementing discontinuous change. Where General Radio, Citibank's Operating Group, and Alpha initiated system-wide changes only after sustained performance decline, Prime proactively initiated system-wide changes to take advantage of competitive/technological conditions. These patterns in organization evolution are not unique. Upheaval, sooner or later, follows convergence if a company is to survive; only a farsighted minority of firms initiate upheaval prior to incurring performance declines.

The task of managing incremental change, or convergence, differs sharply from managing frame-breaking change. Incremental change is compatible with the existing structure of a company and is reinforced over a period of years. In contrast, frame-breaking change is abrupt, painful to participants, and often resisted by the old guard. Forging these new strategy-structure-people-process consistencies and

laying the basis for the next period of incremental change calls for distinctive skills.

Because the future health, and even survival, of a company or business unit is at stake, we need to take a closer look at the nature and consequences of convergent change and of differences imposed by frame-breaking change. We need to explore when and why these painful and risky revolutions interrupt previously successful patterns, and whether these discontinuities can be avoided and/or initiated prior to crisis. Finally, we need to examine what managers can and should do to guide their organizations through periods of convergence and upheaval over time.

THE RESEARCH BASE

The research which sparks this article is based on the abundant company histories and case studies. The more complete case studies have tracked individual firms' evolution and various crises in great detail (e.g., Chandler's seminal study of strategy and structure at DuPont, General Motors, Standard Oil, and Sears[1]). More recent studies have dealt systematically with whole sets of companies and trace their experience over long periods of time.

A series of studies by researchers at McGill University covered over 40 well-known firms in diverse industries for at least 20 years per firm (e.g., Miller and Friesen[2]). Another research program conducted by researchers at Columbia, Duke, and Cornell Universities is tracking the history of large samples of companies in the minicomputer, cement, airlines, and glass industries. This research program builds on earlier work (e.g., Greiner[3]) and finds that most successful firms evolve through long periods of convergence punctuated by frame-breaking change.

The following discussion is based on the history of companies in many different industries, different countries, both large and small organizations, and organizations in various stages of their product class's life-cycle. We are dealing with a widespread phenomenon—not just a few dramatic sequences. Our research strongly suggests that the convergence/upheaval pattern occurs within departments (e.g., Citibank's Operating Group), at the business-unit level (e.g., Prime or General Radio), and at the corporate level of analysis (e.g., the Singer, Chrysler, or Harris Corporations).

The problem of managing both convergent periods and upheaval is not just for the CEO, but necessarily involves general managers as well as functional managers.

PATTERNS IN ORGANIZATIONAL EVOLUTION: CONVERGENCE AND UPHEAVAL

Building on Strength: Periods of Convergence

Successful companies wisely stick to what works well. At General Radio between 1915 and 1950, the loose functional structure, committee management system, internal promotion practices, control with engineering, and the high-quality,premium-price, engineering mentality all worked together to provide a highly congruent system. These internally consistent patterns in strategy, structure, people, and processes served General Radio for over 35 years.

Similarly, the Alpha Corporation's customer driven, low-cost strategy was accomplished by strength in engineering and production and ever more detailed structures and systems which evaluated cost, quality, and new product development. These strengths were epitomized in Alpha's chief engineer and president. The chief engineer had a remarkable talent for helping customers find new uses for industrial fasteners. He relished solving such problems, while at the same time designing fasteners that could be easily manufactured, The president excelled at production—producing dependable, low-cost fasteners. The pair were role models which set a pattern which served Alpha well for 15 years.

As the company grew, the chief engineer hired kindred customer-oriented application engineers. With the help of innovative users, they developed new products, leaving more routine problem-solving and incremental change to the sales and production departments. The president relied on a hands-on manufacturing manager and delegated financial matters to a competent treasurer-controller. Note how well the organization reinforced Alpha's strategy and how the key people fit the organization. There was an excellent fit between strategy and structure. The informal structure also fit well—communications were open, the simple mission of the company was widely endorsed, and routines were well understood.

As the General Radio and Alpha examples suggest, convergence starts out with an effective dovetailing of strategy, structure, people, and processes. For other strategies or in other industries, the particular formal and informal systems might be very different, but still a winning combination. The formal system includes decisions about grouping and linking resources as well as planning and control systems, rewards and evaluation procedures, and human resource management systems. The informal system includes core values, beliefs, norms, communication patterns, and actual decision-making and conflict resolution patterns. It is the whole fabric of structure, systems, people, and processes which must be suited to company strategy.[4]

As the fit between strategy, structure, people, and processes is never perfect, convergence is an ongoing process characterized by incremental change. Over time, in all companies studied, two types of converging changes were common: fine-tuning and incremental adaptations.

CONVERGING CHANGE: FINE-TUNING

Even with good strategy-structure-process fits, well-run companies seek even better ways of exploiting (and defending) their missions. Such effort typically deals with one or more of the following:

- *Refining* policies, methods, and procedures.
- Creating *specialized units and linking mechanisms* to permit increased volume and increased attention to unit quality and cost.
- *Developing personnel* especially suited to the present strategy—through improved selection and training, and tailoring reward systems to match strategic thrusts.
- Fostering individual and group *commitments* to the company mission and to the excellence of one's own department.
- Promoting *confidence* in the accepted norms, beliefs, and myths.
- *Clarifying* established roles, power, status, dependencies, and allocation mechanism.

The fine-tuning fills out and elaborates the consistencies between strategy, structure, people, and processes. These incremental changes lead to an ever more interconnected (and therefore more stable) social system. Convergent periods fit the happy, stick-with-a-winner situations romanticized by Peters and Waterman.[5]

CONVERGING CHANGE: INCREMENTAL ADJUSTMENTS TO ENVIRONMENTAL SHIFTS

In addition to fine-tuning changes, minor shifts in the environment will call for some organizational response. Even the most conservative of organizations expect, even welcome, small changes which do not make too many waves.

A popular expression is that almost any organization can tolerate a "ten-percent change." At any one time, only a few changes are being made; but these changes are still compatible with the prevailing structures, systems, and processes. Examples of such adjustments are an expansion in sales territory, a shift in emphasis among products in the product line, or improved processing technology in production.

The usual process of making changes of this sort is well known: wide acceptance of the need for change, openness to possible alternatives, objective examination of the pros and cons of each plausible alternative, participation of those directly affected in the preceding analysis, a market test or pilot operation where feasible, time to learn the new activities, established role models, known rewards for positive success, evaluation, and refinement.

The role of executive leadership during convergent periods is to reemphasize mission and core values and to delegate incremental decisions to middle-level managers. Note that the uncertainty created for people affected by such changes is well within tolerable limits. Opportunity is provided to anticipate and learn what is new, while most features of the structure remain unchanged.

The overall system adapts, but it is not transformed.

CONVERGING CHANGE: SOME CONSEQUENCES

For those companies whose strategies fit environmental conditions, convergence brings about better and better effectiveness. Incremental change is relatively easy to implement and ever more optimizes the consistencies between strategy, structure, people, and processes. At AT&T, for example, the period between 1913 and 1980 was one of ever more incremental change to further bolster the "Ma Bell" culture, sys-

tems, and structure all in service of developing the telephone network.

Convergent periods are, however, a double-edged sword. As organizations grow and become more successful, they develop internal forces for stability. Organization structures and systems become so interlinked that they only allow compatible changes. Further, over time, employees develop habits, patterned behaviors begin to take on values (e.g., "service is good"), and employees develop a sense of competence in knowing how to get work done within the system. These self-reinforcing patterns of behavior, norms, and values contribute to increased organizational momentum and complacency and, over time, to a sense of organizational history. This organizational history—epitomized by common stories, heroes, and standards—specifies "how we work here" and "what we hold important here."

This organizational momentum is profoundly functional as long as the organization's strategy is appropriate. The Ma Bell and General Radio culture, structure, and systems—and associated internal momentum—were critical to each organization's success. However, if (and when) strategy must change, this momentum cuts the other way. Organizational history is a source of tradition, precedent, and pride which are, in turn, anchors to the past. A proud history often restricts vigilant problem solving and may be a source of resistance to change.

When faced with environmental threat, organizations with strong momentum

- may not register the threat due to organization complacency and/or stunted external vigilance (e.g., the automobile or steel industries), or

- if the threat is recognized, the response is frequently heightened conformity to the status quo and/or increased commitment to "what we do best."

For example, the response of dominant firms to technological threat is frequently increased commitment to the obsolete technology (e.g., telegraph/telephone; vacuum tube/transistor; core/semiconductor memory). A paradoxical result of long periods of success may be heightened organizational complacency, decreased organizational flexibility, and a stunted ability to learn.

Converging change is a double-edged sword. Those very social and technical consistencies which are key sources of success may also be the seeds of failure if environments change. The longer the convergent period, the greater these internal forces for stability. This momentum seems to be particularly accentuated in those most successful firms in a product class (for example, Polaroid, Caterpillar, or U.S. Steel), in historically regulated organizations (for example, AT&T, GTE, or financial service firms), or in organizations that have been traditionally shielded from competition (for example, universities, not-for-profit organizations, government agencies and/or services).

On Frame-Breaking Change

FORCES LEADING TO FRAME-BREAKING CHANGE

What, then, leads to frame-breaking change? Why defy tradition? Simply stated, frame-breaking change occurs in response to or, better yet, in anticipation of major environmental changes—changes which require more than incremental adjustments. The need for discontinuous change springs from one or a combination of the following:

- *Industry Discontinuities*—Sharp changes in legal, political, or technological conditions shift the basis of competition within industries. *Deregulation* has dramatically transformed the financial services and airlines industries. *Substitute product technologies* (such as jet engines, electronic typing, microprocessors) or *substitute process technologies* (such as the planar process in semiconductors or float-glass in glass manufacture) may transform the bases of competition within industries. Similarly, the emergence of industry standards, or *dominant designs* (such as the DC-3, IBM 360, or PDP-8) signal a shift in competition away from product innovation and toward increased process innovation. Finally, *major economic changes* (e.g., oil crises) and *legal shifts* (e.g., patent protection in biotechnology or trade/regulator barriers in pharmaceuticals or cigarettes) also directly affect bases of competition.

- *Product-Life-Cycle Shifts*—Over the course of a product class life-cycle, different strategies are appropriate. In the emergence phase of a product class, competition is based on product innovation and performance, where in the maturity stage, competition centers on cost, volume, and efficiency. Shifts in patterns of demand alter key factors for success. For ex-

ample, the demand and nature of competition for minicomputers, cellular telephones, wide-body aircraft, and bowling alley equipment was transformed as these products gained acceptance and their product classes evolved. Powerful international competition may compound these forces.

- *Internal Company Dynamics*—Entwined with these external forces are breaking points within the firm. Sheer size may require a basically new management design. For example, few inventorentrepreneurs can tolerate the formality that is linked with large volume; even Digital Equipment Company apparently has outgrown the informality so cherished by Kenneth Olsen. Key people die. Family investors may become more concerned with their inheritance taxes than with company development. Revised corporate portfolio strategy may sharply alter the role and resources assigned to business units or functional areas. Such pressures especially when coupled with external changes, may trigger frame-breaking change.

SCOPE OF FRAME-BREAKING CHANGE

Frame-breaking change is driven by shifts in business strategy. As strategy shifts so too must structure, people, and organizational processes. Quite unlike convergent change, frame-breaking reforms involve discontinuous changes throughout the organization. These bursts of change do not reinforce the existing system and are implemented rapidly. For example, the system-wide changes at Prime and General Radio were implemented over 18–24-month periods, where as changes in Citibank's Operating Group were implemented in less than five months. Frame-breaking changes are revolutionary changes *of* the system as opposed to incremental changes *in* the system.

The following features are usually involved in frame-breaking change:

- *Reformed Mission and Core Values*—A strategy shift involves a new definition of company mission. Entering or withdrawing from an industry may be involved; a least the way the company expects to be outstanding is altered. The revamped AT&T is a conspicuous example. Success on its new course calls for a strategy based on competition, aggressiveness, and responsiveness, as well as a revised set of core values about how the firm competes and what it holds as important. Similarly, the initial shift at Prime reflected a strategic shift away from technology and towards sales and marketing. Core values also were aggressively reshaped by Ken Fisher to complement Prime's new strategy.

- *Altered Power and Status*—Frame-breaking change always alters the distribution of power. Some groups lose in the shift while others gain. For example, at Prime and General Radio, the engineering functions lost power, resources, and prestige as the marketing and sales functions gained. These dramatically altered power distributions reflect shifts in bases of competition and resource allocation. A new strategy must be backed up with a shift in the balance of power and status.

- *Reorganization*—A new strategy requires a modification in structure, systems, and procedures. As strategic requirements shift, so too must the choice of organization form. A new direction calls for added activity in some areas and less in others. Changes in structure and systems are means to ensure that this reallocation of effort takes place. New structures and revised roles deliberately break business-as-usual behavior.

- *Revised Interaction Patterns*—The way people in the organization work together has to adapt during frame-breaking change. As strategy is different, new procedures, work flows, communication networks, and decision-making patterns must be established. With these changes in work flows and procedures must also come revised norms, informal decision-making/conflict-resolution procedures, and informal roles.

- *New Executives*—Frame-breaking change also involves new executives, usually brought in from outside the organization (or business unit) and placed in key managerial positions. Commitment to the new mission, energy to overcome prevailing inertia, and freedom from prior obligations are all needed to refocus the organization. A few exceptional members of the old guard may attempt to make this shift, but habits and expectations of their associations are difficult to break. New executives are most likely to provide both the necessary drive and an enhanced set of skills more appropriate for the new strategy. While the overall number of executive changes is usually

relatively small, these new executives have substantial symbolic and substantive effects on the organization. For example, frame-breaking changes at Prime, General Radio, Citibank, and Alpha Corporation were all spearheaded by a relatively small set of new executives from outside the company or group.

WHY ALL AT ONCE?

Frame-breaking change is revolutionary in that the shifts reshape the entire nature of the organization. Those more effective examples of frame-breaking change were implemented rapidly (e.g., Citibank, Prime, Alpha). It appears that a piecemeal approach to frame-breaking changes gets bogged down in politics, individual resistance to change, and organizational inertia (e.g., Sinclair's attempts to reshape General Radio). Frame-breaking change requires discontinuous shifts in strategy, structure, people, and processes concurrently—or at least in a short period of time. Reasons for rapid, simultaneous implementation include:

- *Synergy* within the new structure can be a powerful aid. New executives with a fresh mission, working in a redesigned organization with revised norms and values, backed up with power and status, provide strong reinforcement. The pieces of the revitalized organization pull together, as opposed to piecemeal change where one part of the new organization is out of synch with the old organization.

- *Pockets of resistance* have a chance to grow and develop when frame-breaking change is implemented slowly. The new mission, shifts in organization, and other frame-breaking changes upset the comfortable routines and precedent. Resistance to such fundamental change is natural. If frame-breaking change is implemented slowly, then individuals have a greater opportunity to undermine the changes and organizational inertia works to further stifle fundamental change.

- Typically, there is a *pent-up need for change*. During convergent periods, basic adjustments are postponed. Boat-rocking is discouraged. Once constraints are relaxed, a variety of desirable improvements press for attention. The exhilaration and momentum of a fresh effort (and new team) make difficult moves more acceptable. Change is in fashion.

- Frame-breaking change is an inherently *risky and*

uncertain venture. The longer the implementation period, the greater the period of uncertainty and instability. The most effective frame-breaking changes initiate the new strategy, structure, processes, and systems rapidly and begin the next period of stability and convergent change. The sooner fundamental uncertainty is removed, the better the chances of organizational survival and growth. While the pacing of change is important, the overall time to implement frame-breaking change will be contingent on the size and age of the organization.

PATTERNS IN ORGANIZATION EVOLUTION

This historical approach to organization evolution focuses on convergent periods punctuated by reorientation—discontinuous, organization-wide upheavals. The most effective firms take advantage of relatively long convergent periods. These periods of incremental change build on and take advantage of organization inertia. Frame-breaking change is quite dysfunctional if the organization is successful and the environment is stable. If, however, the organization is performing poorly and/or if the environment changes substantially, frame-breaking change is the only way to realign the organization with its competitive environment. Not all reorientations will be successful (e.g., People Express's expansion and up-scale moves in 1985–86). However, inaction in the face of performance crisis and/or environmental shifts is a certain recipe for failure.

Because reorientations are so disruptive and fraught with uncertainty, the more rapidly they are implemented, the more quickly the organization can reap the benefits of the following convergent period. High-performing firms initiate reorientations when environmental conditions shift and implement these reorientations rapidly (e.g., Prime and Citibank). Low-performing organizations either do not reorient or reorient all the time as they root around to find an effective alignment with environmental conditions.

This metamorphic approach to organization evolution underscores the role of history and precedent as future convergent periods are all constrained and shaped by prior convergent periods. Further, this approach to organization evolution highlights the role of executive leadership in managing convergent periods *and* in initiating and implementing frame-breaking change.

EXECUTIVE LEADERSHIP AND ORGANIZATION EVOLUTION

Executive leadership plays a key role in reinforcing system-wide momentum during convergent periods and in initiating and implementing bursts of change that characterize strategic reorientations: The nature of the leadership task differs sharply during these contrasting periods of organization evolution.

During convergent periods, the executive team focuses on *maintaining* congruence and fit within the organization. Because strategy, structure, processes, and systems are fundamentally sound, the myriad of incremental substantive decisions can be delegated to middle-level management, where direct expertise and information resides. The key role for executive leadership during convergent periods is to reemphasize strategy, mission, and core values and to keep a vigilant eye on external opportunities and/or threats.

Frame-breaking change, however, requires direct executive involvement in all aspects of the change. Given the enormity of the change and inherent internal forces for stability, executive leadership must be involved in the specification of strategy, structure, people, and organizational processes *and* in the development of implementation plans. During frame-breaking change, executive leadership is directly involved in *reorienting* their organizations. Direct personal involvement of senior management seems to be critical to implement these system-wide changes (e.g., Reed at Citibank or Iacocca at Chrysler). Tentative change does not seem to be effective (e.g., Don Sinclair at General Radio).

Frame-breaking change triggers resistance to change from multiple sources change must overcome several generic hurdles, including:

- Individual opposition, rooted in either anxiety or personal commitment to the status quo, is likely to generate substantial individual resistance to change.

- Political coalitions opposing the upheaval may be quickly formed within the organization. During converging periods a political equilibrium is reached. Frame-breaking upsets this equilibrium; powerful individuals and/or groups who see their status threatened will join in resistance.

- Control is difficult during the transition. The systems, roles, and responsibilities of the former organization are in suspension; the new rules of the game—and the rewards—have not yet been clarified.

- External constituents—suppliers, customers, regulatory agencies, local communities, and the like—often prefer continuation of existing relationships rather than uncertain moves in the future.

Whereas convergent change can be delegated, frame-breaking change requires strong, direct leadership from the top as to where the organization is going and how it is to get there. Executive leadership must be directly involved in: motivating constructive behavior, shaping political dynamics, managing control during the transition period, and managing external constituencies. The executive team must direct the content of frame-breaking change *and* provide the energy, vision, and resources to support, and be role models for, the new order. Brilliant ideas for new strategies, structures, and processes will not be effective unless they are coupled with thorough implementation plans actively managed by the executive team.[6]

When to Launch an Upheaval

The most effective executives in our studies foresaw the need for major change. They recognized the external threats and opportunities, and took bold steps to deal with them. For example, a set of minicomputer companies (Prime, Rolm, Datapoint, Data General, among others) risked short-run success to take advantage of new opportunities created by technological and market changes. Indeed, by acting before being forced to do so, they had more time to plan their transitions.[7]

Such visionary executive teams are the exceptions. Most frame-breaking change is postponed until a financial crisis forces drastic action. The momentum, and frequently the success, of convergent periods breeds reluctance to change. This commitment to the status quo, and insensitivity to environmental shocks, is evident in both the Columbia and the McGill studies. It is not until financial crisis shouts its warning that most companies begin their transformation.

The difference in timing between pioneers and reluctant reactors is largely determined by executive leadership. The pioneering moves, in advance of crisis, are usually initiated by executives within the company. They are the exceptional persons who combine the vision, courage, and power to transform an organization. In contrast, the impetus for a tardy break usually comes from outside stakeholders; they eventually put strong pressure on existing executives—or bring in new executives—to make fundamental shifts.

Who Manages the Transformation

Directing a frame-breaking upheaval successfully calls for unusual talent and energy. The new mission must be defined, technology selected, resources acquired, policies revised, values changed, organization restructured, people reassured, inspiration provided, and an array of informal relationships shaped. Executives already on the spot will probably know most about the specific situation, but they may lack the talent, energy, and commitment to carry through an internal revolution.

As seen in the Citibank, Prime, and Alpha examples, most frame-breaking upheavals are managed by executives brought in from outside the company. The Columbia research program finds that externally recruited executives are more than three times more likely to initiate frame-breaking change than existing executive teams. Frame-breaking change was coupled with CEO succession in more than 80 percent of the cases. Further, when frame-breaking change was combined with executive succession, company performance was significantly higher than when former executives stayed in place. In only 6 of 40 cases we studied did a current CEO initiate and implement multiple frame-breaking changes. In each of these six cases, the existing CEO made major changes in his/her direct reports, and this revitalized top team initiated and implemented frame-breaking changes (e.g., Thurston's actions at General Radio).[8]

Executive succession seems to be a powerful tool in managing frame-breaking change. There are several reasons why a fresh set of executives are typically used in company transformations. The new executive team brings different skills and a fresh perspective. Often they arrive with a strong belief in the new mission. Moreover, they are unfettered by prior commitments linked to the status quo; instead, this new top team symbolizes the need for change. Excitement of a new challenge adds to the energy devoted to it.

We should note that many of the executives who could not, or would not, implement frame-breaking change went on to be quite successful in other organizations—for example, Ken Fisher at Encore Computer and Bill Poduska at Apollo Computer. The stimulation of a fresh start and of jobs matched to personal competence applies to individuals as well as to organizations.

Although typical patterns for the when and who of frame-breaking change are clear—wait for a financial crisis and then bring in an outsider, along with a revised executive team, to revamp the company—this is clearly less than satisfactory for a particular organization. Clearly, some companies benefit from transforming themselves before a crisis forces them to do so, and a few exceptional executives have the vision and drive to reorient a business which they nurtured during its preceding period of convergence. The vital tasks are to manage incremental change during convergent periods; to have the vision to initiate and implement frame-breaking change prior to the competition; and to mobilize an executive which can initiate and implement both kinds of change.

CONCLUSION

Our analysis of the way companies evolve over long periods of time indicates that the most effective firms have relatively long periods of convergence giving support to a basic strategy, but such periods are punctuated by upheavals—concurrent and discontinuous changes which reshape the entire organization.

Managers should anticipate that when environments change sharply:

- Frame-breaking change cannot be avoided. These discontinuous organizational changes will either be made proactively or initiated under crisis/turnaround condition.

- Discontinuous changes need to be made in strategy, structure, people, and processes concurrently. Tentative change runs the risk of being smothered by individual, group, and organizational inertia.

- Frame-breaking change requires direct executive involvement in all aspects of the change, usually bolstered with new executives from outside the organization.

- There are no patterns in the sequence of frame-breaking changes, and not all strategies will be effective. Strategy and, in turn, structure, systems, and processes must meet industry-specific competitive issues.

Finally, our historical analysis of organizations highlights the following issues for executive leadership:

- Need to manage for balance, consistency, or fit during convergent period.

- Need to be vigilant for environmental shifts in order to anticipate the need for frame-breaking change.

- Need to effectively manage incremental as well as frame-breaking change.

- Need to build (or rebuild) a top team to help initiate and implement frame-breaking change.

- Need to develop core values which can be used as an anchor as organizations evolve through frame-breaking changes (e.g., IBM, Hewlett-Packard).

- Need to develop and use organizational history as a way to infuse pride in an organization's past and for its future.

- Need to bolster technical, social, and conceptual skills with visionary skills. Visionary skills add energy, direction, and excitement so critical during frame-breaking change.

Effectiveness over changing competitive conditions requires that executives manage fundamentally different kinds of organizations and different kinds of change. The data are consistent across diverse industries and countries, an executive team's ability to proactively initiate and implement frame-breaking change *and* to manage convergent change seem to be important factors which discriminate between organizational renewal and greatness versus complacency and eventual decline.

ACKNOWLEDGMENTS

The authors thank Donald Hambrick and Kathy Harrigan for insightful comments and the Center for Strategy Research and the Center for Research on Innovation and Entrepreneurship at the Graduate School of Business, Columbia University, for financial support.

REFERENCES

1. A. Chandler, *Strategy and Structure* (Cambridge, MA: MIT Press, 1962).

2. D. Miller and P. Friesen, *Organizations: A Quantum View* (Englewood Cliffs, NJ: Prentice-Hall, 1984).

3. L. Greiner, "Evolution and Revolution as Organizations Grow," *Harvard Business Review* (July/August 1972), pp. 37–46.

4. D. Nadler and M. Tushman, *Strategic Organization Design* (Homewood, IL: Scott Foresman, 1986).

5. T. Peters and R. Waterman, *In Search of Excellence* (New York, NY: Harper and Row, 1982).

6. Nadler and Tushman, op. cit.

7. For a discussion of preemptive strategies, see I. MacMillan, "Delays in Competitors' Responses to New Banking Products," *Journal of Business Strategy,* 4 (1984): 58–65.

8. M. Tushman and B. Virany, "Changing Characteristics of Executive Teams in an Emerging Industry," *Journal of Business Venturing* (1986).

38

Time Pacing

Competing in Markets That Won't Stand Still

KATHLEEN M. EISENHARDT
SHONA L. BROWN

Back in 1965, Gordon Moore, a confounder of Intel Corporation, prophesied that the capacity of the microprocessor computer chip would double every 18 months. Moore's Law, as it has since become known, may sound like a law of physics, but it's not. Instead, it's a business objective that Intel's engineers and managers have taken to heart. Over time, Intel has created a treadmill of new-product introductions that have set a blistering pace in its industry. In the decade between 1987 and 1997, Intel generated an astounding average annual return to investors of 44%. Even more impressive, recently Intel's annual earnings equaled those of the top ten personal computer firms *combined.*

Although few companies will ever enjoy a market position like Intel's, managers can learn a key lesson from the world's premier chip maker. Intel is certainly the most visible—but by no means the only—practitioner of *time pacing,* a strategy for competing in fast-changing, unpredictable markets by scheduling change at predictable time intervals. Not only does Intel make Moore's Law a reality through its new-product introductions, but it also time-paces in other key areas. For example, about every nine months, Intel adds a new fabrication facility to its operations. CEO Andy Grove says, "We build factories two years in advance of needing them, before we have the products to run in them

and before we know that the industry is going to grow." By expanding its capacity in this predictable way, Intel deters rivals from entering the business and blocks them from gaining a toehold should Intel be unable to meet demand.

Small and large companies, high and low tech alike, can benefit from time pacing, especially in markets that won't stand still. Cisco Systems, Emerson Electric, Gillette, Netscape, SAP, Sony, Starbucks, and 3M all use time pacing in one form or another. In rapidly shifting industries, time pacing can help managers anticipate change and perhaps, like Intel, set the pace for change. But even in industries in which the rate of change is less than warp speed, time pacing can counteract the natural tendency of managers to wait too long, move too slowly, and lose momentum.

Our understanding of time pacing emerged from almost a decade of research into the drivers of success in high-velocity, intensely competitive industries. One phase of the research took us inside 12 successful companies in different segments of the computer industry—an industry that serves as a prototype for this new competitive reality. We tested the relevance of these ideas in other industries as well, through targeted case studies and consulting work with executives. What we found is that wherever managers were coping

Reprinted by permission of *Harvard Business Review.* From "Time Pacing: Competing in Markets That Won't Stand Still," by Kathleen M. Eisenhardt and Shona L. Brown, March–April 1998. Copyright © 1998 by the Harvard Business School Publishing Corporation; all rights reserved.

with changing business environments, time pacing was critical to their success, helping them resolve the fundamental dilemma of how often to change.

TIME PACING VERSUS EVENT PACING

For most managers, *event pacing* constitutes the familiar and natural order of things. Companies change in response to events such as moves by the competition, shifts in technology, poor financial performance, or new customer demands. Event pacing is about creating a new product when a promising technology comes out of the R&D laboratory, entering a new market in response to a move by a competitor, or making an acquisition because an attractive target becomes available. Managers who event-pace follow a plan and deviate from it only when performance weakens. In markets that are stable, event pacing is an opportunistic and effective way to deal with change. By definition, however, it is also a reactive and often erratic strategy.

In contrast, time pacing refers to creating new products or services launching new businesses, or entering new markets according to the calendar.[1] Even though time-paced companies can be extraordinarily fast, it is important not to confuse time pacing with speed. By definition, time pacing is regular, rhythmic, and proactive. For example, 3M dictates that 30% of revenues will come from new products every year, Netscape introduces a new product about every six months, British Airways refreshes its service classes every five years, and Starbucks opens 300 stores per year to hit the goal of 2,000 outlets by the year 2000. Time pacing is about running a business through regular deadlines to which managers synchronize the speed and intensity of their efforts. Like a metronome, time pacing creates a predictable rhythm for change in a company.

In the companies we studied, time pacing had a powerful psychological impact. Time pacing creates a relentless sense of urgency around meeting deadlines and concentrates individual and team energy around common goals. As one manager says, "It's like running a marathon in 100-yard bursts." Although the tempo may be fast, it is predictable and so gives people a sense of control in otherwise chaotic markets. People become focused, efficient, and confident about the task at hand, which leads to enhanced performance.

In addition to creating a sense of urgency, time pacing disciplines managers to excel at two critical, but often neglected, processes essential to success in changing markets. The first is managing transitions, or the shifts from one activity to the next. The second is managing rhythm, or the pace at which companies change. Companies that march to the rhythm of time pacing build momentum, and companies that effectively manage transitions sustain that momentum without missing important beats.

MANAGING TRANSITIONS

Transitions are notoriously complicated, making them a weak link for companies in changing markets. Common transitions include a shift from one product-development project, advertising campaign, or season of merchandise to the next. Other examples include entering or leaving markets, absorbing new acquisitions, launching new alliances, and bringing volume production on-line.

Transitions typically involve a large number of people, many of whom are not used to working with one another. Because transitions occur less frequently than other activities, managers have fewer opportunities to learn from experience. Communication easily breaks down. Missteps often turn into costly delays. In short, Murphy's Law clearly applies in transitions.

Because major transitions are periods when companies are likely to stumble, we expected to find that managers would devote extra attention to them. The surprise is that they don't. They manage the product development process but not the switch from one project to the next. They spend months analyzing an acquisition but far less time planning the integration. Some managers simply ignore transitions, hoping that somehow they will get from one activity to the next.

When transitions are poor, businesses lose position, stumble, and fall behind. Blockbuster Video is a recent casualty of poor transition management. In an attempt to cut costs, Blockbuster decided to bring its distribution of videos in-house. But Blockbuster made the mistake of switching from its third-party distributor to its own newly designed, automated facility in Texas before its new system was up and running—and the company has been playing catch-up ever since. The snafu has caused repeated delays in getting the latest videos from the warehouse to Blockbuster's local stores, dealing a blow to the company's performance. In 1997, cash flow dropped a precipitous 70%.

In contrast, companies that manage by time pacing learn to choreograph important transitions—and to shorten the time it takes to execute them. Gillette, for example, smoothly executes about 20 new-product transitions per year. Like a pharmaceuticals company, Gillette sees itself as managing a steady flow of products—developing, launching, and harvesting products all at the same time. Gillette manages this balanced product pipeline through a disciplined transition process. It does not release a product prototype into volume production until a mock-up of the next product to follow is available. The wildly successful Sensor razor, for example, was not launched until its successor product, Excel, was in development. In turn, Excel was not launched until its successor product and more than ten candidate products after that were under development. CEO Al Zeien describes Gillette's strategy as "not just reacting to competitors" but as "orchestrating and commanding a business."

Beyond choreographing its transitions, Gillette has worked to slash the time it takes to execute them. After launching the Sensor line in the domestic market, it took Gillette four years to penetrate all of its markets. With its successor line, Excel, Gillette was able to cut that time to three years. Not only does this hasten the company's revenue flow, but it also prevents competitors from copying Gillette's products in one market and introducing them into another before Gillette does.

Gillette has also focused its attention on developing an effective transition process for entering new geographic markets. The company uses its most popular product—razor blades—to establish a beachhead in new countries. During this initial entry, Gillette builds its distribution infrastructure; operating margins are often small and the company may actually lose money. But as other products, such as hair care appliances and toothbrushes, start to fill the warehouses and flow to retailers, Gillette's costs drop and profits rise. These transitions into new markets have been further refined, with variations in the process depending on the level of development in the country. The result is that Gillette consistently hits its target of 40% of sales from new products, a remarkable feat for a consumer-packaged-goods company.

Where Transitions Matter Most

Although transitions are always important, they are especially so in fast-changing markets where, as one manager put it, "transitions are like changing the fan belt while the car is still moving." When the pace is fast there are simply more transitions, and so they command a larger share of managers' time. Moreover, the transitions themselves are more critical because the faster the market is moving, the harder it is to catch up once you stumble. It's like competing in the 4×100 meter relay—the laps are so short that the execution of the baton passes often determines the outcome of the race.

Consider Netscape. To meet its key challenge of running faster than Microsoft and IBM's Lotus, it has shortened transitions of all types. Before Netscape, other companies in the industry typically paced themselves in 12-month product-development cycles, which were followed by beta site testing and then product shipment. Then Netscape streamlined its approach to product launches. The company slashed product intervals (technical guru, Marc Andreessen, wanted three months but settled for six), effectively doubling the number of transitions needed and so upping the ante on executing transitions well. It then shortened the transitions by forgoing the standard practice of using a few major beta test sites. It simply released prototype products onto the Internet and waited for users to give them feedback on problem areas. Suddenly, Netscape had an army of debuggers who could quickly refine its prototype into a finished product—which the company was then able to launch, often for free, on the Web. This fast and smooth transition process helped Netscape maintain its technical lead in browsers.

Effective management of transitions is often critical to companies in markets characterized by constantly shifting opportunities. One global computing company that we studied—we'll call it Andromeda—has a particularly effective process for entering new markets. An executive at the group level is responsible for matching new opportunities with existing businesses. When this executive identifies a new market opportunity or when one bubbles up from below, the transition process begins. In the first month, the group executive develops three or four alternative homes, either in existing divisions or as a new stand-alone venture. The alternative venues are compared according to how well they fit with the opportunity in terms of their technology, markets, manufacturing, and distribution. But Andromeda's managers also consider which of its divisions needs a fresh opportunity to kick-start growth. The choice is made quickly—and within four months from the start of the transition process, resources are formally allocated to the new business, and the top management team is put in place. At that four-month mark, the clock starts ticking, and the team has two years to hit key performance metrics for revenue and profits.

Contrast Andromeda's choreographed process for entering new markets with what we observed at a comparable company we'll call Buccaneer. There managers identified a promising multimedia opportunity but did not have a formal way to enter new markets. Because each opportunity was treated as a unique event, this one required idiosyncratic thinking about whether and how to proceed. Managers needed eight months to "resource" the opportunity. In the interim, three competitors entered the market, preempting Buccaneer and demoralizing the team that had worked on the project.

For companies that attempt to grow quickly through acquisitions, the postmerger integration process is a critical transition. Consider Banc One, a market leader among superregional banks. For a number of years, Banc One bought smaller banks at a measured pace of about ten acquisitions per year, with four to six acquisitions occurring at any one time. The transition process often began on the day that the merger was announced: all employees received a videotape welcoming them to Banc One and explaining what the new affiliation would mean. A team of about 30 Banc One staffers then quickly began a complex process made up of simultaneous activities conducted along multiple fronts. For example, the marketing and retailing departments mapped the affiliate's products onto Banc One's portfolio while the electronic banking department assessed ATM volume. Banc One also assigned the new bank a comparable "mentor" institution that had recently undergone a similar conversion, providing a model for the acquiree of what a postconversion operation should look like. After a 180-day transition process, the final changeover occurred on a single weekend. The old systems were shut down on Friday, and the Banc One system was running on Monday. This choreographed process enabled Banc One to fold

in acquisitions quickly and thus move rapidly into the ranks of the largest and most successful U.S. banks.[2]

The Best Transitions

The best transitions do more than simply take a company from point A to point B. Managers can actually use these transitions to learn, reflect, change direction, and accomplish other goals. Andromeda's process for entering new markets doesn't just let the company deploy resources quickly in order to capture opportunities. It also allows the company to achieve other objectives, such as boosting the performance of flagging operating units. Similarly, while Banc One is integrating its acquisitions, it also exploits the opportunity to skim off new best practices from the acquired banks, which then can be used throughout the Banc One network. The most successful companies use transitions as opportunities for broader-based change.

But the best transitions have little else in common. Our research showed that specific transition processes varied from company to company. In fact, they were surprisingly arbitrary. What made the difference in companies that effectively managed transitions was that they all had clear, choreographed processes that their employees understood. That point became apparent when we did a study of product development at two leading computer companies. Their processes for managing the transition between development projects differed in almost every significant design aspect. In the first company, the transition from one project to the next was led by its technical gurus; in the second, it was led by the marketing managers. One transition took a month; the other took three. Each company had a different set of steps, different timing, different specifications about who should be involved and when. But both transition processes worked because in each case everyone followed a script.

MANAGING RHYTHMS

If transitions sustain an organization's momentum, the rhythms that managers set create that momentum. Rhythm helps people plan ahead and synchronize their activities. The 3M dictum, for example, that 30% of its revenues must come from new products every year lets people gauge what they need to do and when they need to do it.

A Solution for New-Product Development

New-product development is one of the most significant processes for competing in new or shifting markets. In our research on the computer industry, we observed that time pacing had a direct impact on the timeliness and effectiveness of new products. In companies that time-paced new-product development, transitions between projects were fluid and efficient, and products were typically released on schedule. But in companies that let each project unfold according to its own schedule, the development process was often erratic, inefficient, and riddled with delays.

One major computer company we'll call ComputeCo demonstrated all the pitfalls of managing development without time pacing. At ComputeCo, projects started and ended at unpredictable intervals. Schedules varied from project to project, and they often had to be adjusted when specifications were changed to add new product features. As a result, most projects took longer than planned, although some actually ended earlier.

As old projects wound down, developers attempted to land new project assignments on their own. ComputeCo's developers referred to this inefficient transition between projects as "shopping in the parking lot." As one developer said, the transitions were periods to "hang out with anybody else who is in between projects, to see what's happening, and to wait for something to be lined up."

The beginning of new projects was as haphazard and unpredictable as the completion of old ones. When new projects began, they were assigned to whoever happened to be free, with little thought about whether these were the best people for the job. The result was that development expertise was rarely matched to a project's technical needs.

The unexpected beginnings and endings of projects also created delays because not enough people were available to begin new projects. One manager complained, "I have absolutely no way to staff this project, and I have to figure out how to staff it." Caught between a rock and a hard place, her project was eventually late. We also observed instances at ComputeCo when too many developers were free, and so projects were created simply to make work. Describing one such project, a frustrated manager told us, "This project is not a strategic fit. I would rather put our resources into doing something for the business." The further irony was that when critical projects arose without warning, resources could not be freed up fast enough because they were tied up in make-work projects.

Without rhythm, managers tend to be reactive and to see change as an unwelcome surprise. Yet most pay little conscious attention to rhythm. Consider, for example, how many companies are locked into the ritual of annual planning cycles regardless of the actual pace their businesses require for success. A critical dimension of time pacing is setting the right rhythms for change and synchronizing those rhythms both with the marketplace and with the organization's internal capabilities.

Get in Step with the Market

What is the right rhythm? The companies we studied that used time pacing effectively were aligned with important rhythms in the marketplace—such as seasons, suppliers' product development cycles, or swings in customer spending. Surprisingly, we found that although these external rhythms often seemed obvious, their strategic potential was frequently unrecognized by competitors.

Consider one cold-beverage business we studied—we'll call it ThirstCo—for which summer is the peak buying season. ThirstCo decided to exploit this seasonality by creating a rhythm of new-product introductions to coincide with the peak in demand. In retrospect, that seemed like an obvious strategy. But it wasn't at the time, because the standard practice in the industry was to introduce new flavors when they came out of the kitchen, whatever month that happened to be.

In order to execute its rhythm, ThirstCo developed a choreographed process to make the transition to its new products. Now each spring, the company begins by test marketing three or four new flavors, a process that takes about two months. Managers then select the one or two most promising offerings in time for a June product launch. There is even a standard pattern for the launch, with each new product accompanied by a lottery-type promotional game.

A more complex example of setting the right rhythm comes from a large household-goods manufacturer. Managers at this company had traditionally launched new products when they were ready. But the company's key customers, retail giants such as Wal-Mart and Target, relied on regular, seasonal shelf-planning cycles that varied by category (such as school supplies and small housewares). By matching its own product-launch cycles to the retailers' shelf-planning cycles, the manufacturer was able to win more shelf space and thus more sales. Why? Because its newest products and the advertising dollars that accompanied their launch were available when the retailers were re-planning their shelf space. Everyone benefited. The retailers were able to stock the latest and most well-promoted products, consumers were delighted to find products they had just seen advertised, and the manufacturer enjoyed an increase in sales.

Even in seemingly chaotic and volatile markets, there are natural rhythms that can set the tempo for time pacing. One midtier computer company was looking for a way to become a leader in the industry and found the answer in time pacing. As personal computer customers were growing more sophisticated, they were relying more heavily on product reviews from computer magazines, such as those regularly published in *PC World*. So the computer company adjusted its product development cycle to match the length of time between reviews and then synchronized its product releases to come out just before the reviews. The result? Magazine editors wrote about the company's latest and most exciting products, giving them an advantage over competitors' older products. The company then used the favorable magazine reviews in its ad campaigns to give its new-product launches with an extra boost.

Whereas customers may be the most important source of rhythm for a company, external rhythms from suppliers and complementers are also key. Intel's time-pacing strategy, after all, depends on the company's ability not only to execute its rhythm but also to synchronize with others. If the company pumps out chips that are too fast for the complementary products that work with the chips or if it designs chips for which there aren't enough uses, then Intel falters. So to stay in rhythm, Intel must create "new uses and new users"—which is, in fact, the company's slogan for keeping the market in sync with its own pace. Intel executives now show up in Hollywood, strike deals with video game companies, and are almost anywhere that computing power is in demand.

Intel must also ensure that complementers such as software developers and important customers such as personal computer manufacturers are able to keep up with its pace. To that end, Intel gives developers at these companies early access to its new products. And when its technology sprints ahead of the market and threatens the established rhythm, its engineers step in to find solutions, as they did when the speed of Intel's microprocessors outstripped the technology for accessing data from networks. After all, who would want Intel's fast multimedia-processing chips if it took too long to download data from the Internet? So the company moved into the network interface market in 1991 with interface cards. By enhancing the technology and increasing manufacturing efficiency, Intel was able to improve the product, slash prices by about 40%, and create a demand for cheap, fast PC access to networks—and for Intel microprocessors.

For most companies, getting in step with the market means moving faster. Sometimes, however, finding the right rhythm means slowing down, as one chip maker we'll call SiliCo discovered. The performance of some types of semiconductors is primarily driven by the expensive equipment used to make the chips, especially as chip geometries shrink. Suppliers of this equipment tend to operate on two-year development cycles, a cycle twice as long as SiliCo's. By slowing its rate of new-product introductions to match the pace of a key equipment supplier, SiliCo introduced *fewer* products, but each new chip represented a more significant performance advance because it was better designed to leverage the latest equipment from the supplier. By slowing its pace, SiliCo cut its development costs and increased its average revenue per product.

General Management Has Its Rhythms, Too

Time pacing plays a subtle and almost always overlooked role in the general management of any organization. Most managers work around the annual planning-and-review cycle, without questioning whether that's the right interval. But at a major diversified company, managers altered their planning and review process from the traditional annual cycle to one more tailored to the rate of change in specific markets. In businesses like electronic components in which product development time and product life cycles were short, senior executives went to a six-month review cycle. For lines of business such as home appliances in which product life cycles were between one and three years, they stayed with an annual review. For businesses with longer cycles such as heavy industrial equipment, strategic reviews were set for 18 months. These new review periods made more strategic sense. Moreover, the company was able to exploit these changes by having executives from other businesses within the company attend the reviews and influence strategies, particularly around cross-business collaboration opportunities.

In fast-moving segments of the computing and networking industries, the pace is set by executives who manage their companies on incredibly short cycles using real-time information. In the early days of Sun Microsystems, for example, executives monitored the company's performance on a daily basis. The $6 billion networking giant, Cisco Systems, is managed on a fast-time scale as well. Cisco executives watch sales on a weekly basis, a pace that has been impossible for competitors such as Bay Networks to match. The pace at Dell Computer has been termed "Dell-

---

Time-Pacing Basics

The following three sets of questions can help managers put in place the fundamentals of time pacing in their organizations. The questions focus on developing time-based performance metrics, identifying critical transitions that need to be choreographed, and finding rhythms by looking externally.

1. *Performance Metrics.* Most companies use performance measures that focus on costs, profit, or innovation. Do your current performance metrics also include measures based on time, such as elapsed time, speed, and rate? In product development, for example, consider measures such as the number of products launched per quarter, the average time from concept to commercial launch, and the average downtime between projects. In integrating acquisitions, consider tracking the time until the new organizational structure is finalized, the time it takes for the sales growth rate to turn positive after the acquisition, and the number of acquisitions absorbed per year. Every critical transition process should be tracked with at least some time-based measures.

2. *Transitions.* Review the critical transitions in your business. Among the most important are shifting from one product-development project to the next, changing merchandise according to the season, entering new markets, absorbing acquisitions, ramping up to volume production, or launching new strategic alliances. Do you have formal processes for managing each critical transition? Can you simplify or shorten them? Can you accomplish more within a transition than simply getting from A to B?

3. *Rhythms.* List your company's own rhythms, and ask yourself which are really attuned to your business and which are merely habit. Are there important areas with no rhythms at all? For each of your key external relationships—with buyers, complementers, suppliers, and competitors—list the major rhythms driving their businesses. Would getting in sync with any of those rhythms create new opportunities for you? What would it take for your organization to exploit those opportunities?

ocity," a waggish takeoff on the company's focus on speed and timing. The result is no joke for Dell's competitors. As CEO Michael Dell says, his company is "setting the pace for the industry." Companies like Dell and Cisco often deliberately choose a pace that competitors cannot sustain. A number of computing and networking companies are looking to enter the telecommunications business because they believe that their speed will give them a decisive competitive advantage over the industry's incumbents.

Choose a Manageable Pace

Companies can only time-pace as fast as their internal capabilities will allow them to move. After all, time pacing requires not just setting a rhythm but also executing it. How many times has a promising business concept been grounded by an unsustainable pace—for instance, when a national rollout of restaurant outlets exceeds the company's ability to find and train store managers? Companies that time-pace effectively are careful to peg their rhythm to the realities of their internal capabilities. And when that pace falls short of management's ambitions, such companies will ramp up their capabilities.

A fairly simple illustration of how this works is how a credit card company targeted graduating college seniors as customers. The company's managers realized that the optimal time to send direct mail advertising to students was the very brief window between job offers and graduation. If students had job offers in hand, they could be readily evaluated for their financial prospects. And until graduation, the students could easily be reached at their campus addresses. The credit card company decided to execute its direct mail campaign and related card-application processing within this narrow time frame, but doing so required changes in staffing to handle the annual peak work flow.

The principle of matching rhythm to capabilities was the same at Emerson Electric, although the company faced a far more challenging situation. To meet long-term goals for sales growth, Emerson's executives set a target of earning 35% of revenue from the sales of new products—a goal that was initially unreachable because Emerson lacked adequate product-development capacity. So it began a multipronged approach to work up to the rhythm that it had set for itself. It began by streamlining the product develop-

ment process, cutting development cycle time by about 20%. Simultaneously, it strengthened the marketing staff to increase its understanding of what customers wanted—Emerson could no longer rely so heavily on engineering input. A third move was to cut the size of the active product-development portfolio. Managers believed there were too many products under development, or as they put it, "too many cars on the highway," and no clear sense of priorities. The process of upgrading capabilities took several years, but it enabled Emerson to improve its percentage of sales from new products from 21% in 1991 to more than 30% in recent years, and to extend its enviable record of 40 years of earnings-per-share growth.

CHANGING OFTEN ENOUGH

Most of what we've described about time pacing comes from observations of companies that practice it—and from companies that don't. In our work in fast-changing markets, we often see that time pacing helps managers avert the danger of changing too infrequently. By setting a regular pace for change, managers avoid becoming locked into old patterns and habits.

There is also interesting academic work that highlights another common syndrome we have observed—changing too frequently. Computer simulations done by Anjali Sastry of the University of Michigan, for example, show this happening to event-driven players when their environments begin to speed up. Sastry's simulations are programmed with feedback loops and delays: an event takes place, the organization responds by acting, it then gets feedback from the market to which it again may react, and so on. When the simulation mimics a relatively slow market, event pacing works well because it gives managers the time to build competencies that fit the environment.[3] But speed up the rate of change, and event pacing loses its viability. What happens in the simulation is that the organization starts changing *all* the time. It reacts too quickly and never learns to be good at anything.

This research and our own field observations suggest that time pacing can help organizations resist the extreme of changing too often. In rapidly changing, intensely competitive industries, the dilemma of how of-

Modularity's Role in Keeping the Pace

When forced to make a decision about whether to stay, for example, on schedule or meet a product's feature specifications, companies that time-pace by definition choose to stick with a schedule. The essential, but often overlooked, tool that allows them to do so is modularity.

Consider Sony's Walkman, one of the most successful consumer products of all time. The modularity of Walkman's design enables Sony to set the pace in its category with a steady stream of on-time product launches. Based on how different customer groups use the product, Sony designed six basic platforms for the Walkman: playback only, playback and record, playback and tuner, professional playback, professional playback and record, and sports. Then, using standard design elements such as color and styling and distinct components such as batteries, Sony added an assortment of features and technical innovations to the basic platforms with relative ease.

In doing so, Sony made both the actual product design and the process itself modular. The result was that, depending on the time constraints created by the competitive dynamics in a particular segment, the company could choose between a faster but partial redesign or a slower but complete redesign.*

*See Susan Sanderson and Mustafa Uzumeri, "Managing Product Families: The Case of the Sony Walkman," *Research Policy*, vol. 24, 1995.

Modularity is also an important feature of Microsoft's new-product-development process. Although Microsoft is notorious for delays in its operating systems, applications are another story. Here developers design product features as modules and then prioritize them. Because of this modularity, Microsoft can meet release deadlines for products that incorporate the most critical features and roll over those features that are a lower priority to the next time-paced interval.

Modularity is not the province of technology-based companies alone. Consider Japan's 100-year-old Shiseido, now the world's fourth-largest cosmetic company. Japanese consumers are particularly demanding when it comes to refreshed products, sometimes expecting updated offerings as frequently as every month. As Shiseido's president Akira Gemma says, "We see our customers as our own competitors. We need to move ahead not because other brands are doing so but because our customers' needs are changing." Managers at Shiseido modularize their products by separating the development of the products themselves—the shampoos, conditioners, and fragrances—from the packaging. They can then satisfy changing customer demands by refreshing the packaging—by changing the shapes, sizes, and colors of the bottles. They typically change the packaging more often than they change the products themselves.

---

ten to change is acute because the signals for when to change typically are unclear. Does a down month for product sales mean that interest is waning, or is it just a temporary lull? Does a failed initial foray into a market mean that another try will not be successful? If managers change with every signal, then they fail to accomplish tasks and send confusing messages to customers and employees. But if managers don't change, they run the risk of waiting too long and falling too far behind to catch up. Appropriate time pacing helps resolve this dilemma.

Recall Andromeda, the global computing compa-

ny with the streamlined process for moving into new business opportunities. When Andromeda funds a new venture, it requires managers to stick with that venture until an evaluation point at two years. The trial period cannot be cut short. General Electric's Jack Welch describes a similar discipline at GE surrounding organizational changes that just "needed to sit there—like popcorn kernels in a warm pan." It was only later that "suddenly things began to pop." Thus time pacing helps ensure that managers persist long enough to avoid overreacting to the "noise" that accompanies most new ventures. It balances the perseverance neces-

Keeping Up, Gaining Ground, and Setting the Pace

Time pacing opens up strategic options for the companies that use it. They can exploit time pacing to gain competitive ground or even to set the pace of competition in an industry.

KEEPING UP

In the mid-1990s, computer giant Compaq failed to keep up with the pace of change in several of its key markets. In laptops, for example, Compaq lost its rhythm of new-product introductions when it ran into delays for exotic components. Rival Toshiba sprinted by to capture the number-one position in global market share. Even worse, Compaq failed to keep pace with Intel's transition from its 486 microprocessor architecture to the Pentium processor in its corporate desktop and home models. Compaq again lost ground to PC rivals Dell and Gateway.

Since then, Compaq has gotten back in step. It now synchronizes with Intel's developments in microprocessor technology. And to minimize the risk of losing its pace again, Compaq steers clear of unusual components that are subject to erratic supply.

GAINING GROUND

Beyond simply keeping up, companies can use time pacing to gain competitive ground by fully exploiting rhythms and transitions. Consider defense contractor TRW. For its space and defense businesses in the early 1990s, TRW used an annual January-to-January business-planning cycle to budget all its projects in the coming year. But because TRW's prime customer, the U.S. government, was on an October-to-October fiscal year, it was only in the fall that TRW had an accurate picture of all the jobs that the government was putting out to bid. TRW dealt with this uncertainty by setting aside a "reserve" budget in January. Then in October, it used this reserve to bid on contracts that it hadn't anticipated in January.

Simply by changing its planning calendar to match the government's, TRW found it was able to bid on and win more contracts. Instead of holding money in reserve for opportunities that might or might not materialize, TRW could now allocate its entire budget in a more strategic way, placing bets where they were most likely to win. Thus TRW was able to use time pacing to gain ground.

SETTING THE PACE

Since the inception of the Walkman in 1979, Sony has used time pacing to set the pace of both innovation and market segmentation. Most key technical innovations for this product category—in tape drive mechanisms, batteries, and headphones—came from Sony at a pace of one per year. At the same time, with a slavish dedication to meeting launch dates, Sony drove the market with a paced set at 20 new models per year. (For more about how companies achieve this rhythm, see the insert "Modularity's Role in Keeping the Pace.")

The consumer electronics giant also tailored its pacing to particular markets. In Japan, where Sony faced its strongest competition, the company maintained a rapid pace of new-product introductions. Where Sony dominated a particular product category, such as in children's or sports models, it used a slower pace of change. By tailoring its pacing to the competitiveness of its markets, Sony dominates through its model variety even though its average rate of model change was lower than that of the competition. And Sony kept models in the marketplace on average longer than its competitors did.

Sony's ability to set the pace for its industry depended in part on its mastery of critical transitions. Sony was able, for example, to launch products such as the Walkman 2 simultaneously in Europe, Japan, and the United States, preventing competitors from copying the product in one geographic market and from beating Sony to another market with those copycat products.

sary to overcome obstacles along the way with the change that is required when a course of action is failing—a balance that is especially challenging to achieve in rapidly changing markets.

There will always be a place for event pacing in any business that has to cope with inevitable surprises in the marketplace. And although time pacing is not the answer for every business, most companies—especially those in fast-changing markets—cannot afford to ignore it as part of their strategic arsenal. With time pacing, managers can avoid being left behind, gain ground by exploiting rhythms and transitions, and even set the pace of competition.

NOTES

1. For related research on time pacing versus event pacing, see Connie J. G. Gersick, "Pacing Strategic Change: The Case of a New Venture," *Academy of Management Journal,* vol. 37, pp. 9–45.

2. See Gabriel Szulanski, "Appropriability and the Challenge of Scope: Banc One Routinizes Replication," working paper (Wharton School, University of Pennsylvania, 1997).

3. See M. Anjali Sastry, "Problems and Paradoxes in a Model of Punctuated and Organizational Change," *Administrative Science Quarterly,* vol. 42, no. 2, June 1997, pp. 237–275.

39

Implementing New Designs
Managing Organizational Change

DAVID A. NADLER
MICHAEL L. TUSHMAN

CASE

Orient Oil Corporation is a major force in the energy industry. About ten years ago, Orient senior management decided to diversify out of petroleum-based industries into other ventures, some related to the basic business and some completely unrelated. For a while, this seemed to work out. After the first three years of the acquisition strategy, Orient faced problems in managing the different companies within its structure, so it called in a consulting firm, which did an organization study and recommended the establishment of twenty-three individual strategic business units, each with its own president and a complete set of staff functions. The business units were in turn grouped into four major sectors, each headed by a senior corporate executive.

About four years into the strategy, things started to go sour. Many of the management systems, approaches, and methods that had worked so well in the oil business seemed to lead to one disaster after another. For a while, the huge profits of the oil business could be used to cover up the continuing stream of catastrophes in the other units, but finally it became obvious to both insiders and outsiders that Orient was incapable of effectively managing businesses outside its basic industry. A strategic decision was made to start divesting or liquidating the acquisitions and to move back to the base business.

A very senior group was convened to work intensively for several weeks to develop a plan to reorganize the company. They produced a top secret document that proposed reorganizing the company into two major operating units—one focusing primarily on energy exploration and production and the other focusing on refining, distribution, and sales. A third group would hold the non-energy-related business but would be chartered to do itself out of business in two years through divestiture or liquidation.

The policy committee of the corporation met for a full-day session to hear the report of the design task force and, after many hours of debate, decided to go ahead with the group's recommendations. Having worked hard for several hours, the group took a short break at about 4:00 in the afternoon and decided to reconvene at 4:30 to "tie up the loose ends."

As the meeting started again, the discussion moved toward the issue of announcements. Many members of the group were pushing for an immediate announcement. Rumors were flying around the company that something was up, and the group members were concerned about the consequences of possible information leaks. In the midst of this discussion, one of the group turned to the task

From *Competing by Design: The Power of Organizational Architecture,* by David A. Nadler and Michael L. Tushman, pp. 181–203. Copyright © 1997 by Oxford University Press, Inc. Used by permission of Oxford University Press, Inc.

force chairman and said, "Once we make the announcement, what do you want people to do then?" The task force chairman looked around the room for help and saw none. He responded, "Well, there's a lot we haven't figured out yet. We'll just tell people not to worry about it." The questioner came back, "Aren't we just creating problems, then, by announcing this thing? We're just going to disturb people, and nobody will be doing any work." The room was silent.

INTRODUCTION

As with Orient Oil, many managers see their organization design work as completed when "the announcement" is made. Because so much energy may have been expended on reaching an agreement on a design, little thought may have been given to what will happen next. As a result, after the announcement is made, managers suddenly begin to think about how to manage the implementation of the change in design.

In fact, implementing a new design is difficult, as is the implementation of any major change within an organization. Design changes are particularly problematic because it seems so easy to create a design on paper that managers often overlook how truly difficult it is to install a new design and make it work effectively. Truly effective implementation is difficult and often takes a good deal of time.

Many design failures—in which everyone agrees that the reorganization was a disaster—are not failures because of a technically inadequate design but rather are failures of implementation. In practice, an adequate or even mediocre design, if implemented well, can be effective, while the most elegant and sophisticated of designs poorly implemented will fail.

This chapter, then, will be devoted to the question of implementation of organization designs. The underlying issue in design implementation appears to be one of managing organizational change. We will therefore start by providing a way of thinking about changes in organization. Next, we will point out some of the very predictable problems that one encounters when attempting to bring about change. Finally, we will discuss some implications for managing change and outline some specific techniques and action areas for enhancing the implementation of organization design changes.

CRITERIA FOR ORGANIZATIONAL CHANGE

During the past decade, there has been increasing interest in the subject of managing organizational change.[1] One approach to thinking about change that many have found useful was originally proposed by Richard Beckhard and Reuben Harris. They saw the implementation of a change, such as a new organization design, as the moving of an organization toward a desired future state. They saw changes in terms of transitions (see Figure 39.1). At any time, an organization exists in a **current state** (A). The current state describes how the organization functions prior to a change. In terms of our congruence model, we can think of the current state as a particular configuration of the strategy, task, individual, and formal and informal organizations. A change involves movement toward a desired **future state** (B), which describes how the organization should function after the change. In a design, the full set of design documents (strategic design, impact analysis, operational design, and so on) provides a written description of the intended future state.

The period between the current state (A) and the future state (B) can be thought of as the **transition state** (C). In the most general terms, then, the effective management of change involves developing an understanding of the current state, developing an image of the desired future state, and moving the organization through a transition period. In design, we deal with the first two of these steps. Implementation concerns the moving of the organization through the transition period. Typically, as much care needs to be taken in designing the transition as in designing the future state—both are critical.

Several criteria can be used to judge the effective management of transitions. Building on the transition framework just presented, an organizational change, such as the implementation of a new design, can be managed effectively when:

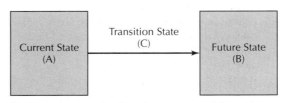

Figure 39.1. Organization change as transition.

1. The organization is moved from the current state to the future state—in which the design is actually installed or implemented.

2. The functioning of the organization design in the future state meets expectations, or works as planned. In the case of design, this meets that the design in practice met the criteria that it was intended to satisfy.

3. The transition is accomplished without undue cost to the organization. This means that the design is implemented without significant disruptions to the business or damage to relationships with customers, suppliers, or regulators. While there is always some cost associated with implementation, the cost should be managed, predictable, and controlled consistent with the estimates done in the impact analysis. "Undue" cost is cost that is unplanned, unpredicted, or uncontrolled.

4. The transition is accomplished without undue cost to individual organization members. Here again, the key operative word is "undue" as defined by the original impact analysis. Much of the cost to individuals occurs more through the manner in which changes are made than through the change itself.

Of course, not every implementation of a new design can be expected to meet all of these criteria consistently, but such standards provide a target for planning implementation. The question is how to maximize the chances that the design will be implemented effectively.

PROBLEMS OF IMPLEMENTING ORGANIZATIONAL CHANGES

What are the issues that must be addressed if managers are to implement effectively? On the broadest level, there are two basic issues—what the change should be and how the change should be implemented. Throughout this book we have been dealing with the first issue as it relates to organization design. We have stressed the importance of diagnosis of problems and causes, followed by systematic work to develop and then choose from alternative solutions that will be responsive to those problems. The second question—how the changes are implemented—is the one on which we will focus now. Observations of changes seem to indi-

cate that there are three types of problems encountered in some form whenever a significant organizational change is attempted.

The Problem of Power

Any organization is a political system made up of various individuals, groups, and coalitions competing for power. Political behavior is thus a natural and expected feature of organizations. Such behavior occurs during the current and future states. In the transition state, however, these dynamics become even more intense as an old design, with its political implications, is dismantled and a new design takes its place. Any significant change (and design changes clearly are significant in terms of power) poses the possibility of upsetting or modifying the balance of power among various formal and informal interest groups. The uncertainty created by change creates ambiguity, which in turn tends to increase the probability of political activity as people try to create some structure and certainty by attempting to control their environment.

Individuals and groups may take political action based on their perceptions of how the change will affect their relative power position in the organization. They will try to influence where they will sit in the organization (both formal and informal) that emerges from the transition and will be concerned about how the conflict of the transition period will affect the balance of power in the future state. Finally, individuals and groups may engage in political action because of their ideological position with regard to the change—the new design, strategy, or approach may be inconsistent with their shared values or their image of the organization.

The Problem of Anxiety

Change in organizations involves the movement from something that is known toward something that is unknown. Individuals naturally have concerns, such as whether they will be needed in the new organization, whether their skills will be valued, and how they will cope with the new situation. These concerns can be summarized in the question that is frequently voiced during a major organizational change—"what's going to happen to me?" To the extent that this question cannot fully be answered (such as in the Orient Oil case at the beginning of this chapter), individuals may experience stress and feel anxious.

As stress and anxiety increase, they may result in a variety of behavior or performance problems. For example, stress may result in difficulty in hearing or integrating information. It may lead people to resist changes that they might otherwise support or in the extreme, engage in irrational and even self-destructive acts. Resistance is a common occurrence, although in many large organizations people may not actively resist the change by openly refusing to implement the new organization design. What does occur is that people passively or subtly resist the change or act in ways that objectively do not appear to be constructive for either the individual or the organization.

The Problem of Organizational Control

A significant change in organization design tends to disrupt the normal course of events within the organization. Thus, it frequently undermines existing systems of management control, particularly those that are embedded in the formal organizational arrangements. An impending change may suddenly make control systems irrelevant or cause them to be perceived as "lame ducks." As a result, it is often easy to lose control during a change. As goals, structures, and people shift, it becomes difficult to monitor performance and make correct assumptions, as one would during a more stable period.

A related problem is that most of the formal organizational arrangements are designed either to manage the current state (the existing design) or to manage the future state (the proposed new design), but those same designs may not be adequate for the management of the transition state. In most situations, they are not appropriate for managing implementation, since they are steady state management systems designed to run organizations already in place. They are not transitional management devices.

IMPLICATIONS FOR CHANGE MANAGEMENT

Each of these three problems lead to some relatively straight-forward conclusions about actions needed to manage change (see Table 39.1). To the extent that a change presents the possibility of significant power problems, the management of the organization's political system must shape the political dynamics associat-

Table 39.1. Change Problems and Implications

Problem		Implication
Power	→	Need to shape the political dynamics associated with change
Anxiety	→	Need to motivate constructive behavior in response to the change
Control	→	Need to systematically manage the transition state

ed with the change, preferably prior to implementation. Second, to the extent that change creates anxiety and the associated patterns of dysfunctional behavior, it is critical to motivate individuals, through communications and rewards, to react constructively to the change. Finally, if a change presents significant control problems, this implication is the need to pay attention to the management of the transition state to ensure effective organizational control during the transition period. The question is how to do this. There appear to be some patterns in the effectively managed changes. While not universal principles, they represent some relatively consistent differences between the actions that managers take in effective cases of change management and the actions taken in ineffective cases.

For each of the three implications for change management, there are four actions that appear to characterize effectively managed changes. On the following pages, each action area will be explained and a list of illustrative techniques associated with each area will be discussed. The summaries of these techniques are listed in Tables 39.2, 39.3, and 39.4, respectively.

Action Areas for Shaping Political Dynamics

The first set of practices concerns the organization as a political system. Any significant change usually involves some modification of the political system, thus raising issues of power. The implication is a need to shape and manage the political dynamics prior to and throughout the transition. This concept relates to four specific action areas.

The first action area involves getting the support of key power groups within the organization in order to build a critical mass in favor of the change. The organization is a political system with competing groups, cliques, coalitions, and interests, each with varying views on any particular change. Some favor the

Table 39.2. Shaping Political Dynamics

Action	Purpose	Technique

Get support of key power groups	Build internal critical mass of support for change	Identify power relationships
		  Key players
		  Stakeholders
		  Influence relationships
		Use strategies for building support
		  Participation
		  Bargaining/deals
		  Isolation
		  Removal

Demonstrate leadership support of the change	Shape the power distribution and influence the patterns of behavior	Leaders model behavior to promote identification with them Articulate vision of future state Use reward system Provide support/resources Remove roadblocks Maintain momentum Send signals through informal organization

Use symbols	Create identification with the change and appearance of a critical mass of support	Communicate with
		  Name/graphics
		  Language systems
		  Symbolic acts
		  Small signals

Build in stability	Reduce excess anxiety, defensive reactions, and conflicts	Allow time to prepare for change Send consistent messages Maintain points of stability Communicate what will not change

change. Some oppose it. Some may be disinterested. But the change cannot succeed unless there is a critical mass of support; several steps can be used to build that support. The first step is identifying the power relationships as a basis for planning a political strategy. This step may involve identifying the key players in the organization, or the individual and/or group stakeholders—the individuals who have a positive, negative, or neutral stake in the change. Frequently, drawing a diagram or creating a stakeholder or influence map may be useful in conceptualizing these relationships. This map should include not only the various stakeholders but their relationships to each other—who influences whom and what the stakes are for each individual.

Having identified the political topography of the change, the next step is to think about approaches for building support. There are several possible methods. The first is participation, which has long been recognized as a tool for reducing resistance to change and for gaining support. As individuals or groups become

involved in a change, they tend to see it as *their* change, rather than one imposed on them.

Participation, while desirable, might not be feasible or wise in all situations. In some cases, participation merely increases the power of opposing groups to forestall the change. Thus, another approach may be bargaining with groups, or cutting deals. In this case, those favoring the change get the support of others by providing some incentive to comply.

A third step is isolation. There may be those who resist participation or bargaining and who persist in attempting to undermine the change. The goal in this situation is to minimize the impact of such individuals on the organization by assigning them to a position outside the mainstream.

In the extreme, the final step is removal. In some cases, individuals who cannot be isolated or brought into constructive roles may have to be removed from the scene through a transfer to another organization or by outplacement. Obviously, participation and bar-

Table 39.3. Motivating Constructive Behavior

Action	Purpose	Technique

Surface/create dissatisfaction with the current state	Unfreeze from the present state and provide motivation to move away from the present situation	Present information on
		  Environmental impact
		  Economic impact
		  Goal discrepancies
		  How change affects people
		  Have organization members collect/present information

Obtain the appropriate levels of participation in planning/implementing change	Obtain the benefits of participation (motivation, better decisions, communication); control the costs of participation (time, control, conflict, ambiguity)	Create opportunities for participation
		  Diagnosis
		  Design
		  Implementation planning
		  Implementation evaluation
		Use a variety of participation methods
		  Direct/indirect
		  Information vs. input vs. decision making
		  Broad vs. narrow scope
		  Expertise vs. representation

Reward desired behavior in transition to future state	Shape behavior to support the future state	Give formal rewards
		  Measures
		  Pay
		  Promotion
		Give informal rewards
		  Recognition/praise
		  Feedback
		  Assignments

Provide time and opportunity to disengage from current state	Help people deal with their attachment and loss associated with change	Allow enough time Create opportunity to vent emotions Have farewell ceremonies

gaining are more desirable and leave a more positive aftermath; however, it would be naive to assume that these first two methods will be successful in all cases.

An important consideration in creating the political momentum and sense of critical mass is the activity of leaders. Thus, a second action area is leader behavior in support of the change. Leaders can greatly shape the power distribution and influence patterns in an organization. They can mold perceptions and create a sense of political momentum by sending out signals, providing support, and dispensing rewards.

Leaders can take a number of specific actions. First, they can serve as models; through their behavior, they provide a vision of the future state and a source of identification for various groups within the organization. Second, leaders can serve as important persons in articulating the vision of the future state. Third, leaders can play a crucial role by rewarding key individuals and specific types of behavior. Fourth, leaders can pro-

vide support through political influence and needed resources. Similarly, leaders can remove roadblocks and, through their public statements, maintain momentum. Finally, leaders can send important signals through the informal organization. During times of uncertainty and change, individuals throughout the organization tend to look to leaders for signals concerning appropriate behavior and the direction of movement in the organization. Frequently, potent signals are sent through such minor acts as patterns of attendance at meetings or the phrases and words used in public statements. By careful attention to these subtle actions, leaders can greatly influence the perceptions of others.

The third action area concerns the use of symbols associated with a change. Such symbols as language, pictures, and acts create a focus for identification and the appearance of a critical mass within the organization's political system. Symbols are used by public and social movements and are similarly relevant to dealing

Table 39.4. Managing the Transition

Action	Purpose	Technique

Develop and communicate a clear image of the future state	Provide direction for management of transition; reduce ambiguity	Develop as complete a design as possible
		General impact statements
		Communicate
		  Repeatedly
		  Multiple channels
		  Tell and sell
		Describe how things will operate
		Communicate clear, stable image/vision of the future

Use multiple and consistent leverage points	Recognize the systemic nature of changes and reduce potential for creating new problems during transition	Use all four organizational components Anticipate poor fits Sequence changes appropriately
Use transition devices	Create organizational arrangements specifically to manage the transition state	Appoint a transition manager Provide transition resources Design specific transition devices (dual systems, backup) Develop a transition plan

Obtain feedback about the transition state; evaluate success	Determine the progress of the transition; reduce dependence on traditional feedback processes	Use formal methods
		  Interviews
		  Focus groups
		  Surveys/samples
		Use informal channels
		Use participation

with the political system within an organization. A variety of devices can be used, such as names and related graphics that clearly identify events, activities, or organizational units. Language is another symbol; it can communicate a unique way of doing business. The use of symbols is a mundane behavior that can, however, have a powerful impact on the clarity of the informal organization. The more focused the informal organization, the less the political turbulence. For example, a particular promotion, a firing, the moving of an office, or an open door, all can serve to create and send important signals. These small but visible signals by the leaders (as mentioned above) can be important in providing a symbolic sense of political movement.

The final action area is that of building stability. Too much uncertainty can create excess anxiety and defensive reaction, thus heightening political conflict to a counterproductive level. The organization must provide certain "anchors" to create a sense of stability within the context of the transition. This can help limit the reverberations of the change and dampen counterproductive political activity. A number of steps, such as preparing people for the change by providing information in advance, can buffer them to a degree against the uncertainty that will occur. Secondly, some stabili-

ty can be preserved—even in the face of change—if managers are careful to maintain the consistency of messages they convey to organization members throughout the period of change. Nothing creates more instability than inconsistent or conflicting messages. Thirdly, it may be important to maintain certain very visible aspects of the business, such as preserving certain units, organizational names, management processes, or staffing patterns or keeping people in the same physical location. Finally, it may help to communicate specifically what will not change—to mediate the fears that everything is changing or that the change will be much greater than what actually is planned.

In summary, the four action areas focus on identifying the political system and then developing a political strategy. Specific action includes using leadership and related symbols to maintain momentum and critical mass in support of the change and building stability to prevent the counterproductive effects of extreme anxiety.

Motivating Constructive Behavior

When a broad, significant change occurs in an organization, the first questions many people ask are "What's in it for me?" and "What's going to happen to me?"

This is an indication of the anxiety that occurs when people are faced with the uncertainty associated with organizational change. Anxiety may result in a number of reactions, ranging from withdrawal to panic to active resistance. The task of management is to somehow relieve that anxiety and motivate constructive behavior through a variety of actions. Some actions are aimed at providing much needed information communicating the nature, extent, and impact of the change. Others are focused on providing clear rewards for required behavior, recognizing and dealing with some of the natural anxiety. There are four specific action areas.

The first action area is to surface or create dissatisfaction with the current state. Individuals may be psychologically attached to the current state, which is comfortable and known, compared to the uncertainty associated with change. A critical step, then, is to demonstrate how unrealistic it is to assume that the current state has been completely good, is still good, and will always remain good. The goal is to "unfreeze" people from their inertia and create willingness to explore the possibility of change. Part of their anxiety is based on fantasies that the future state may create problems, as well as on fantasies about how wonderful the current state is.

Techniques for dealing with this problem involve providing specific information, such as educating people about what is occurring in the environment that is creating the need for change. In addition, it is useful to help people understand the economic and business consequences of not changing. It may be helpful to identify and emphasize discrepancies—the discrepancy between the present situation and the situation as it should be. In critical cases, it may be necessary to paint a disaster scenario, in which people can see what would happen if the current state continued unchanged. It may be helpful to present a graphic image of how the failure to change would affect people. One manager for example, talked very graphically about what would happen if the division did not become successful within eighteen months: "They'll pull buses up to the door, close the plant, and cart away the workers and the machinery." The manager presented a highly graphic image of the consequences of not making the change. An alternative to management's presenting this kind of information may be to involve organization members in collecting and presenting their own perceptions. Participating in the collection and discovery process may make the information

more salient, since it comes from peers in the work force.

There is a need to overcommunicate during change management efforts. Extreme anxiety impairs normal functioning; thus, people may be unable to hear and integrate messages effectively the first time. Therefore, it may be necessary to communicate key messages two, three, four, and even five times to individuals through various media.

The second action area for motivation is to obtain participation in planning and implementing change. Employee participation in the change process yields proven benefits. It tends to capture people's excitement. It may result in better decisions because of employee input, and it may create more direct communications through personal involvement. On the other hand, participation also has some cost. It takes time, involves giving up some control, and may create conflict and increase ambiguity. The question, then, is to choose where, how, and when to build in participation. People may participate in the early diagnosis of the problems, in the design or development of solutions, in implementation planning, or in the actual execution of the implementation. There are many options. Various individuals or groups may participate at different times, depending on their skills and expertise, the information they have, and their acceptance and ownership of the change. Participation can be direct and widespread or indirect through representatives. Representatives may be chosen by position, level, or expertise. Using some form of participation usually outweighs the costs of no involvement at all.

The third action area is to visibly reward the desired behavior in both the future and transition states. People tend to do what they perceive they will be rewarded for doing. To the extent that people see their behavior as leading to rewards or outcomes they value, they will tend to be motivated to perform as expected. It is important to realize that during implementation, the old reward system frequently loses potency and new rewards are not set up as an early step. This results in a situation in which an individual is asked to act in one way but has been rewarded for acting in another way. Sometimes people are punished by the existing measurement system for doing things that are required to make the change successful. Management needs to pay special attention to the indicators of performance, to the dispensation of pay or other tangible rewards, and to promotion during the transition. In addition, there are informal rewards, such as recognition, praise, feedback, or the assignment of different roles, and it is important to carefully manage these to ensure that they support constructive behavior during the transition. It is equally important to reestablish clearly an appropriate reward system for the future state.

The fourth action area directly affects individual anxiety. It is the need to provide time and opportunity to disengage from the current state. People associate a sense of loss with change. It is predictable that they will go through a process of "letting go of," or mourning, the old structure. Management, knowing that this is essential, can greatly assist in this process. A number of specific techniques are possible. One is to provide the appropriate time for letting go, while giving people enough information and preparation to work through their detachment from the current state. Another technique may be to provide the opportunity to vent emotions through an event similar to a wake. This can be done in small group discussions, in which people are encouraged to talk about their feelings concerning the organizational change. While this may initially be seen as promoting resistance, it can have the opposite effect. People will undoubtedly talk about these issues, either formally or informally. If management can recognize such concerns and encourage people to express their feelings, it may help them let go of them and move into constructive action. It may also be useful to create ceremony, ritual, or symbols, such as farewell or closing-day ceremonies, to help give people some psychological closure on the old organization.

Thus, there are four action areas in motivating constructive behavior. One concerns helping people detach themselves from the current state. The second concerns obtaining appropriate levels of participation in planning or implementing the change. The third concerns rewarding desired behavior during the transition, and the final action area has to do with helping people let go of their psychological attachment to the present situation.

Managing the Transition

The third implication concerns the actual and explicit management of the transition state, which is that time period between the current state and the implemented future state. It is frequently characterized by great uncertainty and control problems, because the current state is disassembled prior to full operation of the future state. Managers need to coordinate the transition with the same degree of care, the same resources, and the same skills as they manage any other major project. There are four specific action areas in which managers can work (see Table 39.4).

The first action area is to develop and communicate a clear image of the future state. The ambiguity of change without a focus produces major problems. It is difficult to manage toward something when people do not know what that something is. In the absence of a clear direction, the organization gets "transition paralysis," and activity grinds to a halt. This is caused by uncertainty over what is appropriate, helpful, or constructive behavior. Several specific practices are relevant in this situation. First, there is a need to develop as complete a design as possible for the future state. This may not always be feasible, but to the extent possible, it is important to articulate at least a vision ahead of time. Secondly, it may be useful to construct a statement that identifies the impact of the change on different parts of the organization. Thirdly, it is important to maintain a stable vision and to avoid unnecessary changes, extreme modification, or conflicting views of that vision during the transition.

Finally, there is a need to communicate. As previously indicated, it is important to communicate repeatedly and to use multiple media, be it video, small group discussions, large group meetings, or written memos. It is critical to think of this communication as both a telling and a selling activity. People need to be informed, but they also need to be sold on why the change is important. This may necessitate repeated explanations of the rationale for the change, the nature of the future state, and the advantages of the future. Finally, the future state must be made real, visible, and concrete. Communications should include information on future decision-making and operating procedures. The way in which this is communicated can help shape the vision of the future. For example, one company showed television commercials, both inside and outside its organization, demonstrating the specific types of customer service that it was attempting to provide. The commercials gave people clear, graphic, and memorable images of the future state.

The next area is to use multiple and consistent leverage points for changing behavior. This issue relates to the organizational model underlying this approach to change management. An organization is a system made of tasks, individuals, formal organizational arrangements, and informal organizational arrangements. During a transition, when certain aspects of the organization are being changed, there is a potential for problems arising from a poor fit. An organization works best when all elements fit smoothly. Managers need to use all of these levers for change. Specifically, managers need to think about modifications that need to be made in the work, individuals, formal structure, and informal arrangements. Secondly, there is a need to monitor and/or predict some of the poor fits that may occur when changing any of the organizational components. It is necessary to plan the changes to minimize poor fit among different elements of the organization.

The next action area involves using transition devices. The transition state is different from the current and future states; therefore, there may be a need to create organizational arrangements that are specifically designed to manage the transition state. These devices include: (1) a transition manager; (2) specific transition resources, including budget, time, and staff; (3) specific transition structures, such as dual management systems and backup support; and (4) a transition plan. All of these can be helpful in bringing needed management attention to the transition.

The final area is to obtain feedback and an evaluation of the transition state. The transition is a time when managers need to know what is going on in the organization. There is usually a breakdown in the normal feedback devices that managers use to collect information about how the organization is running. This is particularly serious during a period of change when there may be high anxiety and people hesitate to deliver bad news. Therefore, it is critical to build in various channels for feedback. Formal methods may include individual interviews, various types of focus-group data collection, surveys used globally or with select samples, or feedback gathered during a normal business meeting. Informal channels include senior manager's meetings with individuals or with groups, informal contacts, or field trips. Finally, feedback may be promoted through direct participation by representatives of key groups in planning, monitoring, or implementing the change.

In summary, the initial emphasis in transition management is on identifying a clear image of the future state. Secondly, there is a need to pay attention to the changing configuration of the organizational system and to develop—where needed—unique organizational arrangements to manage the transition period. Finally, there is a need to monitor progress through the development of feedback systems. All of these are important elements in managing a transition.

SUMMARY

Opening Case Revisited

The reorganization at Orient Oil presents the potential for a full range of problems associated with change. This change requires concentrated attention from skilled managers. In Orient, the senior team was exposed to a speaker who raised some of the key issues in managing change and described some new and different methods of change management. As a consequence, the senior group at Orient decided to delay the announcement of the change and appointed a highly respected senior member to head a transition team. This team was dedicated full time to the transition management task. The first assignment was to develop an initial transition plan, which included specific sections dealing with communications; how to get participation in the change; how to sequence the individual changes; how to assign jobs and coordinate moves; how to make the changes in information and control systems; and, finally, what the senior team had to do to lead the change effectively. The senior team reviewed this plan several weeks later and approved it. The change was implemented, led by the senior team, and guided by the transition manager and the transition team. Within six months, all of the major elements of the transition plan had been accomplished. As the Orient Oil chairman reflected, "When I think about all of the things we changed and all of the things we had to accomplish, I never thought that we could have done this so well. I'm amazed."

Why have we placed such an emphasis on change management? The process of implementation is a critical determinant of the success of a new organization design. To develop a design and then not give significant thought, time, and effort to the planning and management of its implementation is to do only part of the job of design.

As we look at organizations over time, we find that changes in design are a normal part of life. They are not one-time events but an ongoing element in the development of an organization. Adaptive organizations are able to respond quickly and effectively to new conditions—they are able to reconfigure to support new strategies as needed. Therefore, organizations that remain effective over time have to develop the capacity to execute change and, in some cases, competently manage accelerated change.

This leads us to our final topic: organizations over time. What are the types of design changes that we might anticipate at different points in time? Moreover, how might managers think ahead and begin to plan necessary changes in organization design in a way that anticipates rather than responds to problems and opportunities? Can creative organization design done in anticipation be an effective competitive tool for the manager?

NOTE

1. R. Beckhard and R. Harris, *Organizational Transitions,* (Reading, MA: Addison-Wesley, 1977); M. Beer, *Organization Change and Development,* (Santa Monica, CA: Goodyear, 1980); N. Margulies and J. Wallace, *Organizational Change,* (Glenview, IL: Scott, Foresman, 1973); D. Nadler, *Feedback and Organization Development,* (Reading, MA; Addison-Wesley, 1977); N. Tichy, *Managing Strategic Change,* (New York: Wiley, 1983); M. Tushman, *Organization Change: An Exploratory Study and Case History,* (Ithaca, NY: NYSSILR, Cornell University, 1974).

40

Beyond the Charismatic Leader

Leadership and Organizational Change

DAVID A. NADLER
MICHAEL L. TUSHMAN

Like never before, discontinuous organization change is an important determinant of organization adaptation. Responding to regulatory, economic, competitive, and/or technological shifts through more efficiently pushing the same organization systems and processes just does not work.[1] Rather, organizations may need to manage through periods of both incremental as well as revolutionary change.[2] Further, given the intensity of global competition in more and more industries, these organizational transformations need to be initiated and implemented rapidly. Speed seems to count.[3] These trends put a premium on executive leadership and the management of system-wide organization change.

There is a growing knowledge base about large-scale organization change.[4] This literature is quite consistent on at least one aspect of effective system-wide change—namely, executive leadership matters. The executive is a critical actor in the drama of organization change.[5] Consider the following examples:

At Fuji-Xerox, Yotaro Kobayashi's response to declining market share, lack of new products, and increasing customer complaints was to initiate widespread organization change. Most fundamentally, Kobayashi's vision was to change the way Fuji-Xerox conducted its business. Kobayashi and his team initiated the "New Xerox Movement"

through Total Quality Control. The core values of quality, problem solving, teamwork, and customer emphasis were espoused and acted upon by Kobayashi and his team. Further, the executive team at Fuji instituted a dense infrastructure of objectives, measures, rewards, tools, education, and slogans, all in service of TQC and the "New Xerox." New heroes were created. Individuals and teams were publicly celebrated to reinforce to the system those behaviors that reflected the best of the new Fuji-Xerox. Kobayashi continually reinforced, celebrated, and communicated his TQC vision. Between 1976–1980, Fuji-Xerox gained back its market share, developed an impressive set of new products, and won the Demming prize.[6]

Much of this Fuji-Xerox learning was transferred to corporate Xerox and further enhanced by Dave Kearns and his executive team. Beginning in 1983, Kearns clearly expressed his "Leadership Through Quality" vision for the corporation. Kearns established a Quality Task Force and Quality Office with respected Xerox executives. This broad executive base developed the architecture of Leadership Through Quality. This effort included quality principles, tools, education, required leadership actions, rewards, and feedback mechanisms. This attempt to transform the entire corporation was initiated at the top and diffused throughout the

Copyright © 1990 by The Regents of the University of California. Reprinted from the *California Management Review*, Vol. 32, No. 2. By permission of The Regents.

firm through overlapping teams. These teams were pushed by Kearns and his team to achieve extraordinary gains. While not completed, this transformation has helped Xerox regain lost market share and improve product development efforts.[7]

At General Electric, Jack Welch's vision of a lean, aggressive organization with all the benefits of size but the agility of small firms is being driven by a set of interrelated actions. For example, the "work-out" effort is a corporate-wide endeavor, spearheaded by Welch, to get the bureaucracy out of a large-old organization and, in turn, to liberate GE employees to be their best. This effort is more than Welch. Welch's vision is being implemented by a senior task force which has initiated work-out efforts in Welch's own top team as well as in each GE business area. These efforts consist of training, problem solving, measures, rewards, feedback procedures, and outside expertise. Similarly, sweeping changes at SAS under Carlzon, at ICI under Harvey-Jones, by Anderson at NCR, and at Honda each emphasize the importance of visionary leadership along with executive teams, systems, structures and processes to transfer an individual's vision of the future into organizational reality.[8]

On the other hand, there are many examples of visionary executives who are unable to translate their vision into organization action. For example, Don Burr's vision at People Express not only to "make a better world" but also to grow rapidly and expand to capture the business traveler was not coupled with requisite changes in organization infrastructure, procedures, and/or roles. Further, Burr was unable to build a cohesive senior team to help execute his compelling vision. This switch in vision, without a committed senior team and associated structure and systems, led to the rapid demise of People Express.

Vision and/or charisma is not enough to sustain large-system change. While a necessary condition in the management of discontinuous change, we must build a model of leadership that goes beyond the inspired individual; a model that takes into account the complexities of system-wide change in large, diverse, geographically complex organizations. We attempt to develop a framework for the extension of charismatic leadership by building on the growing leadership literature,[9] the literature on organization evolution,[10] and

our intensive consulting work with executives attempting major organization change.[11]

ORGANIZATIONAL CHANGE AND RE-ORGANIZATION

Organizations go through change all the time. However, the nature, scope, and intensity of organizational changes vary considerably. Different kinds of organizational changes will require very different kinds of leadership behavior in initiating, energizing, and implementing the change. Organization changes vary along the following dimensions:

- *Strategic and Incremental Changes*—Some changes in organizations, while significant, only affect selected components of the organization. The fundamental aim of such change is to enhance the effectiveness of the organization, but within the general framework of the strategy, mode of organizing, and values that already are in place. Such changes are called *incremental changes*. Incremental changes happen all the time in organizations, and they need not be small. Such things as changes in organization structure, the introduction of new technology, and significant modifications of personnel practices are all large and significant changes, but ones which usually occur within the existing definition and frame of reference of the organization. Other changes have an impact on the whole system of the organization and fundamentally redefine what the organization is or change its basic framework, including strategy, structure, people, processes, and (in some cases) core values. These changes are called *strategic organizational changes*. The Fuji-Xerox, People Express, ICI, and SAS cases are examples of system-wide organization change.

- *Reactive and Anticipatory Changes*—Many organizational changes are made in direct response to some external event. These changes, which are forced upon the organization, are called *reactive*. The Xerox, SAS, and ICI transformations were all initiated in response to organization performance crisis. At other times, strategic organizational change is initiated not because of the need to respond to a contemporaneous event, but rather because senior management believes that change in anticipation of events still to come will provide competitive advantage. These changes are called *anticipatory*. The GE and People Express cases as well as more recent system-wide changes at ALCOA and Cray Research are examples of system-wide change initiated in anticipation of environmental change.

If these two dimensions are combined, a basic typology of different changes can be described (see Figure 40.1).

Change which is incremental and anticipatory is called *tuning*. These changes are not system-wide redefinitions, but rather modifications of specific components, and they are initiated in anticipation of future events. Incremental change which is initiated reactively is called *adaptation*. Strategic change initiated in anticipation of future events is called *re-orientation*, and change which is prompted by immediate demands is called *re-creation*.[12]

Research on patterns of organizational life and death across several industries has provided insight into the patterns of strategic organizational change.[13] Some of the key findings are as follows:

- *Strategic organization changes are necessary*. These changes appear to be environmentally driven. Various factors—be they competitive, technological, or regulatory—drive the organization (either reactively or in anticipation) to make system-wide changes. While strategic organization change does not guarantee success, those organizations that fail to change, generally fail to survive. Discontinuous environmental change seems to require discontinuous organization change.

- *Re-creations are riskier*. Re-creations are riskier endeavors than re-orientations if only because they are initiated under crisis conditions and under sharp time constraints. Further, re-creations almost always in-

volve a change in core values. As core values are most resistant to change, re-creations always trigger substantial individual resistance to change and heightened political behavior. Re-creations that do succeed usually involve changes in the senior leadership of the firm, frequently involving replacement from the outside. For example, the reactive system-wide changes at U.S. Steel, Chrysler, and Singer were all initiated by new senior teams.

- *Re-orientations are associated more with success*. Re-orientations have the luxury of time to shape the change, build coalitions, and empower individuals to be effective in the new organization. Further, re-orientations give senior managers time to prune and shape core values in service of the revised strategy, structure, and processes. For example, the proactive strategic changes at Cray Research, ALCOA, and GE each involved system-wide change as well as the shaping of core values ahead of the competition and from a position of strength.

Re-orientations are, however, risky. When sweeping changes are initiated in advance of precipitating external events, success is contingent on making appropriate strategic bets. As re-orientations are initiated ahead of the competition and in advance of environmental shifts, they require visionary executives. Unfortunately, in real time, it is unclear who will be known as visionary executives (e.g., Welch, Iacocca, Rollwagen at Cray Research) and who will be known as failures (e.g., Don Burr at People Express, or Larry Goshorn at General Automation). In turbulent environments, not to make strategic bets in associated with failure. Not all bets will pay off, however. The advantages of re-orientations derive from the extra implementation time and from the opportunity to learn from and adapt to mistakes.[14]

As with re-creations, executive leadership is crucial in initiating and implementing strategic re-orientations. The majority of successful re-orientations involve change in the CEO and substantial executive team change. Those most successful firms, however, have executive teams that are relatively stable yet are still capable of initiating several re-orientations (e.g., Ken Olsen at DEC and An Wang at Wang).

There are, then, quite fundamentally different kinds of organizational changes. The role of executive

	Incremental	Strategic
Anticipatory	Tuning	Re-orientation
Reactive	Adaptation	Re-creation

Figure 40.1. Types of organizational changes.

leadership varies considerably for these different types of organizational changes. Incremental change typically can be managed by the existing management structures and processes of the organization, sometimes in conjunction with special transition structures.[15] In these situations, a variety of leadership styles may be appropriate, depending upon how the organization is normally managed and led. In strategic changes, however, the management process and structure itself is the subject of change; therefore, it cannot be relied upon to manage the change. In addition, the organization's definition of effective leadership may also be changing as a consequence of the re-orientation or re-creation. In these situations, leadership becomes a very critical element of change management.

This article focuses on the role of executive leadership in strategic organization change, and in particular, the role of leadership in re-orientations. Given organization and individual inertia, re-orientations cannot be initiated or implemented without sustained action by the organization's leadership. Indeed, re-orientations are frequently driven by new leadership, often brought in from outside the organization.[16] A key challenge for executives facing turbulent environments, then, is to learn how to effectively initiate, lead, and manage re-orientations. Leadership of strategic re-orientations requires not only charisma, but also substantial instrumental skills in building executive teams, roles, and systems in support of the change, as well as institutional skills in diffusing leadership throughout the organization.

THE CHARISMATIC LEADER

While the subject of leadership has received much attention over the years, the more specific issue of leadership during periods of change has only recently attracted serious attention.[17] What emerges from various discussions of leadership and organizational change is a picture of the special kind of leadership that appears to be critical during times of strategic organizational change. While various words have been used to portray this type of leadership, we prefer the label "charismatic" leader. It refers to a special quality that enables the leader to mobilize and sustain activity within an organization through specific personal actions combined with perceived personal characteristics.

The concept of the charismatic leader is not the popular version of the great speech maker or television personality. Rather, a model has emerged from recent work aimed at identifying the nature and determinants of a particular type of leadership that successfully brings about changes in an individual's values, goals, needs, or aspirations. Research on charismatic leadership has identified this type of leadership as observable, definable, and having clear behavioral characteristics.[18] We have attempted to develop a first cut description of the leader in terms of patterns of behavior that he/she seems to exhibit. The resulting approach is outlined in Figure 40.2, which lists three major types of behavior that characterize these leaders and some illustrative kinds of actions.

The first component of charismatic leadership is *envisioning*. This involves the creation of a picture of the future, or of a desired future state with which people can identify and which can generate excitement. By creating vision, the leader provides a vehicle for people to develop commitment, a common goal around which people can rally, and a way for people to feel successful. Envisioning is accomplished through a range of different actions. Clearly, the simplest form is through articulation of a compelling vision in clear and dramatic terms. The vision needs to be challenging, meaningful, and worthy of pursuit, but it also needs to be credible. People must believe that it is possible to succeed in the pursuit of the vision. Vision is also communicated in other ways, such as through expectations that the leader expresses and through the leader personally demonstrating behaviors and activities that symbolize and further that vision.

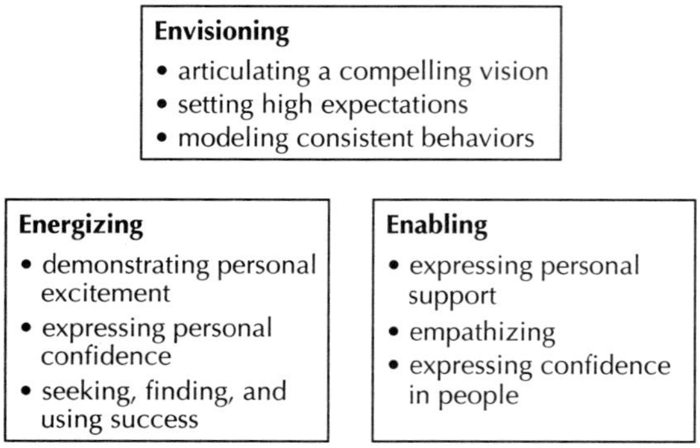

Envisioning
- articulating a compelling vision
- setting high expectations
- modeling consistent behaviors

Energizing
- demonstrating personal excitement
- expressing personal confidence
- seeking, finding, and using success

Enabling
- expressing personal support
- empathizing
- expressing confidence in people

Figure 40.2. The charismatic leader.

The second component is *energizing*. Here the role of the leader is the direct generation of energy—motivation to act—among members of the organization. How is this done? Different leaders engage in energizing in different ways, but some of the most common include demonstration of their own personal excitement and energy, combined with leveraging that excitement through direct personal contact with large numbers of people in the organization. They express confidence in their own ability to succeed. They find, and use, successes to celebrate progress toward the vision.

The third component is *enabling*. The leader psychologically helps people act or perform in the face of challenging goals. Assuming that individuals are directed through a vision and motivated by the creation of energy, they then may need emotional assistance in accomplishing their tasks. This enabling is achieved in several ways. Charismatic leaders demonstrate empathy—the ability to listen, understand, and share the feelings of those in the organization. They express support for individuals. Perhaps most importantly, the charismatic leader tends to express his/her confidence in people's ability to perform effectively and to meet challenges.

Yotaro Kobayashi at Fuji-Xerox and Paul O'Neil at ALCOA each exhibit the characteristics of charismatic leaders. In Kobayashi's transformation at Fuji, he was constantly espousing his New Xerox Movement vision for Fuji. Kobayashi set high standards for his firm (e.g., the 3500 model and the Demming Prize), for himself, and for his team. Beyond espousing this vision for Fuji, Kobayashi provided resources, training, and personal coaching to support his colleagues' efforts in the transformation at Fuji. Similarly, Paul O'Neil has espoused a clear vision for ALCOA anchored on quality, safety, and innovation. O'Neil has made his vision compelling and central to the firm, has set high expectations for his top team and for individuals throughout ALCOA and provides continuous support and energy for his vision through meetings, task forces, video tapes, and extensive personal contact.

Assuming that leaders act in these ways, what functions are they performing that help bring about change? First, they provide a psychological focal point for the energies, hopes, and aspirations of people in the organization. Second, they serve as powerful role models whose behaviors, actions, and personal energy demonstrate the desired behaviors expected throughout the firm. The behaviors of charismatic leaders provide a standard to which others can aspire. Through their personal effectiveness and attractiveness they build a very personal and intimate bond between themselves and the organization. Thus, they can become a source of sustained energy; a figure whose high standards others can identify with and emulate.

Limitations of the Charismatic Leader

Even if one were able to do all of the things involved in being a charismatic leader, it might still not be enough. In fact, our observations suggest that there are a number of inherent limitations to the effectiveness of charismatic leaders, many stemming from risks associated with leadership which revolves around a single individual. Some of the key potential problems are:

- *Unrealistic Expectations*—In creating a vision and getting people energized, the leader may create expectations that are unrealistic or unattainable. These can backfire if the leader cannot live up to the expectations that are created.

- *Dependency and Counterdependency*—A strong, visible, and energetic leader may spur different psychological response. Some individuals may become overly dependent upon the leader, and in some cases whole organizations become dependent. Everyone else stops initiating actions and waits for the leader to provide direction; individuals may become passive or reactive. On the other extreme, others may be uncomfortable with strong personal presence and spend time and energy demonstrating how the leader is wrong—how the emperor has no clothes.

- *Reluctance to Disagree with the Leader*—The charismatic leader's approval or disapproval becomes an important commodity. In the presence of a strong leader, people may become hesitant to disagree or come into conflict with the leader. This may, in turn, lead to stifling conformity.

- *Need for Continuing Magic*—The charismatic leader may become trapped by the expectation that the magic often associated with charisma will continue unabated. This may cause the leader to act in ways that are not functional, or (if the magic is not produced) it may cause a crisis of leadership credibility.

- *Potential Feelings of Betrayal*—When and if things

do not work out as the leader has envisioned, the potential exists for individuals to feel betrayed by their leader. They may become frustrated and angry, with some of that anger directed at the individual who created the expectations that have been betrayed.

- *Disenfranchisement of Next Levels of Management*—A consequence of the strong charismatic leader is that the next levels of management can easily become disenfranchised. They lose their ability to lead because no direction, vision, exhortation, reward, or punishment is meaningful unless it comes directly from the leader. The charismatic leader thus may end up underleveraging his or her management and/or creating passive/dependent direct reports.

- *Limitations of Range of the Individual Leader*—When the leadership process is built around an individual, management's ability to deal with various issues is limited by the time, energy, expertise, and interest of that individual. This is particularly problematic during periods of change when different types of issues demand different types of competencies (e.g., markets, technologies, products, finance) which a single individual may not possess. Different types of strategic changes make different managerial demands and call for different personal characteristics. There may be limits to the number of strategic changes that one individual can lead over the life of an organization.

In light of these risks, it appears that the charismatic leader is a necessary component—but not a sufficient component—of the organizational leadership required for effective organizational re-organization. There is a need to move beyond the charismatic leader.

INSTRUMENTAL LEADERSHIP

Effective leaders of change need to be more than just charismatic. Effective re-orientations seem to be characterized by the presence of another type of leadership behavior which focuses not on the excitement of individuals and changing their goals, needs, or aspirations, but on making sure that individuals in the senior team and throughout the organization behave in ways needed for change to occur. An important leadership role is to build competent teams, clarify required behaviors, built in measurement, and administer rewards and pun-

ishments so that individuals perceive that behavior consistent with the change is central for them in achieving their own goals.[19] We will call this type of leadership *instrumental leadership,* since it focuses on the management of teams, structures, and managerial processes to create individual instrumentalities. The basis of this approach is in expectancy theories of motivation, which propose that individuals will perform those behaviors that they perceive as instrumental for acquiring valued outcomes.[20] Leadership, in this context, involves managing environments to create conditions that motivate desired behavior.[21]

In practice, instrumental leadership of change involves three elements of behavior (see Figure 40.3). The first is *structuring.* The leader invests time in building teams that have the required competence to execute and implement the re-orientation[22] and in creating structures that make it clear what types of behavior are required throughout the organization. This may involve setting goals, establishing standards, and defining roles and responsibilities. Re-orientations seem to require detailed planning about what people will need to do and how they will be required to act during different phases of the change. The second element of instrumental leadership is *controlling.* This involves the creation of systems and processes to measure, monitor, and assess both behavior and results and to administer corrective action.[23] The third element is *rewarding,* which includes the administration of both rewards and punishments contingent upon the degree to which behavior is consistent with the requirements of the change.

Instrumental leadership focuses on the challenge of shaping consistent behaviors in support of the reorientation. The charismatic leader excites individuals, shapes their aspirations, and directs their energy. In

Figure 40.3. Instrumental leadership.

practice, however, this is not enough to sustain patterns of desired behavior. Subordinates and colleagues may be committed to the vision, but over time other forces may influence their behavior, particularly when they are not in direct personal contact with the leader. This is particularly relevant during periods of change when the formal organization and the informal social system may lag behind the leader and communicate outdated messages or reward traditional behavior. Instrumental leadership is needed to ensure compliance over time consistent with the commitment generated by charismatic leadership.

At Xerox, for example, David Kearns used instrumental leadership to further enliven his Leadership Through Quality efforts.[24] Beyond his own sustained behaviors in support of the Leadership Through Quality effort, Kearns and his Quality Office developed a comprehensive set of roles, processes, teams, and feedback and audit mechanisms for getting customer input and continuous improvement into everyday problem solving throughout Xerox. Individuals and teams across the corporation were evaluated on their ability to continuously meet customer requirements. These data were used in making pay, promotion, and career decisions.

The Role of Mundane Behaviors

Typical descriptions of both charismatic and instrumental leaders tend to focus on significant events, critical incidents, and grand gestures. Our vision of the change manager is frequently exemplified by the key speech or public event that is a potential watershed event. While these are important arenas for leadership, leading large-system change also requires sustained attention to the myriad of details that make up organizational life. The accumulation of less dramatic, day-to-day activities and mundane behaviors serves as a powerful determinant of behavior.[25] Through relatively unobtrusive acts, through sustained attention to detail, managers can directly shape perceptions and culture in support of the change effort. Examples of mundane behavior that when taken together can have a great impact include:

- allocation of time; calendar management
- asking questions, following up
- shaping of physical settings

- public statements
- setting agendas of events or meetings
- use of events such as lunches, meetings, to push the change effort
- summarization—post hoc interpretation of what occurred
- creating heroes
- use of humor, stories, and myths
- small symbolic actions, including rewards and punishments

In each of these ways, leaders can use daily activities to emphasize important issues, identify desirable behavior, and help create patterns and meaning out of the various transactions that make up organizational life.

The Complementarity of Leadership Approaches

It appears that effective organizational re-orientation requires both charismatic and instrumental leadership. Charismatic leadership is needed to generate energy, create commitment, and direct individuals towards new objectives, values or aspirations. Instrumental leadership is required to ensure that people really do act in a manner consistent with their new goals. Either one alone is insufficient for the achievement of change.

The complementarity of leadership approaches and the necessity for both creates a dilemma.[26] Success in implementing these dual approaches is associated with the personal style, characteristics, needs, and skills of the executive. An individual who is adept at one approach may have difficulty executing the other. For example, charismatic leaders may have problems with tasks involved in achieving control. Many charismatic leaders are motivated by a strong desire to receive positive feedback from those around them.[27] They may therefore have problems delivering unpleasant messages, dealing with performance problems, or creating situations that could attract negative feelings.[28]

Only exceptional individuals can handle the behavioral requirements of both charismatic and instrumental leadership styles. While such individuals exist, and alternative may be to involve others in leadership roles, thus complementing the strengths and weaknesses of one individual leader.[29] For example, in the early days at Honda, it took the steadying, systems-oriented hand of Takeo Fujisawa to balance the fanatic, impatient, visionary energy of Soichiro Honda. Similarly, at Data General, it took Alsing and Rasala's social, team, and organization skills to balance and make more humane Tom West's vision and standards for the Eclipse team.[30] Without these complementary organization and systems skills, Don Burr was unable to execute his proactive system-wide changes at People Express.

The limitations of the individual leader pose a significant challenge. Charismatic leadership has a broad reach. It can influence many people, but is limited by the frequency and intensity of contact with the individual leader. Instrumental leadership is also limited by the degree to which the individual leader can structure, observe, measure, and reward behavior. These limitations present significant problems for achieving re-orientations. One implication is that structural extensions of leadership should be created in the process of managing re-orientations.[31] A second implication is that human extensions of leadership need to be created to broaden the scope and impact of leader actions. This leads to a third aspect of leadership and change—the extension of leadership beyond the individual leader, or the creation of institutionalized leadership throughout the organization.

INSTITUTIONALIZING THE LEADERSHIP OF CHANGE

Given the limitations of the individual charismatic leader, the challenge is to broaden the range of individuals who can perform the critical leadership functions during periods of significant organizational change. There are three potential leverage points for the extension of leadership—the senior team, broader senior management, and the development of leadership throughout the organization (see Figure 40.4).

Leveraging the Senior Team

The group of individuals who report directly to the individual leader—the executive or senior team—is the first logical place to look for opportunities to extend and institutionalize leadership. Development of an effective, visible, and dynamic senior team can be a major step in getting around the problems and limitations of the individual leader.[32] Examples of such executive teams include the Management Committee established at Corning by Jamie Houghton or Bob Allen's Executive Committee at AT&T. Several actions appear to be important in enhancing the effectiveness of the senior team:

- *Visible Empowerment of the Team*—A first step is the visible empowerment of he team, or "anointing" the team as extensions of the individual leader. There are two different aspects to this empowerment: objective and symbolic. Objective empowerment involves providing team members with the autonomy and resources to serve effectively. Symbolic empowerment involves communicating messages (through information, symbols, and mundane behaviors) to show the organization that these individuals are indeed extensions of the leader and ultimately key components of the leadership. Symbolic empowerment can be done through the use of titles, the designation of organizational structures, and the visible presence of individuals in ceremonial roles.

- *Individual Development of Team Members*—Empowerment will fail if the individuals on the team are not capable of executing their revised leadership roles. A major problem in re-orientations is that the members of the senior team frequently are the product of the very systems, structures, and values that the re-orientation seeks to change. Participating in the change, and more importantly, leading it, may require a significant switching of cognitive gears.[33] Re-orientations demand that senior team members think very differently about the business and about managing. This need for personal change at the most senior level has implications for the selection of senior team members (see below). It also may mean that part of the individual leader's role is to help coach, guide, and support individuals in developing their own leadership capabilities. Each individual need not (and should not) be a "clone" of the individual leader; but each should be able to initiate credible leadership actions in a manner consistent with their own personal styles. Ultimately, it also puts a demand on the leader to deal with those who will not or can not make the personal changes required for helping lead the re-orientation.

- *Composition of the Senior Team*—The need for the senior team to implement change may mean that the composition of that team may have to be altered. Different skills, capabilities, styles, and value orientations may be needed to both lead the changes as well

Figure 40.4. Institutionalized leadership.

as to manage in the reconfigured organization.[34] In fact, most successful re-orientations seem to involve some significant changes in the make-up of the senior team. This may require outplacement of people as well as importing new people, either from outside the organization, or from outside the coalition that has traditionally led the organization.[35]

- *The Inducement of Strategic Anticipation*—A critical issue in executing re-orientations is strategic anticipation. By definition, a re-orientation is a strategic organizational change that is initiated in anticipation of significant external events. Re-orientation occurs because the organization's leadership perceives competitive advantage from initiating change earlier rather than later. The question is, who is responsible for thinking about and anticipating external events, and ultimately deciding that re-orientation is necessary? In some cases, the individual leader does this, but the task is enormous. This is where the senior team can be helpful, because as a group it can scan a larger number of events and potentially be more creative in analyzing the environment and the process of anticipation.

  Companies that are successful anticipators create conditions in which anticipation is more likely to occur. They invest in activities that foster anticipation, such as environmental scanning, experiments or probes inside the organization (frequently on the periphery), and frequent contacts with the outside. The senior team has a major role in initiating, sponsoring, and leveraging these activities.[36]

- *The Senior Team as a Learning System*—For a senior team to benefit from its involvement in leading

change, it must become an effective system for learning about the business, the nature of change, and the task of managing change. The challenge is to both bond the team together, while avoiding insularity. One of the costs of such team structures is that they become isolated from the rest of the organization, they develop patterns of dysfunctional conformity, avoid conflict, and over time develop patterns of learned incompetence. These group processes diminish the team's capacity for effective strategic anticipation, and decreases the team's ability to provide effective leadership of the re-orientation.[37]

There are several ways to enhance a senior team's ability to learn over time. One approach is to work to keep the team an open system, receptive to outside ideas and information. This can be accomplished by creating a constant stream of events that expose people to new ideas and/or situations. For example, creating simulations, using critical incident techniques, creating near histories, are all ways of exposing senior teams to novel situations and sharpening problem-solving skills.[38] Similarly, senior teams can open themselves to new ideas via speakers or visitors brought in to meet with the team, visits by the team to other organizations, frequent contact with customers, and planned informal data collection through personal contact (breakfasts, focus groups, etc.) throughout the organization. A second approach involves the shaping and management of the internal group process of the team itself. This involves working on effective group leadership, building effective team member skills, creating meeting management discipline, acquiring group problem-solving and information-processing skills, and ultimately creating norms that promote effective learning, innovation, and problem solving.[39]

David Kearns at Xerox and Paul O'Neil at ALCOA made substantial use of senior teams in implementing their quality-oriented organization transformations. Both executives appointed senior quality task forces composed of highly respected senior executives. These task forces were charged with developing the corporate-wide architecture of the change effort. To sharpen their change and quality skills, these executives made trips to Japan and to other experienced organizations and were involved in extensive education and problem-solving efforts in their task forces and within their own divisions. These task forces put substance and enhanced energy into the CEO's broad vision. These executives were, in turn, role models and champions of the change efforts in their own sectors.

As a final note, it is important to remember that frequently there are significant obstacles in developing effective senior teams to lead re-orientations. The issues of skills and selection have been mentioned. Equally important is the question of power and succession. A team is most successful when there is a perception of common fate. *Individuals have to believe that the success of the team will, in the long run, be more salient to them than their individual short-run success.* In many situations, this can be accomplished through appropriate structures, objectives, and incentives. But these actions may fail when there are pending (or anticipated) decisions to be made concerning senior management succession. In these situations, the quality of collaboration tends to deteriorate significantly, and effective team leadership of change becomes problematic. The individual leader must manage the timing and process of succession in relation to the requirements for team leadership, so that conflicting (and mutually exclusive) incentives are not created by the situation.[40]

Broadening Senior Management

A second step in moving beyond individual leadership of change is the further extension of the leadership beyond the executive or senior team to include a broader set of individuals who make up the senior management of the organization. This would include individuals one or two levels down from the executive team. At Corning, the establishment of two groups—the Corporate Policy Group (approximately the top 35) and the Corporate Management Group (about the top 120)—are examples of mechanisms used by Houghton to broaden the definition of senior management. This set of individuals is in fact the senior operating management of most sizable organizations and is looked upon as senior management by the majority of employees. In many cases (and particularly during times of change) they do not feel like senior management, and thus they are not positioned to lead the change. They feel like participants (at best) and victims (at worst). This group can be particularly problematic since they may be more embedded in the current system of organizing and managing than some of the senior team. They may be less prepared to change, they frequently have molded themselves to fit the current organizational style, and they may feel disenfranchised by the very act of developing a strong executive team, particularly if that team has been assembled by bringing in people from outside of the organization.

The task is to make this group feel like senior management, to get them signed up for the change, and to motivate and enable them to work as an extension of the senior team. Many of the implications are similar to those mentioned above in relation to the top team; however, there are special problems of size and lack of proximity to the individual charismatic leader. Part of the answer is to get the senior team to take responsibility for developing their own teams as leaders of change. Other specific actions may include:

- *Rites of Passage*—Creating symbolic events that help these individuals to feel more a part of senior management.
- *Senior Groups*—Creating structures (councils, boards, committees, conferences) to maintain contact with this group and reinforce their sense of participation as members of senior management.
- *Participation in Planning Change*—Involving these people in the early diagnosing of the need to change and the planning of change strategies associated with the re-orientation. This is particularly useful in getting them to feel more like owners, rather than victims of the change.
- *Intensive Communication*—Maintaining a constant stream of open communication to and from this group. It is the lack of information and perspective

that psychologically disenfranchises these individuals.

Developing Leadership in the Organization

A third arena for enhancing the leadership of re-organizations is through organizational structures, systems, and process for leadership development consistent with the re-orientation. Frequently leadership development efforts lag behind the re-orientation. The management development system of many organizations often works effectively to create managers who will fit well with the organizational environment that the leadership seeks to abandon. There needs to be a strategic and anticipatory thinking about the leadership development process, including the following:

- *Definition of Managerial Competence*—A first step is determining the skills, capabilities, and capacities needed to manage and lead effectively in the re-orientation and post re-orientation period. Factors that have contributed to managerial success in the past may be the seeds of failure in the future.

- *Sourcing Managerial Talent*—Re-orientations may require that the organization identify significantly different sources for acquiring leaders or potential leaders. Senior managers should be involved in recruiting the hiring. Because of the lead time involved, managerial sourcing has to be approached as a long-term (five to ten years) task.

- *Socialization*—As individuals move into the organization and into positions of leadership, deliberate actions must be taken to teach them how the organization's social system works. During periods of re-orientation, the socialization process ought to lead rather than lag behind the change.

- *Management Education*—Re-orientation may require managers and leaders to use or develop new skills, competencies, or knowledge. This creates a demand for effective management education. Research indicates that the impact of passive internal management education on the development of effective leaders may be minimal when compared with more action-oriented educational experiences. The use of educational events to expose people to external settings or ideas (through out-of-company education) and to socialize individuals through action-oriented executive education may be more useful than attempts to teach people to be effective leaders and managers.[41]

- *Career Management*—Research and experience indicate that the most potent factor in the development of effective leaders is the nature of their job experiences.[42] The challenge is to ensure that middle and lower level managers get a wide range of experiences over time. Preparing people to lead re-orientations may require a greater emphasis on the development of generalists through cross-functional, divisional, and/or multinational career experiences.[43] Diverse career experiences help individuals develop a broad communication network and a range of experiences and competences all of which are vital in managing large-system change. This approach to careers implies the sharing of the burden of career management between both the organization and the employee as well as the deliberate strategy of balancing current contribution with investment for the future when placing people in job assignments.[44]

- *Seeding Talent*—Developing leadership for change may also require deliberate leveraging of available talent. This implies thoughtful placement of individual leaders in different situations and parts of the organization, the use of transfers, and the strategic placement of high-potential leaders.[45]

Perhaps the most ambitious and most well-documented effort at developing leadership throughout the organization is Welch's actions at GE. Welch has used GE's Management Development Institute at Crotonville as an important lever in the transformation of GE. Based on Welch's vision of a lean, competitive, agile organization with businesses leading in their respective markets, Crotonville has been used as a staging area for the revolution at GE. With Welch's active involvement, Crotonville's curriculum has moved from a short-term cognitive orientation towards longer-term problem solving and organization change. The curriculum has been developed to shape experiences and sharpen skills over the course of an individual's career in service of developing leaders to fit into the new GE.[46]

SUMMARY

In a world characterized by global competition, deregulation, sharp technological change, and political turmoil, discontinuous organization change seems to be a determinant of organization adaptation. Those firms that can initiate and implement discontinuous organization change more rapidly and/or prior to the competition have a competitive advantage. While not all change will be successful, inertia or incremental change in the face of altered competitive arenas is a recipe for failure.

Executive leadership is the critical factor in the initiation and implementation of large-system organization change. This article has developed an approach to the leadership of discontinuous organization change with particular reference to re-orientations—discontinuous change initiated in advance of competitive threat and/or performance crisis. Where incremental change can be delegated, strategic change must be driven by senior management. Charismatic leadership is a vital aspect of managing large-system change. Charismatic leaders provide vision, direction, and energy. Thus the successes of O'Neil at ALCOA, Welch at GE, Kearns at Xerox, and Rollwagen and Cray are partly a function of committed, enthusiastic, and passionate individual executives.

Charisma is not, however, enough to effect large-system change. Charismatic leadership must be bolstered by instrumental leadership through attention to detail on roles, responsibilities, structures, and rewards. Further, as many organizations are too large and complex for any one executive and/or senior team to directly manage, responsibility for large-system change must be institutionalized throughout the management system. The leadership of strategic organization change must be pushed throughout the organization to maximize the probability that managers at all levels own and are involved in executing the change efforts and see the concrete benefits of making the change effort work. O'Neil, Welch, Kearns, and Rollwagen are important catalysts in their organizations. Their successes to date are, however, not based simply on strong personalities. Each of these executives has been able to build teams, systems, and managerial processes to leverage and add substance to his vision and energy. It is this interaction of charisma, attention to systems and processes, and widespread involvement at multiple levels that seems to drive large-system change.

Even with inspired leadership, though, no re-orientation can emerge fully developed and planned.

Re-orientations take time to implement. During this transition period, mistakes are made, environments change, and key people leave. Given the turbulence of competitive conditions, the complexity of large-system change and individual cognitive limitations, the executive team must develop its ability to adapt to new conditions and, as importantly, learn from both its successes and failures. As organizations can not remain stable in the face of environmental change, so too must the management of large-system change be flexible. This ability of executive teams to build-in learning and to build-in flexibility into the process of managing large-system organizational change is a touchstone for proactively managing re-orientations.

ACKNOWLEDGMENTS

Don Hambrick and Charles O'Reilly made valuable suggestions on earlier versions of this article. The article is partially based on research conducted under the sponsorship of Columbia University's Innovation and Entrepreneurship Research Center and its Executive Leadership Research Center. A version of this article appeared in M. Tushman, C. O'Reilly, and D. Nadler, eds., *The Management of Organizations: Strategy, Tactics, and Analyses* (New York, NY: Harper & Row, 1989).

NOTES

1. R. Solow, M. Dertouzos, and R. Lester, *Made in America* (Cambridge, MA: MIT Press, 1989).

2. See M.L. Tushman, W. Newman, and E. Romanelli, "Convergence and Upheaval: Managing the Unsteady Pace of Organizational Evolution," *California Management Review,* 29/1 (Fall 1986):29–44.

3. E.g., K. Imai, I. Nonaka, and H. Takeuchi, "Managing the New Product Development Process: How Japanese Companies Learn and Unlearn," in K. Clark and R. Hayes, *The Uneasy Alliance* (Cambridge, MA: Harvard University Press, 1985).

4. E.g., A. Pettigrew, *The Awakening Giant: Continuity and Change at ICI* (London: Blackwell, 1985); J. R. Kimberly and R. E. Quinn, *New Futures: The Challenge of Managing Corporate Transitions* (Homewood, IL: Dow Jones-Irwin, 1984); Y. Allaire and M. Firsirotu, "How to Implement Radical Strategies in Large Organizations," *Sloan Management Review* (Winter 1985).

5. E.g., J. Gabbaro, *The Dynamics of Taking Charge*

(Cambridge, MA: Harvard Business School Press, 1987); L. Greiner and A. Bhambri, "New CEO Intervention and Dynamics of Deliberate Strategic Change," *Strategic Management Journal*, 10 (1989): 67–86; N. M. Tichy and M. A. Devanna, *The Transformational Leader* (New York, NY: John Wiley & Sons, 1986); D. Hambrick, "The Top Management Team: Key to Strategic Success," *California Management Review*, 30/1 (Fall 1987):88–108.

6. Y. Kobayashi, "Quality Control in Japan: The Case of Fuji Xerox," *Japanese Economic Studies* (Spring 1983).

7. G. Jacobson and J. Hillkirk, *Xerox: American Samurai* (New York, NY: Macmillan, 1986).

8. For SAS, see J. Carlzon, *Moments of Truth* (Cambridge, MA: Ballinger, 1987); for ICI, see Pettigrew, op. cit.; for NCR, see R. Rosenbloom, *From Gears to Chips: The Transformation of NCR in the Digital Era* (Cambridge, MA: Harvard University Press, 1988); for Honda, see I. Nonaka, "Creating Organizational Order Out of Chaos: Self-Renewal in Japanese Firms," *California Management Review*, 30/3 (Spring 1988):57–73.

9. Gabbaro, op. cit.; H. Levinson and S. Rosenthal, *CEO: Corporate Leadership in Action* (New York, NY: Basic Books, 1984); Greiner and Bhambri, op. cit.

10. Tushman et al., op. cit.; R. Greenwood and C. Hinings, "Organization Design Types, Tracks, and the Dynamics of Strategic Change," *Organization Studies*, 9/3 (1988): 293–316; D. Miller and P. Friesen, *Organizations: A Quantum View* (Englewood Cliffs, NJ: Prentice-Hall, 1984).

11. D. A. Nadler and M. L. Tushman, "Organizational Framebending: Principles for Managing Reorientation," *Academy of Management Executive*, 3 (1989):194–202.

12. For a more detailed discussion of this framework, see Nadler and Tushman, ibid.

13. Tushman et al., op. cit.; Greiner and Bhambri, op. cit.; Greenwood and Hinings, op. cit.; B. Virany and M. L. Tushman, "Changing Characteristics of Executive Teams in and Emerging Industry," *Journal of Business Venturing*, 1 (1986):261–274; M. L. Tushman and E. Romanelli, "Organizational Evolution: A Metamorphosis Model of Convergence and Re-orientation," in B. M. Staw and L. L. Cummings, eds., *Research in Organizational Behavior*, 5 (Greenwich, CT: JAI Press, 1985), pp. 171–222.

14. J. March, L. Sproull, and M. Tamuz, "Learning from Fragments of Experience," *Organization Science* (in press).

15. R. Beckhard and R. Harris, *Organizational Transitions* (Reading, MA: Addison-Wesley, 1977).

16. See R. Vancil, *Passing the Baton* (Cambridge, MA: Harvard Business School Press, 1987).

17. J. M. Burns, *Leadership* (New York, NY: Harper & Row, 1978); W. Bennis and B. Nanus, *Leaders: The Strategies for Taking Charge* (New York, NY: Harper & Row, 1985); N. M. Tichy and D. Ulrich, "The Leadership Challenge: A Call for the Transformational Leader," *Sloan Management Review* (Fall 1984); Tichy and Devanna, op. cit.

18. D. E. Berlew, "Leadership and Organizational Excitement," in D. A. Kolb, I. M. Rubin, and J. M. McIntyre, eds., *Organizational Psychology* (Englewood Cliffs, NJ: Prentice-Hall, 1974); R. J. House, "A 1976 Theory of Charismatic Leadership," in J. G. Hunt and L. L. Larson, eds., *Leadership: The Cutting Edge* (Carbondale, IL: Southern Illinois University Press, 1977); Levinson and Rosenthal, op. cit.; B. M. Bass, *Performance Beyond Expectations* (New York, NY: Free Press, 1985); R. House et al., "Personality and Charisma in the U.S. Presidency," Wharton Working Paper, 1989.

19. Hambrick, op. cit.; D. Ancona and D. Nadler, "Teamwork at the Top: Creating High Performing Executive Teams," *Sloan Management Review* (in press).

20. V. H. Vroom, *Work and Motivation* (New York, NY: John Wiley & Sons, 1964); J. P. Campbell, M. D. Dunnette, E. E. Lawler, and K. Weick, *Managerial Behavior, Performances, and Effectiveness* (New York, NY: McGraw-Hill, 1970).

21. R. J. House, "Path-Goal Theory of Leader Effectiveness," *Administrative Science Quarterly*, 16 (1971):321–338; G. R. Oldham, "The Motivational Strategies Used by Supervisors: Relationships to Effectiveness Indicators," *Organizational Behavior and Human Performance*, 15 (1976):66–86.

22. See Hambrick, op. cit.

23. E. E. Lawler and J. G. Rhode, *Information and Control in Organizations* (Pacific Palisades, CA: Goodyear, 1976).

24. Jacobson and Hillkirk, op. cit.

25. Gabbaro, op. cit.; T. J. Peters, "Symbols, Patterns, and Settings: An Optimistic Case for Getting Things Done," *Organizational Dynamics* (Autumn 1978).

26. R. J. House, "Exchange and Charismatic Theories of Leadership," in G. Reber, ed., *Encyclopedia of Leadership* (Stuttgart: C.E. Poeschel-Verlag, 1987).

27. M. Kets de Vries and D. Miller, "Neurotic Style and Organization Pathology," *Strategic Management Journal* (1984).

28. Levinson and Rosenthal, op. cit.

29. Hambrick, op. cit.

30. T. Kidder, *Soul of the New Machine* (Boston, MA: Little, Brown, 1981).

31. These are discussed in Nadler and Tushman, op cit.

32. Hambrick, op. cit.

33. M. Louis and R. Sutton, *Switching Cognitive Gears* (Stanford, CA: Stanford University Press, 1987).

34. C. O'Reilly, D. Caldwell, and W. Barnett, "Work Group Demography, Social Integration, and

Turnover," *Administrative Science Quarterly,* 34 (1989):21–37.

35. Hambrick, op. cit.; Virany and Tushman, op. cit.

36. See D. Ancona, "Top Management Teams: Preparing for the Revolution," in J. Carroll, ed., *Social Psychology in Business Organizations* (New York, NY: Erlbaum Associates, in press).

37. Louis and Sutton, op. cit.

38. March et al., op. cit.

39. See also C. Gersick, "Time and Transition in Work Teams," *Academy of Management Journal,* 31 (1988):9–41; Ancona and Nadler, op. cit.

40. See Vancil, op. cit.

41. N. Tichy, "GE's Crotonville: A Staging Ground for Corporate Revolution," *Academy of Management Executive,* 3 (1989):99–106.

42. E.g., Gabbaro, op. cit.; V. Pucik, "International Management of Human Resources," in C. Fombrun et al., *Strategic Human Resource Management* (New York, NY: John Wiley & Sons, 1984).

43. Pucik, op. cit.

44. M. Devanna, C. Fombrun, and N. Tichy, "A Framework for Strategic Human Resource Management," in C. Fombrun et al., *Strategic Human Resource Management* (New York, NY: John Wiley & Sons, 1984).

45. Hambrick, op. cit.

46. Tichy, op. cit.

41

Strategy as Vector and the Inertia of Coevolutionary Lock-In

ROBERT A. BURGELMAN

To examine the consequences of a period of extraordinary success for the long-term adaptive capability of a firm's strategy-making process, this comparative longitudinal study of Andy Grove's tenure as Intel Corporation's chief executive officer (CEO) documents how he moved Intel's strategy-making process from an internal-ecology model to the classical rational-actor model during 1987–1998. His creation of a highly successful strategy vector pursued through an extremely focused induced-strategy process led to coevolutionary lock-in with the personal computer market segment, in which Intel's strategy making became increasingly tied to its existing product market. Intracompany analysis of four new business development cases highlights the inertial consequences of coevolutionary lock-in. The paper examines implications of coevolutionary lock-in in terms of its effect on balancing induced and autonomous strategy processes and exploitation and exploration in organizational learning.

There is a vast literature ascribing the success of a company to the vision, strategy, and leadership approach of its chief executive officer (CEO). Some of these accounts put the CEO at center stage (e.g., Welch, 2001); others put him or her more modestly in the background (e.g., Collins, 2001). Organizational and strategic management researchers, however, have long highlighted the difficulties leaders encounter in aligning organizational action in the pursuit of strategic intent (e.g., Mintzberg, Ahlstrand, and Lampel, 1998). Recent work in organizational ecology (e.g., Barnett and Hansen, 1996), the behavioral theory of the firm (e.g., Levinthal and March, 1993), and neo-institutional theory (e.g., Zuckerman, 2000) continues to illuminate the external and internal limitations facing top management. Yet we still understand little about why some firms have periods of extraordinary success, what the role of the CEO is in heralding and leading the organization through such periods, and what the consequences are of such periods for strategy making thereafter. While organizational researchers are mostly concerned with ordinary states and expect regression toward the mean to wash out fluctuations over time, periods of extraordinary success have potentially important consequences for the strategy-making process as a long-term adaptive organizational capability, that is, spanning multiple generations of CEOs.

Longitudinal field-based research on strategy making at Intel Corporation during Andy Grove's tenure as CEO offered the opportunity to study a period of extraordinary corporate success and its consequences for the company's strategy-making process. Intel seemed a particularly interesting research site be-

Reprinted from "Strategy as Vector and the Inertia of Coevolutionary Lock-in," by Robert A. Burgelman, published in *Administrative Science Quarterly,* Vol. 47, No. 2, by permission of *Administrative Science Quarterly,* Vol. 47, No. 2. Copyright © 2002 by the Johnson Graduate School of Management, Cornell University.

cause it is one of the most important firms of the digital age (Gilder, 1989; Isaacson, 1997), and its evolution highlights the fundamental technological and economic forces that characterize digital industries (e.g., Arthur, 1987). The research could be used to compare Grove's strategy-making approach to that of his predecessor (Gordon Moore) and successor (Craig Barrett) and thus could examine his efficacy as CEO within the context of Intel as an evolving system over time.

Andy Grove succeeded Gordon Moore as CEO in 1987 at the time that Intel was recovering from defeat in its original semiconductor memory business and refocusing on its microprocessor business (Burgelman, 1994). He held the position until early 1998. Between 1987 and 1998, Intel became the clear winner with its microprocessors in the personal computer (PC) market segment. Intel's revenues grew from $1.9 billion to $25.1 billion—an increase of 29.4 percent per annum—and net income grew from $248 million to $6.9 billion—an increase of 39.5 percent per annum. In 1998, however, Intel's growth in the core business slowed down significantly. Also, it had become clear that new business development was relatively unsuccessful during Grove's tenure as CEO. In 1997, Craig Barrett, then Intel's chief operating officer (COO), observed that Intel's core microprocessor business had begun to resemble a creosote bush, a desert plant that poisons the ground around it, preventing other plants from growing nearby. The creosote bush metaphor raised potentially interesting questions about the strategic consequences of Intel's ability to dominate in the PC market segment. It drew attention to the phenomenon of coevolutionary lock-in: a positive feedback process that increasingly ties the previous success of a company's strategy to that of its existing product-market environment, thereby making it difficult to change strategic direction. Despite the attention given to winner-take-all competition in digital industries (e.g., Arthur, 1987) and the role of inertia in organizational and industry evolution (e.g., Hannan and Freeman, 1977, 1984), researchers have paid little attention to how coevolutionary lock-in comes about and may become a significant source of strategic inertia. This study addresses this gap. It seeks to shed light on the role of the CEO in creating a strategy-making process that leads to coevolutionary lock-in and what its implications are for organizational adaptation.

Grove described his approach as "vectoring" In-

tel's strategy-making process. Vector—a quantity having direction and magnitude, denoted by a line drawn from its original to its final position (*Oxford English Dictionary*)—seems an apt metaphor to describe his efforts to align strategy and action. By creating a strategy vector, Grove was able to drive Intel in the intended direction with a total force equal to all the forces at its disposition. The paper examines the long-term adaptive implications of Grove's strategic leadership approach, which seemed to approximate the classical rational-actor model (Allison and Zelikow, 1999; Bendor and Hammond, 1992), and contrasts it with that of his predecessor.

COEVOLUTIONARY LOCK-IN IN FIRM EVOLUTION

Informed by evolutionary organization theory (e.g., Aldrich, 1999; Baum and McKelvey, 1999), earlier research on Intel before Grove became CEO suggested that effective strategy making may be as much about creating an environment in which middle management makes strategic decisions as it is about strategy making in the classical sense and that the role of top management might be to recognize transitions rather than to initiate them (Burgelman, 1994). These findings were consistent with an internal ecology model of strategy making, which was conceptualized in terms of induced and autonomous strategy processes (Burgelman, 1991). Induced strategy exploits initiatives that are within the scope of a company's current strategy and that extend it further in its current product-market environment. Autonomous strategy exploits initiatives that emerge through exploration outside of the scope of the current strategy and that provide the basis for entering into new product-market environments. Intel's strategy making before Grove became CEO resembled an internal-ecology model in which induced (memory-related) and autonomous (microprocessor-related) initiatives competed for the company's scarce resources based on their success in the external competitive environment. This paper documents how Grove's successful strategy vector created a highly focused induced-strategy process, which moved Intel's strategy making away from the internal-ecology model and closer to the rational-actor model. It shows how positive environmental feedback associated with the successful strategy vector caused coevolutionary lock-in and how this can illuminate time-paced evolution (Gersick, 1994; Brown and Eisenhardt, 1997) and the dynamics of competitive intensity (Barnett, 1997).

Strategic Inertia of Coevolutionary Lock-In

This paper's detailed ethnographic data also document new sources of strategic inertia that may be the unintended consequence of coevolutionary lock-in. Systemic sources of inertia associated with coevolutionary lock-in provide additional insight into structural inertia (Hannan and Freeman, 1984). They help elucidate the dynamics of the evolving relative efficiency of internal selection (Miller, 1999; Lovas and Ghoshal, 2000) and external selection (Sorenson, 2000), as a company's product-market environment matures, and of the rate and direction of innovation relative to environmental evolution as firms grow large (SØrensen and Stuart, 2000). Study of the psychological sources of inertia associated with coevolutionary lock-in can be used to assess Prahalad and Bettis's (1986) contention that executives become ingrained with beliefs about causes and effects that may not hold after the environment changes. And they help sort out Audia, Locke, and Smith's (2000) argument that success tends to increase decision makers' feelings of self-efficacy from that of Miller and Chen (1994), who suggest that it causes complacency, understood as drifting without further attempts at improvement. These psychological sources of strategic inertia draw attention to the potential limitations of evolution guided by the strategic intent of the CEO (Lovas and Ghoshal, 2000). Most important for the purposes of this paper, the various sources of strategic inertia associated with coevolutionary lock-in have implications for maintaining a balance between induced and autonomous strategy processes and between exploitation and exploration in organizational learning. They help connect these ideas, which are rooted in evolutionary organization theory (Burgelman, 1991; March, 1991), with related ideas of the modern economic theory of the firm (Rotemberg and Saloner, 1994, 2000).

RESEARCH METHOD

The research reported in this paper is part of a longitudinal multistage, nested case study design (e.g., Yin, 1984; Leonard-Barton, 1990) focused on major periods of Intel's history (Burgelman, 2002). These include Epoch I: Intel the memory company (1968–1985); Epoch II: Intel the microprocessor company (1985–1998); and Epoch III: Intel the Internet building-block company (beyond 1998). These three epochs correspond roughly to the tenure of Gordon Moore, Andy Grove, and Craig Barrett as Intel's CEOs.

Data Collection

INTERVIEW DATA

For this paper, which focuses on Intel's Epoch II, I used data from 63 informants, collected mostly through interviews I and/or a research associate conducted and through informal interactions. Informal interactions sometimes involved a research associate. Others took place in the strategic long-range planning sessions I observed, executive education sessions I taught for senior Intel executives, and working with Intel staff in preparing for executive education sessions. I also had access to transcripts of interviews conducted and tape-recorded by Intel consultants. The list of these informants and their position in the organization is provided in Table 41.1. Managers from different levels, different functional groups, and different businesses were involved. Throughout the research period, I used informal discussions with many current and former Intel employees to corroborate data obtained from the formal interviews. Most interviews lasted between one and two hours and focused on key events, people, and issues. Key events involved, for instance, the introduction of successive generations of microprocessors. Key people were individuals or groups from different functional areas or different hierarchical levels who made critical decisions or made proposals that, while not necessarily implemented, triggered high-level reconsideration of strategic issues. Key issues included, for instance, how to allocate resources to different businesses, how to resolve internal competition between different microprocessor architectures, and how to enter into new businesses. Most interviews were not tape-recorded (exceptions are listed in Table 41.1, below), but the interviewers made extensive notes. Many of the interviews were done together with research associates. Transcripts of the research associates' notes showed agreement on the substantive content of the interviews. This provid-

Table 41.1. Informants Providing Data Concerning Epoch II (1988–1998)

Name and most relevant job during Epoch II	Interview	Informal Interaction
1. Gordon Moore, chairman	X	X
2. Andy Grove, CEO	X	X
3. Craig Barrett, COO	X	X
4. Gerry Parker, executive VP, Technology and Mfg. Group	X	X
5. Paul Otellini, executive VP, Intel Architecture Business Group	X	X
6. Frank Gill, executive VP, Intel Products Group, gen. mgr. Networking	X	X
7. Les Vadasz, senior VP, Corporate Business Development Group	X	X
8. Albert Yu, senior VP, Microprocessor Products Group	X	X
9. Ron Whittier, senior VP, Intel Architecture Labs, Content Group	X	X
10. Andy Bryant, senior VP and CFO	X	X
11. Sean Maloney, senior VP, Sales and Marketing Group		X
12. Dennis Carter, VP, Corporate Marketing Group	X	X
13. Ron Smith, VP, gen. mgr. Chipsets	X	X
14. Patrick Gelsinger, VP, gen. mgr. ProShare	X	X
15. Mike Aymar, VP, Desktop Products Group, Hood River	X	X
16. Mark Christensen, VP, gen. mgr. Networking (late 1990s)	X	X
17. John Miner, VP, Enterprise Server Group		X
18. Hans Geyer, VP, gen. mgr. Flash Products Division		X
19. Patty Murray, VP, Human Resources		X
20. Harold Hughes, VP and CFO mid-1990s	X	X
21. John Davies, VP, Consumer Marketing Desktop Prod. Grp., Hood River	X	
22. Avram Miller, VP, Corporate Development Group, Hood River	X	
23. Jim Johnson, gen. mgr. PC Enhancement Organization (late 1980s)	X	X
24. Claude Leglise, Marketing Director i860 (late 1980s)	X	X
25. Steve McGeady, gen. mgr. Home Media Lab (mid-1990s)	X	X
26. Scott Darling, gen. mgr. Busin. Com. Prod. Grp., ProShare (late 1990s)	X	X
27. Sandra Morris, manager Intel Prod. Grp. (mid-1990s)	X	X
28. Tom Yan, mgr. development OEM Prod. and Syst. Div., Hood River	X	
29. Dick Pashley, gen. mgr. Flash Memory Division (early 1990s)	X	X
30. Warren Evans, Business Process Network, Planning	X	X
31. Renee James, technical assistant to Andy Grove (mid-1990s)	X	X
32. Katherine Yetts, technical assistant to Craig Barrett (mid-1990s)	X	X
33. Michael Bruck, program manager Content Group	X	X
34. Vin Dham, program manager Pentium processor (early 1990s)	X	X
35. Richard Wirt, director Software, IAL	X	X
36. Les Kohn, technical manager, i860 processor (late 1980s)	X	
37. Bruce McCormick, manager, Flash (mid-1980s)	X	
38. Sally Fundakowski, manager, CMG (early 1990s)	X	
39. Tom Macdonald, marketing director for 386 and 486 processors	X	
40. Jim Yasso, mgr. in Desktop Prd. Grp. and Microp. Prd. Grp. (mid-1990s)	X	
41. Don Whiteside, gen. mgr., Digital Imaging and Video Division	X	
42. Lori Wigle, strat. mkting. dir. Digital Imaging and Video Division	X	
43. Tom Willis, manager in Corporate Business Development Group	X	
44. Dave Williams, director Home Media Lab	X	
45. Dave Cobbley, director Home Media Lab	X	
46. Rob Siegel, program manager Hood River	X	X
47. Ganesh Moorthy, mgr., Appliance and Comp. Div. (Deskt. Prod. Grp.)	X	
48. Krish Bandura, engineer, Hood River	X	
49. Roy Coppinger, product mgr. OEM Prod. and Syst. Div., Hood River	X	
50. Eric Mentzer, marketing manager, Chipsets	X*	X
51. Andy Wilhelm, technical manager, Chipsets	X*	
52. Andy Beran, finance manager, Chipsets	X*	
53. Tom Bruegel, finance manager, Networking (mid-1990s)	X*	
54. Dan Sweeney, marketing program mgr., Networking (mid-1990s)	X*	
55. Steve Cassell, engineering mgr., Networking (early 1990s)	X*	

Table 41.1. Continued

Name and most relevant job during Epoch II	Interview	Informal Interaction
56. Kirby Dyess, marketing mgr., PC Enhancemt. Org. (late 1980s)	X*	X
57. Susan Studd, human res. mgr., PC Enhancemt. Org. (late 1980s)	X*	X
58. Gerry Greve, marketing director ProShare (mid-1990s)	X*	
60. Laura Finney, finance manager ProShare (mid-1990s)	X*	
61. Taymoor Arshi, engineering manager, ProShare (mid-1990s)	X*	
62. Mark Olson, product marketing manager Microproc. Prod. Grp.		X
63. John Sutherland, manager, Systems Management Division		X

*These interviews were tape recorded by Intel consultants, and transcripts of the raw recorded interview data were made available to this author.

ed some confidence that the data were valid and reliable.

ARCHIVAL DATA

Archival data, such as documents describing the company's history, annual reports, and reports to financial analysts, were obtained from Intel. Additional archival data were obtained from outside sources, such as industry publications and financial analysts' reports and business press articles about Intel and the semiconductor and computer industries. The archival data could be juxtaposed to the interview data to check for potential systematic biases in retrospective accounts of past strategy.

CASE TEACHING AS A DATA SOURCE

The interview and archival data were used to write several case studies about the role of strategy making in Intel's evolution during the period that Grove was CEO (Cogan and Burgelman, 1991; Steere and Burgelman, 1993a, 1993b; Fine and Burgelman, 1997; Bamford and Burgelman, 1997a, 1997b; Bamford and Burgelman, 1998; Suzuki and Burgelman, 1998; Burgelman, Carter, and Bamford, 1999). Lengthy discussions with the research associates involved in writing these cases provided me with an opportunity at each writing to check whether they thought my interpretation of the data was consistent with theirs, providing an additional check on internal validity (e.g., Dyck and Starke, 1999). Grove taught these cases in Stanford Business School's Master's of Business Administration (MBA) program throughout the research period. This yielded rich additional data as he reflected on Intel's strategic situation in class. It provided a window into the mind of the CEO as strategic thinker that has rarely been matched in previous studies.

Multilevel Comparative Analyses

I adopted the methodology of grounded theorizing (Glaser and Strauss, 1967) to analyze the field data. While grounded theorizing requires care not to use data simply as illustrations of preconceived theoretical ideas, analysis is only possible within a theoretical perspective. With this in mind, I used three interrelated conceptual frameworks generated through grounded theorizing in earlier work. Together, these frameworks form an evolutionary research lens to perform a multilevel comparative analysis of Intel's strategy making during Andy Grove's tenure as CEO. At the company level, the analysis is comparative with respect to time. I examined Intel's strategy making during Epoch II with a framework including induced and autonomous strategy processes (Burgelman, 1991) and compared it with Epoch I. At the company-environment interface level, the analysis is also comparative with respect to time. I examined the coevolution of Intel's strategy with the PC industry during Epoch II, leading to lock-in, with a framework of internal and external forces driving company evolution (Burgelman, 1994) and compared it with Epoch I. The forces taken into account in this framework include the basis of competitive advantage in the industry, the firm's distinctive competencies, its official corporate strategy, its strategic actions, and its internal selection environment. At the intracompany level, the analysis compares new business development efforts during Epoch II. The process model of internal corporate venturing (Burgelman, 1983), which identifies the interlocking key activities of multiple levels of management involved in internal new business development, helped in examining the behavioral details of the development of four cases in the context of Intel's strategy-making process.

Strengths and Limitations of the Research

By concentrating on one firm and tracking one CEO throughout his tenure, I had access to sources with intimate knowledge of the details of the company's strategy making. It also allowed me to become familiar with "the manager's temporal and contextual frame of reference" (Van de Ven, 1992: 181). Because I had virtually unlimited research access to the company throughout the twelve-year research period, I was able to obtain input from different levels of management, which provided a basis for triangulation and made it possible to maintain an appropriate level of distance and neutrality, while capitalizing on the teaching collaboration with Andy Grove. Nevertheless, the research has several limitations. First, it focused on a single high-tech company run by one of the founding team members. Also, during Grove's tenure as CEO, the PC industry expanded enormously, and fortuitous circumstances contributed to giving Intel the opportunity to become a driving force. Finally, during the study, I kept track of the evolving fortunes of Intel's competitors, but it would have been fruitful to study these other organizations systematically if time and access had permitted it.

COEVOLUTIONARY LOCK-IN OF STRATEGY AND ENVIRONMENT

Grove's Strategy Vector

During Epoch II, Gordon Moore remained as chairman and Craig Barrett served as chief operating officer (COO). Looking back in 1999, Andy Grove pointed out that "At no point in Intel's history has it been a solo show. It's never been only one person leading the organization. Our tradition is somewhat of a shared power structure." Nevertheless, many insiders confirmed that Andy Grove drove strategy making during Epoch II. Table 41.2 provides a chronology of selected key instances throughout Epoch II, when it was clear that Grove made the difference in how Intel took strategic action in the core microprocessor business.

The data presented in Table 41.2 show that Grove's role in driving Intel's strategy making relied more on strategic recognition than on foresight. Intel had been lucky to invent the microprocessor and even more lucky to obtain the design win for the IBM PC. But it was ex post facto strategic recognition of the importance of these fortuitous events that set Intel on its highly successful course. An article in the *New York Times* in 1988 pointed out that it was "irksome to competitors . . . that there is a fair amount of luck involved in all of this [Intel's success]." Responding to this, Andy Grove was quoted as saying, "There is such a thing as luck and then you grab it and exploit it" (Pollack, 1988). Grove sometimes also called it "earned luck" (Schlender, 1989). Table 41.2 indicates that the ability to get the organization to follow up on the mandates that he imposed based on his strategic recognition was another defining characteristic of Grove's leadership. Contrasting Grove's strengths to those of cofounder Robert Noyce and his own, Gordon Moore said, "Andy is a true manager. He is very detail oriented. He has strong follow-up—he never trusted that anyone would do what they were asked unless there was follow-up—and he is strongly data driven."

Focusing Intel on the Microprocessor Business
Table 41.2 indicates that toward the end of Epoch I, then-COO Grove recognized that Intel's future lay in microprocessors rather than memory products. To make sure that the organization would be committed to the new microprocessor-focused strategy when he became CEO, Grove made major changes in Intel's senior management. He recalled:

> The Grove leadership approach consisted of trying to persuade and sell the new strategic approach to the management team. . . . After some period of time, the new strategy had traction with some managers and it did not have traction with some others. The people who did not get traction—they may have provided lip service to the new strategy, but their actions were not so supportive—the approach was to remove these people from positions where they could choke progress. We moved them around to other positions where they couldn't impede progress. This worked for a period of time. But when it became obvious that they were in a position that was not so important or influential, several of them left. We didn't actually have to fire anyone, nor were we happy that they left. But they were not happy being in a non-core activity.

Intel's new corporate strategy reflected key lessons that top management had learned from the DRAM (dynamic random access memory) exit. In the context of a case discussion in an MBA class in the early 1990s, Grove said:

> We learned that we had to get around the companies that had subjugated us in DRAM. We learned that high market share was critical for success and that to get market share we had to be willing to invest in manufacturing capacity. Such investments involve big bets because they have to be made in advance of actual demand. We learned that commodity businesses are unattractive, so we didn't want to license out our intellectual property anymore.

General-purpose microprocessors were a disruptive technology (Christensen and Bower, 1996). Microprocessor development was subject to Moore's Law, which posits that computing power doubles every 18 months and is available at the same price. Andy Grove was among the first to recognize that, in contrast to the vertically integrated mainframe and minicomputer industries, the PC industry followed a "horizontal" model in which a component manufacturer's products needed to be able to work with other component manufacturers' products (Grove, 1993, 1996). Grove's "vertical" and "horizontal" were a precursor to what economists call "closed" and "open" models of industry organization (Farrell, Monroe, and Saloner, 1998: 144). Success in the horizontal PC industry was governed by increasing returns to adoption, a new economic force (e.g., Arthur, 1987) that was initially not well understood by most industry participants. Increasing returns to adoption meant that a technological platform, like Intel's x86 microprocessors, became increasingly valuable the more people were using it. Achieving a high installed base was key to creating a virtuous circle. While economies of scale and economies of learning were important determinants of the relative success of different industry participants competing within the same microprocessor architecture, increasing returns to adoption strongly affected competition between different architectures.

RESOLVING THE INTERNAL BATTLE BETWEEN CISC AND RISC

The x86 architecture was based on complex instruction set computing (CISC). During the mid-1980s,

however, Intel's autonomous strategy process generated the development of a microprocessor (the i860) based on a new architecture called reduced instruction set computing (RISC). Internal champions of the i860 had been able to generate support from workstation original equipment manufacturers (OEMs), which were new customers for Intel. During 1989–90, the autonomous and somewhat surreptitious development of the i860 and its initial market success looked like a potentially adaptive variation (Burgelman, 1991). But the new microprocessor soon created significant confusion inside the company that reflected external confusion about the importance of the RISC architecture for the future development of the PC. The internal confusion manifested itself in the emergence of two warring camps within Intel's microprocessor development group (MPG). Each camp had its external supporters. Andy Grove said that Microsoft supported the i860. Compaq, however, strongly supported the x86 architecture. According to Grove, within a short period of time, the RISC camp had been able to claim about 50 percent of the microprocessor development resources because there was no clear corporate strategy regarding RISC (personal communication). Some within Intel proposed to create a transition path from the x86 architecture to the RISC architecture by bringing out two versions of the i486, one called i486c and the other i486r, but this proposal ran into strong resistance from Dennis Carter, Intel's senior marketing executive during most of Epoch II, who feared that it would undermine Intel's brand identity. In part motivated by the negative consequences that a similar battle between CISC and RISC was having within rival Motorola (Tredennick, 1991), Grove eventually resolved the situation. Table 41.2 quotes Dennis Carter on how Grove decided the issue. It also reports Grove's growing concerns about Intel's strategy-making process. The episode strengthened his determination to fully exploit Intel's favorable strategic position with the x86 architecture. He said, "The commitment to the x86 architecture vectorized everybody at Intel in the same direction."

EFFECTIVELY DRIVING STRATEGY MAKING IN THE CORE BUSINESS

The significance of the rise and fall of the i860 microprocessor lies primarily in the effect it had on Grove's efforts to further strengthen Intel's induced strategy process. Table 41.2 shows that Grove had come to the

Table 41.2. Company Level of Analysis: Andy Grove's Impact on Intel's Strategy Making During Epoch II*

Selected key instances	Strategic recognition	Strategic action
	Transition to Epoch II: Focusing Intel on microprocessors as chief operating officer (mid-1980s)	
Ed Gelbach (sales VP and director)†: "In board meetings the question of DRAM would often come up. I would support them from a market perspective, and Gordon [Moore] would support them because they were our technology driver. Andy [Grove] kept quiet on the subject."	*COO Andy Grove:* "I stayed quiet because I didn't know what to do, initially."	Grove removes Carsten as GM Components Division in summer 1985.
	COO Andy Grove: "It's not always clear why you do certain things. You do a lot of things instinctively, without knowing why you're doing it. I knew we had to get out of DRAMs and put all our brightest on microprocessors."	Grove moves Sunlin Chou and the DRAM Technology Development Group to microprocessors.
Jack Carsten (GM Components Division)†: "Grove said: 'Don't worry about the memory business, it is not important to our future.'"	*COO Andy Grove:* "I recall going to see Gordon (Moore) and asking him what a new management would do if we were replaced. The answer was clear: Get out of DRAMs. So, I suggested to Gordon that we go through the revolving door, come back in, and just do it ourselves."	Grove goes to Oregon in October 1985 and tells the organization: "Welcome to the mainstream of Intel."
Another senior executive†: "Grove has been preaching: 'Make the tough decisions! Don't do tomorrow something because you did it today.'"		
	Resolving the battle between i860 (RISC) and x86 (CISC) microprocessors within Intel (1991)	
Dennis Carter (VP Corporate Marketing): "In the end, Andy [Grove] resolved the debate. He essentially did a compromise that favored CISC."	*Andy Grove in February 1991:* "The strategy process reflects the company's culture. You can look at it positively or negatively. Positively, it looks like a Darwinian process: we let the best ideas win; we adapt by ruthlessly exiting business; we provide autonomy, and top management is the referee who waits to see who wins and then rearticulates the strategy; we match evolving skills with evolving opportunities. Negatively, it looks like we have no staying power, we are reactive, try and move somewhere else if we fail; we lack focus."	Grove did not allow the planned introduction of both 486c and 486r processors that would have signaled a planned transition path from CISC to RISC. The i860 business was to continue by that name and was soon halted in early 1991.
		Andy Grove in November 1992: "It was a confusing period for Intel. . . . The i860 was a very successful renegade product that could have destroyed the virtuous circle enjoyed by the Intel Architecture. . . . Intel was helping RISC by legitimizing it. . . ."
	Identifying the magnitude of capital investment as Intel's new differentiator (1993)	
Direct observation during SLRP 1993: In his kick-off presentation, Grove identified Intel's successive key strategic differentiators throughout its evolution: Silicon technology competence (1970s), design competence (mid-1980s), intellectual property (late 1980s), and brand preference (early 1990s). He then suggested that the increasingly large capital investments necessary for next-generation processors had become the new differentiator for the next several years.	*Andy Grove:* Pointing to the great uncertainty associated with these capital investments, Grove posited that they would provide Intel with a new competitive advantage. He asked, rhetorically, "Who is going to invest $5 billion on speculation?"	Grove was willing to make these large bets. During the remaining 4 years of his tenure as CEO, Intel invested $13.5 billion in plant, property, and equipment.
		In 1997, Craig Barrett said, "It's a risk to go out and spend billions of dollars on these manufacturing plants. But if we didn't, we couldn't possibly reap the benefits. We're going down the road at 150 miles per hour, and we know there's a brick wall someplace, but the worst thing we can do is stop too soon and let someone else pass us" (Reinhardt, Sager, and Burrows, 1997: 71).

Resolving conflict around "Intel Inside" between Corporate Marketing and Intel Products Group

Direct observation during SLRP 1993: At the end of SLRP the objectives as stated in 1992 were revisited in light of the discussion during the 1993 SLRP. The third objective in 1992 was "Manage the Intel and Intel Inside brands for significant return and long-term advantage." Grove felt that this objective had to be restated in light of the intense conflicts that had broken into the open between CM (Dennis Carter) and IPG (Frank Gill) during the SLRP 1993 discussions.

Andy Grove: "This is a lame statement. And yet it is the inflection point—[similar] to what happened with the transition from memories to microprocessors. This involves a dialectic. It is a move from a single space to a dual one. This duality is all over the place. It is a continuation of the change from OEM to a distribution channel."

Grove decides: "Dennis [Carter] and Frank [Gill] must rephrase this. It must be words that will affect hundreds of people that work for them and are fighting over it. The new words [must make sure] we get credit for what we do for our [end-user] customers: ease-of-use, richness, upgradability; and who our customers *could be.*"

Supporting Intel's motherboard business in the face of organizational resistance (mid-1990s)

Harold Hughes (former CFO): "Andy was always brilliant at identifying threats to our business. For example, on the motherboards business, Andy and I clashed. I said that we were never going to make any money on motherboards. But they did push adoption of our microprocessors. Our motherboard business allowed the little [OEMs] to stay competitive."

Andy Grove: "I have been rabid about four things in my career at Intel: motherboards, Intel Inside, chipsets, and videoconferencing."

Grove supported the development of the motherboard business in spite of strong opposition of the microprocessor division, whose OEM customers complained vigorously about Intel's vertical integration strategy, and in the face of reservations on the part of the CFO.

Supporting the chipset business to drive industry adoption of Intel technology (mid-1990s)

Several executives pointed out that Andy Grove initially did not support the development of the chipset business based on the new Peripheral Component Interconnect (PCI) bus technology but, rather, wanted to introduce the new technology as an enabling technology into the PC industry with a consortium-based effort.

After the chipset business became very successful, Andy Grove changed his mind about chipsets as a strategic business for Intel.

Grove then began to view the chipset business as an important tool for supporting the corporate strategy. Andy Bryant (CFO) said, "At a time when motherboard pricing was extremely competitive, the motherboard division decided not to use Intel's chipsets because they were more costly than third-party alternatives—even though they provided superior or performance. . . . Grove ruled that the long-term interests of the company required moving advanced technology into the marketplace and that we should forgo short-term returns for the long-term benefits."

Table 41.2. Continued

Selected key instances	Strategic recognition	Strategic action
	Driving Intel to meet the threat of the growth of the low-end of the PC market segment (1997)	
Direct observation during SLRP in September 1997: Grove was very concerned about recent developments in the PC market segment. He felt that Intel's top management was failing to see the strategic implications of the rapid growth in demand for below-$1,000 PCs.	*Andy Grove during his SLRP kick off:* "We say we have a top-to-bottom strategy. But we don't act top-to-bottom, because Intel has low-end phobia. . . . But the low end is not going away. . . . The data about desktop sales at the retail, reseller, and direct level all show a downward trend in price: $500 in about a year! I have not seen that before, And the volumes at the low end are up. So, the good news about segment zero is that we have it on our road map. The bad news is that we don't have an engineered product."	Grove articulated a new mandate, requiring the assignment of a large number of engineers to the task of developing a microprocessor specifically for the low-end market segment.

In about six months the team developed a new product called the Celeron processor, which made it possible for Intel to regain market segment share against AMD in the low end by early 1999.

In early 1999, Paul Otellini observed, "We've made a lot of progress on the low end. One year ago in the sub-$1,000 market our share was about 38 percent. We then lost some ground, but we have regained share, so we're at about 38 percent again." |
| | Looking back: Grove's influence on the PC industry during Epoch II | |
| *Gordon Moore (chairman emeritus) in 1999:* "When he became CEO, he really jumped on the opportunity to organize the industry. I wasn't so inclined to do this. He likes public exposure more than I did, and he has a stronger feeling about where he fits in. . . . Andy has had a tremendous impact on what's going on outside." | | |

*Abbreviations and terms used in this table are as follows: DRAM = dynamic random access memory; RISC = reduced instruction set computing; CISC = complex instruction set computing; and SLRP = strategic long-range planning. The motherboard is the main integrated circuit board in a PC; it contains the microprocessor, the memory, and other support chips. A chipset is the set of support chips for the microprocessor, for example, a chip that controls computer graphics. Bus refers to the set of electrical connections between a microprocessor and the other chips on an integrated circuit board. The speed of communication allowed by the bus affects PC performance. The PCI bus architecture increased speed significantly over the previous bus standard.

†Executive interviewed for Epoch I Study, not listed in Table 41.1.

conclusion that Intel's Darwinian strategy process was perhaps a guise for lack of a clear strategy. His efforts to vectorize everybody at Intel in the same direction in 1991 created an induced strategy process superbly suited for exploiting the rich opportunities in the PC market segment of the microprocessor industry. Several entries in Table 41.2 describe how Grove drove Intel's strategy making in the core business during the remainder of Epoch II. He showed keen insight in the successive strategic differentiators that had formed the basis of Intel's competitive advantage in the past and emphasized the importance of large capital investments for competitive advantage for the remainder of the 1990s. He forced senior executives to resolve the frictions that were emerging between corporate marketing's concerns about protecting the Intel brand and the needs of businesses outside the core microprocessor business. He forced the motherboard business to adopt Intel's more advanced but also more expensive PCI chipset technology in the face of resistance of both the motherboard managers and the finance organization. Toward the end of Epoch II, Grove forced the microprocessor business to face up to the dangerous threat posed by the rapidly growing low end of the PC market. He recognized that Intel's "low-end phobia" was preventing it from meeting the challenge posed by this major environmental shift and directed Intel to engage in a crash effort to develop the Celeron processor to meet it. Finally, as Gordon Moore observed, Grove's strategy vector gave Intel the opportunity to drive its external environment, that is, the development of the PC market segment.

Intel's Narrow Business Strategy

Already in 1989, then-chairman Gordon Moore had observed that CEO Andy Grove had significantly narrowed Intel's strategic focus, but he also predicted that the growth potential of the microprocessor business would not make that a problem in the next twelve years (Burgelman, 1991). Looking back in 1998 and comparing Intel's strategy during Epoch II and Epoch I, Grove said, "The most significant thing was the transformation of the company from a broadly positioned, across-the-board semiconductor supplier that did OK to a highly focused, highly tuned producer of microprocessors, which did better than OK" (Kawamoto and Galante, 1998). Many senior executives confirmed that Grove forced a distinct shift in the

strategy-making process toward a narrow business strategy focused on microprocessors for the PC market segment. Table 41.3 provides evidence of this shift. The views expressed in Table 41.3 touch on various aspects of the strategic leadership approach Grove used to focus Intel's induced strategy process narrowly on the microprocessor business. They include setting clear objectives and establishing a structural context (Bower, 1970; Burgelman, 1983), including strategic planning, organization structure, and resource allocation, to align strategy and action.

UNAMBIGUOUS STRATEGIC OBJECTIVES

Intel's strategic focus became ingrained in the strategy-making process through the setting of clear and consistent objectives. Intel's number-one objective was to strengthen the position of Intel microprocessors in the evolving computer industry. A related objective was to "make the PC it," which became somewhat of a rallying cry. Grove viewed the PC as the ideal tool for computing as well as for communications, and even for entertainment. Intel also made a distinction between "Job 1" and "Job 2." Job 1 encompassed everything that had to do with making the Intel architecture more successful. Job 2 involved the development of new businesses around the core business.

CEO-DRIVEN STRATEGIC PLANNING

Grove said that he had used changes in the company's strategic long-range planning process (SLRP) to redefine the content of the new corporate strategy and get the organization to execute it:

> In 1987, we blew up the SLRP process. Formerly it had been a very bottom-up process, but there was no strategic framework. Each of the different groups was supposed to come up with the strategy for their group, and then we would try to piece them together like a jigsaw puzzle. By '87, I was so frustrated with the whole thing that I started the process of turning the SLRP process on its head. I said, 'I'm going to tell you what the strategy is.' I started with a detailed discussion of the environmental issues, which led to a series of strategic mandates. I did not consult the organization. I did this myself, along with the help of my technical assistant at the time, Dennis Carter . . . I became very directive in prescribing the strategic direction from

Table 41.3. Company Level of Analysis: Views on Intel's Narrow Business Strategy During Epoch II

Gordon Moore (1989):
"Over time . . . Intel has narrowed and narrowed its technological interests. Andy [Grove] has been instrumental in this. . . . We can do variations on present businesses very well. But doing something new is more difficult."

Gerry Parker (1989):
"We could now manufacture everything in one and one-half plants. That's obscene. You need a broad product base—EPROM [electrically programmable read-only memory] is a natural. . . ."

Les Vadasz (1988):
"The system [strategic long-range planning] is now [in the late 1980s] more top-down. A high-level group sets the corporate strategy, and business units operate within that focus. Business units must focus on a few things and do them right. . . . Some managers complain that their 'sandbox' is too well defined."

A senior executive (1995):
"Intel may be too focused too soon. We have narrowed our range of experimentation too fast from 360 degrees to 180 and then to 90. The code words are: You don't have a business plan; your strategy is vague."
"We must narrow down from a 360 degree scan to 20, but even so we still have 20 things to do. Andy [Grove], however, wants a 'laser shot.' "

Frank Gill (1997):
"In 1994–95, Andy [Grove] would tell me 'Frank, I make a billion dollars in profit per quarter and you make a billion dollars in revenue per year. This is all distraction, so focus on Job 1.' "

Another senior executive (1998):
". . . a lot . . . is driven from Job 1, because every six months we have a SLRP [strategic long-range planning meeting]. Andy [Grove] stands up and says . . . here is a problem. And everyone says . . . we can go do wonderful things to solve that problem."

Craig Barrett (1999):
"[During the second epoch] we became much more verticalized behind IA and related businesses. Now we are more broad. . . . This requires less top down management and more P&L and line management."

A third senior executive (1999):
"Barrett is very different from Grove. First, he's encouraging new ideas. . . . Andy wouldn't have let that happen. Craig made it happen. . . . Second is behavior. If you have a good idea, overwhelm it with resources: What do you need? Do what it takes. Come back with a prize. . . . That's a different style."

A fourth senior executive (1999):
"But I am more concerned about Andy [Grove] because of his singular focus. Andy says that PCs are becoming a commodity. So, we must focus on servers and not let Sun [Microsystems] capture this. It is like going back to the old days."
"Barrett at some point will be expected to set the corporate strategy; and if he doesn't, Andy [Grove] will."

the top down. This defined the strategy for all of the groups, and it provided a strategic framework for different groups at different levels of management. It's very hard to reach through several layers of management to communicate the strategy and the vision. SLRP became a tool for doing that.

Typically, Grove's SLRP kickoff speech was followed by a two-hour presentation in which he addressed Intel's strategic challenges, presented his vision of what was happening in the industry, and identified high-level trends. The remainder of the three-day meeting involved presentations by Intel's senior executives concerning specific issues and top-

ics. They worked across product and functional groups to put their presentation together, with the help of a staff member. These executives had been given their assignment without knowing in advance what Grove was going to present. Dennis Carter pointed out that this was viewed as a tough assignment, dreaded by some, and that instances of strategic dissonance surfaced immediately.

CENTRALIZED ORGANIZATION STRUCTURE
During Grove's tenure as CEO, Intel's organization structure became highly centralized. In the words of one senior executive, "Intel was organized around fun-

neling things up to Gordon, Andy, and Craig." Intel was structured as a matrix, with various corporate functions on one side and various product groups on the other. Each product group carried profit and loss responsibility for its respective market, but no product group controlled all of the functional resources needed to execute its strategy. The functional groups were responsible for supporting the product groups and for cultivating necessary expertise across the organization. The functional groups were highly stable so as to develop capabilities, while the product groups were constantly redefined in order to match the evolving product-market environment. Given the importance of microprocessors in Intel's new corporate strategy, and the relentless pace with which new product generations needed to be developed, manufactured, and marketed, coordination among all the groups was critical.

TIGHTLY MANAGED RESOURCE ALLOCATION
The resource allocation process strongly favored Intel's core microprocessor business. As one executive observed in 1999:

> Virtually every single quarter, the requests outweigh the willingness to spend. We would end up ZBB-ing [zero-based budgeting] the lower ROI projects. The larger ROI projects were almost always related to the mainstream CPU [microprocessor] business. Therefore, if you were not part of the mainstream business, you needed to be very spirited and very perseverant to drive your projects through that process every quarter. I knew they were great businesses by any other metric, just not compared to the microprocessor business. . . . If you were in a non-core business, it was tough.

Complementary Strategic Thrusts
Comparing Epoch II with Epoch I, Craig Barrett said in 1999, "We became the industry driving force." Table 41.4 identifies key dynamics of the PC market segment between the early 1980s and 1998. It also identifies several complementary strategic thrusts, briefly discussed below, that made it possible for Intel to drive the PC market segment. These complementary thrusts did not reflect a comprehensive ex ante formulated strategic plan to take control of the PC market segment. Rather, Grove's successful narrow business strategy set in motion a positive feedback process that

extended the number and magnitude of strategic responsibilities that Intel needed to take on to sustain its position as driver of the PC market segment. These, in turn, reinforced the induced strategy process.

SOLE-SOURCE SUPPLIER
The installed base of x86 microprocessors created by IBM's success in the PC market segment (with Intel's 8088 and 80286 microprocessors) had significantly and fortuitously shifted bargaining power in Intel's favor. Understanding the implications of increasing returns to adoption offered Intel the opportunity to become sole-source supplier of microprocessors for the PC market segment as of the 80386 microprocessor generation. Nevertheless, this was a bold move given IBM's still very powerful position in the industry. Looking back, Grove said, "What good is the 386 if IBM doesn't adopt it? . . . We were chewing our nails until 1986, when Compaq adopted the 386. IBM adopted it the next year." Intel was able to keep rival AMD tied up in the courts over intellectual property rights disputes, which allowed it to remain the sole source for the 386 processor for four years. The 386 microprocessor was succeeded by the i486, which was introduced in April 1989. It again took four years (until the summer of 1993) before AMD was able to launch its first 486-compatible processors.

INVESTING IN MANUFACTURING
One of the imperatives associated with the sole-source strategy was that Intel needed to become a world-class manufacturer. Table 41.4 shows the large and rapidly increasing capital investments Intel made during Epoch II. Intel's new manufacturing prowess depended on a new distinctive competence: close integration of the Microprocessor Group's chip designs and process technology and manufacturing competencies within the Technology and Manufacturing Group. Intel became renowned for its ability to optimize the manufacturing process of a new chip design and then to roll out that process to Intel's other plants using the "copy exact" principle.

PACING THE RACE THROUGH PRODUCT LEADERSHIP
Table 41.4 shows the rapid pace of product introductions between 1993 and early 1998: Pentium (1993), Pentium Pro (1995), Pentium MMX (1997), Pentium II (1997), and the Celeron (1998) processors. This

Table 41.4. Company-Environment-Interface Level of Analysis: Highlights of Coevolution of Intel's Narrow Business Strategy and PC Market Segment, Epoch II

					PC market segment			
'81–84	'85	'86	'87	'88	'89	'90	'91	'92
IBM introduces PC/XT/AT with an Intel chip and Microsoft operating system.	Large installed base for IBM PC/XT/AT; Compaq has emerged as a viable competitor; Intel and Microsoft are the fortuitous beneficiaries of a "virtuous circle."	Compaq first with 386 PC; IBM follows.			Clone PC manufacturers are gaining share.			
								Intel strategy
8088 and 80286 chips for IBM PCs; cross-license other chip manufacturers; Intel initially not fully aware of importance of PC for its future.	Decision to be sole source for new 80386 processor and to maintain product leadership; "Red X" end-user marketing campaign.	Court battle with AMD about intellectual property rights for x86 microprocessors prevents AMD from entering the 386 market for 4 years; same for 486.			Intel is sole source for i486 processor; "Intel Inside" end-user marketing campaign; Intel develops an ecosystem; i860 battle resolved; Intel creates IAL to enable the PC industry.			
Revenue ($Billion)	1.4	1.3	1.9	2.9	3.1	3.9	4.8	5.8
Profits ($B)	0.0	–0.2	0.2	0.5	0.4	0.7	0.8	1.1
Cap. Invest. ($B)	0.24	0.15	0.3	0.5	0.4	0.7	0.9	1.2
R&D exp. ($B)	0.19	0.23	0.3	0.3	0.4	0.5	0.6	0.8

time-driven product introduction strategy, however, reflected deep intuition for the feasible pace of development of the PC industry. In an MBA class in fall 1994, Andy Grove revealed that he had learned from studying the data that the peak-to-peak production across microprocessor generations for 386 and 486 microprocessors had been about three years and would be the same for the Pentium processor. Based on this, Grove assumed that the next generation microprocessor, the P6, would follow the same adoption cycle, which informed the timing of Intel's next major capital investment decisions.

BUILDING BRAND WITH END USERS

In April 1990, Intel launched its first "Intel Inside" campaign. Aimed directly at end users, rather than Intel's traditional PC OEM customers, the campaign sought to influence customers to ask for Intel microprocessors specifically when they purchased a PC. Major OEMs such as Compaq and IBM initially refused to participate in some elements because they felt that

Intel Inside decreased their ability to differentiate their products from the competition, but eventually all of them carried the Intel Inside logo on their products, in part, because Intel engaged in massive co-marketing campaigns with the OEMs. From 1990 to 1993, Intel invested more than $500 million in end-user marketing campaigns. Paradoxically, the Pentium flaw crisis of November–December 1994, which according to Grove, "shook Intel to its core," in some ways indicated the powerful impact of Intel's branding strategy on end users.

INTRODUCING INDUSTRY-ENABLING TECHNOLOGIES

Increased competition among a growing number of PC OEMs created intense pressure on their profit margins. Combined with its successful sole-source strategy, this gave Intel the ability to appropriate a large part of the available profits in the PC market segment. This created a positive feedback loop, which increasingly shifted the center of industry influence from the PC OEMs to Intel (and to Microsoft) during the 1990s. Only the

'93	'94	'95	'96	'97	'98
Commoditization of PCs: intense margin pressure for PC OEMs; threat from IBM-Apple-Motorola RISC alliance does not materialize.		Internet emerges: threat of the network computer (NC).		Growth in demand for below-$1,000 PC is a real threat to Intel; NC threat does not materialize.	AMD [Advanced Micro Devices] gains market segment share on the low end.
Intel is sole source for new Pentium processor; Intel vertically integrates into motherboards and chipsets, which are decisively helpful in Pentium launch; Pentium flaw crisis and resolution.		Intel introduces Pentium Pro for workstations with Windows NT; AMD litigation for 386 and 486 settled; Microsoft pressures Intel to stop its native signal processing (NSP) project.		Intel introduces Pentium with MMX and later in the year Pentium II.	Intel introduces Celeron processor to combat AMD on the low end; Pentium II Xeon for workstations/servers.
8.8	11.5	16.2	20.8	25.1	26.3
2.3	2.3	3.6	5.2	6.9	6.1
1.9	2.4	3.6	3.0	4.5	4.0
1.0	1.1	1.3	1.8	2.3	2.7

largest PC OEM customers could afford to do much research and development (R&D). Other OEMs became increasingly dependent on Intel for technological innovation. Intel created the Intel Architecture Labs (IAL) for the purpose of developing new technologies that would remove technological bottlenecks preventing PCs from taking full advantage of the increased processing power of new-generation microprocessors. These technologies were offered to the OEM customers for free or for nominal royalty payments.

CULTIVATING AN ECOSYSTEM OF COMPLEMENTORS

The most important complementary product for Intel's microprocessors was Microsoft's Windows operating system software. Andy Grove described the relationship between Microsoft and Intel as "two companies joined at the hip." While constantly vying for perceived leadership of the PC industry and jealously guarding their own spheres of influence (software for Microsoft and hardware for Intel), most of the time the two companies were able to maintain their symbiotic relationship throughout Grove's tenure as CEO. Intel also invested in creating internal support groups to help other independent software vendors develop applications requiring high processor power to stimulate demand for its next generation processors. Intel provided its partners with advance information about its next microprocessor designs and support products.

FORWARD INTEGRATION INTO CHIPSETS AND MOTHERBOARDS

Intel's chipsets and motherboards made it possible to leverage its strong strategic position in microprocessors by enabling OEM customers, who did not have the resources to develop these system-level products, to introduce PCs with Intel's latest microprocessors. This is turn was helpful in reducing its dependency on the stronger OEMs, in case the latter were reluctant to stay with Intel's road map for developing next-generation microprocessors. This actually happened when some major OEMs initially decided to wait to introduce Pentium-processor-based PCs, and Intel enabled Packard Bell and Dell to take the lead.

Successful Coevolution Turns into Inertia

During Epoch II, in contrast to Epoch I, Intel's distinctive competencies continued to evolve with the basis of competition in the PC market segment of the microprocessor industry, and the official strategy clearly drove strategic action, leveraging both position and distinctive competence. This gave the company great momentum between 1987 and 1997, which is reflected in revenue growth and profit growth (Table 41.4). In late 1998, Intel's stock market valuation surpassed $200 billion for the first time.

LOCK-IN

Intel's narrow business strategy tied its success increasingly to that of the PC market segment. By 1993, 486 microprocessors accounted for 75 percent of the company's revenues of $8.8 billion and 85 percent of its $2.3 billion in net profit. By 1998, 80 percent of Intel's $26.3 billion in revenues and just about all of its $6.1 billion in net profits came from microprocessors. Signaling the company's extreme dependence on the prospects of its product-market environment, revenues grew only 5 percent, and net income declined 13 percent during 1998, in part as a result of the unexpectedly rapid relative growth of the low end of the PC market segment. Table 41.4 shows the increasingly large capital and R&D investments that needed to be made to keep driving the coevolutionary process. Also, Intel's dependence on the OEM customers as a distribution channel for its microprocessor products made forward integration into systems products difficult. Intel's strong interdependence with Microsoft impeded strategic initiatives in the software area. In one widely noted case—Intel's Native Signal Processing (NSP) initiative to augment the microprocessor's video capability (Table 41.4)—Grove admitted that Intel "caved" in the face of Microsoft's displeasure (Schlender, 1996).

INERTIA

By 1997, Intel's road map for the development of next generations of microprocessors determined its long-term development trajectory, which was not easily changed. While Intel had put mechanisms in place that allowed very fast response to short-term contingencies

affecting the road map, Dennis Carter explained that the ability to make quick adjustments, paradoxically, reinforced the company's strategic focus and the lock-in with the PC market segment. The successful crash effort to develop the Celeron processor, however, signaled that while Intel's lock-in with the PC market segment remained strong, the lock-in of the PC market segment with Intel was perhaps loosening. Also, toward the end of 1996, Andy Grove was beginning to worry about the effect Intel's strong influence with its OEM customers was having on its strategy-making process. In an MBA class discussion in fall 1996, Grove said, "There is a hidden danger of Intel becoming very good at this. It is that we become good at one thing only."

COEVOLUTIONARY LOCK-IN AND STRATEGIC INERTIA

Reduced Capacity for New Business Development

By 1997, then COO Craig Barrett did not believe that Intel could sustain its historical growth rate and profitability solely with microprocessors. Barrett realized that Intel's intense focus on microprocessors had made it difficult for new ventures to thrive inside Intel (hence, his use of the creosote bush metaphor mentioned earlier). Different groups in the company continued to explore a multitude of new business ideas (Burgelman, Carter, and Bamford, 1999), but Intel's autonomous strategy process had become less able to exploit new business opportunities. Dennis Carter noted that outbound marketing (delivering a technology to the market) dominated inbound marketing (finding new market needs that could be met by technology). Frank Gill, an executive vice president in charge of Intel's new business development during most of Epoch II, pointed out that Intel's matrix organization did not provide managers with much opportunity to learn to make trade-offs among various functional considerations. This impeded the development of new generations of general managers able to develop new businesses. Also, business-level general managers must resolve the initial ambiguity about the correct strategy of a new business, but in the corporate context this is not sufficient. To continue to obtain corporate support, the process of strategic context determination must be activated, which helps link the new business strategy to the corporate strategy. This explorative, iterative process involves multiple levels of management in building a new strategic thrust for the corporation (Burgelman, 1983).

During fall 1999, Andy Grove reflected on the slowing down of growth in the core microprocessor business and his efforts to develop new businesses during Epoch II: "The old CEO knew that this was coming. He tried like hell to develop new business opportunities, but they almost all turned into [dirt]." Public data support Grove's contention that he knew relatively early on that Intel would have to transform itself again. Already in 1993, he had said:

> Our people have navigated successfully through one transformation, so perhaps it won't be as hard to sign them up for another one. But success can trap you. The more successful we are as a microprocessor company, the more difficult it will be to become something else. To take advantage of some opportunities I see ahead, we're going to have to transform ourselves again. The time to do it is while our business is still strong. (Grove, 1993: 60)

While Grove recognized the need for strategic renewal, difficulties in developing new businesses during Epoch II suggest that he and Intel were subject to sources of strategic inertia associated with coevolutionary lock-in. Table 41.5 identifies these two sources of strategic inertia. The ProShare case shows that the CEO's active involvement in driving new business development is likely to impose the logic of the successful core business in an area in which it may not apply, thereby impeding development of an appropriate business strategy and simultaneously inducing escalation of commitment. The Hood River case shows that even if the CEO is not actively involved, he or she may cast a shadow of influence that also impedes the development of an appropriate strategy for the new business, even though not inducing escalation of commitment. The chipset case shows some of the major difficulties a new business must overcome to get corporate support if the CEO initially views it as an enabler only of the core business. The networking case shows that these difficulties are exacerbated if the link with the core business cannot be easily established, thereby limiting its growth funding to the resources that it can generate

on its own. Table 41.6 summarizes the comparative analysis of these four cases using the process model of internal corporate venturing (Burgelman, 1983). The process model identifies key interlocking activities of different levels of management (corporate, middle, and venture) in the core (definition and impetus) and overlaying (structural context and strategic context) subprocesses of venture development.

Strategic Inertia I: If Strategic, Apply Logic of Core Strategy

THE PROSHARE CASE

The ProShare venture's purpose was to make videoconferencing a standard PC capability, which would help create additional demand for microprocessor power. Grove's strategic intent determined the strategic context for the venture from the start (Table 41.5). His support shielded the venture from the strong selection pressures of the structural context, in particular Intel's rigorous financial reviews. Grove got deeply involved in monitoring the definition of the venture strategy and in authorizing funding of its development (Table 41.6). In a fall 1999 discussion with an MBA class, Grove mentioned that Intel had spent about $750 million on the unsuccessful venture. His insistence on applying the horizontal, frontal assault strategy of the microprocessor business to ProShare reduced the degrees of freedom of the executives in charge of the new business development effort (Table 41.5). Pat Gelsinger's task was to deliver a technology to the market in the same way that Intel delivered next-generation microprocessors to the market. Technical and need-linking efforts were limited in their effectiveness, discipline-instilling product-championing efforts were not required to secure resources internally, and the effectiveness of strategic forcing efforts to secure a fast-growing beachhead in the market was limited (Table 41.6). Frank Gill, the senior executive positioned between Grove and Gelsinger was left—or rather, as he put it, "able to stay"—out of the loop. With Grove performing the role of Gill in the strategic context determination process, the discipline-instilling organizational championing efforts—requiring Gill to convince peers, as well as top management, that the continuation of the videoconferencing venture was in the long-term interest of the corporation—were not required (Table 41.6). Finally, as a consequence of the early and

Table 41.5. Company Level of Analysis: Coevolutionary Lock-In and Sources of Strategic Inertia During Epoch II

Views from below	Intel's strategic intent	Strategic action
	If strategic, apply logic of core business strategy	

Intel's strategy for videoconferencing (ProShare)

Patrick Gelsinger (GM ProShare): "ProShare was viewed as a horizontal capability—that was Andy's [Grove] wish."

"We could have acted on the vertical markets six months sooner if Andy had not had such a strong opinion."

Another ProShare executive: "There wasn't a debate about it, there wasn't even a discussion. . . . Andy had already trained the organization, meaning Intel, that periodically he gets all these flashes of an idea."

Frank Gill (senior executive): "It was not being out of the loop so much as not being sure. . . . [I thought] maybe the throwing of massive resource at it would work. I didn't know for sure and Andy and Pat were quite confident."

Grove's intent was to make videoconferencing an integral capability of the PC. To this end, he favored a frontal assault on the entire PC market segment, rather than targeting vertical segments first.

Grove assigned Patrick Gelsinger, in charge at the time of the next-generation microprocessor development, to ProShare. *Grove:* "Moving Pat off of P6, a product on which the future of our company truly depends, to run this new initiative was a very controversial step. But in many way this is the test of it."

Grove continued to be deeply involved in the strategic decision making until 1996, when he asked Frank Gill to scale down the effort, which involved some 700 people at the time.

Grove in 1999: "We assumed that just because it could be done technically there would be high demand. I was an enthusiastic user and supporter, but I've stopped using it. . . . If we were to do it over again, our approach would be not so much like the Normandy invasion, but more of a vertical focus. . . . We brought a style and conceptual approach to an area where it did not work."

Intel's strategy for bringing the PC into the living room (Hood River)

Rob Siegel (project manager) and his team identified the target applications and uses for the Hood River product. The design called for the use of Intel's 233 MHz Pentium II processor, the highest performance CPU at the time.

By August 1996, Siegel: ". . . we had accomplished a lot. We had Microsoft doing what we wanted them to do, and we had established an impressive customer list. In addition, the Product Line Business Plan presentation went well. We received the highest rating, and Andy Grove came up with the phrase, 'Hijack the TV,' which became our rallying cry."

Andy Grove: " 'The PC is it,' Grove declares. 'That sums up Intel's business plan and rallying cry.' 'Some think the information superhighway will come through their TV,' Grove proclaimed . . . '[But] the information tool of the future is on your desk, not in your living room' " (Burstein and Kline, 1995: 24).

Siegel and his team continued their efforts through the fall of 1996. But they ran into funding problems when the idea of a "network computer" (NC) gained some tracking under the impulse of Oracle's Larry Ellison, and the Desktop Product Group (DPG) reallocated resources to meet the perceived threat to the core business. Siegel was able to get funding reinstated, but the market for Hood River did not develop as planned.

In early 1997, Mike Aymar (GM of DPG) halted the venture.

Aymar: "Originally we expected the venture to . . . generate demand for another 1 million PCs per year. But market projections were for various vendors worldwide to ship only in the tens of thousands of units in '97 and '98. . . . This is insufficient."

Table 41.5. Continued

Views from below	Intel's strategic intent	Strategic action
	If non-strategic, pay as you go	

PCI chipsets as a new business

Andy Beran (finance mgr.): "We never would have gotten into the business if we had to fight for internal capacity. . . . It always would have looked like a lower [return] to the processors."

Beran noted that top management let them keep the cash they generated with old products to fund the development of chipset business: "At the point where that wasn't enough, we were already successful enough to keep going."

Randy Wilhelm (technical mgr.): "There was some doubt, I think, in certain parts of Intel that we were able to push a bus standard, whereas in the past we had always had key OEMs pushing the bus standard."

Eric Mentzer (marketing mgr.): "They said, we don't believe you guys are going to be successful, so we don't want you going into those accounts. . . . The processor division was out telling the field sales force and the customers, don't use this; use the low-risk thing."

Ron Smith (GM chipset business): Regarding his intent to develop the chipset business based on Intel's new PCI technology: "Andy Grove told me that we had no damn business doing PCI. . . . That was early on. He and I had a heated discussion about it. . . . He basically said something to the effect of who do we think we are, a chip company thinking we are going to drive an I/O bus standard?"

Senior Microprocessor Group executives supported Smith's efforts to develop the chipset business. Smith was able to use the new PCI technology to wrest control of chipsets away from PC OEMs and make the chipsets an important tool for supporting the launch of Intel's new Pentium processor. Having succeeded in the face of corporate ambivalence, Grove wrote Smith a note saying, "And I said it couldn't be done." From then on, Grove viewed chipset business as strategically important for the core business.

Networking as a new business

Frank Gill (GM Networking): "First, in the early 1990s, there was Andy Grove's ability to get everybody to focus on Job 1. . . . Any other activity was viewed as a distraction. . . . A second factor was that. . . . Since all the planning activity involving Andy focused on Job 1, he did not have sufficient insight or knowledge to meaningfully contribute to our networking and connectivity businesses."

"In 1994–95, Andy would tell me, 'Frank, I make a billion dollars in profit per quarter and you make a billion dollars in revenue per year. This is all distraction, so focus on Job 1.'"

Mark Christensen (Gill's successor): "For the first six years, from 1991 to 1997, it was basically 'pay your own way' for growth. If you didn't grow, you had the threat of getting downsized. Much of the funding was being funneled into programs that would help microprocessor growth—Job 1."

Grove: "There was a time when I could have flipped a switch between videoconferencing and networking."

"I have been rabid about four things in my career at Intel: motherboards, Intel Inside, chipsets, and videoconferencing. What if I had been equally rabid about networking? Intel could be a very different company."

Reflecting on strategic discussion concerning the networking business with Frank Gill, Grove said, "I am not happy with statements that are somewhat right, but mostly wrong. Maybe I am too good for my own good. I weed out all the weeds, but also some of the potential seeds. . . . Barrett is more comfortable with leaving strategy a bit more murky, undefined."

Grove funded both opportunities, but he said, "Much more funding was going to videoconferencing."

Grove did not allow much time for discussion of the networking business during the strategic long-range planning sessions of the early-to-mid-1990s.

As of 1997, Frank Gill: "Mark [Christensen] clearly got networking better connected within Intel. He came up with the fast Ethernet 'big pipes need big processors' notion and building remote management hooks into the network cards. He also put more focus on OEM customers where Intel had channel power."

After 1997, networking was viewed as part of the corporate strategy, leading to a major acquisition and full corporate support for growing the business.

Table 41.6. Intracompany Level of Analysis: Comparative Process Model Analysis of Four New Business Development Cases During Epoch II

Leadership activities by management level and subprocess*	ProShare	Hood River	Chipsets
Corporate management level:			
Definition: Monitoring	From the start	From the start	Fly under radar
Impetus: Authorizing	From the start	Erratic	Pay as you go
Strategic context: Rationalizing	Premature	Didn't get to	Lagging (link to Pentium)
Structural context: Structuring	Suspended	Strong influence	Strong influence
Selecting (links to structural and strategic contexts)	Suspended	Strong influence	Strong influence
Middle management level:			
Definition: Coaching	Limited	Limited	Strong
Impetus: Strategic building	Didn't get to	Didn't get to	Not necessary
Organizational championing (links impetus and strategic context)	Not necessary	Didn't get to	Strong
Strategic context: Delineating	Premature	Didn't get to	Strong
Structural context: Negotiating	Not necessary	Ineffective	Strong
Venture management level.			
Definition: Technical and need linking	Limited effectiveness	Ineffective	Effective
Product championing (links definition and impetus)	Not necessary	Ineffective	Effective
Impetus: Strategic forcing	Limited effectiveness	Ineffective	Effective
Strategic context: e.g., bootlegging	Little room	Not possible	Anticipate Pentium
Structural context: Questioning	Little room	Ineffective	Work around

	Networking		
Leadership activities by management level and subprocess*	Until 1997	Changes after 1997	
Corporate management level:			
Definition: Monitoring	Little interest	Strong	
Impetus: Authorizing	Pay as you go	Strong	
Strategic context: Rationalizing	Lagging	Link to core	
Structural context: Structuring	Strong influence	Adjusted	
Selecting (links to structural and strategic contexts)	Strong influence	Adjusted	
Middle management level:			
Definition: Coaching	Strong		
Impetus: Strategic building	Limited	Strong	
Organizational championing (links impetus and strategic context)	Give up	Strong	
Strategic context: Delineating	Limited	Strong	
Structural context: Negotiating	Defensive	Strong	
Venture management level:			
Definition: Technical and need linking	Effective		
Product championing (links definition and impetus)	Effective		
Impetus: Strategic forcing	Effective		
Strategic context: e.g., bootlegging	Limited		
Structural context: Questioning	Work around		

*Source: Burgelman (1983).

sustained support from the CEO, the opportunity costs associated with ProShare were not considered until 1996, when Gill was asked to scale the venture down (Table 41.5).

THE HOOD RIVER CASE

The Hood River venture's purpose was to bring the PC into the living room as an electronic entertainment device. Hood River was started as a seed project with initial funding from Intel's Corporate Business Development group in February 1996. The venture's strategy was influenced from the start by Grove's publicly stated strategic intent that the "PC is it," which was taken to heart by Rob Siegel, the project leader (Table 41.5). This drove the technical and need-linking efforts in the Hood River product definition. Since there was no direct and forceful support from the CEO for this project, the selective effects of the structural context were very strong (Table 41.6). This was evident when funding was temporarily cut off without warning in December 1996 to harness resources in the face of the perceived threat of the "network computer" (NC) to Intel's core business. Ineffective technical and need-linking activities made it difficult to collaborate with the consumer electronics OEMs, who had a very different view of the market and the technology required. Siegel tried to pursue product-championing activities, but, as a relative newcomer, he could not exert influence in the network of resource-controlling relationships of Intel's matrix. Strategic forcing never got started, as no consumer electronics OEMs or PC OEMs were willing to adopt the Hood River product concept (Table 41.6). As a result, Michael Aymar, the middle-level executive, had no foundation to build on and could not continue to ask top management for support. He stopped funding Hood River in 1997 (Table 41.5).

Strategic Inertia II: If Non-strategic, Pay as You Go

THE PCI CHIPSET CASE

Intel Architecture Labs developed the PCI bus technology in the early 1990s. Top management's initial intention was to organize a consortium to bring PCI to the PC industry as an enabling technology for the core microprocessor business, as the previous bus standard was too slow to take advantage of increased processing power. Determination of the strategic context of the PCI chipset venture was lagging because Grove was opposed to the idea of turning PCI chipsets into a business (Table 41.5). Ron Smith nevertheless decided to pursue PCI chipsets as a new business. He tried to "fly under the radar" to protect the venture from close top management scrutiny to build a viable business foundation (Table 41.6). He assembled a team of experienced functional managers who were well connected with the rest of the corporation and could access resources that would otherwise not be available. These managers engaged in careful technical and need linking to define Intel's chipset opportunity. Realizing they would not be able to secure scarce manufacturing capacity internally against the more profitable microprocessors, their product championing efforts took the form of contracting with outside manufacturers. Smith convinced his team that winning inside required winning outside through successful strategic forcing (Table 41.6). Each year, the venture delivered more than it had promised, which gave senior executives such as Albert Yu, Paul Otellini, and Craig Barrett a reason for supporting it in the face of Andy Grove's doubts. The chipset venture's potential was sufficiently large that no additional business opportunities needed to be found to reach critical mass. Ron Smith did not have to engage in strategic building, which requires the agglomeration of additional business opportunities through internal transfer of projects and/or through carefully targeted acquisitions, and could focus on coaching the venture team. Also, Smith had anticipated that the PCI chipset would be important for facilitating the launch of the Pentium processor in 1993 and had instructed the team to design the chipset accordingly. Smith's prediction turned out to be correct, which facilitated the determination of the strategic context later on (Table 41.6). Eventually, Grove concluded that the chipset venture was an important business for Intel. His retroactive rationalization concluded the process of strategic context determination. From then on, it had his full support.

THE NETWORKING BUSINESS CASE

In the early 1990s, Frank Gill's charter was to develop new businesses for Intel, but because of the enormous growth of the core business, Andy Grove began to view these efforts as a distraction. Grove felt that Gill was too much focused on the success of the networking business and not enough on that of the core business. Grove also felt uncomfortable with the lack of clarity of the networking strategy (Table 41.5). Gill pointed out that Grove had been totally focused on the core microprocessor business and that the strategic long-range planning process (SLRP) spent little time on businesses that were not considered strategic. Top management looked at networking as an industry enabler, rather than as a new business. Gill gave up on the organizational championing efforts in the face of peer resistance and top management's recalcitrance and focused on short-term financial performance to protect the business (Table 41.6). This created a vicious circle. Unsuccessful organizational championing limited the amount of corporate resources made available for the networking business, which limited the scope of the strategic building activities that Gill could engage in: large acquisitions were simply not permitted. And this, in turn, limited the growth of the business in the fast-growing industry to what could be achieved with the strategic forcing activities based on the internally developed products. Fortunately, these were the result of effective technical and need linking and experienced strong market acceptance. The effectiveness of these activities was at least in part the result of Gill's strong coaching of his team and successful shielding of the networking business from top management. Only in 1997, when a new general manager was able to show the importance of networking for the microprocessor business and for Intel's future growth, was its strategic context determined, and it received full top management support.

DISCUSSION AND CONCLUSIONS

Coevolutionary Lock-In

This study shows how Andy Grove was able to take advantage of the fortuitous circumstances Intel faced in its microprocessor business with the rapid ascendance of the IBM PC and to turn good luck into a strategy vector. He made Intel focus on a narrow business strategy and established an induced strategy process that tightly aligned strategy and action and produced extraordinary success. His deep understanding of the forces that gave rise to the strategy vector also gave him great confidence in dealing with several crises that challenged it. This study, however, also reveals the complex reciprocal causation between Grove's strategic intent and the structures and processes that he put in place and how the very success of the strategy vector resulted in the emergence of coevolutionary lock-in and impeded new business development. Although Grove was a master of strategy, who knew that Intel would have to transform itself again eventually, he and Intel were subject to inescapable evolutionary dilemmas associated with the dynamics of coevolutionary lock-in.

Intel's success as the sole source of the highest value component of PCs made it increasingly able to appropriate the available rents in the PC market segment. But this asymmetry created a positive feedback loop, requiring Intel to make more and more of the investments necessary to enable adoption of next-generation microprocessors. These complementary strategic thrusts helped Intel to control its external environment (Pfeffer and Salancik, 1978), but they also increasingly tied its strategic direction and economic fortunes to the evolution of the PC market segment. Coevolutionary lock-in engendered by strategic dominance entangled Intel in a system of relationships that reduced its freedom of action, a paradox well articulated by J. G. March: "You can have autonomy or you can have power but you cannot have both. Power depends on linkages and linkages destroy autonomy" (personal communication).

As a driving force of the PC market segment, Intel was able to influence the pace of industry change. Such time-paced strategy is a powerful alternative to event-paced strategy (Gersick, 1994; Brown and Eisenhardt, 1997). It allows a company to dictate the pace of strategic change that other players—customers, competitors, suppliers, and complementors—must adhere to. Intel's time-paced strategy, however did not simply try to impose its strategic intent on the product-market environment unilaterally. Grove had learned that there was a natural adoption cycle in the PC market segment, with a period of about three years between the maximum ramp-up for different microprocessor generations. He also knew that Intel could not expect to change that much. At the same time, having put in place the competencies and support infrastructure to deliver new generations of microprocessors to the PC market segment, there was a strong internal drive to do so. Intel's time-paced strategy thus reinforced the lock-in with the PC market segment.

Also, Intel was able to win the two defining battles in the microprocessor market segment—against other Intel Architecture suppliers and against the RISC architecture—that Grove had identified in late 1993. But Intel's competitive intensity increasingly specialized the company's competitive repertoire for the PC market segment (Barnett, 1997), further reinforcing coevolutionary lock-in.

Intel's introduction of the Celeron processor in 1998 to counter AMD at the low end of the PC market segment testifies to the company's relentless competitive intensity. The need for a crash effort to introduce the Celeron processor, however, also suggests that Intel, while continuing to innovate at a high rate with its Pentium processor product family, had begun to produce innovations that were less in tune with evolving environmental demands (SØrensen and Stuart, 2000). Intel seemed to have difficulties recognizing that the importance of the external selection environment relative to the internal selection environment was increasing toward the end of Epoch II (Sorenson, 2000). Intel's difficulties in this respect seem consistent with the observation that in successful organizations there will be a natural tendency for internal selective-retentive processes to dominate external ones (Miller, 1999: 94). Coevolutionary lock-in may thus be an extension and further elucidation of the sources of structural inertia (Hannan and Freeman, 1984).

Extraordinary success associated with coevolutionary lock-in heightened Andy Grove's confidence in the logic of the core business strategy (e.g., Prahalad and Bettis, 1986). But Grove's direct involvement in ProShare made it difficult for the middle-level executive in charge to develop a strategy that was appropriate for the new business and to act in accordance with an objective analysis of the situation. Grove's approach in the ProShare case supports Audia, Locke, and Smith's (2000) suggestion that success may increase a decision maker's feelings of self-efficacy. It confirms that the inertia of success is often best understood in terms of the strength of the decision maker's beliefs in the validity of the current strategy, rather than in terms of complacency or drifting without further attempts at improvement (Miller and Chen, 1994). It also supports Miller's (1994) finding that decision-making styles tend to be more extreme during periods following success than during periods following poor or mediocre performance. Grove eventually came to

realize this, but his strong involvement early on, before major market and technical uncertainties had been reduced, led to escalation of commitment and prevented scaling down or timely exit from the failing business. This raises important questions about the limitations of using top management's strategic intent as a means for guided evolution (Lovas and Ghoshal, 2000). Within Intel's induced-strategy process, guided evolution worked fine: many new projects related to the strategic intent expressed in the microprocessor road map were useful variations that were effectively selected and retained. When Grove tried to use strategic intent to shape new variations that were not commensurate with the logic of the core business, however, the result was misguided evolution.

Much of Intel's R&D investments went into technologies that complemented the microprocessor and thereby offered opportunities to launch new businesses, but the company rarely attempted to do so. One reason for this was that any technology advance that enriched the PC market segment was likely to create more demand for microprocessors, which had very high margins. Thus, it was generally more valuable in the short run to give away technology and quickly disseminate it in the market, rather than try to build a business around it. This suggests the powerful effect that financial strategy and capital market considerations may have on product-market strategy. It also indicates, however, another strong structural inertial consequence of coevolutionary lock-in. As Intel's extraordinary lucrative core business continued to grow very fast in the mid-1990s, Grove began to consider non-core business development as a distraction. Consequently, it was increasingly difficult for non-core new businesses to command top management attention and corporate resources. This was exacerbated by Intel's structural context, which facilitated execution of the core business strategy but was less able to deal with non-core new business development: strategic planning was almost exclusively focused on the core business. New general management talent was not easily developed in Intel's matrix organization. Resource allocation favored the core business, and new businesses were constantly in danger of experiencing random shocks when critical resources were taken away to cope with a perceived threat to the core business. The measurement and reward system was unforgiving for deviations from objectives, even though new business strategies require such flexibility. While many new ideas continued to emerge, the structural context made it difficult to activate the process of strategic context determination necessary to link the new business to the corporate strategy.

Implications for Theory

The causes and consequences of coevolutionary lock-in suggest that this little-noticed process might help illuminate some of the inescapable dilemmas in the natural dynamics of organizational adaptation. It also helps connect ideas about the internal ecology of strategy making, the modern economic theory of the firm, and an evolutionary perspective on organizational learning.

ORGANIZATIONAL ADAPTATION

Previous findings based on a study of Intel's transformation during Epoch I (Burgelman, 1991, 1994) supported the proposition that companies that are successful over long periods of time maintain top-driven strategic intent, through the induced strategy process, while simultaneously maintaining bottom-up-driven strategic renewal, through the autonomous strategy process. Recent efforts by scholars to formalize parts of the induced and autonomous strategy processes framework seem to support this proposition. In Rotemberg and Saloner's (2000) mathematical model, the firm employs a visionary CEO who is consistently biased in favor of certain projects but who leaves the door open for pursuing sufficiently good opportunities outside the existing vision. They have shown that this may offer greater profit-maximizing possibilities than committing to a narrow business strategy (Rotemberg and Saloner, 1994). They showed the important role played by objective middle managers supporting promising projects outside the CEO's vision. Importantly, they also showed that the CEO must not interfere with the autonomy of middle managers in allocating resources to autonomous projects.

The study of Grove's tenure as CEO initially cast doubt on the importance of the autonomous strategy process. Like other great leaders, Grove was able to recognize the unique opportunities facing Intel and to mobilize his organization to exploit them by creating an extremely focused induced strategy process. If the growth of the PC market segment had continued unabated, Intel's induced strategy process would proba-

bly have sufficed to secure continued adaptation, thereby reducing further the relevance of the autonomous strategy process. This would have undermined the validity of the internal ecology perspective on strategy making. Toward the end of Epoch II, however, it became clear that Intel's future growth would also depend on new business development and that the strategies for new businesses might have to be defined by general managers who were closer to the front line. Inertial consequences of coevolutionary lock-in, however, had significantly reduced the effectiveness of Intel's autonomous strategy process. Figure 41.1 provides a schematic representation of the paper's core theoretical idea: a company's relentless and successful pursuit of a narrow business strategy through the induced strategy process may produce coevolutionary lock-in and reduce the effectiveness of the autonomous strategy process, which weakens a company's long-term adaptation.

The heavy lines in Figure 41.1 indicate the reinforcement of Intel's induced strategy process, the creation of the strategy vector, and the coevolutionary lock-in with the PC market segment that it engendered. Figure 41.1 also shows the impact of the sources of inertia associated with coevolutionary lock-in on the autonomous strategy process. Some initiatives that needed to be pursued through the autonomous strategy process were erroneously subjected to the logic of the induced strategy process (Strategic Inertia I); others faced Intel's reduced ability to activate strategic context determination processes (Strategic Inertia II).

Figure 41.1 illuminates inescapable evolutionary dilemmas arising in the natural dynamics of organizational adaptation. Grove's strategic leadership approximated the classical rational-actor model in pursuing Intel's enormous opportunity in the PC market segment, but at the cost of reducing Intel's capability to develop new businesses. Was this a mistake? This study suggests that objective necessities arising from the coevolutionary lock-in of the induced strategy process and the product-market environment were a major cause of the relative neglect of the autonomous strategy process. The resource requirements of pursuing the microprocessor business, especially top management time and attention, did not leave much room for alternative pursuits. And the short-term opportunity costs of pursuing the microprocessor business were perceived as low. Also, it seems quite possible that Andy Grove passed on the CEO baton to Craig Barrett in

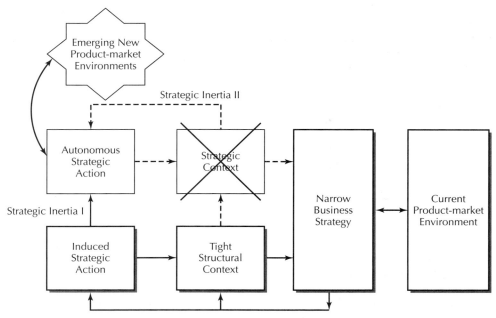

Figure 41.1. Effects of a strategy vector on the internal ecology of strategy making.

early 1998 when he realized that a new, less singularly focused strategic leadership approach was necessary and there was still time to rebuild Intel's new business development capability. Alternatively, might an effort to maintain the internal ecology of strategy making have severely hampered the firm? Does optimal long-term adaptation follow a punctuated equilibrium pattern (e.g., Tushman and Romanelli, 1985), perhaps involving a series of discrete periods, each focused on maximally exploiting the available opportunities, rather than a more continuous evolutionary process of balancing exploitation of available opportunities at a given time with preparing the ground for future growth opportunities? This study cannot definitively answer these alternative questions. Its findings suggest, however, that without major acquisitions, the likelihood of moving instantaneously and discontinuously from one period's opportunity frontier to that of another is low. For instance, it took more than ten years for microprocessors to become Intel's new core business. In 2002, Intel management realizes that large new businesses do not emerge fully formed out of the blue. Recognizing the possibility of alternative developmental paths, this paper's identification of coevolutionary lock-in nevertheless casts new light on the role of strat-

egy making as a long-term adaptive organizational capability. This advance of administrative science provides company leaders responsible for designing the strategy-making process with a conceptual framework for considering more explicitly and sooner the trade-offs involved in balancing induced and autonomous strategic processes and exploitation and exploration in organizational learning.

STRATEGY AND LEARNING

This study's findings raise the question of whether induced and autonomous strategy processes are fundamentally at odds with one another or can be effectively pursued simultaneously. Maintaining the simultaneity of induced (variation reducing) and autonomous (variation increasing) strategy processes may involve difficulties similar to maintaining a balance between exploitation and exploration processes in organizational learning (March, 1991). Both processes compete for limited resources, and company leaders necessarily make trade-offs between them. Given the extraordinary opportunities Intel faced in the core business, focusing on learning that increased its mean performance rather than on learning that could increase the variance of performance seemed rational (March,

1991: 82). Also, Grove's ability to vectorize everybody at Intel in the same direction led to quick convergence of individual beliefs (strategic initiatives) and the organizational code (the corporate strategy) (March, 1991: 75). Intel experienced turnover because the lowest 10 percent of individual performers were systematically replaced, but this also ensured the rapid socialization of new employees to Intel's organizational code because they were keen to understand Intel's performance expectations, which were clearly tied to implementing the core strategy. Overall, Intel's induced-strategy process during Grove's tenure as CEO favored organizational learning that was maximally concerned with exploitation.

Exploration involves experimentation (March, 1991) and is viewed here through the lens of the autonomous strategy process, which dissects exploration into autonomous strategic initiatives and the process of strategic context determination. The strategic context determination process, which depends critically on the general management abilities of middle-level executives, helps companies turn exploration efforts into new exploitation opportunities. The distinction between exploratory initiatives and the strategic context determination process helps explain the mixed record of new business development during Intel's Epoch II. In spite of Grove's efforts to vectorize everybody in the same direction, numerous autonomous strategic initiatives continued to emerge, indicating continued attempts at exploration. The decrease in Intel's capacity to activate strategic context determination processes, however, prevented the company from exploiting the more viable autonomous initiatives. Strategic context determination processes thus appear to be the crucial nexus between exploration and exploitation and key to balancing induced and autonomous strategy processes effectively. Strategic context determination processes complement a company's structural context in important ways. They make it possible to suspend the selective effects of the structural context, which almost unavoidably tends to become fine-tuned for supporting top management's current strategic intent. And they serve to create links between autonomous strategic action and the company's strategy, thereby amending it. The capacity to activate and successfully complete such processes can be viewed as a measure of the intelligence of the company's internal selection environment and may be at the very heart of strategy making as an adaptive organizational capability.

This study's main contributions concern the natural dynamics of organizational adaptation. An evolutionary perspective on strategy making helps bridge and extend related ideas about the benefits and potential opportunity costs of narrow business strategies in the modern economic theory of the firm and ideas about exploitation and exploration in theory about organizational learning. Fine-grained detail of a strategy-making process approximating the classical rational-actor model suggests that the pursuit of focus and efficiency may also become the potential enemy of effective exploration and strategic renewal. Strong positive environmental feedback strengthens the relative importance of the internal selection environment but also causes coevolutionary lock-in, which is a double-edged sword: strategic dominance begets dependence. The relative dominance of the internal selection environment may last a long time, more than ten years in the case of Intel's Epoch II, but eventually, cumulative changes in the external selection environment are likely to reduce its efficiency. Coevolutionary lock-in exacerbates tendencies toward structural inertia in novel and potentially insidious ways because it affects the balance between induced and autonomous strategy processes and a company's ability to develop new businesses and, hence, the long-term adaptive capability of its strategy-making process.

Conclusions from a single case study warrant healthy caution, but by examining a case of extraordinarily successful CEO-driven strategy making that approximated the classical rational-actor model, this paper provides further support for the internal-ecology model of strategy making as an adaptive organizational capability. There is little doubt that companies that find themselves in the fortuitous circumstances that Intel faced in the PC market segment after its defeat in the DRAM business can greatly benefit from a leader with an exceptional ability to capitalize on them. Yet the benefits of the rational-actor model must be tempered by the realization that in dynamic environments, even in digital industries characterized by winner-take-all competition, the relative strength of the company's strategy vector will eventually decline, because the forces that make periods of extraordinary success possible are unlikely to last forever. The inertial consequences of coevolutionary lock-in, however, are likely to linger on if company leaders do not address them. An organization's long-term adaptation, spanning multiple generations of CEOs, may therefore critically depend on maintaining the strategic renewal capability of its internal ecology of strategy making.

ACKNOWLEDGMENTS

The research for this paper was critically dependent on my case writing and teaching collaboration with Andrew S. Grove, Intel's former CEO and current chairman, since 1988. The generous collaboration of Intel Corporation and its managers in this research is much appreciated. James G. March and Ezra W. Zuckerman offered many useful comments on an earlier draft. I am especially indebted to Jim March for drawing attention to coevolutionary lock-in as a phenomenon of organizational adaptation. The ideas of this paper were significantly sharpened as the result of challenging comments and queries of the *ASQ* reviewers and of Christine Oliver, its editor. Thanks also to the managing editor, Linda Johanson, for helpful editorial suggestions.

REFERENCES

Aldrich, H. 1999. *Organizations Evolving.* London: Sage.

Allison, G., and P. Zelikow. 1999. *Essence of Decision: Explaining the Cuban Missile Crisis,* 2d ed. New York: Addison Wesley Longman.

Arthur B. 1987. "Competing technologies: An overview." In G. Dosi (ed.) *Technical Change and Economic Theory:* 590–607. New York: Columbia University Press.

Audia, P. G., E. A. Locke, and K. G. Smith. 2000. "The paradox of success: An archival and a laboratory study of strategic persistence following radical environmental change." *Academy of Management Journal,* 43: 837–853.

Bamford, Raymond S., and Robert A. Burgelman. 1997a. "Intel Corporation: The Hood River Project (A)." Stanford Business School Case SM-49A.

Bamford, Raymond S., and Robert A. Burgelman. 1997b. "Intel Corporation: The Hood River Project (B)." Stanford Business School Case SM-49B.

Bamford, Raymond S., and Robert A. Burgelman. 1998 "Intel's strategic position in the family room, 1998." Stanford Business School Case SM-50.

Barnett, W. P. 1997. "The dynamics of competitive intensity." *Administrative Science Quarterly,* 42: 128–160.

Barnett, W. P., and M. T. Hansen. 1996. "The red queen in organizational evolution." *Strategic Management Journal,* Summer Special Issue, 17: 139–157.

Baum, J. A. C., and B. McKelvey (eds.). 1999. *Variations in Organization Science: In Honor of Donald T. Campbell.* Thousand Oaks, CA: Sage.

Bendor, J., and T. H. Hammond. 1992. "Rethinking Allison's models." *American Political Science Review,* 86: 301–322.

Bower, J. L. 1970. *Managing the Resource Allocation Process.* Boston: Harvard Business School Press.

Brown, S. L., and K. M. Eisenhardt. 1997. "The art of continuous change: Linking complexity theory and time-paced evolution in relentlessly shifting organizations." *Administrative Science Quarterly,* 42: 1–34.

Burgelman, R. A. 1983. "A process model of internal corporate venturing in the diversified major firm." *Administrative Science Quarterly,* 28: 223–244.

Burgelman, R. A. 1991. "Intraorganizational ecology of strategy making and organizational adaptation: Theory and field research." *Organization Science,* 2: 239–262.

Burgelman, R. A. 1994. "Fading memories: A process theory of strategic business exit in dynamic environments." *Administrative Science Quarterly,* 39: 24–56.

Burgelman, R. A. 2002. *Strategy Is Destiny: How Strategy-Making Shapes a Company's Future.* New York: Free Press.

Burgelman, R. A., D. L. Carter, and R. S. Bamford. 1999. "Intel Corporation: The evolution of an adaptive organization." Stanford Business School Case SM-65.

Burstein, D., and D. Kline. 1995. "In the square-off between TV and computer, the smart money might be on the boob tube." *Los Angeles Times,* October 29.

Christensen, C. M., and J. L. Bower. 1996. "Customer power, strategic investment, and the failure of leading firms." *Strategic Management Journal,* 17: 197–218.

Cogan, G. W., and R. A. Burgelman. 1991. "Intel Corporation (C): Strategies for the 1990s." Stanford Business School Case PS-BP-256C.

Collins, J. C. 2001. *Good to Great.* New York: HarperBusiness.

Dyck, B., and F. A. Starke. 1999. "The formation of breakaway organizations: Observations and a process model." *Administrative Science Quarterly,* 44: 792–822.

Farrell, J., H. K. Monroe, and G. Saloner. 1998. "The vertical organization of industry: Systems competition versus component competition." *Journal of Economics and Management Strategy,* 7: 143–182.

Fine, K. M., and R. A. Burgelman. 1997. "Intel Corporation (F): Going beyond success in 1997." Stanford Business School Case S-BP-256F.

Gersick, C. J. G. 1994. "Pacing strategic change: The case of a new venture." *Academy of Management Journal,* 37: 9–45.

Gilder, G. 1989. *Microcosm: The Quantum Revolution in Economics and Technology.* New York: Simon and Schuster.

Glaser, B. G., and A. L. Strauss. 1967. *The Discovery of Grounded Theory.* Chicago: Aldine.

Grove, A. S. 1993. "How Intel makes spending pay off." *Fortune,* February 22: 57–61.

Grove, A. S. 1996. *Only the Paranoid Survive.* New York: Doubleday.

Hannan, M. T., and J. Freeman. 1977. "The population ecology of organizations." *American Journal of Sociology,* 83: 929–984.

Hannan, M. T., and J. Freeman. 1984. "Structural inertia and organizational change." *American Sociological Review,* 49: 149–164.

Isaacson, W. 1997. "The microchip is the dynamo of a new economy driven by the passion of Intel's Andrew Grove." *Time,* December 29: 46–51.

Kawamoto, D., and S. Galante. 1998. "The legacy of Andy Grove." *CNET,* March 26.

Leonard-Barton, D. 1990. "A dual methodology for case studies: Synergistic use of a longitudinal single site with replicated multiple sites." *Organization Science,* 1: 248–266.

Levinthal, D., and J. G. March. 1993. "The myopia of learning." *Strategic Management Journal,* Winter Special Issue, 14: 95–112.

Lovas, B., and S. Ghoshal. 2000. "Strategy as guided evolution." *Strategic Management Journal,* 21: 875–896.

March, J. G. 1991. "Exploration and exploitation in organizational learning." *Organization Science,* 1: 71–87.

Miller, D. 1994. "What happens after success: The perils of excellence." *Journal of Management Studies,* 31: 85–102.

Miller, D. 1999. "Selection processes inside organizations: The self-reinforcing consequences of success." In J. A. C. Baum and B. McKelvey (eds.), *Variations in Organization Science: In Honor of Donald T. Campbell:* 93–109. Thousand Oaks, CA: Sage.

Miller, D., and M.-J. Chen. 1994. "Sources and consequences of competitive inertia: A study of the U.S. airline industry." *Administrative Science Quarterly,* 39: 1–23.

Mintzberg, H., B. Ahlstrand, and J. Lampel. 1998. *Strategy Safari.* New York: Free Press.

Pfeffer, J., and G. R. Salancik. 1978. *The External Control of Organizations.* New York: Harper & Row.

Pollack, A. 1988. "An 'awesome' Intel corners its market." *New York Times,* April 3.

Prahalad, C. K., and R. A. Bettis. 1986. "The dominant logic: A new linkage between diversity and performance." *Strategic Management Journal,* 7: 485–501.

Reinhardt, A., I. Sager, and P. Burrows. 1997. "Can Andy Grove keep profits up in an era of cheap PCs?" *Business Week,* December 22.

Rotemberg, J. J., and G. Saloner. 1994. "The benefits of narrow business strategies." *American Economic Review,* 84: 1330–1349.

Rotenberg, J. J., and G. Saloner. 2000. "Visionaries, managers, and strategic direction." *RAND Journal of Economics,* 31: 693–716.

Schlender, B. R. 1989. "Intel produces a chip packing huge power and wide ambitions." *Wall Street Journal,* February 28.

Schlender, B. R. 1996. "A conversation with the lords of Wintel." *Fortune,* July 8.

Sorenson, O. 2000. "Letting the market work for you: An evolutionary perspective on product strategy." *Strategic Management Journal,* 21: 577–592.

Sørensen, J. B., and T. Stuart. 2000. "Aging, obsolescence and organizational innovation." *Administrative Science Quarterly,* 45: 81–112.

Steere, D., and R. A. Burgelman. 1993a. "Intel Corporation (D): Microprocessors at the crossroads." Stanford Business School Case S-BP-256D.

Steere, D., and R. A. Burgelman. 1993b. "Intel Corporation (E): New directions for the 1990s." Stanford Business School Case S-BP-256E.

Suzuki, O., and R. A. Burgelman. 1998. "The PC-based desktop videoconferencing systems industry in 1998." Stanford Business School Case SM-51.

Tredennick, N. 1991. "1991: The year of the RISC." *Microprocessor Report,* February 6: 16.

Tushman, M. E., and E. Romanelli. 1985. "Organization evolution: A metamorphosis model of convergence and reorientation." In B. M. Staw and L. L. Cummings (eds.), *Research in Organizational Behavior,* 7: 171–222. Greenwich, CT: JAI Press.

Van de Ven, A. H. 1992. "Suggestions for studying strategy process: A research note." *Strategic Management Journal,* Summer Special Issue, 13: 169–188.

Welch, J., with J. A. Byrne. 2001. *Jack.* New York: Warner Business.

Yin, R. K. 1984. *Case Study Research,* Applied Social Research Methods Series, 5. Beverly Hills, CA: Sage.

Zuckerman, E. W. 2000. "Focusing the corporate product: Securities analysts and de-diversification." *Administrative Science Quarterly,* 45: 591–619.

42

Change in the Presence of Fit

The Rise, the Fall, and the Renaissance of Liz Claiborne

NICOLAJ SIGGELKOW

A new framework that addresses how tight fit among a firm's activities affects the firm's ability to react to environmental changes is presented. As part of the framework, a new classification scheme for environmental changes is developed. I argue that fit-conserving change, which leaves the internal fit among a firm's activities intact yet decreases the appropriateness of the set of choices as a whole, poses a particularly difficult challenge for managers. A longitudinal case study of the fashion apparel company Liz Claiborne illustrates the framework.

The last years have seen a remarkable upsurge of interest in the concepts of interaction and fit. Within the management and organization literatures, the notion of fit has a long-standing presence. In particular, the internal fit between the strategy and the structure of firms (e.g., Chandler, 1962; Learned, Christensen, Andrews, and Guth, 1965) and the external fit between the structure and the environment of firms (e.g., Lawrence and Lorsch, 1967; Pennings, 1987) have received much attention. During the late 1980s and 1990s, originally spurred by analyses of Japanese manufacturing methods, researchers revived the topic of fit. The emphasis shifted to studying internal fit at a very fine-grained level of analysis. The importance of replicating entire systems of practices, including production, supply, and human resource policies, rather than single elements, was recognized (e.g., Jaikumar, 1986; MacDuffie, 1995). Expanding the concept of fit beyond manufacturing and ascribing to it a central role in strategy formulation, Porter (1996) stressed the importance of mutually reinforcing activities in creating and sustaining a competitive advantage. Over the same time period, economists as well have become interested in the issues of fit and interdependence among firm choices and have started to create mathematical frameworks that allow rigorous modeling of at least certain types of mutually reinforcing interactions (e.g., Milgrom and Roberts, 1990, 1995).

The common theme of these approaches is that to understand the performance of a firm, one must analyze the firm as a *system* of interconnected choices: choices with respect to activities, policies and organizational structures, capabilities, and resources. Internal fit among choices can lead to a sustainable competitive advantage because it makes imitation difficult (Porter and Rivkin, 1998; Rivkin, 2000). However, the implications of tight fit for the sustainability of a competitive advantage given environmental change are ambiguous. On the one hand, "Firms may have difficulty navigating a changing environment not only because the changes in the environment negate the value of the organization's assets, but also because a tightly cou-

Reprinted from *Academy of Management Journal,* Vol. 44, No. 4, "Change in the Presence of Fit: The Rise, the Fall, and the Renaissance of Liz Claiborne," by Nicolaj Siggelkow. Copyright © 2001 by Academy of Management. Reproduced with permission of Academy of Management via Copyright Clearance Center.

pled organization may have difficulty adapting to such changes" (Levinthal, 1997: 936). Tight coupling requires a firm to modify many choices simultaneously, an inherently difficult task (Nadler, Shaw, and Walton, 1994). On the other hand, tight fit raises the incentive for management to optimally configure and adjust all of its choices. Since each choice influences the payoff of many other choices, the marginal payoff to adjusting each choice in response to some external change is increased in the presence of tighter fit (Porter, 1995). Moreover, tight fit can make a firm more sensitive to environmental change (Weick, 1976). Changes are quickly detected, since the repercussions are felt in multiple areas in the firm.

This article presents a new framework for thinking about the relationship between fit and organizational inertia when a firm is confronted with environmental change. As part of the framework, a new classification scheme for environmental changes is developed. In line with the more recent literature on fit, we examine fit at a very detailed level of analysis—at the level of individual choices. To illustrate the framework, we present a longitudinal study of how a firm that created a system of tightly interconnected choices responded (or failed to respond) to environmental changes. I studied the developmental journey of Liz Claiborne, the largest U.S. manufacturer of women's fashion apparel, from its inception in 1976 to late 1997. I analyze the initial success of Liz Claiborne, the environmental changes it faced in the early 1990s, its first responses, and its subsequent actions in the late 1990s.

LITERATURE REVIEW AND CHANGE FRAMEWORK

Before I examine the historical journey of Liz Claiborne, it will be helpful to briefly review the literature on organizational change that is concerned with changes in systems of interconnected choices. Following the review, I present a new framework for thinking about the relationship between fit and organizational responses given different types of environmental changes.

Logically prior to any theory about *changes* in systems of interrelated parts is the notion that internal fit should not be thought of as "pairwise" associations between variables, but as gestalts, or configurations,

describing sets of elements and their relationships (Drazin and Van de Ven, 1985; Khandwalla, 1973; Miller, 1986; Miller and Friesen, 1984; Nadler and Tushman, 1992). Whereas the term "fit" is used in the literature on configurations to describe the internal relationship among activities, in the contingency literature the term is used to describe the relationship between a firm's choices and its environment. To gain clarity on the concept of fit, I suggest making the distinction between *internal fit* among activities—that is, whether a firm has a coherent configuration of activities—and *external fit,* that is, the appropriateness of the configuration given the environmental conditions facing the firm.

Building on the idea that firms consist of systems of interrelated parts, Miller and Friesen (1982) analyzed the change processes of these systems. They hypothesized and empirically found that quantum changes (changes in many attributes over a short period of time) yielded better performance than piecemeal incremental approaches. Following a similar line of thinking, Tushman and Romanelli (1985) proposed that firms follow a developmental path best described by a punctuated equilibrium model of organizational evolution: Firms engage in incremental changes during most of their history, yet sporadically undergo relatively rapid and fundamental transformations (Gersick, 1991). Empirical support of this developmental pattern has been provided by Tushman, Newman, and Romanelli (1986), Pettigrew (1987), and Romanelli and Tushman (1994).

Intimately tied to the process of change is the issue of firms' inertia. For the purpose of this discussion, I focus on factors that may cause senior management to fail to respond to environmental changes. Hambrick and Mason (1984) proposed a helpful framework for understanding management inertia. In short, managers are thought of as having mental maps that influence both the information they perceive and the way they process it. As a consequence, managers, especially those with long tenure, may be unable to "unlearn" outdated views of the world (Nystrom and Starbuck, 1984). Past success, in particular, reinforces and eventually ossifies mental maps, leading to increased inertia (Murmann and Tushman, 1997). Studies have shown that past success leads to a reduction in information processing (Miller, 1993) and a heightened belief that environmental changes are not going to affect an organization negatively (Milliken, 1990). Moreover, past success can lead to the accumulation of slack resources, which reduce the perceived need to change (Milliken and Lant, 1991), and to the creation of a strong organizational identity or culture. Both past success and strong organizational identities have been found to increase belief in an organization's relative invulnerability to environmental changes (Miller, 1994; Milliken, 1990).

In sum, a variety of psychological reasons have been described in the literature as leading to firm inertia. In the following framework, I develop a link between the work on inertia and the previously described literature on fit. As described by Tushman and Romanelli (1985), inertial forces lead firms along a process of convergence to a specific configuration of strategic position and organizational form. The value of this process has been previously analyzed with respect to two different environmental conditions: stability and turbulence (Miller, Lant, Milliken, and Korn, 1996; Tushman & Romanelli, 1985; Tushman and Rosenkopf, 1996). As long as an environment is relatively stable, convergence, and hence inertial forces, are found to be beneficial. However, in turbulent environments, inertial forces are a liability.

Rather than distinguishing between stable and turbulent environments, the following framework characterizes changes in the environment in terms of their impact on internal and external fit. This characterization scheme can offer new insights into the mediating role that fit plays in the relationship between environmental changes and the ensuing changes (or inertia) at the firm level. In particular, the framework points toward the difficulty of managers' perceiving and reacting to environmental changes that leave the internal fit among the elements within a firm's set of choices intact, yet decrease the value of the set of choices as a whole—that is, destroy external fit.

For the following discussion, the notion of a "performance landscape" is useful. The concept of a performance or fitness landscape was first developed in the realm of evolutionary biology by Sewell Wright (1932). The concept has been further developed and formalized by Kauffman (1993) and has found application in, for instance, studies of organizational adaptation (Levinthal, 1997), organizational variety (Westhoff, Yarbrough, and Yarbrough, 1996), and the difficulty of imitating complex strategies (Rivkin,

2000). In our context, the performance landscape is a multidimensional space in which each dimension represents the values of a particular choice that a firm can make and a final dimension indicating the performance value. For illustration, consider a simple example in which a firm can make only two choices: the breadth of product variety and the flexibility of the production set-up. Imagine the breadth of product variety is on the x-axis, the degree of flexibility is on the y-axis, and the ensuing performance is on the vertical z-axis. The performance landscape maps each pair of variety and flexibility choices onto a performance value (see Figure 42.1a). Similarly, for each set of N choices, the performance landscape would attach a performance value to it in a $N + 1$ dimensional space.

Performance landscapes provide a suggestive way to illustrate the concepts of internal and external fit. External fit—the appropriateness of a set of choices given environmental conditions—is represented by the height of a particular point on the landscape. Environmental conditions encompass all factors that affect the relative profitability of a firm's set of choices, including competitors' actions, customer preferences, and available technologies. As shown in Figure 42.1a, certain combinations of flexibility and product variety lead to higher performance than other combinations.

Consistency among choices—that is, internal fit—is represented by a peak in the landscape. Internal fit corresponds to a peak, because changing any single element (and not changing any other element) within a consistent set of choices leads to a decline in performance. Two examples of consistent sets of choices are the Ford mass production system and the Japanese lean manufacturing system (Milgrom & Roberts, 1990). In our simple two-dimensional example, the mass production system is represented by low variety and low flexibility, and the lean production system is represented by high variety and high flexibility (see Figure 42.1b).

The shape of each peak contains further information: the stronger the degree of interaction among a particular set of choices, the steeper the associated peak. This feature results from the fact that in systems with strong interactions, the performance penalties for misalignments are particularly high because the value of many activities is affected.[1]

Environmental changes can be thought of as changing the landscape: the height, shape, or location

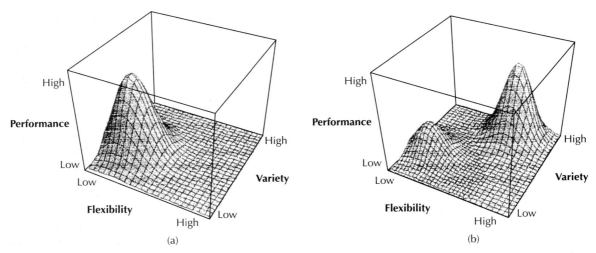

Figure 42.1. Performance landscapes. (a) Early 1900s, the Ford production system (low flexibility, low variety) provides high performance. (b) 1980s, the Japanese production system (high flexibility, high variety) provides better performance, while the value of the Ford production system has decreased.

of peaks changes, new peaks arise, and so forth (Levinthal and Siggelkow, 2001). For instance, in the early 1900s, with the information and production technologies available at the time, the choice of low variety and low flexibility could be implemented very efficiently: the Ford production system represented a high peak in the performance landscape, whereas the high variety–high flexibility choice was technologically very difficult (or even infeasible) to implement for high-volume production. Thus, high variety–high flexibility represented a very low point on the performance landscape (Figure 42.1a). By the 1980s, choosing high variety with high flexibility had become technologically feasible; moreover, it provided substantial advantages in the marketplace. The landscape had changed: the value of the Ford production system had declined, and a new peak, the Japanese production system, had arisen and formed a higher-performance set of choices (Figure 42.1b).

For a firm that occupies a peak, environmental change can affect both external and internal fit. Logically, we can distinguish four cases, which are depicted in Figure 42.2. (1) *No change:* If neither external nor internal fit is affected, the environmental change has no relevance to the firm in question. (2) *Detrimental fit-destroying change:* If both external and internal fit are affected, the firm finds itself at a lower elevation

	External Fit	
	No Change	Change
No Change	No change	Fit-conserving change
Change	Benign fit-destroying change	Detrimental fit-destroying change

(Internal Fit is the vertical axis label on the left, spanning "No Change" and "Change")

Figure 42.2. Change framework.

(lower external fit) and located away from a peak (lower internal fit). (3) *Benign fit-destroying change:* In this case, the firm's performance has not decreased, yet internal fit has been compromised by the environmental change. (4) *Fit-conserving change:* Although internal fit has not been affected, external fit has decreased. In other words, the environmental change has left the internal logic of the firm's system of choices intact while decreasing the appropriateness of the system as a whole.

In sum, with fit-destroying change the firm no longer occupies a peak; with fit-conserving change, the firm still occupies a peak, the height of which has declined, however. The distinction between these two types of changes is important, since firms' reactions to them can differ significantly. After fit-destroying change, a firm will attempt, either through local, incremental search or through long-range search, to change its activities in order to climb onto a new peak. A firm might react quickly in such a situation, since its financial performance has deteriorated (in the case of detrimental fit-destroying change), and internal misfits can be identified. In other words, it is clear that something should be done, and at least some clues as to what should be done might exist, since various elements are misaligned. Moreover, for changes that only nudge a firm away from a peak, one can hypothesize that a firm with a high degree of internal fit reacts faster than a firm with a loosely coupled system. Since peaks are steeper for firms with high internal fit, their incentive to find realignment is large. On a smaller scale, a lean production line provides a good example of tight fit leading to fast response. The absence of inventory (or work-in-process) between individual workstations creates a tightly coupled system. A problem at any workstation is detected very quickly, as the entire line comes to a halt. In addition, incentives to improve each individual production step are high, since the cost of stopping the entire line is large (Womack, Jones, and Roos, 1990).

The situation is different, however, in the case of fit-conserving change: even though the firm's financial performance has declined, no obvious misfits can be detected because the internal logic of the old system remains intact. In this situation, a firm can react in three ways. (1) *Playing the old game:* The firm does not change anything. It keeps its old system of choices, which still displays internal fit though creating suboptimal performance. Graphically, the firm stays on its old, lower peak. (2) *Playing an incomplete game:* The firm changes single elements in its activity system with the consequence of an even further performance decline; the firm moves incrementally away and down from its peak. (3) *Playing a new game:* The firm changes a whole range of its elements and locates on a new and higher peak.

The first two reactions, though destructive, are easily defensible, as managers continue to rely on their old mental maps. Within the landscape metaphor, the term "mental map" is particularly apt: the mental map can be thought of as a manager's map of the performance landscape. In the first option, playing the old game, managers continue to rely on previously successful practices and choices. Moreover, managers may rightly point out that any incremental change would lead to a performance decline. This is the result of their systems already being fully aligned. In a sense, firms are held captive by their existing systems—they have fallen into a competency trap (Levinthal, 1992; Levitt and March, 1988).

Managers who choose the option of playing an incomplete game feel compelled to act, since performance has declined. Yet, in this case, incremental changes only lead to further performance declines. For instance, the American automobile industry recognized that the height of the peak associated with their production system had decreased, even though the internal logic of the mass production system was still intact. Yet, by copying only a few elements of the Japanese production system, the American automobile industry played an incomplete game for many years that did not generate the hoped-for benefits (Hayes and Jaikumar, 1988). In sum, after fit-conserving change, local search and incremental adaptations are not effective.

Only through the third reaction, playing a new game, by comprehensively rearranging a large part of its system of choices, can a firm achieve a significant performance improvement. Graphically, the firm locates itself on a new peak. Such an approach is, however, very difficult to undertake. It requires that managers perceive the systemic nature of the needed changes. Moreover, they need to be willing to act on a broad scale, potentially contradicting some of their past actions. Thus, they have to overcome both their own behavioral "blind spots" (Zajac and Bazerman, 1991) and establish internal legitimacy for their actions (Suchman, 1995). In addition, this broad set of changes has to be implemented successfully; this is a difficult undertaking, as is discussed in the organizational ecology literature on "core changes" (Hannan and Freeman, 1984; Singh, House and Tucker, 1986). Lastly, these changes have to take place over a short period of time for the firm not to experience large performance deficits caused by misfits during the transition period (Miller and Friesen, 1982, 1984). As a result, managers of firms with tightly coupled activity systems face a formidable task—structurally, cognitively, and psychologically—if they are to respond successfully to fit-conserving environmental change.

The following case study illustrates the change framework. After providing a methodological note on the case research, I present a brief sketch of Liz Claiborne's history and then an analysis of the firm's success. I describe Liz Claiborne's choices within five important stages along its value chain: design, production and distribution, the process of selling to retailers, the presentation of merchandise, and marketing. The section concludes with a description of the internal fit within Liz Claiborne's set of choices and a map displaying the interaction among the choices. To use the terminology of the framework, I establish that Liz Claiborne was located on a peak. Moreover, I show that the system of choices had high external fit given the environmental conditions at the time—that is, Liz Claiborne's chosen peak was high. The environmental factors considered are customer taste and demand, retailers' requirements, and the available technology.

In the second section, I describe how these three environmental factors changed in the early 1990s. In other words, Liz Claiborne's performance landscape was shifting. More specifically, Liz Claiborne faced fit-conserving change. The internal logic of its system remained intact, yet the external fit of its system decreased. Moreover, a new peak, which involved a host of different choices with respect to distribution and production, had arisen. The company's management responded to the fit-conserving change by playing an incomplete game: Liz Claiborne attempted to partially change its set of choices, with the consequence of a further performance decline.

In the third main section, I use the same five categories of choices (design, production and distribution, the process of selling to retailers, the presentation of its merchandise, and marketing) to systematically describe the actions, beginning in 1994, of Liz Claiborne's new leadership team, which eventually moved Liz Claiborne to a new peak. This section concludes with another map, displaying the particular choices and the interactions among them. In the final section, I further discuss the framework and outline future research opportunities.

The data for the case study were obtained from several primary and secondary sources. Over a period of one and a half years, between 1996 and 1997, I conducted personal interviews, ranging from one hour to several hours, and shorter follow-up telephone interviews with members of Liz Claiborne's management team. Interviewees included the CEO, the CFO, (chief financial officer), the vice president for corporate planning, and several division presidents. The tenure at Liz Claiborne of the interviewees ranged from one year to ten years. After completing the fact gathering from secondary sources (about 900 articles about Liz Claiborne in trade journals and magazines, in addition to security analysts' reports) and company documents (annual reports, 10Ks, and documents provided by management), a several-hour interview was conducted with one of the founders of the company (Jerome Chazen). Early drafts of the case study were circulated among members of Liz Claiborne's management in addition to Chazen, all of whom provided additions and corrections on factual data in the case. Subsequent discussions with industry experts were used to confirm the outlined changes, in particular those occurring at the industry level.

BRIEF HISTORICAL OVERVIEW

Founded in 1976 with a starting capital of $250,000, Liz Claiborne reached revenues of $116 million in 1981, the year it went public. Five years later, the company became part of the *Fortune* 500 list, the first company started by a woman (the designer Liz Claiborne) to do so. In 1989, *Fortune* reported that Liz Claiborne had achieved the highest average return on year-end equity during the 1980s of all *Fortune* 500 industrial companies: 40.3 percent. In 1991, Liz Claiborne's sales surpassed the $2 billion mark for the first time and its stock price reached record heights: in May of that year, an investment of $10,000 in shares bought at the initial offering had a market value of over $610,000 (see Table 42.1 for financial data).

Beginning in 1992, however, problems in Liz Claiborne's performance surfaced. Its sales stagnated and its net income declined. Over the next three years, Liz Claiborne's market capitalization dropped from $3.5 billion at the end of 1992 to $1.3 billion at the end of 1994. In 1994, Paul Charron, the former executive vice president of VF Corporation, was hired, and he became the new CEO at Liz Claiborne one year later. The implementation of a series of operational and marketing changes led to a marked increase in net income and to a renaissance of Liz Claiborne's stock. By May 1997, Liz Claiborne was trading close to a record high, giving it a market capitalization of $3.2 billion.

LIZ CLAIBORNE'S RISE

How was Liz Claiborne able to achieve its remarkable success in its early years? To summarize, in the late 1970s, Liz Claiborne identified a growing customer group (professional women), and created a new market segment (a segment between moderate and designer sportswear). Unlike the designers of many fashion houses, Ms. Claiborne designed apparel to fit the actual shapes of her customers. She made a mark on the apparel industry with the pronouncement that "the American woman is pear-shaped" (Hass, 1992). Moreover, Liz Claiborne pioneered overseas production for fashion items, thereby allowing it to offer its apparel at lower prices. Lastly, the practice of presenting the lines of apparel as collections within which customers could mix and match made shopping for career clothes easier. As a result, the company garnered the loyalty of customers, who considered Ms. Claiborne to be a personal friend whose taste they could trust when it came to purchasing career clothes (Belkin, 1986). In the words of Liz Claiborne's current CEO, for an entire generation of professional women, Ms. Claiborne provided the imprimatur on clothes acceptable to wear in the workplace (Paul R. Charron, personal communication, February 30, 1997).

In the following subsections, I will describe in detail Liz Claiborne's positioning and the choices its management took with respect to five stages of the company's value chain: design, presentation of its merchandise, selling to retailers, marketing, and production/distribution choices. In the concluding paragraph of this section, I will illustrate the internal and external fit of these choices.

Liz Claiborne's Positioning in a Growing Niche

Liz Claiborne took full advantage of the change in the demographics of the American workforce. In 1960, only 21.9 million American women were employed.

By 1990, 53.5 million American women were working, making up 45 percent of the U.S. workforce. In the mid-1970s, as this process was unfolding, the professional woman did not have much choice with respect to career clothing. There was a large void between the classic dark-blue suit (made, for instance, by Evan-Picone) and the haute couture of, for instance, Carol Horn. Ms. Claiborne, who had spent 16 years as a women's sportswear designer at Youth Guild, a division of Jonathan Logan, was aware of this increasingly expanding niche (Bratman, 1983). In 1976, after Youth Guild closed, Ms. Claiborne decided to pursue this opportunity together with her husband, Arthur Ortenberg, a former consultant in the apparel industry. Within the first months they recruited Leonard Boxer, who had apparel production expertise and connections to overseas suppliers from running production at Susan Thomas Inc., and Jerome Chazen, who knew the marketing side of the women's sportswear industry. With this team of industry experts, Liz Claiborne enjoyed some up-front trust in the industry. Department stores knew Ms. Claiborne's design skills and were willing to give her coveted floor space (Bratman, 1983). In its first year, Liz Claiborne was already generating $2.2 million in sales and operating with a profit.

Design Choices

In 1980, Ms. Claiborne described her offerings as "classic enough that a woman can wear them for several years. They aren't moderate in price, but aren't exorbitant, either" (Ettorre, 1980). In her first collections, no item sold for more than $100. Although the clothes did not fit the formal "dress for success" mold, they were not too far-out to be worn to the office. At the same time, customers perceived the moderately priced Liz Claiborne label as competing against top designers whose clothes cost more than twice as much (Byrne, 1982).

Ms. Claiborne had two goals in mind. She wanted to provide high value to her customers, and she wanted to make shopping easier (Bratman, 1983). It turned out that both could be achieved by an innovative kind of "color-by-the-numbers fashion" that saved the customers both time and anxiety (Traub and Newman, 1985). Ms. Claiborne designed clusters of skirts, shirts, blouses, and sweaters that could be mixed and matched. More precisely, each season's line comprised four to seven concept groups, each of which consisted

Table 42.1. Financial Data for Liz Claiborne[a]

	1996	1995	1994	1993	1992	1991	1990
Sales	2,217.0	2,081.0	2,163.0	2,204.0	2,194.0	2,007.0	1,729.0
Sales growth	(6.5%)	(–3.8%)	(–1.9%)	(0.5%)	(9.3%)	(16.1%)	(22.5%)
Cost of goods sold	1,341.1	1,290.9	1,407.70%	1,452.4	1,364.2	1,207.5	1,030.8
Gross margin	39.52%	37.99%	34.92%	34.10%	37.82%	39.84%	40.38%
Selling, general, and administrative expenses	641.7	600.5	604.4	568.3	507.5	471.1	393.1
Selling, general, and administrative expenses/sales	28.94%	28.85%	27.94%	25.78%	23.13%	23.47%	22.74%
Net income	155.7	126.9	82.9	126.9	218.8	222.7	205.8
Net income growth	(22.7%)	(53.1%)	(–34.7%)	(–42.0%)	(–1.8%)	(8.2%)	(25.0%)
Net income	7.02%	6.10%	3.83%	5.76%	9.97%	11.10%	11.90%
Earnings per share	2.15	1.69	1.06	1.56	2.61	2.61	2.37
Return on equity	15.3%	12.8%	8.4%	13.0%	21.9%	24.5%	28.9%
Cash and securities	528.8	437.8	330.3	309.2	425.6	471.5	431.8
Inventory	349.4	393.3	423.0	436.6	385.9	322.0	265.7
Inventory days	95.1	111.2	109.7	109.7	103.2	97.3	94.1
Long-term debt	1.0	1.1	1.2	1.3	1.4	1.6	15.1
Debt/equity	0.10%	0.11%	0.12%	0.13%	0.14%	0.18%	2.12%
Market value	2,796.8	2,064.9	1,335.0	1,844.1	3,495.0	3,610.6	2,581.8
Share price	38.63	27.50	17.00	22.63	41.63	42.25	29.75

[a]All figures are in millions of dollars, except for earnings per share and share price.

of a balance of items such as blouses, shirts, skirts, and pants. Within each concept group, the mix-and-match design was practiced—that is, each group told a different "color story." Customers could put together an outfit not only in terms of the total look but also in terms of size, by choosing different sizes for tops and bottoms, thereby avoiding the need for alterations. Moreover, sizes were the same across styles, and colors never changed: Navy blue remained the same navy blue, so that a jacket bought in one year would match a skirt or blouse bought two years before.

Presentation Choices

From the beginning, Liz Claiborne focused on selling its merchandise in large, upscale department stores. In 1994, Liz Claiborne's products were offered in more than 9,500 locations in the United States and Canada, yet its four largest customers (Dillard's, the May Department Stores Company, Macy's, and Federated Department Stores) accounted for 44 percent of its sales. For the end customer to reap the benefits of Liz Claiborne's mix-and-match design, it was important that collections be presented together and not split up. Hence, Liz Claiborne pushed for a new presentation format at its retailers. Department stores were traditionally organized around classifications, such as

blouses and pants, but Liz Claiborne required a dedicated space to present its entire collection. Liz Claiborne was actually not the first company that tried to convince retailers to present an entire collection. Chazen had learned that Evan-Picone had put together a small collection of very classic merchandise and had received small dedicated areas from department stores. By and large, however, "Retailers were not sure what to do with these collections and were looking for a complementary resource which would allow them to enlarge the floor space dedicated to collection presentation." (Jerome Chazen, personal communication, October 7, 1997). Consequently, retailers were willing to listen to Chazen when he tried to convince them to present Liz Claiborne's merchandise as a collection.

To help retailers with the presentation of the collections, Liz Claiborne distributed Claiboards or Lizmap diagrams that included sketches, photos, and text showing how merchandise should be displayed in groups. Other innovations included simple measures such as naming the groups and attaching these names to hangers, thus allowing customers to quickly see which pieces of apparel belonged to each group. Moreover, a dedicated staff supported the retailers: Over 20 consultants traveled throughout the country to ensure that clothes and displays were arranged in department

1989	1988	1987	1986	1985	1984	1983	1982	1981
1,411.0	1,184.0	1,053.0	813.0	557.0	391.0	228.0	160.0	116.00%
(19.2%)	(12.4%)	(29.5%)	(46.0%)	(42.3%)	(71.1%)	(42.9%)	(37.0%)	(46.0%)
841.7	758.3	655.6	502.2	341.7	243.8	144.7	109.6	76.2
40.35%	35.95%	37.74%	38.23%	38.65%	37.69%	36.73%	31.50%	34.76%
321.9	255.5	194.7	146.3	97.3	66.3	40.1	27.0	18.2
22.81%	21.58%	18.49%	18.00%	17.47%	16.94%	17.53%	16.88%	15.58%
164.6	110.3	114.4	86.2	60.6	41.9	22.4	14.1	10.2
(49.2%)	(−3.6%)	(32.7%)	(42.2%)	(44.6%)	(87.1%)	(59.2%)	(37.9%)	(64.5%)
11.67%	9.32%	10.86%	10.60%	10.88%	10.71%	9.79%	8.79%	8.73%
1.87	1.26	1.32	1.00	0.71	0.50	0.27	0.17	0.13
26.9%	24.1%	32.0%	34.8%	37.2%	40.1%	34.7%	34.2%	38.1%
372.9	278.3	160.4	104.0	56.2	19.0	11.2		
198.2	168.0	156.4	114.9	72.8	73.4	34.2	21.3	
85.9	80.9	87.1	83.5	77.8	109.9	86.3	70.9	0.0
15.6	14.1	14.5	0.0	10.0	0.0	0.0	0.0	0.0
2.55%	3.08%	4.06%	0.00%	6.15%	0.00%	0.00%	0.00%	0.00%
2,109.8	1,509.1	1,434.4	1,844.0	1,035.4	539.2	357.0	194.6	97.3
24.00	17.25	16.50	21.38	12.13	6.38	4.25	2.33	1.22

stores correctly. These consultants were also engaged in product information seminars for the department stores' sales personnel. In addition, 150 retail specialists who were employed by the stores in which they worked yet received training from Liz Claiborne helped with merchandise presentation, provided instruction for sales help, and relayed customer feedback to Liz Claiborne's headquarters (Better, 1992).

Creating dedicated areas for Liz Claiborne merchandise was a first step toward gaining control over product presentation. Beginning in 1987, Liz Claiborne took its efforts toward product presentation one step further. In Jordan Marsh's flagship store in Boston, Liz Claiborne opened its first store within a store. The 7,200-square-foot LizWorld shop housed Liz Claiborne's full range of merchandise: Liz Collection, LizSport, LizWear, dresses, accessories, shoes, hosiery, eyewear, and fragrance. Within the next few years, Liz Claiborne set up over 200 concept shops within department stores. Moreover, since these shops increased business for retailers, Liz Claiborne successfully argued for the department stores' covering the costs of adding the concept shops. Liz Claiborne's accessories division copied the presentation format and introduced its first concept shop within a department store in 1990. The shop featured a full range of hand-

bags and small leather goods, and Liz Claiborne's latest fashion looks—fully accessorized—decorated the walls.

Selling Process
Since Liz Claiborne believed its merchandise had the greatest impact if presented as a collection, it rejected orders from department stores that were not willing to present the Claiborne line the way Liz Claiborne saw fit. For instance, a store always had to buy a number of tops that matched its order of bottoms (Belkin, 1986). Moreover, buyers were required to purchase an entire group and could not pick and choose among the garments shown.

Liz Claiborne never had a road sales force, making it the only leading garment house in the country that functioned without one (Birmingham, 1985). Retailers who wanted to look at the new Liz Claiborne line had to come to the showrooms in New York,[2] where they were welcomed by a 80–90 person sales force, which won the title "America's Best Sales Force" from *Sales & Marketing Management* in 1987. Its centralized selling location enabled Liz Claiborne to establish relationships at a higher level than would otherwise have been possible. As Chazen explained, "On the road a salesman is lucky if he sees the buyer.

But when retailers come to New York, top management often comes to see the market" (Skolnik, 1985). As a result, although stores' buyers still placed the orders, every major store president in the country visited Liz Claiborne several times a year and met with Liz Claiborne's management.

Liz Claiborne not only demanded the purchase of entire groups, but also enforced a rigid noncancellation policy: if spring merchandise did not sell well in stores, retailers could not cut previous orders for the summer line (Better, 1992). The company created further leverage by pursuing a strict production policy of manufacturing about 5 percent less merchandise than there was demand (orders) for (Hass, 1992). This policy had two effects. First, it increased Liz Claiborne's "sell-through" (the percentage of clothes sold at full price), which some industry observers pegged at 75 percent as compared to an industry average of 50 percent (Deveny, 1989). Second, the policy created a climate of fear among its customers, giving Liz Claiborne a credible weapon with which to ensure that its desires, such as those with respect to retail presentation, were met.

Customer Contact and Marketing

Despite being a company that originally had no direct retailing contact with its end customers, Liz Claiborne sought feedback from them. Its consultants and retail specialists talked to customers daily, and they also arranged, during so-called LizWeeks, in-store events for career women, such as full-blown fashion shows in which 25–30 outfits were shown, and "breakfast clinics" during which women had the chance to see the newest collection and to shop before they went to work. In total, Claiborne sponsored over 100 in-store events each month across the country.

In addition, Liz Claiborne established a point-of-sales data collection system in 1985. Its Systematic Updated Retail Feedback (SURF) system provided management with details on clothes sold in 16 representative stores around the country (Skolnik, 1985).

Owing to its high name recognition and extensive coverage in the editorial pages of many fashion magazines, Liz Claiborne was able to refrain from running expensive corporate advertising campaigns. Moreover, the absence of splashy, "fantasy-driven" advertising campaigns fit well with Liz Claiborne's image as a

"trusted friend." It presented all its products in "co-op ads" produced in conjunction with local department stores.

Production and Distribution Choices

Since its inception, Liz Claiborne had contracted out the production of its merchandise. Moreover, it was one of the first big apparel makers in the 1980s to outsource production across the globe—mainly into Taiwan, Hong Kong, and South Korea. In its first year of operation, Liz Claiborne had used domestic manufacturers exclusively but encountered problems. The domestic suppliers were inflexible and unwilling to work with Liz Claiborne's new designs. Since Leonard Boxer had experience in apparel assembly in the Far East, he started to move production overseas. In 1982 Liz Claiborne was still sourcing about 50 percent of its merchandise domestically, but by 1994 only 14 percent of its merchandise was produced in the United States. Liz Claiborne had contracts with over 500 suppliers in 38 countries, with most of its suppliers being situated in China, South Korea, Sri Lanka, Hong Kong, and Indonesia. Twenty-four percent of its purchases were manufactured by its ten largest suppliers, with none of its suppliers accounting for more than 5 percent.

The company provided some support to contractors, but it did not engage directly in production until 1992. In that year, Liz Claiborne opened its first major production enterprise, a 270,000-square-foot plant in Augusta, Georgia, that annually turned out 500,000 to 1,000,000 pounds of cotton circular-knitted fabrics (jerseys, fleeces, and other types). One advantage of local production lay in response time: this factory was able to fill an order in 20 to 25 days, whereas it took Liz Claiborne's Asian suppliers often as long as 60 days plus shipping (Lee, 1994).

Liz Claiborne also differed from its competitors with respect to how often it offered its merchandise to its retailers. The apparel industry was used to a four-season buying cycle. Liz Claiborne, however, invented two more seasons, pre-spring and pre-fall, to let stores buy six smaller inventory batches of fresh merchandise instead of four larger ones. While reducing inventory costs for the stores, this choice also helped Claiborne's suppliers, who operated more efficiently with two extra cycles filling their slack periods. In addition to offering two more collections, Liz Claiborne offered the collections later than its competitors, with the intent that clothes appropriate for the current season be available in the stores (Birmingham, 1985). Thus, instead of delivering fall goods in July, the company would ship them in late August and September. In other words, Liz Claiborne offered a new season every two months, with, for instance, the clothes delivered in January and February intended to be sold and worn during February and March.

Internal and External Fit

As described in the previous subsections, Liz Claiborne's goal of dressing the professional woman with products that provided high value was implemented through a series of choices that particularly suited its strategy. To systematize the analysis, I grouped Liz Claiborne's choices into five categories: design, presentation, selling, marketing, and production/distribution. Figure 42.3 summarizes the choices within each category and displays the interactions among the choices. The following discussion elaborates on several of the interactions indicated in Figure 42.3, showing the high *internal fit* among Liz Claiborne's choices. A discussion of *external fit* is provided in the second half of this section.

Liz Claiborne's mix-and-match design could only be appreciated if the entire collection was presented together. Hence, it was important (and valuable) to push for a collection rather than a classification presentation. It should also be noted that once a collection presentation was in place, the returns to a mix-and-match design were increased. Thus, formally, collection presentation and mix-and-match design were complementary (Milgrom and Roberts, 1990).[3] The collection-presentation format was supported by a host of other choices, such as concept shops, Claiboards, retail associates, sales consultants, and LizWeek department store presentations. Again, a complementarity existed: the value of these activities was increased by the presence of a collection presentation and, at the same time, the value of the collection presentation was increased

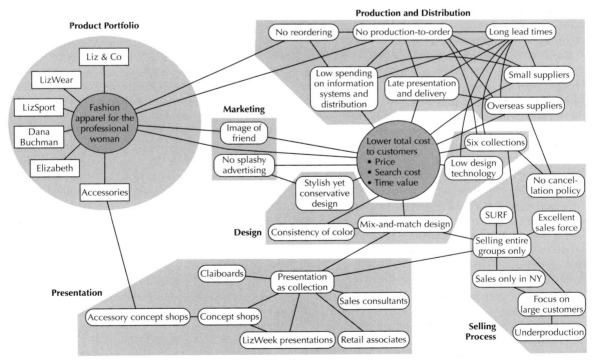

Figure 42.3. Map of interactions among Liz Claiborne's choices in the early 1990s.

by the support activities. Similarly, the apparel could provide its mix-and-match value only if the department store carried the full collection.

In this light, one can understand Liz Claiborne's strict policy of selling only complete groups to its customers. An incidental effect of this requirement was that end customers always saw a full collection in the department store, which strengthened confidence in the brand and increased its perceived value. A consequence of this vending policy with respect to Liz Claiborne's sales organization was that the company had to focus on large buyers. In addition, success with such an inflexible order policy necessitated a high level of trust in its customers. Liz Claiborne's decision to sell only in its New York show room addressed these concerns. On the one hand, senior department store management would come to New York to establish the required trust. On the other hand, the lost customers (those not willing to pay for the trip to New York) were small customers who were not able to buy a full line anyhow. The trust level was further bolstered by an expert sales force and its SURF system, which provided a closer contact with end customers than most other apparel designers could offer at the time. Lastly, Liz Claiborne's decision to offer six collections a year alleviated the inflexibility of being required to buy full lines, since a larger number of lines was offered. The ability to choose from six lines also lessened the impact of the no-cancellation policy, because each order could be smaller than would have been the case with four lines. The no-cancellation policy, in turn, made long-term planning possible, which was important for Liz Claiborne's overseas sourcing strategy. Since its overseas supply system implied longer lead times and an inability to react quickly to demand changes, a steady demand was beneficial. In return, Liz Claiborne could provide high value (and achieve high margins), owing to the lower production costs of its overseas suppliers.

Since Liz Claiborne focused on large buyers, there was a potential risk of being squeezed by its customers. By following a strict underproduction policy, however, the company retained leverage over its customers. Moreover, this strategy had beneficial side effects. By producing slightly below demand, the sell-through was increased, which meant that Liz Claiborne merchandise was less frequently on sale (or was on sale in lower quantities). This in turn fortified the company's "everyday value" claim.

It is important to note that Liz Claiborne's set of choices involved trade-offs. Its decision to use mainly suppliers located in the Far East and to invest little in design, distribution, and information technology all helped to keep costs down but led to three disadvantages: (1) it generated long lead times between the start of design to the delivery of the finished product, (2) retailers could not reorder, and (3) no merchandise could be made to order.

In evaluating the severity of these disadvantages, the external fit of Liz Claiborne's set of choices becomes apparent. All the disadvantages were alleviated by external factors: customer demand, retailers' requirements, available technology, and competitors' strengths. First, the impossibility of reordering was not crucial, since Liz Claiborne faced high customer demand mainly for fashion apparel that was not reordered anyway. Second, the health of Liz Claiborne's primary retail channel, department stores, was relatively solid during the 1980s. As a consequence, department stores were not (yet) concerned with reducing inventory, which would have put pressure on Liz Claiborne to offer reordering. Third, the information and design technology that would allow an efficient reordering system, coupled with shortened design cycles, was only in its early stages of development. As a result, there did not exist a feasible alternative set-up (in other words, a different peak) with which competitors could attack Liz Claiborne's position. Yet imitating Liz Claiborne (trying to climb the same peak and competing on the same terms) was very difficult, because the entire system of choices would have to be duplicated (Porter & Rivkin, 1998; Rivkin, 2000). Consequently, Liz Claiborne enjoyed a strong competitive position that enabled it to easily sell the majority of its output. In turn, with such "guaranteed demand," long lead times and no production-to-order did not pose a problem.

In sum, Liz Claiborne's choices showed high internal fit and—given the environmental conditions at the time—high external fit. In the 1980s, Liz Claiborne had positioned itself on a high peak in the performance landscape. However, during the late 1980s and early 1990s, changes in customer demand, retailers' economic health, and technological advances reduced the external fit of this coherent system: the height of Liz Claiborne's peak started to decrease when a new peak arose in the performance landscape.

LIZ CLAIBORNE'S FALL

Changes in Customer Demand and Product Portfolio

By the early 1990s, the trend towards "casualization" of the workplace had picked up momentum—a development that Liz Claiborne had first underestimated (J. Lewis, president, Liz Claiborne Casual, personal communication, February 30, 1997). More and more companies allowed their employees to dress casually, yet customers could not find an attractive assortment of Liz Claiborne apparel to fulfill this need. Liz Claiborne eventually responded to this shift in customer demand and increased its offerings in the casual and more basic categories. In addition, in May 1992, Liz Claiborne acquired for $31 million Russ Togs, Inc., which had filed for Chapter 11 protection the previous November. Russ Togs manufactured moderately priced women's sportswear under the Russ Togs and The Villager labels. The acquisition was intended to take Liz Claiborne into national and regional chain department stores and the moderate areas of traditional department stores.

These shifts in product portfolio appeared to be natural responses to changes in customer demands, but they had far-reaching consequences. The company increased its presence in apparel categories in which reordering had become a convenience offered by many competitors, yet it was not set up to offer efficient reordering.

Changes in the Retail Channel

During the late 1980s and early 1990s, Liz Claiborne's main distribution channel, the traditional department stores, underwent wrenching change. Several hostile takeovers and leveraged buyouts stretched the liquidity of many department store chains, often to the point of bankruptcy. Prominent examples of this development included Federated Department Stores, which filed for Chapter 11 protection in January 1990, R. H. Macy, which declared bankruptcy in January 1991, and Carter Hawley Hale, which filed for bankruptcy protection in February 1991. As a result, department stores tried to save cash wherever they could.

First, the stores cut down the retail support they provided to their vendors. For instance, much less attention was spent on the presentation and restocking of goods on the floor. Liz Claiborne, being accustomed to having retailers pay for concept shops and presentation support, failed to compensate for this deficit. Since careful presentation of Liz Claiborne's apparel as a collection was essential to its value proposition, the deterioration of shop-floor presentation was particularly detrimental for the company.

Secondly, department stores demanded larger discounts from their vendors. As well as refusing to pay for retailing support, Liz Claiborne refused to cut prices (J. Chazen, personal communication, October 7, 1997). Past success had created a sense of infallibility, coupled with a tinge of hubris, at Liz Claiborne, as it has at many other successful companies (Miller, 1994). In 1989, Jay Margolis, the highest executive at the firm, after the remaining founders, proudly proclaimed: "We like to think of ourselves as the IBM of the garment district" (Deveny, 1989). Liz Claiborne's strong internal culture—the company directory still listed its employees alphabetically by first name—had created a belief in the organization's near invulnerability to environmental changes (Milliken, 1990). Moreover, negative performance was frequently attributed to external factors rather than to internal problems, another common pattern in firms responding to downturns (Ford, 1985). A former Claiborne executive commented as follows: "If the product didn't sell, it was always someone else's fault. The buyer didn't show it right, or it wasn't delivered the right way" (Caminiti, 1994). Yet, Liz Claiborne's apparel, with sagging sales and with lower margins for its retailers than other vendors' apparel provided, became less attractive to department stores and received even less attention and, eventually, less floor space.

Third, to alleviate their liquidity problems, department stores aggressively pursued inventory reduction. Increasingly, they demanded that manufacturers let them reorder items, so they could avoid buying in bulk and having to store merchandise in their stockrooms.

The Old Peak Declines, and a New Peak Arises

In addition to the retailers' demand for reordering, Liz Claiborne faced new competitors who employed a production paradigm allowing them to offer reordering efficiently. Improvements in information, design, and production technology, as well as the spread of standards in bar coding and point of-sales-terminals, had made short reordering cycles, shorter design cycles, and partial production-to-order economically feasible (Abernathy, Dunlop, Hammond, & Weil, 1995). In other words, technological changes had created a new peak in the performance landscape that required a different set of choices. For instance, Jones Apparel, one of Liz Claiborne's strongest new competitors, sourced 55 percent of its products domestically, as compared to 14 percent for Liz Claiborne (D'Innocenzio, 1994). This sourcing strategy, in addition to heavy investments in design technology, allowed Jones to react quickly to new trends in the marketplace.

At the same time, with the demands of retailers and customers shifting, Liz Claiborne's set of choices, although still internally consistent, had become less appropriate to the environment. The company's disadvantages, in particular the long design cycles and lack of reordering and production-to-order, had become more costly. In the 1980s, these disadvantages were small, given the Claiborne product portfolio, but by the 1990s the new requirements of retailers and the decreased costs of a lean production model had magnified the disadvantages: the relative height of Liz Claiborne's peak had declined.

Playing an Incomplete Game

In 1991, faced with increasing demands from retailers for reordering, Liz Claiborne initiated a reordering program for items in its casual division. The company's management followed the path described in the change framework as "playing an incomplete game": Liz Claiborne changed single elements in its activity system, with the consequence of a further performance decline. The firm moved down from its local peak to even lower performance.

The only elements of "quick response"—as these reordering programs became known in the apparel industry—that Liz Claiborne implemented were enabling stores' buyers to submit their orders electronically and promising to fill orders within two weeks. On the production side, no changes were made. The company produced a warehouse full of merchandise and then sold it as orders came in. Since inventory costs had never entered Liz Claiborne's profitability measurements, the inefficiency of this reordering process remained financially hidden (James Lewis, personal communication, February 30, 1997). Moreover, past success had created a buffer of $300–$500 million in cash and securities on Liz Claiborne's balance sheet

(see Table 42.1). With this buffer, Liz Claiborne never experienced the liquidity problems that could have resulted from having funds tied up in inventory. Slack resources had reduced the necessity for Liz Claiborne's management to act upon this inefficiency—a common pitfall of past success, as Milliken and Lant (1991) pointed out.

In addition, allowing department store buyers to place orders (rather than having a vendor-driven continuous replenishment program) caused large swings in the volume of orders, which in turn meant either orders went unfilled or inventory was increased even further. Moreover, department store buyers whose allotted purchasing budget was exhausted often would not reorder at all—even styles which had been sold out—thus leaving popular styles out of stock.

As Figure 42.3 illustrates, the choice of "no reordering" was intimately tied to many other choices Liz Claiborne had made. Simply offering reordering to retailers without making further changes in the system as a whole was bound to create problems. As Hammond (1993) outlined, partial production-to-order and a shortened product development cycle are necessary if a company is to pursue a quick-response strategy efficiently. Otherwise, inventory at the manufacturer starts to accumulate. However, Liz Claiborne's lead times were nine months, about three months longer than lead times of some of its competitors (D'Innocenzio, 1994). Figure 42.3 is also helpful in identifying the reasons for Liz Claiborne's long design-to-market cycle: the location of most of its suppliers in the Far East, the small size of its suppliers, who did not invest in information technology that would have reduced cycle times, and its small investments in technology, such as CAD systems that could reduce time to market. As this example illustrates, incremental changes in a tightly coupled system rarely lead to the desired result. Not until a new management had changed a whole series of choices in the design, distribution, and production set-up, moving Liz Claiborne to a new peak, did performance improve.

LIZ CLAIBORNE'S RENAISSANCE

In 1994, with Liz Claiborne's sales declining and net income plummeting by 35 percent, Paul Charron was hired as new chief operating officer. Charron had previously worked for Procter & Gamble and General Foods and had most recently been executive vice president at VF Corporation, the manufacturer of Wrangler and Lee jeans. In 1995, Charron replaced Chazen as CEO, while Chazen remained chairman of the company. This position was also taken on by Charron in 1996, when Chazen retired.

From the beginning of his tenure as CEO in 1995, Charron pursued three avenues of change within Liz Claiborne: (1) revitalization and modernization of choices within presentation and design that had been neglected over the previous years, (2) a shift in product portfolio, and (3) a wide-ranging restructuring of the company's production and distribution set-up.

Revitalization of Presentation and Design

In 1995, Charron created, under the name LizEdge, a new in-store marketing department. The company hired 125 sales associates, each responsible for instore presentation of better sportswear in four locations. At the same time, Liz Claiborne started to install new in-store fixtures (LizView) in department stores around the country. By April 1997, 200 LizView shops had been installed, and setting up another 400 by the end of 1997 was planned. As had occurred in the mid-1980s with the LizWorld shops, sales increased after the LizView shops were installed, going up an average 19 percent. In addition to providing the new fixtures, the firm began a training program (Liz & Learn) that provided sales support and incentives for department store salespeople.

To obtain a better understanding of the marketplace, Charron commissioned a study on the characteristics and shopping behavior of Liz Claiborne's customers. One of the study's findings was that customer confidence about picking outfits had risen considerably. In the early 1980s, Liz Claiborne's function had been to show what apparel was suitable for the workplace; now, customers asked to be presented with options. In the words of Charron, the customer "has gained confidence to 'put it together' by herself if she is provided with cues" (personal communication, February 30, 1997). These insights were taken into account in designing the new LizView in-store display units.

Another finding of the consumer study was that a typical customer played a large number of roles during the day (professional woman, soccer mom, and so forth) without having much time to change clothes. Hence, versatility of apparel and the ability to dress up or down quickly (for instance, by adding accessories or changing a top) were valued very highly. As a result, Liz Claiborne strengthened its efforts to allow its customers to mix and match across divisions (between LizSport and LizWear, for example).

To ensure that colors were held constant across collections and groups, designers of all units were required to use the same color card, which guaranteed consistency of color. Moreover, meetings among designers from all the companies' businesses were held on a regular monthly schedule; previously, they had met haphazardly.

Changes in Product Portfolio

For the long term, Charron was concerned that the current trend in retailing—the decline of the department stores and the rise of the discount stores such as Wal-Mart—would continue. Concurrent with the consolidation in the retail market, he expected a consolidation in the apparel supply market. As noted, prior to Charron's arrival, Liz Claiborne had acquired Russ Togs. The sales of this division, called the Special Markets Unit, increased to $112 million by the end of 1994 (partly inflated by sell-offs of excess inventory) and decreased to $77.3 million by the end of 1996. Charron decided to enlarge this unit. His vision was to have a different Liz Claiborne brand for every retail channel and every price point: the Russ label for the "budget" segment (to be sold at stores like Wal-Mart); Villager and a new brand, First Issue, intended for the "moderate" segment (to be sold, for instance, at Sears); another new brand, Emma James, for the "upper-moderate" segment (to be sold at stores like Federated Department Stores); the traditional Liz Claiborne Collection and the casual lines, including LizWear, for the "better" segment (to be sold, for instance, at Dillard's); and the successful Dana Buchman line for the "bridge" segment (to be sold, for instance, at Saks Fifth Avenue) (Paul Charron, personal communication, February 30, 1997).

In order to increase general brand awareness, national brand advertising was increased substantially. Using the model Niki Taylor as the centerpiece of its advertising strategy, Liz Claiborne tried to rejuvenate its image, which had grown stale, especially in the eyes of the new generation of professional women. In addition to the public media campaign, at the end of 1994 the company made a statement within the fashion industry by opening a 19,000-square-foot flagship store at 650 Fifth Avenue.

Production and Distribution Changes

Whereas the new initiatives with respect to presentation consisted mainly of the modernization of previous practices, fundamental changes occurred in the way Liz Claiborne orchestrated its production and distribution. In 1995, Charron announced a comprehensive program, LizFirst, which was geared toward increasing efficiency. Its goals were to reduce excess inventories by 40 percent, cut cycle time by 25 percent, and reduce selling, general, and administrative expenses (SG&A) by $100 million over three years. Two ways in which Liz Claiborne sought to fulfill its goals were to reduce the number of suppliers by half and to shift 50 percent of its production to the Western Hemisphere. By concentrating production within larger suppliers who could afford and were willing to invest in information and production technology, and by moving production closer to the region of retail, cycle times could be shortened.

Liz Claiborne also switched back to four instead of six production and design cycles. With six seasons, or a two-month delivery period, none of the merchandise could be made to order. With four seasons, the three-month delivery period allowed the company to produce at least some items to order for the third month of a season. Liz Claiborne also started with some of its clients a vendor-based restocking system, or retail inventory management program (LizRim), in which the firm automatically replenished basic merchandise (mainly jeans, slacks, and shorts) to prior negotiated inventory levels at department stores. This system dramatically lowered "stock-outs" and kept inventory levels at department stores small, without causing huge production and order swings for Liz Claiborne.

One of the pioneers of such a vendor-based system had been Procter & Gamble (in cooperation with Wal-Mart). Later, VF Corporation and Haggar were among the first to adopt a similar system in the basic apparel industry. Charron's prior work experience at Procter & Gamble and VF Corporation provided him with valuable knowledge about the activities needed to support a successful implementation. At Liz Claiborne, the program was spearheaded by the casual

wear division, whose new president had been recruited by Charron from Haggar in December 1994. Charron also brought further expertise in-house by hiring a new chief information officer who had previously been an executive vice president for business systems/logistics at a leading apparel retailer, and a new senior vice president for manufacturing and sourcing who had a background in low-cost private label manufacturing.

By 1997, LizFirst showed good results: Excess inventory had been cut by 47 percent from 1994 levels, its retail management program was in 1,200 stores, operating expenses had been reduced by $82 million, and cycle time in certain key processes had been cut by 40 percent. Moreover, the number of factories Liz Claiborne used had been cut by half.

Internal Fit on a New Peak

Following the structure of Figure 42.3, Figure 42.4 depicts Liz Claiborne's choices as of 1997 in the five categories of design, presentation, selling, marketing, and production/distribution and displays the interactions between the choices. The locations of the five categories on the two maps have been kept approximately constant to facilitate comparison of the choices between the two time points depicted.

We find a familiar cluster of reinforcing choices dealing with the strengthening of the retail presentation. As noted above, Liz Claiborne was rejuvenating its former successful formula: mix-and-match design coupled with a careful presentation strategy involving, among other features, new displays and sales associates. The main changes within these categories were that mix-and-match was extended across divisions and that Liz Claiborne, rather than the retailers, paid for presentation support.

The largest number of new choices clustered around Liz Claiborne's new reordering process (LizRim) and around the system to allow partial production-to-order. Whereas the presentation support was mainly geared toward Liz Claiborne's traditional better sportswear, LizRim was designed to fulfill the requirements of the mass merchants that would carry its budget brands. However, because of its large size, the Liz Casual division, which belonged to the better sportswear division, was initially accounting for the largest use of LizRim. By keeping out-of-stock positions low, LizRim reinforced efforts with respect to the renewed presentation format—the best-trained sales-

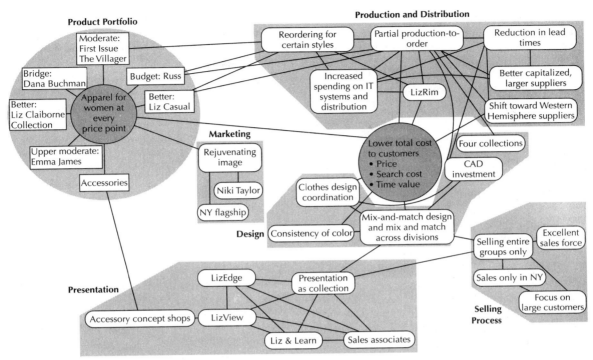

Figure 42.4. Map of interactions among Liz Claiborne's choices in 1997.

people and most cleverly designed display units could not sell merchandise that was out of stock.

DISCUSSION AND CONCLUSION

Why was Liz Claiborne's old management, like many other managements of declining organizations (Cameron, Whetten, and Kim, 1987), unable to respond to environmental changes? The analysis presented above suggests that a major contributing factor was that Liz Claiborne's management faced fit-conserving change. Environmental changes had decreased the value of a part of Liz Claiborne's set of choices (in particular, those concerning production and distribution). Small, incremental changes—exploring the local neighborhood of the current position—no longer sufficed. At the same time, larger, systemic changes lay outside the mental maps of existing management. Different mental maps of the changed performance landscape were required to move Liz Claiborne to a new performance peak.

The purpose of the framework developed in this article is to explore how fit influences the link between environmental changes and ensuing firm change. To this end, I suggested that a useful distinction can be made between environmental changes that affect external and/or internal fit. Whereas environments have been differentiated in the existing literature in terms of stability and turbulence, a distinction based on how *frequently* the performance landscape changes, I instead suggest classifying environmental changes with respect to the *impact* they have on the landscape. The framework thus offers an alternative and complementary classification. With this classification, the effect of environmental change on firms can be described as fit-destroying or fit-conserving—a useful distinction, since managers react differently to these two types of changes. Managers will have a particularly difficult time reacting to fit-conserving change because the internal logic of the existing system of choices remains intact.

The argument outlined in this article finds a parallel in the conceptual approach of Henderson and Clark

(1990), who studied a particular type of environmental change (a technological innovation) and its effects on incumbent firms. They suggest that, rather than distinguishing between incremental and radical innovations (thus measuring the magnitude of change), it is useful to classify innovations with respect to their impact on interactions within existing product systems. Analogously, we argue for the classification of environmental changes according to their impact on internal and external fit, rather than by their frequency. The new distinction Henderson and Clark (1990) introduced is whether an innovation changes architectural knowledge (how parts interact) or component knowledge (how parts work). This distinction allowed Henderson (1993) to explain the inertia of incumbent firms facing innovations in the photolithographic alignment equipment industry. Similarly, it is hoped that the framework proposed here and the distinction between fit-conserving and fit-destroying change will provide a new lens through which the impact of environmental changes on firms with high internal fit can be better understood.

In addition to providing a framework, concerning environmental change I believe that the maps of the firm's choices and their interactions can provide a helpful tool for understanding the structural requirements of change in a system with tight internal fit. For instance, in the present case, Liz Claiborne wanted to offer reordering. As Figures 42.3 and 42.4 illustrate, the choice of whether or not to offer reordering was tied to many other choices. Figure 42.3 can be used to predict the changes that were necessary to implement an efficient reordering process. Directly affected were the previous choices to keep spending on information and distribution technology low and the decision not to produce any apparel to order. One could call these "first-order" changes. However, to produce some merchandise to order, other choices had to be changed: part of the supplier base had to be shifted to the Western Hemisphere, the number of collections had to be reduced to four (which had implications for the design process), the delivery dates had to be moved up in time to allow information gathering early in the season for production delivered late in the season, and lead times had to be reduced. In turn, to reduce lead time, increased investments in design technology, and a shift to larger, better-capitalized suppliers who could invest in information and production technology had to fol-

low. Thus, not only first-order, but also second- and third-order changes were necessary. The mapping of choices and their interactions in Figures 42.3 and 42.4 make these ripple effects clearly visible. At the same time, these maps point out those choices that did *not* have to be changed. For instance, the presentation format, which was mainly connected to the design concept of mix and match, was not affected by changes in the production set-up.

The goal of this study was to outline a new framework and to use an in-depth case analysis for illustration. Clearly, more empirical work needs to be done to illustrate the contrasting effects of fit-conserving and fit-destroying change. For instance, according to the framework, in the face of benign fit-destroying change, firms with tight fit might react faster than firms with loosely coupled systems. On the conceptual side, conditions need to be identified under which fit-conserving and fit-destroying change are likely to arise. A first hypothesis, suggested by our framework and our empirical observations, is that fit-conserving change can be observed if technological change allows rival firms to compete with new *systems* of activities. In landscape terminology, fit-conserving change appears likely if new, high peaks are rising in the landscape. At the same time, moderate fit-destroying change is associated with environmental developments (such as technological improvements) that affect only individual activities.

A further extension of the framework would incorporate a more explicit description of how managers create mental maps of performance landscapes. With faulty representations, new questions arise. For instance, what are the performance consequences of faulty maps, given tight internal fit? What types of misrepresentations are particularly costly, and what are the implications for organizational design? In current work (Siggelkow, 2001), I am pursuing this line of research.

ACKNOWLEDGMENTS

I would like to thank Kim Cameron (the editor), Giovanni Gavetti, Pankaj Ghemawat, Bruce Kogut, Daniel Levinthal, Johannes Pennings, Michael Porter, Daniel Raff, Jan Rivkin, Harbir Singh, Sidney Winter, and three anonymous referees for their helpful comments.

Any remaining errors are mine. Financial support by the Division of Research of the Harvard Business School and the Reginald H. Jones Center for Management Strategy, Policy and Organization at the University of Pennsylvania is gratefully acknowledged.

NOTES

1. For formal models of performance landscapes with these features, see Kauffman (1993).

2. Until 1990, all of Liz Claiborne's domestic sales were performed through its New York showroom. In order to reach smaller specialty stores, Liz Claiborne decided to open two small showrooms in Atlanta and Dallas in 1990 and 1992. However, in these showrooms only dresses, accessories, jewelry, and Liz & Co. better casual knitwear were displayed. The sportswear line was not shown, since the minimum orders were too high for most specialty stores.

3. Two elements, A and B, are complementary if the marginal benefit of A increases with the level of B, and vice versa. This concept can be extended to noncontinuous cases as long as A and B and their combinations can be ordered (Milgrom and Roberts, 1990).

REFERENCES

Abernathy, F., Dunlop, J., Hammond, J., and Weil, D. 1995. The information-integrated channel: A study of the U.S. apparel industry in transition. *Brookings Papers on Economic Activity—Microeconomics:* 175–246.

Belkin, L. 1986. Redesigning Liz Claiborne's empire. *New York Times,* May 4: 1.

Better, N. 1992. The secret of Liz Claiborne's success. *Working Woman,* 17(4): 68.

Birmingham, J. 1985. Claiborne's men. *Daily News Record,* May 28: S11.

Bratman, F. 1983. Liz Claiborne and a landmark. *New York Times,* February 27: 6.

Byrne, J. 1982. Liz, tailor. *Forbes,* January 4: 286.

Cameron, K., Whetten, D., and Kim, M. 1987. Organizational dysfunctions of decline. *Academy of Management Journal,* 30: 126–138.

Caminiti, S. 1994. Liz Claiborne; How to get focused again. *Fortune,* January 24: 85.

Chandler, A. 1962. *Strategy and structure.* Cambridge, MA: MIT Press.

Deveny, K. 1989. Can Ms. Fashion bounce back? *BusinessWeek,* January 16: 64.

D'Innocenzio, A. 1994. Jones, Claiborne tussle for turf. *Women's Wear Daily,* March 23: 8.

Drazin, R., and Van de Ven, A. 1985. An examination of alternative forms of fit in contingency theory. *Administrative Science Quarterly,* 30: 514–539.

Ettorre, B. 1980. Spotlight working woman's dressmaker. *New York Times,* July 6: 7.

Ford, J. D. 1985. The effects of causal attributions on decision makers' responses to performance downturns. *Academy of Management Review,* 10: 770–786.

Gersick, C. 1991. Revolutionary change theories: A multilevel exploration of the punctuated equilibrium paradigm. *Academy of Management Review,* 16: 10–36.

Hambrick, D. C., and Mason, P. A. 1984. Upper echelons: The organization as a reflection of its top managers. *Academy of Management Review,* 9: 193–206.

Hammond, J. 1993. Quick response in retail/manufacturing channels. In J. Hausman and R. Nolan (Eds.), *Globalization, technology, and competition:* 185–214. Boston: Harvard Business School Press.

Hannan, M., and Freeman, J. 1984. Structural inertia and organizational change. *American Sociological Review,* 49: 149–164.

Hass, N. 1992. Like a rock. *Financial World,* February 4: 22.

Hayes, R., & Jaikumar, R. 1988. Manufacturing's crisis: New technologies, obsolete organizations. *Harvard Business Review,* 68(5): 77–85.

Henderson, R. 1993. Underinvestment and incompetence as responses to radical innovation: Evidence from the photolithographic alignment equipment industry. *Rand Journal of Economics,* 24: 248–270.

Henderson, R., and Clark, K. 1990. Architectural innovation: The reconfiguration of existing product technologies and the failure of established firms. *Administrative Science Quarterly,* 35: 9–30.

Jaikumar, R. 1986. Postindustrial manufacturing. *Harvard Business Review,* 64(6): 69–76.

Kauffman, S. A. 1993. *The origins of order: Self-organization and selection in evolution.* New York: Oxford University Press.

Khandwalla, P. 1973. Viable and effective organizational designs of firms. *Academy of Management Journal,* 16: 481–495.

Lawrence, P., and Lorsch, J. 1967. *Organization and environment.* Boston: Harvard Business School Press.

Learned, E., Christensen, C., Andrews, K., and Guth, W. 1965. *Business policy: Text and cases.* Homewood, IL: Irwin.

Lee, M. 1994. Weaving their way home. *Washington Post,* August 25: B9.

Levinthal, D. 1992. Surviving Schumpeterian environments: An evolutionary perspective. *Industrial and Corporate Change,* 1: 427–443.

Levinthal, D. 1997. Adaptation on rugged landscapes. *Management Science,* 43: 934–950.

Levinthal, D., and Siggelkow, N. 2001. *Linking the old and the new: Modular and integrated adaptation to the Internet.* Working paper, Wharton School, University of Pennsylvania.

Levitt, B., and March, J. G. 1988. Organizational learning. In W. R. Scott (Ed.), *Annual review of sociology,* vol. 14: 319–340. Palo Alto, CA: Annual Reviews.

MacDuffie, J. 1995. Human resource bundles and manufacturing performance: Organizational logic and flexible production systems in the world auto industry. *Industrial and Labor Relations Review,* 58: 197–221.

Milgrom, P., and Roberts, J. 1990. The economics of modern manufacturing: Technology, strategy, and organization. *American Economic Review,* 80: 511–528.

Milgrom, P., and Roberts, J. 1995. Complementarities and fit: Strategy, structure, and organizational change in manufacturing. *Journal of Accounting and Economics,* 19: 179–208.

Miller, D. 1986. Configurations of strategy and structure: Towards a synthesis. *Strategic Management Journal,* 7: 233–249.

Miller, D. 1993. Some organizational consequences of CEO succession. *Academy of Management Journal,* 36: 644–659.

Miller, D. 1994. What happens after success: The perils of excellence. *Journal of Management Studies,* 31: 325–358.

Miller, D., and Friesen, P. 1982. Structural change and performance: Quantum vs. piecemeal incremental approaches. *Academy of Management Journal,* 25: 867–892.

Miller, D., and Friesen, P. 1984. *Organizations: A quantum view.* Englewood Cliffs, NJ: Prentice-Hall.

Miller, D., Lant, T. K., Milliken, F. J., and Korn, H. J. 1996. The evolution of strategic simplicity: Exploring two models of organizational adaptation. *Journal of Management,* 22: 863–887.

Milliken, F. J. 1990. Perceiving and interpreting environmental change: An examination of college administrators' interpretation of changing demographics. *Academy of Management Journal,* 33: 42–63.

Milliken, F. J., and Lant, T. K. 1991. The effect of an organization's recent performance history on strategic persistence and change. In P. Shrivastava, A. Huff, and J. Dutton (Ed.), *Advances in strategic management,* vol. 7: 129–156. Greenwich, CT: JAI Press.

Murmann, J. P., and Tushman, M. L. 1997. Organizational responsiveness to environmental shock as an indicator of organizational foresight and oversight: The role of executive team characteristics and organizational context. In R. Garud, P. R. Nayyar, and Z. B.

Shapira (Eds.), *Technological innovation:* 260–278. New York: Cambridge University Press.

Nadler, D. A., Shaw, R. B., and Walton, A. E. 1994. *Discontinuous change.* San Francisco: Jossey-Bass.

Nadler, D. A., and Tushman, M. L. 1992. Designing organizations that have good fit: A framework for understanding new architectures. In D. A. Nadler, M. Gerstein, and R. B. Shaw (Eds.), *Organizational architecture:* 39–56. San Francisco: Jossey-Bass.

Nystrom, P. C., and Starbuck, W. H. 1984. To avoid organizational crises—Unlearn. *Organizational Dynamics,* 12(4): 53–65.

Pennings, J. 1987. Structural contingency theory: A multivariate test. *Organization Studies,* 8: 223–240.

Pettigrew, A. 1987. Context and action in the transformation of the firm. *Journal of Management Studies,* 24: 649–670.

Porter, M. 1995. *Positioning tradeoffs, activity systems, and the theory of competitive strategy.* Working paper, Harvard Graduate School of Business Administration, Boston.

Porter, M. 1996. What is strategy? *Harvard Business Review,* 74(6): 61–78.

Porter, M., and Rivkin, J. 1998. *Activity systems as barriers to imitation.* Working paper no. 98-066, Harvard Graduate School of Business Administration, Boston.

Rivkin, J. 2000. Imitation of complex strategies. *Management Science,* 46: 824–844.

Romanelli, E., and Tushman, M. L. 1994. Organization transformation as punctuated equilibrium. *Academy of Management Journal,* 37: 1141–1166.

Siggelkow, N. 2001. *Misperceiving interactions: Organizational consequences.* Working paper, Wharton School, University of Pennsylvania.

Singh, J., House, R., and Tucker, D. 1986. Organizational change and organizational mortality. *Administrative Science Quarterly,* 31: 587–611.

Skolnik, R. 1985. Liz the wiz; Liz Claiborne Inc. *Sales & Marketing Management,* 135: 50.

Suchman, M. 1995. Managing legitimacy: Strategic and institutional approaches. *Academy of Management Review,* 20: 571–610.

Traub, J., and Newman, M. 1985. Behind all of the glitz and glitter. *Smithsonian,* 16: 30.

Tushman, M. L., Newman, W. H., and Romanelli, E. 1986. Convergence and upheaval: Managing the unsteady pace of organizational evolution. *California Management Review,* 29(1): 29–44.

Tushman, M. L., and Romanelli, E. 1985. Organizational evolution: A metamorphosis model of convergence and reorientation. In L. L. Cummings and B. M. Staw (Eds.), *Research in organizational behavior,* vol. 7: 171–222. Greenwich, CT: JAI Press.

Tushman, M. L., and Rosenkopf, L. 1996. Executive succession, strategic reorientation and performance growth: A longitudinal study in the U.S. cement industry. *Management Science,* 42: 939–953.

Weick, K. E. 1976. Educational organizations as loosely coupled systems. *Administrative Science Quarterly,* 21: 1–19.

Westhoff, F. H., Yarbrough, B., and Yarbrough, R. 1996. Complexity, organizations, and Stuart Kauffman's *The Origins of Order. Journal of Economic Behavior and Organization,* 29: 1–25.

Womack, J., Jones, D., and Roos, D. 1990. *The machine that changed the world.* New York: Rawson Associates.

Wright, S. 1932. The roles of mutation, inbreeding, crossbreeding and selection in evolution. *Proceedings XI International Congress of Genetics,* 1: 356–366.

Zajac, E., and Bazerman, M. 1991. Blind spots in industry and competitor analysis: Implications of interfirm (mis)perceptions for strategic decisions. *Academy of Management Review,* 16: 37–56.

INDEX

ABB. *See* Asea Brown Boveri
Abernath/Utterback model, 35
ABI/Inform, 375
Absorptive capacity, 377–378
Accounting firms, 317
Active inertia, 121–122
Actor network theory, 490
Adaptation
  biological, 278–279
  on the job, 223–224
  organizational, 600–601, 602
  reactive change and, 565
Adaptationism, 129
Adapters, 147–148
Adaptive society, 68–69
Adidas, 215, 216
Adoption cycles, 598
Adtech, 476
Advanced Research Projects Agency
  (ARPA), 272
Affymetrix, 397
Agency theoretic view of the firm, 320
Agilent, 472
Airplane industry, 37
Alcatel, 477
ALCOA, 565, 567, 572, 574
Alfa Romeo, 384
Allied Signal, 284
Alpha Corporation, 532, 533, 536, 538
Amazon.com, 339
Ambassador dimension, 434, 435, 436,
  437–438, 439
Ambidextrous managers, 10–11, 287
Ambidextrous organizations, 4, 8–11,
  12, 29, 276–290
American Airlines, 311
American Bell (AT&T), 277
American Express, 142
American Honda, 258–259
America Online, 135, 140, 370
Amgen, 397
Ampex, 337
Analogies, 496–497, 498
Andersen Consulting, 342, 468, 501, 502
Anticipatory changes, 564–565

Antithetical perspective on balancing
  processes, 184–186
Anxiety, problem of, 554–555, 559, 560
Apollo Computer, 70, 155–157, 531, 539
Apple Computer, 70, 85, 143, 144, 147,
  148, 217, 261, 274, 277, 279–281,
  283, 468
Applied Materials, 284
Appropriability, 322
Appropriation strategy, 370–371
Architectural innovations, 6–7, 9, 11,
  92–106
Architectural knowledge, 94, 622
Architecture, 153, 156, 287–288
Architecture of organizational
  knowledge, 410–411
ARRIS, 397
Arthur Andersen, 468, 502
Ascend, 462–463
Asea Brown Boveri, 203, 287, 288, 289,
  441–456, 472, 479
Ashton Tate, 140, 143, 144
Askus, 478
Assembly line control (ALC) system,
  385
Assets, 318–319
Astra, 468
ASUAG, 45, 46, 47, 50, 51, 54, 278
AT&T, 157, 277, 350, 534, 535, 570
Atari, 140, 147
Attitude of wisdom, 499, 500
Attraction Selection Attrition (ASA)
  model, 237
Audemars Piguet, 47
Autodesk, 145
Automobile industry, 37, 40, 154,
  281–282, 316, 321, 375–390, 424,
  503, 507, 609
Autonomous strategy, 578, 600
Autonomous team structure, 422
Autonomy and power issues, 498

Balancing processes, 183–190
Ballard Power Systems, 271
Banc One, 544

Bankers Trust Company, 155
Bank of Montreal, 476
Bank One, 476
Barnes & Noble, 334, 338, 339, 476
BASF, 4
Battelle, 51
Bayer, 4
Bay Networks, 547
BBC, 461
Behavioral outcome contingencies, 222
Bell Labs, 23, 137, 418, 523–528
Benchmarking, 317, 523–524
Benetton, 404
Bessemer process, 67–68
B. F. Goodrich, 108, 110, 112, 120–121
BHAGs, 214, 215–216
Bienne, 50
Big Red Boat, 462
Binary organizational process model,
  182–183
Biogen, 397
Biotechnology industry, 393, 394–398,
  402–403, 410
Blancpain, 47
Blockbuster Video, 542–543
BOC's Industrial Gases, 195, 196, 197,
  198, 199, 200, 204
Boeing, 98, 211, 215, 216, 217
Bolt Beranek and Newman, 412
Booz-Allen & Hamilton, 458
Borders, 338, 339
Borland, 141, 147–148, 149
Bottom-up processes, 469
Boundary activities, 434–439
Boundary management, 432–439
Boundary objects, 410–411
Boundary spanners, 455
BP. *See* British Petroleum
Brain storming, 237, 243, 483–484, 496,
  497–498, 499
Brand names, 141, 590
Breakthrough innovations, 39
Breguet, 47
Bridgestone, 109, 119
British Airways, 284–285, 542

British Petroleum (BP), 175–177
British Telecom, 350
Brokers, 481, 487
Brown Boveri and Philips, 51–52
Browsers, 543
Bulova, 46, 48
Buying cycles, 614–615, 616, 620

CAD. *See* Computer-aided-design
systems
Callaway Golf, 334, 338
Cambria Company, 67–68
Cambridge University, 370
Cannibalization, 475
Canon, 7, 102–104
Capability Management in Network
Organizations, 477–478
Capability trap, 168–177
Capital budgeting processes, 122
Career clothing, 611–622
Career management, 573
Career paths, 421, 452–454
Careers, 219–231, 500–501, 573
Cargill, 210
Carter-Hawley-Hale, 285, 617
Cartier, 46
Casio, 48
"Casualization" of the workplace, 617
Catallaxies, 403
Catching-up process, 375, 378, 382–384,
387–388, 389
Caterpillar, 530, 535
CBS, 137–138, 141, 142
Celeron processor, 589, 592, 599
Cement manufacturing, 35, 36, 38, 40
Century, 46
Certina, 47
Cetus, 395
Champions, 242, 428
Chandler, Alfred, 108, 123, 404
Chanel, 46
Chaparral Steel, 293, 294, 297, 299, 301,
302
Charismatic leadership, 564, 566–568,
570, 574
Charles Schwab & Co., 334, 339, 458
Chase-Manhattan Bank, 115
Chemicals industry, 174, 229, 293, 294,
297, 298, 300, 301, 513
Chipsets, 591
Chiron, 397
Chopard, 46
Christian Dior, 46
Chrysler Corporation, 286, 311, 506,
532, 537
Churchill, Winston, 215
Ciba-Geigy, 4–5, 11, 194, 195, 196–197,
198, 200, 201, 202, 204

Circuit City, 286, 344
CISC architecture. *See* Complex
instruction set computing
architecture
Cisco Systems, 147, 462–463, 541, 547,
548
Citibank, 531–532, 535, 536, 537, 538
Citicorp, 215, 216
Citizen, 46, 47, 48
City Bank, 215, 216
Civil rights, 263–264
Claris, 144
Clinical trials, 460
CNN, 146, 334
Cobilt, 101
Coca-Cola, 239, 273, 311
Coevolution, 457, 466
Coevolutionary lock-in, 578–579,
600–603
strategic inertia and, 579, 599, 602
of strategy and environment, 582–592
strategy vector and, 598
Coevolving, 457–467
Coexistence, 473
Cognitive processes, 227–228
Cognitive representations, 18, 19, 29
Coherence, 409
Cold-beverage industry, 545–546
Collaboration
as competition dimension, 394–395
cross-business synergies and, 457–467
knowledge and networks in, 393–400
shifting collaborative webs, 459–460
suppliers and, 507
Collaboration creep, 466
Collaborative portfolios, 396–398
Collective beliefs, 188
Collective know-how, 404–405
Collectivism, 243–244, 406–407
Color television, 137–138
Columbia University, 532, 538, 540
Commitment, 240, 424
Commodore, 70
Communication
boundary management and, 436
change transitions and, 559, 560
channels of, 96
Communities of practice, 365, 402,
406–407
Compact disk (CD) technology, 138
Compaq Computer, 70, 82, 141, 333,
334, 343–344, 550, 583
Competence-destroying innovations, 38,
39
Competence-enhancing innovations, 38,
94
Competency traps, 18
Competition, 123, 333, 336, 617–618

Competition-based strategy, 336
Competitive advantage, 3, 307, 308–325,
605–606
Competitive forces approach, 309–310,
312, 324
Complementarities, 475, 615–616
Complementary assets, 318
Complementary products, 141, 144–145,
475
Complementary strategic thrusts, 589,
598
Complex instruction set computing
(CISC) architecture, 583
Component knowledge, 94, 95–97, 622
Components, 93–94
Compulsory cooperation, 343
Computer-aided-design (CAD) systems,
385
Computer-aided manufacturing (CAM)
systems, 385
Computer Associates, 148–149
Computer chips, 541, 546
Computer industry, 343–344, 429–431,
464–465, 514, 517, 518, 546
Conflict patterns, 246–247
Conformity, 236–237, 240
Congruence
assessing, 197–199, 201–203
as managerial trap, 282–283
problem solving and, 194–205
project development and, 295
rules of thumb for, 203–205
Conner Peripherals, 76, 81, 82, 84
Constructed crises, 375, 382, 388–389
Constructive behavior, 558–560
Consumer goods companies, 363–373
Contingency theory, 182
Continuous-aim firing, 59–69
Contract books, 425–426
Contracts, 315, 320–321, 411
Control, 180–183, 555, 568
Control Data, 80, 81, 82, 84, 85–86
Control/exploration relationship,
183–190
Convergence/upheaval pattern of change,
530
Converging change, 533–535, 537
Cooperation, 343
Copier industry, 471
Core capabilities, 292–298, 302–303
Core competences, 307, 314
Core competencies, 3, 18, 95, 161–162
core ideology vs., 213
knowledge and, 403
supplier selection and, 511
Core ideology, 206, 207–213, 216
Core purpose, 209–212, 215
Core rigidities, 18, 298–303

Core values, 207–209, 535–537
Cornell University, 532
Corning, 271, 570, 572
Corporate culture, 317
Corporate ventures, 418
Corum, 46
Cray Research, 565, 574
Creative destruction, 35, 40, 293, 338
Creative tensions, 222
Creativity
    focused, 372
    group, 235
    individual vs. collective, 244
    organizational culture and, 234–235
    weird rules of, 267–275
Crises, 375–376, 378–379
Crisis construction, 375, 382, 388–389
Critical tasks, 197–198
Cross-functional teams, 417, 432–439, 507
Cross-unit groups, 445–446
Cultural inertia, 283
Cultural norms, 236
Culture
    aligning, 198–199
    definition of, 235
    innovation related to, 236–237
    multiple, 288–289
    paradox of, 284
    strong, 234–248, 260–261, 607
Current state, 553, 559, 560
Customers, 83–84, 619

Daewoo, 379, 381
Darwin, Charles, 130
Data General, 70, 272, 538, 570
Dayton Hudson, 461
Decentralization, 417
Decision-making process, 257–259, 511, 599
Deep structures, 120
Defense contracting, 550
Deframing skills, 29
Dell Computer, 141, 161, 547–548, 550
Delphi Automotive Systems, 154
Deregulation, 535
Design competition, 37
Design Continuum, 270
Design implementation, 552–562
Design rules, 151, 153
Development project teams, 417, 419–422
Devil's advocate approach, 240
Dialectical thinking, 413
Digital Equipment Corporation, 70, 148, 158, 535
Digital imaging, 18–30
Digital mobile telephony, 473, 474

Digital printing, 475–476
Dillard's, 612, 619
Discontinuous change, 12, 200, 204, 276, 529, 530–540
    adaptation and, 563, 574
    frame-breaking and, 532
    leadership and, 574
    need for, 535–537
Discontinuous innovation, 7–8, 8–9, 39
Discounting, 145
Discount retailing, 345
Disk drive industry, 7, 70–89, 158
Disney. See Walt Disney Company
Disney Imagineering, 268
Disney Travel Online, 461
Disney World, 462
Dispositional knowledge, 405
Disruptive technological changes, 74–75
Distributive outcomes, 186
Diversification, 325
Divisions of knowledge, 407–408
Divisions of labor, 407–408
Dixie, 50
Dominant designs, 2, 4–6, 33, 37–39, 39–40
    change and, 535
    component and architectural
        knowledge and, 95–96
    technology cycles and, 281–282
Dual core organizations, 186
Dual organizational process model, 183
Duke University, 532
Dunhill, 46
DuPont, 71, 174–175, 222, 503, 532
Durable-goods monopoly, 145
Dvorak Simplified Keyboard, 131, 133
Dynamic capabilities, 3, 29, 307, 308–325
Dynamic conservatism, 33
Dyson Appliances, 270–271

EBAUCHE S.A., 45
Ebel, 46, 47
Ecological pressures, 279
Ecologies of knowledge, 402, 410
Economies of scale, 53
Edison, Thomas, 136–137, 480–481, 490, 502, 503
E. F. Hutton, 260
Electric automobiles, 40
Electric industry, 136–137
Electronic semiconductor (CCD)
    sensors, 23
Electronics industry, 11, 24, 293, 294, 296–297, 298, 299, 300–301, 302, 389, 426, 429, 512, 517, 518–519, 550
Elemedia, 528

Eli Lilly and Company, 397, 398, 463
Emap, 475
Embedded firms, 404
Emergent roles, 455
Emerson Electric, 541, 548
Empowerment, 297–298, 299–300, 570
Enabling leadership, 567
Enhancement launches, 348, 354
Encore Computer, 531, 539
Energizing leadership, 567
Enron, 334, 338
Entrepreneurial organizational
    architectures, 8–9
Entrepreneurial units, 10, 12
Entrepreneurs, 65
Entrepreneurship, 157
Entry strategies, 324–325
Envirogen, 397
Environmental shifts, 534, 606, 607–609, 621
Envisioned future, 206–207, 213–218
Envisioning leadership, 566
Era of ferment, 39
Era of substitution, 37
Ericsson, 468, 469, 471, 472, 473, 474, 475, 476, 477, 478, 479
ESPN, 461, 462
Eterna, 46
EuroDisney, 462
Evan-Picone, 611, 612
Event pacing, 542
Evolution, 279–282
    leadership and, 537–538
    organizational adaptation and, 600
    revolution vs., 139–140, 149
    symbiotic coevolution and, 457–458
Evolutionary change, 287
Evolutionary path, 320
Evolutionary strategies, 139
Evolutionary theory, 131–134
Excludability, 339, 395
Executive sponsors, 429
Expansion strategy, 369–370
Expectations management, 142–143, 149
Explicit knowledge, 377, 408
Exposure effects, 275
External fit, 201, 606, 607, 616, 621
Eye-care medical practices, 459–460

Fabrique d'Ebauches de Sonceboz et
    Ebosa, 47
Failure, 272–274, 553
Failure Mode Effects Analysis (FMEA), 189
Fairchild Semiconductor, 258
Fair outcomes, 344
Fair process, 343

Family values, 111–112, 119, 122
Fannie Mae, 210
FASELEC, 52
Faulty attributions, 169–170
Fax machines, 459
Federated Department Stores, 285, 612, 617, 619
Feedback channels, 561
FHM.com, 475
Financial assets, 318
Financial services industry, 154–155
Firestone Tire & Rubber, 108–124
First-mover advantage, 123, 141
Fiske, Bradley, 64–65
Fit, 605–622
Five-forces framework, 310
Focus, 325
Focused creativity, 372
Ford, Henry, 214, 216, 274
Ford mass production system, 607, 608
Ford Motor Company, 38, 111, 113, 114, 122, 215, 293, 294, 336, 380, 382, 384, 387, 475
Fordson tractor, 38
Formality and informality, 411–412
Formal systems, 533
Frame-breaking change, 532, 535–537
France Telecom, 143
Free-riding, 338–339
French Minitel system, 143–144
FTD, 145
Fuji Xerox, 471, 473, 474, 563, 564, 567
Functional team structure, 420–421
Fundamental attribution error, 170
Future state, 553, 554

Game theory, 310–311
Gatekeepers, 433, 455, 496
Gateway, 550
GCA, 101, 104
GEBN. *See* Michigan State University Global Procurement and Supply Chain Electronic Benchmarking Network
GEC, 468
GE Capital, 459
Genentech, 395, 397
General Automation, 565
General Electric Company, 136–137, 215, 284, 463, 549, 565, 573, 574
General Motors Corporation, 113, 114, 154, 217, 284, 336, 379, 386, 532
General Radio, 282, 283, 530–531, 532, 533, 534, 535, 536, 537, 538
General Tire, 108, 110, 112
GenRad, 283, 531
Gillette, 541, 543
Giro Sport Design, 215

GKN, 385
Glass industry, 36, 38
Global village, 402
Glycomex, 397
Goals, 245, 262
Golf clubs, 334, 338
Goodall, Jane, 270
Goodyear, 2–3, 108, 110, 112, 113
Gould, Stephen Jay, 129–134
Governments, 252
Granite Rock Company, 211
Great Britain, 59–69
Grounded theorizing method, 581
Group age, 228–229
Group cohesion, 235, 239–242
Group creativity, 235
Group processes and effects, 228–229
Groupthink, 239–240
Grove, Andrew S. ("Andy"), 577–603
GTE, 535
Gucci, 46
Guilford, 397

Haggar, 620
Hamilton Watch Company, 46
Harley-Davidson, 161, 258
Harris Corporation, 532
Harvard University, 215, 303
Hayes, 140
Heavy equipment maintenance, 187
Heavyweight development teams, 417, 419, 422–431
Helios medical imaging system, 23–24, 27, 28
Heterogeneity, 245–246, 395
Hetzel, 50
Hewlett-Packard, 141, 206, 207, 208, 209–210, 212, 213, 217, 238–239, 271, 283, 287–288, 289, 293, 294, 297, 298, 299, 301, 302, 355, 408, 409, 423, 458, 460, 471, 472, 473, 474, 477, 479, 539
Hidden design parameters, 153
Hierarchical authority, 259–260
Hierarchy, 445, 455
High-flex firms, 318
High self-monitors, 268
High-strength-low-alloy (HSLA) steel, 98–99
High-technology companies, 187, 189, 434–439
Historical context, 13–14
Hitachi, 276
Hoffman LaRoche, 397
Home Depot, 286, 334, 339
Homophyly, 228
Honda, 7, 48, 215, 239, 258–259, 272, 311, 385, 564, 569–570

Honeywell, 531
Hood River venture, 597
Household-goods industry, 546
Human resources, 198
Hybrid collectives, 406, 407
Hyundai Motor Company, 362, 375, 376, 379–390

IBM, 6, 12, 38, 70, 71, 76, 80, 81, 133, 140, 143, 146, 147, 261, 274, 280, 283, 285, 313, 318, 333, 342, 468, 531, 539, 543
IBM System/360, 151–152, 153
ICI, 564
Idea generators, 455
Identification, 67–68
IDEO, 237, 243, 270, 417–418, 458, 480, 482–503
IKEA, 334, 338
Image sensor technology, 24–25
Imitation, 322
Impetus, 72
Implementation, 241–242, 257, 259–262, 552–562
Improvement, 162–169
Incentives. *See* Reward systems
Incongruence, 195
Increasing insulation, 227
Incremental change, 34, 532, 533–534, 564, 565, 566, 606, 609
Incremental innovations, 6, 8, 92–93, 94, 95, 101, 622
Incumbent inertia, 293, 622
Incumbent organizations, 33
Individualism, 243, 256–257
Individualistic norms, 242–247
Induced strategic processes, 10
Induced strategy, 578, 583, 587, 599, 600
Industrial clusters, 122–123
Industry-enabling technologies, 590–591
Industry leadership, 70, 72
Industry structure, 123
Inertia
    active, 121–122
    cultural, 283
    fit, 606, 607
    frame-breaking change and, 537
    incumbent, 293
    internal competition and, 468
    learning and, 606
    organizational, 18, 19, 29, 388
    psychological sources and, 579
    strategic, and coevolutionary lock-in, 579, 592–598
    structural, 283
    of success, 599

Influence, 262
Informal linking processes, 454–455
Informal relations, 409, 411–412
Informal systems, 533
Information and communication technologies (ICT), 368
Information economy, 402
Information filters, 97
Information-processing capacities, 4 50
Infoseek, 461
Innovation cycles, 33
Innovation streams, 3, 8, 9, 11, 13, 529
Insourcing/outsourcing decisions, 511
Installed base, 145, 146
Institutional assets, 318–319
Instrumental leadership, 568–570
Integrator roles, 446–447
Intel Corporation, 6, 10, 141, 145, 148, 155, 276, 348, 355, 469, 523, 529, 541, 546, 550, 577–603
Intellectual agreement, 242
Intellectual property rights, 141, 322
Intensity of effort, 377
Interac, 147
Interconnection, 147
Interdependence, 395, 443–445, 450
Interfaces, 153
Interfirm networks, 43
Internal competition, 468–479
Internal congruence, 282
Internal ecology models, 578
Internal fit, 201, 606, 607, 615–616, 620–621
Internal routines, 502
Internal structural heterogeneity, 10
Internet, 143, 341, 412, 460, 461
Interneuron, 397
Intuit, 144
Invention, 481
Inventory costs/control, 614, 620
Investment process, 122
Italdesign, 382, 385
ITE hearing aids, 3, 7

Japan
Bridgestone and, 109
coevolution and, 466
global competition and, 336
lean manufacturing and, 607
platform projects and, 424
supplier integration and, 507, 512, 517, 518
watches and, 47–48, 53–54
Japan Telecom, 350
Java, 143
J.C. Penney, 461
Jephthah story, 129

Jet aircraft industry, 98
Job longevity, 219–231
Jobs, Steven, 274, 279, 280
Johnson, Lyndon B., 264
Johnson & Johnson, 206, 207–208, 216, 278, 288, 289, 397
Johnson Controls, 154
Joint technology development, 516
Jones, Jim, 256
Jones Apparel, 618
Jordan Marsh, 613
JVC, 6, 12, 337

Kasper Instruments, 101, 102–104
Kearns, Dave, 563–564, 569, 572
Kia, 381
Kirin, 466
Kissinger, Henry, 257
Kitchen appliances, 494
K-Mart, 286, 461
Know-how, 405
Knowledge
architecture of, 410–411
biotechnology and, 396
collaboration and, 395
communities and, 408–409
core capabilities and, 298
distribution of, 407–408
divisions of, 407–408
explicit, 377, 408
exploitation and, 10, 268, 602
exploration and, 10, 268, 602
leakiness and, 409–410
learning and 377–378
migratory, 378, 388
organizational advantage and, 405–407
organizational blindness and, 408
organizing, 402–413
sticky, 407, 408, 409–410
strategic framework and, 363–373
supplier integration and, 521
tacit, 377, 408
technology issues and, 411–413
within communities, 408–409
Knowledge-based perspective, 402
Knowledge brokers, 410
Knowledge creation, 365, 372
Knowledge domains, 364–365, 372
Knowledge economy, 333–345, 338, 341, 344, 363
Knowledge firms, 402
Knowledge gaps, 364
Knowledge strategies, 366–372
Knowledge transfer, 365–366, 372
Knowledge workers, 307
Kobayashi, Yotaro, 563, 567
Kodak, 21, 119, 149

Land, Edwin, 20–21
Laser printers, 268, 270
Launches, 348, 354
Laura Ashley, 119
Leadership
business units and, 463
charismatic, 564, 566–568, 570, 574
complementarity of approaches and, 569–570
convergent periods and, 534
discontinuous change and, 278, 574
executive succession and, 538
frame-breaking change and, 536
Grove approach to, 582
heavyweight teams and, 427–428
instrumental, 568–570
managing change and, 539
modular, 157–159
organization evolution and, 437–438
power issues and, 254
project, 427–428
strategy vector and, 577–603
support for change and, 557
team leaders and, 438–439
Lean production model, 316, 607
Learning, 10
acquisition process and, 493–494
architectural innovation and, 98
collaboration and, 395, 398–400
crises and, 378–379
crisis construction and, 376–379, 389
dynamic capabilities approach to, 317
inertia and, 606
knowledge and, 377–378
process of, 368
re-orientation and, 573
senior teams and, 571–572
strategy processes and, 601–602
superstitious learning, and 170–173
systems for, 378
technical, 368
Learning-by-using, 494
Lear Seating Corporation, 154
Letters of intent, 511
Leveraging strategy, 367–369
Liaison roles, 445
Library self-check systems, 472
Life-cycle theories of industrial evolution, 123
Lifetime employment, 112, 118
Light-emitting diode (LED) display watches, 49, 56
Lightweight team structure, 421–422
Lincoln, Abraham, 256
Liz Claiborne, 529, 605, 606, 610–622
Lock-in, 592
Loews Corporation, 119
Longines, 46, 47, 50

Lost Arrow Corporation, 210
Lotus, 141, 143, 147, 149
Lotus Development, 273
Low self-monitors, 268
Lucent, 135, 418, 477, 523

Ma Bell culture, 534
Machinery industry, 389
Macy's, 285, 612, 617
Magna International, 154
Mahan, Alfred Thayer, 66, 67
Managerial competence, 573
Manufacturing capabilities, 141
Manufacturing Game, 175
Manufacturing organizations, 507
Marine Stewardship Council, 370
Market assets, 319
Market-based innovations, 7
Market heterogeneity, 475
Market uncertainty, 348
Mars group, 209, 212
Marshall Field's, 461
Mary Kay Cosmetics, 210, 238
MasterCard, 139, 142
Matrix structures, 447–449
Matsushita, 135, 138, 158
Maxtor, 76
May Department Stores Company, 612
M-Bone, 412
McDonald's, 238, 361
McGill University, 532
McKinsey & Company, 210, 501–502
MediaOne, 350
Medical devices industry, 356–357
Medical diagnostic imaging, 320
Medtek, 195, 196, 197, 202
Memorex, 81
Mental maps, 606, 609, 621
Mercedes-Benz, 154
Merck, 206, 208, 210, 212, 214–215,
    216, 217, 397
Mere exposure effect, 268
Mergers and acquisitions, 258, 544
Michelin, 3, 108, 109, 112, 114, 120
Michigan State University Global
    Procurement and Supply Chain
    Electronic Benchmarking Network
    (GEBN), 509
Micropolis, 81, 82, 85–87
Microprocessor industry, 578, 582–583
Microreplication, 502
Microsoft, 6, 11, 135, 138, 139, 140,
    141, 142–143, 144, 145–146, 148,
    149, 155, 261, 277, 280, 336, 338,
    341, 348, 370, 543, 549, 583, 591
Microwave oven industry, 333
Migration path, 144
Migratory knowledge, 378, 388

Minicomputers, 36, 38
Miniscribe, 81, 82
Mission, company, 535
MIT, 25, 303
Mitsubishi, 385, 386, 387, 466
Mobile telephony, 350
Modular analysis, 34
Modular innovation, 94
Modularity, 151–159, 549
Moore's Law, 541
Motherboards, 591–592
Motorola, 206, 207, 211, 276, 422–423,
    583
Multibusiness teams, 463–465
Multiple project assignments, 426–427
Mundane behaviors, 569
Murphy's Law, 542

NASA, 216, 217
National Science Foundation (NSF), 509
Navy (U.S.), 60
NBC, 141
NCR, 564
Netcom Systems, 476
NetGrocer, 370
Netscape, 135, 138, 139, 142, 541, 542,
    543
Network effects, 138
Network elements, 490
Networking, 597–598
Networking industry, 462–463
Network markets, 149
Network production systems, 43, 54,
    55
Network theory, 501
Nevin, John J., 117–119
New Age, 252
New business development, 592–593,
    600
New economics, 336
New economy, 403, 404, 458
New product development, 506–521,
    545
Nike, 210, 212–213, 215, 216, 284
Nikon, 101, 104
Nintendo, 138, 139, 140, 145, 147, 336
Nissan, 284, 385
Nixon, Richard, 254–255
Nokia, 284
Noncancellation policies, 614, 616
Nonrival goods, 339
Nordstrom, 206, 207, 208, 211, 212,
    284, 285
Norms, 242–243
Norm strength, 238
North, Oliver, 259
Not Invented Here (N.I.H.) syndrome,
    229, 230

NovaMed Eyecare Management, 458,
    459–460, 464
NTN, 385
Nucor, 339

OfficeSys example, 459
Oil and chemicals, 515
Omega, 46, 47
O'Neil, Paul, 567, 572
Openness approach, 146
Operating frameworks, 159
Opportunity gaps, 196
Options logic, 347
Oracle, 342, 469
Organizational architecture, 287–288
Organizational boundaries, 319
Organizational change, 553–554
Organizational culture, 235
Organizational ecology, 279
Organizational history, 534
Organizational imprinting, 30
Organizational memory, 492–498
Organizational paradigms, 260–261
Organizational problem solving. See
    Problem-solving strategies
Organizational processes, 316
Organizational process models, 180–183
Organizational technology, 2
Organon Teknika, 397
Orient Oil Corporation, 552–553, 554,
    561
Orthogonal perspective on balancing
    processes, 186–188
Oticon, 2, 12
Overlapping activities, 469
Overlapping communities, 410
Ownership, 424

Palm Computing, 156
Panda's thumb principle, 129–134
Paradigms
    core capabilities and, 302
    organizational, 260–261
    of strategy, 322, 324
Participation in change, 556, 559
Participative management, 231
Passivity, 254
Patching, 462, 464, 474
Patek Philippe, 46, 47
Path dependencies, 28, 319–320
Paths, 315–316, 319–320
Pay for performance, 118
PCI chipset venture, 597
PCS services, 146
Penetration pricing, 142
Pentium, 589–590, 599
People Express, 537, 564, 565, 570
PeopleSoft, 460

Performance
  culture and, 235
  job longevity and, 228
  supplier integration and, 520
  sustained or disrupted, 74–75
  team boundaries and, 435
Performance gaps, 163–164, 196, 389
Performance landscape, 607–608, 610, 618, 621
Performance metrics, 547
Perkin-Elmer, 101, 104
Personal Digital Assistance (PDA) wireless services, 146
Pertec, 81
Pharmaceutical industry, 312, 339, 396–400, 473
Pharmacia, 397, 478, 479
Philip Morris, 208, 215, 216
Philips, 138, 140, 141, 313
Photocopiers, 459
Photography industry, 2, 7, 10
Photolithographic alignment equipment industry, 92, 99–106, 316, 622
Piaget, 46, 47
PIF (Printer In the Field) concept, 23
Piguet, 47
Planning-and-review cycles, 547
Platform launches, 348, 354
Platform teams, 511
Plug-compatible modules, 152
Plus Development Corporation, 84
Polaroid, 2, 7, 10, 12, 18–30, 530, 535
Political dynamics, 554, 555–558
Pooled interdependence, 443
Pope, Alexander, 129–130
Portfolio approach, 307, 347–359
Portfolios, 396–398, 619–620
Positioning options, 347, 348, 350, 352
Positions, 315, 318–319
Positive feedback, 141–142
Power issues, 252–265
  autonomy and, 498
  frame-breaking change and, 536
  senior teams and, 572
  transition state and, 554, 555–558
Preemption, 141–142, 149
Preservative acquisitions, 187
Price Club, 71
Prime Computer, 531, 532, 535, 536, 537, 538
Prior knowledge base, 377
Probing strategy, 271–272
Problem-solving strategies, 97, 204
  congruence approach and, 194–205
  job longevity and, 266–267
  process and, 195–201
  product design and, 497
Process agreement, 242

Process capability, 162
Process conflict, 246
Process development, 161–177
Process discontinuity, 40
Process improvement, 162
Process innovations, 38
Process integration, 513
Process learnings, 368
Process management, 178–190
Process model, 485–492
Process requirements, 179–180
Process switching, 187
Process technology, 518–519
Procter & Gamble, 206, 207, 222, 273, 344, 619, 620
Product design companies, 270
Product development, 292–303
  suppliers and, 506–521
  teams and, 417, 419, 422–431, 432–439
  technology brokering and, 480–503
Product innovations, 38
Production model, 316
Production networks, 42, 43
Product-life-cycle shifts, 535
Product market position, 319
Product platforms, 8
Profitable growth, 335
Project charters, 425
ProShare case, 593, 597, 599
Psychological safety, 222
Punctuated change, 530
Punctuated equilibrium theory, 120, 279, 282, 601, 606
Purchasing, 511, 521
Purchasing managers, 521
Purdue, 303
Pygmalion effect, 300

Qualcomm, 141, 473
Quantum changes, 606
Quantum Corp., 81, 82, 84–85, 86, 158
Quartz analog watches, 49
QWERTY keyboard (typewriter), 130–134

Radial tires, 108–109, 112–114, 119, 121
Radical innovations, 92–93, 94, 97, 622
Rado, 46, 47
Railroad gauges, 135–136
R&D. See Research and development
Rational-actor model, 602
Raychem, 523
Raymond Weil, 46
Raytheon, 276
Razor/blade pricing strategy, 22, 23–24, 26, 28, 29
RCA, 93, 137–138

RCA semiconductors, 276–277, 278, 289
Reach of delivery, 412
Reactive changes, 564
Reactivity, 274
Reality construction, 220
Reality shock, 220
RealNetworks, 135
Rear-guard actions, 147–149
Reciprocal interdependence, 443–444
Reciprocity, 412–413
Reconfiguration, 317–318
Re-creation, 565, 566
Reduced instruction set computing (RISC) architecture, 583, 599
Regeneron, 397
Reinvestment reinforcing loop, 165–167
Related diversification, 325
Relational capability of organizations, 394
Relationship conflict, 246
Relationship development, 507
Remington, 133, 134
Renault, 384
Reordering systems, 618, 620
Re-orientation, 530, 537, 565, 566, 568, 570, 573, 574
Reputation, 141, 318
Research and development
  assembling a strategic portfolio and, 354–356
  biotechnology and, 397, 398
  communication patterns and, 433
  Hyundai and, 386, 387, 388
  Intel and, 599
  portfolio approach to, 307, 347–359
  technological opportunities and, 320
Resilience, 188
Resistance, to change, 536, 537, 555, 556
Resource allocation, 71–72, 79–83, 122, 589
Resource-based perspective, 307, 309, 311–313, 324
Resource dependence, 71, 83–84
Resources, 314
Restaurant outlets, 548
Returns to adoption, 583
Review periods, 547
Revolutionary change, 287
Revolutionary strategies, 139
Reward systems
  coevolving, 465–466
  leadership and, 568
  linking and, 451–452
  new venture divisions and, 525, 527
  team structures and, 439
  technology brokering and, 499–500
  transitions and, 559–560

Rhythms, 544–548
Ricardo Engineering, 386
Riley, Richard, 114, 115–116
RISC architecture. *See* Reduced
    instruction set computing
    architecture
Risk issues, 368–369
    frame-breaking change and, 536–537
    re-creations and, 565
    re-orientations and, 565
    suppliers and, 513–515, 519–520
Risky shift phenomenon, 240
Rival evolutions, 139–140, 149
Rival goods, 339
Rival revolutions, 140, 149
R.J. Reynolds Tobacco Company, 215,
    216
RLL technology, 76–77
Rockefeller, John D., 175
Rockwell, 135, 141, 215
Rolex, 46, 47
Rolm, 438
Room air conditioning industry, 316
Roosevelt, Theodore, 64, 65, 67, 265
Routines, 314, 317, 321, 399, 492–498,
    503
Rover, 284
R. R. Donnelley and Sons, 475
Russ Togs Inc., 617, 619

Saks Fifth Avenue, 619
Sales.com, 460
Samsung, 284
Sanyo Corporation, 351
SAP, 334, 336, 341–342, 344, 541
Sarnoff, David, 137, 137–138
SAS, 564
Schering Plough, 397
Schlumberger, 258
Schumpeter, Josef, 338
Scott, Sir Percy, 61–62, 63
Scott Paper, 119
Scouting dimension, 434, 435, 437–438
Scouting options, 347, 348, 350–351,
    352–353
Sculley, John, 280, 281
Seagate Technology, 79, 80, 81, 82, 84
Sears, 258, 286, 532, 619
SEB, 475, 476, 478, 479
Sega, 147
Seiko, 3, 46, 47, 48, 51, 54, 276,
    277–278
Selective exposure, 227
Self-absorption, 252
Self-confirming attribution error, 171,
    174
Self-organizing systems, 403–404
Selling process, 613–614

SEMATECH, 405
Semiconductor industry, 38, 51,
    100–101, 185, 276–277, 389, 515,
    578
Senior management, 572–573
Senior teams, 11, 12–13, 19, 29,
    570–572
Sequential interdependence, 443
Serendipity, 62
Shakeouts, 40
Sharp, 70
Shipbuilding industry, 389
Shiseido, 549
Sholes, C. L., 132, 133, 134
Shortcuts balancing loop, 166, 167–168
Shugart, 81
Siebel Systems, 460
Siemens, 477
Sims, William S., 63–65, 67
Singer, 532
Singular organizational process models,
    181–182
Situational perspectives, 225
Skandia, 478, 479
Ski resorts, 461, 464
SLRP. *See* Strategic long-range planning
    process
Smart cards, 142
SMH, 47, 50, 54, 340, 341
Socialization, 220–222, 225, 454, 573
Social network theory, 490
Société des Garde-Temps (SGT), 46
Software industry, 402–403
Software sector, 361
Solar cell industry, 351
Sole-source suppliers, 589
Sony, 6, 8, 12, 135, 138, 139, 140, 141,
    147, 206, 207, 208, 210, 215, 216,
    217, 337, 462, 474–475, 541, 549,
    550
Sony Pioneer Spirit, 213
Sophie's Choice scenario, 471,
    473–474
Southwest Airlines, 238, 311, 334
Specialization, 325, 421
Sperry, Elmer, 502, 503
Spirent, 476–477, 479
Ssangyong, 381
S-shaped product life-cycle curves, 8
SSIH, 2–3, 12, 46, 51, 54, 278, 289
Stabilization, 222–223
Staff positions, 452–454, 524–525
Standard Oil, 532
Standards, 153
Standards wars, 135–150
Stanford University, 215, 303, 500,
    581
Starbucks, 338, 339, 541, 542

Statut d'Horlogerie, 45
Steel industry, 389
Steinway, 145
Stepping-stone options, 347, 348, 351,
    353, 354
Sterling Diagnostic, 27
Sticky knowledge, 407, 408, 409–410
Storage technology, 158
Strategic anticipation, 571
Strategic capabilities, 314–315
Strategic change, 324, 564, 566
Strategic conflict approach, 309,
    310–311, 324
Strategic context determination
    processes, 602
Strategic grouping, 441–442
Strategic leaps, 324
Strategic linking, 441–456
Strategic long-range planning process
    (SLRP), 587–588, 598
Strategic management, 308, 324–325
Strategic pricing, 340
Strategic signaling, 310
Strategizing, 308, 322, 324
Strategy focus, 341–342
Strategy processes, 601
Strategy vector, 577, 582–592, 600
Strong cultures, 234–248, 260–261,
    607
Structural assets, 318
Structural holes, 481
Structural inertia, 283
Structural linking decisions, 449–450
Structural partitioning, 187
Structuring, 568
Subaru, 385
Substitute process technologies, 535
Substitute product technologies, 535
Success syndrome, 3, 282–283
Sun Microsystems, 70, 71, 141,
    155–157, 458, 547
Supermarket chains, 253
Superstitious learning, 170–173
Supplier integration, 508–520
Supportive conflict, 239
Support management processes,
    451–452
Survival pricing, 148–149, 149–150
Susan Thomas Inc., 611
Suzuki, 258
Swiss Swatch watch, 46, 47, 54
Swiss watch industry, 42–56
Swiss Watch Industry Federation (FH),
    43–44, 45, 50, 51, 54
Switching costs, 320
Sylvania, 276
Symbols, 557–558
Synergies, 457–467, 536

Synergistic perspective on balancing
  processes, 188–190
Systematic Updated Retail Feedback
  (SURF) system, 614, 616

Tacit knowledge, 377, 408
Tandy, 70
Target, 461–462, 546
Target costing, 340, 512
TAS, 476
Task conflict, 246
Task coordination dimension, 434, 435,
  436, 437–438, 439
Task interdependence, 442–447
TCI, 140
Team building, 438
Team leaders, 438–439
Team structures, 419–422
  multibusiness teams and, 463–465
  reward systems and, 439
Teamwork, 432–439
Technical learnings, 368
Technical literacy, 296–297
Technical uncertainty, 349
Technological assets, 318
Technological change, 2
  assessing rates of, 518–520
  industry structure and, 75–78
  types of, 94–95
  typologies and, 74–75
Technological competence, 87
Technological discontinuities, 5, 36
Technological opportunities, 320
Technology
  institutions and, 404–405
  internal competition and, 469,
    471–474
  knowledge issues and, 411–413
Technology bookshelf, 516–517
Technology brokering
  access and, 487, 490–492
  organizational support and, 499–501
  process model and, 485–492
  product development and, 480–503
Technology cabinet, 495
Technology cycles, 4–6, 8, 33, 35–41,
  36–38, 281–282
Technology innovation, 337, 394
Technology roadmaps, 515–518
Technology sequence, 388
Technology transfer, 481
Telecare Corporation, 210
Tele-Communications, 350
Telecommunications industry, 350, 476
Telstar, 473, 479
Ten-percent change, 534
Texas Instruments, 52, 276, 313
Textronix, 283

Thermo-Electron, 523
Third-wave institutions, 404
3Com, 135, 374
3M Corporation, 206, 210, 211, 234,
  238, 271, 351, 354, 469, 477, 502,
  523, 541, 544
Ticketmaster, 145
Time pacing, 541–551, 598
Time Warner, 146, 272, 464
Timex, 46, 48–49, 55
Tire industry, 7, 108–124
Tissot, 46, 47, 50
Toffler, Alvin, 404
Top-down processes, 469
Toshiba, 70, 276, 550
Total Quality Management (TQM),
  161–162, 182, 564
Toy industry, 270
Toyota, 161, 311, 385, 387
Transaction-cost view, 402, 403
Transcell, 397
Transformation, 317–318
Transition devices, 561
Transition paralysis, 560
Transitions
  criteria for, 553–554
  time pacing and, 542–544, 547
Transition state, 553, 555, 560–561
Translators, 410, 427
TRW, 550
Tuning, 565
Two-sided openness strategy, 146
Typewriters, 130–134

Uncertainty
  employee, 224
  frame-breaking change and,
    536–537
  future state and, 560
  leadership and, 557
  market, 348
  stability during change and, 558
  suppliers and, 519–520
  technical, 349
Uniformity, 237–238
Unilever, 362, 363–373
Uniroyal Goodrich Tire Company, 108,
  110, 112, 121
United Airlines, 311
United Hospitals Inc. (UHI), 239
University of Michigan, 548
UNIX operating system, 156–157
U.S. Robotics, 143, 156
U.S. Rubber, 110
U.S. Steel, 119, 535

Vacuum tube technology, 38
Vail Ski Resorts, 461, 464

Value creation, 337
Value innovation, 307, 334, 335,
  337–345
Value innovators, 334, 336
Value system, 234
Vaporware, 142–143
VCR industry, 6, 281, 333
Venture capital model, 523–528
Vertical integration, 44, 51
VF Corporation, 619, 620
Video recording technology, 337
Virgin Atlantic Airways, 339
Virtual firms, 393
Visa, 139, 142
Visible design rules, 153
Visible information, 158
Vision, 206–218, 260, 564, 566
Volkswagen, 154, 384
Voluntary cooperation, 343
Volvo, 478, 479

Wal-Mart, 208, 210, 215, 216, **286, 334,**
  336, 338, 339, 344, 345, **404, 476,**
  546, 619, 620
Walt Disney Company, 207, 208, 210,
  211, 239, 268, 274, 461, 462
Wang, 565
Warrants, 407, 408
Watch industry, 3, 5, 33, 42–56,
  277–278, 340
Watkins-Johnson, 215
Western Union, 277
Westinghouse, 136–137, 222, **276**
We've arrived syndrome, 217
Window of technology process, **519**
Winner's curse, 142
WomenOnline, 370
WordPerfect, 143, 148
Work ethics, 378, 390
Work harder balancing loop, **164,** 165
Work interdependence, 443–445, **450**
Work-out effort, 564
Work processes, 197–198
Work smarter balancing loop, 164
World Wide Web, 412
World Wildlife Fund, 370
WPP, 475

Xerox Corporation, 93, 188, **268,** **270,**
  272, 277, 362, 405, 408, 451, **479,**
  523, 525, 563–564, 569, 574

Yamaha, 215, 258
Youth Guild, 611

Zenith, 46, 70
Zynaxis, 397